Encyclopedia of
Behavior Modification and Cognitive Behavior Therapy

Encyclopedia of
Behavior Modification and Cognitive Behavior Therapy
volume one

Adult Clinical Applications

Michel Hersen Editor-in-Chief
Pacific University

Michel Hersen
Pacific University

Johan Rosqvist
Pacific University

Editors

A SAGE Reference Publication

SAGE Publications
Thousand Oaks ▪ London ▪ New Delhi

For information:

Sage Publications, Inc.
2455 Teller Road
Thousand Oaks, California 91320

Sage Publications Ltd.
1 Oliver's Yard
55 City Road
London EC1Y 1SP
United Kingdom

Sage Publications India Pvt. Ltd.
B-42, Panchsheel Enclave
Post Box 4109
New Delhi 110 017 India

Printed in the United States of America.

ISBN 978-0-7394-8426-5

Acquiring Editor:	Jim Brace-Thompson
Editorial Assistant:	Karen Ehrmann
Project Editor:	Claudia A. Hoffman
Copy Editor:	Carla Freeman
Typesetter:	C&M Digitals (P) Ltd.
Indexer:	Molly Hall
Cover Designer:	Asya Blue

Contents

Entries

A–Z   *1–622*

Editors

Michel Hersen and Johan Rosqvist
Pacific University

Advisory Board Members

List of Entries

Editors' Note: This list of entries is for Volume I: Adult Clinical Applications only. For Volume II: Child Clinical Applications and Volume III: Educational Applications, please see the List of Entries in the respective volumes.

Reader's Guide

We provide this list to assist readers in locating entries on related topics. It classifies entries into general categories. Some entry titles appear in more than one category.

ASSESSMENT

Behavioral Case Formulation
Behavioral Working Alliance
Behaviorology
Computers and Behavioral
    Assessment
Descriptive and Functional
    Analyses
Intensive Behavior Therapy Unit
Philosophical Aspects of
    Behaviorism
Private Events
Private Practice of Behavioral
    Treatment
Psychoneuroimmunology
Role Playing
Self-Monitoring
Setting Events
Termination
Therapeutic Relationship
Treatment Compliance in
    Cognitive Behavior Therapy

AUTOBIOGRAPHIES AND BIOGRAPHIES

Agras, W. Stewart
Azrin, Nathan H.
Barlow, David H.
Beck, Aaron T.
Bellack, Alan S.
Cautela, Joseph R.
Davison, Gerald C.
Emmelkamp, Paul M. G.
Foa, Edna B.
Franks, Cyril M.
Goldiamond, Israel
Hersen, Michel

Kanfer, Frederick H.
Kazdin, Alan E.
Lazarus, A. A.
Lewinsohn, Peter A.
Marks, Isaac M.
Marshall, William L.
Meichenbaum, Donald H.
Miltenberger, Raymond G.
Paul, Gordon L.
Pavlov, Ivan P.
Skinner, Burrhus Frederic
Suinn, Richard M.
Turner, Samuel M.
Wolpe, Joseph

MAJOR TECHNIQUES

Anger Management
Anxiety/Anger Management
    Training
Applied Relaxation and Tension
Behavioral Approaches to
    Schizophrenia
Behavioral Approaches to
    Sexual Deviation
Behavioral Assessment
Behavioral Gerontology
Behavioral Group Work
Behavioral Medicine
Behavioral Treatment for
    Aggression in Couples
Behavioral Treatment for the
    Addictions
Behavioral Weight Control
    Treatments
Biofeedback
Cognitive Behavior Therapy
Coping With Depression
Coverant Control

Covert Sensitization Conditioning
Dialectical Behavior Therapy
Eating Disorders
Electrical Aversion
Eye Movement Desensitization
    and Reprocessing
Flooding
Functional Analytic
    Psychotherapy
Manualized Behavior Therapy
Memory Rehabilitation After
    Traumatic Brain Injury
Modeling
Motivational Interviewing
Multimodal Behavior Therapy
Operant Conditioning
Organizational Behavior
    Management
Panic Control Treatment
Pharmacotherapy and
    Behavior Therapy
Private Practice of Behavioral
    Treatment
Progressive Muscular Relaxation
Psychoneuroimmunology
Rational-Emotive
    Behavior Therapy
Relapse Prevention
Relaxation Strategies
Role Playing
Self-Control Therapy
Self-Management
Social Skills Training
Stampfl's Therapist Directed
    Implosive (Flooding) Therapy
Systematic Desensitization
Termination
Therapeutic Relationship
Token Economy

About the Editors

Michel Hersen (PhD, ABPP, State University of New York at Buffalo, 1966) is Professor and Dean, School of Professional Psychology, Pacific University, Forest Grove, Oregon. He completed his postdoctoral training at the West Haven VA (Yale University School of Medicine Program). He is past president of the Association for Advancement of Behavior Therapy. He has coauthored and coedited 140 books and has published 225 scientific journal articles. He is coeditor of several psychological journals, including *Behavior Modification, Aggression and Violent Behavior: A Review Journal, Clinical Psychology Review,* and the *Journal of Family Violence.* He is editor in chief of the *Journal of Anxiety Disorders, Journal of Developmental and Physical Disabilities,* and *Clinical Case Studies,* which is totally devoted to description of clients and patients treated with psychotherapy. He is editor in chief of the four-volume work titled *Comprehensive Handbook of Psychological Assessment.* He has been the recipient of numerous grants from the National Institute of Mental Health, the Department of Education, the National Institute of Disabilities and Rehabilitation Research, and the March of Dimes Birth Defects Foundation. He is a Diplomate of the American Board of Professional Psychology, Fellow of the American Psychological Association, Distinguished Practitioner and Member of the National Academy of Practice in Psychology, and recipient of the Distinguished Career Achievement Award in 1996 from the American Board of Medical Psychotherapists and Psychodiagnosticians. Finally, at one point in his career, he was in full-time private practice, and on several occasions, has had part-time private practices.

Johan Rosqvist (PsyD, Pacific University, 2002) is Assistant Professor, School of Professional Psychology, Pacific University, Portland, Oregon. He is completing his postdoctoral training at the Lake Oswego, Oregon, Anxiety Disorders Clinic and at the Portland, Oregon, Psychological Service Center. He is codirector of Pacific University's Solutions for Anxiety Clinic. He has coauthored numerous book chapters on the topic of evidence-based assessment, diagnosis, and treatment of anxiety disorders. He is currently authoring an authoritative text on exposure treatments for anxiety disorders. He has coauthored multiple scientific journal articles on the topic of anxiety and somatoform disorders in peer-reviewed journals such as the *Journal of Anxiety Disorders, Behavior Modification,* and *Clinical Case Studies.* He serves on the editorial board of these journals. In his postdoctoral work, he has continued to research the role of ecologically relevant treatment approaches for complex, resistant, and chronic anxiety presentations. He has continually presented compelling findings about treating refractory cases in naturalistic settings at regional, national, and international conferences and congresses. In his teaching, he has instructed graduate students in the science and art of systematic and scientific assessment, case formulation, and empirically supported treatment planning and interventions. He has continued to supervise and consult on single-case research design, case series methods, and small-N methods. In his spare time, he heads a family-run, self-sufficient, ecologically sustainable farm.

Contributors

Jonathan S. Abramowitz
Mayo Clinic

Ron Acierno
Medical University of South Carolina

W. Stewart Agras
Stanford University School of Medicine

Lynn Alden
University of British Columbia, Canada

David O. Antonuccio
Veterans Administration Medical Center, Reno

Martin M. Antony
Anxiety Treatment and Research Center

Ruben Ardila
National University of Colombia

John G. Arena
Veterans Administration Medical Center-Augusta

L. Michael Ascher
Philadelphia College of Osteopathic Medicine

John Austin
Western Michigan University

Nathan H. Azrin
Nova Southeastern University

David H. Barlow
Boston University

Shawnée L. Basden
Boston University

D. A. Begelman
New Milford, Connecticut

Deborah C. Beidel
University of Maryland

Alan S. Bellack
University of Maryland School of Medicine

Gary R. Birchler
San Diego Healthcare System

Edward B. Blanchard
University of Albany-SUNY

Kirk A. Brunswig
University of Nevada, Reno

Kara Bunting
University of Nevada, Reno

Matthew J. Carpenter
Medical University of South Carolina

Bryan A. Castelda
SUNY at Binghamton

Hewitt B. Clark
University of South Florida

Michael Daniel
Pacific University

Judith R. Davidson
Université Laval, Canada

Gerald C. Davison
University of Southern California

Brett J. Deacon
Mayo Clinic

Douglas L. Delahanty
Kent State University

Dennis J. Delprato
University of Nevada, Las Vegas

John W. Donahoe
University of Massachusetts

Brad C. Donohue
University of Nevada, Las Vegas

E. Thomas Dowd
Kent State University

Barry A. Edelstein
West Virginia University

Kristal Ehrhardt
Western Michigan University

Paul M. G. Emmelkamp
University of Amsterdam, The Netherlands

Brad Evans
Pacific University

William Fals-Stewart
Research Institute on Addictions

Alisha Farley
University of Nevada, Las Vegas

Matthew T. Feldner
University of Vermont

Gene S. Fisch
Yale University

Mark R. Floyd
University of Nevada, Las Vegas

Edna B. Foa
University of Pennsylvania Health System

William C. Follette
University of Nevada, Reno

Cyril M. Franks
Rutgers University

Brian M. Freidenberg
University of Albany

Edward S. Friedman
Western Psychiatric Institute and Clinic

Ann M. Galloway
University of Nebraska Medical Center

Eileen Gambrill
University of California-Berkeley

Christine Hagie
Behavioral Counseling and Research Center

Tyish S. Hall
*University of Maryland and
     University of Nevada, Las Vegas*

Steven C. Hayes
University of Nevada, Reno

Stephen N. Haynes
University of Hawaii, Manoa

Nancy A. Heiser
University of Maryland

Michel Hersen
Pacific University

Sandy Hobbs
University of Paisley, Scotland

Derek R. Hopko
University of Tennessee-Knoxville

Sandra D. Hopko
University of Tennessee-Knoxville

Farrah Hughes
University of Tennessee, Knoxville

Jonathan D. Huppert
University of Pennsylvania

Javel Jackson
Georgia State University

Stanley Jenwick
University of California, Irvine

J. H. Kamphuis
University of Amsterdam, Netherlands

Ruth Kanfer
Arizona State University

Mary E. Kaplar
Bowling Green State University

Paul Karoly
Arizona State University

Alan E. Kazdin
Yale University

Karen Kate Kellum
University of Mississippi

Donald Kincaid
University of South Florida

Jordan T. Knab
University of South Florida

Robert J. Kohlenberg
University of Washington

Lesley Kovan
West Virginia University

Kristine Lake
EMDR Institute

Michael J. Lambert
Brigham Young University

James B. Lane
Pacific University

Marcus T. LaSota
University of Nevada, Las Vegas

Gary W. LaVigna
The Institute for Applied Behavior Analysis

Arnold A. Lazarus
Rutgers University

Craig W. LeCroy
University of Wisconsin

C. W. Lejuez
University of Maryland

Mark Levine
Behavioral Counseling and Research Center

Donald J. Levis
SUNY at Binghamton

Peter M. Lewinsohn
Oregon Research Institute

Noam Lindenboim
University of Washington

Marsha M. Linehan
University of Washington

Thomas W. Lombardo
University of Mississippi

Dani Maack
Pacific University

Jennifer B. Mainka
Eastern Michigan University

Barry M. Maletzky
Portland, Oregon

Richard W. Malott
Western Michigan University

Isaac M. Marks
King's College, United Kingdom

W. L. Marshall
Queen's University, Canada

Corby K. Martin
Pennington Biomedical Research Center

Thomas C. Mawhinney
University of Detroit, Mercy

Marita McCabe
Deakin University, Melbourne

Terry Michael McClanahan
The Permanente Medical Group, Inc.

Nathaniel McConaghy
University of New South Wales, Australia

F. Dudley McGlynn
Auburn University

Alison McLeish
University of Vermont

Donald H. Meichenbaum
University of Waterloo, Canada

Rhonda M. Merwin
University of Mississippi

Catherine Miller
Pacific University

Peter M. Miller
Medical University of South Carolina

William R. Miller
University of New Mexico

Raymond G. Miltenberger
North Dakota State University

Doil D. Montgomery
Nova Southeastern University

Charles M. Morin
Université Laval, Canada

Arthur M. Nezu
MCP Hahnemann University

Christine Maguth Nezu
MCP Hahnemann University

Matthew K. Nock
Harvard University

Raymond W. Novaco
University of California, Irvine

William H. O'Brien
Bowling Green State University

William T. O'Donohue
University of Nevada, Reno

Melanie L. O'Neill
University of British Columbia, Canada

Helen Orvaschel
Nova Southeastern University

Gordon L. Paul
University of Houston

Janet L. Pietrowski
Eastern Michigan University

Ann F. Philips
Dare Family Services

Joseph J. Plaud
Applied Behavioral Consultants, Inc.

Alan D. Poling
Western Michigan University

Roger Poppen
Southern Illinois University-Carbondale

Linda Krug Porzelius
St. Charles Medical Center

Lynn P. Rehm
University of Houston

David Reitman
Nova Southeastern University

Patricia A. Resick
University of Missouri, St. Louis

David C. S. Richard
Eastern Michigan University

Hank Robb
Pacific University

Miguel E. Roberts
University of Mississippi

Sushma T. Roberts
University of Mississippi

Thomas L. Rodebaugh
Temple University

Valerie Romero
University of Nevada, Las Vegas

Sheldon D. Rose
University of Wisconsin

Johan Rosqvist
Pacific University

Barbara O. Rothbaum
Emory University

Brent Rushall
South Dakota State University

Casey Sackett
University of Nevada, Reno

Josée Savard
Université Laval, Canada

Tamara P. Sbraga
University of Nevada, Reno

Carl Schrader
Behavioral Counseling and Research Center

B. J. Scott
Pacific University

Francine Shapiro
Eye Movement Desensitization and Reprocessing Institute

Tom Sharpe
University of Nevada, Las Vegas

Andrea Shreve-Nieger
West Virginia University

Eve M. Sledjeski
Kent State University

Shannan Smith-Janik
University of Virginia

Susan Snycerski
Western Michigan University

Ana A. Sobel
University of Missouri, St. Louis

Linda Carter Sobell
Nova Southeastern University

Stephanie L. Spear
University of Nevada, Reno

Adam Spira
West Virginia University

Melinda A. Stanley
University of Texas Mental Sciences Institute

Tiffany M. Stewart
Pennington Biomedical Research Center

Richard M. Suinn
Colorado State University

Alecia Sundsmo
Pacific University

Bethany A. Teachman
University of Virginia

Wendy Tenhula
University of Maryland, Baltimore

Michael E. Thase
Western Psychiatric Institute and Clinic

James T. Todd
Eastern Michigan University

Jessica J. Tracy
University of Mississippi

Aaron Tritch
Pacific University

Paula Truax
Pacific University

Georgiana Shick Tryon
City University of New York Graduate School

Warren W. Tryon
Fordham University

Mavis Tsai
University of Washington

Samuel M. Turner
University of Maryland

Jerome D. Ulman
Ball State University

E. A. Vargas
B. F. Skinner Foundation

Julie S. Vargas
B. F. Skinner Foundation

Ellen Vedel
University of Amsterdam

David A. Vermeersch
Loma Linda University

Angela E. Waldrop
Medical University of South Carolina

Ricks Warren
Anxiety Disorders Clinic, Lake Oswego, Oregon

William J. Warzak
University of Nebraska Medical Center

Marjorie E. Weishaar
Brown University

Brooke L. Whisenhunt
Southwest Missouri State University

Ursula S. Whiteside
University of Washington

Donald A. Williamson
Pennington Biomedical Research Center

B. Steven Willis
Dare Family Services

Thomas J. Willis
The Institute of Applied Behavior Analysis

Kelly G. Wilson
University of Mississippi

Patricia A. Wisocki
University of Massachusetts

Michael J. Zvolensky
University of Vermont

Preface

This first volume of the *Encyclopedia of Behavior Modification and Cognitive Behavior Therapy* was designed to bring together the expertise and experience of leading researchers and practitioners into a single, expansive overview of novel as well as thoroughly established therapeutic modification techniques for adults. The entries comprising Volume I vary broadly both in length and depth of description of specific strategies, but all are intended to give a range of interested parties immediate insight into the fundamentals of the methods described. Therefore, the collective proliferation of entries all adhere to a more straightforward style of writing and description, which will make even the most complex theories of learning, pathology, and change readily available to readers with less than an expert's knowledge base. Entries cut across a full range of mental health conditions and their respective treatments, with the aim of providing systematic and scientific evaluation of clinical interventions in a fashion that will lend itself to the particular style of treatment common to behavior modification and cognitive-behavioral therapy. The advantage, then, of this broad collection of entries in a single resource is that it provides scholars, researchers, clinicians, students, and other individuals or institutions alike both heuristic value and a solid starting point for any line of inquiry.

This first volume is devoted to adults, as it is the population most commonly encountered by the average researcher, clinician, and graduate student. Even though we limited this volume to the realm of adult interventions, we were still suitably impressed, if not a bit daunted, by the sheer number of methods we felt warranted inclusion. In our efforts to identify the range of topics that justifiably needed entries to make this truly a single resource, we have identified and included more than 150 entries. This rather large number of descriptions may at first seem unwieldy to the reader, but each entry follows a set pattern of outlining the method and particular issues pertinent to it. This leaves the reader with a user-friendly way of quickly identifying the key features and issues of any method of interest, as well as pointing them to more focused and technical resources should it be desired. This standardized format also allows for ready comparisons across methods of interest. The alphabetical listing of the methodologies will facilitate quick maneuvering between specific entries for such comparative purposes.

There are many contributors to Volume I alone, and numerous others have contributed and participated in various ways to its final culmination. First, we feel especially thankful to all of the contributors who graciously agreed to write about their respective areas of expertise. We compliment them on their outstanding quality of entries. Second, we are, as usual, extremely appreciative and impressed by our editorial assistant, Carole Londerée, who with organization and panache made the overarching task of producing this volume feasible. Third and finally, we wish to thank Sage Publications for recognizing the inherent value of the *Encyclopedia of Behavior Modification and Cognitive Behavior Therapy.*

—*Johan Rosqvist, PsyD*
Portland, Oregon

—*Michel Hersen, PhD, ABPP*
Forest Grove, Oregon

Introduction

The Encyclopedia of Behavior Modification and Cognitive Behavior Therapy was designed to enhance the resources available to scholars, practitioners, students, and other interested social science readers. The fact that this three-volume work is needed at this time is a testimonial to the pioneers in this field who only three or four decades ago were fighting the therapeutic establishment to have a voice. Now, of course, behavior modification, behavior therapy, and cognitive behavior therapy are part of the daily lexicon for all. Over the ensuing years, the range of application of all of these therapeutic and modification strategies has proliferated to a point where it literally is difficult to keep abreast of the field. One of the objectives of this encyclopedia, then, is to bring all of the most relevant aspects of the field together in readable, albeit brief format.

This three-volume work provides a thorough examination of components comprising behavior modification, behavior therapy, cognitive behavior therapy, and applied behavior analysis for both adult and child populations in a variety of settings (e.g., outpatient, institutional, and classroom). The specific volumes are as follows: *Volume I: Adult Clinical Applications, Volume II: Child Clinical Applications,* and *Volume III: Educational Applications.* Although the focus is on technical applications, the hundreds of entries also provide historical context to apprise readers of the parameters in which behavior therapists have worked, including research issues and strategies. Entries also contain descriptions of assessment, ethical concerns, theoretical differences, and the unique contributions of key figures in the field. In so doing, there are both biographical sketches and autobiographical sketches for the interested reader.

The entries in this encyclopedia have been written at a level that is appropriate for the educated clinical and social science reader. Indeed, entries have been written in jargon-free fashion, with explanations provided for specialized terminology. Rather than burdening the reader with a plethora of citations within the text, contributors were asked to simply present clear descriptions, but including suggestions for further reading at the end of each entry. The objective here has been to make this work as readable as possible for an interdisciplinary audience.

Major entries for specific strategies have followed a similar format:

1. Description of the Strategy

2. Research Basis

3. Relevant Target Populations and Exceptions

4. Complications

5. Case Illustration

6. Suggested Readings

Biographical sketches have included the following:

1. Birthplace and Date

2. Early Influences

3. Education History

4. Professional Models

5. Major Contributions to the Field

6. Current Work and Views

7. Future Plans

Many individuals have contributed to the fruition of this labor-intensive project. First, I thank my fellow editors, Johan Rosqvist, Alan Gross, Ronald Drabman, George Sugai, and Robert Horner, for their excellent work on this encyclopedia. Second, all of us thank the Advisory Board for their helpful suggestions throughout the process. Third, I thank all of the contributors for taking time out to share their expertise with us and to write in a clear fashion so that all can understand. Fourth, I thank Carole Londerée, my very able editorial assistant (who has made me swear to never again undertake such a complicated project), for keeping things on track. And fifth, but hardly least of all, thank you, James Brace-Thompson, and the terrific staff at Sage for shepherding us through the process. Your wise guidance has been much appreciated.

—*Michel Hersen, PhD, ABPP*
Forest Grove, Oregon

ACCEPTANCE AND COMMITMENT THERAPY

Most adult psychotherapies deal, implicitly or explicitly, with the effect of client thoughts and feelings on overt behavior. In the usual view, certain undesirable emotions or thoughts are believed to produce undesirable patterns of living. On that basis, these thoughts or emotions are targeted for change, control, or elimination. Such a normative focus in psychology is readily revealed both in the way behavioral disorders and their treatment technologies are named (e.g., disorders are "anxiety disorders" or "affective disorders"; treatments are "panic control therapy" or "cognitive restructuring").

In a behavior-analytic view, behavior includes everything that organisms do in interaction with the world, including subtle or private events such as thinking or feeling, but the relation between one psychological action and another always occurs in a historical and situational context. Thus, the question, "What thoughts or emotions control pathological behavior?" is changed to, "What types of contexts produce an undesirable relation between specific psychological activities, such as unhelpful thought-action or emotion-overt behavior relations?"

Acceptance and commitment therapy ("ACT," pronounced as one word, not as initials) is a behavior-analytically rationalized psychotherapy that is based on this core approach. Rather than trying to change private events, ACT attempts to recontextualize them and thus alter how they impact on other forms of activity. Several aspects of the normal social-verbal context for human action are thought to contribute to the establishment of undesirable control by private behaviors, and primary examples include (a) the impact of literal meaning and evaluation, (b) the use of verbal reason-giving as a valid explanation for individual behavior, and (c) social training that cognitive and emotional control can, and should, be achieved as a means to successful living.

LITERALITY

ACT is based on a comprehensive approach to human language and cognition, *relational frame theory* (RFT). According to RFT, the core feature of human language and cognition is arbitrarily applicable relational responding. There are three aspects to this kind of responding: the derivation of a bidirectional relation between events under arbitrary contextual control, combinations of such relations, and contextually controlled changes in stimulus functions due to both of these properties.

For example, by no more than 14 to 16 months, a human child taught to name an object will also orient toward the object given the name. That is, a relation between events learned in one direction will apply in both directions. These kinds of derived relations are based not upon the form of the events related, but rather on arbitrary cues for conventionally trained relational behavior. Once relations of this kind are derived, functions given to one member of a relational network will alter the functions of other events in the network based on the relation between them. If this same child loves to play with dogs and hears someone say "Oh, a dog," the child may approach without ever having responded to such a statement in the past and securing reinforcement.

The verbal community is constantly tightening these relations. This is what is meant in ACT by "the context of literality." In that context, one member of a relational network can be treated almost as if it were another member. Words are used as if they mean or are the things to which they refer. Thus, a word and the situation that it refers to can easily be confused, and many functions that would adhere to the situation become present with regard to the words. Consequently, when humans think something, it is not always obvious that it is even a thought. For example, a person may think, "This is awful." The person may then act as if they are in an awful situation, not in a situation in which they have the thought, "This is awful." This context of literality establishes functions for thought that might be appropriate to the situations constructed, but may not be for the thought itself.

ACT seeks to reduce the context of literality so that the ongoing process of thinking is more evident. The goal is that the products of that process will control less behavior when it is ineffective to do so.

REASON-GIVING AND EXPERIENTIAL CONTROL

A second source of undesirable relations between private events and overt action is reason-giving. People are required to give verbal explanations for their behavior, even if its sources are unknown or obscure. Thoughts and feelings are commonly pointed to in these reasons, an action that is supported by the culture. A person saying, "I felt so anxious I couldn't go" will certainly be thought to have said something reasonable and understandable. He or she may even garner sympathy or reassurance. "I have no idea why I didn't go" will probably receive a much less positive response.

Unfortunately, these rules come to control behavior as people come to believe their own reasons and explanations even when the true historical reasons for action may be remote and inaccessible. Thus, emotions or thoughts may indeed lead to maladaptive avoidance in part because it is "reasonable" to respond to one's thoughts and emotions in this fashion.

As an extension of this context, thoughts and feelings are often directly targeted for change as a means of living a more successful life. For example, a person with an "anxiety disorder" believes that anxiety explains his or her restricted life style and that

changes in living cannot or will not occur until this anxiety is better controlled. Unfortunately, direct attempts at cognitive and emotional control can often be counterproductive. For example, trying not to think negative thoughts tends to increase their frequency and behavior-regulatory power. Avoiding negative feelings likewise increases their behavioral impact.

In place of these contexts, ACT establishes a social-verbal community in therapy in which literal meaning and reason-giving are de-emphasized and experiential acceptance is encouraged. In its place, ACT emphasizes the importance of valued actions. The hope is that by changing these contextual features, unhelpful links between private and other behaviors is undermined and more flexible and effective behaviors will be produced.

SYNOPSIS OF ACT

There are typically at least seven aspects to ACT. These need not occur in any particular sequence, but the following sequence is most typical.

Confronting the System

In the first stage of ACT, the workability of existing solutions is examined. Most clients come into therapy with the general outlines of a "solution" to their problems. Usually, it consists of the elimination of disturbing emotions, thoughts, memories, impulses, and so on. From an ACT perspective, this eminently logical, sensible, and commonsense view of the "solution" is instead one aspect of the core clinical problem. As each previous attempt to "solve the problem" is examined, the underlying experiential-avoidance agenda is highlighted. The client's efforts at emotional and cognitive control are explored in detail, and in each case, the client's experience is considered to see whether this approach solved the problem. The enormous exertion and minimal benefit of previous efforts to solve the problem are emphasized. The sense that the client has of being stuck and the underlying fear that the situation as constructed is hopeless are also brought out and validated. Since the things clients have already attempted are typically logical, commonsense solutions, it becomes clear that some change beyond ordinary verbal logic is needed.

ACT relies a great deal on uses of language that are not linear, such as paradox and metaphor. Specific ACT-relevant themes are at the focus of such metaphorical talk. An example of a metaphor used in this phase of ACT is as follows:

Therapist: Let me give you a metaphor that might help see what I'm saying. The situation you are in is something like this. Imagine that you are blindfolded, given a tool bag, and told to run through a large field. So there you are, living your life, running through the field. Unknown to you, though, there are deep holes in this field. They are fairly widely spaced, but sooner or later you accidentally fall into one. Now, when you fall into the hole, you do the logical thing. You open the tool bag, take the tool you find there, and you try to get out. Unfortunately, the tool inside is a shovel. So you dig. And you dig. But digging is a thing that makes holes, not a way to get out of them. So the hole gets bigger and more elaborate. So you dig differently. You dig fast. You dig slowly. You take big scoops. You take little scoops. But still you are stuck. So maybe you try other things. You might try to figure out exactly how you fell in the hole. "If I just hadn't turned left at the rise, I wouldn't be in here," you might think. And, of course, that might be literally true, but it doesn't make any difference. Even if you knew every step you took, it wouldn't get you out of the hole. So you think, "Maybe I need a really great shovel." That's what you are asking from me. Maybe I have a gold-plated steam shovel. But I don't, and even if I did, I wouldn't use it. Shovels don't get people out of holes—they make them.

Client: So what is the solution?

Therapist: Well, it's not to dig your way out. Let's start with what your experience actually tells you. You know what you've been doing hasn't been working. But what I am asking you to consider is that it *can't* work. Until you open up to that, you will never let go of that shovel, because as far as you know, it's the only thing you've got. But until you let go of it, you have no room for anything else.

Confusion is used deliberately to prevent the client from intellectualizing and compartmentalizing his or her dilemma into the same solutions that have already failed. For example, the therapist might say, "Whatever you hear me saying right now, I want to assure you with 100% confidence that is not what I'm saying." This is actually so, since the client will believe that the therapist is pointing to another way to control or get rid of difficult feelings, when, in fact, it is that entire agenda that the ACT therapist is trying to lay aside.

Trying to Control Private Events Is the Problem

The second goal of ACT is to define emotional and cognitive control as the core problem. By the time the client comes to therapy, he or she has been well trained to view control of private events as both possible and critically important. There are at least four common sources for this view:

1. Direct efforts at control work well in many areas of living, and thus control of private events is likely due to generalization. We are taught to control our environments by deliberate and persistent action ("If at first you don't succeed, try, try again"). This general strategy is beneficial in the world of objects. If one wants to get rid of weeds in the garden, digging them up will work. There seems to be no obvious reason not to apply the same strategy to private events, even though these are historical events that often do not respond well to verbally guided change efforts.

2. Children are told to control emotions ("If you don't stop crying, I'll give you something to cry about") or thoughts ("Just forget it"), with the implication that this is readily done.

3. By hiding their own emotions and thoughts, adults give every indication to children that they can control private events at will. Thus, most people seem to grow up thinking that emotional and cognitive control is workable and even necessary.

4. Attempts to alter private events often seem to work, at least over the short run and when the emotions are relatively moderate. Distraction may remove a negative thought, for example, or relaxation may remove some of the bodily concomitants of anxiety. But if the effort is vitally important (e.g., because

the thought is too terrible ever to think again), these strategies may not work, as well. For example, even if distraction removes a thought, the person will rethink the thought when he or she checks to make sure it has stayed away. Thus, precisely when it is most important to control private events, these efforts are likely to fail.

In this part of ACT, clients are encouraged to examine their own experience to see whether the rule that works in the world of objects ("If you don't like something, figure out how to get rid of it and then get rid of it") has worked in the world inside the skin. ACT therapists suggest that a more accurate rule in this area is, "If you aren't willing to have it, then you've got it." Metaphors are used to make the point:

Therapist: Suppose I had you wired up to a very fine polygraph. It is such a fine machine that there is simply no way you could possibly be anxious without my knowing it. Now, imagine that I have given you a very simple task: Don't get anxious. However, to help motivate you, I pull out a gun. I tell you that to help you work on this task, I will hold the gun to your head. As long as you don't get anxious, I won't shoot you, but if you get anxious, you will be shot. What would happen?

Client: I'm a dead man.

Therapist: Right. But this is the situation you are in right now. Instead of a polygraph, you have something even better—your own nervous system. Instead of a gun, you have your self-esteem or your success in life apparently on the line. So guess what you get?

"I" Versus What "I Do"

The third goal of ACT is to help the client distinguish between the person he or she calls "I" and the problem behaviors that the client wants eliminated. The purpose is to find a psychological place from which it is possible to experience difficult thoughts and feelings without it seeming as though psychological destruction is imminent.

According to RFT, verbal training (particularly "deictic" relations such as here/there, now/then, and I/you) leads to a form of self-awareness that consists

not of the content of verbal reports, but of the perspective or locus of these reports. That is, humans learn not only to observe their own actions but also to do so from a consistent locus or point of view. In one sense of the term, this is what is usually called "I." It is important because it does not change once verbal behavior is sufficiently established. It seems timeless or even spiritual. This sense of "I" thus provides a basis from which acceptance of undesirable emotions does not threaten oneself.

ACT uses various experiential exercises and metaphors to help this sense of "I" come into focus. Most people can experientially recognize the essential continuity between the "I's referred to in the statements, "I went to first grade" and "I am in therapy now," even if many decades have passed from one to the other and virtually everything in the realm of content has changed.

Cognitive Defusion and Mindfulness

Cognitive defusion techniques erode the tight verbal relations that establish stimulus functions through relational learning. A wide variety of techniques are used at this point in ACT to begin to separate thoughts, emotions, and so on from the person having them. For example, we ask clients at least temporarily to adopt a particular verbal style in therapy, saying, "I'm having the thought that I can't go to the mall" (as opposed to simply stating, "I can't go to the mall") or "I'm having the evaluation that I'm a bad person" (as opposed to "I'm a bad person"). Another example of a defusion technique is the repeated word exercise, first used by Titchener. It consists of an exploration of the sensory or perceptual properties of a referent of a short (usually single-syllable) word, followed by a minute of the client and therapist saying that word out loud until it loses all meaning.

Mindfulness exercises are used to contact events in the here and now, without examining them through the filter of evaluative and judgmental language. A variety of mindfulness exercises are used in ACT, such as imagining watching one's thoughts as they float by like leaves on a stream.

Letting Go of the Struggle

In this phase of ACT, clients are encouraged to deliberate experiencing thoughts and feelings that, if taken literally, must be avoided. ACT therapists encourage clients not only to stop struggling, but seemingly to embrace the very things that they most dread.

Many techniques are used in this process, especially "willingness exercises." Avoided private events are brought into the therapy room (via imagery or exercises) and dissembled into component pieces: bodily sensations, thoughts, behavioral predispositions, memories, and so on. In all cases, the goal is not to gain control over them, but to experience them without any attempt to modify or escape them. Avoided events are sought out in vivo, with the purpose of letting go of all avoidance and instead feeling feelings as feelings, sensing sensations as sensations, thinking thoughts as thoughts, and so on.

Values

It is only within the context of values that acceptance, defusion, and overt action come together into a sensible whole. ACT therapists often do values work before other ACT components for that reason. A value is a direction that can be instantiated in behavior but not possessed like an object. ACT therapists ask their clients, "What do you want your life to stand for?" In this phase of treatment, a client is asked to list values in different life domains, such as family, intimate relationships, health, spirituality, and so on.

Various evocative exercises are used to develop more clarity about fundamental values. For example, the ACT therapist may ask clients to write out what they would most like to see on their tombstones or the eulogies they would want to hear at their own funerals. When values are clarified, achievable goals that embody those values, concrete actions that would produce those goals, and specific barriers to performing these actions are identified.

Commitment and Behavior Change

The final goal of ACT is committed action linked to chosen values. The goal is to build over behavioral patterns, linked to values, which are organized into larger and larger behavioral units. Specific behavior change strategies are developed, as in most forms of behavior therapy, but the larger context of ACT is the verbal environment that has been created in therapy that allows no logical escape or verbal defense. The only issue is doing what works. Thus, ACT tries to establish a discrimination between self-rules that

cannot be followed effectively (i.e., rules of emotional avoidance) and self-rules that can be followed effectively and, if followed, will lead to positive consequences (e.g., commitments to behavior change).

—*Steven C. Hayes and Casey Sackett*

See also: *Cognitive Behavior Therapy (Vol. I); Motivational Enhancement Therapy (Vol. I); Motivational Interviewing (Vol. I); Relational Frame Theory (Vol. 1)*

Suggested Readings

Hayes, S. C., Strosahl, K., & Wilson, K. G. (1999). *Acceptance and commitment therapy: An experiential approach to behavior change.* New York: Guilford Press.

AGRAS, W. STEWART

I was born in London, on May 17, 1929. The most important early influence was that of my family, which, being medically oriented, determined my initial career choice. My education history includes Middlesex Hospital, London (now University College School of Medicine, 1950–1956). Because there was no formal psychiatry training program in the United Kingdom at that time, I entered the program at McGill University, Canada (1956–1962). During this time, I completed a residency in adult psychiatry, 1 year of child psychiatry, and 2 years of fellowship at the Montreal Children's Hospital. During my residency, two individuals stood out as professional model influences. The first was Eric Wittkower, a psychoanalyst who was interested in psychosomatic medicine and aroused my curiosity about the interaction between the environment and biological processes. The second was Ewen Cameron, chair of the Department of Psychiatry at McGill, whose seminars concentrating on the nuances of interpersonal exchanges in recorded interactions helped to focus me on the richness of interpersonal behavior. However, the most important influence occurred after I had joined the faculty at the University of Vermont, when I met Harold Leitenberg, who had received his PhD from the University of Indiana in operant conditioning. We worked together applying the principles of operant conditioning to a number of clinical conditions, largely using single-case methodology. This was a rich educational experience in experimental methods. This experience also introduced me to senior individuals in the field of applied behavior analysis, such as Montrose Wolf and Todd Risley, whose research and respect for a collegial approach to research was most important to me. Through their influence, I became editor of the *Journal of Applied Behavior Analysis.*

MAJOR CONTRIBUTIONS TO THE FIELD

From the broadest perspective, I believe my most salient contribution has been, along with a few other pioneering academic psychiatrists, to introduce behavior therapy procedures to the field of psychiatry. Later, I was influential in the development of behavioral medicine in the United States, establishing one of the first behavioral medicine programs and helping to found the Society for Behavioral Medicine, becoming the first president of that organization.

From a research perspective, my first contribution together with Leitenberg and colleagues was to demonstrate that environmental contingencies such as reinforcement were widely applicable across a variety of psychiatric syndromes, such as phobias, obsessive-compulsive disorder, anorexia nervosa, and schizophrenic delusions, using controlled single-case experiments. Moreover, the use of such contingencies was often significantly therapeutic in these disorders. Having demonstrated this important principle, we, together with David Barlow and others, went on to show that exposure to, and practice in, a feared situation was necessary for recovery in all phobic disorders. Isaac Marks and his colleagues at the Institute of Psychiatry in London reported the same finding working with different methods, and the finding has been replicated by others.

I became interested in the use of nonpharmacological treatment for essential hypertension, investigating the effects of relaxation training and weight loss on blood pressure, demonstrating their effectiveness either as a first level of treatment or as an adjunctive treatment to pharmacological management. In the late 1970s, it became evident that the number of patients with bulimia nervosa coming to our clinics for treatment was rapidly increasing. This led our group to conduct some of the first studies using variants of cognitive-behavioral therapy (CBT) for bulimia nervosa, investigating the combination of medication and CBT and extending our findings to binge-eating disorder. Cognitive-behavioral treatment appears to be the most effective approach for both bulimia nervosa and binge-eating disorder, more effective than medication or

other psychotherapies. However, we also showed that interpersonal therapy, although slower to work, appears to be equally effective in the longer term. Other work included laboratory studies investigating the proximal triggers of binge eating. Paralleling these investigations, we have just completed a study of children and their families from birth to 11 years of age aimed at identifying early risk factors for obesity and the eating disorders.

CURRENT WORK

My current work continues my interest in the eating disorders. It includes two multisite studies investigating treatment effectiveness and the mechanisms by which treatment works. To make more definitive statements about the effectiveness of particular treatments, it has become necessary to recruit larger numbers of participants to treatment trials. Hence the need to involve more than one site, so that a relatively large number of participants can be recruited in a reasonable amount of time.

FUTURE PLANS

Having delineated early risk factors for obesity, the next step should be a study in which such factors are altered to determine whether childhood obesity, which is increasing at a rapid pace, can be prevented. I would also plan to follow up on the findings of our present therapy studies. In addition, I will continue to mentor promising young behavioral scientists to ensure a steady flow of new talent to the field.

—*W. Stewart Agras*

See also: Applied Behavior Analysis (Vol. I); Barlow, David H. (Vol. I); Single-Case Research (Vol. I);

ANGER MANAGEMENT

DESCRIPTION OF THE TREATMENT STRATEGY

Providing therapy for persons having recurrent anger problems is a challenging clinical enterprise. This turbulent emotion, ubiquitous in everyday life, is a feature of a wide range of clinical disorders. It is commonly observed in various personality, psychosomatic, and conduct disorders; in schizophrenia, bipolar mood disorders, organic brain disorders, and impulse control dysfunctions; and in a variety of conditions resulting from trauma. The central problematic characteristic of anger in the context of such clinical conditions is that it is "dysregulated"; that is, its activation, expression, and effects occur without appropriate controls.

Cognitive-behavioral therapy (CBT) for anger augments clients' self-regulatory capacities. It aims to minimize anger frequency, intensity, and duration and to moderate anger expression. It is an adjunctive treatment for a targeted clinical problem, seeking to remedy the emotional turbulence associated with subjective distress, detrimental effects on personal relationships, health impairments, and the manifold harmful consequences of aggressive behavior. The main components are cognitive restructuring, arousal reduction, and enhancement of behavioral skills. A key feature of its implementation is therapist-guided progressive exposure to provocation, in conjunction with which anger-regulatory coping skills are acquired.

The term *anger management* has become a rubric for a variety of interventions, as well as becoming common parlance. Therefore, it is useful to distinguish levels of therapeutic intervention for anger, differentiating (a) general clinical care for anger, (b) anger management, and (c) anger treatment. *General clinical care for anger* identifies it as a clinical need and addresses it through various counseling, psychotherapeutic, and psychopharmacological provisions, including client education, support groups, and eclectic treatments, without a formal intervention structure. In contrast, *anger management* typically refers to a structured CBT intervention, which originally was applied as an individual therapy but now is often provided in a group mode, largely psychoeducational in format, such as occurs in court-referred or school-based programs and in general public workshops. Such programs typically follow a topical sequence, covering situational activators ("triggers"), how thoughts and beliefs influence anger, self-observation, various relaxation techniques, problem-solving and conflict resolution strategies, and other cognitive and behavioral coping skills, such as calming self-statements, effective communication, and appropriate assertiveness. There is wide variation in anger management programs, which are now marketed commodities.

Anger treatment, as a cognitive-behavioral therapy, is distinguished from these other levels of intervention by its theoretical grounding, systematization, complexity, and depth of therapeutic approach. It is best provided on an individual basis and may require a preparatory phase to facilitate treatment engagement. Increased depth is associated with thoroughness of assessment, attention to core needs of the clients, greater individual tailoring to client needs, greater specialization in techniques, and the need for clinical coordination and supervision. A specialized form of CBT anger treatment follows a *stress inoculation approach,* which involves therapist-guided, graded exposure to provocation stimuli to facilitate anger control. This occurs *in vitro* through imaginal and role play provocations in the clinic, and *in vivo* through planned testing of coping skills in anger-inducing situations, as established by a hierarchy of provocation scenarios collaboratively constructed by the client and therapist.

People with serious anger problems are often ambivalent about earnestly engaging in treatment, largely due to the value that they ascribe to anger in dealing with life's adversities. Activation of anger may usefully serve to engage aggression in combat and to overcome fear, but in everyday contexts, anger is often maladaptive. Because of the instrumental value of anger and aggression, many clients do not readily recognize the personal costs that their anger routines incur; and because of the embeddedness of anger in long-standing psychological distress, there is inertia to overcome in motivating change efforts. Getting leverage for therapeutic change can be an elusive goal, particularly when referrals for anger treatment entail some element of coercion. This is a salient issue in forensic settings, where clients are guarded about self-disclosure.

Anger is often entrenched in personal identity and may be derivative of a traumatic life history. While many high-anger patients present with a hard exterior, they can be psychologically fragile, especially those having histories of recurrent abuse or trauma or for whom abandonment and rejection have been significant life themes. As anger may be embedded with other distressed emotions, accessing anger is often not straightforward. A "preparatory phase" may be required to foster engagement, develop core competencies necessary for treatment (emotion identification, self-monitoring, communication about anger experiences, and arousal reduction), and build trust in the therapist, providing an atmosphere conducive to personal disclosure and collaboration.

Central to CBT for anger control is the idea that anger is produced by the self-appraised meaning of events and the person's resources for dealing with them, rather than by objective properties of the events. Sometimes anger occurs as a fast-triggered, reflexive response, while other times it results from deliberate attention, extended search, and conscious review. Anger activation is intrinsically linked to perceptions of threat and injustice. Anger control CBT targets the way people process information, remember their experiences, and cognitively orient to situations of stress or challenge. Anger, as an engagement of the organism's survival systems in response to threat, involves interplay of cognitive, physiological, and behavioral components. Cognitive factors include knowledge structures, such as expectations and beliefs, and appraisal processes, which are schematically organized as mental representations about environment-behavior relationships entailing rules governing threatening situations. Arousal or physiological factors include activation in the cardiovascular, endocrine, and limbic systems, and by tension in the skeletal musculature. Anger is affected by hormone levels (neurotransmitters), low stimulus thresholds for the activation of arousal, and diminished inhibitory control. Neurobiological mechanisms involve the amygdala, the prefrontal cortex, and serotonin. Behavioral factors include conditioned and observationally learned repertoires of anger-expressive behavior, including aggression but also avoidance. Implicit in the cognitive labeling of anger is an inclination to act antagonistically toward the source of the provocation. However, an avoidant style of responding, as in some personality and psychosomatic disorders, can foment anger by leaving the provocation unchanged or exacerbated.

CBT anger treatment targets enduring change in cognitive, arousal, and behavioral systems. It centrally involves cognitive restructuring and acquisition of arousal reduction and behavioral coping skills, achieved through changing valuations of anger and augmenting self-monitoring capacity. Because it addresses anger as grounded and embedded in aversive and often traumatic life experiences, it entails the evocation of distressed emotions—fear, sadness, and shame, as well as anger. Therapeutic work centrally involves the learning of new modes of responding to cues previously evocative of anger in the context of relating to the therapist, and it periodically elicits negative sentiment on the part of the therapist to the frustrating, resistive, and unappreciative behavior of the client.

Stress inoculation for anger control involves the following seven key components: (1) client education about anger, stress, and aggression; (2) self-monitoring of anger frequency, intensity, and situational triggers; (3) construction of a personal anger provocation hierarchy, created from the self-monitoring data and used for the practice and testing of coping skills; (4) arousal reduction techniques of progressive muscle relaxation, breathing-focused relaxation, and guided-imagery training; (5) cognitive restructuring of anger schemas by altering attentional focus, modifying appraisals, and using self-instruction; (6) training behavioral coping skills in communication, diplomacy, respectful assertiveness, and strategic withdrawal, as modeled and rehearsed with the therapist; and (7) practicing the cognitive, arousal-regulatory, and behavioral coping skills while visualizing and role playing progressively more intense anger-arousing scenes from the personal hierarchies.

Provocation hierarchy scenarios are designed to capture the client's sensitivities to provoking elements, such as the antagonist's tone of voice or nuances of facial expression. Each scenario ends with provocative aspects of the situation (i.e., not giving the client's reaction), so that it serves as a stimulus scene. The therapist directs this graduated exposure to provocation, knowing the moderating variables that will exacerbate or buffer the magnitude of the anger reaction, in case the scene needs to be intensified or attenuated in potency. Prior to presentation of hierarchy items, whether in imaginal or role-playing mode, anger control coping is rehearsed, and arousal reduction is induced through deep breathing and muscle relaxation. Successful completion of a hierarchy item occurs when the client indicates little or no anger to the scene and can envision or enact effective coping in dealing with the provocation.

An effort is made to anticipate circumstances in the client's life that could be anger provoking and the obstacles to anger control that might arise. People having anger difficulties are often without adequate supportive relationships to provide reinforcement for anger control. Follow-up sessions are typically arranged for relapse prevention to ascertain what coping skills have proven to be most efficacious and to boost treatment in areas in need of further work. Because of the reputations acquired by high-anger people, the reactions of others to them can be slow to change. This can lead to relapse and requires therapeutic attention at follow-up.

RESEARCH BASIS

There is convergent evidence that CBT for anger produces therapeutic gains. Several meta-analytic reviews of treatment efficacy have found medium effect sizes for various CBT interventions, indicating that the large majority of those treated were improved; however, many of the randomized control studies have been done with college students who volunteer for treatment after being identified as high in anger by screening questionnaires. Such samples do not reflect the clinical needs of the angry patients seen by mental health service providers in community and institutional settings. There have been controlled studies with seriously disordered patients, and outcomes in such studies have been positive. The CBT stress inoculation approach to anger control has shown significant effects in controlled studies with adolescents in residential care, adolescent offenders, forensic patients, institutionalized intellectually disabled adults, and Vietnam veterans with severe posttraumatic stress disorder, such as patients having intense, recurrent postwar anger and aggressive behavior.

Meta-analytic reviews fail to include case study reports and multiple-baseline studies with clinical populations for whom CBT and stress inoculation for anger have produced significant clinical gains, for hospitalized depressed patients, child-abusing parents, chronically aggressive patients, emotionally disturbed boys, brain-damaged patients, mentally handicapped patients, adolescents in residential treatment, and hospitalized forensic patients.

Brief CBT anger management, varying across studies from 3 to 16 group sessions, has been successfully used in prisons, but outcome evaluations in these prison-based studies have not been rigorous, and results of efficacy have been uneven. In that regard, the treatment engagement and assessment reactivity issues highlighted earlier are highly relevant.

RELEVANT TARGET POPULATIONS AND EXCEPTIONS

Across categories of clients, the three key issues of appropriateness for CBT anger are: (1) the extent to which the person has an anger-regulatory problem, implying that acquisition or augmentation of anger control capacity would reduce psychological distress, aggression, or other offending behavior, or a physical health problem, such as high blood pressure; (2) whether the person does recognize or can be induced to see the costs of his or her anger/aggression routines and is thus motivated to engage in treatment; and (3) whether the person can sit and attend for approximately 45 minutes. The latter criterion applies especially to hospitalized patients. The stress inoculation approach to anger has been successfully applied to institutionalized mentally disordered (schizophrenia and affective disorders) and intellectual disabled persons (mild to borderline). A treatment "preparatory phase" is often needed for institutionalized patients.

People who are violent are often referred for anger treatment (e.g., incarcerated offenders and spousal abusers or enraged drivers in the community). However, CBT anger treatment is not indicated for those whose violent behavior is not emotionally mediated, whose violent behavior fits their short-term or long-term goals, or whose anger is not acknowledged as having costs. Little is known about the efficacy of CBT anger treatment with psychopaths, but it is doubtful that it would be suitable. As well, persons who are acutely psychotic or whose delusions significantly interfere with daily functioning are not suitable candidates. Persons with substance abuse disorders also require prior treatment to engage in anger therapy.

COMPLICATIONS

For many clients, access to anger treatment often arises through the criminal justice system following acts of violence, which has consequential implications for the client of assessed treatment outcome. Therapeutic engagement in this context will be subject to significant demand characteristics, and such "dynamics" clearly have to be moderated throughout the course of treatment. It is all too easy to refer violent offenders for anger management. Thus, it is crucial to identify whether the violent behavior is a product of anger dyscontrol. Conversely, because current psychiatric diagnostic systems do not differentiate anger as an independent clinical disorder, access to health/social care services for some people may have been impeded.

When anger treatment is conducted within institutions, it must accommodate to the constraints and demands of the custodial environment. Treatment efforts to help the client acquire "normalized" anger expression and coping behaviors need to be tempered in the face of prevailing subcultural norms and practical constraints on personal freedoms and opportunities. The client's immediate circumstances are likely quite distinct from the "problem context" of the original anger difficulties. This presents challenges for baseline and outcome assessment, as well as for the content of in-session treatment and prescriptions for between-session activities.

Many people referred for serious anger problems will also be experiencing a primary comorbid Axis I or II disorder (e.g., substance misuse, schizophrenia, personality disorder), which may directly affect the nature and course of the anger problem. Disentanglement of the comorbidity contribution within the cognitive, arousal, and behavioral domains becomes a key aspect of anger assessment and a significant component of the overall formulation. Treatment content will be required to take these factors into account, either through parallel interventions or synthesis of intervention focus and content.

CASE ILLUSTRATION

"Sandy" was a 26-year-old private in the British Army, whose contact with the Military Psychiatric Services arose following an overdose of medication, which was deemed to be a "cry for help." During the resultant hospitalization, he tended to be generally angry and irritable.

Of specific concern were episodes Sandy reported of "road rage," said to arise from bad driving by miscreants, whom he pursued and confronted. He recognized that such rages were negatively affecting him and his family. Such problems had emerged following two major road traffic accidents during operations in the Gulf and Kosovo, which had rendered him physically incapable of further duties. The situation was exacerbated by his frustration with his "treatment" by the army, compounded by the apparent loss of critical medical documentation regarding these incidents. He was convinced there was a "conspiracy" to deny responsibility and avoid "duty of care" toward him. His physical problems substantially restricted activity and caused daily discomfort. This, in turn, served as a constant reminder of his mistreatment.

Sandy had become increasingly reclusive, so as to minimize anger provocation. He avoided car usage, and barring forays to his local pub, where he regularly drank to excess, he remained at home. He was estranged from his wife and son, who feared his outbursts. His sleep was severely disrupted, and his mood oscillated between anger and "depression."

Formal assessment of posttraumatic stress disorder was negative. Examination of the historical, contextual, and constituent (cognitive, affective, and behavioral) elements of his anger problems gave attention to aspects of anger dyscontrol that might relate to instances of aggressive behavior and the potential influence of comorbid factors, such as alcohol misuse.

The assessment identified long-standing difficulties with anger and aggression. Sandy had grown up in a physically abusive environment, and his enlistment served as a means of escape. Prior to enlisting, he had been involved in a number of violent incidents, one of which had led to a jail sentence of 2 months. A model soldier throughout his career, he viewed his inability to control anger and aggression as a massive failure undermining his reputation as a good soldier.

The severity of Sandy's problems called for individualized anger treatment, and considerable attention was given to building client-therapist trust and engagement. Diary recordings provided real-time critical incidents for exploration, separating cognitive, arousal, and behavioral aspects. Day-to-day driving events readily triggered a prevailing anger schema relating to conspiracy and mistreatment. Social withdrawal recurrently served as an opportunity for "paranoiac" rumination, which maintained high levels of arousal and sensitivity. Therapeutic intervention predominantly focused on changing hostile attribution distortions through enhanced self-monitoring, cognitive restructuring, and reality testing. In parallel, arousal reduction techniques and strategies were adopted to minimize reactivity in provoking situations. Stress inoculation involved rerunning previous provocations and identifying alternative response strategies.

Most significantly, Sandy was able to challenge his "paranoic" worldview, replacing his tendency to see "conspiracy" with more benign appraisals of "fallibility" and "incompetence." This was a springboard for change in other areas. Although bad driving still makes him anxious, his difficulties with rage have all but resolved. During medical discharge from the army, with its associated administrative and logistic provocations, he has managed his anger and aggression, even in the face of high provocation (e.g., theft from his house). He stabilized his relations with his family and friends and reduced his misuse of alcohol. He is much less socially reclusive, and overall, his reported sleep difficulties are much improved. Reflecting on the significance of the gains he achieved, he said that although he would not wish to endure such challenges again, having had to face down his difficulties has "made (me) a better person."

—*Raymond W. Novaco and Stanley Jenwick*

See also: *Behavioral Contracting (Vol. I); Coverant Control (Vol. I); Cue-Controlled Relaxation (Vol. I)*

Suggested Readings

Beck, A. T. (1999). *Prisoners of hate: The cognitive basis of anger, hostility, and violence.* New York: HarperCollins.

Beck, R., & Fernandez, E. (1998). Cognitive behavior therapy in the treatment of anger: A meta-analysis. *Cognitive Therapy and Research, 22,* 63–75.

Chemtob, C. M., Novaco, R. W., Hamada, R., & Gross, D. (1997). Cognitive-behavioral treatment for severe anger in posttraumatic stress disorder. *Journal of Consulting and Clinical Psychology, 65,* 184–189.

Feindler, E. L., & Ecton, R. B. (1986). *Adolescent anger control: Cognitive therapy techniques.* New York: Pergamon Press.

Meichenbaum, D. (1985). *Stress inoculation training.* New York: Pergamon Press.

Novaco, R. W. (1986). Anger as a clinical and social problem. In R. Blanchard & C. Blanchard (Eds.), *Advances in the study of aggression* (Vol. 2, pp. 1–67). New York: Academic Press.

Novaco, R. W. (1997). Remediating anger and aggression with violent offenders. *Legal and Criminological Psychology, 2,* 77–88.

Novaco, R. W., & Chemtob, C. M. (2002). Anger and combat-related posttraumatic stress disorder. *Journal of Traumatic Stress, 15,* 123–132.

Renwick, S. J., Ramm, M., Black, L., & Novaco, R. W. (1997). Anger treatment with forensic hospital patients. *Legal and Criminological Psychology, 2,* 103–116.

Siegman, A. W., & Smith, T. W. (1994). *Anger, hostility, and the heart.* Hillsdale, NJ: Erlbaum.

ANXIETY/ANGER MANAGEMENT TRAINING

DESCRIPTION OF THE STRATEGY

Both anxiety and anger have serious effects on emotional and physical health. High anxiety or stress may reflect disorders such as generalized anxiety disorder (GAD), posttraumatic stress disorder (PTSD), or phobic disorder. Even in reasonably healthy persons, high stress can interfere with performance, such as public speaking or sport performances. Academic work can suffer when there is test anxiety, and reasonable decision making can be difficult when a person is under stress. In a similar way, high anger can lead to negative behaviors culminating in violence to others, self-injury, and even property breakage or destruction. Child abuse and domestic or workplace violence have become serious concerns of society. Interestingly, both anxiety and anger have negative physical health outcomes: High levels are associated with vulnerability to diseases such as respiratory diseases and heart disease and with higher mortality rates. *Anxiety/anger management training* (AMT) is a behavioral intervention that has proven effective for diverse anxiety-based disorders as well as for anger management. AMT is unique in being equally applicable to focused anxiety, such as phobias or test/math/performance anxieties, as well as general anxiety conditions. Similarly, AMT is equally effective in controlling anger that is directional and focused, as well as generalized anger states.

Anxiety/anger management training (AMT) was originally designed in the 1970s as brief behavioral treatment for anxiety, an alternative to exposure or psychotherapy approaches. Unlike exposure, AMT trains the individual in relaxation to eliminate the arousal from the exposure experience. The person therefore has a coping skill to use to directly control the anxiety-arousal state. Basically, relaxation is used to deactivate the emotional arousal. The exposure part of AMT is for the purpose of having the patient experience the emotional arousal in order to practice eliminating the arousal by use of relaxation skills.

AMT also systematically uses steps to increase self-control and self-reliance aspects. Graduated homework assignments assure transferring these skills to real-life settings. The typical AMT session covers six to eight structured sessions, beginning with relaxation training. As the relaxation skill is acquired, AMT sessions then use visualization to recall anxiety/anger, followed by application of relaxation to eliminate the arousal. As the patient demonstrates success, further sessions direct the patient to be able to identify behavioral or cognitive signs that reflect the beginnings of anxiety/anger arousal. The patient is then trained in initiating relaxation when these signs are noted in order to abort the arousal before the anxiety/anger escalates out of control. The total number of sessions depends upon the rate of progress of the patient in acquiring relaxation skills and in the application of relaxation to reduce the anxiety/anger arousal. Initial sessions are characterized by active direction by the therapist, while later sessions involve increased self-direction by the patient in achieving relaxation, experiencing emotional arousal through visualization, and returning to relaxation to reduce and/or eliminate the arousal state.

In 1986, AMT was applied to anger management as the similarities between anxiety and anger were recognized. Both involve emotional arousal, involving physiological changes (e.g., increased sweating during anxiety or increased blood pressure during anger), behavioral changes (e.g., anxious hand clenching or angry verbal outbursts), cognitive changes (e.g., anxious worries or angry thoughts), or subjective feelings (e.g., of panic or blowing up). Both emotions are experienced as powerful impulses that are disruptive and appear out of control. Both emotions may remain ambiguous, as in generalized anxiety or angry outbursts that seem to occur unpredictably. Both can also have a more specific focus: For anxiety, the focus can be specific, such as in phobias; for anger, the focus can also be specific, as in child abuse.

The AMT strategy uses imagery of a previous experience to precipitate anxiety (or anger) arousal during the session. But AMT does not stop with this exposure; the person is then guided to applying relaxation, using relaxation to deactivate the emotional arousal. As control is gained, the individual is then helped to identify personal physiological, behavioral, or thought symptoms present when anxious/angry. The person then learns to use the relaxation as soon as such symptoms signal the beginning stages of anxiety or anger arousal. In effect, such symptoms now become useful cues to trigger the relaxation, thereby aborting the arousal state before it gets out of control.

Each session is tailored to the progress of the individual. Relaxation skills are taught early, and when firmly in place, the arousal is prompted and the person is firmly guided in reinstituting the relaxation until the emotion is deactivated. As the individual's competence and confidence increases, the individual assumes more responsibility for initiating relaxation coping in response to the arousal. Homework moves from practicing relaxation in a quiet environment, to relaxing outside the home (e.g., while riding in a bus/car), to initiating the relaxation to deal with a minor stress (or anger-associated) event, to initiating and maintaining the relaxation control when engaging in a highly stressful/anger-provoking experience. AMT can be completed in six to eight 50-minute sessions.

RESEARCH BASIS

Research studies over 30 years have confirmed the value of AMT for a variety of anxiety-associated problems. These include generalized anxiety disorder, phobic disorder, posttraumatic stress disorder, hypertension associated with anxiety, pain exacerbated by anxiety, and various types of performance anxieties.

AMT has been more effective than no treatment, relaxation training only, and placebo. AMT for phobic conditions is as effective as desensitization, stress inoculation training, or cognitive therapy. However, the positive results of AMT are maintained over longterm follow-up, such as 2 years, with individuals reporting reduction of new anxieties not confronted in the original AMT sessions. This suggests that AMT is actually teaching a skill that is then being applied by the individuals to cope with other stresses. In fact, an important finding was that levels of self-confidence increase following AMT. One study also found AMT more beneficial than psychodynamic therapy for GAD. AMT has also been found effective for both anxiety-related problems and for anger control.

In contrast, desensitization is generally limited to identifiable fears, does not transfer to new fears, and is not designed for self-control training. Also, research confirms that AMT can be delivered in either an individual or a small-group setting.

When ancillary effects of AMT are examined, results show an increase in self-confidence and self-esteem, a decrease in negative thoughts (worries), and an increase in positive thoughts. There is a small literature demonstrating that AMT for anxiety can lead to reduction in mild depressive symptoms. This may be related to the increase in self-efficacy and the decrease of negative-thought schemas.

RELEVANT TARGET POPULATIONS AND EXCEPTIONS

Although initially aimed at GAD patients, AMT has proven effective for many conditions associated with anxiety, such as phobic disorders, PTSD, anxious persons facing stressful medical procedures, and patients with physical disorders relating to stress, such as essential hypertension or pain exacerbated by anxiety.

AMT is also effective for persons with extremely high levels of anger, whether the anger has an identifiable provocation, such as road rage, or the precipitant is ambiguous.

AMT also has been valuable in enhancing patients' use of psychotherapy in a study of chronic schizophrenic patients. Students suffering from test or mathematics anxiety have received benefits from AMT. Although no direct studies have involved ethnic minority populations or children, indirect anecdotal reports suggest AMT should be appropriate. For instance, one research study reported that AMT was useful with Japanese men in Japan, and AMT was successfully incorporated in a stress management workshop for minority adolescents.

Certain individuals may have difficulty progressing in AMT. The ability to experience anxiety/anger arousal is a foundation; an inability to experience this arousal through imagery or recall of a prior event is a problem for training. This can sometimes be handled by determining the reason and resolving the obstacle, for example, if trust in the therapeutic environment needs strengthening or reassurances of safety are needed. Reliance upon recent in vivo experiences can be a solution.

Some individuals may prefer first wanting to identify the situational, interpersonal, or psychodynamic source of their anxiety/anger. AMT may appear to these patients as irrelevant unless they are able to see that emotions often prevent clarity of insight. It might be necessary to explain that by using AMT to reduce the emotion, the patient might be free to pursue core issues. Research has reported that some clients are better able to identify the source of their difficulties after AMT reduces the intensity of their emotional states. In some cases, once the anxiety/anger is under control, individuals are more responsive to other coping-skills training, such as conflict resolution or communication skills.

COMPLICATIONS

Some anxious patients experience an increase in anxiety when introduced to relaxation training. This may represent a fear of loss of control or a fear of unfamiliar experiences. Such an effect is readily identified during the first relaxation training through observation of increase in muscle tension levels and reports of heightened anxiety from the patient. One solution is to provide the patient with greater control over each step

of relaxation training. Our preferred model for teaching relaxation uses the progressive muscle relaxation approach, whereby each muscle group is tensed, then relaxed, while the patient notes the corresponding change in experience. The AMT procedure involves clearly instructing the patient in the procedure and its goals, and identifying the exact muscle sequence (e.g., first the hands, then the upper arms, followed by the forehead, etc.).

When relaxation precipitates anxiety, more time should be taken to describe and explain the progressive relaxation procedure. Furthermore, the patients should be advised that they can stop at any stage for questions. Patients are then asked, rather than told, to try the tension/relaxation cycle with the first muscle group in a familiarization step, then to do the upper arm, and so on. Their cooperation is then sought to again try the hands with their eyes closed and sitting more comfortably. For highly fearful persons, they are then asked to describe the sensations, and their readiness to try the next muscle group is requested, and so on. In each step, the therapist adopts the attitude that the muscle tensing and relaxing is being attempted more as a trial to learn about the procedure. By taking such small steps to approximate actual training, discomfort in patients can be controlled. Once such a comfort level is achieved, then the entire muscle relaxation procedures can be implemented.

CASE ILLUSTRATION

"Jeff" was raised in a rural community, with his being accustomed to high personal independence and few societal restrictions. Formal schooling imposed more regulations and rules than he could tolerate, and he was often sent home for problems with authority. In adult years, the farm was sold to pay family bills, and Jeff moved to the city to seek employment in construction. He remained a social isolate, spending evenings in a bar by himself. Fights with the foreman over being told what to do were interspersed with increasing episodes of violence and property damage.

Enlisting in the Marines, Jeff's quick temper and aggression were channeled into boxing. Upon discharge, he relied upon his ring experience to make a minimal living on preliminary fight cards. However, his fiery temper and uncontrolled physical violence outside of the ring led to brief jail terms and a strain on his finances. His manager counseled him to get a tighter rein on his emotions and frustrations. They were becoming major obstacles to Jeff's future. Jeff agreed to attend an anger management program with a sport psychologist because it was described as training rather than psychological gibberish.

The initial relaxation training went poorly; Jeff resisted fully engaging in the relaxation and failed to practice the technique. It became clear that his resistance stemmed from his perceiving the psychologist as once again someone telling him what to do and how to behave. A less instructional tone and a more collaborative, coaching approach was then adopted by the psychologist, and time was taken to more thoroughly explain AMT. AMT training use with Olympic athletes was described, and the step-by-step procedure of AMT was explained as being similar to learning the fundamentals of boxing skills. This approach improved Jeff's understanding and commitment.

In keeping with the collaborative/coaching orientation, the psychologist began seeking Jeff's advice and input, for instance, on what helped him relax other than drinking. Jeff found Dolly Parton tapes helpful and the positive ways his manager facilitated Jeff's training. By the fourth session, muscle relaxation was again initiated, interspersed with recall by Jeff of his favorite Dolly Parton songs. Steps in each AMT session were always introduced with "Typically, what we would be doing today would be . . ." along with the reason, and followed with, "What do you think, are you ready to try it out?" Feedback following each session covered, "How do you think that went? Is there some aspect we can improve on that would help?"

Anger arousal was achieved through recall and visualization of a recent life event. The scene was: "I was sitting in the Silver Star Bar, listening to Dolly, and hearing someone talking about his shaping up his kids, to do this, do that. I'm feeling the anger this produces in me as I remember being pushed around in my life. . . . Then some other jerk says, "Hey, quite playing that one song. . . . I'm sick of it! I about blew up . . . like a steam boiler inside me pushing to explode."

The AMT sessions would begin with relaxation, then Jeff was invited to visualize being in this scene and to allow himself to feel the buildup of anger. As the arousal occurred, Jeff's physical appearance would change; as his facial and neck muscle would tense, a vein on his forehead would stand out, his breathing would become more rapid and shallow, and his hands would clench into fists. At this point, the psychologist would suggest dismissing the scene and

instead concentrating on relaxing each muscle group, step by step. The Dolly Parton imagery would also be relied up to help Jeff let go of the anger arousal and regain relaxation.

The progression from the first session to completion was deliberately slower than is typical, as Jeff's willingness to cooperate was continuously monitored. Comparisons with boxing helped Jeff view AMT as a type of physical skill training, and soon Jeff was fully committed and eager to progress. He soon was viewing AMT as a way of being in control of his body, instead of his emotions controlling him, and he started to talk about the benefits to his boxing if he fought "more with smarts" and boxed "with control."

Homework assignments now included monitoring his emotional state, especially in the bars. As a boxer, he was used to paying attention to bodily condition and now was learning to attend to his surroundings and how they affected his emotions. He soon learned to identify signs that he was being irritated or upset and relied upon remaining calm by using relaxation or replaying a Dolly Parton melody in his head. As he put it, "Whenever I notice the steam in my boiler building up, I just release it before it cooks over."

—*Richard M. Suinn*

See also: *Relaxation Strategies (Vol. I); Role Playing (Vol. I); Social Effectiveness Training (Vol. I)*

Suggested Readings

Deffenbacher, J. L., & Stark, R. S. (1992). Relaxation and cognitive-relaxation treatments of general anger. *Journal of Counseling Psychology, 39,* 158–167.

Suinn, R. M. (1990). *Anxiety management training: A behavior therapy.* New York: Plenum Press.

Suinn, R. M., & Deffenbacher, J. L. (1988). Anxiety management training. *The Counseling Psychologist, 16,* 31–49.

APPLIED BEHAVIOR ANALYSIS

DESCRIPTION OF THE MODEL

Behaviorism is a philosophical movement begun early 20th century that has given rise to two important applications in clinical settings. One branch derives from the work of Pavlov and Watson and classical conditioning, the other from Thorndike and Skinner and operant conditioning. Clinicians working in the operant behavioral tradition have been known as behavior modifiers or applied behavior analysts, and occasionally, as radical behaviorists. Historically, applied behavior analysts have conducted clinical work in institutional settings with children and adults with developmental disabilities or in schools with typically developing children. By contrast, clinicians working in the classical conditioning paradigm identify as behavior therapists. Practitioners of behavior therapies have been more closely associated with clinical work in adult outpatient settings, especially with anxiety and mood disorders.

The present entry focuses on adult clinical work conducted in the operant conditioning tradition. But first, theoretical issues generic to the behavioral therapies and areas in which applied behavior analysis (or ABA) diverges from behavior therapy (or BT) are described. Finally, following a description of the applied behavior analysis model, case examples of contemporary applications of applied behavior analysis in adult populations are presented.

Theoretical and Philosophical Elements of Behavioral Therapies

Behavioral therapies emphasize pragmatism, empirically based practice, and a present-time orientation, while rejecting unfavorable personality traits or biological deficits as explanations for psychological problems. Pragmatism is a uniquely American philosophy that dictates that therapist and client pursue "meaningful" and achievable goals. It is best summarized by the phrase, "Do what works." Behavior therapies are empirically based in that they demand multi-informant, ongoing assessment, and evaluation of treatment outcome. In assessment, client reports and subjective impressions developed by therapists are checked, whenever possible, against measures of known reliability and validity. In general, direct observation is preferred (where practicable) over subjective ratings, and concrete evidence of behavior change is valued over self-reports.

Whether practiced by behavior therapists or applied behavior analysts, systematic evaluation of a therapy is expected before dissemination. Evidence showing both efficacy (utility in controlled research settings) and effectiveness (utility in clinical practice) is highly valued. The present orientation of behavioral therapies is evident in the emphasis on assessment of the environmental stimuli that are associated with the onset and offset of symptoms. In contrast, insight-oriented therapies have often focused on past or internal facets of experience rather than on contextual factors that may contribute to psychological problems. Finally, behavioral therapies conceptualize psychological problems as "problems of learning" rather than evidence of disease processes (i.e., psychopathology) or personality flaws. By contrast, "symptoms" of psychological problems are described as "adaptive" or "maladaptive."

Distinguishing ABA and BT

Applied behavior analysis can be distinguished from behavior therapy primarily in terms of the research methods used to evaluate treatment effectiveness, the extent to which mediational models of psychological functioning are accepted, and the importance of selectionism as a guiding construct. Relative to behavior therapists, applied behavior analysts have remained committed to the use of "small N" research designs such as the multiple baseline and reversal (ABAB). These "small N" designs permit evaluation of an individual's response to intervention as well as the analysis treatment failures that are obscured in "large N," randomized control trials. By contrast, clinical studies evaluating group treatments have become increasingly popular in behavior therapy, as practitioners have sought to establish the external validity of their treatment protocols (e.g., cognitive behavior therapy, or CBT, for depression).

Similarly, while behavior therapists have become more accepting of verbal report and the introduction of mediational constructs, such as self-efficacy, negative schemas, and cognitive bias, applied behavior analysts working with adults have continued to emphasize behavioral influences that are present in the environment. In addition, applied behavior analysts working with typically functioning adults emphasize contingency-based aspects of their clients' verbalizations. Importantly, neither behavior therapists nor applied behavior analysts deny the importance of thoughts and feelings, but they respond to them in different ways. For example, following the statement, "I'm a terrible father," a behavior therapist/clinical behavior therapist might challenge a client to obtain data confirming (or disconfirming) the statement. By contrast, an applied behavior therapist might note that negative self-statements tend to follow the therapist's suggestions for behavioral change outside of the session.

A hallmark of "debates" between practitioners of behavior therapy/clinical behavior therapy and applied behavior analysis has concerned whether cognitions should be regarded as having a causal role in the genesis and maintenance of psychological problems. While regarded as a mere semantic issue by some, this issue highlights key features that distinguish the behavior therapy and applied behavior analysis traditions. Mediational accounts provided in cognitive behavior therapy or cognitive therapy place a strong emphasis on the causal role of thoughts and perceptions in contributing to human suffering. The conceptualization of thoughts as "causal" serves as the justification for targeting them for change and is central to the rational for change in clinical behavior therapy.

In contemporary applied behavior analysis with nondisabled adults, controversy regarding the causal role of cognitions is sidestepped because behavior analysts view discussions about causality as "useful ways of speaking about reality" rather than describing reality per se. Rather than seeking "the truth," applied behavior analysts pursue accounts and clinical procedures that produce successful outcomes for their clients. As a result, adult work in applied behavior analysis has emphasized understanding of the individual in context. In contrast to popular misconceptions, radical behaviors do not deny the existence of thoughts or feeling; in fact, they are central to treatments intended for adults in outpatient settings.

Assessments derived from the ABA tradition are based on a selectionist model. As originally proposed by Darwin, selection of species characteristics was governed by the consequences associated with various features of the evolving organism. In some environments (contexts), certain characteristics (e.g., hard beaks, curved beaks) were selected over other characteristics based on their relation to fitness (the extent to which the characteristic produced a reproductive advantage). In applied behavior analysis, behavior, like species characteristics, is conceptualized as having variability that can be selected (or not selected, or "extinguished") in a given environment. In functional assessment or its more formal experimental guise, functional analysis (in which the environment is directly manipulated to permit observation of functional relations between the environment and behavior), the therapist attempts to gain an understanding of how the client's behavior "fits" in the setting—put differently, to understand the "purpose" or meaningfulness

of the behavior in terms of it consequences. Consequences are classified as either *reinforcing* (they lead to increases in the behaviors they follow) or *punishing* (they lead to decreases in the behaviors they follow).

In applied behavior analysis, behaviors are often thought of as having a function or purpose. Many behaviors can be thought of as being related to the delivery of attention or material (tangible) reward, or in other cases, the behavior seems to produce its own automatic or sensory rewards. Finally, some behaviors seem to produce escape or avoidance of events. If a behavior is said to have an attention function, it is hypothesized that the behavior produces social attention, a powerful reinforcer for most people. For example, adults in placed in sterile, unstimulating institutional settings may self-injure to obtain social contact. Behaviors that function to produce tangible reinforcers such as access to food, activities, or money can increase problem behavior when they are delivered contingent upon theft, lying, or assault. Other kinds of problem behavior may serve as an escape or avoidance function by removing of painful or distressing stimuli. Examples of escape-motivated behavior include cancellation of dental appointments or failure to resolve family conflicts. Finally, some destructive behavior appears to be maintained because the short-term consequences of the behavior produce potent sensory stimulation (e.g., drugs such as alcohol and crack cocaine), while the long-term consequences of these actions (e.g., automobile accidents, damaged livers, arrest, and prison) are delayed. Finally, it is important to note that reinforcing and punishing consequences can vary from one individual to another, so while alcohol consumption may be powerfully rewarding for one person, it may be of little value or even punishing to another.

Because of the emphasis on the function rather than the structure of behavior problems (as is often associated with very detailed, objective descriptions of behavioral problems), applied behavior therapists have largely rejected *DSM-IV* categories of adult pathology on philosophical grounds. At the same time, behavior therapists and clinical behavior therapists have more readily accepted the *DSM-IV* taxonomy. For example, an individual diagnosed with major depression engages (or does not engage) in a variety of behaviors. They may withdraw rather than approach social situations, cry frequently, evidence sleep disturbances and eating disturbances, verbally report that they are "losers," and perhaps even discuss suicidal intent. While these can be described in terms of structure (and with an even more detailed account in terms of frequency, duration, etc.), they yield no "functional information" (i.e., we do not know what environmental events appear causally related to their display). By contrast, it is a relatively straightforward task to assess whether an individual meets criteria for major depression. To yield a functional account, each of these behaviors (symptoms) would be analyzed in terms of the antecedents (both proximal and distal events that came before) and consequences of these actions. Put somewhat differently, although two individuals may be described as "depressed," the function of the behaviors associated with behaving in this way could be different. For example, social withdrawal for one individual may promote avoidance of social interactions that are anxiety provoking, whereas for another it may yield attention in the form of more frequent visits from concerned relatives. Thus, in ABA, the functional approach to assessment is favored over the structural *DSM-IV* approach because it is believed to promote a more individualized and context-sensitive (idiographic) assessment. A functional account may also be more parsimonious because several behaviors characteristic of a *DSM-IV* syndrome may serve the same environmental function (i.e., they produce the same reinforcers). This kind of conceptualization could lead to more elegant and efficient treatment plans. According to applied behavior analysis theory, more individualized care should prove more effective than one-size-fits-all approaches based on general taxonomies of behavior. Most important, to be fully justifiable as an assessment procedure, functional assessment and analyses must lead to better treatment outcomes (they must be pragmatic).

ABA Fundamentals

Behavioral Assessment

Historically, behavioral assessment has eschewed projective tests (e.g., the Rorschach, self-reports, and developmental interviews) that are the staples of personality-based and insight-oriented therapies. In behavioral assessment, the direct observation of behavior in the setting in which it occurs is favored. Where this is not possible (for a variety of reasons), analogue assessments (e.g., lab or clinic simulations) are used to elicit the relevant information. For example, in functional analytic psychotherapy (FAP), the client-therapist relationship and in-session behavior of the client constitute an important element of the assessment process. Behavioral assessment also tends to be ongoing and recurrent and provides for the evaluation of response to treatment, another core feature of ABA.

Stimulus Control

Fundamental to an understanding of behavior therapy or applied behavior analysis is an understanding of the concepts of stimulus control, reinforcement, and punishment. In contrast to classical conditioning, which emphasizes the association of stimulus events (e.g., the sound of a bell is repeatedly associated or "paired" with the arrival of food), applied behavior analysis emphasizes the concept of contingency. For example, Wilma may respond to Dino's complaints of loneliness by attempting to console him (attention). Her attention to his complaints may tend to increase their frequency (reinforcement). By contrast, talking about loneliness in the presence of Fred is followed by silence, which tends to decrease frequency of complaining in his presence. In this example, attention or the absence of it constitute the consequence, and the people present in the situation become (after many repetitions of the above scenario) discriminative stimuli (stimuli that exert stimulus control). It is important to note that if Fred or Wilma's responses were to change over time, then the likelihood of Dino's complaining in their presence would change as well. Thus, ABA involves assessing contingency relationships that may be very complex (functional assessment) and assisting the behavior in new ways that alter contingencies supporting adaptive and/or maladaptive behavior.

Reinforcement-Based Procedures

Reinforcement-based procedures can range from the very simple to quite complex. In their simplest form, the term describes the presentation of events usually considered pleasant by the client (e.g., praise, tangible things of value to a person, such as money, or the opportunity to escape or avoid an event regarded as unpleasant by the individual). For example, a person may be praised or a therapist may smile when the client makes a positive self-statement. Token economies or behavioral contracts formally outline a plan for the delivery of reinforcers. For example, an employee's compensation for excellent sales performance may include a promotion, increases in salary, as well as "fringe" benefits, such as increased vacation time. There is no end to the number of items that could be included as positive reinforcers, as they are limited only to the imagination of the therapist and client (and the available resources).

While most people associate positive-reinforcement procedures with the delivery of extrinsic or arbitrary incentives such as M&Ms or money, clinical researchers such as Ferster emphasized a distinction between arbitrary and naturally rewarding consequences. For example, if a client demonstrated within-session increases in assertiveness and she had previously been extremely passive, it would be arbitrary to pay her 25¢ for "being assertive" but natural to listen to what she had to say and comply with her request to change next week's appointment. Other clients have been taught to solicit their own reinforcers to increase the rate of social reinforcement in the home or work settings (i.e., natural environments). For example, a man who was unappreciated at work might be instructed to recruit feedback from a supervisor (e.g., "How am I doing?").

Punishment-Based Procedures

Punishment procedures are procedures that can be shown to reduce frequency of "problem behavior." Importantly, ABAs have given serious consideration to the ethics of punishment. In general, the use of punishment is restricted to situations in which positive procedures (i.e., attempts to teach adaptive behavior that eliminates the need for the problem behavior) have been shown to be ineffective and the ongoing display of the problem behavior is dangerous (e.g., self-injury) or has significant long-term costs (e.g., failure to brush teeth). Finally, punishment procedures may have limited applications to adults in outpatient psychotherapy, where the client may readily choose to avoid or terminate therapy rather than submit to punishment. For example, rather than cease drinking, problem drinkers prescribed Antibuse (a drug that induces violent nausea if the user consumes alcohol) generally stop taking the voluntary drug treatment.

A second consideration is that when punishment is used, mild- or moderate-intensity punishments are generally preferred, especially if they are shown to be as effective as punishments of greater intensity. Unfortunately, procedures such as contingent shock

and physical punishment and aversive procedures such as rapid smoking have been heavily publicized and grouped alongside more effective and much milder procedures such as behavior penalty or response cost (e.g., fines for speeding) and time-out (temporary restraining orders or being ejected from a bar for fighting). Like positive reinforcement, punishment procedures work best when they are delivered consistently and immediately. For example, when used as part of a self-management procedure, a man who commits to reducing smoking to three cigarettes a day but smokes four may pledge to donate $5 dollars to his most hated political cause or exercise longer than usual as a consequence. Penalties that are imposed for speeding in automobiles are, in effect, punishment procedures based on response cost. Money serves as the token reinforcer, and fines are expressed in dollars, often with a fixed number of dollars fined for each mile an hour over the speed limit. Also, note that for many, the inconvenience and delay associated with the traffic stop are far more aversive than the fines. Some contingency management systems blend reinforcement and punishment. For example, many government contracts pay a bonus for early satisfaction of contract terms (progressively) but levy penalties for shoddy workmanship or delays. This kind of arrangement is a form of token economy with response cost. In addition, the design of contracts is but one of the many applications of ABA outside of clinical settings that may have great import for its future.

Skill and Performance Deficits (Can't Do or Won't Do?)

Fundamental to ABA is the determination of whether a problem behavior (whether considered an "excess" or a "deficit") results from the absence of "skill" or a lack of "motivation." While the reinforcement and punishment procedures described above are useful for influencing behavior when motivational deficits are apparent, additional techniques may be needed for skills deficits. In general, skill-based teaching in the behavioral tradition involves modeling, role playing, practice (homework), and performance feedback. Each component is described briefly below:

❖ Modeling: For many adults (and children), the opportunity to observe others in demonstration of the skills required for successful performance is vital. Modeling provides the learner with a clear demonstration of the skill to be acquired, thus promoting imitation and enhancing motivation.

❖ Role play: Provides opportunities for the client to "try out" new behaviors in a supportive environment and to obtain feedback that will enhance the quality of the performance. In analogue tests, certain elements of the natural environment are simulated to make performances more realistic and promote generalization of the skill.

❖ Homework: Provides opportunities for additional practice that occur in the natural settings. The provision of homework also provides a basis for the therapist to monitor out-of-session compliance with the treatment regimen and to provide additional feedback on the quality of performance.

❖ Feedback: A function that is vital to acquisition and roughly analogous to reinforcement of appropriate or correct responding. Feedback is usually provided initially by the therapist but may also be solicited by the client in the natural environment. Feedback that is solicited from friends and family at the end of treatment is called *social validity data.* Social validity data may serve as compelling evidence of behavior change.

RESEARCH BASIS

Since its inception, ABAs have been characterized by their dedication to developing an empirically based treatment literature that draws liberally from procedural and conceptual insights arising in laboratory settings. A number of early texts, such as Ullmann and Krasner's *Case Studies in Behavior Modification,* were influential in conveying the viability of the operant approach in clinical settings. In addition, a number of journals publishing work in applied behavior analysis came into existence in the 1960s and 1970s, including the *Journal of Applied Behavior Analysis* and *Behavior Modification.* While these journals continue to publish ABA research, many other journals now publish work that is more specialized.

Experimental Designs for ABA

Mainstream applied psychology is characterized by parametric or group research designs involving large representative samples of individuals, with randomized,

blind assignment to experimental conditions and statistical analysis of group differences. By contrast, ABA emphasizes demonstration of control over a dependent variable by manipulation of the independent variable. For example, in the reversal or ABAB design, individuals in the "A" phase experience "baseline" conditions or the usual environmental conditions. In the "B" or intervention phase, individuals experience the change in the environment. Because the target variable is measured continuously throughout, the effect of the intervention can be assessed by observing (and usually graphing) the changes in the rate of the target behavior as a function of the changes in the environment. Unlike group treatment designs, where changes in the behavior on individuals is obscured (through statistical comparisons of group means), the reversal design makes it possible to observe the impact of the intervention on individuals.

Another design variation, the multiple baseline, makes it possible to evaluate the effectiveness of an intervention by systematically intervening with multiple individuals (or within individuals across multiple behaviors or settings). In this way, no reversal to baseline conditions is required (which in the case of a severely aggressive or depressed individual would be potentially harmful and unethical). Reversal designs and multiple-baseline designs can also be used to evaluate interventions at the community level when groups are treated as individuals. For example, using a multiple-baseline design, rates of exercise among employees could be obtained in three companies. After 1 month of baseline data collection, a "wellness" campaign is begun in Workplace 1, while baseline data continue to be obtained in Workplaces 2 and 3. In the second month, the intervention is introduced in Company 2. In the third month, the intervention is introduced in Company 3. If the intervention were effective, we would expect to see systematic changes in outcome variables such as changes in heart rate, cholesterol levels, amount of exercise each day, and so on as a function of the intervention.

Applications of ABA With Adults

The application of behavior analysis to clinical activities is exceptionally broad, ranging from early work with institutionalized adults with disabilities such as mental retardation and autism to recent developments in adult outpatient psychotherapy. Over the past 25 years, ABA has also been used to facilitate changes at the community level. Research in these diverse areas is highlighted below.

Early Efforts: Developmental Disabilities

Early work based on reinforcement showed that institutionalized patients could be taught simple responses using reinforcement, such as flushing a toilet or the appropriate use of eating utensils. However, efforts to apply operant techniques to teaching increasingly complex behavior grew rapidly. Teodoro Ayllon and Nathan Azrin's work with children and institutionalized adults with developmental disabilities through the introduction of token economies is a good example of early work in the application of the operant conditioning principles to important social problems. In general, these studies showed that operant approaches to ward management based on contingency analyses and the use of contingent reinforcement to promote the development of adaptive skills in institutionalized settings (e.g., self-care and the reduction of self-injury) were superior to existing interventions. More important, research on outcomes associated with contingency management, including the use of token economies, showed that ABA produced levels of independent functioning that were unheard of in other treatment settings. Use of operant techniques such as token systems with institutionalized adults is now the rule rather than the exception.

Individual Outpatient Psychotherapy and Life in the Community

While there was success with adults in institutionalized settings, ABAs encountered more difficulty extending operant conditioning principles to adults without disabilities. As noted previously, within BT, this resulted in the gradual, and then more rapid incorporation of cognitive constructs and, ultimately, in the emergence of CBT. Nevertheless, despite growing dissatisfaction with the model, there were some successes with adults. During the 1970s, Lewinsohn and others found evidence that reinforcement-based approaches could be helpful in the treatment of depression. In the 1970s and 1980s, Jacobson's use of behavioral contracting (a formal procedure in which the delivery of rewards and punishment are agreed to in writing by the participants) in behavioral marital therapy produced therapeutic gains supporting the applicability of reinforcement-based treatments with adults in outpatient settings.

Next-Generation Behavior Therapies

Charles Ferster pioneered efforts to formulate a thoroughly operant model of adult outpatient psychotherapy. Specifically, Ferster's ideas regarding the treatment of depression generated theoretical insights that served as the basis for the formulation of more sophisticated adult ABA models for outpatient therapy. Over time and with a more sophisticated understanding of the subtle differences between BT and ABA, a number of therapies began to emerge that were based upon a more comprehensive extension of Skinner's brand of behaviorism to the adult psychotherapy setting. Skinner's approach is sometimes called "radical (i.e., to the root) behaviorism," and the outpatient work deriving from this tradition has come to be known as "clinical behavior analysis." Among several variants of clinical behavior analysis, a few stand out. Hayes's acceptance and commitment therapy (ACT) emphasizes the importance of verbal behavior, while Kohlenberg's functional analytic psychotherapy (FAP) and Linehan's dialectical behavior therapy (DBT) emphasize the value of the therapist-client relationship. Although additional data are needed to support the effectiveness of all of these therapies, alternative treatments for adult outpatient problems based on ABA are now available. Of the three therapies, DBT for persons diagnosed with borderline personality disorder has the most empirical support. Studies investigating ACT and FAP are ongoing, although the limited data available are supportive.

Community-Based Applications

From the beginning, ABAs have been interested in the application of operant conditioning principles to practical problems (see Skinner's efforts to train pigeons as couriers). Not surprisingly, then, efforts to apply the model beyond the outpatient psychotherapy context have been extensive. In fact, concerns about the social implications of "behavioral engineering" resulted in a backlash against "behavior modification" in the 1970s that still lingers today. Despite these concerns, ABA has been used to address vocational problems (unemployment, absenteeism, underperformance, maximizing productivity, improving adherence to safety procedures, and job satisfaction), hasten medical rehabilitation (e.g., compliance with physical therapy, to manage pain, to improve memory performance), and promote socially important behaviors, such as reducing energy consumption, unsafe driving, and illegal drug use or unwanted pregnancies. ABA procedures have also been used in the areas of sports psychology to promote improved athletic performance and in behavioral medicine and health psychology to promote the adoption of healthy lifestyles.

RELEVANT TARGET POPULATIONS AND EXCEPTIONS

As can be seen above, there are few settings in which the ABA model would not have some application, but some general observations about limitations can be made. First, in settings where ABAs have traditionally had relatively good control (or "influence") over the environment, they have produced excellent results. ABA procedures seem to be especially effective when used to teach a specified set of skills. Reinforcement-based techniques (to address motivational problems) and teaching techniques developed in the laboratory have been very effective in remediating problems where the acquisition of skills has been important. ABA has also been helpful because it requires establishing goals, careful definition of target behaviors, specification of outcome criteria, and frequently, the performance of a task analysis (a very thorough specification of each behavior that is required for successful performance of a task). In many cases, task analysis itself leads to improved training results. Specification of the component steps also provides opportunities to praise gradual approximations to a goal (shaping) and is central to the successful application of the behavioral-training model (e.g., model/practice/role play/feedback). By contrast, one would predict that ABA approaches would be less likely to be successful when more difficult tasks are trained or when the factors that may be influencing a target behavior are extremely complex or capricious.

Another challenge to ABAs has been to promote the generalization and maintenance of skilled or adaptive performances. To the extent that new environments do not support (i.e., provide reinforcers) behaviors learned in the training setting, one might predict that behavior change would not be sustainable. In a multitude of studies, this has proven to be true. To address concerns about generalization and maintenance, ABAs have modified their procedures by training in settings where behavior change is desired and by gradually reducing the extrinsic supports for performance of the adaptive behavior (through fading the cues or consequences used during training). When employed, these modifications appear to be very helpful in promoting generalization and maintenance of change, although the work is difficult.

COMPLICATIONS

One of the most serious problems associated with the adoption of ABA model are perceptions that the methods involve violations of ethical standards or that the model is dehumanizing. To address concerns about ethics, ABAs have developed a very comprehensive statement regarding the right to ethical treatment, which outlines concerns associated with the use of methods described earlier as well as concerns about the failure to use effective treatments. For example, many behavior analysts, including such notables as B. F. Skinner, Murray Sidman, and Jack Michael, have raised serious concerns about the widespread use of punishment. Others have raised concerns about the use of behavior analysis to promote the interests of those in power (the status quo) over the needs of the individuals that behavior analysts have pledged to serve. Yet despite these efforts, persistent misunderstandings still lead some to describe behavioral approaches as demeaning and dehumanizing. Even positive behavioral approaches emphasizing the use of reinforcement have been described as promoting the pursuit of materialist, extrinsic goals at the expense of "intrinsic motivation." In response, ABAs have pointed out sources of behavioral control that already exist within our society (usually based on punishment) and the many instances in which positive reinforcement produces gains in self-confidence, creativity, and motivation.

The behavior-analytic model also requires careful description of target behaviors and the demonstration (where possible) of experimental control. Unfortunately, whether at the individual or community level, it is often difficult to manipulate environmental conditions in a systematic way or to obtain ongoing measurements of relevant behavioral targets. For example, in individual therapy, the therapist typically has only limited, indirect influence on the client's behavior outside of the session. Moreover, target behaviors, such as social skills problems, are frequently difficult to measure reliably.

CASE ILLUSTRATIONS

To provide readers with a sense of the diverse range of applications of behavior analysis with adults, the following examples are offered.

Institutionalized Adult and Self-Injury

The case of "Harry" is a landmark case in the history of behavior analysis. Until he entered treatment, Harry, a 6' 6" self-abusive man, had been self-injurious to the extent that he had caused significant disfigurement of his face. Whenever attempts were made to engage him in instructional activities or attempts were made to remove the restraints designed to prevent further self-injury (e.g., to facilitate taking a shower), he exhibited extreme tantrums. Though he possessed good receptive language and some ability to communicate verbally, he rarely did so. Instead, he alternately screamed and flailed his arms, punctuating these with additional bouts of self-injury. As a result of more than a decade of self-injury and self-restraint, he began regressing developmentally and experienced progressively less frequent contact with his family or the outside world.

Based on a functional assessment of his self-injury, a team of clinicians lead by Richard Foxx determined that Harry's tantrums and self-injury were primarily maintained by escape from tasks. They concluded that his restraints could be used as a reinforcer powerful enough to shape longer and longer periods out of restraint without self-injury (thus creating a larger window of opportunity for skills training). In a very short period, the intervention produced significant reductions in self-injury and time out of restraints. Ultimately, Harry achieved significant gains in functional skills and independence, the acquisition of a job, and much more frequent home visits and contact with the outside community. Importantly, these improvements were documented and sustained over many years.

Outpatient Psychotherapy

Although there is extensive support for cognitive behavior therapy in the treatment of depression, not all clients benefit from the approach. As noted earlier, until recently, there were few alternative treatment approaches for adult outpatient psychotherapy derived from a radical behavioral framework. One such approach, FAP, has been used to supplement CBT methods and provides an interesting contrast in methods.

The client was a 35-year-old, unmarried, unemployed, depressed male experiencing difficulty in social relationships. Previously, this client had experienced a variety of other psychosocial treatments and pharmacotherapy with little benefit. Although some gains had been realized during a 7-week course of CBT, Beck Depression Inventory (BDI) scores had declined from baseline of nearly 30 (clinically significant depression) but stalled in the low 20s (borderline depression). At the eighth session, FAP was introduced to facilitate improvement in the quality of his interpersonal relationships and further reduce his depressive symptoms. In contrast with CBT, FAP emphasizes within-session changes in interpersonal behavior and views the client-therapist relationship as a vehicle for promoting behavioral change. During the CBT intervention, the client was encouraged to record concerns about negative evaluations by others using an "automatic-thoughts record." In addition, the client used CBT techniques such as obtaining evidence and challenging the factual basis of his automatic thoughts. After limited success, however, the client began to find these tasks difficult, and he failed to complete several homework assignments. In contrast to CBT, the FAP therapist engaged the client in a discussion about the client's concerns over negative evaluations (in general) and related these to concerns that the client might have had with respect to the therapist arising from the client's failure to complete the homework assignment. CBT techniques were continued, but the FAP intervention focused on using the client-therapist relationship as a testing ground for hypotheses concerning the client's social functioning outside of the sessions. Introduction of FAP produced an increase in client reports of problematic social situations outside of therapy (on the automatic-thoughts record), yet somewhat paradoxically, a decrease in BDI scores into the midteens. At follow-up, the client reported BDI scores near 10, solidly in the normal range.

FAP is regarded as more consistent with ABA because of its emphasis on within-session behavior and its consequences. FAP therapists look for clinically relevant behavior (CRBs): within-session behaviors that seem to parallel client-reported problems outside of therapy. The therapist makes a concerted effort to respond to the client in ways that will highlight or even evoke CRBs. When these events arise, the therapist assists the client in recognizing the salience of these within-session events and relating them to social relations outside of therapy. In the context of this case study, this involved having the client experience within-session anxieties and fears relevant to confronting the therapist and relating these difficulties to problems confronting his roommate. By encouraging the client to confront the therapist within session (and by the therapist responding in a nondefensive manner that rewarded the client's more assertive behavior), the therapist presumably increased the likelihood that the client would be assertive in both future sessions and in social relations outside of therapy. Ultimately, this client was able to overcome fears of negative evaluation and confront his roommate about his concerns. Therapists with psychodynamic, existential, and acceptance-based training backgrounds would likely find FAP-based conceptualizations and techniques familiar. In any case, the vital component of this ABA-influenced adult psychotherapy involves a careful analysis of within-session social contingencies.

Community Psychology: Injury Prevention

Applications of behavior analysis to the community level sometimes require new terminology, but these efforts generally retain core features such as defining the target behavior (i.e., dependent variable); obtaining baseline behavioral measurement; well-described, replicable manipulations of existing environmental conditions (i.e., independent variable); and ongoing assessment of change in the target following efforts to manipulate the environment. In community-based applications, dependent variables have included seat belt use, driving while intoxicated, exercise habits, and compliance with workplace safety procedures.

A multidimensional intervention designed by Geller and colleagues exemplifies the application of ABA techniques to seat belt use. Sixty pizza delivery drivers in southwest Virginia served as the study participants. The intervention began with a 9-week assessment of the baseline rate of seat belt use, which was initially below 45%. Next, an awareness program (including discussion groups, pledge cards, store signs, and encouragement from supervisors to "buckle up") was introduced, which resulted in an average seat belt use increase of 20%. A second intervention was introduced that added a community component in which drivers became intervention agents and customers were provided with an incentive ("$1 off") if they reminded the dispatcher to tell the delivery driver to buckle up. A third intervention provided extensive training in a safe-delivery program sponsored by the pizza company. Ultimately, seat belt use rose to more than 85%. Importantly, most of the increases in seat belt use appeared to be maintained over time, and turn signal use also appeared to increase, although it was not directly targeted. In addition, while individual responses were aggregated, individual responses to the intervention could also have been analyzed to determine whether individuals responded uniformly or to facilitate the study of "nonresponders."

—David Reitman

See also: Applied Behavior Analysis (Vol. III); Goldiamond, Israel (Vol. I); Schedules of Reinforcement (Vol. II)

Suggested Readings

Azrin, N. H., Philips, R. A., Thienes-Hontos, P., & Besalel, V. A. (1981). Follow-up on welfare benefits received by Job Club clients. *Journal of Vocational Behavior, 18,* 253–254.

Baer, D. M., Wolf, M. M., & Risley, T. R. (1987). Some still current dimensions of applied behavior analysis. *Journal of Applied Behavior Analysis, 20,* 313–328.

Geller, E. S. (1998). *Applications of behavior analysis to prevent injuries from vehicle crashes.* Concord, MA: Cambridge Center for Behavioral Studies.

Hayes, S. C., Strosahl, K. D., & Wilson, K. G. (1999). *Acceptance and commitment therapy: An experiential approach to behavior change.* New York: Guilford Press.

Kohlenberg, R. J., & Tsai, M. (1991). *Functional analytic psychotherapy: Creating intense and curative therapeutic relationships.* New York: Plenum Press.

Linehan, M. M. (1993). *Cognitive-behavioral treatment of borderline personality disorder.* New York: Guilford Press.

Miltenberger, R. G. (2001). *Behavior modification: Principles and procedures* (2nd ed.). Belmont, CA: Wadsworth.

Skinner, B. F. (1953). *Science and human behavior.* New York: Free Press.

APPLIED RELAXATION AND TENSION

DESCRIPTION OF THE STRATEGY

Currently popularized in an array of specific versions, relaxation training has demonstrated its ease of adaptation and flexibility for teaching individuals an effective means to cope with and overcome anxiety, tension, and other stress-related conditions. Since its initial application toward patients by Edmund Jacobson in the 1920s, relaxation training has become one of the most widely prescribed therapeutic exercises employed by mental health professionals. In fact, this technique has been described as the "aspirin of therapy." In its original incarnation, progressive muscle relaxation training (PMRT) sought to teach clients to identify subtle tension sites stored within their skeletal musculature, and by learning to elongate (relax) the specific muscles involved in storing emotional and physical tension, unwanted emotional and mental processes could be corrected. Thus, relaxation was viewed as the means and the end result of treatment.

In the 1950s, Joseph Wolpe adapted PMRT to a briefer form, used in combination with gradual exposure in systematic desensitization, a highly successful behavioral strategy for reducing anxiety and phobias. In its most popular form today, which was highly influenced by the works of Bernstein, Borkovec, and Benson in the 1970s, PMRT is viewed as one component of an effective treatment regimen in therapy. Cognitive-behavioral strategies, such as cognitive restructuring or positive self-talk, are commonly used in conjunction with relaxation training, as there appear to be reciprocal benefits in enhancing the effects of each respective strategy.

Although various alternate versions of PMRT and relaxation training in general are practiced and taught, several common elements exist. All forms are rooted in the basic theory that by bringing about and experiencing sensations that are incompatible with the experience of anxiety (e.g., relaxation, slowing heart rate or breathing, and focusing attention on something other than anxious stimuli), the individual is better able to remain calm and demonstrate control over undesirable, anxiety-provoking situations. It is believed that excessive levels of autonomic arousal are to some extent associated with the client's presenting problems, and, as such, relaxation training is specifically aimed at reducing the arousal level, thereby leading to reduction of the effects (i.e., stress and tension) of the presenting problem. PMRT exercises teach the individual to notice and discriminate degrees of tension, and eventually learn voluntary control of muscular tension. After sufficient practice, the client will be able to easily and quickly achieve a deeply relaxed state.

For the most part, modern PMRT strategies are highly structured yet adaptable and can be taught within 10 sessions. Common to most relaxation techniques, a continuous instructional "patter" is presented throughout the exercises in order to minimize distractions and maintain focus on physical sensations. Most patter consists of a few repetitive cues offered in a loosely structured fashion to remind the client to focus on sensations and appreciate subtle differences between relaxation and tension sensations. (For example, "Notice the difference between tensing and relaxing . . . as if the tension lifted away from you"). The patter is variable, beginning with a normal tone and gradually becoming slower, quieter, and more monotonous. Jacobson's original method dedicated a full session to examining each muscle group in detail, which meant treatment required at least 13 sessions and could last several months. Wolpe abbreviated this method to incorporate 16 muscle groups to be tensed and relaxed within one session, rather than one muscle group per session. This generally remains the standard at present when using PMRT.

PMRT typically begins with a thorough explanation and rationale for its use in treating the client's condition. A detailed outline of how each muscle group will be relaxed, including the sequencing, is offered, and it is important to prepare the client for the prospect of potential complications, such as unfamiliar/unusual sensations associated with the relaxation process. The setting is a dimly lit room, relatively free from outside distractions, where the client is asked to sit in a reclined position with his or her eyes closed. Typically, the client has been instructed to limit excessive movement, loosen restrictive jewelry or clothing, and focus on the therapist's voice, with particular attention given to follow cues signaling tension ("Now"), relaxation ("Okay, relax"), or to signal "yes" responses, as when a client is told to lift his or her index finger to signal whether complete relaxation has been reached.

Beginning with the dominant hand, the client is instructed to tense the muscles only in that hand (demonstrated by therapist in the preparation phase) for a period of 5 to 7 seconds, followed by 30 to 40 seconds of relaxation with attendant patter by the therapist. Although many therapists may choose to alter the specific grouping or sequence, the muscle groups are generally outlined as follows: hand and forearm (dominant first), then each upper arm, forehead, upper cheeks/nose/eyes, jaw, and mouth, neck, chest/shoulders/upper back, abdomen, each upper leg, each calf, and each foot.

Each muscle group receives two cycles at a time unless the client experiences difficulty relaxing. During relaxation of the chest and abdomen, breathing is emphasized and timed so that the client exhales on the "relax" cue. After all groups have been relaxed, the client is asked to signal whether he or she is completely relaxed. If not, then each muscle group is reassessed to determine where tension exists. Following a fully relaxed state, the client is allowed to remain in the relaxed state for a few minutes. Some versions of PMRT also emphasize an imagery component at this point to promote deeper relaxation. The client is gradually brought back to an alert state by counting backward, slowly eliciting greater awareness of surroundings and voluntary muscle control.

Following the exercise, the client is asked open-ended questions, typically regarding whether any aspects were especially difficult or particularly helpful. Clients are instructed to practice this training at home, generally 15 to 20 minutes twice each day, and are sometimes given an audiotape of the session as a model. With continued training, muscle groups become combined so that fewer cycles are required, and the tension stage is eventually phased out so that the client is able to initiate relaxation on command in real-life situations.

Some methods of relaxation training do not use the tensing phase of the training. Passive muscle relaxation, which was credited to Overholser in 1990, is a method that entails having the client focus on relaxation sensations while generating and vividly visualizing the details of a pleasant scene from his or her own experience. The recall of such scenes (with a peaceful beach day being most common) and the effect on relaxation are improved when multiple sensory modalities are enlisted (such as touch, smell, and taste). This method often includes deep-breathing training and guided imagery. Similar to PMRT in terms of process, theory, and methodology, passive muscle relaxation training helps teach the client how to recognize and locate feelings of tension. The effect of this method has been found to be roughly equivalent to PMRT, while also more widely applicable to a greater variety of individuals.

Another popular alternative to PMRT is muscle stretching, which relies on gradually and gently lengthening muscle fibers. This strategy appears to provide a similar tension/relaxation contrast but may be used when the client has physical limitations (such as chronic muscular skeletal pain) that are contraindicated for tension cycles or when the client is unable to detect muscle tension. Other common forms of relaxation training include yoga form stretching, deep breathing, somatic focusing, autogenic relaxation, and meditation.

RESEARCH BASIS

Research dating back more than seven decades has demonstrated that according to electromyography readings, muscular tension and activity are decreased during and following the practice of relaxation-training strategies. Both passive and progressive relaxation techniques have demonstrated a great deal of clinical utility, with the latter receiving the majority of research and clinical attention. Although some research may be mixed, a strong percentage of studies suggest that removing the tensing component in training results in little noticeable difference. As such, research indicates that on a case-by-case basis, each method alone or in combination may prove effective.

PMRT has been studied in depth with a variety of clinical and medical concerns and generally found to be quite successful and readily applicable as at least one component of a treatment package. Simply achieving a relaxed state can add to the effects of other psychological and medical treatment regimens, while also alleviating client/patient distress levels. PMRT methods have demonstrated particular success treating the experience of anxiety and fear in persons with anxious conditions (such as GAD, social phobia, and panic) or other conditions that elicit frequent anxiety or stress. Self-reported anxiety tends to decrease remarkably and quickly with the appropriate application of relaxation methods, although long-standing and chronic (trait) anxiety, which tends to exist as if being a component of the individual's personality, may require longer intervention durations. Relaxation training has been shown to be superior to nondirective therapy and is on par with cognitive techniques for a number of anxiety disorders. Some studies have also shown relaxation training to be effective in the treatment of depression.

PMRT has been used to enhance the treatment effects for a variety of medical and psychological conditions when prescribed in combination with other strategies, such as exposure therapies and cognitive strategies. Evidence suggests that PMRT has lowered problematic arousal levels, decreased self-reported levels of key symptoms, and increased coping skills with pain and discomfort in the following medical and general health concerns: aversion to chemotherapy, chronic pain and aches, tension headaches, chronic tinnitus (decreased ringing annoyance), hypertension, asthma in children, spasmodic dysmenorrhea, conditions of the immune system, insomnia and other sleep disorders, and cardiovascular problems.

RELEVANT TARGET POPULATIONS AND EXCEPTIONS

The majority of persons presenting with mental health complaints are suitable for relaxation training in one form or another. Jacobson promoted PMRT as being applicable for all conditions in which rest is prescribed. With the possible exception of persons experiencing serious thought disorders that may impede their abilities to focus attention on the various aspects of the training and follow directions, no firm contradictions exist. There also does not appear to be an age restriction, as these strategies can be modified for use with persons at a variety of developmental and cognitive levels.

Some versions of relaxation training may not be recommended for application to certain client groups. In such cases, alternative strategies or modifications are required. The tension phase of PMRT may not be indicated for persons who experience difficulty tensing muscles (i.e., initiating or noting sensations is difficult) or for those who experience pain or cramping as a result of tension, with the latter being more common among an elderly population. In these cases, passive muscle relaxation training strategies are recommended. Some clients groups, such as those with extreme forms of GAD or panic disorder, may find the relaxation component anxiety provoking. When clients initially find relaxation to be anxiety provoking, special care is required to gradually ease such individuals into relaxation sensations.

COMPLICATIONS

Several undesirable but not uncommon reactions may occur during relaxation training, the majority of which tend to be related to an interaction of the client's specific background condition and procedural issues. Typically, these concerns may be addressed effectively via adequate preparation, discussion, practice, or modifications of the relaxation protocol or environment. Some of the most common adverse or unintended effects include intrusive thoughts, fear of losing control,

unfamiliar sensory experiences, relaxation-induced anxiety, muscle cramps/spasms, twitches, sleeping, sexual arousal, laughter, and talking.

Intrusive thoughts, when excessive, can be quite disruptive to the relaxation process. These typically indicate that something on the client's mind is interfering with the focusing task. The first step is to redirect the client to focus only on the therapist's voice, which may be possibly accomplished by increasing the amount of patter, and, if necessary, addressing the underlying concern for the client before progressing with training. It should be emphasized that this exercise may seem unusual to some individuals, and in such cases, the initial peculiarities will tend to disappear with frequent practice. In addition, by preparing the client that unexpected sensations or behaviors may be elicited during the first trial, a good deal of anxiety may be allayed should the client experience relaxation sensations as worrisome. Slight twitching of the muscles during relaxation is not uncommon. However, if pain or cramping occurs, alternative strategies or modifications should be employed.

Movement and sleeping can be addressed preventatively through instructions to keep movement to a minimum, get plenty of rest the evening before, and focus on sensations and the therapist's voice. Environmental conditions can also be modified to decrease the likelihood of falling asleep (e.g., add light to room or decrease the comfort of the relaxation position, avoid scheduling sessions early in the morning or after lunch). Laughter and sexual arousal are believed to occur due to the novelty of relaxation sensations and the likelihood for the client's mind to misinterpret subtleties of the context in a humorous or sexual way (e.g., dimly lit room, relaxing tone in therapist's voice, and attention to physical sensations). Both cases will usually diminish with time and, if still present, can be addressed by redirecting the client's focus or exploring the client's underlying impressions or interpretations of the exercise.

Relaxation-induced anxiety, or more accurately, "procedurally induced anxiety," may be due to factors such as a fear of losing control, fear of relaxing sensations, proneness to hyperventilation, and triggering of unpleasant memories. Again, preparation for the possibility of these effects may be helpful. In cases where this anxiety interferes with effective practice of relaxation, the pace and focus on relaxation sensations during training may be either slowed considerably or postponed until the anxiety is more under control.

This may necessitate using other therapeutic strategies to address the underlying content of the anxiety.

CASE ILLUSTRATION

"Patient M," a 52-year-old Caucasian female, presented with the following physical symptoms: nervous stomach, slightly elevated heart rate, frequent urination, and sweating more than usual. She denied worrying and stated that she had faith in God to solve her problems. History was negative for panic attacks or prior anxiety disorders. I told her that relaxation training would be the treatment of choice for her symptoms. When I described the treatment procedures for progressive muscle relaxation training (PMRT), she said that it sounded good except that she had arthritis and was afraid to tense her hand muscles. I told her that we would skip her hands and focus on other muscle groups. We began progressive muscle relaxation, and she responded well to the procedure, tensing and relaxing each muscle group. At the end of the session, she commented that she could feel a dramatic difference between her normal state, the tensed state, and the relaxed state. At the end of the first session, I assigned her homework of practicing twice daily for at least 20 minutes to teach her body how to relax. She promised to practice.

At the start of the second session, Patient M reported having practiced once each day for approximately 15 minutes. She reported becoming aware of "carrying a lot of tension around" all the time. She also reported that although she could relax some during her practice, she was not as successful in achieving relaxation as when I had led her through the procedure. I explained that that was normal and that she should continue her daily practice, increasing to the recommended two 20-minute sessions. In the second session, we repeated the PMRT, and in the last 10 minutes, I introduced some imagery with a description of the sights and sounds of a mountain meadow and a babbling brook. She responded well and vowed to incorporate the imagery into her daily practice.

At the start of the third session, Patient M again reported that working with me was more effective than when she worked alone. I offered to audio tape the session such that she could follow the relaxation and imagery procedure at home. She accepted the offer, and we continued the PMRT, but at her request, we spent more time on imagery. At the start of the fourth session together, she reported that the tape was helpful and she was beginning to feel relaxed on a continual basis. She asked whether it would be acceptable to introduce religious content into the imagery and patter. She gave me examples of her preferred religious content (Psalm 23). We practiced PMRT with imagery and at her suggestion incorporated the religious content into the patter. She responded well to that, and at the end of the session, we agreed she was ready for termination. We scheduled a booster session in 6 weeks, but she cancelled a week ahead of time, stating that she was relaxed, her symptoms were gone, and she did not need a booster session.

—*Mark R. Floyd and Marcus T. LaSota*

See also: Anxiety Management (Vol. II); Applied Tension (Vol. I); Relaxation Strategies (Vol. I)

Suggested Readings

Bernstein, D. A., & Borkovec, T. D. (1973). *Progressive relaxation training: A manual for the helping professions.* Champaign, IL: Research Press.

Bernstein, D. A., & Carlson, C. R. (1993). Progressive relaxation: Abbreviated methods. In P. M. Lehrer & R. L. Woolfolk (Eds.), *Principles and practice of stress management* (2nd ed., pp. 53–87). New York: Guilford Press.

Ferguson, J., Marquis, J., & Taylor, C. B. (1977). A script for deep muscle relaxation. *Diseases of the Nervous System, 38,* 703–708.

Jacobson, E. (1929). *Progressive relaxation: A physiological and clinical investigation of muscular states and their significance in psychology and medical practice.* Chicago: University of Chicago Press.

Jacobson, E. (1938). *Progressive relaxation* (2nd ed.). Chicago: University of Chicago Press.

Jacobson, E. (1978). *You must relax* (4th ed.). New York: McGraw-Hill.

Lichstein, K. L. (1988). *Clinical relaxation strategies.* New York: Wiley.

McGuigan, F. J. (1993). Progressive relaxation: Origins, principles, and clinical applications. In P. M. Lehrer & R. L. Woolfolk (Eds.), *Principles and practice of stress management* (2nd ed., pp. 17–52). New York: Guilford Press.

Overholser, J. C. (1990). Passive relaxation training with guided imagery: A transcript for clinical use. *Phobia Practice and Research Journal, 3,* 107–122.

APPLIED TENSION

DESCRIPTION OF THE STRATEGY

Specific phobias are a common experience in people, and yet relatively few present with these concerns for formal treatment. In this respect, specific phobias differ significantly from other anxiety disorders. People who suffer with a variety of other common anxiety disorders (e.g., social anxiety, generalized anxiety, panic disorder) frequently present themselves for psychological interventions. Interestingly, specific phobias, when treated, often remit faster, and gains endure well over time. This phenomenon may in part be due to the circumscribed nature of specific phobias. Whereas many of the other anxiety disorders may have an insidious fashion of spreading into large parts of a person's life, specific phobias, virtually by definition, are limited to some relatively confined stimulus. In this way, by its very nature, it may also be easier to confine the interference that the fear and anxiety from the specific phobia produces. Indeed, it may be as "easy" as avoiding, for example, flying, certain animals or insects, dental or medical procedures, or the sight of blood. Because the excessive or extreme fear occurs only in the presence of the particular object, animal, or situation, these can usually be avoided almost wholesale.

People are quite adept at building mostly functional lives around avoidance and escape of feared circumstances, and they are typically quite successful with specific phobias, since the accompanying distress is commonly limited to a single or just a few variations of the specific target stimulus. This is quite different from most other anxiety disorders, which typically, when left untreated, will begin to permeate the sufferer's life, regardless of level of impact (e.g., intrapersonal, interpersonal, professional). Indeed, when individuals suffering with specific phobia present themselves for psychological treatment, it is not uncommon to hear that some life circumstances have changed (e.g., a job promotion that requires increased flying or driving, exacerbation of health problems produced by avoidance of medical care). Indeed, such change is forcing them to more directly face their fears, either by sheer necessity or by a desire to not let the fears negatively affect their personal or professional lives. In short, avoidance and escape typically used to cope with the offending stimulus have either directly or artificially been removed from the person's response repertoire.

It has been long recognized and accepted that the common ingredient of many, if not most, behavioral treatments that affect anxiety is exposure to anxiety-provoking stimuli. In fact, through repeated, prolonged exposure to the offending stimulus, anxiety, fear, and other intense negative emotions are reduced. Persons who are exposed to that which makes them feel afraid, and when this is done repeatedly, experience a reduction in their reactions of anxiety. Indeed, through repetition of this general process, the anxiety response can be extinguished. Specific phobias present a unique challenge to this commonly accepted treatment regimen in that some specific-phobia patients exhibit the vasovagal syncope, or fainting, response when faced with their feared stimuli. Such fainting response prevents habituation and, therefore, extinction of the fear response. This is especially common among blood and injury phobias, where fainting is often one of the main symptoms experienced.

When examined critically, it is clear that anxiety produces four typical responses to distressing stimuli. Many people are at least aware of the expression "fight or flight," which represents two of the four anxiety responses. In sequence of utilization, these responses are freeze, flight, fight, and faint (the "four F's"). Each response contains its own unique survival value (i.e., the overarching purpose of anxiety is to promote survival in the presence of genuine threat). These responses are perhaps best exhibited in animals, since people no longer have that many natural predators; nonetheless, they appear as readily in humans under the "right" circumstances.

The first response, freezing, is engaged in the animal kingdom to avoid detection by predators, which primarily see their prey through detection of movement that distinguishes it from the background. Most predators are not gifted with color vision and therefore must rely on movement to discern their individual prey. Some animals have adapted to this through evolutionarily advancing antidetection strategies; for example, zebras' stripes make it more difficult for predators to distinguish one running zebra from another in a herd, decreasing the likelihood that the predator will accurately be able to pick out an individual zebra to kill. Likewise, many other animals of prey (e.g., gazelles and antelopes) are colored in such a fashion as to blend well with grass and brush, making visual detection difficult when they remain still. This freezing response is also often exhibited in people when they are startled, as it is related to a time for orienting to the threat and evaluating what the threat immediately means and requires. People, like animals, are geared to conservation of energy for the purpose of survival. In this sense, individuals will not expend the energy unless they absolutely have to, because if they have to use it later, they will need all excess fuel to optimize chances of survival. In this respect, people are truly like animals.

The second response, flight (i.e., fleeing or running away from threat), is also based in simple survival odds. Simply put, it is easier to increase odds of living by not being hurt or injured. Specifically, running typically represents a lower likelihood of serious injury than fighting does, and therefore flight is preferred to fight when it comes to survival value. Thus, after an animal has been detected, it will flee or run to avoid being killed. People react in the same primitive fashion, as is expressed in the age-old adage "Run away and fight another day."

The third response, fighting, is activated only once the animal has been caught by the predator or the animal simply cannot outrun the predator. Prey still have the capacity to inflict serious injury by kicking or spearing with horns or antlers, and such an injury would potentially be a serious blow to a predator, which depends upon its capacity to kill to survive. A predator with a damaged eye or broken bone will not survive in the wild long, because it cannot successfully kill. The same is true in people, such that most recognize that if it is impossible to run away from a threatening person, the pure odds of surviving a physical attack will be increased by fighting back. It is important to acknowledge that fighting back may not lead to optimal well-being, but it will promote sheer survival.

The fourth, and last response, is to faint, to dissociate, or in any other fashion not be present emotionally during the attack. Indeed, this is the last resort of survival. Predators are typically driven by movement, and once movement stops (i.e., the prey is dead or acts dead), they stop attacking. Therefore, if the prey has been detected, has tried to run away and failed, and cannot sufficiently fight back, then the best chance it has to survive is to, in essence, play dead. Once the animal stops moving further, potentially life-threatening damage can be avoided. Grizzly bear attack survivors often credit their survival to passing out, stopping movements, or simply playing dead. Grizzly bears, like other predators, will often bury their kill to let it season before consuming it. Many grizzly attack survivors indeed report that they were partially buried before the bear left. In a more (unfortunately) common experience, many people respond to the trauma of rape by "catatonic immobility," which is a response akin to not being present in spirit after a realization that all other measures of resistance have failed.

Such catatonic immobility response is related to the vasovagal syncope response in that blood pressure drops, the body goes limp, and the person "checks out," or is present in body only. The vasovagal syncope response is a much stronger drop in blood pressure than that experienced during tonic immobility, and has the common and direct side effect of blood draining away from the head, and fainting frequently results. Unfortunately, this is the primary response mode of a subset of specific phobia patients, primarily those who are blood phobic or phobic to medical/dental/injection procedures. For people who experience this vasovagal syncope response, they respond to their feared stimuli with the unique, diphasic pattern of responding that exemplifies the vasovagal syncope response. While most fears are associated with increased arousal upon exposure to the feared stimuli, these specific phobias are sometimes instead related to this diphasic response mode. First, as with most fears, heart rate and blood pressure increase for a few seconds or minutes. Then, however, there is a sudden decrease in arousal, often accompanied by fainting. The term *vasovagal syncope* is often used to describe this phenomenon, where heart rate and blood pressure suddenly fall and muscle tone is reduced, presumably due to the vagus nerve, a parasympathetic nerve that innervates the chest and upper abdomen. This phenomenon is also a suspected part of a behavioral descriptor of the German term *Platzschwindel,* referring to the sensation of dizziness in public places, or more simply *Platzangst,* which describes fear of open spaces. Such dizziness can often be experienced as a sense of unreality or as if the earth is moving or the body is moving in space. Many specific phobia patients who exhibit the fainting response also often endorse that they feel easily dizzy, shaky, unsteady, and unreal. These symptoms appear to be precursors to the full fainting response.

This fainting response presents a problem in the usual treatment of anxiety. Many versions of anxiety are treated in part with various relaxation procedures aimed at reducing the tension, pressure, and rapid breathing associated with high arousal and high blood pressure commonly experienced in the presence of threat. Indeed, the typical treatment approach for anxiety incorporates some exercises that specifically aim to reduce blood pressure. This is, in fact, contraindicated for a person who already exhibits a low blood pressure problem, like those with the vasovagal tendency. Yet exposure to the feared stimulus is absolutely a necessary component for overall fear reduction and the diminishing of the vasovagal syncope response. The "trick" is therefore to find a way in which sufferers can be repeatedly exposed to the feared situation without fainting, so that they indeed can habituate to the threat and consequently experience a decrease in their reactivity. This is where applied tension plays a pivotal role in the treatment of anxiety.

The primary aim of applied tension is to increase blood pressure and cerebral blood flow. This coping skill is designed to have two parts. The first part consists of teaching the patient how to tense the gross body muscles, and the second is to learn how to identify the earliest signs of dropping blood pressure. Besides reducing risk of fainting, this technique also has the added benefit of decreasing the amount of time that the patient is unconscious should they actually pass out.

The patient is first provided a rationale for the treatment program, after which the skills are demonstrated, and then the patient practices them. The patient practices initially while seated in a comfortable armchair. In the seated position, the patient tenses arm muscles, the torso, and then the legs. This tension is held for approximately 10 to 15 seconds, which typically is long enough for the patient to begin feeling the temperature rise in his or her face. This rising facial temperature and flushing is the sign that cerebral blood pressure is increasing, much like what occurs to a fighter jet plane pilot who is wearing an antigravity suit while performing high-G turns (i.e., the G-suit prevents blackout in pilots by squeezing the legs, arms, and torso of the pilot with increasing G's, to force the blood back into the head). Patients then relax until their bodies feel normal again, which usually occurs within 20 to 30 seconds. They then practice bringing the warmth back to their faces repeatedly, using the same applied-tension technique. The same series of exercises of tensing and relaxing, to produce an increase in blood pressure on demand, is then practiced five times a day. This practice facilitates comfort with increasing blood flow to the head on cue. Once the patient can demonstrate this skill readily and on demand, the typical approach to anxiety treatment begins, namely, exposure. For example, the patient is shown incrementally more and more challenging pictures of injury or bloody scenarios. When patients notice signs of dropping blood pressure (e.g., feeling faint, dizzy, clammy, nauseous, damp),

they then apply the tension skill set to prevent sufficient blood from leaving the head, to ultimately prevent fainting. This is initially done to pictures alone, and then, provided the actual stimulus is possible to experience in vivo, live exercises are continued. Often, this leads up to some actual medical procedure, or the like, that the patient had been avoiding.

RESEARCH BASIS

Research shows that applied tension is superior to the standard exposure treatment (without tension) used for most other anxiety disorders. Lars-Göran Öst and his Swedish colleagues found, for example, that within five sessions, 90% of patients treated with applied tension met the compelling clinically significant improvement standard, whereas only 40% treated in the conventional exposure fashion (without tension) met clinical improvement. This adds support to the central role that the vasovagal syncope response plays for those specific-phobia patients who experience fainting as a primary symptom. Just as fighter jet plane pilots will inevitably black out (i.e., faint) with increasing G's without their G-suits squeezing blood into their heads, so will vasovagal fainting occur without some pressure to keep blood from draining from the head. This can readily be accomplished through applied tension, but it may also be facilitated by keeping the head lower than the heart or assuming a prone position.

RELEVANT TARGET POPULATIONS AND EXCEPTIONS

Most patients who demonstrate the vasovagal fainting response have today been treated effectively with the applied tension technique. The technique was specifically designed to assist this population, and it is of no real use for other populations that do not exhibit this specific fainting response. For people who simply fear fainting but have never actually fainted, it may be an advantage to teach patients the skill set before starting formal exposure treatment, to assist those who may indeed be prone to such a response when avoidance and escape are reduced and eventually stopped. For example, a strong family history of fainting may be an indicator that the person could be prone to such a response. As with any other biophysiological intervention, clearance should be obtained from the patient's medical doctor to ensure that there are no organic contraindications for applied tension.

COMPLICATIONS

The most commonly experienced complication with applied tension is headaches. Should this occur in the patient, it may be a sign that the patient is applying too much tension, thus forcing too much blood into the head, producing a tension headache. This phenomenon is easily combated by having the patient tense and tighten muscles to approximately only 6 or 7 on a 10-point tension scale. Indeed, if the patient is producing tension of 9 or 10 on a 10-point scale, this may be a sure recipe for tension headaches. In describing the rationale and demonstrating the skill set to the patient, the amount of pressure applied should also be described.

CASE ILLUSTRATION

"Joe" was a 36-year-old, divorced, unemployed man, who had been avoiding getting injections or blood draws for many years, primarily because he would on most occasions faint during such procedures. If he remained prone during a blood draw, he would sometimes manage to remain conscious, but his aversive experience with such procedures left him extensively avoiding them. Recently, Joe was referred by his psychiatrist because he is also bipolar and is noncompliant with blood-level checks. During a recent visit with his doctor, it became clear that Joe had experienced some adverse physiological effects due to not maintaining a close check on his blood levels of lithium. Joe had subsequently reported his reluctance for getting the mandatory blood work as being due to the experience of fainting. His psychiatrist subsequently referred him for treatment of this strong vasovagal fainting response so that he could become compliant with his medication-level checks. Because of the new experience of a direct, negative effect on his health, Joe was motivated to learn how to control his fainting so that he could submit to regular blood work. Outside of experiencing new health problems, he may never have presented for treatment.

Treatment began with a rationale for how the fainting response works and why relaxation (which he had been erroneously advised to try before) would not help. The general principles of pressure were explained as they pertained to keeping fighter pilots from blacking out during high-G maneuvers. This response was then explained on a more personal level for Joe, so that he gained insight into why he was fainting. He reported that the principles made sense, and he relayed that when he was prone, the fainting occurred less frequently and he sometimes was able to reduce dizziness by putting his head between his knees. The procedure was then demonstrated, after which Joe began to practice it. After practicing for a week, his capacity to produce color and warmth in his face on demand was assessed. When it was established that he was able to do so, general conversations about blood work procedures ensued. Joe used applied tension when he felt himself getting dizzy and weak. Treatment then progressed systematically through looking at photographs of injections and blood draws, and to the same on video. Once Joe could stand watching these without feeling faint and needed to rely less on the tension technique, the treatment stepped into the in vivo phase, in which Joe and the therapist went to look at the hospital lab. There, they observed other patients getting blood drawn live. Once this became more comfortable, Joe was able to observe, in very close quarters, the therapist getting blood drawn. Following this, Joe was able to get his own blood drawn on a regular basis. Although he did not find the experience of blood draws enjoyable, he was able to submit to regular blood-level checks. He was also able to receive updated vaccinations. At 3-years posttreatment, Joe is reportedly still regularly obtaining blood levels, and he has not suffered any further ill effects of the medications prescribed for bipolar disorder.

—*Johan Rosqvist*

See also: *Anxiety Management (Vol. II); Applied Relaxation and Tension (Vol. I); Breathing Retraining (Vol. I)*

Suggested Readings

Antony, M. M., & Barlow, D. H. (2002). Specific phobias. In D. H. Barlow (Ed.), *Anxiety and its disorders: The nature and treatment of anxiety and panic* (2nd ed., pp. 380–417). New York: Guilford Press.

Antony, M. M., Craske, M. G., & Barlow, D. H. (1995). *Mastery of your specific phobia.* Albany, NY: Graywind.

Graham, D. T., Kabler, J. D., & Lunsfors, L. (1961). Vasovagal fainting: A diphasic response. *Psychosomatic Medicine, 23,* 493–507.

Kleinknecht, R. A. (1994). Acquisition of blood, injury, and needle fears and phobias. *Behaviour Research and Therapy, 32*(8), 817–823.

Kozak, M. J., & Montgomery, G. K. (1981). Multimodal behavioral treatment of recurrent injury-scene-elicited fainting (vasodepressor syncope). *Behavioral Psychotherapy, 9,* 316–321.

Marks, I. M. (1987). *Fears, phobias, and rituals: Panic, anxiety, and their disorders.* Oxford, UK: Oxford University Press.

McLean, P. D., & Woody, S. R. (2001). *Anxiety disorders in adults: An evidence-based approach to psychological treatment.* Oxford, UK: Oxford University Press.

Öst, L. G. (1992). Blood and injection phobia: Background and cognitive, physiological, and behavioral variables. *Journal of Abnormal Psychology, 101*(1), 68–74.

Öst, L. G., & Sterner, U. (1987). Applied tension: A specific behavioral method for treatment of blood phobia. *Behaviour Research and Therapy, 25*(1), 25–29.

Öst, L. G., Sterner, U., & Lindahl, I. L. (1984). Physiological responses in blood phobics. *Behaviour Research and Therapy, 22,* 109–177.

AROUSAL TRAINING

DESCRIPTION OF THE STRATEGY

Arousal training in adults may be used for a range of clinical disorders and may involve interventions to reduce or enhance levels of arousal. Patients need to be trained to detect their levels of arousal and then implement strategies to either increase or decrease these levels. Most particularly, arousal training may be effective for a range of anxiety disorders, where arousal levels need to be reduced, or for sexual dysfunction, where arousal levels may need to be increased. The two disorders that are considered in this entry are panic disorder and male erectile disorder. These two disorders have been chosen because (a) there is a clear association between levels of arousal and the disorder; (b) treatments have been developed to address the arousal symptoms; and (c) panic disorder illustrates high levels of arousal, whereas erectile disorder occurs as a result of low levels of arousal.

PANIC DISORDER

The symptoms of a panic attack include dizziness, sweating, a racing heart, trembling, shaking, and shortness of breath. People who are diagnosed with panic disorder experience recurrent, unexpected panic attacks. They experience high levels of anxiety about the consequences of their panic attacks, as well as concerns about future attacks.

Effective treatment programs for panic disorder help patients tune into their levels of arousal and then implement strategies to reduce their arousal levels before the onset of a panic attack. This may involve breathing retraining, which has a calming effect and serves to prevent the patient from hyperventilating. Cognitive restructuring, which involves a process of altering cognitions about panic attacks and also addressing the automatic thoughts that frequently accompany panic attacks, is also a useful strategy in the treatment of this disorder. Graded exposure to the situation that precipitates the panic attack is also a helpful strategy, particularly for patients who experience panic with agoraphobia. A hierarchy of events can be established, from least arousing to highest in arousal levels, and this hierarchy can be worked though using both controlled breathing and cognitive-restructuring techniques.

MALE ERECTILE DISORDER

Erectile disorder is a common problem among males, with estimates indicating that 40% of men over 40 years of age experience this problem. The disorder is likely to increase with increasing age. It is expressed as difficulty in a man experiencing sufficient levels of sexual arousal to obtain an erection. Erectile disorder may be either partial or complete, with some men experiencing a less robust erection and others experiencing a total loss of erectile capacity. There appear to be both physiological and psychological factors that contribute to the disorder.

Treatment for erectile disorder primarily focuses on variations of Masters and Johnson's sensate focus program. This program involves strategies to increase arousal through systematic desensitization. Essentially, the man is encouraged to focus on the enjoyment of the sexual interaction and not the extent of his erection. Stimulation commences in the general body areas, then moves progressively to the more sexual parts of the body. By taking the focus off performance and shifting the attention to sexual enjoyment, performance anxiety decreases and sexual arousal (and so the degree of the man's erection) increases.

There have been limited recent research studies on psychological treatments for this arousal disorder, since most recent treatments have focused on the use of medical interventions. However, the data that are available suggest that strategies that enhance arousal by taking the pressure off performance are successful in most cases of erectile disorder with a psychological cause.

CONCLUSION

The treatment of the two disorders considered above indicate effectiveness of cognitive-behavioral treatment regimes to address arousal levels for psychological disorders with both high or low levels of arousal. Although the specific target of the treatment and the strategies that are adopted are different, it would appear that addressing levels of arousal is important for effective outcomes for these two psychological disorders.

—*Marita McCabe*

See also: Marshall, William L. (Vol. I); Masturbatory Retraining (Vol. I); Orgasmic Reconditioning (Vol. I)

Suggested Readings

Barlow, D. H. (1988). *Anxiety and its disorders: The nature and treatment of anxiety and panic.* New York: Guilford Press.

Barlow, D. H., & Craske, M. G. (1989). *Mastery of your anxiety and panic.* Albany, NY: Graywind.

Hawton, K. (1993). *Sex therapy.* Oxford, UK: Oxford University Press.

Leiblum, S. R., & Rosen, R. C. (2000). *Principles and practice of sex therapy.* New York: Guilford Press.

ASSOCIATION FOR ADVANCEMENT OF BEHAVIOR THERAPY

ORGANIZATIONAL OVERVIEW

The Association for Advancement of Behavior Therapy (AABT) is a nonprofit organization of health and mental health professionals interested in behavioral and cognitive therapies. The organization is international and seeks to (a) advance the understanding of human behavior; (b) develop, assess, and apply interventions for behavior change; and (c) further the empirical study and advance the theoretical and practical application of behavioral and cognitive therapies. In addition to these general goals, the organization promotes public awareness of behavior and cognitive therapies, operates a therapist locator service, publishes fact sheets, newsletters, and journals, and holds an annual convention that serves an important education and training function.

EARLY INFLUENCES

Though AABT is less than 40 years old, foundations of "behavior therapy" can be traced to laboratory research conducted in the early 20th century. Classical and operant conditioning, the two major forms of learning theory that predominate among AABT members today, rose to prominence during this time. Pavlov's seminal work on conditioned reflexes and John Watson's 1913 treatise on "Psychology as the Behaviorist Views It" were watershed events in the development and dissemination of classical conditioning. The period from 1920 until shortly after World War II was marked by rapid development of learning theories, with significant contributions by Guthrie, Hull, and Mowrer. Along with classical conditioning, the instrumental or operant conditioning theory, developed by Thorndike and further elaborated by Skinner in the 1930s through the 1950s, ultimately prevailed, at least among applied behaviorists.

Although several studies in the 1920s and 1930s indicated that behavioral approaches to clinical problems such as anxiety had promise, widespread adoption of the approach was not forthcoming. In fact, before World War II, the practice of psychotherapy was primarily limited to psychiatrists with psychoanalytic training. Following World War II, however, increased demand for therapists paved the way for clinical psychologists. Furthermore, since proponents of behavioral and learning theories were far more prevalent in postwar academic environments (particularly psychology departments) than in medical schools or general health care settings, the change of the psychologist's role from psychodiagnostician to psychotherapist permitted behaviorally trained psychologists greater access to clinical populations.

As the number of experimentally trained and behaviorally oriented therapists grew, dissatisfaction with psychoanalysis also grew. Leading the chorus of criticisms leveled against psychoanalysis were many of the founding members of AABT. Thus, the origins of behavior therapy and AABT can be traced to the aspirations of a handful of individuals who sought to "advance" alternatives to psychoanalysis that would more readily alleviate human distress and suffering.

MAJOR CONTRIBUTORS

As noted previously, AABT comprises adherents of two major schools of learning theory, classical and operant conditioning. Over the past 25 years, devotees of information-processing theory, often identifying themselves as practitioners of cognitive therapy (CT) or cognitive behavior therapy (CBT), have joined the organization in increasing numbers. Clinicians deriving their behavioral formulations from classical conditioning called themselves "behavior therapists," whereas adherents of operant conditioning referred to themselves as "behavior modifiers" or "behavior analysts." Adherents of both schools of thought have played and continue to play an important role in the organization. Practitioners of CT and CBT have also made vital contributions to the organization.

As noted earlier, founders of the AABT emerged primarily from two seminal groups. The group led by Hans Eysenck met weekly at his home in London. Cyril Franks, AABT's first president, regularly attended. Eysenck's work and the work of his students and colleagues focused on dissatisfactions with traditional psychotherapy and developing a treatment approach based on empirically testable assumptions derived from learning theory. Around this time, discussions about what to call this new therapy arose. The term *behavior therapy* came to refer to the application of learning theory to the treatment of psychological disorders. In 1958, Wolpe and Lazarus traveled to London to share their findings with Eysenck's group. Through his work in London, Eysenck helped Wolpe disseminate his "psychotherapy by reciprocal inhibition" (i.e., systematic desensitization). Among the seminal papers in behavior therapy in the 1950s and 1960s was Eysenck's critical review of the psychotherapy literature that set the stage for greater acceptance of empirically based psychotherapy. His text *Behavior Therapy and the Neuroses* was the first book to use "behavior therapy" in its title.

In 1963, Eysenck and Rachman founded the first journal for research in this new field, *Behaviour Research and Therapy*. For the first time, researchers had a means to efficiently communicate and advance their ideas. Such outlets were important for a growing movement that staked its legitimacy on research and the application of basic science to clinical problems. Wolpe's work was especially important in this regard, as it began with attempts to condition "experimental neurosis" in the laboratory and produced a clinical intervention of considerable effectiveness. Participants in both the London and South African groups thought of themselves as "enthusiastic mavericks" who dared to challenge the psychiatric establishment.

In this sense, founders of AABT seemed acutely aware of and connected to the revolutionary spirit of the times. Their philosophical commitment to social responsibility, idealism, and optimism resulted in a clinical service orientation that was progressive and challenged the status quo.

Adherents of the operant learning tradition trace their intellectual heritage to B. F. Skinner. In 1953, Skinner and Ogden Lindsley began to use the term behavior therapy to refer to the application of operant conditioning principles to the problems of disabled adults and children. In 1965, Leonard Ullmann (AABT past president, 1969–1970) and Leonard Krasner (an AABT founder) contributed *Case Studies in Behavior Modification,* in which the term *applied behavior analysis* was used to refer to the application of operant conditioning techniques such as contingency management to clinical problems. In 1968, *The Journal of Applied Behavior Analysis* was initiated. Many of the early contributors to the applied behavior analysis literature, such as Nathan Azrin (AABT past president, 1975–1976) and Steven Hayes (AABT past president, 1998–1999), have also assumed leadership roles in AABT. Teodoro Ayllon and Nate Azrin's work with children and institutionalized adults with developmental disabilities, as well as the introduction of token economies, were major contributions, as were clinical work and research conducted by Ivar Lovaas, Sidney Bijou, Donald Baer, Todd Risley (AABT past president, 1976–1977), and many others. By the late 1970s, members of AABT, whether identified as behavior therapists or as behavior analysts, had published a significant body of clinical work and research that helped to establish the legitimacy of AABT as a professional organization.

ORGANIZATIONAL HISTORY

Today, AABT is the largest promoter of behavior therapy in the United States and Canada, with more than 4,000 members. While no single person can be credited with founding the organization, two behavioral research groups in the 1950s were instrumental its creation. Hans Eysenck at the Maudsley Hospital (University of London, Institute of Psychiatry) led one group, and Joseph Wolpe (AABT past president, 1967–1968), in Johannesburg, South Africa, led the other. Behavior therapy's initial acceptance in the United Kingdom and South Africa was not accidental. Psychodynamic psychotherapy was not as influential in these countries as in the United States. Clinical work produced by the London and Johannesburg groups in the 1950s and 1960s led to numerous publications and seminal texts on behavior therapy. Although a number of factors appear to have contributed to the formation of AABT, a frequently cited factor was a dearth of publication outlets as well as difficulty getting behavioral research published in traditional clinical journals.

The AABT was founded in 1966 at a meeting in the New York City apartment of Dorothy Suskind, the organization's first executive secretary. Founding members included John Paul Brady (AABT past president, 1970–1971), Joseph Cautela (AABT past president, 1972–1973), Edward Dengorve, Herb Fensterheim, Cyril Franks (AABT past president, 1966–1967), Leonard Krasner, Arnold Lazarus (AABT past president, 1968–1969), Andrew Salter, and Joseph Wolpe (AABT past president, 1967–1968). The first AABT "conference" was held in 1967 in a room borrowed from the American Psychological Association during its annual convention. The program consisted of a business meeting, one symposium, and approximately 20 papers that involved 40 authors. By contrast, the most recent AABT convention in Reno, Nevada (2002), hosted more than 2,100 attendees and 1,100 paper or poster presentations, in addition to numerous workshops, invited presentations, and organizational meetings for 26 special interest groups.

Publication of a newsletter, *The Behavior Therapist,* began simultaneously with the founding of the organization. By 1970, the organization sponsored the publication of the journal *Behavior Therapy,* and in 1994, a second journal, *Cognitive and Behavioral Practice,* was added. In 1973, the organization acquired leased space, and in 1993, it moved to 4,000 square feet of office space in New York City, with nine full-time employees, including an executive director.

CURRENT WORK AND VIEWS

Behavior therapy has developed into an established and respected treatment approach. Members of AABT have played important roles in shaping contemporary clinical work, ranging from assessment to treatment to prevention. With acceptance, some behavior therapists gradually abandoned their commitments to classical and operant conditioning as their sole intervention models. Many, such as Michael Mahoney, Donald Meichenbaum, and Arnold Lazarus, reported feeling constrained by these models. Increasingly, AABT members began to incorporate a more eclectic mix of other therapy models into their treatment approaches and, in particular, elements of cognitive theorizing. While this movement was positively regarded by many AABT members, not all were receptive to this broadening of behavior therapy. Particularly notable was Wolpe's condemnation of cognitive therapy as "watering down and destroying the purity of behavior therapy." Nevertheless, the "cognitive movement" was well under way even as AABT formed. In fact, the first issue of *Behavior Therapy,* in 1970, contained Beck's paper introducing cognitive therapy.

In retrospect, the "cognitive revolution" seemed to capture some of the iconoclastic spirit of the founders of behavior therapy two decades earlier. In 1975, Meichenbaum's *Cognitive Behavior Modification Newsletter* was mailed to 100 people, later growing to 3,000 people in 20 countries. Perhaps these activities and the passionate debate inspired by these dialogues re-created something of the sense of purpose evident among the founders of AABT. Indeed, many of the early proponents of cognitive therapy were criticized for their "heretical views," as had happened to the early behavior therapists. Like their early behavior therapy counterparts, cognitive therapists needed publication outlets, and thus, *Cognitive Therapy and Research* was launched in 1977 by Mahoney. Despite somewhat personal attacks and intellectual challenges, cognitive behaviorists did not leave AABT. Indeed, by the end of the 1980s, many, if not the majority of, AABT members referred to themselves as "cognitive behaviorists."

Throughout the 1980s and 1990s, the organization maintained steady growth. The organization has grown from about 2,000 members in 1975 to more than 4,000 members today. While there were few, if any, publication outlets for behavioral research in the early 1960s, AABT now publishes two professional journals, and a large number of other publications can be identified as behavioral or cognitive behavioral. Prominent behavior therapists have served at state, federal, and international research and social service agencies. Senior AABT members have received numerous honors from the American Psychological Association and other professional societies. Members of AABT are employed by some of the finest universities and colleges in the world. Behavior therapists have been recipients of multi-million-dollar grants investigating the utility of behavioral and cognitive therapies. In general, evaluations of interventions derived from large studies and meta-analyses have established behavior therapy as equally, or in many cases, more effective than other interventions, including pharmacotherapy. The positive findings have been impressive in scope, ranging from work with children and adults across the full range of clinical syndromes found in contemporary psychology. In addition, settings in which behavior therapists find themselves and the range of problems seem to be ever increasing; effective interventions have been demonstrated for diverse problems, ranging from sexual assault to prevention and safety, workplace stress reduction, health psychology, AIDS prevention, bed-wetting, eating disorders, alcohol and drug problems, marital problems, autism, parenting, and child abuse, to name a few.

FUTURE PLANS AND DIRECTIONS

Among the most significant challenges to the membership of AABT are the growing acceptance of behavior therapy, the relationship of science to practice, and threats to the continued acceptance and credibility of behavioral therapies. While the AABT is still a small organization relative to the American Psychological Association and other professional societies, AABT has experienced significant growth in membership, and favorable media coverage has made behavior therapy an important and increasingly well-known treatment option. With greater mainstream acceptance has come a very different set of challenges. For example, increasing numbers of therapists with little formal training or expertise in behavioral psychotherapy are representing themselves as "behavior therapists" or "cognitive behavior therapists." Consequently, concerns have been raised about treatment fidelity and possible abuses of the public trust and credibility of behavior therapy.

Similar to the American Psychological Association, membership growth in AABT has been largely achieved by adding members with an applied focus, as opposed to an academic or scientific orientation. In recent years, some members have questioned the commitment of the organization to science. In contrast to the skeptical, self-critical stance demanded by the science-oriented practitioner is the need to promote the interests of a diverse membership. Wolpe's caution

against the easy acceptance and endorsement of newly developed clinical procedures prior to critical evaluation is a good example of the conservative bias of scientific inquiry. On the other hand, to advance science and practice, the membership of AABT must be cautious about anointing particular treatment procedures as "effective" or evidence based. Continued innovations are requirements for any organization seeking to "advance," and setting evidence standards too high (at least initially) could reduce future innovation in behavior therapy.

In contrast to numerous studies demonstrating "efficacy" (i.e., good evidence of behavior change under controlled conditions), the "real-world" effectiveness of behavioral therapies may be lacking. Some of the most pressing areas for improvement stem from higher rates of treatment underutilization, therapy dropout, and therapeutic failures in disadvantaged and minority populations. Moreover, a behavior therapy that restricts itself to an individual-therapy (talk therapy) treatment model may be unappealing not just to the poor, but to the growing ranks of non-White, non-European clients who might seek counseling. Research suggests potential clients will more readily accept and seek out behavior therapy if it fits their existing worldviews and lifestyles. Simply put, developers of behavioral therapies will need to address diversity.

A third consideration is marketing the behavior therapy model. Because behavioral treatments are problem focused and relatively cost-effective, marketing these therapies in an "outcome-oriented" environment should not be difficult. Some have questioned the need to "sell" behavior therapy, arguing that "data" will prevail in demonstrating the superiority of behavioral and cognitive-behavioral therapies. However, selection or acceptance of a treatment approach is influenced by multiple factors (e.g., prevailing perceptions of effective treatment, the availability of well-trained practitioners, treatment acceptability, cost, and ease of implementation). Given these and other considerations, the widespread acceptance of BT and CBT will be a function of dissemination efforts at the practice level.

Finally, although many individuals remain philosophically opposed to biological solutions to social and interpersonal problems, the position that human suffering and behavior problems result from disease processes with biological or genetic bases is gaining credibility. This may represent one of the most formidable challenges to the future growth of behavior therapy. Sometimes described as the "medical model," this view may be appealing to potential users of behavior therapy because biological approaches offer many of the same advantages as BT and CBT. Namely, pharmacological approaches are generally perceived as efficacious and cost-effective. Unfortunately, this model also suggests that individuals are not "responsible" for their behavior, thus discouraging attempts to cope with these problems. Pharmacological approaches also have the advantage of being symptom- or problem-focused. Interestingly, the pharmaceutical industry spends millions of dollars every year on research, development, and marketing, targeting improvement in symptom relief and reduction of side effects. No comparable effort to systematically develop, improve, and disseminate behavioral therapies exists.

If the above sounds dire, it need not be, as the data clearly suggest that behavioral therapies are generally more effective than other approaches, including biological approaches. In addition, many people are still uncomfortable with pharmacological treatments for behavioral problems and will prefer psychosocial approaches. Indeed, available evidence suggests that the environment changes biology and that effective psychotherapy induces physiological changes that might be similar to and perhaps more long-lasting than the pharmacological approaches. In addition, advances in our understanding of the human genome will highlight the need for behavioral science, rather than render it obsolete. The membership of AABT should continue to play an important role in the development, application, and dissemination of behavioral science in the 21st century.

—*David Reitman and Linda Carter Sobell*

See also: *Applied Behavior Analysis (Vol. III); Behavior Therapy (Vol. II); Franks, Cyril M. (Vol. I)*

Suggested Readings

Cautela, J. (1990). The shaping of behavior therapy: A historical perspective. *The Behavior Therapist, 13,* 211–212.

Fishman, D. B., & Franks, C. M. (1997). The conceptual evolution of behavior therapy. In P. L. Wachtel & S. B. Messer (Eds.), *Theories of psychotherapy: Origins and evolution* (pp. 131–180). Washington, DC: American Psychological Association.

Franks, C. M. (1987). Behavior therapy and AABT: Personal recollections, conceptions, and misconceptions. *The Behavior Therapist, 10,* 171–174.

AUTOGENIC TRAINING

DESCRIPTION OF THE STRATEGY

I. H. Shultz developed autogenic training (AT) in 1932, borrowing from the techniques of yoga and hypnosis. The goal of AT is to decrease stress by self-inducing feelings of warmth and heaviness brought on by lower heart and respiratory rates, as well as decreased muscle tension. There are six phases to AT, including inducing heaviness, inducing warmth, heart practice, breathing practice, abdominal practice, and head practice. The phases are achieved through mentally repeating a series of statements a fixed number of times. For instance, I am completely calm (repeat one time); My right arm is heavy (repeat six times); I am completely calm (repeat one time); My right arm is warm (repeat six times); I am completely calm (repeat one time); My heart beats calmly and regularly (repeat six times); I am completely calm (repeat one time); My breathing is calm and regular, it breathes me (repeat six times); I am completely calm (repeat one time); My abdomen is flowingly warm (repeat six times); I am completely calm (repeat one time); My forehead is pleasantly calm (repeat six times); I am completely calm (repeat one time). As a beginner, it is important to repeat the preceding phrases exactly as specified. Once the technique has been mastered, abbreviations can be made. The session is concluded by instructing the individual to say aloud, "Arms firm, breathe deeply, and open eyes."

Once relaxation has been mastered, personal formalized resolutions (e.g., "I am making good decisions") are repeated between 10 and 30 times. It is important to instruct the individual to concentrate on these statements and to ignore any other thoughts or distractions that may shift attention. The exercises should be completed in a dimly lit room with windows closed, with devices that make noise (e.g., radios, televisions, cell phones) turned off to avoid distractions.

AT can be taught in a relatively short period of time, usually a matter of weeks. For a beginner, the technique should be practiced two or three times daily at 5- to 10-minute intervals. A time schedule for practicing the technique should be emphasized. It is best to initiate AT in the morning, although midday practice of this technique may be spontaneously scheduled to give an added "energy boost" during stressful days.

For persons who suffer insomnia brought on by stress, Dr. Schulze recommends ending the day with this technique to "clear the body and mind tension."

RESEARCH BASIS

AT has demonstrated efficacy when implemented in the absence of other interventions (e.g., psychotherapy, psychopharmacology). However, this procedure has typically been examined when combined with other interventions. Indeed, outcome support for AT has been predominately limited to uncontrolled trials and controlled trials that have incorporated this procedure as an adjunctive component.

RELEVANT TARGET POPULATIONS AND EXCEPTIONS

AT has been shown to be effective in the reduction of stress and mental exhaustion, as well as in treating psychosomatic disturbances such as asthma, chronic migraine headaches and tension, eczema, insomnia, anxiety disorders (panic attacks), inability to concentrate, obesity, high blood pressure, trichotillomania (compulsive hair pulling or twisting), and nightmares resulting from posttraumatic stress disorder (PTSD). Hostility, including lower blood pressure and arterial pressure, have also been reduced consequent to AT. Thus, this procedure is often used in the context of preventative medicine. AT is not recommended for children below the age of 5 and those with mental retardation, because these populations frequently evidence problems attending to the prescribed formulas. Patients who suffer from hypoglycemia or diabetes are advised against using AT due to potential metabolic changes.

COMPLICATIONS

There are several complications in the implementation of AT. These complications include, but are not limited to, staying awake and alert while training, finding places devoid of external distractions and stimuli, concentration difficulties due to central nervous system stimulants and severe stress, and being incapable of suggestion or hypnosis. Patients who suffer from diabetes or hypoglycemia should not participate in AT at home, as heart rate and blood pressure can be affected by AT practice, resulting in unpredictable metabolic changes that may result in danger.

Therefore, persons with these conditions should obtain medical clearance prior to initiating AT. They should also ideally perform all AT practice in facilities where heart and blood pressure may be concurrently monitored. When poor concentration is evidenced during AT, it is advised that the phrase "I am awake and alert" be repeated intermittently throughout the formulas. The latter method may also assist drowsy individuals from falling asleep. Along these lines, deep relaxation and falling asleep sometimes occur during AT. When individuals are identified to evidence these problems, they should be instructed to avoid AT while operating vehicles or other heavy machinery. Strategies that appear to be effective in eliminating external disturbances are to be practiced right after awakening or immediately before bedtime.

When AT fails, it is most often due to the patient's inability to concentrate. If extreme stress and tension are causing the inability to relax and concentrate on the formulas, stop the technique and try another activity to bring about relaxation. When the patient is relaxed, the patient should be instructed to resume AT. It is also recommended that AT be practiced on a moderately empty stomach, as a full stomach often induces drowsiness. Stimulants (i.e., caffeine) should be avoided. If the day has been particularly stressful or tense, a few moments of deep breathing prior to AT may assist in bringing about relaxation.

—*Brad C. Donohue*

See also: *Classical Conditioning (Vol. I); Mindfulness Meditation (Vol. I); Relaxation Strategies (Vol. I)*

Suggested Readings

Farne, M. A., & Jimenez-Munoz, N. (2000). Personality changes induced by AT practice. *Stress Medicine, 16*(4), 263–268.

Haugen, N. S. (2000). The effect of autogenic relaxation on hostility and cardiovascular reactivity in African-American women. *Dissertation Abstracts International: Section B: The Sciences and Engineering, 61*(6-B0, 2988).

Legostaev, G. N. (1996). Changes in mental performance after voluntary relaxation. *Human Physiology, 22*(5), 637–638.

Linden, W. (1994). AT: A narrative and quantitative review of clinical outcome. *Biofeedback and Self-Regulation, 19*(3), 227–264.

Nakamura, N. (2000). The new applicative fields of AT. *Japanese Journal of Autogenic Therapy, 18*(2), 64–67.

Sato, Y., & Matanuga, I. (2002). Examination of "method learning of autogenic training" and "the clinical effects depending on it": The difference between "the direct clinical effects by the way of AT" and "the clinical effects moving it to the place." *Japanese Journal of Autogenic Therapy,* *21*(1–2), 16–23.

Schultz, J. H., & Luthe, W. (1969). *Autogenic therapy: Vol. I. Autogenic methods.* New York: Grune & Stratton.

Takaishi, N. (2000). A comparative study of AT and progressive relaxation as methods for teaching clients to relax. *Sleep and Hypnosis, 2*(3), 132–136.

AVERSION RELIEF

DESCRIPTION OF STRATEGY

Aversive conditioning is intended to produce a conditioned aversion to the target dysfunctional behavior. *Aversion therapy* includes a variety of specific techniques based on both classical and operant conditioning paradigms. An array of aversive stimuli have been used, the most popular of which were electric shock and nausea- or apnea-inducing substances. Covert sensitization also relies on aversive conditioning and is called "covert" because neither the undesirable stimulus nor the aversive stimulus is physically present; they are presented in imagination only. "Sensitization" refers to the intention to build up an avoidance response to the undesirable stimulus.

In *aversion relief,* the subject is enabled to stop the aversive stimulus by performing more appropriate behavior. This cessation, in turn, leads to relief. For example, deviant sexual stimuli (e.g., pictures of nude children) may be the unconditioned stimulus (UCS), followed by onset of shock, the conditioned stimulus (CS), while cessation of shock is preceded by the appearance of pictures of nude adult women. The procedure is intended to condition the pleasant experiences associated with the cessation of shock (aversion relief) to adult females, while the unpleasant experiences associated with the onset of shock are conditioned to children. A typical example of aversion relief therapy is the application of bitter-tasting substances on the thumbs of children who engage in thumb-sucking activity. Thumb sucking will then lead to a bad taste, which will cease as soon as the child withdraws the thumb out of the mouth (aversion relief).

Covert sensitization is also referred to as *aversive imagery.* Before starting the formal covert sensitization procedures, the therapist gathers detailed information of the idiosyncratic characteristics associated with the target maladaptive-approach behavior. This information is essential in order to construe realistic scenes for the patient. Next, the patient is provided with the rationale that his or her problem (e.g., drinking) is a strongly learned habit that must be unlearned by establishing a conditioned link between the pleasurable situation (e.g., drinking) and the unpleasant stimulus (feelings of nausea and vomiting).

To illustrate the covert sensitization procedures, consider the case of a male alcohol-dependent patient. First, the patient is trained to relax. When relaxed, he is asked to close his eyes and to clearly visualize a critical drinking situation. For example, he may be asked to visualize himself in a pub, looking at a glass full of beer, holding the glass in his hand, and having the glass touch his lips. Next, he is asked to imagine that he begins to feel sick to his stomach and that he starts vomiting all over himself and the female bartender; it is important to include as many aversive details as possible. He is told to imagine that he rushes outside or that whenever he is tempted to drink but refuses to do so, the feeling of nausea will remit and that he will feel relieved and relaxed (aversion relief). As a homework assignment, he is asked to repeat these scenarios a number of times per day. Key scenarios can be written on pocket-sized cards, which the patient is instructed to carry with him and to use immediately upon noticing an urge to drink. As a result, much in vivo conditioning occurs in critical temptation situations, during which the patient self-applies the prescribed procedure outside the therapist's office.

RESEARCH BASIS

Aversion relief procedures are rooted in learning theory. When an aversive stimulus is presented immediately after a response and cannot be escaped or avoided, it is considered *punishment.* When aversive stimuli are contingently removed following a desired response, it is termed *negative reinforcement.* When escape responses produce relief from aversive stimuli, the procedure is called *aversion relief.* For example, shock during alcohol sipping could be avoided or escaped by spitting out the alcohol. The aversion relief component of the treatment of alcoholics uses a desirable response (e.g., spitting out alcohol) as a potential positive-reinforcing stimulus, deriving its positive quality from its contiguity with escape. Moreover, cues that initially led to urges will gradually become discriminatory stimuli for avoidance behavior.

Successful outcome of aversion-relief-based procedures has been reported in the treatment of specific phobias, obsessive-compulsive behaviors, obesity, aphonia, torticollis, writing cramp, and various deviant sexual interests. However, most of these reports have been uncontrolled case studies. Controlled studies among anxiety disorder patients (mostly phobic and agoraphobic patients) have been conducted by Solyom and coworkers. Results have been inconclusive, partly due to methodological shortcomings. The only controlled study into the effectiveness of aversion relief with obsessive-compulsive patients found this treatment to be ineffective. Perhaps as a byproduct of the demonstrated effectiveness of exposure in vivo procedures, little interest has since been shown in evaluating the effectiveness of aversion relief in patients with anxiety disorders.

Several studies have evaluated the effects of covert sensitization among alcoholics, but the findings of most of these studies are difficult to interpret due to severe methodological limitations. Also, a number of studies have been reported that used covert sensitization to reduce deviant sexual interest. Generally, results of covert sensitization were positive, but again, a number of issues preclude more definite conclusions. There are reasons to believe that part of the effects of covert sensitization can be explained by expectancy of improvement rather than conditioning factors.

RELEVANT TARGET POPULATIONS

Aversion-based methods have been used in treating maladaptive-approach behaviors such as alcohol dependence, smoking, thumb sucking, specific phobias, obsessive-compulsive behaviors, obesity, aphonia, torticollis, writing cramp, and various deviant sexual interests. More controversially, aversive methods have also been applied to mentally retarded and autistic patients. Aversive stimulation has increasingly become ethically controversial. Furthermore, alternative and less intrusive/objectionable treatments have been found to be at least as effective. For example, in the area of anxiety disorders, exposure in vivo methods are now considered the golden standard, and there is little reason to believe that aversion relief therapy will be able to surpass the effects achieved with exposure in vivo therapy. Likewise, in the area of alcohol dependence, alternative cognitive-behavioral procedures have now been established as effective alternatives.

—Paul M. G. Emmelkamp and J. H. Kamphuis

See also: Emmelkamp, Paul M. G. (Vol. I); Extinction and Habituation (Vol. I); Relaxation Strategies (Vol. I)

Suggested Readings

Azrin, N. H., Nunn, R. G., & Frantz-Renshaw, S. (1980). Habit reversal treatment of thumbsucking. *Behaviour Research & Therapy, 18,* 395–399.

Emmelkamp, P. M. G. (1994). Behavior therapy with adults. In A. E. Bergin & S. L. Garfield (Eds.), *Handbook of psychotherapy and behavior change: An empirical analysis.* New York: Wiley.

Emmelkamp, P. M. G., & Walta, C. (1978). The effects of therapy-set on electrical aversion therapy and covert sensitization. *Behaviour Therapy, 9,* 185–188.

Kapche, R. (1974). Aversion-relief therapy: A review of current procedures and the clinical and experimental evidence. *Psychotherapy: Theory, Research, and Practice, 11,* 156–162.

Lichstein, K. L., & Hung, J. H. F. (1980). Covert sensitization: An examination of covert and overt parameters. *Behavioral Engineering, 6,* 1–18.

Solyom, L. (1971). A comparative study of aversion relief and systematic desensitization in the treatment of phobias. *British Journal of Psychiatry, 119,* 299–303.

Solyom, L. (1972). Variables in the aversion relief therapy of phobics. *Behavior Therapy, 3,* 21–28.

AZRIN, NATHAN H.

BIRTHPLACE

I was born on November 26, 1930, in Boston, Massachusetts, as part of a family that included five siblings, both parents, and grandparents.

EARLY INFLUENCES

My immigrant parents placed the highest priority on education for their children in their view of America as the land of limitless opportunity. As children, we were all expected to obtain paid employment as teenagers, as well as work in the family grocery.

EDUCATION HISTORY

I attended Boston University from 1948, where I majored in psychology, obtaining a BA in 1951, an MA in 1952, and continued in the PhD program in personality and social psychology. Because of my early interest in behavioral psychology, I transferred to Harvard University for the express purpose of studying under B. F. Skinner, receiving a PhD in 1956 from Harvard.

PROFESSIONAL MODELS

Like so many others, my initial interest in the field of psychology was inspired by Freud's writings. An undergraduate course by Dr. Leo Reyna solidified my decision to major in psychology by his elucidation of how quantitative methodology could experimentally evaluate psychological treatments and beliefs. The book by F. Keller and N. Schoenfeld on laboratory-derived principles of reinforcement offered a conceptual model for human applications, as did the studies by Skinner.

At Harvard University, I conducted studies in Skinner's animal lab, where I learned, as I intended, laboratory methodology with animals and Skinner's focus on descriptive analysis. Skinner was interested in my enrolling at Harvard since he had just finished his book *Science and Human Behavior,* the thrust of which coincided with my interest in applying learning theory to practical human problems. The only human research I conducted at Harvard, however, was to serve as Skinner's research assistant in evaluating the effectiveness of the "teaching machine," which Skinner conceived at that time.

Other professional models for me were O. H. Mowrer, for his imaginative animal studies with clinical implications and his development of the first behavioral treatment in the pad-and-buzzer method for enuresis. Kurt Lewin was a model for me of how to conduct human experiments in his group dynamics research.

MAJOR CONTRIBUTIONS TO THE FIELD

A small number of others (Ivar Lovaas, Ted Ayllon, Don Baer, Montrose Wolf, Todd Risley) and myself are generally considered the founders of the field known as *behavior modification* or *applied behavior analysis,* during the late 1950s and early 1960s. Prior to that time, experimental evaluations of clinical and other applied procedures were conspicuously absent, as noted by H. Eysenck, L. Krasner, and others in their writings.

My most popularly known contribution is probably the development of a very rapid and effective toilet-training program for normal children, described in a book still widely used, *Toilet Training in Less than a Day.* I developed this procedure as an extension of my development of effective training programs, including toileting, for profoundly retarded adults who had previously been classified as "untrainable." The other effective training programs I developed for this "untrainable" population were dressing, proper self-feeding, and nighttime continence, all of which are currently in use with this population. The nighttime continence program, known as "dry-bed training," followed the same sequence as the daytime toileting program in that I developed a program for nocturnal enuresis of normal children after having been fortunate in developing a similar program for the "untrainable" retarded.

The second most commonly used contribution of mine is probably the "token economy," also known as a "point system," "level system," or "reward program," which I developed with T. Ayllon. This method of motivating proper conduct and discouraging problematic conduct is now applied extensively by psychologists, parents, teachers, and caretakers in general to normal situations (parent-child, classroom) as well as clinical settings (hospitals, special education classes, attention-deficit/hyperactivity disorder, conduct disorder, etc.).

A third major contribution of mine is the "Job Club" program for assisting job seekers to obtain employment. This program, I have learned, has been and still is widely used and often mandated for job placement by many municipalities, states, and national governments. Its high placement rate of 90% plus has been found with severely job-handicapped populations, including welfare recipients, former mental hospital patients, and so on.

A fourth major contribution of mine is the "habit reversal" method, developed with Gregg Nunn, for treating motor tics, vocal tics, chronic motor tics, Tourette's disorder, trichotillomania, nail biting, and other persistent compulsive habits or movements. In recent clinical reviews, this method has usually been considered the "treatment of choice" in terms of its demonstrated effectiveness for these problems.

A fifth major contribution of mine was the identification of "time-out" in 1960, 1961, 1963 as having motivational properties when arranged as a response consequence, rather than its previous noncontingent use as in the extensive series of studies and comparisons of "spaced versus massed practice." This procedure is now widely used as a child-training procedure in positive parenting.

A sixth major contribution of mine was the "reciprocity counseling" program for marital dysfunction, which formulated several communication procedures, for example, for anger management, positive request, and cognitive restructuring as additives to the several procedures (contracting) developed by R. Stuart.

A seventh major contribution of mine was the community reinforcement method for treating alcoholism as well as drug addiction of youth and adults. In this method, I emphasized teaching incompatible behaviors as well as the above-mentioned communication procedures and reward arrangements.

Another method I developed is the procedure of correction, overcorrection, and positive practice, widely used in parenting and by caretakers. This method arranges as a consequence for errors, misbehaviors, or aggression the requirement that the misbehavior merely be remediated rather than attaching a penalty, reprimand, or loss of privileges. The procedure has been shown to be effective with children, students, and retarded persons and has generally been viewed as a particularly reasonable method of having the person "take responsibility" for his or her actions rather than arranging punishers.

The "regulated breathing" program that I developed with G. Nunn for stuttering is particularly noteworthy for its speed of benefit. A reduction of stuttering is usually attained within one session, additional time being expended primarily for generalization purposes.

OVERALL VIEWS

My overall perspective in developing new treatment methods has been to conduct actual outcome studies rather than speculating or theorizing about what theory is plausible or preferable. I believe that this perspective marks the emergence of clinical/applied psychology as a science-based discipline that now has specific procedural protocols for specific disorders. The substantive content of the procedure is to be discovered or developed for each problem; no general procedure seems to have been proven to be blindly applicable without empirically validated specific variations. My assumption regarding feasibility has been that learning and situational factors can overcome strong biological, societal, family, and medical factors by maximizing the learning and situational influences. I believe that cognitive and affective changes should be made in addition to behavior, which is in contrast with the views of most behavior analysts.

I conducted much of my treatment development research at the Anna State Hospital in Illinois from 1957 to 1980, under an administrative arrangement that I consider a researcher's ideal arrangement. The research was supported in large part by the State of Illinois Psychiatric Training and Research Authority, headed initially by Percival Bailey, MD, and later by Peter Levinson, PhD, both of whom supported my efforts in every way, requiring only that the resulting procedures be of benefit to mental disorders as well as socially appropriate functioning, inpatient or outpatient, at home or in school, in family or in work. The superintendent of Anna State Hospital was R. C. Steck, MD, who had been a family doctor with no special psychiatric or psychological philosophy other than to promote beneficial treatments.

My current/recent work at Nova Southeastern University in Ft. Lauderdale, Florida, has been with Tourette's disorder, insomnia, alcoholism, drug addiction, youth conduct disorder, self-injury of retarded persons, bulimia, and medication adherence of discharged mental hospital patients.

My future plans are to continue to influence psychology to be transformed into a science-based discipline and to continue developing proven methods of improving our functioning. I take great pleasure in looking back at my accomplishments in having developed so many very different procedures for so many difficult human problems, and I feel fortunate to have been blessed by the assistance of so many others and by the many granting agencies that made this possible.

—*Nathan H. Azrin*

See also: *Habit Rehearsal (Vol. II); Job Club Method (Vol. I); Token Economies (Vol. III)*

B

BARLOW, DAVID H.

I was born in Needham, Massachusetts, a suburb of Boston, in 1942, in the midst of World War II, in which my father was killed in action. I attended St. Sebastian's School, a Catholic prep school, graduating in 1960, and the University of Notre Dame, graduating in 1964. At Notre Dame, I became fascinated with literary insights into the often self-defeating behavior of fictional characters. This led to a period of intense study and reading of psychoanalytic characterizations of literary figures, and, ultimately, a vague commitment to a career in psychology. Needing a specific laboratory course in experimental psychology to meet requirements for graduate school, I found a course at Boston College in the summer of 1963, taught by Joseph R. Cautela. That summer, while I was immersed in the laboratories of experimental psychology, Cautela persuaded me that only through a reliance on the slow but inexorable progress of psychological science could the applications of psychology to clinical problems truly advance. Otherwise, applied and clinical psychology would be doomed to a never-ending reliance on fads of the moment. This was a radical idea at a time, when psychotherapy had little or no empirical base, and it was widely believed that none was needed. Rather, it was thought that human behavior and psychological disorders were far too deep and complex to submit to the rigors of the scientific method.

In 1964, after graduating from Notre Dame, I continued my study with Cautela at Boston College. Publication of Joseph Wolpe's book *Psychotherapy by Reciprocal Inhibition,* in 1958, was beginning to create a stir and by 1964 had convinced Cautela that "behavior therapy" might provide the means to realize the application of the principles of psychological science to the clinic. Having met Wolpe, Cautela arranged for me to spend the summer of 1966 working with Wolpe and acquiring firsthand some clinical skills in the fledgling techniques of systematic desensitization, assertiveness training, and direct behavioral modification based on operant principles.

After Beverly Colby and I were married, we left Boston in 1966 to journey to the University of Vermont. Emboldened with a firm belief in the scientific base of clinical psychology but with few, if any, programs espousing that philosophy, I was fortunate to come in contact with Harold Leitenberg, an experimental psychologist at the University of Vermont, who, teaming up with Stewart Agras from the psychiatry department at that university, was beginning an intensive program of clinical research. This program combined Leitenberg's training and experience in laboratories of operant psychology with Agras's deep clinical experience and his desire to be more empirical.

When Stewart Agras decided it was time to accept a chair in psychiatry in 1969, he invited me, just finishing my PhD, to join him in the search. Since most psychiatry departments were dominated in those days by psychoanalytical approaches and were actively hostile to more behavioral conceptualizations, the search took a while. In the fall of 1969, we finally settled on the University of Mississippi Medical Center, where a small psychiatry department with a short history had recently experienced the exodus of a number of existing faculty, leaving mostly open positions and creating the opportunity to shape a more empirically based department of psychiatry. Agras took full advantage of this opportunity by hiring a number of scientifically orientated psychiatrists and psychologists and asking me, fresh out of school myself, to form a clinical psychology internship program. With strong support from Henry Adams at the University of Georgia and the psychology faculty at the University of Mississippi and the University of Southern Mississippi, who supported my notion, unusual at the time, that clinical procedures could derive from the basic science of psychology, three interns were accepted to begin training in the fall of 1970.

This began a productive period of 5 years in which methodologies suitable to clinical research, such as single-case experimental designs emanating from the laboratories of operant psychology, were further developed, resulting in a book published in 1976 with Michel Hersen, *Single Case Experimental Designs*. While at Mississippi, I continued developing my interest in anxiety and sexual disorders and received my first National Institute of Mental Health (NIMH) grant studying the psychological aspects of sexual dysfunctions and deviations. I was promoted to associate professor and then professor of psychiatry in 1974 but had begun to miss my New England roots. When Brown University contacted me in 1974, the interest of the chair of psychiatry at Brown, Ben Feather, was as much in the successful psychology internship-training program as in the program of research. I relocated to Brown University in February of 1975, where I took over psychology programs with a joint appointment as professor of psychiatry and psychology and a charge to initiate the Brown University Clinical Psychology Internship Program.

My research on sexuality and anxiety continued at Brown University, as did the development of my ideas on the integration of science and practice, which ultimately yielded a second book, *The Scientist-Practitioner*, written with Steve Hayes, a former intern at Brown University, and Rosemery Nelson. During this time, I was particularly active in the Association for Advancement of Behavior Therapy (AABT) and was elected president in 1979. Nevertheless, research productivity diminished somewhat at Brown, due to the necessity of attending to administrative and political issues in a large department of psychiatry, and I decided it was time to relocate to a setting that allowed a more complete focus on clinical research. This led to a move to the State University of New York at Albany, joining my friend and colleague from Mississippi days, Ed Blanchard, in 1979, where he was to stay for 17 years. Together with Blanchard, we initiated the Center for Stress and Anxiety Disorders, which became a working research clinic with a large number of grants from the National Institutes of Health (NIH). In this setting, many excellent doctoral students received training in clinical research. Here also, the major themes of my research were fully elaborated: early research on the nosology of anxiety and mood disorders in collaboration with Peter DiNardo and, later, Tim Brown resulted in new conceptualizations of generalized anxiety disorder and panic disorder. These developments were communicated through my service on the anxiety disorders work group for *DSM-III-R* and, later, the task force for *DSM-IV*.

Research on psychopathology focused on the nature of anxiety as evidenced in males, and, later, females, presenting with sexual dysfunction. This particular paradigm afforded an easily quantifiable output of the influence of cognitive and affective components of anxiety in the form of psychophysiological measures of sexual arousal that could be manipulated out of the awareness of the patient. This research resulted in an early model of the process of anxiety manifested as sexual dysfunction. It was also during this time that I developed new treatments for anxiety and related disorders in collaboration with Michelle Craske, Ron Rapee, and others, most notably a new psychological approach to treating panic disorder that has been widely accepted and positively evaluated. Programmatic research on anxiety during the decade of the 1980s resulted in a book, pulling most of these ideas together.

In 1996, after an absence of 30 years, I returned to Boston to become professor of psychology, research professor of psychiatry, director of clinical programs, and director of the Center for Anxiety and Related Disorders at Boston University. The very next year, I had the good fortune to fulfill a long-planned year at the Center for Advanced Study in the Behavioral Sciences, where I updated my theory on the origins of anxiety disorders.

Now approaching the twilight of my career, I expect to devote my remaining years to broadening and deepening my theory of the origins of anxiety and its disorders, and developing a unified treatment protocol for the treatment of emotional disorders.

—David H. Barlow

See also: *Agras, W. Stewart (Vol. I); Behavior Training (Vol. I); Panic Control Treatment (Vol. I)*

Suggested Readings

Barlow, D. H. (1996). Health care policy, psychotherapy research, and the future of psychotherapy. *American Psychologist, 51,* 1050–1058.

Barlow, D. H. (Ed.). (2001). *Clinical handbook of psychological disorders: A step-by-step treatment manual* (3rd ed.). New York: Guilford Press.

Barlow, D. H., & Craske, M. G. (2000). *Mastery of your anxiety and panic: Client workbook for anxiety and panic* (3rd ed.). Boulder, CO: Graywind.

Barlow, D. H., Gorman, J. M., Shear, M. K., & Woods, S. W. (2000). Cognitive-behavioral therapy, imipramine, or their combination for panic disorder: A randomized controlled trial. *Journal of the American Medical Association, 283,* 2529–2536.

Barlow, D. H., Hayes, S. C., & Nelson, R. O. (1984). *The scientist-practitioner: Research and accountability in clinical and educational settings.* New York: Pergamon Press.

Barlow, D. H., & Hersen, M. (1984). *Single case experimental designs: Strategies for studying behavior change* (2nd ed.). New York: Pergamon Press.

BECK, AARON T.

Aaron Temkin Beck, MD, founder of cognitive therapy, was born in Providence, Rhode Island, on July 18, 1921. His parents were Russian Jewish immigrants who valued education and community involvement. His father, Harry Beck, was both the owner of a print shop and a member of the printers' union. Elizabeth Temkin Beck, his mother, had raised her eight younger brothers and sisters after her own mother died and she became the family matriarch. She was president of several local organizations and assertively spoke her opinions at public meetings. According to her sons, it is likely that Lizzie Beck suffered periodically from depression, which began when her only daughter died in the influenza epidemic of 1919. Many family members think that Aaron's birth relieved her depression.

A playground accident and resulting infection nearly killed Beck when he was 7 years old. He attributes his anxieties about surgery and abandonment to this trauma, for he was told that his arm was going to be x-rayed, but instead he was taken to surgery. Moreover, the surgeon began cutting before Beck was unconscious. The infection from his injury required an extended hospitalization, and he missed so much school that he was held back. This, he says, made him feel inferior to his classmates. Following his recovery, he studied so hard that he surpassed his classmates and skipped a grade. He believes this experience taught him how to turn a disadvantage into an advantage, a skill and perspective that would aid him throughout his career.

At Brown University, Beck majored in English and political science and won prizes for essays and oratory. He graduated from Yale School of Medicine, intending to become a neurologist. It was by chance that he entered psychiatry. As a neurology resident at Cushing Veterans Administration Hospital, he was required to do a psychiatry rotation. His earlier studies of psychiatry had left him cold, for he found the Kraepelinian approaches nihilistic and psychodynamic formulations unsubstantiated. As a resident, he struggled with psychoanalytic formulations because he thought they were unscientific. Believing that his pragmatism and rebelliousness interfered with his acceptance of psychoanalysis, he began his own personal analysis, which continued for several years.

Following initial publications on schizophrenia and combat stress, Beck focused on depression and dream research in 1959 in order to substantiate the psychoanalytic hypothesis that depressed individuals experience anger turned inward as the result of an earlier loss of a love object. In this and subsequent studies, Beck found that the themes in the dreams and waking thoughts of depressed persons were rejection, sensitivity to failure, and negative expectations, not hostility or a masochistic need to suffer. Thus, he began to reformulate the model of depression from being based on a person's motivation to how a person processes information in a negatively biased way.

Beck's thinking was influenced by George Kelly, Karen Horney, Alfred Adler, and Harry Stack Sullivan. Kelly's work provided validation for a non-motivational model, and his term "constructs" is like Beck's "schemas." Adler, Horney, and Sullivan were professional models with whom he could identify as he moved away from traditional analysts. Beck found his closest colleagues, however, among psychologists, and in 1963, Beck and Albert Ellis discovered similarities in their formulations, both emphasizing the role of cognition in emotional distress and dysfunctional behavior.

Beck and Ellis, along with Donald Meichenbaum, are often identified as the founders of cognitive behavior therapy. Others, including Albert Bandura, Marvin Goldfried, Gerald Davsion, and Arnold Lazarus, also influenced Beck as part of the "cognitive revolution" in psychology during the 1970s. This movement resulted in a shift from primarily operant models of human behavior to ones emphasizing information processing. Beck made a significant contribution to this change by providing clinical research to support the new, information-processing model, which viewed individuals as actively constructing their experience. In addition to using empirical research to reformulate the theory of depression, Beck developed therapeutic strategies and techniques to treat depression that were congruent with the cognitive model. Thus, he created cognitive therapy: a theory of psychopathology, a research base to support the theory and further test the model, and a system of psychotherapy derived from the theory. Further testing of the techniques and strategies of cognitive therapy demonstrated their efficacy in the treatment of unipolar depression.

Beck's research and theory developed concurrently as he expanded the scope of cognitive therapy from depression to anxiety disorders, personality disorders, substance abuse, suicide, chronic pain, stress, couples' conflicts, anger and violence, and schizophrenia. Among his contributions are several inventories used in research and clinical practice, such as the Beck Depression Inventory, Beck Anxiety Inventory, Scale for Suicide Ideation, Suicide Intent Scale, Beck Hopelessness Scale, Beck Self-Concept Test, Beck Youth Inventories of Emotional and Social Impairment, and the Clark-Beck Obsessive-Compulsive Inventory.

Beck's theoretical contributions begin with his *continuity hypothesis* that human behavior is on a continuum and various syndromes are exaggerated forms of normal emotional responses. He is best known for his theories of depression, anxiety, and personality disorders, which illustrate his *specificity hypothesis* that each disorder has its own specific cognitive content. Interventions for each disorder follow from a cognitive conceptualization based on the core cognitive content and processes for that disorder.

Beck's contributions to psychotherapy include *Socratic dialogue,* the process of asking questions to first understand the client's point of view and then open it to examination; *guided discovery,* or asking a series of questions to uncover relevant information outside the client's current awareness, connect thoughts to deeper beliefs, or synthesize new information; and *collaborative empiricism,* in which the therapist and client work together to identify and test the accuracy and usefulness of the client's beliefs rather than directly challenging the client's beliefs or persuading him or her to adopt the therapist's views. Beck thinks that empirical hypothesis testing is the mechanism of change in cognitive therapy.

His current research interests are the psychopathology of psychiatric disorders, the prediction of suicide, and cognitive therapy of depression and other disorders. He recently developed the cognitive model of schizophrenia. His immediate research is testing a short-term cognitive therapy intervention for high-risk suicidal individuals, most of whom have substance abuse problems and significant Axis II psychopathology. Preliminary results are promising for this new application of cognitive therapy.

—*Marjorie E. Weishaar*

See also: Cognitive-Behavioral Approach to Bipolar Disorder (Vol. I); Cognitive Behavior Therapy (Vol. I); Cognitive Behavior Therapy: Child Clinical Applications (Vol. II)

BEHAVIOR ACTIVATION

DESCRIPTION OF THE STRATEGY

A number of theoretical perspectives have been outlined with regard to factors most critical in understanding the etiology and maintenance of clinical depression; biological theorists implicate decreased levels of the neurotransmitters serotonin and norepinephrine; cognitive psychologists highlight dysfunctional thoughts and maladaptive core schemas; while interpersonal psychotherapists associate clinical depression with impaired interpersonal functioning. From the behavioral perspective provided here, depression results from decreased response-contingent reinforcement for nondepressive (healthy) behavior, a process that results from unavailability of reinforcement in the environment, inability to access reinforcement (e.g., skill deficits), and/or an increased frequency of punishment. Depressive behaviors such as passivity or lethargy also may be maintained through positive (e.g., expressed sympathy) and/or negative reinforcement (e.g., avoidance of responsibilities). In other words, depressed behavior results from some combination of reinforcement of depressed behavior and a lack of reinforcement or even punishment of more healthy alternative behavior.

Based on this model, conventional behavioral therapy for depression was aimed at increasing access to pleasant events and positive reinforcers, as well as decreasing the intensity and frequency of aversive events and consequences. Additional strategies included teaching relaxation skills, social and problem-solving skill training, and a focus on increasing self-control through self-monitoring and self-reinforcement. With increased interest in cognitive theory in the latter quarter of the 20th century, interventions based exclusively on operant and respondent principles, once thought adequate, had begun to be viewed as insufficient to address the complex nature of clinical depression. As such, the treatment of depression began to include direct cognitive manipulations, including cognitive restructuring and self-instructional training.

Within the past decade, there has been a revitalized interest in traditional behavior therapy as conducted without specific attention to cognitive processes and intervention. This resurgence can be attributed to a number of factors, including pressure to develop and implement psychosocial interventions that are both time limited and empirically validated (i.e., in response to managed care organizations), and recent data that suggest significant therapeutic benefits can be achieved without comprehensive cognitive-behavioral treatment packages. In response to these issues, behavior activation research programs have evolved to evaluate the feasibility, effectiveness, and efficacy of purely behavioral interventions for depression.

Behavior activation (BA) may be defined as a therapeutic process that emphasizes structured attempts at increasing overt behaviors that are likely to bring the patient into contact with reinforcing environmental contingencies and produce corresponding improvements in thoughts, mood, and overall quality of life. This strategy is a central component of contemporary behavioral interventions, although the fundamental philosophy and specific behavior activation methods are somewhat distinct across therapies. Neil Jacobson and his colleagues developed a 20- to 24-session behavior activation protocol designed to address the functional aspects of depressive behavior. This intervention focuses on evolving transactions between the person and environment and the identification of environmental triggers and ineffective coping responses involved in the etiology and maintenance of depressed mood. Much like traditional behavioral therapy, this approach conceptualizes depressed behavior (e.g., inactivity, withdrawal) as a coping strategy to avoid environmental circumstances that provide low levels of positive reinforcement or high levels of aversive control. *Behavioral avoidance* is thus a core feature of this treatment model, and the initial treatment objective is to increase a patient's awareness of how an internal or external event (trigger) results in a negative emotional (response) that may effectively establish a recurrent avoidance pattern (i.e., TRAP: trigger, response, avoidance pattern). Once patient and clinician establish recognition of this pattern, the principal objective becomes one of helping the patient to reengage in healthy behaviors through developing alternative coping strategies (i.e., TRAC; trigger, response, alternative coping). Along with increased patient awareness and progression from a TRAP- to a TRAC-based philosophy, the primary therapeutic technique of BA involves teaching patients to *take action.* To reduce escape and avoidance behavior, patients are taught to assess the function of their behavior, and then to make an informed choice to continue escaping and avoiding or instead integrate alternative behaviors into their lifestyles that may improve their moods. Additional treatment strategies used to facilitate development of active coping include rating mastery and pleasure of activities, assigning activities to increase mastery and pleasure, mental rehearsal of assigned activities, role-playing behavioral assignments, therapist modeling, periodic distraction from problems or unpleasant events, mindfulness training or relaxation, self-reinforcement, and skills training (e.g., sleep hygiene, assertiveness, communication, problem solving).

With the dual purpose of adhering to fundamental behavioral theory and with attention to developing a more abbreviated 8- to 15-session protocol, our research group designed an alternative brief behavior activation treatment. In this manualized yet ideographic approach, initial sessions consist of assessing the function of depressed behavior, efforts to weaken access to positive and negative reinforcement for depressed behavior, and introduction of the emotional acceptance-behavioral change treatment rationale. A systematic activation approach then is initiated to increase the frequency and duration of healthy activities to promote increased contact with environmental reinforcement. Patients begin with a weekly self-monitoring exercise that serves as a baseline assessment of daily activities, orients patients to the quality and quantity of their activities, and generates ideas about activities to target during treatment. The emphasis then shifts to identifying behavioral goals within major life areas, including relationships, education, employment, hobbies and recreational activities, physical/ health issues, spirituality, and anxiety-eliciting situations. Subsequent to goal selection, an activity hierarchy is constructed in which 15 activities are rated ranging from "easiest" to "most difficult" to accomplish. Using a master activity log (therapist) and weekly behavioral checkouts (patient) to monitor progress, the patient progressively moves through the hierarchy. For each activity, the therapist and patient collaboratively determine what the weekly and final goals will be in terms of the frequency and duration of activity per week. At the start of each session, the behavioral checkout is examined and discussed, with goals for the following week established as a function of patient success or difficulty with goals for the prior week. Patients identify weekly rewards as incentives for completing the behavioral checkout that they self-administer if their goals are met.

Although consistent with traditional behavioral theory and treatment, novel BA protocols represent important advancements with respect to case conceptualization and intervention components. For example, modern activation approaches are more idiographic, giving more attention to the unique environmental contingencies maintaining an individual's depressed behavior. A related development involves a movement from targeting pleasant events alone to understanding the functional aspects of behavior change. So rather than indiscriminately increasing an individual's contact with events that are presumed to be pleasant or rewarding, this functional analytic approach involves a detailed assessment of contingencies maintaining depressive behavior, idiographic assessment of patients' specific needs and goals, and the subsequent targeting of behavior that, consistent with results of functional analyses, is deemed relevant to improving patients' quality of life.

Finally, it is important to note that BA models acknowledge ongoing controversy surrounding cause-effect relations among biological, cognitive, and behavioral components involved in the etiology and maintenance of clinical depression. As with other models of depression, the importance of cognition in understanding depressive symptoms is not discounted in activation approaches. Cognitive processes are not regarded as proximal causes of depressed overt behavior, however, and therefore are not targeted directly for change. BA procedures address cognitions indirectly by encouraging patients to reengage in rewarding overt behaviors, a process hypothesized to result in more rational and positive cognitions. BA thus addresses the environmental constituent of depressive affect, a component deemed more observable, measurable, and capable of being controlled. It should be noted, however, that the BA approaches do not devalue assessment of cognitions and mood state as measures of treatment progress and outcome. Indeed, if the goal of treatment is for depressed individuals to feel better, then a useful treatment approach must ensure that individuals experience improvement in their thoughts and feelings, even if thoughts and feelings are not directly targeted as change agents.

RESEARCH BASIS

Research evaluating the efficacy and effectiveness of contemporary behavior activation interventions is very much in its infancy. A preliminary outcome study comparing a comprehensive cognitive-behavioral program for depression with behavior activation alone, however, suggested that BA may be just as effective as the comprehensive intervention in terms of overall treatment outcome and the alteration of negative thinking and dysfunctional attributional styles. Importantly, at 24-month follow-up, BA and the comprehensive cognitive-behavioral treatment were also equally effective in preventing relapse. Other outcome data have also been promising. Within a community mental health outpatient setting, for example, the briefer BA protocol was associated with sizable decreases in depressive symptoms among adults with moderate depression. This intervention was also used successfully to treat coexistent anxiety and depressive symptoms, as an adjunct to pharmacotherapy, and was superior to supportive psychotherapy among depressed psychiatric inpatients.

Ongoing research projects into the efficacy and effectiveness of BA protocols involve its implementation among cancer patients with depression in a primary care context, its use as an adjunct to standard smoking cessation treatment, and its utility among patients at high risk for committing suicide. A large clinical trial presently is also being conducted to explore the relative efficacy of BA, cognitive therapy, and pharmacotherapy, with preliminary outcome data indicating comparable efficacy of the three interventions.

RELEVANT TARGET POPULATIONS AND EXCEPTIONS

Behavior activation works well in settings where highly structured, time-limited treatment is a priority (e.g., inpatient units, university counseling centers, employee assistance programs, community mental health facilities). Patients who believe that changing behavior can help change mood and who are worried about the potential side effects of medication also are good candidates for behavior activation. Patients who prefer more emphasis on internal processes (e.g., thoughts, feelings) or insight into developmental factors, or who feel too overwhelmed to work toward directly changing their behavior may benefit from supplementing behavior activation with cognitive therapy and/or medications or an alternative treatment such as psychodynamic therapy. Recent predictor analyses also have indicated that positive outcome of BA is associated with pretreatment (positive) expectancies and inversely related to "reason-giving," that is, the tendency to offer multiple explanations with respect to the etiology and maintenance of depression.

COMPLICATIONS

Further research on the efficacy/effectiveness of BA is required due to several methodological limitations of relevant studies. First, only two of the preliminary outcome studies have included control groups, only one investigation has included a treatment group receiving a comprehensive cognitive-behavioral treatment package, and none of the completed research projects have included comparisons with other psychosocial (i.e., interpersonal psychotherapy) or pharmacological interventions. Second, a major limitation of most studies is the lack of a comprehensive assessment package, with no measurement of potential transfer effects of treatment (e.g., to related anxiety or substance abuse symptoms), evaluation of the effects on functional ability (e.g., quality of life, life satisfaction), or measure of patient satisfaction. With the exception of one case study with favorable results, we also generally are unaware of the potential efficacy of BA as it relates to patients with more complicated clinical presentations, such as those with a coexistent Axis II disorder. Finally, sample size has been quite restricted in several of the studies, and the long-term effects of behavior activation strategies generally remain unevaluated due to the lack of systematic follow-up procedures.

CASE ILLUSTRATION

"Karen" was a 30-year-old divorced Caucasian woman who presented for treatment at a university counseling center. She had a high school education and had been employed as an office manager for 10 years, and she had a history of recurrent depressive episodes and suicidal ideation beginning at age 14. During her present episode of major depression, Karen was experiencing insomnia, increased appetite (she had gained 15 pounds in the previous 2 months), fatigue, and exhibited general anhedonia.

At the initial session, Karen scored in the moderate range on a depression inventory. Her self-monitoring of daily activities indicated that despite regular attendance at work, she did not engage in other desirable and valued activities such as exercising, housework, and social activities. Karen stated that she had low self-esteem and often was not very assertive when certain family members and coworkers requested unreasonable favors. She frequently worked overtime without monetary compensation and expressed distress at the idea of requesting vacation time. Karen's extensive work hours and engagement in strenuous caretaking for her ill father were functional in allowing immediate avoidance of perceived negative consequences of confronting her boss and the guilt associated with "neglecting" her father. Considering the lengthy hours devoted to work and caretaking, access to reinforcement for more desirable behaviors was limited. In addition, Karen was uncertain as to whether the initiation of social interactions would be well received by individuals in her social network. Finally, the delayed benefits of healthy activities (e.g., exercise) appeared to limit their frequency.

Karen's case provides an especially useful illustration of the difference between targeting functionally relevant activities in BA and merely increasing activity. Unlike many other depressed patients, Karen was quite active upon presentation to treatment, yet she had limited contact with fulfilling and rewarding behaviors consistent with life values and goals. Considering the importance of this problem, following assessment of short- and long-term life goals, we began with the construction of her activity hierarchy. Karen's activity hierarchy began with relatively easy goals targeting both necessary life activities, such as organizing her home, and engagement in social activities, such as calling friends on the telephone. Higher-level goals included more strenuous exercise, more social time with friends and family, and improving her occupational circumstances through various behavioral exercises.

Karen was eager to begin treatment and compliant with the protocol throughout. As mentioned above, initial sessions consisted of assessing depressive symptoms, monitoring baseline activity level, and determining value-based behavioral goals and difficulty ratings. Subsequent sessions then followed a common format. First, Karen was given a depression inventory, and any changes in her depressive symptoms were discussed. Second, her weekly monitoring form was reviewed. Goals that she had succeeded in meeting for the week were reinforced by positive feedback from the therapist and a discussion of a pleasant activity she could engage in as a "reward." If she had met a goal at the "ideal" frequency and duration for 3 weeks in a row, it was considered "mastered" and was no longer monitored. Any goals that were not met for the week were discussed constructively, using problem-solving procedures to address obstacles and make any necessary modifications for the following week. For example, if the goal was too difficult, then it was adjusted to a lesser frequency and/or duration. If the problem were due to unassertiveness or perceived social inadequacies, then time was spent facilitating skill development (e.g., through role play). If problematic behaviors were evident within the therapeutic relationship, they were addressed in this context with the objective of promoting generalization to the natural environment. For example, an interesting focus in some of the therapy sessions was Karen's lack of assertiveness toward the therapist. In her relationships with family, friends, and coworkers, Karen admittedly had difficulty saying "no" to certain requests. This problem also periodically manifested during therapy sessions in that she never refused or questioned a behavioral assignment. In one of the last sessions, however, the therapist intentionally asked her to complete a difficult and time-consuming assignment. At first, Karen agreed to make an effort to complete it, but then stated that she would rather not. This observation of increased assertiveness was rewarded via therapist praise. Finally, the typical session ended with determining the following week's goals, which usually consisted of the continuation of some activities from the previous week and some new, slightly more difficult goals adopted from the master activity hierarchy.

In the course of therapy, which consisted of 12 1-hour sessions, Karen's activity level increased until she had met criteria for all of the less difficult and moderately difficult activities, as well as most of the difficult activities. For example, she regularly washed her dishes four times per week (less difficult); she began to walk around her neighborhood on a daily basis, losing 17 pounds over the 12-week period (moderately difficult); and she spent 2 hours per week interacting with her cousin outside her home (difficult). Potentially influenced by lower-level homework assignments designed to increase assertive behaviors, Karen also completed the goal of obtaining new employment with regular hours, health benefits, and paid vacation. Of interest, although negative cognitions were not directly addressed and social and assertiveness skills were discussed at minimum, Karen evidenced a decrease in depressive cognitions and improved mood, as well as greater independence and assertiveness at termination. At termination and a 3-month follow-up, Karen scored in the minimally depressed range on a depression inventory.

—*Derek R. Hopko,*
Sandra D.Hopko, and C. W. Lejuez

See also: *Homework (Vol. I); Manualized Behavior Therapy (Vol. I); Motor Activity and Behavioral Assessment (Vol. I)*

Suggested Readings

Hollon, S. D. (2001). Behavioral activation treatment for depression: A commentary. *Clinical Psychology: Science and Practice, 8,* 271–274.

Hopko, D. R., Lejuez, C. W., LePage, J., McNeil, D. W., & Hopko, S. D. (in press). A brief behavioral activation treatment for depression: A randomized pilot trial within an inpatient psychiatric hospital. *Behavior Modification.*

Hopko, D. R., Lejuez, C. W., Ruggiero, K. J., & Eifert, G. H. (in press). Contemporary behavioral activation treatments for depression: Procedures, principles, and progress. *Clinical Psychology Review.*

Jacobson, N. S., Dobson, K. S., Truax, P. A., Addis, M. E., Koerner, K., Gollan, J. K., et al. (1996). A component analysis of cognitive-behavioral treatment for depression. *Journal of Consulting and Clinical Psychology, 64,* 295–304.

Jacobson, N. S., Martell, C. R., & Dimidjian, S. (2001). Behavioral activation treatment for depression: Returning to contextual roots. *Clinical Psychology: Science and Practice, 8,* 255–270.

Lejuez, C. W., Hopko, D. R., & Hopko, S. D. (2002). *The brief behavioral activation treatment for depression (BATD): A comprehensive patient guide.* Boston: Pearson.

Lejuez, C. W., Hopko, D. R., LePage, J., Hopko, S. D., & McNeil, D. W. (2001). A brief behavioral activation treatment for depression. *Cognitive and Behavioral Practice, 8,* 164–175.

Lewinsohn, P. M. (1974). A behavioral approach to depression. In R. M. Friedman & M. M. Katz (Eds.), *The psychology of depression: Contemporary theory and research.* New York: Wiley.

Lewinsohn, P. M., Munoz, R. F., Youngren, M. A., & Zeiss, A. M. (1986). *Control your depression.* New York: Prentice Hall.

Martell, C. R., Addis, M. E., & Jacobson, N. S. (2001). *Depression in context: Strategies for guided action.* New York: Norton.

Rehm, L. P. (1977). A self-control model for depression. *Behavior Therapy, 8,* 787–804.

BEHAVIOR REHEARSAL

DESCRIPTION OF THE STRATEGY

In the 1950s, what was termed *behavioristic psychodrama* was employed with certain clients who found it unusually difficult to apply assertive behaviors in their day-to-day relationships. Unlike the usual role playing and psychodrama of the day, in which patients acted out their existing attitudes, the aim was to enable the clients to stand up to people who evoked anxiety in them. The therapist would play the role of some person(s) with whom the client was timid or inhibited, the assumption being that appropriate remarks made during this "play" situation would be a stepping-stone toward dealing with the actual people and events. To achieve greater clarity, I introduced the term "behavior rehearsal" in 1966 and emphasized that it is a specific procedure that seeks to replace deficient or inadequate social and interpersonal responses with efficient and effective behavior patterns. Behavior rehearsal can be conducted with a therapist, a friend, or on one's own (e.g., practicing giving a speech in front of a mirror). In some instances, role reversal is an important component, wherein the therapist acts the part of the patient and models the desired verbal and nonverbal behaviors. The use of videos can be especially helpful in monitoring the mode of expression, including tone of voice, inflection, querulous undertones, hesitations, posture, and eye contact.

RESEARCH BASIS

Behavior rehearsal has been applied successfully to various clinical populations (e.g., enabling alcoholic men to cope with problematic situations that tend to trigger excessive drinking, helping nonpsychotic depressed outpatient populations acquire better social skills). It has been implemented in couples therapy where the partners' distress is a result of poor communication styles. This method has also been tested in areas that fall outside the clinical arena. For example, there are many reports in which behavior rehearsal has been used with employees in business and industry (e.g., for managing difficulties with customers). Basically, behavior rehearsal is part of the general field of social skills training, and many different role-playing techniques have been developed to enhance interpersonal effectiveness. Research in the area of "self-efficacy" has demonstrated a clear connection between people's perception of their own self-efficacy in given situations, the course of action they are likely to pursue, and the probability of success or failure. To be unrehearsed and unprepared is unlikely to lead to success. Many people fail in a variety of endeavors simply because they do not know how best to approach others, how to make assertive and not aggressive responses, and how to express their feelings appropriately and adaptively. Talking about these issues and offering good advice seems to produce little change. However, the specially focused role-playing procedures used in behavior rehearsal often prove efficient and effective.

RELEVANT TARGET POPULATIONS AND EXCEPTIONS

Cognitive behavior therapy emphasizes that psychological problems may stem from misinformation (faulty reasoning, dysfunctional beliefs, erroneous ideas) and missing information (skill deficits, gaps in knowledge). Behavior rehearsal targets the second problem area, *missing information.* Clients who lack appropriate and effective responses in specific situations need to acquire the necessary skills. Take, for example, the case of a well-trained professional who is unable to get a good job because his interview skills are deficient, or a person who is at a loss for words when being unfairly criticized. Those are just two of innumerable instances where people suffer the consequences of response deficits. Thus, almost anyone who lacks a necessary skill may benefit from behavior rehearsal. Before venturing into any course of action, a person first needs to feel capable of success. As already stated, individuals' beliefs about their self-efficacy will determine whether they feel optimistic or pessimistic and whether or not it is advisable to expend effort in trying to achieve various goals. Perceived self-efficacy plays a major role in adaptation, coping, and change. Behavior rehearsal procedures can enhance self-efficacy by filling lacunae with knowledge and expertise to bypass needless failure. These findings include clinical situations, educational systems, business organizations, athletic teams, and even urban neighborhoods with violent crime.

What are the exceptions? People suffering from profound depression, extreme anxiety, psychotic thinking, or some personality disorders are unlikely to be good candidates for behavior rehearsal. The success of this procedure calls for one to be able to focus on and attend to a variety of issues while being trained, rehearsed, coached, instructed, and guided toward a desired achievement or end. Those who are unwilling or unable to concentrate and cooperate require different treatment tactics.

COMPLICATIONS

The main untoward events occur when people fail to attain their goals after applying what they had learned and rehearsed. Often, this is because they prematurely attempted to take steps that had not been rehearsed sufficiently. Also, it is impossible to predict the reactions that people may have in response even to the most carefully orchestrated sequence. Thus, I recall rehearsing a young man to confront his often angry and aggressive father about an important issue, and to everyone's amazement, the father reacted as never before: He broke down and cried. This was not the intended outcome of the scenario, and the son emerged feeling guilty rather than fearful—as had been the case before this event.

—Arnold A. Lazarus

See also: *Modeling (Vol. I); Role Playing (Vol. II); Social Skills Instruction (Vol. III)*

Suggested Readings

Bandura, A. (1997). *Self-efficacy: The exercise of control.* New York: Freeman.

Lazarus, A. A. (1966). Behavior rehearsal vs. nondirective therapy vs. advice in effecting behavior change. *Behaviour Research and Therapy, 4,* 209–212.

Lazarus, A. A. (2002). Behavior rehearsal. In M. Hersen & W. Sledge (Eds.), *Encyclopedia of psychotherapy* (Vol. 1., pp. 253–257). New York: Academic Press.

BEHAVIOR THERAPY AND NEUROPSYCHOLOGY

DESCRIPTION OF THE STRATEGY

There have been significant advances in the integration of behavior therapy and neuropsychology since the first accounts of behavioral intervention with brain-injured individuals in the 1970s. Indeed, advent of a "behavioral neuropsychology" recognizes the increasing interdependence of these approaches in the coordinated care of individuals who have experienced brain injury. A neuropsychological approach to patient care emphasizes brain-behavior relationships, whereas a behavioral approach, as embodied by the operant and respondent technologies of behavior modification and behavior therapy, focuses on behavior-environmental relationships. Both approaches may be used to evaluate an individual's cognitive functioning, establish baselines against which progress or decline can be measured, clarify diagnoses, and assist in rehabilitation and treatment planning. Used in tandem, these approaches provide a greater understanding of brain injury than could be obtained through either tradition alone.

Although the conceptual framework underpinning each approach is vastly different, these approaches intersect at the point of observable behavior. Behavior reflects both brain integrity and the influence of the external environment. A behavioral assessment demonstrates reliable and orderly changes in behavior as a function of variables traditionally considered to be influenced by the external environment (e.g., environmental stimuli and contingencies of reinforcement), while neuropsychological assessment focuses on behaviors typically considered to be a function of changes in the internal environment (e.g., central nervous system disruption via anoxic episodes, tumors, gunshot wounds, etc.). In the latter case, patterns of test responses are interpreted within the context of documented injuries and their known sequelae. Although the current state of imaging techniques often yields the extent and location of a brain insult, the heterogeneity of these injuries mandates that the scope of impairment in any particular patient remains speculative until evaluated by neuropsychological examination. Addition of well-established behavioral technology to the practice of neuropsychology brings behavioral principles and procedures to bear upon an individual's functioning while recognizing effects of brain injury on the patient's ability to perceive and respond to his or her environment.

A behavioral approach to brain injury owes much to the tradition of the intensive study of individuals, with attendant operational definitions of target behaviors, procedures for obtaining reliable observation of those behaviors, and recording procedures that capture target behaviors with respect to their relevant dimensions (e.g., frequency, duration, and intensity). Procedures that use subjects as their own controls permit a fine-grain analysis of the effects of environmental events, be they internal or external, on behaviors of therapeutic interest, both in clinic and in vivo. Once functional relations between a behavior and environmental antecedents and consequences have been determined, a treatment plan may be developed to influence occurrence of specific target behaviors. Establishment of behavioral baselines reflective of neuropsychological deficits allows for client improvement or decline to be monitored as a function of pathologic or recuperative processes, as well as medication effects. Therefore, an integrated approach to patient care explores behavior sensitive to brain impairment and environmental contingencies that might affect that behavior, yet each approach has its limitations. That is, while traditional neuropsychological assessment highlights brain-behavior performance at a moment in time, it imperfectly reflects patient performance day by day. In contrast, behavioral assessment samples behavior obtained under different environmental conditions, or contingencies of reinforcement, but may fail to capture the subtleties that often encompass brain injuries. In each case, findings may vary as a function of numerous variables, such as patient age, the nature and location of brain injury, or whether brain insult is an acute or static condition or the result of an acquired or developmental deficit.

RESEARCH BASIS

Behavioral interventions to remediate the sequelae of brain injury have appeared in the literature for more than 30 years. The earliest applications to clinical work with individuals experiencing brain injuries were typically case studies; over time, research has been conducted with small groups of individuals, often within the context of small-N designs. For example, there have been comparisons of behavioral measures obtained during pretreatment to those obtained during treatment (i.e., A-B designs); designs that evaluate treatment through its introduction and subsequent removal (i.e., reversal or withdrawal designs); and designs that evaluate the effects of treatment through its sequential application to multiple behaviors, patients, or settings (i.e., multiple-baseline designs).

Behavioral interventions range from simple contingency management strategies, as might be used to address the disinhibited behaviors common to frontal lobe syndrome, to systematic desensitization and anxiety reduction procedures to address the traumatic sequelae resulting from traumatic brain injury. Cognitive behavior therapy strategies also have been introduced as another component of the therapeutic milieu to address issues that result from brain injury (e.g., affective disturbance, anxiety, and adjustment disorder). In another development, behavioral neuropsychologists have extended behavioral assessment strategies to monitor the ongoing status of individuals who have experienced brain injuries. Using neuropsychological test data as a guide, behavioral measures have been developed that permit ongoing evaluation of patient improvement or decline as a function of time postinjury, medication, therapy, or other environmental effects. Providing family members with behavioral technology to implement treatment or to monitor an individual's status at home exemplifies the integration of behavioral and neuropsychological approaches to patient care.

RELEVANT TARGET POPULATIONS AND EXCEPTIONS

Behavior therapy and applied behavior analysis have long addressed the wide-ranging behaviors of individuals who have experienced brain injuries, but behavioral neuropsychology implies more than simply incorporating behavioral procedures into the armamentarium of those who work with brain-injured patients. Integration of behavioral technology into the assessment and treatment of individuals with brain injuries recognizes that simple extensions of procedures that are successful in remediating the deficits of one population of individuals will not necessarily generalize to the population of individuals who have experienced brain injuries. Behavioral principles have wide generality and will not vary as a function of an individual's injuries; in contrast, behavioral procedures may vary as a function of individual brain integrity, as may be reflected in target behaviors, selection and delivery of reinforcers, the development of therapist prompts, contextual cues, and schedules of reinforcement. Behavioral technology can contribute greatly to an understanding of individual functioning and to rehabilitation planning, but without consideration of an individual's neuropsychological status to assist in identifying relevant cognitive deficiencies that affect adaptive functioning, optimal therapeutic intervention will not be achieved.

COMPLICATIONS

Complications with an integrated approach are most likely to arise when the respective contributions of either discipline are neglected. While both behavioral and neuropsychological approaches intersect at the point of observable behavior, each brings a unique perspective with regard to conceptualizing the causes, consequences, and correlates of a given behavior. Consequently, the limitations inherent in either approach, in isolation, are also present in poorly executed attempts to integrate the two approaches. Behavioral approaches will provide an inadequate account of the brain functioning underlying observable behavior if the contributions of neuropsychology are neglected. Similarly, neuropsychology will provide an incomplete understanding of behavior if the impact of behavioral principles and environmental contingencies on behavior are not taken into account.

A patient's general cognitive functioning is, of course, critical, depending upon the complexity of the task to be performed and the nature of the stimuli required to evoke its occurrence. Receptive language skills and motoric functioning can be similarly important. Patient performance may also be inhibited by factors such as anxiety or fatigue. Finally, ensuring that the target behavior is indeed available in the patient's repertoire and that the prevailing reinforcement contingencies are sufficient to motivate patient performance are crucial to the success of any intervention.

CASE ILLUSTRATION

"M. T." was a 58-year-old, left-handed, Caucasian male who functioned professionally as an orthopedic surgeon. He was self-referred for evaluation due to increasing difficulty recalling recent events and places despite a well-documented lifetime of excellent retention and recall. A comprehensive medical evaluation was unremarkable, with no recent history of illness, injury, or hospitalization. Results of a recent neuropsychological evaluation guided the selection of behavioral tasks for monitoring the status of M. T.'s functioning and development of a behavioral intervention to compensate for current deficits in his recall. Cognitive-behavioral techniques were used to address M. T.'s negative self-evaluations and his overconcern about the evaluations of his peers and colleagues.

Prior assessment of M. T.'s cognitive functioning using the Wechsler Adult Intelligence Scale–III (WAIS-III) suggested that his global cognitive functioning fell within the Superior range (FSIQ = 124). His Verbal Scales, which fell within the Very Superior range (VIQ = 135), were significantly discrepant from his Performance Scales, which fell in the Average range (PIQ = 103). This discrepancy was surprising given his profession, which places a premium on nonverbal memory, visual-spatial relationships, and nonverbal problem solving. M. T.'s General Memory Index on the Wechsler Memory Scales fell in the Average range (SS = 108), somewhat unexpected given his educational and professional history. M. T.'s performance on the Halstead-Reitan Neuropsychological Test Battery for Adults was largely unremarkable except for deficits in memory and constructional tasks. Minor limitations in attention and concentration were also noted. Collectively, this data suggested impairment in areas of visual-spatial organization and recall that were consistent with M. T.'s self-reported difficulty recalling recent events and places.

A series of brief behavioral tasks were constructed to assess M. T.'s functioning across relevant domains identified through neuropsychological assessment (e.g., attention and concentration, verbal and spatial memory, visual-spatial skills). These tasks, administered by family members, were sensitive to improvement or decline in functioning. Moreover, unlike the neuropsychological evaluation, they were relatively brief (i.e., 12–15 minutes total administration time) and inexpensive to administer. Initially, the tasks were administered on a weekly basis to establish baseline functioning. For example, to assess attention and concentration, M. T. was asked to perform on a digits-forward and digits-backward task. On a measure of spatial memory, nine pairs of cards were placed face down in front of M. T., and he was given 60 seconds to match as many pairs as possible. On a task of motor functioning (a control function without known current impairment), M. T. was provided with a string and cup of beads and was instructed to place as many beads on the string as possible in 60 seconds.

In addition to establishing baseline functioning, a behaviorally based intervention was developed to improve M. T.'s ability to "recall" recent places and events. It was recommended that he acquire a "memory book" (e.g., business planner, palm pilot, or other notebook) in which he could record events that he would need to recall later. Given his history of excellent recall, M. T. found using the book frustrating, lamenting that he could neither record all relevant details of each event that occurred during his day nor anticipate which events he would be required to recall at the end of the day. In addition, M. T.'s fear of negative feedback from colleagues and others in his social and professional environment militated against use of the book, resulting in efforts to increase the social reinforcement obtained from family and staff contingent upon using it as well as the development of cognitive behavior therapy procedures to address his social concerns.

Initially, a family member prompted M. T. to use the memory book at home and in social settings when his colleagues were not present, thereby avoiding situations that elicited social anxiety. He recorded information regarding the location and key features of persons, places, and events of the day. He was provided praise and social support for recording, especially for independent use of the memory book, and was alerted to others in his environment who were using similar memory aids. Data were recorded regarding the frequency of M.T.'s unprompted use of the book. Therapeutic efforts in clinic challenged his negative self-evaluation and beliefs that his colleagues perceived him as incompetent and impaired.

At the end of each day, M. T. was prompted to review his memory book and to visualize details of the events he had recorded. A family member questioned him about the people, places, and events entered in his book. High levels of social reinforcement were paired with M. T.'s use of his memory book and accurate recall of its contents. Once he felt comfortable using

his memory book, training was extended throughout his home and work environment. The role of family members in prompting memory book use was gradually faded out, but evening review of the contents of the memory book continued on a daily basis for several weeks. This permitted ongoing evaluation of his recall of events, people, and places relative to his past performance and the degree to which his entries were sufficient to recall the day's events. Over time, M. T.'s independent use of compensatory memory aides increased over time, as did his ability to function effectively in his everyday environment. Ongoing monitoring of other ability areas remained stable, while concerns about the negative evaluations of others declined.

—*William J. Warzak and Ann M. Galloway*

See also: *Behavioral Assessment (Vol. II); Behavioral Gerontology (Vol. I); Behavioral Medicine (Vol. I)*

Suggested Readings

Anderson, C. M., & Warzak, W. J. (2000). Using positive behavior support to facilitate the classroom adaptation of children with brain injuries. *Proven Practice: Prevention and Remediation of School Problems, 2,* 72–82.

Corrigan, P. W., & Jakus, M. R. (1994). Behavioral treatment. In J. M. Silver & S. C. Yudofsky, et al. (Eds.), *Neuropsychiatry of traumatic brain injury* (pp. 733–769). Washington, DC: American Psychiatric Association.

Fluharty, G., & Glassman, N. (2001). Use of antecedent control to improve the outcome of rehabilitation for a client with a frontal lobe injury and intolerance for auditory and tactile stimuli. *Brain Injury, 15*(11), 995–1002.

Khan-Bourne, N., & Brown, R. G. (2003). Cognitive behaviour therapy for the treatment of depression in individuals with brain injury. *Neuropsychological Rehabilitation, 13*(1–2), 89–107.

Park, N. W., Conrod, B., Hussain, K. J., Rewilak, D., & Black, S. E. (2003). A treatment program for individuals with deficient evaluative processing and consequent impaired social and risk judgement. *Neurocase, 9*(1), 51–62.

Rapoport, M., McCauley, S., Levin, H., Song, J., & Feinstein, A. (2002). The role of injury severity in neurobehavioral outcome 3 months after traumatic brain injury. *Neuropsychiatry, Neuropsychology, & Behavioral Neurology, 15*(2), 123–132.

Vriezen, E. R., & Pigott, S.E. (2002). The relationship between parental report on the BRIEF and performance-based measures of executive function in children with moderate to severe traumatic brain injury. *Child Neuropsychology, 8*(4), 296–303.

Warzak, W. J., & Anhalt, K. (2003). Facilitating the psychosocial recovery of youth and adolescents with traumatic brain injury. In K. Hux (Ed.), *Assisting survivors of traumatic brain injury: The role of speech/language pathologists.* New York: Pro Ed Press.

Wesolowski, M. D., & Zencius, A. H. (1994). *Critical issues in neuropsychology: A practical guide to head injury rehabilitation: A focus on postacute residential treatment.* New York: Plenum Press.

BEHAVIOR THERAPY THEORY

Science is equally concerned with understanding and explanation as it is with prediction and control. Prediction has a straightforward understanding; one makes a specific forecast and subsequently determines how accurate it was. Likewise, control also has a straightforward meaning in that one decides upon a desirable change and then attempts to make it so. Understanding and explanation are more complex matters. One might say that we understand something once it has been explained. But what does explanation require? What must one do to properly explain why something occurred, such as why a particular psychological intervention produced the observed outcome or why the outcome did not materialize? No simple answer will suffice here. Theorists vary in that they use different explanatory bases. Behavior therapy theories have employed at least four explanatory bases. The first is the functional analysis of behavior that characterizes operant conditioning explanations that are associated with the experimental analysis of behavior. The second explanatory basis is reciprocal inhibition; it underlies systematic desensitization and related therapies. Cognitive theory provides a third explanatory basis. A fourth network explanatory basis is discerned on the grounds that it recognizes independent emotional nodes that are not the exclusive product of cognitive processing. Each theoretical basis is explained below.

Behavior therapists continue to differ widely with regard to their interests in the scientific basis of their accomplishments. They are split by the differential extent to which they value basic versus applied research. Investigators who value basic over applied research typically value explanation and understanding over prediction and control as their main goals. They use prediction and control in the service of explanation and understanding. Investigators who value applied over basic research typically value prediction and control almost exclusively. They frequently argue that as clinicians, they do not need to understand why their treatments are effective as long as they are skilled at their implementation. A more complete understanding of the science underlying their effective treatments may or may not lead to more effective interventions. Only if it can be demonstrated that a more complete scientific understanding and explanation of behavioral therapeutics leads to new more effective clinical methods are advances in basic science deemed worthy of the time and effort to obtain and the journal space to publish. The possibility that a better understanding of the scientific principles involved may guide the refinement and development of behavior therapies is insufficient justification. This applied science value impedes theoretical development because it denies the necessary intellectual, academic, and financial resources for its development.

Eysenck published a seminal paper in 1952 that augmented the basic and applied science split within psychology by questioning the effectiveness of psychotherapy (see suggested readings). He claimed that the available evidence indicated that treated patients did not improve beyond what could be expected on the basis of spontaneous remission. The burden of proof to demonstrate the effectiveness of psychological interventions was now squarely placed on the shoulders of psychologists. Behavior therapies developed in part as a response to this clarion call for psychotherapy outcome research. Behavior therapists became primarily concerned with getting results: producing outcomes that meet the standards of scientific evidence. It is prudent to first determine whether a treatment works before theorizing about why it works.

LEARNING AND MEMORY

In the 1960s, Eysenck defined behavior therapy as the application of learning theory. Around the same time, Wolpe defined behavior therapy as the application of experimentally supported principles of learning. Both major proponents of behavior therapy correctly understood that (a) behavioral disorders are to some important degree learned, and (b) all behavior therapies presume that effective interventions entail some degree of new learning. That broad theoretical differences remain concerning what is learned and how best to teach what people what they need to learn in order to think, feel, and behave more satisfactorily does not detract from the fact that all behavior therapists, as indeed all psychotherapists of all persuasions, are concerned with learning.

Little consensus emerged regarding this obvious conclusion because of at least two factors: First, learning theory largely meant operant and respondent conditioning, and while they clearly provided core theoretical bases for several behavior therapies, not all behavior therapists were content to limit the scope of their theorizing to these constraints, primarily because of explanatory limitations discussed below regarding the functional analytic basis. Second, psychologists were hotly debating a wide variety of learning theories at the time, and much diversity of theoretical perspective precluded consensus on a learning perspective that the majority of behavior therapists could endorse. Third, the rise of the cognitive revolution within psychology was associated with the decline of research and interest in traditional learning theory. Learning as a basic process was *presumed* by psychologists rather than studied. Basic research into the process of learning was delegated to the newly developing neurosciences. Consequently, behavior therapy theory does not involve learning processes. The next section shows that operant conditioning does not accept even the concept of learning. Formal network theories discussed below are correcting this omission.

Cumulative learning implies some form of memory. Little by way of development or therapeutic progress is possible without a way to preserve changes made as a result of learning. Behavior therapy theories do not explain, or even address, how memories are formed and changed. Formal network theories discussed below are correcting this omission.

THE FUNCTIONAL ANALYTIC BASIS

Learning theory textbooks continue to discuss the theoretical positions articulated by Thorndike, Pavlov, Guthrie, Hull, Skinner, Estes, and Tolman and the Gestalt school. While some aspects of the full spectrum of behavior therapies are traceable to each of these theoretical positions, Skinner's functional analytic operant conditioning approach rapidly formed a core theoretical basis for behavioral assessment and therapy because of its pragmatic concern with the necessary and sufficient conditions for behavior change. Clinicians are chiefly asked to modify behavior. People primarily seek treatment for themselves and/or their children and families because they desire change. Operant conditioning provides a technology for producing change that was readily embraced by

early behavior therapists. The empirical support for principles of operant conditioning is perhaps stronger, arguably much stronger, than for any other behavior therapy.

Learning is understood from this theoretical perspective as a hypothetical construct that cannot be directly observed. We observe behavior and infer that learning has occurred based on systematic changes in behavior. It has been noted that learning has been, and mostly continues to be, circularly defined. Consider the following argument: We observe a behavior change. We offer that change as evidence that learning has occurred. We then use the inference that learning has occurred to explain *why* behavior from which we inferred learning changed. The learning construct is therefore rejected rather than explained. This act makes it unnecessary to explain memory. The recommended alternative explanatory approach is to identify the necessary and sufficient conditions that consistently produce predicted behavior changes and to cite the presence of these conditions when asked to explain why the target behavior changed. This explanatory approach avoids the circular logic problem noted above and advances our therapeutic interventions by clarifying what conditions need to be present, and by implication, which conditions need to be absent, in order for the desired behavior to occur. Left unanswered are questions such as, (a) Why are these the necessary and/or sufficient conditions and not others? and (b) What is/are the plausible proximal causal mechanism(s) that mediate the change process? The first question is frequently regarded as philosophical and beyond the bounds of proper science. The second question is frequently regarded as the province of the neurosciences that are said to possess the proper tools for a scientific answer to this question. The experimental analysis of behavior stands on its methods and believes that its findings form its own coherent discipline. This approach is offered as a model for all psychology and stands in marked contrast to the vast array of inferred psychological constructs found in most introductory psychology textbooks.

Explanations based on this experimental analysis of behavior take the same explanatory form as does Darwin's theory of evolution. The two key concepts are variation and selection. Variation refers to the fact that almost all behaviors are performed somewhat differently upon repetition. The term *operant* means to operate on the physical or social environment in some way. An example of the former is a rat in a Skinner box pressing a lever for food. Operants are theoretical distributions of possible variation in how a behavior might be performed by an individual organism. The rat does not always press the lever for food in the same way. Some lever presses are more forceful than others. Measurements of, say, 1,000 bar presses will form a distribution shaped something like the normal curve, with an average force in the middle and stronger and weaker forces toward each tail. Behaviors have consequences. Some consequences have the property of increasing the probability of behaviors they follow. These consequences are called *reinforcers* because they strengthen behavior in the sense that they make those behaviors more probable. *Selection* is a term that can also be used to describe these events. Dispensation of food is a reinforcer, for bar presses of a certain force or more selects for those bar presses and against weaker ones. Forces below the bar threshold will not sufficiently depress the lever to dispense food, and therefore such behavior will be emitted less frequently in future. Increasing the bar tension will require the animal to press harder to obtain food. This will increase the average force of a bar press in the same way that increasing the average speed by which predators flee is associated with an increase in the average rate with which predators run. Slower predators eat and therefore reproduce less efficiently and so become less representative of the species over time. *Ontogenetic evolution* refers to the evolution of behavior change during an individual's lifetime, versus *phylogenetic evolution*, which refers to structural changes in a species over many life spans. Both processes entail variation and selection. Hence, an operant explanation is quite parallel to a Darwinian explanation in its general form. Both appeal to the interaction of variation and selection over time.

Darwin's theory of evolution was not well received by most biologists of his day because he could not explain the basis of biological variation and how the results of selection during one generation were passed on to the next generation, because the science of genetics had not yet been developed. Darwin proposed a functional theory that lacked plausible proximal causal mechanism information to explain how variation and selection functioned as Darwin proposed. Operant conditioning is also a functional theory that lacks plausible proximal causal mechanism information to explain how variation and selection occur. This is the part that is left to the neurosciences to figure out, and although neuroscientists have done a rather good

job so far, experimental analysis of behavior (EAB) proponents have generally expressed little interest in their findings.

Most psychologists continued to ask questions about mediational processes and were not content with functional statements about necessary and sufficient conditions. They wanted to know more about what happened between the stimulus and the response or, more correctly, between the response (R) and the stimulus (S)—"more correctly," because Skinner was an R-S rather than a S-R psychologist. A main thesis of Skinner's 1932 seminal opus *The Behavior of Organisms* was to distinguish operant (R-S) from respondent (Classical, Pavlovian, S-R) explanations. Skinner focused on the stimulus consequences (e.g., appearance of food) after a response (e.g., bar press), leaving the animal to choose whether to press again or not. Operant conditioning has to do with choice and the conditions that influence what choices are made. Many psychologists were not content to live within these explanatory boundaries. They wanted more by way of explanation and turned to cognitive processes to get it.

THE RECIPROCAL-INHIBITION BASIS

The principle of reciprocal inhibition is a physiological one introduced by Sherrington to describe how a sharp tap on the patellar tendon elicits inhibition of the leg's flexor muscles along with excitation of leg extensor muscles. Wolpe's research on "animal neurosis" convinced him that fear could be reciprocally inhibited by a variety of factors, including muscle relaxation. He developed and popularized a treatment called "systematic desensitization" in his seminal 1958 book, *Psychotherapy by Reciprocal Inhibition*. Systematic desensitization is a multicomponent procedure consisting of relaxation training, hierarchy construction, and visualizing or experiencing each scene while relaxed. He first trained patients in deep muscle relaxation using procedures developed earlier by Jacobsen. A fear hierarchy was created using scenes that ranged from the least to most distressing situations. The patient then relaxed and imagined or experienced each scene. Fear ratings decreased, and this fact was explained on the basis of reciprocal inhibition. Other behavior therapies were developed using the same principle. Sexual arousal was used to reciprocally inhibit anxiety over sexual dysfunction.

Martial arts were used to reciprocally inhibit social anxiety, and so on.

Research has subsequently demonstrated that exposure and response prevention are the two necessary and sufficient conditions for fear reduction. Relaxation training may make patients more willing to expose themselves to fearful scenes, but it is not necessary. Hierarchy construction has the pragmatic advantage of allowing patients to address easy before difficult scenes but is otherwise unnecessary to a successful outcome. Hence, the reciprocal-inhibitory explanatory basis has been discredited.

THE COGNITIVE BASIS

Most original behavior therapists were clinicians who were trained psychoanalytically, rather than experimental psychologists who were schooled in theories of learning and memory, because clinical training was almost entirely dominated by psychoanalytic practitioners at that time. Heinz Hartmann's ego psychology emphasized cognitive processes and problem solving (see suggested readings). Systematic desensitization was described as a coping strategy. Therapists concentrated on helping patients cope with their fears based on approach rather than avoidance.

Automatic negative thoughts practiced since childhood were discovered to underlie emotional distress. These thoughts are organized into schemas and are resistant to change. Cognitive therapy consists of various strategies for correcting this attributional style. Clients are asked to keep records of thoughts, feelings, behaviors, and their consequences to see whether there is any evidence to support their negative conclusions. The reasoning used by clients is examined for logical flaws, and more consistent reasoning is substituted as indicated. This approach was first found to be successful in treating depression but has subsequently been effectively applied to a wide variety of disorders, including anxiety disorders, substance abuse, personality disorders, obsessive-compulsive disorder, eating disorders, and delusions.

Cognitive behavior therapy theories explain behavior disorder on the basis of automatic thoughts, schemas, logical errors, attentional biases, and overvalued ideation. These mediational processes are cited as differentiating factors that explain why one person responds normally to a situation such as riding an elevator, flying in a plane, or giving a speech, whereas another person is too frightened to do so.

THE NETWORK BASIS

Treatment of posttraumatic stress disorder (PTSD) and related disorders has given rise to an informal network behavior therapy theory. Its explanatory basis entails a network of cognitive, emotional, and behavioral nodes that are all highly interconnected. Activation in one area of the network spreads and thereby activates other portions of the network. Hence, thoughts can activate emotions. Emotions can activate thoughts. Each can activate autonomic responses and behaviors, which, in turn, can activate emotions and cognitions. This approach extends the cognitive basis by including independent emotional nodes. Emotion for cognitive theorists derives exclusively from what one thinks. Network theories provide for more independent sources of affect.

A primary limitation of informal network theories is that they lack specificity. While some theorists organize their networks into specified layers, other details of network architecture are lacking, such as how nodes within layers are interconnected and how the layers are interconnected. Activation rules are not specified, which means that predictions in the form of simulated results are not possible. These limitations are addressed by formal network theories.

Formal network theories specify all network parameters in sufficient detail to enable computer simulation of results. Theorists must select one of many different network architectures and one of several different activation functions. Computer software is increasingly available with which to simulate network predictions. Successful simulations presently span the full spectrum of psychology covered by introductory textbooks. A bidirectional associative memory network explanation has been developed that satisfies all published explanatory requirements for an understanding of PTSD.

—*Warren W. Tryon*

See also: *Applied Behavior Analysis (Vol. I); Behavioral Case Formulation (Vol. I); Behavioral Therapy (Vol. II)*

Suggested Readings

McLeod, P., Plunkett, K., & Rolls, E. T. (1998). *Introduction to connectionist modeling of cognitive processes.* New York: Oxford University Press.

McMullin, R. E. (1986). *Handbook of cognitive therapy techniques.* New York: Norton.

Thagard, P. (2000). *Coherence in thought and action.* Cambridge: MIT Press.

Tryon, W. W. (1986). The convergence of cognitive behaviorism and ego-psychology. *Theoretical and Philosophical Psychology, 6*, 90–96.

Tryon, W. W. (1995). Neural networks for behavior therapists: What they are and why they are important. *Behavior Therapy, 26*, 295–318.

Tryon, W. W. (1999). A bidirectional associative memory explanation of posttraumatic stress disorder. *Clinical Psychology Review, 19*, 789–818.

BEHAVIOR TRAINING

DESCRIPTION OF THE STRATEGY

The term *behavior training* can pertain to any type of intervention in which the client develops a set of new behaviors in response to an identified situation. Behavior training is used to build a client's skills where skills are lacking or where maladaptive skills have been used in the past. It is a technique that is highly structured and requires that the client practice the new behaviors outside of therapy sessions. Homework is an essential aspect; homework may involve practicing new skills at home or in real-life situations. The client's progress in therapy is contingent on work done outside of therapy sessions.

Behavior training is an integral part of behavior therapy, a significant aspect of cognitive-behavioral therapy, and may be used in conjunction with a variety of other therapeutic approaches. Behavior training can be used in individual, group, or milieu therapy. This entry will focus on the description, theoretical concepts, and application of behavior training.

In behavior training, the therapist's role is to offer instructions about new behaviors and to promote a set of behaviors that can apply to many situations. The process is interactive; training is designed to meet the needs of each individual. The therapist may reinforce positive behavior with encouragement and approval in addition to highlighting rewards and consequences from the larger environment.

Behavior training is built upon the concepts of operant conditioning. A core premise of operant conditioning is that any learned behavior can be changed through its relationship to reinforcers and punishment. Reinforcers serve to increase identified (target) behaviors. A target behavior increases when presence of positive reinforcers (such as approval or money) is contingent on the target behavior occurring. A target behavior also increases when absence of negative reinforcers (such as nagging, disapproval, or loss) is contingent upon the desired behavior occurring.

To diminish a problem behavior, the process of extinction may be used. *Extinction* refers to the sustained removal of all reinforcers for the behavior. At the beginning of the extinction trial (the removal of enforcers), the problem behavior will increase dramatically for a short time before it begins to diminish. This is called an extinction burst. If reinforcers are actively and consistently withheld in response to a problem behavior, the behavior will continually diminish to extinction.

Punishment refers to an aversive consequence that is used to diminish a problem behavior. Punishment diminishes the problem behavior only during the time punishing conditions are present. It is not effective in the long term, because it does not teach new behavior. Punishment may be completely ineffective if the individual has not yet learned an adaptive response to replace the problem behavior.

One example of behavior training is the token economy, a type of behavior training that is implemented in treatment settings with mentally retarded clients and schizophrenics. The token economy is one in which tokens (which the client can trade in for a reinforcer of choice) are linked to certain target behaviors of the client and used as reinforcers to increase the targeted behaviors. In a residence for mentally retarded adults, for example, a token may be awarded by staff contingent on the client's self-care behaviors, such as laundry or showering. Ideally, the target behaviors will be rewarded by the natural environment as well (e.g., "You look handsome today") and become intrinsically rewarding (e.g., "Being clean feels good").

Other examples of the clinical use of behavior training include relaxation exercises, self-monitoring techniques, self-talk, assertiveness training, and social skills training.

Behavior training emphasizes the relationship between the behavior and the reinforcers of the environment. However, it is generally recognized that behavioral events are mediated by cognition and that cognitive events are behavioral events in and of themselves. Thoughts cannot always be excluded from a therapeutic behavioral intervention.

RESEARCH BASIS

Behavior training is based on several key theoretical concepts. The major theoretical underpinning of behavior training is operant conditioning. Operant conditioning relies on the premise that a volitional behavior exists because it has functioned in the environment in which it was created; the behavior is maintained by the consequences the environment produces in response to the behavior. Problematic behaviors are seen as a pragmatic response to a specific former environment; the behaviors become problematic only when the environment changes and the ingrained behaviors are no longer functional. Simply put, treatment involves changing the relationship between the behavior and the consequences. It involves finding and practicing a behavior adaptive to the current environment (or changing the environment itself); understanding the origins of a problem is not essential to behavior change.

Similarly, behavioral assessment relies on the scientific analysis of the present behavior, rather than on the history of the behavior. The process of analyzing an existing behavior, to find the elements in the environment that serve to sustain the behavior, is referred to as "applied behavior analysis." Applied behavior analysis involves examining the interrelationship between the antecedents (events that stimulate the behavior), the response (the behavior in question), and the consequences or reinforcers of the behavior. After applied behavior analysis is completed, specific pieces of the behavior are identified for change. After specific target behaviors are identified, then the concepts of reinforcement, punishment, extinction, and stimulus control can be used in a behavior-training program.

Studies of the efficacy of reinforcers have been replicated many times. In one study, psychiatric patients (mostly schizophrenics) participated in a token economy targeting self-care skills. (A token economy provides tokens for target behaviors; patients can later cash in their tokens for reinforcers of their choice.) In this study, for example, the patients were rewarded contingent upon the performance of self-care skills, and the patients' performance of self-care routines improved significantly. To study whether the improvement was actually due to the presence of the reinforcer, the researchers altered the patient environment twice more. In the second condition, the patients were rewarded indiscriminately; when the relationship between behavior and reinforcer was intentionally broken in this way, the patients did not perform their self-care routines. In the third condition, when all reinforcers were withdrawn, the self-care

behaviors diminished to one quarter of the level they were during the contingency period. In the context of generations of similar research outcomes, it is evident that making reinforcers contingent on target behaviors is effective for behavior change.

RELEVANT TARGET POPULATIONS AND EXCEPTIONS

Behavior training is used to treat a wide range of psychosocial problems. As long as it has been commonly known that stress plays a significant role in compromising the immune system, information on behavior training has been widely disseminated in popular culture. There are hundreds of relaxation tapes that teach progressive muscle relaxation, breathing, and meditation. Self-help books with behavioral approaches line bookstore shelves. These are books (and tapes) that include instruction on how to handle certain situations and contain exercises for mastery of the skills. Popular books may also include information on self-evaluation: how to tell whether the skills are being mastered. All of these are examples of behavior training.

Behavioral training has proven to be successful in medical settings (this is sometimes referred to as "behavioral medicine"). Behavior training is used for individuals with heart disease, cancer, headaches, chronic pain, and epilepsy. Biofeedback, relaxation, and stress-coping techniques are effective for the majority of people who suffer from migraines. These treatments have been found to maintain effectiveness in migraine sufferers for at least 1 year. Research has also shown that older men and women with high blood pressure have reduced their blood pressure (significantly more than control subjects) when taught to practice transcendental meditation.

Behavior training is used most frequently in the context of cognitive-behavioral therapy. In cases of depression, anxiety, and obsessive-compulsive disorder, cognitive-behavioral therapy is often quite effective. Cognition and behavior are more interdependent than was originally conceptualized. Thoughts are often treated as behavior events in and of themselves. Behavior training can serve to reduce rituals in obsessive-compulsive disorder. Relaxation training and biofeedback are used in treating anxiety.

Social skills training and relaxation techniques can be used for clients with social phobia. These clients can benefit from assertiveness training to improve communication skills and interpersonal effectiveness.

With other phobias, relaxation training is used, often in conjunction with progressive exposure to the feared situation.

A more basic social skills training is used to help mentally retarded adults with self-care and basic conversation as well as social skills. Behavior training has also been used to improve the daily living skills of schizophrenic patients. As mentioned above, the use of token economies is quite effective with this population in inpatient and residential settings.

Recovery from substance abuse requires a great deal of behavioral work, starting with self-monitoring techniques. Sustaining abstinence requires a solid relapse prevention plan that includes a series of behavioral tasks. Smoking cessation and weight loss programs also rely heavily on behavior training (e.g., self-monitoring and exercise). Weight loss programs rely specifically on behavior training to teach self-monitoring of caloric intake.

Psychosocial skills training has been proven effective with habits and coping styles that impinge on adaptive sleep behaviors. Although sleep has biological and acute stress-related causes, maladaptive sleep behavior can exacerbate a sleep problem as well as comorbid mental illness such as depression, bipolar disorder, or schizophrenia. Environmental cues, sleep cognitions, or presleep behaviors may serve to maintain sleep problems that originated with the mental illness.

Behavior training has also been successful in treating sexual dysfunctions in men and women (such as erectile dysfunction, premature ejaculation, hypoactive sexual desire disorder). Sexual intimacy exercises and emotional communication skills training are emphasized. Sensate focus (a series of partner exercises that emphasize touching rather than orgasm) is also used.

Behavior training is used for a wide range of child behavior problems in addition to helping the adults learn parenting skills. However, child and parent interventions are beyond the scope of this article.

COMPLICATIONS

Behavior training is rarely contraindicated or harmful, but it cannot directly address certain clinical issues, such as bereavement, existential issues, and identity issues, for example. Nor would behavior training be used for aiding with a developmental transition or adjustment disorder. Similarly, if a client needs to learn how to build relationships, psychodynamic, interpersonal, or relational therapy would be effective choices. Finally, behavior training will not be successful if a client is ambivalent about changing his or her behavior; behavior training requires that the client be goal oriented and motivated.

A lack of client motivation is the most common reason behavior training fails. Due to limited cognitive development and lack of capacity for insight, behavior training is often indicated for mentally retarded adults and also for children; however, these are generally the clients who are least interested in changing behavior or in working hard to do it. Behavior training requires a strong motivation to change and hard work in order to make a change. It requires that the client spend time doing homework and practicing skills.

Another impediment to the success of behavior training is performance anxiety. Even if a client can perform the behavior, he or she may become anxious at having to perform and to have someone observe the target behavior. Such anxiety can compound the shame the client may feel; clinicians must be careful not to interpret performance anxiety as a lack of motivation or lack of desire to change.

Resistance may also arise from clients who have trust issues and difficulty accepting approval or rewards. These clients may struggle with internal conflicts about approval and judgment from authority figures. For this type of client, it is important to build rapport more slowly and to heighten his or her desire to change the behavior. If this is rushed, behavior training may render the client to be even more resistant to change.

CASE ILLUSTRATION

"Robert" was obtaining poor grades due to his anxiety and lack of skills in presenting papers in class. The contents of his papers were excellent. A behavior therapist, "Dr. Medina," at the university counseling center, had him rate his anxiety, using the Subjective Units of Discomfort Scale, before, during, and after his presentations. His anxiety began to increase the evening before a presentation, peaking after the first 10 minutes of the talk. Dr. Medina suggested that Robert enlist a friend to rate him on eye contact, clarity of speech, and several other public-speaking behaviors Robert had identified as problematic for him.

Dr. Medina and the client then developed a hierarchy of triggers that affected Robert's anxiety related to public presentations. Using a combination of imaginal exposure and deep-breathing techniques, Robert was able to reduce anxiety caused by the triggers. Dr. Medina also provided him with reading material that covered public-speaking skills. First in the therapy session and then with friends, Robert practiced eye contact, projecting to a crowd, and other typical public-speaking techniques. During the semester, Robert presented three more papers. Dr. Medina suggested that Robert's friend continue to rate him during mock and real presentations. Robert achieved success, and his grades improved.

—*Ann F. Philips and B. Steven Willis*

See also: Cognitive Behavior Therapy (Vol. I); Homework (Vol. I); Social Skills Training (Vol. I)

Suggested Readings

Bergen, A. E., & Garfield, S. L. (Eds.). (1994). *Handbook of psychotherapy and behavior change* (4th ed.). Oxford, UK: Wiley.

Hersen, M. (2002). *Clinical behavioral therapy: Adults and children.* West Sussex, UK: Wiley.

Miltenberger, R. G. (2001). *Behavior modification: Principles and procedures.* Belmont, CA: Wadsworth/Thomson.

Pear, J., & Martin, G. L. (2002). *Behavior modification: What it is and how to do it* (7th ed.). Upper Saddle River, NJ: Prentice Hall.

BEHAVIORAL ANALYTIC APPROACH TO SUPERVISION

DESCRIPTION OF THE STRATEGY

With the growing prominence of the empirically supported treatment movement, there has been an increasing emphasis in some training models to base training on diagnosis and selection of treatment from the growing list of supported treatments. Training therapists in empirically supported treatments is still not normative, but the trend appears to be growing. There is no clearly agreed upon method of training therapists in these treatments, but often training follows the pattern of introducing the rationale or theory behind the treatment, observing tapes of the procedure, studying a manual that generally describes what is to be done in each session, and then practicing until the therapist meets some adherence criterion. Adherence to a treatment manual is generally judged

according to some coding system that assesses whether the therapist is engaging in prescribed behaviors for each session. In some instances, coding systems also proscribe certain behaviors not consistent with the treatment model.

In some instances, empirically supported treatment coding systems include measures of competence as well as adherence. *Adherence* refers to conforming to the prescribed elements of the treatment at the correct time according to the protocol. *Competence* refers to the level of skill of the therapist conducting the specific therapy. Competence implies delivering the treatment in a manner to maximize effectiveness of the intervention. However, elements that comprise competence are not well specified.

CLINICAL BEHAVIOR ANALYSIS

In addition to empirically supported treatments gaining prominence, clinical behavior analysis has also evolved over the last 15 years. The scope of behavior analysis has broadened to address clinical issues that have traditionally been the province of clinical psychology. This has presented challenges to the behavior analyst in determining how to apply the principles of contingency management to adult outpatient populations, where the degree of control over the environment is considerably less than in the institutional settings where behavior analysis has traditionally had so much success.

Training therapists in how to apply behavior change principles to more traditional behavioral problems presents interesting challenges. Some supervision issues are the same regardless of the type of therapy or behavior change model employed, while others are uniquely important to a behavior-analytic training model. In any professional training program, therapists can be expected to initially lack confidence and closely follow the advice of supervisors and engage in imitative behavior. Behavior-analytic supervision is particularly attentive to trying to minimize elements of these imitative behaviors. Other stages of training involve the mastery of the basic learning theory and the principles of behavior change, the ability to recognize how these principles manifest themselves in clinical settings, establishing oneself as a mediator of change during therapy, and finally, to analyze and implement change strategies in a flexible manner that is driven by data and an assessment of effectiveness, rather than following highly structured session plans.

Understanding the Principles of Behavior Change

Clinical behavior analysis assumes that behavior change in therapy is accomplished by application of the same learning principles that shape any human learning. Thus, therapists focus on understanding the experimental analysis of human behavior with training in understanding verbal behavior. In addition, the supervision process emphasizes the active role the therapist assumes in the change process. Behavior therapy and cognitive behavior therapy also describe the therapist as taking an active role in therapy, but in those cases, that means that the therapist sets an agenda, assigns homework, and has change as an explicit goal of therapy rather than only insight and understanding. In clinical behavior analysis, it means that the therapist is an active mediator of the reinforcers of behavior change.

Natural Versus Arbitrary Reinforcement

In 1991, Robert Kohlenberg and Mavis Tsai described functional analytic psychotherapy (FAP). FAP was one of the first formal presentations of the application of behavioral principles in the context of an intense therapeutic relationship intended to produce clinical improvement in problems not usually addressed in clinical behavior analysis. One of the key features of that therapy was recognition that the relationship between the therapist and the client was the key means by which behavior change can be produced. While the importance of the therapeutic relationship has been the focus of several schools of therapy, most notably psychodynamic therapies, FAP described how the therapist was potentially an important source of reinforcement for behavior change by virtue of forming a close relationship with the client. That relationship is the vehicle that supports and reinforces behavior change.

The therapeutic relationship is a key factor in mediating behavior change because of the distinction between natural and arbitrary reinforcement described earlier by Charles Ferster. Arbitrary reinforcers are reinforcers contingently delivered by someone (e.g., the therapist) that increase the likelihood of the behavior will occur again but are unlike those in the natural environment that would maintain the behavior. Natural reinforcers are those that support or strengthen a behavior and are like those that function in the natural environment. A simple, nonclinical example is a child putting on his coat when being told to do so by the teacher. The teacher is present, prompts the child to put on the coat, and then says "Good boy." This sequence is an example of arbitrary reinforcement. The behavior is not under the control of contingencies in the natural environment. When the teacher is not present, the controlling contingencies are not present and the behavior is at risk for extinguishing. The natural reinforcer for putting on the coat is being warm when it is cool outside. This is the contingency that operates naturally. That contingent relationship will persist long after the prompt of the teacher is gone. That is not to say that arbitrary reinforcement is not powerful and useful in clinical behavior analysis. Rather, clinical behavior analysis recognizes that only when behavior is under the control of natural reinforcers would one expect it to be robust and resistant to extinction. The emphasis on developing and employing natural reinforcers is one of the main tasks to be developed during behavior-analytic supervision.

Thus, supervision focuses on teaching therapists to identify their interpersonal repertoires in establishing themselves as important reinforcers of behavior change. This position is distinct from most psychotherapy training, where a professional distance is maintained from clients. The result of maintaining distance from a client is that the therapist has to rely primarily on arbitrary reinforcement to create behavior change. The implication is that behavior maintained by arbitrary reinforcement is more prone to extinction as soon as the arbitrary reinforcer is removed.

The therapeutic relation, though allowed to be intense, is bound by ethical canons and is not completely isomorphic with natural relationships. However, the key element is that, where appropriate, the therapist shapes and reinforces clinically important behavior by being pleased, surprised, acquiescent, disappointed, sad, and so on, in a manner much like that which would occur in the natural world if the same behaviors were exhibited by the client. The supervision process focuses on training or permitting (reinforcing) the therapist to respond relatively naturally to client behavior that occurs in a therapy session as if it had occurred in a more natural setting. Certainly, the therapist is taught to recognize that initial attempts by the client to exhibit effective behavior will not be perfect. The therapist has to shape successive approximations of improvement, but even those approximations are reinforced by genuine pleasure at seeing the client try to improve.

Where empirically supported treatments for specific disorders are available, many therapists are taught to adhere to a manualized treatment protocol. From a behavior-analytic perspective, this inadvertently trains rule-governed behavior. Rule-governed behavior is a verbal description of the relationship between a behavior, a situation, and a consequence. For example, therapists may have a rule that says, "When a client is crying (the situation), I should comfort him or her (the behavior) so the client will feel supported (the consequence)." The trouble with rule-governed behavior is that the rule may or may not be correct. That is, in a particular situation, the relationship between the behavior, the situation, and the consequence may be very different from the rule the therapist holds. It is crucial for clients and therapist to accurately describe what the actual relationships are between behaviors, situations, and consequences rather than what the rule each may hold states.

Thus, a second focus of supervision is to train the importance of having the therapist's behavior accurately recognize the functional relationships between behaviors and consequences. It is not true that a behavior is a behavior is a behavior. The same behavior may have very different functions under different circumstances, and it is up to the therapist to identify the actual function of a behavior when it occurs. For example, a client may cry when sad, but he or she may also cry when he or she wants the therapist to stop asking about a particular topic. The therapist may be distracted by the crying and offer comfort (a rule) rather than recognizing that the crying is in a functional class of distracting behavior by the client and realizing that the useful therapeutic response may be to continue to pursue a potentially important topic even when the client finds it upsetting. Recognition that different situations may produce the same kind of response by a client or that different behaviors may occur in same situations to achieve a similar function is a principle (that of functional classes) that therapists must learn as part of the supervision process.

Supervision often focuses on those occasions in therapy when the therapist fails to respond to the function of a behavior rather that the topography (the form of the behavior). It is difficult for many therapists not to reflexively respond to a client being angry or missing a session, because it makes therapists uncomfortable or inconvenienced. However, supervision focuses on training the therapist to discriminate how to respond to the function of these behaviors.

THE SUPERVISION PROCESS

While many types of supervision share common features, some techniques seem particularly useful for achieving the goals believed to be important in providing sound clinical behavior-analytic supervision. One process that helps train therapists to attend to behavioral functions rather than only orienting to their topography is to conduct a functional assessment that results in a case conceptualization. The case conceptualization describes the behavioral problems and positive goals in terms of behavioral principles. For example, a behavior-analytic case conceptualization might contain a problem description such as "Client evidences a manding deficit." A *mand* is an instance of verbal behavior that is generally controlled by some state of deprivation or aversive condition that often specifies its own reinforcer. Clinically, what this means is that the person has difficulty saying when he or she wants something to be different. During therapy, such a problem could look like an assertion deficit, long silences during therapy, or missed sessions, or therapy could seem unfocused because the client isn't able to articulate when something affects him or her. Creating and updating these types of behavioral case conceptualizations provide practice in applying learning principles to complex problems and help therapists to focus on functional classes rather than only the topography of the behavior.

Another procedure that has been useful is to have therapists code each other's therapy tapes. The coding system samples 5- to 10-minute segments of the therapy session using the behavior-analytic case conceptualization the therapist has generated. Each turn of communication between the client and therapist is coded. Whenever an instance of an identified clinically important behavior is observed, the therapist response is coded as to whether the therapist discriminated the behavior as well as whether he or she responded appropriately to it.

One of the issues that contrasts clinical behavior analysis with therapies that follow formal, manualized protocols is that the clinical behavior analyst is trained to recognize that what matters is not precisely how the therapist behaves, but what effect the therapist's behavior has with respect to the goals of therapy.

There is no reason to expect that a young, female therapist and an older, overweight male therapist have the same behavioral repertoires and stimulus properties to effectively reinforce change in the client. That does not mean that different therapists cannot accomplish the same behavior change goal, only that what matters is that the clinical outcome is achieved regardless of how the therapist accomplishes the task. Thus, coding of therapist behavior focuses on effectiveness of their responses to clinically important behaviors exhibited by clients. This exercise trains coders to discriminate relevant behavior on the part of the client and therapist. Likewise, it highlights instances where the therapist did not respond effectively to an important client behavior. It is possible the therapist made a considered decision to overlook one clinically important behavior in order to shape another. The coding and debriefing sessions are excellent training exercises.

In addition to small teams or pairs of peer supervisors, a larger supervision format is useful. In the larger team, the focus of supervision is partly on helping manage cases, but more important, the larger group is a situation where students can observe each other's behavioral repertoire while conceptualizing cases, observing video of sessions, and more important, while each of them gives and takes feedback from each other. Noticing strengths and weaknesses in each other requires the same skill set required for therapy. Once team members notice a strength or weakness, the team format gives the members an opportunity to constructively shape more effective repertoires in each other and to establish themselves as natural reinforcers for supporting behavior change in each other.

For beginning and experienced therapists, it is extremely difficult to avoid developing rule-governed behavior. Therapists believe they learn and can describe a reliable link between a specific behavior they exhibit and an outcome. Much of the time, this produces behavioral inflexibility on the part of the therapist. The challenge is to teach the therapist to attend to the basic tasks of discriminating clinically relevant behavior and to respond effectively. For many years, supervisors have used what is known as the "bug-in-the-ear" procedure. In this procedure, the supervisor observes the therapy session behind a one-way mirror and transmits instructions to the therapist via a radio transmitter to an earpiece (the "bug") the therapist is wearing. While this may be comforting and instructive to the therapist, giving instructions that the therapist do or say what the supervisor suggests would prevent the therapist from drawing from his or her natural repertoire.

One procedure developed to shape therapist behavior while minimizing rule-governance is a modification of the bug-in-the-ear procedure. Behind the one-way mirror, the supervisor watches the session using the therapist's case conceptualization. In the therapy room behind the head of the client is a computer video monitor. The monitor is easily viewed by the therapist but not the client. As the session progresses, the supervisor gives positive or negative feedback that only the therapist can see. This can be in the form of a light bar that rises when the supervisor intends to give positive feedback and goes down when the supervisor believes the therapist is missing an important behavior or responding ineffectively. What is unique is that supervisors do not give any specific information about what they are orienting to when they give increasing or decreasing positive feedback. This requires therapists to attend to what is happening in the therapy session since the in-session behavior is what ultimately influences the supervisor's feedback. Supervisors give no explicit suggestions, which means therapists draw from their own behavioral repertoires in order to be more effective in sessions.

SUMMARY

Behavior-analytic supervision addresses several difficult training issues. It emphasizes theoretical coherence in understanding and changing complex behavior. This is accomplished through readings, behavior-analytically oriented case conceptualization, large and small supervision teams, mutual coding of therapy sessions, and techniques to minimize therapist rule-governed behavior. In contrast to training therapists to follow highly structured manuals, a behavior-analytic approach is flexible in how it allows therapists to accomplish goals.

—*William C. Follette*

See also: *Applied Behavior Analysis (Vol. I); Behavioral Consultation (Vol. II); Behavioral Contracting (Vol. I)*

Suggested Readings

Ferster, C. B. (1967). Arbitrary and natural reinforcement. *The Psychological Record, 22,* 1–16.

Follette, W. C., & Callaghan, G. M. (1995). Do as I do, not as I say: A behavior-analytic approach to supervision. *Professional Psychology: Research and Practice, 26,* 413–421.

Follette, W. C., Naugle, A. E., & Callaghan, G. M. (1996). A radical behavioral understanding of the therapeutic relationship in effecting change. *Behavior Therapy, 27,* 623–641.

BEHAVIORAL APPROACHES TO GAMBLING

DESCRIPTION OF THE STRATEGY

Strategies for treating gambling were derived from behavioral and cognitive models accounting for the development of what is commonly termed *problem, compulsive,* or *pathological gambling.* As gambling on poker machines or racing can result on occasion in immediate or briefly delayed winnings, behaviorists considered that much intermittent reinforcement maintained the behavior, despite its long-term negative consequences. Intermittent reinforcement is established to significantly retard extinction of a conditioned response, compared with invariable reinforcement. As it was considered that gambling is maintained by conditioning, it was suggested that it could also be inhibited by a procedure considered to act by conditioning: aversion therapy. The aversive stimuli usually employed were electric shocks. They were delivered at random to an electrode on the gamblers' arms, at a level sufficiently unpleasant to cause pronounced arm retraction while the gamblers played poker machines continuously. An aversive-conditioned response to gambling cues was considered to result, so inhibiting the wish to gamble. Reports of the procedure gave no attention to absence of retraction of the arm to gambling cues encountered following treatment, the response expected if the procedure acted by conditioning.

Electrical aversion was also used in the form of aversion relief. The subject read aloud a series of cards, at 10-second intervals, each card having a description of aspects of gambling he or she found exciting. An electric shock was given immediately after each card was read aloud. The final card contained a description of an adaptive behavior, such as "Going straight home after work." It was not followed by a shock, with the expectation that the behavior would be reinforced by the accompanying sense of relief. Nausea produced by injections of apomorphine was also used as an aversive agent. Covert sensitization was introduced as an aversive procedure not involving physically aversive stimuli. The subject was instructed while relaxed to visualize gambling, and then to visualize an aversive consequence, such as his wife telling him she was leaving him, or men from whom he had borrowed money attacking him.

Cognitive-behavioral theories emphasized the role of physiological excitement in gambling. A commonly observed behavior of pathological gamblers, which appears to be driven by mounting excitement, has been termed *chasing losses.* Gamblers attempt to recoup losses by increasing the size of the next bet or betting on a horse or dog that in their normal emotional states they would consider unlikely to win. Usually, the chasing cycle ends only when they have spent all their available money. To reduce the excitement associated with gambling, exposure to gambling stimuli combined with response prevention was used. The exposure was usually carried out in reality, commonly termed *in vivo,* in betting facilities. The patient, accompanied by the therapist, remained in the gambling environment without gambling for periods varying from 15 minutes to over an hour. The expectation was that without reinforcement of the urge to gamble, it would diminish by habituation. Exposure with partial-response prevention was also employed, with restrictions on the amount of time and money spent on gambling. Stimulus control therapy required the gamblers to avoid gambling situations completely, aided by limiting their access to money.

A behavior completion theory was advanced to account for the uncontrollable nature of the urge to gamble experienced by pathological gamblers when they attempted not to gamble. It postulated that a representation of habitual behaviors is set up in the brain. When persons encounter cues to complete the behaviors, such as being in situations where they have completed the behaviors previously or if they think about carrying out the behaviors, the brain representation is activated. The arousal system is then excited if they fail to complete behaviors, so that they experience increased tension or excitement, which can be sufficiently aversive as to force them to complete the behaviors against their will. On the basis of this theory, imaginal desensitization was introduced as a treatment for pathological gambling. Subjects were trained to relax and then instructed while relaxed to visualize being in situations that activated the urge to gamble. These situations could include passing near a venue for gambling or being bored at home and thinking of going out to gamble. They were then instructed to visualize not going into the gambling venue, but carrying out an acceptable alternative behavior and to continue to visualize this until they were relaxed. In its original form, it was administered in 14 sessions over a 5-day hospital admission. Subsequently, it has been used with outpatients. They are asked to listen four times a week for at least a month to an audiotape of the procedure, made with the therapist in his or her office.

An alternative theory was that the excitement associated with gambling caused some people, particularly those hypothesized to have addictive personalities, to become addicted to gambling. It was supported by evidence that pathological gamblers showed dependence, with withdrawal symptoms of disturbed mood and behavior, and tolerance, needing to gamble at higher risk to maintain satisfaction. Based on this theory, pathological gambling was treated by relapse prevention, combined with behavioral or other cognitive procedures, usually in a group format. Subjects were trained to identify high-risk situations in which they experienced the urge to gamble. These included places where they had previously gambled, carrying more money than needed, negative emotional states, and social pressures. Subjects were encouraged to develop coping strategies for these situations. These could require training in assertiveness, relaxation, and communication skills, and stress and anger management. Rehearsal, in which the gamblers were instructed to imagine being in high-risk situations and thinking adaptive thoughts and performing adaptive responses, was commonly employed. Having ceased gambling, they were to avoid making apparently irrelevant decisions that could lead to a lapse, that is, a gambling episode. These could include a decision to return to a situation where they had previously gambled, to meet friends but not gamble. If a lapse did occur, the subject was encouraged to accept that it would not inevitably be followed by relapse into prolonged gambling behavior.

As the majority of people who gamble do not become pathological gamblers, it was suggested that false cognitions contributed to the greater liability of some people to continue gambling to their financial disadvantage. These cognitions could include attributing control over their lives to luck, selectively recalling wins rather than losses, or believing they have high levels of skill or possess special knowledge, such as the form of racehorses. An approach aimed at correcting these false cognitions was introduced. Instruction concerning the concept of randomness was

often given a high priority. Subjects were taught that the outcome of each bet was uninfluenced by the outcome of other bets, so that the belief that they would win after a series of losses had no basis, and that no strategies existed to control the outcome.

Most current programs treating pathological gamblers are multimodal, combining cognitive with behavioral procedures. Attendance at Gamblers Anonymous is commonly recommended. Bibliotherapy for gamblers reluctant or unable to access treatment by therapists has been provided by a book describing a self-directed program of imaginal desensitization and cognitive therapy.

Concern at the increased prevalence of gambling and its negative social consequences, resulting from the increased number of gambling outlets approved by governmental agencies, has led to requests that these agencies require the outlets to adopt behavioral strategies to reduce the likelihood of gambling becoming pathological. These strategies include enforced breaks in play, and removal from gambling areas of facilities for gamblers to access funds in their bank accounts.

RESEARCH BASIS

Reviews of outcome studies of treatments of pathological gambling have criticized the small number of subjects usually included, inadequate duration of follow-up, lack of randomization in allocating subjects to treatment versus control procedure, and lack of standardized measures of outcome. Measures employed have included number of criteria for pathological gambling met on the *DSM,* South Oaks Gambling Screen, or the Massachusetts Gambling Screen and changes in perception of control or of self-efficacy, in desire to gamble, or in scores on the Eysenck Personality Questionnaire, the Spielberger State-Trait Anxiety Inventory, the Beck Depression Inventory, the Derogatis Symptom Checklist-90, or Zuckerman's Sensation Seeking Scale. When the focus has been on changes in subjects' psychological states, some studies failed to provide data concerning change in gambling behavior, such as frequency of gambling episodes and time and money spent gambling. Most studies relied on the subjects' self-reports, though some attempted to confirm these by interviewing close relatives or friends. Some studies compared the outcome of gamblers following treatment with wait-list controls. This methodology does not allow for the effect of suggestibility. There is substantial evidence that wait-list patients show a significantly poorer outcome than those treated with an inactive placebo.

The appropriate "intention-to-treat" evaluation was not always employed. With this evaluation, the outcomes for all subjects allocated to treatment or to control procedures are taken into account. Those who were not available for follow-up are included as treatment failures. Dropouts from treatment have consistently been found to have poorer response than those who remain in treatment due to personality differences such as reduced self-control. Of the randomized control studies of treatment of gamblers reported, two failed to use intention-to-treat outcome assessment but nevertheless attracted favorable review. In one, 8 of 22 gamblers who commenced cognitive treatment, including relapse prevention, dropped out. Three of 18 in the control group did not attend for assessment at the time of the posttreatment follow-up. At that time, the 14 subjects who completed treatment showed significantly greater improvement in a number of psychological variables than did the 15 controls. The treated subjects also gambled less often and for fewer hours, but the difference in money spent on gambling by them and the controls was not significant. The control group was maintained for a year, at which time only 9 of the 14 who completed treatment were followed up. Eight of the 9 did not meet the *DSM* criteria for pathological gambling. It was concluded that highly significant treatment gains had been maintained at follow-up, despite the fact that the response of 60% of gamblers who had commenced treatment was unknown. In the second study, 66 gamblers received treatment encouraging adequate perception of randomness combined with relapse prevention. Again, the control group was maintained for 1 year, at which time 28 of the 66 who commenced treatment were available for follow-up at 1 year. Twenty-five of the 28 did not meet *DSM* criteria for pathological gambling. It was again concluded that highly significant treatment gains were maintained at follow-up when the outcome of about 60% was unknown.

An earlier randomized study that used intention-to-treat outcome assessment, but with small subject numbers, found that at 1-year follow-up, of 10 subjects allocated to imaginal desensitization, 2 reported abstinence from gambling, and 5 reported controlled gambling, compared with 2 of the 10 who received aversion relief reporting controlled gambling. Another study using intention-to-treat assessment randomly allocated 64 slot machine gamblers: 16 to individual stimulus control and exposure with response prevention, 16 to group cognitive restructuring, 16 to the two treatments combined, and 16 to a wait-list control. A successful response was defined as abstinence or occurrence of only one or two episodes of gambling using a limited amount of money during the 12 months following treatment. The control group was maintained for 6 months. Fourteen subjects dropped out of treatment but appropriately were included as treatment failures in the evaluation of outcome. At the 6-month follow-up, the responses of the groups who received the individual and group treatment, but not the group who received the combined treatment, were significantly superior to the responses of the wait-list controls. At the 12-month follow-up, 11 of the 16 gamblers who received individual treatment showed successful response, significantly superior to the response of 6 of the 16 in the two groups treated with group cognitive restructuring or the combined procedure.

An outcome study with a longer follow-up period of a mean of 5 years and an adequate number of subjects reported the response of 63 of 120 gamblers who had commenced treatment. Sixty had been randomly allocated to imaginal desensitization, and 60 to other behavioral procedures—20 to electrical aversion, 20 to in vivo exposure, and 20 to imaginal relaxation. At follow-up, 18 classified themselves as abstinent, 24 as controlled, and 21 as uncontrolled gamblers. Twenty-six abstinent or controlled gamblers had received imaginal desensitization, compared with 16 who received the other procedures. The difference was statistically significant. Using intention-to-treat analysis, all the gamblers not followed up at 5 years were classified as uncontrolled. The difference in response of those allocated to imaginal desensitization compared with the other procedures was just less than significant.

The findings of these randomized comparison studies suggest that some behavioral techniques may be more effective than some cognitive procedures. At 1-year follow-up of gamblers who commenced treatment, 70% responded to imaginal desensitization or to individual stimulus control and exposure with response prevention, and 40% responded to cognitive correction and relapse prevention. A finding that needs explanation was that response to individual stimulus control combined with group cognitive therapy was significantly inferior to the response to the individual procedure alone. It raises the possibility that multimodal treatments may be less effective than single treatments. Conclusions from these findings must be tentative, in view of possible differences in the subjects treated and outcome measures used. The finding that at a mean of following treatment, response to imaginal desensitization was better than that to other therapies suggested the effect of its administration over 1 week could persist for this length of time. As all reviews of studies evaluating the treatment of pathological gambling conclude, more randomized comparison studies employing standardized outcome measures are needed. These measures should include frequency of gambling and the time and money spent on it.

In relation to mode of action, successful treatment of pathological gambling may involve reduction of anxiety. In studies evaluating imaginal desensitization, reduction in gambling behavior at follow-up was associated with lower levels of state and trait anxiety. In one study, a lower level of state anxiety 1 month following treatment predicted reduction in gambling urge and behavior at 1 year. In the study of the three groups treated with stimulus control and exposure with response prevention, group cognitive restructuring, or a combination of the two, state and treat anxiety scores fell at the follow-up, but not to a significant extent.

RELEVANT TARGET POPULATIONS AND EXCEPTIONS

Most recent evaluations of behavioral and cognitive treatments of gambling reported that all the subjects accepted for treatment met *DSM* criteria for pathological gambling. Earlier single-case studies reported good responses to treatment of problem gamblers who did not meet these criteria. Hence, failure to meet *DSM* criteria does not exclude the presence of significant gambling problems that respond to treatment. Failure to meet *DSM* criteria may therefore not be appropriate either as an exclusion criterion or as a measure of treatment outcome. Gamblers who have sufficient financial resources can be unable to limit the amount of money they lose when they wish to do so, but they may not meet the necessary five *DSM* criteria. If excluded from treatment, they are likely to lose all financial resources, as their gambling is likely to progress to meet the *DSM* criteria. Other exclusion criteria in outcome studies have included failure to

rate motivation to change at 7 or more on a scale of 0 to 10, failure to score 8 or above on the South Oaks Gambling Screen, or the presence of serious behavioral disorders, mainly alcoholism, psychosis, or bipolar disorder.

COMPLICATIONS

The major complication of treatment of pathological gamblers is that a significant number discontinue some forms of treatment. Not only does this result in these subjects not receiving treatment, but effectiveness of treatment is exaggerated if intention-to-treat outcome assessment is not employed. In three of the randomized studies reviewed, outpatient treatment was used. In the two that used cognitive treatment given over 6 to 11 weeks, about a third dropped out, and 60% were not followed-up at 1 year. A quarter dropped out from the study that compared individual and group treatments administered in weekly sessions over 6 weeks. They were appropriately evaluated as treatment failures at 1 year. All 20 patients who received aversion relief or imaginal desensitization in 14 sessions over a week in hospital completed treatment, and all were available at the 1-year follow-up. All 120 patients treated in hospital over a week with a variety of behavioral procedures completed treatment, though only 63 were available to provide follow-up data at a mean of 5 years. Those who did not were evaluated as treatment failures. Duration of treatment and hospitalization as well as length of follow-up may be factors influencing dropout rates.

Partly influenced by the ideology of Gamblers Anonymous that pathological gambling cannot be cured, but can be arrested through the practice of total abstinence, conflict exists as to whether controlled gambling can be an acceptable outcome. As some gamblers seek treatment not to stop gambling, which they enjoy, but to gamble in a controlled manner, offering them this option can encourage them to accept treatment. In the study that followed up treated gamblers at a mean of 5 years, the state and trait anxiety, neuroticism, psychoticism, and depression scores of subjects who reported abstinence and controlled gambling were in the range of the healthy population, having been in the pathological range prior to treatment. The scores of treated subjects who reported uncontrolled gambling remained in the pathological range. Fifteen of the 18 abstinent and 17 of the 24 controlled gamblers considered their financial positions to be the same or better than that of most people, whereas only 10 of the 21 uncontrolled gamblers did. These findings indicate that some pathological gamblers are able to continue gambling in a controlled manner for several years following treatment. A percentage of the treated gamblers who were abstinent at follow-up reported episodes of severe gambling following treatment, so that such episodes should not be regarded as evidence of failure of treatment.

Significant levels of depression have been found in pathological gamblers, which could be secondary to the consequences of gambling. As pointed out above, depression levels of gamblers fell to within normal limits with a successful response to treatment. Alcoholism, substance abuse, antisocial, narcissistic, and borderline personality disorder, attention-deficit/hyperactivity disorder, and criminal behavior have been reported in more pathological gamblers than controls, and predicted poor response to treatment.

CASE ILLUSTRATION

"Mr. H. S." was 28 years old. He had married 6 years previously and had two children, aged 5 and 3. His childhood and school history were uneventful. He had worked as a salesman since leaving school and had been in his current position 5 years. In adolescence, he commenced gambling on horse racing in betting shops, and though he spent several hours a week in the shops, gambled any available money, and was about $1,000 in debt when he married, he did not consider that he had a gambling problem at that time. After his marriage, he decided he should reduce gambling and initially was successful in doing so. He spent less than an hour and no more than $20 a week gambling, and he paid off his debt. After the birth of his first child, his wife attempted to persuade him to cease gambling as part of an attempt to reduce their expenditures so they could commence saving. His initial response was to gamble more, with the expectation he would win money. As he failed to do so, he commenced borrowing money to continue to gamble at an increased level. As his debts mounted, he persuaded his parents and friends to lend him money. On occasion, he was unable to pay rent on time or give his wife housekeeping money, and he was spending time away from home at weekends gambling. His wife became suspicious and accused him of gambling. He denied this and increased his efforts to borrow money, not informing her of this. He experienced a temptation to take

money from his workplace but was able to resist this. As his debts mounted to over $6,000, he became unable to meet interest payments and revealed the situation to his wife, asking whether her parents could help them financially. She initially threatened to leave him but agreed to remain if he would seek treatment to cease gambling.

When he was interviewed by the therapist, he reported he had not gambled since the confrontation with his wife 3 weeks previously, but was preoccupied with thoughts of how he might get money to recommence. He said he had made repeated efforts in the past to stop gambling and felt restless and irritable when he did so. He had often chased losses, gambling recklessly his remaining money. At times, he had gambled to escape feelings of helplessness, guilt, anxiety, and depression. His condition therefore met the necessary five criteria for a *DSM* diagnosis of pathological gambling. Cues that motivated him to gamble included passing near a betting shop on his way home from work and feeling bored or depressed when at home at the weekend. He reported he had smoked marijuana in adolescence. Currently, he drank on average 10 glasses of beer a week and smoked 20 cigarettes a day. He did not wish to change these behaviors. He had no criminal history. His state and trait anxiety scores were 49 and 54 respectively, and his Beck Depression Inventory score was 22.

An audiotape was made of imaginal desensitization, in which he visualized remaining relaxed while experiencing the cues for gambling. He was instructed to listen to the tape four times a week for 4 weeks. Following this, he reported he had not gambled and experienced minimal urges to do so. He was no longer preoccupied with thoughts of gambling. His state and trait anxiety scores were 32 and 35 respectively, and his Beck Depression score was 6. He was asked to listen to the tape twice weekly for 2 months, then once weekly. He was followed-up monthly for 3 months, then once every other month. After 7 months, he reported he had gambled more than $300 in 5 days, after which he revealed the relapse to his wife. No precipitating cause was apparent. The reason he gave was that he wished to see whether he could gamble a small amount regularly for enjoyment. He decided this was not possible. Temporarily, he listened to the tape more frequently and was seen again monthly for 3 months, and then once every other month for 10 months. He reported no further relapse, and his state and trait anxiety and Beck Depression scores remained in the posttreatment range. He was discharged with the request to return if there was any relapse.

—*Nathaniel McConaghy*

See also: *Behavioral Treatment for the Addictions (Vol. I); Behavioral Treatment of Cigarette Smoking (Vol. I); Self-Control (Vol. I)*

Suggested Readings

Blaszczynski, A. (1998). *Overcoming compulsive gambling: A self-help guide using cognitive-behavioral techniques.* London: Robinson.

Lopez Viets, V. C., & Miller, W. R. (1997). Treatment approaches for pathological gamblers. *Clinical Psychology Review, 17,* 689–702.

McConaghy, N. (1983). Agoraphobia, compulsive behaviours and behaviour completion mechanisms. *Australian and New Zealand Journal of Psychiatry, 17,* 170–179.

Oakley-Browne, M. A., Adams, P., & Mobberly, P. M. (2002). Interventions for pathological gambling (Cochrane Review). *The Cochrane Library, 4,* 1–23. Oxford, UK: Update Software.

Petry, N. M., & Armentano, C. (1999). Prevalence, assessment, and treatment of pathological gambling. *Psychiatric Services, 50,* 1021–1927.

BEHAVIORAL APPROACHES TO SCHIZOPHRENIA

DESCRIPTION OF THE STRATEGY

Schizophrenia is a severe, chronic mental disorder characterized by various behavioral, emotional, and cognitive disturbances. Although the phenomenology of the disorder is highly heterogeneous, common characteristics of the illness can generally be classified into four domains: positive symptoms, negative symptoms, cognitive impairment, and social dysfunction. Positive symptoms include hallucinations, delusions, and disorganization of thinking, speech, and behavior that schizophrenia patients experience. Negative symptoms consist of deficiencies compared with nonpatients, such as a reduced range of emotional experience and expression, social withdrawal, and diminution in goal-directed behavior. In addition to positive and negative symptoms, schizophrenia is associated with diminished life satisfaction, poor social and occupational functioning, neurocognitive impairments, and profound deficits in social competence.

Cognitive impairment is now recognized as a key characteristic of schizophrenia that has a significant (negative) impact on functioning. Finally, social dysfunction is a defining feature of schizophrenia that is stable over time and predictive of the course and outcome of the illness. Cognitive and social deficits are relatively independent of positive and negative symptoms and are not responsive to medication.

Antipsychotic medications play a central role in the treatment of schizophrenia. However, despite striking benefits provided by antipsychotic medication, medication alone does not and cannot be expected to restore premorbid levels of psychosocial function, lead to normative role performance, or produce an acceptable quality of life for most individuals with schizophrenia. As such, behavioral treatment strategies play a key role in the comprehensive care of individuals with schizophrenia. The empirical literature on psychosocial interventions for schizophrenia has expanded dramatically over the last decade, and their acceptance as part of a comprehensive system of care for severally ill patients has grown accordingly. Areas of dysfunction that had seemed immune to psychosocial interventions, including cognitive dysfunction, social avoidance, and psychotic symptoms, are now seen as reasonable targets of treatment. Four of the best supported and most promising behavioral approaches to schizophrenia, each of which targets different aspects of this multifaceted disorder, will be presented in this section: social skills training (SST), cognitive behavior therapy (CBT), cognitive remediation (CR), and token economies (TE). For each of these four key types of intervention, we will provide (a) description of the intervention, (b) research basis, (c) relevant target populations, and (d) complications. Finally, a case illustration of SST will be presented.

SOCIAL SKILLS TRAINING (SST)

Description of the Strategy

The basic technology for teaching social skills was developed in the 1970s and has not changed substantially in the intervening years. Based on social learning principles, SST emphasizes the role of behavioral rehearsal in skill development. Complex social repertoires, such as making friends and dating, are first broken down into discrete steps or component elements. Patients are first taught to perform the elements of each skill, and then gradually learn to smoothly combine them through shaping and reinforcement of successive approximations. The primary modality of training is role play of simulated conversations. The trainer first provides *instructions* on how to perform the skill, and then *models* the behavior to demonstrate how it is performed. A social situation that is relevant to the patient and in which the skill might be used is then identified and the patient engages in *role play* with the trainer. The trainer next provides *feedback* and *positive reinforcement,* followed by suggestions for how the response can be improved. The sequence of role play followed by feedback and reinforcement is then repeated until the patient can perform the response adequately. Training is typically conducted in small groups (6–8 patients), in which case, patients take turns role playing for 3 to 4 trials at a time and providing feedback and reinforcement to one another.

The most widely studied skills-training approach is the UCLA Social and Independent Living Skills Program. This program was designed for ease of dissemination, and it includes carefully crafted videotapes and instruction manuals for both trainers and patient. Training employs standard skills-training techniques (e.g., role play, modeling) and includes modules (curricula) covering seven areas: Medication Management, Symptom Management, Recreation for Leisure, Basic Conversation Skills, Substance Abuse Management, Workplace Fundamentals, and Community Reentry (skills for the transition from inpatient to outpatient environments). Each module can be delivered as a discrete, targeted intervention, or modules can be provided sequentially for a more comprehensive intervention. The UCLA program has been translated into several languages and successfully employed in much of Western Europe and Japan, as well as Canada and the United States.

Research Basis

The basic social skills training strategy was refined and validated in a number of single-case studies and small-group designs conducted in the 1970s and 1980s. These early reports were followed by a series of randomized clinical trials that have provided a clearer picture of areas in which SST is and is not effective. First, SST is not substantially effective for reducing symptoms or preventing relapse. This finding is not surprising. The only reason why SST should affect these domains is by teaching skills that help to reduce social failure that would otherwise cause

sufficient stress to precipitate exacerbations. This stress diathesis model depends on several mediating factors that are themselves unproven (e.g., that social failure produces sufficient stress to precipitate relapse). Second, SST has a reliable and significant effect on specific behavioral skills (e.g., gaze, asking questions, voice volume). Third, SST has a positive impact on social role functioning, although the findings for this outcome domain are not entirely consistent. The results are better for defined skills areas (e.g., medication management, teaching substance abusers how to refuse drugs, HIV prevention skills) than for more general measures of social functioning. Fourth, SST appears to have a positive effect on patient satisfaction and self-efficacy: They feel more self-confident in (targeted) social situations after training. SST is clearly an effective teaching technology that is well received by both patients and clinicians. SST is best conceptualized as a targeted treatment that can achieve important outcomes when applied in conjunction with other critical interventions, including pharmacotherapy, case management, and substance abuse treatment, as well as environmental supports such as housing.

Relevant Target Populations and Exceptions

SST is appropriate as a targeted treatment for social impairment, not as a broad-based treatment for schizophrenia. Studies have generally not examined the use of SST during acute psychotic episodes. The aim of treatment during this phase of the illness is to reduce acute symptoms (primarily positive symptoms). With acute hospital stays often limited to a few days, there is little time opportunity to engage patients in SST (or other systematic behavioral treatment programs). Also, acutely ill patients are not thought to be in a position to attain new skills that would be retained during periods of remission or would generalize to their usual environments. SST is generally conducted on an outpatient basis, but it can be implemented in long-term inpatient settings as well. Given the invariant problem of generalization from training to in vivo application (see below), training, whether formal or informal, should focus on skills that are *currently* relevant to the client's life rather than on skills that might one day be useful. Most of the empirical literature on SST has been devoted to schizophrenia, but the general teaching strategies and style of interaction apply to people with other serious mental illnesses, as well.

Complications

One of the critical questions about SST concerns transfer of training or generalization of newly learned skills to the community. There is scant evidence that there is spontaneous generalization from office-based training to the community. Treatment must bridge the gap between office-based training and the community by systematically prompting and reinforcing desired behavior and/or by engaging significant others in the community to do so. As noted above, neurocognitive impairment is relatively universal among people with schizophrenia, and there is good evidence that these cognitive factors influence social functioning. Several studies have demonstrated that cognitive impairments such as verbal memory, executive functioning, and vigilance influence performance in social skills training. Skills-training techniques are designed to minimize the demands on cognitive capacity, and most patients can benefit from training. However, patients with significant deficits in memory, executive functioning, or attention learn more slowly than patients with more moderate cognitive impairment, and they have difficulty acquiring more complex skills. The goals and pace of training sessions are typically adjusted to accommodate for differences in cognitive impairment and motivation.

COGNITIVE-BEHAVIORAL THERAPY (CBT)

Description of the Strategy

Although antipsychotic medications are generally effective at reducing the positive symptoms of schizophrenia, moderate to high levels of positive symptoms continue to persist among a large number of schizophrenia patients. As many as 20% of patients may not be responsive to medication, and many others are only partially responsive. CBT for psychosis is a verbal therapy that incorporates (a) the establishment of a strong therapeutic alliance characterized by acceptance, support, and mutual goals *before* introduction of behavior change techniques; (b) psychoeducation about the nature of psychosis with the goal of reducing stigma; (c) reduction of stress, anxiety, and depression; (d) use of cognitive-behavioral techniques to help the person cope with psychotic symptoms; and (e) a focus on relapse prevention. Patients are taught to question faulty assumptions about themselves and the world, to accept psychotic symptoms as logical attempts to cope with stress rather than being "crazy" or signs of weakness, and to use coping strategies to control the distress produced by hallucinations and delusions. In most programs, an effort is made to reinforce coping strategies already used by patients and to help them apply the techniques more effectively. Strategies range from simple use of physical or mental distraction (e.g., listening to music on headphones), to calling a friend for support, to logical self-talk (e.g., "This is not a real voice, it is just my imagination. I can control this.") Patients generally receive homework assignments to practice coping strategies and more adaptive ways of thinking between sessions, in order to foster generalization. CBT is typically administered in a one-to-one format in outpatient settings. Therapists in most trials have been doctoral-level clinicians. Treatment duration has varied from 6 to 10 sessions conducted over a few weeks to more than 20 sessions over 9 months or longer.

Research Basis

Since the early 1990s, there has been a growing body of literature on the application of the principles of CBT to address residual psychotic symptoms. The literature is difficult to integrate due to variations in treatment format and duration, control groups, and outcome measures. CBT appears to be most effective for reducing belief in the veracity of delusions, in distress associated with delusions, and in overall levels of symptoms. There is some evidence for its effectiveness in reducing frequency and distress over hallucinations, but the results are somewhat disappointing given that most programs attempt to help patients cope with these symptoms. Similarly, there is some suggestion that CBT is helpful in reducing depression and negative symptoms, but here too, the results are mixed. Conversely, there is replicated evidence that it does not reduce relapse. Follow-up data are also inconsistent, suggesting that the effects of longer-term, more intensive interventions produce durable effects on some, but not all, domains.

There is now a growing evidence base for use of CBT with other psychotic patients, as well. Several large clinical trials have found CBT to be more effective than control conditions, especially including treatment as usual, for decreasing distress associated with delusions and hallucinations.

Relevant Target Populations and Exceptions

Like most psychosocial treatments for schizophrenia, CBT is intended to supplement other services, including pharmacotherapy and case management. Results for acute inpatients have been less impressive than for stabilized (chronic) outpatients with residual symptoms, and longer trials have generally produced better results. Most trials have not recruited patients randomly. Rather, subjects have generally been selected so as to be appropriate for a verbal psychotherapy. Patients with significant cognitive impairment or with substance abuse problems have not been well represented in these trials. It is questionable whether the more abstract, cognitively demanding CBT techniques can work with highly symptomatic patients, cognitively impaired patients, or dually diagnosed patients. As most trials have been conducted in the United Kingdom, CBT has been superimposed on a backdrop of the socialized care provided to serious mental illness (SMI) patients in United Kingdom, rather than the more disjointed approach characteristic of mental health care in the United States. Controlled trials of CBT need to be conducted in the United States with outpatients in order to determine its effectiveness in typical United States public health systems.

Complications

The term *cognitive-behavioral therapy* has been used very loosely in this entry to refer to a wide variety of different treatment techniques. As indicated, they all share some common values and assumptions about the illness and how to relate to patients, but few, if any, would be immediately recognizable as CBT practiced with depressed and anxious patients. In appraising the literature as a whole, it is safer to conclude that there is good evidence for *cognitive-behaviorally oriented* treatment, including the development of a collaborative partnership with the patient, the use of psychoeducation to decrease stigma, developing shared goals, and teaching patients how to cope, rather than for any specific CBT techniques.

COGNITIVE REMEDIATION (CR)

Description of the Strategy

Cognitive impairment is now widely considered to be a central feature of schizophrenia. The vast majority of patients with the illness demonstrate clear deficits relative to healthy controls, most often reported in domains of processing speed, attention, working memory, new learning, and executive/reasoning abilities. Importantly, from the perspective of rehabilitation, (a) a growing body of literature has demonstrated that neuropsychological performance has a significant impact on community functioning, including social competence, independent living, and vocational performance, and (b) optimal pharmacological treatment *offers limited cognitive benefit* and does little to relieve the profound functional disability experienced by patients. These factors have fostered an upsurge of interest over the past decade in the possibility of cognitive remediation in schizophrenia.

The targets of training in cognitive remediation have included verbal memory, problem solving, and executive functions, attention, social perception, and work performance. Some programs have focused narrowly on single domains, while others have targeted a range of functions. Training strategies have been quite diverse, including self-guided practice on computer tasks, self-guided exposure to commercially produced educational software, intensive individual training using paper-and-pencil neurocognitive test materials, and small-group discussions and naturalistic rehearsal of social cognition exercises. Training durations have ranged from 5 weeks to 6 months, usually with multiple training sessions per week. Three prototypical approaches illustrate the similarities and differences among cognitive remediation programs currently described in the literature.

Wykes and colleagues developed cognitive remediation therapy (CRT), an intervention that focuses on executive functioning (e.g., cognitive flexibility, working memory, and planning). The approach employs a sophisticated training model based on principles of errorless learning, targeted reinforcement, and guided practice on cognitive tasks administered in one-on-one therapy sessions. Training media consist of a variety of paper-and-pencil games and neurocognitive tests. An alternative approach introduced by Bell and Wexler capitalizes on the ease of standardization and flexibility provided by computer software. This approach emphasizes repetitive practice of elementary neurocognitive skills (working memory, attention) that are assumed to be the basis for higher-level cognitive processes. In contrast to CRT, there is minimal teaching via interaction between the clinician and patient; patients primarily engage in self-guided practice at computers. Medalia has developed an innovative program called Neuropsychological Educational Approach to Remediation (NEAR), which employs commercially available educational software. These tasks are intrinsically interesting to subjects and have built-in feedback mechanisms to guide performance. The intervention is administered in an open classroom format in which patients attend on an ad lib basis, select tasks they are interested in working on each day, and move at their own pace. Medalia emphasizes self-guided practice, rather than structured training, in order to foster *intrinsic motivation* for learning and to allow patients to enhance their preferred problem-solving styles.

Research Basis

There is an extensive literature documenting that a variety of training techniques can improve performance on neuropsychological tests, and there is a growing literature of more clinically relevant CR programs such as the ones described above. Overall, the data are promising, with most studies generating small to medium effect sizes. A preliminary trial of Wykes's CRT yielded improvement on several neuropsychological measures and modest retention of training effects over a 6-month follow-up interval. A companion fMRI study demonstrated meaningful changes in cortical activation among a subgroup of patients who responded positively to the intervention. Results from the Bell study are among the most impressive to date, with significant changes in several domains of neurocognition. No studies have yet demonstrated a clinically significant effect on community functioning.

Relevant Target Populations and Exceptions

CR has been integrated into supported work programs, day programs, and residential programs for patients with chronic schizophrenia and other serious mental illnesses. Brief CR interventions focused on a single modality (e.g., attention, problem solving) have also been conducted during inpatient hospital stays. As with the other behavioral approaches to schizophrenia discussed here, CR is intended as a supplemental treatment. It is intended to target patients who demonstrate cognitive deficits, but beyond that, it is unclear which patients are most likely to benefit from this type of treatment. CR should not be offered to patients with schizophrenia who do not exhibit cognitive deficits.

Complications

Because most CR programs employ highly individualized treatment models and demand high levels of therapist skill, dissemination of CR approaches presents a challenge that will need to be addressed as the field progresses. Applicability of CR to typical clinical settings, ability of CR to produce clinically meaningful change, and generalization of benefits to community function have not been demonstrated.

TOKEN ECONOMIES (TE)

Description of the Strategy

Social learning programs such as TE are based on the principles of operant conditioning. They are milieu-based programs, typically used on inpatient psychiatric units or in residential settings for patients with chronic mental illness. Tokens or points are distributed as immediate reinforcement when patients perform specified target behaviors. The focus tends to be on behaviors that are adaptive, observable, and operationally defined so that they may be objectively assessed. Target behaviors typically include behaviors such as self-care, basic social interaction, treatment participation, or work activities. Tokens are then exchanged by patients at a later time for individually selected reinforcers, which include various desirable goods or privileges. Use of tokens or points serves to bridge the delay between the performance of the behavior and the opportunity to obtain more meaningful reinforcers. Specific target behaviors, reinforcers, and exchange rates are developed for each program; the specifics are determined by local circumstances and the clinical needs of the particular patient group.

Research Basis

The TE constitutes one the most extensively researched type of behavioral treatment for patients with schizophrenia. Decades of research on TE programs indicate that they are effective in increasing the adaptive behaviors of patients with schizophrenia in institutional treatment environments. For example, when compared with supportive milieu treatment and standard hospital care, a TE for severely debilitated hospital patients yielded significant improvement in 100% of the participating patients compared with 55% in the milieu condition and 33% in the standard care control group. Furthermore, in the TE program,

97% were successfully discharged to the community for at least 18 months compared with 71% in the milieu condition and 45% in the control condition. In addition to improved performance of the target behaviors that are specifically reinforced as part of the program, treatment in a TE has also been associated with improvements in work performance, general ratings of behavior, and negative symptoms.

Relevant Target Populations and Exceptions

Though the focus of this entry is on schizophrenia, principles of operant psychology have been applied to the development of therapeutic interventions for a variety of populations, including patients with other serious mental illnesses, school children, individuals with mental retardation, and delinquents. Among programs for patients with schizophrenia, TE's have been used primarily in long-term inpatient psychiatric settings and residential settings. Studies have generally not examined the use of TE during acute psychotic episodes or brief hospital stays. Though there have been some reports of decreased negative symptoms, such as apathy, psychotic symptoms do not tend to be the focus of TE programs.

Complications

Even though TE is one of the most well-validated, comprehensive psychosocial treatments for schizophrenia, it is not widely in use. Reasons for the lack of current use include shortened hospital stays, which are less well suited to the intervention; the locus of treatment in the community where external control of reinforcers is difficult to maintain; concerns about the ethics of withholding or denying positive reinforcers; and a misunderstanding of the token economy and principles of social learning on which it is based. In addition, the vast majority of studies supporting the token economy were performed more than 20 years ago, contributing to the perception that such an intervention is not feasible or relevant in current treatment settings. Finally, as with SST and CR, the extent to which treatment gains extend or transfer to other settings is not clear.

CASE ILLUSTRATION, SOCIAL SKILLS TRAINING

"Michael S." was a single, White man first diagnosed with schizophrenia when he was 24. He had been working as a clerk in a small store and living with his parents when he first became ill. He had had few friends and dated infrequently. He was 32 when he began to participate in our rehabilitation program. He was living in a group home and had been unable to work since his first psychotic episode. He was described by his case manager as a passive, shy man who was frequently taken advantage of by other residents in the group home and the day treatment program he attended. He was referred to us because of concerns that (a) he needed to be more assertive with other patients, who were "borrowing" his money and personal items and (b) he had expressed an interest in getting a job but was so quiet that he was unable to get past interviews.

Michael was well maintained on medication, did not have significant negative symptoms, and did not manifest behavioral problems that would prevent him from working. Based on the case manager's report and a review of Michael's medical record, we focused our attention on social skills. He was appropriately groomed and did not present himself as a "patient" (e.g., no inappropriate mannerisms, no intrusions of psychotic or tangential thoughts, able to track conversation and provide appropriate responses to questions). However, he had a "deer in the headlights" quality. He seemed quite ill at ease: He scarcely made eye contact, looking mostly at the floor; he seemed to be physically tense; his shoulders were hunched and his head tilted toward the floor; he spoke haltingly in a very soft voice, such that the interviewer frequently had to ask him to repeat what he had said and to speak more loudly. When asked about his case manager's concerns about lending things to peers, he indicated he didn't always want to give away his money and things, but that he was afraid people would get angry with him if he refused. He expressed the desire to return to work as a clerk, especially if the job did not involve much pressure. He reported that he always felt nervous during job interviews even when he thought he could do the work.

In response to our evaluation and Michael's expressed desire to be more assertive and to be able to get a job, we contracted with him to participate in a social skills training group for 3 months. The group included six other patients and met twice per week for 60 to 90 minutes. Michael's program consisted of three interrelated curriculum units: (1) assertiveness training to teach him how to be more effective in refusing unreasonable requests from peers, (2) job interview skills, and (3) drug refusal skills. The unit on drug refusal was based on our concern that Michael was vulnerable to unwanted offers of drugs, and addressed refusal skills (how to say "no") and suggested alternative activities that do not involve drug use. Skills training for all three units consisted primarily of role play rehearsals. A theme was defined for each session (e.g., telling a friend you cannot lend him money), and each patient was prompted to identify a specific situation that had recently occurred or might occur in the near future. Patients then took turns engaging in repeated role plays, in which the therapist portrayed someone in the patient's environment. In Michael's case, he identified other patients who frequently asked him for things, and he rehearsed saying "no" to typical requests. Training Michael in job interview skills was coordinated with efforts by his case manager to arrange for interviews, as training is invariably more effective when it has near-term relevance and the new skills can be practiced in the real world. Training in drug refusal skills proved to be very relevant, as Michael admitted that he was being pressured to use drugs by other patients.

Michael responded well to treatment. He was able to secure a part-time job as a clerk within a few months of training and had maintained the job when we followed up some 6 months later. His case manager reported that he was better able to refuse requests for money, although it was arranged for staff to bank his paychecks and keep a minimal amount of cash on hand, just to be safe. The case manger also reported that urine drug testing was routinely conducted in Michael's group home and that he had been clean each time he was tested.

—*Alan S. Bellack and Wendy Tenhula*

See also: Bellack, Alan S. (Vol. I); Role Playing (Vol. I); Social Skills Training (Vol. I)

Suggested Readings

Bellack, A. S., Gold, J. M., & Buchanan, R. W. (1999). Cognitive rehabilitation for schizophrenia: Problems, prospects, and strategies. *Schizophrenia Bulletin, 25,* 257–274.

Bellack, A. S., Mueser, K. T., Gingerich, S., & Agresta, J. (1997). *Social skills training for schizophrenia: A step-by-step guide.* New York, NY: Guilford Press.

Dickerson, F. B. (2000). Cognitive-behavioral psychotherapy for schizophrenia: A review of recent empirical studies. *Schizophrenia Research, 43,* 71–90.

Liberman, R. P., Wallace, C. J., Blackwell, G., Eckman, T. A., Vaccaro, J. V., & Kuehnel, T. G. (1993). Innovations in skills training for the seriously mentally ill: The UCLA Social and Independent Living Skills Modules. *Innovations and Research, 2,* 43–60.

Medalia, A., & Revheim, N. (1999). Computer assisted learning in psychiatric rehabilitation. *Psychiatric Rehabilitation Skills, 3,* 77–98.

Paul, G. L., & Lentz, R. J. (1977). *Psychosocial treatment of chronic mental patients: Milieu versus social-learning programs.* Cambridge, MA: Harvard University Press.

Rector, N. A., & Beck, A. T. (2001). Cognitive-behavioral therapy for schizophrenia: An empirical review. *Journal of Nervous and Mental Disease, 189,* 278–287.

Twamley, E. W., Jeste, D. V., & Bellack, A. S. (in press). A review of cognitive training in schizophrenia. *Schizophrenia Bulletin.*

Wykes, T., & Van der Gaag, M. (2001). Is it time to develop a new cognitive therapy for psychosis–cognitive remediation therapy (CRT)? *Clinical Psychology Review, 21,* 227–256.

BEHAVIORAL APPROACHES TO SEXUAL DEVIATION

DESCRIPTION OF THE STRATEGY

Programs for the assessment and treatment of sexual deviants have flourished over the past several years, with the majority of these programs focusing on sexual offenders. The media focus on sexual offending has driven a remarkable expansion in North American programs for these offenders from a handful in the late 1970s to 1,784 in 1994. Unfortunately, there appears to have been a reciprocal drop in reports of treatment programs for nonoffending paraphilics. What has emerged has been the development of cognitive-behavioral treatment (CBT) programs for sexual offenders that target a comprehensive range of issues. These programs include a full assessment battery administered before and after treatment, a comprehensive treatment program, and (where possible) postdischarge supervision. The following sections will describe the typical assessment and treatment elements.

Assessment

Five methods involved in the comprehensive assessment of paraphilics will be described. These methods generate data that overlap in many ways, allowing comparisons across procedures. Hypotheses generated to account for any discrepancies can then be pursued by further interviews and testing.

1. *Clinical interview:* The majority of reports describe relatively unstructured approaches to interviews with these men. The client's mental status must be evaluated, as additional psychopathology may suggest different approaches to treatment or a pretreatment intervention (e.g., medication for schizophrenia or severe depression). The major focus of the clinical interview, however, is on the client's life history (including particularly his history of childhood and adult relationships and his sexual history), his attitudes and beliefs, his emotional functioning and coping style, and a variety of aspects of his offense history.

2. *Self-monitoring:* Clients are required to produce daily records of the frequency and intensity of sexual urges, activities, and fantasies. Evidence of pornography and cybersex use should also be collected.

3. *Sexual preference testing:* This has traditionally been one of the central features of the behavioral approach. Phallometric testing (measurement of erectile response to various sexual stimuli) has the longest history and best-established research base. Other researchers have developed visual reaction time (VRT) measures to track the amount of time clients spend looking at and evaluating pictures of clothed adults and children. To date the limited evidence on the value of VRT suggests it may be helpful in identifying the sexual interests of child molesters.

4. *Biological and neuropsychological assessments:* For a small percentage of sexual deviants, disturbances in their sexual steroid or hormonal systems are apparent and may be related to their problem behavior. When the client complains of preoccupation with sex or in other ways appears to be sexually driven, assays of his circulating testosterone are in order. Similarly, when the person's history or evaluation results suggest possible memory, learning, or other cognitive dysfunction, then a full neuropsychological assessment should be completed.

5. *Psychological testing:* Except for evaluating psychopathy, personality testing has not revealed anything significant concerning sexual deviants. Screening for psychopathy is essential, as it contributes to an estimate of future risk to reoffend. Composite actuarial risk assessment instruments form part of a complete assessment of sexual offenders.

Other features that are typically evaluated by psychological tests include sexual interests, dysfunctions, and knowledge; attitudes toward women and children and toward sex; intimacy and loneliness; self-esteem; alcohol and drug use; empathy; assertiveness.

Treatment

It needs to be noted that almost all aspects of treatment with sexual offenders are addressed within a group therapy context. This typically involves two therapists and 8 to 10 offenders engaged in three or four sessions per week in programs running from 4 months to 18 months. The only procedures specifically addressed in individual therapy are those concerned with the modifications of sexual preferences.

At the end of treatment, the client is reappraised and, depending upon his gains, his risk level may be adjusted.

1. *Responsibility:* Clients must take responsibility for their actions and admit to all aspects of their deviance. These issues of responsibility are challenged using some variant of cognitive restructuring in the context of presenting whatever independent evidence (e.g., police records) is available.

2. *Attitudes:* Similarly, attitudes that serve to maintain or justify offending need to be challenged again by a cognitive-restructuring approach. These attitudes can be directly elicited by discussing views of the problem behavior itself, views of women or children and their sexuality, of sex and what constitutes consent, and by considering the costs and benefits of continuing or terminating the paraphilic behavior.

3. *Self-worth:* Since low self-worth inhibits effective participation in treatment, this is an essential early target in treatment. Changing the person's self-statements toward a more positive self-appraisal is effective along with expanding their sources of pleasure and social contacts. Distinguishing clients from their behaviors serves not only to reduce shame but also encourages them to believe they can change.

4. *Coping:* Sexual deviants need to replace sex with more functionally useful ways of dealing with difficulties in their lives. Using a problem-solving approach and distinguishing adaptive coping (i.e., task-focused coping) from maladaptive styles (i.e., emotional-focused or avoidance-focused coping) is an

effective way to move sexual deviants toward a more effective approach to life's problems.

5. *Antisociality:* This is an important issue for sexual offenders, and there are also clear elements of impulsivity in the enactment of other deviant sexual acts. A research-based program has been developed to address these issues; it is usually called "cognitive skills training" and has been shown to add to the effectiveness of the other aspects of sexual offender treatment.

6. *Empathy:* While some sexual offenders have general deficits in empathy, the majority appear to simply lack empathy for their victims. Some of these deficits result from poor emotional recognition skills, while most seem to represent attempts to reduce the offender's guilt or shame and to allow him to continue to offend. Training in emotional recognition is facilitated by having each offender relate to the group an upsetting experience from his life. Each other group member is required to identify the feelings the presenter exhibited as well as his own feelings while listening to the story. This provides extensive direct and vicarious experience in recognizing emotions. Next, all clients are required in group to generate a list of consequences to victims. From this composite list, each client is required to identify harmful effects that are relevant (or might be relevant) to his own victims.

7. *Social skills:* Programs developed in other areas of clinical work have been adapted to address assertiveness, social anxiety, anger, and conversational skills. However, the primary social deficits in sexual deviants concern relationships. The features of effective relationships are outlined as well as the benefits of intimacy and the costs of emotional loneliness. Focused topics include sexual relations, jealousy, communication, nurturing skills, mutual activities, and productive living without a partner. A module on sex education focuses on activities that enhance sexual pleasure, the need for variety and spontaneity, the value of affection, and a concern for mutual pleasure.

8. *Use of intoxicants:* A module adapted from work in the field of addictions is provided. In this module, attention is given to the need to accept responsibility for choosing to abuse a substance.

9. *Sexual interests:* There are two targets in this component of treatment: reduction of arousal to deviant acts and enhancement of arousal to appropriate

activities. Early procedures used to reduce deviant interests involved making various noxious stimuli (e.g., nausea-inducing agents or electric shocks) contingent upon stimuli depicting the deviant acts. More recently, the aversive events have involved foul odors (e.g., rotting meat or smelling salts) or imaginal consequences. Alternatively, satiation therapy requires the subject to masturbate to orgasm and then, during the subsequent refractory period, repeatedly verbally rehearse variations on his deviant theme for at least 10 minutes. This associates deviant thoughts with low sexual responsivity, which reliably produces extinction of arousal to the deviant images.

The most popular procedure for increasing sexual interest in appropriate sexual acts involves having the client replace his deviant thoughts during masturbation with prosocial sexual images. This procedure is called "masturbatory reconditioning." This replacement process requires diligent application by the offender and usually produces slow but progressive changes to the provocative power of the appropriate images. This procedure is typically done in concert with satiation therapy.

10. *Relapse prevention issues:* Clients generate a detailed description of their offense pathways. These pathways include an identification of the background factors (e.g., fluctuating mood, stress, low self-worth, losses, intoxication) that created the psychological conditions predisposing the client to offend. The pathways also describe the circumstances surrounding the offenses and the steps the client took to secure a victim. From these offense pathways and from what has been learned in assessment and treatment, each client produces a set of self-management plans that will avoid, or deal with as they arise, any circumstances (internal or external) that increase the risk of a further offense. To assist the client in enacting his self-management plans, he lists people (both professional and family and friends) who will serve as his support group. Finally, the client provides a set of warning signs that indicate to him and to others that he may be beginning to move toward risk to reoffend.

RESEARCH BASIS

For the assessment and treatment targets outlined above, there is sufficient research or theory to justify including them in the program.

Each component of CBT treatment for sexual offenders has been subject to an evaluation. In each case, the specific component (e.g., empathy training, intimacy enhancement) has been shown to generate the changes aimed for. There is, therefore, research to justify the value of the components of treatment. In addition, a recent meta-analysis evaluated the overall results of 42 methodologically satisfactory treatment outcome studies involving almost 10,000 subjects. The results of this meta-analysis showed that compared with untreated sexual offenders, those who were treated had significantly lower long-term recidivism rates (17% for the untreated subjects, 9% for the treated subjects). A subsequent comparison of the treatment effect size generated by this study with the effect sizes generated by the treatment of other types of offenders, general mental health problems, and physical health problems revealed comparable gains. Finally cost-benefit analyses in terms of victims saved and money saved were also favorable for the treatment of sexual offenders.

RELEVANT TARGET POPULATIONS

Clearly, all persons who commit sexual offenses or who engage in other nonvictim sexual deviances are appropriate candidates for this form of treatment. It is, however, important to note that the present use of the term *sexual deviant* does not include persons whose sexual preferences are directed toward same-sex partners. Cognitive behavior therapists have for many years eschewed the treatment of homosexuals. Within the category "sexual offenders," there are various subtypes, and each subtype (rapists, nonfamilial child molesters, incest offenders, exhibitionists) has been effectively treated.

Many sexual offender program coordinators attempt to engage all possible clients in treatment. Unfortunately, all too many programs refuse to treat sexual offenders who do not take full responsibility for what they have done. A more appropriate perspective might be to see these features of the client's initial presentation as problems in motivation to be addressed by the program.

COMPLICATIONS

The entanglement of sexual offender treatment with the legal and correctional systems has been seen by some as a double-edged sword. The pressure exerted by these systems can provide the leverage necessary to engage reluctant clients. On the other hand, this involvement can hinder treatment progress because of the context (e.g., prison) in which treatment is provided. Despite this caveat, the results of meta-analyses of treatment outcome reveal that institutionally based programs are as effective as community-based treatment.

The problem of most concern in providing treatment in communities is the threat sexual offenders pose while treatment is ongoing. Residential programs go some way to reducing this risk by placing clients on medications to lower their sex drive (antiandrogens) or to increase their sense of control (selective serotonin reuptake inhibitors, or SSRIs).

The fact that in many jurisdictions, treatment providers are required by law to report to the authorities revelations of past offenses, or any imminent risk to attack someone, complicates the role of the therapist. This is an area of treatment provision where the confidentiality that normally constrains therapists from revealing issues expressed by their clients is disrupted. It may be said that sexual offender therapists have at least two sets of clients: sexual offenders and the public. This can cause problems in the effective delivery of treatment.

CASE ILLUSTRATION

"Peter," a primary school teacher, was 33 years of age when he entered treatment. He had been convicted of molesting an 11-year-old girl and admitted to having sexually assaulted five other girls. Peter's assaults began at age 22, although he admitted to having had sexual fantasies of young girls since he was an early teenager.

Peter said his parents were both cold and distant, making him feel rejected and unlovable. From the age of 12 years, Peter began secretly watching his younger sister undress, but he claimed never to have touched her. Peter recalled masturbating several times a day from age 8 years, indicating it was his only childhood source of satisfaction. Although Peter expressed a desire for a sexual relationship with a woman, he had never had one.

Assessment revealed a range of problems. At phallometric assessment, Peter displayed strong, and relatively equal, erectile responses to females of all ages. Similarly, Peter's self-monitoring revealed very high frequencies of strong deviant sexual urges (several every day). His responses at interview (and confirmed by later testing) indicated low self-esteem, shame about his behavior, low intimacy and high loneliness, the use of sex to cope with even minor upsets, a somewhat dysphoric mood, and some degree of state anxiety. Peter also used alcohol in the context of his offenses. He vacillated somewhat about his responsibility for the offenses, which paralleled his fluctuating sense of shame; when shame was strong, he would downplay his role in the offenses, but he would accept responsibility when feeling more confident.

Once baseline responding was established, Peter entered treatment. He was instructed to inhale smelling salts to eradicate deviant urges, and he was told to use masturbatory reconditioning and satiation every time he masturbated. Systematic desensitization reduced heterosexual social anxiety, his self-esteem was enhanced, and he engaged in role plays to increase social skills. Peter was also given relationship training and exposed to a course in problem solving.

Finally, Peter was assisted in developing his pathways to offending and a set of relapse prevention (i.e., self-management) plans. His pathways revealed a typical pattern of feeling lonely, feeling low self-worth, and feeling sorry for himself, leading to increased deviant fantasies and urges, and heightened arousal. Peter then would seek out a victim and offer her money or other gifts. His self-management plans involved strategies for dealing with low self-worth and loneliness, developing relationships with adult females, participating in social activities with adults, and masturbating to appropriate sexual acts. Peter also developed plans to avoid being alone with children and to restrict his use of alcohol to situations in which he could not offend.

Posttreatment evaluations revealed positive changes in all features. Access to a comprehensive national police database revealed that Peter had been offense free for 8 years posttreatment. At a 2-year follow-up evaluation, Peter reported that he had been on two dates with two different adult females. Although these dates did not lead to a relationship, Peter reported feeling satisfied that he had behaved effectively and was optimistic about the future.

—*W. L. Marshall*

See also: *Electrical Aversion (Vol. I); Masturbatory Retraining (Vol. I); Orgasmic Reconditioning (Vol. I)*

Suggested Readings

Laws, D., R., & O'Donohue, W. (Eds.). (1997). *Sexual deviance: Theory, assessment, and treatment.* New York: Guilford Press.

Marshall, W. L., Anderson, D., & Fernandez, Y. M. (1999). *Cognitive behavioural treatment of sexual offenders.* Chichester, UK: Wiley.

Schwartz, B. K., & Cellini, H. R. (Eds.). (1995, 1997, 1999, 2002). *The sex offender* (Vols. 1, 2, 3, 4). Kingston, NJ: Civic Research Institute.

Ward, T., Hudson, S. M., & Laws, D. R. (Eds.). (2003). *Sexual deviance: Issues and controversies.* Thousand Oaks, CA: Sage.

BEHAVIORAL ASSESSMENT

DESCRIPTION OF THE STRATEGY

Behavioral assessment is a flexible system of measurement and judgment that emphasizes principles and concepts of assessment more than the use of specific methods. Behavioral assessment emphasizes the measurement of external environmental factors, such as the social setting in which a client's problem behaviors occur and how others respond to those behaviors; cognitive processes, such as a client's thoughts and beliefs; and overt behavior, such as how a person acts in a particular environment. Behavioral assessment is closely tied to well-established models of learning (such as operant conditioning, classical conditioning, and social learning), and it is strongly influenced by research. For example, the emphasis on the social contexts of problem behavior is derived from many studies that have shown that individuals' social environments can have an influence on the onset, maintenance, magnitude, and cessation of behavior problems, as well as the degree to which treatment goals are achieved.

The guiding principles and concepts of behavioral assessment can be contrasted with those of psychodynamic and personality assessment systems. Unlike behavioral assessment, the latter systems assume that behavioral problems arise primarily from stable, internal, psychological processes, such as unconscious conflicts and dysfunctional personality characteristics. Because in these systems, the main determinants of behavior problems are considered to be internal and stable psychological processes, personality and projective assessment systems emphasize the measurement of internal experiences and personality characteristics by using assessment instruments such as the Rorschach and personality inventories. In contrast, principles of behavioral assessment emphasize measurement through observation, instrumentation, self-monitoring, and behaviorally focused interviews and questionnaires.

Let us begin by reviewing several conceptual foundations of behavioral assessment. The first, as suggested above, is *environmental determinism.* According to the principle of environmental determinism, how an individual behaves (e.g., the likelihood that an individual suffering from depression will engage in self-harm) can often be affected by his or her current situation, as well as how others have responded to certain key behaviors in the past. Learning principles (e.g., reinforcement, punishment, classical conditioning, modeling) are of particular importance in helping us understand these behavior-environment relations. In general, many behaviors, both adaptive and maladaptive, are thought of as responses to specific environmental events that precede, co-occur, and/or follow them.

A second conceptual foundation for behavioral assessment is an emphasis on *empiricism:* the idea that problems can best be understood through the use of scientific methods. When applied to behavioral assessment, empiricism emphasizes use of systematic observation, careful measurement and the formulation of definitions of behaviors and environmental events, the use of well-validated assessment instruments, and control or monitoring of the assessment environment to learn about the form and function of an individual's behavior.

There are several additional characteristics of behavioral assessment. First, the *hypothetico-deductive* method is often used to learn more about a client. In this method of inquiry, an assessor develops hypotheses about the behavior of a client and subsequently designs assessment strategies to test those hypotheses. For example, the assessor may hypothesize that a client may be more likely to injure herself following a confrontation with her spouse. To test this hypothesis, the assessor might request that the client self-monitor marital conflict and instances of self-harm, to see whether there is an elevated chance of self-harm following conflict compared with nonconflict times.

In addition, behavioral assessment stresses the *context of behavior,* the idea that behavior is often influenced by an interaction between the environment and individual differences. The environment might include the physical setting, response contingencies in effect in a particular environment, and the people present. Individual differences might include the unique biological characteristics of the client, his or her culture and ethnic identify, and past learning experiences. Thus, the form and causes of the same behavior problem can differ across persons, as well as across different settings for one person.

An emphasis on the contexts of behavior problems naturally leads to *sensitivity to individual differences.* Thus, behavioral assessment is sensitive to the notion that each client presents with a unique history, physiology, and context. There can be important differences across clients with the same behavior problem simply as a result of differences in culture and ethnicity, age, sex, sexual orientation, and religion, among others. Accordingly, assessment strategies are often customized to reflect these important differences across clients.

Behavioral assessment also places great importance on looking for *multiple and differing causes* of behavior problems. Not surprisingly, a single behavior problem may be the result of a variety of causes. For example, depressed mood can be a consequence of negative life events such as loss of a loved one, negative thoughts about oneself and the future, biochemical changes, and genetic factors. Causes of depressed mood can differ greatly across persons, and often multiple causal factors operate at once.

Reciprocal causation is important in behavioral assessment. A person can affect his or her environment, which can, in turn, affect the person's behavior. For example, a client with generalized anxiety disorder may express her anxiety and level of discomfort to her husband, who may engage in nurturing behaviors and take on responsibility for many of the tasks that his wife finds stressful. This, in turn, may escalate the woman's level of anxiety or prevent exposure to anxiety-provoking situations, thereby reducing the likelihood that anxiety responses will extinguish.

In addition, behavioral assessment assumes that there can be *temporal variability* in behavior problems and their causes. That is, the characteristics and causes of a behavior problem can change over time. This is often observed in differences between factors leading to the onset of a problem (e.g., social stimuli for early instances of smoking), as well as factors that maintain a problem once it is established (e.g., physiological withdrawal effects when a person tries to stop smoking).

Although many types of causes can fit within a behavioral assessment system (e.g., biological, cognitive, early learning, and genetic), behavioral assessment stresses events in *close temporal relations* to behavior problems. Immediate responses by others to a behavior problem, responses to positive alternatives to a behavior problem, the setting in which the person finds himself or herself, stimuli that trigger a response, and what the person thinks in challenging situations are examples of the kind of contemporaneous causal events emphasized in behavioral assessment. Noncontiguous events can be very important (consider the important effects on adults of early childhood physical abuse or the long-lasting effects of spinal cord injury) but are often less amenable to intervention.

Behavioral assessment also emphasizes the *social systems* surrounding a behavior problem. For example, we know that how well an individual is able to cope with loss of a loved one can depend on his or her existing social support network and other contextual factors to which one is exposed. Social system and contextual factors may include physical health and emotional availability of close friends and family members, the stability of one's marriage and family life, the absence of significant economic troubles, and other life stressors.

As outlined below, behavioral assessment focuses on the identification of *functional relations* between behavior problems and their causes. Behavioral assessment goes beyond the description of a behavior problem, such as the typologies of diagnostic systems. It emphasizes the relations, particularly causal relations, among behavior problems and between behavior problems and other environmental, behavioral, and cognitive variables.

The aforementioned conceptual foundations and characteristics have a number of implications for persons who adopt a behavioral assessment approach. First, behavioral assessors must be familiar with learning principles as they apply to the onset, maintenance, and cessation of behavior problems. Second, they must possess the skills required to carefully define and measure behavior and situations. Third, they must be skilled in designing assessment procedures that will permit accurate identification and measurement of complex relations among behaviors and contextual factors. Finally, they must also be well acquainted with the empirical research relevant to their clients.

GOALS AND APPLICATIONS OF BEHAVIORAL ASSESSMENT

One of the primary goals of behavioral assessment is to obtain accurate information about a client's behavior problems and treatment goals, as well as the factors that affect those behavior problems and goals. This primary goal can then be divided into two subgoals: (1) specific measurement of behavior problems, treatment goals, and causal variables (i.e., *description*) and (2) specific measurement of the relations between problems, goals, and causal factors (i.e., *functional analysis*). Regarding treatment applications, the overarching goal of behavioral assessment is to help clinicians better identify the factors that affect clients' responses to treatment, make better judgments about which treatments will be most effective for a given client, and design effective strategies for measuring treatment outcome.

The assessor must first define and specify behavior problems and potential causal factors. Following this, the assessor must design strategies for collecting data on the relations among target behaviors and casual factors. In the sections that follow, we will discuss strategies used to achieve these subordinate goals.

The Definition, Specification, and Quantification of Behaviors and Causal Variables

Once a behavior problem or treatment goal has been broadly identified (typically by the client or the individual who referred the client), the behavioral assessor must then specify and measure as precisely as possible its key characteristics. (It is important to keep in mind that that there are usually multiple problems and treatment goals.) Typically, a specific description includes the qualities of the target behavior, as well as its quantitative dimensions (e.g., rate, duration, and intensity). This level of specificity is useful to the clinician in that it helps him or her better identify the causal variables associated with the behavior problem and track the effects of treatment.

Behavior problems are often composed of three interrelated *modes:* Verbal-cognitive, physiological-affective, and overt-motor. The verbal-cognitive mode includes spoken words as well as thoughts, self-statements, memories, and internal imagery. The physiological-affective mode includes physical responses (e.g., physiological responses, physical sensations) and perceived emotional states. Finally, the overt-motor mode includes observable behavioral responses.

Behavior problems can be extremely complex and difficult to define. For example, an individual who experiences acute anxiety at work may present with many different cognitive, emotional, and overt-motor behaviors. These may include persistent thoughts about his inability to perform his job well, persistent worry about getting fired if he does not complete projects within a certain time frame, a reduction in work efficiency, irritable interactions with other workers, and a variety of physiological symptoms while at work (e.g., accelerated heart rate, sweaty palms, and muscle tension). However, another individual who also experiences work-related anxiety may present with a different configuration of verbal-cognitive, physiological-affective, and overt-motor behaviors.

Once a behavior problem has been described, the assessor must then select the best *measurement dimensions*. Although there are many ways to measure a behavior problem, the dimensions most commonly measured are frequency, duration, and intensity. The dimension selected varies depending upon its relevance to a given client. For example, some clients may report infrequent but long-lasting manic periods, while others may have frequent manic periods that are relatively short in duration.

Following definition and specification of a behavior problem, the assessor must identify the causal variables that affect the client's behavior problems. As noted earlier, important causal variables often fall into two broad modes: social/environmental factors and intrapersonal factors. Social/environmental factors include both interactions with other people and the physical characteristics of an environment (e.g., temperature, noise levels, lighting levels, etc.). In contrast, intrapersonal factors include verbal-cognitive, affective-physiological, and overt-motor behaviors that may exert significant causal effects on a client's behavior. The causal factor measurement dimensions are similar to those used with target behaviors in that frequency, duration, and intensity of contextual factor occurrence are most often measured. Important causal factors may also include systems factors, as noted above.

Several implications emerge from defining, specifying, and quantifying behavior problems and causal factors. First, the process requires that the behavioral assessor think carefully and objectively about the nature of the client's problems and about the factors that might influence their occurrence. This careful approach reduces likelihood that the behavioral assessor will oversimplify, bias, or omit key variables in his or her case formulation. Second, the description and specification process makes it possible for the behavioral assessor to evaluate the personal and social significance of the behavior problem—another important

facet of a case formulation. Finally, this process permits the assessor to evaluate whether the pattern of behaviors presented meet formal diagnostic criteria, as listed in the American Psychiatric Association *Diagnostic and Statistical Manual (DSM-IV)* or other diagnostic systems.

Functional Analysis of the Client's Behavior Problems

Once target behaviors and causal variables have been defined, specified, and quantified, the behavioral assessor then works to develop a *case formulation* depicting the functional relations among the identified variables. This explanatory model of target behavior-causal variable interrelations is known as the *functional analysis*. The functional analysis involves the identification of all important, modifiable causal variables associated with the client's behavior problems and is the primary guide for the development of an individualized treatment plan for the client.

Several variables are typically included in a functional analysis. First, the assessor must estimate which of many possible causal relations are most important in terms of treatment design. The assessor seeks to identify the most important causal relations (i.e., those with the strongest impact on the behavior problem) and the causal relations and variables that are most easily modified. It is important to note that some functional relations are noncausal or correlational, while others are unmodifiable (e.g., consider the causal role of spinal cord damage for a client's depressed mood). In addition, other causal variables exert a very limited impact on the behavior problem and thus may not be the most useful variables upon which to focus treatment. The assessor must become skilled at making these distinctions, because most interventions are aimed at modifying the most important causal variables in order to reduce behavior problems or approach treatment goals.

In identifying important causal relations, the behavioral assessor must examine several factors. First, it is important to look for covariation between a possible causal event and a specified behavior. However, covariation alone does not imply causality. Therefore, the behavioral assessor also seeks to establish (a) temporal order—the changes in the causal variable should precede effects on the target behavior, (b) a logical explanation for the relation (often based on empirical research and theory), and (c) the exclusion of plausible alternative explanations for the observed relation.

Several methods can be used to identify causal functional relations in behavioral assessment. Each method also has its own strengths and limitations in relation to causal inference and suitability for clinical settings. For a more detailed discussion of these assessment methods, see the section of this entry titled "Methods Used to Identify Functional Relations."

Additional Goals and Applications

In addition to the goals reviewed above, behavioral assessment is also concerned with several other goals, including (a) diagnosis and treatment outcome evaluation with clients, (b) the evaluation of mental health delivery systems, (c) informing clients about the assessment and treatment process, (d) research on the causes and covariates of behavior problems, and (e) controlled treatment outcome research.

It is important to keep in mind that behavioral assessment is a conceptually based paradigm; it is based on ideas about behavior and its assessment rather than specific methods of assessment. Therefore, it is easily adapted to a wide variety of contexts. Not only is it useful with individual therapy clients, but it has also been successfully implemented in the assessment of marital and familial relationships, work environments, classrooms and schools, community service agencies, psychiatric units, and medical services, as well as for psychometric evaluation of new assessment instruments.

BEHAVIORAL ASSESSMENT METHODS

Several methods of assessment can be used to identify, specify, and quantify behavior problems and causal variables. Recent surveys of behavior therapists indicate that the most commonly used behavioral assessment methods include behavioral interviewing, rating scales and questionnaires, behavioral observation, and self-monitoring.

Behavioral Assessment Interviewing

Behavioral assessment interviewing differs in structure and focus from other forms of interviewing. Structurally, behavioral interviewing tends tend to conform to the goals of behavioral assessment in that the assessor structures questions that prompt the client to provide specific information about the topography of behavior problems and relevant functional relations. Descriptive queries in the interview direct the client to describe the mode and dimensions of behavior problems and to identify possible causal relations (e.g., "About how many times per week do you have panic episodes?" "How long do they last?" "Can you describe the situations in which they are most likely to occur?").

In terms of focus, client verbalizations are interpreted in two ways. When viewed as a "marker variable," client verbalizations are taken as indicators of behavior problems and causal-factor occurrences. That is, they are viewed as self-report measures of the form of behavior problems and possible functional relations. Sometimes, client behaviors during an interview are treated as a direct occurrence of the target behavior that arose as a function of some causal event present during that moment of the interview. For example, the assessor might note the discussion topics that elicit anger or paranoid ideation by the client. In addition, important functions of the behavioral assessment interview also include (a) maintaining a positive, supportive client-assessor relationship and (b) insuring that clients are fully informed about and agree with the methods and goals of the assessment.

Despite the regularity with which the interview is used as a method of assessment, its psychometric properties are infrequently evaluated. Among research findings published to date, it appears that low to moderate levels of agreement are observed when two different judges listen to interviews and subsequently generate a list of what they perceive to be the most important target behaviors and causal variables. In addition, not only how the interviewer responds to the client's reports but also the degree of similarity between the client and the assessor in terms of race, ethnicity, and sex can sometimes affect the validity of the client's reports.

Behavioral Observation

Behavioral observations can be conducted by both nonparticipant and participant observers. Nonparticipant observers include individuals who have been trained to record the occurrence of behaviors and causal variables but who are not normally part of the client's environment. Because nonparticipant observers are hired and formally trained to conduct observations, they are often able to collect data on an abundance of complex behaviors, causal variables, and behavior-casual variable sequences. Yet despite versatility and potential utility of nonparticipant observation as an assessment method, the costs associated with hiring trained personnel often limit the degree to which assessors are able to take advantage of this method.

Unlike nonparticipant observers, participant observers are part of the client's natural environment. In most cases, participant observers are family members, coworkers, teachers and aides, hospital staff members, or caregivers. Because participant observers are already involved in the client's life, they are able to conduct observations in many different settings across longer periods of time. However, the major drawback associated with participant observation is limited focus: Because participant observers have multiple responsibilities, they are usually able to record only a small number of events. In addition, because they have extensive prior knowledge of the client, they may have difficulty being truly objective and unbiased in their observations.

Behavioral observations can occur within the natural environment, such as at home or in a work setting or in controlled clinical situations. Although naturalistic observation is useful in that it seeks to understand clients' behavior problems in the environment in which they naturally occur, it is nonetheless expensive. Observation in controlled clinical situations, called *analog observation,* is less costly. However, in this type of observation, the generalizability of the resultant clinical judgments to the natural environment can sometimes be problematic.

Self-Monitoring

Using a self-monitoring methodology, clients systematically sample and record their own behavior and sometimes the behavior of others. Because clients, unlike observers, are able to access all three modes of responding (cognitive, affective, overt-motor) across multiple settings, self-monitoring has become a very popular and sophisticated assessment tool. To increase accuracy in recording, target behaviors must be clearly described. Self-monitoring often relies on paper-and-pencil recordings, but some assessors choose to use small handheld computers for this purpose. These computers can be prompted to query the client at specific times with specific prompts, thereby instructing clients to answer specific questions or give specific ratings.

One of the principal limitations of self-monitoring is observer bias. That is, a client may not accurately record target behaviors due to a number of factors, such as expectations for positive or negative consequences, lack of awareness of target behavior occurrence, and application of a criteria for target behavior occurrence that is different from the assessor's. Finally, noncompliance with self-monitoring can also be a problem.

Rating Scales and Self-Report Questionnaires

Self-report questionnaires and rating scales (which may be either paper-and-pencil or computer administered) are inventories that the client completes at various points in time. Rating scales often ask other individuals (e.g., spouse, friend, coworker) to rate or describe the behavior of the client. As an assessment method, rating scales and self-report questionnaires have several strengths. First, they are easily administered and interpreted. Second, the assessor is able to choose from a variety of different self-report questionnaires and rating scales, each of which may evaluate different aspects of a wide range of behavior problems. Finally, questionnaires are also useful in achieving several important behavioral assessment goals, including identification of client behavior problems and strengths, identification of functional relations, and treatment design.

The most significant problem associated with questionnaires is that they often do not take into account the clients' settings or other important environmental factors. For example, many questionnaire items ask clients to rate the degree to which they agree or disagree (e.g., "strongly agree," "strongly disagree") with a variety of general statements about a target behavior (e.g., "I often feel angry"). However, such items ignore the complexity inherent in certain behaviors problems in that they do not account for the way in which behaviors may vary across different situations. These instruments may not ask about more specific situations in which anger is most or least likely to occur, nor about how others respond to angry behaviors. A second problem lies in the fact that many questionnaires and rating scales sum different behaviors, thoughts, and affective states to form a global score. This aggregation of behavioral information is, of course, is not consistent with the emphasis in behavioral assessment on the individualized modes, dimensions, and forms of behavior problems.

Sampling

Several behavioral assessment methods, particularly observation and self-monitoring, involve sampling. As noted above, clients' behaviors can change markedly across time and setting, often because of variation in causal variables. Because one cannot realistically measure all behaviors, in all settings, and at all times, sampling strategies must be used. Therefore, we are able to measure only some behaviors, in some settings, and at some times.

A major consideration in deciding upon a sampling strategy is generalizability. That is, it is important to determine the degree to which the measures can be presumed to be indicative of the actual state of real-world occurrences (i.e., how things really are in the client's natural environment). The behavioral assessor aims to gather data that will permit reasonable inferences about how a client behaves at different points in time (generalizability across time) and in different settings (generalizability across settings), often by measuring a few of many possible behaviors (generalizability across behaviors). Thus, the behavioral assessor must carefully consider what, when, and where to measure behaviors in order to maximize generalizability. Sampling can occur in several ways, as described below.

Event Sampling. Event sampling refers to a strategy wherein the occurrence of a behavior or other event is recorded whenever it is detected. For example, whenever a client experiences a panic attack, he or she might record the time at which the attack occurred, as well as what occurred immediately prior to and subsequent to the attack. It would then be possible to calculate the rate of the behavior and possible causal event to help in its specification, to identify possible causal relations for treatment design, and to monitor changes associated with treatment.

Duration Sampling. Duration sampling measures the amount of time that elapses between the beginning and end of a behavior or causal variable. For example, the same client mentioned above might self-monitor the duration of each anxiety episode.

Interval Sampling. Interval sampling involves dividing an observation session into specific intervals, which can span anywhere from seconds to hours. In partial-interval sampling, an entire interval is recorded as an occurrence if the event is observed during any proportion of the interval. For example, if the anxious client experiences any anxiety attacks within a given period, say 24 hours, then the complete interval is recorded as an occurrence of the behavior. In whole-interval sampling, the event must be observed for the entire period before the interval is recorded as an occurrence. One of the main difficulties with interval sampling is that target behavior and causal variable frequency can be underestimated or overestimated as a function of the duration and frequency of the event.

Real-Time Sampling. Real-time sampling involves recording the time at the beginning and the end of a behavior and causal-variable occurrence. Thus, the client might record that her anxiety attack began at 3:03 p.m. and ended at 3:18 p.m. Real-time recording can provide information about the frequency and duration of target behaviors and causal variables. However, like event and duration sampling, real-time sampling requires that the target behaviors and causal variables have discrete beginning and end points. Thus, this type of sampling may not be appropriate for all behavior problems.

Setting Sampling. In addition to time sampling, the behavioral assessor must decide upon the settings in which the behaviors and causal variables should be sampled. Settings selected are often those in which the events of interest are most likely to occur. Thus, if we are interested in learning more about difficulties in a couple's marital relationship, we might sample in the home at times when it is likely that conflict will be highest.

Subject Sampling. Sometimes, we are able to observe only a few out of many possible assessment subjects. For example, although all members of a support group may exhibit signs of depression, we may choose to sample only a few of those group members. In this case, we presume that our clinical inferences from those individuals whom we observed will be generalizable to other members of that support group.

METHODS USED TO IDENTIFY CAUSAL FUNCTIONAL RELATIONS

The assessment methods described above can provide information about the form of behavior problems and causal variables. They can also provide information about functional relations, an important component of the functional analysis. There are several strategies for estimating functional relations for clients' behavior problems, which will be discussed below.

Marker-Variable Strategy

A marker variable is an easily obtained measure that is reliably associated with the strength of a functional relation in the natural environment. For example, a client's psychophysiological reaction to a short laboratory public-speaking task can serve as a marker for his or her psychophysiological reaction to real-world speaking tasks (e.g., giving a lecture to a class). Empirically validated marker variables can be derived from self-report inventories specifically designed to identify functional relations, as well as structured interviews, psychophysiological assessments, and role-playing exercises. A major advantage of the marker-variable strategy is the ease with which it can be applied. This method enables an assessor to identify many potential causal functional relations with a very limited investment of time and effort.

Generalizability and validity are the most significant problems one must consider when using marker variables. The extent to which unvalidated marker variables (e.g., client reports during an interview or responses to a self-report inventory, responses to laboratory stressors, and observations of in-session setting-behavior interactions) correlate with "real-life" causal relations is often unknown. In addition, for those situations in which empirically validated marker variables are available, the magnitude of correlation between the marker variable and "real-life" causal relations can vary substantially across clients.

Concurrent Administration of Different Assessment Instruments

Concurrent administration of different assessment instruments is a second method that can be used to derive hypotheses about potential functional relations. For example, an assessor may observe that a client reports (a) that several negative life events (e.g., death of a parent) occurred within the past year on a self-report inventory, (b) high daily levels of marital conflict on self-monitoring forms, and (c) symptoms of depression during a behavioral interview. Given these data, it may be plausible to hypothesize that the individual's depression is caused by family difficulties and increased life stressors.

As with the marker-variable strategy, concurrent administration of different assessment devices permits the behavior assessor to identify many potential causal functional relations with a minimal investment of clinical resources. Causal inferences derived from this method must be held very tentatively, however, because the data are correlational in nature. Thus, it is difficult to determine which events came first.

Behavioral Observation and Self-Monitoring of Naturally Occurring Context-Behavior Interactions

A third procedure to estimate causal relations is systematic observation of naturally occurring context-behavior interactions. Most commonly, clients are observed or are asked to self-monitor some dimension (e.g., frequency or magnitude) of a behavior problem, along with one or more contextual or response contingency factors that are hypothesized to affect the target behavior.

Self-monitoring and direct observation of naturally occurring functional relations can yield data that are relevant to causal hypotheses. However, these methods have three practical limitations. First, clients or observers must be adequately trained so that all events are recorded as accurately and reliably as possible. Second, as the number and/or complexity of events to be observed increases, accuracy and reliability often decrease. Third, it is difficult to exclude the possibility that other variables may be affecting the data. Taken together, these limitations suggest that systematic observation methods are best suited for situations in which the behavior and contextual variables are easily quantified and few in number.

Experimental Manipulation

The fourth method that can be used to estimate casual relations is experimental manipulation. Experimental manipulations involve systematically modifying hypothesized causal variables and observing consequent changes in behavior in the clinic or naturalistic settings. Experimental manipulation has received renewed interest in recent years because it can be an effective strategy for identifying response contingencies that may strengthen behavior problems, as well as settings and stimuli that can elicit such problems. Yet despite the potential treatment utility of experimental manipulations, several questions remain unanswered. First, the reliability and validity of some experimental analog observation methods remain unexplored. Second, the incremental benefits of experimental analog observation for treatment design and outcome have not been adequately estimated. Finally, most demonstrations of the treatment utility of analog observation have been limited to a very restricted population of clients who were presenting with a restricted number of behavior problems.

—*William H. O'Brien,*
Mary E. Kaplar, and Stephen N. Haynes

See also: *Behavioral Assessment (Vols. II & III); Virtual Reality Therapy (Vol. I)*

Suggested Readings

Bellack, A. S., & Hersen, M. (1998). (Eds.). *Behavioral assessment: A practical handbook.* Boston: Allyn & Bacon.

Dougher, M. J. (2000). *Clinical behavior analysis.* Reno, NV: Context Press.

Garb, H. N. (1996). *Studying the clinician: Judgment research and psychological assessment.* Washington, DC: American Psychological Association.

Haynes, S. N., & Heiby, E. M. (Eds.). (2003). *Behavioral assessment.* New York: Wiley.

Haynes, S. N., & O'Brien, W. H. (2000). *Principles and practice of behavioral assessment.* New York: Kluwer.

O'Brien, W. H. (1995). Inaccuracies in the estimation of functional relations using self-monitoring data. *Journal of Behavior Therapy and Experimental Psychiatry, 26,* 351–357.

Ramsay, M. C., Reynolds, C. R., & Kamphaus, R. W. (2002). *Essentials of behavioral assessment.* New York: Wiley.

BEHAVIORAL CASE FORMULATION

DESCRIPTION OF THE STRATEGY

The process of providing a clear theoretical explanation for *what* clients do and *why* they do it is termed *case conceptualization.* Case formulation, from a behavioral perspective, implies that the "what" will be observable behaviors and the "why" will be explained by learning principles. Within behavioral theory, both adaptive and maladaptive behaviors are acquired, maintained, and changed through the functional relationships with the events that precede and follow them. More specifically, behavior that is followed by a *reinforcement* is more likely to reoccur, whereas behavior that either fails to be reinforced or is followed by a *punishment* is less likely to reoccur. Furthermore, an individual learns that reinforcement is more likely to occur for certain behaviors in certain circumstances than in others. This means that behavioral case formulation involves a careful assessment of the context within which a behavior occurs, along with developing testable hypotheses about causes, maintaining factors, and treatment interventions.

Behavioral case formulation is, philosophically as well as practically, based in the experimental method. Traditionally, the scientific method has involved four steps: (1) observing a phenomenon, (2) developing hypotheses, (3) testing hypotheses and observing outcome, and (4) revising hypotheses. For the clinician, *observation* mirrors the assessment period; *developing hypotheses* is the treatment-planning phase; *testing hypotheses* is the implementation of the treatment plan; and *revising the hypotheses* is assessing the treatment review. (See Figure 1.)

Observation: Assessment

The assessment phase of behavioral case formulation is integral to behavioral case formulation and involves assessment of both adaptive and maladaptive behaviors along with antecedents and consequences with possible functional properties. The following section addresses a variety of methods for collecting information, identifying observable treatment targets, operationally defining treatment targets, and assessing the behavioral context.

Data Collection Methods

Direct observation of the client's behavior is often touted as the best method of behavioral assessment. Several entries in the volume detail possible methods of direct behavioral observation. Although this type of assessment does reduce the potential bias involved in verbal report, it is rarely used in real clinical settings with adult clients. First, for adult clients who are not intellectually compromised, direct observation is often undesirable. Second, the observer's presence may dramatically change the context of the target behavior. Third, since most behaviors occur in a variety of contexts, observation of all possible permutations is not possible. Finally, and probably most important, direct observation is prohibitively expensive and time intensive. Taken together, these disadvantages to direct observation often lead clinicians to use a number of

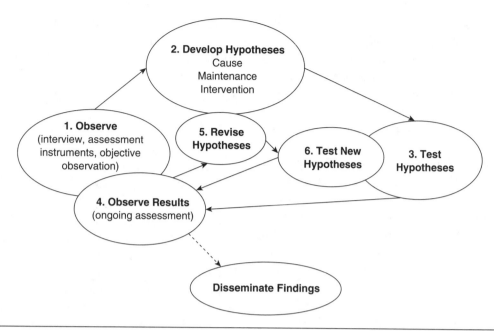

Figure 1   Scientific Method for the Scientist-Practitioner

alternative data collection methods, including the clinical interview, self-report questionnaires, self-monitoring, and naturalistic video or audiotaping.

The *clinical interview,* using either the client or informants, is one of the most common methods. Compared with direct behavioral observation, it is often more desirable, feasible, and cost-effective. It also has the advantage of allowing therapists to observe in-session behavior and begin establishing therapeutic rapport through mutual reinforcement. The primary disadvantage of the unstructured clinical interview is that interrater reliability tends to be quite low. Structured clinical interviews such as the functional analytic interview may increase the reliability of both therapist and client verbal behavior.

Self-report questionnaires often augment the clinical interview. In contrast to the clinical interview, self-report questionnaires represent stable stimuli, and clinician subjectivity is minimized. Questions are asked in the same way each time, and the scores are typically computed according to specific instructions. These questionnaires also allow clinicians to collect a great deal of information with little time and expense as well as providing data regarding how a client compares with published norms for the measures. Although this type of assessment is practical and has increased reliability over interview data collection methods, there are several downsides, including

reliance on client verbal report, loss of validity over repeated administrations, and that many clinicians and clients dislike adding more paperwork.

Despite the fact that observation by an objective observer may be impractical and problematic, teaching non-intellectually-impaired clients to be observers of their own behavior may provide a good alternative. *Self-monitoring* usually involves tracking variables such as the intensity, frequency, duration, context, timing, and so on of a target behavior. Having clients or accessible others observe clients' behaviors is inexpensive and practical and may also have therapeutic value. Researchers have also found that self-monitoring can lead to behavioral change, even when no other treatments are used.

Less frequently used methods of observation include naturalistic or laboratory taping of behaviors, and physiological measures of behavior. Clients may, for example, set up a video to record times when spousal arguments are likely to occur to collect data on antecedents, behavior, and consequences. Both spouses may also wear heart rate monitors to assess physiological reactivity during arguments. These data may aid in assessing possibilities for interrupting the behavioral chain.

Identifying and Describing Target Behaviors

Early behavioral theorists emphasized the importance of focusing only on observable behavioral targets. Internal experiences were discounted in lieu of externally observable behavior. Thus, for a client who reports feeling anxious, the treatment targets might be shaking, sweating, flushing, and avoidance of feared stimuli, rather than the subjective experience of anxiety. More contemporary behavioral theorists such as Aaron Beck and David Barlow have added internal experiences, such as mood and thought, to the list of important behavioral treatment targets. Examples of *externally observable* treatment targets include verbal, nonverbal, and motoric behaviors. More *covert* treatment targets include thinking or believing, feeling, imagining, and physical sensations. Most behavioral case formulations for adults will involve both externally observable and covert behaviors.

With this broadening of acceptable foci for behavioral case formulation, the necessity of accurate *operationalization* has intensified. So, even for internal behaviors, such as mood or thought, externally observable signs often become the focus of assessment and treatment. That is, the *behavioral manifestations* of the internal state will be assessed (e.g., shaking, sweating, avoidance as external manifestations of subjective anxiety), as well as the *frequency, intensity,* and *duration* of internal experiences. Behaviors best depicted by intensity, such as moods or feelings, may be characterized by a 0 to 10 intensity scale. Behaviors best depicted by frequency, such as thoughts or overt behaviors, may be characterized as the average frequency per day or week during that time period. Duration may be assessed using an average (i.e., daily, weekly, monthly) for the duration of episodes of the target behavior. Finally, a timeline should be retrospectively constructed to highlight precipitating events, as well as more immediate antecedents and consequences.

A third step in describing the problem is to decide on the best-fitting *diagnostic category.* Although many behavioral theorists eschew diagnosis because of the negative effects of labeling coupled with a perceived lack of utility in identifying functional relationships, diagnosis remains a centerpiece of treatment planning within the managed-care framework. For these reasons, some basic guidelines for conscientious diagnosis that maximize the potential for benefit and minimize the potential for harm include (a) involving the client in the diagnostic process (i.e., explain how and why; explain that diagnoses are descriptions of behavior rather than illness; diagnoses lead to choices of effective treatments) and (b) making

accurate, careful diagnoses (i.e., use structured interviews whenever possible; make sure that all diagnostic criteria are met; use least severe diagnosis that accurately describes problem; take cultural issues into account).

Functional Assessment: Assessing the Context

The final key assessment area for the Observation Phase of behavioral case formulation is the context within which the target behavior occurs. The context includes past as well as current factors that contribute to the cause and maintenance of the presenting concerns. According to behavioral theory, an understanding of the instrumental variables that precede and follow the target behaviors is essential to developing an effective treatment intervention.

The *remote context* refers to history, especially biological, psychological, or social events that may have been functionally related to earlier episodes or approximations of the current behavior. Although the actual cause of a problem is elusive because it can never be truly known or tested, identifying *setting events* may help in developing hypotheses about current maintenance factors. All aspects of the biopsychosocial assessment are relevant for understanding historical context.

❖ *Learning and modeling.* An understanding of the types of behavior for which the client has been reinforced and punished in the past may help to develop hypotheses about current functional relationships. In addition, knowledge of the behavior of important role models may shed light on current behaviors.

❖ *Life events.* Both recent and past life events may play a significant role in setting the stage for the current behavior. These may be singular or repeated events and may be either traumatic or pivotal in some way. Knowledge of significant events may alert the therapist to important antecedents or consequences for the current behavior. For example, if a woman who experienced panic attacks cued by the smell of cologne had also experienced child sexual abuse by a man who wore heavy cologne, treatment may take a different direction than if no such history existed.

❖ *Genetic factors.* Most research suggests that the likelihood of developing mental health concerns increases when first-degree relatives also have mental health difficulties, even when afflicted parents do not rear the children. Thus, it is important to assess for familial history of psychological and substance abuse problems.

❖ *Physical factors.* Any number of physical factors may be involved in causing, maintaining, and/or exacerbating presenting problems. Depressed mood may, for example, be sequelae of endocrine dysfunction, such as hyper- or hypothyroidism. Panic attacks may be caused or worsened by heart conditions such as mitral valve prolapse. An initial evaluation that includes thorough questioning about possible physical conditions coupled with a recent physical examination and medical records is essential so that serious or complicating physical factors are referred for appropriate care.

❖ *Drugs or substances.* A variety of substances may be related to mental health conditions, including alcohol, prescription drugs, illegal drugs, over-the-counter drugs, and alternative medications. Thorough assessment of current medications in all of these categories is vital to evaluating the extent to which a recent substance initiation, increase, decrease, or discontinuation may fully or partially account for current symptoms.

❖ *Sociocultural factors.* Gender, age, ethnic heritage, religion, socioeconomic status, education, and so on may all be related in idiosyncratic ways to presenting concerns. Behavioral theorists are most interested in the ways that social and cultural factors may affect the learning history and the available punishers, reinforcements, models, and beliefs. Such information may help to form hypotheses about behavioral and cognitive interventions that may be especially helpful.

The *recent context* refers to the current antecedents and consequences that are maintaining the target behavior. More specifically, the context of most interest in behavioral case formulation is the functional relationship between internal and external events that precede and follow the target behavior. The focus of this assessment should be on behaviors as they usually occur and/or a recent, specific example of the behavior. Both may be important in developing hypotheses about treatment.

Antecedents. The events that immediately precede target behavior and increase the probability that the behavior will occur are labeled as antecedents. A stimulus becomes an antecedent when the target behavior has been reinforced immediately following the antecedent in the past and is strengthened with each resultant reinforcement. Much like behavioral targets, antecedents may be internal (physical, emotional, or cognitive) and/or external (behavioral or environmental).

Consequences. The instrumental events that follow the target behavior are labeled as consequences. Consequences are those internal or external events that either increase or decrease the probability that the behavior will occur again. Consequences, like antecedents and target behaviors, may be internal (physical, emotional, or cognitive) and external (behavioral or environmental). At the most basic level, consequences that increase the target are called *reinforcers;* those that reduce the target are called *punishers.* More specifically, reinforcement or punishment can be positive or negative depending upon whether an increase or decrease in the consequence, respectively, leads to a change in the target behavior. That is, with positive reinforcement, an increase in a consequence leads to an increased probability that the target behavior will occur in the future, whereas with negative reinforcement, a decrease in an aversive consequence leads to an increased probability that the target behavior will occur in the future. Similarly, for positive punishment, an increase in a consequence leads to a decreased probability that the target behavior will occur in the future, and with negative punishment, a decrease in a consequence leads to a decreased probability that the target behavior will occur in the future.

It is essential to note here that clients may not always be good observers or reporters of these contingent relationships. First, clients may lack awareness of the actual contingencies. Second, clients' verbal reports may be influenced more by the in-session contingencies than the actual events they are reporting on. Thus, they may be unsure about the contingencies and unwittingly base their responses on actual (e.g., head nods, "uh-uh's") or anticipated (e.g., beliefs about social desirability) therapist reinforcements. Third, clients' beliefs about the consequences of reporting contingencies may also deter them. Clients who receive disability payments for chronic pain conditions may not reveal (or acknowledge to themselves) that these payments provide both positive and negative reinforcement for avoidance. Taken together, these problems highlight the importance of approaching functional analytic interviewing as a hypothesis-generating endeavor rather than a fact-finding mission. This is where it is important for the clinician to have a good grasp of behavioral theory and some probable types of consequences that may be maintaining a behavior to augment the information offered verbally by the client. See the section below on "Developing Hypotheses About Maintenance" for common types of functional relationships with certain presenting concerns.

Observation is classically considered to be the first phase of the scientific method. For practicing scientist clinicians, however, this process continues throughout therapy, as will be evident in the later discussion on "Testing Hypotheses and Revising Hypotheses."

Developing Hypotheses: Treatment Planning

The Observation Phase is followed by the Developing Hypotheses Phase of the scientific method. Once the phenomena or the presenting concerns are observed in behavioral case formulation, then testable hypotheses as to cause, maintenance, and treatment are developed. The goal is a consolidation of information gained during the initial assessment with subsequent data collection (e.g., self-monitoring) and research literature.

Hypotheses About Cause

Behaviorists have often shied away from the concept of cause, focusing instead on currently observable variables. While the value of current behavior and contingencies cannot be underestimated, hypotheses regarding the role of historical events and circumstances may provide important hints about salient contingencies and genetic endowments that might not be available in a present-only-based functional assessment. The variables that would typically be addressed in hypotheses about cause include those assessed in the biopsychosocial assessment, specifically learning and modeling, life events, genetic factors, physical factors, substances and drugs, and sociocultural factors.

Hypotheses About Maintenance

The functional analytic interview is the centerpiece for hypotheses about maintenance. However, because clients may not always be accurate observers of the contingencies for their own behavior, behavioral theory, the empirical literature, and any additional self-monitoring data are also important in generating these hypotheses.

There is an extensive empirical literature on the factors that tend to maintain certain types of presenting concerns. Because depression and anxiety are the most common reasons that adult clients seek help in outpatient psychology clinics, those will be addressed briefly here. Depression tends to be maintained with behavioral factors, such as a reduction in pleasurable or mastery activities or a preponderance of aversive activities (e.g., difficult social interactions, lack of contingent relationship between behavior and outcomes). Behaviors that tend to reduce depression are the reverse of these behavioral deficits or excesses. Cognitive variables that tend to increase depression are unrealistic predictions and labels or standards about self, others, or the world that focus on themes of helplessness, hopelessness, and worthlessness. Anxiety, in contrast, tends to be maintained by the negative reinforcement inherent in escape; when individuals escape the anxiety-provoking stimulus, they experience profound relief. This relief then increases the escape response and reinforces beliefs that the stimulus is catastrophic (e.g., "It was so bad, I had to get out of there or I would have died"; "If I hadn't avoided thinking about it, I would have completely lost it!"). Having knowledge of the empirical findings regarding common contingencies of presenting concerns also may aid in evaluating the accuracy of client reports.

Hypotheses About Treatment

The final step is to develop hypotheses about treatment. These hypotheses should flow logically from information collected in the Observation Phase as well as the hypotheses developed about cause and maintenance. In the behavioral tradition of empiricism, developing hypotheses about treatment also should also take into account the empirical literature on effective treatments. Furthermore, from a pragmatic perspective, good hypotheses about treatment should address cost-effectiveness, affordability, therapist competence, client preference, and client stage of change.

First, the *functional relationship* between the target behaviors and the potential contingencies should be considered. If changing hypothesized contingencies does not lead to a change in the targeted behavior, then these hypotheses are probably in error.

The second step in deciding on a treatment direction is a *literature review of effective treatments* specific to the client's presenting condition. While a comprehensive, critical literature review for each and every client may be beyond the capability of many practicing clinicians, some excellent resources summarizing empirically supported interventions are included in the suggested readings below. The treatment manuals used for these empirically supported interventions are also readily available.

Third, *pragmatically,* any treatment chosen must address priority concerns cost-effectively, affordably, and within therapist range of competence. Treatment choices should aim to maximize effectiveness while minimizing cost. In addition, the treatment must be viable within the client's financial and time constraints, and clinicians must have adequate training and/or supervision in the approaches they use.

Finally, treatment should also be plausible, attractive, and tailored to the client's *readiness to change.* If it is not, the client may be unlikely to either stay in or benefit from therapy. Thus, a treatment plan should address the client's primary presenting concerns first, in the absence of factors that may contraindicate it (e.g., significant risk issues such as suicidal ideation, homicidal ideation, violence, substance abuse, etc.). Similarly, clients' readiness for change should be considered in the choice of interventions. Four basic stages have predictive validity for attrition and therapeutic success: precontemplation (i.e., does not recognize that there is a problem), contemplation (i.e., recognizes that problem exists; unsure whether benefits of change outweigh the costs), action (i.e., ready to change and has already made steps toward changing), and maintenance (i.e., has successfully altered problem and is trying to maintain gains). Clients in early stages of change may benefit most from interventions that focus on increasing awareness of problem behaviors, such as giving feedback about assessments or self-monitoring, whereas clients in later stages of change may make the most change through action-oriented interventions, such as goal setting and cognitive restructuring.

Treatment Plan

After hypotheses about cause, maintenance, and treatment are generated, a treatment plan that defines specific goals, interventions, measurements, and a timeline is developed collaboratively with the client. This collaborative treatment plan should enable clinician and client to test hypotheses regarding treatment.

The treatment plan should include goals that are consistent with hypotheses about treatment and that are sufficiently specific to allow for evaluation of treatment hypotheses. The goals should meet the following SMART criteria: (a) *Specific:* targeting specific variables with observable referents that are relevant to the client's presenting concerns (e.g., intensity of depressed mood; frequency of panic); (b) *Measurable:* including an observable, objective scale of measurement that is meaningful to the client (e.g., on a scale of 0–10; daily frequency); (c) *Anchored:* including the current and desired level of functioning (e.g., intensity of depressed mood will be reduced from a daily average of 9 to a daily average of 5); (d) *Realistic:* considering client's current and past functioning as well as available treatment time; and (e) *Timeline:* including a target date for the goals to be accomplished.

To assess whether hypotheses about treatment are correct, an intervention plan should be outlined, with a clear relationship between goals and interventions. Interventions should target the hypothesized functional relationships and be grounded in the empirical literature, if possible.

Assessment of client progress is essential to both ethical practice and hypothesis testing. Without measurement, clinicians cannot adequately evaluate whether progress is being made. Here again, measurements should have an objective, observable component and directly reflect goals. Both standardized and idiographic measurements are recommended to assess client outcome relative to a relevant population and themselves.

Testing and Revising the Hypotheses: Conducting Treatment

The final stages of behavioral case formulation are Testing and Revising Hypotheses by conducting treatment and measuring outcome according to the plan. If data generated suggest that hypotheses were incorrect or that methods were insufficient to test hypotheses, the client and clinician return to the Observation Phase to develop new hypotheses and a revised plan.

RESEARCH BASIS

Although behavioral case formulation has not been extensively researched as a specific treatment strategy, a plethora of research has addressed the effectiveness of behavioral treatment interventions. These treatment interventions are typically based in behavioral case formulation. Based on the American Psychological Association's criteria for empirically supported treatments (i.e., at least two randomized controlled clinical trials by more than one research group or a series of single-subject designs demonstrating either superiority over a placebo or comparable effectiveness to another well-established treatment with manualized treatments and well-defined subjects), 19 of the 22 well-established treatments for 21 different disorders are behavioral or cognitive-behavioral. This finding suggests that behavioral case formulation may be at the core of effective treatment. In addition, research on functional assessment techniques more exclusively has found success with a variety of adult clients presenting concerns.

RELEVANT TARGET POPULATIONS AND EXCEPTIONS

Behavioral case formulation is a versatile method for formulating a treatment direction and evaluating its effectiveness. This method has demonstrated effectiveness with adults, and older adults at varying levels of psychological, behavioral, and intellectual impairment. Although behavioral case formulation is applicable with most clinical populations, methods may vary according to setting and intellectual capacity of client. Behavioral case formulation with intellectually compromised clients may involve more use of informants and live observation than with nonimpaired clients. Similarly, applying this method in nonclinical settings such as schools or workplaces for problem behaviors that do not reach diagnostic threshold may require omission of clinical diagnosis.

COMPLICATIONS

Although behavioral case formulation is unlikely to result in serious negative consequences for any client, complications that may arise in application include difficulty identifying functional variables, disruption in treatment, or premature treatment planning. First, the central, and perhaps most difficult, element of behavioral case formulation is an accurate definition of the problem and its functional antecedents and consequences. Initial assessment may, for example, point to spousal statements of concern as reinforcers for a client's subjective reports of severe back pain. Only

after a change in spousal behavior fails to change the pain report does it become apparent that the primary functional variables may be positive reinforcement of disability payments and negative reinforcement of relief from work. Second, actual hypothesis testing is often difficult in community settings, because early changes to treatment plans are commonplace due to changes in client report of presenting concern (e.g., client initially reports depression as primary concern and later identifies marriage as focus of treatment); changes in client life circumstances (e.g., client loses job or becomes homeless); crises (e.g., new emergence of suicidal ideation); changes in case formulation (e.g., a variety of life problems originally conceptualized as needing problem-solving training may later appear to be a pattern of worry that would respond best to worry exposure); or attrition. Finally, when the hypothesis-testing approach is adhered to too rigidly, inaccurate hypotheses may be generated prematurely and maintained at the expense of patient care. Although these complications can never be fully eliminated, the steps outlined above are not designed to be finite, mutually exclusive entities. Rather, they are part of a fluid process with overlap and often several iterations.

CASE ILLUSTRATION

Observation of Mr. X

"Mr. X," a 27-year-old, unemployed computer programmer, the married father of three young children, presented with a primary problem of 10 to 15 daily episodes of feeling very panicky and tearful accompanied by hyperventilation, heart racing, nausea, sweating, shaking, dizziness, and feeling that he was going crazy. A secondary problem was a 5-year history of ongoing depression. He requested help with resolving the panic and was ambivalent about treatment for depression. He was participating in current psychotropic treatment for his depression and anxiety when he presented for treatment. He reported that the medication had helped to reduce his depression to a "tolerable level" but that the panic had not been helped.

Defining Target Behaviors

For Mr. X, his panic attacks and depressed mood were operationalized through queries about the behavioral manifestations and impacts, as well as the frequency, intensity, and duration of the depression. According to self-monitoring and the interview, Mr. X reported that the average daily intensity for anxiety and depression was an 8 (on a 0–10 point scale, with larger numbers representing greater severity), with an average of 11 daily panic attacks. An assessment of the historical timeline indicated that within the past 4 years, Mr. X reported five separate episodes of severely depressed mood with durations ranging from 2 weeks to 2 months. Between these episodes, his depressed mood was in the moderate range. Within the past 6 months, his panic attacks had increased steadily from 0 per day to 10 to 15 per day. Diagnostically, the following were identified:

Axis I: 300.21 Panic disorder with agoraphobia

296.33 Major depressive disorder, recurrent, severe without psychotic features, without full interepisode recovery

Axis II: V71.09 No diagnosis

Axis III: Noncontributory physical problems

Axis IV: Unemployment due to depression and panic

Axis V: 50 Functional assessment

Remote Context

Assessment of Mr. X's history suggested that he may have learned or modeled some of his current behaviors. According to Mr. X, his parents' marriage was intact. However, both parents had strict rules and frequently worried about his safety (e.g., curfews, frequent calls to make sure he was okay). His only sibling, a 23-year-old sister, had also been diagnosed with agoraphobia. These life events as well as others may also be setting events for Mr. X's current anxiety and depression. Mr. X reported that his childhood was stressful because his parents were so strict, but he denied any specific events or overt abuse. Instead, he reported his work as a police officer to be traumatic because he often dealt with tragic situations (e.g., hopeless people, car accidents, murders, domestic violence) over which he felt powerless to control. As for genetics, although Mr. X reported that his parents had not been diagnosed with mental health concerns, his description of them suggests his mother and father may both meet criteria for generalized anxiety disorder.

Regarding physical factors, Mr. X was convinced that physical problems were at the root of his problems; however, none of myriad medical tests (e.g., ECG, EKG, CAT scan, blood workup) had revealed any physical problems. Furthermore, substances did not appear to be causal. Mr. X denied any alcohol or illicit drug use. Although he had consumed up to three beers a week prior to the panic onset, he had since discontinued all substance use because he feared that alcohol might elicit an attack. The medication had produced some depression relief; however, the anxiety had been unchanged. Socioculturally, Mr. X's status as a young, middle-income, professional, Caucasian male experiencing depression and anxiety along with recent unemployment had led to some aversive responses from family and peers who expected him to be successfully earning a wage. He also reported some beliefs about himself, based on his perceptions of cultural values for young, professional men, such as, "I must be the primary breadwinner in my family"; "A sign of economic failure is a sign of personal failure"; and "I should deal with this alone and not let anyone see how distressed I am."

Recent Context

Mr. X reported that the panic attacks had begun about 6 months previously and had increased in severity and frequency since then. He could not identify anything unusual about the time that the panic began. He stated that the onset, as well the daily occurrences, seemed to "come out of the blue." Events that were likely to elicit panic attacks were (a) being somewhere where escape was difficult (e.g., mall, store, theater, bus, tunnels) and (b) having very negative thoughts about himself (e.g., "I am worthless," "I am crazy," "I am a bad father," etc.). He reported that his most effective coping strategy was to escape the evocative situation or distract himself as quickly as possible. He reported that the desire to escape was intense and the relief after escape acute.

Depression also had no clear precipitating event other than some reported general difficulty dealing with the "human tragedies" that accompanied his previous job as a police officer. He had been involuntarily retired from his job after being hospitalized for depression 4 years ago. He stated that his depression had been constant since that time. He stated that the depression had worsened since the onset of the panic and that over the past month, he had sat at home because he felt "too depressed to move." He reported depressed mood most of the day nearly every day, accompanied by low interest, difficulty sleeping, feeling very guilty most of the time, low energy, difficulty concentrating, increased appetite, and visible slowing of speech and movements. He admitted to suicidal ideation 4 years ago when hospitalized but denied any current ideation, plan, or intent.

Developing Hypotheses for Mr. X

Hypotheses About Cause

Given the biopsychosocial assessment for Mr. X, it appears that learning/modeling, genetic factors, life events, and sociocultural factors may play causal roles. Examples of hypotheses about cause that may be generated for Mr. X include the following:

❖ Mr. X learned at an early age, through modeling and reinforcement, that the world is dangerous and that cautiousness is rewarded.

❖ Simultaneously, Mr. X's family history of anxiety may have genetically predisposed him to manifest his responses to stress in similar ways.

❖ While Mr. X. was a police officer, he witnessed traumatic events that challenged his central beliefs regarding importance of safety and the role of control (e.g., "As long as I am always careful, I and others can always be safe"). Instead, he learned that there are some events over which he has no control. This led to feelings of panic when not in control.

❖ The majority of men in Mr. X's ethnocultural group are employed and do not have depression or anxiety disorders. Instead, the societal expectation is that young married men will contribute financially to their families and maintain a modicum of mental health. Mr. X may have experienced feelings of shame and fear as a result of not living up to society's expectations for him. These expectations are contributing to the cause of his current intractable depression.

Hypotheses About Maintenance

Although Mr. X reported that anxiety was improved by escape and depression was improved through inactivity, knowledge of the empirical literature as well as typical behavioral conceptualizations of anxiety and depression suggested that the immediate

relief of these strategies was actually exacerbating his conditions long-term. Given these data about Mr. X, the following hypotheses about maintenance were developed:

Mr. X's panic is worsened by:

❖ Occurrence of antecedents in which he has little control
❖ Beliefs that he will die while having a panic attack (e.g., at the first physiological sign of an attack, he says to himself, "Oh no! I really am going to die this time!")
❖ Beliefs that he must be in control at all times
❖ Negative reinforcement (relief) he experiences when he escapes an anxiety-provoking situation
❖ Negative reinforcement (relief) he experiences when dismissed from household and parenting responsibilities

Mr. X's depression is worsened by:

❖ Occurrence of panic attacks
❖ A reduction in pleasurable and mastery activity due to avoidance of anxiety-provoking activities (interaction between anxiety and depression) and low motivation
❖ Beliefs that he should not be experiencing "weak" emotions, such as anxiety and sadness, and that he should be gainfully employed
❖ Positive reinforcement he experiences when his wife inquires compassionately about his sadness
❖ Negative reinforcement (relief) he experiences when dismissed from household and parenting responsibilities

Hypotheses About Mr. X's Treatment

Functional Relationships. For Mr. X, hypotheses about maintenance point to the importance of catastrophic beliefs and avoidance for his panic attacks. Although his depression is more long-standing, it appears that the panic attacks may account for the recent depression exacerbation through the side effects of anxious avoidance (i.e., reduction in activity, unemployment, and reinforcement of beliefs about worthlessness). Treatment, therefore, should address the both behavioral (i.e., avoidance) and cognitive variables (i.e., catastrophic beliefs).

Empirical Literature. With regard to Mr. X's presenting problems, empirically supported interventions exist for both panic and depression. Based on at least one meta-analysis of 43 controlled clinical trials for panic disorder with agoraphobia, treatment packages including education, relaxation, cognitive restructuring, and exposure to the physical symptoms of panic (interoceptive exposure) were the most effective interventions available. Furthermore, interventions involving interoceptive exposure were superior to medication or cognitive-behavioral therapy without interoceptive exposure. Recent reviews of depression interventions suggest that cognitive-behavioral interventions are among the most effective and durable treatments available. The treatment outcome literature on comorbid panic disorder and depression generally supports treating panic prior to treating depression. It appears that depression does not deter panic treatment and, furthermore, that depression symptoms may improve during panic treatment. In the reverse, active panic may actually hinder depression treatment.

Pragmatism. For Mr. X, among the most cost-effective interventions are 12 to 20 session cognitive-behavioral treatments. They are feasible within his insurance allotment of 20 sessions yearly, and the therapist's primary training is in cognitive and behavioral interventions. Mr. X identified a strong preference for targeting his panic symptoms first. Although his depression was severe, he was not experiencing suicidal ideation or other conditions that would mandate priority attention. He expressed tentative interest in later addressing the depressive symptoms if they did not remit in the course of panic treatment. His stage of change was informally identified as action; he had begun making changes in his life to reduce his panic symptoms, including seeing a psychiatrist, beginning regular relaxation practice, and reading self-help books about panic attacks.

After reviewing functional relationships between target behavior and contingencies, empirical literature, and pragmatic concerns, the following hypotheses about treatment were developed along with the treatment plan in Figure 2:

❖ Treatment will be effective if panic treatment precedes depression treatment due to the client preference and empirical evidence supporting the effectiveness of panic treatment with comorbid panic and depression.

❖ Panic treatment that includes education, relaxation, cognitive restructuring, and exposure to the physical symptoms of panic (extinguishing the escape response) will effectively reduce Mr. X's panic symptoms because it:

> is consistent with the hypothesized pertinent functional relationships;
>
> has the best data to support its effectiveness with panic symptoms;
>
> is unlikely to be negatively affected by the depressive symptoms;
>
> is cost-effective and feasible for client and therapist; and
>
> addresses the client's priority concerns first with action-oriented interventions to meet him in the action stage.

❖ Depression symptoms will improve during panic treatment.

Testing Hypotheses and Observing Results for Mr. X

Treatment was conducted according to plan and standardized and idiographic outcomes for depression and anxiety were collected. See Figure 3 for the outcomes.

As can be seen, hypotheses about anxiety and panic were supported, whereas hypotheses regarding depression were not. Consistent with hypotheses, the application of cognitive-behavioral interventions targeted at reducing panic attacks effectively eliminated Mr. X's panic attacks, agoraphobic avoidance, and average daily intensity of anxiety. Contrary to hypotheses, although Mr. X's depression scores diminished somewhat over the 12 sessions, his depression was moderately severe at the conclusion of the treatment plan. Taken together, these findings suggest a need for revising the predictions regarding depression.

Revising Hypotheses

The final phase of the scientific method is often iterative. For Mr. X, the hypothesis regarding the responsiveness of his depression to interventions targeted at panic was unsupported. Therefore, the functional assessment of depression was reviewed. Mr. X reported that his depression had returned to baseline moderate level for the preceding 4 years. A subsequent

Client: Mr. X	Primary Therapist: Dr. Truax	Current Date: 1/5/04	Target Date: 3/23/04

Primary Presenting Concerns:

Panic attacks, anxiety, and depression. Mr. X presents with a 5-year history of recurrent depression without interepisode recovery and a 6-month history of generalized anxiety and panic attacks. Current average intensity for both anxiety and depression is an 8 (0–10 point scale with larger numbers representing greater severity), and he averages 11 panic attacks daily. As a result, his occupational functioning is severely impaired (i.e., he is unemployed) and he avoids nearly all activities that involve leaving the house.

Diagnoses:

Axis I:	300.21	Panic Disorder with Agoraphobia
	296.33	Major Depressive Disorder, Recurrent, Severe without Psychotic Features, Without Full interepisode recovery
Axis II:	V71.09	No diagnosis
Axis III:		Noncontributory physical or medical problems
Axis IV:		Unemployment due to depression and panic
Axis V:		Current functioning = 50

Primary Goals:

1. Reduce frequency of panic attacks from 11 times daily to 3 times daily.
2. Reduce intensity of daily anxiety from an average of 8 to an average of 5.
3. Reduce severity of avoidance from the severe range to the mild range.

Secondary Goals:

4. *Reduce intensity of depressed mood from daily average of 8 to an average of 4.*
5. *Reduce severity of depression from the severe range to the mild range.*

Interventions:

1. Relaxation Training: diaphragmatic breathing, progressive muscle relaxation, cue-controlled relaxation, and recall relaxation (Goals 1 & 2).
2. Cognitive Restructuring: identifying activating events, alarming beliefs, consequences, more reassuring beliefs, and more adaptive coping (Goals 1–5).
3. Interoceptive Exposure: developing a hierarchy and conducting graded exposure to physiological symptoms of panic. (Goals 1, 2, & 3).
4. In Vivo Exposure: developing a hierarchy and conducting graded exposure to avoided situations due to panic (Goals 1–5).

Measurements:	Schedule
Self-monitoring of frequency of panic attacks (Goal 1)	Daily
Self-monitoring of average daily intensity of anxiety on a 0-10 scale (0 = no anxiety, 10 = most anxiety imaginable) (Goal 2)	Daily
Mobility Inventory (Goal 3)	Monthly
Self-monitoring of daily intensity of depression on a 0-10 scale (0 = no depression, 10 = most depression imaginable) (Goal 4)	Daily
Beck Depression Inventory-II (Goal 5)	Monthly

Agreement:

By signing this plan, I agree to complete the above outlined treatment plan. This will entail participating in weekly therapy sessions and regular completion of tasks outside the session. If either client or therapist is concerned about the progress of therapy, the concerned party will address the issue in session as soon as possible.

Prioritized summary and time frame:

12 weekly sessions targeting goals 1–3 (Sessions 1–8: Relaxation Training and Cognitive Restructuring; Sessions 5–12: Interoceptive Exposure; Sessions 8–12: In Vivo exposure

Client Signature:	Therapist Signature:

Figure 2   Treatment Plan for Mr. X

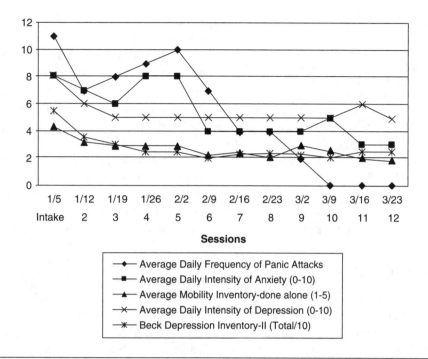

Figure 3   Mr. X's Progress on Standardized and Idiographic Anxiety and Depression Measures

functional assessment of the current depression suggested that important antecedents to worsened depressed mood were inactivity and self-depreciating thoughts regarding competence and unemployment. Based on this functional assessment, Mr. X's preferences, and a review of the empirical literature, new hypotheses regarding Mr. X's depression were generated:

❖ Mr. X's depression is exacerbated and maintained by a paucity of pleasurable and mastery activities (especially unemployment) and thoughts of incompetence and ineptitude.
❖ Interventions should focus on increasing pleasurable and mastery activities while reducing self-depreciating beliefs.
❖ Cognitive-behavioral treatment that includes education, increasing activity through goal setting, career counseling, and cognitive restructuring will effectively reduce Mr. X's symptoms of depression.

SUMMARY

In summary, a framework for behavioral case formulation through applying the scientific method to the clinical setting has been presented. Much like the scientist, the clinician must assess clients (Observation Phase), develop treatment plans (Developing Hypotheses Phase), implement those treatment plans and observe results (Testing Hypotheses Phase), and revise the treatment plans if necessary (Revising Hypotheses Phase). Through conscientious, compassionate attention to pinpointing concerns, understanding contexts, and systematically implementing empirically supported interventions, therapists may offer their clients the maximum opportunity for meaningful improvement in psychotherapy.

—Paula Truax

See also: Applied Behavior Analysis (Vol. I); Behavioral Assessment (Vol. III); Case Conceptualization (Vol. II)

Suggested Readings

Barlow, D. H. (2001). *The clinical handbook of psychological disorders* (3rd ed.). New York: Guilford Press.

Cormier, S., & Cormier, B. (1998). *Interviewing strategies for helpers: Fundamental skills and cognitive-behavioral interventions.* Pacific Grove, CA: Brooks/Cole.

Division 12 Task Force. (1995). Training in and dissemination of empirically validated psychological treatments: Report and recommendations. *The Clinical Psychologist, 48,* 3–23.

Gould, R. A., Otto, M. W., & Pollack, M. H. (1995). A meta-analysis of treatment outcome for panic disorder. *Clinical Psychology Review, 15*(8), 819–844.

Leahy, R. L., & Holland, S. J. (2000). *Treatment plans and interventions for depression and anxiety disorders.* New York: Guilford Press.

McConnaughy, E. A., DiClemente, C. C., Prochaska, J. O., & Velicer, W. F. (1989). Stages of change in psychotherapy: A follow-up report. *Psychotherapy: Theory, Research, Practice, Training, 26*(4), 494–503.

McLean, P. E., Woody, S., Taylor, S., & Koch, W. J. (1998). Comorbid panic disorder and major depression: Implications for cognitive-behavioral therapy. *Journal of Consulting & Clinical Psychology, 66*(2), 240–247.

Nathan, P. E., & Gorman, J. M. (2002). *A guide to treatments that work* (2nd ed.). New York: Oxford University Press.

Stricker, G., & Trierweiler, S. J. (1995). The local clinical scientist: A bridge between science and practice. *American Psychologist, 50*(12), 995–1002.

BEHAVIORAL CONSULTATION

DESCRIPTION OF THE STRATEGY

Principles of operant conditioning have been applied to a wide array of human problems in settings, ranging from homes to large organizations. Application of these principles of learning and related research to consultation services is referred to as *behavioral consultation*. The behavioral consultant has general skills and knowledge plus knowledge of application of principles of operant conditioning to individuals, groups, and organizations. The consultee can range from the administrator of an organization (e.g., school principal, corporate president, hospital administrator) down to an individual within an organization (e.g., student, hospital staff member, worker on an assembly line). However, in most cases, the consultee is an individual who is responsible for the performance of several other individuals.

The behavioral approach to consultation involves both problem solving and teaching. The assumption is that the behavioral consultant's application and/or teaching of principles of operant conditioning will enable the consultee to solve problems that involve behaviors of individuals for whom the consultee is ultimately responsible. These principles may be taught to a single consultee or to members at multiple levels of an organization who are in the position to influence the behavior of organizational subordinates. The consultee is an active participant and not merely the recipient of information. In many cases, the consultee can be considered an extension of the consultant.

One of the tenets of behavioral consultation is that outcome of the consultation should be operationally defined and, ideally, based upon direct observation of behavior. Similarly, planning, decision making, and problem solving should be based on observable behavior. A second tenet is that environmental variables play significant roles in maintenance of behavior and consequently become the focus of interventions designed to change or promote behavior. A third tenet is that behaviors of interest should be repeatedly measured, beginning during the assessment process and continuing throughout the intervention and consultation process.

The general process of behavioral consultation is not unlike that of behavior analysis and modification with individuals. Consultation begins with a meeting between the consultant and consultee, at which time the problem is presented by the consultee. The problem may be unclear at this point, requiring additional inquiry and assessment. Indeed, a consultant might be contacted for the sole purpose of determining the nature and extent of a problem through a thorough functional assessment. This might be followed by an intervention. More often, an intervention is sought to address a problem or series of problems. The consultant conducts a thorough assessment and relies upon the relevant behavioral research base in producing an intervention plan. What tends to differentiate consultation from use of behavior modification procedures with individuals is that consultative services are almost always provided indirectly (i.e., through regular employees of an organization) and frequently address behaviors of many individuals (e.g., classes of students, wards of patients, employees of corporations). Relevant elements of the system in which the problem exists (e.g., direct care nursing staff in a hospital, nursing supervisors, cleaning staff, supply staff, management personnel, hospital administrator, ward architecture, staffing patterns) are considered, and relations between their behaviors and the behavior of interest are analyzed through functional assessment. Assessment continues as the consultant designs an intervention program, oversees the implementation of the program by the consultee, and repeatedly or continuously evaluates the effectiveness of the program.

RESEARCH BASIS

Behavioral consultation can be traced back to the 1960s, when principles of operant conditioning were applied to elementary school classrooms, institutions for the mentally retarded, psychiatric hospitals, and businesses and industry. The early work in psychiatric hospitals and institutions for the mentally retarded typically involved consultation with ward staff with regard to the behaviors of patients. Goals ranged from reduction of problematic behaviors (e.g., aggressive behaviors, self-abusive behaviors) to the strengthening of adaptive behaviors (e.g., independent self-care behaviors, socially appropriate behaviors, participation in scheduled activities). Intervention programs were implemented by staff who were trained by consultants to administer and monitor behavior management programs based on operant conditioning principles. Oftentimes, the behavior of staff members became the target of interventions, as success of programs implemented for the sake of the patients rested on the performance of the staff members. For example, a performance-based lottery was instituted at a residential center for mentally retarded children to improve care of the residents. The appropriate behaviors of staff members (e.g., changing resident clothing) were observed weekly and recorded on slips of paper with the staff members' names. A winner's name was drawn from the weekly slips, and the winner received a reward. The program resulted in increased attention to residents by staff members, more frequent participation in activities by residents, and better health care of residents. Considerable success has been demonstrated over the years in changing the behaviors of both patients and staff members through such applications of operant principles.

Behavioral consultation in business and industry, often included within the domain of organizational behavior management, became apparent in the late 1960s. For the most part, this form of behavioral consultation occurs at the administrative or systems level. Considerable success has been demonstrated in a wide variety of organizational settings with a wide array of significant behaviors, with much of the early focus on performance management. For example, some of the earliest work began at Emery Air Freight, where Edward Feeney demonstrated significant increases in employee performance through application of operant principles.

Behavioral consultation in educational systems has also been very effective. As with business and industry, educational consultation can occur at the administrative level (e.g., with principals), although considerable consultation occurs at the staff, parent, and student levels. Some of the earliest applications of behavioral consultation in school systems focused on the promotion of academic performance. For example, in the late 1970s, the Behavior Analysis Follow-Through project was developed by Don Bushell Jr. to promote the academic performance of more than 7,000 disadvantaged elementary school children in approximately 300 classrooms in 15 U.S. cities. Excellent results were obtained, with performance gains sustained for 2 years after termination of the program.

In recent years, behavioral consultation has been performed in long-term care settings, where the same principles applied in school systems, business, and industry have been applied to older adults and the staff who directly or indirectly provide their care. The present entry will focus on the role of the behavioral consultant in long-term care settings.

RELEVANT TARGET POPULATIONS AND EXCEPTIONS

Many of the entries in this volume describe strategies or procedures that might be used to modify behavior. This entry is distinct from those entries, because the behavioral consultant's primary role is not so much the use of particular techniques, but rather application of behavioral principles to behavior problems that occur within a system, such as a hospital, school, or corporation. In so doing, the consultant might employ the strategies described in other parts of this text. However, the successful application of any of these techniques is largely contingent upon the extent to which the behavioral consultant understands operant principles of behavior.

Within long-term care settings, where residents might exhibit combinations of major mental illnesses, organic mental disorders, and complex medical problems, the behavioral consultant might be called upon to help develop interventions for behavioral excesses (e.g., disruptive vocalization, physical aggression, wandering) or deficits (e.g., low rates of social behavior, physical inactivity, food refusal).

Because behavioral principles are generally applicable, the behavioral consultant services are useful with any population whose behavior is sensitive to changes in the environment. Residents in long-term care settings vary widely in their sensitivity to environmental changes. For example, some residents might have difficulty discriminating between similar stimuli (e.g., between their rooms and other residents' rooms), whereas others might be able to respond differentially to subtly distinct schedules of reinforcement. Although variability exists in the extent to which individuals are sensitive to environmental manipulations, the vast majority of patients in long-term care settings can respond to gross environmental changes along at least one sensory dimension. Residents with relatively intact vision, for example, are generally able to walk around large obstacles that are placed in the middle of a hallway. Similarly, residents with intact hearing and receptive speech are generally able to respond to spoken language. In sum, behavioral consultation can be used with a vast number of target behaviors and populations; it is the job of the behavioral consultant to tailor interventions to specific needs and abilities of both long-term care residents and staff.

COMPLICATIONS

Unfortunately, interventions designed by the behavioral consultant are not always successful. In most cases, the failure of a behavior management plan is due to inappropriate assessment of (a) the variables or environmental contingencies associated with a resident's behavior and/or (b) the variables or environmental contingencies controlling staff members' behaviors. As was discussed above, the behavioral consultant must consider the individual resident and the unique set of contingencies associated with the problem behavior of the resident when preparing to intervene. Indeed, this idiographic approach is a core feature of behavioral interventions. The variables controlling the behavior of the staff members are easy to overlook. Because long-term care staff members are largely responsible for the implementation of the consultants' behavior management plans, the consideration of factors influencing staff behavior is as important to a successful intervention as the consideration of residents' problem behaviors. When attempting to modify a problematic behavior, the behavioral consultant typically identifies the environmental variables controlling that behavior. The same approach is taken when attempting to increase the adherence of long-term care staff to behavior management plans. The consultant must consider potential antecedents to and consequences of staff member adherence and nonadherence.

Antecedents: Setting the Stage for Adherence

Various strategies can be employed to set the stage for staff members' adherence to behavioral protocols. The following section will discuss the manipulation of three important antecedents to adherence: (1) staff members' knowledge, (2) intervention simplicity, and (3) institutional policy.

Staff members' knowledge of behavioral interventions can be an important antecedent to adherence to behavior management plans. One means of increasing staff members' knowledge of the behavioral approach is to provide regularly scheduled in-service training sessions on topics related to behavioral interventions in long-term care. These inservices can include education on the topics of *basic behavioral principles* (e.g., reinforcement, the function of behaviors), *characteristics of common diagnoses* (e.g., depression, dementia), and *preventing staff burnout.* (Note that these topics mirror the emphasis on the needs of both staff and residents.)

The workdays of long-term care staff are often busy and demanding of physical, mental, and emotional resources. Staff members face a seemingly endless list of chores that must be completed within a finite period of time. Given the choice between performing the tasks that are typically perceived as central to their jobs (e.g., delivering meals and medications, bathing residents, assisting with other activities of daily living) and adhering to a behavior management plan, long-term care staff members are more likely to give priority to the former. If the behavior management plan in question is confusing or complex, the odds of adherence are even lower. Thus, to increase likelihood of adherence, behavior management plans are simple in design and wording and require as little behavior from the staff members as possible. In written descriptions of behavior management protocols, simple terminology (avoid using jargon) and sentence structure are used to clearly outline the steps that staff should take to respond to (or ignore) problematic behaviors.

Given that the effects of behavioral interventions are typically monitored through data collection, the behavioral consultant working in a long-term care setting should attempt to make the collection of data as simple as possible. For example, to reduce response cost associated with data collection (i.e., loss of time that could be spent doing other tasks), data-recording materials should be easily accessible, regardless of a staff member's location on a unit. Staff members might be instructed to record antecedents to and consequences of target behaviors on index cards that they carry on their persons; these data can be transferred to official data-recording sheets at the end of a shift.

Administrative support for behavioral interventions is a relatively distal but important antecedent to adherence and nonadherence to behavioral interventions. As mentioned above, behavior management plans can be lost in the shuffle of daily tasks that staff members view as central to their jobs. Frequent and public statements by institutional directors of the importance of adherence to behavior protocols can increase the perceived legitimacy of the work of behavioral consultants. An administrator at one facility at which the authors worked announced that staff members' failure to follow a behavior management plan was equivalent to neglecting to give a prescribed medication. Statements such as this one, which describe medical and psychological care as of equal importance, can be particularly helpful in institutional settings where compliance with medical care is viewed as the primary component of staff members' jobs.

In sum, to set the stage for adherence to behavioral protocols, the behavioral consultant working in long-term care should aim to educate staff members about the rationale for behavioral interventions and to create plans that are elegant in their simplicity and minimize staff member response cost. In addition, clinicians should attempt to gain institutional support for their work, in the form of frequent public endorsements of behavioral interventions. Effectiveness of these antecedents in setting the stage for adherence is enhanced by the thoughtful application of consequences of adherence and nonadherence.

Consequences: Creating an Atmosphere of Accountability

It is important that behavioral consultants reinforce staff adherence to plans they design. This can be accomplished in various ways, and the consultant must determine the reinforcers that are most appropriate for a given institution. For example, in some settings, it is permissible to provide tangible rewards (e.g., cash, gift certificates, etc.) for adherence. In other facilities, however, either institutional policy or budgetary limitations preclude the provision of such consequences. In these situations, the consultant must be especially creative in choosing appropriate consequences for adherence. For example, the consultant might provide public recognition of excellence in adherence by placing names or photographs of adherent staff members on a prominently displayed poster. Alternatively, the consultant can complete letters of

recognition for adherence; one copy can be given to the adherent staff member, and the original can be placed in his or her personnel file. The consultant might suggest to facility administrators that the presence of these letters be considered in decisions regarding staff members' promotions or pay raises.

CASE ILLUSTRATION

At a state-operated long-term care facility for older adults, individual behavior plans designed to manage problem behaviors of older adults were repeatedly failing despite reasonable functional assessments of the residents' behaviors. An informal functional assessment was performed by two behavioral consultants on the recording of problem behaviors and implementation of behavior management programs by nursing staff. Results revealed unreliable data recording and inconsistent behavior management plan implementation by staff members. Attempts to remediate these problems with individual staff members were unsuccessful. Other attempts to bring about control of these behaviors via implementation of aversive consequences by supervisors were equally ineffective. It became clear that a systemic intervention would be needed, as there were no consequences for supervising nurses and other nursing staff for reliable implementation of behavior management plans. However, there were consequences for performance of other nursing duties that were sometimes incompatible with the consistent implementation of the behavior management plans.

To address failures at the supervisory level, a behavior management element was added to a preexisting quality assurance (QA) program for routine medical care, which was coordinated by a QA nurse. There were two components to this intervention, each occurring at different levels of the system. The first component was designed to directly modify protocol adherence of direct-care nursing staff. The QA nurse examined resident records to determine whether behavioral data were being reliably recorded and observed nursing staff responsible for plan implementation. Nursing staff were queried to determine whether they knew and understood each of the behavior plans and recording procedures. Staff who demonstrated an accurate understanding of current behavior management plans were rewarded with certificates of excellence, copies of which were placed in their personnel files. If staff members failed to implement a protocol correctly, they were asked to describe the protocol in question. If staff members were unable to do this, they were given detailed instruction in the plan's implementation until they were able to recite every detail of the plan in question. If they again were observed either neglecting to record behavioral data or neglecting to properly execute a plan, a written reprimand was placed in their personnel files.

The second component was designed to introduce greater accountability into the nursing supervisory system. A biweekly QA meeting was held with the hospital administrator, psychological consultants, social services staff, director of nursing, and other registered nurses in attendance. The QA nurse presented information regarding the reliability of program implementation, direct care staff knowledge of programs, and the effectiveness of these interventions. Presentation of these data in the presence of administrative staff served to increase accountability for program implementation.

—Barry A. Edelstein and Adam Spira

See also: *Behavioral Consultation (Vols. II & III); Private Practice of Behavioral Treatment (Vol. I)*

Suggested Readings

Bergan, J. (1977). *Behavioral consultation.* Columbus, OH: Merrill.

Cassidy, E. L., & Sheikh, J. I. (2002). Pre-intervention assessment for disruptive behavior problems: A focus on staff needs. *Aging & Mental Health, 6,* 166–171.

Hussian, R. A. (1981). *Geriatric psychology: A behavioral perspective.* New York: Van Nostrand.

Hussian, R. A., & Davis, R. L. (1985). *Responsive care: Behavioral interventions with elderly persons.* Champaign, IL: Research Press.

Kratochwill, T. R., Bergan, J. R., & Bergan, J. R. (1990). *Behavioral consultation in applied settings: An individual guide.* Cambridge, MA: Perseus.

Sheridan, S. M., Bergan, J. R., & Kratochwill, T. R. (1997). *Conjoint behavioral consultation: A procedural manual.* Cambridge, MA: Perseus.

BEHAVIORAL CONTRACTING

DESCRIPTION OF THE STRATEGY

Behavioral contracting can be used in a wide variety of contexts. Contracting may be used to increase compliance with treatment itself or to increase compliance with a range of targeted behaviors. Contracting is commonplace in behavior therapies; it also has widespread use by clinicians of diverse theoretical orientations.

The goal of the behavioral contract is to increase frequency of a target behavior. Common behavioral contracts include commitments to attend appointments, maintain a diet, and abstain from drinking or drugs. Contracting involves creating a written agreement between the client and therapist to increase a specific client behavior. Many contracts are based on the "A-B-C" approach, which involves identifying *antecedents* to the behavior, defining the targeted (desired) *behavior,* and identifying the *consequences* (or reinforcers) that will shape and maintain the behavior. Contracts usually operate by implementing new reinforcer(s) designed to increase the target behavior or by altering antecedents.

One of the important parts of behavioral contracting is to define the specific behavior that is a target of change. Contracts will be ineffective and confusing if the target behavior and contingencies are not well-defined and documented. A good contract delineates a very clear expectation. The target behavior must be specific. In a contract focused on managing anger, a target behavior of "Expressing anger in appropriate ways" would be too broad. More effective target behaviors would be "Speak in a calm voice" or "State you are going for a walk, then go for a walk." The behavior should be defined in positive rather than negative terms; people are generally more amenable to increasing a behavior than eliminating one.

To create a behavioral contract, the client may need to first obtain a baseline of the behavior to be changed, that is, the natural frequency with which the problem is occurring. If the baseline is unknown, the client must record each time he or she performs the behavior during a given time period (e.g., hour, day, week). In obtaining a baseline, the client does not try to change the behavior yet; this is a stage of gathering information. Gathering additional information can be helpful, such as documenting the situation in which the behavior occurs and the intensity of the behavior. Sometimes, the baseline is already known; in that case, this step is unnecessary.

The initial goal or target behavior set must be a balance between the client's chance of success and the short-term consequences of not complying. With substance abusers, the initial goal is usually abstinence; noncompliance with this may have severe short-term consequences and will interfere with treatment. In other situations, a contract is designed to increase the target behavior slowly from the baseline so that the client may have an experience of success early on in the treatment. This will increase the likelihood that the client will be motivated to continue to adhere to the contract. For example, in a weight loss program, short-term consequences are not dire; specific target behaviors for diet and exercise may be implemented in a progressive, stepwise manner.

A good behavioral contract has contingencies built into it. The term *contingencies* may be used for anything that is contingent upon the target behavior (i.e., rewards or consequences). A reward or reinforcer is something that increases the likelihood of the target behavior occurring again. Contracts are most effective when contingencies, or reinforcers, are clearly stated. For example, in a controlled environment, such as an inpatient unit, reinforcers are often in the form of privileges on the unit. Consequences in this setting are often a lack of privileges. Often, contracts also have negative consequences in place that are contingent on the desired behavior; if the desired behavior is not performed, these contingencies take effect.

Behavior (or contingency) contracts are most effective when key people are aware of the contract and can help reinforce the contingencies. On an inpatient unit, the patient, nurse, and physician may all sign the contract. In outpatient cases, spouses, relatives, or friends might be made aware of the contract. A contract is most successful when relevant people are aware and in agreement about the content of the contract.

RESEARCH BASIS

Behavioral contracting relies on the principles of operant conditioning and, more specifically, on the concept of the contingency of reinforcement. Operant conditioning involves looking at how voluntary behaviors "operate on" the environment to produce an effect. Operant conditioning relies on the demands of the environment to shape the responses that are elicited. According to operant conditioning theory, one can change behavior by modifying the environment, either before or after the behavior occurs. To intentionally change a behavior to produce a different desired effect on the environment is termed *behavior modification*. The process of analyzing the existing behavior and studying how the behavior could most

effectively produce the desired change is known as *applied behavior analysis*. Applied behavior analysis involves examining the interrelationship between the antecedents (events that stimulate the behavior), the response (the behavior in question), and the consequences or reinforcers of the behavior.

The concept of the contingency of reinforcement is central to behavioral contracting. The *contingency of reinforcement* means that when a desired reinforcer is contingent upon the target behavior occurring, the target behavior will increase. A desired reinforcer is chosen to reward the client contingent upon performing the target behavior. A reinforcer is used until the ultimate target behavior is reached and maintained.

Another important concept is shaping. Shaping is the process of reinforcing a series of successive approximations of the target behavior. When using contracts to shape behaviors, a series of contracts would be used to reinforce a series of target behaviors that lead to the end target behavior. Once the first target behavior is learned, contingencies of the contract are changed, and a new behavior (closer to the ultimate target behavior) is reinforced.

Behavioral contracts serve to document the client's intention to behave in a certain way. Research has shown that verbalizing a commitment to another person increases the likelihood that commitment will be kept. Furthermore, written contracts have been shown to impact target behaviors more effectively than verbal contracts. For example, compliance was examined in a controlled study with three experimental groups. In one group, subjects were not asked whether they planned to comply. In the second group, subjects were asked whether they would comply; these subjects made verbal commitments. In the third group, subjects gave written and verbal commitments to comply. The group with both written and verbal contracts had the best compliance. The group that gave only verbal commitments had greater compliance than the group that gave no commitment.

Research has provided support for efficacy of behavioral contracts. In a 1994 study, for example, two groups of anorexic inpatients were required to gain weight in order to gain privileges on the ward. The target weight gain for Group 1 was higher than the target weight gain for Group 2; there were no other significant differences between the groups, and the contingencies (privileges on the unit) were the same. Group 1 (the group with the higher target weight) gained weight at a significantly faster rate, showing that it was the behavioral contract that had a positive effect on the rate of weight gain.

RELEVANT TARGET POPULATIONS AND EXCEPTIONS

Contracts have proven to be appropriate for clients with a wide range of behavioral goals. Behavioral contracts can be adapted or created to fit any number of different needs; whenever there is a need for a behavior to be more consistently performed, a contract may be useful. Research has shown that contracts have been especially effective with substance abuse, schizophrenia, obesity, anorexia, and student performance.

Contracting has been used extensively and successfully with substance-abusing clients. It has been used to increase attendance to appointments, compliance with treatment, and relapse prevention. Behavioral contracts with family members of substance-abusing clients also increase client compliance and produce better outcomes. Outcomes for dually diagnosed clients (with both substance abuse and mental health issues) have also been more favorable when behavioral contracting was used. Contracts with these clients have been successful in improving compliance to medical, psychiatric, and substance abuse treatment.

Contracts using negative reinforcement or "consequences" are often used with substance-abusing clients. Negative reinforcers are aversive consequences that are removed when the target behavior is performed. Negative reinforcers for substance-abusing clients often include job loss or a probation violation with the threat of returning to jail. Contracts using negative reinforcement have been especially effective with substance-abusing clients who hold positions of responsibility (e.g., medical doctors, psychologists, nurses, etc.). In these cases, the negative reinforcer is often a detailed letter addressed to the licensing board describing the client's substance abuse and surrendering his or her professional license; during treatment, the letter is held by the clinician. If the client is noncompliant with the contract (i.e., the client drinks or uses drugs), the clinician will send the letter to the board of registration.

Positive reinforcers are often used for clients on methadone. Clients with consistent clinic attendance are trusted to take home methadone doses for the following day rather than having to come into the clinic every day. For other substance-abusing clients, positive reinforcers often include simple things clients can give themselves or receive from friends or family members (e.g., free babysitting, rides to therapy and meetings, buying something special, etc.). Positive reinforcers are not effective for abstinence in the short term, but they give clients something to work for while they are developing new habits and finding new ways of spending time.

With schizophrenics and dually diagnosed clients (those with mental illness in addition to substance abuse), behavior contracts have been particularly helpful in compliance and monitoring of psychiatric and medical treatments.

Behavioral contracts are used to increase compliance with weight loss. Behavior contracts may include when, where, or what foods to eat. Reinforcers may include rewards from the client or the client's family. Behavioral contracts are also used to increase weight gain (see example above).

Suicide (or safety) contracts should be used carefully and must not be the primary intervention. It is generally agreed that suicide contracts provide more false reassurance to the clinician than prevention for the patient. With suicidal patients, detailed safety plans, an infusion of hopefulness, alleviation of depression, identification of triggers, and rehearsal of coping skills are more effective. A behavioral contract can be built around one or more of these interventions.

Behavioral contracting is also used extensively for decreasing juvenile probation violations, increasing prosocial behavior in conduct-disordered youth, ameliorating behavior problems in children, and enhancing student performance.

COMPLICATIONS

Several complications can arise when a contract is implemented. First of all, if a contract is developed before there is enough rapport between therapist and client, that contract may become a source of resistance in the therapy. The client may not yet have enough trust in the therapist and may experience the contract as a punishment by the therapist rather than an aid to treatment. This is often a risk in substance abuse treatment, since there is generally a good deal of shame about substance use, and the client may be unable to trust easily.

Contracts can be ineffective and damage the therapy if the tone of the contract becomes angry, punitive, or paternalistic. This may be due either to lack of training or underlying feelings on the part of the therapist. This is especially a risk in mandated treatment or when the therapist (rather than the client, the family, the probation officer, judge, etc.) is in control of the contingency.

Contracts may not be effective if the client is not included in creating the contract. Contracts are most effective if the client chooses the target behavior and wants the behavior change. However, in the case of clients mandated to substance abuse treatment, the client does not often share the same goal. However, it is important to identify something the client is motivated to do (to maintain a job, for example). This goal is clearly related to substance abuse recovery, and the contract will be more effective if this goal is incorporated into the contract.

Just as clients should be included in choosing target behaviors, clients should also be included in choosing reinforcers. The range of items that is reinforcing or motivating varies greatly from person to person. Money and food are primary reinforcers and are reinforcing to almost everyone. However, these reinforcers are not always available, and their use as contingencies is not ethical in many situations. Other, secondary reinforcers vary among individuals. A contract will not be effective if the client is not interested in obtaining the reinforcer.

Neither can contracts be effective if the client does not yet have the skills to perform the behavior. If this is true, then no amount of motivation and no type of contingency will be effective in getting the client to perform the behavior. If the client cannot yet exhibit the behavior at will, then skills training is indicated.

Often, clients merely agree to the contract and are not really invested in the contract or the treatment. In these cases, it is important to thoroughly question clients about their motivation to change. Sometimes when clients appear unmotivated, they are actually experiencing hopelessness; the client does not actually believe the contract will help. In these cases, the therapist must impart confidence that the treatment can work and hopefulness that the client will be able to change.

It is common for spouses and other adult family members to be involved in a client's substance abuse treatment. However, the role of the spouse in the therapy must be clearly defined. It is not the role of the spouse to enforce the contract or to remind the client to behave in a certain way; that is an impossible task, since the spouse does not have control over the client's behaviors. More important, it will create more stress in the relationship and may reinforce an existing dysfunctional pattern. However, the spouse can and should report to the therapist what he or she observes about the client's behaviors.

As noted above, "contracts for safety" (contracts implemented to prevent the client from attempting suicide) are not contraindicated, but they must be used carefully and in conjunction with other intervention in order to be most effective.

CASE ILLUSTRATION (INCLUDING BEHAVIORAL ASSESSMENT)

"Tiffany" was in a psychiatric day program. She had lost more than one job due to her angry outbursts at coworkers. In the past, she had yelled at others, using profane language, and once damaged a cash register by punching it. Tiffany said that she was not sure why she had the outbursts and that they came on quickly. She genuinely wanted to be successful at holding a job and to be better able to provide for her two boys. When Tiffany and her therapist, "Dr. Kim," examined the behavior together, they concluded that it happened almost daily on the first week of a job and lasted about a minute. After the first weeks of the job (if she was still employed), Tiffany's outbursts diminished to about once a week, but were at a higher intensity and lasted up to 5 minutes. Dr. Kim did a behavioral analysis of the antecedents and found out that criticism (be it real or imagined) triggered these inappropriate expressions of anger. The two of them defined some appropriate, assertive responses to criticism, and Tiffany practiced these with Dr. Kim. Tiffany contracted that over the next week, she would practice the skills in the group therapy sessions, practice an assertiveness script with friends, and in addition, she would go into the community twice that week and practice assertiveness exercises.

Tiffany came back to therapy and had met the contracting goals. Dr. Kim expressed warm approval. Tiffany thought she still had a long way to go, but she was proud of herself and more hopeful that she might actually be able to change her behavior after all these years. At this meeting, she and Dr. Kim contracted that she would continue practicing the assertiveness skills in the community; in addition, she would apply for a job in a preemployment workshop.

Once Tiffany had obtained a job in a preemployment workshop, she would be contracting to practice her new skills at the workshop. Her behavioral contract would continue to change weekly, to reflect new goals. The contracting would continue until she was successfully maintaining a job. The therapy would then focus on relapse prevention skills. Tiffany would be contracting to practice skills to prevent her from sliding backward. When that was accomplished, therapy would decrease in frequency until she proved to be stable after 3- and 6-month checkup visits.

—Anne F. Philips

See also: *Behavioral Contracting (Vols. II & III); Evaluating Behavioral Plans (Vol. I)*

Suggested Readings

Bergen, A. E., & Garfield, S. L. (Eds.). (1994). *Handbook of psychotherapy and behavior change* (4th ed.). Oxford, UK: Wiley.

Hersen, M. (2002). *Clinical behavioral therapy: Adults and children.* West Sussex, UK: Wiley.

Miltenberger, R. G. (2001), *Behavior modification: Principles and procedures.* Belmont, CA: Wadsworth/Thomson.

Pear, J., & Martin, G. L. (2002). *Behavior modification: What it is and how to do it* (7th ed.). Upper Saddle River, NJ: Prentice Hall.

BEHAVIORAL GERONTOLOGY

DESCRIPTION OF STRATEGY

Behavioral gerontology is the application of behavioral principles to the problems of older adults. Though considerable work in behavioral gerontology has addressed basic research questions (e.g., the nature of dependency among nursing home residents, extent of new learning among Alzheimer's patients), most efforts in behavioral gerontology have focused on behavioral assessment, behavioral intervention, and a combination of the two. Behavioral gerontology began in the 1960s and early 1970s, with work by individuals such as Cautela, Hoyer, Lindsley, Risley, Baltes, and Pinkston. Though the same principles of behavior are applied to older adults as to younger adults and children, problems addressed with older adults are typically more complex and often unique to older adults. This is particularly the case with older adults who have experienced physical and cognitive decline.

RESEARCH BASIS

A moderate amount of research has been conducted in behavioral geronotology, though many questions remain unanswered. Research areas, target problems, and interventions will be discussed by problem area, with an emphasis on clinical gerontology.

SELF-CARE

Self-care behaviors, including feeding/eating, ambulating, and maintaining personal hygiene may drop from an older adult's behavioral repertoire as a result of the progression of a disease or health problem or simply because these behaviors are no longer reinforced by environmental contingencies. Several studies have demonstrated the effectiveness of employing contingent positive reinforcement (e.g., praise) for eating combined with a time-out procedure for food refusal. Other interventions have incorporated prompting and praise for ambulation independent of a wheelchair and/or reinforcement for distance walked. Employment of token economies has proven effective as a method for reinforcing performance of personal hygiene tasks, including bathing, toileting, and oral hygiene. In addition to interventions based on reinforcement of the self-care behavior, other successful interventions have emphasized skills training involving instruction, modeling, and behavioral rehearsal.

SOCIAL BEHAVIOR

Social Skills

As opportunities for social interaction (e.g., job, school) decrease with age, older adults may find it difficult to interact socially and, as a result, lose social skills that were once a part of their behavioral repertoires. Social withdrawal is also common in older adults due to restraints in mobility or loss of friends and loved ones. Social skills training is a behavioral intervention that involves instruction, modeling of social behavior, behavioral rehearsal or role playing, feedback, and reinforcement of social interaction. Several studies have demonstrated that through social skills training, community-dwelling and institutionalized older adults were able to develop or fine-tune interpersonal skills that enhanced the quality and frequency of interactions with others.

Dependency

Older adults, especially those in nursing homes or institutional settings, must frequently rely on others for assistance with tasks, ranging from transportation to personal hygiene. As dependency on others grows, researchers have found that caregivers may inadvertently reinforce dependency by offering support, such as attention for dependent behavior, while ignoring independent behavior. This, in turn, may act as a catalyst for further functional decline. Behavioral interventions have proven useful as a means of breaking this cycle. Interventions have typically focused on changing caregiver responses to older adults' independent and dependent behaviors, to promote as much autonomy as possible in the older adult. Numerous studies have demonstrated that through caregiver training involving communication skills, knowledge about aging, and basic behavioral principles, caregivers can successfully alter their behaviors, which, in turn, encourages independence in nursing-home residents.

MEMORY AND COGNITION

The aging process is typically associated with decrements in a variety of cognitive abilities. Older adults frequently experience losses in short-term memory, response speed, and ability to learn new information. However, such declines are generally minimal, vary greatly between individuals, and typically do not impact everyday functioning.

Behavioral principles and procedures have been used in attempts to remediate age-related declines in cognitive abilities. Positive reinforcement may be provided for correct responses to improve response speed, accuracy, and risk taking in testing situations. Similarly, modeling strategies have been effective at improving the test-taking performance of older adults. Models may be used to teach older adults effective methods for problem solving, reasoning, and concept formation. Shaping and token economies have also been identified as methods for improving older adults' performance on tests of fluid intelligence.

Reduction of anxiety experienced by older adults in test-taking situations has shown improved performance. For example, highly anxious older adults typically benefit from training in progressive muscle relaxation or stress inoculation prior to memory training.

Cognitive losses associated with organic conditions, such as dementia, may also be amenable to intervention. Imagery techniques for learning words and faces can be effective among older adults with dementia, although the longevity of gains is uncertain. Similarly, spaced retrieval techniques, in which acquired information is repeatedly retrieved at intervals of increasing duration, have been effective at teaching new information and skills to older adults with dementia. Older adults with dementia have been shown to benefit from carrying diaries or wallets with relevant personal information that can be consulted in situations where the information is forgotten.

BEHAVIORAL MEDICINE AND AGING

Behavioral principles and procedures have been effectively applied to the field of gerontological health psychology and behavioral medicine. For example, behavioral interventions have been successful in treating pain, insomnia, and incontinence in older adults.

Pain

Although treatment of persistent pain in older adults typically relies extensively on pharmacological interventions, behavioral interventions offer promising results. Older adults may be particularly susceptible to the reinforcing consequences of pain behaviors, such as grimacing or talking about pain, because these individuals tend to be more isolated and lonely than younger adults. Pain behaviors may be used by older adults to solicit attention and sympathy. Thus, behavioral interventions that provide reinforcement for healthy behaviors and extinction of pain behaviors can be effective at improving activity level, medication intake, pain behaviors, and self-report of pain.

Cognitive-behavioral therapy, involving instruction in techniques such as progressive muscle relaxation, deep breathing, imagery, cognitive restructuring, and problem solving, has been shown to be equally as effective for younger and older pain patients. Specifically, cognitive-behavioral interventions may effectively reduce self-reports of pain, anxiety, depression, medication use, and pain impact. Biofeedback has also been shown to be effective at reducing pain in older adults.

Insomnia

Poor sleep quality and complaints of insomnia are particularly prevalent in aging individuals. Behavioral interventions for insomnia are highly effective with older adults. Many effective behavioral treatments include training in stimulus control, in which older adults are trained to establish regular sleep schedules and use the bed only for sleep. Older adults are often instructed to exit from the bed following a brief unsuccessful attempt at sleep. Furthermore, older adults may be taught to perform a nonarousing activity, such as reading a dull book or listening to the radio, to break previously established sleep-incompatible patterns and prevent cognitive arousal. Instruction in sleep hygiene, imagery, progressive muscle relaxation, and biofeedback have also shown to be effective at treating geriatric insomnia. These behavioral techniques have successfully improved older adults' self-reports and quantitative and qualitative measures of sleep.

Incontinence

Incontinence is a significant problem in both community-dwelling and institutionalized older adults. In addition to an elevated risk of physical complications, incontinence can lead to psychological distress, including embarrassment and anxiety. Incontinence also ranks as one of the leading causes of admission to long-term care facilities. Early treatments for incontinence were aimed at institutional caregivers; nursing staff were trained to implement ongoing behavioral management procedures. Treatments often involved positive reinforcement for dry checks and toileting requests, social disapproval for wetness, and frequent toileting. However, success of such efforts was often limited due to staff turnover, shortages of nurses, and high patient-staff ratios.

Recent behavioral interventions for incontinence have focused on operant conditioning of physiological responses, such as selective contraction of pelvic floor muscles and voluntary inhibition of detrusor contraction, which mediate bladder control. Alone and in combination with scheduled voiding techniques, the effectiveness of biofeedback training has been well documented in incontinent community-living older adults.

PSYCHOPATHOLOGY

Anxiety

Prevalence of anxiety disorders in adults appears to decrease with age. However, recent research has demonstrated that subthreshold anxiety, or a preponderance of anxiety-related symptoms that do not meet diagnostic criteria, is quite common and may prove functionally disabling for many older adults. The sparse behavioral intervention research that exists with older adults has focused mainly on generalized anxiety disorder; a few studies have examined behavioral interventions for obsessive-compulsive disorder. From research that exists, it appears that traditional behavioral interventions for anxiety used with younger adults are efficacious for older cohorts as well. These interventions typically include progressive muscle relaxation, exposure to the anxiety-provoking stimulus, differential reinforcement of "other" behaviors that are incompatible with the anxious behavior/response, response prevention, systematic desensitization, or a combination of these. Further work is much needed to identify effective forms of treatment for the entire spectrum of anxiety disorders as well as subthreshold anxiety in older adults.

Depression

Depression is the most prevalent psychological disorder among older adults. Effective behavioral interventions for depression in older adults typically occur through individual or group psychotherapy. Individual behavior therapy is based on the premise that behavior and mood are linked and when one's positive behavioral experiences increase, mood will improve. As such, most therapies incorporate social reinforcement for increased activity, and the therapist and client may work together to schedule pleasant or enjoyable events into the client's daily schedule. Group therapies are especially effective for older adults, because by the nature of the therapy, loneliness is countered. Indeed, loneliness is a frequent contributing factor to depression. Group therapy takes a psychoeducational approach, with emphasis again on scheduling pleasant activities into the depressed older adult's life. In addition, group members serve as a means of social support and may also aid in decreasing the stigma associated with seeking therapy.

Paranoia

Paranoia is a common psychological problem among older adults, especially for those who suffer from dementia or experience some form of sensory impairment (e.g., blindness, deafness). Research on behavioral interventions for paranoia is largely nonexistent. However, several case studies have demonstrated its potential effectiveness. These studies employed differential reinforcement techniques coupled with selective ignoring. Typically, verbalizations made by the older adult related to delusions and paranoia were ignored, while more appropriate verbalizations were reinforced.

DEMENTIA

Many older adults with dementia exhibit behavior problems, which sometimes vary according to the stage of dementia. Behaviors that are most typically problematic from the perspective of individuals with dementia, their caregivers, and others in the living environment are wandering, disruptive vocalizations, and aggressive behaviors. Several studies have demonstrated effectiveness of behavioral approaches for the assessment and treatment of these problem behaviors.

Wandering

There is little agreement on a definition of wandering, but most conceptualizations include the presence of cognitive impairment and movement through large-scale space. Wandering can constitute a significant problem for caregivers of cognitively impaired older adults. It also represents a potential risk for the impaired older adult who may suffer a fall or become lost in a community, with death as a potential consequence. Cognitively impaired older adults also can become lost in nursing homes or wander in and out of the rooms of other residents, who can become combative when such "strangers" invade their personal space. Several behavioral interventions have been successful with wanderers. Interventions have included, for example, reinforcing behavior that is incompatible with wandering, posting visual cues that previously had been paired with reinforcement or punishment to reinforce appropriate behavior and punish undesirable behavior, and altering the stimulus properties of the environment associated with wandering. In the latter case, for example, one might disguise a door through which someone wanders by placing a poster over the door so that it no longer is associated with exit behavior. Systematic research is sparse, but several case studies have shown promising results.

Disruptive Vocalizations

Verbally disruptive behaviors are vocal behaviors that are disruptive, repetitive, or inappropriate to the circumstances. This is a common problem among older adults with Alzheimer's disease and is often manifested as shouting, screaming, or moaning. The behaviors are disruptive to caregivers and others in the proximity of the older adult. Behavioral interventions have included, for example, positive reinforcement contingent on absence of disruptive vocalizations, time-out for vocalizations, exposure to music, exposure to a family-generated videotape, one-to-one social interactions, ignoring of vocalizations, social skills training, and relaxation training. Most research has been in the form of case studies, although a few group studies also have demonstrated the effectiveness of behavioral interventions. No single intervention has been found effective, with some authors suggesting the need to carefully match treatment to vocalizer.

Aggressive Behavior

Aggressive behavior is common among older adults with dementia and often occurs when caregivers are attempting to provide care or when dementia patients are in the presence of other dementia patients whose behavior is disturbing. A variety of behavioral interventions have been used effectively, including, for example, altering antecedent conditions, altering consequences of aggressive behavior, and differential reinforcement of incompatible behaviors. As with interventions for other problem behaviors, no single approach is effective with all aggressive behaviors. Most of the research has consisted of case studies, with the more effective ones using an initial functional assessment to guide the intervention development and implementation.

COMPLICATIONS

Most of the complications of applying a behavioral approach to the problems of older adults stem from the complexity of many possible controlling variables that are more common with older than younger adults. For example, older adults are more likely than younger adults to experience chronic illnesses, experience limitations due to the illnesses, take multiple medications for these illnesses, experience adverse effects of the medications and their interactions, and have significant sensory impairments that complicate the assessment and intervention processes. For older adults with cognitive impairment (e.g., Alzheimer's disease), the complexities of behavioral assessment and intervention are even more numerous. These "complications" are not intractable and often constitute an intriguing challenge for those who choose to work with older adults.

CASE ILLUSTRATION

"Mr. Adams" was an 85-year-old man with moderate dementia who was recently admitted to a nursing home. Nursing staff noted that he became aggressive when staff members attempted to bathe him. This did not happen consistently. Mr. Adams was in a wheelchair, and he was incapable of communicating effectively due to expressive aphasia. A functional assessment accomplished through direct observation of Mr. Adams's care revealed that his combative behavior diminished in frequency and intensity as he was withdrawn from the bathtub, and further upon being dried. Several initial hypotheses were generated through systematic observations regarding the possible function of the aggressive behavior. First, aggressive behavior could have been emitted to escape water that was too cold. Second, aggressive behavior could have been directed at the person performing the bathing because that person looked like someone disliked by Mr. Adams. Third, Mr. Adams could have been using aggressive behavior to escape the bath because he was embarrassed having an opposite-sexed person bathing him. To test the first hypothesis, the water temperature was increased to two different levels, which produced no change in aggressive behavior. The second hypothesis was judged unlikely, since Mr. Adams was aggressive with several different bathers. To test the third hypothesis, Mr. Adams was first bathed by a woman and then by a man. No aggressive behavior occurred with the man. Another woman and another man each bathed Mr. Adams, and again no aggressive behavior occurred with the man. From then on, only men bathed Mr. Adams, and no further aggressive behavior was observed.

—*Barry A. Edlestein, Andrea Shreve-Nieger, and Lesley Kovan*

See also: *Behavioral Treatment in Natural Environments (Vol. I); Cognitive Behavior Therapy With Religious Beliefs and Practices (Vol. I); Hersen, Michel (Vol. I)*

Suggested Readings

Baltes, M., Neumann, E., & Zank, S. (1994). Maintenance and rehabilitation of independence in old age: An intervention program for staff. *Psychology and Aging, 9*(2), 179–188.

Carstensen, L. (1988). The emerging field of behavioral gerontology. *Behavior Therapy, 19,* 259–281.

Cohen-Mansfield, J., & Werner, P. (1997). Management of verbally disruptive behaviors in nursing home residents. *Journal of Gerontology: Medical Sciences, 52A,* M369–M377.

Fisher, J. E., Swingen, D. N., & Harsin, C. M. (2001). Agitated and aggressive behavior. In B. Edelstein (Ed.), *Clinical geropsychology.* Oxford, UK: Elsevier Science.

Hussian, R. A. (1981). *Geriatric psychology: A behavioral perspective.* New York: Van Nostrand Reinhold.

Karel, M., Ogland-Hand, S., & Gatz, M. (2002). *Assessing and treating late-life depression: A casebook and resource guide.* New York: Basic Books.

Stanley, M., Beck, J., Novy, D., Averill, P., Swann, A., Diefenbach, G., & Hopko, D. (2003). Cognitive-behavioral treatment of late-life generalized anxiety disorder. *Journal of Consulting and Clinical Psychology, 71*(2), 309–319.

BEHAVIORAL GROUP WORK

DESCRIPTION OF THE STRATEGY

Group therapy is a way of working with more than one client at a time in which all the members help one another to establish and achieve treatment goals. In behavioral group therapy (BGT), the major means of intervention are operant, problem solving, or cognitive, and the group is used as an additional tool to enhance effectiveness of these interventions to achieve treatment goals. In this entry, we focus on the benefits of the group and specifically how it is used in assessment, treatment, and generalization planning for adult clients. We also describe how these groups are organized.

Behavioral groups vary considerably. There are groups, not unlike individual therapy, that aim to improve social skills and coping with stress, reduce anxiety and depression, eliminate panic responses, reduce frequency of bulimic behavior, promote weight loss, resolve phobic disorders, ameliorate agoraphobia, manage chronic pain, improve general social functioning, increase abstention from risky sexual activity, and reduce frequency of drug and alcohol abuse. Most of these strategies are supported by empirical research. Groups range in size from 5 to 15 members, although for adults, the norm is 8. They range in duration from 6 to 20 sessions depending on complexity of the presenting problems. Most sessions last from $1\frac{1}{2}$ to 2 hours. There are either one or two therapists. Most groups are closed and time limited. Using similar methods, therapists also organize closed groups in institutions.

Usually, clients in group therapy have shared individual goals in one or several of the above areas. The role of the group is to help members to formulate more specific subgoals and with the help of the therapist and group members to design interventions to achieve those goals.

There are many advantages to treatment in groups. First, because the clients are surrounded by other individuals who are dealing with similar issues, group membership commonly ends the sense of isolation experienced by many clients. The group provides the client with a source of feedback about behaviors that are irritating or acceptable to others and about cognitions that can be viewed as distorted or stress eliciting. We have noted that clients find reinforcement from other group members more powerful than from the group therapist alone. As clients increase frequency of reinforcing others, they note that they are reciprocally reinforced, and group cohesion increases. In groups, clients must learn to deal with the idiosyncrasies of other individuals. They must learn how to offer each other critical feedback and advice in a tactful and helpful manner, both of which are relationship-building skills.

Of course, groups are not without disadvantages. A relevant limitation to be concerned with is that it is more difficult to individualize each client in the group than in one-to-one therapy. Another threat to individualization is the fact that in order for everyone to have a chance to participate actively in every session, limits must be placed on clients who talk more than their share. Confidentiality is more difficult to maintain in groups than in the therapeutic dyad. Confidentiality and consequences of breaches need to be dealt with by the group therapist in pregroup screening and early in treatment.

Assessment in Groups

One important early step in the process of treatment is to assess presenting problems and the resources the individual has for resolving them. In assessment, BGT takes into consideration the environment in which behaviors occur. Most BGT models teach specific skills for defining unique problem situations in such a way that they can be dealt with effectively. Individual testing and pregroup interviews are used. But the group itself is used for assessment by having clients interview each other and observing each other in role plays. As part of assessment, long- and short-term goals are formulated. Each member negotiates his or her own goals with suggestions from the other group members and the therapist.

Group Cohesion

Cohesion refers to the mutual liking of members for one another and the group therapist and their attraction to the program of the group. High cohesion tends to be correlated with high motivation to work on significant problems. In our groups, cohesion of the group can be enhanced by use of group introductory exercises in which members interview each other in pairs and people introduce their partners to the group. It also is a safe way of increasing broad participation and is the first step to self-disclosure. Cohesion is also enhanced by creating opportunities for continued broad participation, protecting members from premature and/or too harsh confrontation, keeping the interaction positive, using variation in the program, using humor occasionally, and developing opportunities for choice and self-decision-making by the members. Level of cohesion is usually monitored at the end of each session on the postsession questionnaire (described below).

Group Goals

Group goals, in contrast to individual treatment goals, refer to a future change in interactive phenomena that will occur in the group. An example of one commonly occurring group goal is that "the attraction of the members to each other (as measured on a postsession questionnaire) will increase from the end of the previous session to the end of the session." Another frequently occurring group goal is that everyone in the group will participate actively in the discussion. Most group goals are proposed to the group by the therapist; their achievement is evaluated by means of member observation and results of the postsession questionnaire (see Table 1). Group goals are important only insofar as their achievement facilitates attainment of individual treatment goals. For example, in an anxiety and depression group in which the group problem was that members rarely provided each other with feedback, the goal was to increase the feedback given to each other.

Table 1   An Example of Questions and Format of a Postsession Questionnaire

1. How useful was this session?

1 ____ 2 ____ 3 ____ 4 ____ 5 ____ 6 ____ 7 ____ 8 ____ 9
not at all   very little   somewhat   quite a bit   extremely

2. How helpful were members to each other during this session?

1 ____ 2 ____ 3 ____ 4 ____ 5 ____ 6 ____ 7 ____ 8 ____ 9
not at all   very little   somewhat   quite a bit   extremely

3. How close did the members feel to each other during this session?

1 ____ 2 ____ 3 ____ 4 ____ 5 ____ 6 ____ 7 ____ 8 ____ 9
not at all   very little   somewhat   quite a bit   extremely

The items in Table 1 represent member perception of the group's usefulness, mutual helpfulness of the members, and group cohesion. Additional items reveal perceived group autonomy and emotional states in the group, as well as satisfaction with the group. Means, discrepancies among the members, and discrepancies between means of the members and the group therapist's observations provide a rough estimate of some of the group phenomena.

Group Problems

Each of the above concepts represents a potential group problem or group resource. The most common group problems are low cohesiveness, uneven distribution of participation, and low self-disclosure. As members increasingly grow to like and trust others in the group, they are increasingly willing to share with others their conflicts, sources of their anxiety, goals, levels of motivation, appraisal of problematic events, and acceptance of feedback and suggestions from others.

Group Interventions

Individual interventions, such as reinforcement, modeling, and cognitive restructuring, are administered in such a way as to encourage members taking leadership roles in helping one another. As such, they become group interventions. Group exercises, modeling by group members, feedback from group members, mutual reinforcement, brainstorming alternative strategies, and ways of appraising situations are, because of their intrinsic reliance on the input of the group, construed as group interventions. Combination of these procedures are often applied to attain group goals or resolve group interaction problems.

Role-played modeling and rehearsal are used to demonstrate new behaviors by leaders or members (modeling), and group members are asked to practice these behaviors (behavioral rehearsal). After a client agrees to try out a new behavior in the extragroup environment, either the therapist or another client demonstrates how the behavior must be performed with appropriate affect. Following one or more brief modeling sessions, the client performs the desired behavior. If it seems to be too difficult, another member will coach the client. These techniques plus group feedback are core activities of social skills training. Some clients are initially reluctant to role-play. But if role play is implemented in a supportive, nonthreatening atmosphere, the activity appears to eventually gain the cooperation of almost all members. Not only do clients who role-play gain increased comfort in the performance of the target behavior, but the cohesion of the group increases.

Group exercises refer to use of structured interactive activities as ways of teaching clients skills that mediate the achievement of therapeutic goals. Introductory exercises to gradually increase group self-disclosure and to enhance cohesion have already been mentioned, as have exercises in the use of positive and critical feedback to analyze problematic situations. Other group interventions include group feedback and use of subgroups to provide independent functioning within the group in order to enhance the breadth of participation.

RESEARCH BASIS

Extensive research on the effectiveness of behavior group therapy has documented the empirical basis of the strategy. Even though many studies do not capitalize on the unique strengths of groups, the group format is often used in research studies because of the efficiency it brings when administering a particular treatment. In general, studies show that certain types of problems are well suited to group therapy. In particular, research has found that problems that are of an interactional nature and problems that can be resistant to change are good candidates for group treatment.

RELEVANT TARGET POPULATIONS AND EXCEPTIONS

BGT has been used extensively with a very broad representation of problems, including depression, anxiety, anger control, parenting, marital difficulties, stress, social skills, assertiveness, grief and loss, obsessive-compulsive disorder, and many others. Its application is congruent with most of the types of problems that clients seek help for. It is best when used with problems that are social interactional in nature. It is not considered a treatment of choice for extremely severe problems.

COMPLICATIONS

Some common complications in the administration of group therapy include confidentiality, client resistance, and therapist ineffectiveness in the group treatment model. Groups do open up the possibility of an individual's privacy being violated when a group member shares something said by another member to a person outside the group. This is a serious issue, and the group therapist must go to great lengths to attempt to protect the privacy of all members involved in group treatment.

Some clients are resistant to being involved in group therapy because they feel uncomfortable sharing aspects of themselves with others. This is unfortunate, because often these are the very clients who could benefit from a group experience. Pregroup interviews are often helpful in preparing reluctant members for a group experience.

Group therapy is not a helpful model to treatment when the therapist conducts the group in a manner similar to individual therapy. When therapists see the dynamics and group processes as incidental or even antagonistic to the therapeutic process, then the benefit of doing group treatment is lost. An effective group therapist must be skilled in techniques and strategies that foster group interaction and shape group behavior and growth.

CASE ILLUSTRATION

The following example demonstrates how a group was used to help one client to formulate and achieve treatment goals in a group for adult men and women with anxiety disorders. The reader should note how group exercises were used to enhance participation and increase cohesion. Also, integration of cognitive and behavioral methods were integrated into the group approach. In the last part of the case, generalization planning with the help of the group is demonstrated.

After a brief overview of the approach, an introduction exercise was enacted (clients in pairs introduced each other and then introduced their partners to the group). A group exercise was then used to train people in the correct formulation of dealing with treatable events. In this exercise, the group analyzed an example of a situation (in terms of a brief background; who, when, where, and what happened; the critical moment; and the behavioral, affective, and cognitive response). After the case example, each client agreed to format a personal situation. "Edna," for example, came to the next session with the following example. As background to her situation, she explained she had trouble getting along with people who put her under stress. Such pressure made her extremely anxious and lowered her self-esteem. When asked by one of the other group members to give a recent example of "being put under stress," she described a situation that occurred at work. "Dave," her coworker, had ordered her to go back to the lab and get some materials that he had forgotten. Dave seemed to have no pressing reason why he could not do this himself (What happened?). This was the critical moment. Edna, who became internally both angry and anxious, nevertheless responded, "Oh sure, okay," and got the materials for him (behavioral response). Edna was annoyed and anxious (affective response) with her passivity. She described herself as a "weak pushover" (cognitive response). She also noted that this was how she usually handled such situations, especially with men (her general pattern). In further examining her thoughts, Edna revealed her desire to be "a nice and helpful person" and "to be liked" no matter what the level of imposition. The other clients, as part of the exercise, evaluated why these were distortions and then changed them into coping cognitions. In the ensuing discussion, other group members suggested that such demands by a colleague indeed represented imposition, and she had the right to refuse. The group, then, generated ideas how she might think in a way that better met her needs and how she might respond differently in that situation. Once she evaluated their ideas, she chose a set of responses with which she felt comfortable. She combined what she said ("No, I'm sorry, I have my own work to finish") with what she thought ("I have the right to refuse when I am clearly being imposed upon, and I don't need to be liked by everyone"). Several others in that session described similar situations, which, in turn, were analyzed by group members.

In a subsequent session, once the plan was developed, "Barry," serving as a model, volunteered to play the role of Edna in telling Dave, in a matter-of-fact tone of voice, that she too was busy and did not appreciate being told, rather than being asked, to be of help. In a stage whisper, Edna (Barry) reminded herself that it was her right to reject Dave's imposition. Another member role-played Dave. After modeling, the group therapist asked Edna if she was ready to do the role play as herself. The role play then was repeated (behavioral rehearsal), with Edna playing her own role, and at the request of the therapist, first, the group gave Edna feedback as to what she did well, and then feedback as to what she might consider doing differently. Edna repeated the role play and incorporated suggestions of the group. She decided that as an extragroup task, the next time anyone else attempted to impose upon her or unfairly put pressure on her, she would respond in a similar way and report back to the group at a subsequent session what happened. Several others in the group who had similar concerns with imposition or authoritarian coworkers also decided on carrying out similar extragroup tasks.

The group lends itself to the facilitation of generalization of change. In one of the later sessions, the principles of generalization were described. Then members designed a generalization plan for a case example. As an extragroup task, clients formulated generalization plans that they reported back to the group at later sessions.

For example, Edna agreed to report back to the group how she had handled experiences with people who imposed on her (using the principles of multiple trials and going public). She informed her friends that she was working on this task, in case they were asked to let her know whether she'd succeeded or failed (going public and ongoing monitoring). She also agreed with a partner in the group, "Rudy," to attend a booster open-treatment session in a month. The therapist made sure that Edna had varied role-playing experiences and extragroup tasks in the course of the group experiences (multiple and varied learning experiences). The therapist also taught members the principles of learning underlying interventions they would be employing. Each client designed a similar plan and shared it with the group.

SUMMARY

In this entry, the process of using behavioral and small-group strategies in the treatment of adults was described. How the group is employed in the process of assessment, intervention, and generalization planning was emphasized. Use of group procedures, especially of small-group exercises, as a means of facilitating the achievement of individual treatment goals and group goals was explained. A method to evaluate level of and achievement of goals in a post-session questionnaire was described. Finally, selections from a case study within the group were presented that exemplify a general approach to behavioral group therapy.

—*Sheldon D. Rose and Craig W. LeCroy*

See also: *Behavioral Family Therapy (Vol. II); Behavioral Marital Therapy (Vol. I); Coercive Cycles in Families (Vol. III)*

Suggested Readings

Bottomley, A., Hunton, S., Roberts, G., Jones, L., & Bradley, C. (1996). A pilot study of cognitive-behavioral therapy and social support group interventions with newly diagnosed cancer patients. *Journal of Psychosocial Oncology, 14,* 65–83.

Fals-Stewart, W., Marks, A. P., & Schafer, J. (1993). A comparison of behavioral group therapy and individual behavior therapy in treating obsessive-compulsive disorder. *The Journal of Nervous and Mental Disease, 181,* 189–193.

Rose, S. D. (1989). *Working with adults in groups.* San Francisco: Jossey-Bass.

Rose, S. D. (1998). *Group therapy with troubled youth: A cognitive-behavioral interactive approach.* Thousand Oaks, CA: Sage.

Telch, F., Agras, W., Rossiter, E., Wilfley, D. T., & Kenardy, J. (1990). Group cognitive-behavioral treatment for the nonpurging bulimic: An initial evaluation. *Journal of Consulting and Clinical Psychology, 58,* 629–635.

BEHAVIORAL MARITAL THERAPY

DESCRIPTION OF THE STRATEGY

Behavioral marital therapy (BMT) has generally been defined as the application of social learning theory and behavioral exchange principles to the treatment of marital distress. During the past decade, BMT has been expanded to include an analysis of cognitive and affective variables that influence or control couple behavior. Social learning theory posits that interpersonal behavior is determined by a combination of variables related to what happens in an individual's social environment and to one's cognitions and perceptions about these events. Accordingly, in regard to marital interaction and satisfaction, the social or interpersonal environment is a primary determinant. These theories suggest that behavior is a function of its antecedents and consequences and that the perceived quality of a relationship is primarily a function of the behaviors exchanged between partners. Therefore, interventions designed to promote rewarding (i.e., positively perceived) behaviors and to reduce or eliminate punishing (i.e., negatively perceived) behaviors would help improve partners' satisfaction with the marriage.

Since its inception in the late 1960s, BMT has incorporated a multimethod assessment approach to the conceptualization and treatment of distressed marriages, followed by interventions inspired primarily by the tenets of social learning theory.

BMT has a fairly distinct tradition of beginning the couple evaluation process by employing at least three different methods of gathering information to understand the problems and strengths of a given relationship and to plan various interventions to accomplish the therapeutic goals. First, there are a series of semi-structured clinical interviews, typically two to three sessions, which often include separate meetings with each partner as well as meeting the couple in a conjoint format. In general, the objectives of these so-called assessment interviews are to (a) screen clients for the appropriateness of couple therapy, (b) determine the nature and course of events related to partners' presenting complaints, (c) determine the goals and objectives of the partners for couple therapy, (d) establish an effective therapeutic relationship, and (e) orient the couple to the therapist's orientation and approach to treatment.

A second fairly unique assessment procedure used in BMT to gather diagnostic information about the couple is the administration of various questionnaires and inventories to learn about specific strengths and problem areas. The discussion of specific measures is beyond the scope of this entry. Suffice it to say that there exist several standardized measures that are designed to assess one or more of the following variables: global relationship satisfaction, communication skills and deficits, areas of change requested by the partners, types of conflict, intensity levels of conflict and styles of conflict resolution, partners' cognitions, expectations, and beliefs about the relationship that may be causing problems, sexual function and dissatisfaction, participation in pleasurable events and rewarding

social activities, and steps toward divorce. BMT practitioners typically ask the couple to complete a selected set of these instruments either before or at the very beginning of the evaluation process. Often, feedback and interpretation of the results are given to the couple regarding their responses.

The third assessment procedure that is routinely associated with the practice of BMT is observation and analysis of a sample of in vivo marital conflict interaction. That is, couples are helped to identify an existing issue about which disagree; they are asked to spend 10 to 15 minutes in the session talking together in a demonstration of how they go about attempting to resolve a conflict. The therapist may or may not leave the room to less obtrusively observe and/or to videotape the communication sample for later review and analysis. The conflict resolution communication sample provides unique and important information regarding the level of problem-solving skills the couple possesses to resolve relationship conflicts and the extent to which improvement in these processes will become treatment goals. The multimethod assessment procedures employed by BMT practitioners provide both converging and diverging types of information that are used in a systematic manner to conceptualize relationship dysfunction and relationship strengths and to formulate a treatment plan (i.e., interventions).

Traditional interventions associated with BMT have included communication and problem-solving skills training and behavioral exchange techniques. While "communication problems" is probably the number one complaint of couples seeking therapy and most therapy approaches work on improving communication between partners in some manner, the hallmark of BMT has been direct training in skill acquisition. Throughout the course of treatment, the therapist employs any number of the following types of interventions to help couples modify their patterns of miscommunication and to acquire improved problem-solving skills: didactic instruction, behavioral rehearsal, coaching and feedback about practicing the skills, videotape feedback, and regular homework assignments to support generalization of the new skills into the home environment. Typically, some variation of the universal problem-solving model is taught, which includes five remedial steps that are designed to modify the couple's maladaptive interaction patterns: agenda building, mutual definition of the problem, brainstorming, implementing the solution, and evaluation or modification of the initial plan.

Usually, concurrent with the communication and problem-solving interventions is the introduction of behavioral-exchange techniques. Emphasis is placed on helping partners to define and instigate increases in positive behaviors and to reduce negative behaviors that are exchanged by partners in their home environment. Using a "bank account" analogy, practitioners of BMT have helped distressed couples to reduce or eliminate what either partner might experience as "withdrawals" from the relationship bank account (e.g., criticisms, starting arguments, inconsiderate or disliked behaviors) and to make positive "deposits" into the relationship account (e.g., initiate quality activities together, increase caring behaviors or other behaviors that partners find pleasing). Over the course of couple therapy, a systematic approach is employed whereby at first, the easiest changes are made, followed by work on the more difficult areas of partner interaction and compatibility.

During the past decade in particular, many clinical investigators have developed models of couple therapy that have expanded the traditional BMT approach to incorporate the identification and modification of important cognitive and affective variables. That is, part of the communication and problem-solving training that is done during BMT may well include helping partners to recognize and alter certain maladaptive cognitions that interfere with the well-being of the relationship. Similarly, it is recognized that affective variables (i.e., feeling reactions) often developed over time within the individual partners may be playing important roles in causing or maintaining relationship distress. Primarily, within therapy sessions, partners can be helped to explore the origins of certain negative, disruptive, or intimacy-inhibiting feelings.

In summary, over three decades of development, BMT has offered a psychoeducational, behaviorally oriented approach to the assessment and treatment of couple distress that has been expanded to include interventions targeting maladaptive behaviors, cognitions, and affective variables and instigating positive changes in these modes of function for the betterment of the couple relationship.

RESEARCH BASIS

In a major review of the empirical literature on BMT in 1998, Donald Baucom and his associates indicated that more than two-dozen well-controlled studies have been performed evaluating the efficacy and effectiveness of BMT. BMT is the most widely evaluated form of marital treatment. For the past three decades, many direct studies and several meta-analytic investigations of multiple studies have confirmed that BMT, as an integrated approach, is a statistically and clinically efficacious treatment when compared with waiting-list control groups and nonspecific treatment or placebo control groups. In general, the research has not found the specific components of BMT (i.e., behavioral exchange vs. communication/problem-solving training) to be differentially effective, nor has BMT been demonstrably more or less effective than other marital therapy approaches to which it has been compared directly. In the past decade, the application of BMT in the treatment of couples where one partner suffers from alcoholism, drug abuse, or major depression has been found to be particularly effective for improving both the targeted disorder and for improving the marital relationship.

Regarding the impact of BMT on couples' lives, reviews of multiple studies have suggested that based on various relationship assessment scores obtained pre- and posttreatment, 56% to 66% of the couples treated with BMT improved significantly, and 35% to 54% reported that their levels of marital satisfaction changed from the clinically distressed to the nondistressed scoring ranges. Follow-up outcome data from these studies suggest that most couples maintain these gains for 6 months to a year, with some relapse indicated 2 to 4 years following treatment. Finally, given the limited data available, it appears that more than 90% of couples treated with BMT find the approach worthwhile and would recommend it to a friend in need; the couple dropout rate for couples entering BMT has been estimated at only 6%. In conclusion, in many empirical studies completed over 30 years of investigation, BMT has been shown to be a valid, efficacious, and effective treatment for marital distress.

RELEVANT TARGET POPULATIONS AND EXCEPTIONS

BMT is most appropriately considered when couple distress is the primary problem or when certain non-relationship factors have caused significant relationship distress and the couple, as a unit, desires and needs therapeutic attention. There are no known restrictions in the application of BMT to diverse ethnic, racial, national, age, gender, or socioeconomic groups. However, regarding couple-specific features,

BMT is thought to be most effective when the partners possess the abilities to collaborate toward mutual objectives of change, to offer support and accommodation to one another while addressing the problems at hand, and, when necessary, to compromise with one another toward resolving their defined problems. When these criteria are met, a combined emphasis on behavior exchange and communication/problem-solving interventions is quite effective. In comparison, because BMT is fundamentally change oriented, the approach may be less effective when the couple's level of relationship distress is very high, one or both partners' commitment to the marriage is low, the issues in conflict are unlikely to change, the couple is invested in maintaining traditional sex roles, or the partners are unable or unwilling to collaborate, accommodate, or compromise with one another. In these cases, while couple therapy may be indicated, an approach less focused on behavior change probably would be more effective.

In terms of exceptions, there are a number of situations for which couple therapy, in general, is not the treatment of choice, at least initially. If either partner's level of individual psychopathology is too severe to be managed or treated in conjoint therapy, alternative treatments should be considered (e.g., hospital inpatient milieu, individual or group psychotherapy, and/or pharmacotherapy). For example, BMT may be excluded, or at least postponed, in cases where either partner is experiencing an active psychosis, a disabling depressive disorder, severe anxiety, or active substance abuse. In addition, cases featuring domestic violence, especially including individuals with antisocial personality disorder, often are not appropriate for BMT. If and when individual problems are treated and improved at least to the point where a relationship focus is appropriate in therapy, then BMT may well be indicated as a concurrent or secondary approach.

COMPLICATIONS

There are few complications regarding the application of BMT, other than the possible exceptions noted above. For BMT to be most effective, however, the couple should be motivated to maintain and to improve their relationship in a change-oriented program. Partners who have other agendas, for example, to end the marriage, to coerce change in their partners without changing themselves, or to maintain the status quo, will find the direct and active BMT approach unhelpful.

CASE ILLUSTRATION

"John" and "Kathy" met about 5 years ago at a dog-training class and dated for 2 years before getting married. Kathy was enrolled in a marine science master's degree program and John was a wholesale food distributor in a large southern California city. During courtship and engagement, they enjoyed traveling, hiking and camping, good sex, and meeting to exercise their dogs. After Kathy graduated, they decided to get married and also to move to a less congested nearby city. Kathy got a good job, and John was attempting to open an expanded site for the distributorship. After 1 year, the couple was able to purchase a fixer-upper home. Over the next 2 years, several stressors affected them: (a) John's job relocation did not succeed, and he eventually quit out of frustration and despair, (b) Kathy's job became more stressful when the company downsized and workload increased, and (c) the couple, having left friends and family in the other city, found themselves socially isolated. When the couple sought marital therapy, their chief complaints emphasized an uncomfortable increase in marital conflict over the past few months. Kathy reported that John did not have a job and financial pressures were mounting. John countered that he was working on various home improvement projects and was planning, when the economy improved, to start his own business. Kathy complained about credit card debt, overreliance on her income, John's daily marijuana use, and that John's attention-deficit disorder (ADD) resulted in his lack of concentration on multiple tasks. John suggested that the couple's fighting episodes coincided with Kathy's menstrual cycle (i.e., PMS). The couple had not contemplated separation or divorce, but they were concerned about the direction and current quality of their relatively new marriage.

In addition to the clinical interviews, assessment inventories indicated continuing strengths in areas of sex and affection, contact and interaction with family and friends, enjoyment of home ownership, and recreational activities. Additional areas for improvement were managing money, communication and decision making, and division of daily chores. The couple provided a 10-minute sample of problem solving about money management in their second evaluation meeting. Observed strengths in communication included focus on the issue, mutual engagement and energy for the interaction, and basic respect for one another (i.e., no contempt, name-calling, or excessive blaming or defensiveness). On the other hand, the couple tended to repeat their respective positions without validation, resolution, or proposals for solution. Each one eventually became frustrated with the discussion and said that, at home, they would have disengaged or deteriorated into arguing and yelling.

John and Kathy were an ideal couple for application of BMT. Entering the process, they possessed good levels of commitment, caring, collaboration, and motivation for change. With their concurrence, the treatment plan included addressing their acknowledged individual issues: John's substance use and ADD and Kathy's PMS. The content issues to be resolved were job issues, money management, sharing household tasks, and socialization. The couple interaction processes to be improved were communication, decision making, and conflict resolution. After three assessment sessions, the couple agreed to eight additional treatment sessions.

Basically, the intervention process and outcomes went as follows: First, their individual problems were addressed. John had been diagnosed with mild-moderate ADD, was not taking medication, but had become lax in using some previously helpful organization and coping skills. Making lists, prioritizing and planning tasks by discussing them with Kathy, and doing fewer things to completion—all were reinstituted and reinforced. John's daily marijuana use was determined to be excessive and related to encouragement from an unemployed neighbor and to his anxiety about work and finances. He agreed to cut back to occasional social use of marijuana. Finally, Kathy's PMS symptoms of irritability and emotional sensitivity had increased since she had gone off the pill to become pregnant. She agreed to consult her physician, institute a previously helpful exercise program, and the couple developed some interactional coping skills to practice during that time of her monthly cycle.

Second, the early sessions were also designed to further strengthen caring behaviors (i.e., individual and mutually rewarding behaviors) and to engage the couple in communication and problem-solving skills training. They learned to increase empathic communication and to reduce conflicts by employing time-outs and a systematic problem-solving model. As these process skills were acquired, the various content areas were addressed and behavioral changes negotiated.

For example, rather than debate money management from positions of frustration and ignorance, they agreed to consult a finance expert regarding things such as consolidating credit card loans into a home equity loan, developing a plan to start a small business, and planning for the baby that they were attempting to conceive. Similarly, given the strengthened caring, communication, and problem-solving behaviors, they were able to negotiate a revised household chores system, develop a plan to organize and finish several home improvement projects, and make a plan to develop local friendships by joining dog-training and -playing groups. Fortunately for this couple, there were no seriously negative character features, deep-seated resentments, mental or physical disorders, or unrelenting substance abuse issues. They terminated therapy successfully after three assessment sessions, seven weekly intervention sessions, and one final follow-up meeting after a break of 6 weeks. Improvements were noted in most of the areas targeted, although, largely due to the struggling economy, John still had not achieved full-time employment. However, Kathy was pregnant, and the couple seemed excited about this event and determined to reach their goals.

—*Gary R. Birchler and William Fals-Stewart*

See also: *Behavioral Family Therapy (Vol. II); Behavioral Group Work (Vol. I); Coercive Cycles in Families (Vol. III)*

Suggested Readings

Baucom, D. H., Shoham, V., Mueser, K. T., Daiuto, A. D., & Stickle, T. R. (1998). Empirically supported couple and family interventions for marital distress and adult mental health problems. *Journal of Consulting and Clinical Psychology, 66,* 53–88.

Birchler, G. R., Fals-Stewart, W., & Magana, C. (2003). Marital dyads. In M. Hersen & S. M. Turner (Eds.), *Diagnostic interviewing* (3rd ed.). New York: Kluwer/Plenum.

Epstein, N. B., & Baucom, D. H. (2002). *Enhanced cognitive-behavioral therapy for couples: A contextual approach.* Washington, DC: APA Books.

Gottman, J. M. (1999). *The marriage clinic: A scientifically based marital therapy.* New York: Norton.

Jacobson, N. S., & Margolin, G. (1979). *Marital therapy: Strategies based on social learning and behavior exchange principles.* New York: Brunner/Mazel.

Notarius, C., & Markman, H. (1993). *We can work it out: Making sense of marital conflict.* New York: Putnam.

Stuart, R. B. (1980). *Helping couples change.* New York: Guilford Press.

BEHAVIORAL MEDICINE

DESCRIPTION OF THE STRATEGY

Behavioral medicine is a term that first arose in the 1960s from the ashes of the psychosomatic medicine and liaison psychiatry movements. Psychosomatic medicine and liaison psychiatry involved the application of Freudian or psychodynamic principles (i.e., psychological forces that interact within an individual and are outside of conscious awareness) to traditionally medical problems. Similarly, behavioral medicine is the application of learning theory principles (i.e., focus on overt, observable behaviors) to traditional medical disorders, such as pain, obesity, and diabetes. The influential Yale Conference on Behavioral Medicine defined behavioral medicine as "the field concerned with the development of behavioral science knowledge and techniques relevant to the understanding of physical health and illness and the application of this knowledge and these techniques to prevention, diagnosis, treatment and rehabilitation." It is our belief that in order to fully understand behavioral medicine, it is essential that the reader have a basic understanding of learning theory.

There are two basic types of learning, classical and operant conditioning, with the crucial thread that holds both together being the belief that behavior is lawful and observable and follows the rules of science. Classical conditioning is also referred to as "Pavlovian conditioning," after the seminal work of the Russian scientist Pavlov in the early 20th century. Classical conditioning can be demonstrated by pairing a neutral stimulus (a conditioned stimulus, CS) in close temporal proximity with another stimulus (an unconditioned stimulus, UCS) that already elicits the desired response (the unconditioned response, UCR). In subsequent presentations of the CS, the organism will emit a new response (the conditioned response, CR) in anticipation of the UCS. For example, the UCS might be food, which elicits the UCR of salivation. The CS, the ringing of a bell, for example, is presented immediately prior to the food UCS. After repeated pairing of the ringing bell with food, the organism will come to salivate in response to the ringing bell.

Operant conditioning postulates that the consequence of a response changes the likelihood that the organism will produce that response in the future. The operant conditioning paradigm is the one most often used in behavioral medicine today. A basic proposition of operant conditioning is that if you wish a behavior to continue or increase in frequency, you reinforce (reward) that behavior. If you wish a behavior to decrease or to stop completely, you do not reinforce that behavior. Thus, within the theoretical framework of operant conditioning, the main way that you strengthen a behavior is to follow it in close temporal proximity with a reinforcer. A reinforcer is any stimulus that occurs following a response that tends to increase the likelihood that the response will be repeated. It is important that the reinforcer follow the desired behavior quickly, such that its presentation is kept to an optimally short delay. As the delay in the reinforcer increases, its effectiveness is generally decreased.

An important procedure in operant conditioning is that of *shaping*. Shaping refers to the learning process by which a predefined target response is achieved through gradual and systematic reinforcement. The shaping process begins with a simple, existing response and lax criteria for reinforcement and gradually moves to more stringent reinforcement criteria in order to achieve more complex responses. After a simple initial response is reliably performed, reinforcement is given contingent on the performance of more complex or difficult responses. This pattern of increasingly stringent contingent reinforcement continues until the final target response is achieved.

Other operant conditioning principles are used in behavioral medicine applications. One of these involves discrimination training, in which the organism demonstrates the ability to differentiate between at least two stimulus conditions by emitting a different response to each stimulus. Another important principle is the concept of generalization: If a response is learned to one stimulus, the organism may also respond to similar stimuli (generalization) but not to a dissimilar stimulus (discrimination).

A BRIEF HISTORY OF BEHAVIORAL MEDICINE

In this section, we give a brief history of behavioral medicine and explain why alternative approaches to traditional medical problems are needed. Behavioral medicine is often subsumed under the general rubric of complementary-alternative medicine (CAM). CAM techniques generally avoid the mind-body dualism of most Western medicine; that is, the belief that the mind and the body function separately, without interchange between the two systems. Behavioral medicine treatments, particularly biofeedback (see below), very explicitly and in a scientific manner demonstrate the interconnectedness between mind and body, showing how mental activity can affect physiological activity and behavior, and vice versa.

Recent years have seen rapid growth in an integrated, holistic approach to health and illness. *Holism,* which dates back to early Greek philosophers such as Plato and Aristotle, refers to a conception of man and nature, viewing the mind and body as an indivisible whole, requiring the study of the entire person rather than isolated parts. It is now well-known that what happens in our minds—our thoughts, feelings, and moods—has a dramatic effect on the onset of many forms of illness and the course of most.

A number of events came together to create the field of behavioral medicine. The first set of events was the application in the late 1960s by some behavior therapists of operant learning theory to the addictions and other traditionally medical problems such as obesity and smoking. The reliability of the interventions allowed growing acceptance by the more biologically but empirically oriented general medicine community.

A second event was the birth of the field of biofeedback in the late 1960s and early 1970s (see below), which led to the development of a technology for reliably changing physiological responses through operant conditioning techniques. Biofeedback was quickly applied to traditionally medical problems, especially the so-called psychophysiological or psychogenic disorders, such as pain. More important, biofeedback was an empirically based and very reliable intervention that appealed to the more empirically based medical community.

A third event was the influential 1977 Yale Conference on Behavioral Medicine. This conference gathered scientists from a diverse number of fields, including psychology, psychiatry, anthropology, sociology and medicine, and it arrived at the definition of the term behavioral medicine given in the first section of this article, which was later refined to emphasize the interdisciplinary aspects of the field and the integration of behavioral and biomedical science.

A fourth event was publication in 1982 of the influential *Journal of Consulting and Clinical Psychology*'s special issue on behavioral medicine, edited by Edward Blanchard. This issue contained a comprehensive overview of the current research and, more important, a number of seminal articles that redefined the field. This issue was considered such a pivotal and important event that it has been updated every 10 years.

A fifth reason that behavioral medicine approaches are increasingly used is the changing nature of the treated illnesses. Modern, mechanistic-based medicine is very effective in dealing with acute illnesses such as infections and accidents. However, modern medicine often fails with chronic illnesses, many of which are influenced by lifestyle choices and are strongly affected by psychological and behavioral factors. It is estimated that as many as 80% of primary care visits are for problems that involve lifestyle and psychological factors.

A final reason for the growth of behavioral medicine treatments is the emphasis on prevention and cost containment in modern health care. Psychological interventions in traditional medical realms have increased at an exponential rate in the past quarter century and have proven effective with a variety of illnesses, such as chronic headache, arthritis, low back pain, irritable bowel syndrome, hypertension, and so on. Today, research points to the targeted use of educational, behavioral, psychophysiological, and psychological interventions in a medical setting as simple, safe, and relatively inexpensive treatments that can dramatically improve health outcomes and reduce the need for more expensive medical approaches.

TREATMENTS

Biofeedback

Biofeedback is especially important to behavioral medicine because it bridges the gap between holistic medicine and traditional medicine in that it combines the scientific rigor of objective outcome and assessment of modern medicine and learning theory with the mind-body integration of holistic approaches. As such, we will spend more time with this intervention than any other.

Biofeedback is a biopsychosocial technique that has been in existence since the seminal work of Neil Miller in the 1960s. The most concise definition of *biofeedback* is probably that of Olton and Noonberg, who characterized it as "any technique which increases the ability of a person to control voluntarily physiological activities by providing information about those activities." In reality, the process of clinical biofeedback training generally involves use of a machine, usually a computer these days, that allows a therapist to monitor the patient's bodily responses (generally surface muscle tension or surface skin temperature, the latter of which is an indicator of sympathetic nervous system arousal and peripheral blood flow). Information concerning the patient's physiological responses are then relayed back to the patient, generally either through an auditory modality (a tone that goes higher or lower depending on, say, muscle tension going higher or lower) and/or a visual modality (now usually a computer screen, where, for example, surface skin temperature is graphed on a second-by-second basis during each minute). Through this physiological feedback, it is hoped that a patient will be able to learn how to control his or her bodily responses through mental means.

Biofeedback has been used quite successfully for chronic pain disorders, especially headaches, anxiety and stress reduction, insomnia, hypertension, urinary and fecal incontinence, and other medical disorders. There are two general theories underlying the use of biofeedback for most chronic benign medical disorders. The first is a direct psychophysiological theory, which attributes the etiology and/or maintenance of the disorder to specific physiological pathology, which biofeedback training modulates in a therapeutic direction. For example, it has traditionally been assumed that tension headache is caused by sustained contraction of skeletal muscles in the forehead, neck, and shoulder regions. Through the use of biofeedback, the patient learns to decrease muscle tension levels, leading to a decrease in headache activity. The second theory is predominantly psychological and postulates that there is a relationship between situational stress and the disorder in question. Through the use of biofeedback, the patient learns to regulate physiological responses such as muscle tension levels or sympathetic nervous system activity, leading to a decrease in overall stress levels, which brings about symptomatic relief. It is not necessary to view these theories as competing; they may be more appropriately viewed as complementary. Most clinicians subscribe to both theories, depending upon the patient's presenting problem, clinical findings, and medical history.

Cognitive-Behavioral Therapy and Behavior Therapy Interventions

Cognitive-behavioral therapies are based on the assumption that an individual's thoughts, emotions, behaviors, and physiology can influence each other.

For example, in pain treatment, cognitive-behavioral interventions generally involve identifying thoughts, emotions, and behaviors that routinely precede or exacerbate pain, with the therapist subsequently teaching patients in a systematic manner to modify these thoughts, feelings, and behaviors.

The most important tool of the cognitive-behavioral therapist is the symptom diary. In cognitive-behavioral procedures, however, the symptom diary is used to monitor more than just the target symptom. For example, in pain treatment, in addition to monitoring pain, the therapist frequently has the patient monitor emotions, behaviors, and cognitive activity such as thoughts or self-statements that occur prior to severe pain or to an emotional event such as anxiety or depression. Patients are then informed that what they think about a situation determines the stressfulness of the situation and that they can learn to control their pain by learning mental strategies for the control of stress. The job of the therapist is to assist the patient to identify unreasonable expectations or beliefs, emotional states, or behaviors that may explain their bodily responses to a variety of stressful situations.

For example, the patient may believe that he or she must be loved by everyone. When experiencing a situation that is interpreted as not supporting this core belief, the patient becomes depressed, which can lead to increases in pain. The therapist aids the patient in examining the logical validity and behavioral and emotional consequences of continuing to hold these maladaptive expectancies and beliefs. Patients are taught to identify these maladaptive cognitions or beliefs in the real world as soon as possible, so as to interrupt the chain of maladaptive thoughts. They are then given coping strategies to implement to counteract the maladaptive thoughts. Typically, these involve reappraisal of the actual risks and consequences of the situation, self-instructions designed at counteracting the specific maladaptive beliefs or thoughts (e.g., "I don't have to be loved by everyone to be a good person"), and biofeedback-assisted relaxation or relaxing imagery (see below) designed to counteract generalized worries and anxiety when there are no immediate or specific performance demands.

Behavior therapy interventions are similar to cognitive-behavioral approaches but focus on events more observable than emotions or self-statements. For example, a behavior therapist will focus primarily on behavior and its effect on the symptoms being treated. Typical behavior therapy approaches for pain are to teach patients how to pace their activities better, how to decrease their pain-related behaviors by not talking about or paying excessive attention to the pain, having others not reinforce the pain (i.e., give attention/sympathy, excuse patients from activities, etc.), decrease secondary gains, and so on.

Relaxation Therapy

Relaxation therapy is a systematic approach to teaching people to gain awareness of their physiological responses and achieve both a cognitive and physiological sense of tranquility without the use of the machinery employed in biofeedback. There are various forms of relaxation therapy. The major types, however, are progressive muscle relaxation therapy, meditation, autogenic training, breathing techniques, meditation, and guided imagery. By far, the most widely used relaxation procedures for headaches are variants of Jacobsonian progressive muscle relaxation therapy and guided imagery, and we will briefly review those procedures now.

Progressive muscle relaxation therapy (or PMRT) has been in existence since the 1920s. It is often called "relaxing through tension release exercises." It is based on the principle that when individuals tense and then release various muscle groups of the body, they will learn to discriminate between a tense state and a relaxed state, as well as the various levels of muscle tension. It is also based on the principle that when you tense and relax muscles of the body, you are in essence forcing the muscles to relax (i.e., go lower than the original baseline muscle tension), but the evidence supporting this assertion is scant. Generally, patients are taught to tense and then release anywhere from 18 to 8 muscle groups initially (holding the tension for 5 to 10 seconds), and then in subsequent sessions, the number of muscle groups is reduced. Finally, to make the PMRT an active coping skill that is portable and applicable in real-world situations, a new type of relaxation, termed *relaxation-by-recall,* is introduced. This type of relaxation, which is built on PMRT, has patients relax by recalling what it was like when their muscles were tense and they let them go. Thus, patients no longer have to tense their muscles, and because relaxation-by-recall is unobtrusive, they can generalize PMRT to everyday situations.

Relaxing, or guided, imagery, with the exception of prayer, is perhaps the oldest of all relaxation techniques. It has been used in the various forms of yoga and Zen meditation to supplement other approaches to relaxation. Just as in ancient times, pleasant nature scenes are the most commonly used subjects for adults in guided imagery today.

The earliest example of imagery being applied in modern times is that of Chappell and Stevenson. Peptic ulcer patients were taught in a group format to use relaxing imagery scenes to counteract anxiety that was assumed to exacerbate their ulcers. At a 3-year follow up, 26 of 28 subjects were still markedly improved, whereas subjects in an untreated control group continued to suffer from ulcers. These days, however, imagery is nearly always combined with other relaxation strategies.

The theoretical logic behind relaxing or guided imagery in the treatment of most medical disorders is straightforward: Through imagining a relaxing scene, one will be able to achieve a state of both mental and physical relaxation that is similar to what the patient would feel if actually experiencing the relaxing event, which would consequently lead to reduction in, for example, pain. If one is imagining an image that has previously been experienced, then relaxing imagery is quite similar to relaxation by recall procedures (i.e., recalling what it was like when your mind and body were calm and relaxed).

Relaxing imagery has one obvious pitfall: Some individuals are simply poor imaginers and may get very discouraged because they are unable to imagine the pleasant scene at all, even after repeated practice. If this happens, clearly the therapist should discontinue the guided imagery and switch to another relaxation technique.

Hypnosis

Hypnosis is a procedure that has been in use since Mesmer in the late 1700s and involves a clinician suggesting that a patient will experience changes in sensations, perceptions, thoughts, and behaviors. After an induction, which typically involves relaxation procedures, the hypnotic suggestions are given. In our opinion, hypnosis has three challenges to overcome. First, not everyone is suggestible and able to enter a deep hypnotic trance. Second, many people come to the therapy session with preconceived attitudes about hypnosis. Sometimes their beliefs are positive, and they are certain that hypnosis can "cure" their problem. However, often people's attitudes concerning hypnosis are negative. Some believe it to be bogus or that they will be under the control of the hypnotist and forced to do things they do not wish to do. Some individuals have religious objections to hypnosis. Finally, hypnosis is rarely used as a sole treatment; rather, it is used as an adjunct to treatment (usually cognitive behavior therapy).

Exercise

Exercise has been touted as a cure for mankind's ills since the beginning of recorded history. Recent empirical research has validated the age-old belief that exercise can significantly increase one's life span and can reduce or prevent a number of illnesses, including chronic pain, diabetes, cardiovascular disease, breast cancer, colon (but not rectal) cancer, hypertension, and obesity. Despite the growing recognition of the utility of moderate to vigorous physical activity in promoting health (and recommendations by the Surgeon General, the American Heart Association, the Centers for Disease Control and Prevention, the American College of Sports Medicine, and other organizations), Americans have been exercising less and clearly getting more obese. Recent research in exercise has stressed exercising in home, occupational, and community sessions. As exercise regimes vary depending on a number of factors, including age of the patient, physical condition, and type of disorder, it is best to individualize the treatment plan. For non-physician providers, it is our strong recommendation to always get the advice and approval of the patient's primary care physician.

CLINICAL USES OF BEHAVIORAL MEDICINE INTERVENTIONS

Stress Reduction

All of the treatments described above have been used for general stress and anxiety reduction, although relaxation therapy and cognitive-behavioral therapy approaches are probably the most commonly used procedures for stress reduction today. Nearly all the research has demonstrated that behavioral medicine techniques are superior to placebo and wait-list controls for the treatment of stress and anxiety. When the various techniques have been compared, which has unfortunately been quite rare, there is generally no difference between the various treatments in terms of their clinical efficacy, with one exception. It does appear that cognitive-behavioral therapy is superior to

relaxation therapy alone for the treatment of generalized anxiety disorder. It should be noted, however, that nearly all frontline clinicians combine cognitive behavior therapy with one or more of the other interventions.

Pain Reduction

When the average primary care physician is asked to name the one area where behavioral medicine techniques have proved their worth, we are certain that most would immediately say pain relief. Reviews of the literature would indicate that this is indeed the case. Because of the importance of pain reduction in the development of behavioral medicine as a field, we shall place more emphasis in this area than in others.

Headache

Benign headache (HA) disorders (that is, HAs that do not arise from identifiable structural causes; the most common are tension-type HA, migraine HA, co-occurring migraine and tension-type HAs, and cluster HA) are perhaps the most commonly occurring pain problems in the United States, leading to millions of lost work days and billion of dollars of treatment expense, including huge sales of over-the-counter analgesics.

There are three well-established, well-researched psychological approaches to the treatment of headache: (1) relaxation training, primarily PMRT and to a lesser degree autogenic training; (2) biofeedback training; and (3) aspects of cognitive-behavioral therapies, especially those that emphasize learning to cope with everyday stressful events. The empirical evidence from randomized clinical trials (RCT) supporting these treatments is fairly large and includes recent direct comparisons of prescription medications to psychological treatment.

Although much of the research has tended to use one or more of the above treatments in relative isolation in order to identify the likely agent of change, the practicing clinician might well use a thoughtful blend of the procedures. It is also a testament to the utility of these treatments that they are routinely available as part of the treatment armamentarium in comprehensive headache specialty clinics.

All three of the treatment approaches (relaxation, biofeedback, and cognitive therapy) have been demonstrated to be individually efficacious with tension-type headache. There is ample evidence that relaxation training, especially as a part of regular between-treatment session homework, adds to the overall efficacy of biofeedback therapy. We should add that the standard form of biofeedback for tension-type headache is electromyographic biofeedback (EMG), with sensors placed either on the forehead (thus detecting muscle activity over the entire face and head) or on the upper back and neck (usually targeting the trapezius muscle). Cognitive therapy, especially as it focuses on helping the patient become aware of daily stresses and then finding new ways to cope with them, is very helpful and usually adds to the effects one can achieve with relaxation alone or EMG biofeedback alone. Although we are unaware of any RCTs evaluating a combination of all three approaches, such a combination would be common in clinical practice.

For the treatment of vascular HA, either migraine HA alone or the poor unfortunate with both migraine and tension-type HA, the most consistent results have been found with a combination of thermal biofeedback (aimed at hand warming) and relaxation training. The latter may well include both PMRT and autogenic training. The combination seems to consistently help a larger proportion of patients than either treatment alone. This effect is more pronounced for patients who suffer from both migraine HA and tension-type HA. Cognitive therapy may add to overall outcome of thermal biofeedback/relaxation combination with the individual HA sufferer. RCTs have not shown a consistent advantage of adding cognitive therapy to the biofeedback/relaxation combination for vascular HA. Cognitive therapy alone is not recommended for vascular HA.

With cluster HA, a distinctly different vascular HA marked by bouts of frequent, relatively brief, extremely intense HAs, there is little data to support the use of strictly psychological treatments.

Lower-Back Pain

A recent review of biofeedback literature for low-back pain concluded that biofeedback appears to hold promise as a clinically useful technique in the treatment of patients with back pain. While the evidence indicates that optimal clinical improvement is clearly obtained when biofeedback is used within the context of a comprehensive, multidisciplinary pain management program, the cumulative weight of the evidence suggests that EMG biofeedback is likely to be helpful, as a single therapy, in the treatment of musculoskeletal low-back pain, obtaining success rates of from 35% to 68% improvement on follow-up.

However, there were many concerns about the literature. Only two studies have directly compared biofeedback to relaxation therapy, and both of these studies were significantly flawed so as to limit definitive conclusions. Direct comparisons of biofeedback to relaxation therapy are clearly needed. Longer (at least 1 year) and larger-scale (at least 50 per group) follow-up studies are required. Evaluations of treatments based on diagnosis (i.e., the cause of the pain) should be conducted. Comparisons of various biofeedback treatment procedures are necessary, such as paraspinal versus frontal electrode placement or training while supine versus training while standing. Finally, further evaluations of patient characteristics predictive of outcome are needed, such as gender, race, chronicity, psychopathology, and psychophysiological reactivity.

Although some type of relaxation therapy is employed in nearly every multidisciplinary pain treatment program, studies that have investigated the unique contributions of relaxation to low-back-pain reduction have been sparse. A review of the literature produced only 14 such studies. Sadly, the relaxation therapy literature for lower-back pain is as methodologically flawed as the biofeedback literature: Only half of the studies reviewed had 10 or more subjects per group, contained any kind of control group comparison, or provided enough information to replicate the relaxation procedures. More important, 10 out of the 14 referenced studies did not include the low-back-pain diagnosis. Overall averaged percentage of improvement for relaxation training for low back pain was 37%, although there was a wide range—from 0 to 100%. Relaxation is generally found to be superior to placebo or wait-list controls, but there is inconclusive evidence supporting the effectiveness of relaxation compared with other behavioral medicine strategies.

Exercise, hypnosis, and cognitive-behavioral therapy techniques have also been used in the treatment of low-back pain. Reviews of the exercise literature, however, demonstrate that nearly all of the studies are confounded by the inclusion of other treatments and have found inconclusive results for the utility of exercise in lower-back pain. There is sparse literature on hypnosis for the treatment of low-back pain, and those few studies are contradictory. There is more evidence for the effectiveness of cognitive-behavioral strategies, but here again, studies are usually confounded by the inclusion of other therapies, especially relaxation.

Myofascial Pain Dysfunction Syndrome

Myofascial pain dysfunction (MPD) syndrome, also known as temporomandibular joint (TMJ) syndrome, is considered a subtype of craniomandibular dysfunction that is caused by hyperactivity of the masticatory muscles. It is characterized by diffuse pain in the muscles of mastication, mastication muscle tenderness, and joint sounds and limitations. Although disagreement exists as to the cause of the hyperactivity (e.g., occlusal problems vs. psychological stress), several researchers have examined the use of relaxation therapy and, especially, EMG biofeedback as treatments, which can provide relief by teaching patients to relax the muscles of the jaw.

Although the majority of the studies have significant limitations, when taken as a whole, they appear to be quite impressive in support of the efficacy of EMG biofeedback and, to a lesser extent, relaxation therapy for MPD syndrome. Most studies find relaxation and biofeedback to be significantly better than no treatment. When relaxation therapy and biofeedback are compared, most studies found no difference between the two procedures. Studies that have combined biofeedback or relaxation therapy with other treatments have found tendencies for the combined treatment to be superior to biofeedback or relaxation alone. Studies that have compared biofeedback or relaxation therapy to more traditional medical procedures, such as occlusal splints, have found the behavioral medicine techniques to be equal or superior to the traditional medical intervention.

Obesity

Obesity is an epidemic in the United States, with estimates that up to 65% of American adults are overweight or obese. Behavioral medicine techniques have led to significant increases in our understanding of the etiology, maintenance, treatment, and prevention of obesity. Obesity can lead to significant decreases in life expectancy; increase the likelihood of getting diseases such as diabetes, hypertension, cardiovascular disease, and colon cancer; and greatly exacerbate other diseases, such as sleep apnea, pain (especially osteoarthritis, lower-back, knee, and neck pain), gastroesophogeal reflux disorder (GERD), and gallbladder disease, as well as many pulmonary diseases.

Behavioral medicine research has been responsible for probably the most important advance in obesity research: the change in treatment goal from getting an individual down to an deal weight to having an individual achieve a healthier weight. Weight losses in the significantly overweight of only 5% to 15% of initial weight are more realistic, as they are easier to maintain and they can frequently lead to significant decreases in the health complications of obesity, including hypertension, diabetes, and cardiovascular disease.

Traditional behavioral approaches to weight control (i.e., decrease portion size, carefully monitor food intake using a food diary, slow down the eating process, etc.) are usually combined with other interventions, including exercise, pharmacotherapy, and surgical interventions. Much remains to be discovered, however, in the search for optimal weight loss strategies, especially examining cultural differences (there is a paucity of research on African Americans, although African Americans are obese at a greater incidence than Caucasians), how to maintain and generalize weight loss, and the effects of weight loss programs through various modalities such as workplace, community (churches, political clubs, etc.), and the Internet.

Smoking Cessation

Tobacco is the number-one preventable cause of death in the United States today. Decrease in smoking rates is one of the most important achievements in the United States in the latter half of the 20th century. On average, rates have gone down in a linear fashion since the Surgeon General's 1964 "Report on Smoking and Health." For example, smoking prevalence among men has fallen from 52% in 1965 to 25.5% in 2001. However, about 23% of adults in the United States still smoke, and this population is quite refractory to intervention. Factors that contribute to the refractoriness of the smoking population are psychiatric comorbidity (such as depression, substance abuse, and schizophrenia), education levels (individuals who did not complete high school have a 3-times-greater risk than those who have graduated college), poverty, motivation level, and amount of nicotine dependence.

The overwhelming majority of tobacco users stop on their own without any intervention. Individual treatment sessions are generally effective but suffer from a number of problems, including high dropout rates, lack of insurance reimbursement, and generally high costs. More important, very few people use individual treatment sessions as a way to stop smoking. Again, research has focused on alternatives to individual sessions, including work site and community-based programs and primary care provider interventions.

Primary care provider intervention would appear to be a very effective way of intervening, as most individuals who quit state that that their physicians' advice strongly influenced them to stop smoking. However, one study found that less than half of all smokers were advised by their physicians in the previous year to quit smoking. One solution may be computer-based clinical reminders. For example, the Department of Veterans Affairs Medical Centers have recently implemented a computer-based alert that requires primary care physicians and staff to inquire about smoking and to offer smoking cessation treatment if the patient is willing to try to stop.

Urinary and Fecal Incontinence

Urinary and fecal incontinence are significant problems in the United States, with over 14 million adults suffering from one or both and more than half of all residents in nursing homes being incontinent. Incontinence is the second leading cause of individuals being placed in nursing care facilities (with the various forms of dementia being the primary cause). Some have estimated the direct costs of incontinence in the United States to be over $50 billion annually. The indirect costs, including the embarrassment, depression, and social isolation caused by both types of incontinence, are impossible to quantify. Thus, incontinence is a significant health problem in the United States today and warrants further research.

Two behavioral techniques, relaxation therapy and EMG biofeedback, have been used to treat urinary and fecal incontinence. Relaxation and strengthening techniques in the form of Kegel pelvic floor muscle exercises have been widely used since the 1940s for urinary incontinence. EMG biofeedback, aimed primarily at reinforcing pelvic floor muscle contractions, has been shown to significantly reduce frequency of urinary incontinence episodes. In the most elegant study to date, 197 women aged 55 to 92 were randomly assigned to a biofeedback treatment, medication, or placebo group. Subjects were given four sessions of EMG biofeedback over an 8-week period. Mean reduction of incontinence episodes were 81% for the biofeedback group, 69% for the drug group, and 39% for the placebo condition. More important, only 14% of

subjects receiving the biofeedback treatment wanted to change to another treatment at the study's end, versus more than 75% in each of the other groups.

Evidence supporting effectiveness of behavioral treatments for fecal incontinence is certainly not as strong as that of urinary incontinence, with conflicting results. It is clear, however, that most of the treatment literature and the standard texts and review articles emphasize the importance of behavioral strategies in the treatment CBT of fecal incontinence, despite the paucity of adequate outcome studies.

Irritable Bowel Syndrome

Irritable bowel syndrome (IBS) is a functional disorder of the lower gastrointestinal (GI) tract characterized by moderate to severe abdominal pain and cramping and altered bowel habits (diarrhea, constipation, or alternating diarrhea and constipation). It affects more than 10% of adult Americans and is a major cause of lost workdays and medical care costs. At present, there are no universally, well-accepted pharmacological treatments for IBS. Antidepressants are sometimes helpful.

There is a reasonable body of research (RCTs) supporting each of the three different psychological approaches to the treatment of IBS: (1) hypnotherapy, (2) brief psychodynamic psychotherapy, and (3) various combinations of cognitive and behavioral treatment procedures. Hypnotherapy focuses on helping the patient to gain control of bowel motility as well as relax. Long-term follow-up shows good maintenance of symptom reduction.

Brief psychodynamic psychotherapy has been shown in three separate RCTs to be of significant benefit in reducing pain and other GI symptoms. Results have been documented to hold up well for a year after treatment. Sometimes a relaxation home practice tape is added to the psychotherapy.

Although there are many more RCTs evaluating various cognitive and behavioral treatment procedures, until recently, most of the trials were relatively small. The typical CBT treatment includes relaxation training, education about normal bowel functioning, and some elements of cognitive therapy, either teaching individuals to recognize stressors and alter the way they think about them and subsequently deal with them or adding more cognitive restructuring and work on cognitive schemas (in the fashion of A. T. Beck's work with depression). Sometimes assertiveness training is added to the mix.

For the most part, these CBT combinations are superior to symptom monitoring. Positive results have been shown to endure up for up to 4-years posttreatment.

There is some evidence that a relatively pure relaxation training alone is efficacious (2 RCTs, one with PMRT and one with meditation). Moreover, the strongest and most consistent results from the authors' laboratories have been with purely cognitively therapy. Three separate small-sale RCTs have shown cognitive therapy alone to lead to clinically significant improvement in 60% to 80% of IBS patients.

At this point, there have been no head-to-head comparisons of these three approaches. There is evidence that they work as well as antidepressants and constitute a viable nondrug alternative.

Insomnia

Primary insomnia (i.e., insomnia believed to be of psychological etiology) is the most common sleep complaint, exceeding by far early-morning awakening and night terrors. Secondary insomnia (that is, insomnia caused by a physical or mental condition) is also quite common. About 12% of adults and 20% of elderly people suffer from chronic insomnia (that is, insomnia of more than 6 months' duration), and women are about twice as likely as men to be insomniacs. Estimates are that in 1999, insomnia's direct medical costs were $14 billion in the United States alone.

Behavioral approaches to primary insomnia have been in use for decades, with most studies finding improvement in self-reported sleep. The major types of behavioral medicine treatments include behavioral strategies such as sleep compression (i.e., restricting sleep to only a few hours in at bedtime); stimulus control (i.e., conducting a sleep ritual before bed, restricting reading, eating, and watching TV in bed, etc.); time-in-bed restrictions (i.e., if one cannot get to sleep in 30 minutes, leave the bedroom and engage in other activities for a specified period of time); progressive relaxation therapy; and cognitive-behavioral therapy (a catchall category that is a combination of relaxation therapy, behavioral therapy, psychoeducation, and therapy aimed at altering dysfunctional attitudes and beliefs about sleep). There is good evidence to suggest that all three treatments reduce latency to sleep onset to under 30 minutes (the standard definition of insomnia is a sleep onset of greater than 30 minutes) in over 70% of patients. Whether objective sleep (i.e., sleep improvement demonstrated by polysomnography data collected during a laboratory sleep study) is improved is in doubt. In most studies, however, sleep duration is also improved by about 30 minutes, and self-reported satisfaction scores are significantly improved by behavioral medicine treatments. There is no evidence yet to support the belief that behavioral treatments lead to meaningful improvement in daytime functioning.

Other behavioral treatments commonly used are paradoxical intention (the patient is told to remain passively awake and give up all efforts to fall asleep), biofeedback, and exercise. There are few studies that have examined the effectiveness of behavioral treatments for secondary insomnia. However, the available evidence does suggest that cognitive-behavioral and relaxation approaches are effective with individuals who suffer from insomnia due to medical or psychiatric conditions.

Anticipatory Nausea in Cancer Chemotherapy

Nausea and vomiting are the most feared side effects of cancer chemotherapy. Two types of behavioral medicine techniques, relaxation therapy and biofeedback, have been used to decrease the negative side effects of cancer chemotherapy, especially the anticipatory nausea. Anticipatory nausea, in which chemotherapy patients begin to get nauseous prior to the actual administration of the drugs, is a significant problem with many types of chemotherapy drugs, and estimates are that about 40% of all chemotherapy patients report at least mild anticipatory nausea. Anticipatory nausea is a curious phenomenon in that it is probably the purest example of classical or Pavlovian conditioning one can find.

While biofeedback-assisted relaxation does seem to help these patients, biofeedback by itself (i.e., not using a relaxation emphasis), while reducing physiological arousal, does not reduce the anticipatory nausea. This is an area where relaxation therapy or systematic desensitization (a behavioral technique that uses relaxation therapy as its primary component) seems to have a clear advantage over biofeedback. For example, in one study, 81 cancer chemotherapy patients were randomly assigned to one of six groups in a 3 (EMG biofeedback/skin temperature biofeedback/no biofeedback) × 2 (relaxation/no relaxation) factorial design. It was concluded that "The findings suggest that relaxation training can be effective in reducing the adverse consequences of chemotherapy and that the positive effects found for biofeedback in prior research were due to the relaxation training that was given with the biofeedback, not the biofeedback alone."

Treatment Compliance

No article on behavioral medicine would be complete without at least mentioning the pervasive and often intractable problem of treatment adherence. Treatment adherence or compliance is frequently referred to as the health care practitioner's version of "the emperor's new clothes," in that nearly all clinicians understand that for treatments to be effective, patients must (a) show up for treatment sessions and (b) adhere to the suggested treatment regimen; however, it is rarely discussed in the literature and usually not addressed directly by the average clinician. Not surprisingly, nearly every study that has examined treatment results has found that treatment outcomes are nearly directly proportional to patients showing up for their treatments and adhering to the regimen. It is clear that treatment compliance/adherence is the biggest problem with behavioral medicine techniques.

Some statistics will both impress and dismay the reader: More than 50% of prescribed medicine is not taken as directed by individuals with chronic illnesses. More than 50% of patients drop out of the average psychology clinic before treatment's logical end. Up to 40% of transplant patients do not adhere to their medication and other aftercare regimens. Among psychiatric patients, 18% did not show up for their first scheduled appointments following inpatient admission. Sixty percent of HIV patients are not compliant with their medication regimens. Compliance with assigned homework in behavioral interventions is also quite low, especially in the addictions.

Treatment adherence is not just a problem for patients. Health care workers are notoriously noncompliant in infection control, with some studies demonstrating woefully poor compliance to hand-washing infection control guidelines, essential to prevent cross-infection.

Adherence is negatively affected by drug and alcohol abuse, psychiatric problems, lower socioeconomic status, motivation levels, memory impairment, regimen complexity, medication side effects, and lack of family support in the treatment regimen. Strategies to combat adherence problems include simplifying treatment regimens, enlisting family support, writing out appointment times and treatment schedules, phoning the patient to remind them of appointments, and tailoring treatment regimens to individuals' lifestyles (often, this means scheduling patients outside of the usual 9-to-5 work hours). In addition, the research is clear that the relationship between the provider and patient significantly improves treatment adherence, while strategies such as blaming the patient for being noncompliant and stereotyping certain types of patients (e.g., "Treating alcoholics is a waste of my time—they're not going to get any better") retards treatment adherence.

Hypertension

Essential hypertension, or elevated blood pressure (BP) in the absence of known physical causes, is another widespread condition that has been the focus of behavioral medicine treatment approaches. At present, the standard recommendation for a newly discovered case of mild hypertension (diastolic BP of 105 mm mercury or lower) is to try nonpharmacological approaches initially for 3 months. Unfortunately, because drugs are potent and rapid in their effects, this may not often be the practice. It seems fairly clear that weight loss in the overweight hypertensive patients has the possibility of noticeably reducing BP. On average, there is a drop in BP of about a millimeter of mercury per kilogram (2.2 pounds) of weight loss. Thus, the first behavioral medicine approach should be weight loss. There may also be an advantage in some hypertensives to alter diet, particularly to reduce sodium (salt) intake.

Some controlled research shows that regular aerobic exercise has a beneficial effect on BP in hypertensive patients. This effect is in addition to the possible weight loss effect that a program of aerobic exercise can produce.

There has been a large amount of research on the use of relaxation training and biofeedback training as treatments for hypertension. For individuals with mild hypertension, both PMRT and meditative forms of relaxation have been shown in several RCTs to lead to modest reductions in BP. In some instances, the improvements have been enough to allow patients to safely discontinue medication while BP remained controlled in the high normotensive range. The two primary biofeedback approaches to hypertension are somewhat different. There was early work, replicated in later studies, showing the efficacy of direct feedback of BP for lowering BP. The other approach has been indirect and involves the use of thermal biofeedback for hand warming (and foot warming). The rationale for this treatment approach is that the successful vasodilation responses arise from a reduction in sympathetic nervous system activity. Again, there are RCTs involving thermal biofeedback that show successful lowering of BP in unmedicated individuals with mild hypertension, with results holding up for a year. There have also been studies that targeted medicated hypertensives that showed that one and possibly two medications can be successfully discontinued.

A major problem in the use of relaxation and biofeedback for lowering BP has been inconsistency of results from one study to another. It appears that some hypertensives are good candidates for these approaches and others are not. Research is needed to identify the good candidates.

Exercise and Depression

While depression is not normally included in articles concerning behavioral medicine, we feel that we would be remiss if we did not at least mention the topic, because so many individuals who suffer from medical problems also have comorbid depression. Cognitive-behavioral strategies have been found to be as effective as pharmacotherapy in most comparisons, without the negative side effects of the SSRIs, such as weight gain, decreased sexual functioning, and dry mouth.

Probably the most exciting data on nonpharmacological treatment of depression involves the effectiveness of a mild to moderate exercise regimen. There is now a growing body of data demonstrating that there is no difference between drug therapy and exercise in the treatment of depression. However, Blumenthal and colleagues have presented exciting data showing that exercise is actually more effective than antidepressant medication in the treatment of mild to moderate major depressive disorder. In this study, 156 depressed individuals 55 or older were matched on depressive symptomatology and randomly assigned into one of three groups: exercise, antidepressant medication, and a combination group. The exercise regimen consisted of brisk walking for 30 minutes three times a week for 16 weeks. There was no difference between any of the groups at the end of treatment, but at 6-month follow-up, the relapse rates were 38% for the drug group, 31% for the combination group, and only 8% for the exercise group. Thus, exercise may actually be superior to pharmacotherapy for mild to moderate major depressive disorder.

FUTURE DIRECTIONS OF BEHAVIORAL MEDICINE

While behavioral medicine is now a mature field, there are a number of areas in which expansion or refinement is necessary. They include the following five areas: (1) alternative methods of treatment delivery, (2) applications of behavioral medicine to new populations, (3) behavioral medicine in the primary care setting, (4) training of health care providers and dissemination of research results, and (5) demonstration of cost-effectiveness of the interventions.

Alternative methods of treatment delivery have already begun to be explored. For many patients with behavioral medicine problems, traditional one-on-one therapy may not be as effective as community-based, workplace-based or group methods. Home or minimal-therapist-based bibliotherapy treatment manuals, sometimes administered through the Internet, have been demonstrated to be of value in a number of behavioral medicine arenas. Even more exciting, tele-health applications through videophone, Internet, and other videoconferencing technology are just now beginning to be explored. Given the large number of individuals who live in rural settings in the United States, such alternative methods of delivery may well be crucial in ensuring equal access to efficacious behavioral medicine interventions.

Behavioral medicine techniques are constantly being applied to novel areas. There is now a growing body of literature exploring psychoneuroimmunology, HIV/AIDS, end-stage renal disease, and organ transplantation. It is clear that behavioral medicine applications in genetic testing will become an emerging area as medical science begins to apply the results of the human-genome-matching project. Established investigators have begun to take behavioral medicine treatments and expand to other, similar clinical problems. For example, in the field of headache, behavioral intervention has been shown to be effective with the elderly, children, and pregnant women. Areas that need to be explored further to determine whether treatment effects can be generalized are headaches in individuals with psychiatric disorders, such as major depression, posttraumatic stress disorder, and generalized anxiety disorder; headaches following cerebral aneurysm; headaches due to eyestrain; posttraumatic headache; and headache in multiple sclerosis patients.

Since the advent of managed care, the primary care provider's role in health care has become paramount. Yet mental health professionals frequently do not effectively interface with primary care providers. This may be due to the academic training model used in the United States, which frequently does not expose students to different disciplines. Behavioral medicine is an interdisciplinary field that requires interfacing with various disciplines. Primary care providers are frequently quite grateful for collaboration with behavioral providers, and establishing such liaisons are quite easy. For example, Arena and Blanchard have described in-depth how to establish a relationship with primary care providers for the treatment of chronic benign headache. Others have done similar things with low-back pain, organ transplants, smoking cessation, and so on. Clearly, primary care interface is essential for behavioral medicine to prosper, and behavioral practitioners are just now emphasizing this growing area of importance.

Dissemination of behavioral medicine treatment results is essential. In our experience, few nonpsychological providers obtain accurate information about behavioral medicine techniques from traditional medical means. Fostering interdisciplinary ties are the best ways to disseminate behavioral medicine treatment results. Interfacing between psychological and nonpsychological providers is fruitful for five reasons. First, the overall health care field benefits by greater dissemination of psychological treatments. Second, many behavioral medicine techniques can easily be taught to the nonpsychological practitioner, who can then use these techniques directly when seeing a patient. Third, demonstration of the efficacy of these techniques to nonpsychological providers leads to those providers disseminating knowledge about behavioral medicine efficacy to their colleagues and students. Fourth, nonpsychological providers interact with patients in the acute phase of an illness and may, through application of behavioral medicine strategies, be able to prevent patients from advancing to chronic states or experiencing the psychological sequelae of medical illness. For example, primary care providers who warn their back pain patients at the onset of pain to avoid falling into the pain-depression cycle (i.e., isolation, decreased social interaction, decreased frequency of pleasurable events) may very well ward off a major depression. Finally, interfacing with interdisciplinary colleagues provides wonderful soil for ideas to grow. Numerous research projects have been stimulated by interdisciplinary collaboration.

Last, cost-effectiveness of behavioral medicine treatments is an area that needs to be explored more fully. There is a paucity of data in this area, which is fraught with methodological difficulty. Psychologically based treatments are especially difficult to analyze from a cost-effectiveness perspective. Issues such as quality of life, positive and negative side effects of treatment, and customer preference are difficult to quantify.

TWO HEADACHE CASE ILLUSTRATIONS

Case Study 1

"Mr. S" was a 51-year-old male with a 7-year history of migraines. He had seen a neurologist, a physiatrist, and a chiropractor for treatment. Despite multiple medication trials, he complained of persistent daily headaches of 2-hour to 2-day duration. He localized the intense throbbing pain to a circumscribed knot at the base of his skull in the left side of the neck that progressed to over the ear and left eyeball. His chiropractor attributed the pain to tension from fused vertebrae.

Mr. S worked four 10-hour days in a supervisory position involving primarily desk work (computing, telephone calls, paperwork). He described his job as "stressful" because "the system bothers me. I'm a perfectionist, and when things don't go a certain way, it bothers me."

His wife recently successfully completed chemotherapy. Also, she and Mr. S have a moderate degree of marital conflict involving other issues.

Mr. S was given 12 sessions of relaxation therapy and thermal biofeedback, as well as simple cognitive-behavioral strategies to help him reframe his cognitions.

Mr. S has always been demanding and suspicious of health care professionals, complaining of insufficient follow-up from physicians. Throughout his treatment involvement, he was politely skeptical, often questioning the rationale for aspects of the therapy. However, he was reliably participatory and eager for information. At treatment completion, he wrote a functional, comprehensive headache prevention/management plan. While it was a significantly statistical/clinical pain reduction success, he focused solely on the benefits of progressive muscle relaxation, saying of

Table 1 Treatment Results for Two Headache Patients

	% Improvement Mr. S		
	1 month	3 months	12 months
Headache index	68	74	53
Headache-free days*	100+	100+	100+
Peak headache rating	20	60	20
Medication quantification scale	40	53	47

	% Improvement Mrs. A		
	1 month	3 months	12 months
Headache index	52	72	80
Headache-free days	125	175	188
Peak headache rating	50	25	25
Medication quantification scale	17	67	75

*Subject had zero headache-free days at baseline (13 days for 1-month and 3-months posttreatment and 6 days for 12-months posttreatment)

biofeedback, "It was interesting to learn, but I can't seem to associate it with pain prevention." His opinions were unchanging, despite multiple previous attempts at explanation of biofeedback utility.

Within a few months of treatment conclusion, the subject's wife called in appreciation of his remarkable improvement. She was extremely grateful for the consistent level of positive impact on Mr. S and described a recent weeklong vacation that for the first time in 7 years was not disrupted by her husband's headaches. Table 1 presents Mr. S's outcome data.

Case Study 2

"Ms. A" was a 27-year-old female with a 15-year history of chronic headaches. During the initial interview, she reported that migraines occurred twice a month, emanated from her left eye, were "pounding/throbbing," and lasted from 2 hours to 2 days. She also described weekly tension headaches characterized by tension and "soreness" at the base of her skull and neck/shoulders. Duration varied from 2 hours to 1 day. Baseline data from 1-month pretreatment charting objectified the frequency of her pain as higher than initially estimated. Only 8 of 28 days were headache free.

Ms. A acknowledged that stress was a contributing factor for her headaches. She held four demanding jobs (including owning her own business), had a toddler, had recently participated in marital therapy, and had constant conflicts with her mother-in-law. Her spouse worked varying hours 7 days a week, held three jobs, and 1 year prior to our session had been jailed for drug use.

Mrs. A was also given 12 sessions of relaxation therapy and thermal biofeedback. From the beginning, Ms. A was highly motivated, inquisitive, and receptive to treatment. She practiced diligently, completed assignments, and generalized training on a multitude of levels. By treatment completion, she was conducting informal relaxation sessions for her friends! Table 1 presents Mrs. A's outcome data.

—*John G. Arena and Edward B. Blanchard*

See also: *Behavioral Treatment for the Addictions (Vol. I); Behavioral Treatment of Cigarette Smoking (Vol. I); Behavioral Weight Treatment Control Therapy With Children (Vol. II); Satiation (Vol. III)*

Suggested Readings

Agras, W. S. (1982). Behavioral medicine in the 1980's: Nonrandom connections. *Journal of Consulting and Clinical Psychology, 50,* 797–803.

Arena, J. G., & Blanchard, E. B. (2001). Biofeedback therapy for chronic pain disorders. In J. D. Loeser, D. Turk, R. C. Chapman, & S. Butler (Eds.), *Bonica's management of pain* (3rd ed., 1755–1763). Baltimore, MD: Williams & Wilkins.

Arena, J. G., & Blanchard, E. B. (in press). Assessment and treatment of chronic benign headache in the primary care setting. In W. O'Donohue, N. Cummings, D. Henderson, & M. Byrd (Eds.), *Behavioral integrative care: Treatments that work in the primary care setting.* New York: Allyn & Bacon.

Blanchard, E. B. (1982). Behavioral medicine: Past, present, and future. *Journal of Consulting and Clinical Psychology, 50,* 795–796.

Blumenthal, J., Babyak, M. A., Moore, K. A., Craighead, W. E., Herman S., Khatri, P., et al. (1999). Effects of exercise training on older patients with major depression. *Archives of Internal Medicine, 159,* 2349–2356.

Burgio, K. L, Locher, J. L., Goode, P. S., Hardin, J. M., McDowell, B. J., Dombrowski, M., et al. (1998). Behavioral versus drug treatment for urge urinary incontinence in older women: A randomized controlled trial. *Journal of the American Medical Association, 280,* 1995–2000.

Burish, T. G., & Jenkins, R. A. (1992). Effectiveness of biofeedback and relaxation training in reducing side effects of cancer chemotherapy. *Health Psychology, 11,* 17–23.

Chappell, M. N., & Stevenson, T. I. (1936). Group psychological training in some organic conditions. *Mental Hygiene, 20,* 588–597.

Dubbert, P. M. (2002). Physical activity and exercise: Recent advances and current challenges. *Journal of Consulting and Clinical Psychology, 70,* 526–536.

Kegel, A. H. (1948). Progressive resistance exercise in the functional restoration of the perineal muscles. *American Journal of Obstetrics and Gynecology, 56,* 238–248.

Olton, D. S., & Noonberg, A. R. (1980). *Biofeedback: Clinical applications in behavioral medicine.* Englewood Cliffs, NJ: Prentice Hall.

Schwartz, G. E. (1982). Testing the biopsychosocial model: The ultimate challenge facing behavioral medicine. *Journal of Consulting and Clinical Psychology, 50,* 1040–1053.

Schwartz, G. E., & Weiss, S. M. (1978). Behavioral medicine revisited: An amended definition. *Journal of Behavioral Medicine, 1*(3), 249–251.

Schwartz, G. E., & Weiss, S. M. (1978). Yale Conference on Behavioral Medicine: A proposed definition and statement of goals. *Journal of Behavioral Medicine, 1*(1), 3–12.

BEHAVIORAL SOCIAL WORK

DESCRIPTION OF THE STRATEGY

Behavioral methods are quite consistent with most of the basic tenants of clinical social work practice and the social work perspective. They were introduced into social work practice in the mid-1960s. Since then, interest in behavioral approaches among social workers has expanded dramatically, as evidenced by the large number of articles with a behavioral orientation in both the clinical and research journals in social work and social workers' contributions to the behavioral psychology literature. Surveys of clinical social workers confirm that behavioral and cognitive-behavioral methods are among the most popular methods subscribed to by social workers. Before presenting behavioral methods commonly used in social work, it is first necessary to be aware of the social work perspective that provides a background sympathetic to the behavioral social worker. In the final part of this entry, a description is given of some of the various fields of practice in social work in which behavioral methods are most commonly used.

THE SOCIAL WORK PERSPECTIVE

The role of the behavioral social worker is both more and less than a behaviorist. This distinction is important in that most social workers practicing behavioral methods do not subscribe to the philosophy of behaviorism. Indeed, the overall success of diffusion of behavioral methods is well tested by examining use of such methods by the social work profession. Many social workers do not have as their primary task treatment of clients. They include community organizers, administrators, policy analysts, and researchers. It is also important to note that many social workers who work directly with clients, either individually or in groups, may not have treatment goals as their focus. Instead, they are focused on organizational or community goals. In the clinical practice of social work, the emphasis has shifted from a psychoanalytic emphasis to ego psychological to a general empirical practice that draws on all the social sciences, and more recently to evidence-based practice. This last perspective is, of course, not limited to behavioral methods. However, as many reviews of literature in social work reveal, most of the empirical or evidence based methods are, in fact, behavioral in orientation. In this shift to behavioral models, the disease model of diagnosis has been replaced by an emphasis on the role of learning.

There has also been a push from funding sources for social workers to be more accountable for their practices. Behavioral methods, because of their specificity and accessibility, lend themselves to the evaluation of outcome. Length of time required to achieve relevant goals, though initially vastly underestimated, is still far shorter and hence more efficient than other approaches previously and presently used by social workers.

If we examine some of the fundamental perspectives of social work, the notion of working with the person-in-environment is underscored. The emphasis on social functioning emerged from social interaction theory and role theory. This is compatible with the assumption that behavior for the most part is evoked and maintained by environmental and cognitive events.

Behavioral theories suggest that performance of one's social role is critical to successful adaptation in society. Most social workers conceptualize their work as needing to understand the demands and life tasks that people encounter if they are to help them realize their personal and social aspirations. To this end, the concept of tasks is used by many social workers in assessing their clients' life situations and plays a key role in the social functioning framework. By asking the question, "What tasks are confronting my client?" the social worker can focus on critical biopsychosocial demands being made in the environment. For instance, as one looks at the tasks confronting a 16-year-old girl who is losing her hair while undergoing chemotherapy, one sees that she must learn to deal not only with the unique demands of being ill and of losing her hair, but she may need help to deal with the impact on her peer group, on her relationship to her boyfriend, and on her school achievement. This young woman, as with every adolescent, is confronting distinct biopsychosocial demands. The social worker must look at these demands and help the young person adapt to her social and biological environment. Some of the help offered is to be found in individual and group treatment with behavioral techniques. The social worker will also look for help in services offered by the community, in the support offered by the family, and possibly by a support group for teenage cancer victims. In addition, the behavioral social worker may use behavioral and cognitive methods to facilitate development of coping skills to deal with the broad range of social problems the above client may have as result of her illness.

Social work today draws heavily on the concept of social justice. The social worker who uses behavioral methods is committed to goals that are compatible with this value. Goals are negotiated with clients that do not result in the "putting down" of other persons or groups. Populations of clients served by social workers are primarily those who are inadequately helped by virtue of their economic status, race and ethnicity, gender, physical, and intellectual challenges (although some social workers do serve the White middle class.). Coping skills are taught that enhance not only the welfare of the client, but also of those with whom the client interacts. An example of such a goal is the writing of a pamphlet by a group of parents of intellectually challenged children to explain to physicians how to talk to their children and to recognize the virtues and strengths of those children.

Focusing on persons and their impinging social environments is likely to lead to the following activities: enhancing the problem-solving and coping and developmental capacities of people, linking people with resources and services, enhancing the delivery of services, and participating in the development and refinement of social policies that impinge on the client's treatment.

Because of this aforementioned array of activities, social workers are often said to work within multiple systems. For example, their practice is at the microlevel system of individuals, the midlevel system of organizations and formal groups, and the macrolevel

system of communities and societies. Strategies that social workers might employ at the various levels include helping individuals find solutions at the microlevel (for example, through the application of parent training methods for child behavior problems), fostering organizational development or facilitating the development of support groups (for example, developing programs of support groups for parents who have attention-deficit/hyperactivity disorder, or ADHD, children) at the midlevel, and coordinating program development or facilitating policy changes at the macrolevel (for example, ensuring that ADHD children receive proper educational services within the school system). The behaviorally oriented social worker primarily, but never exclusively, works within the microsystem of the individual. The behavioral strategies the clinical social worker employs are related to the characteristics and tasks of the specific clients. The specific field of social work in which the social worker is employed lends itself more to some techniques than to others.

FIELDS OF SOCIAL WORK

Thirty-five years ago, social work was organized according to methods, case work, group work, and community work. Presently, the fields of practice are the locus of social work activity, and students often have majors in one or several of these fields. The orientation within each of these fields has been at all three levels or systems. We have selected several of these often-overlapping fields and have identified the major behavioral methods used in each: health, community mental health, child welfare, and school social work.

Health

Social work has had a long-standing relationship with health care since the early 1900s, when social service departments became an established part of hospitals. In the hospital setting, social workers provide direct service to patients and their families, group work for patients with questions such as how to cope with cancer or diabetes, consultation and training of other professionals in interviewing, and discharge planning. Social workers are often involved in planning and policy development within the hospital and sometimes in administration. In these settings, they are especially useful because of their extensive knowledge of community services and their ability to help plan for the transition the patient and family must make when they leave the hospital.

Health promotion has taken place in a variety of community based settings. For example, social workers may provide services in Planned Parenthood, YWCA agencies, public health clinics, or community mental health settings. Prevention and health promotion have become an increasingly large aspect of social work, and many social workers provide such services. A large number of empirically based programs have been developed by social workers that focus on decreasing risk behaviors, such as smoking, and enhancing other life skills: for example, programs designed to impact pregnancy prevention, smoking prevention, substance abuse, and HIV infection.

Community Mental Health

Social workers provide more mental health counseling than any other profession. As such, they have a large impact on the mental health status of this country. Most social workers in this arena work in community mental health clinics, where services such as outpatient care, inpatient care, partial hospitalization, in-home services, substance abuse counseling, family and group therapy, and referrals are a significant part of the work. An increasing number of social workers provide individual, family, and group therapy in private practice settings. Almost all states have some form of licensing for clinical social work services. Social workers in mental health settings also provide services for severely mentally ill adults and homeless individuals and families. Behavioral treatment has been implemented in community-based programs and in inpatient or hospital settings. Both assertive community treatment and family-based treatment target psychoeducational training for families and clients, communication skills for families, problem-solving skills, symptom management, work placement, psychotherapy or counseling, and medication. Inpatient treatment uses standard behavioral principals, such as reinforcement of incompatible behavior to reduce frequency of hallucinations and delusions, contingency management for reducing aggressive behaviors, social skills training to increase verbal and nonverbal skills for interpersonal communication, and self-care, grooming skills, vocational skills, and recreational training.

Child Welfare

Child welfare involves providing social work services to children and adolescents whose parents are unable to adequately fulfill their child-rearing responsibilities or whose communities fail to provide resources and protection that families and children require. Child welfare is a significant part of social work. Social workers provide an array of services within the child welfare field.

The use of behavioral methods in child welfare has been extensive. Perhaps the most clear application has been the use of parent training for child welfare clients. This effort has directly attempted to change parenting behavior and, in particular, reduce or eliminate the use of physical punishment by parents and replace it with reinforcement of alternative behaviors and time-out from reinforcement. Many of the home-based interventions used by social workers in child welfare have as a primary focus teaching behavioral principles to parents as to the use of systematic reinforcement, problem-solving training, behavioral contracting, relaxation training, and anger management. In the child welfare field, social workers have also taught foster parents similar behavioral parenting skills.

More specifically, home-based behavioral interventions inherently found in programs such as family preservation services, "homebuilders," or "home-based services" serve as a good example of how behavioral social work is integrated into child welfare setting. In all of these services, the home is the primary location of treatment. Some of the social work basic principles that guide these practices include treatment of the entire family, use of family empowerment strategies, recognition of families as partners in the change process, attempting to respond to the family holistically, putting child safety first, emphasis on children being reared by their own families, providing a sense of hope, and linking the family with other community-based services. The home-based approach works with families to develop a "problem list," do a functional analysis of the behavior, set goals, draw up contracts, and apply parent training in the methods of reinforcement, differential reinforcement of other behaviors, shaping, extinction, time-out, and response cost. Also taught are family problem-solving strategies that stress open and positive communication among the members. The program includes the development of communication skills, such as carrying out conversations and negotiating with one's children by means of modeling, coaching, rehearsal, and feedback procedures.

School Social Work

School social work is closely linked to child welfare except that the primary setting is the school. School social work involves a broad range of activities that emerge from the interaction of social work and the educational process. In general, school social workers make assessments of the social-interactive needs and behavioral problems of students and develop appropriate programs and services within the school to meet those needs. They also provide direct services to children and consultation to teachers and principles for dealing with problem children and classrooms. They coordinate their efforts with school psychologists, whose tasks often overlap with those of the social worker. Some key functions that a school social worker might perform include working with children in special education. PL94–142, the Education for All Handicapped Children Act, was critical in bringing social workers into the schools. Their tasks include consultation with teachers, linking children and families to community-based services through referrals, mediation of conflicts, and crisis services to individual children and school systems when needed. Dealing with problems of poor attendance is increasingly falling to the school social worker. In addition to dealing with practical barriers to attendance such as transportation and parents who do not wake up in time, parents may be trained in strategies of monitoring homework and in reinforcement of regular attendance at school and at-home behaviors.

Although school social workers make use of individual and family treatment methods, behavioral group methods are employed extensively, because a crucial part of a child's functioning in the school involves relating effectively to other children as well as teachers. Social skills training in groups is frequently carried out by social workers. It is specifically used in the treatment of withdrawn and isolated behavior. Anger management groups have been organized by social workers as well as other staff members in the school to deal with aggressive behavior. Early efforts in the schools by social workers and others to develop group programs for the prevention of teen pregnancy rely heavily on behavioral group methods. Group-based prevention services are also frequently offered as part of school social workers' responsibilities,

for example, in schools with a potential for substance abuse and HIV/AIDs infection. Because many children are impulsive problem solvers in social situations, training in groups in systematic problem solving is an important tool in the social worker's repertoire.

School social workers are often called upon by teachers to help with classroom management problems, using primarily operant methods or assisting the teacher in their use. In addition, school social workers are beginning to employ cognitive-restructuring methods in addition to social skills training to help children deal with their anger and stress.

SUMMARY

In summary, social work subscribes to a person-in-environment perspective that encourages the social worker to analyze how persons function in their social environments. Social workers often assess the difficulty clients are having, not only as an internal problem but also as a problem of not having obtained needed resources to meet demands the environment is placing on such individuals. Therefore, social work emphasizes developing, brokering, and assessing services through referrals that may make a difference in how the individuals function in their roles. This perspective also leads the social worker to consider issues of organizations and communities and recognize that private troubles often become public issues that require social policy solutions. However, within this perspective, much of the day-to-day work of the social worker involves direct service to clients that often involves direct application of behavioral methods to achieve highly specific goals. Several fields of practice were reviewed, and examples were given where such methods have been prominent.

—Sheldon D. Rose and Craig W. LeCroy

See also: *Behavioral Treatment in Natural Environments (Vol. I); Home-Based Reinforcement (Vol. II); Systems of Care (Vol. III)*

Suggested Readings

Gambrill, E. (1995). Behavioral social work: Past, present and future. *Research on social work practice, 5,* 460–484.

Gambrill, E. (1999). *Helping clients: A critical thinker's guide.* New York: Oxford University Press.

Granvold, D. K. (1994). *Cognitive and behavioral treatment: Methods and applications.* Pacific Grove, CA: Wadsworth.

Mattaini, M. A. (1997). *Clinical practice with individuals.* Washington, DC: National Association of Social Worker's Press.

Thyer, B., & Hudson, W. W. (1987). Progress in behavioral social work: An introduction. *Journal of Social Service Research, 10,* 1–6.

BEHAVIORAL SPORT PSYCHOLOGY

DESCRIPTION OF THE STRATEGY

Sport psychology's early years (1900–1960) were primarily concept or cognitive psychology oriented. The conceptual approach focused on discrete topics or the orientations of particular individuals and mainly explained phenomena in terms of theoretical constructs. Little, if any, information was devoted to describing practical procedures for coaches and athletes to follow to alter sport behavior/performance. Cognitive sport psychology was bent more on explanation and description than prescription. To a certain extent, it mirrored the thrust of motor learning, the mainstay of "psychology" in physical activity and education courses of study during that period. Explaining why behavior occurred was more popular than verifying how behavior occurred.

In the early 1960s, and particularly at the Rome Olympic Games, European nations were the sources of involving psychology in athletic arenas. Some good descriptive research on athlete behaviors was provided by practitioners, but their contributions were piecemeal. They did not attract coaches or athletes as being a source of valuable information for improving athletic performances.

B. F. Skinner's publications in the 1960s described a practical deterministic behavior system that attempted to account for all behaviors in all settings. It was labeled *operant conditioning* or, to a lesser degree, *behavior modification,* and popularly as *Skinnerian Psychology.* Today, it is frequently referred to as *applied behavior analysis.* It offered a system that embraced all facets of sporting environments, something that previously did not exist. In the early years, adherents in sport and physical education settings were labeled *Skinnerians.* The proposal of a complete system for behavior explanation was also an original contribution to those fields because it

attempted to be useful in any circumstance. However, it had its detractors because it did not embrace the theoretical, but promoted the variables and procedures for altering behavior/performance. Since many psychologists were both schooled in and adherents of theoretical psychology, the attempt to promote Skinnerian psychology was met with resistance, probably because of the degree of threat it imposed to generally established psychology.

Operant psychology provided a system that contained tenets for explaining and altering all behavioral things. Its adventure into changing behavior fit with a sport model that deemed, "Coaches change athletes' behaviors so that they perform better." This psychology offered a framework for telling coaches how to engage with athletes. It also described research paradigms that focused on single-subject or small-group experimentation and followed procedures that were well accepted in natural science. Sport is also very interested in individuals and small groups rather than populations. This was another attraction about operant psychology. This suggested a system of "applied psychology" that could be useful in sporting environments. In its development over the years, it has come to be termed *behavioral sport psychology.*

RESEARCH BASIS

Behavioral sport psychology deems as largely unacceptable the postulations, assumptions, and procedures of many other forms of psychology. For the study of both covert and overt behaviors, the following are some unacceptable postulates: the phenomenological position, mind-body postulates, psychic expressions and manifestations, and the organocentric postulate.

Behavioral sport psychology limits itself to a series of metapostulates that dictate its investigations and applications. It is interested in data, not "factors/theories/fantasies":

1. *The homogeneity axiom.* The nature and availability of data and events are similar for all scientific fields. They are natural and confrontable. Human inventions, such as labels and theories, are not worthy of study.

2. *The independence axiom.* Each science is concerned with an event field. One cannot borrow the abstractions of other sciences and regard them as

original data (e.g., using communication theory as an analogized explanatory model for motor performance).

3. *The nonreduction postulate.* Events studied should be retained. When functional relationships are obtained, their further reduction is nonsensical. Reducing behaviors to inferred entities (e.g., "self-efficacy," "flow," "motivation") removes important information.

4. *The axiom of construct derivation.* No descriptions can be imposed on original events for investigation. The introduction of extraneous variables or inferred structures into explanations for descriptions is denied. It is common to observe behavior and then have an "expert" add an explanatory label of "why" it occurred. Since such labels cannot be manipulated, they become reasons for justifying all kinds of inappropriate behaviors.

Six further axioms indicate the bounds of inquiry for sport psychology to remain a form of natural science:

1. *Psychological events consist of multifactor interbehavioral fields.* Individuals interact with the environment in measurable and observable forms. The environment is both internal and external to the individual.

2. *Interbehavioral fields are integral and coordinate.* All factors in a specific behavior segment are of equal importance. It is unacceptable to consider one aspect of the total field to be more important than another. For adequate control, the "big picture" should always be contemplated.

3. *Interbehavioral fields are symmetrical and reciprocal.* Behaviors and stimuli occur simultaneously and not as a series of discrete events. Individuals behave to adjust to environmental situations. Behavior is not aroused by some preceding event that is removed before the act is observed.

4. *Interbehavioral fields are evolutional.* Patterns and occurrences of behavior are determined by an individual's history of interactions with the environment.

5. *Interbehavioral fields are outgrowths of ecological behavior.* Psychological behaviors are influenced by the phylogenetic continuum. They are derivations and elaborations of biological activities and are adjustments as part of an evolutionary pattern.

6. *Psychological fields permit investigative analysis.* Interbehavioral fields are open to specific study. Events must be interpreted in perspective to the entire behavioral field, with no special importance being attached to elements within the field.

These postulates allow one to investigate covert and overt behaviors as events within the realm of natural science. One learns much when trying to alter sport behavior as opposed to observing or theorizing about it. "Experimental control" is the catchphrase that indicates a successful attempt to cause behavior. The main hurdle for the observation and control of some events is the technology available. Pseudoscientific work results when the statutes of these tenets are violated for ease and expediency.

The facts of sport are measurable and observable. Any explanation of an observed fact in terms of another entity on another level is unacceptable. To see one player tackle another player is not an indicator of a level of "aggression." No new knowledge is gained by the addition of that abstraction. Terms that imply purpose, drives, creativity, anxiety, and so on are rejected. Constructing abstractions promotes a world that is never directly experienced and therefore cannot be verified. Such an approach is not popular in sport and is possibly why sport psychology has had difficulty in being accepted as important for performance development. For example, coaches will not accept the following:

1. A set of behaviors is observed.

2. The question is asked, "Why did she do those things?"

3. The answer is provided, "Because she was anxious."

4. The explanation is then questioned, "How do you know she was anxious?"

5. The answer is provided, "Because she did those things."

Many traditional sport psychologists never move beyond Step 3 in the above logically circular argument. Until a person's anxiety can be manipulated as an independent variable, it cannot be objectively verified to exist. Until an athlete can be manipulated to perform at 50% of anxiety and then altered to function at 75%, anxiety will remain a useless construct for the practical world of sport. Despite this logical difficulty, constructs such as anxiety continue to be "explored," and "models" of its function are developed and investigated in sport psychology. To a large degree, the study of sport psychology continues outside of sporting environments.

Behavioral sport psychology attempts to study the behaviors of individuals in sport settings. It assumes that behavior is a function of the environment modified by individual characteristics, such as history of reinforcement, rates of behavior emission, stimulus control, and so on. Sport behaviors are many and include frequency and magnitude of physical movements. Following particular instructions, attending practices, the frequency of dropping a ball in a game, and participation in exercise greater than a walk during free time are examples of behaviors studied. The behaviors of interest are defined and reliably measured and observed.

In observing behaviors, contingencies between stimulus events, behaviors, and reinforcers are often discovered. Consistent observations develop to be principles of behavioral sport psychology. Principles such as "Peer reinforcement is stronger than coach reinforcement" are steeped in natural science phenomena. The value of recording observations has developed a number of technologies for describing and classifying events. Observation schedules are popular and useful for describing the levels and consistencies of behaviors in sport and exercise settings.

In the history of behaviorism, overt and covert behaviors were originally considered. However, the more problematical covert behaviors were neglected, largely because experimental subjects were animals, which led to the impression that covert activities were denied as behaviors. The measurement and analysis of covert behavior is possible within a single framework. However, the measurement of covert behaviors (thinking behaviors) is usually beyond the reach of sport science. Current advances in technology are bringing covert behaviors closer to observation and measurement, so the future holds promise for exciting new investigations. Generally, though, one can only infer private events from behaviors; for example, a verbal report is a behavioral response to private events. That interpretation contrasts markedly with the common belief that a verbal report is the sensation of thinking. What an athlete says he or she thinks is not necessarily a duplicate of thinking. Within sport psychology, researchers still attempt to influence thinking behaviors

at a level external to the individual. Popular sport psychology assumes that if the intent of the researcher or therapist is to influence private thinking behaviors, it will occur in the manner desired solely because of that intention. For example, a 1-hour workshop to influence imagery is proposed to produce permanent imagery behavior changes that then will improve performance, which will, in turn, be reflected in the next competition. If a competition is successful, the workshop is the "cause." This is an extreme leap of faith between an unevaluated experience and a much more complex unrelated behavior repertoire in a foreign setting. This is not the stuff of science or a profession. In medicine, it is quackery. At a minimum, the environmental experience has to be shown to produce a related behavior change in the individual(s). A behaviorist answer to this problem is to manipulate external instructions and stimuli that suggest different types of thinking. It intends to determine a functional relationship between the external stimuli and objectively verified outcome behaviors. There is no attempt to describe what occurred privately in a subject, for that is neither observable nor measurable. In the sport behaviorist literature, there are examples of instructing athletes to think in a particular manner and measuring performance outcomes that are usually compared to instructions to think in a "normal" manner and its associated performance levels. In that case, the purpose of the research is to relate the instructions to performance outcomes. Generating explanatory fictions for what occurs inside the head between discriminative stimuli and verifiable responses is a waste of time from the behaviorist viewpoint.

Behavioral sport psychology continues to develop through experimentation. Its language and descriptions have arisen from deductive reasoning. After many observations that produce consistent functional relationships, a principle of behavior is usually espoused. That is demanding and tedious work, but its conclusions are substantial and reliable. That process differs from the inductive process of fantasizing a hypothesis and then supporting or not supporting the fantasy. When results are incompatible with an original prediction, the prediction is "modified" to accommodate the inconsistency. Some people spend their whole lives trying to justify an original guess at what the real world is like. In sports, the concept of "flow" (the internal experience associated with a remarkable performance) is an example. It was produced as a fantasy by someone who had never experienced it.

Its research is descriptive. Rather than work out what is involved with this label-idea, a behaviorist would ask champion athletes what they do when performing remarkably. When verbal descriptions (they are behaviors) have common content, what might be the conduct associated with superior performance is suggested. One original characteristic of "flow" that was popularly espoused was that athletes "see themselves performing in slow motion." If that were so, an implication is that a coach should instruct athletes of lesser ability to image in slow motion while performing, with the expectation that a better performance would result. Unfortunately, such instructions unequivocally produce performance degradation rather than enhancement. The gap between the behavioral and conceptual/cognitive sport psychology is indeed wide.

COMPLICATIONS

Behavioral psychology developed through precise experimentation in which control of extraneous variables was paramount, rather than assigning variability and inaccuracy to a quantity of experimental error, which is a measure that is analogous to a lack of control. The use of statistics to estimate inadequacies of control is not contemplated. In the operant/behavioral experimental paradigm, establishing a reliable baseline to indicate behavior variability and magnitude in a consistent setting is required to establish the comparison base for subsequent observations in manipulated conditions. The more complex the setting and the subject, usually the greater is the time required to "establish baseline." In sport settings, it generally is not feasible to conduct long periods of uninvolved observation when results and changes are required as soon as possible. This led to a shortcut form of observation to establish baseline behaviors. The formation of behavior inventories in the 1970s led to a very accurate method for establishing/predicting baseline behaviors in practical, often time-limited settings. Behavior therapists accepted this measurement technique as a valuable and viable process for measuring behaviors. However, to this day, it has received little attention from "applied" sport psychologists outside the behaviorist orientation.

Behavior inventories are compendiums of descriptions of important situations and related behaviors in sporting environments. Some behaviors are common to all sporting environments. For example, how one sleeps the night before an important competition is general to all sports. On the other hand, some behaviors are specific to each sport. Knowing what an ice hockey goalie reports as a reaction to a forward rush has little relevance for rowing. Behavior inventories include sport-general and sport-specific behaviors. A feature of behavior inventories is the extreme accuracy of their results and interpretations. Behavior inventories are computer analyzed. Each question response is considered, a "diagnostic" redescription of the situation and behavior are queried, and a proposal for coach actions in light of the diagnostic are presented. In the steps involved in developing inventories and associated analyses, the interpreted output is given to each subject, who evaluates the output for what is and is not true for him or her. The acceptability of the diagnostic and suggested coach behaviors is most commonly much greater than 95%. Coaches can rely on this type of information almost without question.

The behaviorist adherence to experimental/treatment effects in applied settings requires a practitioner to conduct entry and exit testing. In the practice of psychology, it is possible to gain real-world insight into the potential effects of treatments and procedures even if control cannot be exerted to a desirable level. It is unacceptable for athletes to be "treated" and beneficial effects to be claimed without evidence of such effects. Typically, a behavioral sport psychologist will use behavior inventories to assess the consistent presence or absence of sport-related behaviors before and after treatments or consultations. Thus, there is a growing database of demonstrated effectiveness of the procedures that adhere to the behavior modification model.

DEVELOPMENTAL PHASES AND PROCEDURAL EMPHASES

The initial thrust of behavioral sport psychology was one of demonstrating that the principles of behavior modification were indeed valid for sport settings. Those demonstrations were mainly experimental studies evaluating the effect of environmental manipulations of sport behaviors. Demonstrations showed that swimmers who publicly recorded their progress through a self-directed training session covered a greater distance than when coached "traditionally" or left alone. The performance of group behavior games illustrated the power of peer reinforcement for controlling troublesome practice behaviors. They were much more effective than coach control. The rate and variety of positive word utterances were increased in a coach by providing consistent contingent feedback. The permanence of the change was also demonstrated by fading the control variable. Athletes increased their productivity at training when they concentrated on being positive in their utterances and interactions with other athletes. After a decade of studies illustrating the methods for attaining experimental control, it was evident that sporting environments were subject to the same principles of behavior as other environments. That was not an earth-shattering conclusion, but was a necessary demonstration to at least silence the initial doubters and alternative theorists.

Once behavioral approaches to sports were generally accepted by the end of the 1970s, teams around the world started to appoint sport psychologists as ancillary support staff. An early approach of some practitioners was to quickly adopt other aspects of behavioral psychology. Established treatment procedures were advocated and employed to solve athlete problems. For example, mild depression was treated with assertiveness training, coping-skills development, desensitization, and thought-stopping. Poor team cohesion was approached with assertive training, attitude change, and sensitivity training. Fears and avoidance behaviors were treated with flooding, implosion therapy, desensitization, self-implosion therapy, and covert modeling. Initially, it was thought that relaxation training was an important part of therapies, but work in the mid-1980s showed clearly that it was unnecessary as a part of any effective treatment.

Late in the 1980s, and particularly after the 1988 Olympics, the newest emphasis was on mental skills training, which persists today. Structured activities that required a package of a variety of experiences and influential factors were advocated for all sports persons. The procedures were common to all sports, with athletes adding specific content for their sports and experiences. Typical mental skills training exercises were structured as discriminative (instructional) stimuli, behavioral steps, the generation of self-reinforcement and the public posting of self-appraisals, and the fading of the exercise to permanently establish the behavior change. The current focus of behavioral sport psychology is on mental skills training. Procedures for shaping covert behaviors are developed with the athlete usually evaluating the behaviors. Public self-reinforcement is applied or withheld depending upon those private appraisals. Packages of mental exercises to promote behavior changes in sport settings exist.

They are promoted by behaviorists and conceptualists/cognitivists alike.

One difference between the classes of exercises is that the behavioral models adhere to the metapostulates of natural science. It usually is unclear what guides the development of the other exercises, although increasingly, they seem to be adopting many of the characteristics of behavioral models. Another difference is what the mental exercises attempt to achieve. Conceptual/cognitivists might attempt to alter "self-efficacy," while the behaviorist would attempt to improve "the frequency and variety of use of self-reinforcing statements." Neither approach allows direct observation of the two outcomes. In the former, an athlete would have to complete a test with an improved score to show a higher level of self-efficacy. The latter would require the athlete to self-report greater use and to provide descriptions of the increased number of positive words used. It might appear that the two outcomes are similar, but there is one difference. The self-efficacy measure is limited to responding to a set of items on a test. All athletes respond to the same stimulus and receive a score. In the latter model, the qualitative and quantitative differences between individuals and within individuals are disclosed and related to real events. It is hard to appreciate self-efficacy even if it is defined. It is easier to appreciate the description of using more positive words, features that did not exist before the mental skills training intervention. In this example, the limits of behavioral sport psychology are approached because of the involvement of private behaviors. In overt behaviors, such as attending practice sessions more regularly, performing more repetitions of an exercise, and adhering to a sequence of activities, the outcomes are unequivocal. They have nothing to do with "increasing an athlete's seriousness for the sport" (a possible conceptualist/cognitivist interpretation).

A feature of mental skills training exercises is they have wide-sweeping effects. They often solve more than one problem. For example, in using thought-stopping to reduce negative thoughts, the requirement to halt the negative and immediately enact a positive thought has two effects. The negative thoughts are reduced, and positive thoughts are increased. As a side effect, the stimuli that originally provoked negative thinking change to provoke positive thinking. Since most athletes are "normal" or "supernormal," clinical treatment procedures or mental skills exercises work very quickly and effectively. Athletes want to change behaviors as soon as they commit to an exercise, which goes a long way toward making the treatment successful. That is one of the reinforcing aspects of being a behavioral sport psychologist.

At the start of the 21st century, with the advent of easy-to-use and inexpensive computer technology, the newest innovation is to place mental skills exercises online to allow anyone access to the resource in the most convenient of situations. Further developments include "personal" attention using the Internet and readily available video technology. It seems that one can be as effective as a behavioral sport psychologist using the Internet as seeing someone in an office or on a practice field. The approach and cooperative behaviors of very compliant athletes allows the use of technology to be effective. One should not expect similar success with resistant clients.

Sport continues to increase its demands on coach, player, and administrator accountability. It is likely that an increase in the last frontier of sport psychology, the mental aspect will receive more attention than in the past, in order to "gain an edge." Behavioral sport psychology is likely to be the framework for achieving acceptance in the real world of specific outcomes and clear contingencies.

—*Brent Rushall*

See also: *Cue-Controlled Relaxation (Vol. I); Self-Instruction (Vol. III); Sports Skills Training (Vol. II)*

Suggested Readings

Day, W. F. (1969). On certain similarities between the philosophical investigations of Ludwig Wittgenstein and the operationism of B. F. Skinner. *Journal of the Experimental Analysis of Behavior, 12,* 489–506.

Dickinson, J. (1977). *A behavioral analysis of sport.* Princeton, NJ: Princeton Book Company.

Martin, G. L., & Hrycaiko, D. (Eds.). (1983). *Behavior modification and coaching: Principles, procedures, and research.* Springfield, IL: Charles C Thomas.

Rushall, B. S. (2003). *Mental skills training for serious athletes.* Available at http://members.cox.net/brushall/mental/ index.htm.

Rushall, B. S. (2003). *Mental skills training for sports* (3rd ed.). Spring Valley, CA: Sports Science Associates.

Rushall, B. S. (2003). *Sport psychology consultation system* (3rd ed.). Spring Valley, CA: Sports Science Associates.

Rushall, B. S., & Siedentop, D. (1972). *The development and control of behavior in sports and physical education.* Philadelphia: Lea & Febiger.

BEHAVIORAL TREATMENT FOR AGGRESSION IN COUPLES

DESCRIPTION OF THE STRATEGY

Intimate partner violence (IPV) remains a pervasive problem in American society, despite more than 20 years of widespread efforts to improve methods of prevention and treatment. As evidenced by several nationally representative surveys, roughly 1 in 5 couples will experience an incident of physical violence from within the dyad each year. IPV appears to have substantial negative consequences for the partners themselves, their children (who have elevated rates of emotional problems and are more likely to assault their intimate partners in adulthood than their counterparts from nonviolent homes), and society in general (resulting from costs related to medical, mental health, police, legal, and social services to victims and perpetrators).

Although historically viewed as a private family issue, IPV is now seen as a broad social problem requiring attention from the treatment community, not to mention legal authorities. Many specialized treatment services for IPV have been developed and proliferated; one of the most common treatments seen in clinical settings grows from a cognitive-behavioral orientation. Cognitive-behavioral approaches are based on the premise that violence-supporting beliefs, a lack of behavioral self-control, and poor assertiveness and relationship skills contribute to IPV. As such, cognitive-behavioral treatment places responsibility for the violence on the perpetrator, because it is the perpetrator who performs the abusive behaviors and who, in turn, can control the underlying cognitive processes leading to such behaviors. Interventions are designed to identify and modify gender-based assumptions and attitudes that can serve as justifications for violence, deficits in social skills and problem solving, and improvements in arousal reduction.

More specifically, to meet these clinical ends, four primary skill areas are often emphasized: (1) relaxation training, (2) cognitive restructuring, (3) self-instructional training, and (4) responsible assertiveness training. Relaxation training is used to help clients identify arousal cues and then use regularly practiced relaxation skills (e.g., deep breathing and self-developed guided imagery) to reduce arousal. Cognitive restructuring consists of examining with perpetrators the antecedents, behaviors, and consequences of their behaviors. In addition, emphasis is placed on identifying, challenging, and replacing automatic thoughts that increase the likelihood of violence (e.g., "She's a liar"; "She'd better listen to me or I will slap her"). Self-instruction requires clients to identify and plan for a recurring stressor, confront the stressor, cope with arousal during engagement, and have a specific plan in place for handling the stressor without violence (e.g., time-out, calm discussion). Assertiveness training includes didactic components to help clients identify aggressive, appropriately assertive, and passive responses in different scenarios. In addition, clients often role-play different situations to practice assertive behavior, with corrective feedback provided as necessary.

Although cognitive-behavioral treatments for IPV have largely been offered in individual or group therapy contexts, it is also important to note that some clinicians have treated IPV in a couples therapy format. In addition to the cognitive-behavioral approaches described above, couples therapy for IPV also focuses on poor partner communication as an underlying factor, as well as the roles of both partners in contributing to violence. Couples therapy for IPV is highly controversial, primarily because some view this approach as implicitly endorsing the notion that victims of IPV are partly to blame for the actions of the partners and, furthermore, may place the victims of IPV at greater risk than treatments that don't include them.

RESEARCH BASIS

A number of studies have evaluated the effectiveness of group- and individual-based treatment programs for IPV. In general, most studies have reported that roughly 50% to 75% of program treatment completers are nonviolent at follow-up (with follow-up periods ranging from directly after treatment completion to 2-years posttreatment). However, these studies have been plagued by very significant methodological problems, including small sample sizes, nonrandom assignment to treatment conditions, inadequate control groups, examination of the outcomes of treatment completers only, and so forth. Recent literature reviews have concluded that the effects of these treatments for IPV are, unfortunately, very small. Although there have been only a handful of studies examining the effects of couples-based treatment for IPV, results suggest it is at least as effective as other treatment formats and, importantly, does not appear

to place partners at comparatively increased risk for violence, as has been hypothesized.

RELEVANT TARGET POPULATIONS AND EXCEPTIONS

Cognitive-behavioral treatment for IPV appears to be appropriate for most couples. The primary exception may be when partners engage in frequent, severe, and highly controlling forms of partner violence. Sometimes referred to as "patriarchial terrorists," these abusers do not appear to respond well to any treatments for IPV. In addition, couples treatment is not appropriate for couples in which one member of the dyad reports having significant fear of his or her partner; in such instances, individual- or group-based IPV treatment may be preferable.

COMPLICATIONS

Cognitive-behavioral treatment is well accepted by most clients who seek help for IPV. However, it is important to note that many clients are referred for treatment by the courts or other agencies within the criminal justice system. In turn, many of these clients may be unmotivated to change their behaviors and may not view the violence toward their partners as particularly problematic. In such instances, efforts to motivate clients to reconsider these beliefs may be necessary before formally engaging in cognitive-behavioral treatment to address their violence.

—*William Fals-Stewart and Gary R. Birchler*

See also: *Behavior Management (Vol. III); Behavioral Group Therapy With Children and Youth (Vol. II); Behavioral Marital Therapy (Vol. I)*

Suggested Readings

Babcock, J. C., & LaTaillade, J. J. (2000). Evaluating interventions for men who batter. In J. P. Vincent & E. N. Jouriles (Eds.), *Domestic violence: Guidelines for research-informed practice* (pp. 37–77). London: Jessica Kingsley.

Hamberger, L. K. (1997). Cognitive-behavioral treatment for men who batter their partners. *Cognitive and Behavioral Practice, 4,* 147–169.

Stith, S. M., Rosen, K. H., & McCollum, E. E. (2002). Domestic violence. In D. H. Sprenkle (Ed.), *Effectiveness research in marriage and family therapy* (pp. 223–254). Alexandria, VA: American Association for Marriage and the Family.

BEHAVIORAL TREATMENTS FOR THE ADDICTIONS

DESCRIPTION OF THE STRATEGY

The behavioral treatment of alcohol and drug addiction has an extensive history, from its humble beginnings emphasizing simple conditioning techniques like aversion therapy to its contemporary emphasis on comprehensive cognitive-behavioral approaches. While recognizing the physiological and genetic aspects of substance use, behavioral clinicians operate under the theoretical notion that addiction is a learned behavior and that treatment techniques based on learning theory can be used to change it.

Behavioral treatment of alcohol and drug abuse typically begins with a functional analysis of behavior, which is, in essence, a complete assessment of the reasons people use and abuse drugs. A thorough functional analysis may take several sessions to complete, and it lays the foundation upon which treatment is built. In determining the patterns of substance use, the counselor inquires with regard to (a) where, when, how much, and with whom does the person use the substance, (b) what triggers episodes of use, and (c) what are the consequences (reinforcers) of use?

The counselor also must determine the expectations of substance use; that is, what effect is expected and desired? Does the person use substances to feel good about himself of herself, alleviate depression, reduce anxiety, combat boredom, reduce cravings, or gain recognition from peers? The functional analysis is not limited explicitly to drug use, but rather examines the skills, strengths, and motivation for change as well.

Self-monitoring is a definite aid to the development of an accurate functional analysis of behavior. In this regard, clients are instructed to keep daily written diaries of cravings and substance use as well as the situations, thoughts, feelings, and people associated with them. To help in this effort, some clinicians ask clients to complete self-rating questionnaires such as the Obsessive-Compulsive Drinking Scale, and others provide clients with handheld computers to record details of addictive behavior.

Once a functional analysis is complete, treatment usually turns toward specific skill development. Coping-skills training can be delivered in a group or individual format, although group delivery is the typical method of choice in most treatment centers. Skills training is based on the notion that substance abuse is a maladaptive way of coping with problems. Skills training provides better methods of interpersonal communication (e.g., appropriate assertiveness), problem-solving skills, and stress management skills. Role playing and assignments to practice these new skills in daily life help to further develop this behavioral repertoire.

Refusal skills training is one of the most common elements of any behavioral approach to treatment. Alcohol and drug dependent individuals are regularly confronted by strong social pressure for continued use. Thus, they are taught not only to assertively reject the substances themselves but also to recognize and avoid the situational environments in which they are found. In this regard, treatment also focuses on the development of new social and recreational activities that are less compatible with substance use.

From a more cognitive framework, treatment entails a discussion of seemingly irrelevant decisions (SIDS). SIDs are small choices that when chained together set the stage for drug use. Each decision by itself may seem minor or irrelevant, but on the whole, the decisions lead the person down a slippery slope of continued drug use. For example, an alcohol-dependent individual may think, "I can go to that picnic and drink soda or something else." Once at the picnic, that thought may lead to "I can have one beer," which may then lead to "I can go out with my friends after the picnic." Each decision, although important in the entire scheme of things, seems irrelevant at the moment. Treatment goals include recognizing, avoiding, and coping with these seemingly irrelevant decisions.

As the individual is able to achieve abstinence, even if for short periods of time, he or she needs specific skills in how to manage urges and craving. Cravings should be "normalized" for the client, with the idea that they are to be expected as part of the recovery process. From a conditioning perspective, drugs are reinforcing in two ways: they provide positive, hedonic effects, but they also relieve withdrawal and craving. Thus, urges and craving are often triggers for relapse and continued use. Dependent individuals are taught to cope with urges using more proactive, healthy strategies.

Based on the notion that environmental and emotional cues are capable of eliciting conditioned responses that may prompt substance use, cue exposure is occasionally used in treatment to extinguish the triggering properties of relevant cues. Using photographic slides, props, or simulated bar settings, clients are repeatedly exposed to cues associated with substance use until cravings diminish in strength. Cue exposure is often used in conjunction with skills training to help clients better cope with the influence of the conditioned stimuli.

Because drug/alcohol dependence is frequently related to broader psychosocial issues, cognitive-behavioral treatment incorporates both interpersonal and intrapersonal skill development. Skills training is built on the premise that the individual lacks the appropriate internal or external resources to manage stressors that often lead to using drugs and/or alcohol. These general life skills may include any of the following: (a) managing negative thinking, (b) promoting self-efficacy, (c) anger management, (d) receiving criticism, (e) nonverbal communication, (f) assertiveness, (g) conversation skills, (h) giving/receiving positive feedback, (i) listening skills, (j) constructive criticism, (k) resolving relationship problems, (l) developing social supports, (m) problem solving, and (n) increasing pleasant activities. As individuals learn and adopt these healthy behaviors, they are better equipped to manage the daily stressors of everyday life.

Inclusion of behavioral marital therapy can significantly enhance the effects of treatment. This strategy helps to identify and resolve relationship problems that trigger substance use and provides the spouse or partner with training in methods of reinforcing sobriety. Behavioral marital therapy reduces treatment attrition and decreases episodes of domestic violence.

Once abstinence is achieved, treatment focuses on relapse prevention. Specific high-risk situations are reviewed, with emphasis on behavioral skills training (e.g., refusal skills), cognitive restructuring, and craving control. Cognitions related to "slips" or temporary episodes of use are discussed from the vantage point of the abstinence violation effect (AVE). The AVE refers to the common cognitive phenomenon in which a lapse is viewed as a total relapse (e.g., "There I go again. I'm off the wagon, and I'll never recover"). The abstinent individual who slips on one occasion develops the perception that because of this slip, abstinence will never be possible. This negative mind-set sets the stage for further lapses. Treatment is geared toward teaching the client to challenge these notions with newly rehearsed, more positive cognitive statements.

Contingency management may also be used as part of the overall treatment plan. This intervention can include the use of monetary incentives to achieve and maintain abstinence. The individual provides urine screens (or breathalyzer samples for alcohol use) that can detect recent drug use. The urine screen can test for a wide variety of illicit substances. If the screen is negative, the individual earns points or monetary reinforcers. Often, the vouchers escalate as the individual provides longer periods of abstinence. For example, the first urine screen, if negative, may result in a voucher for $1, the second $1.25, the third $1.50, and so on. Thus, the individual is reinforced with greater incentives for achieving prolonged periods of abstinence. Accumulated points or vouchers can be redeemed for household goods, reimbursement for bills, and other rewarding items as long as they are compatible with treatment goals (it is unlikely the person is given cash directly). If the urine screen returns positive, the reinforcement schedule is reset to the baseline value, but the individual retains all previous earnings/points. The voucher system may be used independently of or in conjunction with other psychosocial treatment strategies. The efficacy of the contingency management approach has been tested under a variety of reinforcement schedules and with varying magnitudes of reinforcement, and research in this area generally shows positive effects for abstinence, treatment retention, and other psychosocial improvements.

One innovative and comprehensive treatment strategy for drug and alcohol dependence that "puts it all together" is the community reinforcement approach (CRA). This intervention was developed within the alcohol treatment area and has more recently been tested and shown efficacious for opiate- and cocaine-dependent populations. Treatment elements include those listed above (with or without contingency management). In addition to these clinic-based intervention strategies, CRA utilizes community resources to reinforce abstinence. The reinforcement value of drugs/alcohol is replaced by the reinforcing the value of prolonged abstinence. CRA may help individuals find employment, improve or find better housing, engage in community activities, and so on. As the individual finds benefits in vocational areas, family relationships, and social and recreational lifestyles, abstinence is reinforced. Thus, CRA takes treatment out into the community; it is not uncommon to go hiking, to a ball game, or to the mall.

Any discussion of the behavioral treatments for drug/alcohol dependencies must mention the expanding use of pharmacotherapy used in combination with cognitive-behavioral techniques. Medications are useful in conjunction with a comprehensive treatment plan. For example, when combined with behavioral treatment, the opiate antagonist drug naltrexone increases control over alcohol urges and improves cognitive resistance to thoughts about drinking. Thus, the therapeutic effects of cognitive behavior therapy and pharmacotherapy may be synergistic.

RESEARCH BASIS

Behavioral interventions for drug and alcohol dependence have been tested in several controlled clinical trials. In a review of treatment efficacy, cognitive behavior therapy was well supported in comparison to no-treatment controls. In comparison with other active treatment interventions, this review found less consistent results. Some studies demonstrate improved outcomes for cognitive-behavioral treatments, and others demonstrate rates of efficacy similar to other active treatments, such as 12-step programs.

However, it must be noted that even the best-supported treatments for drug and alcohol dependence result in modest efficacy. Many people who struggle with drug dependence do not achieve success (complete abstinence) on their first treatment attempt. Relapse is common to all drugs of abuse, including alcohol. One clear finding from the literature is a dose-response relationship between treatment and success: The more one engages in treatment, the better the chances for successful outcome.

RELEVANT TARGET POPULATIONS AND EXCEPTIONS

Behaviorally based treatments of drug and alcohol dependence are best suited to individuals who adopt a behavioral point of view on their illness. From this perspective, drug and alcohol misuse is considered a habit that can be unlearned, just as it was learned. In contrast, the disease model of addictions is often viewed as being antithetical to cognitive-behavioral approaches. Some individuals are committed to the notion that the only way to recovery is through the fellowship of recovery groups. Though there are some similarities between these approaches, the underlying differences may pose competing messages to those seeking drug abuse treatment.

One particularly large clinical trial (Project MATCH) examined which individuals (diagnosed with alcohol dependence) best respond to which treatments. The study tested more than 20 patient/treatment-matching hypotheses, but few predicted response to treatment. Despite these negative findings, the search continues to determine which individuals benefit most from which treatments. Opiate antagonists in conjunction with behavioral techniques seem to be more effective with more chronic, early-onset addicts than less severe ones.

COMPLICATIONS

As with most other areas of behavioral intervention, treatment of drug and alcohol dependence is often complicated by other psychiatric impairment. Clinical and subclinical depression and anxiety disorders can interfere with one's motivation for treatment and course during recovery. Because drugs and alcohol are often taken to cope with negative mood, addressing underlying depression and anxiety is warranted. Similarly, a significant number of individuals who present for drug abuse treatment may have a history of physical and/or sexual abuse. As such, clinicians often evaluate clients for posttraumatic stress syndrome (PTSD). Often, individuals who enroll in drug abuse treatment services abuse are dependent upon multiple substances. While treatment is complicated by multiple dependencies, the principles of treatment remain the same.

CASE ILLUSTRATION

"Raymond" was a 35-year-old male diagnosed with alcohol dependence, cocaine dependence, and cannabis abuse. His early history was marked by periodic episodes of sexual and physical abuse by multiple perpetrators. His family history was positive for alcohol abuse by both parents. His father left the house when Raymond was 7 years old. He dropped out of high school at age 16, and it was around this time that he began using alcohol and cannabis. At the time of treatment, Raymond was drinking daily, approximately 12 beers per day. He used cocaine intranasally as often as he could afford it (approximately three to four times per week). He reported a past history of intravenous use of cocaine, as well as previous experimentation with heroin. He used cannabis approximately one to two times per week.

Raymond's longest period of abstinence from all drugs was about 1 year, achieved through regular attendance and participation in Alcoholics Anonymous and Narcotics Anonymous (AA and NA) programs. At the time of treatment, he was unemployed and was financially supported by Medicaid. He resided in a trailer with his girlfriend and his sister. He reported that his girlfriend was addicted to benzodiazepines and occasionally used cocaine and alcohol. His sister used cocaine daily. Neither was motivated for treatment.

Raymond's case history highlights the difficulties present in drug abuse treatment. Briefly, pervasive instability and psychosocial stressors mark his history. His limited educational background together with cognitive and reading deficits (dyslexia) presented a challenge throughout treatment. Though he presented for drug abuse treatment, his abuse history suggested the possibility of PTSD and/or clinical depression.

Raymond's personal goals for treatment presented another clinical challenge. At the outset of the treatment, he was motivated to abstain completely from cocaine and to get his alcohol use "under control," but he had little desire to alter his cannabis use. Moreover, the fact that his girlfriend was also drug dependent but not engaged in treatment represented a significant obstacle.

Raymond admitted himself for inpatient treatment for a brief (3-day) medically supervised detoxification. On the day of his discharge, he began an intensive outpatient treatment program. The program consisted of individual and group sessions four times a week over a 1-month period, followed by "step-down" care in which participants attend once per week for variable duration.

Treatment began with a functional analysis of Raymond's drug use. He noted that he used primarily in response to boredom. He would go to the local store, where he would purchase up to five 32-ounce beers; he rarely kept alcohol in his home. He drank at home, often by himself. Neighborhood acquaintances often came by later in the day, at which time Raymond would start using cocaine. It was not uncommon for Raymond to come home and find complete strangers in his house with his girlfriend and sister.

Treatment focused on skills training: learning drug refusal skills, managing urges, developing coping strategies, identifying high-risk situations, identifying seemingly irrelevant decisions, awareness and management of negative thinking, improving self-efficacy and assertiveness, and relapse prevention. Because Raymond drank and abused drugs primarily in

response to boredom, another focus of treatment was to identify and expand interest in other activities. Raymond responded fairly well to treatment. He achieved and maintained abstinence from cocaine for the entire 30-day treatment period. He continued to drink, but with less frequency and amount. Although complete abstinence may have been preferred, this pattern of somewhat-controlled drinking was compatible with stated goals at the outset of treatment. Indeed, in the behavioral treatment field, harm reduction approaches (in which reduced risky alcohol/drug use rather than abstinence is the goal) are gaining increased recognition and use.

Raymond made other significant improvements through treatment. He was able to identify his passive behaviors and, in time, learned to assertively stabilize his home environment. He removed unwanted people from his home and was able to reject visitors whom he knew would tempt him to resume drug use. His sister eventually moved out of the house and enrolled in her own treatment program.

While Raymond made significant improvements both in regard to his personal drug use and his home environment, problems still remained. His girlfriend continued to abuse benzodiazepines and was unwilling to seek treatment. The neighborhood in which he lived remained unstable. Relapse will remain a significant threat for Raymond without continued treatment and significant social and environmental improvements.

—*Peter M. Miller and Matthew J. Carpenter*

See also: *Behavioral Contracting (Vol. II); Behavioral Treatment of Cigarette Smoking (Vol. I); Operant Conditioning (Vol. III)*

Suggested Readings

Anton, R. F., & Swift, R. M. (2003). Current pharmacotherapies of alcoholism: A U.S. perspective. *American Journal on Addictions, 12,* S53–S68.

Azrin, N. H. (1976). Improvements in the community-reinforcement approach to alcoholism. *Behavior Research and Therapy, 14,* 339–348.

Carroll, K. M. (1996). Relapse prevention as a psychosocial treatment approach: A review of controlled clinical trials. *Experimental and Clinical Psychopharmacology, 4,* 46–54.

Higgins, S. T., Wong, C. J., Badger, G. J., Ogden, D. E. H., & Dantona, R. L. (2000). Contingent reinforcement increases cocaine abstinence during outpatient treatment and 1 year of follow-up. *Journal of Consulting and Clinical Psychology, 68,* 64–72.

Kadden, R. M. (2001) Behavioral and cognitive-behavioral treatments for alcoholism: Research opportunities. *Addictive Behaviors, 26*(4), 489–507.

Marlatt, G. A., & Gordon, J. R. (1985). *Relapse prevention: Maintenance strategies in the treatment of addictive behaviors.* New York: Guilford Press.

McCrady, B. S. (1994). Alcoholics Anonymous and behavior therapy: Can habits be treated as diseases? Can diseases be treated as habits? *Journal of Consulting and Clinical Psychology, 62,* 1159–1166.

Meyers, R. J., & Smith, J. E. (1995). *Clinical guide to alcohol treatment: The community reinforcement approach.* New York: Guilford Press.

Onken, L. S., Blaine, J. D., Genser, S., & Horton, A. M. (1997). Treatment of drug-dependent individuals with comorbid mental disorders. *NIDA Research Monograph, 172.* Rockville, MD: National Institute on Drug Abuse.

Project MATCH Research Group. (1998). Matching alcoholism treatment to client heterogeneity: Treatment main effects and matching effects on drinking during treatment. *Journal of Studies on Alcohol, 59,* 631–639.

U.S. Department of Health and Human Services. (2000). *Therapy manuals for drug addiction: A cognitive-behavioral approach: Treating cocaine addiction.* Bethesda, MD: National Institute on Drug Abuse.

BEHAVIORAL TREATMENT IN NATURAL ENVIRONMENTS

DESCRIPTION OF THE STRATEGY

The natural environment has long been an ally for behavior therapy in the production and facilitation of therapeutic change, especially in anxiety disorders and mood disorders. Although behavior therapy more commonly occurs in analog settings (e.g., in office, in hospital, day treatment), ultimately, therapy gains realized in such artificial settings have to be transported, or generalized, to the natural settings in which any given individual patient conducts his or her personal life. This eventuality and necessity have led to relying on natural-environment settings in cases where analog settings alone do not sufficiently produce the desired clinical outcome. This is especially relevant in cases when there are problems with generalizability, or transportability, to settings in which the patient later has to be able to apply the skill sets acquired during in-office treatment to their real-life circumstances.

It is not unusual to see problems of generalizability in treatment-refractory, chronic, and severe cases due

to the role naturally occurring reinforcers and punishers play in the production and maintenance of clinical behavior sets. Indeed, it may be that the naturally occurring information present in the patient's environment, which maintains problems over time, cannot be adequately reproduced in an analog setting. Without access to the genuine, or actual, maintaining variables, it may be that results produced in an artificial setting are general enough that they lack sufficient specificity to adequately mimic what the patient later encounters when he or she returns to the natural cues that historically have produced and maintained the clinically relevant behavior set. This likely, in part at least, accounts for high rates of lapse and relapse realized by many anxiety- and mood-disordered patients upon return to natural settings. That is, skill sets established in the analog setting fail to be relevant enough in natural environments to sufficiently translate across these different settings, thereby leading to a return to the genuine behaviors the natural settings support. This is often referred to as the centrally important issue of ecological relevance.

In fact, some clinical presentations often cannot be adequately treated without direct reliance on the natural environment or naturally occurring cues. For example, treatment of specific phobias often rely on presence of the phobic cues within an exposure paradigm. While some natural cues can readily be brought into an office setting (e.g., a dog), others are not as readily recreated artificially (e.g., heights). Even with a simple cue, such as an animal or an insect phobia, there are commonly more cues than the direct, single stimulus contributing to fear conditioning and avoidance learning. To reduce fear from exposure to a dog, it might have to be a specific dog (i.e., a surrogate is similar, but not sufficient), or it might have to be dogs generally but in a specific location (i.e., there is something specific to the setting that makes the dog, or dogs, especially threatening). Until adequate functional assessments can be conducted of the contributions natural settings might bring to a simple stimulus, it cannot be fully known whether using the stimulus alone in exposure will be sufficient.

The point becomes even more relevant in the treatment of more complex stimuli, such as heights. In those instances, it will typically be necessary to go to the offending stimuli in order for natural or normal habituation and extinction of problematic reactivity to occur. However, many analog versions of heights are being created (e.g., virtual reality), so delivery might be possible in the artificial setting. Virtual reality has been met with mixed results due to the same issue of generalizability from the office setting to the real stimuli. When engaging in an analog version, no matter how technologically savvy, the patient nevertheless knows it is artificial and not genuine or real. In addition, some specific clinical presentations may still necessitate the use of behavioral interventions within the natural environment.

Limitations of patient mobility may also require interventions within natural settings. For example, severe panic disorder with agoraphobia may, by the nature of the disorder, inhibit the patient's perceived ability to travel to an office setting for the delivery of therapeutic services. The helping professional may need to provide both the educational information of the treatment rationale and the behavioral intervention within the natural environment to facilitate treatment. Without the ability to deliver services in such a manner, the patient may refuse clinic-based interventions and feel unable to participate in otherwise efficacious treatment. Similarly, clinically relevant behaviors may occur more exclusively within the natural settings. For instance, individuals who compulsively hoard or who exhibit extensive but specific checking may manifest the behaviors in a number of settings, but typically, the location of worst interference is in personal settings, like the home. Given such circumstances, treatment within the natural environment is not only indicated, but may indeed even be necessary for successful, long-term treatment gains.

Research has historically illustrated in vivo, or live (i.e., real), exposure to be more powerful than any in-imagination version. There are some triggers where it simply is not practical, and perhaps not ethical, to use live or real exposure; however, whenever possible, in vivo is a more powerful agent of change than one with artificial qualities. The natural environment contains important curative components that may be difficult, if not impossible, to recreate artificially, and even if it can be done, ecological relevance may suffer.

RESEARCH BASIS

The research shows that anxiety disorders are the single most commonly presented complaint at community clinics and hospitals alike, and it is known that anxiety is the single most relevant variable in functional impairment. In addition, anxiety disorders are a tremendous financial burden unless resolved, and they account for a greater proportion of total mental health care costs than do either depression or schizophrenia. It is also known that anxiety disorders tend to be chronic and often do not remit without effective treatment. This illustrates that adequate treatment of anxiety-based conditions are paramount on multiple levels (e.g., intrapersonal, interpersonal, occupational, societal).

Adequate utilization of the natural environment to thoroughly counteract fear conditioning and avoidance learning has received much more attention in recent years. Nonetheless, in the United States, due to limitations primarily imposed by managed care, this sometimes critical component of mental health care delivery has been underutilized. Many other regions (e.g., Europe, Scandinavia, Canada) have more commonly used ecological relevance to maximize the impact their treatment delivery provides. (See the suggested readings for some European illustrations.) The view that the natural environment is ultimately a more powerful agent of change is also supported by the literature suggesting that homework facilitates longer-lasting change and prevents relapse more than analog treatment alone. This well-established phenomenon is driven by the fact that most homework is carried out in the patient's natural environment, thereby more readily facilitating an integration of the skill sets learned in an office-to-home environment. It is noteworthy to observe that behavior therapy (and variations thereof) is amongst the most efficacious and effective treatment available for a majority of mental health issues. This is in juxtaposition to many other orientations and modalities that simply do not produce as much, as strong, or as lasting change. Some principal differences can indeed relate to the degree to which the natural environment is directly used in the treatment approaches. Consequently, treatments that rely strictly on an office environment to facilitate change will not be as efficacious as those that include components of ecological relevance.

RELEVANT TARGET POPULATIONS AND EXCEPTIONS

Most patients who demonstrate either an anxiety condition or depression stand to gain substantially more by increased direct contact with natural settings during the treatment process. Many anxiety-disordered patients can be treated without integration of natural cues and settings, but optimized outcomes are more commonly seen with treatment programs that standardly integrate this into their overall treatment packages.

Many hospital-based programs have begun to utilize home-based care provisions in order to more regularly manage the issue of generalizability. This happens not only on an aftercare, transitional basis; in some cases, where a patient perhaps is highly immobilized by fear, it is now not unusual to see home-based care as a precursor to hospital care to facilitate patients being able to come to the hospital under their own efforts. Involuntary hospitalization and being brought to a hospital or office setting with the direct assistance from another person can solidify and confirm many fears typically experienced by chronic, severe, and refractory anxiety-disordered patients. For example, if a patient is fearful of leaving the home but needs to travel through busy streets and crowded areas to an office for treatment, that trip alone may confirm the fears that the outside world is a dangerous place and the home is the only place that is safe. As isolative behavior is typically a core feature that both ignites and maintains depressive symptomatology, clinical depression so frequently necessitates an increased contact with opportunities for reinforcement that natural settings are a self-evident choice for treatment integration.

Natural settings may initially be inappropriate for extremely disordered patients, as the stimuli available in such settings may inherently serve to overwhelm a patient in the early stages of treatment. Consequently, pacing and choice of intensity of natural setting may play an integral role in ultimate treatment success. Nonetheless, patients must learn to function in natural settings; thus, integrating aspects of high ecological relevance are important in reducing future medical utilization. Even in the most severe cases, the treatment must incorporate some element of the natural setting if the individual is ever going to function well in such an environment.

COMPLICATIONS

The most commonly experienced complication with using natural settings for treatment purposes has principally to do with reimbursement issues and liability issues. On a learning theory level, there really are very few true complications, but the pragmatics of treatment provision in nonoffice settings arise with some frequency. First, potentially traveling to deliver treatment in a patient's place of living, working, or some

other natural environment in which he or she experiences difficulties presents unique issues. A health care provider who works out of an office can see patients back-to-back, hour after hour, whereas the helping professional who travels to a patient spends (i.e., wastes) time getting to and back from the location. Outside of having to figure reimbursement for this lost time, there is also a potential issue with wear and tear on personal transportation modes. This can also be viewed as an issue of reimbursement.

Some third-party payers, especially in the United States, will also not reimburse for treatment that is delivered outside of an office setting, and sometimes regardless of the therapeutic necessity. Supervision of therapy (when needed) may also become more difficult when there are multiple settings and long distances involved in the delivery of services. These issues can perhaps be best viewed as problems of a programmatic, policy, and procedural nature.

A second and potentially more potent obstacle to treatment in the natural environment is the possible ethical and liability vulnerabilities. That is, a clinician delivering treatment in an office setting is often within earshot, if not eyesight, of other treatment providers. In-office treatment, therefore, does not as readily lend itself to accusations of malpractice, neglect, and abuse as does working alone with a patient in a natural setting. In the natural environment, it may be the word of a patient against that of the treatment provider. Clinicians can commonly circumvent this situation by delivering treatment in pairs, but this solution obviously increases the financial complication and furthers ethical (i.e., confidentiality) concerns. Another issue of concern may involve the variability of natural settings.

Neither the helping professional nor the patient is able to control all aspects of treatment within the natural environment, and therefore it is important to discuss with the patient the limitations of confidentiality outside of the office. The treatment provider has less control over a natural-environment setting and thus cannot ensure that, for example, the walls in an apartment are soundproof enough, that passersby may not see the patient during treatment, that treatment will not be uninterrupted by distracting phone calls, and so on. Although an open and honest conversation about such risks can clarify many of these complications, the clinician simply cannot anticipate all situations or all patient reactions to the situations. It is vital to collaboratively brainstorm solutions to potential complications, including questions from bystanders or the chance of meeting people familiar with the patient (e.g., coworkers, friends, family members). Use of behavioral interventions within the natural environment does not necessarily dissolve patient concerns regarding confidentiality of treatment; indeed, perceived threats to confidentiality may realistically be magnified. The helping professional needs to attend more closely to issues of confidentiality in the absence of the office setting. Privacy and privilege are patient rights throughout any treatment, despite location, and collaborative conversations regarding how the patient wishes to address such situations is often enough to diffuse possible ethical or treatment complications. Nonetheless, the clinician remains more at risk for ethical and legal recourse should a questionable situation arise.

Not only does professional and legal safety become more complicated in the natural setting, but the clinician's sense of physical safety may also become more in jeopardy. The clinician normally chooses where his or her office is located and thus may consider the safety of its location; however, the clinician cannot choose where a patient lives or works. Treating a patient in a natural setting may put the clinician's physical safety more at risk or at least make the clinician feel more at risk. Some health care providers may have a sense of security when providing treatment in an office setting. However, outside the facility, there may be some awkwardness and difficulty for the clinician to comfortably deliver therapy to patients in a natural setting. Natural-environment treatment is challenging financially, legally, ethically, and personally and therefore demands extensive cost-benefit consideration by the clinician.

CASE ILLUSTRATION

"Jane" was a 53-year-old, divorced, unemployed woman who had, for most of her life, struggled with some specific phobias, namely, heights and driving. She had also experienced depression on and off throughout her life, secondary to anxiety. The fears over the years had insidiously compressed the parts of the world that remained available to her, and she became increasingly withdrawn, isolative, and avoidant. In most ways, she was indeed like a stereotypical specific-phobia patient. Jane had tried a lot of different treatments for anxiety, ranging from past-life regressions to psychodynamic work, but she had never attempted behavior therapy.

In her life as a real estate agent, she depended closely on her ability to show properties to prospective buyers. As her world access became increasingly narrow, she found that she was no longer able to show properties outside of discreet "safe zones," nor could she show properties across the river, as this would necessitate the crossing of bridges. In the end, before she sought behavior therapy treatment, she could also not show a property that was not on the ground floor. She simply would not go into areas where properties were multiple-story heights. This obviously severely restricted her productivity, and before too long, she was fired from the real estate company she had been with for 15 years. Due to her strong limitations, she could not find employment with other agents, as, often, she could not get to their offices for interviews and, more commonly, because she admitted she would not be able to show certain properties if they fell outside of locations she could travel to. Upon discussion of symptoms with her primary care physician, who had prescribed an antidepressant medication, it was suggested to Jane that she could perhaps benefit from an evidence-based treatment for specific phobia. Although fearful of what this treatment would be like, Jane felt she had few other realistic options for improving her functioning.

After a functional assessment was conducted, the behavioral modification plan was presented to Jane, in which models were given for understanding the role of negative reinforcement on anxiety maintenance and how anxiety remits. A thorough discussion followed of how hierarchical, gradual exposure is conducted. With some trepidation, Jane agreed. Over several months, the treatment gently, gradually, but systematically went about exposing her to the naturally occurring cues that sparked her fears, while appropriate response prevention was also practiced.

Gradually, but predictably, Jane's reactivity became decreased systematically to natural situations, to the point where she began to be able to cross all the bridges in town and go up into tall buildings of 12 to 20 floors. She was able to go back into certain areas of town to which she had once been "blocked" from going by excessive and irrational fears. Soon, she was able to begin to make property sales because she was once again able to show them without exhibiting fear and escape behaviors that may have previously prevented sales. In fact, she made a strong point of dropping all safety behaviors in natural settings because she had begun to realize and recognize that others found her behaviors unusual and, at times, ridiculous.

Outside of some basic early in-office work to deliver the principles behind learning theory and exposure, the majority of Jane's treatment was delivered in the natural settings in which she would have to function when she finished treatment. Over the treatment phase, she continued to steadily make notable gains, and at the end of treatment, she was able to travel in ways and to places she had not been in for 15 to 20 years. Most important, she was no longer limited by fear and avoidance, and she was able to obtain a fully functional and more adaptive lifestyle of coping and effectively dealing with life's stressors.

—*Johan Rosqvist, Brad Evans, Dani Maack, Aaron Tritch, and Alecia Sundsmo*

See also: Bell and Pad Bladder Training (Vol. II); Classroom Management (Vol. III); Contextualism (Vol. I)

Suggested Readings

Barlow, D. H. (2001). *Anxiety and its disorders* (2nd ed.). New York: Guilford Press.

Beutler, L. E., Clarkin, J. F., & Bongar, B. (2000). *Guidelines for the systematic treatment of the depressed patient.* Oxford, UK: Oxford University Press.

Boersma, K., den Hengst, S., Dekker, J., & Emmelkamp, P. M. G. (1976). Exposure and response prevention in the natural environment: A comparison with obsessive-compulsive patients. *Behaviour Research and Therapy, 14,* 19–24.

Emmelkamp, P. M. G., van Linden-van den Heuvell, C., Rüphan, M., & Sanderman, R. (1989). Home-based treatment of obsessive-compulsive patients: Intersession interval and therapist involvement. *Behaviour Therapy and Research, 27*(1), 89–93.

Marks, I. M. (1987). *Fears, phobias, and rituals: Panic, anxiety, and their disorders.* Oxford, UK: Oxford University Press.

McLean, P. D., & Woody, S. R. (2001). *Anxiety disorders in adults: An evidence-based approach to psychological treatment.* Oxford, UK: Oxford University Press.

Rice, D. P., & Miller, L. S. (1993). The economic burden of mental disorders. *Advances in Health Economics and Health Services Research, 14,* 37–53.

Rosqvist, J., Thomas, J. C., Egan, D., & Willis, B. S. (2002). Home-based cognitive-behavioral treatment of chronic, refractory obsessive-compulsive disorder can be effective: Single case analysis of four patients. *Behavior Modification, 26*(2), 205–222.

van den Hout, M., Emmelkamp, P., Kraaykamp, H., & Griez, E. (1988). Behavioral treatment of obsessive-compulsives: Inpatient vs. outpatient. *Behaviour Therapy and Research, 26*(4), 331–332.

Willis, B. S., Rosqvist, J., Egan, D., Baney, D., & Manzo, P. (1998). Inpatient and home-based treatment of obsessive-compulsive disorder. In M. A. Jenike, L. Baer, & W. E. Minichiello (Eds.), *Obsessive-compulsive disorders: Practical management* (3rd ed., pp. 570–591). Boston: Mosby.

BEHAVIORAL TREATMENT OF CIGARETTE SMOKING

BIOBEHAVIORAL MODEL OF SMOKING

The most prevalent smoking cessation programs have employed behavioral principles in concert with other strategies. "Typical" behavioral treatment programs focus on antecedents and consequences of smoking and include cognitive techniques that promote coping during and after treatment. The behavioral perspective is that smoking is a learned behavior, originally initiated by psychosocial variables (e.g., adult modeling, curiosity, peer pressure, availability, rebelliousness) and maintained by physiological dependence on nicotine in combination with conditioned environmental stimuli that elicit the urge to smoke once the behavior has been firmly established. In this sense, smoking is a highly overlearned behavior. An average pack-a-day smoker puffs an estimated 160 times each day, providing ample opportunity for internal cues (e.g., anxiety, hunger) and environmental cues (e.g., drinking coffee, talking on the phone) to become associated with the urge to smoke. The act of smoking can also be heavily reinforced operantly by both internal (e.g., pleasure, craving reduction) and external (e.g., social approval from other smokers, handling the cigarette) consequences.

The aversiveness of withdrawal from nicotine must be considered in any model of smoking behavior. Self-monitoring has revealed that coughing, craving for tobacco, feelings of aggression, increased appetite, irritability, nervousness, and restlessness increase in severity during the first week after quitting, followed by a decrease in severity thereafter. Constipation and craving for sweets are at higher levels than baseline for 6 weeks after quitting. Patients who maintain abstinence for 6 weeks experience fewer symptoms during the initial 2 weeks after quitting than those who don't. In addition, at 6 weeks, abstinent patients typically experience symptoms at baseline or lower levels of severity. Clearly, many individuals experience the act of quitting smoking as aversive. The role of expectations in the experience of withdrawal symptoms has yet to be adequately evaluated.

A comprehensive biobehavioral theory of smoking must include biological factors as well. Smokers smoke to cause temporary improvements in performance and affect. There is a periodic pattern of arousal and alertness during smoking, followed by calming and tension reduction after smoking. Smoking stimulates the production of betaendorphins and vasopressin. These neurotransmitters are known to reduce pain, increase tolerance to stress, improve memory, increase concentration, and speed up information processing. Therefore, smoking is maintained by both powerful negative (e.g., reduction of craving) and positive inducements. There may even be an inherited predisposition with regard to susceptibility to these inducements.

DESCRIPTION OF THE STRATEGY

Cognitive-behavioral methods often employ strategies designed to counteract these negative and positive inducements to smoke. These interventions include (a) aversive strategies such as smoke holding, rapid smoking, and noxious imagery, (b) nicotine-fading and controlled-smoking techniques, (c) self-control and self-monitoring strategies that help smokers identify and modify situations, cognitions, feelings, and other cues that promote urges to smoke, (d) partner support, (e) hypnosis, (f) acceptance-based strategies, and (g) relapse prevention strategies.

RESEARCH BASIS

Reports of initial cessation from behavioral programs have ranged from 50% to 100%, with relapse rates of 70% to 80% among studies that provided 3-month follow-up data. This dramatic decline from initial cessation to immediate relapse among the majority of smokers has caused a shift in emphasis toward relapse prevention among smoking researchers. Behavioral approaches have generally been found to be superior to control conditions. Successful treatment approaches, including behavioral interventions, are more successful with light smokers and obtain abstinence rates that range between 25% and 33%. At 6- and 12-month follow-ups, the "average" participant in the "average" smoking control program has a 20% chance of being abstinent. Involvement in one of the more successful programs may increase these odds to between 30% and 40%. It should be noted that most smokers quit without the help of an organized program, perhaps leaving the programs to deal with the smokers who have the most difficulty quitting.

Nicotine gum and transdermal nicotine patches are forms of nicotine replacement that have become standard components of many behavioral treatment programs. Nicotine replacement is featured prominently in the clinical practice guidelines for smoking cessation. One of the difficulties in interpreting the effectiveness of nicotine gum and transdermal nicotine independently of behavioral treatment is that they are designed to be combined with behavior therapy, and the vast majority of published studies include some form of behavioral intervention when nicotine replacement is used. Comparison studies involving nicotine replacement and behavior therapy rarely have single-intervention conditions. This makes it difficult to determine how behavior therapy alone (i.e., without the nicotine replacement or placebo) would fare in a direct comparison with nicotine replacement alone or the combination treatment.

In specialized smoking cessation clinics that included intense behavioral interventions, abstinence rates at 6 months with behavior therapy plus nicotine gum versus behavior therapy plus placebo were 27% and 18%, and the 12-month rates were 23% and 13%, respectively. In general medical practice with "minimal interventions," the results have been less promising, with about 11% quitting with either nicotine gum or placebo gum. These trials demonstrate the benefit of combining nicotine gum with behavior therapy, while use of nicotine gum as the sole intervention is unlikely to be of significant benefit.

In meta-analyses of double-blind, placebo-controlled studies where the nicotine patch was applied as an adjunct to behavioral management, abstinence rates favor the active patch (22% abstinence) as opposed to placebo patch (9% abstinence) at 6-month follow-up. The results with behavior therapy plus transdermal nicotine were generally in the range reported for other successful smoking cessation programs. The optimal duration of transdermal nicotine therapy remains an empirical question, although one review concluded that its use beyond 6 weeks (but no more than 8 weeks) may be indicated only for the most dependent smokers. One study found that behavior therapy combined with 3 weeks of transdermal nicotine therapy resulted in similar outcome (28% abstinence) as behavior therapy combined with 12 weeks of transdermal nicotine therapy (29% abstinence) at 1 month following termination of nicotine replacement. In general, use of the active patch without behavior therapy has been disappointing compared with the placebo patch.

Recently, antidepressants, particularly bupropion, have been added to behavior therapy as an aid to smoking cessation. In a study funded by the manufacturer, 1-year abstinence rates (23%) with buproprion combined with behavior therapy were similar to those found with the patch and behavior therapy. Another study found quit rates as high as 35% at 1-year follow-up when bupropion was combined with the patch and behavioral counseling. As with nicotine replacement, bupropion alone is rarely evaluated, and when it has been, the results have been very disappointing. For example, one study found less than a 5% quit rate at 1-year follow-up when bupropion was utilized without behavioral counseling. Also, bupropion failed to reduce or delay relapse to smoking in smokers who quit while on nicotine patch. So, while there is some evidence that bupropion can aid smoking cessation, there are really too few safety and efficacy studies with long-term follow-up to recommend it as a first-line treatment at this time.

RELEVANT TARGET POPULATIONS AND EXCEPTIONS

No smoker is too young or too old to quit smoking. Dramatic health benefits accrue from quitting even after many years of smoking. Although many patients quit smoking without it, pharmacotherapy can provide an assist. Based on our review of the cessation literature, we offer the following suggestions regarding the addition of nicotine replacement or an antidepressant to behavior therapy for smoking cessation:

1. Encourage compliance with some form of self-help, individual, or group cognitive-behavioral treatment (e.g., "Butt Out," "Quit Smart," "Freedom From Smoking," or "Freshstart" programs) in order to access pharmacological interventions. Such behavioral programs are generally relatively cheap, well packaged, and effective.

2. Build in maintenance sessions and withdrawal from nicotine replacement.

3. Strongly warn patients not to smoke on the patch if for no other reason than it significantly decreases their chances of quitting.

4. Use carbon monoxide monitoring to give feedback, reinforce success, and verify abstinence.

5. Encourage termination of the patch if there is evidence the patient is still smoking after 2 weeks. Have the patient set a new target quit date and try again later.

6. Consider encouraging a 3-week "rapid deployment" nicotine replacement schedule for most patients, because it appears to be cheaper and equally effective as a longer regimen.

7. In all cases, encourage termination of the patch after 6 weeks, because there is no evidence of improved outcome with a longer regimen.

8. Do not routinely prescribe antidepressants, including bupropion, as a smoking cessation aid until more independently generated safety and efficacy data are available.

Following such guidelines will likely make the combination of nicotine replacement and behavior therapy safer, less costly, and more effective.

COMPLICATIONS

As with any drug intervention, there are reasons for caution regarding nicotine replacement. There is the philosophical problem of using a drug to help patients stop using the same drug to which they are addicted. Nicotine replacement is expensive, especially if used as directed for 6 to 12 weeks. Pharmacies currently offer the patch for about $150 for a 6-week supply. Many patients are able to quit without nicotine replacement. Some patients inappropriately put all their eggs in the nicotine patch basket and may not try the behavioral strategies as vigorously.

Some patients use the patch just to cut down and not to quit. More than half of patients continue to smoke while using the gum. Similar smoking rates are found with the patch. In a sample of veterans using behavior therapy combined with the patch, 68% smoked at least one cigarette while wearing the patch. In one minimal intervention study, 55% of patch users were still smoking after 12 weeks of using the patch. In a naturalistic follow-up of elderly patch users, 47% smoked while using the patch, including 20% who smoked every day.

Concomitant smoking has been strongly associated with failure to achieve abstinence. Because many patients do continue to smoke (usually less than 10 cigarettes per day) while on the patch, some may inappropriately get counted as nonsmokers using standard carbon monoxide (CO) levels. Though there is currently no evidence of increased morbidity, case reports suggest there may be a small minority of patients who experience increased cardiovascular risk from smoking on the patch. Although there is the possibility of harm reduction or decreased morbidity from long-term nicotine replacement, this has yet to be demonstrated empirically.

Longer use of the patch may prolong withdrawal too long for some patients. Withdrawal, which can be essentially accomplished in 1 week, may end up taking 6 to 16 weeks or more. Unlike nicotine gum, the patch delivers nicotine constantly to patients whether they want it or not. Some patients have a hard time weaning themselves from the patch. The patch causes skin irritation in some patients and may cause sleep disruption.

CASE ILLUSTRATION

"Joe" was a 54-year-old disabled veteran who had smoked up to 2 packs a day for almost 40 years. He had never before tried to quit smoking. In addressing smoking, his treatment provider considered Joe's stage of quitting. When Joe first came in for treatment, he was among the 15% of smokers who are in the precontemplation stage, and he was not considering quitting. Precontemplators are unaware, unwilling, or discouraged about quitting smoking. They may believe they have their smoking under control. For whatever reasons, they are not considering quitting in the near future, and they are the least likely to benefit from intensive smoking cessation training. To move to the next stage, precontemplators need to identify smoking as a problem, increase awareness of the negative aspects of smoking, and learn to accurately evaluate their ability to quit smoking. Joe's doctor gave him carbon monoxide feedback and showed him that his CO level was in the unhealthy range. As a result, Joe started thinking about quitting smoking, mainly because he wanted to live long enough to see his grandson grow up. This moved him into the contemplation stage.

Contemplators are actively thinking about quitting. Contemplators are interested in gathering information about smoking and how to quit. Contemplators are more upset about their smoking than precontemplators.

They tend to consider the advantages and disadvantages of quitting smoking. They are weighing their options, but they are not quite ready to take action. Contemplators can benefit from advice and information about smoking cessation because it provides the necessary information they need to move to the preparation stage of quitting. Joe's physician began teaching him about the medical consequences of smoking and the medical benefits of quitting. On his doctor's advice, he joined a smoking cessation class, where he learned about the normal stages of quitting and that quitting smoking is not an "all-or-none" phenomenon. He learned how to use "wrap sheets" (structured tracking sheets that wrap around a pack of cigarettes) so he could keep an accurate accounting of his baseline smoking and to reinforce progressive reductions in his smoking rate.

He was given the Reasons for Quitting Scale to evaluate his intrinsic and extrinsic motivation, the Therapeutic Reactance Scale to evaluate his resistance to instruction, the Partner Interaction Questionnaire to evaluate the impact of the smoker's partner, and the Fagerstrom Nicotine Dependence Scale to determine the strength of his addiction. After doing this, he learned that he was motivated primarily by health concerns, that he tended to resist advice to quit, and that he was a heavily dependent smoker.

Joe picked his granddaughter's birthday 3 weeks later as his target quit day. Setting a target quit day moved Joe into the preparation stage. In the preparation stage, smokers feel ready to change. They are about to take action and are in the process of setting goals. It is a good idea to have the smoker pick a target date that is 2 to 4 weeks into the future. Joe was exposed to relaxation and self-hypnosis skills to reduce his anxiety and harness the power of self-suggestion. Joe's wife attended a session and was encouraged to eliminate nagging, shunning, and punishing behaviors, while increasing supportive and reinforcing behaviors. She offered to help Joe in the yard as a way to support one of his favorite hobbies and exercise as an alternative to smoking.

The action stage involves actually changing smoking behavior. Joe began the action stage by practicing some of the strategies designed to limit and eliminate smoking. He was taught strategies for avoiding or altering smoking cues or substituting alternatives to smoking. He decided to practice not smoking while driving his car for a week before his actual quit day. He cleaned his car ashtray in the dishwasher and filled it with sugarless candy. He put his cigarettes in the trunk of his car so he could not possibly give in to an urge to smoke while driving. He paid attention to his urge to smoke while driving, while not giving in to it. He noticed that he could have an urge to smoke but still not smoke and that he didn't go crazy, as he had once feared. He switched brands from Marlboro regulars to Marlboro lights as a "nicotine-fading" strategy in order to reduce his nicotine dependence prior to quit day. He practiced a taste aversion or "smoke-holding" procedure at least once a day to give the cigarettes a bad taste. This involved holding cigarette smoke in his mouth for 30 seconds at a time, without inhaling it into his lungs, while breathing fresh air into his lungs through his nose.

On his quit day, he celebrated by getting his car cleaned, his house cleaned, and his teeth cleaned. He started the 21-mg nicotine patch the same day. Joe began learning strategies to deal with relapse in order to progress to the maintenance stage. He set a short-term goal of quitting for 3 days. He created a written contract to quit for 3 days or send $100 to his least favorite politician, President George Bush. He gave the money in an envelope to his wife for her to hold and mail should he not achieve his short-term goal. His wife, who was also quitting smoking, did the same thing but addressed her envelope to her least favorite politician, Al Gore. Joe achieved his short-term goal and sent the letter without the money. He used the money to take his wife out to a fancy dinner. He switched to the 14-mg patch on the second week of his abstinence and finally to the 7-mg patch on the third week. He highlighted the money he was saving from not smoking by putting it in a jar. At the end of every month, he had almost $200 in the jar, enough for him and his wife to have a glamorous dinner out, something they both enjoyed.

Even months after quitting smoking, he still experienced psychological triggers for an urge to smoke. He filled out the Smoking Self-Efficacy Questionnaire in order to predict the situations in which he was most likely to relapse. He recognized that the holidays would be a high-risk time because his sister, who smoked, would visit with her family. Seeing her smoke was a powerful trigger for him to smoke. Before her visit, he called his sister and politely asked her to help him not smoke over the holidays. She accommodated him by offering to smoke only outside the house during her visit. He purposely avoided alcohol during her visit because he knew that drinking

tended to weaken his resolve. He made it through the holidays without a hitch. About 6 months later, Joe borrowed a cigarette from a friend following a fender bender in his employer's parking lot. He recognized this was a mistake the moment he took the first puff. He decided to frame the experience as an opportunity to learn about another high-risk situation. He told himself that he was not dependent on nicotine after just one cigarette and that going back to smoking would certainly not fix his car. He resolved to practice his relaxation exercises the next time he was faced with such a stressful situation.

—David O. Antonuccio

See also: Behavioral Treatment for the Addictions (Vol. I); Competing Response Training (Vol. II); Positive Behavior Support (Vol. III)

Suggested Readings

Antonuccio, D. O., Boutilier, L. R., Ward, C. H., Morrill, G. B., & Graybar, S. R. (1992). The behavioral treatment of cigarette smoking. In M. Hersen, R. M. Eisler, & P. M. Miller (Eds.), *Progress in behavior modification.* Dekalb, IL: Sycamore.

Critchley, J. A., & Capewell, S. (2003). Mortality risk reduction associated with smoking cessation in patients with coronary heart disease: A systematic review. *Journal of the American Medical Association, 290,* 86–97.

DiClemente, C. C., Prochaska, J. O., Fairhurst, S. K., Velicer, W. F., Velasquez, M. M., & Rossi, J. S. (1991). The process of smoking cessation: An analysis of precontemplation, contemplation, and preparation stages of change. *Journal of Consulting and Clinical Psychology, 59*(2), 295–304.

Fiore, M. C., Bailey, W. C., Cohen, S., et al. (2000). *Treating tobacco use and dependence: Clinical practice guidelines.* Rockville, MD: U.S. Department of Health and Human Services.

Fiore, M. C., Smith, S. S., Jorenby, D. E., & Baker, T. B. (1994). The effectiveness of the nicotine patch for smoking cessation: A meta-analysis. *Journal of the American Medical Association, 271*(24), 1940–1947.

Hughes, J. (1998). Harm-reduction approaches to smoking. The need for data. *American Journal of Preventive Medicine, 15,* 78–79.

Hughes, J. R., Shiffman, S., Callas, P., & Zhang, J. (2003). A meta-analysis of the efficacy of over-the-counter nicotine replacement. *Tobacco Control, 12,* 21–27.

Hughes, J. R., Stead, L. F., & Lancaster, T. (2001). Antidepressants for smoking cessation (Cochrane Review). *The Cochrane Library, 4.*

Hurt, R. D., Krook, J. E., Croghan, I. T., Loprinzi, C. L, Sloan, J. A., Novotny, P. J., et al. (2003). Nicotine patch therapy based on smoking rate followed by bupropiron for prevention of relapse to smoking. *Journal of Clinical Oncology, 21,* 914–920.

Hurt, R. D., Sachs, D. P., Glover, E. D., Offord, K. P., Johnston, J. A., Dale, L. C., et al. (1997). A comparison of sustained-release buproprion and placebo for smoking cessation. *New England Journal of Medicine, 337,* 1195–1202.

Joseph, A. M., & Antonuccio, D. O. (1999). Lack of efficacy of transdermal nicotine in smoking cessation. *New England Journal of Medicine, 341,* 1157–1158.

Kenford, S. L., Fiore, M. C., Jorenby, D. E., Smith, S. S., Wetter, D., & Baker, T. B. (1994). Predicting smoking cessation: Who will quit with and without the nicotine patch. *Journal of the American Medical Association, 271*(8), 589–594.

Klesges, R. C., Ward, K. D., & DeBon, M. (1996). Smoking cessation: A successful behavioral/pharmacologic interface. *Clinical Psychology Review, 16*(6), 479–496.

Lichtenstein, E. (2002). From rapid smoking to the Internet: Five decades of cessation research. *Nicotine & Tobacco Research, 4,* 139–145.

Silagy, C., Lancaster, T., Stead, L., Mant, D., & Fowler, G. (2003). Nicotine replacement therapy for smoking cessation (Cochrane Review). *The Cochrane Library, 3,* 2003.

Yudkin, P., Hey, K., Roberts, S., Welch, S., Murphy, M., & Walton, R. (2003). Abstinence from smoking eight years after participation in randomized controlled trial of nicotine patch. *British Medical Journal, 327,* 28–29.

BEHAVIORAL TREATMENT OF INSOMNIA

DESCRIPTION OF THE STRATEGY

Insomnia involves difficulty falling asleep, problems staying asleep, waking up too early, or nonrestorative sleep, with associated impairment in functioning and fatigue. Insomnia may be situational or acute, follow an intermittent course, or be persistent. It can also be a symptom of another medical or psychological condition or represent a syndrome in itself, as in primary insomnia. Pharmacotherapy is a frequently used treatment option for insomnia. However, behavioral treatments are receiving increased attention, especially for chronic insomnia, because of their efficacy, safety, and patient acceptance.

Insomnia can be viewed as a multidimensional condition. Any given case is likely to involve some combination of predisposing factors (e.g., family history, female gender, older age, hyperarousal) and stressful life events (e.g., personal loss, illness, work stress) that precipitate a bout of poor sleep and a variety

of physiologic, behavioral, emotional, and cognitive factors that maintain the poor sleep. The efficacy of behavioral therapies for insomnia is believed to be due specifically to their ability to alter the main factors that *perpetuate* poor sleep. Perpetuating factors include maladaptive sleep-wake habits, especially sleep scheduling; learned associations of the bed with sleeplessness; and dysfunctional cognitions and other phenomena that prevent sufficient presleep reduction in arousal. Interventions are designed to adjust sleep-wake scheduling to achieve rapid sleep onset and uninterrupted sleep and/or to maximize the association of bedtime with reduced arousal and increased sleep tendency. Some of the behavioral interventions also take advantage of the homeostatic and circadian biological rhythms of sleep tendency, in order to maximize the likelihood of sleep and wakefulness occurring at desired hours.

Behavioral approaches to insomnia generally fall into five categories: stimulus control therapy, sleep restriction, relaxation training, cognitive therapy, and sleep hygiene education.

Stimulus Control Therapy

Through classical conditioning, people with insomnia often come to associate their beds and bedrooms with sleeplessness rather than with sleep. Stimulus control therapy is a brief set of instructions for going to and getting up from bed, designed to maximize the association of the bed with sleepiness and sleep. It also emphasizes a consistent rise time, which helps support the circadian component of the rhythm of sleep tendency. The standard stimulus control instructions are:

- ❖ Go to bed only when sleepy.
- ❖ Use the bed only for sleeping. Sexual activity is the only exception.
- ❖ Leave the bed and the bedroom if you cannot fall asleep within 15 to 20 minutes. Return when sleepy. Repeat this step as often as necessary during the night.
- ❖ Maintain a regular rising time in the morning.
- ❖ Do not nap. (Some clinicians, especially those working with older patients or with patients who have medical conditions, allow a nap of limited duration, e.g., maximum 1 hour before 3:00 p.m., if sleepiness is overwhelming.)

Sleep Restriction Therapy

Sleep restriction therapy is the prescription of a specific amount of time in bed, which is as close as possible to the actual sleep time. This procedure is designed to curtail the time in bed that is spent awake. Some individuals with insomnia spend excessive amounts of time in bed in a fruitless effort to obtain more sleep. Whereas the opposite—restriction of sleep—builds up the biological drive to sleep, it therefore is conducive to a rapid sleep onset and reduced time awake during the night. With this technique, the degree of sleep restriction is gradually reduced as sleep becomes more consolidated. Sleep diaries are used to guide the prescription of time in bed. The steps for sleep restriction are the following:

❖ Calculate mean daily subjective total sleep time, from sleep diaries kept for at least one week.
❖ Time in bed is prescribed as the mean total sleep time or 5 hours, whichever is greater.
❖ Rise time is established by the patient (a time that is sustainable for that person).
❖ Work backward (rise time minus time in bed) to establish the bedtime.
❖ For one week, the individual goes to bed no earlier than the prescribed bedtime and rises no later than the prescribed rise time. This interval is the "sleep window."
❖ Based on sleep efficiency (time asleep divided by time in bed x 100%), adjust the sleep window as follows: (a) If sleep efficiency is greater than 90%, then increase time in bed by 15 minutes; (b) If sleep efficiency is between 85% and 90%, then keep time in bed constant (c). If sleep efficiency is less than 85%, then decrease time in bed by 15 minutes. Adjustments to the window are usually made by altering the bedtime rather than the rise time.
❖ Adjustments are made weekly until optimal sleep efficiency and duration are reached with minimal daytime sleepiness.

Relaxation-Based Interventions

Relaxation techniques for insomnia include a variety of approaches that train the individual to release somatic and mental tension, thereby reducing physiological, cognitive, and emotional arousal that interfere with sleep onset. Several relaxation techniques have been shown to be effective in treating insomnia, including progressive muscle relaxation, imagery, meditation, autogenic training, and biofeedback. Although relaxation-based interventions are commonly used for the treatment of insomnia, they are not the optimal treatment when used alone.

Cognitive Therapy

The goal of cognitive therapy in the context of insomnia is to identify and alter maladaptive thinking patterns that are associated with arousal and the maintenance of sleep difficulty. For example, patients sometimes believe that they must get 8 hours of sleep per night or that if they do not sleep well, they will be unable to function the next day. Such thoughts lead to increased worry and arousal, thereby perpetuating the sleep disturbance. The aim of cognitive therapy is for the patient to replace the maladaptive sleep-related cognitions with ones that are realistic but less worrisome and arousing. The cognitive technique of decatastrophizing is useful, especially in combination with education about interindividual variation in sleep need and explanation of the research findings on the effects of sleep loss on performance. The latter findings indicate that whereas perceived performance deficits may be substantial, objective measures of performance generally show only subtle deficits with sleep loss. Paradoxical intention can be useful for some people who try too hard to fall asleep, believing that they "must sleep." This technique involves instructing the patient to try to stay awake, rather than try to sleep, thereby reducing performance anxiety.

Sleep Hygiene Education

Sleep hygiene education involves provision of information about sleeping conditions and lifestyle habits that promote sleep or minimize sleep interference. A typical set of sleep hygiene recommendations follows:

❖ Avoid stimulants, including caffeine and nicotine, several hours before bed. Caffeine and nicotine can impede sleep onset and reduce sleep quality.
❖ Do not drink alcohol 4 to 6 hours before bedtime. Alcohol can lead to fragmented sleep and early morning awakenings.

❖ Avoid heavy meals within 2 hours of bedtime. These can interfere with sleep. A light snack, however, may be sleep inducing.

❖ Regular exercise in the late afternoon or early evening may deepen sleep. However, exercising too close to bedtime may have a stimulating effect and delay sleep onset.

❖ Keep the bedroom environment quiet, dark, and comfortable.

Treatment Format

Behavioral interventions can be offered as part of individual therapy or offered as group programs. In individual therapy, interventions are often combined to tailor to the set of factors believed to perpetuate that individual's insomnia (based on the assessment). The various interventions are not incompatible, and they can easily be introduced sequentially. However, if only one treatment is offered, then stimulus control therapy or sleep restriction are the best choices. Typically, group programs involve a combination of sleep hygiene education, stimulus control therapy and/or sleep restriction, relaxation techniques, and cognitive therapy. There may be four to seven patients and one or two therapists per group. Group programs have the advantages of lower costs (in therapist time) and mutual support provided by group members.

RESEARCH BASIS

The efficacy of behavioral interventions for chronic, primary insomnia has been well demonstrated. Approximately 70% to 80% of patients achieve some benefit from these interventions. At this time, there is sound empirical support for the efficacy of stimulus control therapy, progressive muscle relaxation, paradoxical intention, sleep restriction, biofeedback and multicomponent cognitive-behavioral therapy in the treatment of chronic primary insomnia. Stimulus control therapy and sleep restriction therapy are particularly efficacious. Sleep hygiene education on its own appears to have limited therapeutic value. However, it seems to be a useful adjunct to the other approaches, reducing some potential complications to the overall treatment process.

On average, with behavioral interventions, patients with chronic insomnia see a reduction of about 30 minutes in sleep onset latency and/or 30 minutes in time awake after sleep onset, bringing these parameters into the nonclinical range in the majority of cases. Sleep duration is increased, on average, by approximately 30 minutes. Patients' ratings of sleep quality and satisfaction with sleep are significantly enhanced. Improvements in sleep are well maintained and sometimes further improved at follow-up, 6 to 8 months after treatment, and there is evidence for maintenance of gains at 2 years after treatment. The limited data on the effect of these interventions on daytime functioning suggest that depressive and anxiety symptoms are reduced, but more research is required on other aspects of functioning, including fatigue levels, cognitive performance, and quality of life.

Patients who participate in group programs achieve results that are broadly comparable to those who participate in individual sleep therapy. Data from self-help programs indicate that this approach is efficacious for many individuals, but therapist-led approaches may be best for individuals with severe or long-standing insomnia or for those who use hypnotics.

Work comparing efficacy of pharmacologic and psychological interventions for the treatment of insomnia demonstrates that both approaches are efficacious; however, the timing of their benefits differs. Whereas medications (e.g., benzodiazepines) function immediately to improve sleep and are useful in the short to medium term (1 day to about 4 weeks), behavioral approaches are useful in the medium to long term (1–2 weeks to at least 2 years). Pharmacologic treatments have some limitations, including alteration of sleep stages, daytime residual effects, potential toxicity when combined with alcohol or other central nervous system depressants, and tolerance and dependence with long-term use. Limited data suggest that patients with chronic insomnia tend to rate behavioral interventions as more acceptable than pharmacologic ones and to express greater satisfaction with behavioral approaches. Methods of educating clinicians and patients about the existence of these methods require further investigation. Despite the empirical evidence for their efficacy, behavioral techniques for insomnia treatment remain relatively unknown and therefore underutilized.

RELEVANT TARGET POPULATIONS AND EXCEPTIONS

The benefits of behavioral treatments for insomnia are well established from research with people who have primary insomnia, are from the community at large, are predominantly women (approximately 60%), with mean age in the early 40s, are healthy, nonusers of hypnotics, with mean duration of insomnia 11 years. However, the range of populations that can potentially benefit from these treatments is quite broad. For example, there is abundant evidence that older adults benefit from these techniques. In addition, it is becoming clear that behavioral interventions are helpful for patients whose insomnia is associated with medical or psychiatric illness. For medical conditions, efficacy of behavioral treatments has been most clearly demonstrated for people with chronic pain and for people with cancer. For psychiatric conditions, the scant literature provides some evidence that patients with anxiety or depressive disorders can benefit from behavioral interventions for insomnia, although modifications may be necessary (e.g., slower adjustment of sleep scheduling), and there may be some degree of residual sleep difficulty. Patients with subclinical anxiety or depressive symptoms have been shown to benefit from behavioral interventions. People with long-standing insomnia and those who use hypnotics also see significant improvements to their sleep with the use of behavioral interventions, although the literature is mixed as to whether the degree of improvement is somewhat reduced with these factors or not.

COMPLICATIONS

Patients with major depression, anxiety disorders, or substance abuse problems need to receive treatment for those disorders as a priority. Also, other sleep disorders, such as sleep apnea, restless-legs syndrome, periodic limb movement disorder, and circadian rhythm disorders need to be screened for and treated, if present. Designing a behavioral treatment can be especially challenging when the patient is a shift worker, as the sleep-wake schedule must fit around the work schedule. Also, for individuals who are using behavioral techniques such as stimulus control therapy and sleep restriction, vacations and travel to other time zones can complicate and prolong the treatment process. For users of hypnotics, decisions need to be made about when and how to withdraw from the medication. It is preferable to implement hypnotic discontinuation in parallel with behavioral treatment. The withdrawal program should be systematic, time limited, and medically supervised. Of course, all the behavioral techniques are dependent on the individual's motivation and ability to carry through with the

techniques. Patients should be informed about the time and commitment required to achieve full benefits of behavioral strategies, so that they can decide whether they wish to opt for this type of treatment.

CASE ILLUSTRATION

"Marilyn" was a 50-year-old, married banker whose main complaint was sleep onset insomnia that had persisted for 9 years. She reported that the problem initially began with a brief bout of sleep difficulty after an eastbound flight. Thereafter, she developed intermittent sleep difficulties, which coincided with her menstrual periods. She started using hypnotics occasionally to deal with these episodes of poor sleep. Over the years, she experienced increasing sleep difficulty despite resolution of the dysmenorrhea through medical treatment and despite her use of various sleeping medications. By the time she came to the clinic, Marilyn was having trouble falling asleep on most nights, and she was taking medication for sleep—either hypnotics or sedating antidepressants or both—7 nights per week. Marilyn expressed great concern and distress about her persistent sleeplessness.

Assessment involved a comprehensive clinical interview for insomnia in conjunction with information obtained from 2 weeks of sleep diaries. During the interview, the clinician examined the history and current nature of the sleep problem; precipitants and consequences of the insomnia; use of hypnotics and other sleep aids; sleep-wake patterns and timing, lifestyle habits, and behaviors and cognitions that perpetuated the sleep difficulty. The interviewer also screened for other sleep disorders, medical problems, medication use, and psychopathology. The following self-report measures were administered: the Brief Symptom Inventory, the Beck Depression Inventory, the State-Trait Anxiety Inventory, and the Dysfunctional Beliefs and Attitudes About Sleep Scale.

Based on the assessment, Marilyn typically retired around 10:30 p.m. and watched television in bed for at least 1 hour. Subjective sleep latency ranged from 30 minutes to 2 hours, with hypnotic medication. (Without medication, she reported taking 5 to 7 hours to fall asleep, or never falling asleep.) Nocturnal awakenings were infrequent and brief, lasting 5 to 10 minutes each. Her last awakening was at approximately 7:30 a.m., at which time she got out of bed promptly. Her average total sleep time was estimated at 6 to 7 hours per night out of 9 hours spent in bed, for a poor sleep efficiency of 76%. Daytime sequelae of the sleep difficulty included listlessness, anxiety, and difficulty concentrating. Marilyn described having a "hyperactive" mind while in bed waiting to fall asleep; and she also described a buildup of anxiety prior to bedtime, in anticipation of sleeplessness. Marilyn's scores on the self-report measures indicated a high level of psychological distress and significant levels of anxiety. Although she reported some depressive symptoms, her depression score was not clinically elevated. On the Dysfunctional Beliefs and Attitudes About Sleep Scale, she strongly endorsed the notions that that she was losing control of her sleep and that she could sleep only with medication. In synopsis, Marilyn's problem was persistent sleep onset insomnia, associated with daytime symptoms of difficulty concentrating and anxiety. The sleep difficulty began with jet lag, became intermittent in association with dysmenorrhea, and worsened over the years, being maintained by hypnotic dependency, conditioned sleeplessness, and anxiety-laden sleep cognitions.

The treatment plan included supervised withdrawal from hypnotic medication concurrent with behavioral treatment to promote sleep-compatible behaviors and to alter dysfunctional sleep cognitions. To follow her progress, Marilyn continued to keep sleep diaries. After some sleep education, stimulus control therapy was introduced in combination with sleep restriction. In collaboration with Marilyn, an initial sleep window was established between 1:00 a.m. to 7:30 a.m. That 6.5-hour window was the only interval in which she could be in bed; and during that interval, she was to follow the stimulus control instructions. After 1 week, her sleep diaries began to show reduced sleep onset latency, and her sleep efficiency climbed to 80%. At the second treatment session, cognitive techniques were introduced, focusing on restructuring Marilyn's beliefs about loss of control of her sleep. She continued following stimulus control instructions with sleep restriction and used cognitive techniques when she found herself becoming anxious about her ability to sleep. After 3 weeks, Marilyn's sleep efficiency had improved sufficiently that her sleep window was now expanded to 12:30 a.m. to 7:30 a.m. She maintained this sleep window and a sleep efficiency of 85% to 90% over the remainder of the treatment period. Because of her success with these procedures, she realized that she had not lost control of her sleep and that it was possible to sleep even while she was tapering the hypnotic medication. Five weeks after the

beginning of treatment, Marilyn reported satisfaction with her sleep. Her sleep diaries and self-report measures showed reduced sleep latency, improved sleep efficiency, improved ratings of sleep quality, and reduced (nonclinical) levels of distress and anxiety. These improvements were still evident at the 1-, 2-, and 6-month follow-ups.

—Charles M. Morin, Judith R.
Davidson, and Josée Savard

See also: *Applied Relaxation and Tension (Vol. 1);*
Biofeedback (Vol. II); Fading (Vol. III)

Suggested Readings

Edinger, J. D., & Wohlgemuth, W. K. (1999). The significance and management of persistent primary insomnia: The past, present and future of behavioral insomnia therapies. *Sleep Medicine Reviews, 3,* 101–118.

Espie, C. A. (2002). Insomnia: Conceptual issues in the development, maintenance and treatment of sleep disorder in adults. *Annual Review of Psychology, 53,* 1–44.

Lichstein, K. L., & Morin, C. M. (2000). *Treatment of late-life insomnia.* Thousand Oaks, CA: Sage.

Morin, C. M., & Espie, C. A. (2003). *Insomnia: A clinical guide to assessment and treatment.* New York: Kluwer/Plenum.

Morin, C. M., Hauri, P. J., Espie, C. A., Spielman, A. J., Buysse, D. J., & Bootzin, R. R. (1999). Nonpharmacologic treatment of chronic insomnia. *Sleep, 22,* 1134–1156.

Murtagh, D. R. R., & Greenwood, K. M. (1995). Identifying effective psychological treatments for insomnia: A meta-analysis. *Journal of Consulting and Clinical Psychology, 63,* 79–89.

Spielman, A. J., & Glovinsky, P. B. (1991). The varied nature of insomnia. In P. J. Hauri (Ed.), *Case studies in insomnia* (pp. 1–15). New York: Plenum Press.

BEHAVIORAL TREATMENT OF MINORITIES

DESCRIPTION OF THE STRATEGY

Diversity is not a treatment or assessment strategy; rather, it is an issue that ought to inform treatment and assessment. Diversity both within the United States and worldwide will increasingly challenge mental health professionals. Within the United States, for example, people of European background have comprised the majority ethnic and cultural group in the United States for some time. However, the demographic patterns in the United States are projected to continue to see a shift from European immigrants to immigrants from Asia, Latin America, and the Pacific Islands, among others. Given current trends, by 2010, more than half the population of the United States will include members of visible racial and ethnic groups who do not share European backgrounds. For example, in 1980, 85% of all immigrants were Asian and Hispanic, and less than 6% were European. Residents of Hispanic origin are projected to replace African Americans as the largest United States minority within the first two decades of the 21st century. Demographic shifts can be seen in many nations worldwide due to cross-immigration and globalization of the world economy.

In addition to issues of race, ethnicity, and culture, clinicians are becoming increasingly sensitive to differences among subgroups within the population that may influence treatment and assessment decisions. For example, some individuals may self-identify as members of the gay and lesbian community. These individuals experience different levels of acceptance from the community at large compared with individuals more identified with the cultural mainstream. Behavior therapists may need to interpret psychological difficulties differently in light of these variations in context. For example, a gay man living openly in a community with strong biases against same-sex intimate relationships may experience harassment and discrimination that could add to the overall experienced life stressors relative to other members of the same community.

Finally, individuals from different regions of the United States and from different socioeconomic backgrounds may show differences in cultural practices and beliefs compared with populations used to norm our assessment instruments and to validate our treatment strategies. For example, in the southern region of the United States, church-centered activities are frequently the center of an individual's social network. Among such groups, solutions from the spiritual community, such as pastoral counseling, prayer requests, and consultation with church elders, may be far more acceptable than seeking professional psychological services. Therefore, members of an individual's social network may view the act of seeking psychological services very differently compared with the same help seeking in another sociocultural subgroup.

Such diversity poses difficulties for psychological assessment. Clinicians make both *Diagnostic and Statistical Manual (DSM)* and International Classification of Disease diagnoses based upon a clustering of signs (what the provider sees) and symptoms (what the client reports). The structure and content of these documents were derived from research done among the dominant ethnic and cultural groups within the industrialized Western world. The fit of these systems to patterns of signs and symptoms seen among other cultures and subcultures is not well established.

Two potential barriers to understanding the difficulties of individuals from populations outside the research base include nontypical clustering of signs and symptoms, and, potentially, wholly distinct disorders. An example of the former can be found among some Asian populations. Both Chinese college students and psychiatric patients are more likely to experience psychological distress as somatic symptoms. Thus, Chinese clients, when depressed, may report fewer psychological complaints, like sadness or hopelessness, and more somatic complaints, like difficulties eating and sleeping.

In addition, we may find some psychological difficulties that are entirely culture bound. For example, *Hwa-Byung* (HB) is a Korean culture-bound syndrome. Koreans link HB to lasting anger, disappointments, sadness, miseries, hostility, grudges, and unfulfilled dreams and expectations. Current Korean beliefs follow that these emotions are not expressed openly and if these same emotions go beyond a threshold, they cannot be kept under control, and as a result are manifested physically in the form of HB. Insofar as symptomatic presentation is often the basis for clinical assessment, understanding the similarity in presentation of mental illness between a given culture or ethnic group and Western mental illness may help clarify the extent to which U. S.-derived assessment instruments should be used as a standard for other cultures.

RESEARCH BASIS

The utility of behavioral treatment strategies for minority populations constitutes a largely unanswered empirical question. However, there are both theoretical and empirical reasons to believe that we will be able to apply behavior therapies to diverse populations. First, behavior therapy has a history of analyzing particular behavioral excesses and deficits in terms of a functional analysis of the relation between the behavior problem and the context in which the problem occurs. Thus, even where a behavioral difficulty is bound entirely within a culture, the behavior therapist's assessment should include an analysis of that problem as it occurs in context. The core analytic strategy includes context, and this would naturally include cultural context. Second, where behavior therapies have been evaluated among minority populations, results have been promising. For example, research has shown that cognitive-behavioral treatment for both depression and anxiety may have good results with Hispanic clients, including trials where treatment was delivered in English, as well as trials where treatment was translated and delivered in Spanish. Several studies have also examined the utility of behavioral treatments for African American clients, with good results.

Although many psychological assessments have not been validated and normed with minority populations, some have. For example, a wide array of norms are available for the Minnesota Multiphasic Personality Inventory. Where no such norms are available, the use of these instruments must be made with caution and close attention to potential cultural differences that might argue for a nonpathological interpretation of responses that might be considered pathological if seen in the cultural mainstream. For example, visions of events that are not seen by others are an accepted aspect of spiritual experience among certain Latino and Native American groups. Thus, we might be less likely to interpret these as hallucinations until we asked additional questions that would provide the context for interpretation.

RELEVANT TARGET POPULATIONS AND EXCEPTIONS

Existing data and theory suggest that we be especially careful in the application of treatment and assessment when we are addressing any client who does not fit readily into the socioeconomic class, ethnicity, and gender that constituted the research population used in the validation of the strategy. However, despite the great diversity of racial, ethnic, and cultural subgroups emerging in the United States, some general conclusions can be made. Behavior therapists must avoid stereotypes and be sensitive to the values, languages, and cultural beliefs of members of minority groups they treat in psychotherapy. While it would be impractical to familiarize oneself with all of the various cultures and subcultures, there may be large groups in a given client catchment area that merit attention. For example, African Americans constitute a third of the population of some southern states. Throughout the southwestern United States, Latinos

of Mexican descent constitute a large proportion of the population. At the same time, we must be careful not to overgeneralize among members of identified groups. Understanding Mexican American culture is not identical with understanding Latino culture. Florida, for example, has many individuals of Cuban descent. Although there are some cultural overlaps, researchers have found important differences between Cuban American and Mexican American subgroups.

Even within a distinct cultural group, we are likely to find members who are more or less socialized to the mainstream culture. Behavior therapists would be remiss not to familiarize themselves with some current and historical cultural context when treating members of these groups. We should be more cautious in interpreting clients' behavior when we are unfamiliar with their cultural backgrounds. Additional inquiry and consultation may provide information that fills in the gaps in our research base.

COMPLICATIONS

There are two major schools of thought about application of therapeutic techniques and assessment. Both approaches have strengths and weaknesses, and it is not entirely clear which ought to guide our actions. The *etic* approach follows that common themes cut across therapeutic interventions and can be applied to any culture with minor modification. Furthermore, culture is regarded as one of variety of factors that influence behavioral expressions of symptoms. The *emic* approach asserts that psychotherapy and counseling must be practiced within the context of the culture, so they seek to understand a behavior of a given culture without reference to outside perspectives. While the emic approach provides detailed data about a particular culture, it lends itself less readily to rigorous scientific comparisons. On the other hand, the etic approach may inappropriately assume that a phenomenon is common across cultures and impose categories that may not be comparable across groups. The resolution of the etic/emic issue is beyond the scope of this essay; however, an etic approach is more consistent with the effort to explore cross-cultural therapeutic universals that have demonstrated utility.

—*Kelly G. Wilson,*
Miguel E. Roberts, and Sushma T. Roberts

See also: *Cultural Differences in Cognitive Therapy (Vol. I);*
Peer Intervention (Vol. II); Peer Tutoring (Vol. III)

Suggested Readings

Butcher, J. (Ed.). (1994). *International adaptations of the MMPI-2: Research and clinical applications.* Minneapolis: University of Minnesota Press.

Dana, R. H. (Ed.). (2000). *Handbook of cross-cultural and multicultural personality assessment.* Mahwah, NJ: Erlbaum.

Hays, P. A. (1995). Multicultural applications of cognitive-behavior therapy. *Professional Psychology: Research and Practice, 26,* 309–315.

Lonner, W. J., & Malpass, R. S. (1994). *Psychology and culture.* Boston: Allyn & Bacon.

Sue, D. W., & Sue, D. (1999). *Counseling the culturally different: Theory and practice* (3rd ed.). New York: Wiley.

Sue, S. (1999). Science, ethnicity, and bias: Where have we gone wrong? *American Psychologist, 54,* 1070–1077.

BEHAVIORAL WEIGHT CONTROL TREATMENTS

DESCRIPTION OF THE STRATEGY

Basic Philosophy of Treatment

Lifestyle behavior modification for obesity is based upon changing eating habits and physical activity to yield negative energy balance, that is, burning more energy than is consumed via eating. During the initial phase of treatment, weight loss occurs at a rate of approximately 1 to 2 pounds (.5 to 1 kg) per week. After this initial phase, the goal of treatment is weight maintenance.

Components of Behavioral Weight Control Interventions

Self-Monitoring. One feature of behavioral weight control interventions is self-monitoring of eating and exercise habits. Self-monitoring involves recording food intake and intentional efforts to increase physical activity. Self-monitoring also involves recording environmental events associated with eating and exercise, for example, place and time of day; cognitive and emotional reactions, such as eating in response to stress; and hunger ratings before and after eating. Self-monitoring enhances awareness of habits and can provide a record of behavior that can be used to evaluate progress and to set goals for reinforcement. Also, the dietary record can be analyzed for the adequacy of the person's nutritional intake across time.

Stimulus Control. Stimulus control procedures alter the relationship between environmental events and eating and exercise habits. Commonly used stimulus control procedures are (a) eating at the same time and place at each meal, (b) slowing eating by putting utensils down between bites, (c) eating on small plates, (d) resisting the urge to have seconds, (e) eating while seated, (f) leaving a small amount of food on one's plate, (g) serving small portions of food, and (h) exercising at the same time each day.

Reinforcement/Shaping. The natural consequences of eating (e.g., the good taste of food and reduction of hunger) facilitate the development of overeating habits, whereas the natural consequences of exercise (e.g., fatigue and muscle soreness) facilitate the development of a sedentary lifestyle. As a person gains weight, the natural consequences of exercise become even more aversive, resulting in less physical activity as obesity increases. Unfortunately, alteration of the natural consequences of eating is essentially impossible without pharmacological or surgical intervention. On a more positive note, the development of healthy physical activity habits makes some of the natural consequences of exercise less aversive over time. Nevertheless, because these natural consequences are so difficult to modify, behavioral programs have typically tried to modify other reinforcers, for example, social reinforcement or material rewards for behavior change. The principle of shaping is generally employed when reinforcement contingencies are formulated. Shaping refers to setting small but reasonable goals at first, and then gradually making them more challenging over the course of treatment.

Goal Setting. Behavioral weight control programs are very goal oriented. These goals might include things such as cessation of eating certain types of foods (e.g., soft drinks), walking up stairs instead of using elevators, or modification of snacks (e.g., eating fruit instead of ice cream).

Behavioral Contracting. To enhance the person's motivation for achieving these goals, a procedure called behavioral contracting is used. Behavioral contracting involves clearly specifying behavioral goals (e.g., "I agree to walk at least 30 minutes per day for at least 5 days per week"). A behavioral contract generally includes some type of reinforcement contingency for successful attainment of the goal (e.g., "if

I meet my exercise goal for this week, I will reward myself by purchasing a copy of my favorite magazine").

Meal Planning. Goals related to nutrient intake may take many forms (e.g., calories, fat grams, or dietary exchanges). Explicit meal plans are most effective. An explicit meal plan might include an actual menu to be followed or the use of prepackaged portion-controlled foods or meal replacements, which consist of shakes, nutrition bars, soups, and entrées.

Modification of Physical Activity. Programs to increase physical activity generally include increasing exercise and decreasing sedentary behavior. Research has found that aerobic exercise is the most effective form of exercise prescription and that compliance is best when the exercise program is incorporated into the person's lifestyle.

Problem Solving. This type of training involves assisting the person to identify problems that are obstacles to successful weight management, define the problem in objective terms, brainstorm about potential solutions to the problem, conduct a cost-benefit analysis for each solution, select a solution and develop a plan of action, and evaluate the success or failure of the plan of action and revise it, based upon this evaluation. This component of treatment is often useful in modifying obstacles that negatively impact compliance with the behavioral program.

Social Support. Social support may be derived from a spouse, family member, or friends. Enhancement of social support is best accomplished by inviting family members and friends to attend some of the therapy sessions. In these sessions, support persons learn to reinforce healthy behavior change and are discouraged from engaging in actions that sabotage progress toward behavior change.

Relapse Prevention. Returning to old, unhealthy habits is a primary cause of relapse and regain of weight that has been lost. Relapse prevention strategies are used to identify situations that place the person at risk for returning to old, unhealthy habits and to develop specific plans to manage these high-risk situations.

Booster Treatment. Booster treatment generally involves periodic therapeutic contact during the period of weight maintenance. This therapeutic contact may take many forms, including face-to-face sessions, scheduled telephone calls, or asynchronous Internet exchanges.

RESEARCH BASIS

Behavioral weight control interventions promote modest weight loss of roughly 9 kg, or 10% of initial body weight. This degree of weight loss significantly improves health and medical conditions associated with obesity (e.g., type 2 diabetes or hypertension). Most of the weight loss occurs during the 6 months following the initiation of therapy. Weight regain is a significant problem that usually begins with the termination of therapy; over one third of lost weight is regained during the year following therapy. Long-term weight loss can be realized, however. Through research, a number of factors have been identified that promote weight loss and weight loss maintenance, and it appears that these factors exert their influence by facilitating and maintaining changes in diet and physical activity habits.

Group therapy is more effective at promoting weight loss than individual therapy, even when people report that they would prefer individual therapy. Weight loss and weight loss maintenance are associated with self-monitoring of dietary intake and physical activity, and problem-solving training is associated with weight loss maintenance. In addition, longer therapy and more frequent therapeutic contact improve weight loss maintenance. Overweight and obesity are chronic conditions that require long-term management; consequently, current behavioral weight loss interventions gradually reduce the frequency of therapeutic contact and incorporate booster treatments that occur months in the future. Given the propensity to regain weight and the chronic nature of overweight and obesity, patients are encouraged to return to therapy should they regain a predefined amount of weight. Returning to therapy should not be viewed as a failure, but rather a necessary step in making long-term lifestyle changes that foster weight loss maintenance.

The most challenging aspect of behavioral weight control interventions is regulation of food intake. Inability to adhere to a meal plan compromises weight loss and will result in weight regain in the long-term. Meal replacements or portion-controlled foods facilitate adherence to meal plans and are associated with weight loss and maintenance. These foods are commercially available and easily incorporated into low-calorie diets. It is important to note, however, that certain diets that use meal replacements require medical monitoring, namely very low-calorie diets (VLCDs), which prescribe a daily energy intake below 800 kcal/day.

The role of physical activity in weight loss is unclear, but its role in weight loss maintenance is undeniable. During therapy, patients are encouraged to gradually increase their levels of physical activity to at least 150 minutes per week. Moderate-intensity activity (e.g., brisk walking) is beneficial for weight loss; therefore, the "No pain, no gain" adage does not apply. Regular physical activity greatly improves the likelihood that weight loss will be maintained.

RELEVANT TARGET POPULATIONS AND EXCEPTIONS

Body mass index (BMI) is used to classify overweight and obesity. BMI is calculated by dividing weight in kilograms by height in meters squared (kg/m^2). A BMI between 18.5 and 24.9 is considered normal weight, 25 to 29.9 is overweight, and a BMI 30 and above is considered obese.

The National Heart, Lung, and Blood Institute (NHLBI) and the National Association for the Study of Obesity (NAASO) published guidelines for selecting weight loss treatment. According to the guidelines, people with BMIs between 25 and 29.9 who have comorbidities (e.g., type 2 diabetes or hypertension) are appropriate for diet, changes in exercise, and behavior therapy. People with BMIs above 29.9 who do or do not have comorbidities should also use these methods. Pharmacotherapy is an additional treatment option for people with BMIs between 27 and 29.9 who have comorbidities and for those with BMIs above 29.9 with or without comorbidities. Finally, weight loss surgery is appropriate for people with BMIs between 35 and 39.9 who have comorbidities and for those with BMIs above 39.9 with or without comorbidities.

Individuals who have BMIs below 25 might be appropriate for behavioral weight control interventions in certain circumstances, though the goal of the therapy might be minimal weight loss or cessation of weight gain. For example, an adult with a BMI below 25 but who has recently gained or is gaining weight might benefit from therapy. In such a case, it is important to determine whether a cause of the weight gain

can be identified and, if so, the extent to which it can be modified. In addition, it is important to determine whether the patient is engaging in behaviors associated with eating disorders (e.g., binge eating, purging) or has a history of an eating disorder. If this behavior is present or such a history exists, alternative treatment is appropriate, since weight control interventions might inadvertently promote disturbed eating behavior. If no such history exists, the goal weight should be clearly stated and should not put the patient at risk of losing too much weight. Monitoring the patient's eating behavior and attitudes about eating and their bodies is necessary to detect behaviors or attitudes associated with eating disorders, should they develop.

The two key components of behavioral weight control interventions are reducing dietary intake and increasing energy expenditure through physical activity. Patients are instructed to initiate and gradually increase physical activity at the outset of therapy, following approval by their physicians. Consultation with a professional in exercise physiology may be beneficial, particularly in the case of patients who have physical limitations. However, physical limitations should not be an insurmountable barrier to physical activity, in most cases. A number of activities are available for those who have impairments in mobility, flexibility, or who suffer from chronic pain (e.g., chair and water aerobics).

COMPLICATIONS

Complications related to behavioral weight control interventions in obese persons vary by the individual. However, common difficulties may include (but are not limited to) motivation for behavior change, difficulty with adherence to behavioral weight control intervention recommendations, difficulty with modification of physical activity, deficit of social support, cultural limitations, and relapse. Obese individuals often present as ambivalent about behavior change. It is important to assess the individual's readiness for change and do what is necessary to aid the individual in actively changing unhealthy habits and prevent relapse.

While individuals are motivated for the results of change (i.e., weight loss), adherence to the behavioral changes necessary for success can be difficult. Adherence to dietary, physical activity, and stimulus control recommendations, in addition to self-monitoring, is particularly important. It is also important to arm individuals with knowledge and problem-solving skills to enable them to continue to work toward their goals. Positive reinforcement is necessary to shape behaviors that will lead to weight loss goals.

Individuals often have difficulty modifying physical activity while maintaining health and safety. Some individuals have difficulty with initiation of activity, while others overdo their efforts, resulting in injury. Working with individuals to find balance in physical activity modification is a key for success of this component of behavioral weight control. Continued encouragement of balance is necessary for accomplishment and maintenance of weight loss goals.

Social support is an important factor for long-term successful weight management. Complications may result if an individual lacks significant social support for their weight loss and lifestyle changes. It is recommended that family members and/or friends be engaged in interventions that promote motivation for and the initiation of behavior change.

Cultural limitations exist regarding the process of lifestyle behavior change and weight loss. Recommendations for behavior change should be viewed as reasonable, and ethnic backgrounds and socioeconomic status should also be considered in the development of a treatment plan. It is important to match recommendations with the person such that the person views the recommendations as reasonable and feasible.

Finally, relapse poses a threat to the effectiveness of behavioral weight control interventions. It is often difficult for individuals who have experienced a temporary "lapse" in their lifestyle change efforts to get back on track and not think that all is lost in their "failure." It is essential to reframe such situations and aid the person in the distinction between a lapse and a relapse, indicating that the person is successful if they resume the intervention as soon as possible.

CASE ILLUSTRATION

"Martin" was a 65-year-old, single, white male who weighed 301 pounds at a height of 5 feet, 7 inches, with a BMI of 47. He had retired as a pilot from the air force due to injury. He reported that he had been more sedentary since his retirement 10 years before the initial assessment. He reported low motivation for exercise or dietary change but was motivated to feel better, improve health, and improve his appearance. Martin reported symptoms of depression co-occurring

with obesity. He reported staying in bed all day and frequent bouts of crying and hopelessness surrounding his inability to do the things he wanted to do. Martin was generally in good physical health other than his obesity. He reported soreness in his knees when he walked.

Clinical interviews found the age of onset of obesity at 45 years. Prior to this assessment, Martin had not attempted to lose weight on his own. Martin reported no family history of obesity. He reported a daily dietary intake of approximately 3,700 calories. Intake consisted of three large meals a day, with few snacks. Dinner was reported to be the largest meal, with eating continuing late into the night while viewing television. Martin's elevated body weight was consistent with high caloric intake and absence of physical activity. Martin's diet primarily consisted of foods high in saturated fat and sugar. He reported eating fried foods regularly and sweets, particularly ice cream. Martin reported no history of alcohol or substance use. From the assessment, it was evident that Martin's obesity had a significant impact on his social functioning, body image, self-esteem, and quality of life.

Martin was seen in group therapy for 1 year. Initially, he was seen once per week, and the frequency of sessions was gradually faded to biweekly and then once per month. Therapy focused upon motivation to help him move from contemplation about habit change to action. Behavior therapy was used to modify portion control through shopping, meal planning, and food preparation, as Martin was prone to buying food in bulk quantities and overconsuming to "get his money's worth." Behavior therapy was also utilized to gradually shape increased physical activity to gain benefit from exercise, but not cause injury. Finally, guidance for enlisting social support from friends in his quest for weight loss was offered, and Martin became more accountable for eating and physical activity behaviors when communicating with friends.

Initially, Martin found difficulty with the concept of gradual and healthy weight loss. After the first week, he wanted the process to go faster, thereby restricting intake and trying to walk further than recommended. As a result, his knees began to hurt and he lost up to 3 to 4 pounds a week for several weeks. He then hit a weight loss plateau and became discouraged. Reasonable goals were reestablished that included a slower rate of weight loss (1 to 2 lbs. per week), and Martin began to meet these goals over time. He was gradually able to increase the duration of physical activity per bout without pain in his knees. He also became disciplined and comfortable with cooking large amounts of food and freezing individual portions so that he developed healthy eating habits but still saved money. By the end of the first year, Martin had lost 80 pounds and was very proud of his progress with eating and his ability to walk places with friends (e.g., the mall). He began engaging in social activities as well as self-improvement activities (e.g., taking care of his skin and hair). During follow-up visits, Martin reported significantly improved quality of life compared with being a "recluse" before his weight loss. He maintained his meal planning and portion control efforts. He also continued to engage in physical activity, such as walking and dancing.

—Donald A. Williamson,
Corby K. Martin, and Tiffany M. Stewart

See also: *Behavioral Medicine (Vol. I); Homework (Vol. I); Behavioral Weight Control Therapy With Children (Vol. II)*

Suggested Readings

Bray, G. A., Bouchard, C., & James, W. P. T. (Eds.). (1998). *Handbook of obesity.* New York: Marcel Dekker.

Jackson, Y., Dietz, W., Sanders, C., Kolbe, L. J., Whyte, J. J., Wechsler, B. S., et al. (2002). Summary of the 2000 Surgeon General's listening session: Toward a national action plan on overweight and obesity. *Obesity Research, 10,* 1299–1305.

National Heart, Lung, and Blood Institute. (1998). Clinical guidelines on the identification, evaluation, and treatment of overweight and obesity in adults: The evidence report. *National Institutes of Health Obesity Research 6*(Suppl. 2), 51S–209S.

Perri, M. G., & Corsica, J. A. (2002). Improving the maintenance of weight lost in behavioral treatment of obesity. In T. A. Wadden & A. J. Stunkard (Eds.), *Handbook of obesity treatment* (pp. 357–379). New York: Guilford Press.

Wing, R. R. (2002). Behavioral weight control. In T. A. Wadden & A. J. Stunkard (Eds.), *Handbook of obesity treatment* (pp. 301–316). New York: Guilford Press.

BEHAVIORAL WORKING ALLIANCE

DESCRIPTION OF STRATEGY

A good working alliance sets the stage for effective cognitive-behavioral therapy. Without it, it is unlikely that clients will cooperate with therapy assignments or even continue in treatment. Thus, it is as important for therapists to establish a collaborative working alliance with their clients as it is for them to know cognitive-behavioral change techniques. Perhaps the most widely accepted definition is Bordin's pantheoretical conceptualization of the working alliance as client-therapist agreement on the goals of therapy and the tasks to be performed to reach those goals coupled with a strong relational bond. This definition is a good fit for cognitive-behavioral therapists, because our theoretical orientation is goal- and task oriented, with an emphasis on close client-therapist collaboration.

Establishing a working alliance is not always easy. While some clients begin therapy with knowledge that they must change their behavior to alleviate their problems, others do not. Some clients blame others for their difficulties, and most have a story to tell about how hard their lives have been. While therapists may have very different formulations of clients' problems, it is not advisable to begin treatment by immediately confronting clients about their behaviors. Clients must first become engaged in the therapeutic process. Such engagement is a precursor of the working alliance.

To become engaged, clients first must believe that therapists truly understand their problems. Therapists can convey understanding to clients by listening closely to what they have to say and responding empathically to their concerns. This initial interaction is one of positive complementarity. The behaviors of clients and therapists complement each other, with therapists following the clients' leads. Clients present their complaints, and therapists seek information and clarification about these concerns. This process may take up much of the initial session. Near the end of the session, therapists summarize clients' concerns and indicate how these problems might be addressed. This interaction is still a complementary one, but at this later juncture, therapists take the lead. Until the end of the session, therapists and clients continue to discuss these initial treatment plans and how they fit with clients' concerns. Clients leave these engagement sessions feeling that therapists understand their concerns and will be able to teach them what to do to ameliorate these problems. The foundation has been set for a good working alliance.

In contrast, a nonengagement session is characterized by symmetrical, rather than complementary, interactions in which both therapists and clients take the lead, but neither follows the other. Sometimes these symmetrical interactions have a negative tone, as well. For example, clients may present concerns that are immediately confronted, challenged, or ignored by therapists. These sessions may conclude with little or no agreement about the clients' problems or the way to address them. This is not the basis for a good working alliance, and, indeed, clients may not even continue in treatment. It should be clear from this discussion that therapists must assume the bulk of the responsibility for initial engagement of clients. They must demonstrate to clients understanding of and sympathy for their concerns. While this is important, the engagement process does not stop with this demonstration. After all, many clients have sympathetic listeners in their lives who have not been able to take away their problems. Therapists must also demonstrate their potential helpfulness by reformulating clients' concerns within a cognitive-behavioral framework and indicating procedures that can be undertaken to address them. Successful engagement sessions may even conclude with homework assignments for clients. These homework assignments should be made in conjunction with clients, thus ensuring agreement on goals and the tasks to achieve them—two components of the working alliance.

After this initial engagement has provided a working base, during the larger, middle phase of therapy, therapists and clients continue their collaboration on treatment. Therapists should structure sessions, and indeed the entire treatment, to ensure that clients attain the maximum success possible when undertaking homework assignments. This can best be accomplished by assigning tasks that are achievable by clients. Therapists impart their knowledge of social learning principles that apply to the concerns being addressed at each session and seek clients' input on goals and tasks to remedy these concerns. Clients report their progress, and therapists praise their accomplishments and encourage them to continue when the going gets tough. In this way, therapists promote clients' self-efficacy. Therapists should indicate that most problems took a while to develop and will, therefore, take some time to eradicate. When both parties are involved in working on clients' problems in this way, a strong working bond develops. This bond coupled with client-therapist agreement on therapy goals and tasks constitutes the working alliance. Without a positive bond with therapists, clients have no reason to trust therapists' judgments about what is best for them. If clients do not agree with goals that

therapists set for them or the cognitive-behavioral tasks they should carry out, they will not comply with treatment.

As therapy progresses, clients will be asked to undertake more difficult assignments. A good working alliance facilitates clients' effecting these assignments; however, in most cases, the alliance will be tested at some point. There will be times when clients resist or fail to perform certain activities. They may indicate that these things are too difficult for them, state a belief that the assignments will not work, or simply say they forgot to perform the activities. These are signs that one or more aspects of the alliance is weakening. Therapists should address this deterioration in the alliance by asking clients to tell them about the difficulties they are having with the assignments. As they did initially in therapy, therapists should follow clients' leads to develop an understanding of why clients are not performing the procedures assigned. Some clients might believe that their therapists do not have a good understanding of their situations. Some clients desire different goals than their therapists. Or some clients may believe that they do not possess the necessary behavioral or emotional tools to carry out the procedures. When therapists understand these impediments, they can formulate cognitive-behavioral activities that address clients' concerns and get therapy back on track.

Disruptions in the working alliance, particularly during the middle phase of therapy, are the rule rather than the exception. Successful resolution of these alliance disturbances can actually strengthen the working alliance beyond what it was initially. Clients, such as those diagnosed with narcissistic or borderline personality disorders who have a history of relationship difficulties, may experience more working-alliance disruptions than other clients. Therapists can reengage these and other clients in the treatment process by focusing on understanding clients' difficulties in carrying out cognitive-behavioral strategies. If therapists do not attend to alliance disruptions, however, clients will not engage in assigned tasks and may leave treatment altogether.

During the termination phase of therapy, a strong working alliance facilitates relapse prevention training, with therapists and clients collaborating on rehearsing responses to possible scenarios that may lead to a posttherapy lapse or relapse. During termination, treatment is reviewed, plans are made for the future, and good-byes are said. Clients and therapists may feel some sadness at ending a good working alliance.

RESEARCH BASIS

There have been numerous studies, summarized in several meta-analyses, linking a positive working alliance with good therapy outcome as assessed by several different instruments. The positive association between working alliance and therapy outcome has been found using therapists of all major theoretical orientations and alliance ratings by therapists, clients, and outside observers. Research results also indicate that establishing a positive working alliance during the first few sessions is crucial to good outcome. Studies suggest that a good early alliance is a better predictor of outcome than a good alliance in the middle phases of therapy, although both predict outcome.

Various theorists have hypothesized that the working alliance changes over the course of therapy in a U-shaped fashion, with higher alliances manifested at the beginning and end of therapy and lower alliances exhibited during the middle phases of therapy, when some of the more difficult therapy tasks are effected. Research on the alliance over time has yielded equivocal results, with some studies finding the U-shaped alliance configuration and others finding other patterns.

Studies generally find significant but moderate (r's in the mid- to upper .30s) correlations between therapist and client ratings of the working alliance, with clients tending to rate the alliance higher than do therapists. This is probably due to the different perspectives of the raters. Therapists have experience with forming alliances with other clients, but therapeutic alliance formation is a new type of relationship for most clients. Despite these differences, ratings by both participants significantly predict outcome, as do ratings made by outside observers.

Researchers have found that forming a working alliance with clients diagnosed with borderline and other personality disorders is more difficult than forming alliances with clients with other diagnoses. Alliance formations with drug-dependent, delinquent, and homeless clients have also been found to be difficult. Generally, clients who find it difficult to form attachments to others have been shown to also have more difficulty forming positive working alliances with their therapists.

Therapists who are empathic and convey understanding of clients' needs have been found to have stronger working alliances with their clients than have therapists who are less empathic and understanding. Therapists who are characterized as cold, distant, critical, and controlling form weaker alliances with their clients. Therapists' experience does not relate to the formation of most working alliances except when clients have histories of difficulty forming relationships. With these clients, therapists who have more experience tend to form stronger alliances. Stronger working alliances are associated with client-therapist positive complementarity.

RELEVANT TARGET POPULATIONS AND EXCEPTIONS

It is important to form positive working alliances with all clients. As indicated, research has found a consistent positive relationship between working alliance and outcome. Research findings suggest that a positive working alliance is itself therapeutic. For many clients, a strong working alliance with a therapist may be among the few good relationships they have. Thus, the working alliance not only facilitates clients' learning and application of cognitive-behavioral coping skills but also provides clients with a model of a good relationship that can be used in their working relationships with others besides the therapist.

COMPLICATIONS

As previously indicated, it is more difficult to form a positive working alliance with some clients (i.e., those diagnosed with personality disorders, those with histories of difficulty forming relationships) than with others. With these clients, it is particularly important for therapists to talk with them about their concerns about becoming involved in a working relationship. Therapists should be sensitive to any relationship difficulties and address them as soon as possible. Otherwise, clients may resist complying with treatment and even drop out.

During the course of therapy, there can also be disruptions in the working alliance. At these times, clients may refuse to do homework assignments, become argumentative, or quit coming to sessions. Therapists should ask clients' reasons for their behaviors, convey an understanding of these reasons, and work with clients to shift to goals and tasks that clients find more doable. Addressing these alliance disruptions may even strengthen the alliance.

CASE ILLUSTRATION

"Susan," a 24-year-old administrative assistant, came to therapy complaining that she was miserable because people continually treated her in an uncaring manner, not listening to her wishes and forcing her to do things that she did not wish to do. The therapist questioned her for more specifics and determined that there were a number of people with whom she displayed subassertive behavior in a variety of circumstances. The therapist shared this formulation with her and reflected her concerns that if she did assert herself with others, they would reject her and she would feel even worse than she currently did. Susan indicated that this was exactly how she felt and that she could see no way out of this dilemma.

The therapist indicated that there are ways of getting one's own way that may not entail rejection by others and that Susan and the therapist might work on some of these, starting with easier situations first. Susan indicated a willingness to try this, and with the therapist's help, she decided to work on a way to get her sometimes-grumpy boss to clarify an assignment he had recently given her. The therapist and Susan took turns role-playing Susan and her boss until Susan was able to confidently produce a request that she and the therapist believed would be effective. Susan's homework was to put this assertive request into effect with her boss. At the following session, she reported that the intervention had worked and that her boss had even apologized to her for not being clearer when he initially gave her the assignment.

The reader will note that the therapist engaged Susan in the therapeutic process by carefully listening to and clarifying her concerns and then presenting her with a way to work on her problems. Susan and the therapist discussed and rehearsed what she would do and reached agreement on the desired behavior (goal) and how it would be carried out (task). Thus, the initial working alliance was established.

There are several instruments that can be used to assess the working alliance. I prefer the Working Alliance Inventory (WAI) by Horvath and Greenberg, because it was designed to assess therapist-client agreement on therapy goals and tasks and the bond between therapist and client. It has a therapist and client form and can be administered at any time throughout the course of therapy. Therapists may find it useful to give the WAI periodically to monitor the alliance.

After completion of this initial assertiveness assignment, Susan continued to work with the therapist on other assertiveness tasks that were progressively more problematic for her. Things proceeded smoothly with Susan, and she developed considerable self-efficacy in handling situations with friends, coworkers, and her boyfriend. At one session, however, when the therapist and Susan were discussing strategies to use to get her parents to be more accepting of her boyfriend, Susan seemed to be less enthusiastic than during other sessions. She cancelled the following week's session, and when she returned for the session after that, she indicated that she had not completed the homework assignment because it was too difficult. This behavior was indicative of a weakening in the working alliance. The therapist discussed with Susan her difficulties with the assignment and with telling the therapist while they were initially discussing the homework that she feared it might not work. The discussion resulted in Susan's learning that she could be more assertive with the therapist. In addition, Susan and the therapist worked on a more graded approach to her parents, and Susan reported that this went well. Thus, the working alliance was strengthened.

Susan continued to use appropriate assertive behaviors in her interactions, and she was increasingly able to confront difficult situations independently. Susan and the therapist decided that she should terminate therapy. At their final session, they summarized their work, examined possible future situations that Susan might confront, acknowledged that they enjoyed working together, and said good-bye.

—Georgiana Shick Tryon

See also: *Behavior Rating Scales (Vol. III); Behavioral Assessment (Vol. I); Role Playing (Vol. II)*

Suggested Readings

Constantino, M. J., Castonguay, L. G., & Schut, A. J. (2002). The working alliance: A flagship for the "scientist-practitioner" model in psychotherapy. In G. S. Tryon (Ed.), *Counseling based on process research: Applying what we know* (pp. 81–131). Boston: Allyn & Bacon.

Horvath, A. O., & Bedi, R. P. (2002). The alliance. In J. C. Norcross (Ed.), *Psychotherapy relationships that work: Therapist contributions and responsiveness to patients* (pp. 37–69). New York: Oxford.

Martin, D. J., Garske, J. P., & Davis, K. M. (2000). Relation of the therapeutic alliance with outcome and other variables: A meta-analytic review. *Journal of Consulting and Clinical Psychology, 68,* 438–450.

Tracey, T. J. G. (2002). Stages of counseling and therapy: An examination of complementarity and the working alliance. In G. S. Tryon (Ed.), *Counseling based on process research: Applying what we know* (pp. 265–297). Boston: Allyn & Bacon.

Tryon, G. S. (2002). Engagement in counseling. In G. S. Tryon (Ed.), *Counseling based on process research: Applying what we know* (pp. 1–26). Boston: Allyn & Bacon.

Tryon, G. S., & Winograd, G. (2002). Goal consensus and collaboration. In J. C. Norcross (Ed.), *Psychotherapy relationships that work: Therapist contributions and responsiveness to patients* (pp. 109–125). New York: Oxford.

Wright, J. H., & Davis, D. (1994). The therapeutic relationship in cognitive-behavioral therapy: Patient perceptions and therapist responses. *Cognitive and Behavioral Practice, 1,* 24–45.

BEHAVIOROLOGY

DESCRIPTION OF THE STRATEGY

Behaviorology is the science of contingent relations between actions and other events. It does not focus on the action, which by itself is mere movement. Neither does it emphasize the stimulus event, for that would make the analysis physicalistic. Behaviorology's unit of analysis is the *relation* between action and event. The functionality of the controls over this relation—including the placement of terms in time—gives it its meaning. For example, with respect to two-term relations, an action and a *postcedent* event that changes the future probability of the class of behavior to which the action belongs defines this relation as *operant,* whereas an action and an *antecedent* event that changes the future probability of the class of behavior to which the action belongs may define this relation as *respondent.* In addition, in two or three or *n*-term contingency relations, controls may ensue from either inside or outside the organism, and the meaning of the relational terms change according to the source of the control—physical, biological, or cultural. No hard-and-fast boundary exists between these relationships and their controls. They blend into one another. Furthermore, they are subsets of one another: Two-term relations occur within three-term, three-term within four-term, and so on, in a widening array of subsystem relationships. The properties of these behavioral relationships constitute the focus of analysis, a *contingency analysis,* with the individual or group as a locus of observation. Such an analysis and

framework of explanation make irrelevant the explanatory term embedded in typical theories of behavior, an agency with dispositional traits such as rationality in economics, free will in theology, and consciousness in psychology.

Though a contingency analysis sorts out properties of behavior relations that are invariant across species (e.g., the similarity of reinforcement-schedule effects in human and pigeon), certain classes of actions specific to a species call for a special analysis, such as echolocation in dolphins, waggle dancing in bees, and verbal behavior in humans. Classes of behavior may be designated by the type of control over them. In human beings, control by direct contact with events both inside and outside the body constitutes one large class. The other large class, verbal behavior, is controlled by that contact being mediated by other people's behavior. B. F. Skinner's theory of verbal behavior, from which a behaviorological analysis of sociocultural behavior derives, drew its concepts from contingency relations discovered in the laboratory, supplemented by observations of everyday cultural events. In the clinical setting, two considerations particularly pertain. First, the therapist does not typically encounter the episodes responsible for the actions that produce emotional and social difficulties, but relies instead on what the client says about past and present events, from which inferences must be made about their continuing effects. Inference creates a number of difficulties, especially epistemological ones. The typography of verbal behavior—mere statement, for example—does not define its meaning; controls do. (The meaning of "I love my job" depends on whether it is said to keep from being fired or as a heartfelt sentiment expressed to a coworker.) Plausible inferences over the controls that lead to particular verbalizations provide direction to effective therapeutic procedures.

Second, a factual description of behavior is not necessarily the most significant type of behaviorological fact, a distinction that goes to the heart of the difference between *tacting* and *referencing.* An individual may appear to be describing some event such as "I saw my father hit my mother," his verbal behavior seemingly under control of that event. But his description is not a tact, only an apparent tact. It is a reference under multiple control of other kinds of verbal relations, heavily influenced by emotional and audience factors. Just as physicians manipulate current physiological relations with medicines and procedures for "guessed-at" outcomes, therapists manipulate both their own and their clients' verbal relations in order to have a current effect both on emotional factors (what clients feel) and on verbal behavior (what clients say to themselves or to others) for later positive outcomes. In dealing with verbal behavior, no agency is involved. Only a straightforward, though complex, set of relations exists between actions, both verbal and nonverbal, and the contingent events, both inside and outside the body, that control those actions.

A number of therapies operate more or less within the behaviorological framework of contingency relations. Their procedures may be more or less contingency based, but their explanations are often agency infused. These therapies differ according to the emphasis and balance given to operant and respondent controls. Therapy may range from (a) simple instruction consisting by and large of maxims on how to be more socially effective through (b) techniques such as desensitization that combine operant and respondent procedures to (c) straightforward respondent-based procedures. In every case, a behaviorological analysis emphasizes the fluid nature of the triangular relations between the actions and statements of the therapist, those of the client, and the histories that both individuals bring into the current setting.

—*Jerome D. Ulman and E. A. Vargas*

See also: Behavior Therapy Theory (Vol. I); Operant Conditioning (Vol. I); Schedules of Reinforcement (Vol. I)

Suggested Readings

Vargas, E. A. (1996). Explanatory frameworks and the thema of agency. *Behaviorology, 4,* 30–42.

Vargas, E. A. (1999). Ethics. In B. A. Thyer (Ed.), *The philosophical legacy of behaviorism* (pp. 89–115). London: Kluwer.

BELLACK, ALAN S.

I was born in New York City, November 27, 1944. An only child, I lived with my parents and maternal grandmother in an apartment building in the Bronx throughout my childhood. I attended public schools and graduated from DeWitt Clinton High School at the age of 16. I was an indifferent student in high school, and while I achieved good grades, I had not developed any strong academic interests or career ambitions. Neither of my parents had attended college, and we all viewed it simply as a logical extension of high school. I applied only to the City College of New York, which was free, a short subway ride from home, and which, coincidentally, had an excellent academic reputation. I selected engineering as my major, for lack of any other defined interest, and to my great dismay soon discovered my lack of facility for calculus and physics. After being put on academic probation, I changed my major to psychology, albeit still without great passion or a real understanding of what psychologists actually did. Nonetheless, my grades and interest in the field improved to the point where I decided to pursue graduate school. With my overall GPA dragged down by my early fiasco with mathematics and hard sciences, I was not competitive for a PhD program, but I was accepted into the master's degree program at St. Johns University. I completed that program with (just about) straight A's and a reasonable facility at projective tests and psychodynamic therapy. The first of a series of serendipitous events that have shaped my career and life than occurred when I decided I liked psychology enough to pursue a PhD (although, to be honest, I still had little idea what real psychologists do). I completed the master's program in January of 1967. That being the Vietnam era, I had a student deferment and would have been drafted if I had waited until September to continue graduate school. The only quality doctoral program that admitted students in midyear was Pennsylvania State University, so I applied there and trundled off to State College, PA, with little idea about what the program was like or what it was like to live away from home.

The years at Penn State were clearly a defining period in my life. I discovered psychology, research, behavior therapy, and big-time college football. More important, I discovered my future wife, Barbara, who was a student in a course for which I was the teaching assistant. The critical academic influences were Robert Stern, a physiological psychologist, who was kind enough to let a clinical student work in his laboratory and learn about science, and fellow graduate students, who were highly critical of the psychodynamic and client-centered approaches promoted by the senior clinical faculty. Behavior therapy was still a nascent discipline at the time, and most of my early education about it came from informal discussions and an odd seminar or two. Nevertheless, something about the behavioral approach struck a chord, and it became a central component of my professional identity and the focal point of the next 20 or so years of my career.

I completed my predoctoral internship at the New York VA Hospital, received my PhD in 1970, and returned to Penn State as a faculty member for 1 year. I then joined the faculty at the University of Pittsburgh. The next major serendipitous event occurred a few years later, when Michel Hersen joined the faculty in the department of psychiatry. Having grown up professionally in an arts-and-sciences world, I had a negative attitude about psychiatry and little experience with or interest in people with schizophrenia. That all changed with Michel's arrival. Having a mutual interest in the emerging area of social skills training, we began a collaboration and friendship that has lasted to this date. Michel was the director of an inpatient unit, which served as our research laboratory. I was primarily interested in behavioral assessment and the behavioral approach to social skills. As there were plenty of people with schizophrenia on the unit, Michel, and later Sam Turner and I, began conducting assessment and treatment trials with that population. During that period, I received a secondary appointment in psychiatry, and my attitudes about it began a gradual tectonic shift that played itself out in subsequent years. I was sufficiently productive during that period to become first associate professor and then professor in 1980. I also served as director of the psychology clinic and then director of clinical training. In addition to opening up the world of psychiatry and severe mental illness to me, Michel also introduced me to the world of academic publishing. The resulting partnership led to joint editorship of two journals, *Behavior Modification* (currently in its 28th year) and *Clinical Psychology Review* (in its 23rd year), and some 29 books, in addition to numerous journal articles and book chapters.

Continuing my shift to a focus on schizophrenia and a home in psychiatry, and stimulated in no small part by my wife's desire to move, I took a position as director of psychology at the Medical College of Pennsylvania (MCP) in 1982. This led to the third major serendipitous event in my career. Under the direction of my new chair and soon to become dear friend Wagner Bridger, MD, MCP, it soon became one of the leading biological psychiatry departments in the country. Working in this environment with world-class biological psychiatrists as colleagues, I became progressively more interested in schizophrenia and in combined behavioral and pharmacological approaches. While maintaining a behavioral view of psychosocial treatment to this day, the behavioral aspect of my work receded into the background over the succeeding 12 years, to the point where I now identify myself as a schizophrenologist rather than a behavior therapist. This shift was an important factor in my 1995 move to the University of Maryland, Department of Psychiatry, one of the leading centers for schizophrenia research in the world. In addition to being director of psychology, I am currently director of the VA Capitol Health Care Network Mental Illness, Research, Education, and Clinical Center (MIRECC). This large, multidisciplinary, VA-funded center focuses on schizophrenia, and its portfolio includes basic neuroscience, psychopharmacology, psychosocial treatment, and health services research. The breadth of the portfolio and its interdisciplinary makeup reflect the complete transition from a hopelessly naive psychology major to a leading clinical scientist with expertise on severe mental illness. A major focus of my work has been and continues to be on developing new psychosocial treatments. Recently, I have developed a very promising behavioral treatment for substance abuse in schizophrenia, and my team and I are currently working on an innovative cognitive remediation intervention.

I am a past president of the Association for Advancement of Behavior Therapy and of the Society for a Science of Clinical Psychology. I am a diplomate of the American Board of Behavior Therapy and the American Board of Professional Psychology, and a fellow of the American Psychological Association, the American Psychological Society, the Association for Clinical Psychosocial Research, and the American Psychopathological Association. I was the first recipient of the American Psychological Foundation Gralnick Foundation Award for my lifetime research on psychosocial aspects of schizophrenia, and I was the first recipient of the Ireland Investigator Award from the National Alliance for Research on Schizophrenia and Depression (NARSAD). I am a coauthor or coeditor of 31 books, and have published more than 150 journal articles and 46 book chapters. I received an National Institute of Mental Health (NIMH) MERIT award and have had continuous funding from National Institutes of Health (NIH) since 1974 for my work on schizophrenia, depression, social skills training, and substance abuse. I am a consultant to the U.S. Justice Department on behavioral treatments and rehabilitation for psychiatric patients and have served on numerous NIMH and National Institute on Drug Abuse (NIDA) review panels. I am coeditor and founder of the journals *Behavior Modification* and *Clinical Psychology Review,* and I serve on the editorial boards of nine other journals, including *Schizophrenia Bulletin.* In reviewing my curriculum vita, it will be apparent by the prevalence of coauthors that I have been blessed with wonderful students and colleagues in Pittsburgh, Philadelphia, and Baltimore.

While my early recognition in the field was as a behavior therapist and expert on social skills, at this point I am much more well-known as one of the world's leading authorities on the psychosocial treatment of schizophrenia. This continues to be the focus of my research. Schizophrenia is a neurodevelopmental disorder marked by subtle neurocognitive impairments that interfere with behavior, learning, and ability to fulfill social roles. While the field has made considerable progress in developing more effective treatments over the past two decades, we have been limited by our lack of knowledge about the basic neurobiological underpinnings of the illness and lack of ability to influence that neurobiology. This serves as a rate-limiting factor on psychosocial treatment. There is great optimism that this will change in the next decade. To the extent that it does and we can pharmacologically enhance learning and performance capacity, there will be great opportunities to develop new and more effective psychosocial interventions. I hope to be an active contributor to this evolution.

—*Alan S. Bellack*

See also: *Behavioral Approaches to Schizophrenia (Vol. I); Behavioral Treatment in Natural Environments (Vol. I); Social Skills Training (Vol. I)*

BIBLIOTHERAPY

DESCRIPTION OF THE STRATEGY

The term *bibliotherapy* refers to reading written material to pursue valued goals. It has been used to pursue a wide range of goals, including educating clients, decreasing anxiety and depression, enhancing social contacts, and developing study skills. There are different kinds of bibliotherapy. One concerns self-help

materials designed to guide the client through assessment and/or intervention in relation to hoped-for outcomes, such as decreasing anxiety or increasing effective study behaviors. Another kind requests clients to read fictional materials or poetry to attain certain outcomes. Yet another encourages readers to read spiritual literature. Many different formats are used, and Internet-based material is likely to increase in use. Surveys of counselors in a variety of professions indicate that they often assign (prescribe) specific readings to clients. Aims may include providing information about a concern, including its prevalence, motivating readers to address it, describing a variety of change options, and helping readers select promising ones. Clinical use differs along the following six dimensions: (1) extent of helper-client contact, ranging from none to extensive; (2) use of individual or group format; (3) development of general versus specific skills; (4) the extent to which readers are requested to "interact" with the written material in terms of completing exercises to test their understanding of content; (5) whether bibliotherapy is used together with other methods; and (6) attention devoted to generalization and maintenance of positive effects. Inclusion of relapse prevention guidelines offers readers information they can review on an as-needed basis. Effective use of bibliographic methods requires generalization and maintenance of valued behaviors. Counselor guidance and support may be necessary. Support also could be provided by group members or "buddies" who are involved in group programs.

Possible benefits of bibliotherapy include attaining desired outcomes with little expenditure of time, money, and effort and accessing accurate information about topics of interest (e.g., social anxiety, depression) and how to achieve valued outcomes (e.g., enhancing self-change skills and decreasing beliefs that hinder self-change). Certain kinds of individuals are more likely than others to profit from self-help formats. People differ in their repertoires of self-change skills and in their histories of using them to attain valued outcomes. Contraindications to use of bibliotherapy include limited reading ability and small probability that the client will follow instructions, perhaps because of personal or environmental obstacles. An advantage of bibliotherapy is that it allows people to achieve desired changes on their own, although some writers point out that use of self-help manuals still ties consumers to therapists, since therapy "experts" are often the authors. Dangers of ineffective self-help materials include an increase in hopelessness and helplessness when desired outcomes do not occur, neglect of other methods that might be successful, such as consulting a clinician, and a worsening of problems.

Compared with the abundance of self-help books and manuals available, the evaluation of these materials is skimpy in terms of whether they do more good than harm. A meta-analysis of 70 bibliotherapy studies by Rick Marrs indicated a positive effect for bibliotherapy. A key concern for future research is the rigorous testing of claims regarding the effectiveness of bibliotherapy in relation to particular outcomes. Given the possible rationing of counselor availability and indications that bibliotherapy can be effective and/or contribute to positive effects at low cost, it is worthwhile to pursue research in this area. The effectiveness of bibliotherapy methods should be enhanced by considering empirical literature describing components of effective self-change efforts and making sure other information provided is accurate.

—*Eileen Gambrill*

See also: *Homework (Vol. I); Instructions (Vol. I); Manualized Behavior Therapy (Vol. I)*

BIOFEEDBACK

DESCRIPTION OF THE STRATEGY

Biofeedback is the process of monitoring some biological event with an instrument designed to provide real-time information about the activity of that event to the person being monitored. In the clinical setting, it is the therapist's responsibility to know what biological event should be monitored and fed back to the client. The therapist must also help the person use the information correctly to change behavior.

The strategy is to use a sensor to measure some biological process. Sensors may be electrodes, such as an EKG electrode, or a temperature probe, or a specifically designed sensor used for detecting an ongoing biological process. Sensors must be able to detect small changes in the physiology in real time and continuously.

The sensor is connected to an instrument through which the physical event is changed into some display that is meaningful to the person being monitored. This display is the feedback signal. It is the task of the person to relate the changes in the display to what they might be doing that is changing their physiology. Today, most instruments use computers and specialized software to generate the display on the video screen and/or generate an audio signal that relates the level of the activity of the physiological event. The necessary feature of the monitoring process is that the equipment is sensitive to small changes in the biological event so that even small changes can be displayed as major changes on the display. An example is the equipment used today to measure finger skin temperature, which can detect a 10th of a degree or smaller change in skin temperature. While most people can tell you whether their hands feel cold or warm, few, unless previously trained in skin temperature regulation, can accurately tell you whether their finger skin temperatures have changed one or two degrees. Yet the sensitivity provided by the system can let persons know not only whether they have relaxed a small amount, which will cause an increase in finger skin temperature, but also that they are starting to do the correct response. The provision of this very sensitive feedback signal allows the person to gain control over the biological process by building on these small changes.

Clinical biofeedback requires accurate measurement of various physiological processes while providing client feedback that is sensitive to small changes in their physiology. It is necessary to also provide instructions to the client about proper interpretation of the feedback signal and to emphasize why changing the physiology will treat the condition. Generalization of what is learned in the clinic to the client's home, work, and social environments is also necessary.

Most biofeedback systems are computer interfaced so the feedback signal can be both visual and auditory. The visual feedback is limited only by the type of graphics available on the computer. The signal can be as simple as a line graph, in which the status of the physiology is depicted by a line that moves across the screen at some predetermined speed and the height of the line carries information about the level of the physiological event. This is one of the simplest types of feedback and looks like a typical graph. In other instances, feedback may be entertaining. This type of feedback is often a video game in which the progress of the game is based upon the level of the physiological event. An example would be to have a puzzle in which the pieces are arranged out of order on the display and the pieces start coming together when the physiological event reaches predetermined levels. In these instances, feedback is not only informative, but provides an incentive for the client to change physiology in order to "play" such games.

Physiological processes that are presently being used in clinical settings are levels of skeletal muscle activity (EMG), finger skin temperature, sweat gland activity (SCA), heart rate, brain wave activity (EEG), and respiration events. Biofeedback of muscle activity is used to reduce sustained muscle activity, which can be the source of pain; increase muscle activity after paralysis; and to reeducate specific muscle control subsequent to an injury to the nervous system, such as following a stroke. Finger temperature biofeedback is often provided as an indicator of general relaxation, since most individuals will have an increase in finger temperature as they go from a stress response to being relaxed. Sweat gland activity is used as a measure of general arousal, especially to cognitive events. Brain wave biofeedback is used to treat disorders such as attention-deficit/hyperactivity disorder (ADHD). When brain wave feedback is used, it is usually based upon research that indicates the person has a specific brain wave that is related to the disorder and that the biofeedback system can detect that type of activity and let the person know when that activity is present. This information allows the person to either increase or decrease that type of activity. Respiration biofeedback is used as a means of teaching correct breathing patterns and as a form of relaxation training.

RESEARCH BASIS

The early research demonstrating biofeedback as a process was based on a controversy in learning theory. This controversy was about the differences between operant and classical conditioning. The operant model postulated that behavior was changed by its consequences. That is, a response could be increased in probability by rewarding it. The typical example is an animal pressing a lever for food or water. The classical model of learning was based on Pavlov's work of conditioning the digestive system through the pairing, in time, of select stimuli. The typical example was the dog coming to salivate to the presentation of a tone after that tone had been paired with food powder. Until the 1960s, no one thought you could change the basic biological systems such as heart rate, salivation, and blood flow through operant conditioning. However, Neal Miller and his colleagues demonstrated systematic changes in heart rate, blood flow, and

gastric motility by rewarding selected changes. When this was discovered, it was then attempted with humans. The research to date has clearly demonstrated that provision of sensitive, continuous feedback of many biological processes can facilitate learning to control the level of the process.

In most clinical applications, it is plausible to conceptualize that the biofeedback process is using both operant and classical conditioning. The operant portion of clinical biofeedback is that information provided by the system is a consequence of the behavior. With proper instructions, the individual will perceive the feedback signal as reinforcement and will perform to bring the reinforcing stimulus into his or her environment. This is especially clear when a signal is contingent upon the individual obtaining a predetermined level of the physiology. An example would be that a certain finger temperature could be set (e.g., 92 degrees) and when that level is reached, music is turned on.

The classical model is when clients are asked to imagine previous events that might have relaxing, emotional memories associated with them. In this case, relaxing imagery elicits changes in physiology, which then will be reflected by the feedback signal letting clients know they are changing their physiology correctly.

RELEVANT TARGET POPULATIONS AND EXCEPTIONS

To present the disorders treated with biofeedback techniques, a table of these disorders was developed. Any listing of disorders must be taken only as a guideline, as it is always biased by the interpretation and experiences of the author. Some applications appear well established by controlled outcome studies of clinical effectiveness and cost-effectiveness, and others are based on repeated single-case studies or multiple studies with relatively small sample sizes. In addition, some applications are based on the clinical literature and the clinical experience of the author. A listing of disorders treated with biofeedback is divided into three categories. The categories are A = well established; B = multiple research support, but not enough to firmly substantiate the application; and C = promising but not established at this time. (See Table 1.)

COMPLICATIONS

The basic requirements when considering clinical biofeedback it that individuals must be able to tolerate

Table 1   Selected Disorders Treated With
                Biofeedback Techniques

A	B	C
ADD/ADHD	Dyschezia (anismus)	Dysmenorhea
Anxiety disorders	Esophageal spasm	Hyperfunctional dysphonia
Asthma	Forearm and hand pain from repeated motion syndrome	Mild to moderate depression
Chronic back and neck pain	Hyperhidrosis	Phantom limb pain
Diabetes mellitus	Insomnia	Tinnitus (associated symptoms)
Essential hypertension	Nocturnal enuresis	
Fecal and urinary incontinence	Specific seizure disorders	
Fibromyalgia	TMJ or MFP	
Irritable bowel syndrome	Writer's cramp	
Motion sickness		
Muscle rehabilitation		
Raynaud's		
Tension and migraine headaches		

application of the sensors, be able to understand the instructions regarding the relationship between their physiology and the feedback signal, and be motivated to change physiology using the feedback signal to facilitate this process. And finally, the individual must be motivated to practice outside the clinic setting what has been leaned in the clinic. Therapists should also be aware that some individuals might experience relaxation-induced anxiety (RIA). While little systematic information is available on incidence of this in clinical practice, it is of concern, as some individuals feel a strong sense of apprehension when a deep state of relaxation is induced.

CASE ILLUSTRATION

A typical application of biofeedback is to facilitate relaxation. When conducting biofeedback-facilitated relaxation training (BFRT), it is first necessary to determine whether the client would benefit from such therapy. General relaxation may be helpful in a variety of conditions, and it may also be useful as an incompatible response during procedures such as

systematic desensitization. BFRT normally takes between 8 and 20 sessions, depending upon the acquisition skills and the distress level of the client before and during therapy. After determination of the need for BFRT, the therapist must explain the rationale for biofeedback therapy, outline the basic aspects of the physiological processes that will be trained, and discuss potential benefits and risks of the training. This author recommends conducting the first BFRT session with frontal EMG feedback, while monitoring other modalities such as finger temperature, SCA, and/or heart rate. The therapist may also find it beneficial to monitor additional physiological events that are connected to the specific conditions being treated. During the first biofeedback session, facial muscle discrimination training should be demonstrated, and the client should be provided time to use his or her relaxation techniques to reduce frontal EMG levels. The therapist should monitor the other modalities during the session to observe the changes that occur as the client tries to reduce frontal EMG levels. An example of the value of monitoring other modalities is that by observing SCA, it can be determined whether the client is engaging in arousing internal dialogue by noting whether there is an increase in SCA level. If so, the therapist can interrupt the session and suggest a change in strategy by the client. During the interruption, the therapist should ask the client what strategy he or she is using and then encourage him or her to select a different strategy, such as diaphragmatic breathing or changes in imagery. In general, the most responsive modality is usually selected as the target of therapy after frontal EMG levels are acceptable.

SUMMARY

To be effective in the clinical application of biofeedback, there must be a measurable physiological process that can be monitored with existing technology, and feedback about the process must be provided with enough resolution and speed to allow the individual to obtain volitional change of the physiological event. Then, this change in physiology must alter the physiological processes causing the targeted disorder. In some instances, the relationship between the monitored physiological event and the disorder is obvious, such as finger temperature for Raynaud's; for others, such as BFRT for asthma and irritable bowel syndrome, the relationship is less obvious. In some instances, training a physiological event indirectly related to the physiology of interest has proven superior to treating the event itself. An example of this is frontal EMG for the treatment of essential hypertension. Therefore, the clinician must be aware of the physiology underlying the disorder and of the literature that relates to the different biofeedback treatments used to treat that disorder. This information must then be combined with the individual's characteristics, such as his or her unique physiological levels and the ability to benefit from the various types of biofeedback techniques available. The clinician must also be skilled in helping the client transfer the control acquired in the clinic to the individual's life situations. Constant advances in computer technology and developments in bioengineering, which provide new sensor technology and signal processing, make the future of clinical biofeedback look very promising.

—*Doil D. Montgomery*

See also: *Behavioral Medicine (Vol. I); Behavioral Pediatrics (Vol. II); Pharmacotherapy and Behavior Therapy (Vol. I)*

Suggested Readings

Evans, J. R., & Abarbanel, A. (Eds.). (1999). *Introduction to quantitative EEG and biofeedback.* New York: Academic Press.

Kasman, G. S., Cram, J. R., Wolf, S. L., & Barton, L. (1998). *Clinical applications in surface electromyography: Chronic musculosketal pain.* Gaithersberg, MD: Aspen.

Schwartz, M., & Andrasik, F. (Eds.). (2003). *Biofeedback: A practitioners guide.* New York: Guilford Press.

BREATHING RETRAINING

DESCRIPTION OF THE STRATEGY

Breathing retraining, also referred to as *diaphragmatic breathing* or *abdominal breathing,* is a successful method used to reduce physiological arousal or anxiety. When anxious, breathing tends to become shallow and rapid. This breathing pattern can perpetuate or even worsen the state of tension in the body by reducing the amount of oxygen being supplied to the brain. In addition, rapid, shallow breathing may result in hyperventilation, which occurs when excess carbon dioxide is in exhaled in relation to the amount of oxygen in the bloodstream. People tend to hyperventilate when they are feeling anxious or tense. However, hyperventilation itself increases symptoms such as dizziness, increased heart rate, and tingling sensations, which serve to further exacerbate the anxiety. Breathing retraining can help reduce

physiological symptoms of anxiety by increasing the oxygen supply to the brain and by triggering the parasympathetic nervous system, which works to restore the body to a calm, resting state. This technique is particularly useful for people who suffer from panic attacks, social anxiety, phobias, or other anxiety disorders.

GUIDELINES FOR IMPLEMENTING THE STRATEGY

The first step in breathing retraining is to learn to distinguish between shallow chest breathing and deep abdominal breathing. One helpful way to identify such difference is by placing one hand on the chest and the other hand on the abdomen right beneath the rib cage. First, one takes a normal chest breath by trying to make the hand on the chest rise and fall while inhaling and exhaling through the mouth. Once able to recognize the sensations associated with shallow chest breathing, the next step involves "retraining" the breathing process by taking deeper abdominal breaths. This is done by inhaling slowly through the nose. Attempt to minimize the movement of the hand on the chest when inhaling by forcing the air deeper into the abdomen, which will cause the hand on your abdomen to rise. It is sometimes helpful to imagine inflating a small set of lungs below the rib cage. While exhaling, the client is asked to breathe out slowly through the nose as the hand on the abdomen falls back down to the resting position. Practice sessions need last only approximately 5 minutes. Some people find it helpful to count slowly to five while inhaling and count backward to zero while exhaling. Counting can serve to slow down the breathing rate, which decreases the chances of hyperventilating. These exercises are easiest to do while lying down at first. After becoming comfortable with the exercises while lying down, the client progresses to a standing position. Ultimately, this technique can be successfully applied while in a sitting position during daily activities (e.g., while driving, at work, in a meeting).

—*Brooke L. Whisenhunt*

See also: *Panic Control Treatment (Vol. I); Progressive Muscular Relaxation (Vol. I); Relaxation Strategies (Vol. I)*

Suggested Readings

Bourne, E. J. (1995). *The anxiety and phobia workbook.* Oakland, CA: New Harbinger.

Zuercher-White, E. (1999). *Overcoming panic disorder and agoraphobia.* Oakland, CA: New Harbinger.

CAUTELA, JOSEPH R.

Joseph R. Cautela was born in Boston on February 21, 1927, a city in which he was to remain his entire life. His parents were immigrants from Sicily, and Cautela grew up in a working-class suburb of Boston, graduating from high school in 1944. After the untimely death of his mother, his father relocated back to their home in Sicily in 1969, where Joseph and his family were to visit him often over the ensuing decades. Early on, Cautela displayed a logical and inquisitive mind and a dedication to hard work that led to marked academic success, and he entered Boston College, graduating in 1949. Following graduation, he began graduate school at Boston University, where, under the mentorship of Leo Renya, he received a PhD in experimental psychology in 1954. While working on his PhD, he taught part-time at his alma mater, Boston College, and also consulted to the Boston Psychopathic Hospital, now the Massachusetts Mental Health Center. Upon earning his PhD, he immediately returned to Boston College as an assistant professor, earning the rank of professor in 1966 and, ultimately, retiring in 1986.

In the early years, Cautela was an extraordinarily busy man. With a growing family to support and a great deal of energy and dedication to his field, he would squeeze every last minute out of every day. He would be up very early in the morning, carving out several hours of writing time.

After concluding his writing, he would commute to his office at Boston College, where he would teach three courses a semester and, most often, another course in the evening school at least one night a week. Cautela also availed himself of other opportunities to teach in the summer and, as an excellent teacher, found no shortage of opportunities. At the end of this very long day, he would then retire to an office in his home, where he would begin seeing private patients from 7 to as late as 11 o'clock or midnight. Despite this punishing schedule, he always seemed to be fresh and always made time for his graduate students at Boston College, whether in his office at school or in his office at home.

As a thoroughly trained Hullian learning theorist, Cautela produced a body of important work on the fundamental properties of learning and conditioning early in his career. Two of the articles emerging from this line of research were "The Effect of Drive on Probability Learning" and "The Problem of Backward Conditioning." But it was the second phase of Cautela's career that was to immortalize him.

His approach to clinical work in those early years was flavored by the prevailing psychodynamic orientation that he had picked up in some clinical training and work-related experiences during the 1950s. But Leo Renya had introduced Cautela to Skinner, Ferster, Lindsley, and later Wolpe when Cautela was a graduate student during the 1950s; and with his strong background in learning theory, he would integrate principles of learning into his clinical work.

In fact, Cautela had read with great interest the work of Joseph Wolpe, first published in 1958, and the subsequent case studies, mostly from England in the early 1960s, heralding the birth of a new approach to therapy called "behavior therapy." Cautela credited Wolpe's book as the inspiration that refocused his career in the early 1960s. At that time, he took a month out of his busy schedule to attend an institute offered by Wolpe. It was during this period that everything came together in Cautela's professional life. With his comprehensive knowledge of the intricacies of the principles of learning and the clinical expertise he had developed through years of experience (he was a superb therapist), Cautela very quickly joined the early ranks of behavior therapists and became one of the 5 to 10 "founding fathers" of this nascent intellectual movement.

With his prolific writing ability and his creative mind, Cautela began publishing innovative and important articles illustrating the use of behavior therapy. As was customary in those early days, many of them were case studies elucidating the process of therapy, including "The Applications of Learning Theory as a Last Resort in the Treatment of Case of Anxiety Neurosis," "Behavior Therapy Treatment of Pervasive Anxiety," and "Behavior Therapy and Geriatrics," all published in the mid 1960s. During these years, he also published on the theoretical basis of behavior therapy articles such as "The Pavlovian Basis of Reciprocal Inhibition Therapy." However, one of his more important papers was titled "Covert Sensitizisation," published in 1967, in which he introduced a provocative new therapeutic technique. In this procedure, patients imaged in detail certain aspects of their behavior vividly associated with consequences that, with practice, would provide a new cognitive "template" for the behavior. This process was surprisingly effective with a variety of addictive behaviors, as well as behaviors associated with negative affect (anxiety-depression). These "self-control" procedures, as Cautela would later refer to them, presaged the development of cognitive approaches to therapy in the 1970s and the subsequent integration of cognitive and behavioral therapy.

In 1972, Cautela married Julie Gleason, and the two of them worked closely together the rest of their lives on scholarly projects and in clinical practice. With his energy and enthusiasm, he consulted widely and rose to prominent positions in many professional associations, including an early stint as president of the Association for Advancement of Behavior Therapy in 1972. With his extraordinarily creative approach to clinical problems, he was able to innovate a variety of new techniques for use with diverse populations. Much of this work was published, some of it in book form or manual form, including his books on covert conditioning and his manual, in collaboration with June Groden, on utilizing calming procedures, such as relaxation, with individuals with severe developmental disabilities.

Throughout his career, Cautela was the model of a caring and committed professional who maintained lasting relationships and friendships with his colleagues and former students. Social gatherings at the Cautela home were eagerly anticipated by large numbers of people in the field as a chance to catch up on developments and share in the excitement of the growing success of cognitive-behavioral approaches over the years. With his extraordinarily punishing schedule, particularly in the early years, Cautela suffered a heart attack in his mid-40s and was to suffer several more over the ensuing years. He attended to his health as best he could by changing behavioral risk factors, lowering stress with his own imaginal procedures, but hardly slowed down in the decades to follow, remaining as productive as ever, much to the amazement of his friends and family. It is ironic that it was cancer to which he finally succumbed on April 28, 1999, at the ripe old age (considering his health) of 72, and this very sad occasion for his wide circle of friends and family was followed the next year, tragically, by the death of his wife, from a similar diagnosis.

At the beginnings of behavior therapy, Cautela and his early pioneering colleagues were accustomed to having their pronouncements on the promise of the application of psychological science to the clinic belittled and ridiculed, and their own personal motivations questioned. Fortunately, he lived to see the triumph of his ideas and nothing short of a revolution in psychological treatments. His memory lives on in the "Joe and Julie Cautela Society," where his friends and former students gather frequently to reexperience the heady and exciting days of the birth of behavior therapy and some of the lingering warmth and love that were so much a part of Cautela's life.

—*David H. Barlow*

See also: *Coverant Control (Vol. I); Covert Rehearsal (Vol. I); Covert Sensitization Conditioning (Vol. I)*

Suggested Readings

Cautela, J. R. (1966). A behavior therapy treatment of pervasive anxiety. *Behavior, Research, and Therapy, 4,* 99–109.

Cautela, J. R. (1966). Treatment of compulsive behavior by covert sensitization. *Psychological Record, 16,* 33–41.

Cautela, J. R. (1967). Covert sensitization. *Psychological Record, 20,* 459–468.

Cautela, J. R. (1969). A classical conditioning approach to the development and modification of behavior in the aged. *The Gerontologist, 9* (Part 1), 109–113.

Cautela, J. R. (1971). Covert conditioning. In A. Jacobs & L. B. Sachs (Eds.), *The psychology of private events: Perspectives on covert response systems* (pp. 109–130). New York: Academic Press.

CLASSICAL CONDITIONING

DESCRIPTION OF THE STRATEGY

Classical conditioning is a procedure used to study behavioral change. The procedure was developed around 1900 by the Russian physiologist Ivan P. Pavlov in the course of his research on the physiology of digestion. The defining feature of the procedure is that the presentation of an eliciting stimulus is dependent upon the prior occurrence of a relatively "neutral" stimulus. In Pavlov's laboratory, food commonly served as the eliciting stimulus, with salivation as the elicited response, and events such as the sound of a ticking metronome or the sight of a rotating black square served as neutral stimuli. After several pairings of the neutral stimulus with the eliciting stimulus, the neutral stimulus began to evoke salivation prior to the presentation of food and during test trials in which the neutral stimulus was presented alone. That is, the ticking sound itself came to evoke salivation. Pairing the neutral stimulus with the eliciting stimulus had produced a new environment-behavior relation: sound-salivation. The procedure is termed *classical conditioning,* because it was the first procedure used to systematically investigate the acquisition of environment-behavior relations. The procedure is also known as *Pavlovian conditioning,* to acknowledge its originator, or as *respondent conditioning,* to emphasize that the behavior is evoked in response to a specified stimulus instead of being emitted. An *emitted response* results from the action of unspecified environmental and intraorganismic events, such as when a novel environment engenders exploratory behavior. The acquisition of environment-behavior relations involving emitted responses is studied with a different procedure known as *operant* or *instrumental* conditioning.

The various stimuli and responses that appear in the classical procedure are designated by technical terms that originated with Pavlov. The neutral stimulus (e.g., a sound) is known as the *conditioned stimulus,* to emphasize that its ability to evoke behavior is dependent upon, or conditional upon, its pairing with the eliciting stimulus. The eliciting stimulus (e.g., food) is termed the *unconditioned stimulus,* to indicate that its ability to evoke the elicited response is independent of the organism's experience with the elicitor in the experiment. The elicited response (e.g., salivation) is known as the *unconditioned response.* The response that comes to be evoked by the conditioned stimulus after pairing is termed the *conditioned response* (also salivation in the example), because its occurrence is dependent upon pairing the conditioned stimulus with the unconditioned stimulus. (The correct English translations of Pavlov's original text are condition*al* and uncondition*al,* not condition*ed* and uncondition*ed,* but the latter terms have persisted because of the faulty initial translation.) Few stimuli are truly neutral—have no behavioral effects—and the responses that initially occur to the to-be-conditioned stimulus are also acknowledged and are known as *orienting responses.* In technical writing, these events are commonly abbreviated CS for conditioned stimulus, US (or UCS) for unconditioned stimulus, UR (or UCR) for unconditioned response, CR for conditioned response, and OR for orienting response.

Many important behavioral phenomena have been discovered using the classical procedure; extinction, discrimination, generalization, spontaneous recovery, and higher-order conditioning are but a few examples. However, the present discussion focuses on the conditions that have been identified with the classical procedure as necessary to produce behavioral change. Beginning with Pavlov, and confirmed in many later studies, a close temporal relation between the CS and the US/UR is essential for learning. As an example, the sound had to immediately precede food/salivation if it was to function as a CS. When the UR has a very short latency (such as an eye-blink elicited by an air-puff), a CS-US/UR interval of less than a second is optimal. When the UR has a longer latency (such as a change in heart rate elicited by electric shock), an interval of a few seconds is optimal. The finding that the CS-US/UR interval is crucial for learning exemplifies the *contiguity* requirement. Until the 1960s, it was generally believed that contiguity of the CS with the US/UR was sufficient for learning with the classical procedure. However, a number of studies, conducted principally by Robert Rescorla, began to call this idea into question. These studies appeared to show that learning could be produced by classical procedures in which occurrences of the CS and US/UR were simply *correlated* with one another: For example, acquisition occurred if the US/UR was more likely during extended time periods containing the CS than during equally long periods in which the CS was absent. These findings encouraged a *molar* conception of learning in which a general relationship between the occurrences of CSs and US/URs was thought to produce behavioral change without specific CS-US/UR contiguity.

Further experiments, conducted principally by Leon Kamin, demonstrated that contiguity was necessary for learning but it was not sufficient. Something else was required. The additional factor was the production of a *behavioral discrepancy* by the US. That is, the UR elicited by the US had to be a behavior that was not already occurring when the CS was presented. The discrepancy requirement is best illustrated by the *blocking experiment.* In blocking, a CS (e.g., a light) is first paired with a US/UR (e.g., food-salivation). After several pairings, the light alone is able to evoke a salivary CR; that is, simple conditioning has occurred. Then, the light is joined by another stimulus (e.g., a tone) that stands in the same temporal relation to food-salivation as the light. Thus, the tone-US/UR relation also satisfies the contiguity requirement. However, when the tone is presented alone, salivary CRs do not appear. The light CS is said to block conditioning to the tone because CRs were already occurring during the light and the US did not produce a *change* in behavior during the tone. The blocking experiment demonstrates that CS-US/UR contiguity produces learning only if, in addition, the US evokes a behavioral discrepancy. In everyday terms, a new environment-behavior relation is acquired only when the learner is "surprised" by the US/UR. Given the findings of blocking experiments, as well as related studies, the molar, or correlation, view of classical conditioning was abandoned. Robert Rescorla and Allan Wagner subsequently advanced an influential account of conditioning that incorporated both the contiguity and discrepancy requirements and accommodated the findings that had prompted the molar view.

The classical procedure enables the experimenter to manipulate the relation of an arbitrary stimulus to the US/UR and is suitable to study acquisition of responses that are evoked by stimuli either because of natural selection (e.g., reflexively elicited responses)

or prior conditioning (e.g., prior CS-CR relations, as in higher-order conditioning). The behavioral component of the CS-CR relation typically includes "emotional" responses (responses mediated by the autonomic nervous system, such as salivary or cardiac responses) but can include other responses (those mediated by the skeletal system, such as the different consummatory responses evoked by grain or water in *autoshaping*). Because emotional responses are often acquired through a classical procedure, variants of this procedure are used in applied behavior analysis to modify dysfunctional emotional behavior, as in the treatment of phobias by *systematic desensitization* and of fetishes by *counterconditioning*. To study the full repertoire of environment-behavior relations, the classical procedure must be supplemented by the operant (or instrumental) procedure.

—*John W. Donahoe*

See also: *Covert Sensitization Conditioning (Vol. I); Electrical Aversion (Vol. I); Pavlov, Ivan P. (Vol. I)*

Suggested Readings

Brown, P. L., & Jenkins, H. M. (1968). Autoshaping of the pigeon's key-peck. *Journal of the Experimental Analysis of Behavior, 11,* 1–8.

Donahoe, J. W., & Palmer, D. C. (1994). *Learning and complex behavior* (pp. 37–49). Boston: Allyn & Bacon.

Kamin, L. J. (1969). Predictability, surprise, attention, and conditioning. In B. A. Campbell & R. M. Church (Eds.), *Punishment and aversive behavior* (pp. 279–296). New York: Appleton-Century-Crofts.

Pavlov, I. P. (1927). *Conditioned reflexes.* New York: Oxford University Press. (Reprinted, New York: Dover, 1960)

Rescorla, R. A. (1967). Pavlovian conditioning and its proper control procedures. *Psychological Review, 74,* 71–80.

Rescorla, R. A., & Wagner, A. R. (1972). A theory of Pavlovian conditioning: Variations in the effectiveness of reinforcement and nonreinforcement. In A. H. Black & W. F. Prokasy (Eds.), *Classical conditioning II* (pp. 64–99). New York: Appleton-Century-Crofts.

COGNITIVE BEHAVIOR THERAPY

DESCRIPTION OF THE STRATEGY

Cognitive behavior therapy (CBT) is a form of psychotherapy that blends strategies from traditional behavioral treatments with various cognitively oriented strategies. It is different from other forms of psychotherapy (e.g., traditional psychodynamic psychotherapies) in that the focus of treatment is on changing the behaviors and cognitions that are thought to be currently maintaining a problem, rather than on helping a client to gain insight into the early developmental factors that may have initially set the stage for developing the problem.

The boundaries of CBT are somewhat unclear. Different practitioners and researchers often use terms such as *cognitive behavior therapy, behavior therapy,* and *cognitive therapy* in different ways. For some professionals, these terms are used interchangeably. For others, they have very different meanings. For the purpose of this entry, the term cognitive behavior therapy is used in its broadest sense, including strategies that are traditionally derived from a behavioral framework, as well as strategies developed by cognitive theorists. Relevant strategies include techniques such as exposure-based therapies for anxiety disorders, cognitive restructuring, behavioral experiments, relaxation training, reinforcement-based treatments, assertiveness training, and many others. Often, combinations of these treatments are used to target different aspects of a client's problem.

The marriage of cognitive and behavioral approaches makes sense in light of the many features they share. For example:

- ❖ Cognitive and behavioral therapies are both conceptually based on established principles from basic psychological science (e.g., learning theory, cognitive science).
- ❖ The effectiveness of cognitive and behavioral therapies can both be understood from a common conceptual framework. For example, exposure therapy (a traditional behavioral treatment for phobic disorders) and cognitive restructuring (teaching people to change negative patterns of thinking) may both work by changing ways in which clients process information.
- ❖ Cognitive and behavioral therapies are both action oriented. That is, they require clients to behave in new ways, in order to change maladaptive patterns of interacting with their environments.
- ❖ Cognitive and behavioral treatments are both typically brief, lasting several months.
- ❖ Both approaches to treatment are problem focused and goal driven. That is, they begin

with identifying particular problems and goals for treatment, and the process of treatment is designed to alleviate the identified problem and to help the client achieve the changes he or she seeks. For example, treatment goals for a person with obsessive-compulsive disorder (OCD) might be to reduce the frequency and severity of obsessional thoughts and compulsive behaviors.

- ❖ Cognitive and behavioral treatments are both transparent. That is, the client is provided with an explanation of the conceptual foundations and practical steps underlying the strategies that are used.
- ❖ Structured homework assignments are an important component of both behavioral and cognitive treatments. Homework may include activities such as practicing particular techniques (e.g., relaxation training), conducting behavioral experiments, and completing cognitive-monitoring diaries.
- ❖ Both approaches to treatment have a strong empirical basis, having been studied in hundreds of controlled clinical trials for a wide range of problems. Therapists are also encouraged to collect data with each client, in order to assess the effectiveness of particular strategies that are being used.

HISTORICAL AND CONCEPTUAL FOUNDATIONS

Modern CBT has its roots in the 1950s and 1960s, when several psychologists and psychiatrists, working in South Africa, England, and the United States, began to study the use of interventions based on principles of learning theory. A growing dissatisfaction with psychoanalysis, as well as increased interest in learning theory among basic scientists in psychology, set the stage for the development and proliferation of behavior therapy. Before long, thanks to the work of pioneers such as Hans Eysenck, Cyril Franks, Arnold Lazarus, Isaac Marks, S. Rachman, G. Terence Wilson, and Joseph Wolpe, behavior therapy became an established form of treatment that included exposure-based strategies, techniques based on classical and operant conditioning, and other strategies aimed at directly changing problem behaviors.

By the early 1960s, the term behavior therapy had appeared in several important publications. Related terms, such as *behavior modification,* also began to be used more frequently during the 1960s. In 1963, the first scientific journal devoted to behavior therapy *(Behaviour Research and Therapy)* was first published, and in 1966, the Association for Advancement of Behavior Therapy (AABT) was formed, with Cyril Franks as the founding president.

In the 1960s and 1970s, several authors began to incorporate cognitive explanations for understanding learning-based phenomena, and this development had a profound influence on the development of specific treatments designed to change negative patterns of thinking and information processing. Although a number of individuals (e.g., Aaron T. Beck, Albert Ellis, Michael Mahoney, Donald Meichenbaum, and others) played important roles in the early advancement of cognitive treatments, Beck and Ellis are most often credited with the development of these treatments. Both of these individuals were originally trained as psychoanalysts, and both described their dissatisfaction with traditional psychoanalysis as fueling their decision to develop new approaches to treating depression, anxiety, and related problems. Ellis called his form of treatment "rational-emotive therapy" (later changed to "rational-emotive behavior therapy"), and Beck called his form of treatment "cognitive therapy." Both treatments were focused on helping clients to shift their beliefs, assumptions, and predictions from being negative, depressive, anxious, and dysfunctional to be more realistic, positive, and adaptive.

With effective behavioral and cognitive treatments becoming more established, researchers in the 1970s and 1980s began to develop protocols that included strategies from both forms of treatment. It was during this period that CBT began to be used more frequently as a way of describing treatments that included both cognitive and behavioral techniques. For most psychological disorders, there are now structured treatment protocols based on CBT principles.

An example of a typical CBT protocol is that for *panic control treatment* (developed by David H. Barlow, Michelle Craske, and Ron Rapee), which includes exposure-based strategies, breathing retraining, and cognitive restructuring for individuals who suffer from panic disorder. In this protocol, exposure is used to reduce avoidance behavior, which, in turn, leads to improved functioning and also helps to change anxious thinking by demonstrating firsthand that most of an individual's fearful predictions do not materialize upon confronting a feared situation. The cognitive strategies used during panic control treatment are designed to help a client to recognize that the symptoms he or she experiences during panic attacks are neither dangerous nor unmanageable. Finally, breathing retraining is included to help clients with panic disorders to slow down their breathing, thereby reducing the frequency and intensity of panic symptoms that may be triggered by hyperventilation or overbreathing.

Professionals who work within a CBT framework assume that psychological problems experienced by an individual are caused and maintained by a number of factors, including:

❖ *Patterns of reinforcement and punishment from the environment.* For example, an individual who receives considerable praise and rewards for being detail oriented, perfectionistic, and hardworking may begin to overvalue the importance of his or her work and may feel devastated when he or she is unable to meet certain arbitrary standards. Similarly, an individual who is criticized and teased frequently while growing up may develop a fear of socializing and of developing intimate relationships.

❖ *Negatively biased thoughts, assumptions, predictions, interpretations, and beliefs.* For example, Aaron Beck hypothesized that depression occurs when individuals hold negative beliefs about themselves (e.g., I am stupid), the world (e.g., People are generally nasty), and the future (e.g., I will never find a job) and when they engage in errors or biases in thinking, such as interpreting events in a negative way despite a lack of evidence supporting such thoughts.

❖ *Behavioral excesses.* These involve engaging in particular problematic behaviors too frequently, giving rise to problems in relationships, work, or other life domains. For example, individuals with bulimia nervosa engage in binge eating and purging, which helps to maintain the problem over time.

❖ *Behavioral deficits.* These are behaviors in which people under engage, to the point of causing disruptions in day-to-day functioning. For example, people who suffer from phobias typically avoid encountering the objects of their fears, thereby keeping their fear levels at a minimal level and reinforcing the fear over time.

❖ *Skills deficits*. For example, an individual who lacks assertiveness skills may frequently find himself or herself being taken advantage of by others, thereby leading to problems with anxiety, depression, or other difficulties.

PROCESS OF ASSESSMENT

For those who practice CBT, assessment has a number of functions. Initially, the purpose of assessment may be to identify particular problems on which to focus during treatment, and perhaps to establish a diagnosis. The assessment process also helps with the process of deciding which treatment strategies are likely to be most beneficial for a particular individual. Finally, the assessment process typically continues throughout treatment, and perhaps even after treatment has ended, in order to measure the outcome of treatment. The structured measurement of outcome is a hallmark of CBT and other evidence-based interventions.

Ideally, assessment occurs through a variety of methods, including direct behavioral observation, monitoring diaries, interviews, and self-report scales. Each of these is described briefly below.

Clinical Interviews

As with almost all forms of psychotherapy, the clinical interview is an important tool for therapists who use CBT. In addition to the usual topics covered during the interview (e.g., history of the presenting problem, personal and family history, etc.), CBT therapists ask questions about particular aspects of the problem that are relevant to the cognitive and behavioral strategies that are typically used. Specifically, they are interested in the types of behavioral excesses and deficits that are associated with the client's difficulties, the triggers and consequences of problem behaviors, and the types of cognitions that are associated with negative mood states such as anxiety, depression, and anger. Often, semistructured interviews are used to ensure a standardized approach to assessment that is unlikely to accidentally miss out on important features of the problem.

Direct Behavioral Observation

Direct behavioral observation involves observing a client in a relevant situation and noting various behaviors and responses of interest. For example, when treating social anxiety disorder using CBT, therapists will often first administer a behavioral approach test (BAT), in which the client confronts a feared situation (e.g., a casual conversation with a stranger, or a brief presentation). During the BAT, the therapist has the opportunity to observe the client in order to note any skills deficits and to observe any avoidance or safety behaviors that are used during the test. After the BAT, clients typically report on the severity of their anxiety and on any anxious thoughts that occurred during the exercise. The BAT can be repeated periodically as a way of measuring change over the course of treatment.

Behavioral observation has the advantage, over other forms of assessment, of being able to identify behaviors or other features of a problem of which a client may be unaware.

Monitoring Diaries

Monitoring diaries are forms that clients complete on a regular basis to measure relevant symptoms or to monitor their use of particular CBT strategies. For example, in CBT-based treatments for substance use disorders, clients are often encouraged to record each time they use the substance, as well as any urges to use the substance that may arise. In the treatment of depression, it is common to have clients monitor their depressive thoughts and to use cognitive diaries to challenge their patterns of negative thinking. Specifically, clients are encouraged to record the evidence supporting their negative thoughts, the evidence that doesn't support their negative thinking, and to arrive at a more realistic conclusion based on the evidence.

An advantage of monitoring diaries is that they avoid problems of retrospective recall bias. By having clients report on their symptoms as they occur, they are more likely to provide an accurate account of the frequency and severity of their symptoms than they might be if they were simply trying to recreate the memory of the symptoms while sitting in the therapist's office several days or weeks later.

Self-Report Scales

Numerous standardized scales exist for measuring the most important features of almost every diagnostic category. For anxiety disorders alone, more than 200 empirically supported scales are currently in use. For example, in the case of panic disorder and agoraphobia, there are scales to measure the frequency of panic attack symptoms, the severity of agoraphobic avoidance, the types of panic-related cognitions held by the client, and the extent to which the client is fearful of panic-related sensations (a hallmark feature of panic disorder). Information obtained on self-report scales can be used to help select targets or goals for treatment, as well as to select the most appropriate strategies for dealing with the problem. Unlike other types of assessment, they are relatively economical to administer in that they require little of the therapist's time.

STRUCTURE OF CBT

Duration, Frequency, and Format of Sessions

Duration, frequency, and format of sessions vary greatly, depending on the type of problem being treated, the therapist's availability, and the client's preferences. Typically, treatment consists of 10 to 20 sessions, usually occurring weekly. However, individuals with complex presentations (e.g., significant comorbidity, personality disorders) may take longer than 20 sessions to treat, and individuals with very focused problems (e.g., specific phobia) can often be treated in a much smaller number of sessions.

Treatment sessions typically last 1 hour, but may last longer (e.g., 90 minutes to 2 hours), particularly if they include therapist-assisted exposure to feared situations. Although CBT sessions usually occur weekly, some treatment protocols are based on a more intensive schedule (e.g., daily sessions for 2 or 3 weeks), and other protocols include less frequent sessions (e.g., every 2 weeks), particularly later in the course of treatment.

The format of CBT varies considerably. Treatment may occur individually or in groups. There is some evidence supporting treatments with minimal therapist contact (e.g., brief treatments, self-help treatments, telephone treatments) for certain types of problems. Although CBT is often administered on an outpatient basis, there are also inpatient and day treatment programs based on a CBT approach.

Structure of a Typical Session

CBT sessions usually begin with the therapist and client collaborating to set an agenda for the meeting. Setting an agenda helps both parties pace the session to ensure that there is enough time to cover the most important topics. Early in the session, some time is also spent reviewing the client's experiences during the previous week and discussing the completion of homework.

The bulk of each session is spent teaching, reviewing, or applying specific CBT strategies to the client's problems. Early in treatment, sessions are often more didactic, with the therapist describing how to use particular techniques. In later sessions, more time is spent actually using the new strategies. For example, the therapist and client may review the evidence regarding negative patterns of thinking. Or the therapist and client may spend time practicing relaxation strategies or confronting feared situations.

At the end of each session, homework is assigned. Clients are encouraged to practice the CBT strategies on a daily basis between sessions.

STRATEGIES USED IN CBT

Psychoeducation

Psychoeducation involves providing clients with information that is likely to facilitate the process of overcoming the problem for which they are being treated. For example, individuals who are being taught to slow down their breathing as a way of relaxing will typically first be taught about the relationship between hyperventilation and anxiety symptoms. Similarly, individuals who receive CBT for an eating disorder are typically also provided with information about a healthy diet and about complications associated with restricting food intake, binge eating, and purging. In fact, dieticians are often included in the treatment of eating disorders, in order to provide the relevant information. Although psychoeducation occurs throughout the treatment, it is often used most extensively during the early sessions and may be supplemented with reading materials, videos, or other educational materials.

Cognitive Restructuring

Cognitive restructuring involves teaching clients to be more aware of their negative thoughts, to evaluate evidence of the extent to which thoughts are accurate, and to replace unrealistic thoughts with more balanced interpretations, predictions, and assumptions. Clients are encouraged to question their beliefs (e.g., Are my thoughts necessarily true? Does this situation matter as much as it feels like it does?) rather than automatically assuming the thoughts are true. Monitoring forms are used to help clients to identify and challenge the thoughts that lead to problems with anxiety, depression, anger, and other negative emotions.

Strategies for challenging negative thinking include:

❖ Becoming educated about relevant facts (e.g., learning about the actual risks of dying in a plane crash in an effort to overcome a fear of flying).
❖ Examining the evidence (e.g., "The fact that my friend often invites me to socialize is evidence that he or she enjoys spending time with me, despite that fact that I believe otherwise when my mood is low").
❖ Examining one's previous experiences (e.g., "Given that I have never fainted before during a panic attack, the odds of my fainting during my next panic attack are minimal").
❖ Shifting perspectives (e.g., "My expectations for my own performance are much higher than the expectations I hold for others or the expectations that others hold for me").
❖ Combating catastrophic thinking by asking "So what. . .?" (e.g., a client who is convinced that not getting a job he or she has just applied for might be encouraged to ask questions such as "What if I don't get the job?" "How could I cope with not getting the job?" "Does not being offered this job mean that I will never find a job?").

Behavioral Experiments

Behavioral experiments (also called hypothesis testing) involve testing out the validity of a particular belief or prediction by conducting an experiment and evaluating the outcome. For example, an individual who is convinced that being the center of attention will lead to horrible consequences might be encouraged to purposely draw attention to him or herself (e.g., speaking in public, dropping keys, spilling a glass of water, etc.) to learn that the actual consequences are quite mild. In reality, it is often quite difficult to get the attention of others.

Exposure-Based Techniques

Exposure is one of the most powerful methods of overcoming fear. It is used routinely in the treatment of anxiety disorders, as well as other problems that include fear as a component (e.g., people with eating disorders who fear eating certain foods). Essentially, clients are encouraged to confront feared objects and situations repeatedly until the fear is no longer a problem. In cases where individuals are fearful of their thoughts (e.g., people with obsessive-compulsive disorder who experience aggressive obsessions; people with posttraumatic stress disorder who constantly try to rid themselves of their traumatic memories), exposure to the feared thoughts and memories can be useful. Similarly, for individuals who are fearful of particular physical symptoms (e.g., people with panic disorder who fear having a racing heart; people with height phobias who fear feeling dizzy in a high place), exposure to the feared physical symptoms (sometimes referred to as *interoceptive exposure*) can be helpful.

Before beginning to use exposure, clients are encouraged to develop an exposure hierarchy. The hierarchy is essentially a list of fear situations (usually 10 to 15), rank ordered by most difficult (at the top) to least difficult (at the bottom). The hierarchy is used to guide the exposure practices throughout the treatment. Clients are encouraged to practice easier items first. As the fear of these items decreases, clients then move on to more difficult items on the hierarchy. Table 1 is an example of an exposure hierarchy for overcoming a phobia of driving.

Exposure is most effective when it is predictable, under the client's control, frequent (daily, if possible), and prolonged (ideally, lasting long enough for the fear to decrease). Clients should be encouraged to practice exposure in different locations and contexts, and with different types of feared objects. For example, a person who fears dogs should practice being around various breeds of dogs, in a variety of locations. During exposure, clients are encouraged not to fight their feelings of fear; they may even be encouraged to purposely intensify the feeling if the fear level is too low to obtain any benefit. Clients are also discouraged from relying on distraction, safety cues, overprotective behaviors, and other subtle avoidance strategies. In the case of obsessive-compulsive disorder, treatment includes prevention of all compulsive rituals. For example, in addition to touching contaminated objects, a person with obsessive-compulsive disorder is also encouraged to prevent all washing, especially after coming into contact with an object that is perceived as contaminated.

Table 1   Sample Hierarchy for Overcoming a Phobia of Driving

Situation	Fear Rating
Driving over the Golden Gate Bridge alone at rush hour	100
Driving alone on the highway at rush hour	90
Driving on the highway with my spouse at rush hour	80
Being a passenger on the highway during rush hour	75
Driving alone on the highway in the middle of the day	65
Driving alone on a city street at midday, when it is raining	65
Driving alone on a city street at midday, when the sky is clear	50
Turning left on a busy city street	45
Driving alone in a busy parking lot	35
Driving alone in an empty parking lot	25

Relaxation- and Meditation-Based Strategies

Relaxation-based strategies have been in use since the development of behavioral treatments. They are most frequently used in the treatment of generalized anxiety disorder and for stress management, but they have also been studied as treatments for other anxiety-based conditions. Common forms of relaxation training include progressive muscle relaxation (involving a series of tension and relaxation exercises), imagery-based relaxation training, and breathing retraining.

Although meditation-based strategies are often included as a component of relaxation training, they have recently begun to receive greater attention in the behavioral literature for their benefits over and above their role in relaxation-based treatments. In particular, a form of meditation called *mindfulness meditation* has been gaining popularity in recent years. Mindfulness meditation teaches an individual to be fully present in each moment, to be aware of his or her thoughts, feelings, and sensations, and to detect symptoms before they become a problem. This form of treatment has been found to be useful for reducing symptoms in anxiety disorder and stress-based medical problems, as well as for preventing relapse in people who have recently recovered from depression.

Social and Communication Skills Training

Social and communication skills training involves teaching individuals particular strategies for increasing the effectiveness of his or her social behaviors. Examples of areas that may be the target of intervention include:

- ❖ Improving eye contact
- ❖ Developing appropriate assertiveness skills
- ❖ Learning to manage conflict effectively
- ❖ Nonverbal communication skills (e.g., body position, personal space, volume of speech)
- ❖ Developing better dating skills
- ❖ Improving presentation skills
- ❖ Enhancing basic skills of daily living

Social and communication skills training involves identifying particular social skills deficits, discussing alternative ways of behaving, modeling appropriate social behaviors, allowing the client to practice alternate behaviors, and providing feedback on the client's performance. Videotaping the client's practices may be used to facilitate the process of providing feedback. Social and communication skills training is often a component of CBT for social anxiety, depression, marital distress, psychotic disorders, and a variety of other problems.

Problem-Solving Strategies

Problem-solving training involves teaching clients a structured, systematic method of solving problems that arise, as an alternative to solving problems impulsively, focusing on the wrong problems, or avoiding dealing with problems all together (e.g., procrastination). Often, individuals have difficulty solving problems because the problems seem amorphous or vague, or because they feel overwhelmed. Problem-solving training helps to get around both of these barriers to the effective resolution of a problem. This strategy has been used to effectively treat a number of psychological problems, including depression, for example. Typically, this type of intervention involves several steps, designed to be completed in sequence:

- ❖ *Assessing, defining, and understanding the problem.* If more than one problem is present, the individual is encouraged to focus on one problem at a time (typically, the issue that is most problematic).
- ❖ *Generating solutions.* This step involves brainstorming a list of as many possible solutions to the problem as possible. At this stage, the client

is encouraged to list all possible solutions, even ones that are impractical or unlikely to be effective. Possible solutions should not be screened or filtered at this stage. Considering solutions that may not be ideal may lead the client to think of another, more useful, solution that he or she might not have thought of otherwise.

❖ *Evaluating the solutions.* This step involves considering the costs and benefits of each solution that was identified in the previous step.

❖ *Choosing the best solution or solutions.* Once the costs and benefits of each solution have been identified, the next step is to select one or more solutions that are most likely to lead to a resolution of the problem.

❖ *Implementing the solution.* The final step in problem solving is to implement the solution that was selected in the previous step. Along the way, barriers to implementation may be encountered, in which case the client is encouraged to use the problem-solving steps to overcome the barriers that arise.

SAMPLE CBT PROTOCOLS

CBT has been found to be an effective treatment for a wide range of problems, including anxiety disorders, mood disorders, psychotic disorders, somatoform disorders, couples' distress, eating disorders, substance use disorders, behavioral problems in children, and certain personality disorders (e.g., borderline personality disorder). For some of these problems (e.g., anxiety disorders), CBT leads to equivalent or superior outcomes when compared with other treatments, such as medication. For other problems (e.g., psychotic disorders, bipolar disorder), CBT is generally thought to be useful only in combination with medication.

To illustrate how CBT is used, a sample session-by-session protocol for treating social anxiety disorder is presented below.

CASE ILLUSTRATION: CBT FOR DEPRESSION

"Cindy" was a 32-year-old high school teacher who had recently begun a leave of absence from her job as a result of feeling overwhelmed and unable to cope with the stress at work. She was married and had two young children. During her assessment, Cindy reported a number of symptoms consistent with a diagnosis of major depressive disorder, including

depressed mood, lack of interest in activities that she normally enjoyed, mild weight loss, insomnia, extreme fatigue, poor concentration, feelings of worthlessness, and passive suicidal thoughts (e.g., feeling that life was no longer worth living). Her depression had begun about a month before, around a particularly stressful period. At the time, work was very busy (numerous exams and term papers to grade), and her oldest child was doing poorly at school. She reported that her husband was not particularly supportive of her when she felt overwhelmed with the stresses in her life. Although this was her first major depressive episode, Cindy had struggled with low self-esteem and occasional depressed mood throughout her life. Her natural tendency when feeling down was to withdraw from her friends and family, to stay in bed, and to avoid dealing with her responsibilities (e.g., paying the bills).

Standard questionnaire measures of depression suggested that her depressed mood was in the moderate range. Cindy reported a number of negative beliefs that were particularly strong when she felt depressed. She reported believing that she was an ineffective teacher and that she was letting down her students and the other staff at school. She also felt that she was a bad parent and spouse and that her family would be better off without her. She believed that others saw her as incompetent, unattractive, boring, and "a drag" to be around. As a result of her depression, Cindy avoided all social contact. She didn't return her friends' phone calls, she avoided going out in public, and she even avoided answering the telephone.

Cindy's treatment began with generating a cognitive-behavioral formulation of her difficulties. Several problem areas were identified, including her depressed mood, social withdrawal (during periods of depression), depressive thinking, tendency to feel overwhelmed by stress, and difficulty being assertive. Treatment included strategies for dealing with each of these problems. After presenting the treatment rationale, several sessions were spent helping Cindy to be more aware of her depressive thoughts and assumptions and to begin to challenge these thoughts using cognitive diaries. Although she was aware that her thinking was biased, it was initially difficult for her to shift her thinking, even after considering the evidence. However, with practice, the cognitive restructuring strategies became easier to use.

In addition, Cindy was encouraged to begin increasing her amount of activity, a process that is often referred to as *behavioral activation.* Despite a complete lack of motivation and energy, Cindy began

Table 2   Cognitive Behavior Therapy for Social Anxiety Disorder

Session No.	Content of Session
1	Assessment of fear triggers, anxious thoughts, avoidance behaviors (including subtle avoidance strategies), typical physical responses to fevgared situations, and other important features. Development of an exposure hierarchy.
2	Presentation of the treatment rational, including psychoeducation regarding the nature of fear and anxiety, a cognitive-behavioral model of social anxiety, and a description of the treatment strategies. Homework: self-help readings on the nature and treatment of social anxiety; monitoring anxiety responses (e.g., anxious thoughts, avoidance behaviors, physical reactions).
3	Review of previous week's homework. Introduction to cognitive therapy—focus on identifying cognitive distortions and biases in thinking. New homework: Monitor anxious thoughts over the coming week.
4	Review of previous week's homework. Cognitive therapy–strategies for changing anxious thoughts. New homework: Practice challenging anxious thoughts over the coming week.
5	Review of previous week's homework. Continue working on challenging anxious thinking. Introduction to exposure-based strategies. New homework: Practice challenging anxious thoughts over the coming week; begin exposure practices between treatment sessions.
6-9	Review of previous week's homework. Continue working on challenging anxious thinking. Practice therapist-assisted exposure and/or simulated exposure role plays using items from exposure hierarchy or other situations. New homework: Over the coming week, (1) practice challenging anxious thoughts and (2) practice exposure.
10	Review of previous week's homework. Continue working on challenging anxious thinking. Introduction to social skills training (e.g., improving eye contact). New homework: Over the coming week, (1) practice challenging anxious thoughts, (2) practice exposure, and (3) practice changing problem social behaviors (as relevant).
11	Review of previous week's homework. Continue use of cognitive therapy, exposure, and social skills training, as necessary. New homework: Over the coming week, (1) practice challenging anxious thoughts, (2) practice exposure, and (3) practice changing problem social behaviors (as relevant).
12	Review of previous week's homework. Continue use of cognitive therapy, exposure, and social skills training, as necessary. Discuss strategies for maintaining gains after the end of treatment. New homework: Continue to use cognitive therapy, exposure, and social skills training as anxiety-provoking situations arise.

to force herself to get out of bed, increase her social contact, and leave the house to shop and to take care of her banking. Within several weeks, these situations became less overwhelming.

Several sessions were also spent teaching Cindy problem-solving strategies for dealing with stress at work and techniques for being more assertive (e.g., being able to ask her husband for emotional support when she felt down). About 4 weeks after treatment began, Cindy's mood had improved somewhat, and she was about to return to work. By the end of treatment (15 sessions), Cindy's mood was much improved. She reported feeling more engaged in her

work and in her relationships. She also reported that her relationship with her husband had improved since she started to express her needs more assertively. Although it is difficult to know for sure whether her improvement was related to her treatment (depression often improves, even without treatment), Cindy was confident that the skills she had learned would be helpful for preventing her depression from returning.

—*Martin M. Antony*

See also: *Beck, Aaron T. (Vol. I); Cognitive Behavior Therapy: Child Clinical Applications (Vol. II); Coping With Depression (Vol. I)*

Suggested Readings

Antony, M. M., & Barlow, D. H. (Eds.). (2002). *Handbook of assessment and treatment planning for psychological disorders.* New York: Guilford Press.

Antony, M. M., & Swinson, R. P. (2000). *Phobic disorders and panic in adults: A guide to assessment and treatment.* Washington, DC: American Psychological Association.

Barlow, D. H. (Ed.). (2001). *Clinical handbook of psychological disorders* (3rd ed.). New York: Guilford Press.

Beck, A. T., Rush, A. J., Shaw, B. F., & Emery, G. (1979). *Cognitive therapy of depression.* New York: Guilford Press.

Beck, J. S. (1995). *Cognitive therapy: Basics and beyond.* New York: Guilford Press.

Burns, D. D. (1999). *The feeling good handbook* (Rev. ed.). New York: Plume.

Clark, D. A., & Beck, A. T. (with Alford, B. A.). (1999). *Scientific foundations of cognitive theory and therapy of depression.* New York: Wiley.

Clark, D. M., & Fairburn, C. G. (Eds.). (1997). *Science and practice of cognitive behaviour therapy.* New York: Oxford University Press.

Greenberger, D., & Padesky, C. A. (1995). *Mind over mood: Change how you feel by changing the way you think.* New York: Guilford Press.

Heimberg, R. G., & Becker, R. E. (2002). *Cognitive-behavioral group therapy for social phobia.* New York: Guilford Press.

Nathan, P. E., & Gorman, J. M. (Eds.). (2002). *A guide to treatments that work* (2nd ed.). New York: Oxford University Press.

Persons, J. B., Davidson, J., & Tompkins, M. A. (2001). *Essential components of cognitive-behavioral therapy for depression.* Washington, DC: American Psychological Association.

Segal, Z. V., Williams, J. M. G., & Teasdale, J. D. (2002). *Mindfulness-based cognitive therapy for depression: A new approach to preventing relapse.* New York: Guilford Press.

Taylor, S. (2000). *Understanding and treating panic disorder: Cognitive and behavioral approaches.* New York: Wiley.

Wells, A. (1997). *Cognitive therapy of anxiety disorders: A practice manual and conceptual guide.* New York: Wiley.

COGNITIVE BEHAVIOR THERAPY WITH RELIGIOUS BELIEFS AND PRACTICES

DESCRIPTION OF THE STRATEGY

In 1956, psychologist Albert Ellis gave up practicing psychoanalysis and psychoanalytically oriented psychotherapy and began what he first called "rational therapy" and what is now called "rational-emotive behavior therapy." However, Ellis continued at least one Freudian tradition. He took a dim view on religion. Nevertheless, within 15 years, papers appeared showing the compatibility between what was by then known as rational-emotive therapy and Christian beliefs and practices.

Even as an adolescent, Ellis had been attracted to philosophy. When he established his new treatment, he incorporated philosophic points of view from around the world. The treatment approach was philosophic because it began by asking, "What is the good life, and what is the means of obtaining it?" His answer was a life based on long-term hedonism, with a particular tip of his cap to the Stoic philosophers, especially Epictetus and his dictum, "Men are not disturbed by events but by the view they take of them," a view that is hardly unique to the Greco-Roman philosophers.

This insight is the basic kernel of all cognitive behavior treatments. Namely, it is the way one construes, cognizes, or "thinks about" a situation that is the crucial factor in determining one's emotional and behavioral response to that event. This remains true whether the event takes place inside or outside an individual's skin and whether the event is also a thought, feeling, or action.

Cognitive therapy, developed by the psychiatrist Aaron Beck, follows this same basic A-B-C method of analysis: There is some *activating event* about which an individual has *beliefs* that lead to emotional and behavioral *consequences* with regard to the original activating event. Beck also had chaffed at the indirectness of psychoanalytic methods. He saw direct examination of what individuals thought and said as the key to understanding and remediating dysfunctional emotions and behavior. He first concentrated his efforts on depression. Unlike Ellis, his approach did not outline any broad philosophic context into which his therapy was to be placed. Rather, it was tacitly understood that no one wanted to be depressed and that which could alleviate depression, especially without the side effects and other problems associated with medications, was a good thing.

By the late 1970s, the "cognitive revolution" was in full swing. Many practitioners who had previously viewed themselves as more strictly behavioral began to take more seriously the idea that "private speech" was just one more type of behavior, as had been maintained by some behaviorists since the time of John

Watson. The old requirements of methodological behaviorism, which held that events about which only one person could make reports, such as thoughts and images, were not eligible for psychological analysis, were largely abandoned. Under that doctrine, what someone said about their thoughts, images, or bodily sensations was admissible to scientific investigation but not the thoughts, images, and sensations themselves. Whatever "cognition" was, it was no longer regarded as existing in the spaceless, weightless, timeless mind-stuff suggested by Rene Descartes. It was more and more regarded as just more empirical or theoretical material of the same ontological type as overt behavior.

Including Religious Values

By the 1980s, the old notion that counseling and psychotherapy could be "value free," a notion that had been most eloquently expounded by Carl Rogers, was also under serious attack. Allen Bergin, among others, pointed out that clients often took on the values of practitioners. Furthermore, as compared with the general U.S. population, a far greater portion of psychologists were, and are, nonreligious. Bergin offered a proposal regarding the desirability of linking psychotherapy and religious values. Ellis responded with an article connecting psychotherapy and atheistic values. The stage was set for the conflict to be addressed empirically.

Bergin soon showed that religious beliefs and practices not only failed to do harm, but there was evidence of their making a positive contribution on a number of health indices. Two knotty problems were left flapping in the wind. First, how could God, or any form of "the supernatural," be subjected to empirical test since, by definition, the supernatural is other than empirical? Second, any attempt to subordinate the supernatural to the empirical, of necessity, does violence to the full majesty of the supernatural. While there have been a number of cautions and apologetics offered on these issues, the problems have not stopped a full bore effort to empirically demonstrate that including religious beliefs and practices in psychological treatment is desirable and beneficial, just as life in all its aspects is made better when it is founded on religious beliefs and practices. Those making this effort have most often been practitioners and researchers who were themselves deeply committed to religious beliefs and practices.

Empirical Therapeutic Tests

Following Beck and his colleagues, Rebecca Propst and colleagues combined the principles of cognitive therapy with Christian beliefs and practices to reduce depression. She showed this could be successfully done. One of her most important findings was that nonbelieving therapists were just as effective in using the combined approaches to reduce depression in Christian clients as were believing therapists. To date, there is no evidence indicating that nonbelievers are less capable of, or effective in, delivering a religiously oriented cognitive-behavioral treatment.

Brad Johnson and various colleagues were able to show that the principles of rational-emotive behavior therapy could also be combined with Christian beliefs and practices to remediate psychological disturbances. To date, there has been no evidence that religiously oriented cognitive behavior therapies (CBT) are more effective than nonreligiously based ones, and virtually all the empirical work has been done using Christian doctrines and practices with Christian clients.

However, it is also certain that some individuals will be more willing to participate in treatment that is consistent with, and related to, their religious beliefs and will do so with greater zeal.

The 1990s saw a number of books published on the inclusion of religious beliefs and practices with psychological interventions, with several published by the American Psychological Association. Ellis publicly acknowledged that religious beliefs and practices were not necessarily a source of disturbance and became the third author on *Counseling and Psychotherapy With Religious Persons*. Those asserting the positive value of religious beliefs and practices and the positive value of including them in psychological treatments were clearly in ascendancy.

Religious Beliefs and Practices Combined With CBT

Because most religious traditions have an articulated set of beliefs and because cognitive-behavioral approaches are based on the notion that reduction in emotional and behavioral dysfunction can be accomplished if clients relinquish certain beliefs and adopt others, it is a relatively straightforward process to identify religious beliefs and practices that are consistent with, or otherwise support, a change from disturbance-associated beliefs to those associated with more functional emoting and behaving. Scriptures can even be used to orient clients to the therapeutic approach. For those with a Christian orientation, Old Testament scriptures such as, "For as he thinketh in his heart so is he," and "I thought on my ways and turned my feet," and New Testament scriptures such as, "Be transformed by the renewing of your mind," or "For I have learned to find resources in myself whatever my circumstances," all provide religious grounding for the basic cognitive-behavioral principle that dysfunctional emotions and behaviors can be changed by focusing on changing beliefs about ourselves and the world in which we live. In practice, it takes very little effort to bring religiously oriented clients to acknowledging that they can be helped by sticking firmly with certain beliefs.

Once oriented, the questions become: (a) Which beliefs are to be retained, (b) Which are to be discarded, and (c) Which alternative beliefs are to be adopted? At this point, certain controversies will appear in the area of means and ends. For example, with an individual whose religious tradition prescribes both monogamy and sexual relations only between married individuals, a goal of avoiding sorrow, guilt, or depression while having sexual relations out of wedlock will be seen as inappropriate and even immoral. Sorrow, guilt, or depression may be seen as the natural outcomes of such behavior and motivators for returning to the way of life prescribed by the religious tradition and avoiding proscribed ways of living.

In principle, a practitioner could point out to clients that they can change their religious beliefs and adopt the view that there is nothing necessarily wrong with nonmonogamous sexual relations or sex relations outside of marriage. However, most authors have argued that even to offer the possibility of changing religious beliefs to clients is unethical because it is beyond the scope of psychological practice to suggest to clients that they might change their religious beliefs. Once the client and practitioner agree, either tacitly or explicitly, that the client intends to stick with the way of living prescribed by his or her religious tradition, the issue of what to do about the sorrow, guilt, and depression will be addressed.

Typically, the practitioner will take the view that sorrow is appropriate when one acts wrongly but that depression is not. The standard cognitive-behavioral intervention will begin, and it will be buttressed by religious doctrine or scripture. For example, if the client is self-condemning for his or her wrong behavior and is a Christian, the practitioner might point out that it is Christian doctrine that individuals are saved by the grace of God rather than through good behavior, and might note New Testament verses such as, "Judge not, that ye be not judged," "For all have sinned and come short of the glory of God," or "God commended his love for us in that while we were sinners, Christ died for us." The practitioner might not only recommend standard cognitive-behavioral homework assignments but also take advantage of religious practices such as prayer or meditation as a means of enhancing them. Thus, clients might be asked whether they believed it appropriate to pray for forgiveness of their misdeeds and for courage and determination to resist doing them in the future. If they answer affirmatively, these activities could be offered as additional homework. When practitioners and clients share the same religious beliefs and religious practices, for example, prayer, then prayer might even be performed in the treatment session.

A similar approach can be taken with anxiety disorders such as panic. There is general agreement that panic is a function of responding to bodily sensations as if they were not only unpleasant and undesired but also catastrophic and unbearable. The standard approach in panic is for clients to engage in activities that either produce bodily sensations similar to those experienced during panic or to have actual panic sensations. This approach is exactly opposite of the activities followed by most panic suffers, who systematically make sustained efforts not to experience these kinds of sensations. Engagement, rather than avoidance, is the first step in treatment.

Once psychologically engaged, the client can notice that such sensations may indeed be quite unpleasant—but that is all they are. In fact, the sensations are not horrible, awful, or terrible, and nothing catastrophic actually happens either during or following the experience of these sensations. Scriptural passages can be identified that underline these points, and depending on their belief system, many believers can be reminded they are never alone in their trial because their deity is with them in their suffering. As before, prayer, meditation or other religiously prescribed practices can be used to assist clients in exposing themselves to unpleasant bodily sensations long enough to experience that if the sensations are not responded to as if they are unbearable and awful but only as unpleasant, the sensations will simply wax and wane. While clients may not come to like or look forward to such sensations, they will also find they no longer fear them, either.

The main problem for the practitioners is to find doctrinal authority, be it scriptural or otherwise, as well as religious practices that support the cognitive-behavioral procedures that have otherwise been shown to be helpful with whatever problem is to be addressed, while, at the same time, finding ways to avoid or neutralize the same type of material that would contribute to or exacerbate the problem. Many have argued that no religious tradition, when properly understood, will be iatrogenic. The rub may come in the "proper understanding." Many authors recommend consultation with clergy or other authoritative sources and insist it is unethical for practitioners to cross the boundary between psychological service for which they are trained and religious guidance and interpretation for which they may not be trained. The psychological practitioner may make use of the religious beliefs and practice the client brings to the session but may not alter or abolish them.

Examples of difficulties are clients who have broken a prescribed standard, such as having had sex outside marriage, an abortion, or being sexually active with members of the same sex, and think themselves utterly worthless and unredeemable. All goes well when religious doctrines and practices can be found that refute the belief that they are utterly worthless and unredeemable, but not so well when religious authorities are cited to show that they are. It is important to note that the problem is not whether these activities are wrong, bad, or mistaken. The religious stance on these matters is assumed to be correct because that is the client's view. Rather, the therapist's problem, to use religious language, is to help the client condemn the sin but not himself or herself as the sinner. To date, the field has not developed criteria that would both discriminate and authorize practitioners to attack religions doctrines and practices that encourage the condemnation of self or others, as well as other disturbance-associated "cognitive errors" when they are asserted to have a religious base. The only agreed-upon practice is consultation with religious authorities with the aim of obtaining authoritative refutation of the client's view that their "cognitive errors" are supported by their religious traditions and practices.

—*Hank Robb*

See also: Behavioral Treatment of Minorities (Vol. I); Cognitive Behavior Therapy (Vol. I); Cognitive Restructuring (Vol. I)

Suggested Readings

Bergin, A. E. (1991). Values and religious issues in psychotherapy and mental health. *American Psychologist, 46,* 394–403.

Johnson, W. B., Ridley, C. R., & Nielsen, S. L. (2000). Religiously sensitive rational emotive behavior therapy: Elegant solutions and ethical risks. *Professional Psychology: Research and Practice, 31*(1), 14–20.

Miller, W. R. (Ed.). (1999). *Integrating spirituality into treatment: Resources for practitioners.* Washington, DC: American Psychological Association.

Nielsen, S. L. (2001). Accommodating religion and integrating religious material during rational emotive behavior therapy. *Cognitive and Behavioral Practice, 8*(1), 34–39.

Nielsen, S. L., Johnson, W. B., & Ellis, A. (2001). *Counseling and psychotherapy with religious persons: A rational-emotive behavioral therapy approach.* Mahwah, NJ: Erlbaum.

Nielsen, S. L., Johnson, W. B., & Ridley, C. R. (2000). Religiously sensitive rational emotive behavior therapy: Theory, techniques, and brief excerpts from a case. *Professional Psychology: Research and Practice, 31*(1), 21–28.

Pargament, K. I. (1997). *The psychology of religion and coping: Theory, research, practice.* New York: Guilford Press.

Propst, R., Ostrom, R., Watkins, P., Dean, T., & Mashburn, D. (1992). Comparative efficacy of religious and nonreligious cognitive-behavioral therapy for the treatment of clinical depression in religious individuals. *Journal of Consulting and Clinical Psychology, 60*(1), 94–103.

Robb, H. (2001). Facilitating rational emotive behavior therapy by including religious beliefs. *Cognitive and Behavioral Practice, 8,* 29–34.

Robb, H. B. III. (2002). Rational emotive behavior therapy and religious clients. *Journal of Rational-Emotive & Cognitive-Behavior Therapy, 20*(3/4), 169–200.

COGNITIVE-BEHAVIORAL APPROACH TO BIPOLAR DISORDER

DESCRIPTION OF THE STRATEGY

Cognitive-behavioral therapy (CBT) has evolved over the past 40 years as an alternative to more traditional nondirective and insight-oriented modes of psychotherapy. The family of cognitive and behavioral therapies includes a diverse group of interventions. Although initially conceived as a therapy for unipolar depression, in the past 20 years, CBT has also been applied to the treatment of bipolar disorder as well.

Environmental Event → Cognitive Appraisal → Emotional reaction (depression or mania) → Behavior

Figure 1   The Classic (linear-processing) Model of CBT

Basic CBT principles that are applied to the treatment of unipolar depression can be modified and adapted to the treatment of bipolar disorder. In general, first and foremost, CBT emphasizes a psychoeducational orientation, by which patients learn about the nature of their illness, resulting problems, and the rationale for use of particular treatment strategies. Second, CBT typically employs homework and self-help assignments to provide patients the opportunity to practice therapeutic methods to enhance generalization of positive therapy effects outside of the therapy hour. Third, objective assessment of psychiatric illness is considered an integral part of treatment, and selection of therapeutic strategies derives logically from such assessments. Fourth, therapeutic methods used are generally structured, are directive, and require a high level of therapist activity. Fifth, CBT interventions are built on empirical evidence that validates the theoretical orientation and guides the choice of therapeutic techniques. Specifically, learning theories (i.e., classical, operant, and observational models of learning) and the principles of cognitive psychology are relied on heavily in constructing cognitive-behavioral treatments. Although classic CBT for unipolar depression is most often a time-limited intervention, CBT for bipolar disorder is also useful as a maintenance psychotherapy.

THE COGNITIVE-BEHAVIORAL MODEL

The basic theories of the cognitive model are rooted in a long tradition of viewing cognitions as primary determinants of emotion and behavior. Cognitive therapy (CT) concepts have been traced back as far as the writings of the Greek Stoic philosophers and have been linked to a number of other influences, including the phenomenological school of philosophy, Albert Ellis's rational-emotive therapy, and the contributions of Adler and other neo-Freudians. However, the greatest impetus for the development of cognitively oriented therapy has been the work of Aaron T. Beck. Figure 1 displays the classic CT (linear-processing) model for understanding the relationships between environmental events, cognition, emotion, and behavior. This model is based on the theoretical assumption that environmental stimuli trigger cognitive processes and the ensuing cognitions give the event personal meaning and elicit subsequent physiological and affective arousal. These emotions, in turn, have a potent reciprocal effect on cognitive content and information processing, such that cascades of dysfunctional thoughts and emotions can occur. The individual's behavioral responses to stimuli and thoughts are viewed as both a product and a cause of maladaptive cognitions. Thus, treatment interventions may be targeted at any or all components of the model.

More recently, Beck and others have expanded the model in recognition of other factors that may be involved in the etiology of mood disorders, especially for patients with bipolar disorder, such as genetic predisposition, state-dependent neurobiological changes, and various interpersonal variables. This more complex model, the "integrative" model of CBT (see Figure 2), more accurately describes the phenomenological course for bipolar disorder. In this model, it is hypothesized that the mood state (depressed, manic, mixed, or hypomanic) leads to changes in thinking and feelings. This leads to changes in behavior that then can lead to impaired psychosocial functioning. There is an increase and worsening of psychosocial problems that lead to emotional duress and the biological changes of sleep loss and the other symptoms of the disorder. Now, the positive-feedback loop is complete, as the worsening biological disturbance results in a worsening of the mood state. These influences must be included in the case conceptualization for CBT treatment of patients with bipolar disorder. It must be emphasized that such an expanded cognitive-biological model, which synthesizes cognitive and neurobiological factors in a combined therapy approach, rests upon a foundation of satisfactory maintenance pharmacotherapy. This point highlights the CBT multimodal approach of addressing each of these "nodes" in the web sequentially or simultaneously. Many current researchers are attempting to understand how best to combine and/or sequence CBT and pharmacotherapy. New developments and modifications of CBT technique will be based upon information from contemporary research in basic and cognitive neuroscience as our understanding of the disorder increases.

Depression or Mania →

← Emotional Duress,   Changes in Thinking and Feeling →
  Sleep Loss, other symptoms
← Psychosocial Problems   Changes in Behavior →
← Impaired Psychosocial Functioning

Figure 2   The Integrative Model of CBT

(Basco & Rush, 1996)

CBT TREATMENT OF PATIENTS WITH BIPOLAR DISORDER

There are several goals of CBT treatment for patients with bipolar disorder. The first is to help the patient accept and understand the disorder and the need for treatment. Second is to help the patient manage life events. Third is to help the patient improve medication adherence and compliance. The fourth goal is to teach better coping strategies for important stressors. And, finally, the fifth goal is to teach the patient skills to prevent relapses of the disorder. The psychoeducational nature of CBT promotes self-monitoring and self-regulation, which are especially crucial to the treatment of this chronic and cycling disorder. Such a treatment strategy also works synergistically to increase medication adherence and compliance, and thus, overall, to help prevent relapse and the social, occupational, and functional impairments associated with being ill.

CBT for bipolar disorders develops out of the integrative model (in Figure 2). Inherent to this model based upon learning is the belief that change is possible. Such change is possible in the realm of the patient's pharmacotherapy and/or psychotherapy—but this depends upon the patient and therapist recognizing the illness state and pattern. The patient is educated about the biological and psychological aspects of depression, mania, hypomania, mixed states, substance abuse, anxiety, and other related disorders. We come to identify the role mood plays in distorting our thinking in either a negative (typical of depression) or a positive (typical of hypomania or mania) bias. This demands a scrupulous monitoring of the symptoms of depression or mania and teaching patients to do so, enabling them to identify and follow the trajectory of this cycling illness—so that adjustments to the treatment plan can be made and new interventions taken. After dysfunctional thoughts are identified and modified, we examine the role of dysfunctional beliefs. Over time, these dysfunctional beliefs are examined for their utility and cost to the patient, possible benefits (and therefore reinforcing elements), and the benefits and difficulties in changing such beliefs. Usually, these discussions lead to an analysis of the rules patients use to formulate their beliefs. We can then examine the origin of the rules patients use and, subsequently, whether they should be modified or amended. This often results in restructuring of their absolute and conditional rules and the institution of new behaviors. These changes in behavior can effect positive changes in psychosocial function, with a reduction of psychosocial problems. The ability to more effectively cope reduces stress and its negative biological effects, making patients more resilient to relapses and recurrences of mood episodes.

CBT with patients with bipolar disorder is generally divided into four phases. The first phase is concerned with socialization of the patient into the CBT model and development of individualized case formulation and treatment goals; this includes education of the patient about medications, symptoms, and their illness patterns. These discussions can be held with the patient and family members, and it is encouraged for all to ask questions and obtain information. This phase generally takes 4 to 6 sessions. In addition, the initial phase of CBT focuses on behavioral treatments to counter predominant symptoms of the illness. At the beginning of CBT, it is important to employ behavioral techniques that reinforce the value of regular sleep, exercise, and a structured daily routine, factors that are typically disturbed in mood illnesses. In CBT with depression, the concern is with behavioral activation strategies to counter symptoms of fatigue, lethargy, poor concentration, and cognitive slowing. This is accomplished through the following techniques: monitoring of daily activities using diaries or mood logs; assessment of mastery and pleasure attained in the process of attending to routine tasks; use of graded task assignments to gradually expand the repertoire of behaviors patients use in their daily tasks, which they apply to problem solving; use of rehearsal to challenge those obstacles to completing tasks that patients employ; and the targeting of specific problems that are amenable to behavioral treatment, such as management of the sleep-wake cycle, nutritional intake, exercise, and so on. Similarly, these same techniques can be applied to bipolar manic, hypomanic, and mixed states to ameliorate negative effects of the disorder upon daily activity and to minimize psychosocial problems and degree of stress the patient experiences.

The second phase of treatment is the skills training phase (Sessions 7–13). The patient continues to learn general coping strategies that foster self-regulation, with a special focus on stabilizing circadian rhythms, as represented by their sleep-activity cycle. Patients are taught more in-depth techniques for self-monitoring of moods, thoughts, behaviors, and how these fluctuate with changes in mood symptoms and/or with stressful events. They are taught to logically analyze dysfunctional thoughts and beliefs and to understand the cognitive and behavioral changes that occur in depression and mania. This is accomplished through exploration of fears, attitudes, and thoughts and by discussions of the advantages and disadvantages of their compensatory behaviors. We work to increase factors that decrease risk and decrease factors that increase risk of relapse: for example, medication and healthy-lifestyle noncompliance, avoidance of substance abuse, and longer-term plans for the management of chronic interpersonal conflict. The third phase (Sessions 14–20) of treatment addresses the patient's defined psychosocial problems. These problems are identified and analyzed. Problem-solving skills that have been learned are applied to the patient's current problems, and adjustments in the patient's attitudes, beliefs, and behaviors are implemented. The fourth phase is the maintenance phase, which continues from monthly to quarterly and focuses on relapse prevention. Stressful events and their personal meanings are examined. A relapse "signature," the characteristic two or three symptoms that are warning signs of relapse, are identified, such as elated mood or irritability, and sleep, energy, or concentration disturbances. In advance of a relapse, the action plans for intervention are reviewed with the patient and family, including plans for contacting the treatment team and crisis management plans for the patients' safety when they do become acutely ill.

RESEARCH BASIS

Over the past 20 years, there have been many anecdotal and case study reports on the treatment of patients with bipolar disorder using CBT. However, there are only three randomized, controlled trials of CBT in patients with bipolar disorder in the literature. In 1984, Cochran and colleagues studied whether CBT improved lithium compliance at 6 and 12 months after treatment compared with a control group. Results indicated no difference in lithium compliance on the self-reports, informant reports, or serum lithium levels, but the physician (who was not blind to which group the patient belonged) reported more compliance. There was a reduction in hospital admissions.

Scott, Garland, and Moorhead have reported results of their pilot study of cognitive therapy in patients with bipolar I ($n = 34$) and bipolar II ($n = 8$) disorders. Half the patients were assigned to immediate CBT or 6-month wait-list control, which was then followed by a course of CBT. At 6-month follow-up, subjects who had CBT showed statistically significantly greater improvement in symptoms and functioning than those in the wait-list control group. In the 29 patients who eventually received CBT, relapse rates in the 18 months after commencing CBT showed a 60% reduction in comparison with the 18 months prior to commencing CBT. Seventy percent of subjects who commenced CBT found it to be a highly acceptable form of treatment. Immediately after receiving CBT, changes in symptoms and functioning were significant, but these changes were not maintained at 6 months after CBT was finished. Interestingly, in the CBT group, reductions in depressive symptoms were more robust than reductions in manic symptoms.

Lam and colleagues examined whether CBT is beneficial in preventing relapse in patients with bipolar disorders who are taking mood-stabilizer medications. They modified classic CBT by (a) utilizing a psychoeducational component that modeled bipolar illness as a stress-diathesis illness, (b) adapting CBT skills to help patients identify the onset of symptoms of bipolar disorder characteristic of their illness patterns, (c) promoting the importance of circadian regularity by emphasizing the importance of routine and sleep, and (d) dealing with the long-term vulnerabilities and difficulties of the illness. Therapy consisted of 12 to 20 sessions and lasted 6 months, and outcomes were measured at 6- and 12-month points. At the end of 1 year, the CBT group had significantly fewer bipolar episodes and fewer days in episode, fewer hospitalizations, and higher social functioning. These patients also showed less mood symptoms on their monthly mood questionnaires and experienced significantly less fluctuation in manic symptoms in the CBT group.

These studies are limited and preliminary, but they are promising. Paucity of clinical studies of bipolar disorder reflects the difficulty in studying this population. Noncompliance with research protocols is exacerbated in this disorder due to its fluctuating between mood states and its relapsing course. These studies were conducted in the context of medication treatment, and this must be sufficiently controlled—a difficult task if the patient is cycling during the study, requiring medication adjustments. Research in this area is hampered by continued discussion in the field as to accuracy of diagnosis, and the heterogeneity of the disorder only confounds this further. There are also basic questions about effectiveness of CBT: What is the optimum way to deliver CBT in this population, and what is the proper intensity, frequency, and duration of CBT treatment for these patients? We need to define the predictors of illness, relapse, and treatment failure. We need to research the effects of CBT treatment on individual psychosocial function and the larger health care utilization costs associated with treating this disorder.

CASE ILLUSTRATION

"Mrs. D" was 32 years old, married, and childless. She grew up in an upper-middle-class family that valued academic and artistic achievement. She had two siblings; one suffered from schizophrenia, but otherwise her family history was unremarkable. She attained a college degree and an advanced degree in architecture. In the past, she had experienced several depressive episodes that responded to psychotherapy, and only brief periods of mild manic symptoms. Prior to her most recent manic episode, she described brief periods of heightened moods and sharpened intuition. She functioned, on the whole, very well and never had been significantly impaired by her illness. She was successful in her career, and she was working at a large architectural firm when, in the past year, she began to experience an increased number of symptoms of mania. These included an increased intuitive sense now bordering on delusional thinking, pressured speech, and ideas of reference (thoughts that others recognized her genius, that conversations were about her), increased energy, elated and grandiose mood, and a significant decreased need for sleep. She

dressed more seductively and appeared unusual to her coworkers, who noted that she was overly intrusive, loud, and hyperactive. Pharmacologic treatment was adjusted, with addition of a mood stabilizer and an atypical antipsychotic medication. She was required to take a leave of absence from work, which upset her usual routine and her biorhythms. Not having to get up in the morning, she would stay up late and night and sleep until early afternoon. She began to slip into a depression characterized by lethargy, lack of motivation, increased appetite and weight, and a sense of helpless, hopelessness, and worthlessness. At her low points, she ruminated about the loss of her job, the loss of her friends, and conflicts with her husband.

She then began a course of CBT. We began with a focus on her behavioral inactivation, teaching her techniques to counteract her lethargy-reinforcing behaviors and replace them with activities. Using a weekly activity schedule, we reviewed her lifestyle and made adjustments to her schedule to take into account the symptoms of her mood state. We scheduled periods of quiet time in which she practiced relaxation techniques and relaxing activities as well as peak times for exercise and directed activities. We reviewed strategies that help her to stabilize her moods—avoidance of too much social stimulation and alcohol or other illegal or stimulating substances. We began to schedule the things she needed to accomplish and create a regular routine, slowly adding more complicated tasks and projects in anticipation of her return to work, closely monitoring her ability to attend to these tasks and stay on focus. We examined her thoughts about her self-esteem: what it meant to her to have experienced manic and depressive episodes; what were the consequences of her illness on her relationships with her husband, friends, and coworkers; and what this would mean about her future. We examined her dysfunctional thoughts and beliefs about these issues and their effects on her behaviors. It was necessary to examine her intense sense of guilt and the belief that she was defective as a result of being diagnosed as having bipolar disorder. We came to see that she had long experienced mild mood states that were unrecognized and ignored, but now these were seen as part and parcel of a larger problem, one that can be managed with medication and psychotherapy.

—*Edward S. Friedman and Michael E. Thase*

See also: *Cognitive Behavior Therapy (Vol. I); Cognitive Restructuring (Vol. I); Coping With Depression (Vol. I)*

Suggested Readings

Basco, M. R., & Rush, A. J. (1966). *Cognitive-behavioral therapy for bipolar disorder.* New York: Guilford Press.

Lam, D. H., Jones S. H., Hayward P., & Bright J. A. (Eds.). (1999). *Cognitive therapy for bipolar disorders: A therapist's guide to concepts, methods, and practice.* New York: Wiley.

Patelis-Siotis, I. (2001). Cognitive-behavioral therapy: Applications for the management of bipolar disorder. *Bipolar Disorders, 3,* 1–10.

Scott, J. (2001). Cognitive therapy as an adjunct to medication in bipolar disorder. *British Journal of Psychiatry, 178*(4), s164–s168.

COGNITIVE RESTRUCTURING

DESCRIPTION OF THE STRATEGY

Cognitive restructuring is an approach to therapy based on learning theories that emphasize the role of cognitions, or thoughts. These theories share much in common with more behaviorally based approaches that focus on the role of environmental stimuli and consequences in the learning process. For example, both behavioral and cognitive theories highlight the role of learning in the development of psychological symptoms and disorders. They also both emphasize an empirical approach, relying on research findings to make conclusions about how psychological problems develop and how best to treat them. However, cognitive theories suggest that learning is mediated by thoughts: People learn to behave in certain ways and to experience particular feelings based on what they *think* is happening in the environment or on their *expectations* about consequences that will occur, rather than on cues and outcomes that actually exist. For example, if an individual believes that "stepping on a crack" will cause some untoward outcome, he or she may be anxious about doing so and try hard to step over cracks in the sidewalk, even though no real connection can be made between this type of behavior and a negative consequence.

Thus, cognitive theories suggest that the primary determinants of behaviors and feelings are thoughts. Accordingly, cognitive therapy (or cognitive restructuring) emphasizes the importance of modifying thoughts to change unhealthy behaviors and feelings. Despite a major emphasis on the role of cognitions, however, cognitive theories also acknowledge the reciprocal impact that behaviors and feelings can have on thoughts. As a result, most variations of cognitive therapy incorporate some attention to direct behavioral change.

Specific versions of cognitive therapy have been developed to address a variety of psychological problems (e.g., depression, anxiety, eating disorders, substance abuse), and each of these varies slightly with regard to the types of approaches used and thoughts targeted (e.g., thoughts about body size and shape in eating disorders, thoughts about pending danger in anxiety). However, all cognitive interventions share a common focus on the identification and change of maladaptive thoughts and the process of thinking. In addition, all cognitive therapy is goal oriented, with a focus on helping patients cope with ongoing problems, rather than on understanding historical events in their lives. The cognitive therapist assumes an active and directive role, working collaboratively with patients to identify and practice new coping strategies. Patients typically are asked to complete homework, usually focused first on increasing their awareness of and ability to identify thoughts that lead to psychological difficulties. Practice exercises in later phases of therapy emphasize the use of coping skills aimed at changing problematic thoughts in situations that produce unhealthy feelings or behaviors. It is important to note that cognitive therapy does not just teach patients to "think positively." Instead, patients are asked to identify irrational or unrealistic thoughts associated with negative feelings or unhealthy behaviors (e.g., "I can't do anything right") and to modify these so that they are more realistic (e.g., "I do some things well and other things not as well"). In addition, cognitive therapy does not typically include attention only to changing thoughts; rather, patients often are asked to try out new behaviors while they practice new ways of thinking.

Two early versions of cognitive therapy probably serve as the basis for almost all currently available cognitive interventions. One of these is Aaron Beck's cognitive-behavioral treatment for depression; the other is Albert Ellis's rational-emotive therapy (RET). In Beck's model, patients are provided, first, with a rationale for the treatment. They are then educated and trained, often with the use of self-monitoring homework assignments, to identify thoughts that represent the negative views of the self, world, and future that characterize depressed mood. Another initial step in Beck's cognitive therapy involves behavioral monitoring, wherein patients are asked to create a record of how they spend their time, rating each activity with regard to the degree of pleasure and mastery experienced. This phase of treatment serves at least two purposes: (1) to provide evidence for disputing certain kinds of beliefs later in therapy (e.g., "I never experience pleasure in anything that I do," or "I'm not good at anything") and (2) to increase the patient's general level of activity. These initial steps in treatment (education, increased awareness, and increased activity) alone can produce reductions in depressive symptoms, but the subsequent phases of treatment are considered the "meat" of Beck's therapy. Here, the therapist teaches patients to take an empirical approach to test the validity of their thoughts, first, by treating thoughts as hypotheses rather than facts and, next, by considering alternative hypotheses (i.e., "What might be another way to look at this situation?") and examining the rationality of thoughts (i.e., "Are my thoughts logical?"). Patients are asked to consider the possibility of logical "errors" in the process of thinking. Common errors include *personalization* (referencing oneself for an outcome that was not under one's control), *all-or-none thinking* (thinking something is "all" bad or "all" good, with no in-between), *selective abstraction* (making a general conclusion based on only one detail of a situation), and *overgeneralization* (making a general conclusion based on one single experience). Other problems in thinking include *overattribution* (assuming excessive personal responsibility for an outcome) and *catastrophizing* (predicting that a behavior or outcome will have overly catastrophic consequences). When patients begin to notice thoughts that represent one or more of these illogical patterns of thinking, they are asked to identify alternative thoughts that are more logical.

Practicing new ways of thinking is not easy. Thus, patients are asked to complete daily homework assignments during this phase of treatment to identify alternative thoughts in situations where they experience negative emotions or outcomes. As they practice, substituting new and more adaptive patterns of thinking becomes easier.

RET is another well-known version of cognitive therapy and uses a more persuasive model of treatment, wherein the therapist tries to convince the patient that his or her thoughts are irrational, as opposed to the more Socratic and empirical style that characterize Beck's model. RET also relies on what is called an A-B-C-D-E paradigm, where A = the activating event or situation; B = the patient's belief; C = the consequence of this belief; D = the "disputing" of the belief by the therapist and patient; and E = the effect of this challenge to the belief. A focus in RET is given to certain types of irrational ideas that are believed to be common across a range of psychological problems in our culture. These beliefs focus on those that incorporate the words "must" (e.g., "Everyone *must* love me at all times"; "My house *must* always be perfectly clean and orderly"), "should" (e.g., "Others *should* follow certain rules at all times"; "I *should* always look my best"), or "awful" (e.g., "It is *awful* if something doesn't turn out the way I want it to"; "It is *awful* if I'm not on time for every appointment").

The similarities in these two approaches to cognitive therapy (restructuring) far outweigh the differences. These models and subsequent approaches derived from them share a common focus on the central goal of helping patients change their thoughts (and oftentimes also behaviors) to improve mood and quality of life. In some cases, cognitive therapy focuses on helping people change thoughts about specific situations (e.g., "I am sure that I'll fail this test"; "I did a terrible job when I made that presentation at work yesterday"). At other times, the goal of cognitive change is to modify more global beliefs (e.g., "I am worthless"; "I cannot function without a man in my life") that seem to guide much of an individual's thinking and behaving. Other techniques of cognitive therapy include *thought-stopping,* which involves helping patients turn their attention away from thoughts that are repetitive and nonproductive, and *self-instructional training,* a strategy that assists people in talking themselves through difficult situations with well-rehearsed phrases (e.g., "I can do this, just one step at a time").

RESEARCH BASIS

Scientific data from a large number of well-controlled studies attest to the utility of cognitive therapy for a wide range of psychological disorders, including depression, anxiety disorders, eating disorders, substance abuse, and marital problems. In fact, cognitive therapy is a primary component of empirically supported treatments for panic disorder, generalized anxiety disorder, social anxiety disorder (for both adults and children), depression, bulimia, pain, smoking, and benzodiazepine withdrawal. In studies of these interventions, treatment is typically conducted in 12 to

20 sessions, and outcomes are generally equivalent or superior to those demonstrated with pharmacological treatment. Particular benefits of a cognitive-behavioral approach are often apparent during long-term follow-up, when relapse occurs less frequently following cognitive therapy than after discontinuation of medication. Empirical data do not always show, however, that adding cognitive interventions significantly increases the benefits of a more behavioral approach nor that cognitive behavior therapy is always superior to alternative models of treatment (e.g., interpersonal psychotherapy, supportive therapy).

RELEVANT TARGET POPULATIONS AND EXCEPTIONS

Although Beck's cognitive therapy was developed initially to target depression, interventions based on this model and on more general approaches like RET have been developed to address a wide range of psychological symptoms and disorders, as noted previously. A number of books have also described the general processes and procedures of cognitive therapy without targeting a specific type of problem or disorder. Cognitive therapy has also been used effectively across the life span, with treatments available for children/adolescents, younger and middle-aged adults, and older people.

To make good use of cognitive therapy, however, patients must have sufficient cognitive capacity to understand the rationale of treatment and to attempt some analysis of their own thinking. As such, the principles and techniques of cognitive therapy are not useful for patients with limited intellectual ability (e.g., those with dementia, mental retardation). Patients also must have some level of motivation for engaging in the treatment, as cognitive therapy requires completion of homework outside of treatment sessions. Even if patients are capable and motivated, however, cognitive therapy is not always optimal. In some cases, a more behavioral approach is warranted. For example, research suggests that a type of behavior therapy called *exposure and response prevention* is optimal for treating obsessive-compulsive disorder and the addition of direct attention to changing thoughts adds little, if any, benefit in outcome. In other cases, clinical formulations of a patient's difficulties may suggest that an alternative approach would be more beneficial. For instance, a patient with serious test anxiety who also has significant deficits in study skills or test-taking

ability would likely benefit little from attempts to change thoughts about his or her expected test performance (since performance will remain poor until skills improve). Instead, an initial course of treatment for such a patient might involve a skills-training approach that focuses on helping the patient learn how to study and how to answer test questions. Cognitive change (e.g., improved expectations for performance) would likely result from a skills-training approach, but a second stage of therapy focusing more directly on cognitive change might be warranted once skills are adequate if anxiety remains excessively high.

COMPLICATIONS

There is some evidence that patients with more severe depression respond more positively to treatment with medication than to cognitive therapy alone. Moreover, some patients fail to agree to a course of cognitive therapy or fail to improve following a typical trial of this treatment. In some cases, booster sessions are needed to maintain gains during long-term follow-up. Cognitive therapy also can be time-consuming and expensive, and most of the data supporting efficacy of this approach come from studies that use highly trained expert therapists, who may not well represent the clinicians who more often treat psychological problems in the "real world." However, empirical evidence is beginning to emerge that briefer versions of cognitive therapy for depression and anxiety can be useful even in more typical health care settings (e.g., primary care clinics, where patients more often present for assistance). Future research will need to focus more on the ability to evaluate outcomes of cognitive therapy in real-world practice and the ease with which these approaches can be integrated into ongoing clinical care.

CASE ILLUSTRATION

"Betty" was a 75-year-old, White, widowed woman who responded to an advertisement for a treatment program to target worry. She reported significant worries about a number of topics: her health, finances, her children's well-being, and others' opinions of her. Although Betty's health was relatively good, she worried that she would become incapacitated as a result of arthritis in her joints or that she might develop a serious illness. She also was very concerned that other people might not like her, despite the fact that she maintained a busy social calendar and quite a few close friendships. Betty also worried that her children were not happy in their relationships, that they were all having serious financial problems, and that she herself might run out of money before she died. In reality, Betty's financial situation was secure. In addition to these worries, Betty reported significant muscle tension in her shoulders and back, serious sleep difficulties, and occasional concentration problems. Despite her busy social calendar, Betty avoided initiating appointments with friends for fear that they would say "no," and she procrastinated when it came to paying bills and examining her financial records for fear that she would realize how little money she actually had. At the time of her initial interview, Betty's symptoms met criteria for generalized anxiety disorder (GAD). She also reported depressed mood, but the associated symptoms were of insufficient severity for a diagnosis of major depression or dysthymia.

Betty reported that she had been a worrier all her life, despite a successful job history and happy family life. Her worries had increased, however, when her husband died 4 years previously. At that time, she had to assume all household and financial responsibilities, and she lost the primary support person in whom she confided her worries. Her husband had served as an effective "worry reducer" in times of increased anxiety.

After initial diagnostic interviewing and assessment of baseline symptom severity using standardized self-report questionnaires (e.g., the Penn State Worry Questionnaire, the Beck Depression Inventory), the therapist and Betty initiated a course of cognitive behavior therapy aimed at reducing her worry and associated physical symptoms and behaviors. First, she was taught progressive deep muscle relaxation, a procedure wherein she learned to alternately tense and relax various muscle groups, in an effort to help her recognize and reduce physical tension associated with worry. This component of treatment was of particular use to Betty when she experienced difficulty sleeping. At these times, she listened to a relaxation tape while lying in her bed. While learning and practicing relaxation exercises, Betty began to monitor her thoughts during episodes of worry and anxiety. With practice, she learned that she had many problematic beliefs, such as, "Everyone needs to like me, and I want to be everyone's best friend"; "All other people are younger, more attractive, and more interesting than I am"; and "My children don't really need me anymore." She was surprised to realize that she thought about herself and others in these ways, but she was able to learn to treat these thoughts as hypotheses (guesses) and to begin to evaluate how "valid" they were. Betty learned that she tended to think in all-or-none terms (e.g., "If all people do not prefer my company all the time, I am not desirable as a friend," or "If my children do not need me in the same ways that they did many years ago, they have no need for me at all"). Although it was difficult for Betty to change these highly ingrained patterns of thinking, she was able to recognize the irrationality of her thoughts and the ways in which they created high levels of anxiety for her.

After Betty began to recognize the illogical ways she was thinking, she started to substitute alterative thoughts, first during practice exercises that she did at least twice a day and later during actual episodes of anxiety as they occurred in her daily life. She slowly began to think "as she went" of possible explanations for events that did not involve as much all-or-none thinking. Once she started to learn new ways of thinking, she was asked to practice new behaviors that involved approaching situations that created some anxiety. In particular, she was asked to begin inviting her friends to accompany her to social events and to complete financial activities on a more regular basis. While doing these activities, Betty used her new cognitive skills to try and think as logically as possible about the outcomes. She was not encouraged to think that all of her friends would accept her invitations each time, but to recognize that it was okay if others declined her invitations. Even if her friends sometimes said "no," Betty was able to think of alternative evidence that these people did indeed want to continue being her friend.

Treatment for Betty was successful. At the end of 15 weekly sessions, Betty reported significantly reduced worry and depressed mood according to standardized self-report questionnaires. She also had fewer physical symptoms of anxiety and was more easily able to initiate social activities with others. Betty maintained some level of anxiety, however, and, in fact, her symptoms still met criteria for a diagnosis of GAD with mild severity. Nevertheless, the quality of her life was significantly improved.

—*Melinda A. Stanley*

See also: *Beck, Aaron T. (Vol. I); Cognitive Behavior Therapy (Vol. I); Cognitive Behavior Therapy: Child Clinical Applications (Vol. II)*

Suggested Readings

Barlow, D. H. (2001). *Clinical handbook of psychological disorders: A step-by-step treatment manual* (3rd ed.). New York: Guilford Press.

Beck, A. T., Freeman, A., & Associates (1990). *Cognitive therapy of personality disorders.* New York: Guilford Press.

Beck, A. T., Rush, A. J., Shaw, F. B., & Emery, G. (1979). *Cognitive therapy of depression.* New York: Guilford Press.

Bond, F. W., & Dryden, W. (2002). *Handbook of brief cognitive behaviour therapy.* New York: Wiley.

Chambless, D. L., Baker, M. J., Baucom, D. H., Beutler, L. E., Calhoun, K. S., Crits-Christoph, P., et al. (1998). Update on empirically validated therapies, II. *The Clinical Psychologist, 51,* 3–16.

Persons, J. (1989). *Cognitive therapy in practice: A case formulation approach.* New York: Norton.

Young, J. E., Klosko, J. S., & Weishaar, M. E. (2003). *Schema therapy: A practitioner's guide.* New York: Guilford Press.

COMPETING RESPONSE TRAINING

DESCRIPTION OF THE STRATEGY

Competing response training is a component of the habit-reversal procedure developed by Azrin and Nunn in 1973. Habit reversal consists of four major treatment components: awareness training, competing response practice, habit control motivation, and generalization training. Substantial research demonstrates the effectiveness of habit reversal for the treatment of habit disorders (nervous habits and tics). Research also demonstrates the effectiveness of a simplified version of habit reversal, consisting of awareness training and competing response practice. Treatment consisting of awareness training and competing response practice is referred to as *competing response training* or *simplified habit reversal.*

In competing response training, the client learns to become aware of each instance of the habit behavior (awareness training) and to use a competing response contingent on the occurrence of the habit behavior or the antecedents to the habit behavior (competing response practice). Competing response training is implemented in one or a small number of outpatient treatment sessions.

Awareness Training

The goal of awareness training is for the client to become aware of each instance of the habit behavior

as soon as it occurs and to become aware of the immediate antecedents to the habit behavior. In this way, the client can use the competing response contingent on the incipient occurrence of the behavior or its antecedents. To develop awareness of the habit behavior, the client first describes the behaviors involved in the habit and then practices detecting each instance of the behavior that occurs in the treatment session.

For motor or vocal tics, habit behaviors that are likely to occur numerous times in the session, the client identifies (verbally or by raising a finger) each instance of the tic that occurs in the session. The therapist praises the client for correctly identifying the tics and points out the occurrence of any tics that the client failed to detect. The therapist and client continue the process until the client can detect each tic as it occurs.

For nervous habits (e.g., hair pulling, nail biting, etc.) that typically would not occur in the presence of the therapist, the client simulates the behavior to enhance awareness. The client simulates situations in which the habit behavior is likely to occur (sitting in a chair watching television) and simulates the behavior exactly as it would occur in the natural setting. As the client simulates the habit behavior, the therapist tells the client to stop at various points in the behavioral movement. For example, if a client engages in hair pulling, the therapist might have the client stop as the hand is being raised up to the head, as the finger first touch the hair, as the fingers isolate a hair to pull, and so forth. By stopping the movements at various stages, the client becomes more aware of the occurrence of the behavior.

The final part of awareness training involves teaching the client to become aware of the sensations, behaviors, or environmental circumstances that precede the occurrence of the habit behavior. The client first describes the possible antecedents and then notes their occurrence as the habit behavior occurs in session. Alternatively, the client may simulate their occurrence in session. Increasing awareness of the antecedents helps the client detect the imminent occurrence of the habit behavior.

Competing Response Practice

In competing response practice, the client engages in a competing response for 1 minute contingent on the habit behavior or the antecedents to the behavior. The competing response is physically incompatible with the habit behavior, easy to engage in, and socially inconspicuous so that the client can engage in the competing response anywhere the habit behavior occurs. For a motor tic, the competing response involves tensing the muscles involved in the tic and holding the body part motionless. The competing response for a vocal tic involves slow, rhythmic breathing through the nose with the mouth closed. For nervous habit involving the hands, the client grasps an object, clasps the hands, puts hands in pockets, or engages the hands in some other behavior incompatible with the habit behavior.

In the treatment session, the therapist instructs the client to practice using the competing response contingent on the habit behavior or its antecedents. For motor or vocal tics, the client engages in the competing response contingent on the tics as they occur naturally in session. For nervous habits, the client simulates the habit behavior and then implements the competing response contingent on the behavior. The therapist praises the client for the correct use of the competing response in the session and prompts the client to use the competing response if the client fails to use it contingent on the habit behavior. After the client demonstrates the successful use of the competing response in session, the therapist instructs the client to use the competing response consistently outside of the treatment sessions to interrupt the habit behavior or prevent its occurrence.

RESEARCH BASIS

Substantial research has established the effectiveness of simplified versions of habit reversal, involving awareness training and competing response practice (competing response training). Research shows that competing response training is effective across a range of nervous habits and motor and vocal tics. Furthermore, research shows that for competing response training to be effective, the client must engage in the competing response contingent on the habit behavior.

RELEVANT TARGET POPULATIONS AND EXCEPTIONS

Competing response training is most likely to be effective for adults and adolescents exhibiting habit disorders. Research has shown that the procedure is less likely to be effective for children and is not likely to be effective for individuals with mental retardation. An important factor contributing to the success of competing response training is compliance with the procedures. Individuals with limited motivation or intellectual abilities are less likely to comply with the procedures.

COMPLICATIONS

Competing response training is relatively straightforward, practically and conceptually, so it is not difficult to use. Nonetheless, factors that might interfere with the consistent use of the procedure are the client's age, intellectual disabilities, severity of the habit disorder (e.g., severe or long-standing trichotillomania), and comorbid psychopathology (e.g., depression).

—*Raymond G. Miltenberger*

See also: Azrin, Nathan H. (Vol. I); Habit Reversal (Vols. I & II)

Suggested Readings

Azrin, N. H., & Nunn, R. G. (1973). Habit reversal: A method of eliminating nervous habits and tics. *Behaviour Research and Therapy, 11,* 619–628.

Azrin, N. H., & Nunn, R. G. (1977). *Habit control in a day.* New York: Simon & Schuster.

Miltenberger, R. G. (2001). Habit reversal treatment manual for trichotillomania. In D. Woods & R. Miltenberger (Eds.), *Tic disorders, trichotillomania, and other repetitive behavior disorders: Behavioral approaches to analysis and treatment* (pp. 171–196). Norwell, MA: Kluwer.

Miltenberger, R. G., Fuqua, R. W., & Woods, D. W. (1998). Applying behavior analysis to clinical problems: Review and analysis of habit reversal. *Journal of Applied Behavior Analysis, 31,* 447–469.

Woods, D. W. (2001). Habit reversal treatment manual for tic disorders. In D. Woods & R. Miltenberger (Eds.), *Tic disorders, trichotillomania, and other repetitive behavior disorders: Behavioral approaches to analysis and treatment* (pp. 33–52). Norwell, MA: Kluwer.

COMPUTER-BASED DATA COLLECTION

DESCRIPTION OF THE STRATEGY

It has been an ongoing challenge for researchers in the psychological, social, and educational sciences to systematically capture the many directly observable behaviors and events inherent to settings in which multiple organisms act and interact. This is particularly true when the focus is upon the direct observation of behavior and when interest is in collecting a relatively inclusive data record of all behaviors and events relevant to a complete description of an experimental setting. For strategy description purposes, *direct observation* is defined as a particular approach to quantifying behavior. Typically, this approach is focused on the collection and analysis of data that pertain to naturally occurring behavior in naturalistic contexts. Primary activity involves operationally defining various behavior types through the development of a behavioral code, and then using trained observers to record instances of behavior occurrences in accordance with those predefined codes. A main component to this type of data collection activity is one of training all observers, or data collectors, to the point that each observer will produce an identical data record given observation of the same behavioral set of events. Essentially, the two main characteristics of behavioral data collection are (a) the use of a predefined coding system and (b) the use of observers trained to an acceptable level of data-recording reliability.

The process of defining and developing a coding system, training observers to acceptable levels of agreement, and collecting a relatively inclusive and complete record of behavior and event occurrences in interactive settings has been historically time-consuming and labor-intensive. Due to time and labor challenges in application, direct observation approaches to the quantitative measurement of behavior occurrences have not been met with widespread popularity in the applied psychological, social, and education sciences. However, without such application, the scientist who proceeds no further than telling others what he or she sees runs the risk of having skeptical colleagues dismiss such narrative reports as anecdotal yarns.

One area of particular interest to the applied analysis of behavior has been in the development of semi-automated computer systems for the collection and analysis of direct observational data in real time. Development has been fomented in large part in answer to time and labor challenges with respect to direct-observation activity, with a variety of computer-based technologies that support the recording and systematic coding of behavior now available commercially. Over the past 20 years, these technologies

have become less expensive, more reliable and user-friendly, and considerably more sophisticated in their data collection and data analysis capabilities. As computer-based data collection and analysis systems continue to develop and evolve, they have the potential to greatly enhance observational activities by improving the reliability and accuracy of recording relative to less capable paper-and pencil-recording methods. They also have the potential to significantly enhance user capabilities in the areas of data calculation and graphing, data reliability and treatment integrity assessments, and recording multiple behaviors and their multiple occurrences in real time for more inclusive and complete observational descriptions. Of particular interest, computer-based data collection and analysis provide opportunity for change agents to inform their clients and other consumers of their services' progress in much more immediate ways, particularly with respect to showing data that support the impact of an intervention. This last feature is of particular appeal when conducting assessments of applied settings with a view toward providing immediate data-based feedback and goal-setting information to clients who are practicing particular skills in those settings.

In concert with computer-based data collection tool development, the manner in which one thinks about how to measure behavior has developed. Largely a function of computer-based data collection capability, multiple discrete measures such as number, rate, duration, percentage, interval, latency, and interresponse time may be readily collected. Also important, these measures may be collected in real time or as they actually occur and without interruption, as opposed to more traditionally accepted momentary time sampling, duration, or interval-time-sampling recording procedures. Finally, a time- and labor-efficient method is made available through computer-based data collection for focusing on the sequential measurement of observational data. Until recently, many of the analysis techniques proposed for sequential data have been in the experimental stages. Computer-supported sequential analysis techniques provide a user-friendly method for implementing log-linear techniques and lag-sequential analyses, the former a multidimensional extension of chi-square tests and the latter based on a conditional probability of occurrence analysis.

What remains is that computer-based tools for direct observation are not widely known to the professional communities that would benefit most from using them and that they oftentimes remain difficult to access to the unfamiliar, though many commercial marketing activities are currently ongoing. One commercially available computer-based data collection and analysis tool, termed *Behavior Evaluation Strategy and Taxonomy* (BEST) software, is described in detail as an illustration of a growing variety of similar tools that exist on the commercial market and in the literature. This example is one of the growing number of tools that are available in a packaged and user-friendly format to professional and scientific communities. In addition, the BEST tool described is representative of the majority of computer-based data collection systems in that it is based on compatibility with IBM Windows operating platforms and includes a variety of features (e.g., interrater reliability, data file merging, data graphing, and sequential-analysis applications) in representing a more inclusive set of computer-based applications that a user might typically have to obtain multiple computer programs to access.

COMPUTER-BASED FEATURES OF BEST

Similar to most computer-based data collection and analysis tools, the BEST software platforms are divided into two separate and distinct data collection and data analysis applications. Both are completely compatible with Windows 95, 98, 200, NT, and XP and operate identically in terms of a Windows-based menu structure, with similar user-friendly features. Computer-based data collection applications facilitate the construction of observation systems by defining alphanumeric keys on a computer keyboard. Up to 36 different behaviors and events may therefore be recorded during an observational session, and each key may also be notated numerically and narratively for additional behavior and event subcategorization. A variety of recording methods are made available via computer-based data collection, including the pressing and holding down of keys to record respective start and stop times of behaviors upon key release and the pressing of a key to record a start time of a behavior and the pressing again of a key to record a stop time. In this way, multiple occurrences of simultaneous or overlapping events may be recorded. By generating a time-based data record with quantitatively measured start and stop times of each recorded event, response frequency, duration, intervals (variable duration), average duration and standard deviations, rate, latency, interresponse time, percentage of observational

time, and time-based measures (such as first, last, span, longest, shortest, etc.) may be extracted using a computer-based data analysis program. Due to the time-based nature of the computer-based data generated, a sophisticated sequential-analysis application is also made readily available. Numerical and text notation features also allow the recording of notes for unique or atypical event occurrences in the time-based sequence in which they occurred. In addition, pause, edit, merge, and a variety of other data management features are made available that permit the interruption and restarting of observational sessions as the need arises; entry errors made while recording may be immediately edited; and multiple data files may be merged in time-based sequence when undertaking complex observational activities from videotape or other permanent records. In relation to the recording of data from permanent records, computer-based data collection apparatus provide for synchronization applications across video record and data collection apparatus startup, ensuring accurate time-based data records and providing sensitivity to onset and termination in relation to when particular behaviors and events occurred.

Computer-based data analysis programs provide a variety of user-friendly options previously thought time- and labor-intensive, including the calculating of response frequency (total number and rate), duration, latency, interresponse time, percentage of observation time and related subintervals, percentage of trials, and conditional probabilities of sequentially based behavior and event relationships. Analysis applications also allow the compartmentalizing of subgroups of behaviors and events to analyze as a logically grouped data file. Options include the calculation of mean and median data, variability in relation to range and frequency distributions, and statistical significance data in relation to sequential analyses. Reliability programs with simple frequency, point-by-point, and Cohen's kappa options are now available to facilitate staff training and interrater reliability check procedures. Graphic analyses include tables, pie charts, temporal records, sequential-analysis tables, and traditional time-series graphs. Statistical applications such as mean, standard deviation, and line of best fit are readily obtainable from computer-based applications as analysis complement to standard graphic analyses. Of additional appeal as computer-based applications evolve are the increasingly sophisticated export features in which both tabular and graphic representations of behavioral data may be compatibly exportable to most commercial graphics programs, such as Windows Paint, Powerpoint, and Delta Graph, and numerical data may be compatibly exported into amenable statistical programs such as SPSS.

Most current computer-based data collection and analysis programs require an IBM-compatible desktop or laptop computer with a minimum 386 processor running a Windows operating platform. The applications have minimal RAM and hard-disk requirements. Data collection applications for handheld PCs are also becoming readily available, as are digital video synchronization applications for data collection platforms. Of additional appeal to the experimental scientist, a variety of remote-data collection apparatuses are now available for those who desire direct hookup to laboratory applications (e.g., bar press, lights, temperature switches, pellet containers, etc.) that obviate the constant presence of a human data collector. Most computer-based data collection and analysis apparatus come in either packaged CD-ROM form or as a direct download from an amenable vendor. Contained in many computer-based systems are example observation systems, example data files, complete and illustrated users' guides, and in some cases a compatible research methodology text. Research text material is helpful in the exploration of a variety of measurement types and analyses made feasible through computer-based support, given that these two areas are evolving as a function of rapid improvements in computer-based capability. Some computer-based packages also include a tutorial in movie-and-sound format, helpful to an initial overview of a software program's many capabilities and applications. Such materials require an Adobe Acrobat reader and a QuickTime movie player, and for those without these applications, they are readily available online via a free download from an appropriate vendor.

Appealing advantages of computer-based data collection and analysis include:

1. Behavioral, quantitative, and qualitative data collection with a push of a button

2. A wide range of sophisticated analyses, including descriptive and predictive statistics, qualitative memo noting, and a variety of graphic and sequential-analysis representations

3. Complete compatibility with a wide variety of statistical and graphics package

4. User customizability to specific data collection and analysis needs

5. Immediate data-based feedback capability in field settings or as an ongoing evaluation tool

6. Built-in reliability application for staff training and interobserver comparisons

7. Data file merging and sorting functions for compiling purposes

General features include:

1. Allowing users to create their own category systems to meet their specific observational needs

2. Storing multiple observation systems for particular applications

3. Recording the start and stop times of multiple events as they naturally occur, providing a variety of descriptive statistics

4. Recording narrative field notes in concert with behavioral and quantitative data

5. Recording information live or synchronized with videotape at almost any location

6. Qualitatively, quantitatively, and sequentially representing and analyzing observational data

7. Providing staff training and ensuring reliability of data collection

8. Interfacing with other software programs for multitasking and remote-site use

9. Being compatible with a range of hardware, including Windows CE handheld computers for data collection in the field

Some specific data collection capabilities include:

1. Recording and categorizing data using complex multiple-event observation systems

2. Using numerical and narrative notations to further delineate event types

3. Recording multiple events simultaneously as they actually occur in time

4. Taking advantage of a user-friendly screen representation when collecting data

5. Facilitating the data collection process with multiple means of recording, including press and hold keys, toggle keys for turning on and off, and remote-key access

6. Pause feature for entering and exiting the same data collection episode at time of exit

7. Editing data collection efforts on the fly and viewing data records as they are collected

8. Automatic recording of response frequency, rates, percentage of total experimental time, shortest and longest event occurrences, event occurrence spans, duration, intervals, time samples, latency, interresponse time, and discrete trials

9. Multitasking when collecting data by assigning keys to perform additional functions, such as starting another software application

10. Taking advantage of MicroSoft CE handheld compatibility when collecting data in particular field settings

Some specific data analysis capabilities include:

1. Identifying frequency, total, and mean duration, standard deviations, rate, and experimental time percentages of each category system event in tabular and graphic formats

2. Identifying time-based information for each category system event, including first- and last-event occurrence, time spans between events, longest and shortest event occurrences, and related means and standard deviations

3. Searching for keywords and memos in narrative notations and representing narrative data within and across data files

4. Processing and comparing multiple data files across one another and across multiple recorded events and measurement types

5. Conducting a variety of reliability analysis functions among data files, including simple frequency, point-by-point, and Cohen's kappa

6. Conducting sequential analyses of the time-based connections among events documented in terms of frequency, conditional probability, and statistical significance (z-score transformations)

7. Merging and time sorting multiple data files enabling comprehensive observational description from videotape

8. Performing event-subgrouping routines to allow a separate analysis of subgroups of events within all program applications

9. Representing data with a host of sophisticated graphing applications for individual data files and for multiple data files across event and measurement type

10. Graphically analyzing mean, standard deviation, and regression across multiple data files and multiple events and measures

11. Printing, saving, and clipboard/pasting data representations into other statistical analysis and graphics-editing software packages

RESEARCH BASIS

Current research shows that computer-based data collection and analysis efforts are more effective than traditional paper-and-pencil and stopwatch methods in providing a more inclusive multiple-behavior and -event record of the direct-observational setting of interest. In addition, computer-based data collection allows recording in real time and the recording of multiple simultaneously occurring behaviors, uncovering previously unknown functional relationships in highly interactive settings. Also largely a function of computer-based data collection and analysis capabilities, reporting of more rigorous data collector training, interrater reliability, and treatment integrity activities and related assessment techniques are more widely seen in the literature. More capable multiple-level statistical analysis of observational records and more sophisticated and thoroughgoing sequential analyses of behavior–event relationships over time have also been realized as a function of computer-based data collection and analysis applications. Enhanced capabilities in measurement and analysis as afforded by computer-based applications have furthered the applied analysis of behavior in particular when research interest has focused on how multiple participants act and interact in a range of social, educational, therapeutic, and clinical settings. In addition, the relative effectiveness of behavioral treatments that include an immediate feedback and data-based goal-setting activity in relation to the training of professionals in educational and clinical settings has been enhanced as a function of computer-based data presentation applications that provide for relatively immediate data viewing and consequent analysis by educator and professional trainee.

RELEVANT TARGET POPULATIONS AND EXCEPTIONS

Computer-based data collection and analysis applications are relevant to research and evaluation populations that have an interest in the more inclusive recording and analysis of multiple behaviors and events as they actually occur in real time. Those with interest in more sophisticated sequential analyses will benefit in particular, given computer-based application feasibility in this area. In addition, those who focus primarily on evaluation and instructional feedback activities, whether operating in professional development sites or in instructional laboratories, will benefit from computer-based data collection and analysis applications due to enhanced immediacy of data viewing and related evaluative interaction based on those data.

COMPLICATIONS

Complications are negligible when implementing computer-based data collection and analysis, with the following exceptions. First, and as computer application development continues, this is becoming less of a consideration, computer-based data collection and analysis instruments are more cost-intensive than traditional data collection and analysis methods. The potential user must weigh increased cost of hardware and software against the additional information gained and the additional application possibilities that may be generated from access to these types of tools. Second, and of particular importance to field-based research and evaluation applications, computer-based data collection is inherently a more intrusive process due to the introduction of such apparatus to an applied observational setting. Additional activity must be implemented to minimize the potentially visually intrusive nature of data collection apparatus to avoid data confounds related to changes in the behaviors of those observed as a function of overt exposure to such apparatus.

CASE ILLUSTRATION

Computer-based data collection has in large measure overcome the traditional argument against use of behavior analysis methods: While quantitative knowledge of specific behavioral activities is important, what has oftentimes occurred through applied behavior analysis methods is the counting of only a few behaviors in isolation and the inappropriate fragmenting of a larger interactive process into discrete elements that are presumed to affect target behaviors or events in some causal way. More capable and inclusive computer-based data collection and analysis strategies have been developed in large part to avoid rendering the study and evaluation of behavioral interactions simplistically generic and to ensure that behavior-analytic approaches remain in the mainstream of applied science. Developmental focus has been on the invention of alternative methods of direct observational data collection and analysis that are capable of quantifying the repeated occurrence of multiple variables and their many setting-specific interactions. Recent developments in the area of computer technologies have significantly added to direct observation research capabilities and facilitated the development of alternative data collection and analysis techniques once thought of only in conceptual terms. Computer-based innovation has facilitated contributions from pioneers in the field of behavior analysis concerning what can and what should conceivably be observed, more capable measurement systems, and methodological and statistical applications for quantifying time-based sequences of behavior.

Education research provides an important illustration due to the challenges of studying multiple participants within highly interactive settings in which multiple behaviors and events are repeatedly occurring. At the first level of educational analysis, an approach might be to ask a teacher to fill out a qualitatively oriented questionnaire (e.g., Likert scale normative data or open-ended response data) and from these responses to provide information on a topic such as job performance or job-related satisfaction by assigning individual scores to the teacher response data gathered. This type of information might then provide general indicators of possible relationships between job performance and relative satisfaction with experiential dimensions (such as a teacher's past professional and personal experiences or particular work setting characteristics). This type of data gathering and analysis effort is probably most frequently cited in the education and social science literature; however, this type of *static-data* measure (i.e., a measure that does not include how events are connected to one another in time) does not tell us much about how a particular teacher interacts with his or her student clientele on a regular basis, nor does it tell us much about how those interactions affect the relative quality of professional behavior (in terms of educational effectiveness or relative personal satisfaction with professional roles). An appealing research and evaluation alternative to learning more about a particular teacher, therefore, may be to describe and analyze the dynamics of how a teacher interacts with his or her students on an immediate and daily basis.

When a researcher uses a direct quantitative observation method to study a particular teacher, the potential contribution of computer-based data collection in relationship to the types of data that may be collected (i.e., a measurement focus that makes the relationships in time between behaviors and events explicit) becomes readily apparent when it is used in addition to the more traditional static measures of the characteristics of teacher and student behavior. When studying a teacher in a classroom situation, for example, a *static* measure (i.e., the discrete characteristics of behaviors and events themselves, such as the relative number of questioning, instructional, feedback, or interpersonal behaviors used) could be collected and the percentage of class time that students are engaged in behaviors (such as skill practice, management and organization, waiting for an opportunity to interact with materials, or active responding) could also be measured. This approach is in line with most behavior analysis techniques and is an approach that would provide important information regarding how a particular teacher and his or her students tend to use their time in a particular educational situation. In addition, many of these kinds of immediately occurring behaviors have been documented as highly correlated with long-term measures of learning and achievement in particular subject matters and skills to be learned. They may therefore be used as relatively effective indicators of the general effectiveness of a particular educational situation. For example, a variety of behavior analysis research has focused on one or two potentially effective teacher behaviors as independent variables and uses a single measure of student behavior, such as the percentage of engagement in practicing an activity. Although some research designs have been developed to examine the behavior of more than one person, rarely have these types of studies focused on

the time-based character of behavior ←→ environment interactions between multiple individuals.

As a function of the enhanced capability of computer-based data collection and analysis, four research and evaluation trends in the education and social sciences are more feasibly pursued as follows. First, behavior ←→ behavior and behavior ←→ environment relationships are a very complex set of phenomena that need to be more thoroughly and inclusively examined. Second, emphasis must be placed on ecological validity or analysis of the functional differences across a variety of settings in which certain relationships are relatively more or less productive. Third, analysis emphasis must be placed not just on the discrete characteristics of behavior and environment events (e.g., number or frequency, percentage of experimental time, rate, etc.) but also, in a complete analysis, on the form and character of the multiple stimuli-and-response relationships among multiple behaviors and events as they actually occur in time in particular situations. Fourth, emphasis must be placed on the discovery of behavior ←→ behavior and behavior ←→ environment relationships that have been repeatedly documented as having predictive therapeutic ends within and across particular professional situations.

This last trend is connected with the appeal of a sequential analysis that computer-based data collection makes feasible. This appeal has partly to do with the inability of the more static approach just illustrated to fully explain the explicit time-based interactive connection between what a particular teacher does in a specific educational situation and how a particular student or group of students respond(s) to the behaviors of that teacher. For example, documenting how often an instructional or organizational behavior is used by a teacher or the relative amount of time a particular student devotes to skill practice does not tell much about how each teacher's and student's behavior are explicitly connected in time-based sequence and may therefore be functionally related. Discrete characteristics of teacher or student behaviors collected without regard for the time-based connection between other behaviors and events also does not tell much about the immediate instructional and social interactions a particular teacher may use to either facilitate desirable student practices or inhibit undesirable student activities. The sequential type of data-based information that a computer-based data collection apparatus may provide is the type of information that may be used to answer the types of information-gathering needs just illustrated. Although study of the characteristics of individual behaviors to discover more about the interactive relationships among humans is important and productive, there is another dimension of human interaction that is as important to explore—the transactions or connections among behaviors that are studied using time-based measures.

A time-based analysis is performed not due to a need to alter a typical behavior-analytic observational coding system in some way, but due to the need for adding an alternative measure to be used in such a way so that the data to be recorded are conducive to capturing behavior sequences. Sequential data provide an additional level of information about an interactive setting under observation, and such data provide information that is not accessible without specifically including a sequential observation lens in the data collection and analysis process. In education research, a sequential data set could, for example, help answer questions about what students tend to do after being exposed to certain types of instruction and whether those teacher behaviors helped to improve student skill practice. Sequential data may also help in answering how certain students might characteristically respond to certain types of interpersonal interactions. Answers to these types of sequentially based questions require a different type of observational lens and an additional way of collecting and looking at observational data. Although nonsequential, or static, behavior data can provide information related to how much instruction or how many interpersonal interactions should be used by a teacher for general effectiveness (based, for example, on a general percentage of student skill practice time), sequential data substantially help in making explicit the specific functional relationship of how a variety of student responses are emitted over time as a function of time-based exposure to different kinds of teacher behaviors.

For several years during and after the contributions of behavior analysis pioneers such as B. F. Skinner and J. R. Kantor, a major criticism of this body of work was that many recommendations for behavior analysis methodology remained at the conceptual stage—without specific data collection and analysis tools to support those recommendations. For example, although an argument that favored looking into the sequential nature of behavior $\leftarrow \rightarrow$

environment interactions was rigorously constructed, and many researchers and clinicians saw the potential importance of this argument, an appealing and user-friendly means of collecting and using this type of data remained largely unavailable. This is no longer the case. Computer-based procedures are now available to be applied to observe and analyze highly interactive applied settings. This type of study involves providing a more inclusive description of multiple behaviors and events, an explicit focus on which behaviors and events tend to precede or follow which other behaviors or events, and a multiple-level descriptive and sequential analysis of which of these sequential connections tend to be most productive in meeting particular educational or therapeutic ends.

—*Tom Sharpe*

See also: *Behavioral Assessment (Vols. I & III); Computers and Behavioral Assessment (Vol. I)*

Suggested Readings

Bakeman, R., & Gottman, J. M. (1997). *Observing interaction: An introduction to sequential analysis* (2nd ed.). New York: Cambridge University Press.

Farrell, A. D. (1992). Computers and behavioral assessment: Current applications, future possibilities, and obstacles to routine use. *Behavioral Assessment, 13,* 159–179.

Kahng, S. W., & Iwata, B. A. (1998). Computerized systems for collecting real-time observational data. *Journal of Applied Behavior Analysis, 31,* 253–261.

Morris, E. K. (1992). ABA presidential address: The aim, progress, and evolution of behavior analysis. *The Behavior Analyst, 15,* 3–29.

Ray, R. D., & Delprato, D. J. (1989). Behavioral systems analysis: Methodological strategies and tactics. *Behavioral Science, 34,* 81–127.

Sharpe, T. L., Hawkins, A., & Lounsbery, M. (1998). Using technology to study and evaluate human interaction: Practice and implications of a sequential behavior approach. *Quest, 50,* 389–401.

Sharpe, T. L., Hawkins, A., & Ray, R. (1995). Interbehavioral field systems assessment: Examining its utility in preservice teacher education. *Journal of Behavioral Education, 5,* 259–280.

Sharpe, T. L., & Koperwas, J. (2000). *Software assist for education and social science settings: Behavior evaluation strategies and taxonomies (BEST) and accompanying qualitative applications.* Thousand Oaks, CA: Sage-Scolari.

Sharpe, T. L., & Koperwas, J. (2003). *Behavior and sequential analyses: Principles and practice.* Thousand Oaks, CA: Sage.

COMPUTERS AND BEHAVIORAL ASSESSMENT

DESCRIPTION OF THE STRATEGY

Computerized behavioral assessment tools include hardware and software applications that enable clinicians to monitor client behavior in ways that would have been impossible 20 years ago. Applications include functional interviews, behavioral questionnaires, clinical case modeling tools, self-monitoring programs, behavior-rating scales and checklists, psychophysiological assessment, and observational systems that utilize symbolic or virtual reality environments. Delivery platforms range from handheld computers (i.e., personal digital assistants, or PDAs) to desktop applications to immersive virtual worlds.

Although the term *computerized behavioral assessment* refers to a broad class of software and hardware applications, the technology rests on a functional foundation. Two variables are functionally related if changes in one variable are associated with, but do not necessarily cause, changes in a second variable. For example, a client's anger outbursts may be exacerbated when she consumes alcohol. Thus, quantity of alcohol consumed may be functionally related to frequency and intensity of the client's anger. One would expect reduction in alcohol consumption to have therapeutically desirable effects on anger modulation.

Computerized behavioral assessment applications distinguish themselves by facilitating assessment of functional relations. For example, a method that has gained increasing acceptance involves use of handheld computers to conduct ecological momentary assessment (EMA). In an EMA assessment strategy, clients use handheld computers to record in their natural environment frequency or intensity of selected target behaviors (e.g., anger intensity) and variables hypothesized to be functionally related to the target behavior (e.g., alcohol consumption). Recording sessions are usually brief and conducted multiple times per day. Advantages to the EMA approach include the following: Handheld computers are ubiquitous and unobtrusive, data are stored in a file for easy analysis, the computer can prompt the client for recording sessions, and feedback can be automatically generated. With regard to the last point, some researchers have gone so far as to develop cognitive behavior treatment modules that are delivered by handheld computer.

However, researchers have noted drawbacks to the EMA approach as well: Clients fatigue over time and may stop entering data, behaviors that occur at high rates may be difficult to code or self-monitor, the value of the data depends upon a priori specification of variables hypothesized to be functionally related, and handheld computers are expensive to replace if lost or stolen.

Computers can also be used to conduct behavioral interviews. Researchers have developed programs to identify client problems and track dimensions of those problems over time. Other researchers have developed structured interviews that are symptom based and focus on diagnostic categorization rather than functional relations. In both cases, the computer is used to collect client information and generate a report that can be used by the clinician to plan and monitor treatment.

Most clients respond well to computerized interviews. While computerized interviews facilitate easy data entry, evidence has accumulated that clients may be more likely to divulge sensitive or embarrassing information to a computer than to a human interviewer. For example, several studies have shown that clients often prefer computerized interviews to human interviews.

In addition, computerized interviews are more reliable in delivering question prompts. Studies have shown that human interviewers may omit 5% or more of questions in a structured interview. However, critics have pointed out that such efficiency is not without cost. For example, a computer cannot monitor nonverbal client behavior, detect subtle inconsistencies in client reports, and can employ only rudimentary data analytic techniques in place of the inferences seasoned clinicians may make.

RESEARCH BASIS

From a research perspective, there have been encouraging results regarding client compliance. For example, one study compared client use of electronic and paper-pencil diaries for pain monitoring. The researchers found that clients in the electronic diary group recorded data more frequently than those in the paper-and-pencil recording group.

Other studies have shown that monitoring of behavior in the natural environment may yield estimates of behavioral frequencies that are not equivalent to clinician ratings. In one study, clients with obsessive-compulsive disorder (OCD) were rated by clinicians using a standard OCD rating scale. Clients then completed the same scale using handheld computers in their natural environments. Results showed that clients' self-ratings were significantly less severe than the ratings made by the clinicians.

A fundamental problem facing use of behavioral assessment technology involves problems in dissemination. Despite burgeoning growth of publications in computerized behavioral assessment, much of the technology has yet to find a place in day-to-day clinical practice. This problem has occurred for several reasons. First, technology can be expensive and difficult to replace. Second, there is a dearth of user-friendly software applications available across different delivery platforms. Third, some behavioral assessment methods, especially methods that are observation-intensive, are logistically challenging and potentially cost-prohibitive. Fourth, with regard to EMA, clients may not have the necessary skill repertoire required to use handheld computers. Fifth, software must not only capture data but also analyze and interpret results. Software that integrates a user-friendly data capture interface, conducts functionally relevant behavioral analysis (e.g., graphing and interpretation), and flexibly aggregates data across collection instances is difficult to write.

RELEVANT TARGET POPULATIONS AND EXCEPTIONS

There are no known population constraints to computerized behavioral assessment. Some researchers have reported that even clients with significant psychotic symptom presentation are able to complete rudimentary computerized interviews. With regard to EMA, both computerized assessment and treatment packages have been used effectively with a variety of diagnostic groups (e.g., panic disorder, agoraphobia, posttraumatic stress disorder, major depression, phobia, OCD, alcohol consumption, etc.). With regard to panic attacks, one study combined both assessment and treatment components so that the client eventually completed a treatment protocol via handheld computer.

Recent research using virtual reality (VR) environments has shown creative new ways of conducting assessment. For example, one group of researchers created autonomous virtual humans, or "avatars," to assess body image perceptions. Another group of researchers has been developing a virtual world that

could help socially anxious individuals interact with avatars. Other researchers have studied sexual preference by using a head-mounted display that projects an image of a naked avatar. Visual exploration of the avatar was measured by a sophisticated algorithm that tracked line-of-sight deviations from specific points of reference on the avatar. As a result, researchers could track the participant's visual scanning of the virtual stimulus. Other researchers have used VR environments to assess and treat a variety of phobias, public speaking anxiety, and a variety of other psychological disorders.

COMPLICATIONS

Because computerized behavioral assessment techniques are largely noninvasive, very few complications may develop as a result of their use. There are, however, certain populations that may not be well suited for computerized behavioral assessment. For example, elderly individuals often do not possess the skills to take advantage of computer technology. Other forms of behavioral assessment that do not require self-monitoring or interfacing with a computer may be more appropriate (e.g., direct observation by a clinician using a handheld computer device).

Other clients may not be good candidates for some computerized behavioral assessment strategies (e.g., EMA) for a variety of reasons. For example, clients diagnosed with antisocial personality disorder and borderline personality disorder and clients with substance use problems may have difficulty completing data collection or returning the handheld computer. Whenever technology is introduced, there is a risk of damage to the equipment, and computerized assessment is no exception.

Overall, research in computerized behavioral assessment has made great strides in the last several years with the development of relevant research journals and the publication of innovative research. The field is faced with two major tasks at this point. First, it is not clear how well these technologies will ultimately be disseminated to practitioners. Second, researchers need to demonstrate *treatment utility* of computerized behavioral assessment. Does the use of computerized behavioral assessment technology lead to client outcomes that are significantly better than if the technology is not used at all? Demonstrating equivalence of outcomes with less sophisticated assessment strategies may not be sufficient if other factors (e.g., cost, logistics, extensive learning curves for software) may prohibit software dissemination and use.

—*David C. S. Richard and Jennifer B. Mainka*

See also: *Computer-Based Data Collection (Vol. I); Behavioral Assessment (Vols. I & II)*

Suggested Readings

Buse, L., & Pawlik, K. (2001). Ambulatory behavioral assessment and in-field performance testing. In J. Fahrenberg & M. Myrtek (Eds.), *Ambulatory assessment: Computer-assisted psychological and psychophysiological methods in monitoring and field studies* (pp. 29–50). Kirkland, WA: Hogrefe & Huber.

Collins, R. L., Morsheimer, E. T., Shiffman, S., Hufford, M. R., Shields, A. L., Shiffman, S., et al. (1998). Ecological momentary assessment in a behavioral drinking moderation training program. *Experimental and Clinical Psychopharmacology, 6*, 306–315.

Gaggioli, A., Mantovani, F., Castelnuovo, G., Wiederhold, B., & Riva, G. (2003). Avatars in clinical psychology: A framework for the clinical use of virtual humans. *Cyberpsychology and Behavior, 6*(2), 117–126.

Hank, P., & Schwenkmezger, P. (2001). Computer-assisted versus paper-and-pencil based self-monitoring: An analysis of experiential and psychometric equivalence. In J. Fahrenberg & M. Myrtek (Eds.), *Ambulatory assessment: Computer-assisted psychological and psychophysiological methods in monitoring and field studies* (pp. 85–99). Kirkland, WA: Hogrefe & Huber.

Herman, S., & Koran, L. M. (1998). In vivo measurement of obsessive-compulsive disorder symptoms using palmtop computers. *Computers in Human Behavior, 14*(3), 449–462.

Jamison, R. N., Raymond, S. A., Levine, J. G., Slawsby, E. A., Nedeljkovic, S. S., & Katz, N. P. (2001). Electronic diaries for monitoring chronic pain: 1-year validation study. *Pain, 91*, 277–285.

Kenardy, J., & Taylor, C.B. (1999). Expected versus unexpected panic attacks: A naturalistic prospective study. *Journal of Anxiety Disorders, 13*, 435–445.

Marks, I. (1999). Computer aids to mental health care. *Canadian Journal of Psychiatry, 44*(4), 548–555.

Newman, M. G., Kenardy, J., Herman, S., & Taylor, C. B. (1995). The use of handheld computers as an adjunct to cognitive-behavioral therapy. *Computers in Human Behavior, 12*, 135–143.

Perez, M., & Reicherts, M. (2001). A computer-assisted self-monitoring procedure for assessing stress-related behavior under real life conditions. In J. Fahrenberg & M. Myrtek (Eds.), *Ambulatory assessment: Computer-assisted psychological and psychophysiological methods in monitoring and field studies* (pp. 51–67). Kirkland, WA: Hogrefe & Huber.

Renaud, P., Rouleau, J. J., Granger, L., Barsetti, I., & Bouchard, S. (2003). Measuring sexual preferences in virtual reality: A pilot study. *Cyberpsychology and Behavior, 5*(1), 1–10.

Richard, D. C. S., & Bobicz, K. (2003). Computers and behavioral assessment: Six years later. *The Behavior Therapist, 26*(1), 219–223.

Richard, D. C. S., & Lauterbach, D. L. (2003). Computers in the training and practice of behavioral assessment. In M. Hersen, S. N. Haynes, & E. Heiby (Eds.), *Comprehensive handbook of psychological assessment: Vol. 3. Behavioral assessment*. New York: Wiley.

Sarrazin, M. S. V., Hall, J. A., Richards, C., & Carswell, C. (2002). A comparison of computer-based versus pencil-and-paper assessments of drug use. *Research on Social Work Practice, 12*(5), 669–683.

Sorbi, M. J., Honkoop, P. C., & Godaert, G. L. R. (2001). A signal-contingent computer diary for the assessment of psychological precedents of the migraine attack. In J. Fahrenberg & M. Myrtek (Eds.), *Ambulatory assessment: Computer-assisted psychological and psychophysiological methods in monitoring and field studies* (pp. 403–412). Kirkland, WA: Hogrefe & Huber.

Stone, A. A., & Shiffman, S. (1994). Ecological momentary assessment: Measuring real world processes in behavioral medicine. *Annals of Behavioral Medicine, 16*, 199–202.

CONTEXTUALISM

DESCRIPTION OF THE STRATEGY

Contextualism is a pragmatic philosophy that uses the ongoing act in context as its model or root metaphor. Acts of this kind are historical, purposive, and situated. For example, "going to the store" implies a historical reason for going (e.g., not enough food in the house), a current purpose (e.g., needing to make the evening meal), and a situational context (e.g., a place to go from and to, money to make the purchase, time to get there). In psychology, philosophies of science based on contextualistic perspectives lead to approaches that emphasize (a) a focus on the whole event, (b) sensitivity to the role of context in establishing the nature and function of an event, and (c) a pragmatic truth criterion; that is, what is "true" is what works in a particular context and with regard to a particular goal. As a result of its pragmatic truth criterion, contextualists adopt a radically psychological epistemology and refrain from ontological declarations of all kinds. What is "true" in one context may not be "true" in another.

Clarity about the goals of analysis is critical to contextualists because goals specify how a pragmatic truth criterion can be applied. There are two broad categories of contextualism in psychology. Descriptive contextualists seek a personal understanding of the participants in the whole event. Psychologists of this kind see psychological science as a field that is similar to history. Narrative psychology, hermeneutics, dramaturgy, Marxism, feminism, and similar approaches are examples. Functional contextualists seek the prediction and influence of events as a single, integrated goal. Psychologists of this kind see psychological science as a pragmatic experimental field. Behavior analysis is an example.

Understanding the contextualistic nature of certain approaches helps make sense of features that would otherwise be mere dogmatism. For example, the "environmentalism" of behavior analysis is a direct result of its goals and pragmatic philosophy. Verbal analyses generate rules for people, not rules for the world. Scientists who seek to predict and influence psychological events must have rules that start with in the environment because that is where the scientists (the rule followers) are with regard to the behavior of others. Thus, factors are sought that are external to the behavior of the individual being studied and are manipulable, at least in principle. Only variables of this kind could lead directly to behavioral influence as an outcome.

Similarly, the behavior-analytic objection to analyses that point to relations between one form of psychological action and another are understandable given the functional contextual nature of behavior analysis. A scientist saying, for example, that thinking leads to overt behavior is pointing to a relationship between two psychological dependent variables. From the point of view of functional contextualism, the analysis must be incomplete until the manipulable context that gave rise to both forms of psychological activity and (importantly) their relation is specified. This is one reason that behavior analysis is often called the *experimental* analysis of behavior, because without manipulation of independent variables, it is difficult to know whether its analytic goals have been accomplished. These independent variables will never be the psychological actions that are being analyzed.

Contextualism is usually contrasted in behavioral psychology with mechanism. In mechanism, parts are primary, not the whole, and the goal is a comprehensive predictive model of the parts, relations, and forces that together make up the "machinery" of human beings. Computer-based information processing

models or their antecedent, S-R (stimulus-response) psychology, are examples. Because of their divergent analytic units and purposes, disagreements between contextualists and mechanists are difficult, or even impossible, to resolve empirically.

—*Steven C. Hayes*

See also: *Acceptance and Commitment Therapy (Vol. I); Behavioral Case Formulation (Vol. I); Behavioral Treatment in Natural Environments (Vol. I)*

CONTROLLED DRINKING

DESCRIPTION OF THE STRATEGY

The first clinical reports of controlled drinking as a treatment outcome for alcohol-dependent individuals appeared in the literature more than 40 years ago. Initially, reports focused on the observation that some alcoholics in abstinence-oriented treatment programs developed a pattern of controlled social drinking as opposed to total abstinence. Thus, in the 1960s, the term *controlled drinking* referred to a treatment outcome as opposed to a specific behavioral treatment strategy. With the landmark studies of Mark and Linda Sobell in the 1970s, behavioral researchers actively pursued specific therapeutic strategies to facilitate a goal of moderate alcohol consumption.

Historically, the term controlled drinking has been poorly defined, referring simply to nonproblematic drinking. Currently, the definition of moderate drinking as a treatment goal is based on drinking guidelines set forth by the National Institute on Alcohol Abuse and Alcoholism (NIAAA). Nonrisky drinking is that which is unlikely to lead to abuse and dependence or to cause or exacerbate alcohol-sensitive medical conditions such as hypertension, gastroesophogeal reflux disorder, and gastritis. Such drinking is defined as no more than 14 drinks a week and never more than 4 drinks on any day for men and no more than 7 drinks a week and never more than 3 drinks on any day for women and all adults over age 65. A standard drink contains about 14 grams (about 0.6 fluid ounces) of pure alcohol. In the United States, this is equivalent to12 ounces of beer, 5 ounces of wine, or 1.5 ounces of liquor.

Behavioral treatment with a goal of moderate drinking is similar to abstinence-oriented treatment in some respects, but different in others. Similar behavioral strategies for either treatment goal include motivational interviewing, coping and social skills training, refusal skills training, cognitive-behavioral treatment, marital therapy, behavioral contracting, relaxation training, community reinforcement, and relapse prevention. However, in the case of controlled-drinking clients, each technique may require alterations to accommodate a nonabstinence goal. For example, refusal skills training would focus on saying "no" to some offers of alcoholic beverages, but not all.

Relapse prevention would focus on strategies to prevent drinking above certain preset limits and would not be implemented unless the client's drinking exceeded the NIAAA daily or weekly guidelines.

In addition to behavioral techniques common to abstinence and nonabstinence goals, controlled-drinking treatment includes strategies specific to the facilitation of moderate drinking. Probably the most basic behavioral method of gaining control over a habitual behavior is self-monitoring. This procedure requires the individual to record daily alcohol consumption (based on number of standard drinks), average time for each drink, situations under which drinking occurs, emotions while drinking (e.g., relaxed, tense, angry), and urges to drink more than the recommended limit. Self-monitoring increases the client's awareness of his or her drinking patterns and provides the therapist with useful information on the functional relationships associated with controlled versus uncontrolled drinking.

Moderation training involves cue exposure, direct instruction, feedback, and modeling of controlled-drinking skills. To provide more realistic environmental cues for drinking, training often occurs in simulated bars, restaurants, or social situations. During training sessions, clients receive instructions and practice in moderate-drinking skills, including ordering mixed as opposed to straight drinks, taking small sips, taking more time between sips, and generally drinking very slowly. Feedback is provided by comments from the therapist or by videotaping sessions for postsession review and critique. Modeling of appropriate drinking skills can be provided using live or videotaped models.

Emotional cue exposure can be used for uncontrolled drinking that is triggered by negative emotional states. During simulated drinking situations, negative moods can be induced through visualization (e.g., encouraging the patient to vividly imagine a recent situation that induced anxiety or anger). After consuming the agreed-upon limit (e.g., one drink), the patient would then be instructed to pour a second drink, look at it, smell it, anticipate its taste, and then pour it out without drinking it. Repetition of this response prevention approach eventually leads to habituation and increased feelings of self-efficacy in emotional situations.

Homework assignments are typically part of moderation training. Clients are instructed to practice controlled-drinking skills at home and at social events. When possible (e.g., drinking at home), clients are told to measure drinks precisely to ensure that a standard drink is within the NIAAA guidelines. In each drinking situation, clients are instructed to set an absolute limit on the number of drinks they will consume prior to drinking. In high-risk situations that trigger uncontrolled drinking, clients may be instructed to avoid drinking altogether. During treatment sessions, the therapist and client can review these assignments and discuss strategies to overcome obstacles to progress.

Recently, the opiate antagonist naltrexone has been used as an adjunctive treatment in behaviorally oriented controlled-drinking programs. Naltrexone reduces alcohol cravings and lowers the risk of relapse to excessive and destructive drinking. The addition of naltrexone to behavioral treatment results in less craving for drinks above the recommended limit. Patients often report that naltrexone reduces the positive effects of alcohol, thus reducing their desire to consume more than one or two drinks.

RESEARCH BASIS

Unfortunately, early studies on the efficacy of controlled drinking were clouded by intense debate and controversy. Objective evaluation of outcome studies was blurred by emotionally charged reports by 12-step proponents that controlled drinking was dangerous in that it gave alcoholics a false sense of hope and encouraged further denial of their problems. This debate still continues today, although it is not as volatile and is limited mostly to the United States. Clinicians in other countries have more readily accepted moderate drinking as a routine treatment option.

Carefully documented studies evaluating abstinence-oriented treatment programs have found that about 25% of patients achieve abstinence, while, despite the total-abstinence treatment goal, 10%

become moderate drinkers. So, regardless of the initial goal of treatment, controlled drinking can be achieved by some. In addition, more than 30 randomized clinical trials of behavioral treatments with moderation as the goal show strong evidence of efficacy for controlled drinking.

While the preponderance of evidence suggests that severely dependent drinkers do better with abstinence approaches, the evidence is clear that a moderate-drinking goal is a viable option for those with less severe problems. In fact, controlled drinking has become part of the routine continuum of care in the prevention and treatment of alcohol use disorders.

RELEVANT TARGET POPULATIONS AND EXCEPTIONS

Controlled-drinking treatments appear to be most suitable for the less dependent, less chronic drinker. Clinical evidence suggests that it is unlikely that individuals showing severe alcohol problems (e.g., above a score of 29 on the Michigan Alcohol Screening Test) are able to achieve or maintain a goal of moderate drinking.

While this is the mainstream clinical opinion, proponents of the "harm reduction" model argue that given the fact that many severely dependent individuals are unable or unwilling to abstain, it is appropriate to try to minimize the harm caused by continued drinking through attempts at controlled-drinking treatments. In this perspective, abstinence is the ideal, but any incremental movement toward reduced harm should be encouraged. While this argument seems plausible, it awaits further empirical justification.

A more recent trend is the application of the controlled-drinking concept to heavy drinkers who are not alcohol dependent. This focus on so-called at-risk drinkers is based on the realization that a significant proportion of problems related to alcohol use (e.g., motor vehicle accidents and injuries, medical problems, family difficulties) occur in drinkers who are not alcohol dependent. Interventions aimed at this population typically occur outside of the traditional alcoholism treatment settings. Since the majority of the population seeks medical treatment on a yearly basis, the primary health care arena has provided a prime setting for controlled-drinking interventions. It is estimated that more than 20% of primary care patients drink at levels harmful to their health. Alcohol screening using questionnaires (e.g., the CAGE and the Alcohol Use Disorders Identification Test) together with alcohol biomarkers (e.g., gamma gluamyltransferase, or GGT, and carbohydrate-resistant transferring, or CDT) have proven to be extremely useful in identifying at-risk drinkers in these settings. More important, brief behavioral interventions, such as motivational interviewing by primary care practitioners, can promote significant reductions in drinking levels in problem drinkers. Most studies have found reductions in consumption and binge drinking of up to 30% over 12 months.

Because of the potential for alcohol-related medical complications, complete abstinence should be the only goal for pregnant women or those trying to conceive, individuals with a contraindicated medication or medical condition, and those with a history of blackouts.

COMPLICATIONS

Comorbid psychiatric conditions such as depression, social anxiety, and posttraumatic stress disorder may complicate treatment and require further evaluation or concomitant psychiatric care. In addition, drug and alcohol abuse often occur together and would lessen the likelihood that a goal of controlled drinking would be successful.

Individuals who have experienced repeated unsuccessful attempts to develop a moderate-drinking pattern may simply be avoiding the necessary choice of abstinence. In all cases, the clinician must carefully consider the possibility that some individuals (particularly severely dependent drinkers) may be denying the inevitability of an abstinence-oriented treatment.

Another treatment complication is related to the possible negative influence of friends and family on the individual's choice to enter into a controlled-drinking program. Friends who strongly believe in the 12-step, disease model of alcoholism may attempt to convince the patient that moderation training is ineffective and dangerous, thereby sabotaging motivation and treatment compliance.

CASE ILLUSTRATION

"Mary" was a 62-year-old widow who was mildly alcohol dependent. While she had been a regular social drinker (about two drinks a day) when her husband was alive, since his death 2 years ago, her drinking had increased. The extent of her alcohol problem surfaced when her primary care physician became concerned about her high blood pressure. Mary had been diagnosed with hypertension 9 months previously, and despite various trials of pharmacological agents, her blood pressure remained uncontrolled. In searching for an explanation, her physician questioned her about her alcohol consumption. Mary admitted to drinking two glasses of wine each afternoon, two cocktails prior to dinner, and a drink of Scotch prior to bedtime to help her sleep. Concerned about the effects of alcohol on her blood pressure, her physician referred her for help in reducing drinking.

During the intake interview, Mary was diagnostically categorized as exhibiting alcohol abuse but not dependence. Apparently, her drinking was exacerbating her uncontrolled hypertension, which was probably related to two falls at home and a recent minor automobile accident. However, she showed no signs of tolerance, withdrawal, or severe dependence. Because of this mild alcohol dependence and her stated desire to reduce consumption rather than abstain totally, a treatment goal of moderate drinking was established.

To obtain a functional behavioral analysis, Mary was asked to keep a written journal of her drinking for a week (including number and types of drinks consumed, amount of each drink, date and time of each drink, cravings for alcohol, and situations, feelings, and thoughts prior to and after drinking). It was apparent that Mary was drinking to excess mostly on days during which she felt bored, lonely, and depressed (a Beck Depression Inventory indicated mild to moderate depression). She rarely consumed more than one drink when she was with family or friends. Also, when drinking alone at home, Mary had little awareness about the size of a standard drink. In fact, as a result of self-monitoring, she soon discovered that her average drink of Scotch and water (poured without measuring) contained approximately 3 ounces of liquor instead of the standard drink size of 1.5 ounces.

Mary agreed to a drinking goal of no more than one drink a day. Treatment involved continued self-monitoring along with instructions, videotaped modeling, and feedback on moderate-drinking skills. She was instructed to always use a shot glass to ensure that her drinks contained no more than 1.5 ounces, take very small sips, and take more time between sips. Drinking was restricted to social situations or prior to dinner at home (but never when alone in the afternoon or prior to bedtime). Her self-monitoring records were evaluated each week, and appropriate feedback and reinforcement were provided.

Treatment also included strategies to help Mary cope with her loneliness and depression. Cognitive-behavioral therapy was used to assist Mary in overcoming her self-doubts and negative self-talk about her ability to cope with life without her husband. Actually, Mary had been a very active and competent woman throughout her life, and it was only since the death of her husband that she had become reclusive. Homework assignments revolved around her becoming more involved in enjoyable activities, especially those that brought her into contact with others. She joined a book discussion club, arranged for travel with friends, and volunteered at the local animal shelter.

Without alcohol before bedtime, Mary experienced difficulty falling asleep. A combination of relaxation training and guided imagery helped her to gradually overcome this problem without the need of a nightcap.

Mary's drinking was successfully reduced to an average of one drink a day. Occasionally, she had two glasses of wine when dining with friends, but this was rare. Her depression gradually lifted, and within 3 months after beginning treatment, her blood pressure was within normal limits.

—*Peter M. Miller*

See also: *Behavioral Medicine (Vol. I); Behavioral Treatment of the Addictions (Vol. I); Self-Control (Vol. I)*

Suggested Readings

Marlatt, G. A., Larimer, M. E., Baer, J. S., & Quigley, L. A. (1993). Harm reduction for alcohol problems: Moving beyond the controlled drinking controversy. *Behavior Therapy, 24,* 461–504.

Miller, W. R., Leckman, A. L., Delaney, H. D., & Tinkcom, M. (1992) Long-term follow-up of behavioral self-control training. *Journal of Studies on Alcohol, 53,* 249–261.

National Institute on Alcohol Abuse and Alcoholism. (2003). *Helping patients with alcohol problems* (NIH Publication No. 03-3769). Bethesda, MD: National Institute on Alcohol Abuse and Alcoholism.

Rosenberg, H. (1993). Prediction of controlled drinking by alcoholics and problem drinkers. *Psychological Bulletin, 113,* 129–139.

Rubio, G., Manzanares, J., Lopez-Munoz F., Alamo, C., Ponce, G., Jimenez-Arriero, et al. (2002). Naltrexone improves outcome of a controlled drinking program. *Journal of Substance Abuse Treatment, 23,* 361–366.

Sobell, M. B., & Sobell, L. C. (1978). *Behavioral treatment of alcohol problems: Individualized therapy and controlled drinking.* New York: Plenum Press.

Sobell, M. B., & Sobell, L. C. (1995). Controlled drinking after 25 years: How important was the great debate? *Addiction, 90,* 1149–1153.

COPING WITH DEPRESSION

DESCRIPTION OF THE STRATEGY

The World Health Organization cites unipolar depression as the most prevalent psychiatric condition currently in the world and predicts that it will become the second most significant cause of global psychiatric disease by 2020. Similar findings have been reported within American society, in that unipolar depression affects between 3% and 13% of Americans annually. It is estimated that between 20% and 55% of American adults will experience a lifetime incident of depression.

The Coping With Depression (CWD) course is based on social learning theory. Lewinsohn was the first to develop the behavioral treatment of depression, and the Coping With Depression course was the product of these efforts. The CWD course has been used to treat various populations and achieved consistent positive outcome in alleviating symptoms of depression.

Depression is assumed to occur when a psychosocial stressor disrupts important behavioral patterns of the individual. This disruption causes a reduction in the rate of response-contingent positive reinforcement. Positive reinforcement is assumed to be related to the availability of reinforcing events in the person's environment, the person's skills (interpersonal and cognitive), and to the person's ability to reverse the effects of the stressor. When the individual fails to reverse the negative balance of reinforcement, an increased self-awareness follows, which can lead to a negative self-evaluation and subsequent depressive state.

Another issue in the etiology of depressive symptoms is the fact that patients who suffer from depression tend to lack social skills, especially during the depressive episode. In addition, according to this model, the patient's familial environment and social networks may inadvertently reinforce depressive behavior by providing increased attention to negative behaviors, such as depressive talk and suicidal behaviors, and thus "maintain" the "depressed" behaviors.

An important part of the behavioral treatment of depression stems from the fact that depressed patients have low rates of engagement in pleasant activities. The *DSM-IV* recognizes this by listing a reduction in pleasurable activities as one of two primary criteria for a diagnosis of depression. Since mood covaries with rates of pleasant and aversive activities, mood improves with increases in pleasant activities and/or a reduction of aversive activities.

The CWD course is a psychoeducational intervention that can be delivered individually or in small groups and has become the most comprehensive behavioral treatment of depression. It focuses on teaching patients techniques and strategies through the extensive use of participant workbooks, a therapist manual, and homework assignments to learn new ways to cope with their depression. Specifically, the CWD course involves helping patients increase the frequency and quality of their engagement in pleasant activities and reduce the frequency of aversive events. The CWD course takes a "smorgasbord" approach to training patients in skills that are most directly related to their depression. The specific skills taught include relaxation, increasing pleasant activities, changing depressogenic cognitions, and social skills.

Treatment sessions are highly structured and use the text *Control Your Depression*, which was designed as a self-help manual. Reading assignments from this text are an integral component of the treatment approach. Studies have shown that clients do well with manuals (i.e., bibliotherapy) but many need the social facilitation and structure provided by the Coping With Depression course. A therapist manual provides session scripts, exercises (homework), and guidelines for the course of treatment. A *Participant Workbook for the Coping With Depression Course* provides the patient with the session syllabi and forms necessary to track and implement various aspects of treatment.

The CWD course is designed to be conducted over twelve 2-hour sessions during an 8-week period. The sessions are held twice weekly for the first 4 weeks and once per week thereafter. Ideally, groups are comprised of 6 to 10 individuals, with one psychotherapist conducting each of the sessions. One- and 6-month "booster sessions" are held to share treatment gains and prevent relapse. Because relapse is common in depression, booster sessions are an integral part of the approach and are incorporated into the patient's initial treatment plan.

RELEVANT TARGET POPULATIONS AND EXCEPTIONS

The CWD course was originally designed to be used to ameliorate depressive symptoms in adults. It has been adapted for use with adolescents, geriatric patients, in prevention efforts, as an adjunct in smoking reduction, with alcoholics, and with delinquent youth.

RESEARCH BASIS

Recent Studies

In a recent meta-analysis of 20 studies (727 participants) conducted between 1984 and 1996, the CWD course was compared with other approaches to treating depression. Of 10 experimental studies that included a control group, the mean effect size ($M_1 - M_2/SD_{pooled}$) of the CWD condition was 0.65, a relatively large effect size. In the other 10 studies where a control group was not used, the effect size (pre- to posttest) was calculated and resulted in a large mean effect size (1.21). In these 20 studies, the large effect sizes were maintained at 1-month, 6-month, 1-year, and 2-year follow-ups.

Another recent study used the CWD course in the treatment of 92 adults with unipolar depression. Multimodal assessment was conducted at pre- and posttreatment, and change was statistically significant at the .0001 level. These effects were maintained at 1-, 6-, 12-, 18-, and 24-month follow-ups. The researchers concluded that the CWD course significantly increased mood, decreased hopelessness, increased social adjustment, and reduced anxiety, which often accompanies depression. This study is of particular interest: The participants were diagnosed with "double depression," a condition that has historically been less responsive to treatment.

The CWD course was compared with a wait-list control group in a multisite study involving 15 prevention departments of community mental health institutions. This study included 143 participants, of whom 43% were diagnosed with current major depressive disorder (MDD) and 80% had a lifetime diagnosis of MDD. The posttest results indicated that the CWD group's depression scores were 50% less than those of the control group. As a result of this project, the CWD course for adults and the CWD for elderly are now available to approximately 80% of the Dutch population.

The CWD course has also been compared to pharmacologic intervention and was shown to be a more efficacious treatment over the long term. For instance, two multisite studies compared the CWD course and amitriptyline, a tricyclic antidepressant (TCA), alone or in combination. The first study included 191 participants, of whom 80% had a diagnosis of major depressive disorder and the remaining 20% had a diagnosis of dysthymic disorder. The participants included 116 participants (71 females) who were treated as outpatients and 75 (49 females) who were treated as psychiatric inpatients. These authors reported that the CWD treatment, when applied alone, was as effective as the TCA applied alone. However, at 1-year follow-up, the CWD course was statistically as effective as the CWD plus the amitriptyline, which were both statistically more effective than the amitriptyline alone.

In a second multisite randomized study, researchers compared the treatment effects of amitriptyline alone or a combination with the CWD course. This multisite study included 155 participants, of whom 75 received the CWD treatment plus amitriptyline (CWD + TCA) and 80 received the amitriptyline alone. It was reported that at posttreatment, the CWD + TCA treatment group yielded 25%-better results in the outpatient sample and a 27%-better result in the inpatient sample on the Beck Depression Inventory and the Hamilton Depression Rating Scale. At 1-year follow up, however, the CWD + TCA was almost twice as effective as TCA alone.

Using Manualized Treatment in Prevention Efforts

The efficacy of using the manualized CWD course in the treatment of depression has been well established. It is therefore logical to apply the principles of CWD in the area of preventing depression. The CWD course has been adapted to treat postpartum depression in women who have recently given birth, by using brief telephonic counseling as a modality of treatment. This approach may be applicable to patients who are too busy or otherwise find it difficult to present to a mental health clinic. Aspects of the CWD could be incorporated into curricula in primary and secondary schools. Efforts should also focus on preventing depression in children of mothers who suffer from depression. Such children are known to be at high risk for depression.

The effectiveness of using the CWD course to prevent depression or relapse in a general outpatient population has also been evaluated. Using a matched-pair design, patients who received the CWD course were 3 times less likely to become depressed during the

6-month pre- to posttreatment period. CWD patients were also less likely to become depressed even when compared with patients who had received antidepressant medication. It was concluded that using the CWD course could be instrumental in the clinical aftercare of depressed patients within the psychiatric outpatient setting.

COMPLICATIONS

There are subsets of medical patients for whom depression is a problem and for whom the CWD course could be an integral part of treatment, for example, patients who present with special needs such as cardiovascular aneurysms or physical limitations (i.e., wheelchair bound, blind, deaf). These patients are presented with special barriers to treatment that must be addressed, and treatment of the depression may have a positive impact on the course of their physical disease.

Modifications to the CWD course can make it suitable for use with ethnic populations. For example, it has been adapted for use with Puerto Rican Americans as well as Chinese Americans, with great success. Work is currently in progress for use with Haitian Americans.

The CWD course should be considered a frontline option and a treatment of choice for unipolar depression and can be used in primary prevention efforts. It can also be used more extensively with medical patients as well as with ethnic minority groups.

CASE ILLUSTRATION

"Jane" was 36-year-old, Caucasian, never married, college educated, and employed as a professional businessperson. At intake with the therapist of record, Jane reported several psychosocial stressors, which included the dissolution of a 10-year relationship. The breakup of this relationship resulted in Jane feeling rejected, lonely, and very despondent over the future.

At the intake appointment, Jane scored a 22 on the Depression–Arkansas (D-Ark) scale, which indicated a "severe" level of depression. She was feeling hopeless over her future and her ability to manage her emotional state; however, she was not suicidal. The manner in which the relationship breakup occurred made her feel rejected.

Treatment involved the Coping With Depression course (CWD), using the *Control Your Depression* text and the *Participant Workbook for the Coping With Depression Course*. During the course of treatment, Jane completed the Pleasant Events Schedule that revealed that she was avoiding many activities that she had previously enjoyed and was not attempting to initiate new activities. Thus, one of Jane's primary presenting symptoms (isolation, withdrawal) was directly related to the low level of positive reinforcement from the environment.

According to the treatment protocol, Jane completed the Daily Tally of Positive and Negative Thoughts, which indicated that she had an average of 50 negative thoughts per day, of which the majority were self-depreciating types of thoughts. Jane stated that many of her negative thoughts had begun in early childhood. Her mother and father withheld positive reinforcement of her accomplishments and also withheld emotional support. These experiences developed into a sense of failure, with Jane questioning her ability to handle challenging life situations. Using the traditional behavioral A-B-C model, Jane was faced with a challenging life event such as the breakup of her long-term relationship (A, activating event). This prompted her to believe that she had a characterological fault (B, belief), which resulted in her feeling badly that she had somehow caused the event. The emotional consequence (C) was lowered self-esteem and ultimately led to depressive symptoms for her.

During the course of treatment, Jane adhered to the treatment regimen (e.g., attending treatment sessions, completing reading and homework assignments). Posttreatment assessment indicated that Jane scored a 3 on the D-Ark, which indicated a minimum level of depressive symptoms. This score was down from a pretreatment score of 22. She also learned to challenge the negative cognitions and to replace these with more positive affirmations.

At 3-month follow-up, Jane reported that had several challenging life situations, but that she "was handling them fairly well." Her D-Ark score was a 4, which indicated minimal severity and was maintained from posttreatment assessment.

—*Terry M McClanahan, David O. Antonuccio, and Peter M. Lewinsohn*

See also: Beck, Aaron T. (Vol. I); Cognitive Behavior Therapy (Vol. I); Cognitive Restructuring (Vol. I)

Suggested Readings

American Psychiatric Association. (1994). *Diagnostic and statistical manual of mental disorders* (4th ed.). Washington, DC: American Psychiatric Association.

Bandura, A. (1977). *Social learning theory.* Englewood Cliffs, NJ: Prentice Hall.

Brown, R. A., Kahler, C. W., Niaura, R., Abrams, D. B., Sales, S. D., Ramsey, S. E., et al. (2001). Cognitive-behavioral treatment for depression in smoking cessation. *Journal of Consulting and Clinical Psychology, 69,* 471–480.

Brown, M. A., & Lewinsohn, P. M. (1984). *Participant workbook for the Coping With Depression Course.* Eugene, OR: Castalia.

Brown, R. A., & Ramsey, S. E. (in press). Addressing comorbid depressive symptomatology in alcohol treatment. *Professional Psychology: Research and Practice.*

Clarke, G. N., Hawkins, W., Murphy, M., Sheeber, L. B., Lewinsohn, P. M., & Seeley, J. J. (1995). Targeted prevention of unipolar depressive disorder in an at-risk sample of high school adolescents: A randomized trial of a group cognitive intervention. *Journal of the American Academy of Child and Adolescent Psychiatry, 34*(3), 312–321.

Cuijpers, P. (1998). A psychoeducational approach to the treatment of depression: A meta-analysis of Lewinsohn's "Coping With Depression" course. *Behavior Therapy, 29,* 521–533.

Hollon, S. D., Muñoz, R. F., Barlow, D. H., Beardslee, M. D., Bell, C. C., Bernal, G., et al. (2002). Psychosocial intervention development for the prevention and treatment of depression: Promoting innovation and increasing awareness. *Biological Psychiatry, 52,* 610–630.

Lewinsohn, P. M., Antonuccio, D. O., Steinmetz-Breckenridge, J. L., & Teri, L. (1984). *The Coping With Depression course: A psychoeducational intervention for unipolar depression.* Eugene, OR: Castalia.

Lewinsohn, P. M., Clarke, G. N., Rohde, P., Hops, H., & Seeley, J. R. (1996). A course in coping: A cognitive-behavioral approach to the treatment of adolescent depression. In E. D. Hibbs & P. S. Jensen (Eds.), *Psychosocial treatments for child and adolescent disorders: Empirically based strategies for clinical practice.* Washington, DC: American Psychological Association.

Lewinsohn, P. M., Muñoz, R. F., Youngren, M. A., & Zeiss, A. M. (1992). *Control your depression* (2nd ed.). Englewood Cliffs, NJ: Prentice Hall.

Muñoz, R. F., Ying, Y. W., Bernal, G., Perez-Stable, E. J., Sorensen, J. L., & Hargreaves, W. A. (1995). Prevention of depression with primary care patients: A randomized controlled trial. *American Journal of Community Psychology, 23*(2), 199–222.

Rossello, J., & Bernal, G. (1996). Adapting cognitive-behavioral and interpersonal treatments for depressed Puerto Rican adolescents. In E. Hibbs & P. S. Jensen (Eds.), *Psychosocial treatments for child and adolescent disorders* (pp. 157–185). Washington, DC: American Psychological Association.

Rossello, J., & Bernal, G. (1998). Treatment of depression in Puerto Rican adolescents. *Journal of Consulting and Clinical Psychology, 67,* 734–745.

Rotter, J. B. (1954). *Social learning and clinical psychology.* Englewood Cliffs, NJ: Prentice Hall.

COVERANT CONTROL

DESCRIPTION OF THE STRATEGY

The word *coverant* is a contraction of covert operant. Thus, it is an internal response that is reinforced (positively or negatively), punished, extinguished, or modeled. However, because the operants are strictly internal (and therefore accessible only by the individual), the consequences must likewise be administered internally. The therapist acts only as an instructor, not as the consequential agent.

There are several types of covert control procedures. Four (covert extinction, covert response cost, thought-stopping, and covert sensitization) decrease frequency of undesirable behavior. Two (covert positive reinforcement and covert negative reinforcement) increase frequency of positive behavior. Covert modeling can be used to either increase or decrease the frequency of a behavior. In using any of these procedures, repetition is very important. People seldom, if ever, learn new thoughts or behaviors after one intervention.

Covert Extinction. The client is instructed to imagine performing an undesirable behavior, called the *target behavior,* and then not being reinforced for that behavior. For example, a client who is unduly forthright would be instructed to imagine herself approaching people too aggressively and being ignored or avoided.

Covert Response Cost. This is similar to covert extinction, but here, clients are asked to imagine that they have no additional reinforcer other than the one maintaining the response. There is a cost because other responses might have provided additional reinforcement. Thus, the aggressive client above would have no way of obtaining the attention she wants and needs.

Thought-Stopping. This was once a familiar technique in the behavior therapist's armamentarium. When the client thinks the undesirable thought or behavior, he is instructed to shout "Stop!" (preferably silently, although occasionally out loud). The client is then instructed to breathe deeply, exhale, and relax. Finally, he is asked to think of a pleasant scene as a reward for terminating the undesirable thought. Sometimes, snapping a rubber band on one's wrist is used rather than the "Stop!" command. This can be useful for clients who ruminate constantly and are disturbed by it.

Covert Sensitization. This is perhaps the best known of the coverant control methods. It is a procedure that pairs an undesirable behavior with an aversive imagery scene. Once the undesirable behavior is reduced or eliminated, so is the aversive image. For example, a client who wishes to stop smoking would be instructed to visualize (in very graphic detail) how sick he becomes when reaching for a cigarette, taking it out of the pack, and putting it in his mouth. As he turns away from the cigarette, he is instructed to notice how much better he feels. Clients who are good at imagery might become quite sick as a result! Theoretically, both classical conditioning and escape conditioning are involved.

Covert Positive Reinforcement. In this procedure, the client is asked to imagine performing a positive target behavior and then to imagine a pleasant scene. For example, a client who has a fear of driving may be asked to imagine herself sitting in a car and driving away, then imagine a pleasant day at the beach. The latter acts as a positive reinforcer for the former.

Covert Negative Reinforcement. In this procedure, the client is asked to imagine an unpleasant aversive situation, then terminate this image and immediately imagine a response to be increased in frequency. For example, a client may be asked to imagine himself arguing with his boss (presumably an aversive event) and to switch immediately to imagining himself being appropriately assertive toward his boss or leaving the situation entirely. Termination of the first image is reinforced by the image of the second.

Covert Modeling. This procedure uses the considerable research conducted by Albert Bandura and his colleagues. The client is asked to imagine a model performing the target behavior and then to imagine this model obtaining either a reinforcing (to increase the probability of the behavior) or a punishing (to decrease the probability of the behavior) consequence. For example, a female client may be asked to imagine a woman model becoming angry at her husband, only to have the husband walk out on her (presumably a punishing consequence). The same client may be asked to imagine the same model acting appropriately assertively toward her husband and the husband engaging her verbally (a reinforcing consequence).

RESEARCH BASIS

A considerable amount of research has been conducted on the effectiveness of various coverant control methods, although not since approximately the mid-1980s. Of these methods, covert sensitization has been investigated the most. The research summarized from the 1970s and early 1980s documented that covert positive reinforcement and (to a lesser extent) covert sensitization were both effective. For example, coverant control was found to be effective in increasing the rate of positive self-evaluations, reducing neurotic depression, and reducing other behavioral problems. But it has been difficult to rule out the possibility of the effects of other causal variables. Joseph Cautela's original theoretical explanations for the results observed appear in retrospect to be rather suspect. Coverant control is at least somewhat effective, but the mechanism of change is not always clear.

RELEVANT TARGET POPULATIONS AND EXCEPTIONS

Coverant control methods are very flexible and can be used with almost anyone desiring greater self-control. However, because the reinforcing consequences must be self-applied, it is important that the client be motivated to change. Thus, coverant control methods may not be appropriate for clients who are referred for therapy by others. In addition, clients who possess significant emotional, mental, or behavioral deficits may lack the requisite ability to concentrate and focus on imagery. People also differ in the degree to which they find imagery work comfortable and possible, and it should not be used with those who do not find it congenial. An assessment of clients' ability to construct involving mental images should be conducted prior to its use.

COMPLICATIONS

Because covert control is self-administered and self-directed, complications are likely to be few. The extreme negative images often created in covert sensitization, however, can be quite distressing to some clients, and those with a high ability to create images may become physically sick. The use of negative images should be monitored carefully and be approved in advance by clients as part of informed consent. Use of positive images is not likely to be risky.

—*E. Thomas Dowd*

See also: Covert Positive Reinforcement (Vol. I); Covert Rehearsal (Vol. I); Covert Sensitization (Vol. I)

Suggested Readings

Bandura, A. (1969). *Principles of behavior modification.* New York: Holt, Rinehart & Winston.

Cautela, J. R., & Kearney, A. J. (1993). *Covert conditioning casebook.* Pacific Grove, CA: Brooks/Cole.

Thoresen, C. E., & Mahoney, M. J. (1974). *Behavioral self-control.* New York: Holt, Rinehart & Winston.

COVERT POSITIVE REINFORCEMENT

DESCRIPTION OF THE STRATEGY

Covert positive reinforcement is an imagery-based procedure used to increase the frequency of both covert and overt behavior. In using covert positive reinforcement, the client imagines his or her performance of the targeted behavior in its typical context, and he or she also imagines the reinforcer, which follows it. The assumption is that the reinforcer functions to strengthen the targeted behavior and increase its frequency in the context described in the "scene."

The first step in implementing this procedure is to ascertain treatment goals, problems interfering with attainment of treatment goals, and behaviors that must be changed to achieve these goals. This is done through a collaborative discussion between the therapist and client. Each element of the process is described as clearly as possible in operational terms.

The second step is to determine the items that might serve as "reinforcers," that is, things that provide some pleasure to the client and function to increase any behavior upon which they may be contingent. These items may be identified by means of an interview,

self-report questionnaires, direct observation, or queries to family and friends. Reinforcers may be tangible (e.g., a glass of wine), intangible (e.g., looking deeply into a lover's eyes and feeling a warm glow, or receiving a compliment after skillfully performing a task), imagerial (e.g., a visualization of standing at the top of a mountain and looking over a scenic view), real, or fantasized.

The third step involves determination of the client's ability to imagine the events described. Thus, the therapist must describe the situational context in which the performance of the targeted behavior is required in a great deal of detail, using as many different sensory stimuli as possible. For example, the situation may be one in which the client is fearful or angry or shy or tempted to do something inappropriate. The targeted behavior may involve the client coping with the fear, calming down, asserting himself or herself, or resisting the temptation. Once the client imagines both the situation and the targeted behavior, he or she also imagines the reinforcer (e.g., making the winning touchdown in a championship football game and having the team hoist the client on their shoulders amid loud cheering.)

The covert positive reinforcement procedure may be employed both for a single response (e.g., a client is reinforced for speaking assertively when his or her rights have been violated) or in a sequential pattern leading up to a desired behavior (e.g., taking a difficult test, being in a situation where the client experiences anxiety on days leading up to the exam, the day of the exam, walking over to the place where the exam will be given, being confronted with the test, struggling with answers to certain questions, handing in the exam, seeing other students finish first, and so forth).

The client's ability to produce the images and experience the scenes in appropriate detail and with appropriate emotion is critical. To assess the client's ability, the therapist may ask the client to rate the scene for its clarity, duration, time to production, and degree of pleasure or displeasure associated with it. The therapist may also ask the client to narrate the scene aloud to get an idea of the detail contained in it. The client is encouraged to try to imagine that he or she is actually experiencing the scene described, not just to picture oneself as a performer in a movie. To achieve the maximum effectiveness, the client strives to imagine the reinforcer within 5 seconds of imagining the targeted behavior.

The therapist and client alternate scene presentations, using a chaining sequence that gradually increases the level of the behavioral requirements by difficulty and complexity. The therapist asks the client to practice the scenes used in the therapy sessions two or three times a day, 10 trials each time. In the beginning of treatment, the therapist presents the reinforcer on a continuous schedule but later presents it only intermittently.

The first published case study in which covert positive reinforcement was described as a treatment intervention was published by Wisocki in 1970. The client was a 27-year-old married woman with two children. Among a series of serious problems, she was especially concerned about her excessively slow performance of household tasks. She spent hours folding clothes, making beds, and putting groceries away. If any family member used the dishes to eat or unfolded clothes to wear or made wrinkles in the bed sheets, she became extremely disturbed. She had been diagnosed with both obsessive-compulsive disorder and schizophrenia.

The problem for which positive covert reinforcement was used was the client's habit of folding clothes several times until they were free of wrinkles. This activity consumed 5 to 10 minutes for each item of clothing, including underwear, sheets, towels, and so on. The client spent an equivalent amount of time putting the item in a drawer, trying to keep it from wrinkling again.

After selecting items to be used as reinforcers, the therapist asked the client to imagine herself in situations in which she refrained from performing the obsessive-compulsive behaviors and in which she made both overt and covert responses that interfered with the obsessive-compulsive behavior. When the designated situation was imagined, the client signaled the therapist, who then spoke the word "reinforcement." This was the cue for the client to imagine one of the predetermined reinforcing items. For example, one scene was the following:

Relax and imagine that you are in the laundry room, standing in front of the day's laundry. You think to yourself that you'll really have to hurry folding these clothes so that you can go shopping with a friend (reinforcement). You impatiently shove the clothes to one side (reinforcement). You fold your daughter's pajamas and quickly put them aside (reinforcement). You take the next item, fold it quickly, and it's a little wrinkled, but you put it on top of other things (reinforcement).

The client was also asked to imagine and reinforce thoughts such as, "I don't care if something is wrinkled; it doesn't matter"; "It's silly to spend so much time folding clothes." Each of the scenes described above are assigned for practice 20 times each day at home.

RESEARCH BASIS

Early reviews of the covert positive reinforcement intervention cautiously concluded that the procedure was generally superior or equal to other interventions used as comparison treatment conditions. A number of concerns were expressed, however, about the quality of the research designs used in the studies. In particular, the studies contained small numbers of participants; they were often lacking in control conditions, such as uniformity in the training of the experimenters, equivalency of the alternate treatment interventions, standardization of the instructions and treatment presentation, and the use of expectancy and/or placebo conditions; and the researchers often relied on self-report or nonvalidated dependent measures to indicate behavioral change. The bulk of the research on covert positive reinforcement was conducted in the 1970s, when the concept of using imagery as a therapeutic venue was innovative and exciting. As is true with any new idea, after it has been touted and preliminarily examined, scientific rigor is required to justify the claims made by the early investigators. This procedure has yet to be exposed to that rigor. Yet it continues to be used successfully in clinical settings for a large range of psychological problems.

RELEVANT TARGET POPULATIONS AND EXCEPTIONS

Covert positive reinforcement has been used with children, adults, and senior clients experiencing a wide range of psychological difficulties. It has also been used with children with autism and mental retardation. In the published literature about this procedure, clinical problems targeted for intervention have included test anxiety, inappropriate social behaviors, disruptive behaviors, weight reduction, fear, and poor self-concept. There were also several studies in which poor attitudes toward particular populations, such as older adults, those with physical handicaps, and those with mental retardation, were modified in a more positive direction by means of the covert positive reinforcement intervention. Finally, in an additional group of studies, investigators tested efficacy of covert positive reinforcement on a variety of isolated behaviors, including yawning, eye contact, circle size estimation, verbal behavior, and tolerance for pain. They reported a differential increase in the behaviors using the reinforcement procedure in comparison with other procedures. Thus, it appears that covert positive reinforcement is relevant for a wide range of problems and populations. No exceptions have been noted.

COMPLICATIONS

As with any imagery-based procedure, it is important when using covert positive reinforcement that the client be actively involved in experiencing the scenes described. As with an in vivo exposure, the contextual scene in which the problem occurs should elicit the emotional response demanded by the event. Likewise, the reinforcing image should be positive, something desired by the client, and effective in producing a change in the required behavior. Some clients have difficulty with this requirement and require more practice in imagery than others. Some never become skilled at visualizing a scene. For these clients, it is better to use in vivo procedures, such as contingency contracting or a token system of reward.

Another problem lies within the scene itself. The scene described to a client must remain intact, just as the therapist designed it, because success with the procedure depends on the way the elements of the scene are arranged. That is, the contextual scene must be visualized clearly as it occurs in a typical life event, the behavior to be increased or strengthened must be visualized in an exact way, and the reinforcer must be visualized within 5 seconds after the targeted behavior is imagined. The overall time for the scene presentation varies with its complexity and the number of different sensory elements involved in the description, but the timing is important. Sometimes clients try to vary the scene elements, and that process could interfere with the success of the procedure.

Anxious clients who are taught covert positive reinforcement to counteract their anxious responses may require more work with the scenes than others. If the client experiences a particularly high level of anxiety when he or she visualizes a contextual scene and his or her response to a situation, it may be necessary to divide the scene into smaller parts than usual and require the client to obtain reinforcers for more actions

that approximate the targeted event. For example, if one has a goal of delivering a speech to 500 people and is anxious about it, scenes will be devised in which reinforcement will occur to many more elements than simply delivering the speech itself. A client will be asked to reinforce himself or herself for thinking calmly about the speech; writing it out carefully; practicing before an audience of various sizes, from a few people to larger numbers of people; and making positive self-statements about the quality of his or her work and ability to do the job. It is also possible that the covert positive reinforcement intervention will contain scenes in which the client makes a mistake with the speech, stumbles over words, or sees someone walk out of the room, all the time making a positive self-coping statement designed to reduce anxiety, which will be reinforced with a selected image.

While the covert positive reinforcement intervention has been used successfully with populations of varied ages, in some cases, the intervention must be adapted. For adolescents with autism, clinical experience has demonstrated a need to shorten the sessions to which a client is exposed, require more frequent sessions, simplify the language used to construct the scenes, and engage in greater probing of the details of the scenes. Many of these same modifications must be made when the client is an older adult. In addition, the scenes may require greater detail to engage the client's imagination, and more trials are needed to produce the desired effect of the procedure.

Finally, to ensure cooperation and to avoid skepticism about use of imagery procedures, it is essential that the client be instructed carefully in the rationale for their use. Occasionally, a client will argue that therapeutic work involving imagery is "not real" and he or she cannot see any benefit in "pretending" or "play acting." For these clients, the therapist reviews the various ways the symbolic presentation of information affects behavior (e.g., the visceral response to a well-written menu when one is hungry; the thought of a plane crashing that makes a person consider taking the train; the added strain and worry produced by imagining negative effects when one is contemplating a difficult task) and explains the learning theory basis underlying application of the covert positive reinforcement intervention in terms of operant conditioning.

—*Patricia A. Wisocki*

See also: Coverant Control (Vol. I); Covert Rehearsal (Vol. I); Covert Reinforcer Sampling (Vol. I)

Suggested Readings

Cautela, J. R., & Kearney, A. (1986). *The covert conditioning handbook.* New York: Springer.

Scott, D. S., & Rosenstiel, A. K. (1975). Covert positive reinforcement studies: Review, critique, and guidelines. *Psychotherapy: Theory, Research, and Practice, 12,* 374–384.

Wisocki, P. A. (1970). Treatment of obsessive-compulsive behavior by covert sensitization and covert reinforcement: A case report. *Journal of Behaviour Therapy and Experimental Psychiatry, 1,* 233–239.

Wisocki, P. A. (1973). A covert reinforcement program for the treatment of test anxiety: A brief report. *Behavior Therapy, 4,* 264–266.

Wisocki, P. A. (1973). The successful treatment of heroin addiction by covert conditioning techniques. *Journal of Behavior Therapy and Experimental Psychiatry, 4,* 55–61.

COVERT REHEARSAL

DESCRIPTION OF THE STRATEGY

The question of whether or not a person can improve his or her performance by means of mentally rehearsing that performance is one that has been studied for several decades. Known by various terms, such as mental practice, visualization, symbolic rehearsal, positive imaging, and introspective rehearsal, covert rehearsal is basically the internal practice of a behavior or sequence of behaviors in the absence of overt or physical movement, with the goal of performance enhancement. Examples of the use of this procedure include both cognitive and overt behavioral tasks. In the cognitive realm, covert rehearsal has long been used to improve memory, such as in studying for a test, preparing to deliver a speech, or trying to memorize a list of some kind. In the behavioral realm, covert rehearsal has been used, for example, to improve performance in sports and musical accomplishment and to prepare a person to communicate or socialize with other people.

Covert rehearsal involves repetition of the material to be learned, and it may be done in a number of different contexts, such as imagining the details of an event or stimulus item, being reminded of the event by an external or internal cue, or reorganizing one's thoughts about an event in a different way. The repetition may be simple, such as continual internal recitation of something one wants to retain in memory, like a list, a poem, or a phone number. Or the repetition

may be elaborate, relating the target stimulus to an image, such as oneself on the basketball court practicing a particular shot, or to a context different from the original one, or attaching it to cues, as in the development of mnemonic devices. In the process of rehearsing, different modalities may be used. These modalities may be imagerial, verbal, or musical. In a therapeutic context, the imagerial modality is used most often in covert rehearsal.

Covert rehearsal is used to either strengthen a correct response or to eliminate an incorrect response. In the first case, the response one might want to strengthen or increase may be the improvement of a sequence of behaviors necessary for smooth performance, such as in a sport or athletic event, sharpening one's debating skills, or the way one communicates to another. In all these cases, the response already exists, and the individual has a certain level of skill in the performance of the response.

In the second case, the targeted response may be an inappropriate or unwanted emotional reaction, such as in the case of anxiety, negative self-evaluation, improper sexual arousal, depressing thoughts, and so forth. In these cases, the desired response (which would counteract or overcome these emotional reactions) may not occur at all, or it may occur at a low frequency. An individual may engage in covert rehearsal in order to learn more effective and more appropriate ways of dealing with situations in which these emotional reactions occur.

The therapist uses the covert rehearsal procedure as a way to help a client identify specific areas of difficulty, practice the behaviors or strategies he or she is trying to learn, and provide "coaching" in the form of suggested alternative behaviors. Covert rehearsal is itself a skill, subject to conscious or voluntary control, whereby a person gains control over the experience.

RESEARCH BASIS

A large number of research studies make it clear that covert rehearsal has a moderate but consistent effect on performance. Covert rehearsal can lead to gains in motor performance, particularly if the task involves simple motor behaviors, but this is not a consistent finding. Tasks that are primarily cognitive, involving memory, organization, and decision making, produce greater gains than those involving physical skill. However, when covert rehearsal or mental practice is compared with physical practice, physical practice is always superior. These findings suggest that covert rehearsal is best used therapeutically in combination with physical practice. For instance, it is probably best to alternate covert rehearsals with physical practice sessions to achieve maximum performance benefits.

The effectiveness of covert rehearsal is also affected by a person's level of prior experience with the task. Those with lesser experience benefit more from covert rehearsal than physical practice when the task is primarily cognitive in nature. Those who have greater experience with a task benefit equally from covert rehearsal on both physical and cognitive tasks.

The evidence also indicates that covert rehearsal is most effective when the interval between rehearsal sessions is short rather than long. While optimum intervals are not known at this time, clinicians typically suggest that clients use covert rehearsal every day in blocks of a minimum of 20 trials for each task at least twice a day. The longer the interval between rehearsals, the smaller the effect of practice.

Finally, there appears to be an ideal amount of time to devote to covert rehearsal. Researchers estimate that a person should not spend more than 20 minutes at any one time on mentally rehearsing a task sequence. Increasing the amount of rehearsal beyond that point produces a smaller and even detrimental effect on performance. Here again, covert rehearsal must be reinforced by actual physical task performance for maximum benefits.

RELEVANT TARGET POPULATIONS AND EXCEPTIONS

Persons of any age or any occupation may successfully employ covert rehearsal as a way to improve or develop task performance, as long as one is able to produce internally the steps one must practice to achieve the goal. The procedure has been used successfully with adults of any age, with a large variety of clinical problems. It has also been used with children and adolescents to help them prepare for various events and tasks. Children and adults with developmental disabilities have benefited from the covert rehearsal procedure as well.

The most well-known use of the procedure today is in the area of sports psychology, in which covert rehearsal is regarded as an essential part of athletic training. A large number of world-renowned competitive athletes attribute at least some of their success to covert rehearsal or mental practice of the various routines they must develop in order to compete

successfully in their respective sports. These athletes compete in sports events such as golf, basketball, football, skiing, high-jumping, tennis, skating, diving, and others.

COMPLICATIONS

The covert rehearsal procedure is not appropriate for individuals who are unable to visualize the behavioral sequence required to achieve the desired goal. As has been said about other imagery-based procedures, the clients must be actively engaged in the visualization process to the extent that they are experiencing the scenes as if they are present in the scenes and not as observers. It is also important that the scene be described in accurate detail, ensuring relevance for the behavior one is practicing, and that each scene contain a number of different sensory stimuli to enhance its reality aspects.

—Patricia A. Wisocki

See also: *Covert Sensitization Conditioning (Vol. I); Self-Control (Vol. I); Self-Control Desensitization (Vol. I)*

Suggested Readings

Driskell, J., Copper, C., & Moran, A. (1994). Does mental practice enhance performance? *Journal of Applied Psychology, 79,* 481–492.

Johnson, R. E. (1980). Memory-based rehearsal. In G. Bower (Ed.), *The psychology of learning and motivation* (Vol. 14, pp. 263–307). New York: Academic Press.

COVERT REINFORCER SAMPLING

DESCRIPTION OF THE STRATEGY

Covert reinforcer sampling is an imagery-based procedure used in conjunction with other treatment interventions when the goal of therapy involves increasing number and range of reinforcing events and items available to clients. After presenting a rationale to the client about the importance of a variety of activities in a person's life and the problems that may develop from a lack of pleasurable experiences, the therapist works with the client to determine what things may be enjoyable to him or her. The interview process is facilitated by use of the Reinforcement Survey Schedule, a list of items including a variety of stimuli that the client is asked to rate according to the degree of pleasure associated with each item. The items of greatest value on this survey for the use of the covert reinforcer sampling procedure are those that involve action, such as attending musical events, sports and recreational activities, hosting parties, and so forth. Any item that the client identifies from this list as at least somewhat pleasurable may be included as an event to be sampled.

The next step is development of a series of images about those events selected for sampling. Some examples of such images include visiting with friends, calling someone on the telephone, taking a drive to the ocean or mountains, playing tennis, inviting friends to a meal at a favorite restaurant, or swimming in the sea. The technique does not involve presentation of either reinforcing or punishing consequences. The client is asked to imagine several of the agreed-upon stimulus events in as much graphic detail as possible several times a day in blocks of 10 to 15 trials each time. Each image should include as many different sensory aspects of the stimulus as possible (e.g., feeling the warmth of the summer air, hearing the surf, seeing the sun setting on the water, and tasting a cold drink). To avoid satiation of the reinforcer, it is important to vary the stimulus material.

Covert reinforcer sampling was adapted from the operant conditioning procedure of reinforcer sampling, to allow for presentation of stimuli through a symbolic rather than physical venue. Reinforcer sampling is itself a variation on the technique of *response priming,* which is any procedure that initiates early steps in a sequence of responses. Reinforcer sampling is used to begin the process of involving a client in a low-frequency activity, with the goal of encouraging the client to increase his or her participation in that activity. For example, if one wanted to increase participation in an exercise class, the client would be taken to visit the class, take in the sensory information from the class, including the music, the colorful clothes, the attention from an instructor, the taste of a healthy juice drink, and so forth. Then, the client might be encouraged to try one of the exercises, simply sit, or stand on an apparatus without exerting any effort. When all aspects of the experience are sampled, the assumption is that the client is more likely to join the exercise class.

In using covert reinforcer sampling, the client relies on self-delivered thoughts or images to rehearse participation in various activities or events. In the example of the exercise class given above, a client using the covert reinforcer sampling procedure is asked to *imagine* him or herself in the midst of an exercise class, feeling one's feet on the treadmill or bicycle, hearing the sounds of the music and the exertion efforts of the class participants, seeing the costumes of the people in the class, tasting a healthy snack, and feeling exhilarated from exercising. The client would be assigned a "homework" task to engage in that imagery exercise several times a day for a fixed period of time. Again, the assumption is that the likelihood of the client actually participating in the class is increased by the sampling of the event in imagination.

The advantages of the covert procedure are (a) it allows for a greater amount of sensory information to be incorporated into the experience, and (b) it allows for a greater number of rehearsal opportunities since it is not necessary to be physically present at the event.

RESEARCH BASIS

Reports of the therapeutic use of covert reinforcer sampling are given in three published case studies. In one case study, covert reinforcer sampling was successfully used to help a socially anxious client explore potentially reinforcing new social activities in order to enhance her range of social skills and increase the quality and quantity of social interactions. Scenes were written for this client that described her participating in a variety of activities, such as hiking in the mountains with a group of people, making conversation at work with colleagues about social events, and singing in a church choir. The client was asked to imagine these scenes several times a day over a 3-month period, after which she significantly increased her engagement in a number of social experiences that she had previously avoided.

The second case involved a 26-year-old man with an addiction to heroin, who also reported feelings of despondency, self-loathing, anger toward his parents, and regret over a painful recent breakup with a girlfriend. At the time he began therapy, he did not engage in any social contact with former friends or make any effort to establish new friendships. After several sessions in which the addictive behavior and the client's self-image were targeted, covert reinforcer sampling was used to reduce the client's fears of interacting with others. He was asked to imagine various reinforcing events, including going to the beach with a girlfriend, playing tennis, seeing a movie, and taking guitar lessons. Several weeks later, he actively participated in all of these events without anxiety.

In the third case, study covert reinforcer sampling was successfully used to reduce the effects of orofacial tardive dyskinesia experienced by a 77-year-old-woman in a nursing home. Following a baseline assessment of frequency of dyskinetic tongue-thrusting movements over nine 5-minute intervals each day for 2 weeks, three interventions were attempted: motivating instructions to try to control tongue thrusting, relaxation training, and covert reinforcer sampling. Motivating instructions had no effect on the target behavior, but both relaxation training and covert reinforcer sampling produced a substantial reduction in the tongue-thrusting incidents. During the covert reinforcer sampling phase, the greatest reduction occurred. A second baseline was taken during which no treatment was provided, and tongue thrusting increased threefold. When the covert reinforcer sampling procedure was reintroduced, frequency of tongue thrusting was reduced by half. In this case, the content of the imagery scenes served to focus the attention of the client on something other than her dyskinetic movements. Discussion about the scenes also stimulated contact with staff and allowed the client to increase the range of pleasurable activities and memories.

One empirical study was conducted in which the differential effects of covert reinforcer sampling and overt reinforcer sampling on the attitudes toward the elderly of a group of 56 college students were examined. After completing an attitude scale, students were divided into four groups. The first was a covert reinforcer sampling group of 15 participants, who were asked to imagine a scene of themselves volunteering in a nursing home, enjoying interactions with the elderly clients, and engaging in a pleasant encounter with an older adult. The scene was read aloud to them three times during each of two 30-minute sessions. The second group consisted of 12 students, who were taken to a nursing home and asked to visit with the residents during two 30-minute blocks of time. The third group of 14 students served as a placebo control; they were asked three times, in two 30-minute periods, to imagine a scene involving themselves working with adults with mental retardation. The fourth group was a no-contact control condition in which 15 students simply completed the attitude scale before and after the study was conducted.

Investigators found a significant increase in positive attitudes toward the elderly for both reinforcer sampling conditions. Those in the overt reinforcer sampling group, however, increased their attitudes significantly more than those in the covert reinforcer sampling group. Interestingly, participants who initially indicated a more negative attitude score responded significantly better to the overt reinforcer sampling procedure, while participants who held more favorable attitudes from the start responded significantly better to the covert reinforcer sampling condition.

RELEVANT TARGET POPULATIONS AND EXCEPTIONS

Covert reinforcer sampling may be used with clients who are depressed, apathetic, dysthymic, or who frequently display a negative outlook on life. Generally, such clients report a low level of reinforcing events in their lives and a lack of interest in a wide range of activities. The procedure is also useful for clients whose living arrangements lack stimulation, such as those in nursing homes, rehabilitation facilities, or institutional settings. It also may be used as a way for people to motivate themselves to perform some task or activity, such as exercising, finishing a job, making a phone call, and so forth.

COMPLICATIONS

No complications have been noted in the published literature with this procedure. It is possible, however, that for some people, the procedure may appear simplistic, and some will refuse to use it for that reason. In such cases, it is important to explain the rationale of the procedure very carefully and thoroughly, emphasizing the effect the symbolic presentation of material (e.g., reading, talking, watching TV, etc.) has on the behavior of an individual.

Those who have difficulty imaging themselves in any kind of activity may also be precluded from using covert reinforcer sampling. The value of the procedure lies in the client's ability to experience the scenes described. Some clients may overcome this obstacle by engaging in imagery practice sessions in which the scenes are described in greater detail than usual and are presented in shorter trials. For those individuals who are not able to produce the required imagery, direct exposure to stimulus events is favored.

—*Patricia A. Wisocki*

See also: *Covert Control (Vol. I); Covert Positive Reinforcement (Vol. I); Covert Rehearsal (Vol. I)*

Suggested Readings

Ayllon, T., & Azrin, N. (1968). Reinforcer sampling: A technique for increasing the behavior of mental patients. *Journal of Applied Behavioral Analysis, 1,* 13–20.

Cautela, J., & Kastenbaum, R. (1967). A reinforcement survey schedule for use in therapy, training, and research. *Psychological Reports, 20,* 1115–1130.

Cautela, J., & Kearney, A. (1986). *The covert conditioning handbook.* New York: Springer.

McInnis, T., Himelstein, H., Doty, D., & Paul, G. (1974). Modification of sampling-exposure procedures for increasing facilities utilization by chronic psychiatric patients. *Journal of Behavior Therapy and Experimental Psychiatry, 5,* 119–127.

Wisocki, P. A. (1973). The successful treatment of a heroin addict by covert conditioning techniques. *Journal of Behavior Therapy and Experimental Psychiatry, 4,* 55–61.

Wisocki, P. A. (1976). A behavioral treatment program for social inadequacy: Multiple methods for a complex problem. In J. Krumboltz & C. Thoresen (Eds.), *Counseling methods* (pp. 287–301). New York: Holt, Rinehart & Winston.

Wisocki, P. A. (1993). The treatment of an elderly woman with orofacial tardive dyskinesia by relaxation and covert reinforcer sampling. In J. R. Cautela & A. J. Kearney (Eds.), *Covert conditioning casebook* (pp. 108–115). Pacific Grove, CA: Brooks/Cole.

Wisocki, P. A., & Telch, M. (1980). Modifying attitudes toward the elderly with the use of sampling procedures. *Scandinavian Journal of Behavior Therapy, 9,* 87–96.

COVERT SENSITIZATION CONDITIONING

DESCRIPTION OF THE STRATEGY

Covert sensitization is a conditioning-based psychotherapeutic and behavioral technique designed to change sexual deviations. Behavioral techniques, such as covert sensitization, olfactory aversion, and faradic or electrical aversion therapy have as their common clinical goal reducing sexual arousal to deviant stimuli through the introduction of aversive events. Covert sensitization is a form of conditioning therapy in which a behavior and its antecedent events are paired with some aversive stimulus in order to promote avoidance of the antecedent events and thereby to decrease the undesirable behaviors. The originator of the procedure, Joseph Cautela, and a colleague defined the conditioning procedure as follows:

Covert conditioning refers to a family of behavioral therapy procedures that combine the use of imagery with the principles of operant conditioning. Covert conditioning is a process through which private events such as thoughts, images, and feelings are manipulated in accordance with principles of learning, usually operant conditioning, to bring about changes in overt behavior, covert psychological behavior (i.e., thoughts, images, feelings) and/or physiological behavior (e.g., glandular secretions).

Covert sensitization involves having a client imagine an undesirable or inappropriate sexual act, followed by imagining negative or aversive consequences. When employing covert sensitization, the negative or aversive stimulus that follows the inappropriate sexual act usually consists of an anxiety-inducing or nausea-inducing image, which may be presented verbally by the therapist or imagined by the client. The aversive scene is individually created and is specific to each client's problem behavior. Covert sensitization has frequently been successfully employed by itself as a behavioral procedure in the treatment of sexual deviance, although oftentimes the procedure is introduced in context of other behavioral management strategies to change or manage sexual deviations. It is important to note that behavioral treatment of sexually offending behavior should be introduced only after a comprehensive functional analysis of the sexual deviance in question. Covert sensitization should be used as a procedure only if the following issues are addressed: (a) implementation of therapeutic behavior change regimens in sexual offending should be individualized to each client in all sexual and general curriculum areas; (b) behavioral responses are best if they are directly measured; (c) behavior patterns should be charted; (d) there needs to be an emphasis on the direct measurement of behavior; (e) functional and descriptive definitions of behavior are the best way to approach the implementation of behavior change regimens; (f) there should be an emphasis on building new and appropriate sexual behaviors as well as general behavioral skills; and (g) a requirement needs to be in place that there will be a behavior-analytic investigation of the impact of environmental influences on each client's behavior.

Covert sensitization is a behavioral approach to changing and managing sexual deviations that is usually employed as one of three tiers of quality behavioral programming, the other two tiers being behavioral skills training, such as social skills, assertiveness skills, communication skills, daily-living skills, and other areas of behavioral skills training, as well as behavioral programming in sexual education. The ultimate goal of a behavioral treatment program, of which covert sensitization is a part, is to achieve behavioral competency skills in all three areas simultaneously and fade advances in each area to the other areas. For example, client achievements in sexual education should be integrated with attainment of appropriate sexual behavior skills for the client in specialized behavioral programming. An example is sexual skills behavior training in which the client is learning appropriate ways to express his sexuality in an interpersonal situation. Furthermore, any major sexual deviancy issues are addressed through implementation of covert sensitization strategies.

The underlying behavioral theory of covert sensitization is best thought of as a combination of classical and operant conditioning processes. The therapist works with a client to develop an aversive image, which will be paired with the precipitative events and with the image of the deviant behavior itself, according to a classical conditioning paradigm. The aversive image serves as the unconditioned stimulus (UCS). The images of the precipitative events, being continually paired with the UCS, become the conditioned stimulus (CS). Both the conditioned response (CR) and the unconditioned response (UCR) consist of a negative reaction, which may be emotional (e.g., fear), physiological (e.g., nausea), or in some other way repulsive. Once the client's deviant behavior has been classically conditioned, he should begin to actively avoid or escape the situations associated with the deviant behavior. The precipitative events, as well as the behavior itself, should elicit a negative reaction, and thus be aversive.

According to the principles of operant conditioning, and specifically of negative reinforcement, the client should behave in ways that would minimize contact with the aversive stimulus, in this case the precipitative events and the deviant behavior. If the client does pursue the deviant behavior further, ideally, the treatments will have at least reduced effectiveness of the reinforcement for that deviant behavior, which should lead to a lower frequency. It would also be possible for classical conditioning to work alone if the CR were so powerful that it rendered the person unable to engage in the deviant behavior or consisted

of a response that was incompatible with the deviant behavior. For example, if the CR were extreme anxiety or fear and the deviant behavior required an erect penis, it may be the case that the CR would preclude possibility of erection and thereby preclude occurrence of the deviant behavior.

Principles of learning and behavior have been integrated into many of the most commonly employed therapy techniques in use today with sexual deviations, or the paraphilias. Some behavioral theorists believed that these deviations were the result of accidental pairings between stimuli that naturally elicited sexual arousal and originally neutral stimuli. One researcher wrote, "Perversion rises through the accidents of our first experience. Gratification remains tied to the form and object once experienced, but this does not happen simply through the force of simultaneous association with that former experience."

Why some individuals choose to incorporate deviant stimuli into their masturbatory fantasies is also explained using a conditioning hypothesis. One factor is the stimulus value of "deviant" stimuli, which is continually strengthened through the pairing of these stimuli with ejaculation. According to a conditioning model, nondeviant stimuli or fantasies, at the same time, undergo extinction (a decrement in responding) as a result of their lack of pairing with ejaculation. Another contributing factor is a common belief held by sexual deviants that a normal sex life is not possible. This belief may develop from a number of different sources, including aversive adult heterosexual experiences or feelings of physical or sexual inadequacy. This leads one to the conclusion that the belief (a covert behavior) may play a precipitating role in the development of sexual deviations (overt behaviors) rather than being an effect of the deviation.

Sexual deviations may be best understood through a combination of classical and operant conditioning processes. Deviant or inappropriate sexual behavior begins with an accidental pairing of an "abnormal" or deviant stimulus with sexual arousal and/or ejaculation, giving this stimulus a high amount of erotic value. Thus, through a classical conditioning process, the deviant stimulus begins to elicit sexual arousal. The deviant stimulus is then incorporated into sexual fantasies during masturbation, which is reinforced by ejaculation. Thus, ejaculation serves as a reinforcer for the covert behavior of deviant fantasizing.

Assisted covert sensitization is a variation of the covert sensitization procedure in which standardized scripts are employed to guide the client though clinically relevant scenarios in which ultimately aversive imaginal consequences are presented. The difference between covert sensitization and assisted covert sensitization is that in the assisted version of the therapeutic procedure, ancillary materials, such as an audiotape or text written onto a card, are used to make the sexual situation and the negative or aversive consequences more structured. Furthermore, covert reenforcement is another variation of covert sensitization in which the client imagines that he has refused to make the inappropriate sexual response and then imagines (or is instructed to imagine) a pleasant or rewarding consequence, thereby covertly reinforcing the appropriate response.

RESEARCH BASIS

There is a wide variety of theories of normal and abnormal sexual behavior, and what is common to these theories is the assertion that at least to some extent, sexual behavior, including sexual deviancy, is learned. It is not surprising that behavioral accounts of sexual behavior advocate this, although these accounts do differ in the extent to which they emphasize classical or operant conditioning, the mediation of cognitive factors, and the role of biological variables in the genesis and maintenance of sexual deviations. Other theories that are not explicitly behaviorally based accounts also rely on the notion that at least to some extent, sexual behavior and arousal are learned. For example, anthropological and sociological accounts of sexual behavior usually claim that individuals learn the range of permissible, and even possible, sexual behavior through a variety of societal and cultural mechanisms. Developmentalists often address critical stages in the learning of sexual behavior and the correlations of age with what is being learned sexually. Feminist accounts of sexuality often emphasize that men learn through a variety of mechanisms in a patriarchal and misogynist society to become sexually aroused to women being battered, dominated, and infantilized. Psychoanalytic accounts of sexual behavior provide a place for the role of trauma to shape and influence sexual behavior. Even physiologists rarely claim that all sexual behavior is completely biologically determined and thus give a role for learning to occur within biological constraints.

In a clinical context, research data on learning and conditioning have had a central role in theories of development, maintenance, and modification of both sexual dysfunctions and sexual deviations. The paraphilias, which generally refer to sexual desires or activities that lie outside the cultural norm and under some conditions are considered mental disorders, have been hypothesized to develop due to early conditioning experiences and to be maintained by their association with orgasm from masturbation to deviant fantasies. Moreover, many behavior therapy programs aimed at modifying sexually deviant behavior use some form of counterconditioning or derivation of a conditioning-based procedure to change or significantly modify the deviant sexual arousal. Covert sensitization is one of the main conditioning-based strategies employed in this regard. Behavioral researchers have emphasized the role of learning in the development of sexual deviations.

Habituation and sensitization are thought to be the simplest and most fundamental forms of learning. These processes are regarded as simple because they involve a two-term relation between stimuli and responses (S-R), rather than a four-term relation found in classical conditioning (CS-US-UR-CR) or a three-term relation thought to be involved in operant conditioning (S^D-R-S^{r+}). Habituation and sensitization are also thought to be more fundamental than classical and operant conditioning because they occur in phylogenetically quite simple organisms and because they are often regarded to be a precondition for the occurrence of other conditioning processes. For example, emotional responding of experimental animals to the experimental chamber must habituate before operant conditioning can take place.

Repeated presentations of a constant eliciting stimulus can result in five possible patterns of responding: (1) response magnitude can systematically decrease; (2) response magnitude can systematically increase; (3) response magnitude can remain constant; (4) response magnitude can be unsystematic; and (5) response magnitude can vary between these in any complex variation. When (1) is not due to physiological fatigue or response adaptation, then habituation is said to occur. When (2) is observed, sensitization is said to occur. In covert sensitization, the learning principles are different than in the traditional sensitization procedure. Covert sensitization is analogous to the operant conditioning procedure of punishment: A negative or aversive consequence for engaging in proscribed sexual behavior is its aim, not the increase of response magnitude as is seen in traditional conditioning studies of sensitization. It is important not to confuse sensitization procedures with the clinical behavior therapy procedure called covert sensitization.

Research has demonstrated that in the treatment of sexual deviations such as pedophilia, it is not necessary to present the subject with children, but only with fantasies involving children. Presentation of covert, fantasy-based stimuli is a key to covert sensitization. Another implication of this finding is that therapists can warn their patients of the conditioning effects of orgasm on the immediately preceding fantasy. Research has also demonstrated that covert sensitization can be used to treat noncontact sexual offenses, such as exhibitionism. The subject in this study was a 37-year-old male who had been exposing himself several times per week. The treatment consisted of covert sensitization techniques, allowing the client to privately expose himself at home to his wife. Before treatment, this client had fantasized about exhibitionism approximately 60% of the time during masturbation and 30% of the time during sexual intercourse with his wife. In the covert sensitization sessions, the subject imagined exposing himself to a woman who would then angrily scold him. As another part of the aversive image, he imagined losing his wife because of the exhibitionism. Thus, the deviant fantasy was paired with two powerfully aversive images. In combination with the covert sensitization procedures, the client was allowed to expose himself two times per week at home with his wife. This private exposure was always followed by either masturbation or sexual intercourse without deviant fantasies. Also, the client was instructed not to masturbate unless his wife was present so that nondeviant sexual fantasy and behavior could be promoted. A posttreatment follow-up indicated that the subject had not publicly exposed himself for 2 years. It would seem that the treatment rendered exhibitionism appropriate, and even socially acceptable, since it occurred in the privacy of the home. Interestingly, the couple even reported that their sex life improved following treatment.

Researchers have also combined classical conditioning and operant conditioning in their covert sensitization treatment approach. Another important part of their treatment consisted of the operant reinforcement of private exposure through orgasm from masturbation or intercourse, both of which took place with the client's wife. Essentially, only the context of the exhibition behavior changed, not the behavior itself. The client learned that the behavior would be reinforced in one situation (at home with his wife), while it would either be extinguished or punished in any other situations.

RELEVANT TARGET POPULATIONS AND EXCEPTIONS

Covert sensitization and its variants are major behavioral treatments for sexual deviations and are relevant to adults experiencing inappropriate sexual urges, as part of a larger treatment regimen described above in the three-tiers analysis. Clients who have developmental disabilities or other significant difficulties with verbal comprehension would not be appropriate candidates for receiving covert sensitization.

Any behavioral intervention strategy should be conducted only after appropriate client consents have been obtained and after a thorough functional analysis of the presenting clinical issues.

COMPLICATIONS

Because covert sensitization is an aversive procedure, clients may feel anxiety, resentment, or anger, and any ancillary cognitive or emotive states should be closely monitored by the therapist. Sometimes using aversive-based behavioral techniques may result in aggressive behavior, which can be managed through basic psychoeducation on the behavioral theory that underlies covert sensitization, as well as the implementation of covert reinforcement strategies in conjunction with the use of covert sensitization procedures.

It is important to note that because covert sensitization is an aversive procedure, all prospective clients should be well-informed concerning the procedure and the potential that the client may feel anxious or resentful as a function of the therapeutic procedure. Sexual behavior should always be functionally assessed and defined for each client through referral source information, record review, direct behavioral assessment, psychometrically validated behavioral self-report measures, and when possible, psychophysiological measurement, such as penile plethysmography. Any type of therapeutic services delivered to those experiencing problems with sexual deviancy should focus on the rights of clients relative to effective, objective, and empirically validated assessment and treatment and to providing the necessary resources to assess sexual arousal and behavior.

CASE ILLUSTRATION

"Tim" was 24 years old. He was originally referred for a physiological (penile plethysmographic) evaluation by a local human service center psychologist in relation to a show-cause hearing for his failure to progress in group treatment at the human service center. This ultimately led to his termination from group therapy. The group treatment focused on psychoeducational issues relating to human sexuality, consent and victim empathy issues, appropriate and inappropriate sexual behavior, and disclosure to other members of the group. Tim chose not to participate actively in any phase of the group treatment. He had an extensive history of sexually abusive behavior. He had earlier pled guilty to a charge of sexual assault and was serving probation at the time of the initiation of therapy services.

According to police records, when he was 19 years old, Tim engaged in sexual activities with a 15-year-old male. The victim reported that he had attempted anal intercourse on approximately 15 occasions. It was reported that Tim ejaculated on a "couple" occasions, though there was no notation of anal penetration, oral sexual contact, or masturbation. The victim also reported on several of these sexual encounters that Tim gained compliance by the victim through purchasing soft drinks and that consent by the victim to sexual interactions was verbally coerced by him. Tim denied engaging in anal intercourse and verbally coercive activities and indicated that the victim engaged in sexual activities, including masturbation, in a mutual fashion.

Tim's penile responses during the course of therapy were recorded by a penile plethysmograph utilizing a Type A mercury-in-rubber penile strain gauge. During the original assessment of Tim's sexual preferences, penile tumescence was continually monitored as he listened to sexually explicit audiotapes. A total of 18 standard audio scripts were presented during the initial assessment. These were descriptions of two adult homosexual interactions, two adult heterosexual interactions, two acts of adult female exhibitionism, two adult female rapes, one male child physical aggression, one female child physical aggression, one male child nonphysical coercion, one

female child nonphysical coercion, three male child fondlings, and three female child fondlings. Tim's subjective reports of sexual arousal were assessed by having him rate how aroused he felt, using a 10-point Likert scale ($0 = not\ at\ all\ aroused$; $9 = extremely\ aroused$).

Results of this assessment component before initiating assisted covert sensitization indicated that Tim was aroused by adult females. However, he also displayed an active pattern of arousal toward stimuli depicting sexual activities with a male child, specifically anal intercourse. Based upon these data, three "deviant" categories that elicited the greatest levels of sexual arousal—fondling a male child (MPF), coercing a female child into sexual activity (FPC), and fondling a female child (FPF)—were noted, and a follow-up recommendation was made for Tim to participate in eight sessions of assisted covert sensitization in addition to being readmitted to group treatment at the local human service center.

Shortly after the initial assessment was conducted, an assisted covert sensitization protocol was begun. Tim was given a consent form and full explanation of the procedure, and all questions were answered concerning the procedure. The initial assisted covert sensitization session was scheduled for the following week. During the week, audiotapes were developed for treatment. These tapes contained 3-minute descriptions of a deviant sexual activity (MPF, FPC, or FPF) followed by a description of a possible negative (aversive) consequence for this type of activity. The consequences were either legal (e.g., being beaten up by the father of the child and then being arrested) or physiological (e.g., feeling very nauseous and vomiting) in nature. The development and implementation of these guided scripts represents the "assisted" component in assisted covert sensitization.

When Tim arrived for the first session, an abbreviated assessment was conducted to obtain baseline measurements of his sexual arousal to MPF, FPC, and FPF stimuli, as well as mutually consenting heterosexual (FAD) and mutually consenting homosexual (MAD) activity.

Following a 10-minute break, the treatment was initiated, involving the presentation of 10 MPF stimuli described above. At the end of the session, Tim was given a copy of the tape and instructed to listen to and visualize the sexual activity as well as the aversive consequences being delivered five times per day. The remaining five sessions were conducted at 1-week intervals apart, beginning with Session 1.

During Session 2, Tim was presented with the same 10 MPF stimuli from the previous session and was again instructed to listen to the tape five times per day until the next session. In Sessions 3 and 4, the same procedures were followed, with the exception that MPF stimuli were presented only two times and FPC stimuli were presented the other times. Tim was again provided with a copy of the new tape and instructed to listen to it five times per day between sessions (with explicit instructions to visualize the stimuli being presented). In Sessions 5 and 6, FPF stimuli were presented six times, MPF two times, and FPC two times each.

After completion of Session 6, Tim returned to the clinic for a 30-day follow-up assessment. The same stimuli from the baseline assessment were used to determine present patterns of sexual arousal. The identical procedure was again followed 3 months later in a final follow-up assessment.

Tim's physiological data for the initial assessment, pretreatment assessment, 30-day follow-up, and 90-day follow-up were calculated and converted to percentages of full erection. This was computed by subtracting his minimum penile circumference for an entire session (e.g., assessment period) from his maximum penile circumference for each trial (the presentation of one audiotaped stimulus represents a trial) and dividing this number by 3. Three centimeters is thought to reflect the circumference change most males undergo from flaccidity (no sexual arousal) to complete engorgement (maximum sexual arousal). This number was then multiplied by 100 to give a percentage of full erection. Thus, percentage of full-erection data give an indication of absolute levels of arousal. In other words, Tim's response to each stimulus was viewed in this manner independently of the other stimuli presented in the session. It was found that the stimuli elicited less arousal each time Tim was assessed during the assisted covert sensitization procedure.

Tim's physiological data for the assessments were next converted to standardized scores (z-scores). Z-scores form a distribution in which the mean of the distribution equals zero (0) and the standard deviation is 1.0. Using this scoring method, Tim's sexual preferences were expressed as positive z-scores, while negative z-scores reflected sexual aversions. The further a score falls from zero, the stronger the preference or aversion. Thus, a score of +2.0 indicates a greater preference than a +1.2, while a score of −2.0 indicates a greater repulsion than a score of −1.2. Z-scores, then, give an indication of relative arousal or preferences and aversions among a group of stimuli. It was found that in the initial assessment, four of the five categories, including the three that were treated, were positive and above 0.50. Looking across the assessments for each of the deviant categories, it was clear that Tim's arousal to these decreased across time, although his arousal to adult mutually consenting sexual activity (FAD) was clearly his most preferred stimulus in all assessments except for the 30-day follow-up, in which mutually consenting heterosexual activity (MAD) was the most preferred stimulus.

Tim's self-report of sexual arousal used the 10-point Likert scale (0 = *not at all aroused;* 9 = *extremely aroused*) for each stimulus category of stimulus across the four assessments, which yields an indication of an individual's subjective experience of arousal that is not always perfectly related to his physiological responding. Once again, it was found that FAD stimuli elicited the greatest levels of arousal, while all others dropped off to 0.

Tim clearly showed clinical progress in both his physiological and self-report of arousal toward sexually deviant stimuli that were the main areas of concern, utilizing the assisted covert sensitization procedure. Recall that the underlying behavior principle of covert sensitization is most often theorized to be a combination of classical and operant conditioning, as described above. Given decrements in physiological arousal and self-report normally observed in covert sensitization procedures, such as in the present case study, it is logical to conclude that the aversive image associated with deviant sexual arousal (the UCS) becomes a CS by virtue of its being contingently paired with the UCS (classical conditioning). Also, it is logical and theoretically coherent to conclude that both the conditioned response (CR) and the unconditioned response (UCR) consist of a negative reaction that may be emotional (e.g., fear), physiological (e.g., nausea), or in some other way repulsive, which further serves to negatively reinforce avoidance or escape behavior (operant conditioning).

—*Joseph J. Plaud*

See also: Covert Control (Vol. I); Covert Rehearsal (Vol. I); Covert Reinforcer Sampling (Vol. I)

Suggested Readings

Abel, G. G., & Blanchard, E. B. (1976). The measurement and generation of sexual arousal in male sexual deviates. In M. Hersen, R. Eisler, & R. M. Miller (Eds.), *Progress in behavior modification* (Vol. 2, pp. 99–133). New York: Academic Press.

Binet, A. (1888). Le fetichisme dans l'amour. *Études de Psychologie Expérimentale, 1–85.*

Brownwell, K. D., & Barlow, D. H. (1976). Measurement and treatment of two sexual deviations in one person. *Journal of Behavior Therapy and Experimental Psychiatry, 7, 349–354.*

Cautela, J. R., & Kearney, A. J. (1990). Behavior analysis, cognitive therapy, and covert conditioning. *Journal of Behavior Therapy and Experimental Psychiatry, 21, 83–90.*

Curtis, R. H., & Presley, A. S. (1972). The extinction of homosexual behaviour by covert sensitization: A case study. *Behavior Research and Therapy, 10, 81–83.*

Dougher, M. J., Crossen, J. R., Ferraro, D. P., & Garland, R. (1987). The effects of covert sensitization on preference for sexual stimuli. *Journal of Behavior Therapy and Experimental Psychiatry, 18, 337–348.*

Gaither, G. A., Rosenkranz, R. R., & Plaud, J. J. (1998). Sexual disorders. In J. J. Plaud & G. H. Eifert (Eds.), *From behavior theory to behavior therapy* (pp. 152–171). Boston: Allyn & Bacon.

Haydn-Smith, P., Marks, I., Buchaya, H., & Repper, D. (1987). Behavioral treatment of life threatening masochistic asphyxiation: A case study. *British Journal of Psychiatry, 150, 518–519.*

Hayes, S. C., Brownwell, K. D., & Barlow, D. H. (1978). The use of self-administered covert sensitization in the treatment of exhibitionism and sadism. *Behavior Therapy, 9, 283–289.*

Hughes, R. C. (1977). Covert sensitization treatment of exhibitionism. *Journal of Behavior Therapy and Experimental Psychiatry, 8, 177–179.*

Jaspers, K. (1963). *General psychopathology.* Manchester, UK: Manchester University Press.

Kendrick, S. R., & McCullough, J. P. (1972). Sequential phases of covert reinforcement and covert sensitization in the treatment of homosexuality. *Journal of Behavior Therapy and Experimental Psychiatry, 3, 229–213.*

King, M. B. (1990). Sneezing as a fetishistic stimulus. *Sexual and Marital Therapy, 5, 69–72.*

Lamontagne, Y., & Lesage, A. (1986). Private exposure and covert sensitization in the treatment of exhibitionism. *Journal of Behavior Therapy and Experimental Psychiatry, 17, 197–201.*

Maletzky, B. M., & George, F. S. (1973). The treatment of homosexuality by "assisted" covert sensitization. *Behavior Research and Therapy, 11, 655–657.*

McGuire, R. J., Carlisle, J. M., & Young, B. G. (1965). Sexual deviation as conditioned behavior. *Behavior Research and Therapy, 2, 185–190.*

McNally, R. J., & Lukach, B. M. (1991). Behavioral treatment of zoophilic exhibitionism. *Journal of Behavior Therapy and Experimental Psychiatry, 22, 281–284.*

Moergen, S. A., Merkel, W. T., & Brown, S. (1990). The use of covert sensitization and social skills training in the treatment of an obscene telephone caller. *Journal of Behavior Therapy and Experimental Psychiatry, 21, 269–275.*

O'Donohue, W. T., & Plaud, J. J. (1994). The conditioning of human sexual arousal. *Archives of Sexual Behavior, 23, 321–344.*

Plaud, J. J., & Gaither, G. A. (1997). A clinical investigation of the possible effects of long-term habituation of sexual arousal in assisted covert sensitization. *Journal of Behavior Therapy and Experimental Psychiatry, 28, 281–290.*

Plaud, J. J., & Martini, J. R. (1999). The respondent conditioning of male sexual arousal. *Behavior Modification, 23, 254–268.*

Rachman, S. (1961). Sexual disorders and behavior therapy. *American Journal of Psychiatry, 118, 235–240.*

Rangaswamy, K. (1987). Treatment of voyeurism by behavior therapy. *Child Psychiatry Quarterly, 20, 73–76.*

Stava, L., Levin, S. M., & Schwanz, C. (1993). The role of aversion in covert sensitization treatment of pedophilia: A case report. *Journal of Child Sexual Abuse, 2, 1–13.*

CUE-CONTROLLED RELAXATION

DESCRIPTION OF THE STRATEGY

Cue-controlled relaxation is a procedure designed to enable an individual to achieve relaxation rapidly through self-produced cues, usually a deep breath that is exhaled and a specific word.

Typically, training in deep diaphragmatic breathing and muscle relaxation (e.g., progressive muscle relaxation) precedes the introduction of cue-controlled relaxation. Once clients master deep muscle relaxation, cue-controlled relaxation is introduced. The specific training in cue-controlled relaxation would begin the session with the same procedures for attaining deep muscle relaxation as in previous sessions. After clients become relaxed during this session, they will be instructed to focus their attention on their breathing. They are instructed to slowly inhale and exhale, with attention to the use of the diaphragm. Upon exhalation, clients are asked to silently repeat to themselves a word such as "relax" or "calm" while the clinician audibly repeats the designated cue word in synchrony with five consecutive exhalations. Clients then repeat the procedure of pairing the exhalation with the cue word about 15 more times. Following this, there is a 60-second period during which the clients are asked to focus on general feelings that accompany their relaxation. Such pairing is then repeated about 20 more times. This is important, as training in cue-controlled relaxation requires repeated pairings of a relaxed state with a designated cue. This training is repeated in session for four to five more sessions.

Clients are also encouraged to practice the cue-controlled relaxation procedure (e.g., 20 pairings) on a daily basis on their own outside of the treatment setting. While it is emphasized initially that these exercises are to be practiced in nonanxiety- or arousal-eliciting settings, clinicians later may also ask clients to practice the pairings in situations where anxiety is elicited, including those that may be of interest for treatment success (e.g., public speaking, test taking, etc.). Related to this, during treatment sessions, clients may be asked to imagine a threatening situation related to their presenting problem until some level of anxiety is experienced, and then to practice the pairings. If relaxation is attained, the clients are asked to use the cue training any time they experience elevations in anxiety outside of the clinical setting.

An innovative variation on cue-controlled relaxation training relates to its optional use with nonverbal externally produced cues that occur on a regular basis. For instance, behaviors such as making the bed, turning on a coffeepot, using keys, and stopping for traffic lights could be paired with relaxation by having the clients perform the deep-breathing exercises and subvocal cuing during their performance of these behaviors. This training can be particularly useful when clinicians are interested in having clients experience the cue-controlled relaxation as part of their daily lives following the conclusion of treatment. While this unique use of cue-controlled relaxation can be useful to clients, it is not necessarily a requirement with cue-controlled relaxation. It is simply an optional, innovative use of the mechanism (i.e., classical conditioning via pairing a cue with relaxation) by which cue-controlled relaxation achieves its goal (eliciting a relaxation response when desired).

RESEARCH BASIS

Cue-controlled relaxation is sometimes referred to as *conditioned relaxation,* given the putative significant role of classical conditioning as the mechanism involved in the training. The rationale behind

cue-controlled relaxation is based on the principles of classical conditioning; it is assumed that following repeated parings of a cue and a relaxed state, an association between the two will be established so that the cue alone develops the potential to elicit feelings of relaxation when warranted, including during anxiety-eliciting experiences. Once this occurs, clients should be able to achieve relaxation upon use of the cue. Subsequently, clients are better equipped to minimize tension during stressful experiences that occur on a day-to-day basis. Mastery of cue-controlled relaxation can result in reductions in general tension and in anxiety experienced at the onset of a stressful event. The end result should be that clients have greater control over tension when confronted with difficult experiences and transient stress.

There are numerous benefits to cue-controlled relaxation. First, it is typically easier to administer and requires less therapy time than some other behavioral interventions (e.g., systematic desensitization). Furthermore, the length of time required for the client to achieve relaxation is relatively brief. Also, the procedure is more readily accessible, portable, and practical than some interventions (e.g., full progressive muscle relaxation, biofeedback). Clients can easily engage in cue-controlled relaxation often and in a variety of situations. In addition, cue-controlled relaxation provides clients a means of reducing tension quickly, as well as discretely. While cue-controlled relaxation has been found to be effective when conducted by mental health professionals, it should be noted that the training has been shown to be effective when delivered by paraprofessionals as well. Finally, there is also a great deal of empirical support for cue-controlled relaxation, which will now be presented.

While target populations for cue-controlled relaxation will be presented shortly, some other empirical findings related to cue-conditioned relaxation will be presented first. Cue-controlled relaxation has been found to successfully alleviate anxiety in general, as well as anxiety specific to a particular circumstance (e.g., public speaking, driving). It has also been shown to reduce stress, as well as compulsive and other anxious behaviors. Improvements in perceived control of anxiety and control in behavior have also been found. In addition, reductions in physical symptoms (e.g., nausea) related to anxiety have been shown following cue-controlled relaxation.

In some instances, cue-controlled relaxation has been found to be just as effective or more effective than progressive muscle relaxation alone, applied-relaxation alone, systematic desensitization, cognitive coping skills training, aromatherapy, rational restructuring, self-monitoring, sensory information, supportive psychotherapy, and no treatment.

Cue-controlled relaxation has been found to generalize to other situations, particularly those involving the presence of stress. Generalization of the relaxation has been found to occur in the treatment of obsessive thinking, as well as specific compulsive behavior problems (e.g., fingernail biting), public speaking, test anxiety, and dental anxiety.

The effects of cue-controlled relaxation seem to be maintained after treatment has ended, suggesting that the procedure has long-lasting effects (2.5 months to 18 months, depending on the study).

RELEVANT TARGET POPULATIONS AND EXCEPTIONS

Uncontrolled research suggests that cue-controlled relaxation is successful in treating numerous conditions. These include, but are not limited to, test anxiety, fear of public speaking, fear of driving alone or at night, snake phobia, flying phobia with and without physical symptoms (e.g., vomiting, fainting), disruptive behavior in people with mental retardation, multiple motor tics, seizure activity (including epileptic seizures), migraine headache, anxiety in general, anxiety with depression, aversion to cancer chemotherapy, obsessive thinking, dental anxiety, and coping problems.

Despite being a resource in the mental health field for more than 30 years, cue-controlled relaxation has been subjected to only a few controlled studies. Controlled research suggests that cue-controlled relaxation is more effective than a no-treatment control group for the following problems: speech anxiety, mathematics anxiety, and excessive anxiety. Controlled research also indicates that cue-controlled relaxation is more effective than attention placebo conditions for speech anxiety.

While studies have shown cue-controlled relaxation to be more effective than no treatment in treatment of test-taking anxiety, other more recent studies have found the training to be equally effective as supportive psychotherapy.

It should also be noted that cue-controlled relaxation has been an integral part of the behavioral treatments of various psychophysiological disorders, such as chronic headache, irritable bowel syndrome, tinnitus, and hypertension. However, it has not been evaluated as a sole treatment for these problems.

COMPLICATIONS

One of the biggest problems related to cue-controlled relaxation is that, as other relaxation treatments, clients may not continue using the techniques on a regular basis following treatment. Yet clinicians could opt to include the optional "nonverbal externally produced cues that occur frequently" component in their treatment designs.

CASE ILLUSTRATION

A married, 37-year-old, Caucasian American female presented with complaints of chronic tension-type headache. She was employed full-time and also was a mother of two school-aged children. She further reported that her life was "filled with stress." When interviewed further, it was determined that the client's headaches tended to be preceded by daily stressors that subsequently caused the client to experience a stiff neck and a feeling of "being stressed." Thus, from a behavioral framework, it seemed that the antecedents were the daily stressors, the behavior was the increase in physical tension (e.g., stiff neck), and the consequences were the headaches themselves. In treatment, the client was exposed to a thorough multi-session relaxation regimen and was instructed to perform daily relaxation exercises at home. She learned to recognize physical tension and to release such tension through progressive muscle relaxation techniques.

Cue-controlled relaxation was presented as part of the final stage of treatment. Following treatment, the client reported that she had been able to incorporate the cue-controlled relaxation training into zher life as a means of coping with daily stressors. Furthermore, she reported that her headaches were less frequent and that they no longer affected her daily functioning. While it is impossible to distinguish the effect of progressive muscle relaxation from the effect of cue-controlled relaxation on outcome (given that the cue-controlled component has been shown to be an integral, highly portable, and practical component in the treatment of tension-type headache only when combined with a relaxation regimen), the client reported that the cue-controlled relaxation component was a very useful part of the overall treatment.

—*Brian M. Freidenberg and Edward B. Blanchard*

See also: *Applied Relaxation and Tension (Vol. I); Relaxation Training With Children (Vol. II); Social Skills Instruction (Vol. III)*

Suggested Readings

Bernstein, D. A., & Borkovec, T. D. (1973). *Progressive relaxation training: A manual for the helping professions.* Champaign, IL: Research Press.

Paul, G. L. (1966). *Insight vs. desensitization in psychotherapy.* Stanford, CA: Stanford University Press.

Paul, G. L. (1966, May). *The specific control of anxiety: Hypnosis and conditioning.* Paper presented at the meeting of the American Psychological Association, New York.

Russell, R. K., Miller, D. E., & June, L. N. (1974). Group cue-controlled relaxation in the treatment of test anxiety. *Behavior Therapy, 5,* 572–573.

Russell, R. K., & Sipich, J. F. (1973). Cue-controlled relaxation in the treatment of test anxiety. *Journal of Behavior Therapy and Experimental Psychiatry, 4,* 47–49.

Russell, R. K., & Sipich, J. F. (1974). Treatment of test anxiety by cue-controlled relaxation. *Behavior Therapy, 5,* 673–676.

CULTURAL DIFFERENCES IN COGNITIVE THERAPY

DESCRIPTION OF THE STRATEGY

One of the greatest challenges facing contemporary behavior and cognitive therapy is to distinguish universals in human mental and behavioral processes from those that are culturally specific. All of the great systems of psychotherapy have incorporated elements of the zeitgeist, the cultural assumptions that form the tacit basis of that particular culture at that particular time, generally without explicit awareness. For example, Sigmund Freud's theory of drive reduction and symptom substitution was based in part on 19th-century mechanics and hydraulics. Symptoms that were suppressed and prevented from entering consciousness would, hydraulically, emerge somewhere else. Discharge of emotional energy led to relief. Even his focus on sexual repression as the source of neurosis can be traced to the heavily sexually repressed culture of 19th-century central Europe. A more contemporary form of psychoanalysis might begin with the "denial of death" instead of the denial of sex.

Thus, where Freud assumed that he had found universals in human mental life, he likely found mostly cultural specifics, bound to place and time.

Later, Carl Rogers's client-centered therapy can be seen as reflecting two cultural aspects of mid-20th century American life: the increasing egalitarianism that reduced the status of the therapist and the increasing material affluence that permitted the leisurely exploration of one's inner life. In today's managed care environment, with diminishing resources available to health care, by contrast, brief therapy in its various manifestations (e.g., solution-focused therapy) is important.

Early behavior therapy was concerned with a mechanized approach to therapy (with one article referring to the behavior therapist as a "reinforcement machine") and may have reflected American fascination with the power of technology and its perceived ability to solve our problems. A similar cultural icon of the period was seen in the gadgets in the James Bond movies. Behavior therapists found that symptom substitution did not, in fact, necessarily occur when symptoms were removed; quite the contrary, there was often a "ripple effect," resulting in better functioning in domains not explicitly addressed in therapy. Behaviorists, however, fell into the same universal trap in arguing that reinforcement was a universal attribute of human motivation. Bandura discovered that the perception of reinforcement was more important than actual reinforcement. Behavior also persisted in the apparent absence of a reinforcer, leading to the creation of ex post facto concepts such as functional autonomy. Adlerians argued that behavior was purposive (anticipatory) rather than reinforced (consequential). The various forms of cognitive therapies were created to explain why reinforcement was not the universal and invariant process it had been thought to be.

The recent interest in constructivistic approaches to therapy may be a result of the clash of cultures caused by increased and rapid transportation and communication, leading to a new appreciation of the relativity of cultural realities.

Cognitive therapy may have created universals of its own from what might turn out to be cultural specifics. It is almost exclusively a North American phenomenon that has translated well to the Americanized societies of Western Europe but perhaps less so to other more radically different societies with different cultural assumptions. This is likely to be true of all cognitive phenomena: cognitive contents (what we say to ourselves), cognitive processes (cognitive distortions), and cognitive structures (core or tacit cognitive assumptions). The latter phenomenon includes cultural knowledge, the tacit or implicit knowledge we all have that is derived from the unspoken (and often unspeakable) rules and assumptions we learn from our cultures. These assumptions are automatically laid down early in life by our constant interaction with our cultures and thereafter only elaborated upon rather than radically changed. They are experienced by people as a "given" so obvious as to require no explanation. If challenged on them, we may say, "But that's just the way things are," "That's just reality," or "Everyone knows that!" If the challenges are serious and sustained, however, individuals may experience a crisis, partially decompensate, feel depersonalized, and begin to lose their sense of identity. This may be expressed by statements such as, "I don't know what's real anymore" or "I don't even know who I am anymore."

Elsewhere, I have discussed acquisition and presence of tacit or implicit knowledge structures and drawn implications for cognitive therapy. Some of these conclusions are as follows:

1. Implicit knowledge is acquired faster than explicit knowledge, especially in emotional situations, and is more resistant to change. This may account for much of the resistance to change noted by every therapist since Freud, even in clients who are quite distressed and seeking therapy.

2. Implicit learning occurs by the tacit detection of covariation when we unconsciously notice which things go together (associationism), in the process forming tacit rules. When faced with new and especially ambiguous situations, we tend to impose our existing tacit cognitive rules on the new situation, thus perpetuating these rules. Thus, we tend to see what we expect to see and find what we expect to find. Even scientists are not immune from this human tendency.

3. Our tacit knowledge structure (including cultural knowledge) tends to be nonverbal (and often preverbal) and therefore cannot easily be discussed or changed. Often, it consists of fleeting images and emotions. It is also more conceptually rich than explicit knowledge.

Tacit or implicit knowledge structures are referred to as *core cognitive schemas* in the cognitive therapy literature, by Aaron Beck, Judith Beck, Jeffrey Young,

and others. They are the unspoken, often maladaptive, rules and assumptions by which we organize and make sense of the world. Two of the more common core cognitive schemas are "I'm unlovable," and "I'm incompetent." Note the striking similarity to Freud's answer to the question, "What should people be able to do well?" He answered, "To love and to work." Perhaps these two human needs are indeed cultural universals.

RESEARCH BASIS

It is very difficult to provide a research basis for this area, at least as research is commonly understood in American scientific psychology. Much of the difficulty derives from the nature of the research enterprise itself; as commonly practiced in North America, it is itself a culturally specific endeavor, relying almost exclusively on the empirical epistemology that has been ascendant since the beginning of the Enlightenment. Other forms of acquiring knowledge may be more appropriate for an investigation of this topic, but these ways have not been traditionally accepted or valued in American scientific psychology. For example, qualitative research designs may be especially useful in conducting cross-cultural research. Most of the literature in this area has been conceptual and anecdotal, discussing issues of concern in practicing cognitive (behavior) therapy with a variety of different minority populations. These have included issues of concern to Orthodox Jewish clients, use of rational-emotive behavior therapy (REBT) with culturally diverse clients, and the use of cognitive behavior therapy with Latinos. Religious clients, especially those of a more traditional kind, are often deeply suspicious of psychotherapy of any type, considering it to be a method of undermining their faith. Because psychologists in general are much less religious than the general population, there may be some validity to this fear. People living in societies only partially affected by Western culture (e.g., Moslem cultures) may have different ways of viewing and making sense of the world and their experiences in it that should be understood before cognitive therapy is attempted.

COMPLICATIONS

Major complications may occur when cognitive behavior therapists operate from the worldview of their cultures and their professional training without understanding the worldviews of their clients. The following are some examples of the problems that might arise using standard cognitive therapy techniques with culturally different clients.

One of the cognitive distortions commonly identified is that of *magnification and minimization:* magnifying the negative and minimizing the positive aspects of oneself. Inherent in the American self-esteem movement is the assumption that it is best to think positively about oneself. But even within the Western Christian tradition, there is a counterassumption that this will lead to a false sense of pride (hubris) or a lack of humility, resulting not only in poorer mental health but less positive social relations, as well. In certain Asian cultures, it is expected that one will derogate oneself, and it is considered in poor taste to flaunt a high opinion of oneself. Asking clients from these cultures to magnify their positives may cause them considerable distress.

One of the early maladaptive schemas identified by Jeffrey Young is that of *enmeshment/undeveloped self.* This is described as an excessive emotional involvement with others at the expense of one's own individualization. But what is excessive? It should be remembered that American society is probably the most individualistic in the world. Other cultures, such as the Italian and some Asian societies, place a much higher value on family and other group connections. They are not expected to separate to the extent Americans do. Buddhist writings speak of the "imposture of the ego" and argue that the self has no real existence at all. True mental health (release from suffering), in Buddhist eyes, involves ending the attachments to possessions, the ego, and one's sense of selfhood. The Buddhist *Second Noble Truth* teaches that the cause of life's difficulties is craving and that humans will continue to suffer until we rid ourselves of this.

Another early maladaptive schema is that of *defectiveness/shame,* the sense that one is defective in important aspects. American culture tends to assume optimistically that humans are inherently good. But the Christian concept of original sin suggests that all of us by nature are defective in fundamental ways. "Confession is good for the soul," as the saying goes, and we become mentally healthier as we confess and acknowledge our defects.

Another complication may occur when the values of the subculture conflict with the values, and sometimes the laws, of the majority culture. An example of this is in the area of child abuse. Certain subcultures, for either cultural or religious (e.g., "Spare the rod and spoil the child") reasons may use corporal punishment in a manner that violates the sensibilities and sometimes the laws of the larger culture. Likewise, women might be encouraged to remain with abusive husbands because of religious strictures. While sensitivity to cultural differences is an important value, it is even more important to adhere to the legal standards of the American society, and therapists cannot violate the law.

CASE ILLUSTRATION

"Anna" was raised in a rather strict, traditional (fundamentalist) Christian household. The family structure was quite patriarchal, with her father setting the rules for the household. The father was also the sole "breadwinner," and Anna's mother had devoted her life to managing the household and raising the children. Anna was the oldest of four children and the only girl. As such, she had been expected from the first to help her mother care for the younger siblings. Much of the family's social life revolved around their church, with most of Sunday, Wednesday evening, and occasionally Saturday devoted to church activities. Most of their friends were involved in the same church. The other evenings were devoted to family activities and studying. Anna did attend her local public school, however, where she had made a number of friends.

Anna was 13 when she began to feel dissatisfied with her life in ways she could not quite describe. Her parents, noticing her distress, took her to a local female therapist who had been recommended to them. Because of the strong family structure, the parents initially met with the therapist and their daughter. At that time, the therapist, being ethically aware, discussed confidentiality issues with everyone and told the parents that she could not ethically tell them what was discussed in therapy and could break confidentiality only in certain specified circumstances. While not entirely pleased, the parents agreed.

Anna and the therapist first identified the sources of her distress. Like many first-generation children of immigrants and members of American subcultures within the majority society, Anna was feeling torn between two cultures. On one hand, she valued the strong support, caring, and social network provided by her family and her church. On the other hand, she envied the greater degree of personal freedom and independent decision making her school friends seemed to possess. In particular, she resented her early curfew and tight control over the friends with whom she was allowed to associate and her constant use as a babysitter for her younger brothers. She had also become increasingly aware of the diversity of religious opinion and belief among her school acquaintances. This included existence of no religious belief at all, a condition that had never occurred to her. She was frightened that she found the latter option somewhat attractive and wondered whether that meant she was going to hell. She appeared to be simultaneously questioning her faith and afraid of losing it.

The therapist, like many psychologists, was quite egalitarian and rather religiously agnostic. She had been trained in the cognitive therapy approach of Aaron T. Beck and Jeffrey Young and identified several cognitive distortions and early maladaptive schemas from those systems. One was all-or-nothing thinking. Anna appeared to think that questioning anything about the faith in which she was raised meant that she was destined for hell. A common self-statement seemed to be, "I must believe everything my faith teaches me or I'm an atheist!" She seemed to hold the following conditional belief: "If I don't believe *everything*, then I can't believe *anything*."

The therapist also thought that Anna was overly enmeshed in her family structure, because almost all of her activities centered around family and church and her parents tightly controlled with whom she interacted, when, and how. Anna did not posses the type of individual identity the therapist thought appropriate for a 13-year-old. Tentative goals might include helping Anna to distance more from family and church and to rationally examine the truth of her belief system against the beliefs of other forms of religion. However, the therapist was also culturally aware and recognized that her own values (including religion) might be influencing her assessment and treatment goals for Anna. In addition, she recognized that developmentally, Anna might be especially open to influence from an outside authority figure such as a therapist, which could lead to an estrangement from her family. Therefore, Anna's therapist sought consultation from a religiously oriented therapist whose own church was close in belief structure to that of Anna's family.

As a result of this consultation, the therapist was able to help Anna examine the values inherent in her strong social and family support network while simultaneously considering ways in which she could discover what sort of person she was becoming. The therapist encouraged Anna to discuss with her parents appropriate ways in which Anna could begin to engage in new activities outside of family and church circles. With Anna's consent, the therapist held several family sessions in which the parents were encouraged to voice their own fears and hopes for their daughter. The therapist, because of her consultation, was able to talk with Anna about the positive role of doubt within the Christian faith and that an examination of basic doctrine could, in fact, lead to a stronger faith. Essentially, the therapist helped Anna reframe the nature of questioning and doubt from a negative attribute to a positive one, designed to deepen and enlarge faith, rather than diminish it.

After a number of sessions, Anna's parents allowed her to attend certain school functions they had been loath to approve earlier. They also agreed to release her from some of the care for her brothers, recognizing that it had become excessive. Anna felt pleased that her concerns had been taken seriously by her parents, and the parents, in turn, felt pleased that Anna was talking to them more. Anna's "enmeshment" with her family, while not perhaps reduced to the level of which the majority culture would approve, was nevertheless reduced. Her all-or-nothing thinking diminished as she began to look at doubt as possessing positive as well as negative features. She began to examine the cultural specifics that all religions contain and to differentiate them from the universal teachings that all religions also contain, recognizing that it is sometimes difficult to distinguish one from the other.

It is difficult to conduct therapy in such a manner as to be respectful of both cultural differences and individual desires/needs. Because this therapist recognized both the existence and relativity of her own value system and the need for consultation, she was able to do it.

—E. Thomas Dowd

See also: *Behavioral Treatment of Minorities (Vol. I); Peer Intervention (Vol. II); Peer Tutoring (Vol. III)*

Suggested Readings

Beck, J. S. (1995). *Cognitive therapy: Basics and beyond.* New York: Guilford Press.

Dowd, E. T. (2002). History and recent developments in cognitive psychotherapy. In R. L. Leahy & E. T. Dowd (Eds.), *Clinical advances in cognitive psychotherapy.* New York: Springer.

Dowd, E. T., & Courchaine, K. E. (2002). Implicit learning, tacit knowledge, and implications for stasis and change in cognitive psychotherapy. In R. L. Leahy & E. T. Dowd (Eds.), *Clinical advances in cognitive psychotherapy*. New York: Springer.

Organista, K. C., & Munoz, R. F. (1996). Cognitive-behavioral therapy with Latinos. *Cognitive and Behavioral Practice, 3,* 255–270.

Paradis, C. M., Friedman, S., Hatch, M., & Ackerman, R. (1996). Cognitive-behavioral treatment of anxiety disorders in Orthodox Jews. *Cognitive and Behavioral Practice, 3,* 271–288.

Randall, E. J. (1994). Cultural relativism in cognitive therapy with disadvantaged African American women. *Journal of Cognitive Psychotherapy: An International Quarterly, 8,* 195–207.

Robin, M. W., & DiGiuseppe, R. (1997). Shoya Moya ik Baraba: Using REBT with culturally diverse clients. In J. Yakura & W. Dryden (Eds.), *Special applications of REBT: A therapist's case book* (pp. 39–67).

Young, J. E. (1999). *Cognitive therapy for personality disorders: A schema-focused approach* (3rd ed.). Sarasota, FL: Practitioner's Resource Series.

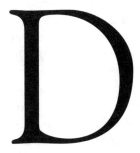

DAVISON, GERALD C.

I was born of second-generation Jewish parents, Aaron and Celia Davison, in Boston, Massachusetts, in 1939, the second of three children. My family and social environments were warm and supportive and placed great emphasis on academic achievement. Like many boys of my background, I attended Boston Latin School for grades 7 through 12. For generations, this school was the way out of several of the Boston ghettos for the children of parents and grandparents who had immigrated from Europe and who saw a rigorous education as the most reliable way for the kids to make it into the mainstream of American society.

Like many of my Boston Latin classmates, I went on to Harvard, where I earned my BA degree in 1961. I did some research with Richard Alpert (years later known as Baba Ram Dass) and wrote my senior honors thesis on perceptual bias under the supervision of Jerome Bruner, a noted cognitive psychologist. Uncertain as to whether to attend law school or to pursue a PhD in psychology, I applied for in my senior year and was awarded a Fulbright Foreign Study Grant to the University of Freiburg, West Germany, going there just one month after East Germany constructed the wall between East and West Berlin. My German *Wanderjahr* afforded me a total immersion in a culture I wanted to understand. Coursework included projective tests, handwriting analysis, dream analysis, and psychoanalysis. I also sang in Freiburg's well-known Russian Chorus. The academic high point of my year abroad was making a presentation *(Referat)* on B. F. Skinner to a class on psychoanalysis.

My remarks were greeted with polite skepticism, and the professor in charge of the course commented wryly—or so it seemed to me—that it had been "interesting" to have me in class that semester.

Upon returning from Germany, I set out for Stanford in the summer of 1962, where I had decided to pursue graduate study in psychology. I did not know which area of psychology I wanted to specialize in, except that I knew it would not be clinical. The reason was that the only clinical psychology I had been exposed to at Harvard and in Freiburg was one or another variant of psychoanalysis, and I just couldn't buy into the epistemology. So I explored social psychology as well as physiological psychology and fell into clinical accidentally when I heard some of the clinical students talking about something called "behavior therapy" and about two members of the faculty in particular, Albert Bandura and Walter Mischel. The proposition that experimental psychology could be relevant to clinical assessment and intervention intrigued me. The decision to switch into clinical became firm when Arnold Lazarus visited for a year from South Africa. I earned my PhD in 1965 with a dissertation on systematic desensitization as a counterconditioning process, did an internship postdoctorally at the Palo Alto VA Hospital, and then went to SUNY at Stony Brook, where an avowedly behavioral clinical program was just starting under the leadership of Leonard Krasner and Harry Kalish.

There, my early cognitive exposure with Bruner manifested itself as I came to appreciate the seminal work of Albert Ellis and Aaron Beck, conducted attribution research with a Schachter-trained social psychologist named Stuart Valins, wrote *Clinical*

249

Behavior Therapy with Marvin Goldfried, and coauthored a textbook on abnormal psychology with John Neale. I also directed the first postdoctoral program in behavior therapy. After 13 years at Stony Brook, the siren call of California drew me back as director of clinical training (1979–1984) at the University of Southern California, where I have been ever since. My administrative work has also included being department chair (1984–1990), interim dean of the Annenberg School for Communication (1994–1996), and a second term as chair beginning in 2001.

I am a fellow of the American Psychological Association (APA) and have served on the Executive Committee of the Division of Clinical Psychology, on the Board of Scientific Affairs, on the Committee on Scientific Awards, on the Council of Representatives, and on the Continuing Professional Education Committee. I am also a charter fellow of the American Psychological Society, on the Advisory Board of the Society for the Exploration of Psychotherapy Integration, and a past president of the Association for Advancement of Behavior Therapy, which I subsequently served as publications coordinator. I am also a distinguished founding fellow of the Academy of Cognitive Therapy. I served two terms on the National Academy of Sciences/National Research Council Committee on Techniques for the Enhancement of Human Performance.

In 1988, I received an outstanding achievement award from APA's Board of Social and Ethical Responsibility; in 1989 was the recipient of the Albert S. Raubenheimer Distinguished Faculty Award from USC College of Letters, Arts, and Sciences; in 1993 won the Associates Award for Excellence in Teaching, a university-wide prize; in 1995 received the Distinguished Psychologist Award from the Los Angeles County Psychological Association; and in 1997 was given the Outstanding Educator Award of the Association for Advancement of Behavior Therapy. At USC, I am a distinguished faculty fellow in the Center for Excellence in Teaching.

Among my many publications, my book *Clinical Behavior Therapy,* coauthored in 1976 with Marvin Goldfried and reissued in expanded form in 1994, is one of two publications that have been recognized as Citation Classics by the Social Sciences Citation Index; it appears in German and Spanish translation. My textbook *Abnormal Psychology,* first published in 1974 with John Neale, was just published in its ninth edition, with Ann Kring as a new coauthor. It is a widely used abnormal text in North America and around the world and is translated into German, Spanish, Italian, and Japanese, with translations into Orthodox Chinese, Portuguese, and Korean in preparation.

Other books include *Case Studies in Abnormal Psychology* (2003, 6th ed.), with Oltmanns and Neale, and *Exploring Abnormal Psychology* (1996), with Neale and Haaga. I am on the editorial board of several professional journals, including *Behavior Therapy, Cognitive Therapy and Research, Journal of Cognitive Psychotherapy, Journal of Psychotherapy Integration, Journal of Clinical Psychology, In Session: Psychotherapy in Practice,* and *Clinical Psychology: Science and Practice.* My publications emphasize experimental and philosophical analyses of psychopathology, assessment, and therapeutic change. My research program focuses on the relationships between cognition and a variety of behavioral and emotional problems via my articulated thoughts in simulated-situations paradigm.

—*Gerald C. Davison*

See also: *Association for Advancement of Behavior Therapy (Vol. I); Relaxation Strategies (Vol. I); Systematic Desensitization (Vol. I)*

DESCRIPTIVE AND FUNCTIONAL ANALYSIS

DESCRIPTION OF THE STRATEGY

Central to behavioral theory is the concept that all behavior, functional or dysfunctional, is the result of learning history. More specifically, behavior that is followed by a *reinforcement* is more likely to reoccur, whereas behavior that either fails to be reinforced or is followed by a *punishment* is less likely to reoccur. Furthermore, an individual learns that reinforcement is more likely to occur for certain behaviors in certain circumstances than in others. Circumstances that signal a probable reinforcing consequence are termed *discriminative stimuli* (S^D). For example, most adults have learned that picking up a ringing phone (S^D) and saying "Hello" (target behavior) will be met with a response of "Hi, this is so and so. . . ." (reinforcement), whereas picking up a phone that is not ringing is unlikely to be followed by a reinforcement. Thus, the phone-answering behavior is unlikely to be repeated with a nonringing phone. Similarly, those who have learned that answering the phone around dinnertime is likely to be followed with the voice of a telemarketer (punishment) are less likely to answer the phone during the dinner hour. In sum, phone-answering behavior is *functionally related* to certain combination of antecedents (ringing, time of day) and consequences (presence of response, nature of response). These factors that control phone-answering behavior may be termed *contingencies*.

Although the factors that control phone-answering behavior appear elementary, a determination of actual factors controlling the behavior may be more elusive than they initially appear. There may be a multitude of factors and combinations of antecedents and consequences controlling any behavior. For example, those in an uncomfortable dinnertime conversation may answer the phone even if they have been regularly punished for this behavior by telemarketing responses in the past. In this case, there are competing contingencies. Although the telemarketer remains aversive, the negative reinforcement (i.e., relief) experienced by avoiding conversation represents a more powerful controlling contingency. Thus, provided that phone-answering was followed by negative reinforcement that outweighs the unpleasant telemarketer, such phone-answering is likely to be repeated under similar circumstances.

Given this theory of behavior acquisition, behavior change falls into three categories: increasing frequency of desirable behavior, decreasing frequency of undesirable behavior, and teaching new desirable behavior. All of these goals require an intricate knowledge of contingencies controlling those behaviors. Two related types of contingency assessment are used for this purpose: descriptive analysis and functional analysis. *Descriptive analysis* requires observation of the naturally occurring antecedents and consequences of target behaviors. This observation then yields hypotheses about the variables responsible for maintaining the behavior. *Functional analysis* requires taking the results from the descriptive analysis (or some other assessment) and testing the hypotheses by manipulating the antecedents and/or consequences and observing whether there is a change in the target behavior. The methods, procedures, and relative advantages and disadvantages of each will be reviewed below.

Descriptive Analysis

Descriptive analysis involves the direct observation of behavior, as it naturally occurs, and the observable events that precede and follow it. The goal of this analysis is to develop hypotheses about important controlling variables for the target behavior. The methods and procedures vary according to the setting, nature of the problem, and age/capability of the patient. The steps involved in a descriptive analysis follow:

1. *Identify and operationally define a target behavior* to increase, decrease, or teach. Target behaviors may be either external or internal. External behaviors are observable by others, whereas internal behaviors are observable only to the person behaving. Many behaviors have both external and internal components. For example, a target behavior may be depressed mood (internal) above an 8 (0 = *no depression;* 10 = *most depressed can imagine*) with concomitant jaw clenching, sighing, statements of low self-worth, and so on (external).

2. *Select the type(s) of observers.* This will depend upon nature of the target, the setting, the availability of observers, and the capability of the patient. When the target behavior is internal, the observer will always be the patient himself or herself. When the target behavior is external, the observer will be either the patient or another person. Patients in institutional settings will usually have therapists, staff, or researchers as observers. Noninstitutionalized adults will often be their own observers or have a spouse, adult child, or another family member as an observer. Therapists may also serve as observers of in-session behavior.

3. *Decide on a schedule of observation.* The most traditional and precise schedule of observation is continuous observation of behavior and potential contingencies using frequency (number of occurrences during the observation period), interval (presence or absence of behavior at specified time intervals, e.g., 30-second intervals), or time sampling (frequency assessed during high-likelihood times, e.g., depressed mood from 7–11 p.m. while at home alone). Less traditional methods include occurrence-based observation.

Continuous observation requires a highly regulated setting in which observers have continuous contact with the patient during the observation period. Occurrence-based observation involves recognizing target behaviors when they occur and identifying events that precede and follow them.

4. *Select a method of observation.* Observation may be live, taped, self-observation, or retrospective report. Live observation is most commonly used in institutional settings by external observers but may also be done by parents, adult children, or caregivers in other settings. Although this is the most accurate of the observation methods, it is often the least practical. Regarding accuracy, videotaped observation is a close second to live observation. While this is most feasible in institutional settings, some researchers have had success having patients in natural settings turn on video or audiotapes when the target behavior is likely to occur (e.g., a distressed couple will turn on the video camera daily after dinner when arguments are most likely to occur). Self-observation is used when patients are observing their own behavior and recording occurrences according to one of the above schedules. This is often the best method available with noninstitutionalized adults. The least reliable method, however the most commonly used, is the retrospective report. Often, clinical interviews are used to gather data based on patient memory of the occurrences of the target behavior and possible contingencies. While a retrospective report may start the questioning regarding functional variables, this should always be followed up with one of the other observation methods.

5. *Conduct the observation.* Observation should continue until several instances of the target behavior have occurred to assess for varied combinations of contingencies.

6. *Develop hypotheses about functional variables.* Results should be evaluated to develop hypotheses about patterns of antecedents and consequences that recur and the potential functional elements that tie these together. Common contingencies responsible for maintaining problem behaviors are positive reinforcement in the form of attention or tangible rewards or negative reinforcement in the form of relief/escape from an unpleasant feeling or task.

7. *Design intervention or functional analysis to test hypothesis.* Hypotheses generated may then be used to design a treatment to change the antecedents and/or consequences that are hypothesized to be maintaining the target behavior. If this treatment were designed to specifically test the hypotheses generated in the descriptive analyses, it would be termed a functional analysis.

Functional Analysis

Although functional and descriptive analyses are based on the same theory of behavioral change, the methods and goals differ. Descriptive analysis is designed to *develop* hypotheses about functional variables, whereas the primary goal of functional analysis is to *test* these hypotheses through manipulating antecedents and/or consequences hypothesized to be functionally related to the maintenance of the target behavior. More specifically, the aims are to (a) identify antecedents that are most likely to precede the target behavior, (b) identify consequences responsible for maintaining the behavior, (c) use identified reinforcing consequences to reinforce alternative behaviors, and (d) identify antecedent or consequential factors that are not reliably related to maintenance of the target behavior. The steps involved in a functional analysis follow.

1. *Develop hypotheses about functional variables.* Several methods of observation may be used to generate hypotheses about variables likely to be functionally related to the target behavior. The method with the most experimental control but the least potential generalizability is observation of the target behavior in the laboratory or clinical setting. An alternative method that simultaneously reduces experimental control while increasing generalizability is to have the patient or other observer collect information about possible antecedents and consequences for the target behavior. Third, knowledge of the factors likely to maintain certain types of behaviors may be used to augment either laboratory or naturalistic observations. For example, anxiety is nearly always accompanied by some kind of avoidance; the relief that follows it usually negatively reinforces such avoidance. Thus, when anxiety is involved, avoidance and relief should be suspected and targeted in baseline assessment. Finally, the most commonly used but least reliable information for functional analyses is the clinical interview. Either the patient or another observer provides a synopsis of the antecedents and consequences of the target behavior.

2. *Identify method of analysis.* The chosen method of analysis must take into account setting, whether single or multiple hypotheses are being tested simultaneously, and level of provocation of the target behavior. Like the hypothesis generation phase, the functional analysis may also take place in a variety of settings, ranging from laboratory and institutional settings to home and school settings. Although multiple hypotheses may be tested simultaneously in highly controlled settings (e.g., presenting randomly ordered stimuli at regular intervals and observing the target behavior), sequential tests of single hypotheses are more feasible in naturalistic settings. The functional analysis may then entail provoking the target behavior by intentionally presenting the hypothesized antecedents or waiting for natural occurrences of the behavior.

3. *Conduct experiment and observe results.*

4. *Integrate results of the functional analysis into a treatment plan.* Variables found to be central to the maintenance of the target behavior are then changed two ways. First, reinforcements for the target behavior are removed, and, second, reinforcements are used instead in response to more functional behaviors. Implementation and results of treatment are evaluated to ensure that the environment is being successfully changed and that changes are corresponding to desired changes in behavior.

RESEARCH BASIS

Functional assessment is, by nature, both philosophically and pragmatically empirical. On an individual basis, success of any descriptive or functional analysis is measured through change in the target behavior. The broader questions are, however, the comparative effectiveness within functional analytic procedures as well as how functional analysis compares with other interventions. Although the research overwhelmingly supports overall effectiveness of functional assessment interventions, these investigations are typically single-case studies or small-sample studies; comparisons with other treatments are rare. The few studies that have addressed this issue have found that in comparison with developmental or standardized assessment, functional assessments are preferred and lead to more targeted interventions. Furthermore, while standardized assessments may enhance performance for a majority of elementary school students, those who fail to respond to the standardized assessment are likely to

improve with more specific functional assessments. Comparisons within functional assessment strategies most frequently find that effectiveness improves as the rigorousness of the strategy and intervention increase. That is, functional analysis tends to be more effective and more specific than descriptive analysis in developing treatment hypotheses. Observational descriptive analysis tends to be more accurate in developing treatment hypotheses than informal or interview data collection. In addition, accuracy of descriptive analyses may be improved by the use of a more structured approach in which the hypothesized antecedent is intentionally presented to increase the target behavior frequency, thereby allowing more opportunity to observe naturally occurring consequences.

RELEVANT TARGET POPULATIONS AND EXCEPTIONS

Research relevant to generalizability addresses both the populations and settings as well as feasibility. The vast majority of the research on functional assessment has focused on intellectually or attentionally (ADD/ADHD) compromised children and adults in schools and institutional settings. Although a small body of research suggests that these interventions can be used effectively with children of average intelligence for problems such as tantrums or dysfunctional eating behaviors in less controlled settings, almost nothing is known about how functional assessment strategies may be effectively generalized to treatment with unimpaired adults. An additional generalizability concern is the feasibility of this very time-intensive procedure. Research suggests that although teachers and parents can be both successfully taught the method and state a preference for its outcome over other options, many are concerned that the costs outweigh the benefits. Some recent advances in creating briefer functional assessments with no apparent loss to accuracy may help to ameliorate this concern.

COMPLICATIONS

Serious complications with functional assessments are rare. The primary problems that arise with functional assessment are difficulties in implementation and generalizability. Because functional assessment strategies tend to involve intensive training and implementation time, caregivers may not have adequate resources or preparation to implement procedures or interventions. Incorrect implementation may then result in either a failure to improve or a worsening of symptoms. For these same reasons, functional assessment may not be generalizable to all settings or populations. In addition, intensive functional analyses resulting in behavior change in the classroom or laboratory may fail to generalize to other settings or similar behaviors.

CASE ILLUSTRATION

"Mr. Aloysius," a 56-year-old married man on disability, was referred to an outpatient behavioral medicine clinic because his reports of intense back pain continued after 10 years of medical and chiropractic care. No medical cause had been identified that explained the pain intensity. In the initial interview, Mr. A demonstrated pain behaviors throughout (i.e., moaning, wincing, howling, grimacing, stating he needed a different chair, clutching his back) and reported that his pain was "always a 10 on a scale of 1 to 10." In addition, he reported that the pain was at its worst in the morning, evening, and after meals, when he had tasks that required movement (e.g., getting dressed, bathing, cleaning up after meals, getting ready for bed, etc.). He noted that his wife was very supportive and helped him whenever he expressed that he was in pain. He stated that he wanted to reduce his pain so he could engage in more pleasurable activities (e.g., going dancing with his wife, traveling, and visiting with grandchildren). In an auxiliary interview with Mr. A's wife, she reported that she was very concerned about Mr. A's pain; however, she was growing weary of doing most of the household chores and their lives being "dominated by his pain." Mrs. A concurred that she wanted to engage in more mutually enjoyable activities as well as getting more household help from Mr. A. She stated that she would be happy to participate in any way in facilitating treatment. Based on observations during the interview and the couple's self-report, the following target behaviors were identified for decrease: severity of subjective experience of pain and pain behavior frequency. Similarly, adaptive-behavior frequency (pleasurable activities and task completion) was identified as a target to increase.

Because maintenance factors for Mr. A's persistent experience of pain were somewhat unclear, a descriptive analysis was used to generate more refined hypotheses for a functional analytic test of these hypotheses. To present a context that might maximize the couple's motivation, the following rationale was provided:

This has been a challenging time for both of you! Experiencing constant pain and a severe reduction of activities has certainly reduced the quality of life for both of you. Because you were both so willing to participate in the extensive evaluation, I think we have some ideas about where to start with treatment to help you feel less controlled by the pain and start enjoying life more. The first thing I would like to propose is that we really get an idea of exactly what makes the pain better and worse as well as what makes the pain severely impact your life satisfaction. To this end, I would like to start with an observation period (describe the steps below).

For the descriptive analysis, three types of observers were used: Mr. A's wife, Mr. A himself, and the therapist. A time-sampling schedule of observation with a combined live (therapist and wife) and self-report method of observation was selected because Mr. A's pain behavior increase appeared to occur at predictable times of day. Furthermore, this method was feasible to implement with this client and observers. The evaluation was conducted in two parts. First, the therapist accompanied Mr. A and his wife during a 4-hour previously scheduled medical evaluation to observe frequency of pain behaviors and possible antecedents and consequences. Second, Mr. and Mrs. A collected data at home during the first hour after awakening, 30 minutes after lunch, and 1 hour prior to bedtime. Mr. A set his watch to beep every 10 minutes during each observation period and recorded his subjective experience of pain. Mrs. A identified all instances of external indications of pain (i.e., pain behaviors) during the observation periods and noted what happened immediately before and after. Mr. A and his wife tracked the frequency of adaptive behaviors based on a list developed by the couple. See Table 1 for results of the descriptive analysis.

Based on this descriptive analysis, the following *hypotheses* were developed:

1. Attention is positively reinforcing pain behavior and adaptive behavior.

2. Relief from pain and unpleasant tasks is negatively reinforcing pain behavior.

Table 1   Mr. Aloysius's Descriptive Analysis

Antecedents	Target Behavior	Consequences
Therapist's observation: Wife or doctor asks Mr. A to move his body or do something uncomfortable such as paperwork or a chore (Mrs. A & therapist) Doctor reminds couples that medical evaluation is required for continued disability coverage (therapist)	Pain behavior (moaning, wincing, howling, grimacing, stating he needed a different chair, clutching his back)	Possible positive reinforcement: Wife pats husband gently and asks if everything is okay (therapist) Wife agrees to stay home from social engagements (Mrs. A) Possible negative reinforcement: Wife offers to do task for husband (Mrs. A & therapist) Doctor eases up on exercise (therapist)
Wife states that she would like Mr. A to join her for a movie and says she won't take "no" for an answer (Mrs. A & Mr. A)	Adaptive behavior	Possible positive reinforcement: Enjoying movie (Mr. A) Wife smiling, hugging, and stating over and over again how much she liked being at a movie with him (Mrs. A & Mr. A) Possible punishment: Increase in pain report the next day (Mr. A)

NOTE: The names enclosed in parentheses represent those who reported that item.

3. Increased pain and discomfort are punishing adaptive activity.

4. Disability payments are negatively reinforcing avoidance of work.

A functional analytic experiment was designed to test these hypotheses. First, although Hypotheses 1 and 2 could be tested independently by having Mr. A engage in unpleasant tasks while attention was systematically increased and decreased, and then holding attention constant while activity was increased and decreased, both were tested simultaneously. The method of analysis chosen was to test Hypotheses 1 and 2 while waiting for naturally occurring instances of the pain behavior in response to the frequently occurring requests to engage in unpleasant daily tasks. Mrs. A was instructed to continue her usual requests to engage in daily tasks and track the frequency of his pain behaviors while she varied her responses according to the following applied behavior analysis (ABA) design. On Monday, Tuesday, and Friday, she was to respond to pain behavior by saying, "I know it hurts, honey. I need your help. I won't be able to finish without your help" (withdrawing negative reinforcement for pain behavior). If pain behavior continued, she would ignore him (withdrawing positive reinforcement for pain behavior). If he helped, she would give him a kiss or hug and thank him for his help (positive reinforcement for adaptive behavior). On Tuesday and Wednesday, she was to respond to his pain behaviors by offering to do the task for him (negative reinforcement for pain behavior) and checking on him to make sure he was okay (positive reinforcement for pain behavior). Mr. A was to continue to track his pain severity throughout this week. The experiment was conducted and results can be observed in Figure 1. Results of Mr. A's Functional Analysis

As can be seen, Mr. A's pain severity and pain behaviors declined when positive and negative reinforcements for them were withdrawn. Likewise, adaptive behaviors increased with positive reinforcement. Thus, results of Mr. A's functional analysis were integrated into a treatment plan to involve continued reinforcement for adaptive behaviors and a lack thereof for pain behaviors. In addition, the treatment plan involved education for a gradual introduction of activity to reduce the probability that adaptive activity would be punished by immediate and residual pain. Monitoring of target behaviors was to continue, and if desired behavior changes were not made or maintained, the descriptive and/or functional analysis would be revisited.

—*Paula Truax*

See also: *Functional Analysis (Vols. II & III); Functional Analytic Psychotherapy (Vol. I)*

Suggested Readings

Calloway, C. J., & Simpson, R. L. (1998). Decisions regarding functions of behavior: Scientific versus informal analyses. *Focus on Autism and Other Developmental Disabilities, 13*(3), 167–175.

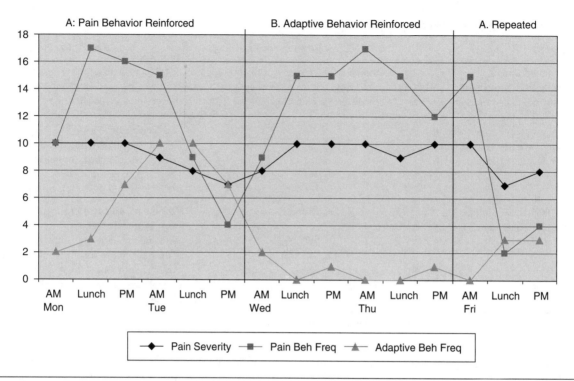

Figure 1   Results of Mr. A's Functional Analysis

Downing, J. E., & Perino, D. M. (1992). Functional versus standardized assessment procedures: Implications for educational programming. *Mental Retardation, 30*(5), 289–295.

Ervin, R. A., Radford, P. M., Bertsch, K., Piper, A. L., Ehrhardt, K. E., & Poling, A. (2001). Descriptive analysis and critique of the empirical literature on school-based functional assessment. *School Psychology Review, 30*(2), 193–210.

Freeman, K. A., Anderson, C. M., & Scotti, J. R. (2000). A structured descriptive methodology: Increasing agreement between descriptive and experimental analyses. *Education and Training in Mental Retardation and Developmental Disabilities, 35,* 55–66.

Haynes, S. N., & O'Brien, W. H. (1990). Functional analysis in behavior therapy. *Clinical Psychology Review, 10,* 649–668.

Iwata, B. A., Sung Woo, K., Wallace, M. D., & Lindberg, J. S. (2000). The functional analysis model of behavioral assessment. In J. Austin & J. E. Carr (Eds.), *Handbook of applied behavior analysis.* Reno, NV: Context Press.

March, R. E., & Horner, R. H. (2002). Feasibility and contributions of functional behavioral assessment in schools. *Journal of Emotional & Behavioral Disorders, 10*(3), 158–170.

Tincani, M. J., Castrogiavanni, A., & Axelrod, S. A. (1999). Comparison of the effectiveness of brief versus traditional functional analyses. *Research in Developmental Disabilities, 20*(5), 327–338.

Toogood, S., & Timlin, K. (2000). The functional assessment of challenging behaviour: A comparison of informant-based, experimental and descriptive methods. *Journal of Applied Research in Intellectual Disabilities, 9*(3), 206–222.

Weigle, K. L., & Scotti, J. R. (2000). Effects of functional analysis information on ratings or intervention effectiveness and acceptability. *Journal for the Association of Persons with Severe Handicaps, 25,* 217–228.

DIALECTICAL BEHAVIOR THERAPY

DESCRIPTION OF THE STRATEGY

Dialectical behavior therapy (DBT) is a comprehensive, multimodal treatment that blends psychotherapy change strategies drawn from cognitive-behavioral approaches with acceptance-based strategies drawn from Eastern meditative (primarily Zen) and Western contemplative practices. These apparently opposing notions, change and acceptance, are integrated within a dialectical framework that guides treatment from case conceptualization to execution of treatment strategies. During the 1980s, Marsha Linehan developed DBT at the University of Washington after finding that standard behavior therapies did not seem effective with the chronically suicidal women she was treating. Linehan, therefore, incorporated a series of acceptance strategies to the treatment together with a set of dialectical strategies aimed at synthesizing the two polarities. DBT later evolved into a treatment for parasuicidal behavior (including both suicide attempts and intentional self-injury) in borderline personality disorder (BPD) and has since been adapted to treat other multidiagnostic, difficult-to-treat populations.

DBT is based on a biosocial theory of the etiology and maintenance of BPD that was developed in an effort to explain BPD criterion characteristics in a manner that is compatible with behavioral theory and consistent with empirical research. The biosocial theory posits that BPD arises from a central dysfunction in the emotion regulation system that develops in childhood as the result of a dynamic transaction between an emotionally vulnerable child and an invalidating environment. The emotional vulnerability is biologically based and manifests as a high sensitivity to emotional stimuli (i.e., lower threshold for emotional response), a high reactivity to emotional stimuli (i.e., stronger emotional response to emotional stimuli), and a slow return to baseline when emotionally aroused (i.e., emotional arousal is long-lasting). People in the child's environment, whether knowingly or unwittingly, invalidate the emotional experience of the child. This, in turn, leads to an escalation of the child's emotional responses or behaviors that attempt to modulate emotions, which can exacerbate the environment's invalidating responses. The biosocial theory maintains that the relationship between the child and the environment is bidirectional and therefore both continuously influence the escalation and deescalation of borderline behaviors.

Accordingly, BPD behaviors are viewed as both the inevitable behavioral outcomes of dysregulated emotions and their display (e.g., changing and unpredictable affective reactions to others or work tasks), as well as maladaptive attempts to regulate emotions (e.g., dropping out of school, promiscuous sex, suicide attempts, etc.). The theory leads to a model of BPD that postulates that (a) BPD individuals lack important interpersonal, self-regulation (including emotion regulation), and distress tolerance skills and (b) characteristics of both the individual and the environment inhibit capabilities that the individual does have and prevent the development of new skills and capabilities. It is therefore essential for the treatment to teach new skills, enhance the skills and capabilities the client already possesses, and improve the client's motivation to use skillful behavior.

As its name suggests, dialectical philosophy is central to DBT. A dialectical framework considers reality as continuous, dynamic, and holistic. Reality, from this perspective, is simultaneously both whole and consisting of bipolar opposites (e.g., atoms consisting of opposing positive and negative charges). Dialectical truth emerges by the process of combination (or synthesis) of elements from both opposing positions (the thesis and antithesis). The primary dialectic in DBT is that of acceptance and change. A therapist may validate clients' perceptions that they are working as hard as they can and yet stress that at the same time, they must work even harder in order to move past their suffering. The acceptance-change balance is modeled both in the treatment strategies of DBT as well as the behavioral skills taught in DBT, with change-based skills such as emotion regulation and interpersonal effectiveness being balanced by more acceptance-based skills such as mindfulness and distress tolerance. From a dialectical perspective, learning to accept is a change in itself, and working to change includes an acceptance of current capabilities.

The therapeutic relationship itself frequently embodies a dialectical tension, with the therapist and the client finding themselves on opposite poles of a certain issue. The process of therapy consists of many attempts to synthesize these opposing views, reaching syntheses from which a new dialectical tension soon emerges. For example, a therapist's position may be that the client's suicidal behavior is the problem; a client's position may be that this behavior is the solution; and a potential synthesis of these positions may be that suicidal behavior is a maladaptive solution to a life of constant suffering. The new point of departure could be working on learning more adaptive skills in order to develop a life worth living. DBT also aims to increase dialectical thinking in BPD individuals, who frequently exhibit extreme dichotomous thinking and behavior (e.g., "I'm the problem" versus "He's the problem").

STRUCTURE AND STAGES OF TREATMENT

DBT is a systemic multimodal treatment, consisting in its standard form of individual behavior therapy, behavioral skills training, as-needed phone consultation, and a case consultation team focused on "treating" the therapist's behavior. Individual therapy focuses primarily on management of crises, strengthening and generalization of skills, increasing motivation to act skillfully while decreasing the motivation for dysfunctional behaviors, and overall treatment coordination and planning. Skills training focuses primarily on the acquisition of DBT skills; phone consultation primarily targets short-term crisis management, generalization of skills and repair of egregious breaks in the therapeutic relationship between sessions; and the case consultation team functions to increase both therapist motivation for treatment and adherence to the treatment protocol, as well as provide backup treatment to clients when necessary. This reflects the fact that DBT is a team-based approach that emphasizes assisting and supporting therapists in treating this population.

DBT conceptualizes the treatment as occurring in stages, each one associated with its own targets goals. Individuals in Stage I have multiple pervasive and debilitating problems, and their behavior is typically out of control. The goals of treatment in Stage I are primarily to help the client achieve stability and control of action, including achieving a reasonable life expectancy (e.g., preventing suicide or other life-threatening behaviors), developing the capacity to connect with and utilize helping individuals, reducing severe impediments to a reasonable quality of life (e.g., homelessness, disabling Axis I disorders), and acquisition of the necessary capabilities to achieve and maintain these tasks. In Stage II, individuals have their actions under reasonable control, and the main goals of treatment are to understand and reduce sequelae of early trauma and to increase clients' capabilities to experience emotions without trauma. In Stage III, clients have mostly done the necessary work of earlier stages, and treatment focuses on the resolution of residual problematic behavior that interferes with achieving other personal goals. While self-respect and self-trust are important throughout treatment, it is in this stage that they take a pivotal role. Many people can be satisfied with resolution of Stage III goals. However, many people may feel a sense of incompleteness; its resolution and the capacity for joy and a sustained sense of personal freedom are the goals of Stage IV. The tasks of treatment at this stage are to help the client achieve expanded awareness, a sense of connectedness to the universe, and spiritual fulfillment.

TREATMENT STRATEGIES

Treatment strategies in DBT broadly fall under acceptance or change categories and can be divided into five sets: (1) core strategies (validation and problem solving), (2) dialectical strategies, (3) change procedures, (4) communication strategies, and (5) case management strategies. In addition, DBT includes a number of specific behavioral treatment protocols covering suicidal behavior, crisis management, therapy-interfering behavior, relationship problem solving and ancillary treatment issues.

Core strategies consist of the balanced application of validation and problem-solving strategies. *Validation* strategies essentially require that the therapist recognize and reflect the sensibility of the client's response. There are six levels of validation specified in DBT: (1) Listening with interest, (2) reflecting an adequate understanding of what is communicated directly, (3) articulating the unspoken ("mindreading"), (4) acknowledging the role of biology and past learning experience as factors causing current client responses, (5) finding and acknowledging the validity of the client's experience and behavior in terms of present circumstances and normal functioning, and (6) responding in a radically genuine manner with the client. *Problem-solving* strategies consist of two main components: behavioral analysis and solution generation, and evaluation and implementation. The behavioral analysis entails a functional analysis of links in the chain of events that include client behavior, environmental factors, and consequences of the client's behavior. The detailed analysis is followed by a solution analysis that functions to generate, evaluate, and implement alternative solutions at each point in the chain of events. It is important to note that in DBT, emotions take a central role in the conceptualization of problem behaviors.

The change procedures in DBT are designed to remediate problems that arise in implementing the new behavioral responses (i.e., the solutions) required to solve problems previously identified in the behavioral assessment. These strategies are primarily adaptations of CBT techniques that emphasize an emotion focus. The four formal change procedures are *contingency management, cognitive restructuring, exposure-based strategies,* and *skills training.* Two communication styles are prescribed in DBT. The modal style is *reciprocal,* marked by warmth, responsiveness to the client's wishes, and self-disclosure of useful information for the client as well as reactions to the client's behavior. Reciprocal communication is balanced by *irreverent communication* style, which functions primarily to push the client "off-balance." It is used when the therapist and the client are "stuck" in some dysfunctional pattern and functions to get the client's attention, change his or her affective response, and get the client to see a completely different point of view. Last, there are three case management strategies in DBT. First, DBT requires that therapists meet regularly with a consultation team, since it is argued that severely suicidal or out-of-control clients are rarely treated effectively alone. In addition, DBT places emphasis on the therapist as a consultant to the client. This strategy stems from the point of view that the therapist's role should primarily teach the client how to interact effectively with the environment, rather than to teach the environment how to interact effectively with the client. It purports to use even distressing difficult situations as learning opportunities and to help teach the client to deal with the world as it is with its imperfections and inequities. However, when necessary to protect the client's life or modify a situation beyond his or her control or when it is the ordinary humane thing to do, the DBT therapist enters and directly intervenes in the client's environment.

Dialectical strategies are woven into all therapeutic interactions. They include the attention to balance of acceptance and change throughout therapy and in every therapeutic exchange. Since one of the goals of treatment is to increase clients' dialectical thinking, a key idea guiding the therapist is that for every position, an opposite position could be held, and the therapist is to bring out the opposites both in therapy and in the client's life, while providing an opportunity for synthesis. This is done by use of stories and metaphors, paradox, ambiguity (when therapeutic), and by drawing attention to changing nature of reality.

RESEARCH BASIS

There is a strong and growing body of DBT research across a variety of populations. Randomized controlled trials have evaluated the efficacy of DBT for the treatment of BPD with current suicidality, BPD and substance abuse, major depression with personality disorder characteristics among the elderly, and binge-eating disorder. As well, there have been a substantial number of controlled, but nonrandomized, trials of DBT in forensic systems, with suicidal

adolescents, on BPD inpatient units, and in other outpatient settings.

Generally, results across the studies indicate that DBT is superior to a variety of non-DBT control conditions in reducing targeted problem behaviors (suicide attempts, substance abuse, treatment dropout, use of psychiatric inpatient hospitalization) and improving both general and social functioning. In less severe populations (perhaps those beginning treatment at Stage II), suicide ideation, depression, and hopelessness are also more effectively reduced in DBT than in control treatments. A study evaluating 3-month inpatient hospitalization has found that the population was divided into a group of clients who have shown remarkable improvement and another group who showed very little improvement. While the investigators have not been able to find post hoc predictors for the responders versus nonresponders, it is possible that DBT is significantly more efficacious for a subtype of BPD population. Further research is necessary. To date, research studies have for the most part evaluated DBT for a period of up to a year. While this period is sufficient for many BPD individuals to move to Stage II of treatment, it is usually not enough time to reach Stages III or IV of treatment, where treatment focuses on major life goals and the capacity for joy and a sense of freedom.

RELEVANT TARGET POPULATIONS AND EXCEPTIONS

DBT was initially developed and evaluated for the treatment of chronically suicidal women meeting criteria for BPD. The bulk of the research support is for this population. It has been adapted for the treatment of BPD and substance abuse, BPD and eating disorders, suicidal adolescents with BPD features, depression among the elderly, and antisocial personality in forensic settings. To date, there are no known populations for which DBT is contraindicated. However, efficacy has not been established for other populations.

COMPLICATIONS

DBT is a multimodal complex treatment, and no research to date has evaluated the components of the treatment. Further research is needed for the mechanisms by which DBT effects change in DBT behaviors. There are some data, however, suggesting that adherence to the DBT treatment protocols may improve outcomes and that egregious violations of protocols may compromise outcomes.

CASE ILLUSTRATION

"Karla" was a White, divorced 28-year-old woman, who, at the time of her referral to the second author, met criteria for BPD, major depression, generalized anxiety disorder, reflex sympathetic dystrophy, and a partially controlled seizure condition. She had had more than 30 psychiatric hospitalizations and parasuicide episodes of varying suicidal intent and degrees of lethality. At the time of intake, conducted while she was on an inpatient unit, Karla was on psychiatric disability and over the last year had engaged in a series of parasuicidal behaviors, including frequent overdoses and episodes of tying a belt tightly around her neck to precipitate unconsciousness. This was, according to her, the only way she could deal with her emotions. According to her self-report, corroborated by hospital and school records and subsequent family meeting, Karla had a long history of an invalidating environment, exemplified by a failed attempt at abortion, physical abuse from her mother toward herself and a sister, an 8-year incestuous and sometimes violent relationship with her father, and a severe learning disability that led to her inappropriately being schooled as mentally retarded when, in reality, she had above average-intelligence. At age 12, she threw herself out of a car, was hospitalized, revealed the incest to hospital staff, who ignored it, and began a series of long inpatient hospitalizations, punctuated by living with former inpatient staff who could not adequately care for her.

Treatment targets in the first few months involved reducing Karla's parasuicidal behavior and forming a strong therapeutic alliance. Behavioral analysis was used to begin tracing the usual sequence of events that led to Karla's suicidal behavior. Using routine monitoring and several behavioral analyses, a characteristic chain of events emerged: (a) a problem (especially involving a sense of rejection), (b) experiencing a painful emotion, (c) images and fantasies of suicide, (d) if still experiencing painful emotion, psychological withdrawal, and (d) if still in pain, overdose or strangulation. It became clear that spending hours at home was correlated with suicidal fantasies and time spent on manual work, particularly home repair for family or friends, was correlated with low misery scores on her monitoring card. Suicidal images also appeared to be linked to anger-producing stimuli as well as to stimuli reminding Karla of previous losses.

Several strategies were used to treat the parasuicidal behavior. First, continuing behavioral analyses were conducted, organizing and articulating the recurring patterns. With each analysis, dysfunctional behaviors were identified, possible alternative more functional behaviors were generated and factors interfering with new behaviors were identified, and therapy focused on reducing those interfering factors. At first, simple crisis survival strategies such as distraction, self-soothing, and figuring out pros and cons of impulsive behaviors were taught and reinforced. Then, treatment focused on teaching and reinforcing exposure to emotional stimuli and experiences, which Karla characteristically avoided, and interpersonal skills to increase positive events in her life and decrease her sense of isolation and loneliness. Mindfulness skills of observing, describing, participating, taking a nonjudgmental stance, attending to the present, focusing on being effective, along with the skills of radical acceptance, were taught and practiced. Third, contingency management was used, both for reducing suicidal behaviors and behaviors interfering with therapy as well as for increasing skillful behavior. Generally, the most powerful reinforcing contingencies were praise, therapeutic warmth, and getting control of the session agenda. After 8 months, strangulation was stopped, and after 18 months, parasuicide was stopped altogether.

Once the sexual abuse was revealed in therapy, the therapist conducted 10 formal exposure sessions (at that time, Karla was at Stage II of treatment, without any parasuicidal behavior). Finding the appropriate cue was challenging, but it was discovered that the size differential (therapist standing on a chair) helped to elicit the appropriate emotional arousal. Karla and her therapist continued to work on coping with Karla's neurological problem and on maintaining high activation level through a volunteer job.

—*Noam Lindenboim*
and Marsha M. Linehan

See also: *Therapeutic Relationship (Vol. I); Trauma Management Therapy (Vol. I); Treatment Failures in Behavioral Treatment (Vol. I)*

Suggested Readings

Koerner, K., & Linehan, M. M. (2000). Research on dialectical behavior therapy for borderline personality disorder. *The Psychiatric Clinics of North America, 23*(1), 151–167.

Linehan, M. M. (1993). *Cognitive-behavioral treatment of borderline personality disorder.* New York: Guilford Press.

Linehan, M. M. (1993). *Skills training manual for treating borderline personality disorder.* New York: Guilford Press.

Linehan, M. M. (1997). Validation and psychotherapy. In A. Bohart & L. Greenberg (Eds.), *Empathy reconsidered: New directions in psychotherapy* (pp. 353–392). Washington, DC: American Psychological Association.

Linehan, M. M. (1998). Development, evaluation, and dissemination of effective psychosocial treatments: Stages of disorder, levels of care, and stages of treatment research. In M. D. Glantz & C. R. Hartel (Eds.), *Drug abuse: Origins and interventions.* Washington, DC: American Psychological Association.

Linehan, M. M., Armstrong, H. E., Suarez, A., Allmon, D., & Heard, H. L. (1991). Cognitive-behavioral treatment of chronically parasuicidal borderline patients. *Archives of General Psychiatry, 48,* 1060–1064.

DIFFERENTIAL REINFORCEMENT OF OTHER BEHAVIOR

DESCRIPTION OF THE STRATEGY

Differential reinforcement of other behavior (DRO) involves the delivery of reinforcement for periods of time during which a target behavior has been absent (e.g., John receives $1 for each day during which he does not hit someone). While this strategy was first used with animals in the early 1960s, it has grown in popularity in applied settings as an alternative to contingent punishment (e.g., time-out, response cost, restitution and overcorrection, and contingent work).

Clinically, there are a variety of ways that a DRO can be implemented. In a *reset DRO,* a "timer" is set for a specified period of time. If the person does not engage in the target behavior during this time, reinforcement is delivered. If the target behavior does occur, the timer is reset. In a *fixed-time DRO,* equal intervals of time are specified (e.g., 10 minutes, 30 minutes, 90 minutes). If the behavior does not occur during an interval, the person is reinforced at the end of the interval for the absence of the behavior. If the behavior does occur, reinforcement is not delivered at that time.

In a *progressive DRO,* otherwise known as a DROP, the procedure is quite similar to the fixed-time strategy but with the following differences. In the DROP, for each consecutive interval during which the target behavior is absent, the reinforcement delivered increases by a specified amount up to a specified maximum. For example, for the first interval without the behavior, the person is given one token; for the

second consecutive interval without the behavior, the person is given two tokens, and so on, up to a specified maximum (e.g., six tokens). As with the other DRO strategies, if the target behavior occurs, reinforcement is not delivered at the end of the interval. The next interval that the person does not engage in the target behavior, the reinforcement is recycled back to the beginning of the progression (e.g., one token) and the progression proceeds as described above. DROP can be particularly applicable when dealing with low-rate behavior (e.g., once a week or longer), with a 1-day DROP interval.

In instances of high-rate, pervasive behaviors (e.g., rocking, self-stimulatory behavior, rumination, twiddling) a *momentary DRO* would be appropriate. This strategy involves observing the person at the end of specified periods of time throughout a day or a session (e.g., 15 minutes, 20 minutes, and 60 minutes) and delivering reinforcement if the target behavior is absent at the "moment" of observation. If the behavior is occurring, reinforcement is not delivered.

There are other ways of implementing a DRO that are beyond the scope of this entry. Some of these include *fixed-time with reset DRO, variable-time DRO,* and *escalating DRO.* With all of these strategies, some rules need to be observed for them to be effective. For example, the size of the DRO interval is extremely important. Initially, the interval size should assure that the person would be successful 50% of the time. Thus, if the person exhibits the target behavior an average of once an hour, the criterion would be 30 minutes without the behavior for reinforcement to occur. Other rules to consider involve how the reinforcers are used. First, what is chosen must be motivating; in other words, it must be worth the effort. Second, the reinforcer should be available only through the DRO strategy (i.e., reinforcer exclusivity). And third, the total amount available should not approach or result in satiation. Care should be taken that the person continues to be interested in the available reinforcer throughout the DRO procedure.

A DRO should not be used in isolation. It is nonconstructive; it does not teach skills; and it suppresses behavior. Thus, a DRO should be used as part of a multi-element support plan that is based on a functional assessment/analysis. The multi-element plan should include ecological strategies designed to improve the "goodness of fit" between the person and his or her living, working, and social environments; positive programming strategies designed to teach functionally equivalent and other critical skills;

focused support strategies designed to gain rapid reduction in the occurrence of challenging behaviors (e.g., antecedent control, stimulus satiation, and reinforcement strategies, including DRO); and reactive strategies designed to reduce the episodic severity of behavioral incidents, thus keeping the person and others safe. DRO and other focused-support strategies can be faded out after the planned ecological changes and the person has learned the critical skills.

—*Gary W. LaVigna and Thomas J. Willis*

See also: *Competing Response Training (Vols. I & II); Differential Reinforcement of Other Behavior (Vol. III)*

Suggested Readings

Donnellan, A. M., LaVigna, G. W., Negri-Shoultz, N., & Fassbender, L. L. (1988). *Progress without punishment.* New York: Teachers College Press.

LaVigna, G. W., & Donnellan, A. M. (1986). *Alternative to punishment: Solving behavior problems with non-aversive strategies.* New York: Irvington.

E

EATING DISORDERS

DESCRIPTION OF THE STRATEGY

Cognitive-behavioral therapy (CBT) for eating disorders is a short-term, semistructured approach in which the therapist and client work collaboratively to address problematic thoughts and behaviors. When treating an individual who has an eating disorder, the therapist first completes a thorough assessment of the client's symptoms and background. Treatment begins by introducing the cognitive model of eating disorders. According to the cognitive model, the core psychopathology in eating disorders is a dysfunctional self-evaluation that is overly negative and based almost entirely upon body shape, weight, and ability to control eating. Overvaluation of appearance and weight contribute to an intense fear of fat, which leads to extreme and rigid dieting.

The cognitive model identifies dieting as a primary cause of binge eating. For most people, extreme dieting attempts cannot be sustained indefinitely. When rigid control is interrupted in any way, often by breaking a dieting rule, the reaction is to temporarily abandon any eating rules, resulting in a complete loss of control over eating. The binge episode allows a brief escape from rigid control and sometimes an escape from negative feelings, which reinforces bingeing. However, shortly after the binge come feelings of guilt, depression, self-loathing, and intense anxiety about weight gain. Purging, most typically through self-induced vomiting, reduces anxiety about weight gain following a binge, which negatively reinforces the purge. Both bingeing and purging contribute to

poor self-esteem, thereby strengthening the negative self-schema. The individual renews her commitment to rigid dietary rules as a means to overcome feelings of inadequacy, and the diet/binge/purge cycle continues.

After introducing the cognitive model, the therapist teaches self-monitoring, a cornerstone of the treatment. Self-monitoring of foods eaten, times, binge eating, purging, moods, and situations provides specific information on antecedents and consequences of bingeing and purging. Using the cognitive-behavioral model as a framework, the therapist incorporates interview and self-monitoring information for a particular client into an individual conceptualization of the problem.

The first stage of treatment includes both psychoeducation and application of behavioral techniques to establish more regular eating habits, decrease rigid dieting, and decrease bingeing and purging. Clients are asked to eat three meals plus two snacks at regular times each day. Weekly weighing provides feedback to the client on how changes in her eating behaviors affect her weight. Self-control strategies, similar to those used in behavioral treatment of obesity, provide the client with tools to refrain from both purging and bingeing. Self-monitoring records help identify cues for binge eating or food restriction. The therapist teaches stimulus control techniques to help the client avoid or change situations that typically trigger a binge. For example, an evening telephone conversation with a young woman's mother is upsetting and often triggers a binge. She learns to substitute an alternative response of calling her good friend after speaking with her mother, which helps her to avoid the binge. Alternatively, she may decide to call her mother in the mornings, when she has less time and opportunity to binge. Self-reward strategies may be used to increase eating for individuals who are overly restrictive or to establish regular eating patterns when eating is chaotic.

The first stage also includes psychoeducation to help reduce dieting, bingeing, and purging. The therapist teaches the client that using laxatives or vomiting as a means of weight control is quite dangerous physically and is not effective in ridding the body of calories. Clients are taught that severe restriction makes people more vulnerable to binge eating and can decrease metabolism, making it increasingly more difficult to lose weight. The therapist and client together talk about what is normal weight for the client and what normal fluctuations in weight can be expected. Clients are encouraged to schedule pleasant events, such as enjoyable hobbies, in order to broaden their activities beyond a narrow focus on food and weight.

Stage 2 of CBT addresses problematic attitudes and beliefs that maintain the disorder, including negative self-beliefs and dysfunctional beliefs about weight, shape, and eating. The negative weight-related self-schema in eating disorders contributes to characteristic negative patterns of thinking, similar to those found in depressed individuals. For example, black-and-white or dichotomous thinking is common, where a woman sees herself as either "fat" or "thin." Foods are either "good or bad," with nothing in-between. First, clients are taught to identify automatic dysfunctional thoughts that can lead to disordered eating (e.g., "I ate that ice cream yesterday. I'm getting fat. I have to skip breakfast and lunch today"). Clients learn to question the validity of these thoughts by finding "evidence" for and against them, then to develop less negative responses (e.g., "I may have gained 1 pound this week, but that doesn't mean I am going to get fat. I am not eating so much that I will gain weight quickly"). Learning to recognize and counter negative thoughts can reduce negative feelings and help to change problematic behaviors. The process of restructuring automatic thoughts should eventually move toward identifying and changing core dysfunctional beliefs or values (e.g., "I need to be thin in order to be liked and respected"). Cognitive techniques address not only weight-related dysfunctional beliefs but also dysfunctional beliefs regarding interpersonal relationships, family life, work, and school.

Exposure techniques are helpful for clients who are avoiding a great number of foods or avoiding anxiety-provoking situations. Distorted cognitions about food and weight often lead individuals to extreme methods of dieting, with many foods identified as "forbidden" because they are "fattening." Avoiding a particular food because of fear of weight gain increases the strength of that fear. Exposure to the food without experiencing the feared consequences of weight gain or purging will reduce fear of the food. Therefore, the client and therapist work to expose the client to a wide range of foods, gradually adding feared and forbidden foods to the diet. Generally, the client is able to eat the foods on her own. When the client is at risk for purging with even a small amount of the food, it may be necessary to first use exposure imaginally during a therapy session. Relaxation may be taught to help the client decrease anxiety. Exposure to feared situations may be helpful to confront situations that have been avoided. Many individuals who have eating disorders avoid situations in which they must wear revealing clothing, such as swimming. Clients may avoid situations in which they must eat in front of others, such as at restaurants or parties. Some clients also avoid many social situations that make them anxious.

During the third stage, the focus turns to maintenance of changes using relapse prevention techniques. Clients develop a detailed list of likely relapse situations and develop a plan for coping with these situations. A detailed, step-by-step plan is written so that the client can refer to it in the future when needed. Clients with eating disorders are likely to think in all-or-none terms, so it is important that they learn to expect setbacks and view them as opportunities for learning.

Like bulimia nervosa, the core psychopathology in anorexia nervosa involves a negative self-schema and an overemphasis on the importance of weight and shape to self-esteem. However, the maintaining factors in anorexia nervosa differ, requiring different treatment techniques. An individual with anorexia nervosa may feel proud of losing weight and maintaining control over hunger. This sense of accomplishment in achieving weight loss goals strongly reinforces food restriction. Dieting and weight loss are negatively reinforced through avoiding the feared stimulus of weight gain. The narrow focus on food and weight may help the individual to avoid dealing with the complexities of their social and emotional lives. The effects of starvation perpetuate the disorder by decreasing metabolic rate, thereby requiring further cuts in calories to maintain the low weight. Starvation also increases rigid food rituals, preoccupation with food, irritability, and social withdrawal.

Treatment of anorexia nervosa typically lasts 1 to 2 years, compared with about 5 months for bulimia nervosa. Individuals with anorexia nervosa typically have very low motivation for treatment. Therefore, the first stage of treatment focuses on developing motivation for change and building a therapeutic relationship. Using a nonconfrontational style, the therapist and client explore the effects of the patient's food and weight choices on emotional and physical functioning. Weight gain must be a primary treatment target because symptoms of starvation can maintain the disorder and because starvation limits the cognitive functioning and the ability to participate in therapy. During treatment, the client slowly works toward eating larger amounts and variety of foods. Meal planning must be addressed in therapy unless the client is also working with a nutritionist. Similar to CBT for bulimia nervosa, the focus of therapy gradually shifts to work on underlying issues related to self-concept, interpersonal problems, and perfectionism. Family involvement is often necessary when treating adolescents. The last stage of treatment focuses on relapse prevention.

RESEARCH BASIS

Several treatment manuals are available for CBT of bulimia nervosa, and more than 50 randomized, controlled studies have compared CBT with other approaches. Studies also support the cognitive-behavioral model of the maintenance of bulimia nervosa. CBT works better than delayed-treatment control groups, supportive-expressive psychotherapy, brief psychodynamic therapy, nutritional counseling, stress management, and pharmacotherapy. CBT is also superior to behavior therapy alone. Interpersonal psychotherapy has shown success rates similar to those of CBT.

Studies find that about half of people who finish treatment achieve a complete absence of binge eating or purging. Most achieve a very low frequency of binge eating and purging by the end of treatment. CBT also improves attitudes toward shape and weight, social functioning, and self-esteem. Those who respond well to CBT appear to maintain changes in the long-term. The strongest predictor of success in CBT is the frequency and severity of bingeing and purging before treatment. Although CBT generally

works well, a small proportion of patients do not benefit significantly from CBT. Clients who fare poorly in CBT do no better in interpersonal psychotherapy. Therefore, recent modifications of CBT for eating disorders were developed with the goal of improving outcomes. The revised CBT offers specific techniques to address low self-esteem, interpersonal difficulties, mood regulation problems, and extreme perfectionistic attitudes.

Relatively few studies have investigated CBT for anorexia nervosa. Research available indicates that CBT is superior to nutritional counseling or pharmacotherapy alone, but nothing is yet known about how CBT compares with other forms of psychotherapy. Although CBT for anorexia nervosa has some research support, dropout rates are high, and many clients still experience some symptoms after treatment.

RELEVANT TARGET POPULATIONS AND EXCEPTIONS

In general, CBT is delivered on an individual basis in outpatient settings. However, research suggests that group format may be as effective as individual CBT. Self-help manuals used with supervision are also effective in reducing binge eating and purging for some individuals. For anorexia nervosa, individual therapy is recommended due to the more intensive nature of the treatment. Inpatient or partial hospitalization is often recommended when medical complications in anorexia nervosa are severe. In particular, individuals who are severely underweight may be best treated in an inpatient setting. Brief, involuntary admissions are sometimes used to restore weight in an individual whose health and safety are at risk.

CBT is also effective in treating individuals with binge-eating disorder who binge regularly but do not use extreme behaviors to control their weight (i.e., self-induced vomiting, laxative or diuretic use, or fasting). Compared with those with bulimia nervosa, individuals with binge-eating disorder are heavier and have less severe concerns about weight and shape. CBT for binge-eating disorder is quite similar to that for bulimia nervosa, with some modifications to help individuals lose weight. Research has found that CBT for binge-eating disorder helps to reduce the frequency and severity of binge eating and to improve body image and self-esteem. However, people who complete the treatment do not usually lose weight.

COMPLICATIONS

For the therapist, treatment of eating disorders, particularly anorexia nervosa, can be very time-consuming and stressful. Eating disorders cause numerous and potentially severe health consequences. Anorexia nervosa has a mortality rate higher than any other psychological disorder. Bulimia nervosa can lead to electrolyte imbalance and cardiac arrest. Thus, patients must be monitored by a physician who is knowledgeable about eating disorders. Often, therapists coordinate a client's care with a physician, dietitian, and family therapist, requiring considerable time outside sessions. When treating children and teenagers, the therapist must also decide on how to involve parents.

In addition to these practical difficulties, many who suffer from eating disorders have a second psychiatric disorder. Anxiety symptoms are common and generally begin before the eating disorder. Anorexia nervosa is frequently accompanied by obsessive-compulsive symptoms and bulimia nervosa by social phobia. Anxiety symptoms may need to be addressed separately in treatment. A substantial proportion of individuals who have bulimia nervosa also have significant problems with substance abuse that may need to be treated before the eating-disorder treatment begins. Presence of a personality disorder tends to predict a poor treatment outcome and may require additional treatment approaches and longer treatment duration. Although depression is frequently present in people who have an eating disorder, it is most likely a consequence of the eating disorder, and it decreases with standard CBT.

CASE ILLUSTRATION

"Kelsey" was an 18-year-old attending her first year of college. She was experiencing difficulties with leaving home and adjusting to college life. She gained 5 pounds in her first few months of eating in the cafeteria, became frightened by her weight gain, and started a restrictive diet regimen. Her diet led to binge eating, then later to self-induced vomiting after the binges. She came to the initial session feeling out of control, shameful, and afraid of weight gain. She reported bingeing and purging on 3 to 4 days per week, usually in the evenings when she was alone in her room. During the first sessions, the therapist obtained information about Kelsey's eating and weight-related symptoms, symptoms of depression and anxiety, psychosocial history, and current functioning. The therapist described the rationale for using CBT and the importance of self-monitoring in directing treatment. Kelsey took home a food record to monitor food eaten, time of day, binges, purges, and situations and emotions leading to binges. It was explained that self-monitoring would provide valuable information about her pattern of binges and purges. The records would also provide a baseline of information so that she could note improvements in the future.

At the next session, Kelsey and the therapist studied the diary and talked about specific antecedents and consequences of binge/purge episodes. An important high-risk situation for Kelsey was being alone in her room in the evenings and feeling anxious, yet bored, while studying. She described a binge/purge episode in which she felt somewhat hungry and began to think about food. She tried not to think about eating but eventually gave in, went down to the basement of the dorm to the candy machine, and purchased 5 candy bars. She took the candy to her room and began eating quickly; tearing the wrappers and hiding them in the garbage, while barely even tasting the candy. She felt fat, ugly, disgusted with herself, and fearful of gaining weight. She felt intense pressure to get rid of the calories and went to the bathroom to make herself vomit. After vomiting, she felt sick, exhausted, and unable to concentrate to study, and went to sleep.

The therapist explained to Kelsey that vomiting does not prevent all of the food and calories from being absorbed and has potentially dangerous consequences. They worked together on a plan to prevent bingeing and purging using self-control techniques. Kelsey worked on changing the high-risk situation of being alone in the evenings. She began making plans with friends to study together in the evenings. She also decided to reward herself at the end of evenings with a phone call to her mother or boyfriend. Kelsey was encouraged to eat regular meals and snacks, so that her food restriction would not set her up for binges. Although Kelsey feared gaining weight if she followed the program, the therapist explained that the number of calories would not result in weight gain and that eating more could actually increase her metabolism, making weight control easier. They agreed to weigh her weekly prior to her therapy session in order to monitor any weight changes.

As weeks went by and she followed the meal plan, she began to trust that she would not gain weight and that she was bingeing much less. To continue decreasing dietary restraint, she was encouraged to slowly increase total number of calories she was eating and to gradually incorporate feared and forbidden foods into her diet. Kelsey created a list of forbidden foods, rating each as to how much she feared and avoided the food. Starting with the least feared food, she introduced approximately one food every week, eating the food with a friend so that she would not purge. As she became more comfortable with a particular food, she took it off of her list of feared foods.

As Kelsey's bingeing and purging became infrequent, the focus shifted from eating to attitudes about weight and appearance. The therapist explained cognitive restructuring and provided a form for recording automatic thoughts. She was able to identify many dysfunctional automatic thoughts, such as "People won't like or respect me if I gain weight." She was also able to identify attributes that she valued in her friends that were completely unrelated to weight and was able to see that her friends valued her for her loyalty, sense of humor, and ability to listen to them. In fact, Kelsey was surprised to learn that her friends did not notice changes in her weight. She began to acknowledge her positive qualities and to view herself in more complex ways, rather than focusing narrowly on weight and appearance. The therapist provided information about cultural pressures on women to be thin and the ridiculously thin ideal promoted by the media.

The final sessions of therapy focused on relapse prevention strategies. Kelsey worked to identify high-risk times that she may face in the future and outlined a strategy for dealing with the plan. For example, arguments with her boyfriend, though infrequent, had always led to bingeing and purging. She decided to write out a specific plan for what she would do to avoid bingeing when they next argued. Her plan listed a number of options, such as calling one of two close friends, getting out of her room and around people, going for a walk, and writing about her feelings in a journal.

Kelsey participated in therapy for a total of 6 months, with breaks for holidays and gradually tapering off toward the end. She was able to completely eliminate bingeing and vomiting. She was able to maintain an acceptable weight while eating three meals per day and exercising regularly. She felt less depressed and was much more active socially. Kelsey also felt good about changes she had made in her self-image.

—*Linda Krug Porzelius*

See also: *Behavioral Medicine (Vol. I); Behavioral Pediatrics (Vol. II); Fading (Vol. III)*

Suggested Readings

Fairburn, C. G. (1995). *Overcoming binge eating.* New York: Guilford Press.

Fairburn, C. G., Cooper, Z., & Shafran, R. (2003). Cognitive behaviour therapy for eating disorders: A "transdiagnostic" theory and treatment. *Behavior Research and Therapy, 41,* 509–528.

Fairburn, C. G., Marcus, M. D., & Wilson, G. T. (1993). Cognitive-behavioral therapy for binge eating and bulimia nervosa: A comprehensive treatment manual. In C. G. Fairburn & G. T. Wilson (Eds.), *Binge eating: Nature, assessment, and treatment* (pp. 383–418). New York: Guilford Press.

Garner, D. M., Vitousek, K., & Pike, K. (1997). Cognitive-behavioral therapy for anorexia nervosa. In D. M. Garner & P. E. Garfinkel (Eds.), *Handbook of treatment for eating disorders* (pp. 94–144). New York: Guilford Press.

Wilson, G. T., & Fairburn, C. G. (2002). Treatments for eating disorders. In P. E. Nathan & J. M. Gorman (Eds.), *A guide to treatments that work* (pp. 559–592). Oxford, UK: Oxford University Press.

EFFICACY, EFFECTIVENESS, AND PATIENT-FOCUSED RESEARCH

DESCRIPTION OF THE STRATEGY

Psychotherapy research has historically been classified into two broad categories: *efficacy* and *effectiveness research.* Efficacy and effectiveness research represent unique yet complementary methods for conducting empirical studies on the effects of psychotherapy and have provided an abundance of evidence that psychotherapies of various kinds are effective treatments for a variety of psychological disorders. The primary differences between the two methods revolve around what is sometimes referred to as the "interpretability/generalizability" dilemma. Efficacy research, which seeks to answer the question, "Does the treatment work under well-controlled experimental conditions?" involves clinical trials of specific therapies. The goal of efficacy research is to maximize internal validity through stringent experimental control, thereby allowing researchers to more confidently attribute findings to treatment rather than to other factors that may have produced the results. In other words, efficacy research strives to ensure the interpretability of results. However, the stringent experimental control in this type of research is rarely, if ever, found in actual clinical practice, thereby limiting the generalizability of results. In fact, opponents of efficacy research and clinical trials have described it as a contextless method used to study context-rich participants and interventions. They argue that efficacy research is the wrong method for empirically validating psychotherapy as it is actually done, because it omits too many crucial elements of what is done in the field. Proponents, on the other hand, claim that efficacy research is the core method for placing treatments on a firm empirical foundation.

Effectiveness research, in contrast to efficacy research, attempts to answer the question, "Does the treatment work in practice?" The goal of effectiveness research is to maximize the external validity or generalizability of results. In other words, there is a high premium placed on studying treatments as they are routinely delivered by clinicians practicing in the field. Accordingly, effectiveness research is generally conducted in less controlled naturalistic or "real world" clinical settings, thereby bridging the gap between science and practice. While providing potentially valuable information to practicing clinicians, effectiveness research also has limitations. Due to the lack of stringent experimental control often present in these studies, results are often subject to many possible interpretations, and numerous replications with greater levels of experimental control are generally required to test alternative interpretations of results from such research. The differences in the objectives of efficacy and effectiveness research (i.e., stringent experimental control resulting in high internal validity allowing for interpretability of results versus less experimental control resulting in high external validity allowing for generalizability of results, respectively) are manifested in the conceptualization, design, and implementation of psychotherapy research studies. While it is sometimes difficult to categorize specific studies as being efficacy or effectiveness research because there is considerable variability and overlap in design features, these two methods typically differ in a variety of ways.

SELECTION OF PARTICIPANTS

In efficacy research, several patient characteristics are often used to determine whether patients are included or excluded from a study. The rationale for establishing inclusion/exclusion criteria that guide selection of participants is based on the need to create a homogeneous group of patients, particularly with regard to diagnosis, that can subsequently be randomized to treatment and control conditions. For example, patients who meet criteria for a single diagnosed disorder are typically selected to participate, while patients with multiple disorders are typically excluded. Diagnostic interviews of potential study participants are conducted using standardized interview procedures with demonstrated reliability, such as the Structured Clinical Interview for Diagnosis (SCID), and the diagnosis is typically made in strict accordance with criteria established in the current edition of the *Diagnostic and Statistical Manual of Mental Disorders.* Furthermore, severity of impairment is often an inclusion/exclusion criterion used in efficacy research. Patients must not only have a single disorder, but the severity of the impairment must fall within a specified range of scores on a particular standardized instrument. In other words, the patient's score on a standardized measure must not be too low, as this might cast doubt as to whether the patient's level of impairment warrants the diagnosis of the disorder/condition that is the focus of the study, but it must also not be too high so as to raise questions about the patient's suitability for participation (e.g., a patient who scores above a specified score on a standardized measure of depression may be experiencing significant suicidal ideation, making the patient unsuitable for the study for ethical reasons). Particular attention is often given to selecting "diagnostically pure" patients for participation in efficacy studies in order to ensure that the disorder of interest and associated symptoms, rather than some other condition or set of problems, are clearly identified. This, in turn, allows for target outcomes to be clearly operationalized (e.g., number of depressive symptoms, number of panic attacks). Age, presence of a specific physical illness, use of medications, concurrent treatment, and substance use are examples of other patient characteristics often used to exclude individuals from an efficacy study for the purpose of creating a homogeneous patient sample. Selecting a homogeneous group of patients, in addition to randomizing them to treatment and control conditions, makes it very difficult to attribute any observed differences between treatment and control groups to differences in patient characteristics.

Effectiveness studies, on the other hand, do not typically exercise significant control over the selection of patients for a study. Inclusion and exclusion criteria are minimal, if at all present, and are driven by clinical necessity and procedures rather than a need for experimental control (e.g., a patient is excluded from participating in an effectiveness study of individual psychotherapy simply because the most appropriate treatment for the patient is deemed to be group psychotherapy). The presence of only minimal inclusion and exclusion criteria allows for a great deal of sample heterogeneity. For example, given that effectiveness studies are typically carried out in routine clinical settings, diagnostic procedures are usually of unknown reliability; practicing clinicians conduct diagnostic interviews that are typically far less structured than the diagnostic interviews conducted in efficacy studies. Consequently, patients with multiple problems or comorbid diagnoses are accepted for treatment and often invited to participate in ongoing effectiveness research. Furthermore, other patient characteristics such as age, presence of a specific illness, and substance use are not typically grounds for exclusion from an effectiveness study. While the allowance of sample heterogeneity raises questions with regard to exactly what disorder or condition is being treated in an effectiveness study, such heterogeneity is highly representative of most clinical service delivery systems, where demographically diverse patients with multiple problems and varying backgrounds often present for treatment.

SELECTION OF CONTROL CONDITIONS

In addition to the treatments under investigation in efficacy and effectiveness research, investigators have the difficult task of deciding which control condition(s) to use. In psychotherapy research, there are essentially four different types of control conditions that can be employed: no treatment, wait-list, attention-placebo, and standard treatment. Patients who are assigned to a no-treatment control condition are administered the assessments on repeated occasions, separated by an interval of time equal to the length of the therapy provided to those in the treatment condition. Any changes seen in the treated patients are compared with the changes seen in the untreated patients.

When treated patients evidence significantly superior improvements over untreated patients, the treatment is credited with producing the changes. This control procedure has desirable features and eliminates several rival hypotheses (e.g., spontaneous remission, historical effects, maturation, and regression to the mean). However, a no-treatment control condition does not guard against other potentially confounding factors, including patient anticipation of treatment, patient expectancy for change, and the act of seeing a therapist, independent of what treatment the therapist actually provided. Although a no-treatment control condition is sometimes useful in the earlier stages of the evaluation of a treatment, other control procedures are preferred.

The wait-list condition, a variant of a no-treatment procedure, provides some additional control. For example, patients in a wait-list control condition have made the step of initiating treatment and may anticipate change due to therapy. The changes that occur for wait-listed patients are evaluated, as are those of the patients who received therapy. Assuming the patients in the wait-list and the treatment conditions are comparable in terms of variables such as gender, age, ethnicity, severity of presenting problem, and motivation, the research may then make inferences that the changes over and above those manifested by the wait-list patients are likely due to the intervention rather than to any extraneous factors that were operative for both the treated and the wait-list conditions. The important demographic and other data are gathered so that statistical comparisons can be conducted to determine condition comparability. Wait-list conditions, like no-treatment conditions, are of less value for treatments that have already been compared with other "inactive" conditions in prior studies. Furthermore, there are potential problems with wait-list controls. Withholding treatment from wait-list patients, particularly for extended periods of time, raises ethical questions. For example, a wait-list patient might experience a life crisis that forces immediate professional attention. For this and other reasons, each control patient's status should be monitored informally but frequently. Independent of pressing distress, wait-list patients are offered the therapy, or an acceptable and effective substitute, as soon as possible after the study is completed.

Attention-placebo (or nonspecific treatment) control conditions are an alternate to the wait-list control that can not only rule out threats to internal validity but also control for the effects that might be due simply to meeting with a therapist. Participants in attention-placebo conditions have contact with and receive attention from a therapist. In addition, these participants often receive a description of the treatment rationale (a statement of purpose and explanation of the treatment procedures offered at the beginning of the intervention). The rationale provided to attention-placebo patients is intended to mobilize an expectancy of positive gains. These nonspecific elements in the therapy (elements separate from the identified treatment strategies) may account for patient change, just as medication placebos and psychological placebos have been found to be effective in some situations. Attention-placebo conditions enable clinical researchers to identify the changes produced by specific therapeutic strategies over and above the effects of nonspecific factors.

Despite their advantage, attention-placebo controls are not without limitations. When long-term therapy is being evaluated, it is questionable from an ethical standpoint to offer some patients contact (placebo) that does not deal directly with the problems for which they have sought therapy. Attention-placebos must be devoid of effective therapeutic techniques while nevertheless providing professional contact and attention and instilling positive expectancies in patients. To offer such an intervention in the guise of effective therapy is acceptable only when patients are fully informed in advance and sign an informed consent acknowledging their willingness to take a chance on receiving either a placebo or a therapy intervention. Even then, a true attention-placebo condition may be very difficult for the therapist to accomplish. In the absence of data to justify the provision of a treatment, clinical researchers accept the ethical mandate to conduct scientifically rigorous evaluations to examine the efficacy of practiced therapies. This may require controlling for nonspecific effects. Of course, following proper evaluations of and positive results from interventions, there is no longer the need for researchers to ask patients (some of whom may have immediate needs) to consent to the possibility of placebo treatment.

Methodologically, it is difficult to ensure that the therapists who conduct attention-placebo conditions have the same degree of positive expectancy for patient gains as do therapists conducting specific interventions. Demand characteristics suggest that when therapists predict favorable outcomes, patients will tend to improve accordingly. Thus, therapist expectancies may not be equal for active and placebo conditions, which could produce confounding factors. Similarly, even if patients in an attention-placebo condition have high expectations at the start, they may grow disenchanted when no specific changes are emerging. When the results suggest that the therapy condition evidenced significantly better outcomes than the attention-placebo control condition, it is essential that the researcher conduct and evaluate patients' perceptions of the credibility of the treatment rationale and their expectations for change (e.g., manipulation checks) to confirm that patients in the attention-placebo control condition perceived the treatment to be credible and expected to improve. Otherwise, differences in treatment outcome are confounded by differences in the credibility of the condition or the expectations for outcomes. Conceptually, it is very difficult to develop procedures believed by researchers to be inert yet still likely to be seen as credible to patients. That is to say, one individual's attention-placebo control condition can be someone else's form of therapy.

Use of a standard treatment (or routine care) as a control condition involves comparing a new treatment with an already-established treatment that is widely accepted and applied in the field. If it is demonstrated that the standard care intervention and the therapy under investigation are equated for nonspecific factors (e.g., duration of treatment or patient and therapist expectancies), this approach enables the researcher to test the relative effects of one type of intervention against a major contemporary competitor. It is, of course, important that researchers ensure that both the standard (routine) treatment and the new treatment are implemented in a high-quality fashion. Standard treatment comparisons should be used only after the standard treatment has been shown to be superior to conditions that control for alternative explanations of outcome. Without these prior tests and an outcome where both the standard and new treatment show improvement, it cannot be determined whether observed changes were due to treatment or due to other factors such as the passage of time or nonspecific factors associated with seeing a therapist. One advantage arises through utilizing the standard treatment control condition: The ethical concerns that arise from the use of no-treatment controls are quelled, given that quality care is provided to all participants in the study; attrition is likely to be kept to a minimum, as all participants receive genuine treatment procedures; and nonspecific factors are likely to be equated.

With regard to selection of control conditions, efficacy and effectiveness research tend to differ, at the very least, in the number and type of control conditions utilized. In efficacy studies, there are often multiple control conditions. It is not uncommon for efficacy studies to include a control group that receives no treatment at all, one that receives some form of attention-placebo, and one or more standard treatment control groups. On the other hand, the practical constraints in applied settings (e.g., established clinical practices, limited resources), where effectiveness research is typically conducted, make the use of multiple control groups difficult, if not impossible. In fact, many effectiveness studies, such as the widely debated *Consumer Reports* study, do not include any control groups. Furthermore, efficacy and effectiveness studies tend to differ in the type of control group(s) used. Efficacy studies are often the "first step" in determining whether a treatment works; indeed, it is reasonable to argue that it is prudent to first evaluate whether a treatment works under stringent experimental conditions before it is determined whether the treatment works in practice. Given that efficacy studies are often the "first step" in the experimental testing of a therapy, it is common for efficacy studies to utilize control groups that receive no treatment at all or attention-placebo in order to determine whether the effects of the experimental treatment exceed the gains made by patients receiving relatively "inactive" (i.e., no-treatment or wait-list controls) or at most only minimally active (i.e., attention-placebo) treatments. Once a treatment has received support for its efficacy, it is then important to test the treatment in practice in order to determine whether the effects of the "efficacious" treatment generalize to practice and, if so, whether these effects are less than, comparable to, or greater than those obtained from standard treatments currently practiced in the field. This is why, in addition to the aforementioned practical constraints inherent in applied settings, effectiveness studies more often include standard treatment control groups rather than no-treatment or attention-placebo control groups.

ASSIGNMENT OF PATIENTS TO TREATMENT AND CONTROL CONDITIONS

After comparison conditions have been chosen, procedures for assigning participants to conditions must be determined. Efficacy and effectiveness research utilize a variety of patient assignment strategies that reflect the underlying objectives of these methodologies. Random assignment of participants may be accomplished by any procedure that gives every participant an equal chance of being assigned to either the control or treatment condition (e.g., assignment by a coin toss). Random assignment of participants to the therapy or control conditions and random assignment of participants to therapists are essential steps in achieving initial comparability between conditions. For instance, random assignment of patients usually eliminates unwanted effects of age or socioeconomic status, because in most cases random assignment does not result in patients in one condition being older, wealthier, or more educated than in the other condition. However, randomization does not guarantee comparability, and appropriate statistical tests are usually applied to examine the comparability of the participants in the conditions.

There can be significant interpretive problems when random assignment is not applied. Consider the situation when the first 30 patients seeking help at a treatment center are assigned to therapy and the next 30 clients are placed on the wait-list. Such assignment is not truly random and may hide subtle selection biases. Perhaps the first 30 patients were exposed to a temporary environmental stress that was no longer a factor when the next 30 patients applied for treatment. Perhaps the first 30 patients sought therapy more quickly due to stronger motivation or more severe symptoms than the next 30. These differences, as opposed to the effects of the treatment under investigation, could plausibly explain any differences between treatment and control conditions. Randomization, then, while not an absolute guarantee for comparability, is clearly a useful strategy for equally distributing characteristics of patients across treatment and control conditions for the purpose of achieving comparability.

Randomized-blocks assignment, or assignment by stratified blocks, represents an alternative strategy (particularly useful for pursuing comparability of conditions) and involves matching prospective clients in subgroups that (a) each contain patients that are highly comparable on key dimensions (e.g., initial severity) and (b) contain the same number of patients as the number of conditions. For example, if the study requires two conditions (a standard treatment and a new treatment condition), patients could be paired off so that each pair is highly comparable. The members in each pair are then randomly assigned to either condition, thus increasing the likelihood that clients across conditions will be comparable while retaining the randomization factor. When feasible, randomized blocks assignment of patients to conditions can be a wise research strategy, especially when a small number of clients are in each condition and when important matching variables are known before beginning the experiment.

Random assignment, being the best strategy for achieving comparability of conditions, maximizes experimental control and internal validity, thereby increasing the confidence with which causal inferences can be made. For this reason, random assignment is an essential component of efficacy research. In fact, it is widely considered that a study that does not employ randomization procedures lacks the experimental control necessary to be considered an efficacy study. On the other hand, while some effectiveness studies utilize random assignment, it is not a necessary requisite of effectiveness research. After all, patients seeking treatment in clinical service delivery systems are not, as participants in efficacy studies, subject to the intrusive process of random assignment to treatment and acquiescence with who and what happens to be offered in the study. To the contrary, patients seeking psychotherapy in the field often get there by active shopping. That is to say, patients enter a treatment with a therapist they screened and chose. This is especially true for patients who select an individual practitioner and at least somewhat true for patients who seek treatment at an outpatient clinic or who have managed care.

Other factors also make randomization of patients a difficult endeavor in clinical delivery settings. For example, there is often a high premium placed on accommodating patient preferences, such as a request to be assigned to a male or female therapist. Furthermore, therapists who are responsible for making case assignments to other therapists (i.e., intake clinicians) often have perceptions of other clinicians' expertise or the lack thereof, which then dictate the case assignments they make, though these perceptions are typically based on clinical judgment rather than empirical evidence. Nevertheless, it is sometimes argued that making a referral to a particular clinician (e.g., student therapist) would be clinically irresponsible, if not unethical, and that inclusion of such a therapist in a study in which randomization of patients is utilized would therefore be inappropriate. Finally, logistical and other factors such as patient and therapist availability, therapists' clinical interests, and limited resources to support research make random assignment of patients in routine clinical settings difficult to achieve.

DELIVERY OF INTERVENTIONS

Differences in the objectives of efficacy and effectiveness research are perhaps most visible in the delivery of intervention(s) to patients in the experimental and control groups. In efficacy research, who, what, and how interventions are delivered to patients are typically stringently controlled. Often, there are clearly defined guidelines dictating the necessary qualifications of therapist participants (e.g., allegiance to a particular theoretical orientation, minimum number of years of professional experience required, educational requirements), and those not meeting such requirements are excluded from participation. Furthermore, in efficacy research, what is being provided to patients in the experimental and control groups is also carefully controlled. When treatments are being provided to experimental and control participants (e.g., in the case of a control group that receives a standard treatment), "manualized" therapies (which dictate therapist actions, usually on a session-by-session basis) are commonly used in efficacy studies, as these are considered to be well-defined. Therapists are often provided training in the manualized treatment they will be providing prior to and periodically throughout the course of the study. Furthermore, what can be said or done by therapists providing "inactive" (i.e., no-treatment or wait-list controls) or minimally active (i.e., attention-placebo) treatments is also well-defined. Formal ratings of therapist actions are also regularly conducted to ensure a sufficient degree of therapist compliance with the treatment manual and other components of the study protocol. Finally, treatments provided to patients in efficacy studies are usually of fixed duration. If patients, for whatever reason, fail to complete participation in the study (e.g., drop out of the study or are excluded during the course of the study), then data gleaned from their participation are often not included in subsequent statistical analyses. All these actions are taken in order to standardize who, what, and how interventions are provided in an attempt to achieve more stringent experimental control over extraneous variables leading to rival interpretations of results.

In effectiveness research, who, what, and how interventions are provided to patients are largely dictated by routine clinical procedures and therefore far less controlled. First, therapist exclusion is rare. Typically, all therapists working in the clinical delivery setting in which the research is being conducted are invited to participate, regardless of theoretical orientation, years of experience, educational background, or standing on other therapist variables. Therapists are usually excluded only if there is some compelling reason that would prohibit their ability to participate in the study (e.g., a clinical supervisor believes a student therapist does not possess adequate clinical skills to participate in the study). Broad inclusion criteria for therapists result in a large degree of therapist heterogeneity. Furthermore, in effectiveness research, interventions are far less controlled. Therapists typically have a great deal of latitude in implementing experimental and control conditions. For example, the standard treatment control group often used in effectiveness research is the "treatment as usual" group. As the name implies, therapists providing treatment to patients in the "treatment as usual" group need only provide clinical services in the manner in which they typically provide services. Therapist compliance to a particular treatment regimen is not typically expected, as therapy is allowed to be self-correcting. In other words, similar to the real world of clinical service delivery, therapists and/or patients are permitted to evaluate how treatment is proceeding and make any necessary changes that would enhance the effectiveness of treatment (e.g., therapist changing technique, patient focusing on a different problem, etc.), a practice that would typically be unacceptable in the context of an efficacy study. Finally, the therapy provided in effectiveness studies is not typically of a fixed duration. Again, similar to the real world of clinical service delivery, patients and/or therapists are left to make decisions about termination, and data gleaned from treatments of widely varying durations are typically included. Consistent with the objectives of effectiveness research, asserting less control over the conditions under which interventions are delivered increases the likelihood that results will generalize to other clinical settings.

ASSESSMENT

Assessment strategies used in efficacy and effectiveness research are almost always vastly different in terms of focus, source, and duration. Given that target outcomes are well-defined and operationalized in efficacy research, assessments tend to focus on multiple yet highly specific domains of functioning. The Beck Depression Inventory, State-Trait Anxiety Inventory, and Fear Questionnaire are all examples of standardized "specific" measures of outcome that are frequently used to assess specific symptom reduction in efficacy studies. Furthermore, assessment data are often gathered from multiple sources. In addition to gathering self-report data from patients by administering them questionnaires, clinicians who are "blind" to which group patients belong to also conduct unbiased ratings of patient status throughout the course of treatment and at follow-up on selected measures. Finally, assessment in efficacy research tends to occur at specified sessions and be of a fixed duration, usually extending beyond termination of treatment. Assessment in efficacy research, then, tends to be focused, highly structured, and quite comprehensive.

In contrast to efficacy research, effectiveness research is almost always focused on improvement in general functioning as well as specific symptom reduction. To this end, "global" measures of outcome designed to assess patient status and functioning in major domains such as symptom distress, interpersonal relationship functioning, social role functioning, and quality of life are often used in effectiveness research. Focusing on the assessment of general functioning is viewed as being consistent with the goals of patients receiving treatment in routine clinical settings, as they are typically seeking to reduce their distress and improve their ability to function in important life roles. In terms of source, effectiveness research is often limited to gathering self-report data from patients. While patient self-report data are limited in a variety of ways, they are the single best source of information available and are typically viewed as more essential than reports from therapists and significant others. Furthermore, given the constraints inherent in clinical service delivery settings, it is simply not feasible to routinely solicit information from others who may be in a position to judge patient progress, such as therapists and significant others. Finally, in effectiveness research, frequency and duration of assessment are often dictated not only by routine clinical procedures but also by patient and therapist preferences, and are therefore highly variable. For example, some patients participating in the study may complete the assessments on a session-by-session basis, while others may fail to complete the assessments on a number of occasions throughout the course of therapy. Rather than eliminating data from patients who fail to complete assessments, effectiveness researchers often utilize, in their subsequent analysis, statistical procedures that allow for and take into account missing observations. In terms of duration, logistical and other factors make the collection of follow-up data quite difficult in effectiveness research.

LIMITATIONS OF EFFICACY AND EFFECTIVENESS RESEARCH AND THE EMERGENCE OF PATIENT-FOCUSED RESEARCH

One very significant limitation associated with both efficacy and effectiveness studies is their emphasis on the examination of the average response of a group of patients without consideration for change of individual patients. Consequently, while efficacy research answers the question, "Does the treatment work under well-controlled experimental conditions?" and effectiveness research answers the question, "Does the treatment work in practice?" both methodologies routinely fail to evaluate the effects of treatment on individual patients and provide therapists with these data. Perhaps this is one reason why practicing clinicians often have little or no interest in research, as they view it as being highly, if not totally, irrelevant to their work with individual patients.

Patient-focused research is a relatively new and additional methodology that seeks to answer the most important question to practicing clinicians, "Is my treatment working for this patient?" and thereby assist therapists in addressing many other practice-relevant questions, such as, "Should I change my treatment plan?" "Should I make a referral?" and "Is it time to end therapy?" Patient-focused research evaluates the effects of treatment on individual patients by monitoring patient progress over the course of psychotherapy and providing this information to a therapist, supervisor, or case manager in order to evaluate therapy gains and improve final outcome. An advantage of patient-focused research is that it places clinicians in the position of monitoring patient progress and modifying treatment according to the patient's specific needs based on this information. This methodology, then, represents a "bottom-up" approach to outcome assessment and builds on the results from past research related to empirically validated psychotherapies. Patient-focused research, then, represents one effort to further bridge the gap between efficacy/ effectiveness research and clinical practice.

Use of this research paradigm is only just beginning to become an expected practice in routine care but has already shown promise in several studies. It may be best regarded as a subtype of effectiveness research, since it emphasizes assessment of treatment response in routine practice with little experimental control. It is generally seen as a quality-assurance methodology for ongoing treatment, a practice that has its focus on integrating research with treatment as it unfolds. Like other effectiveness research, it is usually applied without the use of control groups, patient selection, therapist training, and extensive assessment of patient functioning. In fact, a requirement of such research is usually extremely brief assessment that is undertaken frequently (e.g., weekly). The advantage of such research is the extent to which it can affect and improve practice over a short period of time and the likelihood of obtaining outcome data on an unusually large number of patients who enter treatment. Unlike the typical results of efficacy and effectiveness research, which often take years to complete, publish, and be absorbed by professionals, patient-focused research can be viewed immediately. Its major disadvantage is that the results obtained in such research are usually based on a single, brief, self-report measure, and such research (because of the paucity of controls) cannot be readily used to affect psychological theory.

The research paradigms reviewed here are best seen on a continuum of research strategies aimed at advancing knowledge about effective psychological practice. They are complementary methods that, while overlapping, have distinctly different scientific goals. Advancement of knowledge about effective helping is best accomplished through application of various strategies of formal inquiry.

—*David A. Vermeersch and Michael J. Lambert*

See also: *Empirically Supported Treatment for Childhood Disorders (Vol. II); Evidence-Based Practice (Vol. III); Manualized Behavioral Therapy (Vol. I)*

Suggested Readings

Howard, K. I., Moras, K., Brill, P. L., Martinovich, Z., & Lutz, W. (1996). Efficacy, effectiveness, and client progress. *American Psychologist, 51,* 1059–1064.

Kendall, P. C., Holmbeck, G., & Verduin, T. (2004). Methodology, design, and evaluation in psychotherapy research. In M. J. Lambert (Ed.), *Bergin & Garfields's handbook of psychotherapy and behavior change* (5th ed., pp. 16–43). New York: Wiley.

Lambert, M. J. (2001). Psychotherapy outcome and quality improvement: Introduction to the special section on client-focused research. *Journal of Consulting and Clinical Psychology, 69,* 147–149.

Lambert, M. J., & Ogles, B. M. (2004). The efficacy and effectiveness of psychotherapy. In M. J. Lambert (Ed.), *Bergin & Garfield's handbook of psychotherapy and behavior change* (5th ed., pp. 139–193). New York: Wiley.

Seligman, M. E. P. (1995). The effectiveness of psychotherapy: The *Consumer Reports* study. *American Psychologist, 50*(12), 965–974.

ELECTRICAL AVERSION

DESCRIPTION OF THE STRATEGY

Electrical aversion uses electric shocks to modify urges or behaviors considered unacceptable by the subject treated or others. With one strategy, contingent aversive conditioning, highly painful electric shocks are administered following the carrying out of the behavior. It is used to treat subjects whose behaviors are markedly injurious to others or more commonly to themselves, such as eye gouging or finger biting. When the treatment was introduced, the shocks were commonly administered by a cattle prod directly to the subject's limb, but subsequently they were delivered by remote-control devices. The aim of the shock was to produce immediate cessation of the behavior and prevent its future occurrence.

Other strategies that employed much lower levels of shock at a level determined by the subject to be painful but not unbearable were reintroduced in the 1950s by Wolpe. In one, anxiety relief therapy, subjects were instructed that the shock would be repeated in the treatment sessions and they were to endure it until their desire to have it stop became very strong, when they were to say aloud the word "calm." The shock would then be immediately terminated. After 30 to 60 seconds, the procedure was repeated, 20 to 30 times at a session. The subjects were warned every time a shock was about to be administered, as otherwise some subjects became very anxious between shocks. It was reported that during the treatment, most subjects reported a feeling of relief at the cessation of the shock. This strength of the feeling was sometimes greatly out of proportion to the discomfort that went before. The aim was that when subjects experienced high levels of anxiety in the course of day-to-day experience, they could reduce this by saying to themselves the word "calm."

Wolpe also reported studies using electric aversion to produce avoidance reactions to stimuli that he labeled obsessional. He administered an electric shock to the subject in the presence of the obsessional object, citing the successful use of the procedure in the 1930s for the treatment of both alcoholic addiction and fetishism. As used by Wolpe, the stimulus was presented not directly, but as a mental image, by asking subjects to imagine it. They were instructed to signal when the image was clear, when a severe shock was administered to their forearms. This was repeated 5 to 20 times in a session. Its successful use was reported with a woman with what was termed a food obsession. She found foods with a high salt content or that were fattening irresistibly attractive. Following treatment, she reported that on imagining any such food, she immediately had a feeling of fear and revulsion, accompanied by an image of the shock situation. She no longer experienced the previous misery of hours debating, "Should I eat; should I not?"

In the 1960s, electrical aversion was used mainly with the aim of converting homosexual to heterosexual preference in subjects, mostly men, who sought this. Initially, pictures of nude, same-sex people were associated with electric shocks. In an early study, a classical conditioning format was followed. The shocks were administered to the treated man's feet on about a quarter of the occasions immediately after the picture was shown. If the procedure acted by conditioning, the intermittent rather than invariable reinforcement would make the resultant response more resistant to extinction. Subsequently, it was argued that as photographs symbolized the behaviors to be reduced, words would be equally effective symbols and their use would avoid the necessity of obtaining suitable photographs. Presumably, the adherence to behaviorism then current made the use of mental images unacceptable. It was noted by some therapists that with the aversive classical procedure, as with anxiety relief, when subjects became aware that administration of the electric shocks had finished, they experienced great relief. This relief was added to the aversive procedure in a treatment termed *aversion relief.* With this therapy, subjects were shown a series of words or phrases every 10 seconds. All but the last word or phrase related to the behavior being treated, for example, "homosexual" or "looking at an attractive man." The last phrase related to the behavior to be encouraged, such as "seeing an attractive woman." Each time the subject saw a word or phrase, he read it aloud. In the original form, the subject received a painful shock to the feet, except when the last word was shown. It was reported that subjects quickly learned they received no shock with the last word and experienced marked relief. It was expected this relief would increase the attractiveness of the approved behavior. The series of words were shown five times in a session, which was carried out daily. Electrical aversion in either the classical conditioning or aversion relief format was subsequently used to reduce the likelihood of the treated persons carrying out behaviors they wished to cease, but could not. These included paraphilic behaviors, gambling, obsessive ruminations, and alcohol and other substance abuse.

Other therapists considered an avoidance technique that used partial reinforcement would be more effective than procedures that used a classical conditioning format with invariable reinforcement. They introduced what was termed *anticipatory avoidance conditioning.* Subjects seeking conversion of feelings from homosexual to heterosexual were shown slides of same-sex persons, which they could remove with a switch provided. They were instructed to view each slide as long as they found it attractive. If they left it on for 8 seconds, they were given an electric shock to the calf, which was terminated when they removed the slide. The level of shock employed was that which inhibited their feelings of attraction. On two thirds of occasions, they could remove the slide before 8 seconds, so avoiding the shock, the reinforced trials. On one third of occasions, their attempts to remove the slide in the first 8 seconds were unsuccessful, so they received the shock, the nonreinforced trials. Randomly, on about half the occasions when they removed the slide of the same-sex person, it was replaced by the slide of an opposite-sex person. Another form of contingent electrical aversion was later introduced to treat men who sought conversion of homosexual feelings. They were given shocks contingent on their showing a distinguishable penile circumference response to photographs of males. Up to four further shocks were given at 15-second intervals until penile circumference decrease occurred.

RESEARCH BASIS

It is generally accepted that high levels of contingent shocks act by avoidance conditioning. In one study, their use in 12 profoundly mentally retarded subjects whose behavior resulted in life-threatening self-injuries led to cessation of the behavior in 7 subjects,

so they no longer required to be physically restrained. A further 3 subjects needed the shocks to be administered daily to minimize the frequency and severity of the behavior. A meta-analysis of more than 50 predominantly single-subject studies demonstrated it to be markedly more effective than other procedures used to reduce the frequency of or to eliminate self-injurious behaviors. A 1987 review of aversion therapy by the Council on Scientific Affairs of the American Medical Association concluded the best accepted use of aversive techniques was for the reduction of self-injurious behavior in mentally handicapped subjects, citing evidence that they were successful in 25% of those in whom such behavior was severe. They quoted the conclusion of a national task force convened in 1982 that when behavior was dangerous and had not improved with less intrusive procedures, increasingly aversive techniques up to electric shock for the most severe were appropriate.

The mode of action of electric aversion therapies using lower levels of aversive stimuli has not been established. Anxiety relief was introduced on the basis of animal research studies. A neutral stimulus was repeatedly presented to an eating animal just before withdrawing its food. The stimulus acquired the property of inhibiting feeding even when the animal was in the middle of a meal. Another study found that approach responses were conditioned to a neutral stimulus repeatedly presented at the moment of termination of an electric shock, in contrast to the avoidance that was conditioned to a stimulus that preceded an electric shock. These findings led to the suggestion that a stimulus that consistently coincided with the termination of a noxious stimulus would acquire anxiety-inhibiting effects. The noxious stimulus used with anxiety relief was electric shock. No research has established the superiority of this treatment for anxiety disorders to nonaversive cognitive and behavioral therapies, and it no longer appears to be used for these conditions.

In the 1960s, a number of studies reported the response to various aversive procedures of subjects, mainly men, who sought conversion of their sexual preference from homosexual to heterosexual. The initial report used the intermittent classical format described. The treated man reported great reluctance to use homosexual fantasy with masturbation and continued a new pattern of masturbating to female pictures and fantasies. Subsequent studies reported use of aversion relief. In one, three men treated with aversion relief were followed up at four weeks. Two reported negative feelings to homosexual men or homosexual thoughts, and the third that he had no homosexual desires in situations where in the past he had experienced them. All three reported more heterosexual interest. In a second report, four of six men treated who were having homosexual relations prior to treatment ceased them, finding their homosexual desires easier to control. The sexual feelings of the remaining two were unchanged. It was concluded the treatment did not necessarily awaken sexual interest in women.

A 1-year follow-up of 41 men and 2 women treated with anticipatory avoidance conditioning reported significant improvement in 25, in that they showed ratings of 0 to 2 on the Kinsey 0 to 6 scale, where 0 is exclusively heterosexual and 6 exclusively homosexual. Thirteen of the 25 were heterosexually active, with no homosexual fantasy or behavior. Those with experience of heterosexual activity prior to treatment were more likely to report a successful response. This remains the best response reported in the literature. The poorest was that of 10 men with homosexual feelings treated with electric shock contingent on their showing an increase in penile circumference to photographs of males. At the time of this study, it had not been reported that a percentage of men initially show penile circumference (but not volume) decreases in response to stimuli they find sexually arousing. In such men, arousal to photographs of males would produce temporary penile circumference decreases. Hence, with the contingent procedure, this arousal would not be followed by shock. Their reduced arousal to the photographs of males would result in a temporary penile circumference increase and hence would be followed by shock. One year or more following treatment, 2 and possibly 3 of the 10 reported reduced and 1 no homosexual desire. If the procedure acted by contingent conditioning, administering shocks following reduced homosexual arousal but not increased arousal could have resulted in the inferior response.

Until the end of the 1960s, it was assumed that electrical aversion procedures acted by conditioning. This assumption was then questioned. It was pointed out that the conditioned response to a stimulus reinforced by a painful electric shock to a limb was similar to the unconditioned response to the shock, withdrawal of the limb. The reported responses to aversion procedures were reduction in homosexual feelings and at times, increase in heterosexual feelings. There had been no reports of limb withdrawal. It was concluded that their absence following electrical aversion indicated the reported reduction in homosexual feelings was unlikely to be produced by conditioning. A series of studies were carried out in an attempt to establish the mode of action of electrical aversion in men seeking treatment to convert homosexual to heterosexual preference. In addition to the men's self-reports, their penile-volume responses to 10-second duration moving films of male and female nudes were investigated before and after treatment and at follow-up. There is substantial evidence that penile-volume assessment compared with penile circumference assessment provides a more valid assessment of individual men's stated ratio of heterosexual/homosexual interest. When advantage is taken of its much shorter latency, it is more resistant to modification by the subject.

In the initial study, 40 men were randomly allocated to two procedures. Twenty received apomorphine injections, which produced feelings of nausea as the aversive stimulus while they viewed photographs of nude men. Twenty received aversion relief, using phrases as the cues and shocks delivered to two fingers of their hands as the aversive stimuli. The level of shock administered was that determined by each man as being painful but not unbearable. At 1-year follow-up, half the men considered their homosexual urges were reduced, and half, mainly the same men, that their heterosexual desires were increased. A quarter of the men reported no homosexual relations since treatment, and a further quarter that the frequency of such relations was reduced. There were slight but nonsignificant trends for more men to report increased heterosexual interest following aversion relief and more to report reduced or no homosexual relations following apomorphine aversion. The mean penile-volume responses to the films of men decreased, and those to the films of women increased, both to a significant extent following treatment. However, the magnitude of this change was only sufficient to result in 14 men showing responses indicating a predominant heterosexual orientation. Prior to treatment, 10 men showed responses indicating this orientation.

The increase in the penile-volume responses to films of women was found only in the men who prior to treatment showed negative responses to these films, not in the men who prior to treatment showed positive responses to them. In a follow-up of 1 to 3 years, only

7 of the 40 men considered their sexual orientations had changed from predominantly homosexual to predominantly heterosexual. Other criteria of evaluating responses were also considered to be important. Some men who remained exclusively homosexual and continued homosexual behaviors they found acceptable reported they were no longer continuously preoccupied with homosexual thoughts. They felt more emotionally stable and were able to live and work more effectively. A number of these men were able to control compulsions to make homosexual contacts in public lavatories, which had caused them to be arrested one or more times previously. Six of the nine married men at follow-up stated their marital relationships had markedly improved, including two who had ceased having intercourse with their wives some years prior to treatment.

There were no statistically significant differences in outcome between aversion relief and apomorphine aversion. However, in view of the trends toward slight differences, the study was partially replicated. A further 40 men were randomly allocated, 20 to receive apomorphine therapy as in the first study and 20 to receive the anticipatory avoidance procedure that had been reported to have produced the best results. At the 6-month follow-up, there were no consistent trends for the outcome of the two procedures to differ. Both produced subjective and behavioral responses comparable with those of the first study. Changes in men's penile-volume responses to the films of men and women following the two procedures were also similar and comparable to those found in the first study. The two studies had therefore demonstrated that three markedly different aversive procedures produced apparently identical outcomes. The three procedures used different cues (photographs and words), different aversive stimuli (electric shocks and apomorphine), and different modes of presentation (classical conditioning and intermittent avoidance conditioning). It was considered highly unlikely that they would produce comparable results if they acted by conditioning. To determine this, a further study was carried out.

Forty-six men were randomly allocated to receive electrical aversion in either an anticipatory avoidance, a backward conditioning, or a classical conditioning forward format. Anticipatory avoidance was carried out as in the previous study. The backward-conditioning format approximated the avoidance procedure in terms of frequency and duration of the presentation of the slides of males and females but with the electric shocks preceding rather than following the presentation of the slides of males. With the forward-conditioning format, the men were shown for 10 seconds at 4-minute intervals one of three slides of males they had selected as attractive. For the final second of exposure of each slide and for 1 second following its removal, they received a painful electric shock to two fingers of one hand. At 1-year follow-up, there were no consistent trends for one therapy to be more effective than another. The proportion of men who reported decreased homosexual interest and increased heterosexual interest and related behavioral changes was similar to that in the previous two studies. The change in the sexual orientation of the men as determined by penile-volume assessment was also similar. Backward conditioning is generally accepted to be a relatively ineffective conditioning procedure. The finding that it produced a similar outcome to forms of conditioning accepted to be effective strongly supported the conclusion that the outcome of electrical aversion in influencing homosexual feelings and behavior is not the result of conditioning. Also, if conditioning played a role in the outcome of electrical aversion, it would be expected from conditioning research that the outcome would be greater if more intense shocks were employed. No relationship was found between outcome and the intensity of voltage selected by the men.

In all three studies, the penile-volume increase to films of women was shown only by men who had previously shown negative responses to these films. It was suggested that the aversive procedures produced reduction in homosexual feelings but no actual increase in heterosexual feelings. The increase in heterosexual feelings and behaviors was attributed to their increased awareness of previously existing heterosexual feelings when their homosexual feelings were reduced. A study was carried out investigating whether it was possible to increase the heterosexual feelings of men who sought treatment by a positive-conditioning procedure. With it, they were shown slides of nude women in temporal association with slides of nude men to which they were sexually aroused. Thirty-one homosexual men were randomly allocated, half to this procedure and half to electrical aversion in the classical conditioning format used in the previous study. Both were administered, half in forward- and half in backward-conditioning formats. The men's penile-volume responses were recorded throughout all procedures. No penile response conditioning occurred to the slides of women in the positive-conditioning procedure, although unconditioned penile responses continued to occur to the slides of males throughout treatment. Also, there was no difference in changes in sexual interest or behaviors or penile-volume responses of the men who had received the positive conditioning in a forward as compared with a backward format. These findings indicated that the positive-conditioning procedure had no specific therapeutic effect, but acted as a placebo therapy.

At 3-week and 1-year follow-ups, more men who received the electrical aversion as compared with positive conditioning reported reduction in homosexual interest and behaviors. The differences were statistically significant for reduction in homosexual interest at 3 weeks and reduction in homosexual behavior at 1 year. There was no difference in outcome following electrical aversion given in forward or backward formats. At 3 weeks following both the aversion and positive conditioning, a similar number of men reported increased heterosexual interest and behaviors, but at 1 year, there was a trend for more men to report this following the aversion therapy. It was concluded that the electrical aversion acted specifically to produce reductions of homosexual interest and behaviors significantly greater than the reductions produced by the placebo positive-conditioning procedure. This was the only study in which electrical aversion was compared with a placebo, which appeared to have a suggestibility of effectiveness equivalent to that of electrical aversion.

The changes in the men's penile-volume response assessment to the 10-second films of men and women following the positive conditioning and electrical aversion were similar to the changes in the heterosexual direction that followed the aversive therapies in the three previous studies. If these changes were a specific effect of treatment, they should have been greater following the electrical aversion than the positive-conditioning placebo procedure, since the reduction in homosexual interest and behavior produced by electrical aversion was significantly greater than that which followed the placebo procedure. As the penile-volume changes were comparable following both, it was concluded they were nonspecific and unrelated to the treatment effect. Presumably, they resulted from the men consciously or unconsciously modifying their penile-volume responses to appear more heterosexual. Freund reported in 1971 that 5 (33%) of 15 homosexual men who had previously been tested were able to produce this change without treatment

when requested to attempt to do so. In the four studies discussed, of the men assessed prior to treatment, 117 showed predominantly homosexual and 33 predominantly heterosexual orientation. Following treatment, 53 showed predominantly heterosexual orientation. Hence, 20 (17%) of the men showed the change to predominant heterosexuality, less than the 33% of untreated homosexual men who could produce this change voluntarily. It was concluded that the specific reduction in homosexual feelings and behaviors produced by electrical aversion was not accompanied by any change in the men's sexual orientation as determined by physiological assessment of their sexual arousal to films of males and females.

When it became generally accepted that aversive procedures did not produce a feeling of aversion to the homosexual cues that were followed by aversive stimuli, the outcome was widely accepted to be one of indifference. It was considered that the indifference was due to classical conditioning, even though the expected conditioned response of aversion did not occur. The finding that electrical aversion administered in backward- and forward-conditioning formats produced equivalent outcomes, strong evidence that the procedures could not have acted by conditioning was ignored. Also, findings of some of the studies discussed indicated that indifference was not the outcome of aversive procedures. There was no specific change in the penile-volume responses of the treated men to films of men and women following aversive electrical aversion associated with homosexual cues. Rather than being indifferent to films of men, they continued to show penile-volume responses to them. Lack of indifference was also present in the men who, following aversive therapies, remained exclusively homosexual and continued homosexual behaviors they found acceptable. They reported they were able to resist compulsions to make homosexual contacts in public lavatories, which had caused them to be arrested one or more times previously indicated.

It was pointed out that superficial questioning of subjects who reported a satisfactory response to aversive procedures could lead to the conclusion that they experienced indifference to stimuli that prior to treatment caused them to carry out behaviors or experience feelings that were beyond their control. When questioned in more detail, they reported that when confronted with such stimuli, they still experienced attraction to them. However, the urge to respond behaviorally to the stimuli or to become preoccupied with fantasies concerning them was much reduced or absent. A similar response was reported in studies by a number of therapists. One that used anticipatory avoidance to treat men seeking conversion of feelings from homosexual to heterosexual reported that some men who responded well still displayed an occasional and very slight degree of homosexual interest in directly observing males, without, however, any subsequent fantasy. On the basis of these reports and the findings of the series of studies reviewed, it was argued that aversive procedures produced neither aversion nor indifference, but an ability to control previously uncontrollable fantasies and urges to carry out behaviors considered unacceptable.

A number of uncontrolled studies reported the successful use of electrical aversion in the treatment of pathological gambling. Shocks were delivered at random to an electrode on the gamblers' arms, at a level sufficiently unpleasant to cause pronounced arm retraction, while the gamblers played poker machines continuously. About half the subjects treated reported cessation of gambling. As with the use of electrical aversion for sexual feelings, there was no retraction of the arm to gambling cues noted following treatment, the response expected if the procedure acted by conditioning. A randomized control study compared the use of electrical aversion with a treatment termed *imaginal desensitization*. It was introduced on the basis of a theory suggested by the finding that aversive procedures did not modify sexual preference, but reduced compulsive urges. It proposed that compulsive urges were maintained by neurophysiological behavior completion mechanisms. Two randomized studies found that imaginal desensitization was more effective than aversion relief for pathological gambling. Electrical aversion appears to be no longer used at least in the initial treatment of gambling or indeed of other compulsive conditions. It has largely been replaced by covert sensitization rather than imaginal desensitization.

The replacement did not result from evidence that covert sensitization gave treated subjects greater control than did electrical aversion over urges they experienced as compulsive, but because covert sensitization did not use physically aversive stimuli. Covert sensitization was used initially for men seeking to convert homosexual to heterosexual feelings. They were trained to relax and, while relaxed, to fantasize images such as approaching a man to find he was covered with scabs and gave off a terrible stench that made

them vomit. The only study that compared covert sensitization and electrical aversion found they were equivalent in effectiveness. Twenty men seeking treatment for homosexual urges and/or behaviors they experienced as compulsive were randomly allocated, 10 to each procedure. As it had been demonstrated in the earlier studies discussed that there was no specific change in the penile-volume assessment of sexual orientation in homosexual subjects treated with electrical aversion, this assessment could not provide an objective evaluation of treated subjects' outcomes. Reliance could be placed only on their self-reports. These were obtained in interview by an assessor who took no other part in the study and was blind to the nature of the treatment the subjects received. Subjects were followed up for 1 year. The response to both procedures was similar to that to the aversive procedures found in the studies discussed previously. As imaginal desensitization was shown to be more effective than electrical aversion for compulsive gambling urges, it is possible it would also be more effective than electrical aversion, and therefore also covert sensitization, in reducing compulsive sexual urges. This possibility has not been investigated, and use of covert sensitization to treat these urges, including those of pedophiles and rapists, has largely replaced use of electrical aversion and imaginal desensitization.

The review of aversion therapy by the Amercian Medical Association (AMA) Council on Scientific Affairs emphasized the lack of controlled research in its evaluation. It made no reference to the extensive series of randomized studies that investigated the mode of action of aversion therapies and led to the development and evaluation of imaginal desensitization as superior to electrical aversion and covert sensitization. In regard to the use of aversive procedures in unwanted sexual behaviors, the council decided that the literature contained predominantly uncontrolled multifactorial studies and concluded the most positive results were reported with covert sensitization.

The council review concluded that the evidence supporting the efficacy of electrical aversion in alcoholism was weak and empirical studies evaluating it were limited in number and methodological adequacy. A 1996 review of 339 alcoholism treatment outcome studies reported between 1980 and 1992 found electrical aversion was used in only one study. A probable contributing factor to its limited use was a 1966 report that aversions to tastes were much more easily established in animals by use of malaise produced by ionizing radiation than by electric shock, whereas the reverse was true for aversions to visual and auditory stimuli. Without empirical evidence, subsequent workers decided that to develop aversive control of excessive drinking, malaise produced by stimuli such as rapid rotation was a more appropriate aversive stimulus than electric shock. However, a 1997 study reported a slightly superior abstinence at 6 and 12 months in patients treated for alcoholism with electrical aversion compared with chemical aversion. It also found that patients treated with both procedures had a significantly superior outcome to matched patients from a treatment registry. A 1999 2-year follow-up of 30 patients treated for alcoholism found a combination of electrical aversion and naltrexone to be effective when aversion alone had proved ineffective.

RELEVANT TARGET
POPULATIONS AND EXCEPTIONS

Soon after the reintroduction of electrical aversion in the 1960s, some clinicians expressed ethical and aesthetic objections to the use of physically unpleasant stimuli in aversive therapies. A similar attitude of the wider public was reinforced by the widely acclaimed film of Anthony Burgess's 1972 novel, *A Clockwork Orange,* which demonstrated the forced use of an extreme aversive procedure to produce a disabling aversion to violence in the protagonist. As discussed earlier, electrical aversion does not, in fact, produce aversions, and it was suggested that procedures using aversive stimuli be termed *aversive therapies* rather than aversion therapies. It is unlikely, however, that such a change would lead to increased public acceptance of electrical or other forms of these therapies that use physically unpleasant stimuli.

It is possible the alternative to electrical aversion recommended at the time, covert sensitization, could have more negative effects on treated subjects' self-esteem than the use of electric shocks. As stated earlier, with covert sensitization, men treated to reduce homosexual feelings were asked to fantasize images such as approaching a man covered with scabs who gave off a terrible stench that made them vomit. The possible effect of such visualizations compared with the effect of electric shocks on the self-esteem of the men treated was never investigated when covert sensitization largely replaced electrical aversion. The randomized controlled study discussed earlier found covert sensitization was not superior to electrical

aversion in giving men control over sexual urges experienced as compulsive. A subsequent study compared covert sensitization with imaginal desensitization in the treatment of 20 men with compulsive sexual urges, mainly exhibitionist or homosexual. At 1 year, the men treated with imaginal desensitization reported significantly greater reduction in the strength of the urges and were more likely to cease the compulsive behaviors than those treated with covert sensitization.

Nevertheless, despite the fact that imaginal desensitization does not use negative aversive images, subsequently, covert sensitization rather than imaginal desensitization has mainly replaced electrical aversion in the treatment of compulsive sexual urges, including those of sex offenders, mainly pedophiles and rapists. Despite the belief of most therapists that maintaining or raising the self-esteem of these men is of major importance in increasing their control over deviant urges, the possible negative effect of covert sensitization on self-esteem was not considered. Electrical aversion has been used when other treatments have been unsuccessful. A study that reported the outcome of 30 sex offenders to imaginal desensitization or medroxyprogesterone found that one offender who failed to respond to both treatments showed a response to electrical aversion maintained at 18-month follow-up. Single-case studies have reported long-term responses to electrical aversion of patients with obsessive ruminations who failed to respond to cognitive approaches.

As pointed out earlier, though the AMA Council review concluded the evidence supporting the efficacy of electrical aversion in alcoholism was weak, further positive evidence has been reported in the recent studies reviewed. Additional studies investigating its value would seem indicated. In relation to the treatment of obesity, the AMA Council pointed out the findings of early uncontrolled studies reporting weight loss with aversive procedures were not replicated by later controlled studies. It considered the successes in the earlier studies were due to placebo and expectancy effects. It further concluded that controlled studies showed either no or a temporary effect from aversion therapies for smoking. Occasional case studies of use of electrical aversion for drug abuse have reported positive results, but the AMA Council considered in view of contradictory findings and the inadequacy of many of the studies that no conclusions could be drawn concerning the effectiveness of aversive procedures in drug abuse.

Some people, mainly men, continue to seek treatment to convert homosexual to heterosexual feelings. There is widespread disapproval of attempts to meet their requests rather than encouraging them to accept a gay identity. This issue will be revisited in a forthcoming issue of the *Archives of Sexual Behavior*, in which a number of commentaries will discuss an article reporting successful conversion of homosexual men and women to heterosexuality by what has been termed *reparative therapy*. The research reviewed in this entry found that electrical aversion did not decrease homosexual or increase heterosexual arousal as assessed by penile responses to films of nude men and women. However, it did give treated subjects increased control over unwanted awareness or behavioral expression of homosexual urges, as it did for such awareness or expression of unwanted heterosexual urges. The available evidence from studies in which women and men anonymously report sexual interest and activity by questionnaire indicates that about 20% of the population are or were aware of or expressed homosexual feelings since adolescence. The majority of the 20% are aware of predominant heterosexual feelings, and their sexual activity is predominantly heterosexual. Some of the people, mainly men, with predominant heterosexual feelings and behaviors are among those who seek treatment to cease homosexual behaviors that have become compulsive. Others who seek this treatment want to restrict their sexual activities to a satisfying heterosexual or homosexual relationship. Compulsive behaviors at times put them and their partners at risk of HIV or other sexually transmitted conditions.

Historically, electrical aversion using moderately painful electric shocks was extensively researched to elucidate its mode of action in subjects wishing to convert homosexual to heterosexual feelings and in gamblers. This research provided the major findings that it did not act by conditioning and that though not producing aversion or indifference and not changing the sexual preference of subjects with homosexual feelings, it gave both those subjects and gamblers control over urges they previously had experienced as compulsive. The demonstration that this was possible led to the development of equally or more effective procedures to achieve the same outcome, which, hence, have largely replaced electrical aversion. Unfortunately, the interpretation has persisted that electrical aversion was used only to sexually reorient homosexuals rather than to enable them to cease unacceptable while continuing acceptable homosexual behaviors. This has resulted in widespread failure to utilize the procedures developed from its use, which would enable men with homosexual behaviors who wish to do so to maintain safer sexual practices but are unable to cease unsafe behaviors that they experience as compulsive.

The use of markedly painful stimuli for destructive behaviors remains accepted.

COMPLICATIONS

Soon after the introduction of electrical aversion, there were reports that its use could result in aggressive feelings or behaviors. These reactions were not noted subsequently. I have never observed them in more than 200 subjects in whom I have used electrical aversion. A 1999 criticism of the use of electrical aversion in treatment of people with homosexual feelings stated that the damage it wrought was not considered and that anecdotal evidence suggested it was considerable. The anecdotal evidence was of course post hoc, requiring the illogical assumption that any negative experiences subsequent to an event are a result of that event. No similar criticism appears to have been made of the use of electrical aversion to treat other conditions. The low dropout from electrical aversion of men who sought treatment for homosexual feelings suggests few experienced immediate negative effects. In the five studies reviewed, all 112 men completed treatment, and 110 attended the 2- to 3-week follow-up, which required some hours of their time, as it included penile-volume assessment. Eighty-eight men (78%) attended the 1-year follow-up, which also required this assessment. In the first two studies, the men treated with electrical aversion showed no evidence of disturbed behavior at follow-up 6 months or 1 year later. In the study that compared electrical aversion to positive conditioning, 29 of the 31 subjects attended for the 1-year follow-up. Four had been admitted to psychiatric units for periods of up to 6 weeks in the year following treatment, three following positive conditioning, and one following electrical aversion. All had received psychiatric treatment prior to the study. This finding indicated that if electric aversion produced negative consequences, it was less likely to do so than the nonaversive positive-conditioning procedure that appeared to have acted as a placebo.

CASE ILLUSTRATION

"Mrs. B. L." was a 56-year-old woman who sought treatment a few weeks after she had been charged with stealing goods from a shop. She had been charged with the behavior 9 months previously and had been given a bond to be on good behavior for 2 years, but had then not sought treatment. She was born in Germany and reported an uneventful childhood and schooling. She worked in an office there until she married a man 3 years older, when she was 25. She had a previous relationship of 3 years' duration, which she said was initially satisfactory emotionally and sexually, but she terminated it when her partner commenced drinking excessively. She felt very happy in her relationship with her husband, with whom she migrated to Australia when she was 32, with their son, then aged 2. Her husband was a successful businessman, and she did not work in Australia. She had a daughter, now aged 22. Both children were living at home. She had some concerns about her son, who did not work regularly and had not maintained any long-term relationships. However, she said that prior to the present charge, she was happy with life and enjoyed working at home and had an active social life. Questioned about her sexual life, she said that since menopause, she had had some pain with intercourse, which persisted despite use of a lubricant. It caused her to be reluctant to have intercourse at times, and it had become infrequent. She said her husband accepted this without resentment. I asked whether she would accept gynecological investigation of her pain with intercourse, and when she agreed, I wrote a referral to a female gynecologist, whom I knew would give this problem appropriate attention. She did not smoke or take other substances, apart from alcohol. She said her use of alcohol was low, at most two glasses of wine a day with meals. However, she said prior to the recent episode of shoplifting with which she had been charged, she had had lunch with a friend and had drunk two glasses of wine. She had not told her husband or children about her shoplifting and refused my advice to do so. I pointed out that in my experience, the support of the family was often helpful.

She became tearful at this point in the interview and also when asked to describe her shoplifting behavior. She reported symptoms of depression, with anxiety about the outcome of the court hearing to take place in 7 weeks. She had difficulty getting to sleep and woke frequently thinking about the outcome. Her appetite had deteriorated, and she had lost 3 kilograms in weight. She was no longer enjoying the activities she had enjoyed previously. She asked whether she could be treated without charge additional to the payment made by the national medicare program, as she was concerned her husband might find out the reason if she paid for treatment. When I asked how he would find out, she said the money her husband gave her for housekeeping and her personal expenses was generous but she was reluctant to request additional amounts. She also was determined not to employ a solicitor to defend her, though I pointed out that as she had breached her bail, such help might improve the outcome. She then asked me to provide a report without charge, as she considered this would be sufficient. I asked her whether she was reluctant to spend money on her personal needs and whether this could be a factor in her shoplifting behavior. She denied this, saying she enjoyed buying clothes and was not concerned at their cost. I did not challenge her further at this stage concerning the possible role of reluctance to spend money, in view of the level of her depression.

I suggested that she take paroxetine (20 mg) at night to relieve her depression and that imaginal desensitization be used to control her urge to shoplift. She agreed to accept both procedures. When I saw her 10 days later, she said the paroxetine had relieved the major symptoms of her depression. I then asked about the nature of her shoplifting behavior. She could not identify any prior stresses, but said at the sight of various objects in the shop that she found attractive and might use, she felt an uncontrollable urge to take them, putting them in her purse or pocket. The objects could include items of clothing or household such items as crockery, cutlery, or bottles of preserves. She still felt such urges when shopping but was able to control them in her current state of marked anxiety concerning the outcome of the legal proceedings. When I asked whether she had arranged an appointment with the gynecologist, she said she was postponing this until after the court case.

I then explained the imaginal desensitization procedure in more detail, and we agreed on four scenarios that matched her shoplifting behaviors, such as being in a shop and having an urge to steal attractive items or thinking of going shopping after drinking wine with lunch. Each scenario ended with her visualizing leaving the situation without carrying out the inappropriate behaviors. She was then trained to relax and then, while relaxed, was asked to visualize the scenarios. The session was recorded by tape recorder. She was given the audiotape and told to listen to it three times a week for 4 weeks, in situations where she could sit or lie down and relax. When I saw her after 4 weeks, she said she had listened to the tape as instructed but was still aware of a strong urge to shoplift. In view of the risk of her shoplifting again, she agreed to try the effect of electrical aversion in the form of aversion relief.

Ten phrases describing the unacceptable behaviors, such as, "Feeling an urge to steal an attractive item of clothing" or "Going shopping after drinking alcohol," as well as an 11th statement, "Feeling no urge to shoplift," were written on separate filing cards. The cards were placed upside down in front of the patient, with the card with the 11th statement after the 10 and on top of about 20 blank cards. Electrodes were attached to her first and third right-hand fingers from a device constructed to deliver an electric shock consisting of 1-millisecond pulses every 10 milliseconds, and of 1-second duration. The voltage of the shock to be administered was determined prior to treatment as the level she said was unpleasant but not upsetting. In her case, this was 70 volts. She was then instructed to turn over the first card and read it aloud. Immediately after she completed reading the phrase, she received a shock at the level determined. This procedure was repeated with the following cards every 10 seconds until she had read the phrases on all 10 cards. She then read the final card and did not receive a shock. The 10 cards were then shuffled and the procedure repeated four more times. Shuffling the cards was done in order that she would not realize when she was about to turn over the card with the 11th statement, so that the relief would not be experienced until she saw the phrase. She commenced attending for this treatment twice a week. By the fifth session, she reported that when she had last gone shopping, the urge to shoplift was much weaker in the situations where she had previously experienced it as strong. She was still very anxious about the court case, and I supplied her with a report pointing out as evidence of her motivation to cease shoplifting that she had accepted electrical aversion therapy. It also stated she had become aware of the possible role of alcohol in contributing to her offence and would not drink it before shopping.

At her next session, she reported she had been given 6-months of community service of 10 hours a week. She was working in a Salvation Army shop and was enjoying the work. She had been forced to tell her family, and they had been very supportive. By the 10th treatment session, she said she was experiencing no urge to shoplift, and it was decided to cease the aversion relief. She felt she was no longer depressed, and I suggested she commence to reduce and then cease the paroxetine in a graduated manner. I saw her every few months for the following year, during which time she continued to report no urge to shoplift. I regularly encouraged her to spend money on herself and on outings with her husband and friends and also to make the appointment to see the gynecologist. After a year, we agreed she would terminate her visits but would contact me at the first signs of any return of the shoplifting urge. She still had not contacted the gynecologist.

—*Nathaniel McConaghy*

See also: *Masturbatory Retraining (Vol. I); Orgasmic Reconditioning (Vol. I); Treatment Failures in Behavioral Treatment (Vol. I)*

Suggested Readings

American Medical Association Council on Scientific Affairs. (1987). Aversion therapy. *Journal of the American Medical Association, 258,* 2562–2566.

McConaghy, N. (1977). Behavioral treatment in homosexuality. In M. Hersen, R. M. Eisler, & P. M. Miller (Eds.), *Progress in behavior modification* (pp. 309–380). New York: Academic Press.

McConaghy, N. (1993). *Sexual behavior: Problems and management.* New York: Plenum Press.

McConaghy, N. (1998). Assessment of sexual dysfunction and deviation. In A. S. Bellack & M. Hersen (Eds.), *Behavioral assessment: A practical handbook* (4th ed., pp. 315–341). Boston: Allyn & Bacon.

Wolpe, J. (1958). *Psychotherapy by reciprocal inhibition.* Stanford, CA: Stanford University Press.

EMMELKAMP, PAUL M. G.

I was born in Baarn, a small village in the Netherlands, February 17, 1949, as one of six children in a Catholic family. I was deemed to become a priest but at the age of 16 had to acknowledge that it would give me considerable difficulty to meet the celibacy requirements. Studying (clinical) psychology seemed a logical extension of my earlier priesthood aspirations, albeit without a real understanding of what the study of psychology actually involved.

When I graduated with a master's degree in clinical psychology at the University of Utrecht in 1971, I decided to stay a few years longer at that university. I succeeded in getting a research grant to conduct a PhD project on the behavioral treatment of agoraphobia, which I completed in 1975, under the direction of Walter Everaerd. At that time, I was highly inspired by the work and ideas of Isaac Marks, a psychiatrist at the Maudsley Hospital, in London. In a series of studies, I found that exposure in vivo was much more effective than imaginal exposure. Apart from conducting the studies to be included in my dissertation, I also started research into the behavioral treatment of obsessive-compulsive disorder, a research interest, if not a passion, which would stay with me for the rest of my academic life. There is at least one topic on which I agree with Freud, who noted already in 1926, "Obsessional neurosis is unquestionably the most repaying subject of . . . research."

Starting in 1971, I obtained broad postdoctoral psychotherapy training at the Institute of Medical Psychotherapy in Utrecht. At that time, I was an angry young man who was highly critical about psychotherapeutic methods that were not evidence based, so I gave my teachers and supervisors of the psychodynamic and experiential therapeutic methods a hard time. However, if I learned anything from those clinicians, it was the importance of the therapeutic relationship, which I still pass on to my own students.

In 1994, I moved to the Department of Clinical Psychology at the University of Groningen, which was psychodynamically and experientially oriented. Although my behavioral orientation led to some heavy discussions among the staff, I was allowed to continue my research into the effects of behavioral treatments and, after some time, even to give courses on behavior therapy. In this time, my research interest broadened and included now social phobia, marital distress, and the influence of parental rearing on the etiology of psychopathology. In 1986, I became full professor and head of the Department of Clinical Psychology and head of the Clinical Program at the University of Groningen.

When I was a young man madly running about teaching, doing clinical work, and research, I had no grand scheme in my head as to where research would bring me. Looking back now, my research topics were not so much determined by a major plan or my talents, but much more by being in a particular place at the right time and the possibilities of doing research in a particular area, despite my deficiencies. For example, I started my research projects into the treatment of marital distress after a well-known Dutch systems therapist (Donald MacGillavry) joined our group in Groningen and was enthusiastic about collaborating with me in this area. I moved into research into clinical child psychology when a very nice colleague (Ruud Minderaa) became the head of the Department of Child Psychiatry in Groningen and invited me to do research in his department. After becoming head of the Department of Clinical Psychology in Amsterdam in 1996, my interest in conducting research into addiction was gratified by the hospitality of the Jellinek Clinic. This institute was interested in evidence-based treatments and treatment outcome research. In my Groningen years, my interest in doing research in the addiction field was tempered by the near impossibility to get access to patients in primarily psychodynamically oriented addiction centers.

At the University of Amsterdam, my current research focuses on the etiology and development of psychopathological disorders. In addition, intervention studies are conducted on obsessive-compulsive disorder, posttraumatic stress, burnout, major depression, social phobia and avoidant personality disorder, maritally distressed couples, patients with substance abuse, and children with internalizing and externalizing disorders. Furthermore, research is conducted into endocrine and immunological changes as a result of cognitive-behavioral interventions. I am also involved in studies into therapy through the Internet and virtual reality treatment for a variety of anxiety disorders. I am the principal investigator in many research projects, funded by scientific and governmental institutions.

Failures in treatment have held my interests for a long time. In 1982, Edna Foa and I edited a book about *Failures in Behavior Therapy*, in which a number of factors related to such failure were discussed. I would like to dedicate some of my future time to study the research question relating to which variables determine whether an evidence-based treatment will be effective or not. It seems that scattered over different disorders, there is some knowledge about factors that facilitate or limit treatment effects. Exchange of information across disorders, however, is nonexistent, and theoretical models are lacking.

I am past president of the European Association of Cognitive and Behavior Therapy, editor of *Clinical Psychology & Psychotherapy,* and serve on the editorial board of a number of journals in clinical psychology and psychiatry. In 1996, I was awarded an honorary membership of the Association of Behavior and Cognitive Therapy. In 2001, I was elected as a member of The Royal Academy of Science, and in 2003, I was awarded the senior Heymans award by the Dutch Psychological Association for lifetime achievements.

Last but not least, I am married to Ellen Vedel and am the proud father of five daughters.

—*Paul M. G. Emmelkamp*

See also: *Exposure (Vol. I); Extinction and Habituation (Vol. I); Flooding (Vol. I)*

EVALUATING BEHAVIORAL PLANS

DESCRIPTION OF THE STRATEGY

A behavioral support (intervention or treatment) plan, among other things, aims at reducing a targeted problem behavior. Accordingly, the plan represents the independent variable, while behavioral and other changes represent the dependent variables. In this entry, we discuss many of the considerations that go into identifying and measuring the changes that occur as a result of a plan to evaluate its effectiveness.

The label used to refer to either a single behavior (e.g., *hitting*) or a class of target behaviors (e.g., *physical aggression,* including behaviors such as hitting, kicking, scratching, biting, etc.) is important. The label, first of all, should be physically descriptive; that is, it should describe the physical characteristics (topography) of the behavior. This contributes to more accurate and reliable measurement and unbiased functional assessment and analysis. Mistakenly, people frequently use functionally descriptive labels (e.g., *attention seeking* or *task avoidance*). Functionally descriptive labels call up underlying meanings and prejudices that may compromise measurement and functional assessment/analysis. Furthermore, the conclusions regarding the function or meaning of the target behavior that follow from a functional assessment/analysis are merely considered hypotheses to be tested, at least partially, by the support plan itself. Therefore, it is appropriate to retain the physically descriptive label, even after the assessment/analysis has been carried out.

Other considerations when selecting a label include avoiding the use of terms that have meaning beyond the behavior itself or that are disrespectful. For example, the label *assault* denotes criminal behavior. Similarly, when working with an adult who exhibits a class of behavior that includes the topographies of profanity, crying, screaming, flailing, and throwing objects, it would be more appropriate to use a label such as *outbursts* rather than *tantrums,* since tantrums disrespectfully conveys "childishness."

Given an identified target behavior, how should its changes be measured over time? *Rate measures* are the most common way of describing behavior change over time. Rate is defined as the discrete frequency of behavior during a particular period of time (e.g., 10 times an hour). Data are usually summarized on an outcome graph showing, for example, the daily/weekly/monthly rate of the target behavior during baseline, which is then compared with the changing rate after the initiation of a support plan. To accurately determine its rate, the *cycle* of a behavior must be clearly defined. The cycle is a statement of the criteria for saying an episode has started (i.e., onset criteria) and ended (i.e., offset criteria).

Rate, however, is not the appropriate outcome measure for all behaviors. For example, if the target behavior were the nonperformance of requested activities, rate would not be a meaningful measure, since change in rate would be as much a function of the number of requests made as anything else. For this and similar problems, a better measure would be the percentage of response occurrence, given the number of opportunities. When using percentage of response occurrence measures, it may be unnecessary to record every occurrence. Rather, the behavior can be measured based on a sampling method (e.g., the person's response to a specified, representative set of requests in a day). Furthermore, for behaviors without clear onset and offset criteria (e.g., stereotypic rocking or time on/off task), *whole-interval recording* (presence of the behavior throughout the entire interval, or not) or *partial-interval recording* (presence of the behavior for any part of the interval, or not) or *momentary time sampling* (presence or absence at the end of specified time periods) can be used to measure the increases or decreases in the behavior over time. As a final example, when the behavior is not directly observed, the dependent variable may be defined in terms of a permanent product, such as the number of new wounds found resulting from surreptitious self-injury. Such data might be based on scheduled daily physical examinations.

Table 1   A Comparison of Episodic Severity vs. Measures of Severity Over Time

Target Behavior			Baseline	Intervention
Outbursts				
	Over time	Frequency	10/Week	2/Week*
		Duration	10 Hours/Week	4 Hours/Week*
	Episodic severity	Average duration	1-hr/Episode	2-hr/Episode**
Physical aggression				
	Over time	Frequency	10/Month	3/Month*
		Episodes result in trips to the hospital	7/Month	3/Month*
	Episodic severity			
		Percentage of episodes resulting in trips to the hospital	70%	100%**
Property destruction				
	Over time	Frequency	10/Day	7/Week*
		Cost of repair or replacement	$280/Week	$7/Week*
	Episodic severity	Average cost of repair and replacement	$4 episode	$1 episode

*Improvement

**No improvement

In addition to changes in the occurrence of the target behavior over time, dependent variables may importantly include changes in the severity of the behavior over time. Measures of severity during a particular time period may include, for example, how much time (i.e., duration) the person spends engaging in the behavior (e.g., for outbursts); the cost of repair and replacement (e.g., for property destruction); and, perhaps for physical aggression, the number of episodes that occurred involving the more severe topographies that make up the response class (e.g., stabbing someone with a sharp instrument) or for which the most severe outcomes associated with the target behavior resulted (e.g., the need for medical attention).

While change in severity over time has been measured in the application of behavioral strategies to problem behavior, episodic severity has been overlooked as a dependent variable. Episodic severity is defined as the measure of intensity or gravity of a behavioral incident. Table 1 illustrates the distinction between measuring behavior over time versus episodic severity as a dependent variable. Episodic severity is an important dependent variable, since simply showing a reduction in the rate of a behavior over time or a reduction in the severity of the behavior over time does not guarantee that the severity of individual episodes (i.e., episodic severity) has also decreased; indeed, the opposite is frequently the case. Thus, when the severity of target behavior is of concern, measures of episodic severity may be more useful as a dependent variable than severity for a particular period of time.

However, in addition to changes in target behavior, the clinical validity of a support plan requires that quality of life also be included as a dependent variable. For adults, this would include, but would not be limited to, quantifying and measuring things such as community presence and participation, skill acquisition, increasing independence and productivity, increasing development of a full range of social relationships and friendships, and autonomy and self-determination through the exercise of increasingly informed choice. Such dependent variables, as well as assessing consumer satisfaction, are important, since the reason for targeting a behavior for change is often that its occurrence and/or episodic severity represent a barrier to these quality-of-life outcomes.

It is recognized in the field that this broad range of outcomes and their durability may not be achieved with stand-alone strategies. Rather, based on a comprehensive functional assessment/analysis, multi-element support plans are required. Such plans include strategies designed to improve the person's home, work, and social ecology; strategies designed to teach functionally equivalent and other critical skills; strategies such as antecedent control and differential and time-based schedules of reinforcement to reduce the occurrence of target behavior and the resulting need for reactive strategies; and reactive strategies designed to reduce the episodic severity of behavioral incidents.

Regardless of the dependent variables selected to measure the effectiveness of a plan, the behavior analyst has a responsibility for assuring data reliability and accuracy. This can challenge an analyst whose adult client, for example, may be supported by one staff person collecting data in a community setting for a behavior occurring at a relatively low rate (e.g., 1/month). In such situations, typical methods for assuring reliability/accuracy, in which data collected by two independent observers are compared, don't work because the behavior is unlikely to occur during periodically scheduled dual-recording sessions. The field needs procedures for assessing data reliability/accuracy in such situations. For example, the analyst may record occurrences of the target behavior that become known from incidental reports from staff, from chance direct observation, and from secondary data sources such as formal incident reports and staff communication logs. Periodically, these "incidental" records can be compared with the primary data sheet. If the incidentally recorded occurrences are accurately reflected on the raw data sheets, the analyst may have some confidence in the reliability/accuracy of dependent-variable measurement.

—*Gary W. LaVigna and Thomas J. Willis*

See also: *Behavioral Contracting (Vols. I, II, & III)*

Suggested Readings

Carr, E. G., Doolabh, A., Horner, R. H., Marquis, J. G., McAtee, M. L., McLaughlin, D. M., et al. (1999). *Positive behavioral support for people with developmental disabilities.* Washington, DC: American Association on Mental Retardation.

Favell, J. E. (Chairperson), Azrin, N. H., Baumeister, A. A., Carr, E. G., Dorsey, M. F., Forehand, R., et al. (1982). The treatment of self-injurious behavior (Monograph). *Behavior Therapy, 13,* 529–554.

Fox, P., & Emerson, E. (2002). *Positive goals: Interventions for people with learning disabilities whose behavior challenges.* Cheapside, Brighton, UK: Pavllion.

Hersen, M., & Barlow, D. H. (1976). *Single case experimental designs: Strategies for studying behavior change.* New York: Pergamon Press.

Kazdin, A. E. (1977). Assessing the clinical or applied importance of behavior change through social validation. *Behavior Modification, 1,* 427–451.

LaVigna, G. W., & Willis, T. J. (in press). Episodic severity: An overlooked dependent variable in the application of behavior analysis to challenging behavior. *Journal of Positive Behavior Interventions.*

EXPOSURE

DESCRIPTION OF THE STRATEGY

Since the 1960s and 1970s, it increasingly has been recognized and accepted that the common ingredient of many, if not most, behavioral treatments that affect anxiety is exposure to anxiety-provoking stimuli. Through repeated prolonged exposure to the offending agent, whether situation, event, person, sensation, or place, anxiety, fear, and other intense, associated negative emotions are reduced. In layman terms, exposure is essentially similar to "Facing one's fear" or "Getting back on the horse." No matter what idiom is used, the implication remains the same: Persons are exposed to that which makes them feel afraid, and through facing such fears repeatedly, the reaction of anxiety is reduced.

Although anxiety is a naturally occurring phenomenon and is a normal and adaptive experience in genuinely threatening situations (i.e., it possesses survival value), when anxiety and fear occur within an anxiety disorder, it represents an overly intense, maladaptive, and inappropriate response to what would commonly be deemed a benign threat by others. In this fashion, anxiety-disordered individuals are reacting to non-threatening or benign situations as if they were indeed genuinely threatening. Their perceptions facilitate a belief of threat where either one does not exist or the level of reaction is unwarranted. In fact, these perceptions guide reactions that are maladaptive and misplaced, since they represent inappropriately timed overreactions. Many anxiety-disordered individuals react in this fashion frequently enough so that they appear generally hypervigilant, which frequently leads to needing significantly less "threat" to react with anxiety and fear than their nonanxious counterparts (i.e., they are primed to react). In most anxiety disorders, this leads to a distinct and pervasive pattern of escape from—and eventually avoidance of—anxiety-provoking stimuli. Although this is a natural and common means for coping with threat in both humans and other animals, it prevents individuals from realizing that the stimulus is less threatening than imagined. In the absence of any contrary evidence, however, they do not learn that they have overestimated the threat. Hence, anxiety, fear, and other negative emotions recur each time the threatening stimulus is encountered, and it retains its provocative power. Escape and avoidance are negatively reinforcing, as they at least temporarily reduce perceived distress and therefore increase likelihood of a similar reactive behavior the next time the same or a similar stimulus is encountered. Without evidence to challenge their perceptions and beliefs about the stimulus, individuals cannot change their minds about the "threat," and they remain anxious and fearful of it.

The basic principle of exposure operates exactly on this notion that the overreaction to the stimulus is maintained by continued avoidance and escape. Repeated, prolonged exposure to the stimulus, when combined with prevention of escape and avoidance, sometimes known as *response prevention,* puts the individual in contact with the realistic information about it, rather than the imagined information that has previously been encoded based upon negative reactions. When the stimulus is faced and the feared consequences of remaining in its presence do not occur, repeatedly, new evidence and information can be gathered about its realistic level of threat, and reappraisals can be formed. As the stimulus is repeatedly encountered and the feared consequences continue to not occur, the stimulus becomes viewed as less and less threatening, finally extinguishing the fear. Extinction of fear is typically possible only after habituation to the stimulus occurs. Such habituation process is akin to getting used to something over time, and in the case of anxiety and fear, it is like spending time with something that is thought initially to be dangerous until it is proven otherwise over time (e.g., after spending increasing amounts of time with a dog, the dog phobic comes to realize that it will not bite— a common fear amongst dog phobics—and the dog begins to take on more realistic levels of threat).

Exposure can occur in several ways. The single most effective exposure method is in vivo, or live, exposure, where the individual is faced with the offending stimulus in reality. The closer the stimulus is to the real feared stimulus, the better the result of habituation and extinction will be. Direct experience is indeed best in providing contradictory evidence to threat appraisal and fear conditioning, and repeated, prolonged in vivo exposure seems especially potent in reducing anxiety reactions. Nonetheless, all aspects of fear may not be conducive for live exposure, such as death, AIDS, cancer, harm or violence, and so on. For these kinds of typically unavailable stimuli, in-imagination or fantasy exposures can be used for practical and ethical reasons. In-imagination exposure typically entails exposing the individual to feared or objectionable thoughts, images, or impulses, repeatedly. Individuals with such internal or mentally objectionable stimuli often attempt control of their thoughts and feelings in an effort to reduce contact with unwanted material. All of the best evidence from thought suppression research suggests that such escape and avoidance have the paradoxical effect of increasing the occurrence and intensity of unwanted mental events. Much as in real-life escape and avoidance, the anxiety-disordered individual becomes hypervigilant, or especially sensitive to certain unwanted thought content; paradoxically, by monitoring for this content, it occurs more frequently.

Because most people have all sorts of thoughts and images go through their minds, people who monitor for, or search for, undesirable materials will find them. Unfortunately, once found, such individuals tend to react overly negatively to the content and are typically driven to try to undo, or compensate, for the content. Such mental, compensatory or self-protective behavior is akin to escape and avoidance, in that it consistently supports the individual's perceptions about what is good and bad, or threatening or not. As in the case of live avoidance and escape, mental efforts as such maintain the anxiety sparked by unwanted thoughts. Exposure by loop-tape is often used in conjunction with exposure in imagination to reduce the amount an individual is able to distract from or avoid the cognitive exposure task, whether intentionally or not. Following basic human self-preservative functioning, it is known that when an individual does not engage in flight-or-fight behaviors in response to threat (whether actual or imagined), the common next-response mode is one of disconnecting, or disassociating, from the experience. Therefore, it is not unusual for individuals who are engaged in exposure to report or experience that their minds are wandering or not remaining with the provocative stimulus. Overt, live exposure is harder to inadvertently escape or avoid, but it is much more common for covert or in-imagination exposure to be fraught with distractibility. It is significantly more difficult to not be present during exposure when it is assisted by an audiotape of threat messages playing nonstop. Loop-tapes are also consistently used to burn out reactivity and excessive sensitivity to specific, highly provocative words. Such aversive words have been conceptualized as aversive stimuli by some, and repeated, prolonged exposure has notably been demonstrated as the methodology of choice to reduce such inappropriate reactivity.

The exposure principle is, furthermore, built upon the biological understanding that anxiety is self-limiting; that is, it cannot indefinitely continue. It is physiologically impossible to remain highly aroused and activated indefinitely. In fact, high arousal usually cannot be maintained for more than an hour or two. When individuals are faced with a feared stimulus and they do not avoid or escape it, the experienced anxiety will continue for some time until it gradually begins to decline after feared consequences do not occur or they become accustomed to the sensations that accompany the experience. Such gradual but predictable decline in anxiety is what drives the natural habituation process, which, when repeated, leads to extinction of the fear reaction. All exposure techniques operate on this knowledge that if the individual remains within the feared situation sufficiently, then anxiety will decrease and return toward a more normal level of arousal. It has, however, been debated whether the individual should face the complete, total fear nonstop until all reactivity to the stimulus has seized or whether a gradual series of approximations of the complete fear is as effective. Two variations of exposure seem to dominate this behavior modification technique, namely, flooding or gradual, hierarchical exposure. While both variations ask individuals to face their fear, they differ in how the technique is applied. In flooding, the individual is exposed for long periods of time to stimuli that evoke high levels of anxiety until such fear peaks and begins to decline. Graduated, hierarchical exposure, on the other hand, builds on the premise that new learning about threat is best facilitated by incremental, successive approximations of the ultimate fear. Therefore, gradual exposure does not start with the worst fear, but a lesser approximation of it that typically starts at half the strength of the ultimate fear and slowly works successively up a hierarchy of increasingly challenging stimuli that culminate with the ultimate fear.

RESEARCH BASIS

The research shows that therapist-assisted exposure is more effective than self-directed exposure and computer-assisted exposure. This knowledge delineates the importance of clearly demonstrating what the individual is supposed to do in the exposure and also offers better checks on both intentional and inadvertent avoidance and escape during exposure (both interfere with habituation and extinction). Guided mastery is broadly thought to be more useful than merely assisting in planning what exposures the individual is to do.

In addition, complete response prevention is better than partial or no response prevention. Avoidance, escape, or any kind of distraction or dissociation all interfere with the habituation process by reinforcing that the stimulus is to be feared; the individual's perceptions cannot begin to change until the individual at least acts as though the stimulus is nonthreatening (i.e., remains in its presence fully). Only when completely open to the stimulus can the individual begin to fully incorporate information about the stimulus when the individual is "nondefended."

Last, in-imagination exposure will enhance the effects of in vivo exposure. It is not thought, however, that in-imagination exposure alone to the consequences of not protecting oneself from feared consequences in vivo is effective. Experiencing anxiety while "undefended" is superior, although it is not always possible to experience all scenarios in real life. In-imagination exposure can also be enhanced with real variables of the fear present (e.g., performing imaginal exposures around death and dying in a mortuary or graveyard).

RELEVANT TARGET
POPULATIONS AND EXCEPTIONS

All anxiety disorders have today been treated effectively with exposure techniques. Commonly available, exposure-based treatment manuals exist for specific phobias, panic disorder with or without agoraphobia, social phobia, obsessive-compulsive disorder, generalized anxiety disorder, and posttraumatic stress disorder. In addition, many spectrum conditions, such as body dysmorphic disorder, are amenable to exposure regiments. For younger children, who may not have full insight into the irrationality of their fears, exposure may necessarily occur indirectly within the context of play therapy, because they may not comprehend why the treatment provider would ask them to deliberately face something "dangerous." Likewise, another exception to exposure treatment would be those individuals who do not agree to such treatment after being informed of what it involves. It is known that approximately 30% refuse exposure-based treatment, if it is offered, because of the demands that it puts on individuals, and close to 20% may drop out or end prematurely because the treatment is too challenging. Cognitive therapy may be an acceptable alternative to such individuals, and it may also serve a preparatory function in preparing individuals for the rigors of exposure therapy.

COMPLICATIONS

Clinical depression is known to interfere with the habituation process, especially between sessions. While the individual may habituate in session, there can sometimes appear to be no carryover of new learning between sessions. This will ultimately interfere with the extinction of fear. Depression can further inhibit the individual from attending to all of the cues and information central to reappraisal of feared stimuli. Therefore, it is centrally important that severity of depression be controlled to manage its potential influence on outcome.

While most anxiety-disordered individuals recognize, at some level, the irrationality of their fears, some do not. When individuals do not have insight into the nature of their fears, exposure may not be effective and should not be implemented, for ethical and humane reasons. Psychoeducation and medications may be useful in facilitating insight into irrational fears and the effects of anxiety.

Furthermore, personality disorders are thought to sometimes interfere with the treatment of anxiety. There are likely multiple reasons for this phenomenon, but suffice it to say that if the individual can focus on the anxiety without getting too focused on personality symptoms, treatment can be quite effective. A clear treatment contract may be required to keep exposure treatment on track in such cases.

CASE ILLUSTRATION

"Sue" was a 28-year-old, married, unemployed woman engaged in a broad range of avoidant and compulsive behaviors. Most predominantly, she executed extensive checking rituals that were aimed at relieving obsessive fears that she, by her thoughts or actions, would be responsible for the death of other people. She was also intensely afraid of dying herself. These pervasive obsessions left her practically unable to properly care for herself and her child. In addition, she was grossly impaired in her ability to perform daily household chores, such as grocery shopping, cleaning, and cooking. She was unable to derive enjoyment from listening to music or watching television because she associated certain words, people, and noises with death, dying, and other particular fears. Sue's major complaint was excessive checking and avoidance behaviors, all aimed at preventing disease or death.

At the time of the intake, a thorough behavioral analysis was performed in an effort to define target behaviors precisely and to identify conditions maintaining such target behaviors. This assessment followed a standardized A-B-C cognitive-behavioral model. Using this integrative approach, antecedents (A), or stimulus or setting events, were established. Three kinds of behaviors (B) were observed and measured: (1) covert cognitive (thinking)—attributions, expectations, beliefs, self-talk, images, and so on; (2) overt respondent (physical)—physiological changes occurring within the body; and (3) overt operant (acting)—"voluntary" behavior, whether excess or deficit. Finally, consequences (C), or events that occur during and after a particular behavior, were estimated and explored. This assessment approach was selected as part of a strong effort to more completely understand how Sue's thoughts, feelings, physiology, behavior, and environment interacted to create her individual experience of obsessive-compulsive disorder (OCD). As an outcome measure, the Yale-Brown Obsessive-Compulsive Scale was selected because it provides the most comprehensive narrow-band assessment of OCD.

Treatment involved a systematic hierarchy that exposed Sue to moderately provocative triggers first, and later to progressively more disturbing scenarios. With each level of exposure, she was repeatedly exposed to the same trigger until her reactivity to the stimulus was reduced by at least 50%. Once she achieved habituation to one level of the hierarchy, exposure rose to the next level, so that she was systematically exposed to increasingly difficult OCD triggers after experiencing reduced distress to the previous trigger. As each trigger situation became less and less distressing to her, Sue also combined triggers with moving up the hierarchy. This was partly done to ensure that no single trigger could individually be avoided once it had been passed in the hierarchy. While she remained in the in vivo exposures for at least 90 minutes, she did remain in some trigger situations for up to 3 hours to ensure that her anxiety would sufficiently diminish before she stopped the exposure. These prolonged exposures were done to ensure that she would not escape from the triggers that were the most provocative for her. During all exposures, her anxiety levels and habituation were measured and monitored by use of the Subjective Units of Distress Scale, another step taken to ensure adequate anxiety reduction occurred before stopping any given exposure. When avoidance, escape, and rituals were resisted and Sue faced her fears and withstood her anxiety repeatedly, substantial treatment gains followed.

—Johan Rosqvist

See also: *Exposure and Response Prevention (Vol. II); Extinction (Vol. III); Flooding (Vol. I)*

Suggested Readings

Baer, L., & Minichiello, W. E. (1998). Behavior therapy for obsessive-compulsive disorder. In M. A. Jenike, L. Baer, & W. E. Minichiello (Eds.), *Obsessive-compulsive disorders: Practical management* (3rd ed., pp. 337–367). Boston: Mosby.

Hersen, M. (Ed.). (2002). *Clinical behavior therapy: Adults and children.* New York: Wiley.

Marks, I. M. (1987). *Fears, phobias, and rituals: Panic, anxiety, and their disorders.* Oxford, UK: Oxford University Press.

McLean, P. D., Whittal, M. L., Thordarson, D. S., Taylor, S., Söchting, I., Koch, W. J., et al. (2001). Cognitive versus behavior therapy in the group treatment of obsessive-compulsive disorder. *Journal of Consulting and Clinical Psychology, 69*(2), 205–214.

McLean, P. D., & Woody, S. R. (2001). *Anxiety disorders in adults: An evidence-based approach to psychological treatment.* Oxford, UK: Oxford University Press.

Purdon, C. (1999). Thought suppression and psychopathology. *Behaviour Research and Therapy, 37,* 1029–1054.

Spiegler, M. D., & Guevremont, D. C. (1993). Brief/graduated exposure therapy: Systematic desensitisation and in vivo exposure. In *Contemporary behavior therapy* (2nd ed., pp. 194–225). Pacific Grove: Brooks/Cole.

Spiegler, M. D., & Guevremont, D. C. (1993). Prolonged/intense exposure therapy: Flooding and implosive therapy. In *Contemporary behavior therapy* (2nd ed., pp. 226–250). Pacific Grove: Brooks/Cole.

Steketee, G. (1999). *Therapist protocol: Overcoming obsessive-compulsive disorder: A behavioral and cognitive protocol for the treatment of OCD.* Oakland: New Harbinger.

EXTINCTION AND HABITUATION

DESCRIPTION OF THE STRATEGY

Classical Conditioning

Ivan Pavlov in the early 1900s demonstrated the ease with which a response could be *classically conditioned,* a phenomenon that would ultimately form the basis of behavior therapy. Pavlov repeatedly presented a bell to dogs just prior to the appearance of meat powder. The meat powder was an *unconditioned stimulus* because it naturally made the dogs salivate without any earlier learning. After repeatedly hearing the bell before receiving the meat powder, the dogs learned to salivate in response to the bell, prior to getting the meat. This indicated that the bell had become a *conditioned stimulus* to elicit salivation, and mouth watering was now a *conditioned response* to the bell.

Based on this discovery of the way animals readily learn associations between stimuli, John B. Watson used the classical conditioning model to establish a fear response, like a phobia, in a young boy called "Little Albert." Albert was only 11 months old when Watson conditioned the boy to fear small white rats. For this infant, the rat initially evoked no fear. However, pairing the rat with an unexpected loud noise elicited a clear fear response. Soon, Albert showed fear to all manner of stimuli that resembled white fur, including a Santa Claus mask. Spreading of the conditioned response to related stimuli *(stimulus generalization)* helps explain why an individual with a dog phobia is likely to become afraid of all dogs, and not simply the dog that may have initially bitten him or her.

Classical Extinction

Once a conditioned response has been established by means of repeated pairings of a conditioned stimulus with one that is unconditioned, it is difficult to change the response unless you weaken the association between the stimuli. This process of unlearning is called *classical extinction.* If the conditioned stimulus is no longer paired with the unconditioned stimulus, eventually the conditioned response starts to disappear. In other words, if the bell were repeatedly presented without meat powder, the dogs would gradually stop salivating in response to the bell. In this way, conditioned fear responses or other maladaptive behaviors can be extinguished. Classical extinction does not actually make the conditioned response disappear; rather, it becomes inhibited or suppressed. This is evident from the ease with which the conditioned response can be reinstated or show "spontaneous recovery" over time, indicating that the original learning has not been permanently lost.

Therapies based on classical conditioning are focused on helping the client unlearn the association between the conditioned and unconditioned stimulus, so that the unhealthy response can be extinguished. This unlearning can happen in a number of ways.

Counterconditioning

In *counterconditioning,* the conditioned stimulus is paired with a response that is incompatible with the unhealthy reaction, such as pairing a fear-evoking stimulus with a relaxed feeling. This approach underlies Joseph Wolpe's theory of *reciprocal inhibition,* which involves countering anxiety with a feeling that inhibits the fear response, such as relaxation, sexual arousal, or assertiveness. A healthy behavior eventually replaces the undesirable response. The pairing of the relaxation response with progressively more fear-evoking objects, situations, or images is known as *systematic desensitization.* For instance, an individual who fears heights could be taken to a moderate height and then encouraged to stay at this height while doing relaxation exercises until the fear response diminishes. When the client could remain at the height without feeling much anxiety, he or she would then be ready to move to a more challenging height. Over time, the unhealthy fear response is extinguished through repeated pairing with relaxation, a feeling that is incompatible with fear.

In addition to coupling fear with relaxation, counterconditioning has been used in sex therapy to help treat sexual disorders, such as those related to performance anxiety. In this case, the anxious couple is prompted to pair sexual situations that would normally provoke anxiety with pleasurable feelings, like arousal. In a process known as *sensate focus,* pleasurable touching that does not include intercourse is encouraged, thus reducing anxiety associated with the

pressure to perform and creating positive associations with sexual activity. Similarly, in assertiveness training, the client is taught to respond with confidence in situations that normally evoke anxiety.

Habituation

Even without pairing the negative conditioned response with an incompatible positive response, repeated exposure to a feared situation or image while remaining in that situation will eventually lead to a reduction in the fear response. Reduced strength of the conditioned response following numerous presentations of the evocative stimulus is known as *habituation.* This process forms the basis of a variety of exposure therapies. The common theme involves repeated exposure to the stimuli that evoke the negative response (often fear) and staying in the situation.

By not circumventing the anxiety, the avoidance behavior is not reinforced because the person is challenged to experience the fear. Through exposure, the person learns to tolerate anxiety and experiences mastery. Exposure can be *in vivo* (i.e., to the actual situation, such as touching a live spider) or *imaginal* (e.g., imagining holding a spider) and can be done gradually (e.g., first looking at a picture, then watching a spider from far away, and eventually picking it up) or done through *flooding,* which involves exposure to a highly arousing stimulus for a prolonged period of time. Whatever the form of exposure, clients are encouraged to face their fears and remain in that situation until the fear lessens.

Habituation occurs for a number of reasons. The person gets used to being in the situation and realizes that the imagined catastrophic outcomes do not come true. For instance, a man who is afraid of water learns that he does not drown and can cope even in a frightening situation. In addition to cognitive changes, from a behavioral perspective, the person breaks the established association between the unconditioned and conditioned stimuli. Furthermore, physiological changes occur that naturally lead to a reduction of the conditioned fear response.

When an individual initially becomes frightened, he or she experiences a dramatic increase in fear arousal, produced by the "fight-or-flight" system, which is operated in large part by the body's sympathetic nervous system. The cardiovascular system is activated, and blood is pumped to the skeletal muscles to prepare the body for emergency action. This system is very adaptive when a person is in real danger, because it prepares the body to either escape from the danger or fight the aggressor. However, in anxiety disorders, it essentially acts as a false alarm, because it primes the body to respond to a danger that does not actually exist. Fortunately, this system is designed for emergencies, and our bodies cannot maintain such a heightened state of arousal for an extended period of time. After the initial peak in anxiety, the autonomic nervous system becomes more active to return bodily functions to their normal levels. Thus, the fear response can be extinguished by simply allowing the frightened individual to habituate or become accustomed to the situation.

Aversive Therapy

A conditioned response can also be extinguished by pairing it with another undesirable response. This is useful when the unhealthy behavior is maladaptive but desirable to the person, such as an inappropriate sexual impulse. In this case, the desired behavior can be paired with aversive stimuli to change the positive associations. For example, an individual with pedophilia could be exposed to sexually evocative pictures of young children while simultaneously experiencing brief electric shocks to reduce the pleasurable feelings associated with the pictures. Alternatively, a person who abuses alcohol could pair drinking (an initially pleasurable activity) with a medication that will elicit nausea to reduce the positive associations to alcohol. In this case, it is important that the aversive stimuli be sufficiently negative so that the person does not merely get used to it and habituate.

Operant Conditioning

Even before Pavlov was making dogs salivate through classical conditioning, Edward Thorndike was investigating learning processes in hungry cats that learned through trial and error how to escape from a box to obtain food. When these cats were rewarded with food, they increased the behaviors that enabled their escape. Thorndike labeled the relationship between behaviors and their consequences the "law of effect." In its original version, this law simply states that responses that lead to positive outcomes will increase, while responses that lead to negative outcomes will decrease.

B. F. Skinner was very interested in behaviors that increase or decrease because of the consequences that

follow them and felt that most complex behaviors fit into this category. These behaviors are termed *operant* because they operate on the environment to bring about a given outcome. Skinner noted that behavior would increase if it was followed by a reward (*positive reinforcement,* such as getting dessert after finishing homework) or if it was followed by a negative stimulus being removed (*negative reinforcement,* such as having less homework assigned following good conduct). Analogous decreases in behavior follow positive and negative punishments.

Operant Extinction

Similar to classical extinction, where the association between a stimulus and a conditioned response is weakened, in *operant extinction,* all reinforcers or positive outcomes are withheld from a behavior that was previously rewarded. Accordingly, the undesirable behavior diminishes because it no longer leads to pleasant consequences. For example, an individual with anger management problems who typically gets his or her way after yelling loudly should consistently not be reinforced following yelling. Instead, the person might be reinforced after negotiating in a reasonable manner. In this way, yelling is extinguished, while negotiation is differentially reinforced.

A variation on operant extinction can also occur using punishment, such as instituting "time-outs," where a child who has misbehaved has all reinforcers removed for a period of time. Extinction is most effective when it is consistent (i.e., the positive reinforcement is reliably withheld following the behavior) and alternative desirable behaviors are rewarded. So, although time-outs do involve decreasing a behavior by withholding reinforcers, it is more clearly an example of negative punishment than pure extinction.

RESEARCH BASIS

Classical Extinction Techniques

Applied relaxation in systematic desensitization has substantial support as an adjunct technique in the treatment of a range of anxiety disorders, likely due to the client's increased ability to feel more in control while in the presence of the fearful stimulus. Similarly, sensate focus, concentrating on pleasurable sensations that stem from sensual activities rather than emphasizing orgasm and intercourse, has received considerable support in the extinction of unhealthy responses in sexual arousal disorders.

Habituation-Based Therapies

Exposure therapy has been widely demonstrated as an effective treatment for anxiety, especially when used in combination with other techniques, such as *cognitive restructuring* (changing maladaptive thought patterns). Exposure in conjunction with response prevention has been used to successfully treat obsessive-compulsive disorder (OCD) and, more recently, has shown favorable effects in reducing anger and aggressive behavior. *Satiation therapy* has been used to treat maladaptive sexual arousal and involves prolonged exposure with the expectation that maladaptive arousal will be reduced over time through satiation or boredom with the inappropriate stimuli. While some support exists for this technique, treatments that encourage maladaptive arousal raise a number of ethical concerns.

Aversion Therapies

Aversion therapy has demonstrated favorable short- and long-term results in the treatment of alcohol and cocaine dependence, especially in combination with other treatment modalities, including detoxification and counseling. In contrast, research on aversion therapy to treat maladaptive sexual disorders suggests that such therapies may reduce arousal; however, there are few well-controlled studies and little support for its long-term effectiveness.

Operant Extinction Techniques

Treatments that incorporate principles of operant extinction have been used successfully to treat anger problems, especially in youth. In addition to using positive and negative reinforcement and punishment, such treatments also improve communication skills and attempt to address the client's distorted perceptions regarding social interactions. Operant extinction techniques have shown the greatest support when reinforcement and punishment are consistent.

RELEVANT TARGET POPULATIONS AND EXCEPTIONS

Habituation and extinction techniques provide the foundation for a variety of successful behavioral treatments. For instance, relaxation training and exposure therapy have been used to treat each of the anxiety disorders, including specific phobias and panic disorder. Furthermore, female sexual arousal disorder and male erectile disorder typically improve following sensate focus treatment. Aversion therapy, on the other hand, has historically been used to treat substance dependence and paraphilias, but ethical concerns and questionable long-term maintenance limit its current use.

Operant extinction is frequently used to reduce undesirable behaviors among children with behavioral problems or to lessen repetitive and sometimes harmful behaviors seen in developmental disorders. However, it may not be an appropriate technique for self-injurious behaviors that need to be eliminated quickly, due to a potential increase in either the behavior itself or in aggression when reinforcers are initially withheld (known as an *extinction burst*).

COMPLICATIONS

The principles underlying habituation and extinction have been used to successfully treat the range of anxiety disorders, sexual dysfunctions, and numerous childhood behavior problems. Notwithstanding, the procedures are not without complications. Because of the potential for spontaneous recovery (return of a previously extinguished response), it is important to ensure that the behavior is extinguished across multiple contexts to increase the generalization and maintenance of gains. Other complications include the ethical concerns about using extreme punishments in aversive conditioning. Furthermore, removal of positive reinforcers for operant extinction requires a great deal of control over the environment, which can make it difficult to implement outside of highly restricted settings. Finally, as mentioned earlier, the potential side effects of extinction, such as increases in undesirable or aggressive behavior, make it less ideal for behaviors that need to be terminated quickly, though the risk of these consequences is substantially reduced by combining extinction with other interventions, such as differential reinforcement.

Complications surrounding habituation relate to the need to have clients remain in the situation until the maladaptive response is sufficiently diminished. This can be difficult for therapists who run their practice on a traditional therapy hour. In addition, although rare, there are some individuals whose anxiety increases over time during exposures, rather than showing the usual habituation pattern. This "sensitization" is especially likely if exposures are very brief.

CASE ILLUSTRATION

"Alex," a 63-year-old married grandfather who had recently retired from his position at an accounting firm, sought treatment for OCD. For the past 9 years, he had been concerned with keeping his home exceptionally orderly and spent many hours a day rechecking his accounting work for errors. Cleaning and checking behaviors made him unproductive at work, precipitated his early retirement, and caused numerous arguments with his wife, who felt intense pressure to keep the house immaculate. Although OCD symptoms had been present for nearly a decade, Alex did not seek treatment until his symptoms escalated following retirement.

When Alex left his position, his daughter asked him to help care for his two young grandchildren. Alex adored his grandchildren and was thrilled to spend more time with them. However, with increased responsibility for their care, he felt extremely fearful that his grandchildren might be hurt in some way if his home was not flawlessly clean and organized. Although Alex recognized that his fears were illogical, he spent up to 6 hours a day compulsively cleaning, even combing the fringe on the dining room rug. In addition, Alex did not cook for fear of messing up the kitchen and would not permit his wife to cook or allow his grandchildren to have friends over for fear they would make things untidy and be harmed.

Following a thorough assessment, Alex agreed to start exposure with response/ritual prevention and was gradually exposed to situations that made him anxious. With the therapist's help, Alex prevented himself from cleaning or doing other rituals. A fear hierarchy was developed, starting with relatively easy exposures that centered on different approaches to creating a mess (such as leaving a towel on the floor) and leading to extremely challenging tasks (such as allowing spaghetti sauce to boil over and leaving the mess for 24 hours). In each case, Alex would create the mess, which would evoke anxiety, and then remain in the situation until his anxiety had diminished to at least half of its original strength, with exposures lasting from 30 minutes to 2 to 3 hours. During each exposure, Alex allowed his anxiety to habituate so that the conditioned fear and avoidance responses would eventually be extinguished. His anxiety was regularly monitored throughout exposures using a verbal scale from 0 *(completely calm)* to 100 *(extreme fear,* like panic). After each weekly exposure with the therapist, Alex was instructed to repeat and practice the exposure at least five times during the week (preferably for at least 40 minutes a day) and to ensure that in each case, he remained in the situation until habituation had occurred. After 8 months of regular exposures with repeated practice between sessions, Alex was cleaning only 1 hour a day and no longer exhibited extreme avoidance behaviors.

—*Bethany A. Teachman and Shannan Smith-Janik*

See also: *Exposure (Vol. I); Extinction (Vol. II); Negative Reinforcement (Vol. III)*

Suggested Readings

Barkley, R. A. (1997). *Defiant children: A clinician's manual for assessment and parent training* (2nd ed.). New York: Guilford Press.

Barlow, D. H. (Ed.). (2001). *Clinical handbook of psychological disorders: A step-by-step treatment manual* (3rd ed.). New York: Guilford Press.

Goldstein, E. B. (1994). Basic learning processes. In *Psychology* (pp. 220–271). Pacific Grove, CA: Brooks/Cole.

Laws, D. R., & O'Donohue, W. (Eds.). (1997). *Sexual deviance: Theory, assessment, and treatment.* New York: Guilford Press.

McLean, P. D., & Woody, S. R. (2001). *Anxiety disorders in adults: An evidence-based approach to psychological treatment.* Oxford, UK: Oxford University Press.

Smith, J. W., & Frawley, P. J. (1990). Long-term abstinence from alcohol in patients receiving aversion therapy as part of a multimodal inpatient program. *Journal of Substance Abuse Treatment, 7*(2), 77–82.

EYE MOVEMENT DESENSITIZATION AND REPROCESSING

DESCRIPTION OF THE STRATEGY

Since its introduction in 1989, eye movement desensitization and reprocessing (EMDR) has undergone numerous empirical investigations. Now a widely accepted treatment, EMDR is considered an integrative psychotherapy due to its blending of aspects from different orientations. Therapists from diverse orientations recognize a variety of elements, including nondirective or "free" association, attention to negative beliefs and learning, concentration on physiological sensation, and a client-directed stance.

Since the process of EMDR does expose clients to anxiety-provoking stimuli, some have considered it another form of exposure therapy and have suggested that this would account for its effectiveness. However, since exposure therapy incorporates a habituation and extinction model, positive treatment outcomes are thought to require prolonged, uninterrupted, and undistracted exposure in order for it to be effective. By contrast, EMDR uses very brief (20 to 50 seconds), repeated, client-directed exposures. Also, while exposure therapy prohibits the client from reducing his or her anxiety by "changing the scene" or moving too quickly through a traumatic memory, an integral component of EMDR is nondirective or "free" associating to whatever enters the client's consciousness. Thus, the structure of EMDR directly contradicts the elements that exposure theories purport are necessary for positive outcomes.

Initially, EMDR was known as eye movement desensitization (EMD), as it was assumed that the desensitization of anxiety was the primary result of this approach. However, it was quickly discovered that while targeting a disturbing experience, clients would begin to rapidly associate to earlier, related events. The subsequent changes in distress were accompanied by a reduction of negative attributions and an increase in insight and sense of self-worth. Furthermore, decreasing the disturbance associated with these earlier events was also found to decrease the level of disturbance connected to the present stimulus. It was posited that this decreased disturbance was related to learning that had occurred. Thus, the term *reprocessing* was added, and the information-processing model was developed.

The adaptive information processing (AIP) model is based upon the associative nature of memory and perception and describes pathology as resulting from insufficiently processed events that are dysfunctionally stored in implicit (nondeclarative) rather than explicit (narrative) memory systems. When a person experiences strong negative affect or dissociation as a result of a traumatic event, information processing is impaired and the memory is fundamentally stored with the initial perceptions, physical sensations, emotions, and distorted thoughts as they were at the time of the experience. Because this traumatic memory

network becomes isolated, associative linking with related memories is inhibited and no new learning occurs. A variety of internal and external cues can then trigger the unresolved experience, often leading to nightmares, flashbacks, and intrusive recollections, as observed in individuals diagnosed with posttraumatic stress disorder (PTSD). Since the reexperiencing of this dysfunctionally stored information in future similar events can eventually lead to habitual response patterns, or personality traits, it is reasonable to expect that the resultant disorders would respond well to treatment designed to reprocess this information.

The EMDR protocol is designed to fully access and process the memory components (image, affect, cognitions, sensations), resulting in rapid treatment outcomes consistent with an adaptive resolution. That is, what is useful is learned, stored with appropriate affect, and able to successfully guide the person in the future. Each of the integrative procedures are viewed as contributing to treatment effects; however, some elements introduced in EMDR protocols in 1989 may particularly shed light on possible mechanisms of action: (a) brief client-directed exposure, (b) nondirective "free" association, (c) mindfulness, and (d) eye movements and other dual-attention stimulation.

Through the use of brief client-directed exposure, clients develop the ability to mentally delimit and control disturbing internal stimuli, thereby achieving a sense of mastery and decreasing distress about their symptoms. Also, since short doses of exposure are more tolerable to clients, they are less likely to engage in the avoidance behavior that contributes to pathology.

While attending to the various components of the disturbing memory, clients are asked to be aware of their internal experience, along with the eye movements or other dual-attention stimuli (hand taps or auditory stimuli). During this time, new insights, associations, emotions, and images rapidly emerge into consciousness. The client is instructed to report on anything that comes to mind, and that material becomes the focus for the next set of eye movements. This combined method of "mindfulness" and nondirective or "free" association allows the focus to shift from the original target of distress to other related experiences and information necessary for adequate processing to occur.

Although many of the studies conducted to investigate the eye movement component have been methodologically limited, and further research is needed in order to clarify this issue, recent research has shed some light on their therapeutic contribution. The idea that eye movements are correlated to shifts in cognitive content was proposed in the 1960s. There are a number of hypotheses that attempt to explain how eye movements facilitate the creation of new associative links. One such hypothesis purports that the eye movements or other dual-attention stimulation elicit an orienting response, which is a natural response of interest and attention to a new stimulus.

Through the orienting response, the eye movements appear to disrupt the visual-spatial sketchpad of working memory, thereby reducing the vividness of the image and decreasing the subsequent emotional intensity of the memory. The eye movements act as a distracter or even provoke a relaxation response, which then assists clients as they access material that was once unbearable. As the client becomes increasingly able to tolerate the evoked material, previous associations to negative emotions are interrupted, and new associative links with the dysfunctionally stored information are created. Some compare this process to REM sleep, whereby neurobiological mechanisms integrate episodic memories into the memory network.

EMDR utilizes an eight-phase therapeutic approach to enhance the above-mentioned information-processing system. Though this is a fairly standardized approach, specific protocols have been adapted for use with a variety of clinical issues. The first two phases are dedicated to gathering the information necessary for the selection of suitable targets (including past, present, and future situations) and to providing stabilization techniques, along with education about the client's symptoms and EMDR in general. During the third phase, the image, cognitions (positive and negative), and affect are closely examined, and baseline measures are gathered using the Validity of Cognition scale (VOC) and the Subjective Units of Distress scale (SUD). The negative cognition is formulated in the present tense to highlight the impact of the past event on current self-concept, as well as the irrationality of the belief ("I am powerless" versus "I was powerless"). The empowering positive cognition increases the client's awareness of the cognitive distortion related to the event, enhances motivation, and forges the preliminary links between the dysfunctionally stored memories and emotionally corrective information.

Phases 4 and 5 utilize dual-attention stimulation (eye movements, hand taps, auditory stimuli) to first facilitate adaptive processing, or learning, and then

to enhance the new positive self-assessment. Phase 6 then targets and alleviates any residual physical tension, while Phase 7 assesses the adequacy of the processing during the session and prepares the client for potential spontaneous processing between sessions. During Phase 8, which occurs at the beginning of each subsequent EMDR session, the therapist assesses the client's response to the previously processed targets, and new targets are chosen.

RESEARCH BASIS

Over the years, EMDR has been the focus of much scientific scrutiny and empirical tests. PTSD has been an area of particular interest for many researchers, and after many well-controlled studies, EMDR is now well recognized as an effective treatment for PTSD. In 2000, the International Society for Traumatic Stress Studies officially designated EMDR as an effective treatment for PTSD. In PTSD research, EMDR has been compared to several treatments and controls, including (a) wait-list controls, (b) Veterans Administration (VA) standard care, (c) biofeedback-assisted relaxation, (d) muscle relaxation, (e) active listening, (f) individual psychotherapy in an HMO, (g) exposure therapies, and (h) combinations of exposure and cognitive therapies.

In general, EMDR has been found to be superior to wait-list controls, biofeedback relaxation, active listening, supportive psychotherapy, and standard care (group and individual therapy in a VA hospital and HMO, respectively) on measures of posttraumatic stress. The only randomized study of combat veterans to provide a full course of treatment found that after 12 sessions, 77% no longer had PTSD. Findings of well-designed civilian studies have clearly supported the use of EMDR in the treatment of PTSD, with 77% to 90% of clients no longer suffering from PTSD after 3 to 10 hours of treatment. Randomized controlled studies comparing EMDR and exposure, with and without cognitive therapy, have found treatment outcomes to be relatively equivalent on most measures. However, EMDR treatment was shorter and/or required no homework compared with the 1 to 2 hours of homework per day required for exposure therapy. In fact, the only meta-analytic review to evaluate efficiency found EMDR to be more efficient, reporting fewer sessions than the comparison treatments, with effects maintained at follow-up. Another meta-analytic review found that the more rigorous the study, the larger the treatment effect sizes.

Preliminary research has been conducted to examine the effectiveness of EMDR in treating phobias, panic disorders, and somatoform disorders (chronic pain, phantom limb pain, and body dysmorphic disorder). Some phobia and panic disorder studies failed to provide a full course of treatment and neglected to test the specific EMDR phobia protocol. However, when all of the appropriate procedures were utilized in the phobia studies, positive results were found. Similarly, some positive results have also been found in the use of EMDR with panic disorder (without agoraphobia) and somatoform disorders. Processing the etiological memory using the standard PTSD protocol appears to effectively eliminate the symptoms of body dysmorphia. The same procedures, along with an increased concentration on physical sensations, have been successfully used to treat phantom limb and chronic pain.

As mentioned above, the results of studies designed to investigate the role of eye movements in EMDR have been inconclusive. The results of clinical studies with diagnosed populations indicated a positive though nonsignificant trend, suggesting that eye movements may affect treatment outcomes. However, the dismantling studies with analogue participants (usually normal college students with nonclinical anxiety) found no effect for eye movements. Since the minimal distress of the participants was alleviated with minimal treatment, it was difficult to detect any potential differences between the two conditions (eye movements and non-eye movements). In addition, many of these studies were limited by inadequate sample sizes, insufficient treatment duration, and truncated protocols. To date, seven component action studies, which examined eye movements in isolation, have indicated that eye movements decrease the salience of the memory and its related affect, or increase the associative process.

RELEVANT TARGET POPULATIONS AND EXCEPTIONS

As mentioned above, EMDR has been declared an effective and efficient treatment for PTSD. While clients who have experienced a single-event trauma or a number of related traumas are fairly easy to treat with EMDR, clients who have experienced pervasive trauma (e.g., childhood abuse) will require more

extended EMDR treatment. As mentioned previously, the long-standing nature of this dysfunctionally stored information can lead to the pervasive patterns of responding and interacting. Therefore, EMDR can be used to process memories that are the experiential contributors to the pathology, as well as to incorporate the positive affects and experiences that would have been necessary for healthy growth and socialization.

In terms of defining *trauma,* the Criterion A events used to diagnose PTSD are easy to recognize and can be considered "big-T" traumas. However, the childhood experiences that seem inconsequential to an adult may be very disturbing to the child and can interfere with the information-processing system. These experiences are considered "small-t" traumas.

The inadequate processing and dysfunctionally stored memories related to a disturbing event or trauma can be the cause of many clinical complaints. Therefore, it is reasonable to expect that EMDR would be helpful in reducing or eliminating disorders that follow a distressing event, such as a dog phobia occurring after a dog bite. Though findings to date are inconclusive, preliminary studies indicate that EMDR may be helpful with respect to phobias, some panic disorders, somatoform disorders, and other experientially based clinical complaints. Also, though EMDR is not expected to reverse the effects of biological conditions such as schizophrenia, bipolar disorder, or attention-deficit/hyperactivity disorder (ADHD), it is possible to use this approach to treat the experiential contributors, such as the social and emotional effects of living with these types of illnesses.

COMPLICATIONS

Responses to EMDR treatment can range from mild to high emotional disturbance and may continue between sessions. Therefore, an inability to use self-soothing techniques, major life pressures, cognitive impairment, and an impaired support system are issues that need to be addressed prior to EMDR treatment.

While some people who have struggled with drug and alcohol abuse experience decreased cravings during EMDR treatment, others report an increased desire to use until the trauma memories are fully processed. In cases involving dissociative symptoms, supervised training in this area and a thorough understanding of the appropriate EMDR protocols are strongly recommended.

CASE ILLUSTRATION

A 58-year-old Vietnam veteran was referred for intensive inpatient trauma treatment in a VA hospital after reinitiating treatment following a death in the family. This client had previously received outpatient group and individual treatment during the 1980s. Though he was reporting a good work history, a stable marriage, and no substance abuse issues, this client had also been experiencing disturbing dreams, sleep difficulties, and anger problems. He scored within the moderate range on measures of PTSD symptoms, trauma-related guilt, and depression. Pretest measures indicated a score of 35 on both the PSS-SR and the Beck Depression Inventory (BDI).

After devoting two sessions to client history and preparation, four EMDR sessions targeted four different incidents. Though two major incidents that had occurred during his tour in Vietnam were initially targeted, other memories were identified during the course of EMDR treatment. During the first session, the client recalled his mortar unit being ordered to fire upon specific coordinates. The following morning, it was discovered that some civilians, including children, had been seriously injured. As he recalled this incident, the client reported a personal sense of responsibility for their harm and indicated that his negative cognition was, "It was my fault." He reported his positive cognition as, "I did all I could," though this did not feel believable to him, as his Validity of Cognition (VOC) level was 2 (on the 1-to-7 scale, where 7 is completely true).

The client initially reported a 10 on the SUD scale (0-10). Since by the end of the first session, the SUD level had not decreased beyond a 3, this memory was targeted again during the second session. His SUD level subsequently decreased to 1, and his reported sense of personal responsibility had lessened. However, because the harming of children violates one of his core values, it was not anticipated that this client's SUD level would decrease any further. His reported feelings of guilt were replaced with sadness.

The second targeted memory involved the client's unit being fired upon, for which the client reported a 7 on the SUD scale. He recalled another GI freezing out of fear and being subsequently hit by enemy mortar fire. Though the client initially felt that he should have done more to help him, while processing this memory, he remembered other things that he had had to do and realized that he had done all he could. His final SUD level was 0.

After processing this memory, the client recalled an incident involving a GI who had been forgotten inside a vehicle and had bled to death. This memory became the third target and was processed using eye movements. During the fourth targeted memory, the client recalled his sudden departure from Vietnam and the sadness he felt about leaving men in combat. He had been experiencing long-standing dreams about this incident. His negative cognition was, "I'm not a caring person," and his positive cognition was, "I am a caring person." After processing these memories using EMDR and remembering more details about the events, the SUD levels had decreased from 8 and 10, respectively, to 0.

Overall, a number of behavioral changes were noted during the course of EMDR treatment. The client's sleep increased by 3 hours per night, and his family noticed a decrease in his anger, including fewer arguments. Notably, this client participated in an outing with his family, which was his first in 15 years. Furthermore, after processing the memory involving the children, this client was finally able to grieve the death of his son, something he had not been able to do previously. Though he was still noticing some forgotten memories, they were no longer traumatic and appeared to be merely more details of memories. In fact, he is now able to experience positive feelings when he thinks of leaving Vietnam. Posttest measures indicated scores of 4 on the PSS-SR and 3 on the BDI.

After experiencing such positive results, this client expressed some confusion about why he had not been able to access the pertinent information during his prior treatment. He also felt disappointed about all of the "wasted" years he had spent suffering. The client compared the process of being able to access the necessary positive information to finding missing puzzle pieces and noted that "Some of the pieces are good ones."

It is posited that the nondirective "free-association" process aids in the memory retrieval. In addition, neuropsychologists and a few recent studies have posited that the accessing of salient memories and associations occurs because the bilateral activation inaugurates a process similar to that which occurs in REM sleep.

—*Francine Shapiro and Kristine Lake*

See also: *Exposure (Vol. I); Manualized Behavioral Therapy (Vol. I); Modeling (Vol. I)*

Suggested Readings

Carlson, J. G., Chemtob, C. M., Rusnak, K., Hedlund, N. L., & Muraoka, M. Y. (1998). Eye movement desensitization and reprocessing for combat-related posttraumatic stress disorder. *Journal of Traumatic Stress, 11,* 324.

De Jongh, A., Ten Broeke, E., & Renssen, M. R. (1999). Treatment of specific phobias with eye movement desensitization and reprocessing (EMDR): Protocol, empirical status, and conceptual issues. *Journal of Anxiety Disorders, 13,* 69–85.

Kuiken, D., Bears, M., Miall, D., & Smith, L. (2001–2002). Eye movement desensitization reprocessing facilitates attentional orienting. *Imagination, Cognition, and Personality, 21*(1), 3–20.

Maxfield, L., & Hyer, L. A. (2002). The relationship between efficacy and methodology in studies investigating EMDR treatment of PTSD. *Journal of Clinical Psychology, 58,* 23–41.

Perkins, B., & Rouanzoin, C. (2002). A critical evaluation of current views regarding eye movement desensitization and reprocessing (EMDR): Clarifying points of confusion. *Journal of Clinical Psychology, 58,* 77–97.

Ray, A. L., & Zbik, A. (2001) Cognitive behavioral therapies and beyond. In C. D. Tollison, J. R. Satterthwaite, & J. W. Tollison (Eds.), *Practical pain management* (3rd ed., pp. 189–208.). Philadelphia: Lippencott.

Rogers, S., & Silver, S. M. (2002). Is EMDR an exposure therapy?: A review of trauma protocols. *Journal of Clinical Psychology, 58,* 43–59.

Shapiro, F. (2001). *Eye movement desensitization and reprocessing: Basic principles, protocols, and procedures* (2nd ed.). New York: Guilford Press.

Shapiro, F. (2002). *EMDR as an integrative psychotherapy approach: Experts of diverse orientations explore the paradigm prism.* Washington, DC: American Psychological Association Books.

Shapiro, F. (2002). EMDR twelve years after its introduction: Past and future research. *Journal of Clinical Psychology, 58,* 1–22.

Stickgold, R. (2002). EMDR: A putative neurobiological mechanism of action. *Journal of Clinical Psychology, 58,* 61–75.

FLOODING

DESCRIPTION OF THE STRATEGY

Flooding procedures can be subdivided according to cues presented (*psychodynamic* cues vs. *symptom-contingent* cues). In implosive therapy as originally developed by Stampfl, the therapist presents a complex of conditioned stimuli to the patient without primary reinforcement and without allowing an avoidance response. The therapist tries to maximize anxiety throughout treatment, which eventually leads to *extinction.* Sessions are continued until a significant reduction in anxiety is achieved. It is essential to the implosive approach that the patient be exposed to aversive stimuli assumed to be underlying the patient's problems (hypothesized-sequential cues). *Hypothesized cues* are defined as "those which are not directly correlated with symptom onset but which represent 'guesses' as to the remaining components of the avoided CS [conditioned stimulus] complex." These hypothesized cues may concern dynamics such as aggression, guilt, punishment, rejection, loss of control, and oral, anal, or sexual material.

Almost all controlled studies have conducted implosive therapy with symptom-contingent cues without the psychodynamic ones. Since therapeutic procedures used differ considerably from the implosive therapy as originally developed by Stampfl, the term *flooding* will be used further.

Apart from psychodynamic cues, flooding therapy for phobias got wide attention from behavior therapists. Flooding can be carried out in imagination or in vivo, but the earlier studies and clinical applications consisted of imaginal flooding. With flooding in imagination, patients have to imagine situations and experiences that they find most frightening for a prolonged period of time. One of the most important variables in determining effectiveness of flooding appears to be duration of exposure to the stimulus variable within each session. Too early termination of flooding sessions may lead to exacerbation instead of a reduction of fear. In fact, the patient is then allowed to escape the fearful situation (either in imagination or in vivo), which may lead to an immediate anxiety reduction (negative reinforcement).

RESEARCH BASIS

Flooding procedures are theoretically founded on animal research into the conditioning and extinction of fear. According to Mowrer, anxiety is attached to previously neutral cues through classical conditioning. In the second stage of learning, the animal terminates the aversive stimulus by making escape responses, thereby reducing the anxiety it experiences. Based on this two-factor theory, flooding is held to work to reduce anxiety by extinction. A number of studies have addressed issues relevant to humans, such as the duration of flooding, and imaginal versus in vivo flooding. Continuous flooding has been shown to be superior to interrupted flooding, both in nonclinical anxious subjects *(analog research)* and phobic and obsessive-compulsive patients. It is noteworthy that in most studies with clinical patients, much longer exposure duration has been used than has typically been done in analog research. In the analog studies, flooding sessions lasted from 20 to 60 minutes. In contrast, in clinical studies where flooding has been found to be effective, flooding lasted up to several hours.

The process of anxiety reduction during flooding in imagination sessions has been studied in several studies. Results showed that habituation of subjective anxiety occurs within sessions. Most often, it follows a curvilinear pattern. In addition, evidence was provided for habituation across sessions. Several studies investigated whether habituation of physiological arousal occurred during flooding in imagination. Generally, after an initial increase in arousal, arousal decreases, thus showing a curvilinear habituation curve. Such results were found on heart rate and on skin conductance measures.

In flooding in vivo in agoraphobic patients and obsessive-compulsive patients, there is usually little decrement in heart rate and subjective anxiety during the first hour of exposure. During the second hour, heart rate and subjective anxiety decline substantially. Studies on specific phobics also found habituation of physiological arousal and subjective anxiety during prolonged exposure in vivo. Here, heart rate was found to decrease much earlier than with agoraphobics and obsessive-compulsives.

Flooding in fantasy evoked less tachycardia than exposure in vivo. Even after habituation to imaginal stimuli had occurred, patients responded with much tachycardia when exposed to the phobic stimuli in vivo.

As to biochemical changes during flooding in vivo, there is some evidence that anxiety induced by flooding led to growth hormone response. However, flooding did not lead to change in prolactin levels; furthermore, almost no cortisol elevations were found. Normally, biochemical changes are shown in response to stressors on these indices.

Although cognitive changes are presumably of paramount importance in the process of flooding, these factors have received relatively little attention. A number of studies have investigated the influence of expectancy of improvement on the outcome of flooding in imagination. Most effects achieved with flooding in imagination can be attributed to such cognitive factors, since flooding in imagination has not been shown to be effective independently from nonspecific variables as expectancy of therapeutic gain. Results with respect to the influence of expectancy factors on the effects of flooding in vivo are inconclusive.

Another continuing debate in the flooding literature concerns the stimulus content during flooding. Some therapists have used actual depictions of the feared situation. Others have employed depiction of horrifying scenes, often including adverse consequences to the patient, based on the notion that anxiety evocation was necessary before extinction could occur. For example, during flooding, one can have a car-phobic patient imagine that he is driving a car on a busy motorway or have him imagine that he is involved in a terrible car accident. Even if adverse consequences to the subject are excluded, the content of a flooding scene may differ considerably. For instance, flooding scenes can contain either coping statements or helplessness statements. In other studies, even reassuring statements with phobic subjects have been used: Flooding along these lines may be better conceived of as cognitive procedures. Several studies compared flooding with and without horrifying scenes. Results of these studies are equivocal, but most studies found pleasant flooding to be more effective. Thus, inclusion of horrifying stimuli during flooding in imagination does not enhance effectiveness.

Several studies have investigated effects of anxiety evocation during exposure in vivo. In the early days of exposure in vivo, it was thought to be essential that anxiety should be maximized during exposure in vivo before extinction or habituation could occur. Patients were encouraged to confront their symptoms during exposure in vivo; therapists' reassurance was minimized. Instead, throughout the exposure in vivo procedure, the therapist tried to induce anxiety by statements such as, "Imagine yourself feeling worse and worse, giddy, sweaty, nauseated, as if you are about to vomit any moment. . . . You fall to the floor half conscious, people gather round you, someone calls for an ambulance." Studies comparing high and low anxiety provocation during flooding in vivo found both procedures equally effective. Thus, deliberately inducing anxiety during exposure in vivo did not enhance improvement. In speech anxiety, delivering a speech without anxiety provocation was even more effective than when anxiety was deliberately provoked by a "booing" audience.

Several clinical studies have been conducted comparing flooding in imagination with flooding in vivo. Most studies found flooding in vivo to be superior to flooding in imagination. However, results of most studies are difficult to interpret since flooding in imagination was conducted by means of a tape recorder, which is usually less effective than when given by a life therapist.

Emmelkamp and Wessels compared three different flooding procedures in severe agoraphobics: (1) 90 minutes of flooding in vivo, (2) 90 minutes of flooding in imagination, and (3) 45 minutes of flooding in imagination immediately followed by 45 minutes of flooding in vivo. Flooding in vivo proved to be superior to flooding in imagination, whereas the effects of the combined procedure were in-between those of exposure in vivo and exposure in imagination.

Finally, the role of response prevention should be stressed. When patients are exposed to the phobic stimulus, they are prevented from responding with escape and avoidance. In contrast to what was expected theoretically, research has shown that escape during flooding is less detrimental than once thought. Nevertheless, it remains therapeutically wise to prevent escape and avoidance responses during flooding, including cognitive avoidance as distraction or dissociation.

RELEVANT TARGET POPULATIONS

Most research has been conducted on agoraphobic patients, obsessive-compulsive patients, and patients with posttraumatic stress disorder. In agoraphobic patients and obsessive-compulsive patients with clear rituals, prolonged exposure in vivo is more effective than imaginal flooding. However, in checking rituals, imaginal flooding appears to be as effective as in vivo exposure. This could be explained by the fact that it is more difficult to expose patients with checking compulsions to situations they fear. For example, in patients who have to carry out all kinds of checking actions for fear of a disaster (for example, a war or something dreadful happening to their families), it is easier to have these scenes imagined than to apply flooding in vivo. Other good candidates for imaginal flooding are patients with pure obsessions, patients with thunder phobias, and bereavement, since exposure in vivo is usually not feasible.

COMPLICATIONS

Although behavior therapists tend to devote little attention to the quality of the therapeutic relationship, this relationship is vitally important for flooding. If there is not a trusting bond between patient and therapist, flooding is not recommended, since patients may perceive this aversive therapy experience as punishment. In children, flooding is also not recommended, but a more gradual approach is to be preferred. Finally,

given the high anxiety and panic that accompany flooding, this treatment is also not recommended in cases with potential medical complications (e.g., cardiovascular problems, high blood pressure, and pregnancy).

CASE ILLUSTRATION

"Susan" was a 27-year-old female suffering from fear of dying. She was subject to obsessions in which she saw herself dying. Cue selection plays an essential part before the actual flooding is begun. Questioning yielded the following information: The patient was afraid of illnesses that lead to a sudden death (e.g., cerebral hemorrhage, tumor, heart attack). Because of this, she also had body sensations (e.g. hot head, stifling, shortness of breath, a burning pain in the chest and arms). Death was always sudden (no long illnesses), and she was terrified of her housekeeping being criticized after her death. She visualized the funeral vividly. It was important to include all these cues in the scenes to be used during prolonged exposure in imagination. The following was a scene used during the treatment.

Imagine you're at home, the weather is fine, but you don't feel well. You have a headache and you think: "I'd better take an aspirin to make it go away." You lie down in bed but it doesn't pass. It is a very strange feeling, a different kind of headache. You get up . . . you feel dizzy, warm in your head, and then you think—if this only turns out all right—you feel even stranger, can no longer tell where you are . . . you have to go the neighbor . . . you think you're having a seizure . . . she has to phone the doctor . . . you ring the neighbor's bell . . . she opens the door: "What's the matter with you?" she asks. But you can no longer say anything—you fall down, just like that . . . and then you feel that you are going to die . . . then it's over . . . you're dead . . . on the neighbor's step. David dashes home . . . your parents as well. They do not understand: "How is this possible, she is only 27?" Your mother is crying, your father is trying to console her—you can never speak to them again, never go out with them—you are dead. Then there's the funeral: You are lying in your coffin . . . at the front of the church . . . everybody is there . . . the whole family . . . your friends . . . and then the reverend says that it is so incomprehensible that such a young woman should be snatched away in the prime of her life, and the people cry, then go to the graveyard . . . you are lying in your coffin in the grave . . . slowly, the coffin is lowered, your mother is crying, David is crying, and then for the last time, they wish you good-bye, then they leave . . . they leave you behind in the graveyard. After the funeral, Iris and Martha go to your house to prepare dinner for the family. Iris opens the kitchen cupboards and says to Martha: "What a mess, just look at that, she had little to do, and still the place is a mess." They tell the family what a mess the place is . . . Iris wipes her fingers across the windowsill, sees all the dog's hairs on the floor, and shows the others . . . that you could be so untidy.

It is important to correspond to patient's factual thought in these scenes and not to exaggerate. The best way to present the scenes is in a matter-of-fact tone. Dramatization usually leads to ridicule and offers an opportunity for cognitive avoidance: "This is not real—this is not how it happens in real life." Recording of these scenes is not advised, because such a method of presenting a situation generally has little effect.

The therapist is constantly on the look out for outward signs of anxiety to discover whether certain items especially evoke anxiety. Such an item can then be offered repeatedly until habituation has occurred. With exposure in imagination as well, it is useful to score patients' subjective anxiety levels after each scene. Care must be taken, however, that no breaks are introduced in the actual exposure, since such breaks obstruct habituation. For the same reason, it is not sensible to ask for further information during an exposure session; this should be done before or after the exposure session. Duration of exposure sessions depends on whether anxiety has diminished; therefore, there are no general rules to be given. After 1 1/2 hours, however, it becomes impossible for most people to continue concentrating on scenes. It is advisable not to introduce new material or variations at the end of the exposure session, as the chances are that little time will remain for reducing the anxiety. Such a mistake was made with Susan during the second exposure session. Anxiety had decreased on presentation of scenes so much that the patient was made to describe the scenes herself. As a result of such variation, the anxiety level increased again. This caused the patient to suffer some days of anxiety and led to justified feelings of guilt in the therapist.

Variation of scenes is necessary to prevent patients from habituating to the text instead of to the situation.

When patients have difficulty in identifying themselves with their roles, it helps to have them describe the scenes aloud. The therapist should pay attention to subtle avoidance behavior. In the example mentioned above (Susan), the patient kept referring to "it," when, in fact, she was referring to herself or the coffin. The therapist must correct this, for example by asking, "Who is lying in the coffin?" After some time, if exposure sessions have been successful, the patient may be given exposure for homework. The patient must make the time, once a day for at least an hour, to go through the scenes until anxiety has decreased. If the patient cannot do this (too threatening) alone at home, it may help to use successive approximation to achieve this.

—*Paul M. G. Emmelkamp*

See also: *Emmelkamp, Paul M. G. (Vol. I); Extinction (Vol. III); Flooding (Vol. II)*

Suggested Readings

Emmelkamp, P. M. G. (1990). Anxiety and fear. In A. S. Bellack, M. Hersen, & A. Kazdin (Eds.), *International handbook of behavior modification and therapy.* (2nd ed., pp. 283–305). New York: Plenum Press.

Emmelkamp. P. M. G., & Wessels, H. (1975). Flooding in imagination versus flooding in vivo. A comparison with agoraphobics. *Behaviour Research & Therapy, 13,* 7–16.

Miller, C. M. (2002). Flooding. In M. Hersen & W. Sledge (Eds.), *Encyclopedia of psychotherapy* (Vol. I, pp. 809–813). New York: Academic Press.

Mowrer, O. H. (1960). *Learning theory and behavior.* New York: Wiley.

Turner, S. M., Beidel, D. C., & Long, P. J. (1992). Reduction of fear in social phobics: An examination of extinction patterns. *Behavior Therapy, 23,* 389–403.

FOA, EDNA B.

I was born in Haifa, Israel, on December 28, 1937, and received my undergraduate education in Israel, coming to the United States for my graduate education in 1966. My entire career as an academic professional has been in Philadelphia, first at Temple University, then at the Medical College of Pennsylvania, and since 1998, at the Department of Psychiatry at the University of Pennsylvania Medical School. In 1979, I founded the Center for the Treatment and Study of Anxiety, where, with the collaboration of many colleagues, I have been conducting all my research and clinical activities.

EARLY INFLUENCES AND EDUCATION HISTORY

I was drawn to psychology as an adolescent, when I discovered the writings of Sigmund Freud and became fascinated with psychoanalysis. After graduating from high school, I went to a Normal School to train to work with delinquent children. My teacher of psychology there was a trained psychoanalyst who encouraged me to write my final thesis on the Freudian explanation of childhood delinquency.

After working 2 years in a boarding school for delinquent children, I continued to study psychology at Bar Ilan University, where I received my BA in 1962. At Bar Ilan, my clinical psychology teachers all represented psychoanalytical or psychodynamic orientations; none of them thought that psychotherapy can or should be studied empirically. However, in Bar Ilan, I was also exposed to research in experimental and social psychology and became extremely interested both in the science of psychology and in empirical research. This interest was fostered by my late husband, Uriel G. Foa, who was then the chair of the department of psychology and a distinguished researcher in social psychology.

My first contact with behavior therapy and behavior modification occurred at the University of Illinois, where I received my MA in 1970, under the supervision of O. H. Mowrer. In the 60s, the clinical program in the Department of Psychology at Urbana was one of the strongholds of behavior therapy and modification; their faculty included Leonard Ullmann, Leonard Krazner, and Gordon Paul, to name only a few. There, I first become acquainted with the work of Joseph Wolpe and with the integration of experimental psychology concepts into psychopathology and treatment. The educational experience at the University of Illinois together with Uriel Foa's mentoring in research methodology marked the beginning of my professional career.

After completing my PhD in 1970, at the University of Missouri at Columbia, I was awarded a National Institute of Mental Health (NIMH) postdoctoral fellowship to work with Wolpe at Temple University, the mecca of behavior therapy at the time. There, I had the opportunity to meet leaders in the field, many of whom influenced my conceptual and empirical work. Of particular importance for me was the influence of Peter Lang and Stanley Rachman.

PROFESSIONAL MODELS

At the University of Illinois, I was introduced not only to behavior modification and behavior therapy but also to the clinician-researcher model; and it is this model that is reflected in the development of my own career. I began my research examining the efficacy of behavioral treatments for anxiety disorders and identifying the active processes involved in these treatments. I soon discovered the limitations of behavior therapy: Not all patients were helped, and many remain quite symptomatic. This realization motivated me to examine the failures more carefully. Consequently, I embarked on an inquiry into treatment processes that distinguish patients who benefit from behavior therapy from those who do not. This led me to editing a book titled *Failures in Behavior Therapy* (1983), designed to draw attention to exploring variables that predict success and failure in behavior therapy.

Pursing this line, I extended my interest from the study of treatment processes to the study of what it is that treatment should correct. Hence, I have been conducting studies that aim to elucidate the mechanisms involved in pathological fear and anxiety. Thus, my work emphasizes the relationship between three areas of research: therapy outcome, therapy processes, and psychopathology. Most recently, and continuing in the spirit of the clinician-researcher model, I have been much concerned with disseminating the effective treatment that my colleagues and I have developed for obsessive-compulsive disorder (OCD) and posttraumatic stress disorder (PTSD) and by means of lectures, workshops, and also by systematic study of the efficacy of these treatments in the hands of clinicians in community-based clinics, who are not experts in cognitive behavior therapy.

MAJOR CONTRIBUTIONS TO THE FIELD

Most of my academic activity has been concerned with research on the psychopathology and treatment of the anxiety disorders, primarily OCD, PTSD, social phobia, and to a lesser degree, panic disorder with agoraphobia, as well as specific phobia. This research has been theoretically driven so that my theory has informed the direction of research, and the empirical findings have, in turn, led to further development of the theory.

Theoretical Work

My interest in the psychopathology and treatment of anxiety has produced a number of theoretical papers that are widely cited. Perhaps the best known is "Emotional Processing of Fear: Exposure to Corrective Information," which develops a theory on the processes involved in pathological anxiety and its treatment. Emotional processing theory conceives the anxiety disorders as reflecting distinct pathological fear structures that include associations among representations of the feared stimuli, the feared responses, and their meaning. Accordingly, the goal of treatment for any given anxiety disorder is to form a modified structure in which the stimuli are the same as in the original structure, but the pathological elements have been corrected. Successful therapy achieves this goal by activating the pathological structure and, at the same time, introducing corrective information that can be incorporated into the modified structure.

Treatment Outcome Studies

In a series of studies, I have been developing and systematically investigating the active ingredients of exposure and ritual prevention (EX/RP) for OCD. At the same time, I have been investigating the efficacy of various medications, both alone and together with cognitive behavior therapy, in ameliorating OCD symptoms. These studies have helped to provide the knowledge of how to conduct cognitive behavior therapy for OCD and how to combine such therapy with medication. The treatment program that emerged from this research has been disseminated to therapists and clients via treatment manuals and even more widely disseminated via a self-help book entitled *Stop Obsessing*. As chair of the *DSM-IV* Subcommittee for OCD, I also had the opportunity to incorporate empirical research findings into the diagnostic criteria of OCD.

Since 1983, I have been studying PTSD, pursuing both outcome studies and psychopathology research. As in the earlier work in OCD, my colleagues and I have been developing and systematically studying several different short-term cognitive-behavioral treatment programs for PTSD. This research was summarized in a book presenting the theory and practice of cognitive behavior therapy for PTSD, titled *Treating the Trauma of Rape: Cognitive-Behavioral Therapy for PTSD*. The influence of these studies on the field has been such that

the treatment program we have developed, known as *prolonged exposure,* is considered by many experts to be the treatment of choice for PTSD. In 2002, this treatment was recognized by an award from Substance Abuse and Mental Health Services Administration (SAMSHA) as a model treatment to be targeted for dissemination among clinicians.

Treatment Processes Research

As a complement to my interest in developing effective treatments for pathological anxiety, I have been systematically concerned with understanding the processes that make the treatment work. In this endeavor, I was first influenced by conditioning theory and later on by the theoretical framework of information processing. For example, in several studies, we found that patients who fail to show fear activation during exposure to their feared situation or memory (where fear is measured by self-report, physiological responses, and facial expressions) and who fail to habituate between sessions do not benefit from treatment as much as those who do. Other process variables that I found to influence treatment outcome for PTSD include organization of the trauma narrative during repeated reliving of the trauma and changes in the schemas of "world" and "self."

Psychopathology Research

In investigating mechanisms underlying pathological anxiety, I have been concerned with applying methods of experimental psychology to clinical research, as well as carrying out more descriptive psychopathology studies. Specifically, I have used a variety of cognitive experimental methods (e.g., dichotic listening, emotional stroop) in order to elucidate information-processing biases that characterize the anxiety disorders. In studying the psychopathology of these disorders, I have developed a number of measures of OCD and PTSD severity. My self-report measure of PTSD, the Posttraumatic Diagnostic Scale (PDS), is being widely used around the world.

CURRENT WORKS AND VIEWS

I continue to conduct research on OCD, PTSD, and social phobia. In OCD, my colleagues and I are currently studying the augmentation effects of exposure and ritual prevention in patients (both children and adults) who are partial responders to medication. In PTSD, we are conducting several studies that measure processes and outcome of exposure therapy. Some studies reflect my current interest in treating anxiety disorders that are comorbid with another disorder (e.g., PTSD with alcohol dependence, social phobia with depression). Other studies reflect my interest in understanding the relationship between psychological and biological factors underlying PTSD as well as the influence of prolonged exposure on each of these domains and their interrelations. Still other studies reflect my current enthusiasm for disseminating our treatments to clinicians in the community who do not have expertise in cognitive behavior therapy.

FUTURE PLANS

My future research will continue to emphasize the relationship between therapy outcomes and its dissemination, therapy processes, and psychopathology. Within this framework, together with my junior colleagues, I am embarking on new projects, which include (a) developing treatment for PTSD related to abuse by partners; this treatment will focus on helping women to access psychological and environmental resources as they attempt to leave their abusive partners; (b) exploring programs for maximizing remission from PTSD; and (c) conducting experiments to study how to change cognitive biases (e.g., attentional, interpretation) in social phobia, in order to develop new paradigms for treating this disorder.

—Edna B. Foa

FRANKS, CYRIL, M.

To span three continents, 50 years of behavior therapy, hundreds of professional publications and formal addresses worldwide, plus decades of postdoctoral training and administration in less than 1,300 words is a formidable undertaking.

Born in Wales, in the United Kingdom, in 1923, and raised in a pleasant Welsh seaside town, I attended an elite state-financed grammar school from 1935 until 1941. Latin and classical Greek were compulsory, and, for the few Jewish students, after-school Hebrew classes and Jewish cultural programs were

optional for those who, like me, so chose. In addition, weekly Welsh language classes were compulsory for all students despite the fact that virtually no one in our community used Welsh, if they understood it at all, as their primary tongue. Thus, I was expected to become familiar with three very different alphabets (Greek, Hebrew, and English) and learn a total of five languages in addition to the customary core of intensive academic education and my elected specialization in applied science. This was compounded by a plethora of escalating wartime stresses and necessary restrictions due to mounting food shortages and more.

Little of the above seemed to have interfered significantly with my ability to make the best of circumstances until nightly bombing of my town began. On two occasions, near misses damaged our family home. Soon afterward, our magnificent 300-year-old school building was totally destroyed, and 10% of my schoolmates and two teachers were killed or injured. Regardless, classes continued on the grounds of my ravaged school.

After grammar school graduation, I was directed to enroll in an accelerated University of Wales Applied Science Program. Upon graduating in 1943 with a BS in electronics and applied physics, I was immediately assigned to an appropriate research and development company near London.

Shortly afterward, the war ended. But by then, while still science oriented, my future career path had shifted to the burgeoning new field of clinical psychology, about which I then knew virtually nothing. Having no formal training in psychology, I had to take several years of basic university courses and pass the university-prescribed psychology equivalent examination.

At this point, I began my search for appropriate doctoral training in clinical psychology. Apparently, in those times, the late 1940s, all clinical psychology training programs worldwide, and these were few, were unequivocally Freudian and totally devoid of data and accountability. Perhaps worse yet, in those days, only physicians were sanctioned by the medical establishment to practice therapy, and private practice by psychologists did not yet exist. Parenthetically, in sharp contrast, in both the United Kingdom and the United States, any qualified mental health professional, including PhD clinical psychologists, can now engage in any kind of legally sanctioned therapy, and in both countries, the major issue now concerns the circumstances under which qualified psychologists should be legally permitted to prescribe medication. We have come a long way.

Around 1949, I found the only clinical training program in either the United Kingdom or North America that seemed to offer promise of meeting all my needs. This was a program created by Professor Eysenck, then rapidly becoming the leading figure in British Psychology. At the University of London Institute of Psychiatry, Eysenck offered two programs, a 1-year clinical internship and a 3- to 4-year PhD program in experimental/clinical psychology. Prior to final acceptance, I had to take additional psychology courses elsewhere because of my unusual proposed entry into the field.

The goal of this still-evolving PhD program was to supplement, and eventually replace, the prevailing Freudian paradigm with a totally different behavioral model directed first to psychologists and, much later, to many psychiatrists. Ideally, the projected new paradigm was to be a totally different way of conceptualizing clinical psychology: a stimulus-response, testable, learning-theory-based paradigm with demonstrably effective assessment and treatment procedures.

During this period of exploration at the Institute of Psychiatry, we strove to develop a maximally appropriate learning theory model but were forced to settle on a less than ideal, but adequate, Pavlovian-Hullian classical conditioning model. From this vantage point, slowly and painfully, we developed a few minimally cost-effective, non-Freudian conditioning procedures that met our unrealistic criteria, although I did not accept these as unrealistic at the time. These criteria included good reliability, accountability, outcome evaluation, client and clinician satisfaction, and follow-up. Progress was inevitably slow, acceptable procedures few and rarely of major clinical importance, and throughout, resistance from most physicians remained massive.

During this period, I took a year off to complete a master's degree at the University of Minnesota, where I met my wife, Violet, then a master's-level clinical psychologist. We went back to London, where I received my PhD in 1954, closely related to our developing new paradigm. In 1959, Violet received her PhD in London. Later, she became known as the originator of the now widely accepted concept of non-sexist therapy.

For me, my proudest accomplishment in London was the opportunity to make use of both my technical and psychological backgrounds, designing and constructing what turned out to be the world's first soundproof human-conditioning laboratory for the understanding, assessment, and treatment of psychological disorders, described in detail in a 1955 article in the prestigious British journal *Nature*. But overall, feeling discouraged despite receiving early tenure at London University, progress was slow due both to continued resistance from the mental health establishment and our excessively rigorous and unrealistic criteria for all new behavioral clinical procedures. But by now, on the positive side, the new concept behavior therapy was becoming more accepted.

In 1957, Violet and I moved to Princeton, New Jersey's Neuropsychiatric Institute in search of a more receptive climate. In the United States, the situation was only marginally better, but I did manage to have a similar conditioning laboratory built in Princeton, with the emphasis again on a Pavlovian classical conditioning rather than Skinner's operant conditioning. Skinner, it might be noted, was not a clinician and worked predominantly with animals.

Eventually, I gathered around me a small group of kindred spirits, and, in 1966, we created the AABT, the Association for the Advancement of Behavior Therapy, its name suggested by me because of my long involvement with the British Association for Advancement of Science. In both instances, the focus was firmly upon professional and not personal advancement.

From then on, events moved rapidly. In 1966, I was elected the AABT's first president and appointed founding editor of the AABT's flagship journal, *Behavior Therapy*. My first book, on conditioning techniques in clinical practice, appeared in the 1960s, and soon after, the term *conditioning therapy* had been abandoned in favor of *behavior therapy*. Son afterward, my second, edited, book directly used the term behavior therapy and ran into three printings. Behavior therapy was becoming recognized increasingly worldwide.

In 1970, I moved to nearby Rutgers University; and after 21 years of doctoral and postdoctoral administration, teaching, behavioral research, and clinical practice, I retired in 1991 as distinguished professor emeritus, after 2 yearlong sabbaticals in Australia.

Over the years, ongoing events compelled me to ease my rigid requirements for the one "true" behavior therapy. Behavior therapy had become increasingly cognitive, with many diverse interpretations of the notion "cognitive," but for the most part, learning theory based. In 1981, concerned, I wrote an article plaintively titled "2081—Will We Be Many or One or None?" It was around this time, when the majority of clinical psychologists and even many psychiatrists had grudgingly accepted the new paradigm, that a number of highly respected data-based psychologists developed increasingly recognized behavior therapy systems of their own, all viable reflections of the new paradigm and most including more than behavior alone: cognition, conditioning, behavior, affect, and more, with a variety of learning theory cores and all with demonstrable effectiveness.

By then, my professional activities, like those of many others, began to reflect more and more the realization that not only was there no one "true" behavior therapy but that, as the earlier Freudian paradigm became passé, behavioral science methodology and the new paradigm became increasingly relevant and timely. However, the term behavior therapy, an understandable foundation for earlier times, is now an oversimplification. Cognition, conditioning affect, and behavior are now inseparable components of the new paradigm, and there seems to be no one "true" behavior therapy.

As for myself, to the extent that circumstances will permit, I plan to continue editing the journal I founded 26 years ago, *Child & Family Behavior Therapy* and, in conjunction with my colleagues, to continue to explore systematically the many parameters of the still-evolving new behavior therapy, perhaps under the guise of a more acceptable name.

—*Cyril M. Franks*

See also: Association for Advancement of Behavior Therapy (Vol. I); Classical Conditioning (Vol. I); Pavlov, Ivan P. (Vol. I)

FUNCTIONAL ANALYTIC PSYCHOTHERAPY

DESCRIPTION OF THE STRATEGY

Functional analytic psychotherapy (FAP) is a psychological treatment that draws on the therapist-client relationship to provide powerful in-therapy learning opportunities. This treatment is derived from B. F. Skinner's radical behaviorism, which accounts for our external actions, private feelings, and beliefs in

terms of the types of past experiences that shape us. FAP produces change through the natural and curative contingencies of reinforcement that occur within a close, emotional, and involving therapist-client relationship.

Psychologists R. J. Kohlenberg and M. Tsai began to conceive of such a treatment after noticing that some of their clients treated with conventional cognitive and behavioral therapy techniques showed dramatic and pervasive improvements that far exceeded treatment goals. They noticed that these improvements occurred in those clients with whom they had particularly intense and involved client-therapist relationships. These intense relationships were not created intentionally, but seemed to emerge naturally over the course of therapy. As a result of these observations, Kohlenberg and Tsai used behavioral concepts first to develop a theory about the resulting dramatic improvement from intense therapist-client relationships, and then to identify the steps therapists can take to facilitate such relationships. The result was FAP, a treatment in which the client-therapist relationship is at the core of the change process.

In FAP, the therapist concentrates on the opportunities for therapeutic change that occur when the client's daily life problems are manifested within the therapeutic relationship. Although informed by behaviorism, FAP's emphasis on the therapist-client relationship also has some unexpected similarities to the Freudian concept of transference, defined as the client's reaction to the therapist, as if the therapist were someone important in the client's past. FAP can be used as a stand-alone treatment or, as illustrated later, can be used to enhance other approaches.

FAP underscores the importance of "therapist-client relationship learning opportunities," that is, when problems in the client's daily life actually occur in interactions with the therapist. This concept, that the best way to learn is by doing (in vivo), is a well-accepted notion. For example, it is easier to learn to drive a car while actually driving with an instructor than via classroom instruction. Likewise, it is initially easier for a client to engage in appropriate forms of responding when the therapist is present to provide feedback than when they are between sessions, in a difficult situation, and trying to remember what their therapist has taught them. Experience has shown that these in-session improvements will almost always generalize to daily life.

CLINICALLY RELEVANT BEHAVIORS

The two main types of FAP learning opportunities are client *problems* that occur in the session and client *improvements* that occur in session. In vivo occurrences of the client's problems are "real" and are distinguished from the "role playing" or "behavioral rehearsal" that are sometimes used in behavior therapy. In FAP, in vivo occurrences of the client's problems are referred to as *clinically relevant behaviors, type 1* (CRB1s).

On the other hand, *clinically relevant behaviors, type 2* (CRB2s), are actual improvements that occur in session. Consider a male client, depressed because he feels he has no friends. He avoids eye contact during therapy, answers questions in an unfocused and tangential manner, and gets angry with the therapist for not having all the answers. All of these are possible CRB1s (problems). If the client subsequently increases his eye contact with the therapist and is more accepting of the therapist's limitations, these are CRB2s (improvements). In FAP, it is crucial that the therapist have an understanding of CRBs, is able to recognize them when they occur, and knows how to nurture the development of CRB2s.

APPLYING FAP

FAP has three primary therapeutic strategies: (1) Watch for CRBs; (2) evoke CRBs; and (3) reinforce CRB2s.

Strategy 1: Watch for CRBs

This strategy is the most important aspect of FAP. The more proficient a therapist is at recognizing CRBs, the better will be the outcome. It is hypothesized that following Rule 1 will lead to increased intensity and stronger emotional reactions between therapist and client. If Strategy 1 is the only rule that a therapist follows, it alone should promote a positive outcome. In other words, a therapist who is skilled at observing instances of clinically relevant behavior as they occur is also more likely to react in a therapeutic manner to these instances. Thus, a therapist following Strategy 1 is more likely to naturally reinforce, punish, and extinguish client behaviors in ways that foster the development of behavior useful in daily life.

Strategy 2: Evoke CRBs

Since the occurrence of CRBs is required to do FAP, how can a therapist facilitate that occurrence?

Client problems that are reenacted during role playing, as pointed out earlier, are not the same as naturally occurring CRBs. Furthermore, feigning evocative situations, such as coming late to a session or getting angry with the client, are not recommended, because such behaviors are incongruent with the close and honest relationship called for in FAP.

As it turns out, regardless of the type of therapy, the structure of most therapy sessions naturally evokes CRB. For example, all therapists set appointments and require fees for treatment. These procedures can evoke CRBs relating, for example, to the client making and keeping commitments, being punctual or being too compulsive or feeling like they are so worthless that they need to pay someone to listen to them. Similarly, the universal therapist request of a client to be open and to express both positive and negative feelings could evoke the client's problems in forming close relationships. CRBs are ubiquitous in all therapies but frequently are overlooked by therapists who are not trained to recognize them.

Strategy 3: Reinforce CRB2s

Reinforcement means that the therapist should nurture and strengthen in-session improvements. A well-known aspect of reinforcement is that the closer in time and place the behavior is to its consequences, the greater the effect of those consequences. Treatment effects will be stronger, therefore, if clients' problem behaviors and improvements occur during the session, where they are closest in time and place to the available reinforcement (consequences) from the therapist. It is best to rely on the therapist's natural reactions to the client rather then to gratuitously use phrases such as "That's terrific" or "Great," which the client may view as insincere. Therapists who are skilled in FAP are aware of CRB2s as they occur and are genuinely and spontaneously reinforcing. One way that therapists can become more naturally reinforcing is by seeking opportunities to sincerely reinforce others for desirable behavior in their everyday lives.

Therapists who are not aware of CRBs may inadvertently punish CRB2s (improvements). For example, a woman sought help for depression that was related to her lack of assertiveness with her husband. The therapist attempted to teach her to be more assertive by using role play. The client expressed discomfort with role play and asked whether there was another way to approach the problem. The therapist then suggested to the client that by resisting the role play, she was being avoidant, and pressured her to role-play anyway. The FAP analysis of this incident is that the client's expression of her reluctance to role-play was itself a CRB2, since she was being assertive with the therapist, which is the very real-life skill that the therapist was attempting to teach. The therapist, however, did not reinforce this assertiveness and may even have unintentionally punished it by accusing her of being avoidant and insisting that she do the role play. If the therapist had been aware that a CRB2 were occurring, he would have recognized the in vivo therapeutic opportunity and nurtured the client's assertiveness by pointing out to her the value of expressing her feelings and respecting her wishes to not do the role play. We hypothesize that this "here and now" experiential assertiveness would be more likely to generalize to real life than would the role play.

ENHANCING OTHER APPROACHES: USING FAP TO ENHANCE COGNITIVE THERAPY FOR DEPRESSION

Cognitive therapy (CT) for depression, developed in 1979 by Aaron Beck and his colleagues, is an effective treatment for major depression. As with any treatment for depression, however, there is room for improvement. In particular, some clients are resistant to the methods and rationale of cognitive therapy, and outcome is endangered by what is known as a *rationale-client mismatch*. Examples of mismatches include clients who experience that their feelings rule no matter what thoughts they have, who are looking for a more intense and interpersonal therapy, or who want to understand how their problems are related to their family histories. In an attempt to more effectively address the diverse needs of clients, reduce mismatches, and yet retain the value that cognitive therapy has for many clients, a combined FAP and CT treatment was developed. The new treatment is referred to as *FAP-enhanced cognitive therapy* (FECT).

FECT contains two enhancements to standard CBT. The first is an expanded rationale for the causes and treatment of depression. The expanded rationale includes several possible causes for depression, in addition to the cognitive therapy hypothesis that depression results from dysfunctional thoughts and beliefs. For example, clients are told that depression can be related to losses that need to be grieved, to family-of-origin or historical issues, to a dearth of experiences that bring a sense of mastery and pleasure, to anger turned inward, or to not having intimacy skills. This

expanded rationale allows for better treatment-client matching. Improved treatment matching has been shown to reduce dropouts and improve outcome.

The second enhancement emphasizes the therapy-client relationship as an in vivo opportunity. For example, the therapist may tell the client, "It will be helpful for us to *focus on our interaction* if you have issues or difficulties that come up with me that also come up with other people in your life, such as coworkers, friends, and your spouse. When you express your thoughts, feelings, and desires in an authentic, caring, and assertive way, you are less likely to be depressed." These enhancements may make FECT sound similar to psychoanalysis.

RESEARCH BASIS

FAP research has involved case studies and treatment development studies. Kohlenberg and Tsai presented a number of case studies in their 1991 treatment manual, *Functional Analytic Psychotherapy*. These studies support their hypothesis that an in vivo focus during therapy leads to significant clinical improvement. Other case studies by other clinicians on exhibitionism, drug abuse, and personality disorder have also supported the efficacy of FAP.

In 2000, Kohlenberg and colleagues Tsai, Parker, Kanter, and Bolling completed a National Institute of Mental Health treatment development study using FECT for clients with major depression. This treatment development study demonstrated that experienced cognitive therapists could learn how to do FECT competently. Both FECT and CT had positive outcomes, with FECT faring slightly better (79% of FECT clients and 60% of CT clients responded to treatment) on measures of depression. However, FECT clients showed considerable improvement on measures of interpersonal functioning when compared with CT. This finding is consistent with the increased focus on interpersonal relationships in FECT. Although this study did not have long-term follow-up, improved interpersonal functioning is known to prevent depression relapse.

Although preliminary findings are favorable, FAP is a new treatment, and the types of empirical studies conducted to date reflect its early stage of development. However, controlled studies of the effectiveness of FAP are needed. To this end, Kohlenberg and colleagues will next conduct a randomized clinical trial in which patients with major depression will be assigned to receive either CT or FECT for major depression. This will be the first empirical study to assess the utility of FECT by comparing it with CT.

RELEVANT TARGET POPULATIONS AND EXCEPTIONS

FAP and FECT have been used primarily to treat adult depression, but these techniques can be useful for other populations. FAP is currently being used in research studies at the University of Nevada-Reno to treat tranquilizer and nicotine dependence. Researchers at the University of South Carolina, Greensboro, reported that FAP improved treatment outcome in a group therapy for depressed adolescents.

One must proceed carefully with FAP, however, because it is an intense treatment. Despite this, FAP has been effective for clients who were emotionally quite reactive, as described in a case reported by Kohlenberg and Tsai of a suicidal female diagnosed with borderline personality disorder. In addition, Callaghan (San Jose State University) successfully treated an individual with histrionic and narcissistic personality behaviors. FAP, a powerful treatment by itself, is also an integrative approach that can be combined with almost any other type of therapy to improve outcome. For example, a case study by R. H. Paul (University of Oklahoma) reported benefits of using FAP as an addition to other treatment for a pedophiliac.

COMPLICATIONS

The intensity of the client-therapist relationship can be an exceptional tool for treatment. However, therapists must be provocative enough to evoke CRB1s, but not so provocative that they overwhelm and immobilize the client. Fortunately, the therapist receives immediate feedback: the client's reaction. In most cases, a therapist should initially focus on problems that occur outside the session before targeting the more sensitive in-session problems.

The therapist must always remember that in identifying CRB1s, one is making a hypothesis whose clinical relevance and empirical verity need to be demonstrated, not just assumed. FAP does not provide a theoretical basis for deciding what specific behaviors should be in the repertoire of a person based on race, gender, sexual orientation, age, physical disabilities, or membership in any other group. FAP also does not give models of what a healthy person should look like

or what kind of goals the client should have. There is always the risk that therapists can impose their own values on the client in a damaging way. This risk highlights the importance of consulting with other therapists (e.g., reviewing session videos, discussing client matters).

CASE ILLUSTRATION

One of the coauthors, Dr. Tsai, treated "Joanne," a bright, compassionate, and sensitive woman who came into therapy troubled by symptoms consistent with posttraumatic stress disorder: constant anxiety, insomnia, and flashbacks and nightmares of being raped by unknown persons. She also avoided and had difficulty in close, intimate relationships. Joanne had been emotionally and sexually abused by her father, though she had no specific memories of such abuse. The following example illustrates a CRB1 related to the client needing to ask for what she wants (i.e., the therapist wants her to recognize that her needs are important and deserve attention).

As with almost all survivors of sexual abuse, Joanne was reinforced for giving her father what he wanted but was severely punished for "wanting" for herself. Thus, she had poor contact with those private stimuli commonly known as "needs" and, furthermore, had little opportunity to develop an ability for asking or requesting others to act in ways that satisfied these needs. Currently, she experienced herself as not being entitled to expect anything from others, frequently not knowing what she wanted, and on those occasions when she was in contact with wanting something from others feeling that this "wanting" was "bad."

During therapy, Dr. Tsai encouraged her to "want" by attempting to reinforce any contact that Joanne had with desires concerning their relationship. An important incident occurred about 4 months into her therapy, when the client called Dr. Tsai at 11:30 p.m. in the middle of a flashback. Joanne was panicked and shrieking. The therapist recognized this call as a CRB2 in which she was contacting an unpleasant state that she wanted help with. Dr. Tsai asked Joanne if she wanted to meet for a session right then; she said yes. Later, Joanne said it was very difficult for her to say yes because of her past history of being rejected and otherwise punished in such circumstances, but she was terrified and really wanted to be with her therapist. By responding to her expressed need, the therapist reinforced her verbalizations of "wanting." Subsequently, Joanne learned to ask for extra sessions and telephone time when she needed them, and this behavior of stating her wants and needs eventually generalized to other relationships. As the strength of these CRB2s increased, there was a corresponding change in her feelings about "wanting" being acceptable and her needs being important. This example may seem extreme because therapists and others cannot meet all of a client's needs; however, it illustrates the FAP process. The therapist and Joanne had several discussions about how her needs were important even if the therapist or someone else did not meet them, and it did not mean she was "bad" for having them. Toward the end of therapy, Joanne understood the importance of taking responsibility for getting her needs met and balancing her needs with the needs of those who were close to her. She gradually improved in almost every problematic aspect of her daily life during her treatment.

In summary, FAP posits that the therapist-client relationship is a social environment with the potential to evoke and change actual instances of the client's problematic behavior. FAP underscores the importance of in vivo learning opportunities, the actual occurrences of the client's daily life problems in client-therapist interactions. Change is produced through the natural and curative contingencies of reinforcement that occur within a close, intense, and emotional therapeutic relationship.

—Ursula S. Whiteside,
Robert J. Kohlenberg, and Mavis Tsai

See also: Behavioral Analytic Approach to Supervision (Vol. I); Functional Analysis (Vols. II & III)

Suggested Readings

Follette, W. C., Naugle, A. E., & Callaghan, G. M. (1996). A radical behavioral understanding of the therapeutic relationship in effecting change. *Behavior Therapy, 27,* 623–641.

Kohlenberg, R. J., Kanter, J. W., Bolling, M. Y., Parker, C. R., & Tsai, M. (2002). Enhancing cognitive therapy for depression with functional analytic psychotherapy: Treatment guidelines and empirical findings. *Cognitive and Behavioral Practice, 9,* 213–229.

Kohlenberg, R. J., & Tsai, M. (1991). *Functional analytic psychotherapy: A guide for creating intense and curative therapeutic relationships.* New York: Plenum Press.

Kohlenberg, R. J., & Tsai, M. (1994). Functional analytic psychotherapy: A behavioral approach to treatment and integration. *Journal of Psychotherapy Integration, 4,* 175–201.

Kohlenberg, R. J., & Tsai, M. (1994). Improving cognitive therapy for depression with functional analytic psychotherapy: Theory and case study. *The Behavior Analyst, 17,* 305–320.

Kohlenberg, R. J., & Tsai, M. (1995). I speak, therefore I am: A behavioral approach to understanding the self. *The Behavior Therapist, 18,* 113–116.

Kohlenberg, R. J., & Tsai, M. (1998). Healing interpersonal trauma with the intimacy of the therapeutic relationship. In F. R. Abueg, V. Follette, & J. Ruzek (Eds.), *Trauma in context: A cognitive-behavioral approach.* New York: Guilford Press.

Skinner, B. F. (1974). *About behaviorism.* New York: Knopf.

GENERALIZATION

DESCRIPTION OF THE STRATEGY

Generalization occurs when behavior in one environment changes by virtue of reinforcement contingencies imposed on that behavior in a second environment that has stimuli in common with the first. As a laboratory example, if pecking a green disk by a pigeon is followed by food, pecking will also increase somewhat if the disk becomes blue or yellow. Pecking the blue or yellow disk exemplifies generalization along the physical dimension of wavelength (color). Similarly, if saying "ball" by a child is praised when a red ball rolls across the floor, saying "ball" may also occur when a yellow ball is presented or, perhaps, even when an object such as a candle rolls across the floor. The shape of the ball provides the common stimuli in the first case, the movement of the object in the second. In either case, the environmental guidance of behavior is altered in an environment that differs in some way from the one in which the behavior was conditioned. Generalization can occur following conditioning with either a classical or an operant procedure.

Here, we focus on two issues: the variables that affect the extent of generalization and the behavioral processes involved in generalization. The extent of generalization is affected by the physical similarity between environments and by the history of the organism. The history includes both the history of the species of which the organism is a member (natural selection) and the history of the individual (selection by reinforcement). As an example of the first, consider food reinforcement for pecking a green disk when a medium-pitched tone is also present. If the color of the disk is then changed but the pitch of the tone remains the same, pecking declines progressively as the color departs from green. However, if the pigeon is tested when the pitch of the tone changes but the color of the disk remains green, pecking is unchanged. Generalization occurred along the color dimension but not the pitch dimension, although pecking was reinforced as frequently during the medium-pitched tone as during the green disk. This difference occurs in part because pigeons have an evolutionary history of natural selection in which visual stimuli reliably guided consummatory behavior but auditory stimuli did not. With a nocturnal animal for which consummatory behavior has been guided over evolutionary time by auditory instead of visual stimuli, the opposite could occur.

The most important determinant of generalization is the history of the individual organism. As a laboratory example, if pecking a green disk is reinforced during a medium-pitched tone but not when the tone is absent and the disk remains green, generalization now occurs along the pitch dimension and less so along the color dimension. Differential reinforcement of responding along the tone dimension causes the history of selection by reinforcement to override the history of natural selection. Stated broadly, if behavior has different consequences in different environments, then the strength of responding varies systematically as the environment departs from the environment in which the behavior was reinforced. That is, stimulus generalization occurs.

What behavioral processes produce generalization? Environments that differ from the environment in which the behavior was reinforced may control behavior if they share stimuli in common with the training environment and these common stimuli were present when the behavior was reinforced. For example, if responding is reinforced when a disk is green but not when it is red, then responding generalizes more to blue than to yellow. Blue is more similar to green (the stimulus present when reinforcement occurred) and is less similar to red (the stimulus present when extinction occurred), whereas the reverse is true of yellow. The conclusion that generalization reflects the reinforcement history of the learner is most clearly seen with procedures in which different responses are conditioned at two points along a stimulus dimension and generalization to an intermediate stimulus is assessed. For example, suppose that rapid responding is conditioned to a blue stimulus and slow responding to a yellow stimulus. This can be accomplished by reinforcing responses during blue only when they occur within brief intervals after a previous response and during yellow only after longer intervals since the previous response. (Technically, such procedures reinforce responses that have different *interresponse times*). Following differential conditioning, generalized responding is measured to an intermediate green stimulus. The overall rate of responding during green is intermediate between the rapid responding conditioned to blue and the slow responding conditioned to yellow. However, a moment-to-moment analysis of responding during green reveals that the moderate overall rate is the result of oscillations between the fast responding conditioned to blue and the slow responding conditioned to yellow. That is, generalized responding is a mixture of the environment-behavior relations previously conditioned to elements of the blue and yellow stimuli that are shared with the intermediate green test stimulus. (Green light stimulates some of the same visual receptors that are stimulated by blue and yellow light.) In short, generalization is not a new and distinct behavioral process. Instead, generalization results from the conditioning process itself and occurs to the extent that the new environment contains stimuli that evoke behavior previously conditioned to the common stimuli. Furthermore, the behavior that occurs during generalization is restricted to the specific responses that were previously conditioned to these common stimuli.

The dependence of generalization on prior conditioning has important implications for applied behavior analysis. Behavior therapy attempts to provide experiences that alter the client's behavior in the natural environment. If the effects of therapy are to generalize from the therapeutic situation to the natural environment, then the behavior of interest must be brought under the control of stimuli that are likely to occur in the natural environment. This can be accomplished in two basic ways. First, therapy can arrange for stimuli from the natural environment to be present when appropriate behavior is reinforced and dysfunctional behavior is extinguished. As an example, if social stimuli arouse fear responses that compete with desired behavior, the client may be exposed to such stimuli with effective responses reinforced and adverse consequences eliminated. The greater the similarity of the stimuli present during the therapeutic intervention to those occurring in the natural environment, the greater the efficacy of the therapy. So-called in situ training and role playing, in which behavior is modified in approximations to the natural environment, capitalize on what is known from the experimental analysis of the generalization. The second basic way by which the effects of therapy can generalize to the natural environment is to reinforce behavior in the presence of stimuli not previously present in the natural environment and then to introduce those stimuli into the natural environment. Cognitive-behavioral therapy implements this implication of generalization research when effective behavior is brought under the control of stimuli from subvocal speech ("thoughts") and then the subvocal speech is brought under the control of stimuli from the natural environment. For example, in the therapy situation, a relaxation response may be conditioned to saying the word "relax" aloud and then subvocally. Next, stimuli from the natural environment can be established as discriminative stimuli for the subvocal response "relax," with the result that the relaxation response occurs in the natural environment and competes with dysfunctional fear responses.

Finally, it should be noted that behavior in the natural environment can arise from processes other than generalization on the basis of physical similarity, that is, through functional similarity from the formation of equivalence classes.

—*John W. Donahoe*

See also: Behavioral Treatment in Natural Environments (Vol. I); Generalization (Vols. II & III)

Suggested Readings

Bickel, W. K., & Etzel, B. C. (1985). The quantal nature of controlling stimulus-response relations as measured in tests of stimulus generalization. *Journal of the Experimental Analysis of Behavior, 44,* 247–270.

Donahoe, J. W., & Wessells, M. G. (1980). *Learning, language, and memory* (pp. 176–189). New York: Harper & Row.

Hanson, H. M. (1959). Effects of discrimination training on stimulus generalization. *Journal of Experimental Psychology, 58,* 321–334.

Jenkins, H. M., & Harrison, R. H. (1962). Effect of discrimination training on auditory generalization. *Journal of the Experimental Analysis of Behavior, 5,* 434–441.

Stokes, T. F., & Baer, D. M. (1977). An implicit technology of generalization. *Journal of Applied Behavior Analysis, 10,* 349–367.

GOLDIAMOND, ISRAEL

Israel (Izzy) Goldiamond was born on November 1, 1919, in a little village in Russia near Kiev, in the Ukraine. His family immigrated to the United States in 1923 when he was 3 years old and settled in Brooklyn, New York, where he spent most of his childhood. After graduating from Brooklyn College with a bachelor's degree in English, he enlisted in the army and served during World War II in military intelligence until his discharge in November of 1945.

He and Betty Johnson married in February 1946, and they moved to California so that he could attend the University of California in Berkeley. With the goal of eventually entering the graduate program in psychology, he proceeded to take the necessary undergraduate courses in that subject. However, after a year and a half, an opportunity came for him to work at the Chicago Institute of Design, known as the "New Bauhaus." This occurred as an outgrowth of his life-long interest and considerable skill in cartooning and drawing. The Goldiamonds moved with the full expectation that this new path would lead him to a career as a designer. However, in the fall of 1948, he realized he preferred to study and work in the field of psychology.

It was at this time that he enrolled at the University of Chicago. However, still not having sufficient undergraduate credits to qualify for the psychology graduate program, he again took courses as a general student. When he finally qualified for the graduate program, he never looked back, not even bothering

with a master's degree, but going straight for his PhD. This he achieved in 1955 when his sharply honed 27-page dissertation, a psychophysical study in the field of visual perception, was submitted and accepted.

At this point, Goldiamond still had not been introduced to behavioral approaches, a subject then avoided at the university. It was Howard Hunt who introduced him to operant conditioning, but it was his first teaching job at Southern Illinois University at Carbondale that turned out to be fortuitous. It was there that he met Nate Azrin, who had studied with Skinner at Harvard. A close and lasting friendship was formed between the two around long conversations about behavior analysis; Goldiamond immediately grasped how the operant paradigm could be used for purposes of experimental analysis and replication. Fred Keller, Murray Sidman, Ogden Lindsley, and Charles Ferster were also early influences.

The operant paradigm became the conceptual framework for Goldiamond's work as he moved to Arizona State, Johns Hopkins, the Institute for Behavior Research (as director), full circle back to the University of Chicago as full professor in 1968, and eventually as professor emeritus in psychology and psychiatry. He taught the university's first courses in behavior analysis and programming.

Goldiamond's contributions not only included his work in basic behavioral research and its applications but also involved the very founding of the field of applied behavior analysis (ABA). In 1968, he served on the first editorial board of the *Journal of Applied Behavior Analysis,* and he, with Jerry Mertens, organized the very first ABA conference in 1974. An outcome of the conference was the formation of the Midwest Association for Behavior Analysis (MABA), of which Goldiamond became the first president. MABA evolved into the Association for Behavior Analysis in 1976, with Azrin its first president and Goldiamond as its second.

To reflect on Goldiamond's brilliant contributions is to reflect on genius itself. While these contributions include various studies in the experimental analysis of behavior, he reveled in ABA. His still-cited contributions include, but are not limited to, research on the development of speech and speech fluency and operant applications to self-control. In fact, Goldiamond's personal interest in self-control was first prompted by a weight problem during his undergraduate years. (His "self-control" of this problem also led to a lifelong interest in proper nutrition; he later taught nutrition students at the University of Chicago how to use operant methods to get their clients to comply with healthful eating regimens.) His contributions to the self-control literature, dating from 1965, were to play a poignant role in his life.

In 1970, an auto accident left him paraplegic and dependent on a wheelchair. Experiences with rehabilitation hospitals and professionals led to his conclusion that progress was dependent on application of operant principles to his own behavior. This he did with his characteristic enthusiasm, courage, and humor. What he learned, he shared, making a lasting impact on the self-control literature and the field of rehabilitation itself. It also led to his investing much of his time over a 25-year period advocating for psychologists, students, and others with physical disabilities to have access to educational and work settings. This activity included participating on the American Psychological Association's Task Force on the Handicapped, aimed at increasing accessibility for psychologists and psychology students.

What Goldiamond brought to rehabilitation was his constructional approach, which, in contrast to the pathological model, cast the person with a disability as the central character in facilitating recovery. This was accomplished by identifying the target behavioral repertoire, the current relevant repertoire, the procedures for change, and the contingencies to support change. Applications to rehabilitation were only one area in which his constructional approach has made a substantial contribution. In fact, it is likely that the full influence of his seminal articles on "constructional approaches and alternative sets" is yet to be realized. While the influence of these articles on clinical practice is apparent in the professional literature, both nationally and internationally, the most visible influence to date may be on the development and dramatic growth of positive practices in the area of challenging behavior.

The contributions to positive behavioral supports include an emphasis on comprehensive functional assessment/analyses, that is, identifying the current relevant repertoire by understanding the target behavior as functional for the person as part of complex nonlinear relationships between both the target behavior and relevant alternative behaviors and the environment. The contributions also include an emphasis on constructional efforts to develop alternative, adaptive repertoires that are functionally equivalent to the maladaptive repertoires. Positive practices derived from the constructional model are being applied not only with people who are disabled but also increasingly with large populations of typical children in school-wide systems.

Goldiamond had the opportunity to see his influence on the beginning of this revolution before he died at the age of 76, on November 19, 1995. However, his life was filled with more than his work. His days were enriched by his lifelong addiction to drawing and cartooning, and he enjoyed reading (especially science fiction) and travel. He avidly read, studied, and loved discussing the Bible and biblical commentary. He spoke several languages and always had dictionaries nearby in English, Russian, Hebrew, Portuguese, Spanish, French, and Arabic, the latter of which he was required to learn as a boy when he was sent to study in Israel for a period of time. Access to these books and his renowned memory made him a formidable opponent in the debates he loved to have with his friends and family regarding the etymology and use of words.

He was also a family man and is survived by his loved wife Betty, their three children and, by current count, five grandchildren, one of whom, at 17 months, was born after his death. He is also survived by the many students whose lives he changed and who consider it a privilege to introduce his work to a new generation. I am thankful to be among them.

—*Gary W. LaVigna*

See also: *Azrin, Nathan H. (Vol. I); Behavioral Assessment (Vol. II)*

Suggested Readings

Goldiamond, I. (1973). A diary of self-modification. *Psychology Today, 7*(6), 95–102.

Goldiamond, I. (1975). Alternative sets as a framework for behavioral formulations and research. *Behaviorism, 3*(1), 49–86.

Goldiamond, I. (2002). Toward a constructional approach to social problems: Ethical and Constitutional issues raised by applied behavior analysis. *Behavior and Social Issues, 11*(2), 108–197. (Original work published 1974, *Behaviorism, 2*, 1–85)

GROUP BEHAVIORAL THERAPY FOR DEPRESSION

Depression is one of the most common mental health problems, affecting approximately 17 million Americans per year and costing more than $43 billion per year in death, lost productivity, work absenteeism, and treatment. Although the most extensively researched treatments available (cognitive/behavioral individual therapy and pharmacological interventions) have recovery rates between 50% and 60%, the cost for these treatments remains out of reach for many sufferers and service providers. This need to provide effective, affordable treatment has motivated an upsurge in group treatments for depression. In addition, many of the auxiliary benefits of group participation may be particularly beneficial for depressed clients. The most commonly researched and implemented group interventions for depression typically involve both behavioral and cognitive interventions.

DESCRIPTION OF THE STRATEGY

Group cognitive behavior therapy (CBT) originated with Peter Lewinsohn in the late 1960s and was later titled the "Coping With Depression" course. Although many minor variations have been integrated by clinicians and researchers, the basic group CBT conceptualization and interventions have remained the same since that time. The CBT conceptualization of depression suggests that depression is a product of both behavioral and cognitive errors. Behaviorally, depression is seen as the result of a downward spiral fueled by a synergistic relationship between a lack of activities and low motivation. Thus, depression can develop when an individual foregoes activities that would normally be pleasurable or provide a sense of accomplishment. Not participating in activities increases depression and reduces motivation to participate in other activities. This increased depression further reduces participation in activities, and so on. In addition, depression can be caused or exacerbated by a preponderance of aversive activities, such as negative interactions with family members. Cognitively, depression is conceptualized as the product of depressogenic automatic thoughts about self, the environment, and the future (e.g., I will fail the test; Others will reject me because I have failed; I will always fail), arising from core schematic beliefs (e.g., If I don't succeed at everything I try, I am a failure as a person) that may have developed in childhood. Group CBT for depression uses the group environment to facilitate the development of behavioral and cognitive coping skills to reduce depressive symptoms.

Group CBT for depression is typically time limited and structured. Sessions are structured with agendas, and methods of change include education, modeling,

in-session practice, feedback, and homework. Although these groups may span between 4 and 20 sessions, most traditional CBT depression groups last approximately 12 sessions. Usually, group CBT for depression begins with a focus on behavior change, followed by cognitive change strategies. Behavioral interventions typically include the group leaders presenting the downward-spiral rationale (The less you do, the worse you feel, the worse you feel, the less you do. . . .) coupled with each group member developing specific, measurable, and attainable goals for increasing pleasurable and mastery activities. In addition, some CBT group protocols target skills deficits with assertiveness training, social skills training, and/or relaxation training. Cognitive interventions begin with the group leaders presenting the cognitive model of depression that highlights how extreme, unhelpful, or rigid thinking can cause or exacerbate depression. Group members then learn how to identify the role of their own distorted beliefs in maintaining negative views of the self, the environment, and the future. In particular, group members identify thinking errors that include overgeneralization (e.g., Because I failed the test last week, I am a failure); catastrophizing (e.g., Everyone will reject me if I fail the test); all-or-nothing thinking (e.g., Either I pass the test or I am a failure); mistaking possibilities for certainties (e.g., I will fail the test); and using extreme words (e.g., never, always). Then, group members learn to challenge their beliefs with questions such as: What is the evidence that the automatic thought is true or not true? Is there an alternative explanation? What's the worst that could happen? Could I live through it? What's the most realistic outcome? Through this questioning, alternative more helpful beliefs are identified and practiced. Behavioral experiments may also be designed to challenge some beliefs (e.g., deliberately fail a quiz and observe the actual consequences). Some groups include cognitive interventions for identifying and challenging overarching beliefs or core schemas that may predispose members to experience depressogenic automatic thoughts. An example of a core schematic belief for a client who demands constant perfection from himself or herself may be, "If I do not succeed at everything I do, I am completely worthless."

Although the interventions described above can easily be implemented in individual treatment, group interventions offer many unique advantages to the depressed client. First, the group environment is rich with natural reinforcers and punishers for client behaviors. These contingencies may help shape more functional behavior as well as increase client awareness of problematic behaviors. Second, there are many opportunities to practice and master skills prior to trying them out in the real world. Third, group interventions provide a normalizing challenge to the frequent client belief that they are alone in their concerns. Fourth, group interventions also provide built-in social supports for isolated clients to bridge the gap to more independent external social supports. Fifth, social support doubles as a motivator, providing a strong reinforcement potential for successfully completing homework and group tasks. Finally, and perhaps most obviously, group interventions are cost-effective, thus allowing more clients to benefit from fewer health care dollars.

RESEARCH BASIS

Treatment outcome research suggests that behavioral group depression treatment is an economical alternative to individual therapy and pharmacotherapy, with largely comparable outcomes. A recent meta-analysis of group treatments for depression suggests that group depression treatment is clearly superior to no treatment, with 85% of treated clients being better off than untreated clients. In addition, comparisons between group CBT and individual therapy or pharmacotherapy suggest negligible differences in posttest outcomes. At follow-ups, however, both group and individual CBT interventions have been repeatedly shown to maintain their gains better than pharmacological interventions; and at least one socioeconomic cost-effectiveness analysis suggests that group CBT for depression is more than $6,000 cheaper than fluoxetine (Prozac) over a 2-year period. Furthermore, when CBT groups are compared with other depression treatment groups, CBT group interventions have a slight advantage over other group interventions for depression. In sum, the research supports the use of group CBT for depression.

RELEVANT TARGET POPULATIONS AND EXCEPTIONS

Behavioral group depression interventions are applicable to a wide range of depressed clients. Although adaptable to most depressed populations, some clinical situations such as the following may be inappropriate for groups: when group is used as the sole intervention for a client in suicidal crisis who needs careful monitoring; when group is the first intervention for a depressed client with significant social phobia; when a client expresses a strong preference against group; or when a client's cognitive, interpersonal, or emotional abilities are mismatched to either the group content or the other group members. In addition, some research suggests that severely and/or chronically depressed clients may be best suited to a multifaceted intervention that includes group treatment, pharmacotherapy, and individual therapy.

COMPLICATIONS

Serious complications are rare in behavioral depression groups. The most likely complications are treatment failure (30%–50%) and attrition (40%–50%). These complications may be avoided or remedied through careful monitoring of client progress and modifying the treatment content or modality when clients fail to make expected improvements.

—*Paula Truax*

See also: *Coping With Depression (Vol. I); Evidence-Based Practice (Vol. III); Manualized Behavioral Therapy (Vol. II)*

Suggested Readings

Antonuccio, D. O., Thomas, M., & Danton, W. G. (1997). A cost-effectiveness analysis of cognitive behavior therapy and fluoxetine (Prozac) in the treatment of depression. *Behavior Therapy, 28,* 187–210.

Brown, R. A., & Lewinsohn, P. M. (1984). A psychoeducational approach to the treatment of depression: Comparison of group, individual, and minimal contact procedures. *Journal of Consulting and Clinical Psychology, 52,* 774–783.

Dobson, K. S. (1989). A meta-analysis of the efficacy of cognitive therapy for depression. *Journal of Consulting and Clinical Psychology, 57,* 414–419.

Evans, M. D., Hollon, S. D., DeRubeis, R. J., Piasecki, J. M., Grove, W. M., Garvey, M. J., et al. (1992). Differential relapse following cognitive therapy and pharmacotherapy for depression. *Archives of General Psychiatry, 49*(10), 802–808.

Greenberg, P. E., Stiglin, L. E., Findelstein, S. N., & Berndt, E. R. (1993). The economic burden of depression in 1990. *Journal of Clinical Psychiatry, 54,* 405–418.

Lewinsohn, P. M, Hoberman, H. M., & Rosenbaum, M. (1988). The Coping With Depression course: Review and future directions. *Canadian Journal of Behavioural Science, 21,* 470–493.

Lewinsohn, P. M., Weinstein, M., & Alper, T. (1970). A behavioral approach to the group treatment of depressed persons: A methodological contribution. *Journal of Clinical Psychology, 26,* 525–532.

McDermut, W., Miller, I. W., & Brown, R. A. (2001). The efficacy of group psychotherapy for depression: A meta-analysis and review of the empirical research. *Clinical Psychology: Science & Practice, 8*(1), 98–116.

Shapiro, D. A., Rees, A., Barkham, M., Hardy, G., Reynolds, S., & Startup, M. (1995). Effects of treatment duration and severity of depression on the maintenance of gains after cognitive-behavioral and psychodynamic interpersonal psychotherapy. *Journal of Consulting and Clinical Psychology, 63,* 378–387.

GUIDED MASTERY

DESCRIPTION OF THE STRATEGY

Guided mastery is a therapeutic method of assisting clients in raising their self-efficacy (i.e., perception that a task can be accomplished) so they are motivated to attempt, and subsequently accomplish, progressively more difficult tasks that are involved in the implementation of behavioral therapies. As proficiency and flexibility of performance are accomplished, therapeutic assistance is gradually withdrawn. For instance, exposure to progressively greater anxiety-provoking situations is the treatment of choice for individuals who evidence problems associated with anxiety disorders (e.g., panic disorder with agoraphobia). In the utilization of guided mastery, a therapist might encourage and assist the individual in accomplishing a situation that is associated with a low degree of anxiety (e.g., walking in the shopping center with a friend) prior to attempting a situation that evokes slightly more anxiety (e.g., walking in the shopping center without a friend). In the latter situation, the therapist would conduct various cognitive-behavioral strategies to increase the individual's self-efficacy during the exposure trials (e.g., encourage objective thinking, praise effort, teach relevant coping skills).

There are several strategies involved in guided mastery, including performing tasks jointly, modeling, overcoming problematic subtasks, graduating tasks, setting proximal goals, graduating the treatment setting, and giving physical and mechanical support. Performing tasks jointly is important when attempting to improve self-efficacy, because people often feel more capable when a trusted companion is present.

Indeed, in performing tasks jointly, clients feel confident that assurance and assistance are available; thus, they will attempt greater accomplishments. Another technique to improve self-efficacy is to model successful accomplishment of therapeutic tasks, verbally describing behavior or showing a video of behavior in order to give concrete guidance relevant to the execution of the behavior. Modeling is especially useful when attempting to eliminate defensive behaviors or awkward performance and may also be used jointly with other techniques. A small aspect of an activity that is troubling may significantly lower self-efficacy for the entire activity, thus restricting efforts to attempt the respective task. Therefore, focusing on overcoming problematic subtasks can be a powerful technique in guiding the client to mastery.

Another alternative is to graduate tasks so that they become progressively more difficult. In this strategy, the client first attempts a strategy for which self-efficacy is relatively high, and upon accomplishing this task feels more prepared to accomplish the next task, and so on. The latter strategy is enhanced by setting proximal goals. In this method, a goal is set for each task involved in the hierarchy of tasks to be accomplished. Thus, accomplishment of each goal provides a feeling of accomplishment and preparedness for the upcoming task of greater perceived difficulty. Graduating treatment settings involves attempting related tasks in settings that are perceived to be increasingly more difficult. Thus, the client improves self-efficacy through the generalization process. Physical or mechanical support might include manually guiding an individual in the accomplishment of a task (e.g., holding the bicycle seat while a child first learns to ride). As with the other methods of guided mastery, assistance would be gradually withdrawn (e.g., holding the bicycle seat with less support as the child's riding improves).

People believe themselves to be capable not solely on the level of performance they are able to master but also their ability to perform the activity proficiently in varied ways, and without restrictions. Therefore, in utilizing guided mastery, it is important to ask clients whether there is anything special they do to cope with threatening situations. It may be necessary to clarify by providing examples of common defensive maneuvers such as muscle tension, gripping an object tightly, or holding one's breath. Although it is important to correct defensive mechanisms the client may have developed, this should not be the main focus of the treatment and should begin only after the client has maintained a fairly high level of performance. After the client can perform a given task, even if it is done using some defensive behaviors or self-restrictions, performance of the next task in the hierarchy should be encouraged, because proficiency and flexibility for that task are typically increased as a by-product.

After the client is able to perform the desired behavior proficiently and with flexibility, it is important to assist the client in functioning independently. The principles for fostering independent performance include using the least amount of assistance needed, withdrawing assistance as soon as possible while sustaining progress, and training people to be their own therapist (e.g., teaching the client to utilize empirically based problem-solving methods). This helps to promote a generalized sense of self-efficacy and to allow clients to master their fears using self-treatment efforts after therapy has ended.

RESEARCH BASIS

Pure exposure-based interventions with guided mastery in patients with agoraphobia and other specific phobias have been examined in a few controlled-outcome studies. These studies have generally indicated that guided mastery significantly improves behavioral functioning, reduces performance anxiety, and increases self-efficacy levels. Indeed, empirical research suggests that guided mastery is an effective component in the treatment of some specific phobias within just two sessions. Moreover, the self-efficacy model upon which guided mastery is founded has consistently been shown to be positively related to improvements in phobic behavior.

RELEVANT TARGET POPULATIONS AND EXCEPTIONS

Guided-mastery treatment may be used to treat a broad range of phobic conditions, including agoraphobia, specific phobias, and multiphobic conditions. The method is appropriate for children and adults of all ages and developmental levels, including low-functioning individuals, who often require graduated assistance. No exceptions for its use have been identified in the literature.

COMPLICATIONS

The client may refuse to attempt an assigned task in the therapy office or in a naturalistic setting. In these cases, as consistent with the guided mastery method, the level of assistance should be increased and/or an easier task should be assigned. In the latter strategy, the hierarchy may need to be adjusted to permit more tasks that are perceived to be increasingly more difficult. The therapist should also show concern, while providing statements of hope (e.g., "You can do it").

—*Brad C. Donohue*

See also: *Behavior Activation (Vol. I); Behavioral Treatment in Natural Environments (Vol. I); Virtual Reality Therapy (Vol. I)*

Suggested Readings

Hersen, M., Eisler, R. M., & Miller, P. M. (Eds.). (1990). *Progress in behavior modification.* Newbury Park, CA: Sage.

Hoffart, A. (1995). A comparison of cognitive and guided mastery therapy of agoraphobia. *Behavior Research and Therapy, 33,* 423–434.

Hoffart, A. (1998). Cognitive and guided mastery therapy of agoraphobia: Long-term outcome and mechanisms of change. *Cognitive Therapy and Research, 22,* 195–207.

Williams, L., Dooseman, G., & Kleifield, E. (1984). Comparative effectiveness of guided mastery and exposure treatments for intractable phobias. *Journal of Consulting and Clinical Psychology, 53,* 237–247.

Williams, L., Turner, S., & Peer, D. (1985). Guided mastery and performance desensitization treatments for severe acrophobia. *Journal of Consulting and Clinical Psychology, 52,* 505–518.

Williams, L., & Zane, G. (1989). Guided mastery and stimulus exposure treatments for severe performance anxiety in agoraphobia. *Behavior Research and Therapy, 27,* 237–245.

H

HABIT REVERSAL

DESCRIPTION OF THE STRATEGY

Azrin and Nunn developed *habit reversal* in 1973. The intervention includes four phases, including awareness, competing response, motivation, and generalization. The goal of the awareness phase is to increase the client's awareness of the target behavior, either a tic or habit. First, the client is instructed to describe the target behavior in detail. This is often done with the client looking in a mirror and reenacting the tic or habit. The client is then instructed to spontaneously acknowledge the target behavior when it occurs during the session. The therapist assists in identifying tics or habits that the client fails to acknowledge and teaches the client to become aware of the early signs or sensory preconditions of the target behavior. The therapist concludes the awareness phase by assisting the client in identifying situations in which the tic or habit occurs most frequently. Thus, the client describes all the situations, persons, and places in which the target behavior occurs. The client also describes how the behavior is enacted in each situation.

After the client has become fully aware of the manifestations of the target behavior, the competing response phase is initiated. The goal of the competing response phase is to teach the client to engage in a behavior that is incompatible with the target behavior. The competing response must (a) be the opposite of the target behavior, (b) be maintained for several minutes, (c) produce an isometric tensing of the muscles involved in the target behavior, (d) be socially inconspicuous and compatible with usual ongoing activities while still incompatible with the target behavior, and (e) strengthen the opposing muscles. The client and therapist mutually determine the appropriate competing response for each specific target behavior. The client is instructed to perform the competing response when the target behavior occurs or, ideally, at first awareness of the early signs of the tic or habit.

In the motivation phase, the client is encouraged to continue to implement the awareness and competing response phases. However, three motivation techniques are additionally employed: habit inconvenience review, social support procedure, and public display. In the habit inconvenience review, the client reviews all the problems, embarrassments, discomforts, and inconveniences that are caused by the target behavior. It is also important for the client and therapist to discuss the advantages of eliminating the target behavior. The social support procedure is presented after the client has displayed control of the target behavior in the therapy sessions. Family and friends are taught to praise the client for nonoccurrence of the target behavior and to remind the client to practice the competing response technique when they notice occurrences of the target behavior that are not recognized by the client. In the public display, the client is taught to demonstrate control of the target behavior in front of a friendly audience (e.g., family, friends).

The final phase of generalization training consists of symbolic rehearsal. Enhancing generalization of the results of the above procedures to all areas of the client's life is the goal of this phase. In symbolic rehearsal, the client is instructed to imagine one of the situations discussed during the situation awareness training technique. The client imagines detecting an early sign of the target behavior and consequently performs the competing response.

RESEARCH BASIS

Habit reversal has been shown to be effective in the treatment of tic disorders, trichotillomania, stuttering, and other "nervous habits." Nervous habits include body-focused stable and repetitive behaviors, for example, skin picking, oral-digital habits, nail biting, hair pulling, persistent scratching, bruxism (teeth grinding), and chewing on one's own skin. Abbreviations of Azrin and Nunn's original procedure have demonstrated effectiveness and always include awareness training and competing response training.

Though research has shown habit reversal to be effective, it is not yet considered a "well-established" empirically validated treatment by the American Psychological Association's Division 12 Task Force on Promotion and Dissemination of Psychological Procedures. This task force was formed to present guidelines for determining whether a psychological procedure has acquired sufficient support to be deemed "empirically validated." Presently, the task force has two classifications, "probably efficacious" and the more rigorous "well-established." Habit reversal has been denoted "probably efficacious" by the task force, as controlled comparisons of habit reversal with placebo and other interventions have been scarce.

RELEVANT TARGET POPULATIONS AND EXCEPTIONS

Habit reversal may be effectively implemented with children, adolescents, or adults experiencing any of the following disorders or difficulties: any type of tic disorder, including transient tic disorder, chronic motor or vocal tic disorder, Tourette's disorder, and tic disorder not otherwise specified. Stereotypic movement disorder (stereotypy/habit disorder), trichotillomania, stuttering, and "nervous habits" are also appropriately treated with habit reversal. Habit reversal is not appropriate for use with individuals who evidence borderline intellectual functioning or are mentally retarded (i.e., IQ below 70).

COMPLICATIONS

There are several complications in the implementation of habit reversal. These complications include, but are not limited to, issues of compliance and interpersonal difficulties in social functioning. Indeed, when habit reversal fails, it is most often due to the client failing to implement the habit-reversal procedures as protocol dictates. Reasons for noncompliance include a lack of motivation, impaired intelligence, or the existence of competing activities. Two strategies appear to be effective in the development of treatment compliance. The first strategy entails the use of contingency management procedures (establishing rewards contingent on performance of behaviors that are compatible with the habit-reversal procedure). Of course, these programs are usually best implemented by persons who are able to exert greatest influence on the client (e.g., spouse). Such programs help to strengthen the correct implementation of the competing response procedure. Self-monitoring and monitoring by the social support person may also assist in treatment compliance.

When the client is engaging in the competing response only in the presence of the support person, that person should be instructed to covertly observe the client. If the support person witnesses the client engaging in the competing response, the support person should provide praise. If the support person observes that the client is not engaging in the competing response, the client should be reminded to perform the competing behavior.

Difficulties in social functioning can hinder the effectiveness of habit reversal. First, it should be determined whether the difficulty in social functioning is due to a social skills deficit or is a direct consequence of the disorder. If the disturbance is determined to be a result of a social skills deficit, the clinician will need to first implement social skills training. If the disruption appears to be a result of a negative peer group reaction to the child's problem, then peer group education should be performed to help decrease biases and stereotypes.

CASE ILLUSTRATION

"Sam" was a 31-year-old male who presented with a shoulder-jerking tic. The tic was defined as a sudden upward jerk and then an immediate fall of the right shoulder. Sam's spouse reported that he had repeatedly engaged in the tic for the past 2 years.

In Sam's first therapy session, he defined his tic behavior and was asked to demonstrate the behavior. During the session, Sam was instructed to point out any time he was aware of an occurrence of the tic. If a tic occurred that Sam did not acknowledge, the therapist would point it out to him. This continued until Sam acknowledged the occurrences of the tic without the assistance of the therapist. Sam and the therapist discussed presence of any early signs. Sam acknowledged having a "feeling" in his shoulder prior to the tic behavior. He was subsequently taught to become more aware of this feeling and to alert the therapist during the session if he became aware of this early sign. Sam and the therapist made a list of the situations and places in which the tic occurred, as well as any persons around whom the tic occurred. Each of the situations, places, or persons was described in detail, and it was determined that the tic was most frequent during meetings with his boss and colleagues at work, because he noticed he became "very nervous" when in meetings.

In the next session, Sam was taught to engage in a competing response for 3 minutes when he noticed the early signs of the tic or after a tic had occurred. The competing response for Sam was to isometrically hold down his shoulders in order to strengthen the opposing muscles of his upward jerking tic. Sam was to perform this competing behavior during the next week whenever he was aware of an early sign or after any time that he became aware of a tic behavior.

The following session was designed to increase Sam's motivation in eliminating the tic. First, Sam and the therapist made a detailed list of all of the inconveniences, embarrassments, and distresses that the tic had caused or been causing. For Sam, this list included items such as "not wanting to go out with other couples" and, more specifically, "feeling like an embarrassment to my wife" when a tic occurred while out with friends. Another list was constructed that consisted of various advantages or positive outcomes that would result from a reduction, or elimination, of the tic behavior. This listed included the possibility of "going out with other couples and people from work" (something that was very important to Sam) and "not being, or feeling like, an embarrassment to my wife." Also during this session, the social support procedure was introduced. Sam's spouse had been in attendance at most of the sessions, thus making her easily accessible for this next technique. Sam's wife was taught to encourage any tic-free periods, as well as the use of the competing response technique. Specifically, she was instructed to provide praise ("I have not noticed any tic in the last 10 minutes. That's great, Sam!"

or "Great job in using your competing response technique!"). His wife was also taught to gently remind Sam of any instances in which she noticed an occurrence of the tic in which he did not engage in the competing response. The therapist, Sam's wife, and Sam identified a reminder relevant to performing the competing response (i.e., "Sam, I noticed that you had a tic but didn't do your exercises. Don't forget to do your exercises now"). They also decided that if she noticed the tic behavior in a situation where others were present, she would inconspicuously get Sam's attention, and then pull on her left ear. This would be a signal to Sam that he had forgotten to use his competing response exercise. Both Sam and his wife were instructed to use the techniques that they learned in this session during the next week.

In the final session, symbolic rehearsal was used to help Sam in generalizing the techniques outside the therapy office. Sam chose the situation of having dinner at a restaurant with his wife and another couple. He imagined that he was at a very fancy restaurant eating dinner and that he sensed "feeling" the tic coming on. He imagined that he performed the competing response technique and that the tic did not occur. This process was repeated with other situations that were listed during the situational awareness training. A brief review was given for all of the techniques that were taught during the past sessions. Sam and his wife were told that the therapist would call them once a month for the next 3 months to monitor treatment progress and that additional sessions would be scheduled, if needed.

—*Brad C. Donohue and Alisha Farley*

See also: *Applied Behavior Analysis (Vol. II); Azrin, Nathan H. (Vol. I); Habit Reversal (Vol. II)*

Suggested Readings

Azrin, N. H., & Nunn, R. G. (1973). Habit reversal: A method of eliminating nervous tics and habits. *Behaviour Research and Therapy, 11,* 619–628.

Rothbaum, B. O., & Ninan, P. T. (1999). Manual for the cognitive-behavioral treatment of trichotillomania. In D. J. Stein, G. A. Christenson, et al. (Eds.), *Trichotillomania* (pp. 263–284). Washington, DC: American Psychiatric Association.

Woods, D. W. (2001). Habit reversal treatment manual for tic disorders. In D. W. Woods & R. G. Miltenberger (Eds.), *Tic disorders, trichotillomania, and other repetitive behavior disorders: Behavioral approaches to analysis and treatment* (pp. 97–132). New York: Kluwer Academic.

Woods, D. W., & Miltenberger, R. G. (1995). Habit reversal: A review of applications and variations. *Journal of Behavior Therapy and Experimental Psychiatry, 26*(2), 123–131.

Woods, D. W., & Miltenberger, R. G. (1996). A review of habit reversal with childhood habit disorders. *Education and Treatment of Children, 19*(2), 197–214.

HERSEN, MICHEL

I was born on a snowy day on January 14, 1940, in Brussels, Belgium. When I was only 16 weeks old, my parents traversed Belgium, France, and Spain, eventually reaching Portugal, to avoid the invading Nazi armies. Finally, in May of 1941, the Hersens (then Herszhowicz) reached New York City, where I had my initial education. Early influences were my parents, who stressed the importance of a broad education, including music, the arts, philosophy, science, and history. Beginning as a classically trained violinist at the Julliard School of Music, I entered Queens College in New York in 1957 and by my sophomore year in college had decided to become a clinical psychologist. This occurred after observing the psychological evaluation of a child with mental retardation. I then marched into Gregory Razran's office (the chair and famous Pavlovian) and announced to him that I was going to become a professor of psychology. After 10 minutes, he stopped laughing.

After obtaining the BA from Queens College in 1961, I received my MA from Hofstra University. There, I was influenced by Julia Vane, who stressed the import of testing, and Harold Yuker, who felt psychologists should be broadly trained. I then started my doctoral work at the State University of New York at Buffalo (affectionately referred to as SUNY, Buffalo) and finished my PhD in February of 1966. My major influence there was B. R. Bugelski, the learning theorist, who always took on a few clinical students. I conducted my first piece of research with him (published in the *Journal of Experimental Psychology* in 1966), the verbal-conditioning study being run with the able assistance of my now publisher at Taylor and Francis: Dr. George Zimmar. This was a memorable day for many reasons, being November 22, 1963, the day JFK was assassinated.

My only formal training in behavior therapy consisted of attending two lectures by James Geer at Buffalo, who had recently familiarized himself with systematic desensitization. After Buffalo, I moved to Connecticut and did my postdoctoral training in the Yale program at the West Haven VA. This training was primarily existential and psychoanalytic from the theoretical perspectives. At the West Haven VA, I was supervised by Charles Zigun, MD, and he invited me to join his practice in Fairfield, Connecticut. This is where my conversion to behavior therapy took place, after a series of successes in helping school phobic children overcome their fears using carefully orchestrated operant strategies. From 1969 to 1970, I worked at Fairfield State Hospital and was fortunate to have D. A. Begelman as my boss, who further encouraged my interests in behaviorism. While at Fairfield Hills Hospital, I pursued my interests in verbal conditioning and also the study of fear in schizophrenics. All of these studies eventuated in publications.

From 1970 to 1974, I had the pleasure of being associated with Stewart Agras, David Barlow, Edward Blanchard, Gene Abel, Richard Eisler, and Peter Miller, among others, at the University of Mississippi Medical Center, in Jackson, Mississippi. Working with these illustrious colleagues was an eye-opener and further cemented my interests in the application of behavioral strategies to difficult clinical problems. Many complicated single-case studies were conducted and published in a variety of behavioral and psychiatric journals. There too, I wrote my first book with Dave Barlow *(Single Case Experimental Designs)*. With Dick Eisler and Peter Miller, we developed strategies to assess and treat social skill deficits for a variety of populations. We also initiated the yearly and sometimes twice-yearly series, *Progress in Behavior Modification*. In addition, Peter Miller and I established a new journal, *Addictive Behaviors*. In Mississippi, I cofounded a behavioral internship training program with Dave Barlow, which still exists.

From 1974 to 1992, I was professor of psychiatry at Western Psychiatric Institute and Clinic, University of Pittsburgh School of Medicine, where I initially worked closely with Alan Bellack and Sam Turner. This fruitful collaboration involved the application of social skill strategies to depressed women, unassertive children, and schizophrenics. Later, I worked with Vincent B. Van Hasselt and Robert Ammerman, applying behavioral strategies to a variety of child populations. A number of journals were founded in Pittsburgh by my colleagues and me, including *Behavior Modification, Clinical Psychology Review, Journal of Family Violence, Journal of Developmental and Physical Disabilities,* and *Journal of Anxiety*

Disorders. In 1979, I was elected the 14th president of the Association for Advancement of Behavior Therapy, following an illustrious group of individuals, such as Cyril Franks, Joseph Wolpe, Arnold Lazarus, Joseph Cautela, Gerald Davison, Nathan Azrin, Alan Kazdin, and David Barlow. It was quite an honor. In Pittsburgh, I founded a behavioral internship training program with Sam Turner that still is in operation.

In 1992, I moved to Nova Southeastern University, Florida, where I became director of the Community Clinic for Older Adults and, for a short period, interim dean of the program. Two new journals, consistent with my research interests at the time, were founded: *Journal of Clinical Geropsychology* and *Aggression and Violent Behavior: A Review Journal.*

Turning my attention to the broader problems of full-time administration, in 1997, I became dean of the School of Professional Psychology at Pacific University, in Oregon. Consistent with the mission of a professional school, I founded yet another new journal *(Clinical Case Studies),* to provide an outlet for publication and reading for our more clinically oriented colleagues. I also developed separate postdoctoral training programs in clinical research with adults and children, both of which are extent.

Over the years, I have continued to review and organize material in our exponentially growing field and have written and edited some 140 or so books. I have published 224 articles and 95 chapters.

Future goals involve further establishing the reputation of the behavioral aspects of our MA in Counseling Psychology and PsyD in Clinical Psychology at Pacific University, encouraging junior faculty to research and publish, and continuing to review interesting developments in the field of psychology in general.

—*Michel Hersen*

See also: *Association for Advancement of Behavior Therapy (Vol. I); Single-Case Research (Vol. I); Social Skills Training (Vol. I)*

HISTORICAL ANTECEDENTS OF BEHAVIOR MODIFICATION AND THERAPY

DESCRIPTION OF THE STRATEGY

Behavior modification and behavior therapy have a short history of a few decades (four or five), but a long past. It goes back to the first thoughts concerning human nature, health and illness, and mental disorders and their etiology and their treatment. In modern times, it begins with the applications of learning theory, of the procedures of classical conditioning and operant conditioning to clinical and educational problems.

This is an area of knowledge that began humbly at the end of the 1950s, but which grew tremendously in the decades of the 1980s and 1990s. Today, this has become an essential pillar; it is part of the mainstream of clinical psychology and of psychiatry, and it has changed from being a controversial approach to being an "orthodox approach." All of this happened in a few decades, the last ones of the 20th century.

REMOTE ANTECEDENTS

In the first registered civilizations, the explanations of "different" behavior were based in demonology. People who acted in an abnormal way were supposed to be possessed by bad spirits, and exorcism was the treatment to eliminate those spirits. In Greece, Rome, Christianity, and the first American civilizations, this was the accepted view. In the Middle Ages, demonology became the dominant explanation of maladaptive behavior.

Only in the Renaissance and the years following it did biological explanations start to be considered. This led to a more humane rather than harsh treatment and to an important reorganization of the treatment institutions. In the following centuries, above all, in Europe, they continued with this tradition of biologically explaining the so-called mental illnesses. This identification of psychological disorders with organic pathology had a great influence.

However, that "medical model" of mental illnesses, as it came to be known much later, received a lot of criticism. There were many gaps in our knowledge of causes, development, evolution, and treatment of mental illnesses. The organic causes were not clear in the majority of the cases, and for most of the mental illnesses, no evidence existed of organic pathology.

The alternative movement was to find psychological causes and psychological treatments. Hypnosis, suggestion, and Mesmerism developed treatment strategies and were very popular. It was considered that neuroses could be treated with methods such as suggestion or Mesmerism. Within this tradition, psychoanalysis appeared, mainly due to Sigmund Freud

(1856–1939). This made up a very broad and influential effort to understand deviate behavior.

Psychoanalysis adopted an intrapsychic-disease model of abnormal behavior. The psychological processes of action were proposed as an explanation of the maladaptive behavior and of the psychological symptoms. The system was broadly developed, although the bulk of psychoanalytic theory was not readily open to scientific verification. Its therapeutic efficiency was also brought into question, its value as an explanation, and the fact of ignoring the cultural and sociological variables that limit its applicability.

Behavior therapy was initially presented as an alternative to psychoanalysis and to the organic explanations. It came from basic research in psychology and in laboratory situations with animals and with human participants. It had solid scientific backing. It emphasized overt behavior and was applied not only to psychiatric patients but also to retarded children, clinical populations in a broad sense, and so on.

DIAGNOSIS, THERAPY, AND ITS DISCONTENTS

When applying the medical model to abnormal behavior, the need was seen to design methods to identify the concerns or disorders that were going to be treated. This was done based on the classification of mental illnesses and the psychiatric diagnosis.

It was considered that identifying specific disorders could contribute to the discovery of their causes, thus enabling one to choose treatment procedures and to be able to predict their results. The diagnosis had proven its usefulness in medicine, and that did not have to be different in the area of psychopathology. Several diagnostic systems were proposed, some simple and others more complex. At present, the most widely used are the International Classification of Diseases (ICD) and the *Diagnostic and Statistical Manual of Mental Disorders (DSM)*. The latter is highly elaborated and has periodically been revised to include new developments in assessment and evaluation. The most recent edition is the *DSM-IV*, published in 1994 by the American Psychiatric Association.

Criticism to psychiatric diagnosis was strong. First, classification of abnormal behavior as disease was questioned. Thomas Szasz insisted that mental diseases were problems in coping with life that individuals experience as result of stress. They wouldn't be diseases in the literal sense, such as influenza, syphilis, or tuberculosis.

Second, the reliability, validity, and usefulness of diagnosis were questioned. Reliability (agreement between evaluators) was very low, and most of the diagnosticians did not agree on the labels they assigned to patients. The little validity in relation to the outcomes of the disorder was another important criticism, also related to the value of the psychiatric diagnosis.

Finally, a broader criticism referred to the objection of labeling individuals as "mentally ill": that giving them a diagnosis produced discrimination and errors in self-perception and led them to accept their labels and, as a result, to behave the way they were "supposed to."

The diagnostic instruments were much attacked, above all, the projective techniques.

On the other hand, the criticism of psychotherapy did not take long. Up to the beginning of the 1950s, no one had criticized the effectiveness of psychotherapy, nor had it been submitted to a thorough evaluation. It was Hans J. Eysenck (1916–1997) who researched whether rigorous evidence existed for the proposition that psychotherapy was effective. From his work, Eysenck concluded that the cure rate was approximately of the same magnitude as remission without treatment (spontaneous remission). In other words, the effectiveness of psychotherapy was no longer tenable.

BEHAVIOR THERAPY AS AN ALTERNATIVE

Due to the little validity of psychoanalytical therapies, the criticism of the "medical model" of mental illnesses, and the wariness of psychiatric classifications that did more damage than good to the patient, an alternative rooted in experimental psychology was proposed, which came to be called "behavior therapy."

This therapy had as direct forerunners classical conditioning (Pavlov), learning theory (Thorndike), behaviorism (Watson), and the experimental analysis of behavior (Skinner). There were attempts to apply learning theory to problems of a clinical nature. Watson's papers were especially important. So was the research of Wolpe. We can state that the most influential books in the origin of behavior therapy were Skinner's *Science and Human Behavior* (1953), and Wolpe's *Psychotherapy by Reciprocal Inhibition* (1958). The first one provided the fundamentals to understand behavior in terms of operant conditioning. Wolpe's book offered a conceptualization of human neurosis in terms of Pavlovian and Hullian earning theory. Another influential book was Eysenck's *Behavior Therapy and the Neuroses* (1960).

From the organizational and professional point of view, the founding of the Association for the Advancement of Behavior Therapy (AABT) in 1966 and the Association for Behavior Analysis (ABA) in 1974 had great importance. The first journal about behavior therapy, founded by Eysenck in England in 1963, was *Behaviour Research and Therapy*. The founding of the *Journal of Applied Behavior Analysis (JABA)* in 1968 was also noteworthy.

All this movement that emerged from experimental psychology attempted to apply the knowledge coming from laboratory research to clinical and educational problems. Several names were used, which could be defined as follows. *Behavior therapy* is the application of a large number of techniques that employ psychological principles (especially learning) to change human behavior constructively. *Applied behavior analysis,* on the other hand, refers to applications to broad areas such as mental illness, education, child rearing, crime, education, and retardation, and it basically makes use of the findings of operant conditioning. Finally, *behavior modification* is an even wider field that has the following features:

1. Focus upon current rather than historical determinants of behavior

2. Emphasis on overt behavior change as the main criterion by which treatment should be evaluated

3. Specification of treatment in objective terms so as to make replication possible

4. Reliance upon basic research in psychology as a source of hypotheses about treatment and specific therapy techniques

5. Specificity in defining, treating, and measuring the target problems in therapy

For many authors, these differences are not very important and do not merit the differentiation between behavior modification, behavior therapy, and applied behavior analysis. In contrast, for other authors, the differences are important, and it is pertinent to talk about the different fields, although they are very closely related.

The most important techniques used are assertion training, relaxation, systematic desensitization, modeling, operant conditioning procedures, self-control, biofeedback, and aversive conditioning.

—*Ruben Ardila*

See also: Behavior Therapy Theory (Vol. I); Kantor's Behaviorism (Vol. I); Skinner, Burrhus Frederic (Vol. II)

Suggested Readings

Ardila, R. (1980). *Terapia del compotamiento, fundamentos, técnicas y aplicaciones* [Behavior therapy, foundations, techniques, and applications]. Bilbao, Spain: Desclée de Brower.

Ardila R. et al. (Eds.). (1998). *Manual de análisis experimental del comportamiento* [Handbook of experimental analysis of behavior]. Madrid, Spain: Biblioteca Nueva.

Bellack, A. S., Hersen, M., & Kazdin, A. E. (Eds.). (1990). *International handbook of behavior modification and therapy* (2nd ed.). New York: Plenum Press.

Kazdin, A. E. (1978). *History of behavior modification.* Baltimore: University Park Press.

Martin, G., & Pear, J. (1999). *Behavior modification. What it is and how to do it* (6th ed.). Upper Saddle River, NJ: Prentice Hall.

Plaud, J. J., & Eifert, G. H. (Eds.). (1998). *From behavior theory to behavior therapy.* Boston: Allyn & Bacon.

Wolpe, J., Salter, A., & Reyna, L. J. (Eds.). (1964). *The conditioning therapies.* New York: Holt, Rinehart & Winston.

HOMEWORK

DESCRIPTION OF THE STRATEGY

Homework assignments are designed to engage clients in activities outside of the therapeutic context that facilitate movement toward accomplishing treatment goals. This technique is utilized by mental health professionals from various therapeutic backgrounds, and it can be employed in the treatment of a wide range of disorders. Research shows that the completion of homework between therapy sessions is related to a more positive therapeutic outcome. This chapter will address the following areas: the nature of homework, research on its effectiveness, populations on which it can be used, and considerations for incorporating this technique into therapy.

Homework refers to therapeutic assignments given to a client by a therapist that are to be completed between therapy sessions. Most homework assignments fall into one of three categories: written assignments, self-monitoring procedures, and skills practice.

The type of assignments given to a particular client can vary depending on the theoretical orientation of the therapist and the presenting problems of the client.

The practice of assigning homework to clients became widespread as a result of the increased popularity of the cognitive-behavioral theoretical orientation, which focuses on identifying and changing clients' specific thoughts and behaviors that are seen to be problematic. The concept of assigning tasks for a client to complete between therapy sessions appeared as early as 1936 but was not formally operationalized until 1981, when John L. Shelton and Rona L. Levy produced a treatment handbook that established specific guidelines for homework assignments. This work supplemented the writings of Aaron Beck and colleagues during the late 1970s and early 1980s that emphasized homework assignment as an important component of cognitive-behavioral therapy.

Despite the origins of homework assignment as a therapeutic technique, its application is not limited to treatment conducted by cognitive-behavioral therapists. Homework techniques are utilized by therapists endorsing a wide range of theoretical orientations, including psychodynamic, family systems, humanistic, interpersonal, and eclectic approaches. Of 221 master's- and doctoral-level psychologists surveyed in New Zealand, 98% incorporated homework techniques into their practices and assigned homework in an average of 57% of their therapy sessions. Although more than half of the psychologists surveyed identified themselves as cognitive-behavioral in their therapeutic approach, 43% endorsed other theoretical backgrounds.

Homework assignments vary in form depending upon a number of client and therapist variables. However, there are some elements of homework implementation that can be used as guidelines. Generally speaking, assignments should be clear, specific, and concrete and should increase in difficulty as treatment progresses. The purpose of the homework should be explained to the client, and his or her concerns and attitudes toward each assignment should be solicited. It may also be helpful to outline each assignment in writing, which serves to create a formal record of the homework and to remind the client of the specific details of each assignment. In the case of weekly sessions, each therapy session should begin with a review of the client's progress in completing previously assigned homework and end with a summary of the assignment for the upcoming week. This allows the therapist to systematically reward the client's efforts in completing the previous assignment and outline the specific details of the next assignment.

Homework assignment adds many essential features that help facilitate positive therapeutic outcome for the client. Homework is a cost-effective way of extending therapeutic contact outside of the standard treatment setting. A client who completes homework assignments multiplies the amount of time spent working toward treatment goals. Homework also allows the client to apply skills or techniques learned in therapy sessions to real-life situations, in order to test whether or not these skills will actually be adaptive within the client's daily environment. Such application is thought to improve the level of emotional and cognitive processing the client experiences and to facilitate generalization to other situations within the client's environment. Once therapy terminates, the client must apply the knowledge and skills gained in therapy sessions to real-life situations in order to be successful. Homework allows the client to practice and receive guidance on this integration while still in therapy. Often, homework assignments can involve cooperation of friends and family members, who can provide a supportive context for the completion of the client's assignments. The opportunity to practice skills learned in the clinic in a realistic context also allows the client the opportunity to provide the therapist with feedback on obstacles to the completion of assignments. Then, the therapist can assist in problem solving or can reevaluate the client's situation and alter the assignment accordingly. Homework assignments can serve to provide continuity between sessions for the client, as the discussion of homework at the beginning and end of every session adds an element of consistency and linearity to treatment. For the therapist, compliance with homework assignments can provide an indication of how motivated the client is to improve, as well as supply valuable information about the client's ability to face challenges and accomplish goals within the context of daily life.

RESEARCH BASIS

Over the last two decades, much research has been conducted to determine the effectiveness of homework assignments in increasing the likelihood of positive therapeutic outcome. Studies have differed with regard to research design, types of homework, assessment techniques, and types of samples selected. While numerous studies have found that homework assignments either produce or are associated with more positive therapeutic outcomes, some studies have failed to discover significant effects or relationships. On the whole, however, it is highly likely that using homework techniques in therapy can have a positive impact on symptom reduction and therapeutic outcome.

Research Design and Methods

Overall, two main types of outcome research have been conducted. The first focuses on determining the correlational relationship between assignment of homework and therapeutic outcome. The second consists of experimental studies that investigate causal effects of homework assignment in therapy. Correlational studies give limited information, because they cannot show causation or whether or not a third variable is operating to produce the observed effects. Possible third variables responsible for moderating the effect of homework assignment on treatment outcome include the client's motivation level, openness to change, optimism, or symptom severity. By contrast, experimental studies can speak to the directionality of the homework-outcome relationship. These usually include two groups of participants: those receiving homework as a part of therapy and those receiving therapy that does not include homework assignments.

Besides varying on design, studies investigating the nature and effectiveness of homework differ as to the nature of assignments, methods used to measure compliance, and intervals at which homework compliance is evaluated. While many studies do not specify the exact nature of homework assignments, some have been limited to specific types of assignments, such as exposure to feared objects or situations, practice of relaxation techniques, or development of assertiveness skills. While some studies measure homework compliance though objective electronic equipment, others use subjective therapist and/or client ratings to gauge the client's level of compliance with assignments. There also is variation among studies with regard to the intervals at which homework compliance is assessed. While some studies measure homework compliance at weekly intervals, others measure compliance only after the completion of treatment.

Finally, studies also vary on participant samples used. Many focus on samples of people suffering from a particular disorder, such as major depression or panic disorder. Findings on the therapeutic impact of homework on outcome from the latter studies are limited in their generalizability to other client populations.

Research Findings

Nikolaos Kazantzis reviewed all research specifically designed to investigate whether homework improved therapeutic outcome. He suspected the reason several studies failed to find positive effects of homework on treatment outcome was that they had insufficient power in their analyses. Power, as it relates to research, has to do with the chances that a particular study will detect the effect of the variable of interest. In this case, that variable is the effect of homework on treatment outcome. Factors that influence power include the number of participants in the study, the actual size of the effect, and the threshold probability level set by the experimenter that determines whether or not a finding is significant. A power analysis on 27 studies with either significant or nonsignificant findings determined that on average, studies conducted between 1980 and 1998 had insufficient power to detect treatment effects. Average power to detect small effects was .11, meaning that researchers had only an 11% chance of detecting a small treatment effect. The average power was .44 for detecting medium effects and .71 for large effects. The generally followed guideline established by Jacob Cohen is to ensure one's power level is .80 or greater before conducting a study, giving a researcher at least an 80% chance of detecting a medium existing effect.

Kazantzis later conducted a meta-analysis on these 27 studies to determine the overall finding of studies investigating homework effectiveness. Based on his analysis of the reports, he determined the size of the effect of homework on therapeutic outcome to be .36. Although this effect is in the small to medium range, it still means that the incorporation of homework into therapeutic practice has a real and measurable positive effect on the client's outcome. Kazantzis's analysis of studies that utilized a correlational design calculated the effect size for the relationship between homework compliance and treatment outcome as .22. He also examined moderating variables, such as types of homework, assessment techniques, and types of samples selected. However, he could not confidently conclude that these variables significantly impacted the relationship between homework assignment and therapeutic outcome. The results of this meta-analysis lend great confidence to the notion that the use of homework has an impact on the extent to which clients improve in therapy.

RELEVANT TARGET POPULATIONS

There are virtually no restrictions on the application of homework in therapy. Guidelines for using homework as a therapeutic technique for a wide range of diagnoses and client populations exist within the treatment literature base. Specific guidelines for homework assignment have been suggested for a wide range of client conditions and problems, including mood disturbances, specific phobias, generalized anxiety disorder, social phobia, panic disorder, posttraumatic stress disorder, alcohol dependence, body image disturbances, delusions and hallucinations, Tourette's disorder, social skills deficits, loneliness, and personality disorders. Guidelines have also focused on designing homework techniques for specific client populations, such as children and adolescents, older adults, and clients receiving marital or family therapy.

CONSIDERATIONS

Planning and client preparation in the assignment of homework are crucial. Client understanding of and compliance with homework are goals that can require development of skills. Assignments that are relevant, practical, and understood by the client are more likely to be accepted and completed. To optimize levels of client compliance, several considerations must be made by the therapist when designing and presenting homework assignments.

Before assigning homework to a particular client, the therapist should consider individual client variables that will impact the nature of potential assignments and affect homework compliance. The therapist must be sensitive to client characteristics, such as cultural background, religious beliefs, and socioeconomic status, in order to ensure the homework assignment is appropriate within these contexts. For example, a therapist designing homework to increase a client's level of assertiveness must be aware and respectful of that client's cultural background, especially if a culturally based value is held that group cooperation is more important than individual autonomy.

The therapist should evaluate whether or not potential homework assignments are directly relevant to the particular client's treatment goals. The therapist is responsible for providing a clear rationale to the client

as to the purpose of each assignment. If a clear association between an assignment and the client's therapeutic goals is made, the client is more likely to value assignment completion. It is also important for the client to have the opportunity to negotiate the terms of each assignment, so that the final assignment reflects a collaborative effort and is agreeable to both parties.

Finally, it is important for the therapist to frame the attempt of the client to complete homework assignments as clinically useful regardless of whether or not the client succeeds or fails in this attempt. Homework assignments with unsuccessful outcomes can be viewed as learning opportunities for both client and therapist and can lead to the adjustment of future assignments based upon client feedback. It is important that the therapist consistently reinforce attempts made by the client to complete assignments, as this will increase the likelihood of future homework compliance.

CASE ILLUSTRATION

"Josie" was a 22-year-old college undergraduate who crashed her SUV, resulting in the death of "Sally," a passenger who was her best friend. She developed posttraumatic stress disorder, including phobic avoidance of driving, panic reactions while riding in cars, flashbacks of the accident, intense guilt, and several other problems. Resulting social and academic performance impairments led her to seek help. We used progressive muscle relaxation training (PMR) and both imaginal and in vivo exposure to reduce her anxiety and fears, and we used cognitive restructuring and exposure to reduce her guilt.

In the initial session, we explained that homework assignments were critical to rapid improvement and that they would serve two roles. First, self-monitoring of avoidance and guilt-related thoughts would help us understand the content of her problems and the behavior chains that led to them. Second, practicing procedures and skills learned in therapy in the context of her everyday life would extend her treatment throughout the week and to the environments where she most needed help.

Josie liked the collaborative structure of this treatment approach. Following a comprehensive assessment of problems, including a structured clinical interview and a test of her anxiety when encouraged to drive a short distance and while riding in a car as a passenger, we taught her PMR in the first session. We also showed her how to make an A-B-C diary of her guilt-related thoughts, with the A's (antecedents), B's (behaviors), and C's (consequences) representing any thoughts, feelings, situations, or behaviors that occurred before, during, and after her intense guilt episodes. We gave her an A-B-C form and, by getting a description of her last guilt experience, guided her to fill this in as a practice example. She described that upon seeing Sally's boyfriend, she told herself she was to blame, cried, and wished she had pulled over for the cell phone call that led to the crash. Her first homework assignment was to record in her A-B-C diary twice a day and to practice PMR in her dorm room using the audiotaped recording made in the session to guide her. As agreed, we phoned Josie 2 days later to assess her homework progress and problems. She revealed that she had trouble with PMR practice in the dorm with her noisy roommate, so we guided her in problem solving, and she arrived at using a small library study room.

For the second and subsequent sessions, we reviewed her homework at the start of each session and gave her assignments at the end. Her diary showed that guilt episodes occurred when she ran into friends of Sally, and this was resulting in her avoidance of their mutual friends. This information led us to role-play a dialogue with Sally's friends, and, by reversing roles, Josie began to perceive the possibility that these friends could have support for her rather than anger. Her homework for this issue then became challenging her self-blame thoughts and setting small steps toward actively approaching these people and engaging them in conversation instead of running away.

Homework following up on the imaginal exposure in sessions consisted of two forms of self-exposure. One form was for Josie to continue to imagine herself in the crash whenever she had intrusive thoughts about it in her bed at night, instead of trying to avoid these thoughts. A second form was graduated self-exposure to driving in which she would drive her new SUV for increasingly longer distances. In later sessions, after driving was easier, we modified her assignments by suggesting that she drive increasingly closer to the accident scene. For all of these homework assignments, we negotiated how much Josie would attempt to do on her own, and we often had to reduce the excessive demands she placed on herself in session in order to limit her failure experiences. With achievable homework goals, which Josie regularly met, we were able to routinely praise her accomplishments.

When Josie had shown considerable improvement in all areas, we mutually terminated her treatment sessions. However, we gave her a final homework assignment; she was to try to generalize the concepts and procedures she learned in therapy to other aspects of her life.

—*Thomas W. Lombardo and Jessica J. Tracy*

See also: *Behavior Rehearsal (Vol. I); Behavioral Treatment in Natural Environments (Vol. I); Manualized Behavior Therapy (Vol. I)*

Suggested Readings

Addis, M. E., & Jacobson, N. S. (2002). A closer look at the treatment rationale and homework compliance in cognitive-behavioral therapy for depression. *Cognitive Therapy and Research, 24,* 313–326.

Coon, D. W., & Gallagher-Thompson, D. (2002). Encouraging homework completion among older adults in therapy. *Journal of Clinical Psychology, 58,* 549–563.

Dattilio, F. M. (2002). Homework assignments in couple and family therapy. *Journal of Clinical Psychology, 58,* 535–547.

Freeman, A., & Rosenfield, B. (2002). Modifying therapeutic homework for patients with personality disorders. *Journal of Clinical Psychology, 58,* 513–524.

Hudson, J. L., & Kendall, P.C. (2002). Showing you can do it: Homework in therapy for children and adolescents with anxiety disorders. *Journal of Clinical Psychology, 58,* 525–534.

Kazantzis, N. (1999). Psychologists' use of homework assignments in clinical practice. *Professional Psychology: Research and Practice, 30,* 581–585.

Kazantzis, N., Deane, F. P., & Ronan, K. R. (2000). Homework assignments in cognitive and behavioral therapy: A meta-analysis. *Clinical Psychology: Science and Practice, 7,* 189–202.

Kazantzis, N., & Lampropoulos, G. K. (2002). Reflecting on homework in psychotherapy: What can we conclude from research and experience? *Journal of Clinical Psychology, 58,* 577–585.

Schultheis, G. M. (1998). *Brief therapy homework planner.* New York: Wiley.

Tompkins, M. A. (2002). Guidelines for enhancing homework compliance. *Journal of Clinical Psychology, 58,* 565–576.

I

INFORMED CONSENT TO TREATMENT

DESCRIPTION OF THE STRATEGY

The doctrine of informed consent requires that a client be informed of potential benefits and risks of contemplated treatments, expected prognosis with and without treatment, and any possible alternative treatments, prior to entering treatment. Underlying the doctrine of informed consent is the principle of autonomy, the idea that a client's life and treatment should be self-determined.

Three elements are necessary for consent to be truly informed, and all three elements must be present for consent to be valid. The three elements are intelligence, knowledge, and voluntariness. *Intelligence*, sometimes referred to as competency, is defined as a client's legal capacity to comprehend and evaluate the specific information that is offered. Unless otherwise deemed by the courts, adults are considered legally competent to understand information and to make medical decisions concerning their health. Children, on the other hand, typically are not considered competent and cannot give valid informed consent. Instead, consent for treatment of a minor must be obtained from a legal guardian or parent. It should be noted that some state statutes recognize the mature-minor exception, granting the right to consent to treatment to minors near the age of majority or mature enough to understand and weigh treatment options.

Knowledge, the second element of valid consent, is defined as a client's ability to appreciate how the given treatment information applies to him or her specifically. Knowledge is not a presumed legal capacity to comprehend information, but instead must be assessed by the clinician with each individual client throughout treatment.

Voluntariness, the third element of valid consent, suggests that a client's consent may not be coerced or enticed by the treating agent. For example, clinicians may not promise miraculous cures, nor should they offer financial incentives for participating in treatment. Clinicians should also inform their clients that they may withdraw from treatment at any time. Finally, there are ethical constraints as to the extent to which a client can voluntarily consent. For example, a therapist cannot justify sexual acts with a client by claiming that the client voluntarily agreed to these acts as part of treatment.

LEGAL AND ETHICAL BASES OF INFORMED CONSENT

Initially, informed consent was a legal concept applying only to physicians and surgeons, requiring doctors to tell patients the type of treatment recommended. Within the medical community, the concept eventually was expanded in scope, requiring physicians to provide information about all available treatments so that patients could make educated decisions as to whether to accept a particular form of treatment. Largely because psychotherapeutic techniques lack the physical invasiveness inherent in surgery and many other medical procedures, informed consent initially was not required for psychotherapy. However, as psychotherapy increasingly has become accepted as a legitimate medical procedure by third-party payers and the law, legal requirements such as informed consent to treatment have been imposed on therapists to the same extent as on other health care providers.

Even prior to legal mandates, ethical codes developed by the American Psychological Association (APA) and the American Counseling Association (ACA) required clinicians to obtain informed consent for treatment. The overarching principles espoused in these ethical codes are that clinicians must consider each client's best interests, autonomy, and self-determination.

Failure to obtain informed consent from a client increases the risk of a civil lawsuit, an ethics complaint, or both. To win a suit based on a failure to obtain informed consent, the client must prove all of the following five points: (1) that the risks involved with a therapy should have been disclosed, (2) that the risks were not disclosed, (3) that the risks materialized, (4) that the materialized risks resulted in injury, and (5) that the client would not have accepted the therapy if he or she had known of the risks involved. It is true that such lawsuits are uncommon and difficult to prove currently. More frequently, clients file ethics complaints with state licensing boards, citing lack of voluntary consent or lack of sufficient information. Unlike civil lawsuits, no harm to the client need materialize. Instead, a psychologist will be found in violation of the ethics code if he or she neglected reasonable informed consent procedures.

HOW TO OBTAIN INFORMED CONSENT

Although legal requirements and ethical principles demand that clinicians obtain informed consent prior to treatment, exactly how much information should be provided to each client is unclear. Two major standards have been employed by the courts to determine whether a client has received adequate information prior to treatment. The first is called the *professional standard,* and it requires that the professional present the same amount of information to a client as other professionals in the community typically provide. The professional standard has been criticized for being somewhat paternalistic in that professionals determine the extent of the information provided to clients. The second standard is called the *reasonable client standard* and is the one preferred by both the courts and professionals currently. This standard requires professionals to give as much information as a reasonable client would need to make treatment decisions. The major problem with this standard is the difficulty

in quantifying the exact amount of information a reasonable client needs to make an informed decision. Within psychotherapy, no consensus has been reached as to the ideal amount of information to provide to each client. Most clinicians favor an individualized and ongoing process of informed consent.

Given the difficulty in predicting outcomes of psychotherapy, as well as the need to present complex information while developing rapport, clinicians should adopt a process model rather than an event model of obtaining informed consent. Ongoing discussions with clients throughout the treatment process are necessary to ensure that they have sufficient opportunities to ask questions and have information clarified. At the initiation of therapy, clinicians should provide general information on the nature of therapy, such as therapist qualifications, limits of confidentiality (e.g., mandated reporting of child abuse), and general client rights (e.g., right to withdraw from therapy at any time). Logistical information should also be given, such as scheduling practices and fee structures. Currently, there is a debate but no consensus on whether other types of information (e.g., financial incentives that might influence treatment recommendations) should be included in this initial discussion. All such information should be given at the beginning of the very first session, prior to obtaining potentially sensitive information, conducting assessments, or implementing any treatment techniques. Clinicians may want to employ a written information sheet that is read and signed by the client. If utilizing such a form, clinicians should ensure that it is written in plain language that is free of jargon or legalistic phrases. Whether or not a written form is used, any questions or discussions of information should be documented in a progress note to demonstrate client knowledge.

The informed consent process should continue each time specific treatments are proposed. When discussing treatment plans, clinicians should provide information on the purpose of the proposed treatment, any possible discomforts or harms, and any potential positive benefits. In addition, clients must be told about alternative treatments available and the possible risks and benefits of these treatments. Standard-of-care issues now dictate that clinicians employ empirically supported treatments. If a clinician decides to employ an unusual or experimental treatment, he or she should thoroughly document that the client has been fully informed about standard treatments as well as possible risks and benefits of the experimental treatment.

Finally, clients must be informed that "no treatment" is an option and must be informed of the possible consequences of opting out of treatment. Clinicians should carefully document in progress notes all discussions of treatment options.

It is likely that providing more information to clients reduces risk of exploitation of clients by informing them of rights and expectations. In addition, it is likely that utilizing informed consent procedures may align client and clinician expectations of therapy, resulting in a better therapy outcome as well as fewer lawsuits or ethical complaints for clinicians. Clearly, research on effects of informed consent procedures should be conducted.

—*Catherine Miller*

See also: *Behavior Therapy Theory (Vol. I); Electrical Aversion (Vol. I); Punishment (Vol. II)*

Suggested Readings

American Psychological Association. (2002). Ethical principles of psychologists and code of conduct. *American Psychologist, 57*(12), 1060–1073.

Appelbaum, P. S. (1997). Informed consent to psychotherapy: Recent developments. *Psychiatric Services, 48*, 445–446.

Beahrs, J. O., & Gutheil, T. G. (2001). Informed consent to psychotherapy. *American Journal of Psychiatry, 158*(1), 4–10.

Gross, B. H. (2001). Informed consent (for psychotherapeutic treatment). *Annals of the American Psychotherapy Association, 4*(5), 24.

Koocher, G. P., & Keith-Spiegel, P. (1998). *Ethics in psychology: Professional standards and cases* (2nd ed.). New York: Oxford University Press.

Miller, C. A. (2002). Informed consent. In M. Hersen & W. Sledge (Eds.), *Encyclopedia of psychotherapy* (pp. 17–24). New York: Academic Press.

Petrila, J. (2003). The emerging debate over the shape of informed consent: Can the doctrine bear the weight? *Behavioral Sciences and the Law, 21*, 121–133.

Zuckerman, E. L. (1997). *The paper office* (2nd ed.). New York: Guilford Press.

INSTRUCTIONS

DESCRIPTION OF THE STRATEGY

In the context of behavioral analysis, verbal and written instructions are utilized to facilitate positive behavioral change by describing or prompting desired behaviors that are likely to be rewarded. In this way, instructions serve as discriminative stimuli to signal which behaviors will receive desired consequences, when to initiate prompted actions, and how to complete the responses.

There are four instructional prompts commonly employed by most behavior analysts (i.e., verbal, environmental, physical, and behavioral). Each of these prompts may be used alone or in combination with the others. Verbal prompts are clearly stated statements indicating what the individual is expected to do and, ideally, when the response is to be performed (e.g., "Joe, grab the rake with your hand now"). Environmental prompts are cues in the environment that remind individuals to perform behaviors (e.g., a sign indicating that it is necessary to wash hands prior to working in a restaurant). Physical prompts (i.e., physical guidance) involve physical direction or assistance in performing desired behaviors (e.g., placing one's hands over an autistic person's self-abusive fist and gently guiding the hand back to his lap). Physical prompts are often used to teach self-help skills to individuals with developmental disabilities, such as teaching an adult who is both deaf and blind self-feeding skills by guiding the hand holding the utensil from the plate to her mouth. Finally, behavioral prompts involve the recognition of one behavior cuing the performance of another. For instance, a woman's cue to engage in relaxation exercises (e.g., deep breathing) may be recognition of her voice tone rising in anger.

Self-instructional therapy, developed by Donald Meichenbaum, is a cognitive instructional intervention that has demonstrated effectiveness in controlled-treatment outcome studies. In this method, the individual is taught to employ subvocal instructions that act to guide self-initiated behavior. There are several steps in this approach, including identification of stimuli (e.g., intoxicated spouse) and self-statements (e.g., "I'm scared") that produce stress, initiation of instructional self-statements to cope with the stressful situation (e.g., "I just need to get out of this room quietly when my husband isn't looking. I'm walking toward the door. I need to open the door softly"), and initiation of self-reinforcing statements when coping skills are successful (e.g., "I knew I could get to my friend's house safely. I did a great job, and I'm proud of myself").

RELEVANT TARGET POPULATIONS AND EXCEPTIONS

Instructional feedback may be used to facilitate community efforts (e.g., use of seatbelts, encouragement of recycling) and assist in the acquisition of skills that assist in the treatment of various clinical problems. For instance, an adult with attention-deficit hyperactivity disorder might be taught to utilize the self-instructional statement, "Stop," whenever an impulse to blurt out a question in college occurs. Similarly, substance-abusing adults can be taught to initiate self-statements that assist them in withdrawing from stimulus events that have been associated with drug use in the past (e.g., "I need to walk away from this dance club"). Instructions are also useful in teaching individuals to cope with stressful situations that would otherwise be overwhelming (e.g., using self-instructions to guide an individual through the requisite steps of a calculus problem during a major examination). In parent-training interventions targeting child misconduct, it is customary to teach parents methods of giving their children instructions that are likely to bring about increased compliance (e.g., using "please," giving only one or two instructions at a time, proper voice tone, keeping vocabulary age appropriate).

Although the use of instructions alone may assist in the acquisition of behavioral skills, studies have consistently indicated that the maintenance of behavior is dependent on its reinforcement. Indeed, if the individual does not perceive that the targeted behavior will be rewarded or the individual is incapable of executing the targeted behavior, instructions are likely to be ineffective.

COMPLICATIONS

If behavior is not changing in the desired direction or is not being performed consistently, in a behavior modification program, one of the first things to examine is use of prompts or instructions. Of course, instructions need to be succinct, clearly stated, specific, state when the request is expected to be performed, and reflect vocabulary that is understood by the individual. As indicated above, compliance to instructions is often dependent on the strength of the resulting reinforcement. If reinforcement is weak, the prompted behavior will often not occur or will be inconsistent with transient effects. Instructions are designed to initiate performance. Whether performance is sustained and behavior improves depends on the consequences that follow.

—*Brad C. Donohue*

See also: Direct Instruction (Vol. III); Feedback (Vol. II); Homework (Vol. I)

Suggested Readings

Kazdin, A. E. (1994). *Behavior modification in applied settings* (5th ed.). Pacific Grove, CA: Brooks/Cole.

Martin, G., & Pear, J. (1999). *Behavior modification: What it is and how to do it.* Upper Saddle River, NJ: Prentice Hall.

Spiegler, M. D., & Guevremont, D. C. (2003). Stimulus control and reinforcement therapy. In *Contemporary behavior therapy* (4th ed., pp. 113–120). Belmont, CA: Wadsworth.

INTENSIVE BEHAVIOR THERAPY UNIT

DESCRIPTION OF THE STRATEGY

The key component of the intensive behavior therapy unit (IBTU) is a weekly incentive program within a prison that monitors personal hygiene and grooming, sanitation, compliance with general rules, such as not engaging in assaultive behavior, and socialization activities. Appropriate compliance with these activities is recorded on a checklist that is completed on a daily basis by an officer who oversees the unit. Incentives are distributed or withheld based on each inmate/participant's performance and progress. The goal of IBTU is to promote prosocial behavior through external rewards, with the hope that the problematic behavior will eventually become extinguished as the inmate/participant comes to feel intrinsically rewarded by behaving in an appropriate manner.

Each IBTU inmate has a comprehensive behavioral plan (CBP) completed by the assigned IBTU counselor upon admission to the program. The CBP outlines the problem behaviors to be eliminated, as well as establishing baselines and setting long-term and short-term goals with target dates. The IBTU inmates are required to participate in community range meetings, socialization groups, activity therapy, individual counseling sessions in which self-monitoring is encouraged, CBP meetings, and monthly psychiatric rounds with the mental health team (psychiatrist, psychiatric nurse, and IBTU counselor).

The incentive component of the IBTU program rewards inmates on a weekly basis based on cumulative ratings by the unit officer, IBTU counselor, activity therapist, and another member of the treatment staff. The inmates are rated based on hygiene, sanitation, activity attendance, participation, and targeted behaviors. Points are given daily for each satisfactory hygiene and sanitation item, one point for courtesy and nondisruptive behavior, and one point for each day the inmate does not receive an infraction from the unit officer. Rewards include a predetermined amount of cigarettes, candy, chips, juice, or personal hygiene items depending on the total number of points they have accumulated by the end of the week.

IBTU consists of two levels, Level I and Level II. All participants enter as a Level II, which is the most restrictive level. The inmates remain on this level for a minimum of 3 to 5 weeks. Inmates on Level II are on room restriction and are supervised when they are out of their rooms. When Level II inmates are impulsive and unpredictable, their treatment plan states that they will be handcuffed when they are outside their rooms. Level II inmates are allowed one phone call per month, one hour of recreation Monday to Friday, and no visitation or store privileges. A significant period of stability in behavioral change is required for advancement to Level I. It is anticipated that behavior change will be followed by a period of consolidation of new skills. When inmates are promoted to Level I, they are on range restriction, which includes use of the phone and 2 hours of television privileges. If improvements in an inmate's behavior are not maintained while the inmate is on Level I, he or she will be demoted to Level II. A significant period of stability in behavioral change is required before an inmate will be promoted from IBTU.

RESEARCH BASIS

IBTU is a successful program because it is based on solid behavioral therapy techniques that originate in the clinical application of learning theory. It is a behavioral-contingency program that emphasizes self-reward and social reward. The contingencies aid in the participant learning the appropriate and desired behaviors.

RELEVANT TARGET POPULATIONS AND EXCEPTIONS

IBTU is currently for people who have a difficult time making it in prison. They are prisoners within the Georgia Department of Corrections, thus demonstrating that they have not been able to make it in society. Often, they display in prison behaviors similar to the ones they displayed in society. In addition, they are on the mental health caseload, meaning that they have been assessed to have some type of Axis I disorder or a severe Axis II personality disorder. Therefore, IBTU provides treatment in a structured therapeutic environment for mental health/mental retardation inmates who are unable to perform in a less restrictive environment. This unit provides programs, security, and individual behavioral plans in a controlled atmosphere that allows for behavior treatment plans to be implemented while security is also maintained.

The criteria for admission to IBTU includes those inmates who are presenting behaviors that are disturbing to themselves or disruptive to the community in which they live. Second, they have displayed longstanding problematic behavior that is resistant to the usual and customary attempts to assist inmates in containing their behavior. In addition, IBTU includes inmates who are unwilling or unable to participate in the usual program activities that are offered by the institution. Customary treatment services and disciplinary procedures should be utilized and exhausted prior to an IBTU referral.

COMPLICATIONS

The IBTU has a due process committee that oversees a prisoner's refusal to accept IBTU placement. If the committee finds reasonable grounds to adhere to the prisoner's refusal, the prisoner will not be eligible for any type of incentives and the refusal will be reflected on his or her parole review summary. In addition, it may be necessary for the inmate to be placed in lockdown for the "safety and security of the institution" if he or she is extremely aggressive or impulsively assaultive.

CASE ILLUSTRATIONS

In the case of "Julia," she was an inmate who was transferred from another institution due to her significant problematic behavior. She refused to keep up her personal hygiene by refusing to shower, refusing meals, and not keeping her room sanitary based on institutional standards, and she was extremely hostile and aggressive toward staff and other inmates. She had never been to prison before and also did not have a mental health diagnosis. Her weight dropped 20 pounds in a month and a half; therefore, she was evaluated and viewed as being psychotic and unable to care for herself. She was provided with a psychiatric intervention, a prolixin injection, due to being a danger to herself and others. Slowly, over the next few weeks, she began to participate in the IBTU program. Within

3 months, she was medication compliant, nonviolent, and kept her hygiene and sanitation requirements at the expected levels. She then graduated from the program and was able to comply with the rules and regulations of the institution.

In the case of "Jane," she was sentenced to prison and came in as a diagnostic inmate. The previous year, she had been a resident of a mental hospital. This inmate on a daily basis engaged in at least one extreme self-injurious behavior. Jane would throw herself down stairs, and cut her face and throat with glass in an attempt to gain attention from others. She also would swallow elongated objects, such as antennas, pens, spoons, and toothbrushes. Following several surgeries to remove these items, it was observed that she would constantly reopen and remove her sutures. A staffing was conducted, and it was determined that the best placement for her would be IBTU. While on the unit, she was placed on 24-hour camera observation to monitor self-injurious attempts. Behavioral interventions used included modeling, cuing for her to articulate her needs in an appropriate manner, and ignoring negative attention-seeking behaviors. Positive behaviors were rewarded with weekly incentives, verbal praise, and special activities, such as watching television. When her attention-seeking and self-injurious behaviors had subsided for 3 months, as a reinforcer, she was allowed to have her lights cut off at night and was not being subjected to 24-hour camera observation. After 10 months, she was promoted to a less restrictive environment, where no further incidents of the problematic behaviors resurfaced.

—*Javel Jackson*

See also: Applied Behavior Analysis (Vol. I); Behavioral Approaches to Schizophrenia (Vol. I); Token Economy (Vol. I)

Suggested Readings

Jacobson, N. (Ed.). (1987). *Psychotherapists in clinical practice: Cognitive and behavioral perspectives.* New York: Guilford Press.

Klein, S. (1987). *Learning: Principles and applications.* New York: McGraw-Hill.

Rachlin, H. (1976). *Introduction to modern behaviorism.* San Francisco: W. H. Freeman.

J

JOB CLUB METHOD

DESCRIPTION OF THE STRATEGY

The Job Club method utilizes the usual behavioral psychology format for skill acquisition, treating the job search as a sequence of skills to be learned, practiced, and performed under the supervision of the group counselor. The job seekers meet as a group of 6 to 12 persons, every day obtaining job leads, contacting potential employers, preparing resumés, rehearsing, telephoning, and so on until a job is obtained, with no limit in the number of sessions. Standard forms and scripts are provided and individualized for each person. The job seekers are taught to obtain their own job leads. The program provides assistance and instruction in the following areas: (a) supplies and services, (b) telephone, (c) scripts for telephone contacts, (d) sample letters to possible employers, (e) group support, (f) buddy system for individual support, (g) skill in uncovering unpublished job openings, (h) supervision in utilizing posted employment notices, (i) mutual transportation assistance, (j) interview rehearsal, (k) contacting one's family for support, (l) self-recording of job contact efforts as a progress motivator, (m) emphasis on communicating job-relevant personal/social skills in addition to job skills, (n) maintenance of a group listing of job openings uncovered by other group members, and (o) instruction in emphasizing job-related skills obtained apart from paid job experience.

The group counselor adopts the same style as is used in behavioral group therapy: positive, interactive, rehearsal, self-recording, obtaining significant-other support, modeling, written forms, group support, and a structured-session protocol. The group counselor follows a rotation format, speaking to each member for approximately 1 minute, giving praise for the evidence of appropriate search behaviors, as well as providing instructions regarding revisions or additional efforts to be made prior to the next contact by the counselor. The counselor directs the attention of other group members to notable successes of an individual, such as arranging several interviews for that afternoon.

Attendance occurs every day except when the member goes to an interview, each session being directed entirely to arranging these interviews. A self-recording "after-interview" checklist is filled out by the job seeker after each interview and reviewed by the counselor subsequently. The checklist lists the suggested desirable aspects of the interviewer's conduct (e.g., on time, appropriate dress, eye contact), describes one's relevant work experience, describes one's relevant positive and social attributes (e.g., a "team player," "takes responsibility," "willing to work overtime," "well-liked by fellow employees," etc.), arranges a "callback" within a week, and so on. The group meets for one half day each day, the remainder being taken up by the interviews arranged.

The method differs from most other methods of job finding instruction in the following respects: (1) the job seeker performs the job search in the session rather than searching after the session; (2) the method emphasizes uncovering job leads as yet unpublicized; (3) the emphasis is on personal contacts (relatives, friends, acquaintances) as the source of job leads versus formal job-opening listings; and (4) the program provides and/or assists with all aspects of the job search, including (a) typing of a resume; (b) photocopies; (c) postage;

(d) telephone availability; (e) transportation; (f) advice regarding dress appropriateness; (g) using each job lead contact to generate other job leads; (h) utilizing the personal information network; (i) utilizing the Yellow Pages as a major initial source of leads; and (j) providing relocation information when the local area has very severe unemployment, as in a one-industry town when that industry leaves.

In controlled-outcome studies comparing the Job Club method with normal job seeking, the average time taken to obtain a job by the Job Club members has been about 2 weeks. The average number of interviews before a job was obtained has been about 3 weeks. The usual percentage of successes has been in excess of 90%. Salaries have usually been higher than for those job seekers not in the Job Club condition. Retention has been excellent in that follow-up shows that the members find other jobs even if they leave the one initially obtained.

RESEARCH BASIS

The method has been evaluated in several controlled-outcome studies with randomly assigned control/comparison group job seekers and is one of the only methods of job placement to be evaluated in this manner. The results have consistently shown 90% or greater rate of full-time employment with diverse and extreme job-handicapped populations.

RELEVANT TARGET POPULATIONS AND EXCEPTIONS

The Job Club has been found effective for obtaining employment in different studies and reports with high school students, the elderly, the visually impaired, the intellectually handicapped, the chronically mentally ill, professionals, unskilled, semiskilled, hearing impaired, workforce programs, physically handicapped, welfare recipients, state hospital patients, halfway house and outpatient mental patients, alcoholics, drug addicts, those with psychiatric disorders, and criminal offenders and in several foreign countries.

The Job Club method also has been found empirically to decrease depression and to increase feelings of self-efficacy, indicating its value in improving one's psychological state as well as in obtaining employment.

The general assumption of this method is that everyone is potentially employable and therefore strives for 100% employment. Some clear exceptions seem to be the severe or profoundly retarded, the bedridden, and the severely psychotic, none of these having been reported as being attempted.

The most common setting for the Job Club is that of welfare programs of cities, states, and counties, which attempt to avoid welfare costs that would be necessary for the unemployed. Other settings are existing programs for the specific populations listed above, such as the elderly, mentally disturbed, colleges, ex-offenders, college graduates, and so on.

COMPLICATIONS

The Job Club method requires a group leader who is familiar with the component job-counseling procedures of the method. Also required is a facility with sufficient telephone, photocopying, and usual office resources. Contrary to a connotation of the "Job Club" name, the program is not a self-help or recreational endeavor. The most common problem seen in self-designated "Job Clubs" is the adoption of a support group format in which the members exchange thoughts and experiences about their current and past problems in obtaining employment. The Job Club format is the antithesis of this; the members spend their time in the sessions actively locating job leads and arranging interviews, rather than discussing past failures in doing so.

—*Nathan H. Azrin*

See also: *Applied Behavior Analysis (Vol. I); Azrin, Nathan H. (Vol. I); Homework (Vol. I)*

Suggested Readings

Azrin, N. H., & Besalel, V. A. (1980). *A Job Club counselor's manual: A behavioral approach to vocational counseling.* Austin, TX: Pro-Ed.

Azrin, N. H., & Philip, R. A. (1979). The Job Club method for the job-handicapped: A comparative outcome study. *Rehabilitation Counselors Bulletin, 25,* 144–155.

Azrin, N. H., Philips, R. A., Thienes-Hontos, P., & Besalel, V. A. (1980). A comparative evaluation of the Job Club program with welfare recipients. *Journal of Vocational Behavior, 16,* 133–145.

Elksnin, L. K., & Elksnin, N. (1991). The school counselor as job search facilitator: Increasing employment of handicapped students through job clubs. *School Counselor, 38,* 215–220.

Jacobs, E. (1984). A skills-oriented model facilitating employment among psychiatrically disabled persons. *Rehabilitation Counseling Bulletin, 28,* 87–96.

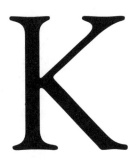

KANFER, FREDERICK H.

Frederick H. Kanfer was born on December 6, 1925, in Vienna, Austria, the only child of Oscar and Anna Kanfer. He lived in Vienna until 1938, when wartime conditions prompted the family to flee Austria. Enduring several years of hardship, the family eventually made their way to a new life in the United States.

EARLY INFLUENCES

Kanfer and his family settled in New York City, where he mastered English in high school and then pursued his interest in science and engineering at the Cooper Union School of Technology. As a result of America's involvement in the Second World War, Kanfer's schooling was again interrupted for 2 years, during which he served combat duty in the U.S. Army in Europe and the Pacific. Returning to New York after the war, Kanfer enrolled at Long Island University, earning a BS degree (cum laude) in 1948. Although Kanfer thought seriously about pursuing a medical degree, his abiding interest in the complexities of the human condition led him to psychology as a career. He entered the clinical psychology program at Indiana University in 1949, taking his master's degree in 1952 and his PhD in 1953. His experiences at Indiana strengthened and nurtured his interests in the principles of learning as a means of understanding human distress and dysfunctional action within a framework that was both precise and testable.

PROFESSIONAL HISTORY

Kanfer's first academic position was in the Department of Psychology at Washington University (1953–1957).

This was followed by professorships at Purdue University (1957–1962), the University of Oregon Medical School (1962–1969), the University of Cincinnati (1969–1973), and the University of Illinois at Urbana-Champaign, where he served as director of clinical training, became a university scholar in 1990, and an emeritus professor in 1995. In addition to his work in the United States, Kanfer's unique skills and broad humanitarian interests led him to play a major role in the development of clinical/behavioral psychology in Europe, particularly in Germany, where he engaged in collaborative research, program development, and clinical training. For example, he helped develop the first behaviorally oriented clinic in Germany in 1976.

PROFESSIONAL MODELS

Among his graduate school mentors, one whom he particularly admired was J. R. Kantor, whose "interbehavioral psychology" sought, among other things, to create a more seamless link between clinical theory and clinical practice, a cause that Kanfer championed and advanced throughout his career. His early work with George Saslow and Joseph Matarazzo was important in establishing the legitimacy of behavioral principles in psychiatry and of analogue laboratory research in clinical science.

MAJOR CONTRIBUTIONS TO THE FIELD

From the beginning of his career, Kanfer believed that the promise of behavioral theory for the clinical practice of psychotherapy lay in transcending the nonmentalistic stimulus response (S-R) theory of his day toward a fuller appreciation of the role of language and of the dynamic process by which clients can ultimately take control of and responsibility for the conduct of their lives: self-regulation. In a career spanning more than four decades, Kanfer pursued his dream of creating a richly textured, transactional model of human adaptation, adaptive disorder, and clinical intervention, a perspective he shared with students and colleagues in his 10 volumes (written in English, German, and Spanish), more than 150 articles, and countless consultations with colleagues around the globe.

Kanfer's contributions to behavior modification and cognitive behavior therapy fall roughly into three main areas: (1) behavioral assessment/diagnosis, (2) research into the mechanisms involved in self-regulation and self-control, and (3) delineation of the client and therapist skills needed to facilitate change and enhance the therapeutic alliance.

Behavioral Assessment

During his years at Oregon, Kanfer developed a unique and productive relationship with a senior colleague, the psychiatrist George Saslow. In 1965, the duo published a paper in the *Archives of General Psychiatry* on "behavioral diagnosis" that introduced a groundbreaking behavior-analytic alternative to traditional psychiatric classification. In this classic work, now familiar concepts, such as behavioral excesses and deficits, motivational assessment, and the need to contextualize the clinical decision-making process (in time, place, interpersonal settings, and cultural conditions), were articulated with force and clarity. In 1969, Kanfer and Saslow developed a seven-part history-taking and interview guide to aid clinicians in the functional assessment and remediation of problem behavior. In subsequent decades, Kanfer and his students and colleagues further refined and elaborated the behavior-analytic approach.

Self-Regulation and Self-Control

Kanfer's early work on verbal conditioning, conducted in collaboration with Matarazzo, Saslow, Albert Marston, Pryse Duerfeldt, and Jeanne Phillips, established the premise that verbal-ideational modification was central to long-term adjustment and that complex cognitive mechanisms would do their job most efficiently when the patient came to believe in himself or herself as the major agent of change. Ultimately, *self*-guidance would need to supplant external guidance. When, in 1970, Kanfer and Phillips published their highly influential text *Learning*

Foundations of Behavior Therapy, the empirical groundwork for a science of self-regulation was being effectively established. The Kanfer and Phillips volume, along with Albert Bandura's (1969) *Principles of Behavior Modification,* became the conceptual cornerstones of the cognitive-behavioral movement that was to flower in the 1970s and 1980s and inspire several generations of researchers and practitioners in psychology, social work, and education.

The 1970s and 1980s saw Kanfer and his associates (Paul Karoly, Larry Grimm, Sue Hagerman, Bruce Schefft, and others) apply his Skinnerian-inspired model of self-change under conditions of conflicting contingencies (i.e., *self-control*) to topics such as children's resistance to temptation (delay of gratification) and to child and adult tolerance of fearful or noxious stimulation. Moreover, the theoretical structure of the interplay between self-directedness and external mediation and its implication for the nature of personal freedom were topics that continually engaged Kanfer's attention, encouraging him to refine and expand his heuristic models over the years.

Therapist Skills and the Helping Process

Never the ivory-tower theoretician, Kanfer sought to develop conceptually based, testable, and teachable methods of clinical intervention. Many of his books, including the four editions of *Helping People Change* and the volume *Maximizing Treatment Gains* (both coedited with Arnold Goldstein); the German text *Selbsmanagement: Ein Lehrbuch fur die Klinische Praxis (Self-Management: A Textbook for Clinical Practice),* with his colleagues Dieter Schmelzer and Hans Reinecker; and his 1988 text, *Guiding the Process of Therapeutic Change* (with Bruce Schefft), were manuals for interpersonally and socially sensitive treatment. Kanfer's career and balance of contributions to science and practice attest to his lifelong commitment to the scientist-practitioner model.

—*Ruth Kanfer and Paul Karoly*

See also: Behavioral Assessment (Vol. I); Self-Management (Vol. I); Self-Monitoring (Vol. II)

KANTOR'S INTERBEHAVIORISM

MAJOR CONTRIBUTIONS TO THE FIELD

The intellectual movement that gave rise to behaviorism, the foundational perspective of behavior modification and cognitive behavior therapy, was based on the idea that it was possible to take a natural science approach to human psychological events. J. R. Kantor (1888–1984) worked to advance an objective science of psychology as an independent member of the family of natural sciences. Kantor offered an advanced form of behaviorism that contained little of the remnants of earlier thinking that troubled most other behavioral postulate systems. The greatest roadblocks to an authentic behavioral psychology have their basis in the dualistic position that separates behavioral occurrence into separate and distinct physical (or behavior) and mental (or psychological) components. Kantor provided a nondualistic psychology that incorporated the distinctly psychological components (e.g., emotive and cognitive events) into a framework that remained consistent with the dictate that the subject matter of science is always part of the natural world (i.e., spatiotemporal occurrence).

Behavior therapists (e.g., Cyril Franks) occasionally have argued that behavioral therapy's tendency to ignore philosophical and theoretical issues has hindered progress toward central goals such as professional practice that is soundly based on science. In answer, Kantor's interbehaviorism is a complete approach to behavior that begins with historical and philosophical analysis, proceeds through theoretical foundations for psychology, continues with analysis of scientific research operations, and ends up with postulates for applied work. In this way, interbehaviorism is very much consistent with the foundational behavior therapy position that theory and practice are interrelated and of equal importance and that behavior therapy is not merely a collection of deductively derived techniques or relegated to the arena of technological application.

Interbehaviorism is distinguished from other behavioral perspectives by its *field* (or *system*) orientation. Kantor argued that despite the many scientific advances associated with behaviorism, its failure to take more of a systemic perspective left it open to further emendation, adding the prefix *inter-* to behaviorism. This prefix was designed to communicate explicitly that behavior must always be described in system terms. Nonsystemic versions of behavioral theory rely on one or more versions of linear thinking and analysis. Examples include direct S→R conditioning, cognitive mediation in the form of S→cognition→R, and the Skinnerian three-term contingency of discriminative stimulus→operant response→consequence. In all of these cases, cause proceeds in

a linear and one-directional fashion to effect. Furthermore, this classic form of causal thinking underlies reductionist attempts to understand behavior, according to which biological structures and processes are independent causes of behavior.

Interbehaviorism's systemic approach to causality, on the other hand, is nonlinear. The empirical fact of temporal sequencing of events is not taken as prima facie evidence of linearity in the functional relations between events. For example, the fact that a distinctive stimulus compound is consistently followed by anxiety-like responses does not imply that the stimulus compound creates the subsequent response pattern and that knowledge of this relation is the end point of behavior analysis. Behavior therapists routinely adopt the nonlinearity principle, but their conventional nonsystemic behavioral frameworks fail to provide a coherent perspective from which to generally apply the principle of nonlinearity and to communicate it to trainees.

The core contribution of J. R. Kantor lies in his explicit advocacy of *field systems theory*. He argued that despite the many scientific advances associated with behaviorism, its lack of a systems character mandated further development. Kantor's term *interbehavior* was primarily designed to emphasize not only an isolated response to stimulus-function, but the multiplistic connections among organisms, organismic action, setting factors, and other relevant enabling and impeding conditions operative in a particular setting. In relation, the term *field* stems from Kantor's holistic approach to behavioral psychology and the assertion that the behavioral sciences must become increasingly ecological and contextually bound in analysis. In this regard, a field is interpreted as involving a thorough accounting of observable events that conceivably operate within a given setting. Adding the term *system* provides emphasis on the dynamic and reciprocal interaction of the many elements contained within a field. A systemic dimension accentuates the presence of at least two or more behaviors or events that share varying degrees of enabling or constraining influence on one another and consequently force the field system into a constant state of flux. An *interbehavioral field system,* therefore, is defined as a relatively unique, constantly changing, spatial and temporal confluence of multiple behavioral and setting events. This orientation also contributes to advocacy of an inductive research process, in which theory is defined as inductive integration of systemic observations. Psychology as a science has a long history of attempting deductively driven theoretical research. Examples include Pavlovian neurologizing of classical conditioning mechanisms, and Hull and like-minded learning theorists who spent a large portion of their scientific writing on theory construction and the empirical evaluation of hypotheses generated from these theories. Kantor's interbehaviorism indirectly promotes a construction of theory that begins with data collection, builds toward inductive integration, and only then becomes directive to more research. This approach is recommended not so much because it derives hypotheses, but because it illuminates where our current knowledge is insufficient.

To appreciate Kantor's interbehaviorism both evolutionally and in the context of its future viability, it is useful to summarize how scientific thinking has changed over the centuries.

HISTORICAL ANALYSIS

Historical analysis of scientific thought reveals three general stages. The first stage assumed that natural events acted under self-contained powers. During the time of Galileo, for example, the learned view was that there existed things that completely, inherently, and necessarily possess what was termed *Being*. Within this school of thought, theorists invoked various substances with unique and inherent properties to account for heat (e.g., caloric), combustion (phlogiston), light (ether), biological functioning (e.g., vital force and entelechy), and human psychological behavior (e.g., soul, spirit, and mind). This initial stage is referred to as substance theory, substance property, or a self-actional stage of scientific thought.

The second stage of scientific thought, linear mechanism, is associated with the advent of modern science. This stage retained substances; however, interpretation of natural phenomena was organized in terms of a defined force operating between unalterable objects. Newton's gravitational laws connecting the motion of the earth with the action of the sun are illustrative of this stage of thinking. Mechanism advanced the construct of energy as a substance that was basis for transformational descriptions—descriptions typically expressed using statistical and correlational procedures. Causal determinism and reductionism were characteristic of this stage, with the fundamental explanatory model illustrated by linear cause→effect.

Though linear mechanics continues to provide a dominant model for much scientific thinking and

application, the transition from classical mechanics to Maxwell's equations was a critical development toward the third stage of scientific thought. An illustration from physics provides an example. When explaining electrical charges, a mechanical theorist would attempt to describe the action of two electric charges only by concepts referring to the two charges themselves. However, a system (field) theorist finds it necessary to include the field between the two charges in order to understand them; the charges are components of a broader system.

DESCRIPTION OF INTERBEHAVIORISM

According to Kantor's system theory, the psychological event is a collection of things and conditions operating as a whole. It is not the reacting organism alone that makes up the event but also the stimulating things and conditions, as well as the setting factors. The system alternative to the terms *cause* and *effect* of traditional language is articulation of an entire set of conditions and that this set represents the cause of an event. Linearly acting determining cause is replaced by factor participation within the interbehavioral model. The systemic principle of participation, for example, means that biological conditions are not ultimate determiners even in cases heavily influenced by biology. Behavior therapists who have worked with senile dementia and schizophrenia, for example, know that biological factors are participants, not linear causes, in behavior, but a nonlinear perspective helps us to coherently and effectively confront the interrelations between different classes of factors that contribute to behavioral events.

Kantor added the prefix *inter-* to behaviorism to communicate that psychological events always comprise interdependent participating factors. Thus, a minimum of two variables is always involved, one pertaining to actions of organisms, the other to actions of at least one set of conditions with which the organism's actions are coordinated. However, a more complete conceptual description of the psychological event (PE) requires more factors, as specified by the equation:

$$PE = C(k, sf, rf, hi, st, md)$$

In this formulation, k symbolizes that all psychological events are unique, sf represents stimulus-function, rf stands for response-function, hi is the historical process through which the correlated sf and rf developed, st recognizes that sf←→rf coordinations always take place in particular settings and represents the medium by which the organism contacts the physiological and physical correlates of sf (e.g., light is a medium of contact for visual interactions), and C communicates that the PE consists of an entire system of interdependent factors.

In interbehavioral terms, a stimulus in the three-term equation posited by B. F. Skinner's *Behavior of Organisms* provides a discriminative stimulus setting an occasion for an opportunity to respond, while not mechanically impelling or causing the response. Next, a response is an instance of operant or choice-making behavior and not simply a reflex as a function of the presence of a stimulus. Finally, a consequence of a particular response is viewed as either a functionally reinforcing or punishing stimulus for responding. What remains missing to this model, according to Kantor, are (a) description and analysis of the larger system of behaviors and events operating around the three-term relationship under investigation that provide context and (b) the important time-based measures of those behavior and event occurrences that provide a functional and structural analysis of the contextual field of events. Taking an example from Morris, if you saw a man running down the streets of a particular city without the larger analysis that Kantor recommends—in other words, knowledge of the contextual and time-based meaning of the function and form of the behavior of running—the man could be running for a train, training for a run, or engaged in any other form of running behavior, with the behavior of running operating as a stimulus, response, or consequence to the larger contextual system of behaviors and related structural and topographic events in which it is operating.

Essentially, Kantor provided an alternative to the simple linear model of Skinner's three-term contingency to provide more complete and more accurate description and understanding of behavior in context. The term interbehavior makes explicit that it is the entire set of behavior and event conditions that are operative within a particular situation, and it is their reciprocal time-based interactions that provide analytic information as to what causes a particular behavior or event occurrence. Modeled another way, a systems approach provides the addition of a double-headed arrow to signify the bidirectional and interactional nature of stimulus ←→response relationships;

and the additional alphanumeric indicator for each portion of the three-term contingency, as illustrated below, is designed to highlight the view that multiple stimuli, responses, and consequences are operating within a particular field system:

$$1\text{-}n \quad 1\text{-}n \quad 1\text{-}n$$

STIMULUS ←→
RESPONSE ←→ CONSEQUENCE

The interbehaviorism of Kantor focuses on the mutually interdependent actions of an organism and a cue (stimulus, object, or signal). Instead of a simple one-directional sequence from signal to action separated by a period of time, focus is on the ongoing interactions over time among action and signal as they operate within, and are functionally and structurally impacted by, a larger system of behaviors and events.

According to Kantor, a field system is the totality of behaviors and events contained within a particular situation under study. A field system is dynamic and continuously changing and is considered relatively unique to each individual operating within a particular setting. A behavioral system under study at a given point in time is also characteristically dependent on previous systems and on the behavior and setting factors that have influenced individuals under study at previous points in time. Conceptually, Kantor's contributions make a distinction between the principles of demonstration and discovery as related to the experimental and applied analysis of behavior. Currently, the activity of discovery remains less well understood in both the philosophy of science and in behavior analysis methodology, largely due to the greater challenges when attempting to teach and to learn the principles of discovery. For example, discovering the complex set of conditions that control negatively impacting behavior in a marriage relationship and consequently altering those conditions toward long-lasting therapeutic ends may take more time and energy than simply demonstrating that a particular behavior change technique (e.g., time-out from marital interactions when conflict arises) may reduce the number and length of a particular undesirable behavior (e.g., episodes of marital conflict). Scientifically, teaching for discovery involves the challenging task of bringing professional caregiver behavior under the control of client behavior within particular situations. In other words, a Kantorian recommendation is designed to get professional caregivers to understand complex behavioral repertoires to the point of effectively choosing a particular set of behavioral interactions as a function of what a particular situation or clientele warrants, rather than simply demonstrating a particular treatment in a rule-governed manner or in some generalized sense as a function of having learned that particular treatment. This is what an interbehavioral methodology is designed to accomplish. In contrast, when operating within a demonstration orientation to behavior analysis, the behavior of the professional caregiver and the client need be demonstrated only as present or absent as a function of the presence or absence of a particular treatment in relative isolation from the larger system in which treatment and desired outcome operate. While a demonstration approach is time- and energy efficient in relation to applied behavior analysis research design, it is not always the approach most beneficial to an understanding, or effective use, of the complex form and function of particular behaviors that are operating in particular situations.

Operating within an interbehavioral framework also provides the opportunity to view the Skinnerian aim of causal prediction and control in a less austere and more inclusive manner. An interbehavioral framework makes explicit the position that all one can really attempt to accomplish is to describe in inclusive ways what may functionally impact on certain behaviors in certain situations, hence, relatively increasing or decreasing their probability of occurrence given a similar system of circumstances at some future point in time. This is a matter of methodological emphasis, in contrast to simply demonstrating in some isolated manner that a particular behavior or event causes the presence or absence of another without taking into account the larger system of behavior and event occurrences in which a demonstrated relationship operates.

The interbehavioral postulate that psychological events are always functional affairs at times is taken as self-evident to many behavior therapists. Indeed, functionality is the basis of Wolpe's early stimulus-response analysis, and others, such as Lazarus, pointed out how sometimes we had to remove structural blinders to identify the "why" of presenting complaints. However, in the absence of an overriding philosophical and theoretical orientation, structural analysis frequently obscures analysts' appreciation of the inherent functionality of psychological behavior.

For example, modification of the structure of response$\leftarrow\rightarrow$stimulus relations, as is promoted by manualized treatments, is to rely on actuarial structural-functional relations, a point not always stressed in presentations of treatment manuals. On the other hand, behavior therapists have long recommended flexible application of treatment manuals, in part, to effectively address functionality. It is likely that relaxation training's rate of decline as an uncritically applied structural-based intervention would have been accelerated if a behaviorism based on coordinations between stimulus-function and response-function had been more prominent.

CONTEMPORARY CONTRIBUTIONS

Perhaps the most significant contribution of interbehavioral psychology to adult behavior modification and cognitive behavior therapy has been its often unrecognized role in the very evolution of the discipline. In the first *Annual Review of Psychology* article on behavior therapy, Krasner noted that by the end of World War II, Kantor's work, along with that of others (e.g., J. S. Mill, Thorndike, Pavlov, Mowrer), had helped establish a "behavioristic" scientific psychology that would form the foundation for behavior therapy. One of the earliest applications of behavioral principles to a human behavior disorder was reported by Paul R. Fuller. Fuller's report of his work with a severely developmentally impaired adult was so unique when it appeared in an established experimental psychology journal; there were no outlets devoted to clinical behavioral work at the time (1949), and there would not be until many years later. In 1973, Fuller discussed the crucial role Kantor played in the groundbreaking work. Others who have made important contributions to behavior therapy have explicitly acknowledged Kantor's contribution to their work. This list includes B. F. Skinner, F. H. Kanfer, J. B. Rotter, S. W. Bijou, and R. G. Wahler. J. V. Brady, an experimentalist who has done noteworthy research related to behavioral pathology, has additionally shown how Kantor's approach to emotion can be effectively applied in the behavioral biology of emotion.

Two issues of great attention and importance have been how to handle what the "person on the street" refers to as "thoughts," and the associated cognitive and cognitive-behavioral movement. Goss documented how early behaviorists were considerably more sophisticated than is revealed in frequent pejorative presentations of Watson's views, and reviewed how Kantor, along with others, anticipated later developments in behavioral conceptualizations of complex behavior by means of verbal mediating responses and stimuli. Furthermore, interbehaviorism anticipated the movement in cognitive behavior therapy from rationalist therapies (based on linear mechanism) to constructivist therapies. Systemic theory provides the fundamental assumptions of the latter (e.g., systemic causality, embodied mind).

One of the factors in Kantor's systemic psychological event is setting. This recognizes that functional behavior is always situated or contextualized. In practice, setting factors are relatively long-term intra-organismic and extraorganismic conditions. The chemical state of the behavior's body, a recently completed verbal dispute, and concurrent social circumstances are common examples of conditions that can function as setting factors to thereby modulate stimulus-function and response-function coordinations. Like many of Kantor's other ideas, psychologists from time to time have not doubted that context is important. But interbehaviorism supplies an organized framework for including context, as demonstrated by how Wahler incorporated setting factors into clinical work with families.

Although sometimes overlooked, behavior therapy has long endorsed self-management as the goal of therapy and at least implicitly thereby recognized behavior as inherently under self-control as opposed to external regulation. Self-regulation is inherent in the system outlook. This contrasts with how linear mechanism handles behavior control. According to the cause→effect model of mechanism, control is one-way, from cause to effect. Stimulus→response psychology is a faithful translation of such thinking: Response (behavior) is caused by an independent agent (e.g., environmental stimulus, biological state). In the systemic approach, control is intrasystemic, which means one part of a system does not cause other parts because the system comprises interdependent components. This possibly abstruse idea to some is actually taken into account whenever the behavior therapist asks how the behavior of the client contributes to his or her plight—which may appear to be out of the individual's control.

Kantor's systemic behaviorism goes far toward providing an organized framework for another aspect of behavior that is obvious to clinicians but is difficult to reconcile with linear mechanism. This is the observation that responses are organized and interdependent, not independent. Responses show patterned, nonrandom relations when two or more are measured over the same time period or over different time windows. It is the functional interdependence of responses that underlies event relations that are labeled *symptom substitution*. The fact that artificial restraints (of whatever form) on one-response topography are followed by occurrences of collateral responses follows from the systemic and functional nature of behavior organization. Response patterns or response covariation reflect the systemic nature of behavior at the level of the behaver's action component. This is in line with movement away from a linear approach in which possible experimental solutions to an immediate concern are sought through examination of a very limited number of treatment and measurement variables, with scientific results temporally and contextually constricted and overlooking potentially functional systemic interdependencies among behaviors and events.

Standards of practice in behavior therapy call for assessment in three channels whenever possible. Measurement in domains of the overt motoric, physiological, and self-descriptive is a step toward taking into account the systemic nature of behavior. However, the interbehavioral perspective points to a greatly expanded approach to assessment to address the multivariate and dynamic nature of behavior. Systemic assessment does not force behavior into the linear independent-variable→dependent-variable model provided by mechanism. Instead, the behavior-system-oriented clinician adopts methods to the need to assess multiple interacting events in real time. The goal of behavioral systems analysis is to detect predictable patterns in covariations of events over the same time period and in event transitions across time. Statistical-mathematical models continue to be developed and scientifically accepted to facilitate this type of analysis, including Markov chain analysis, information theory, cross-spectral analysis, grammatical inference, lag-sequential analysis, and the most frequently used sequential behavior analysis. Such dynamic multievent analysis can be extremely labor-intensive and expensive. However, as event recording and analysis technology advances, we are witnessing increased applications of time-based, multievent methodology in family therapy, marital therapy, behavioral medicine, interpersonal skill therapy, and anxiety disorders. A recent text by Sharpe and Koperwas, for example, *Behavior and Sequential*

Analysis: Principles and Practice, traces the authors' route from interbehavioral theory to data collection and analysis procedures, and to consequent application of data in professional training and clinical activity.

Social, educational, and psychological scientists are now regularly contributing to respective scientific literatures in relation to the systems character of behavior over time. These contributions have been categorized under a variety of terms to include dyadic interaction, interactional rhythms, structural linguistics, systems theory, concurrency analysis, ecobehavioral analysis, and behavioral systems analysis. Examples of application are also found in the physical sciences and in cybernetic theory. Productive use of behavior systems analysis includes applications in family therapy and marital interaction, clinical psychology, school psychology, and health delivery services; general interpersonal skills; and animal communication. Sequential and systems-oriented methods have been used in each of these disciplines to produce scientific information that has served to better train a variety of professionals toward effective practice and to have a positive impact on the clients served by those trained professionals. Although much remains in the statistical development and validation of interbehavioral analyses as rigorous research methods, many contemporary behavioral scientists agree that such methods provide meaningful insights into the organization, structure, and function of complex interactive behavior patterns among multiple individuals.

Kantor provides an important theoretical foundation and related descriptive-analytic perspective to the analysis of behavior to which many contemporary scientists subscribe. To Kantor, the Skinnerian three-term contingency relationship model needed further measurement development, with his major contribution being the recommendation to measure behavior and event occurrences according to the time-based functional and structural system in which they operated. Some remain concerned about behavior therapy because of its roots in science. Cultural tradition places science and human behavior in different categories, a division that can appear to be reinforced when behavior therapists highlight the importance of behavior principles derived from nonhuman research. Delprato has shown how interbehaviorism is an authentic humanism, a point that might help counter claims that behaviorism conflicts with the human experience, and Kantor has provided a set of theoretical principles upon which contemporary scientists may rely when integrating an interbehavioral approach to research and practice.

—*Tom Sharpe and Dennis J. Delprato*

See also: *Behavior Therapy (Vol. II); Behavior Therapy Theory (Vol. I); Skinner, Burrhus Frederic (Vol. I)*

Suggested Readings

Bakeman, R., & Gottman, J. M. (1997). *Observing interaction: An introduction to sequential analysis* (2nd ed.). New York: Cambridge University Press.

Brady, J. V. (1975). Toward a behavioral biology of emotion. In L. Levi (Ed.), *Emotions—Their parameters and measurement* (pp. 17–45). New York: Raven Press.

Delprato, D. J. (1995). Interbehavioral psychology: Critical, systematic, and integrative approach to clinical services. In W. O'Donohue & L. Krasner (Eds.), *Theories of behavior therapy: Exploring behavior change* (pp. 609–636). Washington, DC: American Psychological Association.

Delprato, D. J. (2003). J. R. Kantor's interbehavioral psychology and humanism. *The Psychological Record, 53,* 3–14.

Einstein, A., & Infeld, L. (1938). *The evolution of physics.* New York: Simon & Schuster.

Franks, C. M. (1998). Forward: The importance of being theoretical. In J. J. Plaud & G. H. Eifert (Eds.), *From behavior theory to behavior therapy* (pp. ix–vxiii). Boston: Allyn & Bacon.

Fuller, P. R. (1973). Professors Kantor and Skinner: The "grand alliance" of the 40's. *The Psychological Record, 23,* 318–324.

Goss, A. E. (1961). Early behaviorism and verbal mediating responses. *American Psychologist, 16,* 285–298.

Kantor, J. R. (1953). *The logic of modern science.* Chicago: Principia Press.

Kantor, J. R. (1959). *Interbehavioral psychology.* Granville, OH: Principia Press.

Kantor, J. R. (1969). *The scientific evolution of psychology* (Vol. 2). Chicago: Principia Press.

Kantor, J. R., & Smith, N. W. (1975). *The science of psychology: An interbehavioral survey.* Chicago: Principia Press.

Krasner, L. (1971). Behavior therapy. *Annual Review of Psychology, 22,* 483–532.

Morris, E. K. (1992). The aim, progress, and evolution of behavior analysis. *The Behavior Analyst, 15,* 3–29.

Ray, R. D., & Delprato, D. J. (1989). Behavioral systems analysis: Methodological strategies and tactics. *Behavioral Science, 34,* 81–112.

Sharpe, T. L., & Koperwas, J. (2003). *Behavior and sequential analyses: Principles and practice.* Thousand Oaks, CA: Sage.

Skinner, B. F. (1938). *The behavior of organisms.* New York: Appleton-Century-Crofts.

Wahler, R. G., & Dumas, J. E. (1989). Attentional problems in dysfunctional mother-child interactions: An interbehavioral model. *Psychological Bulletin, 105,* 116–130.

Wampold, B. E. (1992). The intensive examination of social interactions. In T. R. Kratochwill & J. R. Levin (Eds.), *Single-case research design and analysis: New directions for psychology and education* (pp. 93–131). Hillsdale, NJ: Erlbaum.

KAZDIN, ALAN E.

I was born in Cincinnati, Ohio, in 1945. I completed my BA at San Jose State University in 1967 and received my doctorate in psychology (clinical/experimental psychopathology) from Northwestern University in 1970, where I remained as an assistant professor for 1 year. In 1971, I took a position as assistant professor of psychology at Pennsylvania State University, where I remained until 1979. In 1980, I became professor of child psychiatry at the University of Pittsburgh School of Medicine, where I directed an inpatient treatment service for disturbed children. In 1989, I moved to Yale University, where I have been professor and chairman of psychology and director of the Yale Child Conduct Clinic, an outpatient treatment service for children and families. In 2000, I became John M. Musser Professor of Psychology. In 2002, I assumed the position of chair, department of child psychiatry and director of the Child Study Center at Yale University School of Medicine. The Child Study Center is the only freestanding department of child psychiatry in the United States.

From 1974 through 1978, I worked on a project commissioned by the National Academy of Sciences to document the evolution of scientific findings and theoretical approaches leading to the development of behavior modification. The product was published in a book, *History of Behavior Modification: Experimental Foundations of Contemporary Research* (1978). This was the only large-scale historical effort to chart the development of behavioral modification. In 1977 to 1978, I spent a year at the Center for Advanced Study in the Behavioral Sciences (Stanford, CA) and collaborated with a group of colleagues (Stewart Agras, Nathan Azrin, Walter Mischel, Stanley Rachman, and G. Terence Wilson) on the status, accomplishments, and limitations of behavior therapy. Two of the products of this collaboration were *Evaluation of Behavior Therapy: Issues, Evidence, and Research Strategies* (1978) and *Behavior Therapy: Toward an Applied Clinical Science* (1979).

I have served as editor for a number of professional journals, including *Behavior Therapy* (1979–1983), *Journal of Consulting and Clinical Psychology* (1985–1990), *Psychological Assessment* (1989–1991), *Clinical Psychology: Science and Practice* (1994–1998), and *Current Directions in Psychological Science* (1999–present). I have served on the board of editors of more than 40 journals. I have also edited an annual book series on *Advances in Clinical Child Psychology* (1977–1992, with Benjamin Lahey) and a book series, *Developmental Clinical Psychology and Psychiatry* (1983–2002). In addition, I was editor in chief of the *Encyclopedia of Psychology* (2000), an eight-volume work under the auspices of Oxford University Press and the American Psychological Association. Currently, I edit a book series, *Current Perspectives in Psychology*, for Yale University Press.

I have received several honors: a Research Scientist Award and a MERIT Award from the National Institute of Mental Health; Award for Distinguished Scientific Contribution to Clinical Psychology (1992), Award for Distinguished Professional Contribution to Clinical Child Psychology (1995), and a Distinguished Scientist Award (1999) from the American Psychological Association; and an Award for Outstanding Research Contribution by an Individual (1998) from the Association for Advancement of Behavior Therapy. I have served as President for the Association for Advancement of Behavior Therapy (1977–1978).

My research has focused primarily on the development of behavioral and cognitive-behavioral interventions. During my graduate training, I worked in a treatment and rehabilitation facility for emotionally disturbed and mentally retarded children, adolescents, and adults and was given the task to develop interventions. This contributed to my interest in behavioral interventions in home, school, institutions, and the community at large. This interest was reflected in subsequent writings, including *The Token Economy* (1977) and *Behavior Modification in Applied Settings* (6th ed., 2001).

At Pennsylvania State University, my research focused on interventions for children in the schools and institutions for the mentally retarded and for adults with social withdrawal and anxiety. When I moved to the University of Pittsburgh School of Medicine, my research focused more exclusively on childhood psychopathology. I began a series of studies on depression and antisocial behavior in clinically referred youths. The studies led to additional work on suicidality, hopelessness, child abuse, fire setting, and anxiety disorders.

The majority of my work has focused on treatment of aggressive and antisocial children referred for inpatient or outpatient treatment. This work has spanned a period of approximately 20 years. A series of studies evaluated the effectiveness of problem-solving skills training and parent management training with children (aged 2–13), the factors that contribute to therapeutic change, models of delivering treatment to optimize treatment effectiveness, and the processes through which change occur. Among the main findings are that variants of treatment produce clinically important change in such children at home and at school and those factors predict treatment outcomes, including severity and scope of child dysfunction, parent psychopathology stress, and socioeconomic disadvantage. Several factors that influence outcome, including parent perceptions of treatment, parent relationships with the therapist, and stress during the course of treatment, are of special interest because efforts to address these in therapy are likely to influence participation in and adherence to treatment and clinical outcomes. My writings have focused on evaluation of child and adolescent psychotherapy more broadly, including recent works lamenting the paucity of theory, the endless proliferation of unevaluated treatments (550+), and the need for different ways of conducting treatment research. These are outlined in papers and a book, *Psychotherapy for Children and Adolescents: Directions for Research and Practice* (2000), and *Evidence-Based Psychotherapies for Children and Adolescents* (2003), coedited with John Weisz.

Over the years, my writings and research program have generated more than 500 publications, including more than 35 authored or edited books. Many of these writings have focused on methodology and research design. During graduate training, I imprinted on the notion that the answers to critical research questions depend quite heavily on the methods and statistics used to evaluate them. My writings have attempted to elaborate the practices, methods, and foibles of the ways in which research is planned, executed, and reported. This emphasis is illustrated in *Single-Case*

Research Designs: Methods for Clinical and Applied Settings (1982), *Research Design in Clinical Psychology* (4th ed., 2003), and *Methodological Issues and Strategies in Clinical Research* (3rd ed., 2003). My contributions reflect the melding of intervention research with these interests in evaluation methodology more generally. Key to this is my emphasis on the importance of evaluation in intervention work, whether in research or clinical practice.

—Alan E. Kazdin

See also: *Applied Behavior Analysis (Vol. II); Association for Advancement of Behavior Therapy (Vol. I); Behavioral Assessment (Vol. III)*

Suggested Readings

Agras, W. S., Kazdin, A. E., & Wilson, G. T. (1979). *Behavior therapy: Toward an applied clinical science*. San Francisco: W. H. Freeman.

Kazdin, A. E. (1977). *The token economy: A review and evaluation*. New York: Plenum Press.

Kazdin, A. E. (1978). *History of behavior modification: Experimental foundations of contemporary research*. Baltimore: University Park Press.

Kazdin, A. E. (1982). *Single-case research designs: Methods for clinical and applied settings*. New York: Oxford University Press.

Kazdin, A. E. (Ed.). (2000). *The encyclopedia of psychology* (Vols. 1–8). New York/Washington, DC: Oxford University Press/American Psychological Association.

Kazdin, A. E. (2000). *Psychotherapy for children and adolescents: Directions for research and practice*. New York: Oxford University Press.

Kazdin, A. E. (2001). *Behavior modification in applied settings* (6th ed.). Belmont, CA: Wadsworth/Thomson Learning.

Kazdin, A. E. (Ed.). (2003). *Methodological issues and strategies in clinical research* (3rd ed.). Washington, DC: American Psychological Association.

Kazdin, A. E. (2003). *Research design in clinical psychology* (4th ed.). Needham Heights, MA: Allyn & Bacon.

Kazdin, A. E., & Weisz, J. R. (Eds.). (2003). *Evidence-based psychotherapies for children and adolescents*. New York: Guilford Press.

Kazdin, A. E., & Wilson, G. T. (1978). *Evaluation of behavior therapy: Issues, evidence, and research strategies*. Cambridge, MA: Ballinger.

LAZARUS, ARNOLD A.

I was born on January 27, 1932, in Johannesburg, South Africa. The youngest of four children, I attended the University of the Witwatersrand, where I majored in psychology and sociology and went on to receive a PhD in clinical psychology in 1960. I went into full-time private practice and was a part-time lecturer at the Witwatersrand Medical School in Johannesburg.

In 1963, I accepted an invitation from the Department of Psychology at Stanford University and joined their faculty as a visiting assistant professor. With my wife, Daphne (whom I married in 1956), I journeyed to California with our two children, Linda, then aged 4, and Clifford, aged 2. We all returned to South Africa in 1964, where I returned to my private practice and part-time teaching position. With my nuclear family, I subsequently immigrated to the United States in 1966, when I was appointed director of the Behavior Therapy Institute in Sausalito, California. In 1967, I joined the faculty of Temple University Medical School as a full professor. In 1970 to 1972, I was a visiting professor at Yale University and director of Clinical Training, and in 1972, I accepted an offer from Rutgers University, where I received the rank of distinguished professor of psychology. I taught there from 1972 to 1998 and then retired as a distinguished professor emeritus of psychology. In addition to my private practice, I now work with my son, Clifford N. Lazarus, PhD, director of Comprehensive Psychological Services in Princeton, New Jersey. Father and son are also developing a Center for Multimodal Psychological Services.

As former president of several professional associations and societies, I have received many honors and awards for my contributions to clinical theory and therapy. These include the Distinguished Psychologist Award from American Psychological Association's (APA) Division of Psychotherapy, the Distinguished Professional Contributions Award from APA's Division of Clinical Psychology, the Distinguished Service Award from the American Board of Professional Psychology, and two Lifetime Achievement Awards, one from the California Psychological Association and the other from the Association for Advancement of Behavior Therapy. I am also the recipient of the first Annual Cummings PSYCHE Award. This honor, in addition to a $50,000 tax-free prize, included a bronze statue of the Greek goddess Psyche and a large framed calligraphy certificate outlining my many contributions. I have been inducted, as a charter member, into the National Academies of Practice as a Distinguished Practitioner in Psychology.

With 18 books and more than 300 professional and scientific articles to my credit, I am widely recognized as an international authority on effective and efficient psychotherapy and have given innumerable talks and workshops both here and abroad. In addition to my academic and scholarly activities, as a licensed psychologist and a diplomate of the American Board of Professional Psychology, I have maintained an active psychotherapy practice since 1959.

I coined the terms "behavior therapy" and "behavior therapist," which first appeared in a professional publication in 1958, and went on to innovate and develop many behavior therapy techniques. Professor Cyril M.

Franks, who founded the Association for Advancement of Behavior Therapy, described my broad-based, multi-modal orientation as "behavior therapy in one of its most advanced forms."

One of my current interests is in examining the impact of licensing boards and ethics committees. This concern was spawned circa 1993, when two of my colleagues were severely censured by state licensing boards for transcending minor boundaries. I also grew alarmed when some of my students helpfully went beyond the call of duty on behalf of some of their clients and were reprimanded by authoritarian supervisors for "stepping outside accepted boundaries." I have published several articles and coedited a book on the benefits that can accrue when certain boundaries are transcended. I have been serving as an expert witness in court cases involving colleagues whom I feel have been unfairly rebuked.

"Arnold Allan Lazarus" is listed in *Who's Who in America* and in *Who's Who in The World.*

—*Arnold A. Lazarus*

See also: Multimodal Behavior Therapy (Vol. I); Systematic Desensitization (Vol. I); Wolpe, Joseph (Vol. I)

LEWINSOHN, PETER M.

I was born in Berlin, Germany, in 1930. With my parents and my brother, Tom, I immigrated to Shanghai, China in 1941, where I lived throughout World War II. I then immigrated to the United States in 1947. After I received my BS from Allegheny College in 1951, I went on to obtain a doctoral degree from the Johns Hopkins University in 1955. Six years later, I received my diploma in clinical psychology from the American Board of Examiners in Professional Psychology. While I completed postdoctoral training at the Philadelphia Child Guidance Clinic between 1958 and 1959, I met my future wife, Cynthia Stiefel. We were married and have two sons, David and Mark, and are now the proud grandparents of five grandchildren.

I served on the clinical staff of numerous organizations, including the State Hospital in Osowatomie, Kansas, the Eastern Pennsylvania Psychiatric Institute, St. Christopher's Hospital for Children, and LaRue D. Carter Memorial Hospital in Indianapolis, Indiana, where I remained until 1963. Throughout my career, I have been a faculty member of various educational institutions, including the Department of Psychiatry at the Indiana University Medical School, the Department of Psychology at the Southern Illinois University, and the Department of Psychology at the University of Oregon. I am currently professor emeritus of psychology at the University of Oregon and an Adjunct Professor of Psychiatry at the Oregon Health and Science University.

Issues with significant clinical relevance have encompassed my research interests. My first study, published in 1956, dealt with psychosomatic disorders, and subsequent works include the creation of the Pleasant Events Schedule, the Unpleasant Events Schedule, and the Life Attitudes Schedule. Since 1964, my research has concentrated on depression across the life span and related phenomena, such as suicide, eating disorders, bipolar disorder, cigarette smoking and physical disease, subthreshold conditions, effects of brain damage, and continuing education for psychologists.

The psychological treatment of depressed individuals has always been a primary focus of my research. Starting with a behavioral formulation of depression, my associates and I derived a number of cognitive-behavioral strategies for individual and group treatment. These treatments have been adapted for use with depressed adolescents and elderly individuals. Depression is probably unrivaled in the breadth of issues that it raises. It can easily raise all, or almost all, of the clinical, theoretical, and methodological issues that are of importance in psychotherapy research. Its study and treatment involve interactions among cognitions, emotions, and overt behavior; among psychophysiology, brain chemistry, and environmental influences; and among developmental issues. Depression is the most common mental disorder, especially if one considers that it occurs by itself and also in conjunction with many other mental and physical disorders. Thus, depression is an extremely broad condition that can be used to focus on many theoretically and clinically challenging questions.

My focus on depression was strongly influenced by Charles Ferster. Focusing on the passivity (i.e., low behavior rate) of depressed individuals, it was a relatively small step to postulate that they must be on an extinction schedule, that is, that a lack of, or a reduction in, response-contingent positive reinforcement might be an important antecedent for the occurrence of depression. This approach led me to formulate what later became known as the "behavioral model of depression" and to develop specific interventions based on this model. If people become depressed because their behavior no longer leads to reinforcement, then one needs to help them change their behavior and their environment. These studies were designed at first for use with individual patients and later for use with groups.

My original model of depression did not assign a causal role to depressotypic cognitions, assuming them to be consequences of the depressed state. An important supplement to the behavioral position was that the social environment provides reinforcement in the form of sympathy, interest, and concern for depressive behaviors, thus increasing the rate of depressive verbal behaviors. Social skill was seen as an area of deficit especially important in the development of depressive behaviors. On the basis of empirical studies, the theory was expanded to incorporate a relationship between aversive events and depression. Specifically, it was hypothesized that depressed individuals are more sensitive, experience a greater number of aversive events, and are less skillful in terminating aversive events.

My move to the University of Oregon in 1965 was important. Being a member of the clinical faculty and participating in the clinical supervision of graduate students gave me the necessary control over a clinical setting where I could combine clinical training and supervision with research.

A turning point in my career began with a phone call from Dr. Arthur Ulene, who was interested in using the strategies described in a self-help book I and my colleagues had written in my television program (*Feeling Fine*). Specifically, he asked me to assist him in the treatment of depressed individuals as the basis for a miniseries on depression, which, it was hoped, would prove useful for depressed people. With some trepidation, the four colleagues (Toni Zeiss, Mary Ann Youngren, Ricardo Munoz, and Peter Lewinsohn)

treated these individuals (in a hall in San Francisco rented by NBC) using our book, *Control Your Depression,* as the basis for the "course." At the end of the treatment, the patients appeared improved, and the resulting 10- to 4-minute segments were aired during a 2-week period in late 1978.

My work, in collaboration with Greg Clarke, Harry Hoberman, Hy Hops, and Paul Rohde, developed the "Adolescent Coping With Depression" course, a cognitive-behavioral treatment for use with depressed adolescents. The course has been translated into German, Dutch, and Spanish.

In 1985, my colleagues and I began an ongoing longitudinal study, the Oregon Adolescent Depression Project, which followed a large cohort of high school students from the general community from adolescence into young adulthood. The study design includes both the parents and the children of the probands, and the study's overall goal is to increase current knowledge about the epidemiology of adolescent depression, risk and protective factors, etiology, the course of adolescent depression over time, and the continuity of psychopathology from childhood through adolescence.

Among many professional awards, I have received the 2000 award in recognition of the best paper on eating disorders, the 1996 Nathan Cummings Foundation Award from the American Academy of Child and Adolescent Psychiatry, the Distinguished Scientist Award from the Society for a Science of Clinical Psychology in 1996, the Joseph Zubin Award from Society for Research in Psychopathology in 1991, and the Mental Health Association of Oregon Professional Award in 1978.

—*Peter M. Lewinsohn*

See also: *Behavioral Assessment (Vol. I); Cognitive Behavior Therapy (Vol. I); Setting Events (Vol. I)*

M

MANUALIZED BEHAVIOR THERAPY

Treatment manuals for psychological disorders are written materials that identify key concepts, procedures, and tactics for the delivery of a clinical intervention. Treatment manuals are specifically designed to help modify the factors and processes believed to produce, maintain, or increase the magnitude or frequency of problematic behavior. There is considerable diversity in regard to the level of specification in a particular manualized therapy, which is a function of the type of treatment being employed and the manual's stage of development. Nonetheless, all manualized therapies provide rules pertaining to how therapists are to prepare for treatment, describe what they should do during the session itself, and characterize how the process of therapy is to proceed over time.

HISTORICAL CONTEXT

At least initially, the primary aim of developing and implementing manualized therapies was to improve the evaluation of particular treatment strategies and entire treatment programs. Indeed, manuals served to specify in abbreviated form the nature of the treatment and articulate in detail how it was to be delivered. Thus, researchers would have available a precise and standardized clinical methodology that could be used in the evaluation of a particular treatment's efficacy. In addition, manuals provided researchers with the opportunity to standardize training of a specific treatment so as to increase the chance that the therapy would be delivered in the manner designated by, and consistent with,

the theoretical underpinnings of the approach. Today, the development and utilization of manualized therapies reflects an important breakthrough in the larger history of developing and evaluating psychosocial treatments for psychopathology specifically and psychological dysfunction more generally.

Reasons for Implementing Treatment Manuals

With the advantage of hindsight, it is easy to identify a number of key reasons why manualized therapies originally emerged in the mid- to late 1970s. Prior to having standardized treatment methods and procedures, researchers often were left in the dark in regard to how a particular treatment was delivered. In the best-case scenario, questions about the effects of a clinical trial could be directed at how well a particular treatment was delivered. In the worst-case scenario, it was possible to question whether a particular treatment was really delivered at all or at least whether the key components of that therapy were implemented. Other types of common concerns were aimed at issues such as whether the therapy under investigation was delivered in a consistent fashion across study participants. Still other concerns were aimed at how well the results could be replicated across independent research sites. All of these questions, and others similar to them, essentially reflect questions of *treatment integrity*. A prerequisite for adequately addressing questions of treatment integrity from a scientific standpoint is to have a methodology that identifies the treatment of interest and guides its delivery in a step-by-step manner. In fact, treatment manuals are virtually a de facto requirement in treatment efficacy research.

Today, the development and utilization of manualized behavior therapies have far exceeded the boundaries of research circles. Indeed, the use of manuals in clinical contexts with no clear research objectives has been spurred on by health care policy changes demanding that psychological services follow guidelines for relatively brief treatments that have an empirical basis for outcome. Also, treatment manuals often are used as a basis for training psychologists and other mental health professionals in training programs, and they have become increasingly involved in clinical practice. Thus, despite the fact that manuals have helped to improve the quality of large-scale clinical trials in accordance with their original intended purpose, it is perhaps not surprising that they have been the subject of controversy and intense debate. In fact, the use of treatment manuals has called attention to clinical issues that strike at the very heart of what treatment should be considered clinically useful and in what contexts it should be implemented.

Empirically Supported Therapies and the Use of Treatment Manuals

Psychosocial treatment development and dissemination are based upon the influential stage model used by the Food and Drug Administration for the approval of drugs. Briefly, there are three primary units, each reflecting different stages in treatment development. Stage 1 reflects technological refinement and pilot research aimed at developing theory-based treatment strategies that can usefully be applied to a specific type of psychopathology. Stage 2 is concerned with demonstrating that a particular treatment can produce positive behavior change in a controlled evaluation. In addition, in Stage 2, research can be aimed at ascertaining the mechanisms of action for a particular treatment (how it works). Stage 3 is field research involving larger samples of patients for the evaluation of treatments that already have shown initial success in Stage 2. An important, often misunderstood, point related to treatment manuals within the larger context of the stage model is that the roles and content of manuals should evolve with the stage of development of a specific treatment. That is, treatment manuals develop as the treatment itself develops in various stages, from initial basic outlines to highly elaborate and sophisticated systems appropriate for use with diverse clinical populations.

The movement to develop lists of empirically supported therapies for target populations defined by diagnostic categories has been pioneered by the Division 12 Task Force on Promotion and Dissemination of Psychological Procedures. The primary objective of the task force has been to critically review the existing empirical treatment literature in an effort to identify those psychosocial interventions that have shown promise in alleviating specific types of psychological problems. The criteria for demonstrating efficacy are categorized as either "well-established treatments" or "probably efficacious treatments." Although it is not possible to review the criteria for each of these domains in their entirety, "well-established therapies" generally have demonstrated superior outcomes compared with a control condition (e.g., placebo) or another treatment on two separate occasions by independent investigators. In contrast, "probably efficacious treatments" generally indicate that a treatment results in greater improvement than that observed in persons who desire psychological treatment but are on a waiting list for such treatment.

The empirically supported treatment (Division 12) task force evaluates all manualized therapies according to their *efficacy;* that is, demonstrations that an intervention improves psychological status in well-controlled, experimental studies. This research differs slightly from questions of *effectiveness,* defined as the relative degree of utility of a treatment to produce positive outcomes in the context in which treatment most often is sought (naturalistic studies). Typically, large-scale clinical trials are used to evaluate and demonstrate the efficacy of psychological interventions. Such evaluations are outcome oriented; they are an evaluation of a particular type of therapy compared with some type of control group (e.g., placebo, other form of "active" therapy).

Once potentially efficacious treatments are identified and agreed upon, the task force disseminates this information through established mechanisms (e.g., journal articles). It is important to understand that the task of charting efficacious treatments is an ongoing, dynamic process, as researchers are continuously examining therapies, refining their components, and assessing their utility across different populations, sites, and time periods. Nearly all therapies that are evaluated by the task force have been manualized so as to facilitate the understanding and evaluation of the treatment's key concepts, procedures, and delivery tactics; that is, manuals help codify and systematize the treatment procedures. The use of manualized treatments in clinical practice is a relatively recent change in mental health work, but despite its short history, it already has had far-reaching implications for the field of psychotherapy.

Perhaps the most obvious asset to the development and use of treatment manuals in clinical practice is that the treatments have been evaluated within the context of controlled studies. Unlike many traditional forms of psychotherapy, manuals focus and structure treatment; typically, the intervention itself is time limited. Such a focused approach provides a relatively "tight" therapeutic context whereby the rationale, goals, and therapeutic exercises are clearly portrayed. Moreover, the ongoing evaluation of progress is implicitly conducted as a part of therapy, helping ensure a reasonable degree of behavior change and standard of care. Aside from the benefits of providing clients with treatment options with empirical support, treatment manuals have also facilitated the training of therapists in specific types of clinical procedures and assessment strategies.

Behavior Therapy's Contributions to the Manualization of Empirically Supported Psychosocial Treatments

Since its inception, behavior therapy has been committed to empirical evaluation and the development of effective, time-efficient therapeutic strategies. It is therefore not surprising that behavior therapists have been at the forefront of the major developments in the movement toward empirically supported treatments and their associated manuals. In fact, the majority of empirically supported treatments can be considered "behavioral" or "cognitive-behavioral" in their theoretical foundations, content, and implementation procedures. Whereas behavioral interventions were initially based on operant and classical conditioning principles, cognitive treatment components have increasingly been added to these therapies. This evolution of behavior therapy reflects the growing recognition that cognitive factors and information processing characterize many important aspects of psychological dysfunction and human suffering. Thus, it is not surprising that contemporary behavioral interventions can be best described as *multicomponent strategies,* which contain treatment elements based on both basic learning principles and more recent developments in cognitive science. Although the vast majority

of manual-based treatments have been cognitive behavioral, they are by no means limited or restricted to a single theoretical orientation. Indeed, the main distinguishing feature of treatment manuals is not theoretical orientation, but the implicit commitment to clinical guidelines and protocol-driven practice—an explicit attempt to ensure a certain standard of care.

Contemporary Issues Related to the Use and Acceptance of Manualized Treatments

Although manualized treatments have increased exposure, including public access, to efficacious treatments for a wide variety of mental health problems, they have not necessarily been wholly embraced by the field. Critics of manualized therapies have cited numerous concerns related to their use, the vast majority of which have originated from the practice community. The main issues surrounding the use of manualized treatments generally rest on questions concerning their relative clinical utility as applied to "real-world" behavior problems (as opposed to controlled-test trials) and, to a lesser extent, professional issues pertaining to the level of training and experience that is necessary to contribute to effective treatment. For the purposes of the present entry, only a select number of the most common concerns will be described. It is important to note that while these debates historically have rested on theoretical arguments, they increasingly have been studied from a scientific perspective. The empirical research that has emerged in such domains has been, and will continue to be, critical in terms of comprehensively addressing the issues at the heart of manualized-therapy debates.

One of the most common concerns about manualized therapies pertains to the degree to which they impede, de-emphasize, or obstruct clinical decision making. Specifically, some scholars have suggested that manualized therapy undermines and restricts clinical judgment of individual therapists in the practice setting. From this perspective, it has been argued that the manualization of treatments could be problematic, because most clinicians are highly sensitive to the individual needs and characteristics of their patients. Furthermore, it has been suggested that greater degrees of flexibility often are needed to deliver treatment in the "real world" relative to when treatments are developed and initially tested in clinical trials conducted in research settings; in brief, expert clinical judgment optimizes therapeutic activities. Such concerns about the utility of clinical judgment must be weighed against the background of a large body of evidence that suggests personal judgments typically are worse, or at the very least not better than, statistical prediction based upon scientific analyses of persons with the same or similar type of problem. Moreover, the value of clinical judgment often rests on recognizing the limitations of subjective judgment and the ability to use the available empirical evidence, rather than intuitive forms of thinking. Manualized treatments based upon scientific testing guide therapists in implementing what research, rather than clinical judgment, suggests is the most clinically appropriate activity to carry out. Thus, the available evidence suggests that utilizing manuals will be a more successful and clinically helpful activity across therapists.

Another concern raised about manualized therapies is that they often are developed from studies involving a group of patients with a homogenous diagnostic profile yet are clinically implemented with patients exhibiting multiple behavior problems. This argument has been based on the assumption that practitioners treat individuals with higher rates of comorbidity compared with those involved in clinical test trials. Empirical research has, again, seriously challenged this argument, as many of the efficacy studies do include samples with multiple behavior problems. Indeed, most studies using manuals have indicated that patients demonstrate high rates of comorbidity, severe psychopathology, and histories of failed therapy (both psychological and pharmacological). It also is important to note that the degree to which comorbidity affects treatment outcome appears to be a function of the specific presenting problem (disorder), co-occurring psychopathology, and the type of treatment being employed. In fact, some research suggests that although comorbidity is associated with more severe psychopathology, it does not necessarily predict treatment success or dropout. Although the generalizability of controlled trials using manuals will naturally need to be evaluated using effectiveness studies, there is little reason to suspect that manual-based therapies will perform less well than treatment as usual. Another issue related to comorbidity and the use of manuals pertains to the extent to which treatments focused on a specific disorder can result in globalized improvement and clinically significant reduction in comorbid problems. Again, a growing body of evidence

related to this issue indicates successfully treating a single psychological disorder often produces marked improvements in psychological functioning, including comorbidity.

A third issue related to the use of manuals concerns the degree to which the adoption of manualized treatments will stymie the development of novel therapeutic approaches. Although there has been a serious and systematic attempt to make sure manualized therapies can be used to produce meaningful and reliable behavior change, these treatments are, by definition, a "work-in-progress." Of course, the degree to which a specific therapy is effective for a particular problem will be a function of a combination of factors, including, but not limited to, knowledge of the disorder. As a result, manualized therapies are some of the most well-studied therapies and have been shown to produce clinically relevant change in rigorous (controlled) evaluations. However, these therapies are not a panacea, and therefore future work is needed to enhance existing approaches and develop alternative, perhaps more powerful, methods of change. Thus, there is nothing inherent to manualized therapies that will impede the development of innovative clinical strategies. Moreover, because manualized therapies prompt therapeutic innovation based on empirical, rather than anecdotal evidence, they increase the quality standards used in the future development of therapeutic interventions. In other words, extensive evaluation involved in manual development places a premium on accountability, which enhances innovation of clinical procedures.

A final issue that is relevant to the use of manuals is the degree to which they may affect the therapist's contribution to treatment. Specifically, given the increasing availability and use of treatment manuals, some scholars have questioned whether skilled therapists will be replaced by technicians who have relatively less knowledge, training, and expertise. Therapist effects on the outcome of treatment have been well documented; however, the specific characteristics or behaviors of therapists that produce behavior change have not been identified. The utilization of manuals should offer a greater degree of standardization in terms of therapeutic strategies but not in the personal characteristics or behavior of therapists. In contrast, in nonmanualized or nonstandardized treatments, both therapist and treatment effects are confounded, and hence, there is no way to understand the unique contribution of either factor in clinical outcome. Thus, manualized-treatment research offers an important and exciting opportunity to better understand the role of the therapist in terms of treatment outcome. Also, it is important to note that available studies suggest the use of manualized treatments in terms of enhancing motivation about behavior change requires the skilled involvement of therapists. Indeed, research suggests that manual-based treatment is associated with a high degree of positive therapeutic alliance.

FUTURE DIRECTIONS

The initial efforts of the Society of Clinical Psychology (Division 12) task force on psychological intervention have focused on developing lists of empirically supported interventions as a way to increase accountability in clinical science and practice. A second "wave" of efforts sought to disseminate information about effective therapies for mental health problems to various constituencies, including practitioners, researchers, third-party payers, and the general public. This second movement has also played a critical role in integrating empirically supported treatments in training programs at the predoctoral and internship levels. There are now readily available resources about "effective treatments," such as *A Guide to Treatments That Work,* edited by Peter Nathan and Jack Gorman, which have dramatically increased access to empirically supported interventions. Other similar types of activities have grown outside of the Society of Clinical Psychology (Division 12), including special issues of journals, conferences, and professional work groups (see suggested readings for examples).

Although there has been astounding progress made in forwarding manualized therapy in a relatively short amount of time, a number of key issues will need to be addressed for this movement to continue to grow in the future. John Weisz and his colleagues (see suggested readings) have articulated an important "next phase" of development in the use of manualized therapies. These scholars suggest that empirically supported treatments will need to pursue a three-part agenda. The first part involves the continued evolution of review and classification procedures, with an emphasis on reliability across reviewers as a way of enhancing the "clinical merit" of various therapeutic procedures. The second part of the agenda involves the continued evaluation of available work to promote improved levels of research. The third and final part of

the agenda involves the development of an integrated dissemination program that can make information on manualized therapies readily accessible to practitioners, researchers, policymakers, and the public at large. Over time, such efforts will help link the science and practice communities of clinical psychology and other mental health fields (e.g., psychiatry) within a web of evidence-based practice and training.

CASE ILLUSTRATION

We now provide a clinical case description of an individual with panic disorder with agoraphobia to illustrate the use of a treatment manual.

Case Description

"Darlene" was a 43-year-old Caucasian woman with four children (ages ranging from 7–21). She had been married for 11 years and was employed as a floor manager in a large retail store. An unstructured clinical interview revealed that she was experiencing three to four panic attacks per week, which arose "out of the blue." The attacks were occurring in various settings, including at work, in the home, and at various times throughout the day. She noted that she was not enjoying her life due to the chronic worry about experiencing one of these anxiety attacks. Furthermore, she had not been able to participate in activities that she previously enjoyed, such as sexual activity with her husband, long-distance driving, flying, and going out in public (e.g., shopping, bus rides). She had been "feeling down" and "blue" as a result of these functional limitations. Despite her emotional distress, Darlene reported no history of mental health treatment.

We administered the Anxiety Disorders Interview Schedule for the *Diagnostic and Statistical Manual-Fourth Edition* (ADIS-IV) to further evaluate her anxiety-related psychological functioning. Information gathered via the structured interview revealed that Darlene was experiencing three unpredictable and uncued panic attacks per week, high levels of worry about the next attack, and moderate to severe avoidance of situations believed to trigger an attack. Moreover, the attacks were not due to drugs and were not better accounted for by another Axis I disorder. In addition, Darlene was experiencing major depressive episodes, which we conceptualized as secondary to the development of panic disorder.

Manualized Therapy for Panic Disorder

A current "well-established therapy" for panic disorder and agoraphobia termed *panic control therapy* (PCT) is a multicomponent cognitive-behavioral intervention guided by the use of a treatment manual titled *Mastery of Your Anxiety and Panic-III* (MAP-III), which articulates the procedures for PCT in a step-by-step fashion. Manual-based therapies like the MAP-III also include self-report and behavioral assessment tracking instruments that can be readily employed to evaluate treatment progress of individual patients across different time frames.

MAP-III contains a number of key components, including exposure to bodily and environmental situations associated with fear and panic, relaxation and breathing retraining, psychoeducation, and cognitive interventions. Briefly, exposure to interoceptive bodily events is achieved through exercises that produce somatic sensations similar to sensations experienced prior to and during a panic attack (e.g., head spinning, breathing through a straw, hyperventilation). Situational exposure involves contacting feared environmental stimuli without escaping from them, if panic symptoms occur. For instance, a person with panic disorder with agoraphobia who fears crowds might be asked to go to a shopping center and stay there for a specified period of time or until potentially high levels of anxiety have subsided. Relaxation training refers to exercises that serve to decrease basal levels of autonomic arousal. Breathing retraining refers to having patients breathe diaphragmatically at a rate of approximately 15 breaths per minute (depending on the individual client) in an effort to optimize the balance between oxygen and carbon dioxide in the patient's blood. Cognitive strategies typically are aimed at (a) correcting misappraisals of bodily sensations as threatening, (b) helping patients to predict more accurately the future likelihood of panic attacks, and (c) helping patients to predict more accurately and rationally the likely consequences of panic attacks.

Treatment Process With Manual

In the case of Darlene, the MAP-III helped to guide the delivery of psychoeducation, which taught her about the nature of panic attacks and panic disorder. The MAP-III self-monitoring exercises indicated that Darleen's panic attacks were primarily characterized by feelings of unreality, sweating, difficulty breathing, increased heart rate, and a fear that she was dying or going crazy. To further assess the nature of Darlene's panic attacks, we chose to use initial exposure exercises outlined in the MAP-III that would closely mimic the panic sensations she was reporting, in order to evaluate whether these events were leading to her panic attacks. We chose an exercise that involved staring at a spot on a wall for an extended period of time, which is known to elicit feelings of unreality. We also conducted a hyperventilation exercise that elicits increased heart rate and sweating as well as difficulty breathing. Darlene's responses to these exposure exercises were characterized by multiple complaints of somatic symptomotology resembling her panic attacks, followed by rapid increases in anxiety ratings, suggesting that these sensations she was reporting were, in fact, important triggers for her panic attacks.

In combination, psychoeducation, self-monitoring, and initial exposure exercises resulted in Darlene learning a number of key issues related to her panic problem: (a) Fear and panic are not dangerous per se; (b) panic is more likely on stressful days; (c) certain sensations (e.g., rapidly beating heart, feelings of unreality) are more likely to accompany and elicit panic attacks; and (d) avoidance of anxiety-inducing situations, such as a trip to the mall, prevent panic attacks in the short term but do not constitute a sound long-term strategy. At this point in treatment, the MAP-III prompts therapists to help clients develop alternative coping strategies in order to reduce reliance on avoidant strategies. Darlene learned to breathe diaphragmatically and use progressive muscle relaxation to lower general levels of arousal. We then worked on developing an awareness of antecedents to panic and the consequences of these antecedents. For example, Darlene was taught to monitor her panic responses to sexual activity to illustrate for her that although sexual activity results in bodily arousal, such activity is not a good predictor of her panic attacks.

The final component of the MAP-III program is exposure. Although exposure can be done in a variety of ways, the key aspect is eliciting emotional distress. Choosing an exposure exercise is a perfect example of how a manualized treatment can be conducted in an idiographic fashion. We chose to use the hyperventilation and wall-staring exercises because during the assessment phase of treatment, they functioned to elicit sensations resembling those experienced during Darlene's panic attacks. We also conducted exposure exercises in an unpredictable (e.g., switching randomly between the two exercises) manner in order to elicit maximum distress. The MAP-III also teaches clients to self-expose in vivo in an idiographic fashion. For example, Darlene was prompted to go to the mall, a context she had previously avoided, until her anxiety decreased.

Taken together, the components to panic treatment outlined in the MAP-III manual resulted in clinically significant reductions in panic attack frequency, worry about future attacks, and associated depressive symptomotology. More important, Darlene was able to resume participation in daily life activities toward the end of treatment, improving her quality of life. All treatment gains have been maintained at 12-month follow-up assessment.

SUMMARY

In summary, treatment manuals are written materials that identify key concepts, procedures, and tactics for the delivery of a clinical intervention. In this manner, treatment manuals are designed to help modify clinically relevant variables and processes involved with problematic behavior. Although manuals are quite diverse, all provide guidance pertaining to how therapists are to prepare for treatment, describe what they should do during the session itself, and characterize how the process of therapy is to proceed over time. Manuals have greatly helped with efforts to improve the evaluation of particular treatment strategies by specifying the nature of the treatment and articulate how it is to be delivered, and they offer a promising approach to studying therapist variables that affect therapy. More recently, manualized therapies have become increasingly utilized in clinical service contexts, calling attention to clinical issues that strike at the very heart of what treatment should be considered "clinically useful" and in what contexts it should be implemented. Although the use of manuals has been controversial in a number of respects, few would challenge the contention that manuals likely will retain an important and influential role in the continued evolution of psychological treatment in upcoming years.

—*Michael J. Zvolensky,*
Matthew T. Feldner, and Alison McLeish

See also: *Dialectical Behavior Therapy (Vol. I); Homework (Vol. I); Role Playing (Vol. I)*

Suggested Readings

Carroll, K. M., & Nuro, K. F. (2002). One size cannot fit all: A stage model for psychotherapy manual development. *Clinical Psychology: Science and Practice, 9,* 396–406.

Chambless, D. L., Sanderson, W. C., Shoham, V., Bennett-Johnson, S., Pope, K. S., Crits-Chiristoph, P., et al. (1996). An update on empirically validated therapies. *The Clinical Psychologist, 49,* 5–18.

Garfield, S. L. (1996). Some problems associated with "validated" forms of psychotherapy. *Clinical Psychology: Science and Practice, 3,* 218–229.

Kendall, P. C., & Chambless, D. L. (Eds.). (1998). Empirically supported psychological therapies [Special section]. *Journal of Consulting and Clinical Psychology, 66,* 3–167.

Nathan, P. E., & Gorman, J. M. (Eds.). (1998). *A guide to treatments that work.* New York: Oxford University Press.

Task Force on Promotion and Dissemination of Psychological Procedures. (1995). Training in and dissemination of empirically validated psychological treatments: Report and recommendations. *The Clinical Psychologist, 48,* 3–23.

Weisz, J. R., Hawley, K. M., Pilkonis, P. A., Woody, S. R., & Follette, W. C. (2000). Stressing the (other) three R's in the search for empirically supported treatments: Review procedures, research quality, relevance to practice, and the public interest. *Clinical Psychology: Science and Practice, 7,* 243–258.

MARKS, ISAAC M.

I was born in Cape Town, South Africa, in 1935, and qualified in medicine there in 1956. I trained as a psychiatrist at the University of London at the Bethlem-Maudsley Hospital from 1960 to 1963. I was a founding member of the Royal College of Psychiatrists in 1971 and became a fellow in 1976. I conducted clinical research at the Institute of Psychiatry, University of London, and the Bethlem-Maudsley Hospital from 1964 to 2000, becoming honorary consultant psychiatrist there in 1968, and professor of experimental psychopathology there in 1978. In 2000, I became professor emeritus there and senior research investigator at Charing Cross Hospital Campus, Imperial College, University of London, where I established a computer-guided self-help clinic. I have been a fellow at the Center for Advanced Study in the Behavioral Sciences in Stanford, California; Salmon lecturer and medalist at the New York Academy of Sciences; Sackler Scholar at the Advanced Studies Institute, University of Tel Aviv; consultant to the World Health Organization and the National Institute of Mental Health, and the National Institute for Clinical Excellence in the United Kingdom; visiting professor to universities in six continents; chairman of the British Association for Behavioural Psychotherapy; and president of the

European Association of Behaviour Therapy. I am on the editorial boards of many professional journals, have won the Starkey Medal and Prize of the Royal Society of Health, and have been on many professional committees. I have published 12 professional books, including *Fears, Phobias, and Rituals,* which was also translated into Spanish; *Living With Fear,* which was translated into 10 languages; and *Innovations in Mental Health Care Delivery,* in addition to 430 scientific papers. My research has included evolutionary influences on human behavior; the origins, features, and treatment of anxiety, phobic, obsessive-compulsive, and sexual disorders; interactions between drugs and behavioral psychotherapy; development of a national nurse therapist training program; community care of serious mental illness; and health care and cost-effectiveness evaluation. I have developed computer aids for the evaluation and delivery of psychiatric treatment, which is now a focus of my research.

Early influences on my research on behavior therapy were Michael Gelder and Jack Rachman, with whom I published research papers (when at the Institute of Psychiatry/Bethlem-Maudsley Hospital in London). My views on the nature of the scientific process that shaped my research were molded by writings of the philosophers of science Karl Jaspers, Carl Hempel, and Thomas Kuhn. My major contributions to the field include identification of the value of exposure as a unifying factor of many forms of anxiety reduction in behavior therapy and showing how exposure therapy could be effective given as self-help. I have shown in a series of studies how behavior therapy of various kinds can be effective when guided by several computer interfaces. Recently, I found that anxiety was reduced reliably by a few non-exposure therapies, as well. I pointed out the considerable uncertainty about the main therapeutic ingredients responsible for the efficacy of treatments for anxiety and depressive disorders, whether these therapies are behavioral, cognitive, interpersonal, or of a problem-solving nature. To facilitate identification of effective ingredients of therapy, I recently started working with a task force of the Association for Advancement of Behavior Therapy and European Association for Behavioural and Cognitive Therapies to evolve a common language of psychotherapy procedures. I have long been active in working toward the most cost-effective ways of delivering effective therapy for anxiety and depressive disorders, given that the majority of sufferers in the community are

untreated. My work on computer-aided self-help is an example of this.

—*Isaac M. Marks*

See also: *Exposure (Vol. I); Flooding (Vol. I); Response Prevention (Vol. I)*

MARSHALL, WILLIAM L.

I was born in Perth, Western Australia, on July 30, 1935. I left school at age 15 years, that being the earliest age permitted in Western Australia. I worked in various clerical jobs until age 26 years, when an opportunity was presented to attend university as a mature-age entrant. My undergraduate degree (B. Psych., 1967) at the University of Western Australia provided an excellent grounding in experimental psychology, particularly in perception and learning, which proved to be very useful. My research supervisor A. J. (Tim) Marshall (unrelated) provided excellent guidance. A master's of science at the University of London (1969) was spent in both study and extensive clinical experience at both Maudsley and Bethlem Royal Hospitals. Stanley (Jack) Rachman was my clinical supervisor. Jack was the ideal scientist-practitioner model, and his influence has been felt ever since. I then went to Canada to do my doctoral degree at Queen's University, which I completed in 1971.

When I started work with sexual offenders in 1969, there were very few others interested in this area of work. Isaac Marks and John Bancroft in England and Gene Abel and Nick Groth in North America all provided support and encouragement as we struggled to determine the most effective treatment methods for these problematic clients. As a devoted behaviorist in the early 1970s, I found the neophyte Association for Advancement of Behavior Therapy and its members to be excellent models, and supportive. In particular, the friendship and encouragement from David Barlow, Michael Mahoney, Joe Wolpe, Alan Kazdin, and Michel Hersen were very valuable.

Since the late 1960s, I have devoted most of my clinical and research efforts to sexual offenders. I have more than 270 publications, including 12 books, and I have been on the editorial board of 16 international journals. In the mid-1970s, I developed satiation therapy, which proved to be one to the most popular and effective procedures for reducing deviant sexual preferences. In 1971, I published a description of a program for sexual offenders that included for the first time treatment targets involving social and relationship skills. Shortly thereafter, I published the first description of a phallometric procedure for assessing rapists. With my colleague Howard Barbaree, I published in 1984 a theory of the development of sexual offending, which has continued to evolve and has been somewhat influential. Recently, my colleagues and I have documented the role of the therapist in generating treatment changes.

I was president of the Association for the Treatment of Sexual Abusers from 2000 to 2001, and in 1993, I received that association's Lifetime Achievement Award. In 1999, I was awarded the Santiago Grisolia Prize from the Queen Sophia Centre in Spain for my worldwide contributions to the reduction of violence, and in 2000, I was elected a fellow of the Royal Society of Canada.

My current work includes continued research into factors that characterize sexual offenders, including shame and guilt, empathy, self-esteem, coping, intimacy and loneliness, and deviant sexual interests. Also, recently I have examined the reliability and validity of the diagnosis sexual sadism, and I am continuing my investigations of the childhood and adolescent antecedents of sexual offending.

I construe sexual deviance as a complexly caused and maintained behavior that serves to inappropriately meet a variety of needs (e.g., sexual, intimacy, approval, power) of people who are otherwise unable to meet these needs in prosocial ways. I remain optimistic about the value of treatment and endeavors to be compassionate and respectful toward all sexual deviants (offenders and nonoffenders) and their victims.

My future plans involve continuing my work with sexual offenders, which I consider to be an exciting and fulfilling task, until I am no longer able to contribute. I consider it a privilege to have the opportunity to help people in need and to prevent further victimization.

—*W. L. Marshall*

See also: *Arousal Training (Vol. I); Masturbatory Retraining (Vol. I); Squeeze Technique (Vol. I)*

MASTURBATORY RETRAINING

DESCRIPTION OF STRATEGY

Masturbatory retraining, also termed *masturbatory* or *orgasmic reconditioning,* was introduced to treat people, usually men, who sought to convert their sexual preference from homosexual to heterosexual. More recently, it has mainly been used to treat sex offenders, usually male rapists and pedophiles. It aims to condition the man's sexual arousal to stimuli considered appropriate by instructing him to masturbate to ejaculation while using fantasies, such as making love to an adult woman or man or watching slides or listening to audiotapes. He is to totally avoid deviant fantasies, such as those of children or aggressive sexual behaviors. It was expected that he would become sexually aroused to the appropriate stimuli and his interest in inappropriate stimuli would diminish. Subsequently, a procedure aimed at reducing his inappropriate interest by satiation was added. The man was instructed after ejaculating, having used the conditioning procedure, to continue to masturbate for a prolonged period, usually about an hour, while fantasizing aloud every possible variation of his deviant activities. It could be carried out by the man at his home, where he recorded his verbalizations, for the therapist to check that he was following instructions.

RESEARCH BASIS

Most of the empirical studies of masturbatory retraining reported its use in one or a few patients with no or inadequate controls. To assess changes in sexual preference, usually the man's penile circumference responses to appropriate and deviant stimuli prior to and following the procedure were measured. The validity of these responses as measures of sexual preference has been increasingly questioned. As they require 2 minutes to develop, the man investigated has time to modify his responses by using fantasies differing from the stimuli shown him. Nevertheless, changes in these responses following masturbatory retraining were accepted as evidence of the treatment's efficacy. Some workers pointed out that it seemed inappropriate to attempt to reduce sexual arousal to deviant fantasies by encouraging men to masturbate to nondeviant fantasies if they were already strongly sexually aroused by the nondeviant fantasies. Some pedophiles and most rapists are strongly attracted to adult women. Also, evidence was advanced questioning the conditioning rationale for masturbatory retraining. Penile volume responses to sexual stimuli have been shown to provide a much more valid assessment of sexual preference than do penile circumference responses, presumably because volume responses occur within 10 seconds, allowing the subject much less time to modify them. Penile volume responses to films of men who sought treatment to reduce homosexual feelings were assessed. Married men who had repeatedly experienced orgasm in the presence of cues of women, their wives, showed no evidence of increased penile volume responses to films of women or decreased penile volume responses to films of men, compared with single men with no history of heterosexual intercourse. This finding that associating orgasm with stimuli considered appropriate failed to increase sexual arousal to those stimuli indicates the need for studies using penile volume assessment to evaluate the efficacy of masturbatory retraining. Sex offenders are commonly under considerable social and often legal pressure to comply with treatment. Insistence that they masturbate for long periods while verbalizing deviant fantasies would seem likely to be experienced as demeaning by many offenders whose self-esteem is usually already low. Until there is adequate evidence that these procedures change sexual preference, their inclusion in treatment programs seems questionable on ethical grounds.

—*Nathaniel McConaghy*

See also: *Marshall, William L. (Vol. I); Orgasmic Reconditioning (Vol. I); Squeeze Technique (Vol. I)*

Suggested Readings

Laws, D. R., & Marshall, W. L. (1991). Masturbatory reconditioning with sexual deviates: An evaluative review. *Advances in Behaviour Research and Therapy, 13,* 13–25.

McConaghy, N. (1993). *Sexual behavior: Problems and management.* New York: Plenum Press.

McConaghy, N. (1998). Assessment of sexual dysfunction and deviation. In A. S. Bellack & M. Hersen (Eds.), *Behavioral assessment: A practical handbook* (4th ed.). Boston: Allyn & Bacon.

MEICHENBAUM, DONALD H.

I was born in New York City in June 1940 and attended public schools in New York, culminating in a BA from City College of New York in 1962. I attended the University of Illinois, in Champaign, where I received my PhD in clinical psychology in 1966. I then took a position as assistant professor at the University of Waterloo in Waterloo, Ontario, Canada, where I remained until I took early retirement in 1998. I am currently distinguished professor emeritus and spend my winters in Florida, where I am research director of the Melissa Institute for Violence Prevention and for the Treatment of Victims of Violence in Miami, Florida. The Melissa Institute is designed to bridge the gap between scientific findings and public policy and clinical and educational practices.

I am one of the founders of cognitive behavior therapy. My contributions to the field have been noted by North American clinicians in a survey reported in the *American Psychologist.* I have been voted "one of the 10 most influential psychologists of the century." My 1977 book, *Cognitive Behavior Modification: An Integrative Approach,* is a Citation Classic. This initial book was soon followed by a series of authored, coauthored, and edited books that reflect my broad interest in applying cognitive-behavioral intervention to a variety of clinical problems. These books include *Stress Inoculation Training* (1985); *Pain and Behavioral Medicine* (1983); *Facilitating Treatment Adherence: A Practitioner's Guidebook* (1987); *Nurturing Independent Learners* (1998); and two clinical handbooks, *The Assessment and Treatment of Individuals With Posttraumatic Stress Disorder* (1994) and *Treating Individuals with Anger-Control and Aggressive Behaviors* (2001).

I am editor of the Kluwer-Plenum series on stress and coping, have served as coeditor of *Cognitive Therapy and Research,* and have served on the editorial boards of more than a dozen journals. I have received many honors in recognition of my contributions, including being the honorary president of the Canadian Psychological Association and the recipient of the Research Award of the American Psychological Association.

I have consulted and presented training workshops worldwide. My current commitment is to work on reduction of violence, so my grandchildren will inherit a safer world.

—*Donald H. Meichenbaum*

See also: *Cognitive Behavior Therapy (Vol. I); Self-Monitoring (Vol. II); Self-Statement Modification (Vol. I)*

MEMORY REHABILITATION AFTER TRAUMATIC BRAIN INJURY

DESCRIPTION OF THE STRATEGY

Memory functioning is often impaired when individuals experience traumatic brain injury (TBI). Techniques designed to improve memory functioning are drawn from cognitive theories that attempt to explain how learning and memory work. Since different types of injuries affect memory functioning differently, rehabilitation methods attempt to integrate conceptualizations such as levels of processing and stages of memory to take advantage of specific areas in which functioning is spared. As part of a comprehensive rehabilitation plan for such patients, the goals of memory rehabilitation are to decrease maladaptive behaviors resulting from memory impairment and increase adaptive functioning in patients' daily environments. Specific techniques for memory rehabilitation may be divided into three categories: (1) external aids, (2) internal-compensatory approaches, and (3) direct retraining of memory. Each of these will be discussed in turn.

External aids attempt to decrease the need for patients to accurately retrieve memories by placing the information to be recalled outside of the individual. Environmental cues, such as large signs posted near appliances with instructions for use, are one type of external aid. Alternately, environmental modifications may be made (e.g., disconnecting all but one stove burner and placing a colorful sticker near the corresponding knob). In addition, the home might be organized so that important materials (e.g., keys, wallets, family schedules, telephone messages) are kept in a central place. Cues also may be provided via checklists (e.g., on the door, detailing what to check before leaving the house). Other external aids include electronic devices to locate keys and pillboxes with alarms that are set to go off when it is time to take medications. A common external aid is the memory notebook, sections of which might include a calendar, to-do list, journal, events log, telephone numbers and addresses, and space to record things forgotten as well as successful remembering. Electronic memory notebooks are used similarly and have the added benefit of programmable alarms to remind the patient of certain tasks, including checking the notebook. Patients must be extensively trained to use most external aids.

Training in the use of internal-compensatory strategies capitalizes on usually preserved procedural memory and implicit memory to teach domain-specific skills. For example, patients may be taught to remember which medications to take or to learn certain names. Generalization does not usually occur with this approach. Strategies for internal compensatory training include mnemonic techniques, the vanishing-cues method, and errorless learning. Mnemonic techniques involve rehearsal and elaboration of information to be remembered (e.g., using visual imagery). When training using the vanishing-cues method, maximum cuing is initially provided, with the amount of cuing slowly reduced over learning trials. Errorless learning involves providing patients with answers versus allowing them to guess during the learning phase, and the patient is encouraged to respond only when sure of the answers. Errorless learning appears to lessen interference due to remembering incorrect responses during the learning phase.

Direct retraining focuses on teaching techniques to encode information in such a way that there is a greater likelihood of remembering it. For example, educating patients about metacognitive strategies and helping the person attend to semantics, meaning, and organization of the material may be used. Patients may visually imagine new material or otherwise elaborate on it and relate it to existing information. Prospective memory training is a type of direct retraining in which patients are asked to think about future events (e.g., to perform a given task at a specified time), with the intervening time span beginning at a few seconds and gradually lengthening. Distractions are added as the patient achieves successes.

RESEARCH BASIS

Systematic research with TBI patients is difficult to conduct due to significant variability in type of memory impairment among subjects, and research in this area is limited. As would be expected, greater successes have been found when subjects have mild versus severe memory impairment. When tasks are relevant to daily functioning, modest improvements have been achieved using external aids and internal-compensatory strategies. The use of a memory notebook is among the most effective rehabilitation methods. In many studies, improved functioning does not continue past the training period, while in some cases, improvements are maintained for up to 6 months. These improvements do not usually generalize. In the absence of other viable rehabilitation options, these methods appear the most promising at this time. In contrast, most direct retraining strategies have not produced significant results. In general, only prospective memory retraining looks promising, but more research is needed in this area.

COMPLICATIONS

In general, recovery of memory functions after TBI is difficult to achieve. It is important to note that TBI usually affects interrelated brain functioning, such as ability to sustain attention and awareness of deficits. Since attention to information is necessary for memory processes to function, many apparent memory deficits are likely secondary to impaired attentional abilities. In these cases, memory functioning is better addressed through treatments aimed at increasing attention. For other patients, attention and awareness deficits must first be addressed in order to effectively proceed with memory rehabilitation.

Impaired ability to read and write severely limits some patients' abilities to use external cues such as memory notebooks. Rehabilitation of older individuals may be further complicated due to age-related differences in brain functioning and recovery. Therefore, a thorough assessment is necessary in order to understand patients' strengths versus deficits so as to take advantage of memory and other cognitive processes that are better preserved. The most effective rehabilitation strategies are tailored to patient strengths and take into account patients' daily needs and specific problems in the environment. For this reason and because generalization tends to be difficult, community- based services are especially useful. Initially, the best method of choosing treatments may involve maintaining flexibility and pursuing a series of trials using different approaches to see which has the more favorable effect. In the end, a combination of approaches may have the greatest utility for most patients.

—*Michael Daniel and B. J. Scott*

See also: *Behavioral Assessment (Vol. I); Generalization (Vol. I); Instructions (Vol. I)*

Suggested Readings

Carney, N. C., Maynard, H. M., & Patterson, P. H. (1999). Effect of cognitive rehabilitation on outcomes for persons with traumatic brain injury: A systematic review. *Journal of Head Trauma Rehabilitation, 14*(3), 277–307.

Cicerone, K. D., Dahlberg, C., Kalmar, K., Langenbahn, D. M., Malec, M. F., Bergquist, T. F., et al. (2000). Evidence-based cognitive rehabilitation: Recommendations for clinical practice. *Archives of Physical Medicine and Rehabilitation, 18*(12), 1596–1615.

Leon-Carrion, J. (1997). Rehabilitation of memory. In J. Leon-Carrion (Ed.), *Neuropsychological rehabilitation: Fundamentals, innovations, and directions.* Delray Beach, FL: GR/St. Lucie Press.

Mateer, C. A., & Raskin, S. A. (1999). Cognitive rehabilitation. In M. Rosenthal, E. R. Griffith, J. S. Kreutzer, & B. Pentland (Eds.), *Rehabilitation of the adult and child with traumatic brain injury* (3rd ed., pp. 254–270). Philadelphia: F. A. Davis.

Raskin, S. A. (2000). Cognitive remediation of mild traumatic brain injury in an older age group. In S. A. Raskin & C. A. Mateer (Eds.), *Neuropsychological management of mild traumatic brain injury* (pp. 254–268). New York: Oxford University Press.

Raskin, S. A. (2000). Memory. In S. A. Raskin & C. A. Mateer (Eds.), *Neuropsychological management of mild traumatic brain injury* (pp. 93–112). New York: Oxford University Press.

Sohlberg, M. M., & Mateer, C. A. (2001). *Cognitive rehabilitation: An integrative neuropsychological approach.* New York: Guilford Press.

MILTENBERGER, RAYMOND G.

I was born in St. Louis, Missouri, on April 29, 1956. The earliest and most enduring influence on me came from my parents. I was the second oldest of eight children, with a father who worked in manufacturing and a mother who worked in the home (which was hard work, with eight kids). I learned many things from my parents, Ed and Ginny, some of the most important being the value of hard work, independence, and achievement. Ed and Ginny supported all of their children's efforts and valued their accomplishments. In essence, they used behavior modification principles to set the occasion for successful behavior and reinforce achievement.

The earliest influence on me professionally came in an undergraduate psychology course taught by Peter Bankhart at Wabash College. Although the course was titled "Adjustment," we used the Whaley and Malott text, *Elementary Principles of Behavior,* which covered the basic principles of behavioral psychology. From my first in-depth exposure to behavioral principles in this course, I developed an abiding interest in behavioral psychology and decided to pursue a graduate degree in behavioral psychology at Western Michigan University.

EDUCATION HISTORY

I obtained a bachelor's degree in liberal arts, with a major in psychology, in 1978, from Wabash College, Crawfordsville, Indiana.

I obtained a master's degree in 1981 and doctoral degree in 1985, in clinical psychology with a behavioral emphasis, from Western Michigan University, Kalamazoo, Michigan.

My predoctoral internship in behavioral pediatrics and developmental disabilities (1984–1985) took place at the Kennedy Institute of the Johns Hopkins University Medical School, Baltimore, Maryland.

PROFESSIONAL MODELS

My first professional model was Peter Bankhart, my academic advisor and professor in a number of undergraduate classes. From Peter, I experienced my first exposure to behavioral psychology. In addition, Peter modeled how to teach undergraduate classes in a way that generated student interest and how to develop rapport with students and function as an effective advisor.

The next individuals I consider to be influential models were three professors in my graduate program at Western Michigan University: Wayne Fuqua, Alan Poling, and Jack Michael. These three individuals showed how to make graduate classes interesting (and demanding) and how to motivate students to be successful. In addition, through his work as my research mentor, Wayne Fuqua showed me how to be a successful researcher and an effective mentor myself. All three helped put the fire in my belly for an academic career in behavior analysis.

MAJOR CONTRIBUTIONS TO THE FIELD

My major contributions to the field involve both teaching and research. As a teacher at the graduate level, my goal is to prepare students for careers as researchers or practitioners in applied behavior analysis. I accomplish this goal primarily by mentoring graduate students in my research program and to a lesser extent, through classroom instruction. As a teacher at the undergraduate level, my goal is to get students excited about behavior analysis in the hope that they will pursue further study in the area. I accomplish this goal by demonstrating the utility of a behavioral approach in classes and by mentoring students in my research program. As one indication of my commitment to teaching, I wrote an undergraduate textbook titled *Behavior Modification: Principles and Procedures* (originally published in 1997), which is now in its third edition.

The focus of my research program is in the areas of habit disorders and safety skills training. In the habit disorders area, I have published research evaluating treatments for habit behaviors such as tics, trichotillomania, thumb sucking, nail biting, and stuttering. This work has focused on establishing the effectiveness of simplified habit reversal, the limits of simplified habit reversal, and the utility of adjunct treatments. In addition, some of my research has focused on evaluating the function of habit behaviors and the effectiveness of functional treatments. In 2001, I published an edited text with Doug Woods, *Tic Disorders, Trichotillomania, and Other Repetitive Behavior Disorders: Behavioral Approaches to Analysis and Treatment,* which reflects the research I have done in this area.

In the safety skills area, my published work centers on the evaluation of behavioral skills training procedures for teaching safety skills such as sexual abuse prevention skills and abduction prevention skills to children and to adults with mental retardation. In this research, I have investigated assessment issues (the correspondence between verbal reports, actual skills, and the transfer of skills to naturalistic situations), training issues (the relative effectiveness of behavioral skills training versus educational approaches), and generalization issues (the importance of actual practice of skills in naturalistic situations).

CURRENT WORK AND VIEWS

My current work is an extension of my safety skills training research to the area of firearm injury prevention. Hundreds of children are killed or injured each year by other children who find loaded guns and play with them. My current research focuses on teaching children safety skills to prevent gunplay. My research team has conducted a number of studies demonstrating the effectiveness of individual and group behavioral skills training procedures emphasizing an active learning approach. This research has also shown that standard educational approaches (involving instructions, modeling, and discussion, but no active rehearsal of the skills) are not effective in teaching skills and producing transfer of those skills to naturalistic situations in which a child finds a gun. These findings, and the findings of my other research in safety skills training, have implications for how best to teach important safety skills to children. In my view, educators focus too much on providing information about safety skills and assume that increases in knowledge will translate into increases in the use of the skills. Furthermore, most programs used in schools to teach a variety of safety skills are never evaluated to establish their effectiveness. My research suggests that educational approaches do not result in skill acquisition and transfer and that behavioral skills training approaches are needed if we want children and adults with disabilities to acquire and be able to use important safety skills.

FUTURE PLANS

My plans for the future are to continue research in habit disorders and safety skills training, focusing in the immediate future on skills training to prevent firearm injury in children. Furthermore, I plan to continue revising my behavior modification textbook at periodic intervals so it continues to be a current resource in the field.

—*Raymond G. Miltenberger*

See also: Applied Behavior Analysis (Vols. I, II, & III)

MINDFULNESS MEDITATION

DESCRIPTION OF THE STRATEGY

Clinical interventions based on mindfulness meditation are appearing with increasing frequency in the empirical literature. Such interventions have been developed to reduce distress and improve quality of life in individuals suffering from a wide range of physical and mental disorders, including chronic pain, cancer, eating disorders, anxiety disorders, mood disorders, and substance abuse. The literature contains terminology referring to a number of related concepts and techniques, including "mindfulness training," "mindful practice," "mindfulness-based" interventions, "mindfulness meditation," and, most simply, "mindfulness." To complicate matters, there is a similar, but distinct, social psychological construct of "mindfulness" with a different origin and separate theoretical and research literature, which will not be addressed in this entry.

Mindfulness meditation is distinct from concentration meditation. Together, they represent the two major forms of meditation practice. A brief account of the origins and function of mindfulness meditation in Buddhist thought and practice provides a useful context

for understanding its varying uses in cognitive and behavioral practice.

"Mindfulness" is the common English translation of the Pali term *sati* (Pali is the ancient Indic language of the oldest Buddhist literature). It is one aspect (right mindfulness) of the Noble Eightfold Path, which the Buddha outlined as the means of liberation from suffering or mental anguish. In this context, "mindfulness" is the capacity to attend fully to the content of experience as it occurs in the immediate present and to remain in contact with the experience for its duration, without attempting either to terminate or to prolong it and without judgment or other verbal commentary. Mindfulness meditation refers to the specific practices intended to develop our capacity for mindfulness. With diligent practice under the guidance of a teacher, mindfulness meditation is said to facilitate the discovery and rectification of the causes of mental anguish that arise from the practitioner's own mental processes.

Concentration meditation refers to practices involving sustained, focused attention to a single object, such as a mental image, a mantra, or an external physical object. Instruction in mindfulness typically involves exercises to develop concentration, which is a necessary but not sufficient condition for mindfulness. However, mindfulness itself attends to any experiences that enter the field of awareness, with equal attention given to bodily sensations, thoughts, and emotional experience.

Mindfulness is the core stance of the various meditative practices in all the principal forms of Buddhism. However, because its Buddhist origins potentially are a barrier to its acceptance in Western health and behavioral health contexts, interventions based on mindfulness meditation typically are presented to clients without reference to their origins, except in cases in which these origins might enhance credibility and acceptability for cultural reasons.

Training in mindfulness utilizes both formal and informal practices. Traditional formal practices include meditation in the familiar sitting position but also include standing, recumbent, and walking meditation. Contemporary applications of mindfulness in therapeutic contexts often include mindful participation in movement exercises, such as hatha yoga, as a formal practice. The four traditional objects, or "foundations," of mindfulness meditation are bodily sensations, feelings (not emotions, but rather the positive, negative, or neutral valence of one's immediate response to current experience), state of mind (mood or general condition of consciousness at a given moment), and mental contents (the specific contents of consciousness at a given moment, including images, thoughts, and emotions).

Formal practice begins with the teacher or therapist providing instructions in session, often in a group setting. The initial exercise may involve mindfulness of bodily sensation in general ("body scan") or may focus more narrowly on the physical sensations of breathing. Instructions for seated meditation on breathing call for sitting either in a chair or on a cushion on the floor, with the back erect and unsupported, but not tense. The instructor then directs the client's attention to the physical sensations of breathing, either the rising and falling of the abdomen or the touch of the breath as it enters and leaves the nostrils. Additional instructions direct the client to note any distractions and to refocus on the breath. As the client develops a higher level of concentration, the focus of mindful awareness expands to include the four foundations of mindfulness, the full range of bodily, cognitive, and emotional experience.

An essential feature of this approach is a commitment by the client to formal daily practice, typically for 45 minutes per day. The therapist typically provides recorded instructions to aid in daily practice.

Informal practices facilitate the generalization of mindfulness to everyday activities, including situations that are problematic for the client. They also are potentially useful when client characteristics, such as acute distress or affective dyscontrol, preclude using the more intense formal practices. Informal practice involves participating in an everyday activity, such as eating, showering, or housecleaning, with the same purposeful attention to present experience and nonjudgmental attitude cultivated in formal practice. Some programs incorporate brief (3-minute) periods of mindfulness of the breath or bodily sensations that can be used throughout the day to foster generalization.

Opinion is divided regarding whether clinicians using mindfulness must engage in formal mindfulness meditation practice. However, anyone considering the use of informal mindfulness techniques with clients should at least have experience applying these techniques in his or her own daily life. Clinicians should not attempt to teach formal meditation practices without having had a period of formal practice under the guidance of a qualified teacher, for at least two reasons. First, meditation often presents challenges that are best understood and worked with on an experiential level, which will be unfamiliar to an inexperienced clinician. Second, the therapist's own mindful approach to working with the client will model the characteristics of mindfulness thought to be of benefit to the client.

An elaborate Buddhist psychology, the *Abhidhamma* of the Pali Canon, provides the rationale for the effectiveness of mindfulness meditation. However, the processes and effects of mindfulness meditation probably are best couched in language compatible with Western psychological theory if it is to be integrated into psychological practice. In this regard, it is useful to speak of the processes and effects of mindfulness in terms of first-order and second-order mechanisms of change. *First-order change mechanisms* refer to processes that bring about change in the content of overt behavior or private experience. Most cognitive and behavioral techniques target first-order change. *Second-order change mechanisms,* on the other hand, refer to processes that change the context or meaning of behavior or experience.

Proposed first-order change mechanisms of mindfulness include relaxation, covert exposure, incompatible response, and enhanced self-management.

Relaxation is a well-documented effect of meditation, but the relationship between mindfulness meditation and relaxation is more complex than this general finding suggests. The purpose of mindfulness meditation is to teach nonjudgmental observation of one's current experience, rather than to induce relaxation. Increased relaxation frequently occurs, but the actual experience that is the object of mindfulness meditation may include autonomic arousal, muscle tension, troubling thoughts, and other phenomena considered to be incompatible with relaxation. The apparent contradiction results from failing to distinguish relaxation as a state of low physiological arousal from the sometimes tranquil, nonreactive cognitive stance that characterizes mindfulness. Thus, relaxation may be more appropriately considered a secondary benefit of mindfulness than a primary therapeutic mechanism.

Exposure to avoided stimuli is a core element of behavioral treatments of anxiety disorders. Mindfulness meditation provides covert exposure to feared stimuli through mindful attention to relevant thoughts and images. In addition, the basic stance of mindfulness is incompatible with the various cognitive-avoidance strategies that might otherwise prevent habituation.

A related proposed therapeutic mechanism depends on the finite cognitive bandwidth that characterizes human information processing. Mindfulness meditation appears to occupy cognitive resources sufficient to be incompatible with worry, rumination, castrophizing, and other cognitive symptoms, thus providing symptomatic relief.

Several authors have proposed that the improved control of attention and more accurate self-observation developed through mindfulness practice lead to enhanced self-management. Increased attention to and awareness of the cognitions, emotions, and physical sensations that are early signs of problems may prompt the use of previously learned coping skills before a problem is fully developed, when coping skills are most likely to interrupt the problem sequence. Examples in the literature include coping with pain and stress, adaptive responding to early signs of depressive relapse, and recognition of satiety cues in binge eaters.

Self-management may also be enhanced through attention to and recognition of the actual consequences of behavior, rather than to one's habitual attributions about what contributes to one's distress.

A final proposed mechanism by which mindfulness meditation enhances self-management involves the nonjudgmental recognition of one's private, subjective experience for what it is, rather than as a necessarily accurate reflection of reality (see discussion of second-order change mechanisms below). This recognition facilitates a less automatic, less reactive mode of behavior, characterized by a shift in control of behavior from mood and reactive thinking to the person's values and desired goals.

Proponents of mindfulness-based interventions place greater emphasis on second-order change mechanisms relative to the first-order mechanisms described above. Proposed second-order mechanisms include cognitive change, exposure and desensitization to private experience, and acceptance. These mechanisms are closely interrelated and may best be considered as differing perspectives on the same process.

Several authors propose that mindfulness promotes a change in attitude toward private experience, sometimes characterized as taking on a "decentered" or "deliteralized" perspective. Thoughts are perceived as "just thoughts," emotions as "just emotions," and bodily sensations as "just feelings," rather than as realities that require corrective action, escape, avoidance, or other typically maladaptive coping strategies.

An alternative formulation of this mechanism is that mindfulness facilitates exposure and desensitization to aversive private experiences. Mindfulness meditation promotes sustained, nonjudgmental observation of thoughts, emotions, and bodily sensations that typically are avoided or that serve as triggers for other problematic phenomena. Prolonged exposure in the absence of escape or strategies to attenuate the experience facilitates habituation to the experience. For example, mindful observation of anxiety-related bodily experience may lead to habituation of the emotional reaction to anxiety symptoms that characterizes panic attacks.

A widely discussed second-order change process that is closely associated with mindfulness is acceptance. Indeed, acceptance is considered one of the cornerstones of mindfulness practice. As is the case with mindfulness itself, there is no generally agreed-upon operational definition of acceptance, but descriptions in the literature overlap considerably with those of mindfulness. Such descriptions emphasize experiencing events, both overt and private, fully and willingly. This characterization overlaps with the emphasis on nonjudgmental awareness in discussions of mindfulness. All descriptions of mindfulness-based interventions include an emphasis on the acceptance of a full range of cognitive, emotional, and bodily experiences without trying to avoid, escape, or change them. Examples include physical pain, anxiety symptoms, urges to use psychoactive substances or to binge eat, and maladaptive cognitions. Thus, one important therapeutic mechanism of mindfulness mediation may be the acquisition of acceptance skills.

RESEARCH BASIS

Research in mindfulness-based intervention is in its infancy. Treatment outcome studies have shown such interventions to be effective in variety of behavioral medicine and mental health contexts. However, such treatments typically include a number of mindfulness-related activities and other components, such as education about the condition being treated. No component analyses or dismantling studies have identified the necessary and sufficient components of therapeutic change. Nor have there been studies of client, therapist, or treatment variables that moderate change.

Similarly, studies of the processes that mediate the effects of mindfulness are just beginning. Early studies have demonstrated that mindfulness training does increase "metacognitive awareness," the decentered or deliteralized attitude toward private experience discussed earlier. However, this process is not specific to mindfulness, as clients in cognitive-behavioral therapy also show such increases in metacognitive awareness.

In the absence of such clarifying research, clinicians should be cautious in expanding the use of mindfulness-based interventions to conditions beyond those already described in the literature.

RELEVANT TARGET POPULATIONS AND EXCEPTIONS

Mindfulness has been used both as a general approach to stress management and as a specific treatment targeted at aspects of disorders that are conceptualized to be especially amenable to its effects. The first published study of an intervention based on mindfulness meditation described its efficacy in the management of chronic pain. Other behavioral medicine research has shown that a mindfulness-based intervention was effective in decreasing mood disturbance and stress symptoms in patients with a variety of cancer diagnoses and stages of illness and in decreasing the duration of phototherapy required to reach therapeutic response in psoriasis.

Research with mental disorders has demonstrated the efficacy of mindfulness-based interventions in reducing symptoms in patients with a variety of anxiety disorders and in reducing the risk of relapse in patients with recurrent major depression. An effective treatment protocol for borderline personality disorder includes training in mindfulness skills, and this intervention also has been utilized with some efficacy in eating disorders.

Recent theoretical papers have presented models of generalized anxiety disorder and relapse in substance abuse treatment that support the inclusion of mindfulness-based treatments for these conditions. However, no efficacy studies have been published to date.

Mindfulness-based interventions are demanding of the client's time and effort. They are unlikely to be effective for clients unable or unwilling to organize sufficient time for practice. Work with clients at risk for dissociation or decompensation should begin with informal practice and progress to more formal practices only after such clients demonstrate tolerance of, and some benefit from, the informal practices.

There are no published studies utilizing mindfulness-based interventions with children.

COMPLICATIONS

No adverse reactions to mindfulness meditation have been reported in the empirical literature. It is likely that some clients will have difficulty tolerating the distress frequently evoked by observing bodily sensations, thoughts, and emotions. Many such clients will respond well to a consistent mindfulness-based approach that supports the client in mindfully observing the distress itself. The more serious risk for mindfulness-based approaches may be inadequate therapist fidelity to the model. That is, the therapist may respond to client distress by shifting to a strategy aimed at escaping, avoiding, or reducing the distress, thus undermining the effects of mindfulness.

—*James B. Lane*

See also: Autogenic Training (Vol. I); Classical Conditioning (Vol. I); Relaxation Strategies (Vol. I)

Suggested Readings

Breslin, F. C., Zack, M., & McMain, S. (2002). An information-processing analysis of mindfulness: Implications for relapse prevention in the treatment of substance abuse. *Clinical Psychology: Science and Practice, 9*, 275–299.

Campos, P. E. (Ed.). (2002). Special series: Integrating Buddhist philosophy with cognitive and behavioral practice. *Cognitive and Behavioral Practice, 9*, 38–78.

Gunaratana, H. (2002). *Mindfulness in plain English* (Updated and expanded ed.). Boston: Wisdom Publications.

Hayes, S. C., Jacobson, N. S., Follette, V. M., & Dougher, M. J. (Eds.). (1994). *Acceptance and change: Content and context in psychotherapy.* Reno, NV: Context Press.

Kabat-Zinn, J. (1990). *Full catastrophe living: Using the wisdom of your body and mind to face stress, pain, and illness.* New York: Dell.

Kabat-Zinn, J. (1994). *Wherever you go, there you are: Mindfulness meditation in everyday life.* New York: Hyperion.

Linehan, M. M. (1993). *Cognitive-behavioral treatment of borderline personality disorder.* New York: Guilford Press.

Roemer, L., & Orsillo, S. M. (2002). Expanding our conceptualization of and treatment for generalized anxiety disorder: Integrating mindfulness/acceptance-based approaches with existing cognitive-behavioral models. *Clinical Psychology: Science & Practice, 9*(1), 54–68.

Segal, Z. V., Williams, J. M. G., & Teasdale, J. D. (2002). *Mindfulness-based cognitive therapy for depression: A new approach to preventing relapse.* New York: Guilford Press.

MODELING

DESCRIPTION OF THE STRATEGY

People learn by watching other people. Throughout history, writers, educators, and social leaders have extolled the importance of providing a good example for others and, conversely, for basing one's own behavior on the conduct of particularly virtuous or accomplished individuals. Modeling procedures take advantage of observational, or vicarious, learning to teach people more adaptive responses. Modeling involves having an observer watch another person, the model, engage in specific behaviors that demonstrate effective ways to respond to problem situations. The modeled segments are structured and are systematically and repeatedly presented until the observer displays the desired behavioral outcome.

Observing the behavior of others, which we will call *modeling,* produces three general effects. First, modeling can help people acquire new behaviors and emotional responses, a process called *observational learning.* Modeling is particularly useful in teaching complex or intricate behaviors, such as effective social behavior or an academic skill. In addition, watching the emotional reactions of others can produce similar emotional responses in observers. Thus, a child may develop a fear of thunderstorms from watching her mother's fearful behavior during storms. Such acquired fears may persist for years. An important clinical extension of this principle is that anxiety can also be reduced or eliminated by observing others approach the feared object or situation without suffering harmful effects. This process is sometimes called *vicarious extinction.*

Second, observing another's behavior and the consequences of that behavior for the model can *inhibit* or *disinhibit* existing behavior. Thus, a child who observes another child being ridiculed for speaking in class may become less willing to try to answer questions. In contrast, observing a bully receive approval for aggressive behavior may encourage other children to display aggression.

Finally, modeling can lead to *response facilitation.* Here, a person uses the behavior of another as a cue as to when to engage in specific behaviors. At a social function, for example, a person may watch whether others shake hands or bow, or when they begin to eat, so that he or she can match the behavior displayed by people who know what to do. Observational techniques are used in cognitive-behavioral treatments to produce all three types of outcomes.

Two of the most common clinical uses of modeling are as components of treatments designed to overcome maladaptive anxiety and to teach effective interpersonal behavior. An example of the use of modeling

to overcome anxiety is found in the treatment of obsessive-compulsive disorder, a condition marked by unshakable intrusive thoughts and repetitive, unwanted behaviors. Treatment generally begins with the therapist and patient developing a hierarchy of feared objects or behaviors that are organized from least to most anxiety provoking. Patients are then exposed to the feared events using *participant modeling,* a technique in which the therapist first models the feared behavior, followed by the patient. Participant modeling begins with the least anxiety-provoking item of the hierarchy and moves to more anxiety-provoking items as lower items come to elicit less anxiety. Take the example of a person who fears contamination from touching light switches or doorknobs. First, the therapist will touch the "contaminated" object, and then the patient will be encouraged to do so. Observing the therapist touch the object without harm takes advantage of vicarious extinction to reduce patient anxiety, which, in turn, reduces avoidance of feared objects in real life.

As described above, when treating anxiety-related conditions, it is generally more effective to present the feared objects or situations in a graduated fashion. Beginning with a situation that evokes a high level of anxiety may reduce the person's motivation to perform the feared action and can even increase fear. In addition, it is essential to prevent the person from engaging in *safety behaviors,* that is, actions that prevent full exposure to either the model or the feared event. For example, people with obsessive-compulsive disorder might look away when the therapist touches the object or rub their hands on their clothes to reduce the imagined contamination that comes from touching it. People will even engage in such "decontamination" responses when observing the therapist touch feared objects. Patients must be taught to prevent themselves from taking actions that nullify the effect of exposure. Each exposure to the feared object or situation must be of sufficient duration to allow anxiety to dissipate, and each item in the fear hierarchy should be repeated until new presentations elicit little anxiety. The final step in the procedure is to assign "homework" exposure exercises in which the person touches feared objects at home. Again, a graduated approach is important.

An example of the use of modeling to teach more effective interpersonal strategies is found in treatments for aggressive behavior. In these treatments, people are first asked to monitor themselves and to identify situations that trigger anger and aggressive responses. They then watch videotaped or live models demonstrate nonaggressive ways to defuse those situations. The models often begin the segment by verbalizing cognitive strategies to reframe the situation so as to reduce anger. They then tell their plans for managing the event. Such *cognitive modeling* has been shown to enhance the observer's mastery and retention of the new behavior. Next, the model demonstrates socially effective nonaggressive behavior, after which the patient rehearses the behavior with the therapist or members of a treatment group. Following in-session rehearsal, patients try the new behaviors in their daily lives.

As with anxiety, presenting situations in a graduated fashion increases treatment effectiveness. In addition, to maximize learning, complex behavior must be broken into smaller components. Ideally, the model begins by illustrating relatively straightforward behaviors and moves to more complicated responses only when the patient masters the basic behavioral building blocks. After observing each modeled segment, the patient rehearses the demonstrated behavior, and the therapist provides feedback on the patient's performance. It is particularly important that positive features of the observer's performance be noted. Social reinforcement helps people recognize which elements of their performance are effective, increase motivation, and contribute to their mastery of the behavior. The therapist and patient then work together to identify any deficiencies in the person's performance, and new behaviors that specifically address those deficiencies are demonstrated. In this way, behavior is shaped to become increasingly more effective. Behavioral rehearsal significantly increases the likelihood of treatment success. Thus, patients should practice new behaviors until they feel a sense of comfort and mastery before trying them in their daily interactions.

RESEARCH BASIS

In the treatment context, modeling is seldom used alone, but instead is integrated with exposure or behavioral-rehearsal techniques. Participant modeling, where the patient performs the desired behavior after the model, is significantly more effective in reducing anxiety than simply observing a model. As noted earlier, in-session rehearsal of modeled behaviors increases learning and retention. Rehearsal also

increases performance, that is, the likelihood that the person will try the new behavior in real-life situations.

The characteristics of the model affect the outcome of observational procedures. People more readily learn from models whom they perceive to be similar to themselves. Thus, similarities in age, appearance, and social class between observer and model all facilitate modeling. An example of this principle is the *coping model.* In contrast to the *mastery model,* who flawlessly demonstrates the desired behavior on the first try, the coping model initially appears uncertain, fearful, or inept but then goes on to master the situation. Fearful or low-self-esteem individuals are believed to respond better to coping models because they identify with the model's initial uncertainty. Another example of the similarity principle is found in *peer modeling,* a technique that is often used in academic or work settings. Here, the person is paired on a task with a similar other, for example, a classmate or coworker. Peer modeling offers the person the opportunity for naturalistic observation of how a similar person handles a difficult situation. On the whole, models who appear to have authority, social status, and success are more readily imitated than low-status models. Live models are more effective than videotaped, or *symbolic,* models. Finally, modeling effects are enhanced through the use of multiple models, as opposed to a single model.

Another key factor to treatment success is the outcome produced by the modeled behavior. Models who are visibly rewarded are more effective than models who do not receive rewards or are punished. Indeed, observing a model receive a negative outcome has been found to completely inhibit the observer's motivation to perform the behavior. In a similar vein, if the observers' first real-life attempts are punished, they are unlikely to repeat the adaptive response, whether it is approaching a feared object or trying a new behavioral strategy to manage a difficult situation. Therefore, it is important that homework assignments begin with behaviors and situations where the person will be successful.

RELEVANT TARGET POPULATIONS AND EXCEPTIONS

Modeling is used to treat many types of problem behavior. As noted earlier, modeling is an integral part of treatment for the anxiety disorders. In addition to obsessive-compulsive disorder, modeling is used in treatments for the phobias. One such example is social phobia, a condition marked by excessive anxiety in social situations. Videotaped or live models are used to demonstrate effective patterns of social behavior for the phobic person, which are then practiced. Modeling not only teaches the person new skills to handle unfamiliar social events, but observing the model handle criticism or be assertive reduces the anxiety such events often produce in people with social phobia. Social-phobic people are also encouraged to observe others in real life. Naturalistic observation not only teaches responses that are appropriate to the person's life situation but also corrects these individuals' inaccurate assumptions that they alone display signs of anxiety or behave awkwardly in social situations. Thus, observational techniques can be used to correct the mistaken beliefs that fuel social anxiety.

Modeling is used as part of treatments for other anxiety spectrum conditions, as well. For example, treatment regimens for some sexual disorders incorporate observational learning. Thus, a person for whom anxiety inhibits sexual arousal or orgasm might watch videotapes of couples engaging in sexual intercourse. Observing the taped models reduces anxiety and helps the person and his or her partner learn effective sexual behavior.

Observational procedures are also widely used in educational settings, both in routine teaching and in helping people overcome learning problems. Modeling is used in occupational settings to teach work-related skills, ranging from simple motor behaviors to effective conflict resolution. In health care settings, videotaped models are used to reduce patients' fears about upcoming medical procedures and to teach them how to manage pain.

An advantage of modeling is that it can be used with young children, who may have difficulty with verbal information or following complicated procedures. Indeed, modeling is commonly used to treat phobias and maladaptive aggression in children and adolescents. Modeling is also a central part of treatment programs for autistic children. Here, therapist modeling is used to shape speech and social behavior. In building language for example, the therapist will model a sound and then reward the child for imitating the sound. The therapist gradually moves toward verbalizing a complete word. The child, in turn, is rewarded for closer and closer approximations until he or she says the word. This modeling and shaping procedure takes considerable time but is one of the few demonstrably effective techniques for overcoming some of the deficits found in autism.

COMPLICATIONS

Modeling procedures require that participants have the capacity to devote attention to modeled stimuli and the ability to discriminate relevant cues. Both attentional focus and discrimination can be reduced by lack of motivation and by cognitive impairment. Observers can also be limited by heightened emotionality, as when anxiety is so great that the person is unwilling to observe the model or has difficulty focusing on or identifying the relevant stimuli. Finally, people with some types of personality disorders may not use their newly learned behavior in the way that was intended. For example, psychopaths can use the social skills they learn from modeling procedures to manipulate others rather than to build genuine relationships.

CASE ILLUSTRATION

"Mary" was a 37-year-old single woman employed as a secretary-clerk. She came to treatment seeking help for anxiety in social situations. Mary reported that she had no close friends and few contacts other than her parents. Although she was active in her church, she felt tense, shaky, and uncomfortable talking to other church members. She seldom talked to coworkers and was particularly distressed about a woman coworker whom she felt criticized and made fun of her. Mary also had difficulty disagreeing with others and expressing her opinions. Finally, she believed that others could see her anxiety and that they did not respect her or want much to do with her. In general, she led a lonely life, working by herself during the day and watching television at night.

Four methods were used to assess key problem areas. First, a behavioral interview was conducted to develop a list of situations that produced social anxiety. Mary's typical thoughts and physical symptoms were identified for each problem situation, as well as her behavioral response to the event. Second, she and her therapist role-played several problem situations. These situations were videotaped and reviewed to rate her anxiety and behavior. Particular attention was devoted to identifying safety behaviors, small behaviors used to reduce anxiety or prevent anticipated criticism. Third, she monitored daily life events and rated her anxiety in each social encounter using a 100-point subjective distress scale (SUDS). She also noted the safety behaviors that she used to reduce anxiety in daily life. For example, she noted that she tried to avoid looking at people, spoke softly, and left rooms when groups of coworkers were talking. She also found that she tended to agree and laugh along when the problem coworker bullied her. Finally, structured questionnaires were given to measure assertiveness, anxiety during social interactions, and dysphoric mood.

The primary treatment goal was to encourage Mary to engage in more active, prosocial, and assertive interpersonal behaviors. Treatment began by presenting a videotape in which models demonstrated assertive, nonassertive, and aggressive behavior patterns. After each segment, the tape was stopped, and Mary and her therapist enacted the event. Following this, situations calling for assertive behaviors were selected from her self-monitoring and were role-played. Some of the role plays were videotaped and reviewed to identify things she had done well and ways to strengthen her behavior, such as speaking up and looking directly at people.

As a result of her self-monitoring, Mary recognized that her avoidant behavior discouraged other people from talking with her. To address this pattern, Mary and her therapist identified behaviors that conveyed friendliness and interest in others. Behavior rehearsal was used to increase her comfort smiling, maintaining appropriate eye contact, greeting others, and responding to small talk. Information from her self-monitoring was used to target key situations. For each situation, Mary was first asked to identify behaviors that would communicate friendliness. She then practiced the situation and reflected on whether she was satisfied with her behavior. Whenever she was uncertain what to do, her therapist would demonstrate several ways to handle the event, and she would try again. At each step, Mary was encouraged not to mimic the therapist, but to adapt the modeled behavior to her own style. As she became increasingly confident in her performance, she began to apply the new behavioral strategies to life events, beginning by talking to church members and coworkers who appeared friendly. She was surprised to discover that other people became more talkative and interested in her after she changed her behavior.

Naturalistic observation techniques were used to increase her understanding of the workplace social environment. She was first assigned to observe other people during meetings to see whether they ever displayed anxiety. She found that virtually everyone occasionally stumbled over their words, appeared anxious, or didn't know what to do. Another assignment was to watch how coworkers handled the office bully. She was amazed to discover that the woman was as critical and difficult with others as with herself. This discovery reduced Mary's belief that the bully picked on her because she was anxious or in some way defective. She found herself expressing support for a timid coworker, who also received ridicule, and the two began to go for coffee. The realization that she was not alone and the social support provided by the coworker led her to eventually tell the bully that she "did not appreciate being laughed at." Another coworker chimed in to agree, and the tide turned against the aggressor. By the end of treatment, Mary was routinely having coffee and lunch with her two coworkers, and they occasionally socialized outside of work, two changes that significantly improved her quality of life.

—Lynn Alden

See also: *Modeling (Vol. II); Peer Tutoring (Vol. III); Social Skills Training (Vol. I);*

Suggested Readings

Bandura, A. (1997). *Self-efficacy: The exercise of control.* New York: Freeman.

Bandura, A. (1986). *Social foundations of thought and action: A social cognitive theory.* Englewood Cliffs, NJ: Prentice Hall.

Barratt, P. M. (1998). Group therapy for childhood anxiety disorders. *Journal of Clinical Child Psychology, 27,* 459–468.

Spiegler, M. D., & Guevremont, D. C. (2003). Modeling therapy and skills training. In *Contemporary Behavior Therapy* (4th ed.). Belmont, CA: Thomson-Wadsworth.

Webster-Stratton, C., & Hammond, M. (1997). Treatment of children with early-onset conduct problems: A comparison of child and parent training interventions. *Journal of Consulting and Clinical Psychology, 65,* 93–109.

MOTIVATIONAL ENHANCEMENT THERAPY

DESCRIPTION OF THE STRATEGY

Motivational enhancement therapy (MET) was originally developed as one of three treatment methods tested in Project MATCH, a multisite clinical trial funded by the National Institute on Alcohol Abuse and Alcoholism and the largest study ever conducted with psychotherapies for alcohol use disorders. Project MATCH aimed to compare three treatment methods with very different conceptual-theoretical bases. MET was adopted as a treatment focused on increasing clients' intrinsic motivation for change. It was compared with cognitive behavior therapy intended to teach coping skills for relapse prevention and with a 12-step facilitation therapy designed to engage clients in the spiritual program of Alcoholics Anonymous.

MET combines two intervention methods: the clinical style of motivational interviewing and structured personal feedback from pretreatment evaluation. Prior to Project MATCH, this combination had been termed a "drinker's checkup," in which a comprehensive evaluation was followed by a session in which the client received individual feedback of findings, delivered in an empathic and nonconfrontational counseling style. The drinker's checkup was subsequently adapted for use with various other target concerns, including tobacco smoking, marijuana use, heroin and cocaine use, and marital counseling (a "relationship checkup").

The clinical style of *motivational interviewing* (MI) is described in a separate entry in this volume. In essence, MI is a client-centered yet directive counseling method for helping people to resolve ambivalence and strengthen motivation and commitment to change. The MI counselor avoids arguing for change and instead elicits the client's own desire, reasons, perceived need and self-efficacy for change. Within MI, clients in essence talk themselves into change. In contrast to a deficit reduction view of clients—that they lack knowledge, skills, insight, or motivation that the therapist must install—MI assumes that the necessary motivations for change are already within the client, waiting to be evoked. MI does not, in itself, involve the use of formal pretreatment evaluation or personal feedback for clients. It is the addition of structured assessment feedback that differentiates MET from MI.

Although the treatment that was tested in Project MATCH required a prescribed set of alcohol-related assessment measures, the method of MET is not tied to particular measures. It could include nearly any reliable and valid measure that is pertinent to the target clinical issue. The Project MATCH intervention assessed drinking levels, blood alcohol (intoxication) peaks, ethanol tolerance and dependence levels, negative consequences of drinking, liver function tests, and

neuropsychological tests sensitive to alcohol's early effects on cognitive functioning. For smokers, the pertinent dimensions might include carbon monoxide levels, lung capacity, cigarette consumption, and nicotine dependence level. In couples counseling, the checkup component could assess each partner's relationship satisfaction, communication style, sexual satisfaction, mood states, and shared pleasant events. A "spiritual checkup" could be devised using psychometrically sound measures of constructs such as meaning in life, concept of God, values, spiritual practices and experiences, and altruistic love. Other checkup formats are easily imagined for diet and exercise, psychological well-being, physical health, and quality of life.

To be useful in MET, scores from such assessment measures must be interpretable. The client's individual score can be compared with established standards for clinical interpretation (such as cut-scores for mild, medium, substantial, or severe dependence) or with norms for general or clinical populations (ideally adjusted for gender and perhaps age). The clinician reviews each finding with the client, explaining the meaning of the measure, the client's own score, and that score's significance relative to norms. With regard to drinking or drug use, for example, we have quantified clients' own levels of use and then compared them with national norms to determine each client's percentile placement (e.g., the percentage of other men or women who use the same amount of the drug, or more). Comparison of self with relevant social norms has a well-established track record in effecting behavior change and is one example of more general processes of self-regulation whereby people adjust their behavior in response to goals and feedback.

One can imagine a wide range of clinician styles for delivering assessment feedback. Within MET, the information is clearly explained, but the counselor avoids directly telling the client what to think or do about it. Instead, the counselor asks the client for his or her reactions and responds to these with the MI style of reflective listening, paying particular attention to the client's self-motivating statements of concern, desire, reasons, need, or commitment to change. The period of assessment feedback is often preceded and followed by open-ended MI, to elicit the client's intrinsic motivations for change above and beyond information provided in the feedback.

The counselor then draws together all of the client's "change talk," including responses to the assessment feedback, in a transitional summary and then opens the door for the client to suggest what the next step might be. The MET counselor does not abruptly shift into a prescriptive mode, but instead follows the client's lead toward a change plan that is acceptable and to which the client is willing to commit.

RESEARCH BASIS

The research basis described for MI is pertinent to MET. There is also a large motivational literature demonstrating that behavior change is motivated when people receive feedback of status that is discrepant with their own goals and values. There is reason, therefore, to expect that both MI and personal feedback can exert separate effects in promoting behavior change. Their combination in MET has been tested in more than a dozen clinical trials for substance abuse alone. When added to treatment, MET has been found in several studies to double posttreatment abstinence rates. When delivered at the beginning of treatment, MET also has been found to increase treatment retention and adherence and to increase client motivation for change in ways that treatment staff can reliably perceive though unaware of which clients had received MET. Clinical trial support has also been published for a marijuana checkup. One large clinical trial with clients seeking treatment for heroin and cocaine dependence failed to show a beneficial effect when MET was added to treatment as usual. Other studies, however, have reported beneficial outcomes of MET with illicit drug users.

RELEVANT TARGET POPULATIONS AND EXCEPTIONS

As with motivational interviewing, the intended target population for MET is people whose low level of motivation is an obstacle to their undertaking needed behavior change. Within the transtheoretical model of change, these would be contemplators (ambivalent about change) and precontemplators (seeing no need for change). MET may be particularly useful (compared with MI) with precontemplators, where what is needed in order to progress to the next stage of change is to create ambivalence. MI and MET appear to be differentially effective with clients who are less motivated for change or who show higher levels of anger and resistance about change at the outset of consultation. For those who are already well along in readiness

for change, MET may add no benefit, because its primary purpose is to enhance motivation for change.

COMPLICATIONS

Beyond complications of motivational interviewing itself, MET introduces complexities related to assessment and feedback. One of these is additional time required to obtain the assessment information needed for MET. A possibility here is to rely on the assessment data already collected before treatment begins, thus avoiding the need for additional data collection and the associated time. Often, however, the standard intake evaluation does not include a sufficient range of psychometrically sound measures on the basis of which people can be given reliable feedback. In this case, it may be worth the investment of additional assessment time. To the extent that paper-and-pencil or computer-administered measures can be used, the demand on professional time is diminished but still adds to client time burden before treatment begins.

The MET interviewer also needs thorough familiarity with the assessment instruments and their interpretation. Questions usually arise with regard to how scores are determined, what they mean, and their validity. The therapist should be able to answer these comfortably and factually. This adds to the amount to be learned before one is prepared to offer MET.

There are also times when the assessment feedback component of MET comes into conflict with the overall clinical style of MI. In general, the goal within MI is to evoke increasing client readiness for and commitment to change and to minimize resistance to change. For some clients, the process of providing assessment feedback engenders resistance, and the client begins backing away from problem recognition and change. If this occurs, it is wise not to persist in reviewing feedback, but instead to attend to and reflect what the client is experiencing. It is generally countertherapeutic to push ahead with feedback or a change plan when the client is obviously resisting it. A better course would be falling back to a broad MI style, building willingness to hear the feedback, continuing to explore, and considering the possibility of change.

CASE ILLUSTRATION

"Gloria" was a 38-year-old supervisor at a retail department store, who came for an evaluation of her drinking at the urging of her family. Her husband in particular had watched her drinking accelerate over the years, to the point that she was consuming large amounts of alcohol daily. She could not remember the last time she had gone for an entire day without drinking, and she consciously avoided situations in which alcohol was not available. When the family went camping in the mountains of New Mexico, she took along an ample supply of wine and tequila. She sometimes went out drinking with women friends after work or on weekends, but usually, she just came home and disappeared into her workroom to spend time telephoning friends or surfing the Internet. She drove the children to school in the morning, and her husband picked them up after school and cared for them in the evenings while she was drinking.

The crisis began one night when her husband threatened to divorce her and obtain full custody of their three children. The choice he put to her was to go get help or to move out. She was stunned, but she agreed to be evaluated. He called the clinic the next day, and we saw her that afternoon.

Consultation began with a 45-minute session of motivational interviewing, in which the therapist focused on understanding the situation from Gloria's perspective. She was obviously uncomfortable talking about her drinking, and embarrassed to have been pushed into counseling. The therapist acknowledged these feelings with empathic listening, and within a few minutes, she seemed to relax a bit. She acknowledged one concern that she had about her own use of alcohol—frequent lapses of memory (blackouts) during later evening hours. When the therapist continued to respond with acceptance and reflective listening, she began to divulge more. The therapist's goal for this session, beyond establishing rapport, was to gain her agreement to complete a 2-hour thorough evaluation of her drinking and related problems. When he raised this toward the end of the first session, she blurted: "But I'm not an alcoholic, am I?"

"To be honest," he said, "I'm not particularly interested in labels. I don't even know enough to be very helpful to you at this point. What matters, I think, is what's happening in your life in relation to alcohol, and what, if anything, you want to do about it. That's where this evaluation could be useful. Are you willing to spend the time?" She agreed.

She had, in fact, been drinking far more than even her family knew. She was surprised at the amount herself when the interviewer (an assessment technician) helped her, during the evaluation, to reconstruct her alcohol use for the prior 3 months. She had been averaging nearly 11 standard drinks per day (the amount of alcohol that is contained in about 10 cans of beer, or in her case, in a quart of wine plus a double shot of tequila). Also evaluated were her negative life consequences from drinking, her level of alcohol dependence, her mood states, and her motivations for drinking. Some neuropsychological tests were administered that are particularly sensitive to alcohol's early effects on cognitive functioning, and a blood test was drawn to examine liver function tests.

A few days after completing this assessment, Gloria came back for a third visit. Following an initial check-in (no significant changes had occurred), they reviewed together the findings from her evaluation. The therapist first explained the "standard drink" unit, and she was clearly startled by the calculation that she had been averaging 76 drinks per week. "I realized it was a lot when I was going through the interview," she said, "but that seems awfully high."

"It surprises you," the therapist reflected. "You hadn't really ever thought about how much you were drinking."

"I was kind of aware of it, but I had no idea it was so much."

The therapist went on to compare her drinking with that for adult women in the United States. She was above the 99th percentile: Fewer than 1 in 100 women drank as much as she did.

"Most of my friends drink as much as I do," she said.

"What do you make of that?"

"I guess we're an elite group," she said, and smiled for the first time.

They continued reviewing the results of the evaluation. Her blood alcohol level, in the course of a typical evening of drinking, was probably exceeding 200 mg% (.200), which explained the memory problems. Given the rate of alcohol metabolism, it also meant that she had been driving her children to school while still legally intoxicated (the limit in New Mexico was .08). Although she had not had any alcohol since the night before, had she been pulled over, she could have gone to jail. It shocked her. "That must be why I feel so bad every morning at work," she offered.

She had accumulated a substantial number of negative consequences of drinking, even by her own self-report. It was, in fact, about the average level of lifetime consequences for people entering treatment for alcohol problems. She met diagnostic criteria for alcohol dependence, and her level of dependence fell into the "substantial" range. "Am I alcoholic?" she asked again. The therapist explained that "alcoholism" had been abandoned as a formal diagnosis in the United States in 1980, and he described the pattern of dependence in which alcohol gradually, over time, takes on an ever more central role in a person's life.

According to a mood questionnaire, Gloria was decidedly depressed, which opened up a short discussion of alcohol as a depressant drug. She showed mild elevation on one liver enzyme and impairment on two of the cognitive tests that are sensitive to alcohol's effects.

"So, what do you make of all this?" the therapist asked when they had finished.

"I don't know," Gloria said. "I guess my husband was right. I don't like to admit it, but this is pretty depressing."

"So what are you thinking about drinking at this point?"

"To tell you the truth, I'm thinking about *having* a drink or 10," she said with a nervous laugh. "I guess I need to do something—for my family, for myself."

From there, they developed a treatment plan that involved joint outpatient counseling for Gloria and her husband, while their children stayed with friends. By her fourth session, which her husband attended, she had cut down to two to three drinks per day and had 2 days of complete abstinence. The therapist began cognitive behavior therapy focused on her mood and drinking. The next week, there were 2 days with some drinking and 5 days of abstinence.

On her sixth visit, Gloria had had only one drink, and therapy began to focus on couple counseling. The topic of drinking came up, though. Her husband was upset that Gloria was "still drinking." The therapist reframed: "She's gone from 76 drinks a week to 1, and at the same time you're still understandably nervous because this is so new." They talked about how much better she looked and felt and how she was spending more time with her family rather than in her workroom. "The kids are noticing, too," he said. "They're always on her lap now, and want to be with her." She beamed. The next week, she had had no alcohol at all, and that's how it stayed for the rest of 4 months of outpatient treatment.

—*William R. Miller*

See also: *Behavioral Case Formulation (Vol. I); Motivational Interviewing (Vol. I);*

Suggested Readings

Agostinelli, G., Brown, J. M., & Miller, W. R. (1995). Effects of normative feedback on consumption among heavy drinking college students. *Journal of Drug Education, 25,* 31–40.

Babor, T. F., & Del Boca, F. K. (Eds.). (2003). *Treatment matching in alcoholism.* Cambridge, UK: Cambridge University Press.

Holder, H. D., Cisler, R. A., Longabaugh, R., Stout, R. L., Treno, A. J., & Zweben, A. (2000). Alcoholism treatment and medical care costs from Project MATCH. *Addiction, 95,* 999–1013.

Miller, W. R. (Ed.). (1999). *Enhancing motivation for change in substance abuse treatment* (Treatment Improvement Protocol Series, No. 35). Rockville, MD: Center for Substance Abuse Treatment.

Miller, W. R., Zweben, A., DiClemente, C. C., & Rychtarik, R. G. (1992). *Motivational enhancement therapy manual: A clinical research guide for therapists treating individuals with alcohol abuse and dependence* (Vol. 2, Project MATCH Monograph Series). Rockville, MD: National Institute on Alcohol Abuse and Alcoholism.

Project MATCH Research Group. (1997). Matching alcoholism treatments to client heterogeneity: Project MATCH post-treatment drinking outcomes. *Journal of Studies on Alcohol, 58,* 7–29.

MOTIVATIONAL INTERVIEWING

DESCRIPTION OF THE STRATEGY

Most forms of cognitive behavior therapy presuppose an adequate level of client motivation for change. They are characteristically directive and prescriptive, recommending particular changes in client behavior and cognition, and often involving homework assignments for the client to carry out between sessions. As with many other therapies, adherence to treatment prescriptions is a significant problem in cognitive behavior therapy, particularly with certain populations and target problems.

Motivational interviewing (MI) was predicated on the assumption that many people with current behavior problems are at best ambivalent about changing them, even when entering treatment. If this is so, then it would not be surprising that directive prescriptions for behavior change are met with fluctuating compliance. MI was designed to address ambivalence directly, enhancing clients' intrinsic motivation for and commitment to change. It was originally intended as a prelude to therapy, enhancing treatment adherence and thereby improving outcomes. There is evidence (discussed below) that MI does, in fact, enhance adherence and outcomes when added to other treatment. It became apparent quite early, however, that MI alone can also trigger behavior change and that in some circumstances, MI is itself a psychotherapeutic intervention.

MI is heavily rooted in the humanistic client-centered counseling methods developed and tested by Carl Rogers and his students and might be regarded as an evolution of client-centered therapy. Many of the specific methods used within MI are drawn directly from the work of Rogers, and in a real sense, one cannot competently deliver MI without first developing proficiency in client-centered counseling.

Where, then, does MI depart from a client-centered approach? The principal point of departure is that MI is consciously directive, whereas client-centered counseling has usually been described as nondirective. Within MI, the therapist seeks to elicit and differentially reinforce particular types of client speech, tipping the balance of ambivalence toward intrinsic motivation for and commitment to change. Rogers maintained that his own responding to clients was noncontingent and unconditional, although his student Charles Truax published data suggesting that, in fact, Rogers selectively reinforced certain kinds of client statements. MI assumes that therapists necessarily select the client statements to which they will respond, as well as their own responses to those statements, in a nonrandom manner. Such selective reinforcement is a conscious process in MI, directed toward specific change goals. This means that MI is useful when there is a particular behavior change goal, especially when the client is ambivalent about achieving the goal.

MI was originally described in 1983 as a method for working with problem drinkers. To say that a client is ambivalent is to assume that he or she simultaneously wants to change and wants to stay the same. Both forms of motivation are present within the ambivalent client. If the therapist takes up the pro-change side of the argument (e.g., "You have a drinking problem, and you need to quit"), the ambivalent client predictably responds with counterchange arguments (e.g., "No I'm not, and I don't want to"). Such acting out of the client's ambivalence might be therapeutic were it not for the fact that people tend to be persuaded by what they themselves say. If counseling is done in a way that elicits counterchange arguments from clients, they are in essence talking themselves

out of changing. MI intentionally seeks to elicit from clients their own intrinsic motivations for and commitment to change. When MI is done well, clients literally talk themselves into change.

Recent descriptions of MI have emphasized its underlying spirit, a set of basic assumptions within which the method is practiced. MI is, first of all, an eliciting approach. Prescriptive psychotherapies often proceed from the underlying assumption that "I have what you need" and seek to provide the client with new knowledge, coping skills, insight, or patterns of cognition. Within MI, the starting assumption is that "You have what you need," and the therapist's task is to draw it out from the client. It is more listening than telling, more evoking wisdom than installing it. MI is also a collaborative approach. Counselor and client work in partnership, recognizing that clients are the experts on themselves. It is a respectful expert-to-expert collaboration, rather than an expert-to-recipient approach. Finally, MI respects client autonomy. Ultimately, it is the client who chooses his or her own path, behavior, and lifestyle. Much as therapists might wish to make choices for their clients, ultimately, they cannot. It is noteworthy that these underlying assumptions of MI overlap much more with the humanistic-existential "third force" in psychology than with the historic perspectives of behavior therapy.

Within this underlying spirit of the approach, there are four general guiding principles of MI:

1. Express empathy

2. Develop discrepancy

3. Roll with resistance

4. Support self-efficacy

Empathic reflective listening is as fundamental to MI as it is to client-centered counseling. The therapist seeks primarily to understand the client's own perspectives, while directively strengthening, by emphasis, certain of those perspectives. With a particular behavior change goal in mind, the therapist seeks to develop discrepancy in the client's consciousness between the status quo (behave as usual) and the client's own higher goals and values. "Resistance" is understood simply as the client's voicing of the status quo, the other side of ambivalence about change, and the goal is to "roll with" resistance rather than opposing (and thereby strengthening) it. Finally, commitment to change depends both upon perceived importance and perceived ability to change. Therefore, attention is given in MI both to eliciting the importance of change (desire, reasons, need) and to strengthening self-efficacy for change (ability).

Two phases of MI are recognized. In Phase 1, the therapist's primary task is to elicit and strengthen the client's own intrinsic motivations for change by exploring desire, ability, reasons, and need. In Phase 2, the therapist helps the client consolidate these into commitment to a specific plan for change. Knowing when to shift from Phase 1 (enhancing motivation) to Phase 2 (strengthening commitment) is a key judgment call and is driven by attention to particular signs of client readiness for change.

RESEARCH BASIS

A large evidence base now supports both the efficacy of MI and its theorized mechanisms of change. To date, the strongest support for MI's efficacy remains in the treatment of alcohol and other drug problems. Positive clinical trials have also been published, however, in the treatment of pathological gambling and in the management of chronic diseases, including diabetes, hypertension, and cardiovascular disease. It has been applied effectively both in reducing problem behavior and in promoting health behaviors. A majority of trials have found MI to be significantly more effective than no intervention or psychoeducational control conditions.

MI has also been tested as an add-on to other treatment methods, usually by providing a session or two of MI prior to or early in treatment. Interestingly, the specific effects of MI on outcome appear to be somewhat larger when it is added to another treatment than when it is tested against no treatment. This seems counterintuitive in that in the former design, MI must exert an effect over and above that of the treatment to which it is being added. Perhaps the easiest way to understand this finding is as a synergistic effect of MI and the concomitant treatment. MI has been found to increase treatment retention and adherence, which, in turn, are related to improved outcomes. Program therapists unaware of which patients had been randomly chosen to receive MI at intake have reliably rated MI patients as more motivated, working harder, and having better prognoses relative to no-MI patients. In sum, even a session or two of individual MI at the beginning of treatment appears to increase client motivation for change in a way that is easily perceptible to their therapists and that is associated with better treatment outcomes.

While treatment outcome research has been accumulating, so has knowledge about how MI works. There is clear evidence that therapists differ significantly from one another in their effectiveness in using MI. Early studies demonstrated a strong positive relationship between the therapist's level of skill in accurate empathy (reflective listening) and more positive treatment outcomes with alcohol use disorders. Other research demonstrated a negative relationship between therapist confrontation and client abstinence. Therapists with a more confrontational style reliably elicit higher levels of client resistance, which, in turn, predicts less behavior change. A direct comparison of MI with "nondirective" client-centered therapy showed greater behavior change with MI, supporting the importance of the directive component of MI.

A significant problem for the theory of MI, however, was a repeated finding of no relationship between client "change talk" and subsequent behavior change. As theorized by the progenitors of MI, clients' voicing of pro-change motivation during MI should increase the probability of behavior change. Yet no such predictive relationship was found.

A breakthrough came with careful psycholinguistic analyses of MI session tapes by Dr. Paul Amrhein. He differentiated between client statements that signaled five categories of motivation: ability, commitment, desire, need, and reasons to change, all of which had previously been combined and analyzed as "change talk." He found that only one of these five commitments robustly predicted behavior change (in this case, abstinence from illicit drugs). He also found that it was not the frequency of commitment language, but rather the strength of commitment that mattered. Furthermore, it was not the overall level (mean) of commitment strength before or during MI that mattered, but rather the pattern (slope) of commitment strength during an MI session. Behavior change occurred when clients showed a pattern of increasing strength of commitment over the course of an MI session. The other four kinds of change talk—ability, desire, need, and reasons—all predicted commitment strength but did not themselves predict behavior change (see Figure 1).

To restate this in clinical language: Successful behavior change (drug abstinence) occurred when clients voiced their ability, desire, need, and reasons

Client verbalization of:
Desire
Ability
Reasons
Need

Figure 1   Hypothesized Causal Chain for the Efficacy of Motivational Interviewing

for change (Phase 1), which, in turn, led them to make stronger verbal commitment to change (Phase 2). They talked themselves into change. The pattern became clear only when "change talk" was differentiated into its component parts. Voicing one's ability, desire, need, and reasons for change did not lead to behavior change without a verbalized commitment. In retrospect, the crucial importance of client commitment makes sense clinically and is consistent with cognitive psychology findings that behavior is more likely to be enacted when people voice specific "implementation intentions." Emphasis on commitment was also what distinguished Phase 2 from Phase 1 in original descriptions of MI.

The pressures of managed care have naturally led to the question of whether MI can be offered effectively in group therapy. It is clear, at least, that translating MI from individual to group format is by no means a straightforward process. Whereas studies of individual MI have produced reasonably consistent evidence of beneficial effect, the outcomes of group MI have been far more variable. In a few studies, group MI appeared to backfire. Those receiving group MI showed less behavior change than those in a control group, who, in turn, showed less change than those given individual MI. If the causal chain in Figure 1 does account for the effectiveness of MI, it is easy to see how group MI could be challenging. If the engine of MI is to evoke from each individual enough positive change talk (and to minimize resistance) to lead to personal commitment language, groups pose a special challenge because each client gets much less "airtime" for sustained exploration.

Other research has explored how clinicians learn MI. It is clear that proficiency in MI can be increased substantially by training (based on analyses of therapy session tapes before and after training) and that increased skillfulness maintains over time (based on analyses of tapes up to a year later). MI-consistent therapist behaviors increase, and MI-inconsistent responses decrease. Perhaps more important, clients show increased levels of change talk and commitment

language after their therapists have been trained in MI, the pattern that predicts subsequent behavior change. Nevertheless, there remains substantial variability in the acquisition of MI proficiency by clinicians, and optimal methods for teaching this approach need to be clarified.

RELEVANT TARGET POPULATIONS AND EXCEPTIONS

MI was originally intended to increase intrinsic motivation in clients who were not yet ready for or committed to change. The prototypic client was the problem drinker who did not see sufficient reason to do anything about her or his drinking. Within the transtheoretical stages of change described by Prochaska and DiClemente, these would be people in the "precontemplation" (not even considering change) or "contemplation" (ambivalent) stages. Some studies have found precisely that clients who are less ready for change (precontemplation or contemplation stage) respond differentially well to MI compared with action-oriented, cognitive behavior therapy. In essence, MI addresses these clients where they are: in the process of deciding whether to make a change.

There is also evidence that clients who are more resistant or angry at the beginning of treatment respond particularly well to MI compared with action-focused therapies. Again, MI was specifically designed to reduce resistance to change, and so it is sensible that it would be particularly effective for less motivated clients.

Equally sensible is the finding that MI is not differentially beneficial for clients who have already decided and committed themselves to behavior change. In fact, there is some evidence that MI can be detrimental when clients are ready for action. Imagine being ready for change and asking a therapist for advice, only to be met with reflective listening. This is as much a mismatch of styles as is an action-focused therapist with an ambivalent client. This is not to say that one should abandon an empathic style once a client is ready for action. There is evidence that empathic counselors are more effective behavior therapists. When a client is ready for change, however, it may not be optimal to spend a lot of time reflecting on the reasons for change.

The cross-cultural applicability of MI appears to be good. Beyond the United States, it has been used successfully in places as diverse as Africa, Australia,

China, and Scandinavia. U.S. studies have shown similarly good response to MI among Hispanic, African American, and non-Hispanic White Americans and differentially better response to MI among Native Americans (compared with cognitive-behavioral or 12-step treatment for alcohol problems). Because the MI therapist focuses so much on understanding the unique perspectives and motivations of the client, MI may be particularly helpful when therapist and client come from different cultural backgrounds.

COMPLICATIONS

By virtue of its underlying philosophy, MI can clash with authoritarian values and systems. Particularly in the treatment of certain populations, such as offenders and people with substance use disorders, some programs espouse a strongly authoritarian and confrontational approach that assumes the client to be unable or unwilling to make responsible choices. Such programs may embrace a highly directive and restrictive approach predicated on "We know what is best for you." Caregivers operating within such systems often find that an MI approach clashes with the authoritarian program philosophy. Similarly, clinicians who are accustomed to a highly prescriptive counseling style may find it difficult to understand and develop proficiency in MI. The reflective, accepting style of MI (and of client-centered counseling more generally) may be mistaken for approval or endorsement of clients' behavior.

The practice of MI can also be complicated when there are conflicting professional roles, as when one is a representative both of the client and of society. Probation officers face this challenge. They are, on one hand, advocates and counselors for their offender-clients; yet they also, as agents of society, have responsibility and authority to enforce laws as well as the conditions set by the courts. It is not impossible or undesirable for probation officers to practice MI, but the dual professional roles do increase complexity.

MI can also prove vexing for clinicians who have trouble detaching from their clients' choices. Personal investment in or identification with clients' lives can make it difficult to honor client autonomy and to maintain the balanced and empathic outside perspective that characterizes MI.

Another complexity is how to combine MI with other therapeutic approaches. As noted above, there is good evidence that MI can exert a synergistic effect in combination with other treatment methods. Its empathic style can also be a relational foundation on which to construct other approaches. Complexity here has to do with timing and the smooth shifting of gears from MI to what is often a more prescriptive method. Some clinicians have difficulty suspending their didactic styles long enough to provide effective MI. Others are quite comfortable with the client-centered style of MI but struggle when it is time to shift into a more specifically prescriptive phase. In practice, client ambivalence emerges and resurfaces throughout the course of behavioral counseling, and the flexible therapist shifts back and forth between styles, responding to the client's cues.

MI is not easily acquired through a onetime clinical workshop or by reading books or viewing videotapes. As with any complex skill, proficiency in MI is gained over time through practice with feedback. A complication is that clinicians who attend a day or two of training often leave persuaded that they have acquired and are now practicing MI or, indeed, that they were "already doing it" even before training. Studies of training indicate that these self-perceptions of competence are statistically unrelated to actual skillfulness in MI as measured from clinical practice. Another challenge, then, is for clinicians to continue learning and gaining proficiency with MI after initial training.

CASE ILLUSTRATION

"Manuel" had been caught. Working the night shift as a janitor, he kept a flask of vodka in his locker and tended to drink throughout the evening, particularly after he had completed his early round of emptying the office wastebaskets and buffing the tile floors. He had the building largely to himself after 11. Even the workaholics had gone home, and only the night supervisor and security guard would swing by once or twice. The guard was an *amigo* and didn't mind sharing a drink or two. It was the supervisor he had to watch out for. This time, he misjudged. The super had already been by once, and Manuel fell asleep on a couch around 2. At 3, the supervisor shook him awake, found the flask, and sent him home in a taxi. When Manuel came to work the next night, a urine cup was waiting for him. The test came back positive for marijuana.

The following day, Manuel found himself in the employee assistance program (EAP) office. He had protested but was told that the alternative was to be fired on the spot. Even before Manuel spoke, the EAP counselor could see that he was angry. "Looks like you're not too happy about being here," she said. Then she invited him to tell her the story of what had happened.

As he slowly recounted the night he had been caught, the counselor was particularly interested in what Manuel's own concerns were. First and foremost, he wanted to keep his job. His wife was ill, and besides the income from his job, they needed its health care coverage. She also asked what he thought the supervisor's interests were and explored some concerns that family members had expressed about his drinking. In each case, she wanted to understand Manuel's own perspectives and why he thought that these other people might be concerned about his use of alcohol. By the end of the first session, she had a beginning understanding of how he saw his situation and a pretty good list of his own points of concern. She decided, however, that he wasn't quite ready to discuss what to do, so she scheduled another appointment later in the week to continue to process.

When he came back, Manuel said that he had been talking to his wife about his drinking. She had expressed concern before, but now she was very upset that he could lose his job and wanted him to quit drinking altogether. The counselor integrated this into a summary reflection that included his own reasons for concern from the prior session and asked whether he had thought of any other disadvantages of his use of alcohol and marijuana. "I guess I don't feel so good when I wake up," he said, "but that's probably just a hangover, and not getting enough sleep." The counselor was immediately tempted to disagree or educate, but instead, she stuck with an MI style and tested the readiness waters:

So this all started when your supervisor made an extra round that night and found you sleeping with your flask. That led to the drug test and the additional problem of a positive test for pot. Your family had expressed some concerns about your drinking before, but if it weren't for that night, you probably wouldn't be here talking to me. If I understand you right, your main concern is to keep your job, and that's a big concern for your family, too, especially because of health coverage. You're worried about your wife's health, and you definitely want to be

there for her. You've also noticed that you feel bad in the morning, and you suspect that it has something to do with alcohol at least. And sometimes you've wondered about your drinking at night and on the job, if that's the right thing to do. Mostly though, you want to keep this job, because you like it and you need it. Have I missed anything?

Manuel agreed that it was a good summary of his situation. Then, the counselor tested the waters for Phase 2, to move toward commitment to a particular change plan: "So what are you thinking, at this point, about drinking and pot? What are you considering as options?"

Manuel said that he needed to stop drinking at night and at work. With regard to marijuana, he wanted to know how long it stays in the body, and the counselor explained that it can turn up on a test weeks later. He was angry about this perceived intrusion into his privacy (which she reflected) but acknowledged that given repeated urine tests, he would need to stop using pot altogether. Together, they discussed what support he might find useful, beyond that of his family, in making these changes, and he agreed to come back for two more sessions with his wife to discuss this.

The understatement within the counselor's summary above is characteristic of MI, as is her letting it be up to the client to make a decision about what to do. Certainly, these contrast with a counseling style of telling clients what to think and do. The assumption is that the ambivalent client has at least some intrinsic motivation for change and ideas about how to proceed. The counselor provides his or her expertise as needed and requested, but focuses primarily on evoking the client's own reasons and plans for change.

—*William R. Miller*

See also: Behavioral Case Formulation (Vol. I); Motivational Enhancement Therapy (Vol. I)

Suggested Readings

Miller, W. R. (in press). Motivational interviewing in the service of health promotion. *American Journal of Health Promotion.*

Miller, W. R., & Mount, K. A. (2001). A small study of training in motivational interviewing: Does one workshop change clinician and client behavior? *Behavioural and Cognitive Psychotherapy, 29,* 457–471.

Miller, W. R., & Rollnick, S. (2002). *Motivational interviewing: Preparing people for change* (2nd ed.). New York: Guilford Press.

Project MATCH Research Group (1997). Project MATCH secondary a priori hypotheses. *Addiction, 92,* 1671–1698.

Rollnick, S., Mason, P., & Butler, C. (1999). *Health behavior change: A guide for practitioners.* New York: Churchill Livingstone.

MOTOR ACTIVITY AND BEHAVIORAL ASSESSMENT

DESCRIPTION OF THE STRATEGY

Actigraphy is the term used to describe the instrumented measurement of activity level. Older actigraphs used a sensor that identified presence of movement above a designated threshold and accumulated frequency counts to computer memory locations at the end of specified epochs, such as 1, 5, 10, 15, or 30 minutes, depending upon the device. Newer actigraphs use an accelerometer to detect small changes in the rate of movement. Our limbs are jointed and therefore move in arcs. These curved movements are associated with continuous changes in acceleration. Modern actigraphs frequently discern at least 255 levels of acceleration. They either digitize and then integrate these acceleration measurements or integrate the analog output of accelerometers before storing the result in memory at the end of a user-defined epoch. Frequently, this is set to 1 minute and typically ranges from 5 seconds to 15 minutes. An epoch length of 30 seconds is frequently used in sleep research. The integral of acceleration with respect to time is velocity. Hence, actigraph measurements are proportional to movement velocity, which corresponds to movement intensity. Actigraph measures form a ratio scale with an absolute-zero point: complete inactivity. They quantify movement intensity up to a maximum beyond which the device saturates and is no longer responsive. Actigraphs typically connect to a personal computer through the serial port. Each manufacturer provides software to initialize the actigraphs to begin at a designated day, hour, and minute. This is possible because actigraphs contain a clock that regulates the time they begin recording and governs when data are written to memory. Data can be displayed graphically and analyzed numerically either through software provided by the vendor, or the files can be exported to Excel, SPSS, or some other data-analytic package for processing.

Actigraphs measure their own movement. This will be the same movement as that produced by the person at the site of attachment. Hence, wrist activity level differs from waist activity level, which differs from ankle activity level. In general, activity level is measured at a specified site of attachment. It is therefore incorrect to speak of activity level as though one value described the entire individual. One must carefully choose the site of attachment. The wrist is the preferred site of attachment for sleep because prior research has shown that when an individual is awake, the wrist is the most frequently moving body part. The waist is the preferred site of attachment when estimating caloric expenditure because the center of gravity of one's body is located near the waist. Vertical movements of the center of gravity expend energy in direct proportion to moving a lead weight of the same mass as the person the same vertical distances. Sometimes it is desirable to monitor two or more sites in order to obtain a more complete picture. The ankle is the least studied site of attachment largely because the repeated impacts caused by walking and running are hard on the actigraphs.

Clinicians deserve the same high-quality data as researchers because they are making important decisions that affect the lives of their clients. The growing commercial availability of actigraphs and the widespread availability of personal computers make use of self-report and human observation of activity level obsolete. People are still the best at appraising the quality and social appropriateness of behavior. They should leave quantifying magnitude of energy associated with behavior to instruments.

Behavioral Assessment

Behavioral assessment involves two major areas. One facet of behavioral assessment concerns what is called the *topography of behavior,* which includes the frequency, intensity, and duration of behavior. The assessment of motor activity pertains exclusively to this facet of behavioral assessment. The other facet of behavioral assessment entails conducting a functional analysis of behavior. The next several sections discuss the reasons why knowledge of frequency, intensity, and duration of motor activity is relevant to practitioners of behavior modification and therapy by reviewing its relevance to initial assessment and diagnosis, process assessment, and outcome evaluation.

Initial Assessment and Diagnosis

Behavior modification and therapy differ in their approach to behavioral assessment, including their emphasis on formal diagnosis. Behavior modifiers are typically concerned almost exclusively with determining the topography of the target problem and conducting a functional analysis of it so that they can design an intervention based on their assessments. This is because their objective is to change the target behavior in specified ways. Assessing frequency, intensity, and duration of a target behavior enables one to determine whether the presenting problem constitutes a behavioral excess or deficit. The clinical objective in the case of behavioral excess is to reduce frequency, intensity, and/or duration of the target behavior. The clinical objective in the case of behavioral deficit is to increase frequency, intensity, and/or duration of behavior. A functional assessment seeks to determine what antecedent social and physical stimuli set the occasion for the emission or omission of the target behavior and what consequent social and physical stimuli maintain the emission or omission of the target behavior.

Formal diagnosis, based on a system such as the *Diagnostic and Statistical Manual* of the American Psychiatric Association, currently in its fourth edition and known as the *DSM-IV,* may lead to selecting a manualized treatment. It also may lead to selecting a class of medication but otherwise does not lead to specific treatment because it is not an etiological-based system. Its initial purpose is to categorize mental illnesses for the purpose of statistical reporting. Its main research purpose today is in selecting what are thought to be homogeneous patient groups for the purpose of conducting manualized-therapy outcome research. Motor activity is a surprisingly relevant target behavior because it pertains to the inclusion and/or exclusion criteria of 48 *DSM-IV* disorders.

Psychological/Behavioral Disorders

The affective disorders range from major depression through mania in a finely graded way. Instruments are better designed than human observers to monitor and systematically record activity measurements at prescribed intervals over days, weeks, and months. Current diagnostic practices based on human judgment impose categories on this continuous spectrum. Instruments can better reflect quantitative differences in activity level. People with major depression tend to be inactive during the day and to have disturbed sleep. Clinical severity appears to be directly proportional to diurnal inactivity and nocturnal activity. Wrist activity has been well validated against polysomnography (PSG), the gold standard measure of sleep. Wrist actigraphy has been empirically shown to track sleep improvements associated with successful hospital treatment of persons with major depression. Manic persons tend to be hyperactive both day and night; the greater the motor excess, the more severe the disorder.

Medical Diseases

The original case definition of chronic fatigue syndrome stipulated a 50% decrease in activity level as a major inclusion criterion. This definition was based on the fact that severe fatigue makes people feel that they no longer have the energy to go to maintain their desired lifestyles, including work, shopping, and social/recreational activities. Lowered activity level is the final common pathway for all of these decisions. While it is possible to ask people to keep detailed records about their activity levels, it is both simpler and more objective to directly measure it via actigraphy. When instructed to observe their own behavior, people tend to deviate from instructions and change criteria over time. Such observer drift even characterizes the behavior of trained observers. Actigraphs are instruments and as such are not subject to these problems, although they come with their own limitations, such as battery life and periodic malfunctions that can be repaired.

Activity-level decreases seem to be the body's way of conserving energy with which to fight infection. Hence, people tend to sleep more and do less while acutely ill. For example, persons with AIDS experience recurrent health crises of this sort. Continuous motor-activity-level monitoring will reflect variability in their functional limitations. Cardiac disease decreases activity level due either to painful angina or fatigue. Chronic obstructive pulmonary disease decreases activity level due to oxygen deprivation. Arthritis can decrease activity level due to joint swelling and discomfort. Actigraphy can assess the degree to which these disorders impose functional limitations on the patient.

Sleep Disorders

Sleep onset is a gradual rather than discrete process that involves a series of behavioral and physiological changes that occur in a fixed sequence. Three general sleep onset phases can presently be discerned. The first phase entails quiescence and immobility. We settle down and become inactive before going to sleep. Wrist actigraphy determines sleep onset toward the end of this phase. The second phase entails muscle relaxation and EEG changes. EEG sleep onset was initially validated by the fact that people dropped handheld objects as they fell asleep. The third phase entails auditory threshold increases and perceived sleep onset as reported by sleep logs.

Systematic differences between actigraphic-measured and polysomnography-measured sleep parameters are well documented but permit clinical and research application in cases of depression and in various sleep disorders. For example, sleepwalking entails ambulation at night for which the individual has no memory. Actigraphy can document to within 1 minute or 30 seconds, or less if desired, when the person began to ambulate and can measure with the same temporal precision how long ambulation occurred and the time when inactivity resumed. Circadian rhythm sleep disorder typically entails some combination of less than normally active diurnal periods and more than normally active nocturnal periods. This disorder can arise from shift work, jet lag, and Alzheimer's dementia. Because much of the basic laboratory research in animals on circadian rhythms entails activity measurement, it is especially appropriate to measure activity level in people with this problem. Sleep state misperception is a disorder in which the patient claims not to have slept at all—but objective means, either polysomnography or actigraphy, reveal that the person has, in fact, slept most of the night. Some objective sleep measure is required to make this diagnosis, and actigraphy is a desirable choice because it can be used for many nights while the person sleeps in his or her own bed, thereby generating a large pertinent behavioral sample, versus sleeping three nights in a sleep laboratory, where the problem may not occur at all.

Process Evaluation

All of the applications of actigraphy described above can be used in an ongoing way to determine how treatment is progressing. For example, actigraphy can determine how well medication and/or behavioral intervention controls hyperactivity in children with the combined form of attention-deficit/hyperactivity disorder (ADHD). Actigraphy is sufficiently sensitive that it can detect the daily rebound, motor activity increase, at 6 p.m. from a stat dose of medication at 8 a.m. Actigraphy can evaluate the extent to which the newer time-release form of medication, which continuously releases medication over time, moderates these behavioral shifts.

Actigraphy can track recovery from major depression or mania or chronic fatigue syndrome by tracking the return of normal circadian rhythm. Actigraphy can track recovery from major surgery, which reduces activity level to zero during the surgery and acute recovery. Patients are encouraged to ambulate as soon as possible and are not discharged from the hospital until they can effectively do so. Wrist and waist actigraphy can track this recovery process. It can also evaluate the extent to which normal sleep returns.

Outcome Evaluation

All of the applications of actigraphy described above can be used to evaluate final therapeutic outcome by determining the extent to which diurnal and nocturnal activity levels have returned to normal, meaning premorbid levels. Outcome needs to be assessed over meaningful time periods. Actigraphy can be continued for extended periods of time. One actigraph model can record behavior every minute of the day and night for up to 88 days before filling memory. A similarly large behavioral sample could be repeated if necessary.

RESEARCH BASIS

Laboratory research indicates that actigraphs are highly reliable and valid. They provide ratio scale measurements that have absolute-zero and equal-measurement intervals, thereby allowing proportional inferences (see suggested reading by Tryon and Williams for further details). The operating characteristics of actigraphs are best studied under laboratory conditions, because only with machines can movements be carefully repeated. Large and small pendulums have been used, because their movements are reproducible and change in known ways. Spinners have also been used, because acceleration changes as a function of rotation. Studies have shown that repeated measurements from actigraphs are typically within 5% of full scale of each other. Actigraphs can be calibrated so that average device differences can be removed. That is, systematic differences can be deleted, leaving only random measurement error. Some investigators attempt to study actigraph reliability and validity by placing them on people and instructing them to perform certain tasks. The problem with this approach is that people cannot repeat movements with the same degree of accuracy that pendulums and spinners can. Results are therefore confounded within and between participant behavioral variability with actigraph variability. This can substantially underestimate both the reliability and validity of actigraphs. Investigators who insist on using people to evaluate instrument reliability and validity often cite the artificial nature of pendulum and spinning movement relative to human behavior. However, human behavior arguably contains complex combinations of these elemental movements, and humans cannot guarantee repeatability with regard to the exact composition of these complex composites. We calibrate thermometers against ice and boiling water and are not troubled when taking a patient's temperature. A similar approach is recommended when measuring accelerated movement.

Both correlational and analysis of variance procedures normally used to evaluate the reliability and validity of psychological tests cannot be used to assess the reliability and validity of actigraphs, because the variability among actigraphs is so much less than the variability among participants that strange and incorrect results emerge. For example, correlational-based methods produce reliability coefficients near zero when all devices completely agree. This is because interdevice variability, which corresponds to interpersonal variability, approaches zero. Actigraphs should therefore be evaluated by engineering criteria such as dividing the standard deviation of repeated measurements by their mean value.

Actigraphy has been used successfully in a wide variety of medical and psychological studies to evaluate intervention effects on sleep and waking behavior. Motor activity pertains to the inclusion or exclusion criteria of 48 disorders described by the *DSM-IV*. Actigraphy research has been conducted with many of these disorders.

RELEVANT TARGET POPULATIONS AND EXCEPTIONS

Ankle actigraphy has been used with infants to document the development of normal sleep and evaluate the benefits of cosleeping with parents. Wrist and waist actigraphy have been used successfully with children and adults, including the frail elderly in nursing homes. Actigraphy is suitable for use with persons in all cultures, though care must be taken when interpreting results.

COMPLICATIONS

Wrist actigraphy can become tiresome, especially with older actigraphs that were larger and more cumbersome than newer models. Battery failure and device malfunction are problems that are fortunately becoming less frequent. No social complications have been noted with children wearing actigraphs to school.

CASE ILLUSTRATION

This case concerns a 45-year-old White female who complained of fatigue and was diagnosed with chronic fatigue syndrome. She wore a waist and wrist actigraph for 14 consecutive 24-hour periods and kept a log of daily activities. A simple graphic display was sufficient to reveal that her waking (diurnal) periods were associated with minimal activity due primarily to the fact that she frequently felt too tired to engage in as many activities as she wished to. As important, actigraphy revealed that her sleeping (nocturnal) periods contained considerably more activity than that demonstrated by a control person, who was a woman of similar age but not seeking treatment of any kind. This persistent nocturnal activity corresponded well with her complaint that sleep was not restorative. These data can be used as a point of reference to evaluate subsequent clinical change.

—*Warren W. Tryon*

See also: *Applied Behavior Analysis (Vol. III); Behavioral Assessment (Vols. I & II)*

Suggested Readings

Tryon, W. W. (1991). *Activity measurement in psychology and medicine.* New York: Plenum Press.

Tryon, W. W. (1998). Behavioral observation. In M. Hersen & A. S. Bellack (Eds.), *Behavioral assessment: A practical handbook* (4th ed., pp. 79–103). Boston: Allyn & Bacon.

Tryon, W. W. (1998). Physical activity. In M. Hersen & B. B. Van Hasselt (Eds.), *Handbook of clinical geropsychology* (pp. 523–556). New York: Plenum Press.

Tryon, W. W. (1999). *Behavioral model.* In M. Hersen & V. B. Van Hasselt (Eds.), *Advanced abnormal psychology* (pp. 93–123). New York: Plenum Press.

Tryon, W. W. (2002). Activity level and *DSM-IV.* In S. Turner & M. Hersen (Eds.), *Adult psychopathology and diagnosis* (4th. ed., pp. 547–577). New York: Wiley.

Tryon, W. W., & Williams, R. (1996). Fully proportional actigraphy: A new instrument. *Behavior Research Methods Instruments & Computers, 28,* 392–403.

MULTIMODAL BEHAVIOR THERAPY

DESCRIPTION OF THE STRATEGY

What constitutes a broad-based and perhaps all-encompassing design for effective therapy? Clearly, there are essential behaviors to be acquired—acts and actions that are necessary for coping with life's demands. The control and expression of one's emotions are also imperative for adaptive living. It is important to correct inappropriate affective responses that undermine success in many spheres. Untoward sensations (e.g., the ravages of tension), intrusive images (e.g., pictures of personal failure and ridicule from others), and faulty cognitions (e.g., toxic ideas and irrational beliefs) also play a significant role in diminishing the quality of life. Each of the foregoing areas must be addressed in an endeavor to remedy significant excesses and deficits. Moreover, the quality of one's interpersonal relationships is a key ingredient of happiness and success, and without the requisite social skills, one is likely to be cast aside, or even ostracized.

The aforementioned considerations led to the development of *multimodal behavior therapy.* Emphasis was placed on the fact that at base, we are biological organisms (neurophysiological/biochemical entities) who *behave* (act and react), *emote* (experience affective responses), *sense* (respond to tactile, olfactory, gustatory, visual, and auditory stimuli), *imagine* (conjure up sights, sounds, and other events in our mind's eye), *think* (entertain beliefs, opinions, values, and attitudes), and *interact* with one another (enjoy, tolerate, or suffer various interpersonal relationships). By referring to the seven discrete but interactive dimensions or modalities as *behavior, affect, sensation, imagery, cognition, interpersonal,* and *drugs/biologicals,* the convenient acronym BASIC I.D. emerges from the first letter of each one. The BASIC I.D. or multimodal framework rests on a broad social and cognitive learning theory.

The polar opposite of the multimodal approach is the Rogerian or person-centered orientation, which is entirely conversational and virtually unimodal. While, in general, the relationship between therapist and client is highly significant and sometimes "necessary and sufficient," in most instances, the doctor-patient relationship is but the soil that enables the techniques to take root. A good relationship, adequate rapport, and a constructive working alliance are "usually necessary but often insufficient." Many psychotherapeutic approaches are trimodal, addressing affect, behavior, and cognition—ABC. The multimodal approach provides clinicians with a comprehensive template. By separating sensations from emotions, distinguishing between images and cognitions, emphasizing both intraindividual and interpersonal behaviors, and underscoring the biological substrate, the multimodal orientation is most far-reaching. By assessing a client's BASIC I.D., one endeavors to "leave no stone unturned."

METHODS OF ASSESSMENT AND INTERVENTION

The elements of a thorough assessment involve the following range of questions:

B: What is this individual doing that is getting in the way of his or her happiness of personal fulfillment (self-defeating actions, maladaptive behaviors)? What does the client need to increase and decrease? What should he or she stop doing and start doing?

A: What emotions (affective reactions) are predominant? Are we dealing with anger, anxiety, depression, or combinations thereof, and to what extent (e.g., irritation versus rage, sadness versus profound melancholy)? What appears to generate these negative affects—certain cognitions, images, interpersonal conflicts? And how does the person respond (behave) when feeling a certain way? It is important to look for interactive processes: What impact do various behaviors have on the person's affect, and vice versa? How does this influence each of the other modalities?

S: Are there specific sensory complaints (e.g., tension, chronic pain, tremors)? What feelings, thoughts, and behaviors are connected to these negative sensations? What positive sensations (e.g., visual, auditory, tactile, olfactory, and gustatory delights) does the person report? This includes the individual as a sensual and sexual being. When called for, the enhancement or cultivation of erotic pleasure is a viable therapeutic goal.

I: What fantasies and images are predominant? What is the person's "self-image?" Are there specific success or failure images? Are there negative or intrusive images (e.g., flashbacks to unhappy or traumatic experiences)? And how are these images connected to ongoing cognitions, behaviors, affective reactions, and the like?

C: Can we determine the individual's main attitudes, values, beliefs, and opinions? What are this person's predominant "shoulds," "oughts," and "musts"? Are there any definite dysfunctional beliefs or irrational ideas? Can we detect any untoward automatic thoughts that undermine his or her functioning?

I.: Interpersonally, who are the significant others in this individual's life? What does he or she want, desire, expect, and receive from them, and what does he or she, in turn, give to and do for them? What relationships give him or her particular pleasures and pains?

D.: Is this person biologically healthy and health conscious? Does he or she have any medical complaints or concerns? What relevant details pertain to diet, weight, sleep, exercise, alcohol, and drug use?

The foregoing are some of the main issues that multimodal clinicians traverse while assessing the client's BASIC I.D. A more comprehensive problem identification sequence is derived from asking most clients to complete a Multimodal Life History Inventory. This 15-page questionnaire facilitates treatment when conscientiously filled in by clients as a homework assignment, usually after the initial session. Seriously disturbed (e.g., deluded, deeply depressed, highly agitated) clients will obviously not be expected to comply, but most psychiatric outpatients who are reasonably literate will find the exercise useful for speeding up routine history taking and readily provide the therapist with a BASIC I.D. analysis.

In addition, there are three other important assessment procedures employed in MMT–Second-Order

BASIC I.D.: *assessments,* a method called *bridging,* and another called *tracking.*

Second-Order BASIC I.D. Assessments

If and when treatment impasses arise, a more detailed inquiry into associated behaviors, affective responses, sensory reactions, images, cognitions, interpersonal factors, and possible biological considerations may shed light on the situation. For example, a client was making almost no progress with assertiveness-training procedures. He was asked to picture himself as a truly assertive person and was then asked to recount how his behavior would differ in general, what affective reactions he might anticipate, and so forth, across the BASIC I.D. This brought a central cognitive schema to light that had eluded all other avenues of inquiry: "I am not entitled to be happy." Therapy was then aimed directly at addressing this maladaptive cognition before assertiveness training was resumed.

Bridging

Let's say a therapist is interested in a client's emotional responses to an event: "How did you feel when your father yelled at you in front of your friends?" Instead of discussing his feelings, the client responds with defensive and irrelevant intellectualizations: "My dad had strange priorities, and even as a kid, I used to question his judgment." It is often counterproductive to confront the client and point out that he is evading the question and seems reluctant to face his true feelings. In situations of this kind, bridging is usually effective. First, the therapist deliberately tunes into the client's preferred modality—in this case, the cognitive domain. Thus, the therapist explores the cognitive content: "So you see it as a consequence involving judgments and priorities. Please tell me more." In this way, after perhaps a 5– to 10-minute discourse, the therapist endeavors to branch off into other directions that seem more productive: "Tell me, while we have been discussing these matters, have you noticed any sensations anywhere in your body?" This sudden switch from cognition to sensation may begin to elicit more pertinent information (given the assumption that in this instance, sensory inputs are probably less threatening than affective material). The client may refer to some sensations of tension or bodily discomfort, at which point the therapist may ask him to focus on them, often with an hypnotic overlay: "Will you please close your eyes, and now feel that neck tension. (Pause). Now, relax deeply for a few moments, breathe easily and gently, in and out, in and out, just letting yourself feel calm and peaceful." The feelings of tension, their associated images, and cognitions may then be examined. One may then venture to bridge into affect: "Beneath the sensations, can you find any strong feelings or emotions? Perhaps they are lurking in the background." At this juncture, it is not unusual for clients to give voice to their feelings: "I am in touch with anger and with sadness." By starting where the client is and then bridging into a different modality, most clients then seem to be willing to traverse the more emotionally charged areas they have been avoiding.

Tracking the Firing Order

A fairly reliable pattern may be discerned of the way that many people generate negative affect. Some dwell first on unpleasant sensations (palpitations, shortness of breath, tremors), followed by aversive images (pictures of disastrous events), to which they attach negative cognitions (ideas about catastrophic illness), leading to maladaptive behavior (withdrawal and avoidance). This S-I-C-B firing order (sensation, imagery, cognition, behavior) may require a different treatment strategy from that employed with, say, a C-I-S-B sequence, an I-C-B-S, or yet a different firing order. Clinical findings suggest that it is often best to apply treatment techniques in accordance with a client's specific chain reaction. A rapid way of determining someone's firing order is to have him or her in an altered state of consciousness—deeply relaxed with eyes closed—contemplating untoward events and then describing their reactions.

A Structural Profile Inventory (SPI) has been developed and tested. This 35-item survey provides a quantitative rating of the extent to which clients favor specific BASIC I.D. areas. The instrument measures action-oriented proclivities (behavior), the degree of emotionality (affect), the value attached to various sensory experiences (sensation), the amount of time devoted to fantasy, day dreaming, and "thinking in pictures" (imagery), analytical and problem-solving propensities (cognition), the importance attached to interacting with other people (interpersonal), and the extent to which health-conscious habits are observed (drugs/biology). It has been shown that when clients and therapists have wide differences on the SPI, therapeutic outcomes tend to be adversely affected.

In multimodal assessment, the BASIC I.D. serves as a template to remind therapists to examine each of the seven modalities and their interactive effects. It implies that we are social beings who move, feel, sense, imagine, and think and that at base, we are biochemical-neurophysiological entities. Students and colleagues frequently inquire as to whether any particular areas are more significant, or more heavily weighted, than the others. For thoroughness, all seven require careful attention, but perhaps the biological and interpersonal modalities are especially significant.

The biological modality wields a profound influence on all the other modalities. Unpleasant sensory reactions can signal a host of medical illnesses; excessive emotional reactions (anxiety, depression, and rage) may all have biological determinants; faulty thinking and images of gloom, doom, and terror may derive entirely from chemical imbalances; and untoward personal and interpersonal behaviors may stem from many somatic reactions, ranging from toxins (e.g., drugs or alcohol) to intracranial lesions. Hence, when any doubts arise about the probable involvement of biological factors, it is imperative to have them fully investigated. A person who has no untoward medical/physical problems and enjoys warm, meaningful, and loving relationships is apt to find life personally and interpersonally fulfilling. Hence, the biological modality serves as the base, and the interpersonal modality is perhaps the apex. The seven modalities are by no means static or linear, but exist in a state of reciprocal transaction.

A question often raised is whether a "spiritual" dimension should be added. In the interests of parsimony, I point out that when someone refers to having had a "spiritual" or a "transcendental" experience, typically their reactions point to, and can be captured by, the interplay among powerful cognitions, images, sensations, and affective responses.

Multimodal therapists have treated a wide range of afflictions, including maladaptive habits, fears and phobias, stress-related difficulties, sexual dysfunctions, depression, eating disorders, and obsessive-compulsive disorder.

The multimodal approach is not a unitary or closed system. It is basically a clinical approach that rests on a social and cognitive learning theory and uses technical eclectic and empirically supported procedures in an individualistic manner. The overriding question is mainly, "Who and what is best for this client?" Obviously, no one therapist can be well versed in the entire gamut of methods and procedures that exist. Some clinicians are excellent with children, whereas others have a talent for working with geriatric populations. Some practitioners have specialized in specific disorders (e.g., eating disorders, sexual dysfunctions, posttraumatic stress disorder panic, depression, substance abuse, or schizophrenia). Those who employ multimodal therapy will bring their talents to bear on their areas of special proficiency and employ the BASIC I.D. as per the foregoing discussions and, by so doing, possibly enhance their clinical impact. If a problem or a specific client falls outside their sphere of expertise, they will endeavor to effect a referral to an appropriate resource.

Follow-up studies that have been conducted since 1973 have consistently suggested that durable outcomes are in direct proportion to the number of modalities deliberately traversed. Although there is obviously a point of diminishing returns, it is a multimodal maxim that *the more someone learns in therapy, the less likely he or she is to relapse.* In this connection, circa 1970, it became apparent that lacunae or gaps in people's coping responses were responsible for many relapses. This occurred even after they had been in various (nonmultimodal) therapies, often for years on end. Follow-ups indicate that this ensures far more compelling and durable results.

—*Arnold A. Lazarus*

See also: *Behavioral Assessment (Vol. I); Lazarus, Arnold A. (Vol. I)*

Suggested Readings

Fay, A., & Lazarus, A. A. (1993). On necessity and sufficiency in psychotherapy. *Psychotherapy in Private Practice, 12,* 33–39.

Herman, S. M. (1991). Client-therapist similarity on the Multimodal Structural Profile Inventory as predictive of psychotherapy outcome. *Psychotherapy Bulletin, 26,* 26–27.

Herman, S. M. (1998). The relationship between therapist-client modality similarity and psychotherapy outcome. *Journal of Psychotherapy Practice and Research, 7,* 56–64.

Lazarus, A. A. (1992). Multimodal therapy: Technical eclecticism with minimal integration. In J. C. Norcross & M. R. Goldfried (Eds.), *Handbook of psychotherapy integration* (pp. 231–263). New York: Basic Books.

Lazarus, A. A. (1997). *Brief but comprehensive psychotherapy: The multimodal way.* New York: Springer.

Lazarus, A. A. (2000). My professional journey: The development of multimodal therapy. In J. J. Shay & J. Wheelis (Eds.), *Odysseys in psychotherapy.* New York: Irvington.

Lazarus, A. A. (2001). From insight and reflection to action and clinical breadth. In M. R. Goldfried (Ed.), *How therapists change* (pp. 163–181). Washington, DC: American Psychological Association.

Lazarus, A. A. (2001). Multimodal therapy in clinical psychology. In N. J. Smelser & P. B. Baltes (Eds.), *Encyclopedia of the social and behavioral sciences* (pp. 10193–10197). Oxford, UK: Elsevier Press.

Lazarus, A. A. (2002). Client readiness for change, cultural concerns, and risk taking: A multimodal case presentation. *Clinical Case Studies, 1,* 39–48.

Lazarus, A. A., & Lazarus, C. N. (1991). *Multimodal life history inventory.* Champaign, IL: Research Press.

Lazarus, C. N., & Lazarus, A. A. (2002). EMDR: An elegantly concentrated multimodal procedure? In F. Shapiro (Ed.), *EMDR as an integrative psychotherapy approach* (pp. 209–223). Washington, DC: American Psychological Association.

Palmer, S., & Lazarus, A. A. (2001). In the counselor's chair: Multimodal therapy. In P. Milner & S. Palmer (Eds.), *Counselling: The BACP counselling reader* (pp. 94–98). London: Sage.

NEGATIVE COGNITIONS

DESCRIPTION OF THE STRATEGY

The idea that reality is relative is not a new concept and was discussed at length by no less a notable than Plato. Even proverbial phrases like "Seeing the world through rose-colored glasses" and "The glass is half-full or half-empty" imply the existence of alternative views of the same reality. About 100 years ago, Sigmund Freud related this construct to psychopathology when he alluded to "overly" accurate perceptions of some patients prone to depression. Inasmuch as this concept has an extensive history, it is surprising that awareness of negative cognitions as a distinct and direct treatment strategy has been embraced only relatively recently.

The construct of negative cognitions has its foundation in the understanding that environmental interactions are often neutral or at least open to interpretation. We perceive and evaluate information in cognitive structures referred to as *schemas,* which are formed through our histories. That is, our early experiences provide the basis upon which we shape our views and expectations of ourselves, our future, and the world with which we interact. It is not the world that is positive or negative, but our interpretation of that world (or our perception of events) that has valence. The individual attributes meaning to events and interactions on the basis of preexisting schemas. Out attributions are central to how we experience our personal world, and these attributions have a direct bearing on our affect and behavior.

By way of illustration, a man running to catch a bus collides with another person, dropping his briefcase. The event can be viewed as an intentional act of aggression by the other party, resulting in anger and possibly aggression. The event can also be viewed as confirmation of personal clumsiness and, further, the man's sense of embarrassment and worthlessness. Alternatively, the event may be seen as positive if the other party is a woman the man finds attractive and he views the incident as an opportunity for the two to get acquainted. Another example is that of a woman asked to give a presentation at work. The event may be viewed as an opportunity to demonstrate knowledge and mastery of a particular subject, thereby a positive experience; or the event is anticipated as an occasion for failure and public humiliation, clearly a negative experience. It is not the event, but the expectations that are positive or negative.

Our perception of events, rather than the events themselves, mediate response. An individual who perceives events as negative will experience negative affect related to the negative cognitions and will behave in consonance with these affects (and cognitions). If events are neutral and our perceptions are not, then an individual can learn to modify what is perceived, leading to altered (improved) affect and behavior. The treatment strategy assumes that an individual can be taught awareness of these (conscious and identifiable) negative cognitions. Through a process of collaborative empiricism, these dysfunctional thoughts can be examined, challenged, and altered, leading to positive change in how one feels and behaves. The therapist's Socratic questioning provides a mechanism for the individual to learn a "new truth" in the search for a more functional (and positive) reality.

RESEARCH BASIS

Evidence for the relationship between negative cognitions and subsequent affect and behavior is extensive. Research has found that individuals with mood and anxiety disorders have specific negative cognitions associated with these pathologies and that treatments designed to focus on altering these cognitions result in improvements in presenting psychopathology. Several studies have reported results with cognitive strategies for these disorders that are equivalent or superior to the use of medications, particularly for mild and moderate major depressions and anxiety disorders. In addition, research has suggested that cognitive strategies with mood and anxiety disorders provide a prophylactic benefit superior to those of antidepressants generally used with these psychopathologies. Apparently, patients who are able to benefit from cognitive interventions learn to alter their thinking, such that they are able to apply what they learn over time and in new situations, resulting in relapse prevention. The positive findings associated with cognitive therapies extend over more than three decades and have led to the use of similar strategies with additional patient populations (e.g., substance abuse, eating disorders, personality disorders). While promising, efficacy in these latter domains awaits definitive conclusions.

RELEVANT TARGET POPULATIONS AND EXCEPTIONS

The populations found most likely to benefit from the modification of negative cognitions are those who suffer from depression and from anxiety disorders such as panic and agoraphobia, social phobias, post-traumatic stress disorders, and, to a somewhat lesser extent, generalized anxiety disorders. The use of cognitive strategies with depression and anxiety disorders do vary somewhat.

Depressed individuals often present with negative concepts about the self. While growing up, they form views that they are unworthy, that the world will not treat them well, and that this will always be true. Their information processing becomes faulty, so that failures are noted, while successes are overlooked (selective abstraction). Their perceptions can become self-fulfilling, and they often feel incapable of changing their circumstances, leading to feelings of helplessness and hopelessness.

Anxious individuals tend to view the world as frightening or dangerous. As a result, they are hypervigilant in their attention to potential perils, and they

perceive themselves as lacking the ability to overcome them. A world seen as filled with danger and the self-perception of inadequacy to overcome these dangers results in escalating anxiety.

The depressed individual looks to the world to confirm an internalized view of unworthiness, while the anxious individual looks to the world to confirm an internalized view of threat. Neither feels up to the task of mastering their quandaries. Both have detrimental perceptions, negative attributions, and feelings of helplessness. While elements of these negative cognitions differ, treatment strategies are similar. Cognitive distortions are identified, examined, and challenged. Treatment teaches awareness of the reality that was created and its consequences and assists with the reconstruction of the past, in order to create a more adaptive worldview.

Some exceptions to these targeted groups should be noted. For example, individuals with specific phobias often respond to simple behavioral interventions and therefore do not need to examine their cognitions. In addition, far less data are available for those suffering from dysthymia. This chronic condition is often treatment resistant, and therapeutic recommendations are likely to be more tentative. Finally, severe depressions and mood and anxiety disorders that resist cognitive interventions may benefit from adjunctive medications found to be effective with these disorders. Often with treatment-refractory cases, the use of cognitive therapy is more beneficial once the psychotropic medications have had an opportunity to initiate the healing process.

COMPLICATIONS

Before initiating efforts at cognitive interventions, the depressed or anxious individual should be evaluated for appropriateness. A level of cognitive ability is needed that demonstrates the capacity for abstract thinking in order for this strategy to be effective. Without the intellectual and cognitive aptitudes required, the individual may be unable to understand and generalize the concepts of distorted cognitions and may lack the capacity to benefit from therapeutic tasks such as role playing. In addition, homework is viewed as an integral part of cognitive treatment, as it facilitates and reinforces the learning process. Patients who are uncooperative in the work required or who sabotage treatment by being passive or avoidant must be brought into compliance so that the work may proceed.

Finally, cognitive treatments were designed to be time limited, often between 12 and 16 weeks. However, some studies have found that while symptom relief is often achieved within this time frame, functional impairments and recoveries that include factors such as work performance often take weeks or even months longer. Such issues should be given fuller consideration when attending to an individual's cognitions in relation to the treatment of some disorders.

—Helen Orvaschel

See also: Cognitive Behavior Therapy (Vol. I); Self-Monitoring (Vol. I); Self-Statement Modification (Vol. I)

Suggested Readings

Beck, A. T., Rush, A. J., Shaw, B. F., & Emery, G. (1979). Cognitive therapy of depression. New York: Guilford Press.

Elkin, I., Shea, M. T., Watkins, J. T., Imber, S. D., Sotsky, S. M., Collins, J. F., et al. (1989). NIMH treatment of depression collaborative research program. I: General effectiveness of treatments. Archives of General Psychiatry, 46, 971–983.

Evans, M. D., Hollon, S. D., DeRubeis, R. J., Piasecki, J. M., Grove, W. M., Garvey, M. J., et al. (1992). Differential relapse following cognitive therapy and pharmacotherapy for depression. Archives of General Psychiatry, 49, 802–808.

Finch, A. J., Nelson, W. M., & Ott, E. S. (1993). Cognitive-behavioral procedures with children and adolescents: A practical guide. Boston: Allyn & Bacon.

Freud, S. (1917). Completed psychological works: Vol. 14. Mourning and melancholia (J. Strachey, Ed.). New York: Hogarth Press.

Hollon, S. D., DeRubeis, R. J., Evans, M. D., Wiemer, M. J., Garvey, M. J., Grove, W. M., et al. (1992). Cognitive therapy and pharmacotherapy for depression. Archives of General Psychiatry, 49, 774–781.

NONCONTINGENT REINFORCEMENT

DESCRIPTION OF THE STRATEGY

In recent years, researchers have demonstrated that undesired operant behaviors exhibited by people with developmental disabilities can be reduced by delivering the reinforcer for those behaviors under purely time-based (usually fixed-time) schedules. Such schedules often are referred to as noncontingent reinforcement (NCR), although that description is inaccurate, as discussed below, under "Complications." Using NCR typically involves three steps, described as follows.

Step 1: Functional Assessment

Initially, a functional assessment should be conducted to identify the reinforcer(s) for the problem behavior. Depending on the time and resources available, the reinforcer(s) can be isolated by direct observation, interviews with knowledgeable caregivers, or experimental functional analysis in which the target behavior is measured under different experimental conditions. In most published studies, attention was the reinforcer for the troublesome behavior, although other reinforcers also have been identified.

NCR typically is most useful when the reinforcer for the behavior to be reduced is a stimulus that can be identified and delivered by caregivers. Studies have, however, shown that the response-independent delivery of stimuli believed to be important to clients (e.g., attention) will sometimes reduce undesired behaviors even though those behaviors are not maintained by those stimuli. Frequently, attending to a person who is self-injurious may, for instance, reduce self-injury, even if attention is not the reinforcer for the behavior. Response-independent delivery of edibles and attention may be worth considering as techniques for reducing hard-to-manage behaviors in clients with severe developmental disabilities, even under conditions where the reinforcers that maintain those behaviors in the everyday environment cannot be isolated or manipulated.

Step 2: NCR

NCR involves delivering to the client the stimulus that was delivered in Step 1 as the reinforcer for the target behavior or delivering another stimulus thought to be valuable to him or her. This stimulus is presented each time a specified period of time elapses, regardless of whether or not the behavior occurs. This arrangement is technically labeled a fixed-time schedule. If, for example, a psychiatric inpatient's screaming is reinforced by attention from staff, NCR would involve having a staff member attend to the patient at specified intervals regardless of whether or not the patient screamed. The time the staff attends to the patient should be similar to the period of attention that was revealed to be reinforcing during functional assessment.

Initially, the interval between presentations of the stimulus should be very brief. In fact, NCR often starts with continuous stimulus presentations. The interval is gradually increased across time until a value that can be sustained over long periods is reached. In most published studies, the maximum interstimulus interval attained typically is in the neighborhood of 5 minutes. No one knows whether substantially longer intervals are effective in reducing behavior. It appears, however, that success at longer intervals may require a very gradual increase in the interstimulus interval and perhaps an increase in stimulus duration or amount. Moreover, adding a "protective" requirement, such that stimulus delivery cannot occur until a specified period has elapsed without occurrence of the target behavior, may increase effectiveness. Under such an arrangement, each occurrence of the target behavior would reset the interstimulus interval. Although this possibility has not been systematically evaluated, arranging variable time rather than fixed time, stimulus presentation is another strategy for increasing treatment effectiveness when a long interstimulus interval is required. Reinforcing desired alternatives to the response targeted for deceleration is another strategy that merits consideration.

There is no generally accepted formula for increasing the interval between stimulus presentations. In general, the interval should be increased slowly (e.g., by no more than 25% each time an increase is arranged), and increases should occur only when the client's behavior is adequately controlled at the existing interval. Although caregivers are wise to develop an algorithm for changing the interstimulus interval prior to implementing NCR, the client's behavior must ultimately guide treatment decisions.

Step 3: Evaluation

Before NCR is implemented, staff should select and implement a measurement system that accurately quantifies the problem behavior. The data obtained are essential to making decisions regarding the utility of NCR in general and about the specific interstimulus interval that is appropriate at a given point in time. In addition to quantifying the target behavior, caregivers should be sensitive to adverse changes in other behaviors, including a general reduction in responding, that might arise during NCR.

RESEARCH BASIS

Over the last decade, more than 40 published studies have reported the successful use of NCR to reduce troublesome behaviors. Those studies provide compelling evidence of the potential effectiveness of the procedure, although they are limited in several significant regards, as discussed under "Relevant Target Populations and Exceptions."

RELEVANT TARGET POPULATIONS AND EXCEPTIONS

In published studies, NCR typically was used to reduce self-injurious, aggressive, and disruptive behaviors exhibited by persons with developmental disabilities. These behaviors occurred at relatively high rates prior to intervention, and the reinforcers that maintained them could be isolated through functional assessment. The range of clients and behaviors with which NCR is effective has yet to be determined, but it appears that the procedure is best suited for managing high-frequency and high-intensity troublesome behaviors that have proven refractory to treatment with other interventions.

With few exceptions, published studies involving NCR have been conducted in contrived settings during brief (15 minutes or less) experimental sessions. NCR does not appear to be well suited for reducing troublesome behaviors over long periods in clients' everyday environments, unless the time between deliveries of the scheduled event (e.g., attention) can be gradually increased to a manageable level (e.g., 15 minutes) without loss of effectiveness. Moreover, repeated deliveries of attention or other stimuli under an NCR arrangement may (through satiation) reduce the capacity of those stimuli to reinforce desired behaviors. Finally, NCR as typically arranged does not increase appropriate behavior.

COMPLICATIONS

Behavioral psychologists typically define reinforcement functionally, as an operation or process in which the occurrence of a behavior is followed by a change in the environment (reinforcer), and as a result, such behavior subsequently increases in rate or is otherwise strengthened. If the reinforcer is produced by the response, reinforcement is termed *response-dependent, response-contingent,* or simply *contingent.* If, however, behavior is strengthened by a reinforcer that follows but is not produced by the response in question, reinforcement is termed *response-independent, not-response-contingent,* or *noncontingent.* Response-independent reinforcement is also sometimes labeled as *superstitious* or *adventitious* reinforcement.

When time-based presentations of a stimulus only reduce the frequency of behavior, as is the case when so-called NCR is effective in therapeutic applications, the operation should not be referred to as reinforcement.

Nevertheless, the term noncontingent reinforcement is firmly entrenched in the literature and undoubtedly will continue to be used to refer to procedures in which behavior is weakened through response-independent delivery of stimuli known or thought to be reinforcers in other contexts.

At least three behavioral processes may be responsible for the response-reducing effects of NCR. One is satiation, in which repeated delivery of the stimulus that reinforces undesired behavior reduces motivation to gain access to that stimulus. Another is extinction, in which the reinforcing temporal relation between undesired behavior and a stimulus that existed prior to NCR (e.g., self-injury is regularly and shortly followed by attention) is broken. A third is evocation of behavior incompatible with undesired responding. If, for example, a staff member gives a client an edible

every 15 seconds, the client may spend her or his time chewing, swallowing, and orienting toward the caregiver, not in scratching or biting other residents.

—Alan D. Poling and Kristal Ehrhardt

See also: *Behavior Management (Vol. III); Behavior Therapy (Vol. II); Behavior Therapy Theory (Vol. I)*

Suggested Readings

Carr, J. E., Coriaty, S., Wilder, D. A., Gaunt, B. T., Dozier, C. L., Britton, L. N., Avina, C., et al. (2000). A review of "noncontingent" reinforcement as treatment for the aberrant behavior of individuals with developmental disabilities. *Research in Developmental Disabilities, 21,* 377–391.

Tucker, M., Sigafoos, J., & Bushell, H. (1998). Use of noncontingent reinforcement in the treatment of challenging behavior. *Behavior Modification, 22,* 529–547.

OPERANT CONDITIONING

DESCRIPTION OF THE STRATEGY

Operant conditioning is based on the premise that behavior is a function of its consequences. Unlike Pavlov, who took a stimulus-response (S-R) approach, Skinner took a response-stimulus (R-S) approach. He theorized that consequences of behavior at time T_1 modify probability of emitting the same or similar behavior in the same or similar circumstances at time T_2. Skinner suggested that behavior evolves ontogenetically through variation and selection in a manner rather parallel to how Darwin viewed organisms to evolve phylogenetically. The strategy in applying operant conditioning concerns the therapeutic direction of this ontogenetic evolutionary process and entails the following steps.

The first step is to identify a target behavior that is central to the client's complaint. This step is sometimes more difficult than one might expect. Clients rarely formulate their problems in terms of specific behavioral complaints. They more frequently present with evaluative and emotional statements, such as "My spouse/children no longer love(s)/respect(s) me." Or "I feel sad and depressed." Or "I am anxious and stressed and want to feel better." Clinicians need to explore with clients what particular changes in their behavior or the behavior of other people would help them achieve their goals. For example, one might ask, "What it is that your spouse does or does not do that makes you feel that he or she no longer loves you?" What you or others do not do is as important as what you or they do. The object of this first step is to identify a target behavior.

The second step is to conduct a behavioral assessment, which entails two phases. The first phase concerns assessing topography of the target response. The clinician needs to determine frequency, intensity, and/or duration of the target behavior. Clinicians are largely dependent upon adults to observe their own behavior. Occasionally, a spouse or significant other person can be enlisted to observe the frequency, intensity, and/or duration of the target behavior, but mainly, the person ends up observing himself or herself. Behaviors that occur too frequently, too intensely, or with too great a duration constitute behavioral excesses. Behaviors that do not occur frequently enough, not intensely enough, or with too short of a duration constitute behavioral deficits.

The second phase of behavioral assessment is to conduct a functional analysis of behavior, where for each instance of the target behavior, antecedent and consequent events are also recorded. Antecedent conditions, known technically as discriminative stimuli, are the conditions that set the occasion for the emission or omission of the target behavior. The target behavior is not thought to be reflexively elicited by these conditions in the Pavlovian sense, but rather, these are the conditions that are typically associated with the occurrence of the target behavior. Some of the consequent conditions may function as reinforcers and strengthen the target behavior. Not all consequent conditions function as reinforcers, so care must be taken to identify the ones that actually reinforce and make behavior stronger or more probable.

The third step is to create a behavioral treatment plan based on results of behavioral assessment. Target behaviors that constitute behavioral excesses are to be

Table 1   Taxonomy of Operant Conditioning[a]

		Consequent Event Unsignaled			Consequent Event Signaled		
		Onset or Increase	No Change	Offset or Decrease	Onset or Increase	No Change	Offset or Decrease
Response emission	Positive reinforcer +	$E^+\uparrow$ Reward[b]	$E^+\downarrow$ Extinction	$E_+\downarrow$ Penalty	$sE^+\uparrow$ Signaled reward	$sE^+\downarrow$ Signaled extinction	$sE_+\downarrow$ Signaled penalty
	Negative reinforcer −	$E^-\downarrow$ Punish	$E^-\downarrow$ Extinction	$E_-\uparrow$ Relief	$sE^+\downarrow$ Signaled punish	$sE^-\downarrow$ Signaled extinction	$sE_-\uparrow$ Signaled relief
Response omission	Positive reinforcer +	$O^+\downarrow$ Omission reward	$O^+\uparrow$ Omission extinction	$O_+\uparrow$ Omission penalty	$sO^+\downarrow$ Signaled omission reward	$sO^+\uparrow$ Signaled extinction	$sO_+\uparrow$ Signaled omission penalty
	Negative reinforcer −	$O^-\uparrow$ Omission punish	$O^-\uparrow$ Omission extinction	$O_-\downarrow$ Omission relief	$sO^-\uparrow$ Signaled omission punish	$sO^-\uparrow$ Signaled extinction	$sO_-\downarrow$ Signaled omission relief

a. A taxonomy of operant conditioning first published by Woods (1974) and expanded by Tryon (1999). Reproduced here with minor modification with permission.

b. The term *conditioning* is assumed to follow each table entry.

SOURCE: Table 1: A taxonomy of operant conditioning first published by Woods (1974) and expanded by Tryon (1999). Reproduced here with minor modification with permission.

reduced, and behaviors that constitute behavioral deficits are to be increased. More complex situations where two incompatible reinforcement contingencies operate simultaneously indicate that one or the other needs to be discontinued.

RESEARCH BASIS

The principles of operant conditioning have been extensively investigated under laboratory conditions since approximately 1930 and in clinical contexts since around 1940. These principles are among the most well-replicated findings in psychology and provide the basis for an empirically informed practice. Table 1 summarizes the basic principles of operant conditioning.

To avoid circular reasoning, it is necessary to first determine whether a stimulus is a positive or a negative reinforcer. The word *reinforce* means "to make stronger." We are said to strengthen behavior when we increase its frequency, intensity, and/or duration. The operational definition of a reinforcer is that it strengthens behavior it follows. One can turn stimuli "on" or "off." We identify a positive reinforcer if turning the stimulus "on" contingent upon emission of a behavior strengthens the behavior. This implies that the stimulus

was "off" for some time prior to the emission of the target behavior. We identify a negative reinforcer if turning the stimulus "off" contingent upon emission of a behavior strengthens the behavior. This implies that the stimulus was on for some time prior to the emission of the target behavior. Negative reinforcement is not punishment. Punishment entails the contingent onset of a negative reinforcer (see Table 1).

Three manipulations of positive and negative reinforcers are recognized. One can onset or increase them, offset or decrease them, or not change them at all. The four combinations of onset-offset vs. positive-negative reinforcer form a 2 x 2 table that defines four types of consequences (operant conditions), which have predictable effects on a target behavior. The "up" arrow indicates that the designated condition increases the frequency, intensity, and/or duration of the target behavior. The "down" arrow indicates that the designated condition decreases the frequency, intensity, and/or duration of the target behavior. Reward conditioning is defined by the onset of a positive reinforcer. This condition assumes that the positive reinforcer is "off" prior to its onset. Food pellets are frequently used in the laboratory. Depriving the organism of access to food for 24 or 48 hours or restricting food access until the organism weighs 80% of its free-feeding weight are two preconditions used to make food onset have functional properties. Well-fed animals will frequently not work at tasks that produce access to more food. Consumption of a food turns the positive reinforcer "off" by removing food from the environment.

Penalty conditioning is defined by offset of a positive reinforcer. For humans, this occurs when a fine is paid or when tokens previously earned are forfeited. This condition assumes that the positive reinforcer is "on" prior to its offset, as is the case when money or tokens are earned through prior behavior. Punishment conditioning is defined by the onset of a negative reinforcer. Stimuli that increase behavior when turned "off" decrease behavior when turned "on." Punishment suppresses behavior only under the circumstances in which it occurs. This operant condition assumes that the negative reinforcer is "off" prior to its onset. Relief conditioning is defined by the offset of a negative reinforcer. Chronic nagging that terminates contingent upon some behavior is an example. Relief conditioning presumes that the negative reinforcer is continually "on" and is only briefly turned "off." The coercive family process described by Gerald Patterson and his colleagues includes adults who modify each other's behavior using relief conditioning. The term *coercive* reflects the psychological impression that one has little option but to give in.

These four fundamental conditions are replicated within another 2×2 table defined by whether the target behavior is emitted or omitted versus whether the consequence was signaled or not. The top half of Table 1 covers the case where consequences are conditional on the emission of the target behavior. Notice that the arrows for "Reward" and "Relief" conditioning point upward as they strengthen behavior. Notice that the arrows for "Penalty" and "Punishment" conditioning point downward as they weaken behavior. The bottom half of Table 1 covers the case where consequences are conditional on the omission of the target behavior, which includes the emission of any other behavior and not behaving at all. Time sampling entails observing for some period, say, 10 seconds, and recording for the next 10 seconds, repeating this cycle for the duration of assessment. If the target behavior has not taken place during a particular interval, then it is possible to deliver one of the four fundamental consequences described above. Rewarding people for not smoking or not drinking or not eating are other examples of omission conditioning. Notice that the arrows associated with the lower omission portion of Table 1 point in the opposite direction from

the arrows associated with the upper portion of this table. "Omission reward conditioning" and "Omission relief conditioning" now decrease the frequency, intensity, and/or duration of the target behavior whereas "Omission penalty conditioning" and "Omission punishment conditioning" now increase the frequency, intensity, and/or duration of the target behavior.

Extinction is a fifth fundamental condition. It is more complex than the others in that it is defined by the absence of change in positive and negative reinforcers contingent upon either the emission or omission of behavior. There must be a complete lack of relationship between what the organism does with regard to the target behavior and what happens to it. Performing or not performing the target behavior cannot change any stimulus that has positive or negative reinforcing properties. Extinction is simple to implement in the laboratory but very difficult to implement clinically. Experimenters simply deactivate the feeder in the laboratory. Pressing the lever or not pressing the lever or performing any other behavior will not produce food. Extinction is a helpless condition. One might be instructed to ignore some irritating behavior, perhaps humming, by one's spouse on the basis that absence of social reinforcement, extinction, will cause it to disappear. This presumes that the behavior is not intrinsically rewarding; performing the behavior is its own reward. It presumes that no one else in the house comments on it; negative attention can reinforce, or strengthen, behavior. It may become too difficult to ignore the humming as it become louder and continues longer. Increased intensity and behavioral variation that organisms typically demonstrate under extinction conditions can temporarily exacerbate the behavior being extinguished. Conditions such as these can set the occasion where extinction ceases and the person either returns to his or her previous response mode or behaves differently and quite possibly in a less constructive manner.

Reinforcers can be scheduled in many different ways, and each method has a somewhat different behavioral effect depending upon how it is scheduled. Continuous reinforcement means that a reinforcer is always given contingent upon emission or omission of a response. Reinforcers can be scheduled using a counter in either a fixed or variable way; these are called *fixed-* and *variable-ratio schedules*. A fixed-ratio schedule provides reinforcement after every N response, where N represents a fixed number. A variable-ratio schedule provides reinforcement after an average of N responses;

sometimes fewer and other times more responses are required. Reinforcers can be scheduled using a timer in either a fixed or variable way; these are called *fixed-* and *variable-interval schedules*. A fixed-interval schedule provides reinforcement for the first response after T seconds have elapsed. A variable-interval schedule provides reinforcement for the first response after an average of T seconds have elapsed. Reinforcers can be scheduled on the basis of response rate. *Differential reinforcement of high rate* entails providing reinforcement when the number of responses per unit time exceeds a set value. *Differential reinforcement of low rate* entails providing reinforcement when the number of responses per unit of time is less than a set value. It is possible to monitor and provide consequences for two or more behaviors, such as when left and right levers are presented to the organism. Separate reinforcement schedules can be assigned to each lever. Other reinforcement schedules are possible. The major point here is that the way reinforcers are associated with behavior is as or more important in determining behavior than what the reinforcers are. A thousand food pellets given out to separate organisms by each of these methods against the same target behavior will produce predictably and remarkably different behaviors.

Noticeably absent from the material presented above is any discussion of why these principles work as they do, how they change the organism, what makes a reinforcer reinforcing, or related questions. This is primarily because operant conditioning seeks a functional understanding of behavior and limits inquiry to this approach. The suggested readings below by Donahoe show how *parallel distributed processing connectionist neural network theory* is being used to provide a deeper understanding of operant conditioning.

RELEVANT TARGET POPULATIONS AND EXCEPTIONS

Principles of operant conditioning are phylogenetically general. This means that they have been shown to hold for a variety of species, including humans (adults and children), rats, mice, pigeons, dogs, cats, fish, and other life forms. Hence, operant conditioning is applicable to all people from all cultures regardless of any mental or physical handicaps they might have. This wide applicability means that operant conditioning can be applied in situations where many other treatments cannot and is one of the reasons why behavior therapists favor this approach.

COMPLICATIONS

A primary complication is that like gravity, principles of operant conditioning can create problems as well as provide therapeutic intervention. The suggested reading by Martin and Pear contains "pitfall" sections that describe how operant conditioning principles can be used to inadvertently reinforce undesirable behaviors. For example, interrupting in midsentence during a social gathering may be socially reinforced by a spouse, who subsequently may be surprised to find that this same behavior occurs during a marital argument. Strengthening behavior in one situation can cause it to generalize to other situations where it is far less desirable. This problem can be addressed by discrimination training that either reinforces the behavior in one situation and extinguishes it in the other or punishes in the other situation for greater contrast. Couples sometimes revert to punishment or relief conditioning to get their way in a particular situation. The other person may be tempted to respond in-kind but more intensely, and, if successful, this countermove is strengthened and will become more probable in future to where it is the first choice in how to respond. This coercive family process can transform a positive caring and courting relationship into an aggressive and destructive relationship, where each person struggles for the upper hand and dominating the other becomes an independent and primary objective that can include domestic violence.

CASE ILLUSTRATION

This case concerns a 25-year-old single, White female living in New York City who was fearful of the subway and did not take it despite obvious transportation benefits. This problem was long-standing and had recently become problematic when she needed to travel more for her job. The target behavior in this case was a sequence of behaviors, a behavioral chain, that entailed walking down into the subway, paying the fare, waiting for a train, entering the train, riding the train, exiting the train, and exiting the subway. Interviewing rapidly revealed that these behaviors did not occur, thereby establishing a behavioral deficit. Antecedent setting conditions were all circumstances that required her to travel to places that are conveniently accessible by subway and more difficult to get to by other modes of transportation, including driving; she owned a car. Consequent events were not observed because she did not ride the subway. No traumatic history of riding the subway could be found. She had heard stories about accidents and crimes that occurred in subways but had not experienced any of these events herself.

It would have been unreasonable to expect her to be able to engage in all of the desired behaviors at one time. Hence, intervention was based on shaping, a process of gradual approximation. She thought of the subway as a dirty place and therefore chose to wear gloves while performing the following behaviors. Allowing her to wear gloves increased the probability that she would engage in the initial behaviors in the specified behavioral chain and was therefore deemed clinically advisable. That it was winter made wearing gloves more appropriate. She was instructed to enter the subway in a confident and assertive manner, to approach the fare box, to turn around and return to the surface, and then to reinforce herself for this behavioral sequence with positive self-statements about her success and growing self-control over her ability to use the subway. She was instructed to repeat this sequence until she could do so comfortably. She was then instructed to proceed past the fare box, onto a local subway, proceed one stop, exit the subway, and to reward herself in the same way described above. She then had an option of either taking a cab or bus back to where she began, walking back, or riding the subway back. When she was able to ride down and back one stop, she was asked to ride down and back two stops, then three, four, and so on, until she could ride any chosen number of stops. She was then instructed to ride different subway lines to promote response generalization. She progressed systematically over a 10-week period and can now ride the subway, but still does not find this mode of transportation especially appealing. Perhaps that will abate with time, provided that she does not have any bad experiences and finds this mode of transportation cost-effective and time-efficient.

—*Warren W. Tryon*

See also: *Behavior Therapy Theory (Vol. I); Behavioral Treatment in Natural Environments (Vol. I); Operant Conditioning (Vols. II & III)*

Suggested Readings

Donahoe, J. W. (1997). The necessity of neural networks. In G. E. Stelmach & P. A. Vroon (Series Eds.), J. W. Donahoe & V. P. Dorsel (Vol. Eds.), *Advances in psychology: Vol. 121.* *Neural-network models of cognition: Biobehavioral foundations* (pp. 1–19). Amsterdam: Elsevier.

Donahoe, J. W., & Palmer, D. C. (1989). The interpretation of complex human behavior: Some reactions to parallel distributed processing (J. L. McClelland, D. E. Rumelhart, & the PDP Research Group, Eds.). *Journal of the Experimental Analysis of Behavior, 51,* 399–416.

Martin, G., & Pear, J. (2002). *Behavior modification: What it is and how to do it* (7th ed.). Englewood Cliffs, NJ: Prentice Hall.

Tryon, W. W. (1998). Behavioral observation. In M. Hersen & A. S. Bellack (Eds.), *Behavioral assessment: A practical handbook* (4th ed., pp. 79–103). Boston: Allyn & Bacon.

Tryon, W. W. (1999). Behavioral model. In M. Hersen & V. B. Van Hasselt (Eds.), *Advanced abnormal psychology* (pp. 93–123). New York: Plenum Press.

Tryon, W. W. (2002). Expanding the explanatory base of behavior analysis via modern connectionism: Selectionism as a common explanatory core. *The Behavior Analyst Today, 3,* 104–118.

ORGANIZATIONAL BEHAVIOR MANAGEMENT

DESCRIPTION OF THE STRATEGY

Organizational behavior management (OBM), also known as performance management, involves the systematic application of behavior analysis techniques to improve the functionality of organizations and their members. The principal publication outlet for OBM has been the *Journal of Organizational Behavior Management* (*JOBM,* Haworth Press), which was founded in 1977. The first editor of *JOBM* was Aubrey C. Daniels, with Larry Miller as managing editor. The professional organization that represents the field of OBM is the OBM Network. The OBM Network is a special-interest group of the Association for Behavior Analysis and was founded in 1982.

Skinner, in 1953, was among the first to suggest applications of behavior analysis to improve organizational productivity. Articles began to appear on the topic during the 1950s and 1960s, but the field was not formally established until the late 1970s. OBM techniques have produced effective results in a wide variety of settings, including large and small organizations, nonprofit and for-profit organizations, publicly and privately held organizations, and unionized and nonunionized work cultures. Studies have targeted a variety of organizational behaviors and results for improvement, including productivity, quality, customer satisfaction and service, safety, and health. The most commonly used OBM interventions include performance feedback, verbal praise, goal setting, monetary rewards, nonmonetary tangible rewards, training, antecedents (i.e., job aids, prompts), punishment, and systems redesign.

As most practitioners and researchers in OBM are trained in applied behavior analysis, OBM work is highly pragmatic, so practitioners and researchers tend to assume a problem-solving role. Organizational problems are typically addressed at one or more of three levels: the performer level, the process level, and/or the organizational level. The performer level is perhaps the most common of these in the research literature. Problems at this level involve performance problems of employees and employee groups. Performer-level interventions involve changing worker behavior to achieve more valuable organizational results. Performer-level interventions are most clearly informed by the known effective techniques of applied behavior analysis. The process level involves how people go about doing the work within a series of interdependent tasks that culminate in creation of products or services important to the organization. Intervention at the process level involves improving efficiency with which tasks are completed, reducing complexity and redundancy in processes, and engineering effective management and workflow systems. Process-level interventions are most clearly informed by general systems theory and behavioral systems analysis. The organization level involves the mission and strategy of the organization and functioning of the total organization in relation to its immediate (i.e., the local community and industry competitors) and distal environments (i.e., the legal, economic, and cultural environment and global competition). Organizational-level interventions are most clearly informed by general systems theory and organizational theory and strategy.

RESEARCH BASIS

Results of empirical OBM research show that when antecedents clearly specify conditions under which preferred work behavior will be highly correlated with clearly specified consequences (e.g., feedback and tangible or social rewards), the typical effect is substantial improvement in the targeted behavior and in the organizationally relevant results. As stated above, particular techniques and applications in OBM vary widely. However, most OBM research activities have focused on changing behavior and results (the outcomes or products of behavior) at work. The most frequently utilized technique of behavior change in OBM has been delivery of performance feedback. Performance feedback should be specific, individualized, and delivered immediately before or after the target behavior. It can involve verbal reports of performance or graphic representations of performance over time. Feedback is most effective if delivered immediately and individually; however, research shows that delayed and group feedback are also effective in many cases. Feedback can be delivered by peers, by supervisors, or by the target individual through self-monitoring of performance. Feedback is most effective when delivered frequently (i.e., daily or many times each day), but it may also work when delivered on a weekly or monthly basis, depending on the performance targeted. More complex skills typically require more frequent and more specific feedback than do less complex skills. Comparisons of intermittent and frequent feedback suggest that employees prefer frequent feedback but that frequent feedback does not necessarily produce more durable behavior change.

Contingent reinforcement is another highly effective technique frequently used in OBM. Contingent reinforcement can be tangible (usually involving a low-cost item), verbal (often called "praise"), or monetary. Research on monetary incentives suggests that it is the contingency between the payment amount and the target behavior that determines effectiveness of the incentive, rather than amount of the incentive paid.

Goal setting is an antecedent strategy often used alone and/or in conjunction with feedback and reinforcement. Effective goals should be challenging, yet attainable. That is, effective goals should be difficult for the performer to attain: They should be set at a level that is somewhat higher than current levels of performance. However, goals must also be attainable: They should be set at a level that has been achieved by the performer some time in the past. Perhaps the best heuristic in setting goals is to set the goal at the level of the highest point during baseline (pregoal setting) performance. Depending on the context in which goals are specified, whether the effectiveness of goals is due to their signaling the availability of reinforcement or to their ability to alter the function of stimuli in the performance environment remains a subject of debate among researchers.

RELEVANT TARGET
POPULATIONS AND EXCEPTIONS

Work-related behavior of virtually any individual or group within a bona fide formal organization could be targeted for behavior and results improvement through applications of OBM-based interventions. Interventions have occurred among individuals at the shop floor level, among supervisors, among managers and even among top-level organizational executives, including the CEO. They have been applied in a basic materials foundry, among caregivers and staff in mental/developmental and physical health care agencies/facilities, in universities (from an admissions office to a chemistry lab), in doctors' offices, in government agencies, in *Fortune 500* companies, in an amusement park, in a game arcade, in a roofing company, in real estate offices, in retail sales outlets, in telemarketing facilities, in a necktie factory, in a food-processing plant, in small machine shops, in large and small factories (in the U.S. and Russia), in the hospitality industry (banquet operations and hotel room cleaning and maintenance), in pizza outlets (safe-driving practices among pizza delivers), in numerous and various organizations (targeting safe work practices), at the front desk operations of an Australian police station, and other venues too numerous to list here. While OBM applications are designed for individuals and groups in virtually any formal organizational context, OBM is not the basis of individual therapeutic interventions to treat individual cases of maladaptive behavior of a purely personal nature. It is not, for example, involved in treating individuals with phobias or drug dependencies. However, it may be used to improve the functioning of organizational context responsible for delivering such services. OBM has, for example, been used to improve efficiency of administrative functions in doctors' offices, while not becoming involved with the performance of any medical treatments per se. On some occasion, but with less frequency than the targets listed above, OBM methods have been used to test whether certain elements of a socially desirable change initiative (e.g., increasing use of buses versus individual car driving, smoking reduction in a community) can effect socially desired changes at the level of a whole community.

COMPLICATIONS

Complications are more often than not associated with ensuring that intervention effectiveness data are not compromised in terms of their reliability and validity.

For example, organizational leaders who must approve and make monetary investments in OBM interventions as part of their organizational development efforts are not inclined to the approve use of a powerful experimental design such as the ABAB reversal design. Generally, OBM researchers are forced to use multiple-baseline designs and even simple AB designs with systematic replications, when such replications are possible. Thus, what appears in journals that require published research results to meet rigorous standards of data reliability and validity with respect to intervention effects presents a censored record regarding OBM interventions that have been put in place. Thus, effectiveness of the average intervention is unknown, while effectiveness of those reported in scientific research publications, such as *JOBM,* does not represent a random sample from the population of OBM-based interventions. That, of course, is because the editorial board of reviewers discriminates against intervention efforts that fail to produce results or provide poor evidence concerning reliability and validity of the intervention data. Their presumption is that readers are concerned with learning about interventions that can be expected to work in their organizational settings should they replicate the interventions in their work settings.

Complications also arise when an intervention depends on presence of OBM researchers to ensure maintenance. For example, unless an intervention irreversibly changes some practice or includes an enduring or self-sustaining maintenance component (i.e., a change in the system per se), a reversal toward the baseline performance level is likely to coincide with departure of the research or practitioner team. Fortunately, there are numerous OBM-based interventions that produce behavior and performance changes that are resistant to reversal and for which the multiple-baseline design is ideally suited to the task of establishing reliability and validity of intervention effectiveness.

Another complication associated with published research record on OBM intervention effectiveness is rooted in what makes OBM an attractive organizational behavior and performance change strategy. When an OBM intervention arranges for powerful reinforcers to be delivered contingent on a specified behavior or its result in a work setting, that behavior and result will often exhibit a rapid increase in rate of occurrence. This makes specification of desired behavior and results upon which such reinforcement will be contingently delivered a critical step in the intervention process. If, for example, specification fails to require quality as well as quantity of work done in order to obtain reinforcements, typically quality will suffer while quantity shows a dramatic increase. If, on the other hand, specification includes a quality standard that is far greater than required to meet customer specifications or desires, quality may rise at the expense of quantity and efficiency (i.e., costs will rise with quality). But this complication is not a fault of the principles of operant behavior reinforcement upon which many OBM interventions rely. The fault in such cases resides with the skill and competence of OBM practitioner or scientist; that is, the fault is in identifying targets that are either (a) not important to the organization's mission or strategy and/or (b) produce some detrimental imbalance in the organizational system. Once again, how many such complications occur in applied field settings is not likely to be learned, because those practitioners and applied scientists, with few exceptions, engage in a practice of self-censorship (i.e., they do not attempt to publish their failures).

Another complication that can compromise even the most meticulously planned intervention or organizational development effort is a powerful shift in the competitive or social environment of the organization in which an OBM intervention has begun. Imagine, for example, what might occur in a state-funded health care system if the state's governor announced that a budget crisis might require a significant reduction in the system's staffing levels. Or suppose an OBM intervention was well under way in an air passenger corporation when the industry was deregulated. Dramatic declines and/or improvements might occur in response to news of this sort. But dramatic changes not associated with an ongoing OBM intervention would compromise the data concerning effects of the intervention.

CASE ILLUSTRATION

It is difficult describe any typical OBM case, because the problems, settings, and resultant treatments vary so widely, as described above. Therefore, presented below are seven steps that characterize the course of the typical OBM case, irrespective of problem, setting, and treatment.

1. *Find the mission.* The typical OBM case solution is one in which the practitioner or researcher first works with managers to identify the mission (i.e., the most important result that the job, department, or organization should accomplish) of the targeted job, department, and/or organization.

2. *Find the pinpoints.* After the mission is made obvious, the OBM practitioner then works with managers and/or employees to determine the important behavior and results needed to accomplish the mission. These behaviors and results are often called "pinpoints," or "targets."

3. *Develop a measurement system.* The OBM practitioner then helps the target audience to develop an accurate and reliable means of measuring the pinpointed behavior and results. In many instances, this measurement system will involve tracking costs associated with the pinpoints as well. The purpose in this case is to get an idea of the current levels of the important behaviors and results and to provide a baseline comparison that can be later used to evaluate the effects of solutions.

4. *Select an evaluation design.* If it is possible to evaluate effects of the solutions that are to be implemented, then the practitioner, manager, and employees should attempt to do so. The most commonly used evaluation strategy is a multiple-baseline design, in which baseline data are collected for one or more tasks, individuals, jobs, departments, or locations, and then similar solutions are implemented, in a staggered fashion, for each of the baselines over time. Reversal and multi-element designs are also used, though they are less common, because each involves removing a potentially effective solution for the purposes of demonstrating its efficacy. There are occasions in the practice of OBM in which it is not possible to rigorously evaluate the efficacy of solutions. In these cases, it is recommended to at minimum use an A-B (i.e., baseline-treatment) design so that one can see whether any positive effects appear to result from the solution.

5. *Diagnose the problem.* In this phase, the practitioner asks questions and conducts observations of work completion and the work environment to determine the cause(s) of the performance deficiencies. Typically, such functional assessment involves asking questions and collecting data about four broad areas of potential causes: Antecedents, knowledge and skills, equipment and processes (including a systems analysis), and consequences.

6. *Develop and implement a solution.* Based on results of the functional assessment, the practitioner

should work with managers and employees to help them develop and implement a set of solutions that address the identified deficiencies. In practice, employees and managers are trained to implement on their own and to maintain the practices specified by the solution once the practitioner withdraws from the organization.

7. *Evaluate the effects.* Results are typically measured before, during, and after solution implementation. At least three types of results are of interest to the OBM practitioner and researcher: behavior change results, treatment acceptability, and cost-benefit results. Behavior change results are of interest for obvious reasons, including that the practitioner wants to be sure that the solution changed the intended behaviors and produced the intended outcomes. Treatment acceptability is very important in OBM, as the solution will not be maintained if employees and management find it to be unpalatable. Finally, cost-benefit results are important in order to calculate return on investment figures. These figures tell the practitioner and managers how many dollars were earned or saved by the organization for every dollar spent on the OBM efforts.

OBM interventions involve changing the behavior of people in jobs rather than shifting people among jobs in attempts to fit them with work they can perform, given that their current behavioral repertoires are fixed rather than malleable. So, OBM interventions are devised to change behavior of a given workforce that has been determined to possess the aptitude for skills improvement and potential for behavioral shaping required to achieve results that support achievement of the organization's mission, goals, and performance (e.g., goods production or service delivery).

—*John Austin and Thomas C. Mawhinney*

See also: Behavioral Consultation (Vol. I); Behavior Management (Vol. III); Behavior Management for Improving Academic and Classroom Behavior (Vol. II)

Suggested Readings

Abernathy, W. B. (2000). *Managing without supervising: Creating an organization-wide performance system.* Memphis, TN: PerfSys Press.

Braksick, L. W. (2000). *Unlock behavior, unleash profits.* New York: McGraw-Hill.

Daniels, A. C. (1989). *Performance management: Improving quality productivity through positive reinforcement.* Tucker, GA: Performance Management Publications.

Daniels, A. C. (1994). *Bringing out the best in people.* New York: McGraw-Hill.

Daniels, A. C. (2001). *Other people's habits.* New York: McGraw-Hill.

Frederiksen, L. W. (Ed.). (1982). *Handbook of organizational behavior management.* New York: Wiley.

Gilbert, T. F. (1978). *Human competence: Engineering worthy performance.* New York: McGraw-Hill.

Hayes, L., Austin, J., Houmanfar, R., & Clayton, M. (Eds.). (2001). *Organizational change.* Reno, NV: Context Press.

Johnson, C., Mawhinney, T. C., & Redmon, W. (Eds.). (2001). *Handbook of organizational performance: Behavior analysis and management.* Binghamton, NY: Haworth Press.

Luthans, F., & Kreitner, R. (1985). *Organizational behavior modification and beyond.* Glenview, IL: Scott, Foresman.

O'Brien, R. M., Dickinson, A. M., & Rosow, M. P. (Eds.). (1982). *Industrial behavior modification.* New York: Pergamon Press.

Rummler, G. A., & Brache, A. P. (1995). *Improving performance: How to manage the white space on the organization chart* (Rev. ed.). San Francisco: Jossey-Bass.

ORGASMIC RECONDITIONING

DESCRIPTION OF THE STRATEGY

Imagery during masturbation and during interpersonal sexual activity is of paramount importance in treating the sexual offender. Fantasy sustains urge; thus, gaining access to such fantasies can be crucial in understanding sexual desires and reactions. However, clients' fantasies remain very much a private reserve of information, inaccessible to the treatment provider unless and until full trust is established. Therefore, the techniques described here must be approached cautiously only after building full rapport with the client. This is of special importance in working with the sexual offender, who, most often, does not enter treatment on an entirely voluntary basis.

Orgasmic reconditioning (OR), also called masturbatory reconditioning, has been described as a series of techniques for treating sexual offenders, the vast majority of whom are males. (In keeping with the standard nomenclature in this literature, clients will be referred to in the male gender only.) These methods can be applied, with some imagination, to female offenders and to other disorders, such as the sexual desire, arousal, and orgasmic disorders. However, in this description, its applications to sexual offenders will be emphasized inasmuch as it is within this population that these techniques have been developed and best studied.

Because OR employs a client's own sexual fantasies to reduce or eliminate deviant arousal and behaviors, it is usually introduced into treatment when sufficient trust has been established to discuss masturbation fantasies. It forms but one set of treatment methods generally employed among a number of techniques (described elsewhere in this volume), such as assisted covert sensitization, aversive conditioning, and relapse prevention, in an overall treatment program for the sexual offender.

Three types of orgasmic reconditioning techniques have thus far been employed for sexual offenders: directed masturbation, masturbatory satiation, and masturbatory fantasy change. In *directed masturbation,* the client is simply asked to masturbate to nondeviant fantasies or depictions, such as photographs, as often as daily and to avoid masturbation to any deviant fantasies. This assignment may continue for a period of 2 to 4 months or more. As with all OR techniques, these masturbation sessions are considered private and are usually carried out in the client's home when he is alone. (Compliance may be checked with homework audiotapes, as described below.) Theoretically, the link between appropriate fantasies, such as sexual activity with an adult female, and the pleasure of self-stimulation and, eventually, orgasm, should eventually strengthen nondeviant arousal. Moreover, abstinence from masturbation to deviant fantasies should weaken interests in those directions.

However, most sexual offenders are already aroused to normal stimuli in addition to possessing deviant attractions. Therefore, increasing arousal to nondeviant stimuli is a goal reserved for those offenders who lack sufficient normal arousal. For the majority of offenders, it is of more crucial concern to reduce deviant arousal. Therefore, *masturbatory satiation* has assumed a place of even greater importance than directed masturbation in the repertoire of treatment techniques for the sexual offender.

In masturbatory satiation, the client is asked to masturbate to fantasies or pictures of sexual activity with an appropriate stimulus (such as a same-aged female) until he reaches climax. At that point, he is directed to continue to try to masturbate for anywhere from 15 to 60 minutes to his deviant fantasies (such as images of sexual activity with a young girl or boy, or rape scenes). Although 60 minutes has been recommended by some authors, a 30-minute period may be easier for the client to accept and hence may encourage greater compliance. Again, audiotapes may help

ensure some measure of compliance. The client is usually asked to perform this technique each time he masturbates, but not less than three times each week.

Theoretically, this technique relies on the finding that sexual arousal and desire are at their lowest levels immediately following ejaculation. Therefore, the client is being asked, in this technique, first to masturbate to nondeviant fantasies to climax (actually, the first technique mentioned above, directed masturbation), then to try to masturbate to his abnormal fantasies at the time of lowest sexual drive, thereby associating these deviant interests with minimal arousal. Indeed, to have to masturbate then is quite likely an aversive event. Moreover, masturbating at this time and for an extended period thereafter, for example, 30 minutes, is reported by offenders to be physically painful to a mild degree and, more to the point, boring, as it almost never leads to further arousal, an erection, or ejaculation. For this purpose, some clinicians stress that the offender repeat the same deviant scenes again and again during this period of lowest sexual drive. It is this boring, repetitive nature of the technique that has led therapists to refer to it as masturbatory *satiation,* although it is by no means clear that satiation is the only, or even major, mechanism by which this method exerts its effects.

Thus, although included among reconditioning techniques, elements of aversive conditioning and cognitive change are obviously relevant as well in explaining the benefits of masturbatory satiation. These benefits have been demonstrated in a number of reports in the literature, both clinical and research based (see suggested readings, below). In fact, some case reports have indicated eradication of deviant arousal with this technique alone, although almost all programs employ it as one among a number of additional cognitive and behavioral methods in their arsenal. It would appear to harbor twin components, both of perhaps equal value:

1. Masturbation to climax to nondeviant fantasies at the time of maximum arousal (the directed masturbation component)

2. Masturbation thereafter to deviant fantasies at the time of minimum arousal

Further work is indicated to separate and test each component. However, from a clinical point of view, this procedure has proven remarkably effective in reducing deviant arousal, which, in turn, has been demonstrated to be a key element in decreasing the risk that any offender will commit another sexual offense. Thus, it has formed an integral component of most sexual offender treatment programs in this country and abroad. Indeed, this technique has generated a similar, less intrusive, and nonorgasmic approach, termed *verbal satiation,* in which the offender simply repeats aloud (often into a tape recorder) his particular deviant fantasies over extended periods of time. Here, satiation and boredom are the key elements believed to be responsible for reductions in interest and arousal to the deviant material.

In the third component comprising the OR techniques, *masturbatory fantasy change,* the client is asked to masturbate to deviant fantasies until the point of ejaculatory inevitability is reached. At that immediate point, he is asked to switch abruptly from deviant fantasies to fantasies or pictures of nondeviant sexual activities, thus associating these more normal fantasies and images with the pleasure of climax. In subsequent masturbatory sessions, he is asked to make this switch slightly earlier each time, until he is finally masturbating to nondeviant fantasies and materials alone. The optimum time course for these sessions is individualized for each offender, with three such sessions each week usually required over a period of several months to achieve a complete switchover from deviant to nondeviant fantasies. As with the other OR techniques, sessions can be tape-recorded to facilitate compliance, and all sessions can be conducted by the client in the privacy of his home.

In this technique, theory holds that as the offender builds up sexual pleasure by masturbating to deviant fantasies and materials at first, by having to switch to normal imagery just at the moment of greatest pleasure, the orgasm, he is building a growing association between nondeviant fantasy and arousal, which will be further enhanced by making this switch earlier and earlier during the process of masturbation. Thus, this technique combines elements of directed masturbation with the advantages inherent in the deviant arousal already present in most sexual offenders.

While this particular technique involves greater participation and control on the part of the client than the other OR techniques mentioned above, greater risks are inherent in it, as well. The client must make an often difficult leap across a wide conceptual gap; if too difficult to achieve, he may simply not comply or, worse, may reach climax while continuing to fantasize about deviant images. This difficulty underscores the need to establish trust before implementing this method.

However, it also emphasizes the need to check compliance with all the OR techniques. While the client can be asked to describe how he performs these procedures, both in group or, preferentially, in individual sessions, most therapists insist that clients also tape-record some of their masturbation sessions as well. Thereafter, these recordings can be reviewed with the client. While this does not guarantee authenticity, skilled therapists can often detect falsifications and provide redirection. These recordings can also be used for further clarification and scene collection when employing related techniques, such as assisted covert sensitization.

It is important to again emphasize that masturbation and its associated fantasies are intensely private events. Even though identified sexual offenders are most often required by law to undertake treatment, and despite the fact that most therapists would agree that their most important task is to guarantee community safety by reducing the risk that another sexual crime will be committed, all treatment providers must endeavor to respect their clients' privacy and confidentiality. Fortunately, these techniques, proven to reduce deviant arousal and thereby to reduce the chance an offender will create another victim, can be applied with both sensitivity to clients' needs and yet appreciation of their powerful effects.

RESEARCH BASIS

Over the past two decades, a number of studies have demonstrated clinical success employing the three techniques described above. However, the majority of reports have focused on masturbatory satiation. Nonetheless, case reports utilizing directed masturbation and masturbatory fantasy change have described positive results as well. Improvements, in terms of both self-reports of lower deviant interests and more objective plethysmograph tracings of reduced deviant arousal, can often be seen within several weeks of initiating these procedures, although elimination of deviant arousal can take many months and, in some cases, may never be fully achieved. Still, reductions in this direction can be helpful, particularly as these OR techniques must be considered as only part of the full arsenal of treatment methods employed in a comprehensive sexual offender treatment program.

Unfortunately, the scientific basis for proving efficacy of any of these techniques is weakened by the following limitations within the present literature:

1. Almost all studies fail to distinguish among types of sexual offenders. Treatment response has been shown to be quite different within subgroups of offenders. For example, situational offenders against a single girl have proven to have a more positive response to treatment than predatory homosexual pedophiles or rapists.

2. None of these techniques has been tested in isolation; treatment results are generally reported for a total program, encompassing a variety of techniques. Thus, the individual efficacy of any OR technique is uncertain.

3. Individual studies often report impressive results but include only limited numbers of subjects. Larger studies and meta-analyses are needed; fortunately, several are currently under way in this field (see suggested readings).

RELEVANT TARGET POPULATIONS AND EXCEPTIONS

A crucial distinction must be kept in mind when considering the treatment of sexual offenders as opposed to most other groups of clients: These individuals most often are in therapy against their will. As such, trust building is of crucial importance before implementing such intrusive techniques. Also, as indicated above, some sexual offenders are more amenable to any treatment techniques than others. Research shows markedly positive results utilizing these methods in situational offenders, but their use should not be confined to that group. More dangerous offenders, such as those who repeatedly seek out and molest young girls or boys or who serially rape women, should also be exposed to these techniques, as they often will benefit as well. In addition, these techniques can be extended to the growing population of female sexual offenders, who can be asked to utilize masturbation and imagery in a fashion similar to their male counterparts. However, application of these intrusive techniques to a population of juvenile offenders has proven controversial, as many therapists and social scientists believe adolescents may be too fragile in their sexual development to comprehend and participate in OR procedures. Others experienced in this field disagree

and have reported success in applying such techniques to teenage offenders without harmful effects. It remains for future larger trials to resolve this contentious issue.

Another potential concern arises in the application of these techniques to those offenders who suffer from a psychiatric illness. Certainly, the therapist must ensure that these individuals have access to treatment, both medical and psychotherapeutic, and are not acutely ill, before instituting these intrusive techniques.

Some clients may object on religious or moral grounds to performing masturbation, while others may insist that they never masturbate. The latter can usually be induced to carry out these procedures with trust building and encouragement, but the former have a sometimes valid objection. Nonetheless, the therapist can often convince such offenders that follow-through actually enhances their safety to be at large and hence occupies the higher moral ground. Not infrequently, the client's religious leader can be asked to participate in encouraging compliance. Overall, the vast majority of sexual offenders have been found to be appropriate for these techniques and to have benefited from their deployment.

COMPLICATIONS

It might appear that many clients would object to such highly intrusive methods, and hence, their application could encourage a hostile atmosphere in therapy, especially since most sexual offenders enter treatment under less than voluntary conditions. In the experience of most therapists, however, OR techniques can actually encourage a closer relationship with the therapist if they are broached after sufficient rapport has been established. Most such clients, after several months of working with a therapist, can share their innermost fantasies, although we have no way of rigorously determining their veracity. Thus, one potentially serious complication is the falsification of fantasies and the consequent misapplication of these techniques. Trust building, in association with, paradoxically, the penile plethysmograph and the polygraph, can help in ferreting out truths from fictions in this regard.

A second complication arises from quite a different quarter: Nonprofessional, support, administrative, and correctional personnel may misinterpret the intent or application of such techniques. Social service workers, family members, parole and probation officers, and program administrators must be included in planning treatment programs and should be informed about the scientific basis for implementing these techniques. Their views, sometimes hostile, must nonetheless be taken into account. In the experience of most treatment providers, once aware that OR procedures have been empirically validated to reduce risk, these participants in the offender's program are happy to allow treatment to proceed and actively participate in the treatment program.

CASE ILLUSTRATION

"Mr. E," a 45-year-old government administrator, had been attracted to young boys, particularly in the 9- to 13-year age range, since his adolescence. Early life experiences combined with constitutional factors were believed to be responsible, although etiology for these disorders remains to be determined. E had developed some attraction to adult men as well, although this was weaker than his fondness for boys. He harbored no attraction to females. Despite his deviant desires, E had led a rather conventional life, working steadily, advancing in his job, and even contributing volunteer time to his community in areas other than working with youth.

However, his attraction to boys led him increasingly to be involved with them, particularly in leading outings for his church youth group and in assisting with coaching sports in a local middle school. His habit was to befriend a boy and his family, then ingratiate himself with them by taking the boy on trips and buying him and his family expensive gifts. He would gradually proceed to discuss sexual matters with the boy, then initiate some fondling and oral sex. Despite the fact that E had carried out these activities with several boys throughout his 20s and 30s, he had not been reported to authorities until his early 40s.

Following a 2-year prison sentence, E was mandated into an outpatient sexual offender treatment program. Plethysmograph testing revealed greatest arousal to boys, followed by some arousal to men, with little arousal to females or aggressive sexuality. The polygraph was helpful in eliciting further disclosures about additional victims. A variety of actuarial tests, including the Static-99 and the SORAG, indicated that E still posed some risk to be at large as he entered treatment; he had received no treatment in prison.

Following much trust building in individual therapy combined with some confrontation in group,

E was deemed ready to undertake more intrusive procedures. These included individual cognitive restructuring, relapse prevention, and empathy training, along with the behavioral techniques of assisted covert sensitization, pletyhsmographic biofeedback, and vicarious sensitization. In the midst of this strenuous regimen, at about the fourth month of therapy, E was introduced to OR techniques.

Masturbatory fantasy change was believed to be within E's capacities and was elected after discussions with E and his parole officer. E was first asked to masturbate in the privacy of his home three times each week to deviant fantasies of sexual activity with young boys; then, as he reached the point of ejaculatory inevitability, he was asked to immediately switch his fantasy to sexual activity with an adult male. (E had previously agreed that exclusively adult homosexual arousal was an appropriate treatment goal.) After E was able to make this switch successfully for 1 week, he was asked to perform the switch earlier during masturbation each week, over a period of 13 weeks, until he was masturbating entirely to nondeviant adult male fantasies. E was also asked to tape-record these sessions, and he and his therapist reviewed the tapes weekly. While initially embarrassing to him, E realized that these reviews helped him understand his feelings during masturbation and helped him to complete the assignments more faithfully.

During these weeks, E was asked by his therapist to also vary his masturbation sessions by once each week, masturbating to nondeviant fantasies first until climax; he was then to continue masturbating to deviant fantasies of sexual activity with young boys for 30 minutes thereafter, thus accomplishing masturbatory satiation. E reported that both techniques seemed to help lessen deviant arousal.

Indeed, after 19 weeks of intensive cognitive and behavioral work, E's plethysmograph showed no deviant arousal, but continued arousal to adult males. Following a further year of cognitive work and behavioral booster sessions, E remained free of deviant arousal and claimed to have lost all attraction to boys. In addition, a legal-records check revealed no additional charges. Unfortunately, only time will tell whether E can remain free from harmful sexual behaviors. However, he has scored well on the SONAR, a test designed to measure progress in treatment through an assessment of dynamic as well as static risk factors, and he appears to have markedly benefited from his therapy program. In addition, he has initiated a relationship with another adult male, a positive sign.

The extent to which OR techniques contributed to apparent treatment success in this case is unknowable, confounded by the application of so many other approaches. Nonetheless, serial plethysmograph measurements seemed to indicate that the most rapid decline in deviant arousal occurred with the initiation of these OR methods. While any single case cannot prove treatment efficacy, E's progress in treatment is not unusual, and his response to the masturbatory techniques employed is fairly typical of many sexual offenders in treatment. Ideally, further advances in this field will allow us to learn more about the individual efficacy of such techniques and enable us to apply them with ever greater skill and sensitivity.

—*Barry M. Maletzky*

See also: *Barlow, David H. (Vol. I); Behavioral Approaches to Sexual Deviation (Vol. I); Masturbatory Retraining (Vol. I)*

Suggested Readings

Dempster, R. J., & Hart, S. D. (2002). The relative utility of fixed and variable risk factors in discriminating sexual recidivists and nonrecidivists. *Sexual Abuse: A Journal of Research and Treatment, 14,* 121–138.

Hanson, R. K., Gordon, A., Harris, A. J. R., Marques, J. K., Murphy, W., Quinsey, V. L., et al. (2002). First report of the collaborative outcome data project on the effectiveness of psychological treatment for sex offenders. *Sexual Abuse: A Journal of Research and Treatment, 14,* 169–194.

Johnston, P., Hudson, S. M., & Marshall, W. L. (1992). The effects of masturbatory reconditioning with nonfamilial child molesters. *Behaviour Research and Therapy, 30,* 559–561.

Laws, D. R. (1995). Verbal satiation: Notes on procedure, with speculations on its mechanism of effect. *Sexual Abuse: A Journal of Research and Treatment, 7,* 155–166.

Laws, D. R., & Marshall, W. L. (1991). Masturbatory reconditioning with sexual deviates: An evaluative review. *Advances in Behavior Research and Therapy, 13,* 13–25.

Maletzky, B. M. (1985). Orgasmic reconditioning. In A. S. Bellak & M. Hersen (Eds.), *Dictionary of behavior therapy techniques* (pp. 157–158). New York: Pergamon Press.

Maletzky, B. M. (1991). *Treating the sexual offender* (pp. 102–109). Newbury Park, CA: Sage.

Maletzky, B. M. (2003). A serial rapist treated with behavioral and cognitive techniques and followed for 12 years. *Clinical Case Studies, 1,* 1–27.

Maletzky, B. M., & Steinhauser, C. (2002). A 25-year follow-up of cognitive/behavioral therapy with 7,275 sexual offenders. *Behavior Modification, 26,* 123–147.

Marshall, W. L. (1979). Satiation therapy: A procedure for reducing deviant sexual arousal. *Journal of Applied Behavior Analysis, 12,* 377–389.

OVERCORRECTION

DESCRIPTION OF THE STRATEGY

Overcorrection is an empirically derived method of punishment. Briefly, after an undesired behavior occurs, the perpetrator is instructed to "correct" the undesired behavior (i.e., restitution). The perpetrator is then directed to engage in an effortful response that more than corrects the effects of the inappropriate behavior (i.e., restoration of the immediate environment to an improved condition). Instructions to perform desired behaviors must occur immediately contingent upon occurrence of the undesired behavior. For instance, if a mentally retarded adult threw a bowl of cereal on the floor, the staff instructor would first instruct this individual to assist in cleaning the cereal from the floor (restitution). The person would then be required to assist in mopping the kitchen floor or scrubbing the table (overcorrection). If an adolescent slammed her door in anger, the parent could instruct her to practice shutting the door softly several times. She could also be instructed to adjust or check the hinges of the door as another overcorrection strategy. In the latter example, restitution would involve shutting the door once. The overcorrection component is often unnecessary when the undesired behavior is nonhabitual (e.g., happened for the first time) or relatively benign. Thus, in the previous example, the adolescent might be instructed to shut the door softly only once if she had slammed the door for the first time.

RESEARCH BASIS

Research has shown that unlike other punishment procedures, overcorrection not only suppresses inappropriate behavior but also develops positive practice behaviors. Indeed, most commonly employed punishment techniques (e.g., response cost, restriction of privileges, corporal punishment) are focused on suppressing the undesired behaviors. The distinguishing feature of overcorrection in relation to these techniques is that this procedure focuses on improving the appropriate behavior that is incompatible with the undesired response. Thus, overcorrection shifts attention to desirable behaviors that need to be developed, which is the priority of any behavior change program.

Outcome studies involving overcorrection have indicated rapid and long-lasting therapeutic effects for this intervention. Indeed, overcorrection has ameliorated various behavior problems for which other techniques (e.g., time-out, reprimands, reinforcement of other behavior, physical restraint) have been shown to be ineffective. Although definitive statements about the relative efficacy of alternative punishment techniques cannot be made at this time, overcorrection appears to be very effective in its own right. In addition, evidence suggests that parents, teachers, and instructional staff members view overcorrection as a punishment procedure that is more acceptable than other potential alternatives.

RELEVANT TARGET POPULATIONS AND EXCEPTIONS

Overcorrection was originally developed by Nathan Azrin and Richard Foxx to decrease the frequency of harmful, self-destructive, and self-stimulatory behaviors, such as hand-flapping. Later, overcorrection was expanded for use with parents of children who evidence noncompliance to parental commands, as well as other oppositional behaviors (e.g., vandalism, cursing). Overcorrection alone or in combination with other procedures has also been shown to reduce toileting accidents, tantrums, nail biting, and poor table manners. The learning-based emphasis of overcorrection makes it a particularly valuable intervention for use with mentally retarded, learning disabled, and autistic populations.

It is important to assess the feasibility of overcorrection prior to its implementation. Indeed, effort-based punishments (e.g., overcorrection) sometimes interrupt ongoing activities and are time-consuming and impractical. For instance, it may not be possible to implement overcorrection with a toddler while engaged in a job interview. Moreover, perpetrators of inappropriate behaviors may resist instructions to perform desired behaviors in the restitution or overcorrection phases. For these individuals, an incentive program should be employed. Briefly, when noncompliance first occurs, the perpetrator must be told that failure to perform the desired behavior will result in a more severe negative consequence that is within the instructor's control (e.g., restriction of privileges, time-out from reinforcement). If the latter warning fails to elicit performance of the desired behavior, the consequence would need to be initiated immediately. Prompting and physically guiding the perpetrator through the desired behavioral response chain, shaping (e.g., rewarding successive approximations toward the desired behavior), and the instructor's attributing external circumstances to performance of the undesired behavior (e.g., "I think the traffic must have caused you to come home past your curfew") have also been shown to increase the perpetrator's likelihood of performing the desired behaviors when motivation is wanting.

—Brad C. Donohue

See also: *Competing Response Training (Vol. I); Error Correction (Vol. III); Overcorrection (Vol. II)*

Suggested Readings

Kazdin, A. (1994). *Behavior modification in applied settings* (5th ed.). Pacific Grove, CA: Brooks/Cole.

Kerr, M. M., & Nelson, C. M. (1998). Stereotypic behaviors. In *Strategies for managing behavior problems in the classroom* (3rd ed., pp. 307–311). Englewood Cliffs, NJ: Prentice Hall.

Malott, R. W., Malott, M. E., & Trojan, E. A. (2000) *Elementary principles of behavior* (4th ed.). Upper Saddle River, NJ: Prentice Hall.

P

PANIC CONTROL TREATMENT

DESCRIPTION OF THE STRATEGY

Panic disorder (PD) is characterized by the sudden onset of intense fear or discomfort accompanied by various, and often intense, physical sensations that develop abruptly and reach their peak within 10 minutes. Although it is necessary for these attacks to be both recurrent and unexpected in order to meet diagnostic criteria for PD, it is clear that even after an initial attack, most people begin to associate the physical sensations they experience with a particular event or situation. For example, if an individual experiences "unexpected" heart palpitations and shortness of breath in the morning, they are more likely to associate those symptoms with the large cup of coffee they drank for breakfast rather than make no association. Similarly, if an initial panic attack is experienced while on a crowded subway during the stress of an early morning rush hour commute, it is likely that the situation may be subsequently avoided or endured with dread.

Thus, when people are fearful of activities or events, they will tend do things that they feel will prevent the events from occurring. The result is that many individuals with panic engage in elaborate safety and avoidance behaviors, such as keeping medications on hand or leaving a situation before the anxiety can begin. Because the feared situation is avoided or tolerated with the aid of a safety behavior, the individual will usually assume that when the feared event does not occur, it is the result of these actions rather then the event's rarity.

For many individuals, the process of experiencing an "unexpected panic attack" in particular situations is followed by the subsequent avoidance of those situations in an attempt to prevent the recurrence of unpleasant physical sensations. This cycle often results in debilitating avoidance and eventual treatment-seeking behaviors. Therefore, it comes as no surprise that the most effective forms of treatment for PD with/or without agoraphobia are ones in which the somatic symptoms of panic are reproduced and experienced acutely by the individual in such a way that they can reality test the actual danger of these symptoms, termed *interoceptive exposure*. This form of treatment is in contrast to the typical treatments for PD, which tend to focus solely on external situations that evoke panic symptoms (situational exposure).

Thus, much as agoraphobia is avoidance of external fears and situations, interoceptive avoidance is defined as the avoidance of situations or activities, such as exercising or drinking caffeine, in which the individual is likely to experience feared somatic sensations.

As a result of this new concept and new research aimed at understanding the importance of interoceptive cues and avoidance in individuals with PD, Barlow and Craske developed a new psychological treatment for PD they called "panic control treatment" (PCT), which has interoceptive exposure as a central component of its treatment model and has been met with wide acceptance by fellow clinicians and sufferers of panic attacks.

Fundamentally, PCT combines the principles of traditional situational exposure with the newly developed interoceptive exposure and psychoeducation about the physiology of panic, which all work to modify cognitive misconceptions. Thus, the three components of panic targeted by PCT are (1) physical sensations, (2) cognitions, and (3) behavioral avoidance. In addition, PCT relies heavily on work, including exposure, in which the client engages outside of the therapeutic environment.

Physical Sensations

The physical sensations of panic include shortness of breath, heart palpitations, chest pain, sweating, and dizziness. During PCT, the individual is first educated about the underlying cardiovascular and hormonal systems that are involved in producing these physical sensations. This is generally introduced within the context of the fight-flight response. The fight-flight response is the way the body responds in order to enable individuals to escape danger or defend themselves if escape is not possible. To accomplish this, a host of rapid changes occur within the body that act to increase an individual's ability to fight or flee. For example, blood is routed away from the gut and into the limbs, and the heart races in an attempt to get more oxygen to the muscles. Clients are shown that although this response is adaptive and generally helpful, panic attacks are inappropriate reactions that occur when there are no real threats in the environment and thus are maladaptive. The therapist's goal for this portion of the treatment is to help the client to understand why the physical sensations occur, for example, helping the client to realize that a pounding heart is the result of his or her body's natural fear response rather then a sign of an imminent heart attack.

Also in this module of the treatment, the therapist will introduce hyperventilation as a possible source of uncomfortable sensations that occur during an attack. This is often further demonstrated by having the client participate in a voluntary hyperventilation experiment. During this experiment, the client is asked to stand and breathe very fast and very deep, as if blowing up a balloon. This exercise is continued for approximately 90 seconds or at such time that the client feels that he or she cannot continue. After the completion of the exercise, the therapist will question the client about the sensations he or she experienced during the exercise. If these sensations are similar to those experienced during a panic attack, the therapist will help the client to understand that some of the symptoms experienced during a panic attack may be due to overbreathing. Often, clients will notice that although they

experience similar physical sensations as those that they experience during panic attacks, they are not fearful. This is to be expected, as this exercise is completed within the safe therapeutic context. To help the client to avoid overbreathing during a panic attack, the therapist instructs the client on controlled diaphragmatic breathing.

The final component of this module of PCT is the introduction of the concept of interoceptive conditioning and the implementation of interoceptive exposure. The therapist begins by first conducting a series of symptom induction tests that serve to identify sensations that have become triggers of anxiety and fear in the client. These tests include the following: shake head from side to side (30 seconds); head between knees (30 seconds) and then lift quickly; run in place (1 minute); hold breath (30 seconds); complete body muscle tension (2 minutes); spin in chair or twirl in place (1 minute); hyperventilate (1 minute); and stare at a light (1 minute), then read a paragraph. Each exercise is meant to simulate sensations the client may experience during an actual panic attack. Clients are asked to rate both the intensity of any sensations they may experience and the amount of fear and anxiety they experience as a result of those sensations.

Once the therapist and the clients have identified those sensations that the client associates with fear and anxiety, the therapist will proceed with the hallmark of PCT, interoceptive exposure. It is essential at this point in therapy to identify and prevent any safety behaviors and subtle avoidance behaviors that clients may use to decrease their anxiety exposures. The rationale of interoceptive exposure is to allow the client to face the feared sensations repeatedly, until it is no longer able to evoke fear. This has the ultimate effect of reducing both anxious thoughts and the conditioned fear reaction. During interoceptive exposure, the client is asked to engage in a specific exercise repeatedly (at least three repetitions), pausing between repetitions in order to allow the anxiety to dissipate, while recording both the appearance of physical sensations and the amount of anxiety they produce.

Cognitions

Conducting interoceptive exposures allows the clinician to begin to introduce the cognitive module of PCT. Individuals who suffer from panic often misinterpret the physical sensations they experience as a sign of an imminent catastrophe. For example, during a panic attack, an individual may believe that he or she is having a heart attack or dying. Although clients learn in the first module of PCT that the physical sensations they experience can be explained by the body's natural reaction to a perceived threat through the fight-flight response, cognitive work is also needed in order to correct any irrational misattributions in which the client may still engage. The therapist begins by having the client identify any automatic thoughts that occur in the course of interoceptive exposure. Automatic thoughts may occur out of awareness and may influence emotions and behavior. The automatic thoughts of individuals who experience panic often involve negative interpretations and predictions about a particular situation. For example, a client may think that he or she may have a panic attack while driving and cause an accident. Because automatic thoughts are often unconscious, the clinician may have to probe in collaboration with the client in order to fully identify the ways in which they are influencing the client's emotions and behaviors. The therapist may ask questions such as "What do you imagine happening that would be terrible?" and "What would be so bad about that happening?"

Although these consequences may seem inevitable to the client, the therapist will try to normalize the experience. An individual's perceptions about any particular event depend upon the likelihood that the event will occur and then how bad the consequences would be. Individuals with panic tend to engage in probability overestimation, which is characterized by overpredicting that an unlikely event will occur. For example, when predicting that something bad will happen, such as getting into a car accident in the middle of a snowstorm, experiencing anxiety and fear would be quite appropriate. However, when experiencing fear and anxiety after predicting a car accident in the summer on clear roads where an accident is very unlikely, the anxiety and fear are inappropriate.

To counteract probability overestimation, the client is encouraged to objectively evaluate the likelihood of the event in question occurring, a method that requires analysis of facts rather than feelings. For example, consider the following automatic thought offered by a female client experiencing panic attacks: "If I have a panic attack while away from home, I will faint and be very embarrassed." The therapist will encourage her not to accept this thought as fact, but rather to be skeptical and test it out in systematic fashion. The

client should ask herself how many times the predicted event actually happened under the exact or even similar circumstances. She should also consider whether there is any other evidence to support her prediction, such as a propensity to faint. The ultimate goal of this exercise is not to reassure the client that the feared event will not occur, but rather to allow the client to arrive at a realistic, appropriate estimate of the events likelihood.

People with panic often engage in another form of negative thinking called *catastrophic thinking*. Catastrophic thinking is an error in thinking in which an individual perceives the consequences of an event occurring as catastrophic when actually, they are not. Common catastrophic thoughts displayed by individuals with PD include "I will lose control," and "I will faint in a public place." The client is encouraged to understand that although there are negative consequences of events such as this occurring, they are not as disastrous or terrible as he or she would automatically assume. Similar to countering probability overestimation, the goal of countering catastrophic thoughts is to be able to realistically assess how bad it would be if a feared event actually occurred. Clients are encouraged to imagine the worst possible consequence of a feared event and to evaluate their ability to cope should it occur.

Behavioral Avoidance

The third component or module of PCT focuses on an individual's behavior predispositions that are influenced by anxiety. As previously mentioned, people who experience panic attacks in particular situations tend to avoid or escape those situations or develop safety behaviors. The behavioral component of PCT requires the client to confront the anxiety-provoking situations and is referred to as *exposure therapy*. The first step in this component is to establish an exposure hierarchy, which requires clients to list feared situations and rate the degree of anxiety they think they would experience if they entered those situations alone and without any safety behaviors. Clients also rate the likelihood that they will avoid the proposed situation under those conditions. This hierarchy will serve as a guideline for situational-exposure exercises.

The goals of situational exposure are to help individuals realize the realistic dangers of particular situations, as well as their realistic ability to cope with such events. Exposure helps to weaken conditioned fear reactions and create more healthy associations. Finally, exposure leads to a decrease in avoidance and impairment, which serves to disrupt the panic cycle. While most of the exposure exercise takes place outside of the therapeutic setting, it is essential that the client continue to identify anxious thoughts and use countering cognitive activities in order to fully embrace the treatment.

This is a critical point in therapy for agoraphobic patients, and it is essential that the therapist express this to the client, as the client's natural inclination is to avoid these feared situations.

During a situational exposure, the therapist instructs the client to remain in the situation until his or her anxiety decreases to a significantly low level. This decrease in anxiety is called *within-session habituation*. The client should notice that the within-session habituation time decreases with continued exposure to the feared situation. In addition, between-session habituation should occur. This is evident by a between-session decease in the initial level of anxiety experienced at the start of the next exposure exercise. Because individuals with panic do not simply fear the situation but also the occurrence of "scary" physical sensations in the situation, it is essential that while doing situational exposures, the client experience these sensations. Although this may happen naturally if the task is difficult enough, the therapist may often increase the sensations by introducing symptom induction during the exposure. For example, consider a client who avoids riding on the subway for fear of experiencing a panic attack. The therapist may instruct the client to ride the subway repeatedly on separate occasions, until the anxiety he or she experiences is significantly lower the usual. The therapist may also instruct the client to hyperventilate during a subway ride, in order to amplify the positive effects of situational exposure.

SUMMARY

Panic disorder (PD) is a debilitating condition in which individuals experience unexpected panic attacks and then become very anxious that they will happen again. They avoid external situations associated with panic attacks, as well as situations that may produce physical sensations of an attack. Panic control treatment (PCT) utilizes the traditional components of situational exposure therapy, in which sufferers confront situations associated with panic attacks (such as crowded public places) and psychoeducation about the nature of panic.

PCT also adds the new component of interoceptive exposure in an effort to target the prevalent and often debilitating avoidance of situations and activities that induce physical sensations of panic. This treatment has been designated by the National Institute of Mental Health as the treatment of choice for panic disorder.

—*Shawnée L. Basden and David H. Barlow*

See also: *Evidence-Based Practice (Vol. III); Guided Mastery (Vol. I); Relaxation Training With Children (Vol. II)*

Suggested Readings

Barlow, D. H., & Craske, M. G. (2000). *Mastery of your anxiety and panic: Client workbook for anxiety and panic* (3rd ed.). Boulder, CO: Graywind.

Barlow, D. H., Gorman, J. M., Shear, M. K., & Woods, S. W. (2000). Cognitive-behavioral therapy, imipramine, or their combination for panic disorder: A randomized controlled trial. *Journal of the American Medical Association, 283*, 2529–2536.

Barlow, D. H., Raffa, S. D., & Cohen, E. M. (2002). Psychosocial treatments for panic disorders, phobias, and generalized anxiety disorder. In P. E. Nathan & J. M. Gorman (Eds.), *A guide to treatments that work* (2nd ed.). New York: Oxford University Press.

Carter, M., & Barlow, D. H. (1993). Interoceptive exposure in the treatment of panic disorder. In *Innovations in clinical practice: A source book* (Vol. 12, pp. 329–336). Sarasota, FL: Professional Resource Exchange.

Craske, M. G., & Barlow, D. H. (2000). *Mastery of your anxiety and panic: Client workbook for agoraphobia* (3rd ed.). Boulder, CO: Graywind.

Craske, M. G., Barlow, D. H., & Meadows, E. A. (2000). *Mastery of your anxiety and panic: Therapist guide for anxiety, panic, and agoraphobia* (3rd ed.). Boulder, CO: Graywind.

PARADOXICAL INTENTION

DESCRIPTION OF THE STRATEGY

Of the techniques that fall into the classification of therapeutic paradox, paradoxical intention has been the most common to appear in the literature of behavior therapy and cognitive behavior therapy. This popularity is perhaps due to two factors: It is effective with a wide variety of anxiety disorders, and it is easily incorporated as a primary or ancillary procedure into behavioral treatment programs.

The procedure requires individuals, paradoxically, to intend to do the very thing that they are trying not to do. A common example of its use occurs with some clients complaining of sleep onset insomnia. The paradoxical intention instruction requires, when they go to bed, that they remain awake as long as possible. The instruction is simple, but the preparation is considerably more complex.

All paradoxical therapeutic procedures have two things in common. The first is that they contradict received opinion or common sense. That is, therapists' suggestions oppose clients' expectations. This is similar to the "punch line" of a joke. A good joke leads listeners to imagine possible endings of the story that would not be particularly funny—and instead, surprises them with something that they did not expect, thus producing laughter. The second common element is the goal of the surprising request. In essence, clients are asked to stop "trying" to change and instead to remain as they are with respect to their target behaviors. Of course, in trying to change, clients, in fact, actually are remaining the same. The paradoxical suggestion allows them to cease struggling and thereby forms a platform on which improvement can potentially be based.

Most problems that clients bring to therapists are accompanied by what may be called *serious concern*. That is, the individuals view their complaints with apprehension and alarm; they believe that unless resolved, their problems can potentially lead to significant negative life changes; in the extreme, some consider their difficulties to be life threatening. Therefore, people who invest sleep, for example, with a disproportionate amount of importance will not willingly agree to give up even 1 hour of sleep, much less one or more nights of sleep. It is for this reason that the preparation and the manner of presentation of the paradoxical instruction are critical to the success of the procedure.

There is a considerable literature on the administration of psychotherapeutic paradox; one area focuses on the use of humor. A number of therapists have discussed the importance of humor and absurdity in reducing the serious concern with which clients invest their problems. When individuals develop a more realistic perspective of their problems, it becomes possible to involve them in experiences that can serve to move them in the direction of their goals. For this reason, paradoxical techniques rely on the element of surprise, which, when successfully administered, introduces humor into the therapeutic situation.

RESEARCH BASIS

Paradoxical procedures have been described in psychotherapeutic literature since the 1920s. Until relatively recently, reports of success have largely appeared in the context of uncontrolled case studies. Since the late 1970s, data from research incorporating more sophisticated designs have generally supported suggestions of the efficacy of paradoxical intention with a variety of anxiety disorders or anxiety-based difficulties, when used as part of a behavioral treatment program. In addition, several studies have failed to find differences between paradoxical intention and other conventional behavioral procedures with specific complaints.

Other paradoxical procedures have largely been ignored as targets of empirical investigation. This neglect is principally due to the fact that the procedures are typically administered in a spontaneous manner, making it difficult to incorporate them into designs that require deliberate, predictable, and invariant presentation.

RELEVANT TARGET POPULATIONS AND EXCEPTIONS

The wide variety of paradoxical procedures offer a fair amount of flexibility to the psychotherapist. As a result, the procedures have been employed with all combinations and permutations of psychotherapeutic subjects, particularly by family- or systems-oriented therapists. However, because of the uncommon nature of the procedures, therapists must be particularly careful in their use.

Of course, as is the case with all therapeutic techniques, a context of good rapport and considerable therapist experience forms the basis for success with these techniques. Therapists who are generally inexperienced or lack experience with paradoxical procedures specifically should be particularly cautious in their initial trials with these techniques. The clients with whom the procedures are initially employed must be sufficiently resilient to withstand any problems in administration; and their behavioral targets, while of significance to these clients, should be of a variety that allow for second chances in the event of iatrogenic errors.

—*L. Michael Ascher*

See also: *Assertiveness Training (Vol. II); Behavioral Momentum (Vol. III); Motivational Enhancement Therapy (Vol. I)*

Suggested Readings

Ascher, L. M. (1989). *Therapeutic paradox.* New York: Guilford Press.

Frankl, V. E. (1975). Paradoxical intention and dereflection. *Psychotherapy: Theory, research and practice, 12,* 226–237.

Frankl, V. E. (1985). Logos, paradox, and the search for meaning. In M. J. Mahoney & A. Freeman (Eds.), *Cognition and psychotherapy.* New York: Plenum Press.

Haley, J. (1973). *Uncommon therapy: The psychiatric techniques of Milton H. Erickson, M.D.* New York: Norton.

Watzlawick, P., Weakland, J., & Fisch, R. (1974). *Change: Principles of problem formulation and problem resolution.* New York: Norton.

Weeks, G. R., & L'Abate, L. A. (1982). *Paradoxical psychotherapy: Theory and practice with individuals, couples, and families.* New York: Brunner/Mazel.

PAUL, GORDON L.

My parents lived on an Iowa farm at the time of my birth, September 2, 1935. I was born in nearby Marshalltown, where I grew up following our loss of the farm in 1939. I was the only surviving child of Leon D. Paul and Ione Hickman (Perry), but a large extended family of cousins, aunts, uncles, and maternal grandparents were major influences as well. Nonacademic life, choices based on irrelevant factors, and chance events have all contributed to my intellectual approach, accomplishments, and ultimate status as a research scientist, teacher, and clinician.

Nobody had much money during my formative years. I was the first to graduate college. My father ended schooling in the sixth grade. He toiled as a factory worker until his death in 1954 at age 40. He was an "anti-snob," for whom friendships were more important than career. My mother taught for years in one-room schools on an associate's certificate, earning her BA in 1961. Advanced study and acclaim in both special and sex education later followed. She retired in 1991 after 54 years in the classroom. Now in her 92nd year, she continues to teach piano and tutor students at home.

Parents, extended family, and close family friends modeled a strong work ethic that prized excellence, personal responsibility, and compassion for others. I also gained firsthand experience with many of life's tribulations, including alcoholism, child abuse, failed marriages, suicide, and severe emotional problems.

Extremes of values and behavior on many dimensions were part of growing up. Family reunions were enjoyable events demonstrating tolerance, conflict resolution, and selective avoidance of problem topics based on respect for one another, all useful lessons. Developmental experiences with family and friends instilled a firm belief in the importance of friendships and of the positive role of social supports. They also resulted in a desire to understand the distressing actions, thoughts, and emotions of troubled and troubling people.

Education through high school was in the Marshalltown public schools. Although always employed in outside jobs, I was elected to several class offices and regularly received high grades. Music and drama became major interests after football injuries precluded further participation in sports. I gained my adult height (6' 4") by age 13. This allowed me to work in traveling dance bands, which provided many maturing experiences. Committed to a career as a musician, I ran several combos and dance bands during my last years of high school and first year of college. I graduated high school with honors in 1953. After a year at Marshalltown Community College, I was accepted into the U.S. Naval School of Music in Washington, D.C., as a contract musician.

En route from basic training to the Navy music school, I renewed contact with Joan M. Wyatt in Marshalltown. We were married on Christmas Eve, 1954, following a whirlwind courtship. Jo Paul has been my lover, partner, and best friend ever since, participating in those decisions that most influenced my personal and professional development. Our sons, Dennis and Dana, were born in Navy hospitals. Our daughter, Joni, was born just after we left the Navy to resume college.

During 4 years with Navy bands, I gained a year of college credits in music school and San Diego City College. My first psychology courses were fascinating. Psychoanalytic theory became an avocation that I pursued through self-study while preparing an Olympics band on a seagoing flagship. Traveling with show bands and later serving as service school command bandmaster helped change my career focus. The major job that I enjoyed as a musician was big-band jazz. As this required too much traveling for a family man, psychology became the fastest route to a BA.

I applied only to the University of Iowa because tuition and housing in "tin-hut" barracks were cheap enough to be covered by the GI Bill and it was near our extended families. Soon having three children, Jo's major job became child rearing, along with home typing. I worked at a shoe store while taking classes, earning my BA with highest honors in psychology and mathematics in 1960. Our hard work was rewarded by election to the Phi Beta Kappa Society.

Most psychology courses at Iowa nicely packaged my avocational interests, but I hated all the emphasis and courses in research and methodology. More applied courses were smuggled from the medical school and the Child Welfare Research Station. Ron Wilson, a young assistant professor, guided additional clinical studies and arranged for me to work briefly as an aide at the state mental hospital. The push for theoretical laboratory research and derogation of clinical work by the senior professors had a paradoxical effect. I became committed to a neo-Freudian, ego-analytic approach and a clinical career in psychiatry or clinical psychology. I had enjoyed the medical school physiological and anatomy courses, and all clinical training in psychology seemingly required research as a "necessary evil." Even so, applied research with people rather than rats seemed preferable to "wasting" 3 years on "cuts and bruises." Clinical psychology it would be.

Although Iowa faculty offered unsolicited admission and financial support, my selection criteria for graduate school required a more active clinical training program as well. I applied to the strongest programs closest to Iowa City and received offers from both. Jo and I chose the University of Illinois at Urbana-Champaign because of cheaper moving and housing costs.

At Illinois, raising our three children continued as Jo's major job, adding preschool day care to home typing to assist finances. I worked on assistantships in research and in the department clinic, with additional paid jobs at the counseling bureau and nearby VA Hospital. During my final year, I obtained a National Institute of Mental Health (NIMH) fellowship and a federal grant for support, completing the PhD with distinction in 1964, with a clinical major and physiological and educational psychology minors.

The 4 years of 80-hour workweeks in graduate school provided intense education and training experiences from 36 influential figures in psychology and allied departments, hospitals, and institutes. Tom D'Zurilla, Ron Krug, Rick Schulte, and I formed a study group, from which the arguments, discussions, and mutual support were major developmental influences.

I chose Charles (Erik) Eriksen, a strict methodologist, as advisor for both master's and doctoral projects' line of advisors tracing back to William James. Other members of my doctoral committee, Wes Becker, Lloyd Humphreys, Merle Ohlsen, Don Shannon, and Jerry Wiggins, all served as strong models.

Most clinical training at Illinois was based on Freudian, Rogerian, or neo-Freudian theories and associated insight-oriented approaches, and I loved it! The evidence-based content courses, however, regularly failed to support the fundamental principles underlying our clinical training. I hated that and became determined to demonstrate the "basic truth" of psychodynamic concepts. Drawing on my forced training in research methods at Iowa and Illinois, I became expert at identifying research errors in studies that challenged psychodynamic constructs. I also designed my MA thesis and other studies to properly test them. To my dismay, findings of my own studies consistently supported alternative explanatory principles instead of my cherished beliefs!

Several clinical students asked Erik to offer a seminar in which we could examine claims that insight-oriented therapy did not work and that this new approach called "behavior therapy" did. We concluded that the new approach had promise and that flawed studies failed to support insight-oriented therapy, but they did NOT show it was ineffective. A well-designed study was needed.

Again drawing on my forced research training, I developed design requirements to yield cause-effect evidence for the comparative effectiveness of any treatment approach, the nature of questions to be asked, and the domains and classes of variables requiring measurement, manipulation, or control. My dissertation was intended to be a model study that would clearly demonstrate the superiority of insight-oriented therapy, not only to behavioral treatment but also to all relevant control conditions. The superiority I had hoped to demonstrate for insight-oriented psychotherapy with real-life performance anxiety was nowhere to be found; attention-placebo treatment did as well, and systematic desensitization was far more effective.

Combined with accumulating evidence, these findings forced me to discard beliefs in the active unconscious and in any "school" approach dependent on articles of faith rather than proof, a paradigm shift in which I explicitly adopted a utility criterion for guidance. That is, among sets of principles that might explain any clinical phenomenon, use the simplest set with firm evidential support that also gives direction for bringing about change. So far, principles of learning and performance, including biological and social contexts, provide the best working hypotheses for the great majority of clinical problems, ranging from "anxiety" to "schizophrenia."

Having enough supervised clinical hours to skip a predoctoral internship, Illinois faculty encouraged me to take a research university appointment. I still planned a clinical career, however, and wanted more experience with psychoses and hospitals before leaving the trainee role. Len Ullmann joined the Illinois faculty during my last year and guided me to Stanford University Press to publish my dissertation. He also introduced me to Len Krasner, who was helpful in arranging a postdoctoral year at the VA Medical Center in Palo Alto, California. Still short of funds, we packed up the family and our worldly goods in a converted school bus and trekked off to Palo Alto.

The postdoctoral year at VA Palo Alto involved two rotations. The first was on the Menlo Park campus in the token-economy program for chronic patients, run by Jack Atthowe and Len Krasner. Bill Fairweather's social milieu unit was a few buildings away. Visits by a stream of behaviorally oriented psychologists and psychiatrists added to our daily discussions of applied learning theory, reinforcing my shift in orientation. The second rotation was on the Palo Alto campus in a milieu ward for acute patients. Jack Shelton, a psychiatrist whose Szaszian "mental illness is a myth" approach was quite compatible with my own, ran this ward. Otherwise, drug treatment predominated, and most professionals endorsed psychodynamic orientations. This provided many opportunities to argue and clarify positions. Jerry Davison joined us as a trainee at the end of the year. Jack, Jerry, and I regularly asked challenging questions during weekly grand rounds when unsupported opinions were asserted as facts, further reinforcing use of the utility criterion.

During my postdoctoral year, I also attended weekly seminars with several influential Stanford University Faculty, including Al Bandura, and spent a few hours each week with private clients and consulting. Gossip about my dissertation led to rapid entry into the talk circuit and many job offers. After seeing the range of mental health settings, I reluctantly concluded that universities were the only places to support all major activities I had come to value, clinical research, training, and practice. Jo and I had decided

that a smaller town with more traditional values would be the best place to raise our children, when I was invited to return to Illinois. I joined the Illinois clinical faculty in 1965, thinking that a 2-year trial would be good test for job satisfaction.

We remained at the University of Illinois at Urbana-Champaign for 15 years. With a series of able students, I supervised clinical practica and taught graduate courses in behavior disorders and interventions—twice receiving awards for Excellence in Graduate Training. A strong faculty provided collegial support, and several behavioral clinicians were added over time. For several years, I continued research on anxiety-related problems, a private practice, and hospital consulting.

Symposia in the 1960s resulted in networking with others engaged in what we now see as the "behavioral revolution." Job offers, invited chapters, and positions of influence on review panels and policy committees were early career consequences. Such networking ultimately resulted in my consulting to more than 200 organizations and service on many task forces, study sections, review, and policy-making groups at regional, state, and national levels. I eventually served on the editorial boards of 7 major clinical journals and became a frequent consulting editor for 19.

My early years at Illinois were productive enough that I received tenure after 2 years and promotion to full professor 3 years later. Major contributions to the literature during that time were empirical studies and reviews of treatment for anxiety-related problems as well as methodological pieces on research design and tactics, many of which became citation classics.

My formulation of the "ultimate clinical question(s)" to summarize the domains and classes of variables needing description, measurement, or control in treatment research has been identified as a marker for the start of the evidence-based movement in psychology. The question, "What treatment, by whom, is most effective for this individual, with that specific problem, under which set of circumstances, and how does it come about?" has guided investigators and practitioners for more than three decades. The extension of the question and organizational scheme to inpatient and biomedical treatments, as well as entire facilities and systems of service, has also proven useful.

During the past 35 years, my research has emphasized application of the utility criterion to treatment of psychoses, institutionalized populations, and observational assessment, supported by nearly $5 million in grants and contracts. For 16 years, I directed the

Psychosocial Rehabilitation Units and, later, the Clinical Research Unit at the Adolph Meyer Mental Health Center, Decatur, Illinois. Jo and I remained in Illinois until 1980, when I was appointed the Hugh Roy and Lillie Cranz Cullen Distinguished Professor of Psychology at the University of Houston. Having a dislike for cold and snow, we moved to Texas, where this work has continued as a collaborative effort with a host of talented students, ex-students, and colleagues in Texas, Missouri, Florida, and Illinois.

Many contributions emerged from the work we began at the Meyer Center. Theoretical formulations and principles similar to those found most useful for anxiety-related problems are also best for understanding and treating those problems that are classified under the rubric of schizophrenia. Major contributions from this line of clinical research include the development and refinement of two sets of technology, a comprehensive residential treatment program that works, and a system for ongoing assessment and monitoring of patient, staff, and program functioning.

The Social Learning Program with integrated aftercare is the treatment program. It has been documented to be the "treatment of choice" for severely disabled people with mentally ill diagnoses. With 3 times better cost-efficiency than alternatives and requiring no greater staffing than most existing operations, implementation is already under way in several states. Under the direction of Tony Menditto, Fulton State Hospital in Missouri is furthest developed.

The Computerized TSBC/SRIC Planned-Access Observational Information System is the assessment and monitoring system. It has been documented to provide the ongoing practical and objective facts needed to maximize the effectiveness and cost-efficiency for any adult inpatient program (medical, drug, or psychosocial) for mentally ill, developmentally disabled, or alcohol/substance abuse clientele. It is also necessary to implement the Social Learning Program. Reviewers have likened the TSBC/SRIC System to the cloud chamber in physics and the electron microscope in biology, in which "the technical gain may be a difference in kind, not merely a difference in degree." The upgrades needed for efficient, user-friendly implementation are now being completed under the direction of Mark Licht, in Florida, and Paul Stuve, in Missouri.

These research developments have received numerous awards, including the Distinguished Scientific Contributions to Clinical Psychology award of the American Psychological Association Society of Clinical Psychology. Our group's endeavors have resulted in my election to fellow status in several national organizations and in around 40 honorary biographical publications, elected offices, and expert listings, including *Good Housekeeping's* "Best Mental Health Experts (Schizophrenia)."

Hoping never to completely retire, I continue to teach in the graduate clinical program, supervise student practica and research, provide editorial service, and maintain a limited consulting and treatment practice. Service also continues as an advisor to several government and professional groups and to advocacy organizations on behalf of people suffering from severe emotional, behavioral, and mental disabilities. Future plans for all of these endeavors include influencing others to apply the utility criterion and always evaluate the evidence, especially regarding putative disease entities and labels. My major future plans for our research group are to complete the needed materials and undertake widespread dissemination of the Social Learning Program and TSBC/SRIC System so that the mental health field can benefit from this technology.

—*Gordon L. Paul*

See also: *Token Economy (Vols. I, II, & III)*

Suggested Readings

Paul, G. L. (2001). The active unconscious, symptom substitution, & other things that went "bump" in the night. In W. T. O'Donohue, D. A. Henderson, S. C. Hayes, J. E. Fisher, & L. J. Hayes (Eds.), *A history of the behavioral therapies: Founders' personal histories* (pp. 295–336). Reno, NV: Context Press.

PAVLOV, IVAN P.

Ivan Petrovich Pavlov (1849–1936) was a Russian physiologist who developed one of the two basic procedures used to study behavioral change in the laboratory. His procedure is variously called *Pavlovian, classical,* or *respondent conditioning.* In the Pavlovian procedure, the learner is presented with a "neutral" stimulus, followed closely in time by a stimulus that already elicits behavior. In Pavlov's laboratory, the neutral stimulus was commonly the ticking sound of a metronome, and the eliciting stimulus was food that elicited salivation. After a number of pairings of the ticking sound with food, the sound alone could evoke salivation. Thus, the procedure produced a new relation between the environment and behavior: the sound-salivation relation. The second procedure used to study behavioral change is called *operant* or *instrumental conditioning* and was independently developed by Edward L. Thorndike at about the same time, around 1900. In contrast to Pavlov's procedure, in the operant procedure, a behavior instead of a stimulus precedes the eliciting stimulus. Outside the laboratory, elicitors are typically preceded by both stimuli and behavior, as when seeing and then eating ice cream are followed by stimulation of receptors in the mouth and elicitation of salivation. As a result, the sight of ice cream comes to control both salivating and eating.

Pavlov began to study behavioral change after incidental observations during his studies of digestion. Using his skills as a surgeon—he was ambidextrous—Pavlov had been able to expose nerves controlling the heart, and ducts secreting digestive juices during food intake. For this work, he would receive a Nobel Prize for medicine in 1904. However, a few years before receiving the prize, Pavlov noticed that the salivary glands would often begin to secrete before food was introduced into the mouth. For example, salivation might be evoked by the sound of the footsteps of the caretaker who normally fed the dogs or by the mere sight of food. Instead of regarding these events as unwanted intrusions into his study of digestion, Pavlov realized that he had inadvertently identified a method to study learning in the laboratory. Accordingly, he dropped his study of the neural control of digestion and—against the advice of colleagues—turned his attention to what he called "psychic reflexes." In 1903, his first paper on conditioning was presented to the 14th Medical Congress in Madrid, in which he described the basic phenomena using terminology that is now standard in the field. Among the phenomena were extinction, discrimination, generalization, spontaneous recovery, and higher-order conditioning. Higher-order conditioning demonstrated that new environment-behavior relations could be selected not only by innate eliciting stimuli (e.g., food-elicited salivation) but also by learned elicitors (e.g., a light that was paired with only the sound of a metronome would come to evoke salivation if the sound had previously been paired with food). Thus, the range of possible elicitors that served as reinforcers could expand with experience.

After the Communist Revolution in Russia, the Soviet government continued to support Pavlov as one of their most famous scientists. However, Pavlov resisted the intrusion of politics into science. When his status entitled him to special food rations, he refused unless members of his institute also received them. When admission to the university was about to be denied to an applicant because he was the son of a priest, Pavlov responded that he also was the son of a priest. When political figures were proposed for membership in scientific societies, Pavlov alone opposed them. Pavlov remained scientifically productive throughout his long life, devoting his later years to the application of conditioning for the alleviation of mental illness.

—*John W. Donahoe*

See also: *Classical Conditioning (Vols. I & II)*

Suggested Readings

Babkin, B. P. (1949). *Pavlov.* Chicago: University of Chicago Press.

Pavlov, I. P. (1906). The scientific investigation of psychical facilities or processes in the higher animals, *Science, 24,* 610–619.

Pavlov, I. P. (1927). *Conditioned reflexes.* New York: Oxford University Press. (Reprinted, New York: Dover, 1960)

Pavlov, I. P. (1941). *Conditioned reflexes and psychiatry.* New York: International Publishers.

Yerkes, R. M., & Margulis, S. (1909). The method of Pavlovian animal psychology. *Psychological Bulletin, 6,* 257–273.

PERSON-CENTERED PLANNING

DESCRIPTION OF THE STRATEGY

Person-centered planning (PCP) is a term used to describe an approach utilized to assist individuals in planning for their futures. The goal of PCP is to aid an individual in developing meaningful life goals based on his or her strengths and talents, utilizing individual, natural, and creative supports and services.

PCP is a process for defining the life a person wishes to live and then describing what needs to be accomplished to assist that person in moving toward that life. It is rooted in values, goals, and outcomes important to the person but takes into account other critical factors that have an impact on his or her life, for example, family and agency views, a person's disability, funding, and community supports.

PCP has developed and evolved as practitioners worked with individuals with different types of disabilities to improve the quality of their lives. Although there are various approaches to PCP, they share the following characteristics:

1. They view the individual as a person first, rather than as a diagnosis, behavior problem, or disability.

2. They use everyday language, pictures, and symbols, rather than professional jargon.

3. Planning centers around defining each person's unique strengths, interests, and capacities within the context of living in the community.

4. The process gives strength to the voices of the people and those who know them most intimately in accounting for their histories, evaluating their present conditions in terms of valued experiences, and defining desirable changes in their lives.

PCP is not a single technique, but a term used to describe a collection of techniques, each with its own defining features and distinct history. These techniques were developed out of a community of practice in the early 1970s to mid-1980s by North Americans who were applying the principle of normalization to improve services to people with developmental disabilities. By the late 1970s, the work in this arena had spread to Britain, thus developing into a transatlantic movement in the field of developmental disabilities. The term person-centered planning was commonly used by 1985, and within the next decade, 12 distinct approaches had been identified. Common PCP approaches used today include Making Action Plans, known as MAPS, Personal Profiling, Group Action Planning, known as GAP, Personal Futures Planning, Essential Lifestyle Planning, and Planning Alternative Tomorrows with Hope, known as PATH.

PCP is a collaborative activity whereby a group of relevant people are brought together to meet with an individual. The group or team usually comprises family members, friends, teachers, community members, and agency personnel who are interested in, knowledgeable of, and committed to the well-being of this individual. The team meets at least once, but preferably on an as-needed basis, to gain a better understanding of the individual, build relationships and trust with the individual, and create plans with the individual for his or her future. They examine the individual's past, present, and future, focusing on the individual's strengths and interests. Through the use of a group facilitator and graphic displays (usually words, pictures, and symbols recorded on flip chart pads), an individual is encouraged to describe the kind of life he or she wants to live. The process permits the team to understand the past life of the individual, see the individual's current life, and envision an improved life for the individual's future. A final outcome is a comprehensive plan for the individual's future that outlines short-term and long-term goals, necessary supports and services, and identified roles for the individual team members.

The rationale for using PCP techniques, as opposed to other traditional service planning techniques, lies in their focus on personal goals and futures planning at an individual level. These techniques are designed to explore future options for an individual, reflecting on individual dreams and aspirations, rather than on deficits and weaknesses. The techniques are person centered rather than system centered. With ownership in the process, individuals who engage in PCP are more likely to buy into the process and collaborate on the resulting plans. System-centered approaches are controlled by professionals who provide a continuum of services that may or may not meet the needs of a given individual, with results that are likely to be sabotaged by the individual. PCP approaches result in decisions and outcomes that are controlled by the individual with a disability and those closest to him or her.

During the 1990s, PCP was aligned with another developing parallel approach to supporting individuals with disabilities, known as *positive behavior support.* Positive behavior support is an applied science that grew out of applied behavioral analysis. It addresses an individual's challenging behavior in seeking an enhanced quality of life through redesign of the individual's living environment. These two approaches share common values, philosophies, and techniques for supporting individuals with disabilities to live in typical home, school, and community settings. During the last decade, there has been a melding of these two approaches to provide a person-centered and comprehensive support approach for individuals with disabilities who also have particularly challenging behavior.

Although PCP is often considered more of an art than a science, investigators are beginning to establish an empirical base of support for its use. The majority of research to date has been done in the qualitative arena, as there are difficulties in operationally defining the independent and dependent variables in this process. It is often difficult to separate the process from the outcomes in such a planning process. PCP is considered a paradigm shift in how services are planned and delivered to persons with disabilities. Unlike traditional service plans, such as rehabilitation plans and individual care plans, which focus on the services the system can offer, PCP is based on positive underlying values, such as choice, respect, self-determination, and positive approaches to addressing problem behaviors. This approach has been strengthened greatly by the scientific, technically sound intervention strategies of positive behavioral support.

Many investigators and practitioners consider PCP to be a philosophy as much as a practice. It is deeply rooted in the core individual values of self-determination and quality of life. As such, there is a risk in having such practices mandated by policies in the mental health and education arenas—for example, practitioners may adopt abbreviated versions of such planning techniques or utilize undertrained staff to meet the requirements of such mandates. Such practices would inevitably compromise the depth, energy, and creative ability that are core to effective PCP.

Although PCP may not be a panacea for all populations and individuals, its reputation as a planning tool in the disabilities arena has enjoyed much acclaim. Rooted in the field of developmental disabilities, the use of PCP techniques has become quite widespread in educational and therapeutic milieus. These PCP planning approaches are utilized in educational and community planning for young children and in defining career and community aspirations for youth, young adults, and adults with challenges such as behavioral/emotional difficulties.

—Hewitt B. Clark, Jordan T. Knab,
and Donald Kincaid

See also: *Contextualism (Vol. I); Individualized Education Program (Vol. III); Multisystemic Therapy (Vol. II);*

Suggested Readings

Clark, H. B., & Davis, M. (2000). *Transition to adulthood: A resource for assisting young people with emotional or behavioral difficulties.* Baltimore: Paul H. Brookes.

Holburn, S., & Vietze, P. M. (2002). *Person-centered planning: Research, practice, and future directions.* Baltimore: Paul H. Brookes.

Kincaid, D. (1996). Person-centered planning. In L. K. Koegel, R. L. Koegel, & G. Dunlap (Eds.), *Positive behavioral*

support: Including people with difficult behaviors in the community* (pp. 439–465). Baltimore: Paul H. Brookes.

Mount, B. (1987). *Person futures planning: Finding directions for change* (Doctoral dissertation, University of Georgia). Ann Arbor, MI: UMI Dissertation Information Service.

Mount, B., & Zwernick, K. (1988). *It's never too early, it's never too late: An overview on personal futures planning.* St. Paul, MN: Governor's Council on Developmental Disabilities.

O'Brien, J., Mount, B., & O'Brien, C. (1990). *The personal profile.* Lithonia, GA: Responsive Systems Associates.

Pearpoint, J., O'Brien, J., & Forest, M. (1996). *Planning alternative tomorrows with hope: A workbook for planning possible and positive futures.* Toronto, Canada: Inclusion Press.

Smull, M. (1997). *A blueprint for essential lifestyle planning.* Napa, CA: Allen, Shea & Associates.

Vandercook, T., York, J., & Forest, M. (1989). The McGill Action Planning System (MAPS): A strategy for building the vision. *Journal of the Association for Persons With Severe Handicaps, 14,* 205–215.

PHARMACOTHERAPY AND BEHAVIOR THERAPY

DESCRIPTION OF THE STRATEGY

In general, pharmacotherapy involves the use of drugs to improve behavior, whereas behavior therapy involves the use of procedures based on principles of learning to achieve the same objective. Drugs that are intended to improve mood, cognitive status, or overt behavior are termed *psychotropic* drugs. Since the 1950s, when the first generally effective antipsychotic drug, chlorpromazine (Thorazine), was introduced, psychotropic drugs have played a major role in treating adults with a wide range of behavior disorders. Dozens of different psychotropic drugs currently are available, and millions of prescriptions are written for them. With few exceptions, pharmacotherapy is under the control of psychiatrists and other physicians.

Not surprisingly, therefore, discussions of pharmacotherapy often are couched in terms of a medical model, in which a patient's signs and symptoms are assumed to be indications of an underlying disease that involves a neurochemical aberration. A deficiency in serotonergic activity, for example, is widely assumed to be responsible for the signs and symptoms of depression. Effective psychotropic drugs are assumed to alter the neurochemical processes responsible for the disease, which, in turn, leads to improvements in behavior. For example, effective antidepressant drugs increase serotonergic activity. They also improve mood and overt behavior in most people diagnosed with depression.

Since the 1960s, behavior therapy has been widely and successfully used to treat many different behavior disorders. Behavior therapy comprises many different therapeutic techniques. Although most contemporary behavior therapists acknowledge the role of neurochemical events in controlling behavior, they typically do not emphasize events at this level of analysis. Instead, they concentrate on how learning contributes to the genesis and maintenance of behavior disorders and how procedures based on principles of operant and classical conditioning can be used to treat them. For example, a real or perceived decrease in the quantity or quality of reinforcement that a person receives can lead to the signs and symptoms of depression. Interventions that enable patients to increase reinforcement and to avoid negative and erroneous evaluative statements are effective in treating most people with depression.

Interestingly, there is growing evidence that effective behavior therapies produce changes in brain activity comparable to those produced by effective psychotropic drugs. Behavior therapists do not, however, index therapeutic gains in terms of changes in central nervous system activity, but rather in terms of overt behavior, which is important in its own right and as an index of affect and cognitive status. Physicians also use behavior change to index clinical effectiveness, and the general approaches used by physicians and behavior therapists to treat behavior disorders are similar. With both therapeutic modalities, treatment is most likely to be effective when:

1. The treatment is appropriate for the patient and behavior problem of concern. The results of well-controlled studies provide the best rationale for matching patients to treatments.

2. The treatment is individually tailored to the patient and administered consistently in the intended fashion. Failure of patients to be exposed consistently to intended interventions is a serious issue with respect to both pharmacotherapy, where it is known as *medication noncompliance,* and behavior therapy, where it is known as *inadequate treatment integrity.*

3. The treatment is evaluated carefully. Treatment evaluation requires clear specification of goals, collection of accurate data directly relevant to those goals, and data-based decisions concerning the costs and benefits of treatment.

4. The treatment is altered until success is attained. If outcome data indicate that the initially selected intervention is not producing the desired effects, the treatment should be altered and reevaluated. Changes in treatment may involve altering some aspect of the initial intervention (e.g., adjusting drug dosage or the frequency of therapy sessions), moving to an alternative intervention (e.g., substituting a tricyclic antidepressant for a serotonin-specific reuptake inhibitor in treating a patient with depression, substituting response cost for time-out in treating a physically assaultive patient with severe mental retardation), or adding a treatment component (e.g., prescribing an antidepressant medication to a patient with depression being treated with cognitive behavior therapy, or vice versa).

5. The treatment is integrated with other kinds of interventions to best serve the needs of the patient. Many adults who are candidates for treatment with a psychotropic drug or behavior therapy have problems in several areas of their lives. Such individuals often benefit from the services of a number of professionals (e.g., a psychologist, psychiatrist, social worker, and religious leader), as well as from the support provided by family and friends. Steps taken to ensure open communication and collaborative problem solving among all of these individuals go far in optimizing benefits for the patient, who, of course, participates in the process.

RESEARCH BASIS

Pharmacotherapy and behavior therapy encompass so many specific treatments and are used to treat so many behavior disorders that it is impossible to review the relevant research in a brief document. In general, there is abundant evidence of the effectiveness of each treatment strategy. For instance, there is compelling evidence that most patients suffering from obsessive-compulsive disorder or depression will derive benefit from either pharmacological or behavioral treatment, if well designed and executed. There also is some, although often less compelling, evidence of the value of the two in combination. Although there are many noteworthy exceptions, the majority of published clinical studies of psychotropic drugs have utilized between-subjects experimental designs and statistical analysis of data. Measures of behavior often are indirect, involving rating scales or global clinical impressions. Most of the research evaluating behavior therapy, in contrast, has involved within-subject experimental designs, visual data analysis, and direct measures of behavior. Neither strategy is superior in a general sense, but they do differ in the kind of information that they provide and in the difficulties they pose for researchers. Randomized-groups designs with double-blinds and placebo controls, for example, are the "gold standard" for research in clinical psychopharmacology. It may, however, be difficult to obtain access to enough participants to allow for the use of such designs, especially when protected populations, such as people with mental retardation, are of interest. For this and other reasons, several scientists have suggested that the small-N research methods widely used by behavior therapists may be invaluable in certain areas of clinical psychopharmacology and should be more widely used.

It is important to recognize that the quality and quantity of the evidence in support of the effectiveness of pharmacotherapy or behavior therapy depend on the condition and specific therapy or therapies under consideration. Even in situations where there is clear evidence of treatment effectiveness, however, it cannot be assumed that every treated individual will exhibit a favorable response. Good outcome data increase the likelihood that patients can be matched with useful treatments, but the accuracy of the match can never be assumed. In every case, it is essential that treatment effects be evaluated in each patient. To determine effectiveness of any treatment for a behavior disorder, three questions must be answered: (1) What are the desired effects of the intervention? (2) Were those effects obtained? and (3) Were there any significant adverse reactions? Although these questions seem relatively straightforward, answering them can be complex, especially in the context of everyday treatment evaluation. At minimum, assessment of therapeutic efficacy requires well-defined treatment goals, objectively measured behavioral outcomes, and data-based decision making.

PATIENT TARGET POPULATIONS AND EXCEPTIONS

Many conditions, such as depression and anxiety disorders, can in most cases be treated effectively with either pharmacological or behavioral interventions. In such cases, the treatment modality that is better for a specific patient depends on several factors, including patient preference, historical response to particular treatments, current availability of treatment options, and likelihood of compliance with pharmacological and nonpharmacological interventions. As noted previously, matching patients to treatments, whether pharmacological or behavioral, is one quintessential part of good clinical practice.

With respect to some behavior disorders and perhaps in general, the proportion of people treated by physicians rather than psychologists has increased over time. For example, Mark Olfson and his colleagues reported in an article published in the January 9, 2002, *Journal of the American Medical Association* that 87.3% of outpatients with depression received treatment from physicians, whereas 19.1% received treatment from psychologists. In 1987, 68.9% and 29.8% received treatment from physicians and psychologists, respectively. From 1987 to 1997, the percentage of such patients who received medication rose from 44.6 to 79.4. Factors contributing to the relative popularity of pharmacological treatments versus behavioral treatments are both complex and controversial.

Even with respect to conditions where pharmacotherapy is generally effective and popular, as in the case with depression, a minority of patients do not respond favorably to drug treatment. Such patients may, however, respond favorably to behavioral interventions. In addition, some patients who respond favorably to particular medications may be sufficiently troubled by side effects to prefer a nonpharmacological alternative. For example, a depressed man treated with a serotonin-specific reuptake inhibitor (SSRI) might show dramatic improvements in mood and overt behavior but experience enduring difficulties in producing and maintaining an erection. Such an individual might well prefer an alternative, and perhaps a nonpharmacological, intervention.

Just as some individuals do not respond favorably to pharmacological treatment, others do not respond well to behavior therapy. For some disorders, with schizophrenia as a prime example, pharmacological interventions are generally acknowledged as first-line treatments. Even when this is true, however, behavior therapy can be valuable in helping to ensure that patients comply with intended treatment protocols, which is a second quintessential part of good clinical practice. Behavior therapy can also be useful in helping patients to acquire new repertoires (e.g., to learn vocational skills), which medications cannot do. Medications may, however, increase a patient's sensitivity to behavioral interventions, allowing for learning that would otherwise not occur.

For certain patients, optimal results are produced by a combination of pharmacological and behavioral interventions. For instance, there is some evidence that integrated pharmacological and psychosocial interventions may be especially useful in treating individuals who abuse alcohol and that a combination of behavior therapy and pharmacotherapy is valuable in treating depression refractory to either type of intervention alone.

COMPLICATIONS

There are clear medical contraindications to the use of certain drugs. For example, recent evidence suggests that the antipsychotic drug thioridazine (Mellaril) may cause serious cardiotoxicity and should not be prescribed for patients with clinically significant cardiac disorders. Potentially harmful drug interactions also may limit the use of certain psychotropic agents. As a case in point, the SSRI antidepressant sertraline (Zoloft) should not be given to patients receiving monoamine oxidase inhibitors, drugs sometimes used to treat depression, or pimozide (Orap), an antipsychotic medication.

Medical conditions rarely limit use of behavior therapies. Other patient characteristics may, however, do so. For example, acceptance and commitment therapy, which relies heavily on verbal interactions between the patient and therapist, is inappropriate for patients with serious cognitive deficiencies.

Failure to monitor treatment effects adequately is a common problem when psychotropic medications are prescribed for adults with developmental disabilities, who may be unable to describe how they are reacting to medications. Development and widespread adoption of valid and practical medication-monitoring systems for use with this population are badly needed.

For many patients, financial considerations, including limits of insurance coverage, place limits on the kind and intensity of therapy that is available to them. For example, someone may be unable to purchase an expensive psychotropic drug or to pay for enough therapy sessions to derive significant benefit. Such considerations may complicate selection of the initial therapy and limit the extent to which treatment can be individualized to the patient.

Patient misconceptions concerning particular therapies may complicate the use of those therapies. For example, some people view reinforcement-based therapies as bribery and object to them on that basis or believe that it is improper "to reward people for doing what they ought to do anyway." Other people hold the erroneous belief that seeking any sort of help in dealing with behavioral problems is a sign of weakness that is to be avoided or that psychotropic drug treatments always produce significant side effects. Gently disabusing patients of erroneous conceptions about treatments that may benefit them sometimes is a necessary, but difficult, part of effective service provision.

CASE ILLUSTRATION

This hypothetical case example is based loosely on the results of a study reported by Normal Schmidt and his colleagues in the February 1997 issue of *Military Medicine*. The patient is a 20-year-old man who joined the army 2 years ago. A skilled drummer, he was assigned to his unit's marching band, a role that he initially relished. Over time, however, he became increasing uncomfortable during band practices and especially during performances, which he eventually came to avoid whenever possible. Thoughts of making errors and fear of the resulting ridicule became recurrent, to the point of disrupting his sleep and everyday activities unrelated to music, which led him to seek help from one of the base physicians. After two meetings, the physician ascertained that the patient met the diagnostic criteria for panic disorder and prescribed clonazepam (Clontril) at a dose of 1 mg per day to treat the condition. To provide an empirical index of the initial severity of the condition, the patient completed the self-report version of the Liebowitz Social Anxiety Scale before treatment was begun. This widely used scale requires little time to complete and is acceptable with respect to validity and reliability. To quantify possible treatment effects, he also completed it at weekly intervals thereafter.

These data, like the overall impressions of the patient and physician, suggested that 1 mg clonazepam was of real but limited value. Over time, the physician titrated the dosage upward to 2 mg, then to 3 mg. Therapeutic effects were not enhanced at higher dosages, and somnolence became a problem at 3 mg. Therefore, the dose was reduced to 2 mg. After a month on this dose, the patient's problems persisted, and the physician referred him to the base psychologist.

The psychologist arranged brief cognitive-behavioral treatment for the panic disorder. The treatment comprised education, training in cognitive reappraisal, and interoceptive and in vivo exposure to band practices and performances. Liebowitz Social Anxiety Scale scores, like self-reports of subjective status and avoidance responding, indicated substantial benefits after eight weekly treatment sessions. At this time, the patient, psychologist, and physician met to discuss the possibility of terminating clonazepam and decided to do so. Cognitive-behavioral treatment continued for 4 more weeks, at the end of which both the patient and the psychologist deemed it successful. Nearly 2 years later, the patient is successful as a musician and a soldier in general, although a "refresher" course of cognitive-behavioral treatment was required 8 months ago, prior to a major performance.

Although a behavioral intervention appeared to be more effective than a pharmacological one in this example, it is important to emphasize that this certainly is not necessarily the case. Moreover, the sequence in which treatments were arranged and the procedures used to obtain outcome measures, although typical of those that could be used in everyday situations, are inadequate to support strong statements about treatment effectiveness.

—*Alan D. Poling and Kristal Ehrhardt*

See also: *Multimodal Behavior Therapy (Vol. I);* *Multisystemic Therapy (Vol. II); Systems of Care (Vol. III)*

Suggested Readings

Bezchlibnyk-Butler, K. Z., & Jeffries, J. J. (Eds.). (2001). *Clinical handbook of psychotropic drugs*. Kirtland, WA: Hogrefen & Huber.

Hersen, M. (Ed.). (2002). *Clinical behavior therapy: Adults and children*. New York: Wiley.

Matson, J. L., Bamburg, J. W., Mayville, E. A., Pinkston, J., Bielecki, J., Kuhn, D., et al. (2000). Psychopharmacology and mental retardation: A 10-year review (1990–1999). *Research in Developmental Disabilities, 21,* 263–296.

Schatzberg, A. F., Cole, J. O., & DeBattista, C. (2003). *Manual of clinical psychopharmacology*. Washington, DC: American Psychiatric Publishing.

Spiegler, M. D., & Guevremont, D. C. (1998). *Contemporary behavior therapy*. Belmont, CA: Brooks/Cole.

PHILOSOPHICAL ASPECTS OF BEHAVIORISM

DESCRIPTION OF THE STRATEGY

Psychological science seeks to develop comprehensive explanations of the behavior of organisms. The form they should take has long been a contentious issue within the discipline. Even behaviorists have disagreed among themselves about the approach that should prevail. In addition, the technological challenges of the laboratory have divorced psychology from its parent discipline, philosophy. The rupture has not been uneventful: The two disciplines have often distanced each other like receding galaxies. One eminent philosopher has characterized psychology as "experimental methods and conceptual confusion," while psychologists deem much philosophical commentary about their discipline to stem from ignorance of its methods and goals.

TYPES OF BEHAVIORISM

Since John B. Watson coined the term "behaviorism," the movement, at various points in its development, renounced reliance on the subjective, mentalist, cognitive, introspective, dualistic, indefinable, private, or mediating variables. All the same, there are several problems in defining behaviorism. First, it is difficult to provide a formulation that encapsulates all of its historical forms while avoiding triviality. Accordingly, characterizing behaviorism minimally as an approach that anchors the database in observable dependent and independent variables may sometimes fail to distinguish it from other nonbehavioristic psychologies. Second, extruded mentalistic concepts are not always coextensive. Depending upon how a theorist construes them, mental states are not always "inferred," mental predicates do not always refer to private processes, mentalism does not always imply dualism (as Jerry Fodor has persuasively argued), mediating variables are not always indefinable, cognitive variables do not always run an inductive risk, radical behaviorism does not renounce the study of private events, and so on. Third, many "behaviorist" programs have increasingly embraced internal variables as cognitively oriented theorists and clinical practitioners continue to make inroads into the discipline. In *radical behaviorism,* "operant conditioners," like B. F. Skinner and his followers, have abandoned reliance on things such as desires, motives, intentions, feelings, sensations, judgments, volitions, purposes, consciousness, and the like in causally explaining human behavior. They seem to have been outnumbered by others—grouped in the past under the umbrella term *methodological behaviorism*—calling only for observables at requisite points in theory construction. Indeed, the chosen emphasis in applied fields is now dubbed the *cognitive-behavioral orientation.*

Philosophers, despite their older enchantment with behavioristic formulations in the philosophy of mind, have lately turned their attention to the study of consciousness, especially as this bears on the resolution of the mind-brain problem. Despite the team effort, they appear to be virtually confounded by the challenge to explain consciousness in terms of brain states. "Mysterians," like the philosopher Colin McGinn, have despaired of any likelihood of a solution—principally because they cannot conceive what form it could possibly take.

Despite the inroads made by cognitive theory, it should be kept in mind that if the emphasis in selective therapeutic interventions is on the prediction and control of behavior, it is unclear why an explanatory need for mentalistic concepts must always figure importantly in designing curricula of behavior change. While radical behaviorists may have misconceived the role of cognitive and mediating variables in wider explanatory schemas, their critics may overestimate reliance on such variables when the task involves, for example, enriching the verbal repertoires of autistic children. Accordingly, the relevance of any chosen philosophy of science may depend upon what arena of endeavor is the focus of professional effort.

PRIVATE EVENTS

Private events for behaviorists in psychology and philosophy seem to have been a springboard for generating controversy. Psychologists of all persuasions generally assume that mental events are private, inferred entities. Yet the *logical behaviorism* of philosophers, like Gilbert Ryle and Ludwig Wittgenstein, in attempting to "rectify the logical geography of mental-status concepts," challenged this common assumption. Both philosophers held that many mental predicates do not refer to private or internal events, but to the predominantly public ways we are disposed to behave. For them, to feel emotion, for example, is not to infer at some inductive risk the occurrence of a private psychological event, process, or object, but to behave in certain ways—verbally and otherwise—in observable, albeit special circumstances.

Even considering its relevance for a surprising number of mental-status concepts lending themselves to a dispositional analysis, the problem with Ryle's program consisted precisely in his failure to reconcile

logical behaviorism with events like sensations or *qualia* (i.e., the broad range of subjective raw feels) that are indisputably private to persons experiencing them. In addition, his assault on "the ghost in the machine" involved an attack on metaphysical dualism (i.e., the Cartesian theory that mind was made of different "stuff" than physical events). However, other philosophers have faulted Ryle's attempt to parlay a program involving the redeployment of mental-status terms into a metaphysical thesis about the nature of reality. Many of the same critics also feel Wittgenstein's theory that all philosophical problems are the result of linguistic confusions was overdrawn.

On the other hand, for radical behaviorists like Skinner, mental-status terms, however defined, point inferentially to private events of a noncausal nature. It is quite in the idiom of Skinner to declare that "Smith did not behave that way because he was angry, but because he was reinforced for doing so." It is not altogether clear whether radical behaviorists on occasion (a) deny the existence of mentalistic entities, in the manner of eliminative materialism; (b) acknowledge their existence, although consider them redundant in a behavioral analysis; or (c) regard them as prescientific concepts that can be translated into observable behavioral terms. The three slants are on quite different explanatory wavelengths. The last-named version is reminiscent of a theory proposed by Rudolph Carnap, a logical positivist and original member of the Vienna Circle. He felt that mental concepts could be recast as physicalistic ones by means of "reduction-sentences." One of his colleagues, Carl Hempel, originally sympathetic to the "recasting" of mental terms, subsequently abandoned this point of view.

Radical behaviorists (i.e., Skinnerians) conceive the reduction or elimination of mentalistic terms as a one-way street. Suppose the process went in the reverse direction, and a behavioral analysis could not even be conceived without the introduction of mentalistic concepts? The following might serve as an illustration.

An experimenter undertakes to place a pigeon on a schedule of reinforcement under which the latter is made contingent on the number of responses emitted (ratio scheduling). Accordingly, reinforcement is delivered every third response (fixed ratio or FR3 scheduling). There is nonetheless an undetermined interval schedule (reinforcement based on the time elapsing between responses) that *fits* the FR3 schedule already specified. This is because the latter is denotatively the same as an unspecified variable-interval schedule (VI) overlapping it. Thus, if the pigeon takes 10 minutes to emit the first three responses before reinforcement, 5 minutes to emit the next three responses before reinforcement, and 2 minutes to emit the following sequence of three responses before reinforcement, a VI schedule also describes its history of reinforcement. (In the unlikely event that the time elapsing between reinforcements after three responses was always the same, say 5 minutes, the overlapping schedule would be an FI5 one.) The question then arises: Has the pigeon been placed on a FR or VI schedule? If the answer is "both," no ultimate distinction can be drawn between ratio and interval schedules of reinforcement, since both types describe the same facts.

In the manner of a distinction drawn by W. V. Quine, we might say that both types of scheduling *fit* the facts, but the experimenter's arrangement *guides* the scheduling in question. However, since "guiding" in Quine's sense involves a causal relationship, why should the FR schedule be considered the preferred causal account in contrast to the VI schedule denotatively identical to it? The only deciding factor here in determining schedule type is the experimenter's *intention,* a mentalistic concept. The conclusion, hardly a comforting one for behaviorists who wish to extrude mentalistic concepts from explanatory schemas, is that some behavioristic concepts cannot even be operationally defined without the introduction of mentalisms like *intentionality!*

Quine, a behavioristically oriented philosopher sympathetic to Skinner's views, likewise felt "intentionality" was either an irreducible concept requiring a "science" all its own or an idiom without scientific foundation. He opted for the latter alternative. On the other hand, Hempel's renunciation of the physicalism of the Vienna Circle was based on the realization that there can be no recasting of mentalistic into physicalistic terms without the subsequent reintroduction of the former somewhere along the line.

Many behavioral psychologists, especially in the therapeutic area, rely on private events as a central feature of their applications. Clinical techniques such as Joseph Wolpe's systematic desensitization, Joseph Cautela's covert sensitization, Lloyd Homme's coverant control, and forms of cognitive-behavioral techniques favored by Aaron T. Beck, Albert Ellis, Donald Meichenbaum, and Michael Mahoney, focusing upon internal cognitions, have enjoyed popularity. Even Skinner has insisted that providing an adequate explanatory treatment of private (not mental!) events is at the heart of his radical behaviorism.

Skinner adopted what might be called a third-person perspective on private events, or those occurring "under the skin." Acknowledging such realities as sensations, he construed the acquisition of verbal self-descriptive repertoires about them as reinforced by the verbal community. Thus, self-awareness about private states is a social product: Others reinforce our self-statements about our sensations on the basis of their overt behavioral manifestations. The statement "I have a toothache" is thus acquired through mentoring from the outside, as it were.

The radical behaviorist theory may founder on the failure to draw an essential distinction. Does "self-awareness" pertain to correctly speaking about one's pains, or experiencing them, or both? It is patent that our sensation language must be learned and is therefore subject to error: We are not born knowing how to use certain terms. However, do we feel pain only on the condition that we get a little help from our friends?

Skinner, in addition, was skeptical about knowledge of private events. He has averred, "Everyone mistrusts verbal responses which describe private events." Yet some reasons he supplies for his skepticism do not validate the generalization. He has stated, for example, "The individual who excuses himself from an unpleasant task by pleading a headache cannot be successfully challenged, even though the existence of the private event is doubtful." But the boy who cries wolf once too often is, as a cultural practice, frequently and successfully challenged. Moreover, when we are in the dark about the existence of headaches in sometime liars, the skepticism arises from our doubting the reliability of these persons, not because what they report is a private event. We can also harbor doubts about their reports of public events, and there are circumstances in which it would be absurd to doubt their private sensations, as when they report them as they howl under a dentist's relentless drill or when an anvil is dropped on their foot.

According to Skinner, the verbal community is in a disadvantageous position with respect to reinforcing statements about occurrences it was not privy to because of their inaccessibility. Yet such a concession renders his theory counterintuitive. Suppose "self-awareness" covered experiencing sensations and the verbal community-reinforced first-person statements about pains incorrectly. Would it then be possible to experience pains without actually having them or have them without being aware of them? How does one manage to have a severe headache without being aware of it or experience a toothache without having one? Yet on a given interpretation of Skinner's views, such absurd consequences would appear to be a possibility.

Alternatively, the upshot of faulty instruction by the verbal community may result merely in a cockeyed use of sensation terminology, hardly affecting the private sensations we harbor. The family of paradoxes surrounding sensation statements was dealt with at great length in the later writings of Wittgenstein—with a rather different outcome than Skinner's treatment of the problem.

MORAL PHILOSOPHY

Behaviorists sometimes take a characteristic tack on value judgments, including moral appraisals. They have held that statements containing terms like "good," "ought," "rights," "values," and the like implicitly assert something about reinforcement. The thrust of this view is succinctly expressed in Skinner's dictum that "A list of values is a list of reinforcers." The doctrine is actually a scion of an older moral tradition called "Naturalism," the theory that statements about what "ought" to be are derivable in one form or another from statements about what "is." This "is-ought" dichotomy was discussed by the 18th-century philosopher David Hume, who argued for the impossibility of deriving "ought" statements from factual propositions because of the categorical disparity between the two. His position has been adopted by most contemporary philosophers. What is their beef with the behavioristic formulation?

According to many antinaturalistic philosophers, just because the way some individual has behaved prompts others to judge his action as "right" or "wrong" does not justify contending that what is meant by the terms is a descriptive property of his behavior, implicit or otherwise. Hence, prescriptive terms are not translatable into behavioral terms. Arguing that "good" functions as a name, or oblique reference, to empirical properties of behavior or its reinforcing consequences because a pattern has occasioned moral judgment is tantamount to suggesting that the number 2 admits of a behavioral analysis because it occurs in the verbal behavior of those categorizing human events numerically!

There is no denying that events subject to behavioral analysis play a role in occasioning value judgments. Indeed, behavior is the grounding upon which moral statements or arguments are sustained or justified. However, this is a far cry from the theory that the virtual meaning of prescriptive terms is behavioral data or that the former can be "reduced" to the latter. Consequently, we cannot maintain, as does Skinner, that "You ought to tell the truth" means "If you tell the truth, you will be reinforced for doing so." Does "You ought to racially discriminate" mean "If you racially discriminate, you will be reinforced for doing so"? It seems obvious that whether discrimination is right or wrong cannot be decided by reviewing the history of who was reinforced for practicing it. As a matter of historical record, many moral reformers we revere were punished, not positively reinforced, for ideas they felt obliged to popularize. They did not regard their treatment by society as a yardstick of their moral stance, and this is often taken as evidence of the stature and probity of such figures.

THEORY AND APPLICATION

Despite the contentious nature of discussions about behaviorism on the meta-theoretical level, there is no denying its progress in so-called therapeutic applications.

The creation of techniques to change the plight of disabled populations, persons with psychiatric disorders, and innovations in the educational curricula of normal populations have been too numerous to mention. Recent research on compromised clinical populations has indicated a degree of overlap when it comes to the therapeutic efficacy of treatment procedures inspired by differing orientations in psychology. However, behavioral techniques have a distinct advantage in connection with intellectually compromised clinical populations, pervasive developmental disorders and autism, learning disabilities, depression, specific fears, panic disorder, speech dysfluencies, obsessive-compulsive disorder, and types of sexual dysfunction.

All the same, the nature of the connection between theory and application has received little attention. Behavior therapists, for example, often speak about their clinical armamentarium as a set of "experimentally derived treatment techniques." What sense of the term *derived* is functioning here?

In a study authored by C. B. Truax, it was discovered that Rogerian therapy, in contrast to representing "unconditional positive regard," was actually selectively reinforcing clients' verbal behavior. An impartial observer might conclude that what he or she was privy to was not client-centered therapy, but another form of behavior therapy. One might describe the therapeutic transaction as "unintentional behavior therapy," since the Rogerian therapist was unaware of the selective nature of his approach. Had the therapeutic ministration been effective, its success could therefore be explained in behavioristic terms.

The epiphany is that the therapeutic success of many forms of psychotherapy can be explained—or at least analyzed—in behavioristic terms. (And no wonder: If the latter is presumed to account for human behavior in general, professional therapeutic behaviors naturally fall within their purview.) Since behavior theory has a wide explanatory compass, are therapeutic regimens of sundry types "derivations" if this framework can explain their success? The answer, it seems to the present author, is a simple one. "Derivations" are simply those applications practiced by professionals who self-consciously use a special vocabulary and inventory of concepts to explain their effectiveness. Considering the wide compass of behavior theory, it is difficult to envision how it might fail to "explain" the success of most treatment techniques. Consequently, effective psychotherapies can be construed as "derivable" from behavior theory in the sense that the latter is consistent with or embraces a set of therapeutic results. The practitioner in question need only play a certain theoretical language game.

Even failed psychotherapies can be explained behaviorally. In the Truax experiment, the client-centered interventions turned out to be selective reinforcements of verbal behavior. Yet if "unconditional positive regard" remained true to form, it could be analyzed as "noncontingent reinforcement of verbal behavior."

The failure of behaviorally oriented social experiments like the *Walden-II*-style "utopias" in Virginia and Mexico hardly document a failure of behaviorism or its philosophy of science; they only imply misappropriations of concepts like "reinforcement," "aversive control," or "extinction." Such concepts are more advantageously viewed as explanatory principles embracing a wide variety of techniques rather than as names of specific interventions in parochial armamentaria. Theoretical orientations in psychology do not specify roadmaps or blueprints for particularized therapeutic techniques deducible from them, but only an inventory of concepts and principles embracing whatever applications are in fact developed. That the opposite viewpoint has enjoyed popularity is more a matter of historical than logical significance.

CAUSALITY AND FREEDOM

Determinism is often construed as the philosophical theory that every event has a set of causally sufficient conditions that necessitate it. Some commentators regard it more as a guiding or heuristic principle in the conduct of scientific inquiry—for good reason. It is hardly challenged or falsified by the failure to isolate the causes of any particular event, while the causation of most human behaviors has not been demonstrated. Other philosophers regard determinism, as well as arguments for it, as incoherent or badly in need of clarification. Be that as it may, determinism does not really warm up in philosophical circles until it squares off with freedom and moral responsibility, notions often regarded in behaviorist psychology as "figments," "scientific fictions," or "relics of autonomous man."

Behavioral psychology's purge of freedom and responsibility frequently goes hand in hand with attributing to the environment those achievements traditionally reserved for persons. Many philosophers would consider this to be a case of double standards in behavioral psychology. If Jones is not responsible for his achievements because his environment "caused" him to behave the way he does, why isn't he responsible for Smith's behavior if something he does causes Smith to behave in a certain way? Moreover, if "responsibility" is nullified once the causes of a particular event are demonstrated, how can environments be held responsible for human patterns when they are likewise the causal result of a set of prior conditions? When mentalistic psychologies are criticized because they tend to invoke environmentally unanchored, independent variables, no formulation—including behaviorism—meets the proposed criterion of explanatory adequacy. Carrying the logic to an extreme, it might be argued that neither persons nor environments could be held responsible because of a problem of infinite regress.

In philosophy, the determinism/free will controversy is far from resolved, and there are philosophers who believe that freedom and moral responsibility are not precluded by determinism, even if the latter were true. They are called "compatibilists," or "soft determinists." Some of them have even held that human freedom requires causal necessitation, since the alternative is indeterminism, for them an even more serious threat to cherished concepts.

Despite the conceptual difficulties in some forms of behaviorism, programs of effective behavior change can be undertaken by sidestepping philosophical issues.

These programs, especially on the therapeutic level, can move ahead without underlying metaphysical assumptions and on the basis that efforts to help clients take a recognizably efficacious form. Psychologists who are flawed philosophers often make promising agents of desirable behavior change, while impeccable philosophers tend to leave the world exactly as they find it—an accomplishment that is nothing to write home about.

—*D. A. Begelman*

Author's Note. The author wishes to thank Professor Edward Walter for his constructive comments.

See also: Applied Behavior Analysis (Vol. III); Behavior Therapy Theory (Vol. I); Paradigmatic Behavior Therapy (Vol. II)

Suggested Readings

Carnap, R. (1953). Testability and meaning. In H. Feigl & M. Brodbeck (Eds.), *Readings in the philosophy of science* (pp. 47–92). New York: Appleton-Century-Crofts.

Ferster, C. B., & Skinner, B. F. (1957). *Schedules of reinforcement.* New York: Appleton-Century-Crofts.

Fodor, J. (1968). *Psychological explanation: An introduction to the philosophy of psychology.* New York: Random House.

Hempel, C. (1980). The logical analysis of psychology. In N. Block (Ed.), *Readings in the philosophy of psychology* (Vol. I, pp. 14–33). Cambridge, MA: Harvard University Press.

Hume, D. (1973) *A treatise of human nature* (A. Selby-Bigge, Ed.; Book 3, Pt. 1, Sec. 1. L.). Oxford, UK: Clarendon Press.

McGinn C. (1993). *The problem of consciousness.* London: Blackwell.

Quine, W. V. (1972) Methodological reflections on current linguistic theory. In D. Davidson & G. Harman (Eds.), *Semantics of natural language.* (pp. 442–454). Dordrecht, Netherlands: D. Reidel.

Ryle, G. (1949). *The concept of mind.* New York: Barnes & Noble.

Skinner, B. F. (1953). *Science and human behavior.* New York: Free Press.

Truax, C. B. (1966). Reinforcement and non-reinforcement in Rogerian psychotherapy. *Journal of Abnormal Psychology, 71,* 1–9.

Wittgenstein, L. (1953). *Philosophical investigations.* New York: Macmillan.

PRIVATE EVENTS

DESCRIPTION OF THE STRATEGY

Stated simply, private events are those events occurring "within the skin" of a person or other organism. That is, private events involve stimuli and/or behaviors to which only the behaving organism has direct access. Although many private events have overt behaviors or stimuli that they typically accompany (e.g., the swelling of a sprained ankle is observable to others), the private event (e.g., the pain) is not perceivable by external observers. Thinking, imagining, remembering, feeling, understanding, knowing, and perceiving bodily states are all events that only the organism experiencing them may contact directly.

Behavior analysis has been widely misrepresented as excluding or ignoring private events. Although there are exceptions, many early behaviorists, including J. R. Kantor and B. F. Skinner, along with most contemporary behaviorists, make no such restriction. The faulty belief in the behaviorist rejection of private events has several origins. For example, position of behavior analysis is often confused with other behavioral positions emerging during the same historical period. Inclusion of private events as open to direct scientific analyses distinguishes the radical behaviorism of B. F. Skinner from the methodological behaviorism of individuals such as Clark Hull. The latter behaviorists insisted exclusively on inclusion of data that were subject to interobserver agreement. Although interobserver agreement is seen as important in contemporary behavior analysis, it does not define the limits of behavioral science.

The belief that behavior analysts deny the existence of private events may also stem from the refusal of behavior analysts to consider private events as the causes of overt behavior (e.g., thoughts causing action). However, exclusion of private events as explanatory causes of behavior does not exclude such events from being the subject of study. For the behavior analyst, private events are always the dependent variables that one explains, rather than the independent variables that explain behavior. When private events, such as thoughts of self-efficacy, are seen to be highly correlated with performance, the behavior analyst seeks to understand the environmental conditions that lead to (a) the thoughts of self-efficacy, (b) the overt performance, and (c) the relation between the thought and performance.

RESEARCH ON PRIVATE EVENTS

The belief that behaviorism is ill equipped to analyze private events may also result from the relative lack of empirical research concerning private events from a behavior-analytic perspective. In dealing with the analysis of the behavior of simple organisms in simple environments, variability in overt behavior could be analyzed without analyses of private events. This is also essentially the case in experimental analysis of the behavior of individuals when extreme control of the environment is possible, such as among institutionalized individuals. Thus, because the empirical analysis of private events was both unnecessary and methodologically troublesome, private events were largely ignored. However, as behavior analysis expands into adult clinical populations and problems, the need for analysis of private events has become more acute. These analyses have begun to appear in greater numbers in the behavioral literature. This is particularly the case with basic research concerning rule-governed behavior, stimulus equivalence, and issues of self. For example, recent literatures have emerged examining phenomenon such as self-discrimination, self-control, the participation of private events in equivalence relations, and rule following. Likewise, in the clinical behavior analysis literature, private events have emerged as a topic of central empirical and theoretical concern.

RELEVANT TARGET POPULATIONS

The empirical analysis of private events becomes increasingly important to the extent that we have less capacity to exert control over the day-to-day environment of treated individuals. Analyses of private events are also likely to be more important in higher-functioning populations for whom primary reinforcers, such as food, may not be the central reinforcing events. For example, if we organize an environment that is noncoercive and rich in opportunities for primary reinforcers for individuals with profound mental retardation, they will be relatively happy. However, for noninstitutionalized adults and children, we may find ourselves somewhat limited in our ability to carefully organize such an environment. In these instances, we need to understand the relationship between private events, such as an individual's sense of life purpose and direction (i.e., potentially distal and symbolic reinforcers) and the maintenance of both overt behavior and a positive attitude toward such activities in less than optimal conditions. For example, a school teacher may find meaning and worth in his or her experience of teaching even in a suboptimal teaching environment, and we may be able to assist the teacher in maintaining psychological contact with this reinforcer even when it may not be apparent in the objective, immediate environmental circumstances.

COMPLICATIONS

While the investigation of private events is theoretically coherent and methodologically possible, their study carries with it many complications. It is simply easier to study behaviors that are subject to interobserver agreement. Pain provides an excellent example. If an individual fails to report pain, we have difficulty ascertaining whether pain was not felt or merely not reported. If it was not reported, we must wonder whether the failure was a matter of deception or a failure to discriminate the relevant state. No laboratory test can tell us whether an individual is feeling pain or not. In the area of back pain, for example, one may find observable injury with no reported pain and pain with no observable injury. Thus, while theoretically coherent and empirically possible, private events remain a challenging research domain.

—Kelly G. Wilson and Karen Kate

See also: Autogenic Training (Vol. I); Cognitive
    Restructuring (Vol. II); Establishing Operations (Vol. III)

Suggested Readings

Hayes, S. C., Barnes, D., & Roche, B. (Eds.). (2001). *Relational frame theory: A post-Skinnerian account of human language and cognition.* New York: Plenum Press.

Hayes, S. C., Wilson, K. G., & Gifford, E. V. (1999). A contextualistic perspective on consciousness and private events. In B. A. Thyer (Ed.), *The philosophical legacy of behaviorism* (pp. 153–187). Dordrecht, Netherlands: Kluwer.

Moore, J. (1980). On behaviorism and private events. *The Psychological Record, 30,* 459–475.

Parrott, L. J. (1984). Listening and understanding. *The Behavior Analyst, 7,* 29–39.

Skinner, B. F. (1945). The operational analysis of psychological terms. *Psychological Review, 42,* 270–277.

Taylor, I., & O'Reilly, M. F. (1997). Toward a functional analysis of private verbal self-regulation. *Journal of Applied Behavior Analysis, 30,* 43–58.

Wilson, K. G., & Hayes, S. C. (2000). Why it is crucial to understand thinking and feeling: An analysis and application to drug abuse. *The Behavior Analyst, 23,* 25–43.

PRIVATE PRACTICE OF BEHAVIORAL TREATMENT

I have been involved in the private practice of behavior therapy since I completed my internship in 1980. In 1985, I started a private practice anxiety disorders clinic, which now includes four licensed psychologists, two licensed clinical social workers, and one professional counselor. We also have a psychiatric nurse practitioner in our office suite, to whom we often refer clients who need medication evaluations or pharmacotherapy. In addition, I am currently supervising a psychology resident, who has extensive experience in behavior therapy and operates on a sliding scale.

In our brochure, we state that "The Anxiety Disorders Clinic is committed to the goal of using treatment techniques that have been empirically validated and shown to be effective in the treatment of anxiety disorders." We are thus publicly committing to primary care physicians, other health care providers, and to consumers that we strive to conduct an evidence-based practice.

THERAPEUTIC RELATIONSHIP

While in the early days of behavior therapy, the importance of the therapist-client relationship was de-emphasized, current behavior therapists view the quality of this relationship as quite important to successful treatment outcome. For example, David Burns has shown in his research that clients' perceptions of the therapist's empathy contribute significantly to the outcome of cognitive-behavioral therapy (CBT) for depression. Compared with therapists of other therapeutic orientations, however, behavior therapists do not see the therapeutic relationship as *the* most important factor, but rather they still believe that specific behavioral interventions are most important. Clearly, in our private practice, we try to establish a solid therapeutic working alliance. In addition to the possibility that this may be therapeutic in itself, we believe that such alliance is often necessary to get clients to engage in therapeutic tasks that are uncomfortable and time-consuming, including exposure and response prevention for obsessive-compulsive disorder (OCD).

BEHAVIORAL ASSESSMENT

As for behavioral assessment, we rely primarily on reliable and valid self-report measures. Most of these measures have been used in randomized controlled trials (i.e., efficacy research), conducted at clinical research centers around the world. This allows us to compare the outcome of our behavioral treatments with results of studies conducted by the experts in the field. Most of these measures are brief and quickly

scorable, saving both client and therapist time. In addition, we have both clinical and nonclinical norms available, which allows us to determine the clinical significance of treatment results. Fortunately, practitioners' guides to empirically based measures of anxiety and depression are now available.

Our assessment packet currently contains the following self-report measures: the Fear Questionnaire, Mobility Inventory, Body Sensations Questionnaire, Agoraphobic Cognitions Questionnaire, Anxiety Sensitivity Index, Penn State Worry Questionnaire, State-Trait Anxiety Inventory, and Beck Depression Inventory II. We use additional measures depending on the specific anxiety disorder we want to measure, for example, the Yale-Brown Obsessive-Compulsive Scale for OCD.

In addition to self-report measures, we also use self-monitoring measures, such as the Panic Attack Record and Weekly Progress Record, to measure panic attack characteristics and daily mood. As for measures of overt behavior, we use clients' progress on exposure hierarchies and informal behavioral tests when treating specific phobias, such as snake, spider, and bird phobias, as well as claustrophobia. We do not typically use psychophysiological measures.

TREATMENT MANUALS

When treatment manuals are available for a specific disorder, we use these them in a flexible manner. While some clinicians are skeptical about the value of conducting manualized treatments, we find treatment manuals quite useful. Our experience suggests that these manuals can be used quite flexibly, with ample opportunity for therapist use of clinical wisdom and creativity and attention to achieving a strong working alliance with our clients. When crises or other problems in addition to the disorder being treated arise, we shift our attention to these concerns as clinically indicated, but then return to where we left off in the therapy manual. We find that the manual provides structure but not a straightjacket for therapy. Sometimes treatment sessions are similar in number to those reported in the efficacy literature, while at other times, it takes much longer to finish the manualized treatment, particularly when there are comorbid disorders.

In addition, most of our clients report liking to have the manual to refer back to for review both during therapy and afterward. As an interesting illustration, one of my early panic control treatment clients, with whom I was using Barlow and Craske's *Mastery of Your Anxiety and Panic*, reported during a long-term follow up assessment that someone walking in front of her house appeared to be quite frightened and was apparently hyperventilating during a panic attack. My former client stopped this person, invited her into her house, went over relevant portions of the treatment manual with her, and showed her how to do slow diaphragm breathing!

RESEARCH BASIS

In our private practice, we have conducted ongoing outcome research on empirically supported treatments (ESTs). As most of the research supporting these treatments has been efficacy research, our private practice research is effectiveness research. Here, we are able to ask the question whether treatments conducted by experts who developed the treatments, conducted in university settings under tightly controlled conditions with highly selected populations with extensive disqualifying characteristics, generalize to the private practice setting. We have examined this issue with panic control treatment (PCT) for panic disorder, exposure and response prevention for OCD, cognitive-processing therapy for posttraumatic stress disorder (PTSD), and group CBT for social phobia. In each of these cases, we have collaborated with graduate students working on their theses or dissertations at the School for Professional Psychology at Pacific University.

Our research has found that each of the ESTs mentioned above have been effective in our private practice setting. In general, our results are quite comparable to those obtained in the efficacy studies. As an illustration, consider our research on the treatment of panic disorder.

In July 2001, we presented the results of a long-term follow-up of our panic disorder patients at the World Congress of Behavioral and Cognitive Therapies in Vancouver, British Columbia. Jon Strand, a graduate student at the School of Professional Psychology (SPP) at Pacific University, conducted this research for his master's thesis. The CBT was Barlow and Craske's panic control treatment. One hundred consecutive private practice referrals entered treatment, and 77 completed treatment. Of this group, 45 (32 females and 13 males) participated in the follow-up assessments. Patients had completed an average of 14.4 hours of treatment, provided by a licensed psychologist, psychology resident, licensed professional counselor, or psychiatric nurse

practitioner. Length of follow-up ranged from 3 months to 6.7 years, with an average of 2 years.

Results indicated that at follow-up, 87% of patients were panic free, and 66% obtained high-end state functioning. To obtain high-end state functioning, patients had to score within the normal range on 5 of 6 measures of panic disorder and agoraphobia (in addition to being panic free). As with our earlier study, results of this long-term follow-up study are consistent with results obtained at research centers throughout the world. In addition, our study appears to be the longest follow-up of panic control treatment reported in the literature. We concluded that panic control treatment is highly adaptable to private practice when delivered by trained professional specializing in the treatment of anxiety disorders.

ETHICAL ISSUES

While the private practice of behavior therapy is subject to the same American Psychological Association (APA) code of ethics as any other theoretical approach, there are some specific ethical issues that may more commonly arise in the practice of behavior therapy. These issues center around the use of in vivo exposure techniques and other out-of-office therapeutic activities. In my own practice, I have used in vivo exposure with clients with OCD, panic disorder with and without agoraphobia, specific phobias (e.g., driving, birds, claustrophobia, fear of flying), and social phobia. Fieldwork with these clients raises a number of issues that behavior therapists should be aware of and address. Therapists must be cognizant that the potential for dual-role issues to develop may be higher than in usual office-based practice, as accompanying clients to relevant exposure experiences may be more similar to both client and therapist experiences in more nonprofessional roles. For example, being with a pareuretic client in a public restroom, riding in the car with a driving phobic, practicing hyperventilation at the mall, or conducting exposure and response prevention in the client's home remove both client and therapist from the office setting, where both roles may be under stimulus control.

In today's culture, where risk management and ethical practice often appear blurred, it may be tempting for the behavior therapist to avoid in vivo therapeutic work. Here, the ethical principle of client welfare seems most relevant. In this case, if research has shown that the empirically supported treatment for a particular disorder includes in vivo exposure, then the ethically correct course of action is to venture outside the confines of the office.

This, of course, raises interesting questions about informed consent and use of third-party payments. Therapists need to check with clients' insurance companies to see whether out-of-office therapy will be covered. The answer to this question, then, becomes relevant to informed consent. In other words, clients need to be clear about what out-of-pocket expenses in vivo exposure treatment will incur and realize that travel time to and from the exposure destination will be their expense.

Therapists should also be intentional about what they will charge clients in certain particularly sticky situations. I recall an experience early in my private practice career when I scheduled a home visit to observe a child's behavior at the dinner table. When I arrived at the client's home, I was invited to dinner, and I accepted, thus becoming a participant observer. Understandably, in retrospect, the mom was confused and angry when I billed her for my services. An appropriate informed consent clarifying my role and rationale for the home visit and a rational for my *not* eating dinner with the family, that is, being an observer but not a participant, would have been more prudent.

Informed consent should also include limits to confidentiality that may arise if the client or therapist sees someone he or she knows while on a therapeutic outing. Informed consent should also include the rationale for in vivo work and why it confers an advantage over in-session-only activities. This may not only enlist client motivation and willingness to confront uncomfortable situations, but may foster clarity of the therapist and client roles.

Risks of in vivo procedures should, of course, be included, for example, limits to confidentiality, discomfort upon facing feared situations, potential side effects such as a temporary increase in anxiety, intrusive thoughts, nightmares, or panic attacks. In all cases, careful documentation of out-of-office activities is, of course, essential.

ADVERTISING

Advertising is not unique to the private practice of behavior therapy, but some of the approaches that I have found most useful might be noted. Overall, we have received few clients from Yellow Page ads or taking other health care providers to lunch. One of our main sources of advertising, in addition to satisfied clients referring friends and family members, has been visibility derived via conducting workshops for both professionals and laypersons. Probably our best form of advertising, however, is the regular newsletter we send to physicians and nurse practitioners.

By presenting workshops, sometimes paid, other times for free, we have continued over the years to remind the community that we are anxiety disorders specialists. In our newsletter, we discuss disorders that we most commonly treat and, when available, outcome data. This empirical orientation is stated in our newsletter and appears to garner respect from other health care professionals. Given the significant percentage of patients who present to physicians with anxiety and depression, they are usually grateful for a respected source of referral.

We have sent copies of abstracts of conference presentations to managed care companies as well. These organizations appear increasingly aware of the relevance of behavior therapy and managed care concerns: use of ESTs, relatively short-term treatment focus, goal-oriented, measures of improvement, and so on.

SUPERVISION

Behavior therapy supervision has been another component of our private practice. We have supervised practicum students in counseling and residents in clinical psychology. Here, we pass on our Boulder model and training in the administration of ESTs. This has also allowed us to offer treatment to low-income, uninsured clients on a low-cost, sliding-scale basis. Supervisees have also been very helpful in assisting with various in vivo exposures activities.

TEACHING

As an adjunct professor at SPP, I have been reinforced for continuing to stay current on ESTs for the most common clinical problems. As well as being intrinsically rewarding, contact with other faulty and students also increases our visibility in the community and fosters collaboration with students for our private practice research. In addition, students' class papers and research with other faculty members provides me with up-to-date information on the current state of research on treatments for clinical problems that are not within my own area of expertise, thus broadening my awareness of when I might make referrals to colleagues who provide these treatments.

COURT TESTIFYING

Another aspect of my private practice of behavior therapy has been testifying as an expert witness in cases of PTSD. Having an empirically oriented practice and a resumé with numerous publications is appealing to attorneys. Similarly, the American Board of Professional Psychology (ABPP) in behavioral psychology allows me to be referred to as "board certified," which appears to have enhanced my credibility in the courtroom setting. Specializing in the anxiety disorders has also allowed me to respond to attorney questions and forensic reports not only from my clinical experience but also from my knowledge of empirically supported conceptual models and treatments. For example, in a recent case, I was asked to respond to an evaluation of a PTSD client by an examiner who stated in his report that the client's panic disorder could not be related to stressful events at work and stated,

> This lack of any causal connection to the work place is also clinically consistent with the nature of panic disorder; by definition, panic attacks are not associated with external or situational triggers. In other words, they occur out of the blue and are unprovoked/unprecipitated events.

To the contrary, I suggested that there is a well-known association of increased life stress in the 6- to 12-month period preceding onset of panic attacks. In addition, as stated in *DSM-IV-TR,*

> Although a diagnosis of Panic Disorder definitionally requires that at least some of the Panic Attacks be unexpected, individuals with Panic Disorder frequently report also having situationally bound or situationally predisposed attacks.

In addition, while this PTSD case superficially did not seem to meet the Criteria A requirement of being a threat to one's life or physical integrity, upon further exploration, I found such perception of threat. Another case involved a blind client who fell in an uncovered manhole at a construction site and suffered a concussion and amnesia for the accident, but developed full PTSD symptomatology when he heard an eye witness account of his fall. In my judgment, this client met PTSD criteria similar to cases where one develops PTSD upon hearing about a traumatic event happening to a loved one.

—Ricks Warren

See also: Behavior Consultation (Vol. II & III); Manualized Behavior Therapy (Vol. I)

Suggested Readings

Antony, M. M., Orsillo, S. M., & Roemer, L. (Eds.). (2001). *Practitioner's guide to empirically based measure of anxiety.* New York: Kluwer Academic/Plenum.

Fishman, S. T., & Lubetkin, B. S. (1983). Office practice of behavior therapy. In M. Hersen (Ed.), *Outpatient behavior therapy: A clinical guide.* New York: Grune & Stratton.

Hayes, S. C., Barlow, D. H., & Nelsen-Gray, R. O. (1999). *The scientist practitioner: Research and accountability in the age of managed care* (2nd ed.). Boston: Allyn & Bacon.

Last, C. G., & Hersen, M. (1985). Clinical practice of behavior therapy. In M. Hersen & C. G. Last (Eds.), *Behavior therapy casebook.* New York: Springer.

Nezu, A. M., Ronan, G. F., Meadows, E. A., & McClure, K. S. (Eds.). (2000). *Practitioner's guide to empirically based measures of depression.* New York: Kluwer Academic/Plenum.

Thomas, J. C., & Hersen, M. (Eds.). (2003). *Understanding research in clinical and counseling psychology.* Mahwah, NJ: Erlbaum.

PROBLEM-SOLVING THERAPY

DESCRIPTION OF THE STRATEGY

Problem solving (often referred to as "social problem solving," to emphasize that such activities occur in social or interpersonal contexts) is the cognitive-behavioral process by which a person attempts to identify or discover effective or adaptive solutions for stressful problems encountered during the course of everyday living. Problem-solving therapy (PST) provides for systematic training to help individuals cope more effectively with such stressful events by teaching them to apply a variety of skills geared to help them either (a) alter the nature of the problem (i.e., *problem-focused* goals, such as overcoming obstacles to a goal), (b) change their distressing reactions to the problem (i.e., *emotion-focused* goals, such as accepting that a problem cannot be changed), or (c) both.

Within a cognitive-behavioral framework, problem-solving outcomes are viewed as being largely determined by two general but partially independent dimensions: (a) problem orientation and (b) problem-solving style. *Problem orientation* is the set of cognitive-affective schemas that represent a person's generalized beliefs, attitudes, and emotional reactions about problems in living and one's ability to successfully cope with such problems. This orientation can be either positive or negative in nature. *Positive orientation* is the constructive, problem-solving set that involves the general disposition to (a) appraise a problem as a "challenge" (i.e., opportunity for benefit or gain), (b) believe that problems are solvable ("optimism"), (c) believe in one's personal ability to solve problems successfully ("self-efficacy"), (d) believe that successful problem solving takes time, effort, and persistence, and (e) commit oneself to solving problems with dispatch rather than avoidance. In contrast, *negative problem orientation* is a dysfunctional or inhibitive cognitive-emotional set that involves the general tendency to (a) view problems as significant threats to one's well-being, (b) doubt one's personal ability to solve problems successfully ("low self-efficacy"), and (c) become frustrated and upset when confronted with problems ("low frustration tolerance").

Problem-solving style refers to those core cognitive-behavioral activities that people engage in when attempting to cope with problems in living. Three differing problem-solving styles have been identified, one being an adaptive style, whereas the other two reflect maladaptive ways of coping.

Rational problem solving is the constructive problem-solving style that involves the systematic and planful application of certain skills, each of which makes a distinct contribution toward the discovery of an adaptive solution or coping response. Specifically, the rational problem solver carefully and systematically gathers facts and information about a problem, identifies demands and obstacles, sets realistic problem-solving goals, generates a variety of possible solutions, anticipates the consequences of the different solutions, judges and compares the alternatives, and then chooses and implements a solution while carefully monitoring and evaluating the outcome.

Impulsivity/carelessness represents one ineffective problem-solving style that involves a generalized response pattern characterized by impulsive, hurried, or careless attempts at problem resolution. An impulsive/careless style is often associated with individuals who have a low tolerance for uncertainty, distress, or negative emotions. *Avoidance style,* a second maladaptive coping pattern, is characterized by procrastination, passivity, and dependency. Individuals with a strong avoidant style prefer to distance themselves from problems rather than confront them, put off solving problems for as long as possible, wait for problems to resolve themselves, and attempt to shift the responsibility for solving their problems to others.

The overarching goals of PST include (a) enhancing individuals' positive orientation and application of specific rational problem-solving tasks (i.e., defining problems, generating possible solution ideas, making decisions to order to develop a solution plan, carrying out the plan, monitoring its effects, and evaluating the outcome) and (b) minimizing their negative orientation and tendency to engage in dysfunctional problem-solving style activities (i.e., impulsive or careless attempts to cope with problems, avoidance of problems). PST strategies include didactic explanations, role play training exercises, practice opportunities, and homework assignments geared to foster practice between training sessions.

Problem Orientation

A variety of training approaches can be used to foster a positive problem orientation. One technique is the *reverse-advocacy role play strategy.* According to this strategy, the therapist pretends to adopt a particular negative belief and asks the patient to provide reasons why that belief is irrational, illogical, incorrect, and/or maladaptive. Such beliefs might include the following statements: "Problems are not common to everyone, so if I have a problem, that means I'm crazy"; "There must be a perfect solution to this problem"; "I'll never be the same again." At times when the patient has difficulty generating arguments against the therapist's position, the counselor then adopts a more extreme form of the belief, such as "No matter how long it takes, I will continue to try and find the perfect solution so that I can make everybody happy and no one can get mad at me!" This procedure is intended to help patients identify alternative ways of thinking and then to dispute or contradict previously held negative beliefs with more adaptive perspectives.

Other related cognitive-restructuring and cognitive-therapy-based techniques are also useful in helping the patient to overcome specific distortions or deficiencies in information processing that may underlie a negative problem orientation, such as negative attributional style, negative appraisals, cognitive distortions, and irrational beliefs.

Patients are also taught to view feelings or emotions as *cues* that a problem exists and to use a visual image of a red traffic stop sign as a signal to *STOP and THINK,* in other words, to recognize problems as problems and to label them as such. Doing so serves to inhibit the tendency to act impulsively or automatically in reaction to such situations. It also facilitates the tendency to approach or confront problems rather than to avoid them.

Problem Definition and Formulation

Problem definition can be likened to "mapping" a guide for the remainder of the problem-solving process. The major focus of this task is to better understand the nature of the problem and to set clearly defined and reasonable goals. Training in this task focuses on the following activities: (a) gathering available information about the problem, (b) using clear and unambiguous language, (c) separating facts from assumptions, (d) identifying the factors that make the situation a problem, and (e) setting realistic problem-solving goals.

Generation of Alternatives

When generating alternative solutions to a problem, PST encourages broad-based, creative, and flexible thinking. In essence, patients are taught various brainstorming strategies (e.g., "The more the better"; "Defer judgment of ideas until a comprehensive list is created"). This helps to increase the likelihood that the best or most effective solution ideas will be discovered.

Decision Making

Once a list of alternative options has been generated, the problem solver begins to systematically and thoroughly evaluate the potential for each solution to meet the defined goal(s). Training in this component helps the patient to use the following criteria to conduct a cost-benefit analysis based on the utility of each alternative solution: (a) the likelihood that the solution will meet the defined goal, (b) the likelihood that the person responsible for solving the problem can actually carry out the solution plan optimally, (c) the personal (i.e., effects on oneself) and social (i.e., effects on others) consequences, and (d) the short-term and long-term effects.

Solution Implementation and Verification

This last rational problem-solving task involves first carrying out the solution plan and then monitoring and evaluating the consequences of the actual outcome. PST encourages the patient to practice the performance aspect of solution implementation as a means of enhancing the probability that it will be carried

out in its optimal form. Once the plan is under way, the patient is encouraged to monitor the actual results. Using this information allows the problem solver to evaluate the results by comparing the actual outcome with his or her expectations or predictions about the outcome.

If this match is satisfactory, the patient is encouraged to administer some form of self-reinforcement, self-statements of congratulations, or tangible gifts or rewards. However, if the match is unsatisfactory, then he or she is encouraged to recycle through various aspects of the problem-solving process once again. In this troubleshooting process, particular care needs to be exercised in differentiating between difficulties with the performance of the solution plan and the problem-solving process itself.

Supervised Practice

After the majority of training has occurred, the remainder of PST should be devoted to practicing the newly acquired skills and applying them to a variety of stressful problems. Beyond actually resolving such problems, continuous in-session practice serves three additional purposes: (a) The patient can receive "professional" feedback from the therapist; (b) increased facility with the overall PST model can decrease the amount of time and effort necessary to apply the various problem-solving tasks with each new problem; and (c) practice fosters maintenance and generalization of the skills.

The number of "practice" sessions required after formal PST training often is dependent upon the competency level a patient achieves, as well as the actual improvement in his or her overall quality of life. Of the research protocols that have found PST to be an effective cognitive-behavioral therapy intervention, the number of included sessions has ranged from 8 to 12 sessions.

RESEARCH BASIS

Based on the literature regarding the efficacy of this intervention strategy, PST appears to be flexible with regard to treatment goals and methods of implementation. For example, it can be conducted in a group format, on an individual and couples basis, as part of a larger cognitive-behavioral treatment package, and even over the phone. It has also been applied as a means of helping patients to overcome barriers associated with successful adherence to other medical or psychosocial treatment protocols, such as in the treatment of obesity.

RELEVANT TARGET POPULATIONS AND EXCEPTIONS

PST has been shown to be effective regarding a wide range of clinical populations, psychological problems, and the distress associated with chronic medical disorders. These include unipolar depression, geriatric depression, distressed primary care patients, social phobia, agoraphobia, obesity, coronary heart disease, adult cancer patients, schizophrenia, mentally retarded adults with concomitant psychiatric problems, HIV-risk behaviors, drug abuse, suicide, childhood aggression, and conduct disorder. It is unlikely, however, to be effective for specific phobias or obsessive-compulsive disorder. PST strategies have been incorporated in various behavioral marital therapy programs and as part of a larger treatment protocol for borderline personality disorder.

COMPLICATIONS

Presence of severe anxiety or panic symptoms would tend to limit the ability of a patient to understand and engage in the various in-session problem-solving exercises. Behavioral stress management techniques, such as relaxation training, should be applied if this should occur.

Naive therapists may have the tendency to focus on superficial problems be somewhat "mechanical" in their teaching of the problem-solving skills, and/or focus more on the rational problem-solving skills and less on problem orientation training. PST, although a skills-oriented protocol, should be conducted within the context of a positive therapist-patient relationship.

CASE ILLUSTRATION

"Karen" was a 29-year-old, unhappily married, unemployed woman who felt depressed, hopeless, and a "failure at being a wife and mother." Her sense of self-efficacy was rather low, usually leading to avoidance of confrontation with her husband, whom she characterized as very lazy, uninvolved, and verbally abuse. She tended to be very uncreative in thinking of differing options in reacting to life's problems, often stating, "What's the use, things never change?" Although she did have two close female friends, they were usually the

ones to initiate social activities outside the home. Karen had started junior college right after high school but soon dropped out when she became pregnant with the first of three children. Although she stated that she loved them, she often felt "trapped" without a future, feeling bitter about never finishing school. Whereas she never attempted suicide because of the children, she frequently fantasized about feeling numb. This caused her additional concerns, as she felt she had begun drinking too much during the past 6 months.

An initial case formulation was based on information obtained during several intake interview sessions, as well as completion of relevant questionnaires that assessed levels of depression, hopelessness, anxiety, as well as an evaluation of her problem-solving abilities (e.g., Social Problem-Solving Inventory-Revised). This assessment yielded the following problem-solving profile: significant negative problem orientation, the tendency to avoid facing problems when they occurred and to act impulsively at times to avoid negative feelings (i.e., "going for the quick fix"), an inability to generate alternative solutions, deficient social skills, which further discouraged her from carrying out any solutions, and a strong tendency to minimize any attempts to cope with difficulties.

PST focused on overturning Karen's negative problem orientation and improving her rational problem-solving skills. Based on her answers to the SPSI-R and information obtained during the intake interviews, her negative orientation revolved around the following core beliefs: "My life will never change, so better not to try anything—otherwise I'll just get more upset"; "Even though my friends say they care, they can't understand what I'm going through, so it's better to keep it inside"; and "It's better to feel nothing than to feel bad." Such beliefs became important targets to change. To accomplish this, she was taught to better understand how her thoughts, feelings, and behavior greatly affected each other and that such a strong negative orientation almost "guaranteed that her life would become a self-fulfilling prophecy." With careful daily monitoring of these three variables, she began to see how she "kept herself in a personal prison." The important initial insight occurred when Karen observed her oldest daughter, Anne, react in a similar avoidant manner when confronted with difficult schoolwork. Karen began to be very concerned that her own negative philosophy would be adopted by Anne, as well as by her other two children—a situation that she was scared would happen unless she changed.

To combat her negative problem orientation, Karen was initially taught to perceive negative emotions, cognitions, and physical sensations as signals that "something is wrong" (i.e., as the discriminative stimulus that a problem exists), rather than to react to such negative stimuli as if they were the "end product" of a series of events that she was unable to cope with. As such, she learned to use the *STOP and THINK* technique to become more aware of the problems to be solved, rather than simply feel depressed or hopeless. Karen particularly liked this conceptualization, feeling that "There is something else to look forward to rather than being depressed!"

In addition, PST involved repeated trials of the reversed-advocacy role play strategy specifically that focused on changing Karen's negative core beliefs. Earlier in treatment, this focus was conceptualized by the therapist as "planting the seeds of a more positive problem orientation," knowing that the strength of her negative orientation necessitated continued therapeutic attention. Although Karen did not display significant problems with defining problems, she did have difficulties in setting realistic goals for herself. Initially, she tended to identify unrealistically high goals (e.g., "I'm going to go back to school, a great school, and finish in record time—that's how important it is to me!") for herself, making it very difficult to achieve and therefore more likely for her to feel depressed, hopeless, and incompetent. As such, training in this rational problem-solving skill focused heavily on helping her to delineate more reachable and realistic goals ("I can take one course next fall and use this experience to help better find out about how to make realistic plans for finishing in the future").

Also, based on the initial assessment, training Karen to be more effective in generating alternatives was considered crucial. Continued evaluation revealed that the major difficulty resided not so much in her ability to think of possible options, but in automatically judging that "Nothing can really work!" Teaching her to defer judgment until a later time was a major focus of treatment at this point. In addition, Karen was taught additional brainstorming strategies in order to develop new alternatives. One of the strategies she found especially helpful in producing a large pool of options was visualizing how one of her "heroes" would solve a particular problem. Realizing that she had a much wider range of options to specific problems as well as "life in general" significantly improved her earlier feelings of hopelessness and pessimism.

Initial training in decision making revealed that Karen continued to have difficulty "giving up" some of the long-held beliefs about her own abilities. Specifically, although she might rate a particular alternative as having a strong likelihood of helping to reach her goal, she consistently rated her own ability to optimally carry out the solution as "very poor." Based on previous work with her, it was apparent that such evaluations were not a realistic appraisal of a given's alternative's value, but rather the influence of her poor self-efficacy beliefs. As such, the therapist "circled back" to the problem orientation training once again and engaged Karen in several more reversed-advocacy role plays. In addition, she was encouraged to try to carry out certain solutions in less stressful problems (e.g., getting a new babysitter) in order to "test out" the assumption that she would fail. As a result of this focus, Karen began to evaluate potential solutions to more difficult problems (e.g., improving communications with her husband as a means of determining whether her marriage was able to be improved) in a realistic manner. Although she was beginning to feel more confident in her coping and problem-solving abilities, the therapist began training in the last rational problem-solving skill, solution implementation and verification, by teaching her additional tools for self-motivation to carry out a solution plan. For example, Karen was taught to identify as many of the potentially positive consequences to solving her problem and compare that list with one that contained the negative consequences likely to occur if she did not implement her solution. Preparing these lists helped Karen to concretely see evidence that it was in her best interests to implement a solution plan.

After the sessions devoted to teaching Karen the various problem-solving skills, much of the remainder of therapy focused on applying such skills to a wide variety of problems that she was experiencing, as well as those she predicted were likely to occur in the future (e.g., her husband might react negatively to her increased sense of competence and overall improvement in her well-being). As a result of PST, Karen felt more confident in her overall coping abilities and experienced significant improvement in her depression.

—*Arthur M. Nezu and Christine Maguth Nezu*

See also: *Homework (Vol. I); Problem-Solving Consult Model (Vol. III); Problem-Solving Training (Vol. II)*

Suggested Readings

D'Zurilla, T. J., & Nezu, A. M. (1999). *Problem-solving therapy: A social competence approach to clinical intervention* (2nd ed.). New York: Springer.

D'Zurilla, T. J., Nezu, A. M., & Maydeu-Olivares, A. (2002). *Social Problem-Solving Inventory-Revised (SPSI-R): Technical manual.* North Tonawanda, NY: Multi-Health Systems.

D'Zurilla, T. J., Nezu, A. M., & Maydeu-Olivares, A. (in press). What is social problem solving? Meaning, measures, and models. In E. C. Chang, T. J. D'Zurilla, & L. J. Sanna (Eds.), *Social problem solving: Theory, research, and training.* Washington, DC: American Psychological Association.

Nezu, A. M. (in press). Problem solving and behavior therapy revisited. *Behavior Therapy.*

Nezu, A. M., Nezu, C. M., Felgoise, S. H., McClure, K. S., & Houts, P. S. (in press). Project Genesis: Assessing the efficacy of problem-solving therapy for distressed adult cancer patients. *Journal of Consulting and Clinical Psychology.*

Nezu, A. M., Nezu, C. M., Friedman, S. H., Faddis, S., & Houts, P. S. (1998). *Helping cancer patients cope: A problem-solving approach.* Washington, DC: American Psychological Association.

Nezu, A. M., Nezu, C. M., & Lombardo, E. R. (2001). Managing stress through problem solving. *Stress News, 13,* 11–14.

Nezu, A. M., Nezu, C. M., & Perri, M. G. (1989). *Problem-solving therapy for depression: Theory, research, and clinical guidelines.* New York: Wiley.

PROGRESSIVE MUSCULAR RELAXATION

DESCRIPTION OF THE STRATEGY

Relaxation training is a set of procedures used in clinical practice to alter an individual's physiological, behavioral, cognitive, and emotional functioning. Relaxation is often incorporated into treatment to allow clients to respond to life events with increased physical and emotional self-control and with a more positive phenomenal experience. Although several variations of relaxation training exist, the most commonly used approach is progressive relaxation that involves learning how to regulate muscle tension through the systematic tensing and releasing of major muscle groups throughout the body.

Progressive relaxation training originated in the early part of the century, when Edmund Jacobsen applied relaxation skills with his clients suffering from tension disorders. He conceptualized relaxation as a way to limit the amount of energy expended when skeletal muscles become overactive. In turn, adenosine triphosphate (ATP), one of the body's principal energy sources, would be conserved, and fatigue could be reduced. Consistent use of relaxation skills would therefore increase the likelihood that bodily functioning would remain at a more optimal level.

Further physiological explanations for the utility of relaxation often refer to reduced activation in the sympathetic branch of the autonomic nervous system. By using relaxation skills in response to perceived stressors, an individual may reduce excessive skeletal muscle activity that creates the experience of tension. Progressive relaxation may also activate the parasympathetic branch of the autonomic nervous system, which leads to reduced arousal. This explanation is often referred to as the *relaxation response.*

ASSESSMENT

Clinical assessment is most useful when it informs effective treatments that fit the unique needs of each client. For relaxation training to serve as an effective treatment tool, it is crucial for several issues to be addressed during the assessment phase. First, the clinician should determine whether a medical condition, like untreated hypertension, primarily accounts for the client's presenting symptoms. It is often appropriate for clients to have a medical evaluation in order to rule out organic bases for presenting complaints. In addition, the clinician should assess the client's frequency and amount of stimulant use, because use of stimulants may contribute to increased physiological activity as well as muscle tension. If possible (e.g., not part of a medical prescription), a plan to decrease stimulant use should be made. Second, several factors may contribute to reports of anxiety and tension that can be appropriately targeted through relaxation training. Such areas include autonomic overactivation reflected in quality of sleep, drug/alcohol use, adherence to rituals, withdrawal from others, change in appetite/sex drive, interpersonal problems, feeling fatigued, depressed, or in pain. Third, clinicians should note the degree to which clients are able to concentrate during sessions. To acquire effective relaxation skills, it will be necessary for a client to be able to focus on bodily sensations and be as free from cognitive distractions as possible. Finally, antecedents contributing to and consequences resulting from anxiety or tension should be discussed. Once clients are able to understand the role environmental factors play in the maintenance of anxiety and tension, they may be more likely to intervene appropriately. In fact, it is possible for a subgroup of highly anxious clients to experience increased subjective distress and physiological arousal when they reach a relaxed state. Clinicians may at this point consider using another type or relaxation procedure or inform the client that relaxation training will initially serve as an exposure exercise to the aversive sensations and thoughts and eventually move toward its intended use, to induce relaxation. It is important for clinicians to discuss with clients their expectations regarding treatment to be sure that expectations are reasonable before treatment begins. The clinician may also recommend to clients that they practice self-monitoring to increase awareness of the frequency and severity of muscle tension or anxiety as the associated environmental factors.

The presentation of Jacobsen's abbreviated progressive relaxation training consists of six phases. The client is introduced to the rationale and procedure for abbreviated progressive relaxation (APR) in the first phase. The procedure is presented as obtaining a set of skills not unlike other sets of skills (e.g., bike riding) that the client develops. Highlighting the importance of practice and active participation in skill development for example, is a crucial component of this first phase.

In the next phase, the client is presented with the 16-target muscle groups (list included at end of entry), and relaxation techniques are presented. Before beginning relaxation procedures, the client should be in a reclined and comfortable position. At this point, the client is instructed to breathe slowly and regularly and then tense the muscle for 5 to 7 seconds, to release the tension quickly, and to allow the muscle to relax for 30 to 40 seconds. The client is instructed to continue to breath when muscles are tensed. Each muscle is tensed and relaxed two times. During the second trial, the relaxation period is extended to 45 to 60 seconds. The goal of this exercise is to have the client focus his or her attention on the changes in sensations as muscles are tensed and relaxed. At this point, the client is asked to signal with a finger whether the particular muscle group feels relaxed. If the client reports feeling relaxed, the clinician progresses to the next muscle group. If the client does not signal relaxation, the procedures are repeated. After the first session, the clinician discusses with the client any reactions that he or she may have had to relaxation training as

well as problems that either occurred in the session or those that may occur outside of sessions. This discussion will assist in creating the plan for at-home practice.

Most clients typically report an ability to achieve deep relaxation using the procedure after three sessions. After relaxation is achieved using the 16 muscle groups, muscles are consolidated into 7 groups, and then into 4 groups. The initial training phase is followed by a phase in which clients begin to pair sensations that occur during relaxation with cue words such as "Okay, relax," which continues for 30 to 45 seconds. If relaxation does not occur through recall, the initial procedure is practiced again. Once cue control is obtained, attempts to increase depth of relaxation occur by introducing counting with recall of muscle groups, and ultimately by counting alone. The goal of the advanced sessions is to program for generalization of the relaxation skills. Clients are more likely to engage in sufficient practice outside of session if the skills can be applied discretely and when time is limited. Practice is necessary for training to be effective in such a way so that clients can implement the skills without the clinician's aid, in increasingly distractible areas, and with less required cues.

RESEARCH BASIS

Since Jacobsen's pioneering research, other investigators have closely examined the effectiveness of the progressive relaxation procedure. The use of relaxation procedures across clinical problems has led to reductions in physiological activity (e.g., blood pressure) and in reported tension and anxiety at posttreatment and follow-up. Treatment-dismantling studies sought to answer questions regarding the relative effectiveness of relaxation alone or in combination with other treatment components. A great deal of this type of research has focused on the use of relaxation training as a component of cognitive-behavioral treatment packages for anxiety disorders. The research suggests that relaxation is most effective when used as a component of a larger treatment package. Finally, researchers have focused on research efforts toward determining the number of sessions necessary for relaxation skills to be adequately acquired. Researchers sought to create an abbreviated protocol because clinicians were concerned with the significant amount of time required by Jacobsen's original relaxation-training procedures. Empirical findings suggest that the average number of sessions necessary for clients to acquire prescribed relaxation skills is between five and six.

Empirical studies have also demonstrated that factors such as the therapist-client relationship and therapy room environment can contribute to the success or lack of success of relaxation training. Findings from these studies suggest that a therapist teaching relaxation skills should be empathic and procedurally flexible. The therapeutic environment should be free of excess noise and distractions, as well as kept at a comfortable temperature.

RELEVANT TARGET POPULATIONS

Relaxation training has been used to treat a wide range of clinical problems. The majority of the research on relaxation has focused on the treatment of specific types of anxiety (e.g., speech anxiety and social anxiety) and phobias, as well as generalized anxiety. Relaxation training has also been used to treat side effects of cancer chemotherapy, depression in postpartum women, insomnia, hypertension, asthma, and chronic pain conditions such as tension headache. Relaxation training is appropriate for these populations because physiological sensations often contribute to psychological problems. Through the use of relaxation techniques, an individual may become more aware of the sensations and learn how to mediate the impact of them in order to effectively alter his or her behavioral, cognitive, and emotional functioning.

COMPLICATIONS

Although adverse effects resulting from relaxation training occur infrequently in the general clinical population, it is important to consider factors likely to impede treatment. Despite the fact that relaxation-training produces effective results in many anxiety-based clinical problems, the procedure has also been found to induce anxiety and panic in some clients. For these individuals, a state of decreased arousal and vigilance (e.g., relaxation) is responsible for the onset of panic. Clients with histories that cause sensations resulting from relaxation to induce fear are also not likely to benefit from relaxation as a form of treatment.

Relaxation training may also be difficult for individuals who are unable to maintain adequate concentration during the procedure. It is not uncommon for clients to experience intrusive thoughts as they begin to relax. The clinicians can suggest that the client focus on the clinician's voice if necessary, to assist with concentration. In addition, clients who experience physical pain from muscle tension may not be well suited for relaxation training. The procedure is also not appropriate for individuals who cannot learn to observe and report on muscle tension after several sessions. It is important for a clinician to consider these obstacles, because if unattended to, the negative experience may lead the client to cease seeking treatment for his or her clinical problem. Finally, individuals with skills deficits in areas that contribute to anxiety require intervention targeting skill acquisition before relaxation training is appropriate. A client with inadequate study skills, for example, is likely to experience anxiety when tested. However, after instructing the individual how to better study for exams, anxiety may decrease without the need for relaxation training.

CASE ILLUSTRATION

"Dan" was a 40-year-old data programmer seeking services for chronic headaches. He received a referral for psychological services from his physician after all medical tests indicated the absence of an organic cause for the tension and pain. Dan stated that his supervisors placed a great deal of pressure of him to work quickly and accurately. He reported difficulty falling and staying asleep, had a small appetite, and drank caffeinated beverages throughout the day to stay alert. He reported feeling fatigued most of the time, which caused him to stay home and had limited his interactions with friends and family. He stated that he struggled to maintain concentration while at work as well as when at home. Even when at home, he could not get himself to "wind down" and finally received comfort from headaches once he managed to fall asleep. Dan was unable to describe specifically what brought on the tension that he experienced. The clinician asked that Dan complete questionnaires.

Given Dan's report of symptoms, it appeared that he was a good candidate for relaxation training. It would be useful to present self-monitoring as a tool to increase awareness during the first session so that over the course of the week, Dan could begin to notice the antecedents and consequence related to the tension that he experienced. A plan to decrease caffeine intake that Dan considered reasonable and was able to adhere to was recommended.

In the second session, the clinician presented the rationale and procedure for relaxation training. In Dan's case, relaxation would allow him to become more aware of tension as the process began and intervene appropriately and effectively. The skills would be of particular use for him when he became pressured to meet a deadline or before going to bed. They discussed his expectations for treatment and brainstormed possible obstacles that might get in the way of using relaxation techniques. Dan was instructed how to tense and relax large muscle groups in order to repeatedly experience and discriminate sensations associated with tension and relaxation. Muscle groups were consolidated, and relaxation cues became less specific in an effort to make the relaxation procedure amenable to use in a wide range of situations, whether he was at work or when alone at home. Dan was encouraged to practice the procedure at least two times a day.

Dan initially had difficulty maintaining concentration during in-session training. He occasionally talked to the clinician and she suggested that Dan focus on her voice as she moved through the procedure and avoid conversation unless he had a concern related to the procedure. Several trials were required before Dan reported relaxation of the first group of muscles. The clinician continued with the procedure until Dan reported relaxation in all muscle groups. Over the course of the next sessions, the clinician progressed to the use of cue-controlled and counting relaxation procedures. Before termination, the clinician administered questionnaires that asked Dan to report on his current level of tension and other psychological symptoms related to sleep and depression that he reported as problems in his first session.

TARGETED MUSCLE GROUPS

1. Dominant hand and forearm: make a tight fist

2. Dominant upper arm: push elbow down against chair

3. Nondominant hand and forearm: same as dominant

4. Nondominant upper arm: same as dominant

5. Forehead: raise eyebrows as high as possible

6. Upper cheeks and nose: squint and wrinkle nose

7. Lower face and jaw: clench teeth and pull back corners of mouth

8. Neck: pull chin toward chest and try to raise it simultaneously

9. Chest, shoulders, upper back: pull shoulder blades together

10. Abdomen: make stomach hard

11. Dominant upper leg: tense muscles on upper side and lower side

12. Dominant calf: pull toes toward head

13. Dominant foot: point toes downward, turn foot in, and curl toes gently

14. Nondominant upper leg: same as dominant

15. Nondominant calf: same as dominant

16. Nondominant foot: same as dominant

EXAMPLE OF SCRIPTED PROCEDURES

I want you to start the relaxation procedure by taking a deep breath and holding it . . . and letting it out. This will help you to relax. And another . . . and hold it . . . and let it out. Good. Imagine that with each breath, you inhale not only air but also relaxation, and that this relaxation spreads from your lungs throughout your body, and that as you exhale, you push out any tension in your body. Take another deep breath and hold it . . . and let it out. Good.

Let's begin by tensing the muscles of the right hand and arm by clenching your fist and bending your arm at the elbow, as if to show off your biceps. Tense these muscles now. Good. Hold it . . . feel the tension . . . feel the tightness . . . relax. Let go of all the tension. Let your hand and arm fall down to a comfortable position. Feel the relaxation as it spreads through your fingers . . . hand . . . lower arm . . . and throughout your upper arm to your shoulder. Notice the difference between the feeling in your right hand and arm and your left hand and arm. These are the pleasant feelings of relaxation.

Okay, let's again tense the muscles of . . .

—*William T. O'Donohue and Stephanie L. Spear*

See also: *Applied Relaxation and Tension (Vol. I); Relaxation Training With Children (Vol. II); Self-Management (Vol. III)*

Suggested Readings

Benson, H. (1975). *The relaxation response.* New York: William Morrow.

Bernstein, D. A., & Borkovec, T. D. (1973). *Progressive relaxation training: A manual for the helping professions.* Champaign, IL: Research Press.

Carlson, C. R., & Bernstein, D. A. (1995). Relaxation skills training: Abbreviated progressive relaxation. In W. T. O'Donohue & L. Krasner (Eds.), *Handbook of psychological skills training: Clinical techniques and applications.* Boston: Allyn & Bacon.

Hillenberg, B., & Collins, F. (1982). A procedural analysis and review of relaxation training research. *Behavior Research and Therapy, 20,* 251–260.

Hyman, R. B., Feldman, H. R., Harris, R. B., Levin, R. F., & Malloy, G. B. (1989). The effects of relaxation training on clinical symptoms: A meta-analysis. *Nursing Research, 38*(4), 216–220.

Jacobson, E. (1970). *Modern treatment of tense patients.* Springfield, IL: Charles C Thomas.

Jacobsen, E. (1977). The origins and development of progressive relaxation. *Journal of Behavior Therapy and Experimental Psychiatry, 8,* 119–123.

Smith, J. C. (1985). *Relaxation dynamics: Nine world approaches to self-relaxation.* Champaign, IL: Research Press.

Wolpe, J. (1958). *Psychotherapy by reciprocal inhibition.* Stanford, CA: Stanford University Press.

PSYCHONEUROIMMUNOLOGY

DESCRIPTION OF THE STRATEGY

Historically, the immune system was thought to operate autonomously, without input from other bodily systems. However, interdisciplinary research in the 1980s began to suggest interactions between the nervous and immune systems, thus leading to the development of the field of psychoneuroimmunology (PNI). Research in the area of PNI examines the interrelationships among brain, behavior, and immunity. The finding that immune system activity could be altered by external influences led to studies demonstrating that both increases and decreases in immune activity could be conditioned. Subsequent research has begun to examine the extent to which interventions could be developed to positively impact immune system activity in various disease populations such as cancer and HIV patients. Furthermore, the immune system has been repeatedly examined as a mechanism through which behavioral interventions (e.g., relaxation

therapy and cognitive-behavioral stress management) may slow disease progression. The present entry will review the literature examining the impact of behavioral interventions on immunity, focusing on studies in which immune components are used as the primary dependent variables as well as studies examining immunity as a mechanism for altered disease progression.

OVERVIEW OF THE IMMUNE SYSTEM

Prior to reviewing the PNI literature, it is necessary to first provide a brief overview of immune system functioning. The immune system is extremely complex, involving the interplay of numerous cellular and chemical components. Therefore, a comprehensive review of the workings of the immune system is well beyond the scope of this entry. Rather, we will briefly review the activity of the immune cells and components that are most commonly examined in the PNI literature.

The primary purpose of the immune system is to fight against infection and disease by identifying and eliminating foreign pathogens (e.g., bacteria, fungi, viruses) and mutated self-cells. This is accomplished through the activity of the two branches of the immune system: acquired (specific) and innate (non-specific) immunity. Although these branches are discussed separately, they do not operate independently. The two branches communicate with each other, influence each other, and to some extent, control each other.

Innate Immunity

The innate immune system represents the first line of defense against invading pathogens and mutated self-cells. Cells of the innate immune system (e.g., macrophages, neutrophils, natural killer cells) serve primarily a surveillance function in the body. These cells are capable of destroying cells they recognize as non-self, without any need to have encountered the foreign invader previously. Macrophages are an integral component of an immune response, serving to attack, break down, and display components of the invading pathogen to other immune cells in order to quickly mount an effective immune response (see below). Natural killer (NK) cells are large, granular white blood cells with demonstrated antitumor and antiviral activity. They are commonly measured in

PNI research because they are easily quantified in peripheral blood samples and because they appear to be reliably affected by psychosocial variables (e.g., distress, depression).

Perhaps the most efficient way of reviewing immune system activity is to trace how the immune system would respond to invasion by an *antigen* (antibody generator). A typical innate immune response to an initial infection involves phagocytosis of the pathogen by macrophages or other innate immune cells. After engulfing the antigen, the macrophage breaks it into its constituent proteins. These proteins are then displayed on the membrane of the macrophage so that cells of the acquired immune system can recognize the invading antigen. At this point, the macrophage is referred to as an *antigen-presenting cell* (APC). Upon engulfing and displaying the antigen, macrophages release chemical messengers (cytokines) that communicate with other cells of the immune system to inform them of the infection. One such cytokine is Interleukin-1 (IL-1), which serves to stimulate the acquired immune system response.

Acquired Immunity

The role of the acquired immune system is to identify and eliminate specific antigens in the body. In contrast to innate immunity, acquired immunity involves a specific cascade of reactions to a particular antigen, and the magnitude of response to this pathogen increases with each successive exposure, referred to as *memory*.

Once the APC presents the antigen on its membrane, antigen-specific T lymphocytes recognize the presented antigen and initiate the acquired immune defense process. The acquired immune response is typically divided into cell-mediated and humoral immunity. Cell-mediated immunity is carried out by T lymphocytes, which are a group of immune cells that mature in the thymus. Alternatively, humoral immunity is mediated by antibodies produced by B lymphocytes, which in humans mature in the bone marrow.

The release of IL-1 by the APC stimulates helper T cells (also referred to as CD4 cells) specific to that antigen to begin replicating. Helper T cells also secrete cytokines such as IL-2 and interferon (IFN), which stimulate cytotoxic T cells (CD8 cells) to destroy infected cells. T-helper cells also activate the humoral immune response by secreting IL-4. IL-4

activates B lymphocytes and initiates the process of antibody formation. As with T cells, specific B cells respond to specific antigens such that upon encountering an antigen, B cells specific to that antigen are rapidly produced.

B cells provide the body with two important defenses against foreign invaders. B cells both secrete antibodies designed to kill the specific antigen and attract other white blood cells to destroy the antigen. Antibodies are also referred to as *immunoglobulins* (Ig). There are five classes of immunoglobulins: IgG, IgM, IgA, IgE, and Ig D. IgG is the most common immunoglobulin and primarily acts to neutralize bacteria and viruses. IgM aids in the lysis of foreign cells, while IgE plays an important role in eliminating parasites. The role of IgA is not as well-known, but due to its prevalence in mucous membranes, it is thought to protect the skin from microorganism penetration. Similarly, little is known about the role of IgD; however, it is thought to function during fetal development of the immune system.

In addition to producing antibodies, B cells also differentiate into memory cells. Memory cells have the same specific receptor sites as the parent B cell; however, they are not activated during the initial interaction with the antigen. Rather, these cells "remember" the antigen and, upon subsequent contact with the same antigen, aid in earlier identification and more rapid elimination. Memory cells are responsible for the effectiveness of immunizations. When individuals are immunized against a particular virus, they are exposed to low levels of inactive antigen so that upon subsequent encounters with the virus, their immune systems can mount faster, more effective responses.

MEASUREMENT OF IMMUNE ACTIVITY

The ability to examine the effects of stress and outside influences on immune activity has been contingent upon the development of reliable techniques for assessing the number and activity of immune cells. Quantification of immune cells is typically accomplished by first isolating lymphocytes from peripheral blood samples. Flow cytometry can then be used to determine the number of cells of a particular type, providing the percentage of cells of that type in the blood sample. If it is necessary to obtain a sample of a particular type of cell, a fluorescence-activated cell sorter (FACS) can separate and collect cells of similar typology together. However, simple increases or decreases in number of peripheral lymphocytes may or may not result in consequent differences in activity against pathogens. Therefore, PNI research also typically involves the measurement of immune activity.

The most commonly used functional measures in PNI research include assays of lymphocyte blastogenesis, NK cell functioning, and latent antibody titers. When lymphocytes encounter their specific antigens, they undergo blastogenesis, or, in other words, the cells proliferate in response to the antigens. The most common method of measuring blastogenesis is through in vitro exposure of the lymphocyte to nonspecific antigens called *mitogens*. The number of lymphocytes produced (i.e., the extent to which the lymphocytes proliferate) as a result of mitogen stimulation can then be used as a measure of lymphocyte activity. Typical mitogens used to activate T lymphocytes include phytohemaglutinin (PHA) and concanavalin A (ConA), while pokeweed mitogen (PWM) is often used to assess B lymphocyte activation.

NK cell activity is evaluated through a 4- to 5-hour chromium release assay. As previously mentioned, one function of NK cells is the destruction of tumor cells. To assess NK activity, tumor target cells are labeled with radioactive chromium and then incubated with known amounts of NK cells isolated from a participant's blood sample. As NK cells lyse the tumor cells, chromium is released into the surrounding medium. The amount of radioactivity present in the supernatant then serves as a marker for NK activity; the greater number of tumor cells lysed, the more chromium released and the more radioactive the supernatant.

The previously discussed measures of immune activity have focused on assessing activity of specific immune cells. These measures may not accurately reflect how the numerous components of the immune system work together to destroy antigens. One way to assess how the cellular immune system is functioning in general is to measure antibody titers to latent viruses such as herpes viruses and Epstein-Barr virus. The cellular immune response plays a pivotal role in maintaining virus latency and reactivation, and levels of antibody titers to latent herpes viruses are thought to reflect cellular immune system competence. Approximately 85% of the population is infected with these latent viruses. In a healthy individual, these viruses lie dormant, and the immune system does a sufficient job of keeping the virus in check with minimal effort. In other words, relatively low antibody levels are necessary to keep the virus dormant in a healthy individual. However, in a stressed or immuno-suppressed individual, the immune system may have to work much harder (reflected in much higher antibody levels) to suppress viral activity.

Whereas simple quantification of immune cells does not provide information as to the activity of cells or how effective these cells will be at attacking foreign pathogens, activity measures alone are also difficult to interpret. Increased activity may reflect an upregulation of the activity of existing cells, or increased activity may be due to simply increased number of peripheral cells in the blood sample. Therefore, most PNI studies incorporate both quantitative and activity measures of immunity.

Conditioned Alterations of the Immune System

The possibility of a link between the brain and the immune system was first noted in early observations that immune reactions could be classically conditioned. In the early 1900s, Russian researchers demonstrated that artificial roses and pictures of hay fields could induce allergic responses in sensitive patients. Despite lacking relevant controls, these findings suggested that the immune system could be classically conditioned to respond to neutral stimuli.

However, subsequent research largely ignored these findings until 1975, when Ader and Cohen conducted a landmark study in which they elegantly demonstrated conditioned immunosuppression in rats using a taste aversion paradigm. The prevailing zeitgeist at the time was that the immune system was autonomous, operating without input from other bodily systems. However, Ader and Cohen's findings led to the birth of the field of PNI and hundreds of subsequent studies examining myriad ways in which immune activity could be altered by outside influences.

Ader was examining the phenomenon of conditioned taste aversion in rats when he serendipitously discovered that immune alterations could also be classically conditioned. In the original study, rats were given the novel taste of saccharin (the neutral-conditioned stimulus) and then were administered cyclophosphamide (CY), which made the animals ill. Surprisingly, a large number of the animals (especially those receiving the highest doses of saccharin) died during the protocol. In addition to inducing illness,

CY causes immunosuppression. Ader subsequently hypothesized that along with conditioning taste aversion, he was also conditioning immunosuppression, and his immunosuppressed subjects were succumbing to opportunistic agents in the laboratory. Ader and Cohen's subsequent study supported this hypothesis and demonstrated that the pairing of a neutral stimulus with an immunosuppressive agent could result in conditioned immunosuppression. Hundreds of studies have since replicated and extended these findings in both animal and human subjects. Given early anecdotal reports of correlations between levels of distress and illness, the majority of studies in PNI have examined the impact that stressors exert on the immune system.

Physiology of Stress

It is unknown exactly how stress affects immunity, but it appears that a number of mechanisms may be responsible. Stress may indirectly affect immunity and health by negatively impacting health behaviors. Stress has been associated with poorer diet, decreased exercising, poorer sleep, delay in seeking medical treatment, and a number of other poor health behaviors. Alternatively, stress may directly impact immune activity through the release of stress-related hormones, such as glucocorticoids and catecholamines. The typical stress response consists of the activation of two systems, the *hypothalamic-pituitary-adrenocortical axis* (HPA axis) and the *sympathetic nervous system* (SNS). Activation of these systems results in many physiological changes, including increased cardiovascular activity, heightened arousal, and improved attention and cognitive function. Activation of the SNS leads to the release of catecholamines, such as epinephrine, norepinephrine, and dopamine, while activation of the HPA axis leads to the release of corticosteroids, such as cortisol. Stress hormones have been shown to directly affect immune system activity. Increased epinephrine is associated with increased release of immature lymphocytes into circulation, while increased levels of norepinephrine have been associated with increased NK cell activity. In contrast, corticosteroids have been shown to suppress immune functioning through reductions in number and activity of lymphocytes, macrophages, and NK cells, and decreased antibody formation. Given that both SNS and HPA axis hormones are elevated during stress, the relative concentration of these hormones, the timing

of their release, and differences in pharmacokinetics may account for findings that different types of stress differentially impact immune activity.

Impact of Stress on Immunity

Acute Stress

Numerous laboratory studies have been conducted examining the effects of acute stressors on various measures of immunity. Acute stress studies have examined the impact of a very heterogeneous group of stressors ranging in type and duration and have differed with respect to what immune system components were examined. Therefore, it is not surprising that findings have differed depending on the duration, frequency, controllability, and type of stressor. However, a few consistent findings have emerged. In general, studies of the impact of acute stress on immune cells have consistently found increases in number of most cellular immune components. Although counterintuitive, an increase in number of cells in peripheral blood is often seen with a concomitant decrease in the activity of the same cells. This pattern of findings is consistent with the hypothesis that during stress, immune cells are released in large numbers into the periphery from stores in immune organs. However, these cells are immature and unable to effectively fight invading pathogens. Therefore, the actual number of cells in peripheral blood increases, while the overall activity of cells decreases. These results further reinforce the importance of assessing both quantitative and qualitative measures of immunity.

Although most immune cells display this pattern of responding to acute stress, research examining the activity of some immune components has not been as consistent. For instance, studies of the impact of acute stress on NK cells have produced mixed results. While the number of NK cells consistently increases during acute stress, some studies have reported increased NK cell activity and others have reported decreased activity following exposure to acute stress. These contradictory findings may be due to differences in timing of blood sampling. Studies finding increased activity typically examined NK cell functioning during and immediately following stress exposure, while studies that found decreased activity typically examined functioning at later time points (hours and days later). This suggests that the effects of stress on NK cell activity may follow a biphasic pattern, whereby activity increases during the stressor and then decreases below baseline, and further reinforces the importance of timing of immunological sampling in the interpretation of PNI studies.

Laboratory studies of the impact of acute stress on immunity allow for strict controls over the type, duration, timing, and intensity of the stressor. However, the extent to which results of these studies generalize to naturalistic stress exposure is questionable. Furthermore, it is unknown whether immune changes observed in laboratory settings are clinically significant; that is, are changes in immunity of great enough magnitude to result in increased risk for disease onset or faster disease progression? Kiecolt-Glaser and colleagues have attempted to rectify this shortcoming by examining a standard naturalistic acute stressor, academic examinations. Their typical protocol involves sampling blood from students during exams and, again, soon after a vacation. In a series of studies examining a number of immune variables, they found that during examinations, there were distinct alterations in cell-mediated, humoral, and innate immunity. More specifically, during exams, students had reduced number and activity of T lymphocytes, decreased NK cell activity, and an increased number of antibodies to latent viruses, suggesting overall suppression of the immune system. The observed relationships between stress and immunity persisted after controlling for the effects of poor health habits typically observed during examinations (poor diet, lack of exercise, sleep deprivation). Furthermore, Kiecolt-Glaser and colleagues were able to demonstrate that the immune alterations observed during finals may have clinical relevance. Participants who reported more stress during the examination period were significantly more likely to self-report being sick during the exams, suggesting that stress-related immunosuppression may be related to increased risk for contracting illness.

Chronic Stress

Fewer studies have examined the impact of chronic stress on immunity, perhaps due to the logistics involved in recruitment and retention of individuals experiencing a persistent stressor. Chronic stressors that have been studied include stress associated with the Three-Mile Island nuclear power plant accident, unemployment, diagnosis with a chronic illness, and caregiving for chronically ill relatives. Overall, research examining chronic stress and immunity has found stress to result in immunosuppression of a wide range of immune measures. Kiecolt-Glaser and colleagues examined the effects of caregiving for patients with Alzheimer's disease on immune system functioning in the caregiver. Across a number of studies, caregiving was associated with lower absolute numbers of T lymphocytes and increased antibody titers to latent viruses.

Similar results have been reported in individuals experiencing bereavement, marital separation, and divorce. Prospective studies examining the impact of losing a spouse on the surviving spouse's immune levels have revealed that bereavement is associated with lower T cell proliferation and decreased NK activity. However, as mentioned, it is unclear as to the extent to which observed immune changes are clinically relevant or to what extent immune alterations translate to increased risk for the onset or progression of disease.

Stress, Immunity, and Health

We have briefly reviewed the PNI literature and demonstrated that distress is associated with reliable changes in immunocompetence. However, few studies have attempted to determine whether stress-related immune alterations are associated with increased risk for contracting disease or increased risk for faster disease progression. Research examining the impact of stress on disease has consistently shown stress to be related to poorer health outcomes (i.e., faster progression of immune-related disorders such as cancer and HIV/AIDS, slower wound healing in healthy individuals, and greater incidence rates of the common cold and upper-respiratory infections). This relationship was thought to be a consequence of the direct impact that stress has on the immune system. However, only a few studies have examined stress-related immunosuppression as a mechanism by which stress could impact physical health.

Wound Healing

Kiecolt-Glaser and colleagues have addressed this question using a novel wound-healing paradigm. In one study, dental students received a standardized biopsy wound during a period of low stress (summer vacation) and, again, during a period of high stress (examinations). Wound healing was tracked over several days. During the high-stress period, students took an average of 3 days longer to heal compared with during their summer vacations. In addition, students had significantly lower IL-1β levels (a proinflammatory cytokine involved in the initiation and progression of wound healing) during the examination period. These findings suggest that chronic stress can affect health through immune-mediated changes during a relatively mild period of stress. A similar study involving a more chronic stressor (caregiving for a family member with dementia) produced comparable findings: Caregivers took longer to heal and had significantly lower levels of IL-1β compared with matched controls. Although stress was correlated with immune levels and wound healing, these studies did not directly test a mediational model of stress, immunity, and health, limiting the ability to conclude that stress-related immunosuppression was responsible for the observed differences in wound healing.

Cancer

Cancer is a heterogeneous group of diseases characterized by uncontrolled, abnormal tumor growth. Several studies have examined how the immune system can mediate the impact of psychosocial stress on cancer development, progression, and mortality; however, they have produced inconsistent results. Research examining the relationship between self-reports of stress and onset of cancer is largely flawed due to retrospective designs and biased reporting (a recent cancer diagnosis may alter the way in which a participant recalls prior stress levels). However, based on methodologically sound examinations of the relationship between stress and cancer onset, researchers largely agree that there is no evidence to suggest that stress may be associated with the development or onset of cancer.

On the other hand, the evidence for a relationship between stress and faster cancer progression or shorter disease-free intervals is much stronger. Early research found psychosocial factors such as loneliness, depression, suppressed expression of emotion, and low social support to be related to faster cancer progression and increased mortality. Due to its antitumor properties, NK cell activity has been the most studied immune measure in psychobiological cancer research. Levy and colleagues suggested that psychosocial factors (such as adjustment to illness, anxiety,

and depressive symptoms) might impair NK cell activity, thus leading to faster cancer progression or tumor growth. In a cross-sectional study, adjustment to illness, overall distress, fatigue, and NK cell activity were measured in 75 women recently diagnosed with breast cancer. Results revealed that lower NK cell activity was related to lack of social support and higher levels of fatigue/depression. Lower NK activity was also related to worse cancer prognosis at a 3-month follow-up assessment. These findings suggest that psychosocial factors impact cancer-related immunity and may have consequent effects on disease progression.

HIV/AIDS

The human immunodeficiency virus (HIV) is a retrovirus that specifically invades, destroys, and is propagated through the reproduction of CD4+ or T-helper cells. HIV can be spread through sexual contact, intravenous drug use, or contact with infected blood. Similar to research in cancer, research has begun to examine the effects of psychosocial factors and stress on HIV progression. Outcomes typically measured include reactivation of latent viruses (which can facilitate HIV progression) and number of CD4 cells. These studies have also produced mixed results, with some research showing psychological distress to be related to poorer immune functioning and others finding that distress is associated with enhanced immune functioning. Undergoing testing for HIV has been demonstrated to be a potent stressor, associated with impaired lymphocyte proliferation in individuals who ultimately test negative. In contrast, individuals who tested positive for HIV antibodies did not display any differences in immune activity during the prenotification period, despite reporting higher levels of distress than seronegative individuals, questioning the extent to which stress is related to immunosuppression in people with HIV.

Furthermore, the impact of distress on immunity and HIV progression is unclear. In an initial study, Temoshok and colleagues found that less psychological distress, greater fitness/exercise, greater physiological reactivity, and greater emotional control were associated with increased CD4 cell counts. However, in a subsequent larger-scale longitudinal study, increased anxiety, less emotional control, and greater loneliness were significantly related to higher percentages of CD4 cells. It has been hypothesized that these contradictory findings may be due to differences in stage of illness between study samples. In sum, conclusions regarding the relationship between stress, immunity, and HIV progression are hindered by equivocal findings. However, research examining the impact of psychosocial interventions in HIV-positive individuals has produced more consistent results (see below).

Summary

Research examining the extent to which stress-related changes in immunity are associated with clinically significant health outcomes have produced mixed, but suggestive, findings. Across a variety of diseases, distress has been associated with faster disease progression, greater morbidity, and increased mortality. Given these suggestive findings, researchers have begun examining whether one can intervene to decrease stress and block stress-related immune deficits and disease progression.

BEHAVIORAL INTERVENTIONS AND IMMUNITY

Based on previously mentioned findings linking stress-related immune deficits to disease progression, researchers hypothesized that interventions designed to decrease stress might result in positive changes in immune activity and consequent slowing of disease progression. These interventions have typically been conducted in samples with immune-related disorders such as cancer and HIV-positive patients. However, a few studies have examined the effects of interventions on immunocompetence in healthy individuals.

Healthy Individuals

Despite mixed findings, the majority of studies have found that behavioral interventions are effective at decreasing distress, improving quality of life, and positively affecting immune functioning and consequent health in relatively healthy individuals. One such study examined the impact of relaxation training and social contact intervention on immunological functioning in elderly individuals. Participants were assigned to a relaxation group, a social contact group, or a no-treatment control group. The relaxation intervention consisted of instruction and practice with relaxation techniques three times per week for 1 month. The social contact intervention consisted of

being visited in their homes three times a week for 1 month by a college student. NK cell activity and antibody levels to herpes virus were measured before and after the intervention as indices of immune system functioning. Results revealed that the relaxation group had significantly increased NK cell activity and decreased antibody levels, while there were no significant changes in the social contact or control groups. These results suggest that relaxation training, a component of many cognitive-behavioral interventions, may effectively increase immune functioning in healthy older adults.

Kiecolt-Glaser and colleagues conducted a similar intervention in which they randomly assigned medical students during examinations to either a stress management intervention or a control condition. In contrast to the findings with older adults, there were no differences in immune activity (percentage of helper T lymphocytes, NK cell activity) between the control and intervention groups. However, frequency with which intervention participants practiced the relaxation techniques was positively correlated with the percentage of helper T cells. These results suggest a dose-response relationship, whereby greater use of the relaxation techniques is necessary to positively impact immunity.

These studies suggest that behavioral interventions can have a positive impact on immunity. However, as is common when examining interventions that have many components, it is unclear what parts of the intervention are the most effective, although relaxation training has been consistently associated with higher immune activity in healthy participants.

Similarly, a number of methodological limitations hinder conclusions regarding the impact of behavioral interventions on immunity and subsequent health. First, interventions in "healthy" stressed individuals typically have not followed participants for a long enough time to determine whether immune alterations have an impact on health. Second, most studies have relied on only one or a few measures of immune activity. Given the complexity of the immune system, it is unclear the extent to which single immune measures represent overall immune functioning. Many researchers have questioned the clinical significance of immune alterations in response to behavioral interventions, as observed levels often fall within the normal range of immune functioning in healthy individuals. Therefore, it is unclear whether stress-related decreases in immunity increase risk for disease onset or progression and whether buffering these decreases through interventions conveys protection against this risk. However, whereas the clinical significance of immune changes have been questioned in healthy adults, researchers have hypothesized that changes of a magnitude seen in most studies may have clinical significance in chronically ill or immunosuppressed individuals.

Behavioral Interventions in Disease Populations

Cancer

In one of the most cited studies of behavioral interventions in a disease population, Spiegel and colleagues found slowed disease progression and decreased mortality in late-stage metastatic breast cancer patients assigned to a psychosocial intervention versus controls. Participants receiving the intervention met as a group weekly for 1 year. During these sessions, patients learned about adaptive coping techniques to reduce anxiety, depression, and pain associated with their illness. In addition, the women in the therapy group formed strong social bonds to further buffer the negative effects of their chronic illness. Results revealed that the intervention significantly increased length of survival in intervention participants (mean = 36.6 months, SD = 37.6) compared with controls (mean = 18.9 months, SD = 10.8). These findings were replicated in two other randomized studies that examined the impact of psychotherapeutic interventions on survival in individuals with lymphoma, leukemia, or melanoma.

However, other studies have been unable to replicate Spiegel's findings. For example, Gellert and colleagues examined the impact of a psychosocial support program on length of survival in women with breast cancer. Patients in the treatment condition received weekly cancer peer support, family therapy and individual counseling, and training in positive imagery. After controlling for appropriate prognostic factors, there were no significant differences in length of survival between the intervention group and the controls. These inconsistent findings could be due to the differing intervention protocols employed in these studies. For instance, in Speigel's study, the intervention was designed to increase adaptive coping strategies and decrease psychological distress specifically related to their illness, whereas Gellert's study may

not have directly focused on issues related to patients' cancer experiences.

Although research has suggested beneficial effects of interventions on survival from cancer, these studies did not examine immune activity as a possible mechanism through which the intervention may impact disease progression. Fawzy and colleagues have examined the impact of a psychosocial intervention on immune functioning in participants with malignant melanomas. Participants in the intervention condition received 6 weeks of health education, stress management, problem-solving skills, and psychological support. Results revealed that the intervention group had significantly increased percentages of NK cells and increased NK cell activity compared with controls 6 months following the intervention. Furthermore, participants who received the intervention were more likely to have survived their cancer compared with controls 6 years later. However, the findings of the Fawzy studies underscore one of the previously mentioned shortcomings of the PNI literature: the inability to demonstrate that stress-related immune alterations result in health consequences. Although intervention participants had higher levels and activity of NK cells 6 months after the intervention and had higher 6-year survival rates than control participants, NK measures were not related to survival. In summary, the majority of studies have found that psychosocial interventions slow disease progression and may increase survival time in cancer patients. However, the extent to which intervention-related immunological changes serve as a mechanism for slowed progression remain unclear. Studies examining distress, immunity, and disease variables typically do not find that stress-induced alterations in immunity fully mediate the impact of stress on disease. However, this may be because existing studies typically assess one or two immune components, and this may not adequately address the complex interplay of cellular and chemical components that constitute a body's immune response. Future intervention research in which multiple immune indices are measured are necessary to allow interpretation of the extent to which immune alterations may be responsible for the beneficial health effects seen in intervention research.

HIV/AIDS

Perhaps the best way to test the efficacy of behavioral interventions at increasing immunity and improving health is to examine diseases characterized by immunodeficiency. The progression of HIV is marked by decreases in levels of CD4 cells, and demonstrating that behavioral interventions result in slower progression or an increase in CD4 cell number would be a strong argument for the utility of these interventions. Unfortunately, results of studies examining whether behavioral interventions enhance immune functioning in HIV-positive individuals have been equivocal. Several studies have employed the use of a variety of interventions in an attempt to improve immune functioning, with limited success. Early research failed to produce increased immune functioning in men with HIV who received training in relaxation techniques and stress management skills. Although intervention recipients reported less distress, less depression, and increased quality of life, there were no differences in immune measures or disease-related symptoms between intervention and control groups. However, recent research has proved more promising. Over the past decade, Antoni and colleagues have conducted several large-scale studies examining the effect of a variety of behavioral interventions on immune functioning in HIV-positive individuals. One of their first studies examined the effect of physical exercise on immune function. Healthy (seronegative) gay males at high risk for contracting HIV were recruited. Participants were randomly assigned to the intervention condition (aerobic exercise three times a week for a month) or a no-contact control condition. Following the intervention, results revealed that exercise significantly increased CD4 (helper T) cells and B cells and increased lymphocyte activity in individuals who tested seronegative. However, the exercise intervention did not enhance immune functioning in seropositive individuals, again questioning the extent to which psychosocial influences can impact immunity in HIV-positive individuals. However, this intervention did not directly target the negative psychological sequelae, such as depression and anxiety, that are typically associated with HIV-positive status. As a result, a more tailored intervention was designed to target the psychological and physical distress associated with HIV and AIDS.

In this study, Antoni and colleagues examined the effects of a cognitive-behavioral stress management intervention (CBSM) on distress levels and immunological functioning following notification of HIV-positive status. Healthy gay men were recruited and randomly assigned to an intervention group or a control group 5 weeks prior to HIV status notification. The intervention was an intensive 5-week, group-based intervention that consisted of weekly sessions of relaxation-training techniques, exercise, and various cognitive-behavioral techniques, such as cognitive restructuring, identifying cognitive distortions, coping-skills training, anger management, HIV risk behavior education, and social support strategies. Baseline levels of psychological distress and immune functioning were measured 1 week prior to notification, and follow-up measurements were collected 1 week following notification. Men who were notified that they were seropositive for HIV were analyzed separately from those who were notified that they were seronegative. Among seropositive individuals, participants in the CBSM intervention group had significantly lower depression levels than control participants. In addition, the intervention significantly increased lymphocyte cell counts (CD56 and CD4) and proliferative responses to pokeweed mitogen in seropositive men, while the control group did not exhibit any change in immunity from baseline to follow-up. These findings provided initial evidence of the efficacy of a behavioral intervention targeting issues faced by individuals with HIV at buffering the negative effects associated with HIV status notification.

More recently, Antoni and colleagues conducted a randomized study examining the effects of CBSM on anxiety and immune functioning in 73 HIV-positive gay men. Participants were randomly assigned to either a 10-week intervention or a wait-list control group. The intervention group reported significantly lower anxiety, anger, and perceived stress levels post-treatment compared with the control group. In addition, the intervention group had significantly higher T-cytotoxic/suppressor cell counts compared with controls 6 to 12 months after the intervention. Within-group analyses revealed a significant decline in T-cytotoxic/suppressor cells over time for participants in the control group, whereas cell counts were stable up to 1 year later for participants who received the intervention. These findings are promising and suggest that multimodal interventions may not only increase psychological well-being but may also inhibit the progression of HIV in seropositive individuals.

CONCLUSIONS AND FUTURE DIRECTIONS

Although the field of PNI is relatively new, there is much evidence for an interrelationship between brain, behavior, and immunity. As reviewed above, a number of studies have demonstrated a link between stress and disease progression. Furthermore, stress has been shown to result in reliable alterations in immune activity. However, the extent to which stress-related immune alterations are associated with clinically relevant health outcomes is still unclear. Many studies have attempted to demonstrate that immune alterations mediate the relationship between stress and health, with limited success. This may be due to the enormous complexity of the immune response and our current techniques for assessing individual immune components in peripheral blood. These measures may not adequately reflect an in vivo immune system response to foreign pathogens or disease. In addition, the relationship between stress-induced immunosuppression and health has not been tested using the appropriate statistical analyses and methodological designs. Longitudinal studies using mediational modeling are necessary to properly test the extent to which observed immunological changes are responsible for differences in disease course.

Nevertheless, interventions designed to improve immunocompetence in response to stress and disease have been promising. At the very least, these interventions have improved quality of life for patients and in some cases have resulted in longer survival and disease-free intervals. However, there is a need for replication and additional research using more standardized interventions that can be tested across patient samples, allowing comparison of results across studies. Elucidation of effective components of psychosocial interventions will also result in more efficient therapies. Although in its infancy, research examining mechanisms through which behavioral interventions may impact disease has provided very suggestive findings regarding the role that the immune system may have in mediating the impact of stress on disease progression.

—*Douglas L. Delahanty and Eve M. Sledjeski*

See also: Behavioral Pediatrics (Vol. II); Early Risk Screening (Vol. III); Memory Rehabilitation After Traumatic Brain Injury (Vol. I)

Suggested Readings

Ader, R., Felten, D., & Cohen, N. (2001). *Psychoneuroimmunology* (3rd ed., Vols. 1 & 2). San Diego, CA: Academic Press.

Antoni, M., Schneiderman, N., Fletcher, M., Goldstein, D., Ironson, G., & Laperriere, A. (1990). Psychoneuroimmunology and HIV-1. *Journal of Consulting and Clinical Psychology, 58,* 38–49.

Garssen, B., & Goodkin, K. (1999). On the role of immunological factors as mediators between psychosocial factors and cancer progression. *Psychiatry Research, 85,* 51–61.

Kiecolt-Glaser, J. K. (1999). Stress, personal relationships, and immune function: Health implications. *Brain, Behavior, and Immunity, 13,* 61–72.

Maier, S. F., & Watkins, L.R. (1998). Cytokines for psychologists: Implications of bidirectional immune-to-brain communication for understanding behavior, mood, and cognition. *Psychological Review, 105,* 83–107.

O'Leary, A. (1990). Stress, emotion, and human immune function. *Psychological Bulletin, 108,* 363–382.

R

RATIONAL-EMOTIVE BEHAVIOR THERAPY

DESCRIPTION OF THE STRATEGY

In 1956, Albert Ellis presented his new approach to psychological treatment at the annual meeting of the American Psychological Association. He called it "rational therapy." Immediately attacked as rationalistic and unconcerned with the emotional aspect of human life, he soon changed the name to "rational-emotive therapy." After many years of being urged to take official note of the clearly behavioral aspects of the theory and practice, Ellis renamed his approach "rational-emotive behavior therapy" (REBT) in the early 1990s.

Ellis did not set out to be a psychological practitioner. He was driven in that direction by one of his long-standing interests: human sexuality and human sexual behavior. His development of REBT was greatly shaped by another of his long-standing passions: philosophy. Having focused on business as an undergraduate, he pursued graduate training in psychology from Columbia University because of the interest and his already developed expertise in human sexuality. His doctoral committee allowed him to pursue a dissertation on the sexual behavior of Columbia University coeds. However, when the data were reviewed, his committee felt the findings were too controversial for publication. He competed a second dissertation, this time on issues in psychological measurement.

Ellis readily accepted the reigning psychoanalytic ethos of his day and completed his own analysis with a psychoanalyst trained in the tradition of Karen Horney. He practiced psychoanalysis and psychoanalytically oriented psychotherapy. However, his interest in sexual dysfunction and the utilization of couples treatment formats showed him that direct, explicit instruction was often more effective and efficient. Reaching back to his lifelong interest in philosophy, he fashioned what was, then, a strikingly different approach to psychological intervention. He especially focused on the insight offered by the Stoic philosopher Epictetus, "Men are not disturbed by events, but by the view they take of them." He first called his approach rational therapy because he took the position that human disturbances (e.g., anger, anxiety, depression, and guilt) were related to irrational beliefs, while more functional, if still negative emotions (e.g., annoyance, concern, sorrow, and regret) were related to rational beliefs.

Ellis made clear from his earliest work on this new theory that he considered human beings to be simultaneously sensing, thinking, emoting, and behavior organisms. While all these functions occurred more or less simultaneously, it was also true that one may be more dominate at any moment. Thus, a person is more often a sensing, THINKING, emoting, behaving individual when, for example, playing chess than when watching her child, the first person in her family to receive a college diploma, walk across the stage at graduation. Then, that person is more likely a sensing, thinking, EMOTING, behaving individual.

Ellis put his treatment approach squarely in the center of an overall philosophy for living that strongly tipped toward hedonism. He held that humans were constantly tempted by short-term pleasures to act against their long-term interests. Thus, from its inception, Ellis encouraged those he served and those he trained to build a high tolerance for frustration. By doing so, each individual could focus on his or her long-term interests rather than giving in to what might feel good at the moment but that also sowed the seeds of later pain and suffering.

In 1950s America, Ellis was iconoclastic in calling for nothing less than a sexual revolution in which sexual pleasure between consenting adults was to be constricted only by avoiding long-term problems such as unwanted children or the transmission of disease. Like Freud before him, Ellis took a very dim view of religious strictures and especially religious sexual prohibitions. Influenced by Karen Horney's "tyranny of the shoulds," Ellis spoke out strongly and forthrightly against absolutistic "shoulds, oughts, and musts" that functioned to deny human enjoyment and fulfillment in this earthly life. He made clear that in his view, this was the only life any human beings were going to have. Standing against both behaviorism and psychoanalysis, and offering blistering attacks on the latter, his approach was an early member of what came to be called the "third force" in psychology.

THE BASIC APPROACH

Then, as now, Ellis offered a simple mnemonic for individuals to grasp the theory, the ABC's of REBT. "A" stands for the activating event. "B" stands for the beliefs we hold about A. "C's" are the emotional and behavioral consequences of B combining with A. When C is dysfunctional (i.e., consists of disturbed emotional responses and self-defeating behavior), the individual is encouraged to D, dispute the irrational beliefs that are believed to be the source of these dysfunctional C's. Effective disputing leads to E, the new, more effective philosophy of living.

IRRATIONAL AND RATIONAL BELIEFS

In the early years, Ellis offered a number of what he labeled "irrational beliefs." Eventually, he saw such lists could become almost endless and set about to determine the core source, or sources, of disturbance. Continuing to focus on absolutistic shoulds, oughts, and musts, he labeled three forms of demandingness as the core sources of disturbance: (1) I must, (2) you must, and (3) the world, or conditions, must. To these, he eventually added three additional sources of disturbance

that he held were derivatives of demandingness. The first is "awfulizing": the notion that since certain things must, or must not, be, it is awful if they might appear or actually do appear. "Awful" was further defined as worse than could possibly be or much worse than actually exists. The second is "frustration intolerance" or "I-can't-stand-it-itis": the notion that since certain things must, or must not, be, it is literally unbearable if they might appear or actually do appear. The third is "person rating" or "downing self and others": The notion that since certain things must, or must not, be, one's human worth goes up if one does as he or she must do and down if he or she does not.

Every irrational belief has its rational counterpart. Ellis recognized a difference between what absolutely must be and what contingently must be. Thus, it is one thing to insist, "I must pass this required class if I am to graduate" and another to insist, "I absolutely must pass this class or absolutely must graduate." "Contingent must's" are rational in the sense that one can check and see whether they are, in fact, true. "Absolute must's" are different. Ellis remains fond of referring to "Jehovahian commands and demands," noting the individual had assumed the role of a god. As an atheist, he also gave short shrift to the notion that any commands are demands that had ever been issued by supernatural beings. Similarly, one may have many reasons why it would be preferable if I, you, or the world went in a certain direction. However, because something is reasonable or desirable does not mean it absolutely must exist.

Ellis was quick to admit that many things were indeed bad, meaning we do not like them or we prefer something different. However, it is one thing to maintain that things are bad and another to insist they are worse than can possibly be or much worse than they actually are. He noted that "I don't like it" may be quite true, but it is a far cry from "I can't stand it." Finally, while human beings may have many kinds of worth (e.g., worker worth, mate worth, parent worth, friend worth, etc.) and while these worths may vary from high to low, one's membership in the human family, their human worth, does not vary. Either one is a human being or one is not. Even a human being with very low social worth is still a human being. Even if a person has a genetic defect, he or she remains a human being, albeit one with a genetic defect. In this sense, REBT is profoundly humanistic. There are not good humans or bad humans. All are equal in their humanity.

FUNCTIONAL AND DYSFUNCTIONAL EMOTIONS AND BEHAVIORS

Rational beliefs were asserted to be related to functional emotions and overt behaviors, while irrational beliefs were asserted to be related to dysfunctional emotions and overt behaviors. Functional emotions are not necessary positive in the sense of pleasant. For example, when one acts badly and feels regret, the emotion is negative. However, that regret is also helpful in getting one to change one's behavior. Thus, regret is negative but functional. The functionality comes from getting the individual to focus on what was done wrong and how to do otherwise in the next instance. This can be contrasted with guilt. Here, the individual behaves as if he or she has not only done a bad thing, but has become a bad person. Only doing penance, including feeling guilty for "long enough," can restore one's self to the status of "good." What one focuses on is not the badness of the act, but the badness of self. Once self is redeemed, one is just as likely to act badly again, because no focus has been placed on the badness or wrongness of what was done in terms of the practical, bad effects associated with the action. Thus, guilt is negative and dysfunctional.

A similar analysis can be given for positive emotions. When one performs well at an activity and believes, "This is great," one is likely to feel good. However, if one believes, "I am great," one is likely to feel personally superior and act condescendingly toward those who perform less well. While such feelings of superiority may feel good, they are not functional in long-term human interactions, and often not even in short-term human interactions. Thus, positive emotions also can be functional and dysfunctional.

Theoretically, at the time of any given activating event (A), both rational and irrational beliefs are engaged. These lead to tendencies toward functional emotions and behaviors and dysfunctional emotions and behaviors. The emotions and behaviors actually produced are determined by the relative strength of the related beliefs. Thus, one might feel sorry, but also somewhat guilty. A therapist responding to a client in such a situation would affirm the rational beliefs and functional sorrow related to them while also encouraging the client to recognize the irrational beliefs associated with guilt. These irrational beliefs would then be disputed in an attempt to produce a more effective philosophy for living and the elimination of guilt.

COMPLEX ANALYSIS

While the basic A-B-C-D-E components of the theory are relatively simple and straightforward, they also offer the possibility for complex analysis. This is because REBT recognizes that individuals may have secondary problems as a result of their reactions to their original reactions. Thus, an individual could fail or think about past failures, respond strongly with the belief, "This is awful and unbearable," and respond weakly, or not at all, with the belief, "This is unfortunate and too bad," and produce emotional consequences of mainly depression and, possibly, some sorrow. However, the same individual could treat this first-level emotional C as a new activating event (A_2). To this A_2, the individual could respond strongly with, "This tendency to get depressed proves me worthless," and quite weakly, or not at all, with the belief, "This tendency to get depressed is just one more human fallibility but doesn't make me any more or less human." The likely result is greater depression or depression over being depressed and, possibly, some sorrow. While the dysfunctional C in both cases is depression, the irrational beliefs are different. In the first round, the source is awfulizing and frustration intolerance. In the second round, it is self-downing. Third-level disturbance is also a possibility. The second dysfunctional C becomes yet another activating event (A_3). To this A_3, the individual responds strongly with, "It will be awful and unbearable if my future were to continue with depression, so it absolutely must not be in my future," and weakly, or not at all with, "If I have depression in my future, that will be unfortunate, but unfortunate things can happen to me." The likely result is anxiety and possibly concern. This type of anxiety is labeled "discomfort" anxiety and contrasted with "ego anxiety," which would be produced by predictions of becoming a "louse," "worm," "crumb," "no-good-nick," or whatever the individual's terminology for "would fall on the scale of humanity." An observer would see the individual with both anxiety and depression. However, the theoretical analysis would show there are two levels of depression and a third level of anxiety. The first level depression is related to actual and current failure in the world or to thoughts about past failures through awfulizing and frustration intolerance. The second-level depression is related to the depression sensations themselves through self-rating. The third-level anxiety is related to the possible continuation of bodily sensations, namely, depression sensations, rather than to events outside one's skin, such as anxiety related to thoughts of possible failure of a marriage or on a test. The means by which this anxiety is related to the depression is by discomfort anxiety (i.e., awfulizing and frustration intolerance), rather than ego anxiety (i.e., self-downing). It is important to note, as is apparent from this example that anything, such as thoughts, images, sensations, events outside one's skin, or whatever, can serve as an activating event. Activating events are not limited to any particular event category.

DISPUTATION

The theoretical analysis guides the disputing process. Offering disputes for ego anxiety when the irrational belief is actually discomfort anxiety is unlikely to be effective. Furthermore, if both ego anxiety and discomfort anxiety were involved, then separate disputes for each would need to be offered. Similarly, disputes for awfulizing and frustration intolerance of past failures that are related to depression will not address depression related to self-downing over past or current failures.

There is also a theorized order of operations for disputing, namely, disputing first takes place at the last level of disturbance and works backward to the first level. Thus, in this hypothesized case, anxiety would first be addressed, then depression related to self-downing, and finally depression related to awfulizing and frustration intolerance. Intuitively, it might seem that successfully disputing the primary level irrational belief(s) would automatically end the sequence of disturbance. However, metaphorically speaking, it is as if each level of disturbance is piled one on top of another so that secondary and tertiary disturbance hold the primary disturbance fast under their weight. It is for this reason that "blocks of disturbance" are removed in reverse order of their production.

PHILOSOPHIC CHANGE

Almost from the beginning, REBT was viewed as an approach to human suffering to be made accessible to all. Ellis aimed not merely at the reduction of particular symptoms, but at deep philosophic change. By the early 1960s, he and Robert Harper had coauthored self-help books aimed to help ordinary people apply the principles to reduce their own disturbance, live more fulfilling lives, and deal more effectively and humanely with the disturbances of those around them.

Physician Maxi Maultsby adapted the principles of REBT especially to the problems of alcohol misuse and labeled his approach "rational behavior therapy." Paul Hauk also wrote a number of the early self-help books, and his contributions continued for several decades. By the mid-1960s, Ellis had established a center in New York City that not only had the function of training practitioners but also of encouraging what he viewed as a more humane and rational approach to living. From then until today, virtually no Friday night has passed at what is now the Albert Ellis Institute without public demonstrations applying the principles of REBT to problems of daily living brought to the stage by volunteer clients. Philosophically, REBT puts forth a positive agenda encouraging values such as self-interest, social interest, self-direction, high frustration tolerance, flexibility, commitment to creative pursuits, acceptance of uncertainty, scientific thinking, self-acceptance, risk taking, long-range hedonism, and acceptance of imperfectability of self, others, and the world.

PRACTITIONER STYLE

A word must be said about the often irreverent, acerbic, and profane language used by Albert Ellis. In short, it is a style adopted for its effect. There is nothing in REBT that requires this style and if evidenced as not useful with a particular client, even Ellis quickly drops it. REBT is not defined by the style of the practitioner, but by the application of the A-B-C-D-E process to client concerns. The style with which it is presented varies with the effectiveness of that style with the client at hand and the predilections of the practitioner. At no time is style intended to trump substance. On the other hand, REBT is often intentionally evocative, because when clients experience their disturbances with the practitioner in the consultation room, they can work directly on the beliefs associated with those disturbances and experience the immediate result. In such cases, treatment is not about something that happens somewhere else, but addresses events immediately present, at least psychologically, in the consultation room.

INNOVATIVE ADJUNCTS TO TREATMENT

Ellis made readings part of the treatment process and incorporated tape recordings addressing various topics when the technology became available. He also made tapes of client sessions, which clients took home with them to review as part of their away-from-session homework, though most practitioners of REBT do not follow this practice. Homework has been an essential aspect of REBT from the beginning and harks back to Ellis's early days of making explicit homework assignments to couples receiving treatment for sexual and other difficulties. Today, there are literally hundreds of self-help books pamphlets and tapes relating the principles of REBT to the problems of living. For a few years, the center sponsored a school that aimed at bringing rational-emotive principles into the classroom. This work was later forwarded by a number of authors, most prominently Anne Vernon and Michael Benard. Despite Ellis's atheism, the principles of REBT have been expanded to the areas of religion and spirituality.

THE NECESSITY OF AN EMOTIONAL BOND

This emphasis on self-help and the presumed capability of individuals to make changes through their own efforts is importantly related to the REBT view of the relationship between client and practitioner. Namely, REBT views a strong emotional bond between client and practitioner as often desirable in treatment but not a necessary requirement for change. It recognizes that many individuals have made important, useful, and even profound changes in their lives based on lectures or talks they have heard or materials they have read.

TYPES OF BELIEFS

In the early 1980s, Ruth and Rick Wessler suggested distinctions be drawn between three different types of beliefs: perceptual, inferential, and evaluative. Consider a couple sitting on a couch. Two observers could argue as to whether one member of the couple had her arm around the other or whether it lay on the couch behind. This would be a disagreement about *perceptual beliefs*. Having agreed that one member had her arm around the other rather than on the couch behind, one of the observers might infer that one member of the couple was upset and the other was offering comfort. The other observer might infer that one was making a sexual advance toward the other. This would be a disagreement about *inferential beliefs*. Finally, the observers could agree that one member had her arm around the other rather than on the couch behind and that a sexual advance was being

made rather than comforting being offered, and disagree in their evaluations. One might evaluate such behavior as bad while the other evaluated it as good. This would be a disagreement about *evaluate beliefs*. The point was strongly made that REBT disputing is initially and primarily made toward evaluative beliefs. Thus, in the example cited above, a practitioner would focus on whether the individual evaluating the overt behavior and inferred meaning as "bad" did not escalate from "bad" to "awful" or from "good" to "absolutely perfect." Alternately, the practitioner might check to see that the individual did not escalate from "What is being done is a bad act" to "The person has become a bad person." This emphasis distinguished REBT from approaches that attempted to show individuals that such thoughts such as "Every body hates me" were factually mistaken. Rather, REBT focused on disputing the notion that "Life is awful and unbearable if people do as they must not and all hate me." It is not perceptual thinking errors that are the focus of REBT, but evaluative ones, because the latter were hypothesized to be associated with dysfunctional emotions and behavior. Once clients are no longer disturbed, they often are encouraged to check as to whether they might also be factually mistaken.

SYSTEMATIZATION OF DISPUTING

Disputing has been systematized largely by Ray DiGiuseppe and colleagues. Four types of disputes have been identified: logical, empirical, functional, and alternative rational belief. *Logical disputes* are problematic because many individuals simply do not understand what it is to commit a logical fallacy. For example, logic requires that there be two premises that can be connected in such a way that a conclusion can be drawn. A classic example is, "All men have Y chromosomes. This individual is a man. Therefore, this individual has a Y chromosome." Thus, it is illogical to conclude that "Because I do not like something, it must not exist, because a conclusion is drawn from only one premise." Alternatively, there might be two premises, but not related in such a way that a conclusion can logically be drawn. For example, "A bad thing was done. John did it. Therefore, John is a jerk." In this case, there are two premises, but the conclusion does not logically follow. To use logical disputes, the person with whom they are to be used must already be sensitive to logical fallacies or must first be taught to be sensitive to them.

A second type of dispute is empirical. *Empirical disputes* are often easy to misunderstand and misuse. Their use underlines an important distinction between REBT and certain other cognitive-behavioral approaches. Consider a client who feels depressed and reports thinking or overtly states, "Everyone hates me." One notion of empirical disputing would be to have the individual actually check with all those in her environment to determine whether, indeed, everyone does hate her. The therapist makes this assignment assuming the facts would show there are some people in the client's environment who do not hate her. Thus, she would be encouraged to change her assertion and reduce her depression. As noted above, this is not the REBT approach.

Empirical disputing in REBT takes a different approach, because it is directed at irrational beliefs. This is not to say that the individual might not be wrong about her assessment of how the world actually is. People do make such mistakes, and an REBT therapist would eventually get around to checking on the accuracy of these beliefs. However, the basic REBT premise is that it is not things, but our view of them that causes our emotional problems. Thus, REBT disputing does not start with the A, or activating event. It assumes, for the moment, the client is correct, and goes on to look at what irrational beliefs the individual might hold about the A. Thus, the therapist would look for beliefs such as, "When every one hates me, as they absolutely must not, it is awful, unbearable, and proves me no good." Only then would any empirical disputing begin, and it would be directly targeted at the irrational beliefs.

Thus, in classical Ellisonian disputation style, "Where is the evidence that when everyone hates you it is awful?" "Where is the evidence that someone absolutely must like you?" "Where is the evidence that you cannot bear everyone hating you?" "Where is the evidence what when everyone hates you, then you become utterly worthless and no good?" In fact, there is no evidence for any of these assertions. However, what clients assume to be evidence must also be addressed.

A common response is what is sometimes termed *emotional reasoning*. A client might assert, "The fact that I am depressed proves it (the activating event) is awful." "No," the therapist could respond. "It only proves that when you stick with insisting that things you do not want to happen are awful, you then feel depressed. Being depressed doesn't prove the things

are, in fact, awful. It just proves that when you believe something is awful, you get depressed."

"Well, they certainly feel awful," the client might respond. "Yes," the therapist could reply, "but many things feel or seem to be a certain way. That doesn't prove they are that way. It certainly looks, feels, or seems that the sun rises and sets, but it doesn't. The earth turns. That certain things look or feel or seem a certain way does not prove that is how they actually are." Thus, empirical disputing in REBT shows clients there is no empirical or factual evidence on which to base their irrational beliefs, though there may or may not be evidence to back up their views of various activating events.

Functional disputes look at the function of sticking with certain irrational beliefs and show clients that by changing their beliefs, they more likely could have emotional and behavioral responses they desire. Here is an example. "So, when you stick with, 'I must please other people, and it will be awful if I do not,' you end up feeling anxious over the possibility that you might not please them, right? Thus, if you would like to be less anxious, you could work to give up the notion that you absolutely must please other people and that it will be awful if you do not." With functional disputes, the relationship between irrational beliefs and unwanted C's is underlined. The client is shown that if she does not want a certain outcome, she can achieve it by relinquishing its cause, namely, the irrational belief, or beliefs, associated with it.

Alternative rational beliefs are considered a kind of dispute, because by showing clients what they could believe instead of their irrational beliefs, the clients are encouraged to give up those beliefs. As previously noted, REBT takes the notion that for every irrational belief, there is also a rational belief, just as for every dysfunctional emotional and behavioral response, there is a functional, if not perfect, response. With regard to awfulizing, a little creative thought will show that no matter how bad things are, they could be worse, and usually a lot worse. Thus, one could be in a vehicular crash and be paralyzed from the neck down and in constant pain for 20 years. It is also possible that several loved ones could be burned and maimed in the crash and go on suffering long after the accident. Almost all individuals agree that since they would be conscious of their loved ones' suffering, their situation would be even worse. Most of the things individuals actually suffer pale in comparison to this scenario. While it may be true that this or that thing feels or seems awful, REBT maintains a clear distinction between how things feel or seem and how they actually are. An alternative rational belief for awfulizing is, "Even with this bad thing in my life, things could be worse and, likely, a lot worse."

When individuals stick with the notion that something is unbearable, the REBT therapist can point out that as a matter of fact, they actually are bearing it. Until we die or escape some other way, we stand anything. The only real question is how well we stand it: well or less than well. Sticking with the notion that we cannot bear something that we are bearing or might bear leads only to bearing it less well. Thus, "I do not like something" may, indeed, prove that "I do not like it." However, not liking something does not prove that "I cannot bear it." An alternative rational belief for frustration intolerance is, "I don't like it, but I can stand it."

As a lyric for one of his famous "rational songs," Albert Ellis once penned, "Demandingness will land you less than what you really want." In so doing, he provided a functional dispute to absolutistic musts. It is his insistence that outside the world of definitions there are no absolutes that has caused Ellis and REBT to receive so much criticism. REBT makes all actions relative to the deepest desires of the client and to no one else and nothing else, including religious or other social authorities.

It is a well-known philosophic truism that "About taste, there is no argument." If you like something, you like it, and that is all that can be said. However, there may be quite a bit to be said about indulging your preference because of the practical consequences of doing so. Thus, there certainly are "contingent must's." If you want this, then you must do that. If you do not want that, then you must not do this. It is too bad to want things that are incompatible with other desires, but we often do, and that is just part of the human predicament. Often, we just cannot have it all. REBT recognizes both preferences and "contingent musts" and shows individuals that some courses of action are wiser than others relative to the individual's deepest desires. By attending to the contingencies operating in the world and in themselves, individuals can also work to get what they want and avoid what they do not want. However, none of us is running the universe, and thus none can effectively issue a godlike, Jehovahian command that "The world must go my way." That includes only and always desiring what we want to desire and never desiring what we don't

want to desire. Similarly, there may be 5 or 500 very good reasons for the world to go a certain way, either from our individual perspectives or the perspective of the entire human race. But just because something is judged by one or all to be wiser, preferable, or desirable does not mean that it absolutely must exist. Just because something is judged by one or all to be foolish or detrimental does not mean that it absolutely must not exist. An alternative rational belief for demandingness is that "I, or humanity in general, can run some things, but not every thing" or "Because I, or humanity in general, want it doesn't mean I, or we, must get it."

DISPUTATION STYLE

Disputes can also very in the way they are presented. They may be presented didactically: "It is not true that the world must go your way even if you have very good reasons for wanting it to go your way." They may be presented Socratically: "Is it really true that the world must go your way even if you have very good reasons for wanting it to go your way?" They can be presented metaphorically: "Even Superman can't make other people desire to do what he wants them to." They also can be presented humorously: "Did God really call you up and say, 'I'm busy. Would you mind running the world for awhile?'"

REBT is almost alone in its long advocacy and systematic use of humor in psychological treatment. This can be seen in audacious, irreverent quips such as, "Masterbation means self-abuse" or "You are not a worm for acting wormily." It is also found in rational humorous songs that are a staple of public presentations and demonstrations of REBT. The offering below illustrates poking fun at awfulizing about the problems of being a parent and is sung to the tune of "Santa Claus Is Coming to Town."

My child doesn't work
As hard as I wish.
No other Mom (Dad)
Has trouble like this?
How dare my kid(s) make trouble for me!
S/he's (They're) hard to teach
As s/he (they) MUST NOT be.
Children SHOULD be EASY on me.
How dare my kid(s) make trouble for me!
It's such a crying shame now,
That I have what I've got.

I'm living with a child now,
What I need is a RO*BOT.*
So I'm g'onna get mad,
And maybe depressed,
Scream and yell, and
Beat my chest.
How dare my kid(s) make trouble for me!

As with all forms of disputing, the intention is to reduce the controlling role of irrational beliefs and increase the controlling role of rational beliefs. While the practitioner humorously ridicules the irrational beliefs and encourages the client to do the same, the practitioner explicitly works against individuals ridiculing themselves or others for having their irrational beliefs or experiencing the dysfunctional emotional and behavioral responses associated with them. This distinction between using humor to ridicule irrational beliefs, but not to ridicule the person holding them, is fundamental to the philosophical stance of REBT and thus to effective disputing. Human beings are viewed as fallible. That is the way they are. Using a religious inflection, one can learn to hate the sin but not the sinner.

TREATMENT SEQUENCE SUMMARY

The rational-emotive behavior therapy treatment sequence has been summarized by Windy Dryden, a British psychology professor and private practitioner, who has now written, cowritten, and edited more books on this form of treatment than even its founder, Albert Ellis.

Step 1: With the client, identify why certain emotional and behavioral reactions are problematic and why changing them is desirable. *Tom comes in because he is depressed over his wife threatening to leave him due to his overdrinking alcohol and failing to follow up on home and work responsibilities.*

Step 2: Have the client to give at least one specific example of the problematic emotional/behavioral reaction. *Tom went drinking after work last night instead of coming home for dinner and going to one of his children's school plays.*

Step 3: Determine specifically which part of the activating event your client responded to with an irrational belief. Assume the client's view of the activating event is accurate and explore what he or she believes about it. *Tom maintains that his day at work was difficult and he must be able to take a break when he needs one. Drinking helps him relax.*

Step 4: Determine whether there is a secondary or tertiary emotional problem (i.e., a problem about having the emotional/behavioral problem that is targeted for change) and also determine whether the emotional/behavioral problem that is targeted for change is itself a secondary or tertiary emotional problem. *Tom sees that his behavior hurts his marriage, and he blames and condemns himself for acting stupidly. He not only feels sad, but depressed and angry at himself.*

Step 5: Teach the general principle that beliefs are the source of emotional and behavioral reactions to activating events. *Tom is shown that if he thought there was $1 million waiting for him at home, he would have skipped drinking and gone home, even though when he arrived, he found there was no money. Thus, his beliefs about the world, rather than the world itself, would be controlling the way he operates in the world.*

Step 6: Determine which specific rational beliefs and irrational beliefs the client holds that are relevant to the emotional and behavioral consequences and, if possible, express them in both specific and general terms. *Specifically, Tom believes that after a hard day at work, he must be able to relax by drinking. Generally, Tom believes that he simply must have certain things in life that he wants. Specifically, Tom believes that when his drinking produces bad results, he becomes a bad person and should be blamed and condemned for his drinking and its bad results. Generally, Tom believes that when people do things that are bad, they become bad people and should be blamed and condemned.*

Step 7: Show the client how holding these specific believes in specific instances leads to disturbance. *Tom is shown that if he only preferred to relax but did not demand it, he would not feel compelled to drink. Tom is also shown that if he condemned bad acts but did not condemn those who do bad acts as bad people and then blame and condemn them, then he would not experience depression and self-anger.*

Step 8: Use factual, logical, and pragmatic disputes and alternative rational beliefs presented Socratically, didactically, humorously, and metaphorically to undermine adherence to irrational beliefs. *Tom is shown that the world does not HAVE TO go his way no matter how much he wants it to or how many good reasons he has for the world to go his way, because he is not running the world, and whatever the world runs on, it is not reason. Tom is shown he can stick with his preferences but give up his demands. He is shown that even though something is unpleasant in the moment (forgoing drinking after work), he can make himself do it for the sake of something he holds to be more important (better relations with his wife). He is shown that even when he has strong urges in his skin, he does not have to go along with the notion that he absolutely must follow his urges. Rather, even when strong urges are present, he does not lose control of his hands, feet, and mouth. Because something is hard to do does not make it impossible. Tom is also shown that he can "Condemn the sin but not the sinner." He can stop putting himself down for his bad behavior, because bad behavior does not make him a bad person. It only makes him a person who acted badly. Sorrow for bad behavior can help to change that behavior in the future, but depression and self-hatred are unnecessary to live a life that is fulfilling.*

Step 9: Show the client that "knowing" the right answer is not the same as having a deeply held conviction and that the latter will take work and practice but is the truly important change to make. *Tom is asked to say, "I am a banana." When he does, he is asked if he really believes he is a banana. His "no" helps him see that words are not the same as deeply held convictions. Becoming more convinced is related to making himself act in the new way and allowing the consequences of the new action to convince him that the new way of acting really is better than the old way. "Willpower" to follow his new direction goes up by making himself follow the new direction. "Willpower" is not something that he must first have to start moving in that direction.*

Step 10: Encourage the client to turn the new learning into a deeply held conviction using *cognitive* (written or taped disputes, rational self-statements, teaching others, audio or bibliotherapy), *emotive* (rational-emotive imagery, emotive self-presentation of self-dialogue and self-statements, shame-attacking exercises, parables and wise sayings, rational humorous songs or poetry), and *behavioral* (exposure,

fixed-role, "as if" therapy, assertive training, using rewards and penalties) methods as well as inference testing to practice, practice, practice new ways of responding. *Tom is encouraged to go over his disputes and alternative rational beliefs several times a day. He is encouraged to keep track of his thoughts and his urges and notice that he does not have to go along with either the thought, "Going drinking would be pleasant, therefore I MUST go," or the urge to drink. While with his practitioner, he goes over how to respond more effectively using visual imagery. He is encouraged to do the imagery of more effective actions several times a day. He is encouraged to keep records and bring them in. He is given a tape of his session to go over while commuting to and from work.*

Step 11: Check up on homework assignments to ensure compliance. *When Tom comes in for future sessions, his records are reviewed and he is asked about listening to his tape between sessions.*

Step 12: Facilitate the working-through process by encouraging the client to take on new homework assignments and continue to work on adopting a new philosophic outlook on life, recognizing that backsliding and nonsensical thinking are a common part of human existence and accepting that our best hope is to deal with them effectively when they occur rather than maintain the hope that we will some day eliminate them. *Tom is encouraged to begin working against his awfulizing and low frustration tolerance about workplace situations so that at the end of the day, he is not so exhausted and distraught. He is also encouraged to simultaneously look for a new, more satisfying, work situation.*

—*Hank Robb*

See also: *Behavior Therapy (Vol. II); Negative Cognitions (Vol. I); Social Skills Instruction (Vol. III)*

Suggested Readings

Dryden, W. (Ed.). (2003). *Rational emotive behaviour therapy theoretical developments.* East Sussex, UK: Brunner-Routledge.

Dryden, W., & DiGiuseppe, R. (1990). *A primer on rational-emotive therapy.* Champaign, IL: Research Press.

Ellis, A. (1994). *Reason and emotion in psychotherapy: Revised and updated.* Secaucus, NJ: Birch Lane Press.

Ellis, A., & Dryden, W. (1987). *The practice of rational emotive therapy.* New York: Springer.

Nielsen, S. L., Johnson, W. B., & Ellis, A. (2001). *Counseling and psychotherapy with religious persons: A rational emotive behavioral therapy approach.* Mahwah, NJ: Erlbaum.

Walen, S. R., DiGiuseppe, R., & Dryden, W. (1992). *A practitioner's guide to rational-emotive therapy* (2nd ed.). New York: Oxford University Press.

REINFORCEMENT

DESCRIPTION OF THE STRATEGY

Reinforcement is the process by which experience changes behavior or, stated more fully, the process by which experience changes the environmental control of behavior. Reinforcement plays a role in the emergence of complex behavior that is analogous to the role played by natural selection in the evolution of species. That is, through the cumulative effects of reinforcement, the behavior of the newborn is shaped into the behavior of the adult. Reinforcement is a fundamental focus of the experimental analysis of behavior and is basic to the interpretation of behavior in the natural environment. In experimental analysis, behavior is studied under highly controlled circumstances, usually in the laboratory, where, essentially, all of the variables that control behavior can be manipulated and all of their relevant effects measured. In interpretation, behavior is explained, but through the exclusive use of principles uncovered by experimental analysis when circumstances do not permit experimental analysis. Complex behavior, including much adult human behavior and applied behavior analysis, is the province of interpretation. The experimental analysis of reinforcement is emphasized here, because understanding reinforcement is key to interpreting and modifying behavior in the natural environment.

At the behavioral scale of measurement, reinforcement occurs when a stimulus that elicits a response is introduced into an ongoing stream of environmental and behavioral events. The eliciting stimulus may be the product of either natural selection, as when food elicits salivation, or of prior reinforcement, as when a tone elicits salivation after being paired with food. An eliciting stimulus that increases the environmental control of behavior is said to function as a reinforcing stimulus, or *reinforcer.* An eliciting stimulus that decreases the strength of an environment-behavior relation is said to function as a punishing stimulus, or *punisher.* When a stimulus has become an elicitor through natural selection, it functions as an *unconditioned,* or *primary, reinforcer.* When a stimulus becomes an elicitor through prior reinforcement, it functions as a *conditioned,* or *secondary, reinforcer.*

EXPERIMENTAL ANALYSIS OF REINFORCEMENT

In the laboratory, two basic procedures are used to investigate reinforcement: the classical procedure and the operant procedure. In the classical procedure, the reinforcing stimulus is introduced after an environmental event, and that environment acquires control of the response elicited by the reinforcer. For example, if a tone is regularly followed by a food stimulus (which elicits salivation), then the tone comes to control salivation. In the operant procedure, the reinforcing stimulus is introduced after a behavioral event, and the environment acquires control of that behavior as well as the elicited response. For example, if a rat sees and presses a lever and the press is regularly followed by a food stimulus, then the sight of the lever acquires control over lever pressing as well as salivation. In the classical example, food strengthened the tone-salivation relation. In the operant example, food strengthened both the tone-lever press and the tone-salivation relation. The present treatment of reinforcement focuses on the operant procedure because an arbitrary behavior (e.g., lever pressing) may be brought under the control of the environment, whereas the classical procedure allows only elicited responses (e.g., salivation) to come under environmental control. The full behavioral capabilities of the learner are modifiable only with operant procedures.

TEMPORAL RELATIONS WITH THE REINFORCER

The first factor identified in the effort to formulate an experimentally grounded principle of reinforcement was *contiguity.* Contiguity in the operant procedure refers to the time interval between the behavior and the reinforcer (and, perforce, between environmental stimuli accompanying the response and the reinforcer). The general conclusion from studies using a variety of operant procedures is that the reinforcer most strongly strengthens control by the environment of whatever behavior immediately precedes the reinforcer. Studies of the effect of contiguity are complicated in the operant procedure because other behavior has an opportunity to intrude into the time interval between the critical response and the reinforcing stimulus as the interval increases. Other environment-behavior relations can then occur closer in time to the reinforcer and be strengthened more than the relation of interest.

Although a reinforcer selects the environment-behavior relation that immediately precedes it, experienced organisms give the appearance of tolerating longer intervals until the reinforcer. For example, when a sound has previously been paired with food, lever pressing can be acquired with an appreciable delay until food if lever pressing is immediately followed by the sound. The sound functions as an immediate conditioned reinforcer. Human behavior that appears to be maintained by delayed reinforcers is typically sustained by immediate conditioned reinforcers. Conditioned reinforcers can be provided by environmental stimuli, such as immediate approval by a coworker for work that is not compensated with money for days. Conditioned reinforcers can also be provided by stimuli produced by the learner's own behavior, as when a behavior produces stimuli that have previously been paired with a reinforcer, for example, a work product that is discriminated as "well-done."

B. F. Skinner stressed the importance of contiguity between the behavior and the reinforcer—what he called the "moment of reinforcement." In his words, "To say that a reinforcement is contingent upon a response may mean nothing more than that it follows the response. . . . Conditioning takes place because of the temporal relation only." Note that Skinner used the term *contingency* in its dictionary sense: "(a) an event that may but is not certain to occur; (b) something liable to happen as an adjunct to . . . something else" (Merriam-Webster). To hold that a reinforcer is contingent on behavior is simply to say that these events occurred together in time on at least one occasion. Of course, a number of such moment-to-moment contingencies are often required to have the cumulative effect of strengthening an environment-behavior relation.

BEHAVIORAL DISCREPANCY AND REINFORCEMENT

Until the late 1960s, it was thought that contiguity with the reinforcer was all that was required to strengthen an environment-behavior relation. However, using first the classical procedure and then the operant procedure, experimental analysis demonstrated that reinforcement required the reinforcer to elicit a response that constituted a change in ongoing behavior. This second factor is known as the *behavioral-discrepancy* requirement. As an illustration of the discrepancy requirement, suppose that lever pressing is reinforced with food only when a light is on. Consistent with the contiguity requirement, when the light is present, the sight of the lever acquires control over pressing because the immediate presentation of food serves as a reinforcer. (A stimulus-response-reinforcer sequence exemplifies a *three-term contingency*.) Suppose that the light is then accompanied by a tone and that lever pressing continues to produce food as before. Note that the tone-press relation now also meets the contiguity requirement (i.e., the light-press relation is followed by food). If contiguity were all that was required for reinforcement, then the tone should also acquire control over lever pressing. However, when the tone is presented alone without the light, lever pressing does not occur! This finding demonstrates that contiguity is not enough. What else is required? Research revealed that an environment-behavior relation is reinforced by an eliciting stimulus only if the eliciting stimulus evokes a response that differs from ongoing behavior. Because the light already evoked salivation because it had previously been paired with food during lever-press training, the response elicited by food during the tone did not constitute a change: The animal was already salivating when the food arrived. Thus, for reinforcement to take place, the environment-behavior relation must immediately precede an eliciting stimulus that evokes a response that is not occurring at that moment. In nontechnical terms, the learner must be "surprised" by the reinforcer. As an everyday example of the discrepancy requirement, praise from an overly indulgent parent would not be an effective conditioned reinforcer because praise is fully expected.

In summary, the current understanding of the principle of reinforcement based on experimental analysis is that the environmental control of behavior changes when behavior is immediately followed (the contiguity requirement) by a stimulus that elicits a behavior that is not occurring at that moment (the discrepancy requirement). This principle applies equally well to environment-behavior relations produced with either the classical or operant procedure and, for that reason, is called the *unified reinforcement principle*. In the classical procedure, the environment acquires control over the reinforcer-elicited response. In the operant procedure, the environment acquires control over the response that precedes the reinforcer as well as the reinforcer-elicited response.

RELATED FORMULATIONS OF THE REINFORCEMENT PRINCIPLE

Before the contiguity and discrepancy requirements were fully understood, several other empirical formulations were proposed. These formulations remain useful for some purposes and can be reconciled with the unified reinforcement principle. Research by David Premack demonstrated that a response could be reinforced if it was immediately followed by the opportunity to engage in a stronger response. As an illustration, running by a rat in an activity wheel (a lower-probability response) could be strengthened by the opportunity to drink a sweet liquid (a higher-probability response). Reinforcement with this contingency is anticipated; sweet-tasting liquids strongly elicit drinking. However, more noteworthy was the finding that reinforcement could also occur when the contingency was reversed: Drinking could be strengthened by the opportunity to run if conditions were arranged such that running was more probable than drinking. For example, running could be made more probable by reducing access to the running wheel prior to the experiment, and drinking could be made less probable by reducing the sweetness of the liquid. The reversibility of the reinforcing contingency led to the formulation of the probability-differential hypothesis of reinforcement, or the Premack principle: Reinforcement occurs if a lower-probability response is followed by the opportunity to engage in a higher-probability response. This formulation provides a useful, but not infallible, rule of thumb for applied behavior analysis. The therapist can determine the baseline levels of various activities in which the client normally engages and then institute contingencies whereby lower-probability desirable behavior is followed by stimuli that permit higher-probability behavior. For example, 10 minutes of homework (a lower-probability response) could be followed by the opportunity to play a video game (a higher-probability response). Note that the conditions that satisfy the probability-differential hypothesis also meet the contiguity and discrepancy requirements. The stimulus that controls the higher-probability response is immediately presented after the lower-probability response, and the higher-probability response represents a change in ongoing behavior.

Experimental analysis conducted by William Timberlake and James Allison subsequently demonstrated that reinforcement could occur under conditions that violated the probability-differential hypothesis. Specifically, the opportunity to engage in a *lower*-probability response could reinforce a higher-probability response if the learner had been deprived of the opportunity to engage in the lower-probability response. As an example, a low-probability response such as running in an activity wheel could increase a high-probability response such as drinking when the animal had been precluded from running in the wheel as often as when access to the wheel was unrestricted. Stated differently, the opportunity to engage in a response of any probability could serve as a reinforcer if the learner had been deprived of the opportunity to engage in that response to its normal baseline level. This finding led to the response-deprivation hypothesis of reinforcement. Note that the response-deprivation hypothesis is also consistent with the unified reinforcement principle. Deprivation of the opportunity to engage in a response increases the strength of that response when the stimuli that permit it become available. Thus, response deprivation causes stimuli that control the contingent response to become effective eliciting stimuli, thereby producing a larger behavioral discrepancy when these stimuli occur immediately after the operant (noncontingent) response.

REINFORCEMENT AND PUNISHMENT

Reinforcement and punishment seem very different phenomena; the first refers to strengthening an environment-behavior relation and the second to weakening a relation. However, the unified reinforcement principle indicates that the two phenomena can be different consequences of the same process. When a behavioral discrepancy occurs in an operant procedure, the environment acquires control over two classes of responses: the behavior that precedes the reinforcer and the elicited response that is evoked by the reinforcer. If components of the elicited response are incompatible with the behavior preceding the eliciting stimulus, then the strength of the operant can be reduced. Consider the case in which food-reinforced lever pressing is followed by shock. Shock elicits escape responses that cause the animal to withdraw from the stimuli that control lever pressing and, in that way, reduces the strength of lever pressing. Lever pressing cannot occur when the animal is escaping from the environment that controls lever pressing. When operant responses and elicited responses compete, the net effect of the same process that strengthens behavior can cause the operant to weaken. If the environmental control of competing elicited responses extinguishes, the operant behavior that precedes the elicitor recovers its strength. However, if the environmental control of elicited responses persists, the behavior remains weak. The interaction between operants and elicited responses reveals itself in other ways. For example, when pecking a disk by a pigeon produces grain as the reinforcer, pecking responses include opening the beak as if to consume grain. When pecking the disk produces water as a reinforcer, operant pecking includes throat movements that occur during drinking. In applied behavior analysis, possible interactions between operant and reinforcer-elicited responses must also be considered. For example, if a developmentally disabled child is being taught to reach for a toothbrush using a treat as a reinforcer, obtaining the treat should not require limb movements that are incompatible with those required to reach for the toothbrush.

SCOPE OF A BEHAVIORAL ANALYSIS OF REINFORCEMENT

In the experimental analysis of reinforcement, the responses elicited by the reinforcer are usually expressed at the behavioral level and measurable (e.g., salivation elicited by food or escape responses elicited by shock). However, in the natural environment, reinforcers may not elicit easily observed responses, yet reinforcement occurs nevertheless. For example, what are the behavioral responses elicited by effective conditioned reinforcers such as a friend's smile? Most often, reinforcement in the natural environment does not satisfy the conditions required for experimental analysis, nor need them. In the natural environment, reinforcement is used for the interpretation of behavior, not for its experimental analysis. As such, unmeasured reinforcer-elicited responses may be assumed to occur even when they are undetectable at the behavioral level. Obviously, behavior can occur independently of its being observed. To deal with events that are not observable at one scale of measurement, experimental analysis typically moves to a finer-grained level—here, from behavior to neuroscience. Observations at the level of neuroscience do not replace a behavioral analysis; they supplement it. For

most purposes, a principle of reinforcement formulated at the behavioral level is quite satisfactory, as in much of applied behavior analysis. However, a thoroughgoing experimental analysis supplements behavioral observations with those from neuroscience. As a case in point, electrophysiological observations of activity initiated in certain midbrain neurons by unconditioned reinforcers (such as food) reveal that activity of these same neurons increases when conditioned reinforcers occur (such as a light that has been paired with food). At the neural level, unconditioned and conditioned reinforcers produce similar responses even though conditioned reinforcers may not evoke responses that are readily measured at the behavioral level. A more general reason to explore the neural mechanisms of reinforcement is that appreciation of the full power of reinforcement may await the discovery of its biological mechanisms, as occurred with genetics in the history of natural selection.

SOME IMPLICATIONS OF REINFORCEMENT

The study of reinforcement has focused on experimental analysis of the process and, as such, has employed relatively simple three-term contingencies among stimuli, responses, and reinforcers. Here, several implications of reinforcement in more complex situations are mentioned. Recall that reinforcers cause environmental stimuli to acquire control over two classes of responses, those elicited by the reinforcer and those of the operant itself. Accordingly, stimuli that arise from acquired reinforcer-elicited responses and that precede the operant can participate with environmental stimuli in the control of the operant. That is, the operant can come under the joint control of environmental stimuli and stimuli from acquired reinforcer-elicited responses. If acquired reinforcer-elicited responses are extinguished, then the operant can be weakened even though the operant itself has not undergone extinction. As an example from applied behavior analysis, extinction of conditioned fear responses can weaken avoidance behavior even when the avoidance behavior has not been directly extinguished.

Finally, the present discussion has been confined to operant procedures in which a single occurrence of a response in the presence of a discrete stimulus produced the reinforcer. In the laboratory and especially in the natural environment, reinforcement can occur under much more complex circumstances. Many of these circumstances have been examined under the headings of *discrimination* formation and *schedules of reinforcement*. For example, when multiple responses are required to produce a reinforcer, higher rates of responding are selected than when only a single response is necessary. Thus, variations in behavior, such as its rate, that are conventionally attributed to "motivation" can result from different response-reinforcer contingencies. Also, studies have uncovered orderly relations between variables that are defined over longer periods of time than the moment-to-moment relations of the three-term contingency. For example, when an organism has access to two environments that have different response requirements for a reinforcer, the rates of responding in those environments often match their associated rates of reinforcers. This orderly relation is known as the *matching law*. Integrating findings based on variables defined over longer periods of time (i.e., molar variables) with findings from moment-to-moment analyses of reinforcement remains an active area of ongoing research.

—*John W. Donahoe*

See also: *Applied Behavior Analysis (Vols. I, II, & III)*

Suggested Readings

Baum, W. M. (1974). On two types of deviations from the matching law. *Journal of the Experimental Analysis of Behavior, 22,* 231–242.

Catania, A. C. (1971). Reinforcement schedules: The role of responses preceding the one that produces the reinforcer. *Journal of the Experimental Analysis of Behavior, 15,* 271–287.

Donahoe, J. W., Burgos, J. E., & Palmer, D. C. (1993). Selectionist approach to reinforcement. *Journal of the Experimental Analysis of Behavior, 58,* 17–40.

Donahoe, J. W., Crowley, M. A., Millard, W. J., & Stickney, K. A. (1982). A unified principle of reinforcement. *Quantitative models of behavior* (Vol. 2, pp. 493–521). Cambridge, MA: Ballinger.

Estes, W. K., & Skinner, B. F. (1941). Some quantitative properties of anxiety. *Journal of Experimental Psychology, 29,* 390–400.

Ferster, C. B., & Skinner, B. F. (1957). *Schedules of reinforcement.* New York: Appleton-Century-Crofts.

Herrnstein, R. J. (1970). On the law of effect. *Journal of the Experimental Analysis of Behavior, 13,* 243–266.

Jenkins, H. M., & Moore, B. R. (1973). The form of the auto-shaped response with food and water reinforcement. *Journal of the Experimental Analysis of Behavior, 20,* 163–181.

Premack, D. (1959). Toward empirical behavioral laws: I. Positive reinforcement. *Psychological Review, 66,* 219–233.

Rescorla, R. A. (1991). Associative relations in instrumental learning: The eighteenth Bartlett Memorial Lecture. *Quarterly Journal of Experimental Psychology, 43B,* 1–23.

Schoenfeld, W. H. (1950). An experimental approach to anxiety, escape, and avoidance behavior. In P. H. Hoch & J. Zubin (Eds.), *Anxiety* (pp. 70–99). Oxford, UK: Grune & Stratton.

Schultz, W. (1997). Adaptive dopaminergic neurons report the appetitive value of environmental stimuli. In J. W. Donahoe & V. P. Dorsel (Eds.), *Neural-network models of cognition: Biobehavioral foundations* (pp. 317–325). Amsterdam: Elsevier Science Press.

Shimp, C. P. Optimal behavior in free-operant environments. *Psychological Review, 76,* 97–112.

Skinner, B. F. (1948). "Superstition" in the pigeon. *Journal of Experimental Psychology, 38,* 168–172.

Timberlake, W., & Allison, J. (1974). Response deprivation: An empirical approach to instrumental performance. *Psychological Review, 81,* 146–164.

vom Saal, W., & Jenkins, H. M. (1970). Blocking the development of stimulus control. *Learning and Motivation, 1,* 52–64.

RELAPSE PREVENTION

DESCRIPTION OF THE STRATEGY

Alan Marlatt and Judith Gordon developed relapse prevention (RP) as a response to their concerns over the steadily plummeting survival of treatment gains once clients discontinued alcoholism treatment if no further intervention was implemented. Their observations revealed that treatment, with all of its costs and benefits, was attenuated over time. A significant number of clients who responded to a variety of treatments for addictive behaviors could expect to reach abstinence for a certain period to time, only to lose control of the target behaviors again following cessation of treatment.

Thus, the primary assumption of RP evolved: It is problematic to expect the effects of a treatment that is designed to moderate or eliminate an undesirable behavior to endure beyond the termination of treatment. Hunt, Barnett, and Branch found that within 1 year of ending alcoholism treatment, more than 80% of clients would resume drinking (treatment failure) and two thirds of these relapses would occur in the first 3 months. Standard abstinence treatments involve an intense but limited period of time during which clients are brought into contact with new influences or experiences, information, and contextual components that aid in creating changes in their behaviors. In addition, these therapies include accountability and a regular dose of treatment given reliably over a period of time in a restricted environment. Once accountability and dose elements are significantly reduced or removed (typically after the client has reached his or her treatment goals), the treatment is terminated, and the client must learn to implement the skills and knowledge learned in a new context in an old context with little or no assistance. In fact, clients often enter environments in which their demonstration of treatment gains may be punished. For example, a cocaine addict who is trying to learn new ways to cope with difficult situations may be cajoled for becoming "boring." Generalizing the skills to varied situations and across time poses a significant challenge, and many treatment failures are the result.

Marlatt and his colleagues believed that treatment failures could be analyzed in order to discover internal and external variables that increased risk for relapse. They further reasoned that knowing events such as situational factors, mood states, and cognitions would identify individualized targets of change for clients, targets focused not on the acquisition of quitting behavior, but the maintenance of that behavior. Based loosely on Albert Bandura's social learning theory, the RP model proposes that at the cessation of a habit control treatment, a client feels self-efficacious with regard to the unwanted behavior and that this perception of self-efficacy stems from learned and practiced skills. Over time, the client contacts internal and external risk factors, such as seemingly irrelevant decisions (SIDS) (also called seeming unimportant decisions, or SUDs) and/or high-risk situations (HRS), which threaten the client's self-control and consequently his or her perception of self-efficacy. According to the model, if clients have adaptive coping skills to adequately address the internal and external challenges to their control, they will not relapse. However, if their skills are not sufficient to meet challenges, a lapse or relapse may occur. In response to a resumption of the undesirable behavior, the client has a reaction that either increases attempts to implement adaptive coping skills—or fails to cope effectively and consequently engages in the undesirable behavior, perhaps because it provides immediate gratification. Marlatt's supposition that the targets of RP are cognitions and behaviors that are collectively referred to as "coping skills" is embedded within this framework. Marlatt and colleagues' treatment therefore employs cognitive-behavioral techniques to improve the retention, accessibility, and implementation of adaptive coping responses following the termination of treatment.

In the short period of time since its introduction, RP has evolved in numerous directions. It has been applied to new problem areas such as overeating and sexual offending. It has also come into use as a full program of treatment and lifestyle change, instead of simply a supplemental intervention strategy. In its many manifestations, RP addresses high-risk situations, the avoidance of those situations, the management of those situations, and skills for recovery after encountering those situations. The recognition that these goals are useful not only for treatment maintenance but also for the initial learning phase has led to the use of RP as a treatment gains approach for a variety of habit control problems. RP is also emerging as a bona fide theory of compulsive habit patterns and the processes of relapse. It should be noted that RP is most widely used with behaviors deemed volitional in origin (e.g., behaviors of consumption); however, some practitioners have applied RP in problems behaviors where the volitional element is less clear (e.g., schizophrenia, depression). The future of RP includes motivational interviewing, stepped care, and harm reduction, as well as further clarification of the theoretical underpinnings, mechanisms, and outcomes of RP.

In general, RP's foci are, first, identification of high-risk situations and, second, teaching the client to employ appropriate self-control responses. High-risk situations are determined by an analysis of past offenses and by reports of situations in which the client feels or felt "tempted." Examples of these high-risk situations may be a bar or tavern for smokers and drinkers, playgrounds and shopping malls for sexual offenders, and casinos for gamblers. Appropriate responses are those behaviors that lead to escape or avoidance of high-risk situations or, if remaining in a high-risk situation, behaviors that foster controlled actions. For example, a smoker might learn to avoid frequenting convenience stores for any reason due to the strong presence of smoking products at the cash register. D. R. Laws suggests that responding with an appropriate coping response in high-risk situations will lead to increased self-efficacy and a decreased probability of relapse. He also indicates that if appropriate coping responses are not utilized or not in the behavioral repertoire, there will be a decrease in self-efficacy and increased likelihood of positive outcome expectancies (perception of positive experiences resulting from engaging in maladaptive behavior), a lapse, and an increased probability of future lapses and relapses.

High-Risk Situations

This component involves the ideographic assessment of high-risk situations. The client and clinician work together to identify the situations in which the client has previously engaged in problematic behavior and those situations in which the client is likely to engage in problematic behavior in the future. One technique often used requires the client to describe the thoughts, feelings, and behaviors that occurred before, during, and after each relevant instance of the undesired behavior. This data set can then be used to discern common elements that can be identified as precursors of high-risk situations and reinforcers of losses of control. The client will be asked to generate a list of low-risk situations and what aspects of those situations differentiate them from high-risk situations. The treatment focus is to train the client to recognize themes and commonalties in their high-risk situations so that they can generalize the ability to assess level of risk in novel situations. The therapist works with clients to ensure that they are realistic in their assessment of the level of risk in a variety of hypothetical situations.

❖ Lapses are occurrences of the problem behavior in the context of a behavior reduction or elimination plan (e.g., a drink for the alcohol cessation client).

❖ Relapses are the return to baseline levels or near pretreatment levels of the occurrence of the problem behavior (e.g., returning to a pack-a-day habit for the tobacco cessation client).

❖ The "acceptability" of lapses and relapses is dependent upon the behavior (e.g., sexual offenders may have more consequences for a lapse or relapse than a smoker has).

❖ All relevant previous occurrences of the problem behavior are analyzed in terms of thoughts, feelings, and behaviors before (triggers), during, and after these occurrences.

❖ Similarities across affect, cognitions, and behaviors that tend to co-occur reliably with the problem behavior are identified.

❖ High-risk situations can be internal (affect, cognitions), external (victim types, locations), or interactive (given certain internal conditions, external conditions may make an occurrence of the problem behavior more likely).

❖ A chain of behaviors that probabilistically lead to lapse or relapse is constructed (e.g., emotional and cognitive settings events set up decisions and behaviors that place the client in a situation in which he or she is likely to lapse).

In addition to identifying the high-risk elements of the behavior chain, the client is assisted in employing appropriate self-control responses (interventions) acquired through treatment. Thus, skill training is critical to RP. These behavioral alternatives can be implemented at any point in the behavior chain, ideally before the client reaches a high-risk situation at the end of the chain. Appropriate self-control responses are those behaviors that lead to avoidance of, management in, escape from, and debriefing after, when faced with an element of a high-risk situation. Typically, the client will prepare avoidance, escape, and control responses in anticipation of contacting the fairly inevitable HRS. For example, if a sexual offender finds himself fantasizing about a young child, he may, through treatment, learn to avoid looking at children's clothing advertisements that lead to those thoughts, "urge surf" (i.e., tolerate the uncomfortable thoughts and feelings until they naturally subside), distract himself by going to the gym to interrupt (escape from) the deviant fantasy, and then journal about the event to perhaps modify his response strategies for the future.

Cognitive Distortions

Another component of RP is the identification and challenging of cognitive distortions, self-statements that operate as permission givers for engaging in offensive behaviors. Therapists trained in cognitive-behavioral therapy often find it necessary to address the client's cognitive distortions in treating problems of self-control. Clients typically view these rationalizations as both accurate representations of the world and adequate justifications for engaging in the unwanted behavior. Examples of cognitive distortions can be seen in Steen's *The Adult Relapse Prevention Workbook,* as well as Brunswig and O'Donohue's *Relapse Prevention for Sexual Harassers.* Some common cognitive distortions are victim blaming, entitlement, minimizing, rationalizing, projection, magnification, victim stance, catastrophizing, overgeneralizing, all-or-nothing, negative bias, positive bias, and personalization. Jenkins-Hall describes the steps for changing cognitive distortions as identifying the thoughts that lead to maladaptive behavior, analyzing the validity and utility of the thoughts, and implementing an intervention designed to change the cognitive distortions into more adaptive cognitions. The therapist first assists the client in developing alternative interpretations for his or her initial thoughts. The client is then asked to evaluate whether the past thinking made it easier to commit the problematic behavior and begins to develop skills to analyze the logic and evidence behind certain types of thinking. Finally, the client is assisted in disputing and challenging these thoughts in therapy and generalizing these skills to his or her natural environment. With respect to RP, clients are assisted in examining how cognitive distortions affect the prevention of relapses and are aided in challenging their thinking as it relates to the above elements of RP.

❖ Identify the relevant cognitive distortions and SIDs with your client.
❖ Use techniques such as analyzing the validity and utility of the thoughts, develop alternative interpretations, directing clients to dispute and challenge their own thoughts, and other similar rational-emotive behavior therapy, cognitive-behavioral therapy, and cognitive therapy techniques.

SIDs/SUDs

Seeming irrelevant decisions (SIDs) (also called seeming unimportant decisions, or SUDs) are those behaviors that might not lead directly to a high-risk situation, but are early in the chain of decisions that place the client in a high-risk situation. For example, if the client reports that he is more likely to engage in the problematic behavior after drinking, a SID would be agreeing to attend a luncheon with a coworker who is known to drink alcohol heavily at lunch. Lunching with the coworker is not the high-risk situation. However, the introduction of alcohol is likely to increase the potential of the individual finding himself in a high-risk situation.

In addressing SIDs, the therapist works with the client to determine the types of decisions that lead to high-risk situations. Once the client can identify many

potential SIDs, the client learns and practices effective decision-making skills. The therapist works with the client to ensure that the generated solutions and skills are adequate and appropriate. In addition, therapists may also role-play situations with the client to allow the client a chance to practice their intervention skills in hypothetical high-risk situations.

PIG

PIG refers to "the problem of immediate gratification." In essence, individuals acting in such a way as to receive immediate positive consequences will often suffer larger, more aversive consequences at a later date. However, there is a disconnect between pursuing the immediate positive reinforcement and considering future negative consequences of doing so. With smokers, the immediate relief from withdrawal symptoms provided by a cigarette is the proximal consequence, while emphysema, lung cancer, and death are more distal consequences. Offending, or the problematic behavior, is a "quick fix" to feeling better.

Psychoeducational approaches that teach the client how to create a decision matrix are often employed to combat the PIG. The therapist assists the client in developing a matrix, which is a concise, written representation of the positive and negative outcomes for engaging or not engaging in the problematic behavior, and then assigning probabilities (0.0 to 1.0) of that outcome actually occurring. This is done in both an immediate and short-term time frame. The therapist challenges any unrealistic or improbable outcomes until the client is able to generate more realistic ones. The therapist then directs the client to analyze past situations in which they engaged in the problematic behavior and to compare the immediate gratifications against the long-term consequences. Clients are then encouraged to utilize this decision matrix when encountering novel situations. Many sessions may be dedicated to role-playing situations to overlearn this process. Moreover, many clients carry a small version of the decision matrix with them to have it available in case they contact a high-risk situation and have problems coping effectively.

Outcome Expectancies

The client is asked to construct a decision matrix: on one dimension, the choice of offending versus not offending, on the second dimension, the positive and negative outcomes, and on the third dimension, the short- and long-term consequences. Often, the client will not generate accurate outcomes and is instructed in more realistic outcomes for their offending and nonoffending behaviors. Another component in some manifestations of RP is enhancing victim empathy. Clients are asked to do a variety of tasks, such as watching a video tape of victims telling of the effects of their victimization, imagining how the client and a loved one would feel if victimized, and writing a letter from the victim's point of view.

AVE

The abstinence violation effect (AVE) may occur when a client fails to cope effectively in a high-risk situation, lapses, and views the lapse as so severe that he or she may as well fully relapse. The reasoning recognizes a small failure, focuses on it as evidence that behavioral control is not possible, and indulges the desire for the immediate positive reinforcement that comes with enacting the problem behavior. For example, an overeater may have an AVE when expressing, "One slice of cheesecake is a lapse, so I may as well go all out and have the rest of the cheesecake." The individual's belief is that since she has violated the rule of abstinence, she "may as well" get the most out of the lapse, resulting in relapse.

The AVE occurs when a client is in high-risk situation and views the potential lapse as so severe that he or she may as well relapse. In a case such as this, the client and therapist practice identifying and coping with lapses. The treatment is not lapse prevention; lapses are to be expected, planned for, and taken as opportunities for the client to demonstrate learning. It is *relapse* prevention. Most often, relapse tends to be construed as a return to pretreatment levels of occurrence of the targeted behavior.

Treatment in this component involves describing and predicting the AVE and working with the client to learn alternative coping skills for when a lapse occurs, such that they are more confident in responding appropriately to lapses at any point in the behavior chain. This also affords an opportunity for the client to anticipate the AVE and include interventions for the AVE as a part of the RP plan. This is done through practice sessions in which the client and therapist identify lapse situations and practice the implementation of intervention skills. It must be emphasized to the client that lapses are to be expected and can be

handled if planned for in advance. Clients who recognize that lapses are normal and expected are less likely to use a minor instance in a rationale to relapse.

Social Skills

Another common problem in some self-control problems relates to deficits in social skills. Clients' losses of control are sometimes associated with interpersonal problems. An ideographic assessment can be used to learn which, if any, key social skills deficits are present. The clinician should address relative deficits in perception, interpretation, response generation, enactment, and evaluation. In conducting social skills training with these clients, clients and therapists typically discuss the abstract principles of the particular class of social skills. The therapist then models the specific set of social skills. The client and therapist then role-play a situation that emphasizes the specific social skills relevant for the client. For example, for a client working sexually inappropriate behavior in the workplace, the client and therapist may role-play joke-telling situations, socializing, or other critical situations common at the workplace. The therapist would then provide feedback for the client regarding the skills present and absent during the role play.

Planning for Lapses and Utilizing a Support Group

As indicated earlier, clients should be informed that lapses are to be expected and can be better handled when they are anticipated. To plan for lapses, clients should know how they would handle and intervene in situations in which they feel at risk for engaging in the problematic behavior. This is referred to as development of a *relapse prevention plan*. The creation of this plan is a dynamic and iterative process in which the triggers, distortions, high-risk situations, and interventions are planned for, documented, and evaluated after their occurrence. While some clients have often presented voluminous plans (one has even presented his in a collection of three-ring binders), plans that can accompany clients everywhere they go will often be more likely to be used. A useful plan outlines strategies for avoiding, managing, escaping, and debriefing high-risk situations; recognizing and intervening in cognitive distortions, SIDs/SUDs, the PIG, and the AVE; seeking help from an identified support group should the need arise after therapy; and modifying the RP plan based on feedback, successes, and failures of the plan. One way to do this is for clients to learn and practice all of the requisite skills beforehand and continually review and update their RP plans based on their use in real-life situations. In addition, clients can be assisted in developing cue cards, which can be used to refresh and prompt them on their RP strategies as needed.

Maintenance and Aftercare

Eventually, there is a gradual reduction of the role of therapy and therapist in the client's life. To enhance the gains made in therapy, as well as assist clients in the implementation of their RP plans, sessions are often faded from biweekly, to monthly, then bimonthly in order to provide the clients time and opportunity to generalize their new skills with support, accountability, and assistance in revising the RP plan if necessary. As many of the problems addressed with RP are enduring behavior problems, practitioners employing RP typically inform their clients that they will struggle with the problems for life and they will likely never be "cured." To combat this and assist in the maintenance of problem-free behavior, sessions may continue annually for years. The purpose of these sessions is to act as boosters to the primary therapy and to assist the client in updating and reviewing the RP plan with the knowledge gained through experience. New triggers for old behaviors inevitably appear. Constant revision keeps the RP plan fresh and useful.

As with any therapeutic intervention, therapists are obligated to design a plan for aftercare, and RP is no exception. While the goal of RP is the prevention of the occurrence of problematic behavior, the client's lifestyle must also be addressed for the most effective process of change. The RP model speculates that lifestyle imbalance, that is, a lack of balance between positive and negative activities, is a major contributor to succumbing to potential losses of control. Therefore, development of positive addictions or positive alternative behaviors is also emphasized. Positive alternatives are healthy behaviors and enjoyable hobbies (e.g., reading, bowling, and fly-fishing) in which the client can engage without experiencing adverse consequences. It is crucial that the therapist work to avoid recommending previously paired triggers and positive alternatives (e.g., bowling for the smoker who smoked while bowling), as those alternatives may work as

conditioned triggers for the problem behavior. Prior to the fading of sessions, the therapist assists the client in identifying and getting involved in enjoyable alternative activities that support the developed RP plan.

RESEARCH BASIS

In general, there is some evidence that RP can be a moderately effective program of interventions to prevent the reoccurrence of many problematic behaviors, including substance abuse, overeating, gambling, smoking, and sexual offending. However, there exists a disconcerting lack of data to support the theoretical foundations of RP and its hypothesized mechanisms of action. For example, there has not been a clear demonstration of the necessary and sufficient internal and external conditions that will predict instances of lapses and relapses. Efforts to gather increasingly specific treatment outcome data are extensive and ongoing. The active, essential ingredients of what has evolved into a multifaceted program of CBT techniques are unknown. Investigations have been hampered by the extensive variety in treatment interventions that are called RP. What the field does have is a bevy of clinical experience across a broad domain of client problems, all suggestive that RP is plausible as well as popular with both clients and therapists.

RELEVANT TARGET POPULATIONS AND EXCEPTIONS

In the short period of time since its introduction, RP has evolved in numerous directions. In many venues, it is used as it was originally designed, as a booster treatment. However, its scope has expanded. It is no longer viewed as solely a supplemental intervention strategy, but is now being applied and utilized as a full program of treatment in areas such as smoking cessation, overeating, and sexual offending. RP is also emerging as a bona fide theory of compulsive habit patterns and the processes of relapse. It has been applied for a variety of treatment targets, typically for problems often viewed as issues of self-control or compulsivity, such as alcohol abuse, nicotine use, eating-related difficulties (overeating, self-restriction), and undercontrolled sexuality (e.g., sexual offending, sexual "addiction," and sexual harassment). Thus, for clients with problems in these domains, RP may be a beneficial intervention. Furthermore, RP will likely be the treatment of choice for clients presenting with problems of sexual misbehavior (e.g., sexual harassment and sexual offending) and risky sexual behavior. It is also likely be the preferred treatment for clients presenting with "habit" or "self-control" problems (e.g., substance abuse); and in addition, it continues to be a maintenance program for a variety of other interventions, including CBT for depression and anxiety, and substance abuse. RP should be avoided in cases in which the client's ability to recall historical data or verbally process new information is impaired (e.g., mental retardation/developmental delay, organic injury) due to RP's reliance on verbal processing. There may be other media through which RP instruction could occur, though the effectiveness of alternative approaches has not been thoroughly evaluated. While significant numbers of developmentally delayed sex offenders are receiving treatment, RP is often a small element in a comprehensive treatment program.

COMPLICATIONS

The effective application of RP is complicated by the lack of a cohesive testable theory, tentative empirical basis, and pragmatic considerations. RP theory fails to explain how the core features of the relapse process interact, ignores the complexity of high-risk situations, combines cognitive and conditioning perspectives to explain lapses, combines several psychological theories in the conceptualization of the AVE, and proposes that two competing processes occur simultaneously after the lapse or relapse (the biphasic effect and AVE). As noted above, good treatment outcome studies have been hampered by the diversity of approaches known as RP (with overlapping core features and many additional CBT interventions), by the ethical issues introduced by withholding treatment from a control group, and by measurement issues surrounding lapses and relapses. Reliance on self-reported losses of control is unrealistic for obvious reasons. Last, RP is complicated by practical concerns. RP is usually offered in a group treatment format, requiring clients to reveal information about their losses of self-control to strangers. Consequently, many candidates for RP may decline the treatment. It may be offered years after a habit-controlled problem has emerged, making it difficult to identify many causal factors. RP often involves the treatment of substance abuse or the substance use that surrounds another problem (e.g., gambling). Being a highly cognitive approach that relies on memory and information processing, RP may well be impeded by the situational, short-term, and long-term effects of drug use. Last, a primary assumption of RP is that aversive emotional experiences set the stage for a lapse or relapse. Relapse prevention addresses feelings through distractions, a technique that has been shown in related literatures to set up recurrences of unwanted emotions and associated thoughts.

CASE ILLUSTRATION

"Robert" is a 36-year-old, college educated information technology (IT) specialist at a moderately sized company in a city on the West Coast. He has worked for the company for 6 years, recently promoted from IT assistant to specialist and having previously worked in a similar capacity for small companies across the southwestern United States. He is married, and his wife of 4 years is expecting their first child. Three separate complaints have been made to the human resources department related to Robert's behavior. One the first occasion, he brushed his arm across the breasts of a coworker under the guise of solving a computer problem. The second report details Robert's placing a hand on a female coworker's thigh under the guise of lifting himself from a seated position on the floor under her desk. In the third complaint, he again placed his hand on a female coworker's thigh while lifting himself from the floor, only to have his hand "slip" to her pubic area; and while trying to "steady" himself, he surreptitiously grabbed her breast with his other hand. Robert presents in your office after the company recommends that he seek professional intervention as part of a probationary period while the allegations are under investigation.

In the interview, you discover the following: Robert reveals that he and his wife have been having financial difficulties related to the pregnancy. As a result, Robert reports that he has been less attracted to his wife. Your review of the records indicates that all of the three complainants were temporary workers, young, and had brunette hair. Robert has told you that in his work with each of three victims, he had engaged in banter that had contained occasional sexual innuendo.

For Robert's situation, we'll define the terms as they relate to him:

Lapse: engaging in banter that contains sexual innuendo.

Relapse: inappropriate physical contact with coworker.

High-risk situation: being in close quarters with dark-haired, young, female temporary workers.

Setting the stage: not feeling attracted to his spouse.

SIDs: deciding to be seated on the floor to address the computer problem and deciding to stand in such a way as to necessitate a reach across his victim.

PIG: For Robert, it probably felt better to have the immediate gratification from touching the attractive young temp than to address the problems he was having at home with his spouse.

AVE: Having already touched the thigh of a coworker, Robert escalated into touching both her pubic area and breast.

Offense chain: In looking at Robert's case, we can see that his problems at home set the stage for his offense. This is one area of intervention. Second, we see that Robert tends to be most at risk when in close quarters with attractive, dark-haired temporary workers. Third, Robert's SIDs makes his high-risk situations even more dangerous, as he sets himself up to make touching easy. He also previctimizes his coworkers by assessing their willingness to engage in sexual talk. We also notice an escalating pattern of behavior from the early report to the third report.

—*William T. O'Donohue, Kirk A. Brunswig, and Tamara P. Sbraga*

See also: *Generalization (Vol. I); Relapse Prevention (Vol. II); Schedules of Reinforcement (Vol. III)*

Suggested Readings

Brunswig, K. A., & O'Donohue, W. (2002). *Relapse prevention for sexual harassers.* New York: Kluwer Academic/Plenum.

Laws, D. R. (Ed.) (1989). *Relapse prevention with sex offenders.* New York: Guilford Press.

Laws, D. R. (1995). A theory of relapse prevention. In W. O'Donohue & L. Krasner (Eds.), *Theories of behavior therapy: Exploring behavior change.* Washington, DC: American Psychological Association.

Laws, D. R., Hudson, S. M., & Ward, T. (Eds.). (2000). *Remaking relapse prevention with sex offenders: A sourcebook.* Thousand Oaks, CA: Sage.

Marlatt, G. A. (1998). *Harm reduction: Pragmatic strategies for managing high-risk behaviors.* New York: Guilford Press.

Marlatt, G. A., & Gordon, J. R. (Eds.). (1985). *Relapse prevention.* New York: Guilford Press.

Sandberg, G. G., & Marlatt, G. A. (1991). Relapse prevention. In D. A. Gravlo & R. I. Shader (Eds.), *Clinical manual of dependence.* Washington, DC: American Psychiatric Press.

Ward, T., & Hudson, S. (1996). Relapse prevention: A critical analysis. *Sexual Abuse: A Journal of Research and Treatment, 8,* 177–199.

RELATIONAL FRAME THEORY

DESCRIPTION OF THE STRATEGY

Relational frame theory (RFT) is a comprehensive behavioral approach to human language and cognition. The theory, while based in behavior analysis and backed up by scores of human operant studies, nevertheless affirms the importance of topics that are not traditionally associated with behavior analytic research, such as thinking, feeling, planning, and reasoning. RFT differs significantly from B. F. Skinner's approach to the topic, offering an alternative operant account.

Research with verbally able humans has demonstrated that given a relationship between two novel stimuli A and B, human beings will derive a relationship between B and A, even though this relation has not been directly trained. For example, a human who has learned to pick B from an array of stimuli given the presentation of A will now be likely to pick A from an array given the presentation of B. Nonhumans do this with great difficulty, if at all (although this point has not been resolved in the literature), but even human infants 16 months of age (and perhaps younger) show this performance, which is part of a larger set of similar derived behaviors called *stimulus equivalence.* Humans without at least some spontaneous receptive language, however, do not show this effect, which is one of several findings that implicate derived stimulus relations as a core process in human language and cognition.

RFT research has shown that the specific relations between novel arbitrary stimuli need not be only equivalence relations, they can also be comparisons, such as "bigger than" or "better than," or temporal relations, such as "A comes before B." For instance, a verbally able human who is told "A is bigger than B" will derive "B is smaller than A" without having this relationship explicitly stated. In RFT, the derived bidirectionality of such stimulus relations is termed *mutual entailment.* What is crucial is that stimulus relationships of this kind are not dependent on the formal nature of the related events: They can be controlled by arbitrary cues. A dime is "bigger than" a nickel, for example, simply because the "bigger than" relation has been assigned to dimes relative to nickels by social whim and convention. The physical size of dimes relative to nickels is not what is at issue.

Relations are also derived in more complex networks of stimuli. If a human is told A = B and B = C, A = C will be readily derived. Given relational networks like "A is bigger than B" and "B is bigger than C," human beings will also derive "A is bigger than C" and "C is smaller than A." RFT terms these types of relations *combinatorial entailment.* Relational networks may be very complex and lead to a wide variety of derived stimulus relations. Since humans can then relate entire relational networks (examples include metaphor and analogy), even a few trained relations can lead to myriad derived relations.

When stimuli are framed relationally in this manner, altering the function of one stimulus may cause alterations in the other stimuli in the relational network based on the derived relation between them, a property RFT calls the *transformation of stimulus functions.* A commonplace example is the way that words such as *anxiety* may invoke a corresponding emotional response. It appears that the psychological functions associated with the emotional events transfer in part to the words that name them. The transformation of stimulus functions is itself under contextual control. For instance, all the functions of an apple do not transfer to the word *apple.* One can taste an apple given the written word *apple,* but one would be unlikely to try to eat the word.

It is this last property that makes derived relational responding so important and so relevant to clinical concerns. For example, a person who has had a panic attack while "trapped" in a restaurant may generalize this feeling to other events that may lead to being "trapped" (e.g., elevators, conversations, jobs, marriages). What brings this set of events together is not their formal properties, but their participation in a verbal/cognitive network.

To put it succinctly, relational frames are patterns of arbitrarily applicable relational responding that show the contextually controlled properties of mutual entailment, combinatorial entailment, and transformation of stimulus functions. According to RFT, these relational responses are (a) learned, operant behavior and (b) at the core of human verbal events. A body of research has tested these two claims, so far with supportive outcomes.

RFT offers an account of the complex features of human language and cognition that is based on fairly simple learning principles. It has been used to construct accounts of a wide variety of verbal phenomena, including humor, metaphors, storytelling, problem solving and rule governance. RFT has important clinical implications as well.

Derived stimulus relations help explain both the utility of human language and cognition and its role in psychopathology. The bidirectional nature of human language means that if an incorrect choice is made, verbal evaluation of that choice will alter the function of the original environment when it is next encountered so that the more effective choice might be made. Bidirectionality also makes self-awareness painful, however, because verbal awareness of past painful events can occasion pain once again. Unlike nonhumans, humans cannot avoid pain by avoiding the situations in which it has occurred, since language allows pain to occur in almost any situation through derived relations. As a recourse, humans begin to try to avoid the painful thoughts and feelings themselves, even when doing so causes harm; that is, they show *experiential avoidance.* Experiential avoidance is one of the most pathological psychological processes known, but RFT suggests that it is built into human language and cognition.

In much the same way, the verbal problem-solving abilities that give such an advantage to humans can be turned against them. Relational frames of time and evaluation will permit human beings to construct futures that have never been experienced and to compare these futures with desired ends. This process can lead humans to generate useful rules for control of their environment, but it can also enable anticipatory anxiety, existential meaninglessness, self-blame, and similar processes. From an RFT perspective, psychopathology is often problem solving gone awry, in which the "solution" is at the core of the problem due to an overextension of the avoidant, temporal, and comparative functions that are built into language.

Fortunately, RFT suggests a possible solution. In an RFT conception, relational frames are contextually controlled by two aspects of the situation: features that regulate derived relations and those that regulate the transformation of stimulus functions through them. RFT suggests a contextualistic way to deal with the pervasiveness of human pain: Change the contexts that support a thought –> action or emotion –> action relation. Acceptance, mindfulness, and cognitive defusion strategies are examples of such methods. Acceptance and commitment therapy, dialectical behavior therapy, mindfulness-based cognitive therapy, and similar cognitive-behavioral procedures use such techniques in an effort to change the function of previously avoided cognition and emotion. RFT thus helps explain some of the recent transition toward more "Eastern" methods in CBT.

—*Steven C. Hayes and Kara Bunting*

See also: *Behavioral Family Therapy (Vol. II); Contextualism (Vol. I); Functional Relation (Vol. III)*

Suggested Readings

Barnes-Holmes, Y., Hayes, S. C., Barnes-Holmes, D., & Roche, B. (2001). Relational frame theory: A post-Skinnerian account of human language and cognition. In H. W. Reese & R. Kail (Eds.), *Advances in child development and behavior* (Vol. 28, pp. 101–138). New York: Academic.

Hayes, S. C., Barnes-Holmes, D., & Roche, B. (2001). (Eds.). *Relational frame theory: A post-Skinnerian account of human language and cognition.* New York: Plenum Press.

RELAXATION STRATEGIES

DESCRIPTION OF THE STRATEGY

The root word, *lax,* from the Latin, simply means "loose." Thus, *relaxation* means "loosening," "release," or "abatement." It implies a prior condition of tension, restraint, or rigidity, which then is diminished. In physiology, relaxation refers to inactivity in muscle fibers, resulting in reduced tonus and movement. All of these considerations are relevant for the technical use of the term within the behavioral therapies.

Clinically, relaxation refers to a condition of calmness, repose, or tranquility, both physical and psychological, which contrasts with states of tension, stress, or emotional upset, which are detrimental to an individual's functioning. Relaxation also refers to steps a person takes to achieve such equanimity.

A variety of relaxation-training methods have been developed, but there are some common features. Training is conducted by an expert, regarded as having special knowledge and skills, with a client who expects some benefit beyond that which could be achieved by simple "rest." Training customarily is carried out one-on-one, though small groups sometimes are employed. Clients usually are encouraged to practice outside the training setting and to apply their skills in upsetting circumstances. Relaxation training may be the sole mode of treatment or, more often, a component of multifaceted treatment programs that may involve cognitive restructuring and systematic exposure. In addition, various relaxation-training methods may be combined in a simultaneous or sequential fashion.

The most influential or popular relaxation-training techniques are described briefly, in an approximate historical sequence, followed by a description of assessment methods.

Progressive Relaxation

In the 1930s, Edmund Jacobson developed the method of tense-release muscle relaxation. The client lies in a recumbent position and is instructed to engage in an activity that increases tension in an isolated muscle group, for example, extending the right index finger. The client is instructed to attend to the sensations of tension, in this case, a portion of the right forearm, and then to return the finger to a resting position and note the sensations of relaxation. This is repeated for the flexors of the index finger. Training is conducted for scores of individual muscle groups throughout the body, requiring dozens of sessions extending over many months.

In the 1950s, Joseph Wolpe introduced relaxation to behavior therapy. He modified Jacobson's procedure so that a larger number of muscle groups are covered simultaneously, greatly decreasing training time. For example, all five fingers of the right hand are extended and then relaxed, rather than each individually. Wolpe regarded relaxation as antithetical to anxiety and incorporated it into his systematic desensitization procedure, in which clients are trained to engage in relaxation in the presence of anxiety-evoking cues.

In the 1970s, Douglas Bernstein and Thomas Borkovec further abbreviated the number of exercises. For example, the right hand and forearm are incorporated into one exercise by making and releasing a fist.

There are 16 such "individual" muscle groups; these are combined into 7 and then into 4 areas of the body in a fixed sequence. Training takes 10 sessions to complete the entire sequence. This standardized format is widely employed in research programs in order to administer participants a specific "dose" of training.

The goal of all progressive relaxation procedures is to increase clients' awareness of unnecessary tension anywhere in their bodies and their ability to turn it off. A variation, termed *applied relaxation,* is often employed, in which the client relaxes parts of his or her body while carrying out activities of daily living or confronting difficult situations.

Biofeedback

Biofeedback gained currency in the 1970s as a procedure to teach control of specific physiologic systems related to particular symptoms or for training generalized relaxation. Biofeedback requires electronic equipment that measures physiologic activity and provides the client with an auditory or visual signal reflecting minute changes in that activity. By learning to control the signal, the client gains control over the activity. The most popular methods are electromyographic (EMG) biofeedback for muscle systems and thermal biofeedback for vascular systems, but many other organ systems and functions also are targeted. Training times vary from three to a dozen or more sessions. Home-training equipment may be employed, and "weaning" the client from the machine often is a final phase of training.

Meditation

Also in the 1970s, interest in ancient yoga and Zen philosophies and practices became widespread. Herbert Benson, in a secular analysis of meditation, outlined four components. The first element is a *quiet environment,* a setting free from intrusions and distractions. The second element is a *mental device,* typically a simple syllable, word, or phrase that is repeated to oneself, either silently or aloud. (In religious settings, this is termed a *mantra,* a secret sound given by a "guru" that has special significance for the trainee.) The utterance typically is paired with each respiratory exhalation. In another variation, a visual stimulus, such as a candle flame, may be employed as a focus of attention. The third element is *passive*

attitude. This is achieved by instructions to not worry about performance, to let distracting thoughts go, and return to the mental device. The fourth element is a *comfortable position* that prevents cramping or falling asleep. The "lotus" position, sitting, or kneeling are recommended. Initial instruction typically is accomplished in a single session, but clients continue to meet with their trainers or groups of meditators in repeated sessions to increase proficiency.

Verbal Induction Procedures

There are several procedures in which the trainer verbally describes events that the client then attempts to experience, usually covertly. These became clinically popular in the same era as meditation.

Hypnosis has a long history, with many connotations of special power exerted by the hypnotist. Clinically, it is viewed as susceptibility to suggestion, and the trainer simply describes a series of bodily sensations and experiences. In standardized induction procedures, items are scaled from those that most people achieve readily (such as eye closure) to those that relatively few people experience (such as anesthesia). Training is accomplished in one or a few sessions and usually is conducted in a setting for a particular purpose, such as preparation for a medical procedure. Self-hypnosis, in which a person focuses on experiences previously trained, may be used for home practice.

Guided imagery is a procedure in which the trainer describes a pleasant scene that the client imagines himself or herself passively experiencing. In addition to visual suggestions, auditory, olfactory, and kinesthetic cues often are employed. Like hypnosis, training takes few sessions and often is conducted to distract or calm the client in an aversive situation. Recorded imagery descriptions may be given to the client for home practice. Alternatively, clients may be encouraged to construct their own scenes.

Autogenic training involves the trainer reciting a series of specific phrases related to bodily sensations characteristic of a relaxed state, such as warm hands and a cool forehead. The client repeats the phrases silently and simultaneously attends to the sensations described. There are about two dozen phrases, and it takes several sessions to go through them all. The phrases may be recorded for home practice, or the client may memorize them.

Behavioral Relaxation Training

In the 1980s, Roger Poppen analyzed the behaviors that result from various relaxation-training procedures and devised a method to teach these behaviors directly. Ten postures and activities are taught through instruction, modeling, and performance feedback to a client seated in a reclining chair. Training typically is accomplished in 2 or 3 sessions but may take as many as 10, depending on how quickly the client achieves mastery of the items. Variations include training in an upright, seated position and "mini-relaxation" of areas of the body while engaged in activities of daily living.

Breathing Training

Breathing is an element in progressive relaxation, meditation, autogenic training, and behavioral relaxation training, but exclusive focus on breathing for panic and other disorders related to hyperventilation expanded in the 1980s. Diaphragmatic breathing at a slow pace is the most common technique. Clients are made aware of their breathing patterns by placement of their hands on chest and abdomen, or biofeedback instruments may be employed. Instruction can be completed in a single session, but repeated practice is necessary for proficiency.

Assessment of Relaxation

There are many ways to measure the effects of relaxation training. Some assessment methods arise from particular training methods, but most can be employed with all training techniques. There are three major categories of assessment: self-report, external observation, and physiological measurement. Multiple measures within and across these three domains provide the best evidence of training effectiveness.

Self-report by the client is the easiest and most widespread measure of relaxation. Clients may comment spontaneously on their subjective experience or may be prompted by the trainer to do so. Numerical scales rating the degree of relaxation often are employed. Relaxation inventories are available, in which clients endorse items that describe relaxed feelings. Clients may be advised to keep records of the frequency or duration of their home practice. Where the target of training is a particular symptom, such as anxiety or pain, clients may be instructed to keep diaries that rate the frequency or intensity of the problem.

External observation typically is performed by the trainer during the training session. Often, this is informal, and the trainer relies on his or her clinical experience to assess the client's progress. A combination of self-report and trainer observation is employed in hypnosis to mark which items a client successfully completes on a susceptibility index. The Behavioral Relaxation Scale is a systematic observation procedure that is a component of behavioral relaxation training, but its reliability and validity have been demonstrated with other training procedures as well. Besides the trainer, other people in the client's environment, such as a spouse or parent, may be solicited to make observations of the client's practice or symptoms.

Physiological measurement is an integral part of biofeedback procedures but is also employed with other training methods. There are two general classes of physiological assessment: muscles (usually by means of EMG) and organs innervated by the autonomic nervous system. In *muscular assessment,* which muscles are chosen depends upon the focus of treatment. General relaxation should result in lowered activity in muscles throughout the body, but those of the face or shoulders are regarded as particularly useful sites. Specific symptoms are assessed by measuring activity in muscles related to the problem; for example, forehead muscles for tension headache, lumbar muscles for low-back pain, and forearm muscles for hand tremor. *Autonomic assessment* is of interest because of the role of the autonomic nervous system in emotional arousal and stress disorders. General relaxation may be indicated by respiration rate or pattern, or oxygen consumption levels. Measures related to specific symptoms are commonly employed; for example, heart rate and blood pressure for hypertension and peripheral vasodilation for Raynaud's disease.

RESEARCH BASIS

Tens of thousands of studies, ranging from case reports to clinical trials, document the arousal-reducing potency of relaxation training and the treatment efficacy of therapy programs that include relaxation. Continuing research is directed toward improving the efficiency of therapy programs and increasing the proportion of recipients who achieve clinical success.

Some empirical consensus exists as to which training procedures are best with particular disorders, but much more research is needed.

Another area of research concerns the relationship between behavioral and medical treatments. Many studies show that relaxation programs often are successful for persons for whom medication or surgery is prohibitive, ineffective, or iatrogenic. Medical procedures usually are seen as the primary mode of treatment, and "alternative" methods are employed only when they fail.

There are beginning efforts toward developing a theoretical rationale to organize existing data and guide future research. A general view is that there are categories of relaxation and related categories of problems, and matching the correct type of training and symptom will be most effective. Some categories that have been proposed include a dualistic approach (cognitive and somatic), a tripartite approach (cognitive, muscular, and autonomic), and a four-modality approach (motoric, visceral, verbal, and observational).

RELEVANT TARGET POPULATIONS

Specific and social phobias are the target for systematic desensitization, which employs progressive muscle relaxation as a key element. Relaxation is less important in exposure procedures, in which clients' experience of arousal and dissipation of anxiety is a therapeutic element. However, relaxation continues to be a significant component of coping-skill approaches to psychological disorders such as agoraphobia, anger, depression, obsessive-compulsive disorder, social phobias, and specific phobias.

Relaxation is a primary ingredient in programs for a wide variety of stress, pain, and other medically related disorders. Programs of muscle relaxation, often combined with EMG biofeedback, are effective with adult and pediatric tension headache, chronic back pain, temporomandibular-joint disorder, and essential tremor. Relaxation programs, often including thermal biofeedback, are effective with adult and pediatric migraine headache, hypertension, and Raynaud's disease. Programs of muscle relaxation, imagery, and hypnosis procedures are effective with pain and worry from chronic medical conditions, such as cancer or severe burns in both adults and pediatric populations, nausea related to cancer chemotherapy, and phobic avoidance of dental or invasive medical procedures.

COMPLICATIONS AND EXCEPTIONS

Relaxation training usually is benign, but there are some individual exceptions. Occasionally, early in training, a client may experience one or more of a variety of unpleasant sensations, termed *relaxation-induced anxiety;* these include sudden jerking, heart palpitations, dizziness, tingling, feelings of unreality, breathing irregularities, and nausea. Persons with generalized anxiety disorder or panic disorder are more likely to have such reactions. Other complaints include fear of losing control and discomfort with being watched. While no hard-and-fast rules exist for dealing with these problems, usually reassurance, a slower pace, and, in some cases, a change to another training method are sufficient.

Populations with limited intellectual capacity, such as mental retardation or brain injury, often have difficulty understanding the rationale or following the instructions for certain relaxation procedures. Also, people with mental illness, such as paranoid schizophrenia, may have bizarre ideation that interferes with training. Recent research with behavioral relaxation training indicates that it can be adapted to meet the needs of special populations.

The tensing phase of progressive relaxation may be contraindicated for some individuals with disorders related to muscle tension, such as low-back pain. More passive procedures provide a useful alternative.

CASE ILLUSTRATION

"Clara" was a 47-year-old woman with a graduate degree who was very active in church and community affairs. She was married to a locally prominent figure and had two sons. Six months prior to referral, Clara was diagnosed with neurofacial pain in the maxillary region of the trigeminal nerve; this diagnosis followed 3 months of medical treatment for sinusitis. Large daily doses of prescription and over-the-counter pain medication were ineffective. A maxillary nerve block provided short-term relief, and nerve ablation surgery was offered. She decided to try a less invasive procedure before surgery.

Assessment included a structured interview that detailed the antecedents and consequences of her pain. Clara reported that pain was exacerbated by worry, tension, and anger related to stressful events, such as illness of family members, demands from her volunteer commitments, and family caretaking responsibilities. Pain was accompanied by depression and irritability and interfered with her daily activities. A muscle scan revealed high EMG levels in her right-side jaw and neck muscles. She reported continuous pain on the right side of her face, described as burning and throbbing, with occasional blurred vision. She rated her pain four times daily on a 0 to 5 scale; ratings ranged from 3 *(moderate)* to 5 *(incapacitating)*.

Treatment consisted of behavioral relaxation training, with home practice and self-monitoring between office sessions. Approximately one third of each session was devoted to training, with the balance spent in discussion of application in her daily life. Clara achieved training criterion on the Behavioral Relaxation Scale in the reclined position within two sessions, and in the upright position within three additional sessions. In the final two sessions, a five-step mini-relaxation program was devised: Stop and sit, close eyes, inhale deeply, drop jaw, and exhale. These comprised a set of self-instructions that she employed at transitions between activities during her busy day. A plan to include EMG biofeedback training was not necessary. There were two intervals during treatment in which family illness prevented Clara from attending training or practicing. These "unplanned reversals" were accompanied by increased pain and reinforced her belief in the relationship between relaxation and relief. By the final session and at a 2-month follow-up, she demonstrated proficiency on the Behavioral Relaxation Scale, her pain ratings had declined to 1 (barely noticeable), medication use decreased markedly, and facial EMG levels were low and symmetrical.

Clara presented a clear picture of a "driven" person, focused on meeting her responsibilities to family and community and unable to take time for herself unless pain forced her to stop. Although generally aware of the relation between stress and pain, self-monitoring and discussion with the therapist helped her see specific instances. Furthermore, relaxation provided her with a means for dealing with stress and became part of a lifestyle change. She reported increased awareness of tension and used her skills to break the stress-pain cycle. Clara also saw the unreasonable demands that she placed on herself and, without specific cognitive therapy, took steps to alter them.

—Roger Poppen

See also: *Anxiety/Anger Management Training (Vol. II); Applied Relaxation and Tension (Vol. I); Self-Management (Vol. III)*

Suggested Readings

Benson, H. (1975). *The relaxation response.* New York: William Morrow.

Bernstein, D. A., & Borkovec, T. D. (1973). *Progressive relaxation training.* Champaign, IL: Research Press.

Blanchard, E. B., & Andrasik, F. (1985). *Management of chronic headaches.* New York: Pergamon Press.

Jacobson, E. (1938). *Progressive relaxation.* Chicago: University of Chicago Press.

Lehrer, P. M., Carr, R., Sargunaraj, D., & Woolfolk, R. L. (1994). Stress management techniques: Are they all equivalent or do they have specific effects? *Biofeedback and Self-Regulation, 19,* 353–401.

Lichstein, K. L. (1988). *Clinical relaxation strategies.* New York: Wiley.

Poppen, R. (1998). *Behavioral relaxation training and assessment* (2nd ed.). Thousand Oaks, CA: Sage.

Smith, J. C. (1989). *Relaxation dynamics: A cognitive-behavioral approach to relaxation.* Champaign, IL: Research Press.

RESPONSE PREVENTION

DESCRIPTION OF THE STRATEGY

Response prevention refers to a practice in which a learned behavioral reaction to a stimulus or event is blocked or inhibited. The purpose of response prevention is to break the association between the learned behavioral reaction, which typically is one that is harmful or maladaptive in the case of response prevention, and the antecedent or consequent events that maintain the response. Decades of theoretical and empirical work on the principles of associative learning have demonstrated that behaviors are influenced by the events that precede and follow them and that adding, removing, or changing these events will modify behaviors. In some instances, however, it is not possible or desirable to change the antecedent or consequent events. Therefore, it may be necessary to prevent the behavior from occurring altogether.

Response prevention is commonly used in the behavioral treatment of intense anxiety, perhaps most often in the treatment of obsessive-compulsive disorder (OCD). According to the cognitive-behavioral model of OCD, certain types of thoughts (e.g., contamination by dirt or germs) may become aversive through the process of classical conditioning. Subsequently, the individual may perform compensatory behaviors that decrease the anxiety or discomfort associated with the aversive thoughts (e.g., self-cleaning to rid oneself of the perceived contamination). If these behaviors do, in fact, decrease anxiety or discomfort, they are likely to increase in frequency and intensity via negative reinforcement. Over time, with repeated reinforcement, these compensatory behaviors can become very frequent and intense and often take the form of specific "rituals" performed to ward off the obsessive thoughts and experienced anxiety. The performance of such ritualistic behaviors will decrease the probability that an individual's anxiety will subside naturally, as the individual never learns that these behavioral responses are not necessary to decrease the experienced anxiety.

In the behavioral treatment of OCD, the individual is repeatedly exposed to the feared stimulus or event for a prolonged period of time. Through this repeated exposure, the individual learns that the perceived consequences of confronting the feared stimulus do not occur, and thus he or she obtains new information regarding the nonthreatening nature of that stimulus. For this exposure to occur and ultimately result in the extinction of the individual's fear, all attempts to escape from the feared stimulus or engage in compensatory behaviors must be blocked or prevented. Therefore, in the treatment of OCD, response prevention, or "ritual prevention," allows the individual to learn the stimulus is not dangerous, and the experienced anxiety will decrease naturally, without the performance of such responses.

Although response prevention is most commonly associated with the treatment of OCD, this procedure also has a place more generally in the treatment of other anxiety disorders and nonanxiety-related behavior problems. Indeed, exposure to feared stimuli is a major component of the behavioral treatment of all anxiety disorders. Whenever such exposure is performed, it is important that the individual's attempts to escape or avoid the feared stimulus are prevented, so that habituation to the stimulus can occur and anxiety can decrease. Thus, the clinician must employ response prevention to block escape and avoidance from exposure situations. Response prevention may also be used in the treatment of nonanxiety-related behavior problems. For example, in the treatment of impulsive or aggressive behaviors, a major component of many treatments is teaching the individual to inhibit impulsive or aggressive responses to perceived provocation in favor of no response or a less aggressive response.

Response prevention can take one of several forms in actual practice. Early uses of response prevention procedures involved the clinician physically blocking the performance of the individual's response (e.g., turning off the water supply to the individual's bathroom or holding the individual's arms). Response prevention methods involving physical restriction by the clinician are now generally considered extreme, and typically are not necessary to facilitate cooperation. Although clinicians may still use physical prevention of the behavioral response in some cases (e.g., not allowing a child into the bathroom to wash his or her hands after an exposure early in the course of treatment), it is considered most desirable to implement response prevention with as little physical restraint as possible. This will maximize the generality of the treatment effects, as the individual ultimately must learn to prevent the response outside of the clinician's presence. Therefore, methods of response prevention in which the clinician verbally coaches the individual through not engaging in the learned response first in the office and, ultimately, alone outside the office are considered most likely to lead to treatment generality and maintenance.

Given the individual is not engaging in the initial, maladaptive learned response, one might ask: What then, should they do? If the goal of the intervention is habituation to the feared stimulus (as in the treatment of anxiety disorders), any behavior that does not function to avoid or escape the feared stimulus and associated anxiety and distress should be reinforced. If the goal of the intervention is the performance of a more adaptive response (as in the treatment of aggressive behaviors), any behavior except the initial learned response should be reinforced, with the ultimate goal of shaping adaptive alternative behaviors that are incompatible with the initial learned response. For instance, if an individual commonly punches those who deliver unwanted feedback, the individual may first be rewarded for not performing the initial learned response and, ultimately, for responding in a calm and nonphysical manner.

RESEARCH BASIS

There is well-established research support for the efficacy and effectiveness of treatment protocols incorporating response prevention procedures, primarily in the treatment of OCD. Cognitive-behavioral treatment approaches combining exposure and response prevention procedures are currently the most effective treatments for OCD. A comparison of response prevention only, exposure only, and a combination of the two in the treatment of OCD revealed that response prevention only was associated with a decreased urge to ritualize, exposure only was associated with decreased anxiety in the presence of the feared stimuli, and the combined treatment was superior to either component alone on virtually all outcome measures. Thus, although response prevention can be effective when used alone, the combination of exposure with response prevention is considered the treatment of choice for OCD. Although response prevention is an important component of treatments for other behavior problems, it has not been evaluated as an individual treatment component outside of the OCD literature.

Complete prevention of the learned response is more effective than partial response prevention in decreasing anxiety and associated compulsive behaviors. If an individual is permitted to engage in some part or variant of the initial learned response, that individual may not learn that the response is not necessary for anxiety to dissipate. Thus, complete response prevention is necessary for full treatment effects to occur.

It is also notable that the effectiveness of exposure-plus-response prevention procedures in the treatment of OCD has been demonstrated in laboratory as well as clinical settings when administered daily versus twice weekly, and regardless of amount of clinician experience (e.g., 1 year vs. more than 9 years) in using these procedures. Thus, response prevention appears to be effective across settings, clinicians, and treatment parameters.

RELEVANT TARGET POPULATIONS AND EXCEPTIONS

Response prevention procedures are a central component of behavioral treatments for OCD and also play a large role in the treatment of other anxiety disorders and nonanxiety-related behavior problems. Generally speaking, response prevention is an appropriate intervention component whenever an undesirable response follows some identifiable stimuli. For this reason, response prevention commonly appears in treatment manuals for OCD and related disorders (e.g., trichotillomania), panic disorder, social anxiety disorder, simple phobias, alcohol and substance use disorders, as well as treatments for impulsive and aggressive behaviors. Moreover, the efficacy of treatments using

response prevention has been demonstrated across samples including adults, adolescents, and children. Although the content and delivery of response prevention procedures will vary depending on the developmental level of the individual, the behavioral principles involved remain the same.

COMPLICATIONS

Perhaps the greatest complications associated with the use of response prevention in clinical settings are avoidance and nonadherence from the individual seeking treatment. The prospect of being barred from engaging in safe, familiar behaviors, often in the context of exposure to highly feared stimuli, is understandably very frightening and overwhelming to many people. As a result, approximately 30% of individuals offered exposure-based treatments refuse to engage in such therapies, and an additional 20% terminate treatment prematurely. In addition, individuals involved in treatments including response prevention often to fail to adhere fully to the treatment protocol during sessions and especially outside of sessions, which may limit treatment gains.

Special attention should be given to these potential complications whenever administering treatments containing response prevention procedures. Several techniques are likely to decrease treatment refusal, dropout, or nonadherence. First, careful and comprehensive education about the nature and effectiveness of response prevention should occur early in the course of assessment and treatment. The clinician should regularly "check in" with the individual to ensure he or she is comfortable adhering to the proposed treatment plan throughout the entire course of treatment. Second, the clinician should actively involve the individual in planning the structure and pace of the intervention as well as in helping to problem solve any obstacles or barriers to treatment that may arise. Third, it is often helpful to enlist the support of the individual's family members or significant other when providing psychoeducation, behavioral assessment and monitoring, and intervention efforts in order to actively deal with potential avoidance or resistance to response prevention procedures.

Some studies have reported decreased efficacy of treatments, including response prevention procedures, in the treatment of OCD when there is a comorbid depressive illness; however, these findings have been somewhat inconsistent. Overall, there is evidence that those with a comorbid depression often benefit a great deal from such treatments but may have smaller treatment gains than those without a comorbid depressive illness. Of course, clinicians should always consider the implications of comorbid behavior problems with developing and implementing their interventions.

CASE ILLUSTRATION

"Nicole" was a 30-year-old, single, African American woman who presented to an outpatient psychological services clinic with a primary complaint of engaging in frequent washing and cleaning behaviors that interfered with her ability to work and complete household chores and had begun to interfere with her romantic relationships. Nicole, who was working as an accountant, reported she had always been a "neat freak" but that her need to wash her body and ensure the cleanliness of all things with which she came into contact had become a problem and had prompted her boyfriend to insist she seek treatment. At the time of Nicole's presentation to the clinic, she reported spending approximately 3 hours per day cleaning her body (including showering, hand and feet washing, teeth brushing, and grooming) and an additional 2 hours per day cleaning objects in her home (including clothes, towels, bed sheets, furniture, and appliances).

During Nicole's first two clinic visits, a thorough behavioral assessment was performed. This assessment drew from multiple informants (i.e., clinician, Nicole, and her boyfriend) and measurement methods (i.e., interview, rating scales, and direct behavioral observation) to develop a detailed case formulation and behavioral treatment plan. Each component of the assessment focused on obtaining specific information about the frequency, duration, and intensity of Nicole's obsessive thoughts and compulsive behaviors; the amount of associated distress and impairment; information about objects, situations, and places that evoked her obsessions and compulsions; and information about her attempts to avoid or escape these settings.

The assessment revealed that Nicole experienced daily obsessive thoughts of germ contamination, ranging from brief thoughts that she had come into contact with potentially harmful dirt particles to intense, elaborate, and persistent fears about having contracted a fatal virus due to contact with some contaminated object. These thoughts typically intensified over time and dissipated only if she engaged in compensatory washing and cleaning rituals. The rituals ranged from washing her hands and arms for 15 minutes and changing her underwear at work to taking 1-hour showers and repeatedly washing all of her clothes and bed sheets. Nicole reported she had to engage in these behaviors in order to make sure she would not become ill or even die from her contact with germs or viral agents. However, she acknowledged these behaviors were problematic given they interfered with her productivity at the office and her ability to keep up with household chores and interact with her boyfriend.

Treatment involved providing psychoeducation about the nature of obsessions and compulsions, and the efficacy of exposing Nicole to her feared thoughts and situations and preventing her engagement in compulsive behaviors. Nicole was initially apprehensive about participating in this treatment, but agreed to "give it a try." Nicole and her therapist developed a hierarchy of increasingly distressing contamination situations, ranging from touching a dusty desktop, to sitting on a toilet at the bus terminal, to touching a dead animal lying in the street. Over the course of treatment, Nicole and her therapist worked their way up the hierarchy, exposing Nicole to these increasingly distressing situations. It was vital to her treatment that after engaging in each exposure exercise, Nicole was prevented (via verbal instruction and an agreement with her clinician) from engaging in any compulsive response behaviors. That is, she was prevented from washing or cleaning herself after each exposure in order to allow her anxiety to decrease naturally, without escaping from the situation or engaging in safety behaviors. At several points during her treatment, her boyfriend reported and the clinician observed that Nicole had begun to engage in alternative compulsive behaviors, such as rubbing her hands together and wiping her hands on her clothes as an apparent proxy behavior to washing with soap and water. Nicole was questioned about this and admitted to doing so in an attempt to "get rid of the germs." In each instance, Nicole was reminded of the treatment model and the importance of preventing all compulsive behaviors. At each point, she responded well to such redirection and ceased the compulsive behaviors. Instead, during the exposure exercises, Nicole kept her hands at her sides and focused on the feared stimuli throughout the exposure period.

It was important to develop guidelines for "normal/ acceptable" washing and cleaning behaviors for Nicole to follow at work and at home. For instance,

Nicole was allowed to wash her hands for no more than 30 seconds, five times per day, and could shower only once per day for 15 minutes. Thus, only repetitive, excessive washing behaviors were prevented in this treatment, and adaptive washing behaviors were taught and rewarded. Once all compulsive behaviors were successfully prevented, the frequency, duration, and intensity of Nicole's obsessive and compulsive symptoms began to slowly decrease, and her level of social and occupational functioning increased significantly.

—*Matthew K. Nock*

See also: *Extinction and Habituation (Vol. I); Massed Practice (Vol. II); Preventing Escalated Behavior (Vol. III)*

Suggested Readings

Foa, E. B., & Franklin, M. E. (2001). Obsessive-compulsive disorder. In D. H. Barlow (Ed.), *Clinical handbook of psychological disorders* (3rd ed., pp. 209–263). New York: Guilford Press.

Foa, E. B., Wilson, R., & Wilson, R. R. (2001). *Stop obsessing: How to overcome your obsessions and compulsions* (Rev. ed.). New York: Bantam Doubleday Dell.

Hersen, M. (Ed.). (2002). *Clinical behavior therapy: Adults and children.* New York: Wiley.

Kazdin, A. E. (2001). *Behavior modification in applied settings* (6th ed.). Belmont, CA: Wadsworth.

Kozak, M. J., & Foa, E. B. (1997). *Mastery of obsessive-compulsive disorder: A cognitive-behavioral approach.* San Antonio, TX: The Psychological Corporation.

March, J. S., & Mulle, K. (1998). *OCD in children and adolescents: A cognitive-behavioral treatment manual.* New York: Guilford Press.

McLean, P. D., & Woody, S. R. (2001). *Anxiety disorders in adults: An evidence-based approach to psychological treatment.* New York: Oxford University Press.

Steketee, G. (1999). *Therapist protocol: Overcoming obsessive-compulsive disorder: A behavioral and cognitive protocol for the treatment of OCD.* Oakland, CA: New Harbinger.

ROLE PLAYING

DESCRIPTION OF THE STRATEGY

Role playing emerged as a form of behavioral assessment in the late 1970s. At the time, it was presented as the best means to estimate a patient's assertiveness skills in naturalistic settings. In a role play, an individual practices an observable behavior in the presence of a therapist as a means of assessment or intervention.

In role play assessments, the aim is to determine the individual's skill level when engaging in the target behavior. In an intervention, a role play provides an opportunity for behavioral rehearsal and feedback to shape behavior in the desired direction.

As an assessment tool, role plays have the benefits of being brief and easy to implement, and they require few resources. Role playing eventually became popular as a form of intervention, primarily to enhance social skills in depressed and schizophrenic patients. The role play format provides a rich opportunity for patients to practice new methods of interaction. It allows an individual to repeatedly engage in new strategies of interpersonal behavior in the presence of a therapist, who can provide immediate feedback. Depending on the problem it is designed to address, role play may also serve as a formal exposure to cues that trigger anger, anxiety, or drug cravings.

Role playing, when used as an intervention, relies on a process of ongoing observation and feedback to help a client gradually shape his or her behavior. When role playing is used as an assessment tool, the client may be asked to respond to a simulated situation, often involving a confederate or actor, that parallels an area in which skills are anticipated to be somewhat deficient. For example, a role play assessment for a person with alcoholism might present a scenario in which the participant is being offered a drink by a friend and the participant is expected to employ drink-refusal skills.

At first, the target person may report that role playing feels artificial and awkward. However, after completing a few role plays with the therapist, clients usually become increasingly comfortable engaging in the role and accepting feedback. To encourage participants to become as engaged as possible, the therapist must give negative feedback in a gentle and sensitive manner and be sure to comment on any improvements the client makes in each iteration of the role play. Typically, a good rule of thumb is to precede each critical comment with a complimentary comment on some aspect of the role play that was successfully accomplished.

Videotaping allows a client to review his or her performance in a role play; however, more immediate, ongoing feedback from the clinician is also helpful, because specific suggestions for alternative behaviors can be made, providing excellent feedback. A comparison of pretreatment and posttreatment videotapes of client role plays may provide valuable feedback about treatment gains. *Role reversal* is a technique that may be helpful when a patients finds a scenario particularly difficult. In this technique, the therapist plays the patient, and the patient plays the role of the other person in the scene. This approach allows the therapist to model appropriate behavior while allowing the patient to act out his or her expectations of how the other person might react. The therapist then has the opportunity to address the patient's potentially distorted or extreme expectations, and the patient may be more able to understand the other person's perspective on the situation.

RESEARCH BASIS

There has been a great deal of research on the use of role playing as an assessment tool and somewhat less regarding role playing as an intervention. The argument for using role playing as a behavioral assessment tool is that it may provide a more valid indicator of functioning than self-report measures. This is particularly likely to be true in individuals with very limited insight, who may lack the ability to provide valid self-reports of functioning, including individuals with thought disorders or significant cognitive impairment.

The research supporting the external validity of role play assessments estimating everyday functioning is inconsistent. Validity of the strategy seems to rely in part on the type of administration used, with highly structured role plays achieving greater reliability, but lower real-world (i.e., external) validity. Thus, procedures that use more structure and briefer assessments tend to be more reliable. For example, providing a confederate with a number of predetermined statements and asking the target individual to provide only one response to each statement is likely to provide some consistency across test periods, but does not mimic the reciprocal nature of most human interactions. The alternative might be to give the confederate a more flexible framework within which he or she may work and to require a conversation of at least a few minutes' duration between the target and the confederate. Some would argue that this approach provides more validity, but likely decreases reliability across assessments. Despite the critiques of role play assessments, some role play formats have achieved significant interrater reliability and test-retest reliability.

The Simulated Social Interaction Test (SSIT) is among the more structured and psychometrically validated role play measures. The SSIT consists of eight brief situations that are read by a narrator. A confederate provides verbal prompts, and trained judges make global ratings of social skill and anxiety exhibited by the target person. The Behavioral Assertiveness Test-Revised (BAT-R) is also relatively structured, with 16 interpersonal situations for patients to role-play with a confederate. The sessions are videotaped, and judges provide global ratings on assertiveness. In contrast to the SSIT and BAT-R, the label Role Play Test (RPT) encompasses a number of role play assessments that also rely on a narrated scenario and a confederate but with varying degrees of structure. More structured formats require the confederate to participate minimally in a 2- to 5-minute interaction. Less structured forms of RPT are more naturalistic, with simple instructions for the target person and confederate to talk normally for up to 12 minutes. Raters may score micro- (e.g., seconds of eye contact) or macrolevel (e.g., overall anxiety) responses.

RELEVANT TARGET POPULATIONS AND EXCEPTIONS

Role playing was first used as an assessment tool to measure assertiveness skills. Its uses have now broadened to include many populations for assessment and intervention. One benefit of role playing interventions is that their successes do not rest on a significant degree of insight from patients. The role play format relies on practicing observable behaviors shaped by feedback and modeling. To make treatment goals more attainable for patients with significant limitations, macrolevel skills (e.g., making conversation) can be broken down into their component parts (e.g., making eye contact, tone of voice), then eventually combined as the patients' skills improve.

When role plays are used as an assessment tool, research suggests that they are most externally valid when they obtain global ratings rather than specific behavioral ratings of skill or anxiety (e.g., eye contact, posture). Validity, of course, is determined by how well the outcome of the procedure matches the goals of conducting the procedure. Clinician's instructions to clients in role play assessments should be tailored to meet the goals of the assessment. For example, if the goal is to determine the client's usual level of social functioning, the client could be told to act as he or she normally would. If the goal is to determine the maximum skill level of the client, he or she might be asked to perform as a very skilled person might behave.

Role playing may be used as a formal or informal assessment tool to provide a starting point for intervention. *Social skills training* is a phrase commonly used to broadly define the treatments in which role play assessments and interventions are used. The term *social skills* encompasses an enormous range of human behaviors. Role playing has been used to treat diagnoses such as anxiety disorders, avoidant personality disorder, and unipolar depression. It has also been used to increase social skills among thought-disordered patients, a population that typically suffers from significant deficits in social functioning. Patients who are substance abusing or substance dependent have been treated with role play interventions to increase skills in refusing substances and enhance positive social functioning as a means of decreasing likelihood of relapse. Among adolescents and adults at risk for sexually transmitted diseases, role play assessments and interventions have been developed to teach better assertiveness skills to counter coercive behaviors from potential partners and to increase negotiation skills to encourage safer-sex behaviors.

Another domain of social skills training is anger management. Role plays can be used to play out hypothetical situations so that anger triggers can be identified and addressed. By practicing skills in session, a patient has the opportunity to "call a time-out" or to test several potential responses without the same emotional intensity that is present in real social interactions. Role plays have also been used for anger management among specific groups, such as athletes, as a way to help them keep their attention focused and improve performance.

Finally, role play interventions have been used to enhance prosocial skills among delinquent adolescents and incarcerated adults. These interventions tend to focus on increasing interpersonal problem-solving skills and anger management. Among adolescents who have been involved in delinquent behaviors, role plays may also be used to develop the ability to firmly refuse to engage in delinquent behaviors (e.g., turn down an offer of drugs, avoid a fight).

In treatment, role plays are usually one component in a larger cognitive-behavioral or behavioral treatment approach. Patients eventually are expected to practice in their everyday lives the skills they learned in during in-session role plays.

COMPLICATIONS

Some clients may not readily agree to engage in role playing as a part of treatment, particularly if their presenting complaints include social anxiety related to a fear of negative evaluation. Group interventions appear to work well for treatment of social anxiety, probably in part for their normalizing effects and the development of supportive relationships among group members.

It is important to keep in mind that because role plays are not perfect analogues for actual social interactions, they are not perfect indicators of skill level. If an individual does not perform a skill well in the role play assessment, he or she is unlikely to demonstrate that skill in a natural setting. However, if a person exhibits a skill in the assessment, he or she is not necessarily likely to exhibit it in real life in novel situations. Therefore, role play assessments may be more accurate in detecting deficits than strengths in social skills.

CASE ILLUSTRATION

"Dave" was a 46-year-old male who had been arrested once for engaging in oral sex with an adolescent girl. He voluntarily sought treatment after being released from jail. During treatment, Dave admitted to having engaged in sexual acts with other adolescent girls over a number of years. Following the initial intake session, the therapist used Alan Marlatt's relapse prevention model as a framework for understanding and identifying triggers that might increase Dave's risk for reoffending. A behavioral analysis revealed that areas contributing to risk included financial stress, discontent with work, low self-confidence, and feelings of loneliness. In conceptualizing the case, it became clear that Dave had social skills deficits that adversely affected his functioning in both occupational and social spheres. Dave's low self-esteem and lack of confidence when interacting with adult women seemed to be significant motivators for his seeking sexual contact with teenage girls. He maintained that he felt sexually attracted to adult women but feared that they would reject him.

Dave had had few romantic relationships or close friendships over the years. He described himself as a "late bloomer." Despite his difficulties, Dave chose to work in a commission-based sales job requiring extensive interpersonal contact with coworkers and customers. According to Dave's own report, he became defensive and hostile when offered constructive feedback at work. Dave's customers seemed to take advantage of his lack of assertiveness to broker deals that ultimately led to his earning relatively low commissions.

In the first phase of treatment, Dave learned to enhance his coping responses to financial and work stressors. He provided weekly self-reports of any contact he had with children and any occurrence of sexual fantasies that included images of children. In the second phase of treatment, the weekly monitoring continued to be an integral part of treatment, but the primary focus of treatment was on social skills training. Dave was treated with a cognitive-behavioral intervention that included role plays as a means to enhance his confidence and skill level in social situations with adult peers. During this phase of treatment, Dave's level of risk for reoffending was evaluated in every session with questions that targeted each of his areas of risk: financial, occupational, self-confidence, and loneliness. The therapist engaged Dave in role plays of increasing complexity, beginning with simple skills such as making a friendly comment to a stranger (e.g., a comment on the weather). The content of the role play scenarios became increasingly complex as Dave developed new skills and his confidence increased. As a key component of treatment, Dave was asked to practice the new skills he learned in each session by practicing them two to three times in the following week.

Each session began with a review of homework in which Dave described interpersonal interactions in which he practiced new skills. After the therapist provided feedback and support regarding areas for improvement and progress made in the homework, the discussion turned to targeting a new social skill. A role play would be conducted, with the therapist and patient both able to interrupt at any time with the signal "Time-out." This signal was chosen jointly by the patient and therapist because the patient enjoyed spectator sports and indicated that he would not feel hurt if the therapist used this signal to stop the role play. During and after the role play, the therapist used humor and a gentle and encouraging tone to provide feedback on verbal and nonverbal skills, such as speed and content of speech, eye contact, hand gestures, and so on. The following role play illustrates a typical in-session interaction:

Therapist: There is an attractive woman about your age in front of you in the line at the grocery store. You would like to start a conversation with her. Let's role play the situation, and I will pretend to be her while you play yourself. You begin.

Client: It sure is a beautiful day.

Therapist: It is, isn't it?

Client: I think I will go for a run today. I used to work with a national track team that was very successful. I still work out with them sometimes, just to help out. I think I have a gift for coaching young people. I really connect with them.

Therapist: Time-out. Good job starting up the conversation with a casual comment. She might be able to get more involved in the conversation if you ask a question about her. How about giving that a try?

Client: Okay. I guess I could ask her if she has plans for the afternoon.

Therapist: Say it as if you are talking to her.

Client: Do you have any plans for the afternoon?

Therapist: I think I will probably go for a walk or something to enjoy the fresh air.

Client: I was thinking of going for a run, but maybe we could go for a walk together.

Therapist: Time-out. That was great, especially the way that you gave a friendly smile as you talked and kept good eye contact. One suggestion, though, would be to ease into an invitation a little more slowly. For example, you might want to introduce yourself first, so that she can feel more comfortable. Let's try the scene again.

Role play scenarios focused on identified problem areas such as assertiveness skills at work, social interactions at church gatherings, and initiating and following through on a date with a woman. Dave eventually was able to initiate dates with adult women, avoiding those women who had any minor children. At the time of termination, he had started to consider establishing a more serious relationship with a woman he was dating. He had not reoffended against a child or adolescent for 2 years. He reported increased confidence and satisfaction at work, in church, and in his dating life.

—*Angela E. Waldrop and Ron Acierno*

See also: *Augmentative and Alternative Communication (Vol. III); Modeling (Vol. I); Role Playing (Vol. II)*

Suggested Readings

Bellack, A. S., Morrison, R. L., Mueser, K. T., Wade, J. H., & Sayers, S. L. (1990). Role play for assessing the social competence of psychiatric patients. *Psychological Assessment: A Journal of Consulting and Clinical Psychology, 2,* 248–255.

Donohue, B., Acierno, R., Hersen, M., & Van Hasselt, V. B. (1995). Social skills training for depressed, visually impaired older adults. *Behavior Modification, 19,* 379–424.

Haynes, S. N. (2001). Clinical applications of analogue behavioral observation: Dimensions of psychometric evaluation. *Psychological Assessment, 13,* 73–85.

Hersen, M., Bellack, A. S., & Himmelhoch, J. M. (1980). Treatment of unipolar depression with social skills training. *Behavior Modification, 4,* 547–556.

Patterson, T. L., Moscona, S., McKibbin, C. L., Davidson, K., & Jeste, D. V. (2001). Social skills performance assessment among older patients with schizophrenia. *Schizophrenia Research, 48,* 351–360.

S

SCHEDULE-INDUCED BEHAVIOR

DESCRIPTION OF THE STRATEGY

Schedule-induced or *adjunctive behavior,* first reported by John Falk in 1961, is generally defined as excessive behavior produced by a schedule of intermittent reinforcement but not required by the schedule. Although several types of schedule-induced behavior have been reported in a wide variety of organisms, including drinking and air licking in rats, aggression in pigeons, and movement and eating in humans, the prototypical example of schedule-induced behavior is schedule-induced polydipsia (excessive drinking) in rats. In a standard experimental preparation, food-deprived rats are fed small, 45 mg food pellets approximately once per minute in a Skinner box with water freely available. Over several sessions, rats gradually develop a robust stereotyped pattern of postfood water consumption, in which a drinking bout of 5 to 30 seconds in length occurs a few seconds after the consumption of each pellet. Rats can drink 15 to 30 ml of water in 30 minutes and half their body weight in 3 to 4 hours. A domestic Norway rat normally drinks about 10 to 20 ml of water in a 24-hour period.

In most studies, only the total amount of induced responding is measured. Yet each adjunctive response has several distinct characteristics: magnitude, duration, probability, and postreinforcement latency. During acquisition, the magnitude and duration of the response generally do not change greatly, the probability increases to a plateau—sometimes occurring after 100% of food deliveries—and the latency decreases to just a few seconds. Food deprivation is

not required, but greater deprivation generally produces faster acquisition and a higher response probability. Adjunctive responding is most likely when food pellets are delivered once each three minutes. Under some conditions, however, such as when interpellet interval lengths are varied within sessions, strong adjunctive drinking bouts, clearly distinct from ordinary drinking bouts, can occur under interpellet intervals as long as 16 minutes and can also be seen when sessions include only a single-pellet delivery trial and no schedule at all. The type of food can affect drinking, with powdered and most liquid food producing little adjunctive responding relative to dry food pellets. The size of the meal does not seem to have a definite relationship to probability of the adjunctive response. The fact that rats will lick an airstream in place of water suggests that the rats are not drinking due to the mouth-drying effects of food. Moreover, induced aggression in pigeons has the same general characteristics as drinking in rats and cannot be attributed to ingestive factors.

The origin and function of adjunctive behavior have not been resolved. It is not superstitious, maintained by contingent reinforcement, or conditioned by Pavlovian processes. Some suggest that adjunctive behavior serves timing functions or reduces anxiety or frustration due to interruption of eating. In terms of topography and development during acquisition, adjunctive behavior resembles sensitized elicited responding—behavior that is strengthened by repeated elicitations. This makes evolutionary sense. The reduction of drinking through habituation by repeated consumption of small meals would lead to dehydration. Sensitization would result in the extra hydration necessary to process food consumed in this way. Aggression in pigeons, similarly, might arise because smaller, spaced meals might imply a shortage of resources requiring strengthened defensive responses relative to situations with sufficient food. Excessiveness, therefore, might not be a fundamental feature of adjunctive behavior. Excessiveness is due to the repeated elicitation of discrete, strengthened reflexive responses.

The significance and existence of adjunctive behavior in humans has been debated. Some have suggested that schedule-induced behavior is a model for alcoholism, drug abuse, and large-scale ritualistic behavior in humans; these unneeded behaviors arise as side effects of schedules of reinforcement maintaining other behaviors. Others complain that the experimental literature contains few, if any, true examples of human induced behavior. Humans do not exhibit the reinforcer-response specificity, strength, persistence, stereotyped topography, and gradual acquisition of induced responses exhibited in nonhumans. Excessiveness alone, critics suggest, is a superficial basis for comparing induced behavior in animals to alcoholism and large-scale rituals in humans.

Despite possible weaknesses as a model of drug abuse and rituals in human behavior, some research now points to adjunctive behavior as a model of aspects of obsessive-compulsive disorder (OCD) in humans. Giving selective serotonin reuptake inhibitors (SSRIs) to polydipsic rats on reinforcement schedules for bar pressing will reduce water consumption but leave bar pressing relatively unaffected. SSRIs given to humans with OCD will often reduce the incidence of compulsive behavior without affecting most other responding. The highly specific, stereotyped adjunctive responses seen in animals are similar in general topography and persistence to certain kinds of stimulus-bound compulsive responses in humans (sometimes said to have a "ritualistic character"). Indeed, induced responses do not require an ongoing schedule; once established by intermittent stimulation, they can be elicited any time by an appropriate stimulus presentation. Polydipsic rats, like humans with compulsions, will go to great lengths to engage in the behavior. Rats will press a lever up to 50 times for a postfood drink. In a runway where food and water are separated by a meter or more, rats will run back and forth, adjusting running speed to minimize the time between eating and drinking. When the distance becomes too great, drinking becomes less probable, as human compulsions do under certain response prevention situations. Response prevention, exposure, and other interventions that address compulsion

directly are similar to interventions known to reduce sensitized responses, such as strongly reinforced alternative responses, counterconditioning, and high response cost.

Conceiving of compulsive responding as induced responding arising through sensitization could explain some aspects of OCD, promote a rethinking of the role of anxiety and stress in OCD, and suggest new therapeutic interventions. Although compulsions are typically normal behaviors, because they are exhibited excessively and inappropriately, the controlling conditions and functions of compulsive episodes are not obvious. If compulsions are induced, engendered by intermittent stimulation in the past and elicited in the present, determining the cause of compulsive episodes would be a matter of identifying antecedents. The psychological function or meaning of the compulsion, if any, would be secondary and provide an ineffective avenue for therapeutic intervention. The induction model also suggests why interventions that assume that the anxiety- or stress-reducing properties of compulsive responding are critical to maintaining the compulsion are less effective than behavior therapies (e.g., response prevention and exposure)—which directly address the compulsive responses. Anxiety and stress responses may be not be important mediating events at all; they may be secondary effects or perhaps even additional induced responses. Exploring the effectiveness of behavioral interventions known to reduce sensitized elicited responding is an obvious implication of this theory. Examining the correspondences between central mechanisms of induced responding and compulsions, including those in lateral hypothalamus and associated structures, might lead to the discovery of compounds, which, like SSRIs, have a selective effect in reducing compulsive responding.

For decades, schedule-induced behavior has been a laboratory curiosity with few clear implications for human behavior. If the correspondences between sensitization, schedule induction, and OCD are real, it is possible that a wide variety of seemingly anomalous human behaviors—OCD and perhaps drug abuse—could be explained by known behavioral processes and additional effective behavior therapies developed using laboratory-tested principles.

—James T. Todd and Janet L. Pietrowski

See also: *Applied Behavior Analysis (Vols. I & II); Schedules of Reinforcement (Vol. III)*

Suggested Readings

Falk, J. L. (1977). The origin and functions of adjunctive behavior. *Animal Learning and Behavior, 5,* 325–335.

Falk, J. L. (1992). Drug abuse as an adjunctive behavior. *Drug and Alcohol Dependence, 52,* 91–98.

Overskeid, G. (1992). Is any human behavior schedule-induced? *Psychological Record, 42,* 323–340.

Riley, A. L., & Wetherington, C. L. (1989). Schedule-induced polydipsia: Is the rat a small furry human? (An analysis of an animal model of human alcoholism). In S. B. Klein & R. R. Mowrer (Eds.), *Contemporary learning theories: Instrumental conditioning theory and the impact of biological constraints on learning* (pp. 205–236). Hillsdale, NJ: Erlbaum.

Wetherington, C. L. (1981). Is adjunctive behavior a third class of behavior? *Neuroscience and Biobehavioral Reviews, 6,* 329–350.

Woods, A., Smith, C., Szewczak, M., Dunn, R. W., Cornfeldt, M., & Corbett, R. (1993). Selective serotonin re-uptake inhibitors decrease schedule-induced polydipsia in rats: A potential model for obsessive-compulsive disorder. *Psychopharmacology, 112,* 195–198.

SCHEDULES OF REINFORCEMENT

DESCRIPTION OF THE STRATEGY

Schedules of reinforcement describe the rules for arranging reinforcers. Reinforcers are stimuli (physical events) that strengthen behaviors that precede and typically produce them. Behaviors that are strengthened by reinforcement are termed *operant,* because they operate on the environment to produce an important change. The response-strengthening effects of reinforcement typically involve an increase in the future rate or probability of operant behavior under similar circumstances in the future, although other changes in behavior (e.g., a decrease in latency or increase in amplitude) can also be indicative of reinforcement.

Schedules of reinforcement may specify temporal requirements, response requirements, or both. A huge variety of schedules can be arranged in controlled settings. Although several variables influence performance under a given schedule, basic research makes it clear that rates and temporal patterns of responding are strongly influenced by the way in which reinforcers are arranged. Schedules of reinforcement also influence choice and resistance of behavior to disruption (e.g., by extinction). Exposure to one kind of schedule may influence subsequent patterns of responding under another schedule. Finally, schedules of reinforcement play an important role in establishing control of behavior by antecedent discriminative stimuli.

Although the distinction is not particularly useful, it is convention to distinguish between positive and negative reinforcement. Schedules of positive reinforcement specify the requirements for adding something, termed a *positive reinforcer,* to the environment. If, for example, a therapist regularly praises a depressed client for making positive statements and more such statements are made as a result, then praise is functioning as a positive reinforcer and the therapist has arranged a schedule of positive reinforcement for making positive statements.

Schedules of negative reinforcement specify the requirements for removing something, termed a *negative reinforcer,* from the environment, or for postponing or presenting the delivery of such a reinforcer. It is standard practice to distinguish escape behavior, which is evident when responding is strengthened because it terminates or reduces the intensity of a stimulus, from avoidance behavior, which is evident when responding is strengthened because it prevents or postpones the presentation of an otherwise forthcoming stimulus. If, for example, a baby cries each night unless allowed to sleep in her parents' bed, her parents may move the baby to their bed after it cries as escape behavior, or before it cries as avoidance behavior. In both cases, the baby's crying is a negative reinforcer. "Negative" in this sense does not refer to the value of the increase in behavior produced by reinforcement or to the ethical or practical value of a particular reinforcement procedure. Neither negative nor positive reinforcement automatically produces desired or undesired changes in behavior, and although the majority of clinical applications involve positive reinforcement, both can be used to therapeutic advantage. Although negative reinforcement frequently is confused with punishment, which weakens behavior, it is important to recognize that both positive and negative reinforcement strengthen the designated operant response.

Because of their powerful effects on behavior, schedules of reinforcement potentially are of great clinical importance. By arranging appropriate schedules of reinforcement, it frequently is possible to increase appropriate responding. In general, people fail to behave in desired ways because they do not know how to do so or because their everyday environment does not arrange sufficient reinforcement to maintain appropriate behavior. For example, a woman with severe cognitive impairments may fail to make her bed because she has not been taught to make it or because there are no significant consequences (reinforcers or punishers) regardless of whether or not her bed is made. In the former case, contrived schedules of reinforcement could be used as part of a training program involving shaping and chaining. In the latter, contrived schedules could be used to engender and maintain appropriate responding. For example, each time her bed was made by 8 a.m., the woman might receive praise and have a magnetic star attached to the metal headboard of her bed. When five stars were earned, they could be exchanged for a desired object or activity. Failing to make her bed by 8 would result in the loss of a star. This arrangement, which could be construed as a schedule of reinforcement, might well lead to consistent bed making.

Schedules of reinforcement can be used to reduce or eliminate troublesome behaviors, as well as to increase desirable behaviors. One schedule that can be effective in reducing troublesome behavior is usually, but misleadingly, termed the *differential reinforcement of other behavior* (DRO) schedule. Under a DRO schedule, the reinforcer is presented dependent on the passage of a specified time during which the target behavior does not occur. For example, if a DRO 1-minute schedule of food delivery were arranged to reduce self-injurious scratching by a person with severe mental retardation, the person would receive food each time 1 minute passed without scratching. Each episode of scratching would reset the interval. If effective, this schedule would decrease how often scratching occurred. No other behavior is required to produce food delivery, and no other behavior is necessarily strengthened under DRO schedules. In fact, in nearly all published studies involving DRO, data are presented only for the response targeted for reduction. Therefore, the designation "DRO" is misleading. A better description is *differential reinforcement of pausing* (DRP), because pauses are what are required for reinforcer delivery and pauses are what increase when such schedules are effective. People can learn to omit, as well as emit, behavior, and they learn the former under DRP schedules.

In addition to their value as tools for changing behavior, schedules of reinforcement are important because naturally occurring schedules frequently are responsible for the maintenance of troublesome

behaviors. Existence of such schedules can be revealed through functional assessment, which comprises a set of techniques used to isolate lawful antecedents and consequences of responses of clinical significance. For example, studies have revealed that troublesome student behaviors in school settings often are maintained (reinforced) by attention from adults or other students.

RESEARCH BASIS

Hundreds of studies have examined schedule-controlled behavior in nonhuman subjects. For instance, a recent search of the PsycINFO database using "schedule of reinforcement" and "animal" as subject terms yielded 335 relevant publications. Basic research with nonhumans convincingly demonstrates that behavior is strongly influenced by schedules of reinforcement. For example, fixed-ratio (FR) schedules deliver a reinforcer following every "nth" response (e.g., fifth under an FR 5). Such schedules typically generate relatively high and stable response rates, with pronounced pauses following delivery of each reinforcer. These pauses vary directly with the length of the upcoming ratio. Variable-ratio schedules, in contrast, arrange for the delivery of a positive reinforcer following every nth response, on average, although the number of responses required to earn each reinforcer varies. Such schedules usually engender high and relatively stable patterns of responding, with little pausing after reinforcers are received.

An especially compelling example of the exquisite sensitivity of behavior to scheduled consequences involves performance under concurrent variable-interval (VI) variable-internal (VI) schedules of positive reinforcement. Concurrent schedules simultaneously and independently arrange reinforcers for two or more different behaviors. Under VI schedules, a reinforcer becomes available once a specified interval that varies around a known mean value elapses and is delivered dependent on a designated response. For example, under a concurrent VI 1-minute VI 2-minute schedule of food delivery, a pigeon's pecks on the left-most of two plastic disks (keys) would produce grain on average once each minute, whereas pecks on the right key would produce grain on average once every 2 minutes. Under such conditions, the number of responses (or amount of time) allocated to each component schedules (e.g., VI 1-minute and VI 2-minute) is proportional to the number of reinforcers earned under those schedules. This relation, which is codified in the generalized matching equation, provides clear evidence of the exquisite sensitivity of living creatures to the consequences of their actions and the specific schedules under which those consequences are arranged.

Far fewer basic-research studies have examined schedule-controlled behavior in humans than in non-humans. For example, when "human" was substituted for "animal" in the literature search described above, only 30 relevant publications were found. With some exceptions, described later, humans and other species appear to respond in similar fashion to particular schedules of reinforcement.

Moreover, and importantly, a sizable number of studies have demonstrated the feasibility of using reinforcement schedules to produce clinically significant changes in a substantial range of target behaviors. Descriptions of useful schedules and instructions for arranging them are standard fare in applied behavior analysis textbooks.

RELEVANT TARGET POPULATIONS AND EXCEPTIONS

Almost all humans are sensitive to the consequences of their behavior and, hence, to schedules of reinforcement. The primary exceptions are individuals with extreme central nervous system damage, who are not sensitive to any sort of psychological intervention. Schedules of reinforcement have been used to deal with a substantial range of behavior problems in a variety of client populations. Nevertheless, most published studies have involved people with developmental disabilities. The primary reason for this is that the circumstances of their lives often make it relatively easy to isolate effective reinforcers and to arrange appropriate schedules.

A significant problem in the therapeutic use of schedules of reinforcement is isolating effective reinforcers that can be manipulated to produce the desired schedule. Practical and ethical considerations make it difficult for therapists and other caregivers to control the objects and events that serve as reinforcers for most adults in their everyday settings. Moreover, effectiveness of most stimuli as positive reinforcers requires that motivation to receive those stimuli is high. Environmental variables that alter the capacity of stimuli to function as reinforcers are termed

motivational operations (MOs), which are divided into *establishing operations* (EOs), which increase reinforcing effectiveness, and *abolishing operations* (AOs), which reduce it. Unless appropriate EOs are in effect naturally or can be arranged artificially, schedules of reinforcement are not likely to produce the desired effects. Even when effective reinforcers can be isolated and appropriate EOs put in effect, arranging and maintaining a schedule of reinforcement may prove difficult or impossible, especially when there is need for the intervention to be in place across time and settings.

COMPLICATIONS

In some cases, the behavior of verbal humans is influenced to a greater degree by rules, or instructions, describing consequences of their behavior than by the actual manner in which those consequences are arranged. For example, college students instructed to "work fast" often do so, even though they would receive more reinforcers by responding slowly. Students instructed to "work slowly," as students given no instructions at all, are more sensitive to the consequences of particular rates and patterns of responding.

In therapeutic settings, clients may generate rules that reduce their sensitivity to scheduled events. Rules are descriptions of relations between stimuli and responses. Consider, for example, a wife and husband who are seeing a marital therapist, in part because his style of lovemaking is, in her words, "brief and brutal." The therapist encourages them to experiment in various ways, with the woman providing verbal encouragement (e.g., "That feels good, keep going") when the man behaves in ways that stimulate her. The therapist posits that her praise will reinforce appropriate interactions, but no matter how much the man loves and wants to please his wife, this is unlikely to occur if he follows the rule "Women want it hard." No matter how that rule was generated, its control over the man's sexual repertoire must be abolished before the intervention is effective. Rule-governed behavior is cognitive behavior, and altering counterproductive cognitions sometimes is necessary for schedules of reinforcement to produce desired effects. In addition, generating rules that are consistent with the actual consequences of behavior is apt to maximize sensitivity to those consequences.

Several authors have suggested caution in referring to schedules of reinforcement in describing many complex relations between behavior and its consequences that occur naturally for humans or are arranged therapeutically to improve their behavior. These arrangements bear little resemblance to schedules of reinforcement as studied in the laboratory, and viewing them as comparable is apt to be misleading. For example, in the scenario of lovemaking just described, what schedule is the woman arranging, and what is gained by referring to a schedule of reinforcement in describing the consequences that she arranges?

CASE ILLUSTRATION

"Jim" is a young adult diagnosed with mild mental retardation who lives in a group home. He has recently secured a job in a local fast-food restaurant, where his primary responsibility is cleaning trays. Although he comes to work on time and is generally well behaved, Jim does not work fast enough to suit the establishment's owner. To increase Jim's speed, the owner arranges a bonus system where Jim receives, in addition to his hourly wage, a check mark on a blackboard for every 20 trays he cleans. At the end of the week, the check marks can be exchanged for menu items, at an exchange rate agreed upon by Jim and his boss. This arrangement constitutes an FR 20 schedule and should increase Jim's speed, given that conditions have been arranged such that check marks are effective as conditioned reinforcers and the food items for which they can be exchanged are reinforcing for Jim. Whether or not the intervention is effective could be easily ascertained by comparing the number of trays cleaned per hour before and after the schedule was implemented.

—*Alan D. Poling and Susan Snycerski*

See also: *Applied Behavior Analysis (Vols. I & II); Schedules of Reinforcement (Vol. III)*

Suggested Readings

Miltenberger, R. (2001). *Behavior modification: Principles and procedures.* Pacific Grove, CA: Brooks/Cole.

Shull, R. L., & Scott, L. P. (1998). Reinforcement: Schedule performance. In K. A. Lattal & M. Perone (Eds.), *Handbook of research methods in human operant behavior* (pp. 95–129). New York: Plenum Press.

SELF-CONTROL

DESCRIPTION OF THE STRATEGY

The term *self-control* has been most often employed, within the domain of behavior modification, to describe varied forms of self-guided treatment that seek to alter the probability of habitual, preferred, or readily reinforced behaviors, thoughts, or emotional responses when their long-range consequences are at odds with their immediate effects (that is, when they involve *conflicting contingencies*). Mechanisms underlying self-directed habit change include the systematic (re)deployment of attentional resources (e.g., focusing on the frequency of one's self-defeating actions and/or their consequences), realistic goal setting, nondefensive appraisal of perceived discrepancies between desired and current states, verbal self-instructional skills, and the self-administration of positive or negative consequences. Change instigated via self-imposed treatments is expected to persist over time, not because varied self-control mechanisms, such as those noted above, continue to be enacted, but rather because practice, positive outcome expectancies, a belief in one's abilities (self-efficacy), and environmental support structures (cues and reinforcing consequences) enable the individual to "automate" the newly strengthened and presumably more adaptive response pattern.

The targets of self-control efforts may vary, but typically fall within two broad categories. Some habitual responses that are in need of change are associated with immediately pleasant or rewarding consequences but unpleasant, costly, legally proscribed, or unhealthful long-term outcomes. Examples are cigarette smoking, excessive alcohol consumption, viewing child pornography, overeating, and the like. The self-control of such responses requires a strategy for lowering the probability of approaching the highly rewarding immediate response—such as by rendering that response aversive through the self-administration of criticism. Alternatively, some actions or patterns of thought are immediately unpleasant, anxiety provoking, time- or resource intensive, and low in probability (e.g., studying for an exam when one's friends are out partying, participating in a painful medical examination, meeting new people when one is extremely shy, etc.) but nevertheless valuable over the long haul. The self-control of such patterns requires ways of rendering immediately unlikely responses more probable—such as by bringing rewarding consequences to bear, contingent on their emission. In both cases, the individual lacking self-control skills is said to act *impulsively,* motivated by attention to short-term gains or losses and by the tendency to discount possible future consequences. In fact, impulsivity, a predisposition toward rapid, error-prone, unthinking action, is often cast as the opposite of self-control.

Self-control is best understood a special case of the broader construct of *self-regulation,* which refers to the process of guiding oneself toward distant and often difficult goals in the relative absence of situational prompts and contingent rewards. Whereas self-regulation pertains to processes underlying goal persistence or attainment, the objective of self-control efforts is *self-* or *habit change.* In both cases, the achievement of the ultimate objective (directional maintenance or directional change) is a matter of degree rather than being an all-or-nothing outcome. Similarly, the "causal" elements involved are never completely internal or external, but instead are the products of a complex interplay between inner and outer forces. Thus, self-control and external control are not polar opposites.

Readers should note that although self-control tactics are often learned with the help of parents, teachers, and skilled clinicians and can be augmented, in certain cases, by the use of pharmacologic agents and external social supports, a key defining dimension of self-control therapies is their emphasis on personal initiative, active decision making, and client responsibility for program enactment. Self-controlled interventions possess the twin virtues of being performed in places and at times selected by the client as most appropriate as well as being capable of targeting private responses to which only the client has direct access. A corollary of these interventive advantages is the further assumption that self-controlled treatments represent a cost-effective means of maximizing the maintenance (stability), transfer, and generalization of therapeutic effects.

It is particularly important to appreciate that *self-control therapy* is not a single technique, but an organizing term applied whenever self-change is the primary clinical objective. In fact, over the years, a host of techniques have been used in the field of behavior modification to facilitate client control over problematic habits. A fair number of the externally managed treatments described in this encyclopedia that ostensibly rely upon "passive conditioning" to achieve their effects have been translated into *self-administered versions* for the sake of ceding greater behavioral and decisional authority to the client. For example, a phobic individual could create his or her own hierarchy of feared stimuli, learn to relax via self-instruction, and then pair relaxation with phobic stimuli in imagination. However, the usual format for the self-administration of traditional behavior therapies, such as systematic desensitization, is sequential, involving therapist-guided treatment, followed by fading of therapist management, and culminating with the client taking on the lion's share of the responsibility for program implementation.

Self-control interventions can likewise be initiated at the outset of treatment, based on the presumption that the target problem can be most efficiently eliminated under a client-controlled regimen. Client-controlled treatments are built upon a conceptual model that specifies the components, stages, or constituents of self-directed change. Surprisingly, operant conditioning, the prototype of "externally managed" or "coercive" behavior control, was among the first to provide insights into the components of self-control. In the 1950s, B. F. Skinner proposed that by prearranging the appropriate cues and consequences, humans could take on the roles of experimenter and subject for the purpose of managing their own response patterns. When an operant researcher seeks to shape the behavior of an animal or human subject, that researcher must (a) place the subject in a controllable environment, (b) deprive the subject of access to valued rewards, (c) decide on what the subject is required to do in order to earn reinforcement, (d) monitor and record the subject's ongoing actions, (e) determine whether the subject has met the standard or criterion for receiving a reward, and then (f) arrange to administer a reward, contingent on the appropriate action pattern. These steps, when carried out by a solitary human seeking to unobtrusively shape or control himself or herself, translate into the frequently applied tactics of (a) stimulus control (environmental management), (b) self-deprivation, (c) goal setting or standard setting, (d) self-monitoring or self-observation, (e) self-evaluation of whether the standard has been achieved, and (f) contingent self-presentation of consequences (e.g., self-reward or self-punishment). Note that the self-mediated version of the operant model is predicated upon non-Skinnerian mechanisms such as the capacity for self-awareness, forethought, and discrepancy detection.

Because self-control essentially involves a change in the probability of behavior built upon an altered set of preferences, it is possible to adopt a pure or "radical" behavioral account of self-control that does not directly invoke mental mechanisms or covert processes (such as self-reflection or the covert comparison of one's actions against symbolized standards). The noncognitive view requires an analysis only of overt actions and their reinforcement/punishment contingencies conducted over time and in context. Such an approach, called *teleological behaviorism, molar behaviorism,* or *hyperbolic discounting theory,* contends that self-control is nothing more (nor less) than the choice between an immediate versus a delayed consequence. Moreover, it is a choice that depends upon a small number of objective parameters, such as the value or frequency of both the delayed and the immediate consequences and the temporal extent of the delay. Response preference can, in fact, be mathematically specified by the *matching law,* which states that the ratio of values of two rewarding response alternatives that differ in delay and amount is equal to the product of the ratio of the amounts multiplied by the inverse ratio of the delays. When rewards are in conflict, the prototypical case illustrating this choice-based model of self-control is *delay of gratification.* It involves the selection of a larger but later (LL) reward over a smaller, sooner (SS) reward. When aversive (punishing) consequences are at issue, self-control is defined as the selection of the SS negative consequence over the LL negative outcome.

Notably, from the perspective of a choice-based model, the tactics for achieving preference change (self-control) have typically involved experimenter-based manipulation or specification of performance feedback, delay times, the relative magnitudes of the incentives, time allotted for reward consumption, and/or other relevant information about the operative contingencies. Hence, the discounting model presumes that a person can be shaped or conditioned into making the nonimpulsive choice under controlled conditions and will, at other times and in other places, remain behaviorally committed to the acquired preference. Since the 1970s, behavioral investigators have become increasingly comfortable with the less tangible and more abstract reward-and-punishment systems that characterize proactive, free-ranging humans and with the explicitly cognitive or symbolic aspects of the self-control process as it unfolds in the natural environment (including the specification of covert targets of change, such as thoughts, emotions, physiological

reactions, and images). Consequently, the boundaries of self-control, both as a process and a clinical objective, have widened considerably. Among the cognitive-behavioral strategies now associated with self-control therapy are precommitment, self-instructional training, self-statement modification, covert conditioning, cue-controlled relaxation, thought-stopping, bibliotherapy, and biofeedback.

Although no standard self-control strategy exists, many of the procedures employed in the last 30 years have included (a) the presentation of a rationale for why self-managed change is desirable, (b) the presentation of a simplified model of self-control, (c) training in the self-monitoring and self-recording of the problematic response(s), (d) the specification of a detailed habit change plan based on a functional analysis of the "to-be-controlled" response, (e) explicit training in and practice of self-control methods, and (f) training in the self-administration of valued incentives contingent upon the implementation of program components.

RESEARCH BASIS

Self-control, by definition, is enacted in "risky" situations, those in which people are confronted by frequent and often unavoidable temptations (e.g., to take drugs, to avoid feared situations, etc.). Therefore, would-be self-controllers must contend with formidable contextual, biological, and psychological forces that threaten to undermine their most heartfelt intentions and best-laid plans. In other words, self-control tactics, as they are performed in the laboratory or the consulting room, may not fully represent self-control as it is played out over protracted periods in the natural environment. Moreover, because self-control therapies often involve combinations of self- and therapist-managed interventions as well as educational components, many of which can be justified by alternative conceptual models, it is not easy to state with precision that a particular self-control treatment or treatment package has proven its clinical effectiveness.

Nonetheless, controlled group experiments and single-case (time-series) experiments have been conducted to evaluate the efficacy of complex therapy packages featuring multiple techniques or components of self-control that are either compared with each other, with externally managed behavioral interventions, or with no treatment. When the influence of self-control methods is estimated using between- or within-subjects designs, combinations of self-control techniques (e.g., self-monitoring, verbal self-guidance, self-administered consequences, goal setting, and the like) often perform as well as contingency management, relaxation, or some other established intervention; sometimes better (over the long term); and occasionally not as well. Self-control therapies are typically more powerful than no treatment, particularly when self-monitoring and self-statement components are included. In addition, multiple self-control components applied over extended time periods tend to yield better outcomes than single-component treatments applied for shorter intervals. Unfortunately, experimenters have rarely been able to rule out the change-inducing effects of factors that are common across all the treatment components in a comparative analysis, such as therapist attention, knowledge and acceptance of the therapy rationale, positive expectations for treatment success, and therapist-patient relationship factors. Long-term follow-ups are not always included in research designs, although in recent years, more attention has been paid to program adherence and persistence. At present, then, the question of whether multicomponent self-control packages are independently curative and meaningfully sustained remains open. Similarly, our knowledge is extremely limited of which specific components of the typical self-control protocol are effective in isolation from the other components. Nevertheless, the research findings, to date, can be interpreted as encouraging.

RELEVANT TARGET POPULATIONS AND EXCEPTIONS

Self-control treatments have been applied across a variety of clinical targets, including eating disorders, cigarette smoking, alcohol and other substance abuse or addiction problems, study skills and school performance deficits (e.g., writing, mathematics), hyperactivity, autism, sleep disorders, phobic avoidance, aggressiveness, depression, pain (e.g., migraine headaches, arthritis), sexual dysfunction, chronic disease management/ adherence issues, and many others. Not much research attention has yet been paid to determining the most or least appropriate targets for self-managed intervention, although problems ostensibly reflecting "impulse control" deficits are the most common in the clinical literature. Self-control methods have been used with children, adolescents, adults, and elderly populations, with generally good short-term results and increasing evidence of sustained effects.

As self-control tactics require a fair degree of comprehension and communication skill as well as the capacity to focus upon and recall internal events and to anticipate future occurrences, it has not been a treatment of choice for preverbal children or for adults requiring significant external supervision. However, with appropriate program simplification, tailoring, prompting, corrective feedback, and fading, even these groups can be taught the rudimentary skills of self-control. Finally, self-control efforts may not take hold if potential clients are unwilling to tolerate the short-term discomforts associated with altering self-defeating but otherwise highly rewarding action patterns.

COMPLICATIONS

Attempts to use thought-stopping or other means of suppression to control unwanted thoughts or images can sometimes yield an increase rather than a decrease in the target thoughts (presumably because when a person has a lot on his/her mind, the process of searching for instances of unwanted thoughts outweighs the process of seeking acceptable alternatives). Another complication arises because behaviors associated with impulse control disorders (cigarette smoking, eating forbidden foods, displays of temper, etc.) tend to be "primed" by ubiquitous situational cues that capture attention; therefore, the unwanted behaviors are often emitted before the person can put self-control tactics into effect. Also, because individuals rarely pursue only one goal at a time, they may on occasion lose track of their multiple intentions, again precipitating self-control failure. Program noncompliance in such circumstances can be demoralizing, sometimes precipitating wholesale abandonment of self-change efforts (as in "I ate one potato chip, so I might as well eat the whole bag"). In short, the continued mobilization of effort (e.g., concentration, recall of program details and goals, self-deprivation, etc.) associated with the use of self-control tactics can take an emotional toll on individuals not adequately prepared for the stresses of self-managed treatment. Moreover, when the target of control is a feeling or expressive state, the individual must also be prepared to modulate the thoughts and behaviors that tend to accompany the to-be-controlled emotion.

CASE ILLUSTRATION

"Jack" was a 43-year-old renal dialysis patient referred by his physician because of continued failure to follow medically established restrictions concerning fluid intake. Despite his awareness of the serious long-term health consequences of his excessive fluid intake (including the possibility of high blood pressure, congestive heart failure, or premature death), he nevertheless consumed several liters more than the recommended daily maximum. Although family members tried to manage Jack's water and other fluid intake while he was at home, they could not oversee his dietary activities when he was at work or otherwise away from the house. Jack, who claimed to be "strongly committed" to staying healthy, described himself as lacking the "willpower" to eat without drinking or to suffer with thirst for more than a few hours at a time. "Human beings need food and water," he would say. "It just seems unnatural to do what the doctor wants me to do."

The unexpected death of a close friend also on dialysis preceded Jack's admission to a self-control training program. The first part of the training involved the provision of a model of self-control that emphasized three essential ingredients: self-observation, self-evaluation, and the self-administration of rewards. Jack was taught to keep a diary of his fluid intake and the conditions that surrounded his drinking. He was then asked to cut down gradually on his drinking, with successively smaller amounts allowed on successive days. He soon noted that there were times when it was easier to comply with the program; and he was encouraged to reward himself for adherence by purchasing small items for his collection of Civil War memorabilia. When he failed to do so, which was also frequent in the early days of treatment, he was taught to withhold a pleasurable activity (such as watching TV).

Over the course of treatment, Jack was taught stimulus control techniques that could be used to reduce his exposure to situations that prompted heavy fluid intake, and he was given practice in informing friends and coworkers about his medical condition and in eliciting their assistance and support. Although Jack was initially reticent about appearing "needy" to others, he eventually realized that the goal of appearing strong and independent was something "left over from his 20s" and not as important as maintaining his health and being with his family.

In less than 8 weeks, Jack's daily fluid intake achieved medically acceptable levels. He reported feeling "in better charge" of himself. Treatment was terminated, with the understanding that Jack would continue his diary keeping and use whatever self-control tactics he deemed necessary to reestablish

appropriate drinking should the fluid levels again fall into a dangerous range. At 6 months, Jack reported three program lapses but relatively rapid recovery of control.

—Paul Karoly

See also: *Kanfer, Frederick H. (Vol. I); Self-Management (Vol. I); Self-Monitoring (Vol. III)*

Suggested Readings:

Bandura, A. (1986). *Social foundations of thought and action: A social cognitive theory.* Englewood Cliffs, NJ: Prentice Hall.

Delprato, D. J. (1989). A paradigm shift in behavior therapy: From external control to self-control. In W. A. Hershberger (Ed.), *Volitional action: Conation and control* (pp. 449–467). Amsterdam: North Holland.

Febbraro, G. A. R., & Clum, G. A. (1998). Meta-analytic investigation of the effectiveness of self-regulatory components in the treatment of adult problem behaviors. *Clinical Psychology Review, 18,* 143–161.

Kanfer, F. H., & Gaelick-Buys, L. (1991). Self-management methods. In F. H. Kanfer & A. P. Goldstein (Eds.), *Helping people change: A textbook of methods* (4th ed., pp. 305–360). New York: Pergamon Press.

Karoly, P. (1995). Self-control theory. In W. O'Donohue & L. Krasner (Eds.), *Theories of behavior therapy: Exploring behavior change* (pp. 259–285). Washington, DC: American Psychological Association.

Kazdin, A. E. (2001). *Behavior modification in applied settings* (6th ed., chap. 10). Belmont, CA: Wadsworth.

Metcalfe, J., & Mischel, W. (1999). A hot/cool system analysis of delay of gratification: Dynamics of willpower. *Psychological Review, 106,* 3–19.

Rachlin, H. (2000). *The science of self-control.* Cambridge, MA: Harvard University Press.

Robinson, T. R., Smith, S. W., Miller, M. D., & Brownell, M. T. (1999). Cognitive behavior modification of hyperactivity-impulsivity and aggression: A meta-analysis of school-based studies. *Journal of Educational Psychology, 91,* 195–203.

Watson, D. L., & Tharp, R. G. (2002). *Self-directed behavior: Self-modification for personal adjustment* (8th ed.). Belmont, CA: Wadsworth.

SELF-CONTROL DESENSITIZATION

DESCRIPTION OF THE STRATEGY

Self-control desensitization (SCD) is a variation of systematic desensitization (SD) that was developed by Marvin Goldfried in 1971. It is based on a somewhat different theoretical model than SD and provides for more procedural control to clients. Classical systematic desensitization as developed by Joseph Wolpe is based on a counterconditioning model and relies on a hierarchical procedure of gradual anxiety extinction. Two aspects are important. First, fear-producing situations must be arranged on a graduated hierarchy, from those involving the least anxiety to those involving the most. Second, the anxiety-producing scenes must be paired with relaxation such that the relaxation is stronger than the anxiety. It was considered important to immediately terminate the anxiety-producing scene should anxiety occur, so that anxiety did not overwhelm relaxation, rather than relaxation reducing anxiety. The therapist is in charge of this procedure, instructing the client and presenting the anxiety-producing scenes in ascending order and with the appropriate timing.

In self-control desensitization, however, the theoretical model of counterconditioning is replaced by a coping-skills model. Rather than an automatic weakening of a psychological bond taking place, a method of active coping is learned. The rationale provided to clients is that they have learned through past experience to react to certain situations with anxiety. They are told that the relaxation and breathing control techniques that they will learn will help them cope with these situations with less anxiety and avoidance. In addition, in accordance with a more mediational paradigm, clients are told it is not as important that a strict anxiety hierarchy be constructed and followed. The therapist works with clients to include items from a variety of different anxiety-producing situations. In presenting the anxiety-producing scenes, the therapist may encourage the client to stay with it until the anxiety diminishes, rather than terminating it as soon as anxiety appears. This practice is contrary to that considered optimal according to the counterconditioning model.

The treatment program is as follows. Clients are given the coping-skills rationale and are taught relaxation and deep-breathing skills. They are instructed to pay attention to their internal sensations as a way of acquiring information about their progress in coping and to use these skills to relax away anxiety and practice covert cognitive rehearsal for situations they may face. Anxiety-producing scenes from a variety of situations are constructed jointly by the therapist and client, and the client is asked to imagine them for 10 to 15 seconds if there is no anxiety response. If there is an anxiety response, however, the client is instructed to remain with the scene and gradually to relax the anxiety away or use other coping strategies to reduce the anxiety. Only if anxiety becomes unmanageable should the client terminate the scene. It is not necessary that the scenes be presented in a hierarchy, and scenes should be repeated until the client can handle the anxiety without difficulty or until it has been eliminated. Once clients have learned relaxation and other coping strategies, they can then use them in actual anxiety-producing situations. In fact, for ultimate success, it is important that clients practice these techniques outside of the therapy situation, in a sort of homework assignment. Research by Aaron Beck and his colleagues has shown that client completion of homework assignments in cognitive therapy correlates significantly with therapeutic outcome. It is likely the same would be true with other therapeutic interventions.

Self-control desensitization illustrates nicely the proposition that the positive results obtained by a therapeutic technique may have little or nothing to do with the theoretical rationale upon which it is based. Indeed, in some ways, self-control desensitization appears to be based on a rationale contradictory to that of classical systematic desensitization. The model is active and coping rather than passive and automatic. A hierarchical presentation is not necessary. Several anxiety-producing situations are presented instead of one. Clients are encouraged to remain in an anxiety-producing situation rather than terminate it immediately. Clients are also encouraged to practice their new skills in real-life situations, rather than assuming the imagery counterconditioning will be sufficient. In essence, human learning is assumed to take place by an active and continuing coping practice, rather than by an automatic instillation of new behavior. It should be noted that another anxiety reduction technique, flooding (or implosive therapy), is also based on a procedure contradictory to that of classical desensitization, in this instance, beginning at the top of the hierarchy and reducing anxiety by continued exposure. Exposure therapy, which is conceptually based on the flooding model, has been shown to be very effective in treating a variety of anxiety disorders.

RESEARCH BASIS

Most of the research on self-control desensitization itself was conducted in the 1970s and early 1980s, with some doctoral dissertations conducted in the late 1980s. Self-control desensitization has also been combined with other related techniques, such as applied relaxation and Richard Suinn's anxiety management training (AMT). An early study by Marvin Goldfried found that a cognitively oriented technique (rational restructuring) was somewhat better, especially on generalization, than self-control desensitization in reducing interpersonal anxiety. Jerry Deffenbacher has conducted a series of studies on SCD, one of which found self-control desensitization to be somewhat more effective than traditional systematic desensitization. Two later follow-up studies found (a) SCD to be similarly effective when compared with AMT in reducing test anxiety as well as other anxieties in college students after 15 months and (b) relaxation as self-control and modified desensitization to be equally effective in treating targeted and nontarget anxieties 1 year later. A relatively recent case study used a combination of techniques (self-monitoring, relaxation training, coping imagery, self-statements) along with self-control desensitization to successfully treat generalized anxiety disorder in a 34-year-old male. Significantly, the authors claimed that in-depth cognitive therapy was not employed, presumably because it was not needed.

Like many other therapy techniques, the research has shown that self-control desensitization is effective when compared with no-treatment control groups. However, there is scant evidence that it is more effective than other credible treatments, and, in fact, it is now used in conjunction with other techniques, rather than alone. SCD may be somewhat more effective than traditional, therapist-administered desensitization, perhaps because clients are invested with more control and self-direction. There also is no evidence that the use of a graduated hierarchy is really necessary. The mechanism of effectiveness appears to be the gradual acquisition by clients of coping strategies, perhaps accompanied by the therapeutic nonspecific effects of hope, optimism, self-confidence, and a personal sense of efficacy and mastery.

RELEVANT TARGET POPULATIONS AND EXCEPTIONS

Self-control desensitization has been primarily employed in the treatment of anxiety disorders, including related problems such as phobias and vaginismus. However, SCD and variations of it have also been applied to the treatment of anger problems, alcoholism, primary dysmenorrhea, the development of socially relevant behavior in children, smoking reduction, and pain reduction. Self-control desensitization is intrinsically an arousal-reducing intervention, so it might be especially applicable to disorders that involve heightened arousal as a component. However, the self-control aspect may be useful in treating all problems where impulsivity or lack of self-control is an aspect. This is a fruitful area for future research.

Self-control desensitization has been applied largely to adults, with occasional use with children. A search of the literature indicates it has not been applied to the treatment of other than neurotic-type disorders. It may be counterindicated with individuals who lack basic self-control and socialization skills, such as those with mental retardation or psychosis. SCD relies heavily on client collaboration with therapists and client exercise of initiative and for this reason may be unsuitable for those who lack these characteristics. Because it relies on client ability to use and feel comfortable with imagery, it may not be suitable for clients who cannot use imagery well or who are not comfortable with it. Dowd has discussed the presence of significant individual differences in imagery ability and its implications for therapy.

COMPLICATIONS

Because self-control desensitization involves the active installation of coping skills and is partly or largely client self-directed, it is unlikely that significant complications will arise. Indeed, for these very reasons, SCD depends heavily on client motivation and therapist social influence. Unmotivated clients may not participate well in the in-therapy exercises and are even less likely to perform these exercises outside of the therapy setting. Unless the felt distress is great, clients may not possess the motivation to expose themselves deliberately to anxiety-producing imagery and to remain with it. They have learned over time that the easiest and quickest way to reduce their anxiety is to avoid anxiety-producing situations, either in reality or in imagination. Thus, it may be difficult for therapists to persuade clients to directly face what they very much fear.

CASE ILLUSTRATION

"Steve" sought therapy because of a debilitating anxiety that had begun to seriously interfere with his occupational functioning. Steve had always had difficulty dealing with demanding supervisors and other authority figures in his life. But his current boss, "George," was particularly demanding and rather obnoxious, in addition. George appeared to cover his own insecurities and deficits by being especially hard on Steve and requiring unreasonably quick turn-arounds on job tasks and near-perfect performance as well. George's motto seemed to be, "If you can't or won't do *what* I want, *when* I want it, for as *long* as I want it, then get out and make way for someone who can and will!" Even though Steve recognized this and was able to discuss it with the therapist, he was still unable to deal with George's demands and place them in context. George was quickly able to reduce Steve's verbal behavior to a series of apologetic stammers, a feat he seemed to relish.

The therapist first conducted a behavioral assessment. While Steve was anxious whenever he was around George, he was especially anxious in two situations: when George was giving him new assignments and when George scolded him about his performance. Therapist questioning also revealed that in those situations, Steve looked at the floor, slumped, and had great difficulty verbally responding. Thus, both his verbal and nonverbal behavior radiated powerlessness and defeat.

Steve and the therapist then jointly constructed several detailed images of the two situations in which he had particular difficulty responding to George. First, the therapist asked Steve to close his eyes and imagine himself receiving a new assignment from George. Furthermore, Steve was asked to look directly at George and to stand erect. The therapist then asked Steve to feel the anxiety but to stay with that scene until the anxiety began to diminish. He was instructed to breathe deeply and slowly as an aid to relaxation and anxiety reduction. Assertive behavior, as demonstrated by a more erect posture and maintaining eye contact, was also described and used as an anxiety reduction technique. Once Steve's anxiety began to diminish, he was asked to terminate the scene. This procedure was repeated until Steve had less difficulty reducing his anxiety.

Steve was then asked to imagine being scolded by George for not completing his assignment fast enough and perfectly. This was a more difficult task. He was again instructed to stand erect and look George in the eye, then feel the anxiety and gradually relax it away by deep, slow breathing. This procedure was repeated, and Steve was instructed to not respond to George until he was able to reduce his anxiety within a reasonable time. Then, the therapist and Steve constructed several sentences that Steve could use to respond to George, such as, "It is difficult for me to do a good job when I don't have enough time" and "I don't think my standards are unreasonable." These and other sentences were constructed to be reflective of what Steve thought, rather than accusatory, in order to reduce George's possible defensive behavior.

The therapist then asked Steve again to close his eyes and imagine George scolding him for inadequate performance. He was then asked to repeat the constructed sentences to George at appropriate times while looking him in the eye, standing erect, and relaxing. Because Steve was now required to exercise several tasks simultaneously, more practice was required before he was able to reduce his anxiety within a reasonable time.

Once Steve was able to reduce his anxiety in these exercises, he and the therapist discussed ways that he might use his new skills while actually talking to George. He felt somewhat comfortable practicing these skills with George while receiving an assignment, but not while being scolded. Therefore, the first task was mutually agreed upon as homework because Steve was scheduled to receive a new work assignment the following day. He completed his homework task better than he expected (the therapist prepared him for a less-than-perfect performance) and was quite pleased. He said that he felt an increased sense of power and even reported that George seemed a little taken aback by his new behavior. The therapist and Steve together developed a homework plan that prepared Steve to interact with George in other situations (at Steve's initiative) using his new behavior.

Eventually, Steve felt confident enough to use his new skills and prepared sentences to deal with George's scolding behavior. Curiously, however, Steve reported that George did not say as much about his (Steve's) task completion and did so with less scolding behavior. Steve and the therapist discussed the possibility that Steve's newly assertive verbal and nonverbal behavior had the effect of reducing George's scolding behavior. They discussed additional sentences Steve might use in defending himself without attacking George if necessary.

This case example illustrates the major themes of self-control desensitization. Work began with situations that caused the client the most difficulty. Anxiety reduction was facilitated by relaxation, deep breathing, and assertive behavior. The new skills were practiced repeatedly until the client was able to reduce his anxiety in a reasonable amount of time. As an example of successive approximations to desired behavior, graduated assignments were given so the client was able to have success and mastery experiences. The new skills were eventually applied in real-life situations but only when the client felt ready. Because perfection may have been a theme in the client's life (not just with his boss), the therapist prepared him for less-than-perfect performances in these therapeutic tasks, just as he prepared him for dealing with his supervisor. The therapist realized that practice, perhaps considerable practice, was necessary as the client learned new skills.

—E. Thomas Dowd

See also: Self-Control Therapy (Vol. I); Self-Management (Vol. I); Systematic Desensitization (Vol. I)

Suggested Readings

Borkovec, T. D., & Whisman, M. A. (1996). Psychosocial treatment for generalized anxiety disorder. In M. R. Mavissakalian & R. F. Prien (Eds.), *Long-term treatments of anxiety disorders* (pp. 171–199). Washington, DC: American Psychiatric Press.

Costello, E., & Borkovec, T.D. (1992). Generalized anxiety disorder. In A. Freeman & F. M. Dattilio (Eds.), *Comprehensive casebook of cognitive therapy.* New York: Plenum Press.

Deffenbacher, J. L., & Michaels, A. C. (1981). Anxiety management training and self-control desensitization: 15 months later. *Journal of Counseling Psychology, 28,* 459–462.

Deffenbacher, J. L., & Michaels, A. C. (1981). Two self-control procedures in the reduction of targeted and non-targeted anxieties: A year later. *Journal of Counseling Psychology, 27,* 9–15.

Dowd, E. T. (2000). *Cognitive hypnotherapy.* Livingston, NJ: Jason Aronson.

Goldfried, M. R. (1971). Systematic desensitization as training in self-control. *Journal of Consulting and Clinical Psychology, 37,* 228–234.

Goldfried, N. M. R., & Goldfried, A. P. (1977). Importance of hierarchy content in the self-control of anxiety. *Journal of Consulting and Clinical Psychology, 45,* 124–134.

Kanter, N. J., & Goldfried, M. R. (1979). Relative effectiveness of rational restructuring and self-control desensitization in the reduction of interpersonal anxiety. *Behavior Therapy, 10,* 472–490.

SELF-CONTROL THERAPY

DESCRIPTION OF THE STRATEGY

Self-control therapies are strategies for teaching people skills and techniques for controlling their own behavior when striving to achieve long-term goals. It is usually assumed that people employ self-control strategies implicitly in their efforts to change behavior, such as when starting a diet or exercise program or attempting to quit smoking. Self-control therapies attempt to teach these strategies in an explicit way. A number of self-control models are used as the basis for self-control theories. One example is the self-management therapy (SMT) program for depression developed by the author.

SMT is a structured, manualized, cognitive-behavioral group therapy program for the treatment of depression. The program is currently presented in 14 weekly, 1 1/2-hour sessions. Each session includes a didactic portion, a discussion period, in-session paper-and-pencil exercises, and weekly homework assignments that are reviewed at the beginning of the next session. It is an illustration of self-control therapies in that it is "transparent" to the participants. They are told the targets of the intervention; they are instructed in applying the intervention on their own; and the theoretical rationale for the intervention is explicitly presented. Participants are consciously applying psychological principles to change their own behavior.

SMT can be thought of in three ways. First, it is targeting specific components of depression and teaching the participants self-change techniques for modifying each target behavior. Second, it can be thought of as teaching principles of self-change in the context of depression. Third, it can be seen as teaching behaviors that are the opposite of depression (i.e., positive self-esteem and self-control behaviors). People with positive self-esteem are people who accurately view their world, have a realistic sense of their abilities, set reasonable standards and goals, and are able to control their behavior with feedback to themselves.

The first session of the SMT program serves to introduce the participants to one another and to the program. The nature of depression is described and related to the symptoms presented by the participants. A brief overall description and rationale for the program are presented by the therapist. Homework for this first session involves keeping track of daily mood by rating average mood for each day on a scale of zero to 10, where zero is the worst, most depressed day ever and 10 is the happiest day ever. The purpose of the assignment is to focus on daily variations in mood and to get participants used to the mood scale.

In the second session, homework is reviewed with emphasis on participants' observations on their mood variability during the week and any correlates of their moods that they might have observed (e.g., felt better on days when they were busy). The didactic presentation in this session conveys a central premise of the program. The program asserts that mood is influenced by behavior and cognition (i.e., activities that people engage in daily and the "self-statements" they make to themselves about what they do). While the relationship may go both ways, the program assumes that depressed participants can change their daily moods and thus their depression by changing activities and self-statements. In various ways, the rest of the program involves strategies for increasing positive activities and positive self-statements. The homework assignment is to continue monitoring mood and, in addition, to list positive activities and self-statements each day. This self-monitoring assignment is continued throughout the program, with a variation in focus with each new topic.

In the third session, the relationship between mood and events is demonstrated to participants by graphing their week's homework. For each day of the week, the mood rating is graphed with a connected line. Then, the total number of activities and self-statements for each day are graphed on the same form. Parallel lines illustrate the relationship between mood and activity. The homework assignment is to continue the self-monitoring logs daily.

The topic covered in the next session is the idea that any event has both positive and negative immediate and delayed consequences. When people are depressed, they tend to focus on immediate consequences to the relative exclusion of long-term consequences of their behavior. Activities can be positive either because they are immediately pleasurable or because they produce some delayed or long-term positive outcome. Eating ice cream is immediately pleasurable, while mowing the lawn may be a positive activity because the end product of a nice-looking lawn is pleasing. The homework assignment is to list each day at least one positive activity that is positive because it has a delayed positive effect. Each time such an activity is listed, participants are instructed to list a positive self-statement identifying the positive long-term effect of their behavior (e.g., "I made my yard look much better").

Having covered the effects of activities, the next few sessions focus on their causes. Depressed persons are seen as making external, unstable, and specific attributions for positive events. "That was nice, but it wasn't my doing. It was just luck and may never happen again." Exercises in the session teach the participants to realistically take credit for positive activities. The exercise includes having participants take positive events from their self-monitoring logs and examine their causes. The homework assignment is to include in each day's self-monitoring log one positive self-statement recognizing credit for a taking responsibility for a positive activity.

In a parallel session, the idea is presented that depressed people tend to blame themselves for negative events. For a negative event, depressed persons tend to make internal, stable, and global attributions. In effect, they are saying, "It was my fault. I always fail in this way, and I fail in everything else of this type." Again, an exercise takes participants through a series of examples teaching them not to take excessive blame for negative effects, but instead, to see that some of the reasons for negative events are external, unstable, and specific. The homework assignment is to write a self-statement daily that realistically diminishes blame from oneself for negative events.

Goal setting is the focus of the next sessions. Depressed people tend to be disconnected from long-term goals, and they often set goals poorly. Drawing from the behavioral literature on goal setting, good goals should be positively stated, concretely defined, in the person's control, and attainable. Participants are asked to choose a goal of intermediate range that they can work on for the next few weeks. With a goal-setting form, they are guided through an exercise to define the goal and to establish a list of component subgoals necessary to reach the main goal. The homework assignment is to include the accomplishment of subgoals on the daily self-monitoring log list of positive activities. The intent of the homework is for participants to acknowledge to themselves progress toward the distal goal.

Following the goal-setting topic, the idea of self-reward as a means of motivating oneself to pursue the goal is introduced. Essentially, a person can increase the probability of accomplishing difficult subgoal behaviors by setting up contingent rewards for their completion. Participants construct a list of pleasurable activities that they could use to reward themselves with when they accomplish difficult subgoal behaviors. For example, when completing shopping for the materials necessary for the goal of completing some home repairs, the participant might self-reward with a stop at a favorite donut shop. The homework here is to list the subgoal activities accomplished on the self-monitoring log and also to record contingent reward activities.

The final topics of the program deal with the way in which depressed people talk to themselves. Depressed persons typically talk to themselves in ways that are punishing and diminishing of motivation. For example, "Why should I try to do this? I'll never succeed. I always make a fool out of myself by failing at things like this." The idea presented is that talking to oneself in realistically more positive ways can increase rather than decrease motivation. In one exercise, participants are asked to make a list of comfortable statements that acknowledge a positive accomplishment. As one person might say to a friend, "You did a great job with that task," the person might list for himself or herself, saying, "I did a great job with that task." The corresponding homework assignment is to consciously practice contingent self-rewarding statements daily and to record them in the self-monitoring log as positive self-statements.

The final sessions of SMT allow for continued practice of the lessons taught in the program and review of the ideas involved. The therapist is given some latitude in deciding when to go on to a new topic during the weeks of the program. The extra sessions may be spent early to go over a topic that the therapist feels needs further effort, or they may be saved for continuation.

RESEARCH BASIS

Results of therapy outcome studies indicate that SMT is superior in reducing the severity, frequency, and duration of complaints common in those who meet the criteria for depression compared with nonspecific therapies, no-treatment, and wait-list control conditions and is equal to or superior to other forms of cognitive-behavioral therapy for depression. SMT has been investigated in a number of studies with adult outpatients by Rehm and his colleagues and by other psychotherapy researchers.

In addition, a number of studies have supported the underlying assumptions of the SMT program. For example, depressed persons tend to view themselves as experiencing more negative and fewer positive events than realistic observers. They tend to prefer small, immediate over larger, long-term rewards. They make negative attributions for positive and negative events and set perfectionistic standards for themselves. Research on goal setting suggests that depressed people set unrealistic goals, which sometimes are seen as the only way to achieve happiness. They self-punish more and self-reward less.

RELEVANT TARGET POPULATIONS AND EXCEPTIONS

The SMT program has been adapted for a variety of populations and age ranges, including renal dialysis patients, veterans with posttraumatic stress disorder, prisoners, psychiatric inpatients, psychiatric day treatment patients, battered women, the elderly, and children. In each case, the manual has been modified to employ appropriate examples and, in some cases, to adapt the teaching methods to the population.

Other forms of self-control therapy have been used primarily for problems of self-control, such as weight control, quitting smoking, and moderating alcohol intake. Self-control strategies are also used for establishing new positive behaviors, such as healthy eating, developing and maintaining an exercise program, or consistently following a pattern of taking medication on an appropriate schedule.

COMPLICATIONS

Complications for SMT include additional comorbid psychological problems. Studies of therapy for depression find that coexisting conditions such as posttraumatic stress disorder (PTSD) and alcohol use lead to less effective participation. It is common clinical management to refer depressed persons for substance abuse treatment first before attempting therapy for depression. There is a small literature on the effects of severity of depression that suggests that psychological therapies may be less effective for more severe depression. Certainly, participants in any psychological therapy approach must be sufficiently able and motivated to carry out the program. Some very severe patients may be virtually immobile and unmotivated, and psychotic symptoms may make the person unavailable to psychological interventions. At most levels of depression, however, psychological approaches seem to be effective.

CASE ILLUSTRATION

"Mrs. L" was a 48-year-old divorced woman working as a secretary in a small law office and living by herself in an apartment. She described herself as having episodes of depression since high school, but that it was much worse since her divorce a year ago. She characterized her life as getting to work each morning with great effort, putting a false smile on her face to get through the day, and then returning to an untidy apartment, where she did little but watch TV. Weekends were even worse, with little to do and an intensified sense of loneliness and self-pity.

In a structured diagnostic interview, Mrs. L met criteria for a major depressive disorder. Her Beck Depression Inventory score was 26, indicating a moderate to severe depression. On a Pleasant Events Schedule, her responses indicated a low number of positive activities with little enjoyment of them. On the Self-Control Questionnaire for Depression, she scored well below the mean for positive self-control habits and beliefs.

Mrs. L began SMT with some reluctance, saying that she did not think anything would help her. At the second session, her mood ratings were generally low (between 2 and 4), but she noted that it was a surprise to her that she noticed variation from day to day. At the next session, she had two to five positive activities listed for each day and no positive self-statements. Her mood and events graph showed a fairly close relationship, although in the discussion, she expressed the opinion that it was her moods that influenced how may pleasurable things she did each day, not the other way around.

After learning about immediate and delayed consequences, she began doing a few things to reestablish contact with people. She called her sister in a distant city and promised to write her. She went to church on Sunday and felt better that day. In the sessions having to do with attributions for positive and negative events, she felt that depressive attributions were very characteristic of her. She noted that she always felt to blame for anything that went wrong at the office and never believed praise or complements. During the week, she worked on daily self-statements about her accomplishments at work and about not taking too much blame when a problem arose she had to deal with.

In the goal-setting exercises, she chose a goal having to do with increasing her contact with people outside of work. Her subgoals included finding out about leisure learning classes in her area and talking to the minister of her church about volunteer work she might do. During the next week, she enrolled in a photography class and began assisting in the church library. She wrote a number of positive self-statements in her homework about her pride in doing these things.

Mrs. L found the idea of saying positive things to herself as rewards foreign. At first, she felt it was prideful and bragging but was able to be convinced that if she said it to herself, it was not bragging. She was also able to identify and list several characteristics of herself that were positive: She was conscientious at work, always polite with people, and was a loyal friend.

In the last few weeks of the therapy program, Mrs. L was rating her daily moods in the 7 to 9 range, and she was listing 10 to 15 positive activities or self-statements daily. She was more animated in talking about her life and felt optimistic about her future. Her Beck Depression Inventory score at the end of therapy had dropped to 5, she was expressing more positive self-control behavior and attitudes, and she no longer met criteria for depression. She asked for extra blank copies of the therapy forms so that she could continue working on things on her own.

—*Lynn P. Rehm*

See also: *Self-Control (Vol. I); Self-Management (Vol. I); Self-Monitoring (Vol. I)*

Suggested Readings

Rehm, L. P. (1977). A self-control model of depression. *Behavior Therapy, 8,* 787–804.

Rehm, L. P. (1985). A self-management therapy program for depression. *International Journal of Mental Health, 13*(3–4), 34–53.

Rehm, L. P., Fuchs, C. Z., Roth, D. M., Kornblith, S. J., & Romano, J. (1979). A comparison of self-control and social skills treatments of depression. *Behavior Therapy, 10,* 429–442.

Rehm, L. P., Kaslow, N. J., & Rabin, A. S. (1987). Cognitive and behavioral targets in a self-control behavior therapy program for depression. *Journal of Consulting and Clinical Psychology, 55,* 60–67.

Rehm, L. P., Kornblith, S. J., O'Hara, M. W., Lamparski, D. M., Romano, J.M., & Volkin, J. I. (1981). An evaluation of major components in a self-control therapy program for depression. *Behavior Modification, 5,* 459–490.

Rehm, L. P., & Sharp, R. N. (1996). Strategies in the treatment of childhood depression. In M. Reinecke, F. M. Dattilio, & A. Freeman (Eds.), *Comprehensive casebook on cognitive behavior therapy with adolescents* (pp. 103–123). New York: Guilford Press.

Reynolds, W. M., & Coats, K. I. (1986). A comparison of cognitive-behavioral therapy and relaxation training for the treatment of depression in adolescents. *Journal of Consulting and Clinical Psychology. 54*(5), 653–60.

Rokke, P. D., Tomhave, J. A., & Jocic, Z. (2000). Self-management therapy and educational group therapy for depressed elders. *Cognitive Therapy & Research, 24*(1), 99–119.

Stark, K. D., Reynolds, W. M., & Kaslow, N. J. (1987). A comparison of the relative efficacy of self-control therapy and a behavioral problem-solving therapy for depression in children. *Journal of Abnormal Child Psychology. 15*(1), 91–113.

SELF-MANAGEMENT

DESCRIPTION OF THE STRATEGY

Ineffective Natural Contingencies

Grandma's Wisdom: The problem with you members of today's younger generation is that you must have instant gratification; you cannot delay your gratification.

The Behavior Analyst's Wisdom: The problem with people who have poor self-control, who have poor impulse control, is that they choose smaller, immediate reinforcers instead of larger, delayed reinforcers.

This makes sense to most behavior analysts because of the gradient of delayed reinforcement: the greater the delay between the response and the reinforcer, the less the impact of that reinforcer, and the less the increase in the future frequency of that response as a result of that reinforcer. In fact, the delay gradient is so steep that there has been no clear demonstration of reinforcement when the reinforcer is delayed by more than a minute or so with nonverbal organisms, whether they are nonhuman animals or nonverbal human beings. The delay gradient is so steep that in working with nonverbal autistic children, no behavior analyst would delay the reinforcer by more than a few seconds and preferably by no more than a fraction of a second. The quicker, the better; and if the delay is greater than a minute or so, there will be no reinforcing effect at all.

But when extrapolating from this basic, behavior-analytic research to the typical self-management problems of adults, there is a confound between two causal variables: For example, if you overeat, you will gain excess weight—a delayed, aversive consequence of the overeating. Grandmother would say you overeat because you cannot delay your gratification. However, the confound is that not only is that weight gain delayed but also the amount of permanent weight gain from a single instance of overeating is insignificant. Only as a result of a large number of instances of overeating will you experience the aversive outcome of significant weight gain.

Most obese people in the United States know the rule describing that contingency: If you repeatedly overeat, you will become overweight. The problem is, knowing the overweight rule does not suppress this one instance of eating that delicious fudge sundae topped with the whipped cream and the maraschino cherry, because a single instance of eating this dessert will cause no significant harm and will, indeed, taste great. So, knowing the overweight rule does not help the masses of Americans who have or are on their way to having gradually slipped into obesity, one fudge sundae at a time. Knowledge of this rule describing the natural contingency exerts little control over gluttony.

But do we fail to follow the overweight rule because our behavior is not controlled by delayed consequences, as grandma accuses? Suppose the dieter had agreed to donate $5, $20, or, if need be, $100 to a despised charity each time he ate a single bite of a fudge sundae. And suppose the dieter were working with a performance manager who would reliably enforce the penalty specified in this behavioral contract. Then, it is unlikely that the dieter would ever eat another fudge sundae, even though the payment of the penalty might be delayed by a day, week, month, or year. As long as the contract is in effect, knowledge of this performance management contingency will suppress fudge sundae gluttony.

So, we have trouble managing our own behavior when each instance of that behavior has only an insignificant outcome, though the outcomes of many repetitions of that behavior will be highly significant. And we have little trouble managing our own behavior when each instance of that behavior has a significant outcome, though that outcome might be greatly delayed.

But the outcome of our behavior also needs to be probable. Many people have trouble following the "buckle-up" rule, even though they might have a serious auto accident as soon as they pull onto the street. Even though the delay between the failure to buckle up and the accident could be only a few seconds, they fail to buckle up because the probability of the accident is so low. However, if they were driving in a dangerous auto race or a dangerous stunt-driving demonstration, they would always buckle up, because the probability of a serious accident would be fairly high.

Preaching about the cumulative effect of eating fudge sundaes is an ineffective strategy, as is preaching about the law of large numbers and the probability that sooner or later, you will wish you had buckled up. Our behavior is controlled by the outcome of each individual response, not by the cumulative size and not by the cumulative probability of the outcome of a large number of those responses. The *natural contingency* between a response and its outcome will be ineffective if the outcome of each individual response is too small or too improbable, even though the cumulative impact of those outcomes is significant. And once the delay exceeds a minute or so, further increases in the delay are of little importance.

Performance Management Contingencies

A small percentage of people self-manage sufficiently well that they actually follow the rules describing the natural consequences of good dieting and good buckling up, even though the natural consequence of any individual instance of appropriate behavior is infinitesimally small or only infinitesimally probable. However, such people seem to have unique behavioral histories, perhaps behavioral histories that cause them to say supplemental self-management rules to themselves, rules involving supplemental values not typical of most people. For example, *Any instance of my violating the healthful-diet rule means I have weak character. Any instance of my failing to buckle up means I'm a poor mother who doesn't mind risking the chance that her children will be motherless. Any instance of my being promiscuous means I'm a sinner and will not enter heaven. Any instance of my taking a single sip of alcohol means I will start the inexorable drift back into the state of drunkenness it took me so many years to work my way out of.*

These supplemental rules describe sizable, probable outcomes that are contingent on each instance of the behavior of concern; therefore, they will control the behavior of the small percentage of people who both believe the rules and say them to themselves, when the occasion arises. However, most people neither believe the rules nor hold the values those rules imply. As a result, many people in the United States are becoming obese, killing themselves on the highway, getting divorced, and failing to maintain their recovery from alcoholism. Furthermore, it appears that people who have not acquired a belief in such rules and their implied values in childhood can never acquire those beliefs and values in adulthood; at least, there is little clear evidence that they can.

When it is logistically feasible, the easiest, most reliable way to manage the behavior of an adult is to involve an external performance manager who observes the problem behavior and adds a performance management consequence: for example, the policeman who gives a ticket to anyone who fails to "click it." (The probability of buckling up increases sharply as a function of the probability of a ticket for failing to do so, even though the price of a ticket is trivial compared to the "price" of the injury resulting from a serious accident.) Another example of an external performance manager is the parent, spouse, or friend who monitors and will chastise the glutton, the philanderer, and the recovered alcoholic if they give in to temptation.

But often, such omnipresent, external performance managers are not logistically feasible. Either the policeman is not there or the parent, spouse, or friend also gives in to the temptation. In such cases, the person must be a *self-manager:* The person must self-monitor and, if need be, provide the performance management consequences.

The Steps of Self-Management

Analyze the Natural Contingency

What is the ineffective natural contingency failing to control your behavior (Why do you want to change your behavior)? *I eat too much, so I weigh too much, and I am not healthy enough* (real issue: *I no longer look good in a bikini, and I feel like a loser*). *I don't exercise enough, so I'm not healthy enough (I no longer look good in a bikini, and I feel like a loser). I'm not writing enough, so I'm not contributing enough to the well-being of humanity (I won't get promoted, and I feel like a loser).*

Specify the Goal

I will eat no more than 1,250 calories per day until I weigh 147 lbs; then, I will eat no more than 2,300 calories per day. I will work out for 2 hours, 6 days a week. I will write 2 hours every day. It is also of value to specify benefit measures, such as weight, dress size, miles run, fastest mile, cardiovascular fitness, maximum pounds lifted, pages written, pages published, grades, and subjective happiness.

Design the Intervention

Monitor and Record Your Behavior. Usually, we are unaware of how many times we comment sarcastically to someone we love, pollute our psychic environment by swearing, bite our nails, light a cigarette, speed, fail to buckle up, drink enough fluids, take our vitamins, or smile. So simply monitoring and being aware of our own behavior may be enough to allow us to manage it. But it is difficult to become aware of each instance of our behavior, especially habitual behavior, unless we attempt to record each instance, ideally, when it occurs or should have occurred.

For frequently occurring behaviors, it is important to always carry a convenient recording device: a 3×5 card, a small notebook, pennies in your left pocket at the beginning of the day so you can transfer one to the right pocket after each behavior, a ring you move from one finger to the other, a pack of cigarettes with the number of cigarettes specified at the beginning of the day, a golf counter, a personal digital assistant, or the back of your hand. You can record behaviors that occur only daily on a calendar, notebook, or computer: for example, whether you exercised, wrote, called your mother, or got to bed, up, and to work on time. However, even in these cases, it is often important to record at the time of the behavior; for example, right after you finish writing, you should record how many hours you actually wrote. Immediate recording will attenuate our rose-tinted nostalgia, even for events that are only a few hours old.

It then helps to graph your data, at least once a week. One convenient type of graph is a year-at-a-glance graph, where the x-axis is marked with the 52 weeks of the year (to give you a pretty big picture) and the y-axis indicates the total number of responses for each week (or the average of a benefit measure, like weight or blood pressure). You can also eliminate a step by recording each day's totals directly on your year-at-a-glance graph. For example, after Monday's 2-mile walk, you can make a mark at 2 above the appropriate week; and after Tuesday's 3-mile walk, you can make a mark at 5 (Monday's 2 plus Tuesday's 3), so that at the end of the week, your graph shows the total number of miles you walked that week.

A daily or weekly mark on a calendar can also provide an alternative visual summary of your performance. For example, you can mark each successful day with a green highlighter; and to rub it in, you can mark each failure with red, if you are so inclined.

Add a Performance Management Contingency. Though merely observing your behavior or observing and graphing that behavior may be all you need do in order to manage that behavior, often, you may need more; often, you may need to add a performance management contingency. For example, *Every day I eat no more than 1,250 calories, I will give myself $5 to spend frivolously.*

That performance management contingency may work if you have sufficient self-management skills to refrain from robbing your own bank and spending $5 on frivolous living despite your having just consumed 4,000 calories. And a few people who need added performance management contingencies to control their dieting will not need the help of such added contingencies to control their robbing the bank, but most will need some help. However, that help should not take the form of giving an external performance manager $100 with instructions to pay back $5 for each perfect day, unless $100 was all you had in your bank.

Another problem with this contingency is that it allows for procrastination. You can gorge today and do the $5-producing 1,250-calorie diet tomorrow; that only means it will take you 11 days instead of 10 to earn the $50 you need to buy that frivolous new blouse.

Generally, a better contingency would be, *Every day I eat more than 1,250 calories, I will give someone else $5 to spend frivolously,* like a despised roommate or despised charity.

The previous contingency is an analogue to a penalty contingency, an analogue because the actual loss of the $5 will normally occur more than 1 minute after exceeding the 1,250-calorie limit. Such analogue penalty contingencies are effective in decreasing undesirable behavior. And to increase desirable behavior, an analogue to an avoidance contingency works well: *Every day I exercise for one hour, I avoid paying a $5 fine.* But, if you have not finished your hour by midnight, you must pay the $5.

Implement the Self-Management Procedure

It is easy to fantasize about what we wish to change in ourselves and the specific goals we wish to achieve.

It is even easy to design an intervention; but for us procrastinators, it may be hard to actually initiate our interventions, our self-management procedures. We can always start it next week or the week after. Therefore, it helps to set a specific implementation deadline, ideally, a deadline someone else will monitor.

Evaluate the Results

Your behavior graph and your benefits graph tell the story. Either you are sticking to the 1,250-calorie diet reliably enough or you are not. Either you are losing weight or you are not. Check once a week to be sure, but do not let an occasional bad week discourage you.

Recycle

The Goals and Benefits. There is a good chance that eventually, your performance will deteriorate to the point where you need to recycle your intervention. Perhaps your goals were unrealistic. Instead of writing 4 hours per day, you can more realistically shoot for 2 hours per day, which is still much better than your pre-self-management zero hours per day. Or perhaps you are not getting the benefits you had anticipated, and you need to add an exercise contingency to your diet contingency.

The Performance Management Contingency. It is also possible that the contingency is simply not working. The first reaction is to say that the $5 fine is not large enough (and for me, that is the case); but $20 usually works. However, you should not increase the size of the fine to the point that the aversiveness of paying the fine is greater than the aversiveness of cheating, lying, or refusing to pay the fine, thus risking the loss of a potentially effective intervention.

An alternative to increasing the fine is to make the contingencies more fine grained. *If any of my meals exceed 400 calories, I'll pay $5.* Now you do not end up having consumed 1,200 calories by noon and thus dooming yourself to late-evening failure. *If I do not exercise by 9 a.m., I'll pay $5.* Now you do not need to futilely try to get yourself to exercise after work when you are too tired to do anything but sit in front of the TV.

Accountability. Get a little help from your friends. But the most common problem is that you are not implementing your self-management procedure with sufficient integrity: You have stopped recording your data every day. Or you have stopped paying your fines reliably. Things fall apart.

The solution is to get a performance manager, someone to whom you report daily, or at least weekly, and perhaps someone to whom you pay your fines, or at least who monitors your paying the fines.

Then, the most common problem is that your performance manager is not monitoring, and perhaps enforcing, your self-management procedure with sufficient integrity: When you fail to give them your daily or weekly call or e-mail, they let it slide. When you fail to pay your fines, they do not notice. Things fall apart.

Then, the solution is to get a more reliable performance manager, if need be, someone you pay for their help, ideally, someone you formally meet with, face-to-face every week, like a supervisee or supervisor, a counselor, clinician, or behavior analyst. Sometimes, roommates, friends, and spouses will work, but usually not. And least reliable of all is the spouse whose sexual favors are part of your performance management contingency: Many have tried; few have succeeded.

Even though you have help from your friends, you are still carrying the bulk of the burden. You are still using a self-management procedure.

RESEARCH BASIS

Although most laboratory research on self-control and self-management has been done with preschool children and some applied research has been done with mentally handicapped adults, most applied research has been done with normally verbal adults, including college students—adults wanting to manage a specific behavior or circumscribed set of behaviors. Typically, the applied researchers have been practitioners working with clients and college professors working with students in their classes.

Many people succeed in many aspects of their lives without explicit self-management procedures, for example, effectively dieting, exercising, quitting smoking, and maintaining high productivity in unstructured contexts (e.g., writing). But most people have several areas in need of explicit self-management procedures, though few make use of such procedures. However, research with both mild behavior problems and clinically serious behavior problems has demonstrated the effectiveness of these procedures.

RELEVANT TARGET POPULATIONS

Self-management procedures have been successful in the following areas:

1. In behavioral medicine, to increase aerobic conditioning, weight training, yoga, meditation, flossing, eating healthy food, drinking fluids, taking vitamins, taking medications, and staying on a diabetic diet regimen. And to decrease smoking, alcohol consumption, excess calorie consumption, scratching, nail biting, hair pulling, teeth grinding, and face picking.

2. At work, to increase work attendance; work productivity; completing unfinished work; filing; using a daily organizer; returning phone calls; spending the time needed to learn computer programs; writing articles, chapters, and books; complimenting coworkers; saying "no" when appropriate; and asking questions when appropriate. And to decrease time on personal phone calls.

3. In the university, to increase thesis and dissertation writing and completion, textbook reading, homework completion, and speaking up in class.

4. In the home, to increase reinforcement of appropriate and extinction of inappropriate child behavior, making positive comments to the children, spending quality time with the children, and doing domestic chores.

5. And in the enhancement of life quality, to increase practicing musical instruments, listening to music, leisure reading, writing letters to friends and family, and writing letters to a dying friend.

Self-management procedures require that the participant have language skills and be willing to implement the procedure. However, it is not unusual for people desperately wanting to achieve a particular goal to be unwilling to commit to changing their behavior or else to using self-management procedures to do so. For example, some obese people may be unwilling to start a diet and exercise regime. Or they may be unwilling to use a self-management procedure to do so, arguing that they have the willpower to do it without the constraints of such a procedure and will probably start exercising that willpower next week on their own.

COMPLICATIONS

Some simple self-managed behaviors eventually become habitual and no longer need the support of self-management procedures, for example, buckling up. Some eventually become habitual enough to need only a small amount of support, like including flossing in the early morning routine of washing and shaving. And others eventually can be maintained by daily recording and graphing with explicit performance management contingencies no longer needed, like early-morning jogging. But still others will require perpetual self-management with added performance management contingencies, like writing 2 hours every day.

However, there are great differences among individual as to how much explicit self-management is needed both to initiate and to maintain the desired behavior changes; for example, some productive professional writers maintain a daily writing regimen by setting aside several hours of writing time the first thing every morning, though some also self-impose a daily quota of words or pages but with no other performance management contingency.

Some people maintain self-management procedures for years, though they may be in a continuous state of fine-tuning and recycling. However, many people are unable to sustain the use of self-management procedures even though they may want to; for example, when their behavior analysis course is over, most college students drop their self-management procedures even though they were applying those procedures to behaviors of special concern to them and even though they anticipate that their performance will deteriorate.

Self-management procedures seem easiest to apply to relatively short-term projects, like writing a thesis or dieting before getting fitted for the wedding gown, than to lifelong projects, like perpetual diet management. Also self-management procedures seem easiest to apply to episodic events, like daily exercise, than to continuous events, like smoking abstinence or diet management.

And, though the procedures are self-management, many, or perhaps most, people will have more success at implementing and maintaining those procedures with the help of an external performance manager to whom they report at least weekly, a difficult relation to maintain.

CASE ILLUSTRATION

At the age of 29, an assistant professor was having trouble getting his writing done for a book he was coauthoring; so he contracted to write 4 hours a day or pay $1 for each hourly shortfall. But then he had trouble actually writing during those hours; so he fed himself a bite of pizza for each sentence he wrote. With the help of such self-management procedures, that book and eventually others were written. At the age of 30, he was moving into that post-grad-school, pre-middle-age spread, so he contracted with his secretary to pay $1 for each serving of junk food he ate. In addition, each day he was above the day's goal weight, he had to clean the pigeon cages in the psych lab. At the age of 31, he put a loose rubber band around his wrist, which he snapped each time he made a negative, critical, or sarcastic remark. At 32, he began pulling the hairs out of his fashionably long beard, leaving a 50-cent-size bald spot on his chin (trichotillomania); merely recording each instance of the behavior with a golf counter reduced the frequency to zero. At 40, he contracted to floss twice a day, adhere to a strict low-fat, low-sugar, low-cholesterol diet and to run 3 miles per day. At 66, each day, the full professor records his performance data in an Excel spreadsheet, noting whether he met his contracts of getting up by 4 a.m., weighing less than 150 lbs, getting to the fitness center by 5:30 a.m. (to run, spin, lift weights, and stretch), checking his Outlook calendar and to-do list, starting writing by 10 a.m., writing 2 hours, e-mailing his self-management spreadsheet to his hired performance manager by 12 p.m., eating a healthful diet, not exceeding his calorie limit, eating no unauthorized desserts, not speeding, not surfing the Web during the weekdays, and going to bed by 9 p.m. He typically has $20 self-management contingencies only on writing, calories, desserts, and Web surfing.

As a result of these self-management procedures, at the age of 66, his health, weight, and fitness are excellent. His scholarly productivity is above average. He still often dessert binges on the road, but rarely at home. He has gotten only one speeding ticket in the last 5 years (he had previously lost his driver's license). He no longer falls asleep in the middle of one-on-one meetings with his graduate students. Only rarely does he unintentionally miss a meeting. Only four times in the previous 6 months has his average weekly intake exceeded 2,300 calories, though once it reached 3,800. Over the 2 previous years, he accumulated 1,100 hours of writing—somewhat loosely defined, 75% of his goal—though too much of that has been episodic and driven by postdeadline panic; for example, finishing this entry is requiring 8 hours per day for both weekend days to avoid a fine of $20 per missing hour.

This costs him about $1,500 a year in $20 penalties, a few hundred dollars a year for a performance manager and spreadsheet programmer, and a few minutes every day for the spreadsheet updating and spreadsheet-generated graph monitoring, cheaper and more effective than talk therapy.

—Richard W. Malott

See also: *Self-Control (Vol. I); Self-Control Therapy (Vol. I); Self-Statement Modification (Vol. I)*

Suggested Readings

Malott, R. W. (1984) Rule-governed behavior, self-management, and the developmentally disabled: A theoretical analysis. *Analysis and Intervention in Developmental Disabilities, 4,* 199–209.

Malott, R. W. (1986). Self-management, rule-governed behavior, and everyday life. In H. W. Reese & L. J. Parrott (Eds.), *Behavioral science: Philosophical, methodological, and empirical advances* (pp. 207–228). Hillsdale, NJ: Erlbaum.

Malott, R. W. (1989). The achievement of evasive goals: Control by rules describing contingencies that are not direct-acting. In S. C. Hayes (Ed.), *Rule-governed behavior: Cognition, contingencies, and instructional control* (pp. 269–322). New York: Plenum Press.

Malott, R. W., & Harrison, H. (2003). *I'll stop procrastinating when I get around to it.* Kalamazoo, MI: DickMalott.com.

Watson, D. L., & Tharp, R. G. (2001). *Self-directed behavior: Self-modification for personal adjustment* (8th ed.). Monterey, CA: Brooks/Cole.

SELF-MONITORING

DESCRIPTION OF THE STRATEGY

Self-monitoring refers to the process of systematically attending to one's current actions, thoughts, emotions, or physiological reactions and/or to their immediate antecedents or consequences over a sufficient period of time to allow for comprehensive and reliable sampling. Immediacy, continuity, and relative precision distinguish self-monitoring from typical retrospective self-reports (which are implicitly built upon the accurate recall of prior *unsystematic* self-monitoring). Self-monitoring, also called *self-observation,* serves a dual function within clinical behavior therapy in that it refers both to a discovery-oriented technique for self-assessment (e.g., "How many cigarettes per day do I smoke?") and a method of altering the frequency of monitored activities (e.g., "I shouldn't be smoking that many cigarettes!").

As a means of self-assessment and self-induced change, self-monitoring is widely employed. In a recent survey, for example, 83% of behavior therapists reported using self-monitoring with 44% of their patients. Yet the clinical impact of self-monitoring is difficult to examine in isolation from other regulatory mechanisms, such as postperformance self-evaluation, expectancy, mood, memory, and selective attention. Moreover, the dual nature of self-monitoring functions may be problematic to the extent that the change-inducing or "reactive" aspect of the process compromises the accuracy of the self-assessment aspect.

Self-monitoring is often used as a synonym for *self-recording,* the process of manually, mechanically, or electronically counting and tabulating the frequency or intensity of an emitted response, its antecedents, or its consequences. Clearly, the process of directing one's attention inward or outward and discriminating among perceived stimuli is quite distinct from that of making a permanent record of monitored events. Nonetheless, many investigators consider the observational and recording processes to be the two defining components of self-monitoring. A third "duality" associated with self-monitoring (in addition to its dual functions and its dual components) refers to the twofold nature of its potential clinical targets—that is, the observation and recording of positive/desirable events (such as the implementation of a treatment strategy or the display of adaptive behavior) versus negative/undesirable ones (e.g., symptoms, countertherapeutic thoughts, etc.).

To complicate matters somewhat, the term *self-monitoring* is regularly employed in social and personality psychology to denote an individual-difference variable that reflects the extent to which people observe and control their expressive self-presentations and are sensitive to cues regarding appropriate interpersonal behavior. Without denying its potential relevance to behavior modification, the social psychological meaning of self-monitoring will not be considered further.

Self-Monitoring as an Assessment Strategy

As an alternative to costly or potentially impractical external surveillance of problem behaviors, self-monitoring offers the client the possibility of frequent and immediate feedback about problem behaviors. When clients do not recall, or choose not to recall, actions, thoughts, or feelings that may render them vulnerable to distress or to interpersonal conflict,

self-monitoring holds up a "mirror" to a troublesome reality. For the clinician, self-monitoring can supplement the data obtained via diagnostic interview or questionnaire, potentially providing a more complete analysis of symptom frequency, duration, intensity, quality, and the like, as well as information about the subtle functional links between symptom expression and the cues and contingencies of everyday life. For clients with vague complaints or multiple problems, self-monitoring can assist in the selection and sequencing of clinical change targets. Self-monitoring is especially recommended when collecting information about clinical targets that are private (e.g., thoughts, images, urges, impulses, cravings, etc.), relatively infrequent, naturally occurring, socially proscribed, or embarrassing. In contrast to retrospective self-reports, self-monitored data can be more reliable, less biased, and, under appropriate conditions, can also be subjected to statistical analyses expressly designed for single-case repeated (time-series) measures. Finally, after treatment has begun, self-monitoring can provide a direct and useful method of gauging the degree of treatment implementation and/or treatment progress.

After selecting appropriate targets for assessment via self-monitoring, which should include not only problem behaviors but also alternative, "healthy" responses, the clinician must ensure that the response dimensions and sampling procedures used are consistent with the nature of those targets. For example, discrete, time-limited events (such as cigarette smoking or shoplifting) usually entail *frequency* counts. Extended events (such as arguments with one's coworkers or periods of avoiding work) may require that *duration* be assessed in addition to frequency. The display of temper tantrums or arguments may likewise call for the monitoring of stimulus or behavioral *intensity* and/or *response latency* (time from provocation to onset of action). After specifying the *formal* or *topographic characteristics* of the response to be monitored, a decision must be reached as to when data are collected. Sometimes it is important to count every instance of an activity (such as suicidal or homicidal thoughts or urges, panic attacks, or episodes of migraine headache). *Event sampling* is the method designed to capture all occasions of a to-be-monitored activity and is particularly useful when the events in question are comparatively infrequent or unpredictable. *Interval recording* is the preferred method of sampling when the to-be-monitored behavior occurs frequently or cannot (or need not) be counted on an instance-by-instance basis. An example of interval recording would be a self-assessment of chronic hostility or aggressiveness at work through the use of a diary form that divides the workday into eight 1-hour periods and requires the one who is self-montoring to note the occurrence or nonoccurrence of an aggressive act during each 1-hour interval. Accurate, proximate, and consistent interval recording of this kind require that the monitoring individual be attentive to the starting and ending of the successive hourly intervals. One the other hand, when using unobtrusive, automatic counting devices (such as pedometers that continuously record the number of steps a person takes), an individual can achieve an event sampling of a relatively frequent act without having to be consistently attentive. Although of relatively recent vintage, a procedure called *momentary time sampling,* involving a signaling device that randomly or systematically prompts the individual to self-attend and self-record, is also available as an alternative to interval sampling.

The medium of self-monitoring has always tended toward the simple, direct, and portable and includes *recording devices,* such as index cards, wrist counters, punch cards, rating scales and checklists, tape recorders, and the like; *signaling devices,* such as pagers and beepers; and *timing devices,* such as stopwatches. To assist in the functional assessment of some clinical targets, a *structured diary* is another self-monitoring method that has frequently been called into service. In contrast to an open-ended, narrative diary, a structured diary is usually marked off into at least three columns: one labeled *antecedents,* the second labeled *behaviors,* and the third labeled *consequences* (yielding the so-called ABC's of behavioral analysis) and is to be completed in close proximity to the problem behavior, thought, or feeling. After a few days, an examination of the ABC's of an individual's diary-assessed action patterns might reveal unnoticed triggering stimuli or potent reinforcing consequences that could serve as targets for change. It is not unusual for diary keepers to learn a great deal about the circumstances of their problems: for some, the sobering reality of problem pervasiveness and for others, the encouraging realization that adjustive difficulties are confined to specific places and times.

Self-Monitoring as a Treatment Strategy

Self-monitoring as a mechanism for therapeutic change may be understood from several perspectives.

Within a behavioral or cognitive-behavioral framework, self-monitoring is the traditional starting point for self-directed change or *self-control.* After attending to, counting, and recording instances of excessive problem behavior (smoking, drinking, gambling, and the like), the individual may learn to de-automate habitual patterns, evaluate the monitored behavior as undesirable, set higher standards for his or her conduct, and/or become increasingly willing to take the initially difficult steps toward a reduction in the frequency or quality of the problematic pattern. The synoptic *three-phase model of self-control* (i.e., self-monitoring, self-evaluation, and self-delivery of consequences) tends to emphasize the motivational aspects of the self-change process. By contrast, self-observation can also be construed as a cognitive or meta-cognitive activity, akin to the concept of *mindfulness.* That is, when people decide to pay attention to their inner experience, their emitted behavior, or to the connection between features of a situation (e.g., the presence of an attractive person) and their reaction (e.g., blushing), they are likely to notice things or to draw conclusions or to make distinctions that they had not previously. Such *mindful* processing of information is believed to enhance people's sensitivity to their surroundings and to increase their likelihood of accepting or constructing new interpretations of themselves, others, or the world. The mindfulness interpretation of self-observation, although decidedly cognitive, is not at all incompatible with the motivational view; and both can assist therapists in helping clients to modify maladaptive habits. A key aspect of both perspectives on self-monitoring as a treatment strategy is the idea that beyond sensing and recording, the individual must examine, store, retrieve, and make sense of the accumulated self-referenced data in a manner that facilitates change.

As is the case for self-monitoring as an assessment strategy, use of self-monitoring as an intervention usually requires some form of training. Effective training capitalizes on components such as explicit education regarding its theoretical and practical rationale, in-office role playing, practice in the deployment of mechanical/electronic recording devices or data-recording formats, accuracy checks (e.g., by trained, unobtrusive external observers), and some form of reinforcement for correct and timely data collection.

Its often dramatic and immediate clinical impact on target responses notwithstanding, self-monitoring as the sole mechanism for inducing change is not generally recommended, simply because its reactive, informational, and/or reinforcing effects tend to dissipate. Owing to its diminishing returns over time, it is important that clinicians seeking to exploit self-monitoring as a treatment strategy combine it with other, powerful change techniques such as self- or other-presented reward for appropriate behavior or response cost for inappropriate action.

RESEARCH BASIS

Behavioral research in self-monitoring has focused mainly upon the therapeutic effects of self-monitoring, sometimes alone, but more often in combination with other behavior management strategies. In fact, self-monitoring has become a basic ingredient in much of contemporary cognitive-behavioral treatment. Unfortunately, empirical evaluation of self-monitoring as a clinical intervention is typically nonspecific, owing to the fact that it usually comes bundled with other active treatment strategies within multicomponent therapeutic packages. Other relevant research on the topic has been directed at methods for improving the accuracy and reliability of self-monitored data and at procedures for enhancing the therapeutic or reactive effects of self-monitoring as a component of self-management programs. Determining sensitivity of self-monitored data to treatment-based change has also been explored. In addition, investigators in clinical psychiatry and psychology have been interested for more than a decade in exploring the links between self-monitoring deficits and various neurological problems, including a hypothesized self-monitoring deficit in schizophrenia. Recently, research has emerged that examines the use of the Internet as a vehicle for the delivery of self-monitoring and self-change programs (so-called telemonitoring and Web-based therapy) as well as the utility of automatic counters, handheld computers, and sophisticated long-distance measuring devices for convenient (albeit costly) ambulatory assessment of physiological responses.

In all of these domains, findings appear to support the continued and expanded use of self-monitoring methods and principles. Although failures of self-monitoring have been noted, they have often resulted from poor response definition, excessive monitoring requirements, or contamination by subjective, retrospective recall rather than from intrinsic defects of the self-monitoring process per se or its method of pairing with other behavior modification techniques.

Despite the acknowledged successes and untapped promise of this strategy, a number of conceptual and practical issues remain to be addressed. For example, given the range of reactive effects associated with self-monitoring, the study of individual differences in reactivity merits careful empirical attention. Research is needed that concentrates on factors such as personal values, goals and self-regulatory patterns, cognitive skills, and environmental conditions as potential moderators or mediators of therapeutic change. The need for methods of improving the accuracy of self-monitoring, particularly when children are involved, continues to be a priority. Furthermore, the long-term effects of self-monitoring as a treatment or assessment strategy have not yet been adequately investigated across diverse populations and clinical problems.

RELEVANT TARGET POPULATIONS AND EXCEPTIONS

Self-monitoring methods are appropriate for a variety of problems and clients. Self-observational approaches have been especially valuable in classroom settings, where they have assisted students to track and manage their learning and performance problems, and as applied to clinical disorders for which direct external observation methods would have proven either impractical or socially unacceptable (e.g., the assessment and treatment of sexual disorders, sleep patterns, antisocial acts, and the like). Self-monitoring has been successfully used with intellectually challenged children and adults, with individuals classified as severely mentally ill, with clients whose problems encompass medical or physiological symptoms (such as headaches and eating disorders), and with elderly persons.

However, clinicians must be cautious about that to which they ask clients to pay special attention via self-monitoring. It is generally inadvisable to ask depressed individuals to record all of their negative thoughts for extended periods, to require persons diagnosed with obsessive-compulsive disorder to further ritualize their introspectiveness via systematic event monitoring, or to reinforce obese patients' concerns about their appearance by asking them to record their weight on a daily basis. Because self-monitoring is designed mainly to permit useful self-assessment and to encourage healthy lifestyle change, it should be avoided (or judiciously applied and, if need be, discontinued) whenever the possibility arises that enhanced self-directed attention will exacerbate clients' self-defeating habits, feelings of inadequacy or hopelessness, or preoccupation with past or present failures.

COMPLICATIONS

Even when applied carefully and thoughtfully, self-monitoring methods can be problematic. The most discussed complicating factor is, of course, the possibility that the reactive or change-inducing aspects of the process will adversely affect the accuracy of self-monitoring during the diagnostic or assessment phase(s) of treatment. Accuracy can also be compromised by having clients monitor too many targets (called *monitoring overload)* or attend only to undesirable responses. Interestingly, although monitoring overload is a recognized problem, research has also found that unwanted reactivity can be reduced when multiple targets are monitored, rather than one. Similarly, when self-monitoring becomes too complex or time-consuming, procedural compliance tends to decline, even for highly motivated clients.

Although popular as an intervention strategy with children, self-monitoring is nonetheless subject to various complications when children's developmental needs or limitations are inadequately addressed. For example, young children's suggestibility can eventuate in self-recorded data about events that never happened. And even older children and adolescents may be unwilling to self-monitor socially proscribed responses. Thus, it is not unusual to find discrepancies between the self-monitoring records of children (particularly children under the age of 5) and the observational records of parents and teachers. Therapists should remain mindful of the potential limitations imposed by children's truncated attention spans, their narrow and sometimes literal understanding of the treatment rationale, and their tendency to discontinue activities that are no longer seen as "fun and interesting."

CASE ILLUSTRATION

Three 8-year-old boys in an elementary school tended to use their teacher-assigned independent writing time for nonacademic or "off-task" pursuits, such as wandering around the room, gazing out the window, eating and drinking, and the like. Working independently on poetry or story writing did not appear to be a valued goal for any of the boys during the baseline external-observation period. To help these three children become better self-managers, a program consisting of self-monitoring plus goal setting was sequentially introduced by means of a multiple-baseline-across-subjects design. The students' level of "on-task" behavior during daily half-hour writing periods was targeted for change. To gauge program success, a clear set of performance criteria were established, allowing classroom observers to record both appropriate on-task and inappropriate off-task behavior.

After baseline data were collected on each child, the formal training began. Each child was informed about the importance of staying on task during the writing period and was provided a precise description of the on-task behaviors targeted for improvement. Each child was provided with a tape recorder and a self-recording sheet to be kept on his desk. At the beginning of each session, the student wrote an answer to the question, "What does the teacher want me to do?" at the top of the recording sheet. The tape recorder produced a quiet signal every 30 to 90 seconds, after which the child was required to indicate whether he was or was not on task at the time. After the writing session, the child tallied his "yes" responses and graphed them. Goal setting was introduced after a stable level was achieved for self-monitoring. After reviewing the accumulated records, the child and his teacher jointly determined a reasonable goal for the next session.

The results were quite positive for all three boys. Whereas baseline on-task behavior averaged about 45%, the self-monitoring intervention yielded an average of 90% on-task activity. The goal-setting component maintained the gains, which remained high during a stimulus fading and a follow-up period.

—*Paul Karoly*

See also: Behavioral Assessment (Vol. I); Kanfer, Frederick H. (Vol. I); Self-Control (Vol. I)

Suggested Readings

Baird, S., & Nelson-Gray, R. O. (1999). Direct observation and self-monitoring. In S. C. Hayes, D. H. Barlow, & R. O. Nelson-Gray (Eds.), *The scientist-practitioner* (2nd ed., pp. 353–386). New York: Allyn & Bacon.

Bornstein, P. H., Hamilton, S. B., & Bornstein, M. T. (1986). Self-monitoring procedures. In A. R. Ciminero, K. S. Calhoun, & H. E. Adams (Eds.), *Handbook of behavioral assessment* (2nd ed., pp. 176–222). New York: Wiley-Interscience.

Cone, J. D. (1999). Introduction to the special section on self-monitoring: A major assessment method in clinical psychology. *Psychological Assessment, 11,* 411–414.

Elliot, A. J., Miltenberger, R. G., Kaster-Bundgaard, J., & Lumley, V. (1996). A national survey of assessment and therapy used by behavior therapists. *Cognitive and Behavioral Practice, 3,* 107–125.

Foster, S. L., Laverty-Finch, C., Gizzo, D. P., & Osantowski, J. (1999). Practical issues in self-observation. *Psychological Assessment, 11,* 426–438.

Gomez, E. J., Caceres, C., Lopez, D., & Del Pozo, F. (2002). A Web-based self-monitoring system for people living with HIV/AIDS. *Computer Methods and Programs in Biomedicine, 69,* 75–86.

Jackson, J. L. (1999). Psychometric considerations in self-monitoring assessment. *Psychological Assessment, 11,* 439–447.

Korotitsch, W. J., & Nelson-Gray, R. O. (1999). An overview of self-monitoring research in assessment and treatment. *Psychological Assessment, 11,* 415–425.

Langer, E. J., & Moldoveanu, M. (2000). The construct of mindfulness. *Journal of Social Issues, 56,* 1–9.

Moore, D. W., Prebble, S., Robertson, J., Waetford, R., & Anderson, A. (2001). Self-recording with goal-setting: A self-management programme for the classroom. *Educational Psychology, 21,* 255–265.

Watson, D. L., & Tharp, R. G. (2002). *Self-directed behavior: Self-modification for personal adjustment* (8th ed., chap. 3.) Belmont, CA: Wadsworth.

SELF-STATEMENT MODIFICATION

DESCRIPTION OF THE STRATEGY

Self-statement modification (SSM) dates from Donald Meichenbaum's groundbreaking 1977 book that was one of the precursors of cognitive behavior therapy (or modification). Variously labeled as "the internal dialogue" (Meichenbaum), "automatic thoughts" (Beck), "irrational beliefs/thoughts" (Ellis), or "rational restructuring" (Goldfried), modification of these negative beliefs or self-statements forms a major part of the armamentarium of modern cognitive behavior therapy in all its manifestations. Self-statement modification is rarely attempted as a complete treatment, however; rather, it is typically used as one component of a comprehensive treatment package that includes a number of other cognitive-behavioral ingredients. Automatic self-statements can be construed as *cognitive contents* or the "what" of human cognition. They are our self-talk and are involved in ruminative processes, conscious or otherwise.

Meichenbaum based his original conceptualization on the work of Alexander Luria and Lev Vygotsky in investigating cognitive development and self-regulation of behavior in children. They found that children's self-statements (positive or negative) are first overt and modeled on the overt statements of significant adults in their lives. These self-statements, then, gradually become covert as the child grows and develops. They eventually become automatic and nonconscious. Cognitive behavior modification reverses this procedure. Automatic self-statements are first assessed and brought into consciousness, evaluated for their veridicality, and then overtly modified as needed. These overtly modified, more positive self-statements then ideally become automatic in turn.

Meichenbaum describes three phases in his cognitive behavior modification. The first phase is that of observation, in which clients become aware of the contents of their own verbal behavior. The second phase consists of the training in, and subsequent emission of, incompatible verbal behavior (self-statements), which is more positive. The third phase consists of the development of new cognitions about change itself, as clients begin a new internal dialogue about their changes. For example, they may begin to think about their new social interactions as evidence for greater prosocial abilities and thus begin to think differently about themselves. The implication is that behavior (including verbal) change may precede cognitive change, rather than the reverse. People may talk to themselves differently (and more positively) if their behavior changes in a more positive direction. For example, they may begin to say to themselves, "Gee, I'm not so bad at . . . after all!" Or they may say, "Hey, it worked! Maybe I can succeed at . . . after all!"

There are two aspects of self-statement modification. First, maladaptive self-statements are assessed. Second, these maladaptive self-statements are gradually replaced by more adaptive self-statements.

Dowd (1995) has described a variety of self-statement assessments. Interview-based methods include "thinking aloud," "thought-listing," "prompted recall," and "imagery assessment." There are also methods based on constructed questionnaires, which have the advantage of standardization. These include the Assertive Self-Statement Test (ASST), the Social Interaction Self-Statement Test (SISST), the Automatic Thoughts Questionnaire (ATQ), the Dysfunctional Styles Questionnaire (DSQ), and the Irrational Beliefs Test (IBT). The last three have been used considerably in cognitive behavior therapy research and practice.

Once maladaptive self-statements have been identified, clients are taught more adaptive self-statements in place of these. For example, thoughts like, "I'll never be able to do this!" might be replaced by, "I can do this if I plan well." Thoughts like, "I'm just not smart enough!" might be replaced by, "There's no evidence I'm more stupid than any one else."

The form that the modification of these negative self-statements takes depends considerably on the therapist's theoretical orientation and personal style. Ellis favors a vigorous and forceful disputing of the irrational beliefs identified as mediators between events and the client's subsequent emotions. He has identified approximately 12 irrational beliefs (sometimes called "The Dirty Dozen") that he argues lie behind emotional upset. Beck, on the other hand, prefers a more collaborative approach, where the therapist works with the patient as an equal to identify the more idiosyncratic negative thoughts that may cause or mediate emotional problems. Some second-generation cognitive behavior therapists, such as Arthur Freeman, may work more with the belief structures underlying specific self-statements and that organize these self-statements into themes. Others, such as Christine Padesky, may work with "hot cognitions," those with significant emotional loading. More recently, J. S. Beck has used imagery methods in self-statement modification, and E. Thomas Dowd has integrated it with hypnosis.

RESEARCH BASIS

Research on self-statement modification is often difficult to disentangle from research on cognitive (behavior) therapy (modification) because SSM is such an important part of the cognitive behavior therapy treatment package. The large body of positive research findings in cognitive behavior therapy in part speaks to the efficacy of SSM. However, more specific research on self-statement modification alone has also been conducted. For example, two meta-analyses were published, in 1983 and 1989, on adults and children. Although the effect was less pronounced for children, self-statement modification produced a greater effect size than no-treatment or placebo controls (in that order). Self-statement modification has also been found to be effective in preparing clients for stressful medical procedures, as well as in anger management, social skills training, and assertion training.

RELEVANT TARGET POPULATIONS AND EXCEPTIONS

Self-statement modification can be used with virtually everyone. All people have an internal dialogue of some sort, and part or much of it tends to be negative. Only those individuals who have strong reservations about self-exploration of any kind may not benefit, and they are not likely to be good candidates for psychotherapy of any kind.

COMPLICATIONS

If conducted with a modicum of sensitivity and skill, self-statement modification is unlikely to result in complications. Premature exposure of some negative self-statements, especially certain "hot cognitions," may result in emotional distress, but this can be reduced or eliminated by appropriate pacing of therapeutic interventions.

—*E. Thomas Dowd*

See also: *Cognitive Behavior Therapy (Vol. I); Cognitive Behavior Therapy: Child Clinical Applications (Vol. II); Meichenbaum, Donald H. (Vol. I)*

Suggested Readings

Beck, J. S. (1995). *Cognitive therapy: Basics and beyond.* New York: Guilford Press.

Dowd, E. T. (1995). Cognitive career assessment: Concepts and applications. *Journal of Career Assessment, 3,* 1–20.

Dowd, E. T. (2000). *Cognitive hypnotherapy.* Livingston, NJ: Jason Aronson.

Dush, D. M., Hirt, M. L., & Schroeder, H. E. (1983). Self-statement modification with adults: A meta-analysis. *Psychological Bulletin, 94,* 408–422.

Dush, D. M., Hirt, M. L., & Schroeder, H. E. (1989). Self-statement modification in the treatment of child behavior disorders: A meta-analysis. *Psychological Bulletin, 106,* 97–106.

Meichenbaum, D. (1977). *Cognitive-behavior modification.* New York: Plenum Press.

SETTING EVENTS

DESCRIPTION OF THE STRATEGY

In its early form, behavior analysis dealt with three key variables, namely discriminative stimulus, response, and reinforcing stimulus. These three categories did not cover all experimental variables. Some procedures were undertaken that were not incorporated into the functional analysis. For example, experimental animals were routinely deprived of food, thus increasing the likelihood that food pellets would be effective reinforcers. However, deprivation was not given a central place in the functional analysis. When concepts from the experimental analysis of behavior were applied to human behavior in natural settings, some researchers saw a need for an additional type of variable. Two approaches were adopted.

One was to take over the label "setting factors or events" from interbehavioral psychology. This was applied to stimulus operations that could affect stimulus-response relationships. These included hunger and satiation, age, and health, as well as the presence or absence of other people. Thus, "setting event" is a broad and somewhat imprecise category. However, its use alerted researchers to the need to take account of the many antecedent factors that might have an impact on the effectiveness of intervention. The setting event concept is used particularly in client assessment. For example, the Setting Events Checklist has been developed to identify possible antecedents of challenging behavior. Items include negative social interactions, unusual sleep patterns, menstrual period, and changed medication.

In addition, a setting event itself might be the focus of intervention. Two cases illustrate this. The first is a biological example. It was observed that a client showed an increased frequency of self-injuring behavior during periods of menstrual discharge. Intervention involved procedures aimed at reducing such discomfort, for example, by providing a hot-water bottle and by reducing the consumption of acidic food. The second is an environmental example. A young woman showed high levels of disruptive behavior at school. It was observed that levels of this behavior seemed to be associated with her journey to school by car. When the route followed required a high number of stops (for example, at traffic signals), her subsequent disruptive behavior was also high. A route was planned that required fewer such stops. This resulted in greatly reduced levels of disruptive behavior.

A second approach to dealing with the power of antecedent events other than discriminative stimuli was to employ the category of "establishing operations." Establishing operations are stimuli that increase the effectiveness of some reinforcers and evoke the behavior that has in the past been followed by those reinforcers. There is no consensus yet on the relations between the concept of setting event and the concept of establishing operation. Some writers seek to distinguish between the two, and others regard establishing operations as a subcategory of stimulus events. Use of the term establishing operations seems to be becoming more common. This arises from a need to deal more precisely with the impact of background factors. Establishing operations are easier than setting events to incorporate into a functional analysis.

—*Sandy Hobbs*

See also: *Applied Behavior Analysis (Vols. I, II, & III)*

Suggested Readings

Iwata, B. A., Smith, R. G., & Michael, J. (2000). Current research on the influence of establishing operations on behavior in applied settings, *Journal of Applied Behavior Analysis, 33,* 411–418.

Luiselli, J. K., & Cameron, M. J. (Eds.). (1998). *Antecedent control: Innovative approaches to behavioral support.* Baltimore: Paul H. Brookes.

McGill, P. (1999). Establishing operations: Implications for the assessment, treatment, and prevention of problem behavior, *Journal of Applied Behavior Analysis, 32,* 393–418.

SHADOWING

DESCRIPTION OF THE STRATEGY

Behavioral problems in adults with mental health and/or developmental disabilities are a primary causative factor in the exclusion of these individuals with challenges from mainstream education, leisure, employment, and independent-living opportunities. While interventions based on the principles of applied behavior analysis have, for the most part, been effective in remediating behavioral difficulties, implementation of these procedures can be both time-consuming and unreliable.

Shadowing is a strategy developed to help program staff consistently implement behavior change programs. The technique is defined by its most salient characteristic, the provision of a mediator to provide extra support to a challenged individual, typically, but not necessarily, in the form of 1:1 training and supervision. In practice, shadowing encompasses a process of observation, assessment, skill training, and feedback provided by a mediator assigned to a specific consumer. Shadowing procedures can be implemented singly or in small groups, for the entire day or just during particularly difficult periods, within one or across several sites, and in close proximity or from a reasonable distance.

Shadowing as a change technique has numerous advantages. First and foremost is the flexibility that it provides to program implementers. The shadow staff can teach critical behaviors in the setting and time that they are actually required rather than relying upon teaching sites that do not exist in the natural environment or times that do not correspond to the riskiest periods for the individual with challenges. Given the difficulty that this population has with generalization of learned skills to the target environment, the usefulness of having a support mediator available who can model the desired behavior and provide immediate feedback cannot be overestimated.

Shadowing also provides support for consumers to help them function in less restrictive environments. Often, individuals with behavioral challenges are relegated to more segregated, less stimulating environments where staff will "put up with challenging behaviors." In many cases, this leads to a "challenge match," with consumers competing for staff attention in an ever-escalating cycle of negative behaviors. Shadow staff can alter this situation by providing additional support within mainstream activities to ensure consumer participation, while insuring the safety of all those in the immediate environment.

Finally, presence of a shadow staff can increase the efficiency and efficacy of desired behavior. This is accomplished through mediator-provided cues that provide the consumer with information about what to do and, importantly, when to do it. In addition, the ability of shadow staff to provide immediate reinforcement and/or corrective feedback increases the efficacy (effectiveness) of the desired behavior. Research supports the idea that the easier a behavior is to perform (efficiency) and the immediacy of the reinforcement it receives (efficacy) play a primary role in whether a given behavior is demonstrated. Presence of a shadow staff can be instrumental in increasing both the efficiency and efficacy of desired alternative behaviors, with corresponding decreases in interfering challenging behaviors.

Shadowing begins with an in-depth functional analysis that provides data-based information on specific challenging behaviors, including triggering and setting events, maintaining consequences, related skills deficits, and the strengths of the individual. A particular emphasis is placed on "high-risk" situations, defined as the times, settings, people, and activities that place the individual at high risk for the occurrence of challenging behaviors. An analysis of the support options available during these risky periods is also performed.

Once the functional analysis is completed, a behavioral support plan is generated that addresses the communicative function of the challenging behavior. Using this communicative message as a guide, behavior analysts then design a specific change program that targets alteration of problematic antecedents, the teaching of replacement behaviors, and provision of consistent feedback for both the occurrence and nonoccurrence of the challenging behavior. Ideally, the behavior plan is generated without regard to existing mediator support, focusing instead on the specific needs of the consumer and the best practices in the field. The decision to provide additional support should come from a team of professionals serving the consumer and should be based on a realistic appraisal of the current staffing pattern and staff's ability to implement the proposed plan.

If the decision to provide additional support is made, the next step in the process involves the design of a "shadow plan." Such a plan delineates the goals and objectives of the intervention, including the specific expectations of the persons selected to provide shadow services (e.g., proximity to the consumer, type and frequency of feedback), the strategies to be implemented, and the plan to fade the shadow staff as progress is demonstrated. In general, shadows have a primary role in implementing the components of the behavior plan: altering triggering events, teaching prosocial skills, and delivering positive and corrective feedback, as needed.

Prevention of behavioral challenges is an important component of the work of the shadow staff. Prevention is most effectively accomplished through altering known triggering events that put the consumer at risk. These triggering conditions often relate to cooperating with instructions, transitioning across activities and/or environments, and coping with the perceived or actual provocations from others. The role of shadow staff in these situations should be determined by the shadow plan but typically includes eliminating the triggering events (e.g., eliminating a specific activity or instruction), altering the antecedent (e.g., preparing the individual for transition), and cuing the consumer to engage in previously learned coping skills (e.g., using communication strategies).

While prevention is essential, it is not typically sufficient to achieve all desired behavior change outcomes. Skill training is the second important function of the shadow staff. Presence of a shadow in the actual environment in which the particular skill must be exhibited enables the individual with challenging behaviors to be cued or prompted to perform desired alternative behaviors, to observe a model of the performance of the behavior, and to obtain immediate feedback on the correctness of the response. Since shadow staff can focus on one individual rather than the whole group, skill-training opportunities can be created across the day, and the target individual can be taught to engage in incompatible behaviors and perform alternative skills on an in vivo basis. Critical social and communication skills are often the focus of behavioral interventions, and shadow staff play a key role in teaching and reinforcing these skills. Skill training in areas such as self-management, self-advocacy, and problem solving is an important part of the role of shadowing, particularly since it is the acquisition of these and related skills that will enable the shadow staff to fade their presence as self-control and social skills are demonstrated.

An additional component of the shadow position is the ability of the dedicated staff to encourage the consumer to participate in available activities within his or her community. Engagement is critical to reduction of challenging behaviors. Rates of engagement are inversely correlated with challenging behaviors; as engagement rates increase, behavioral challenges decrease. Behavioral-change programs that focus on increasing engagement often succeed in creating a situation wherein challenging behavior is "crowded out," since it is difficult to engage in two incompatible behaviors at the same time. Shadow staff are often instrumental in helping individuals with challenges to remain engaged in high-interest activities and subsequently avoid challenging behaviors.

Finally, availability of shadow staff to implement consequence-based programming makes the use of positive reductive schedules of reinforcement possible. Many behavior change programs rely upon differential reinforcement of other behavior (DRO), differential reinforcement of incompatible/alternative behavior (DRI, DRA), and differential reinforcement of low rates of behavior (DRL) to effect change. While these schedules are often effective, they are highly labor intensive. Once again, the dedicated staff member can often adhere to schedule demands without the inconsistencies that plague these procedures and compromise their effectiveness.

RESEARCH BASIS

Research indicates that challenging behavior is the primary factor affecting the ability of individuals to partake fully in educational, employment, and leisure activities. Usefulness of having a dedicated or shadow staff to provide the consumer with difficult behaviors with additional support and training has been demonstrated in numerous research reports with both children and adults. Shadow staff are most useful when they encourage the consumers to participate in their environment in a manner that crowds out challenging behaviors. Multiple studies also point to the effectiveness of prevention strategies such as antecedent management in minimizing the impact of challenging behaviors.

Behavioral-change strategies that focus on teaching consumers replacement behaviors that have the same function but a different form than the challenging behavior are now considered state of the art within the field of applied behavior analysis. The importance of teaching communication, social, self-management, and related skills as alternatives to challenging behaviors is acknowledged by most practitioners. Shadow staff, whose primary job involves implementing these strategies, have been shown to play an integral role in integrating consumers with challenges into least restrictive settings.

RELEVANT TARGET POPULATIONS AND EXCEPTIONS

Shadow staff have been employed with both children and adults with challenging behaviors in school and community settings. All diagnostic populations have been served, including individuals with autism spectrum disorders, Down syndrome, conduct disorder, and neurological challenges of all types. Behaviors addressed are often of high intensity and/or frequency and include aggression, self-injury, property destruction, elopement, and extreme withdrawal. To be maximally effective, shadow staff must provide services in a manner that avoids stigma to the individual and focuses on skill acquisition rather than punitive approaches. In general, the consumer must be agreeable to the shadow arrangement in order to reduce oppositional behavior.

COMPLICATIONS

The primary complication in the use of shadow support is the potential dependency of the individual with challenging behavior upon the staff member. Such dependency typically manifests itself in reduced instructional control of all other staff, behavioral challenges being decreased only in the presence of the shadow staff, and overly extended support periods related to the difficulty in fading services once initiated.

Strategies that have been employed to address these potential complications include using multiple staff as shadows, developing a fade plan at the time the shadow-staffing arrangement begins, teaching the consumer self-management strategies, and developing an environment that is stimulating and crowds out problematic behavior.

CASE ILLUSTRATION

"John" was a 21-year-old man with autism who was attending a fully included classroom in a "transition" program. He spent part of his day at a local community college and the remainder of the day at a job site at a local restaurant with other students from his special education class. While at the college, John was integrated with nonhandicapped students in several electives, including art, music, and physical education, and his primary challenging behavior was aggression. A functional analysis performed on this behavior indicated that John was most at risk for aggressive behavior when there were unexplained changes in his schedule, when he was asked to engage in an activity he disliked, and whenever he was given corrective feedback. John's aggression was quite serious, and he had injured several peers and staff during outbursts both at college and at the job site.

To assist John in learning to manage his problematic behaviors, a shadow aide was employed. After a period of observation, the team convened to develop a shadow plan to delineate the responsibilities of the aide and other staff in the classroom and to discuss how the positive behavior support plan would be implemented. To facilitate generalization and reduce the likelihood of dependence, it was agreed that the shadow aide function would be filled by all staff on a rotating basis. The day was divided into activity periods and a plan developed for each period, which included suggested proximity between the aide and John, skills to be cued, and reinforcement strategies to be employed.

It was agreed that the support staff assigned to John each period would help him to develop a schedule that would specify his responsibilities for that period as well as the reinforcement that he could expect for successfully negotiating the activity. In addition, all shadow staff were instructed in strategies to help him learn to ask for assistance when needed and to ask for a break when he was feeling tired or not interested in work assignments. Finally, John was placed on a DRO schedule in which he was reinforced with money for every 15-minute block that he remained aggression free.

This plan led to a rapid reduction in aggressive behavior along with increases in spontaneous language and work output. Once success was achieved, the DRO interval was increased by 15 minutes after each 10-consecutive-day period without aggression. Within 3 months, John's DRO interval had been increased to 1 hour, and after 6 months, John was being reinforced just once in the morning and once at the completion of the day.

At this point, the shadow aide position began a planned fade. Fading was accomplished by systematically removing the shadow for 5 minutes out of every hour interval. As long as John maintained his behavior at low levels, fading continued. Over the course of the next year, the shadow aide was removed, while existing staff took over the implementation of the program without a significant decrement in John's performance.

—*Carl Schrader, Christine Hagie, and Mark Levine*

See also: *Behavioral Assessment (Vol. I); Social Skills Training (Vol. I)*

Suggested Readings

Cuvo, A. J., & Davis, P. K. (1998). Establishing and transferring stimulus control: Teaching people with developmental disabilities. In J. K. Luiselli & M. J. Cameron (Eds.), *Antecedent control: Innovative approaches to behavioral support* (pp. 347–372). Baltimore: Paul H. Brookes.

Lucyshun, J. M., Olson, D. L., & Horner, R. H. (1999). Building an ecology of support for a young woman with severe problem behaviors living in the community. In J. R. Scotti & L. H. Meyer (Eds.), *Behavioral intervention: Principles, models, and practices* (pp. 269–290). Baltimore: Paul H. Brookes.

Marks, S. U., Schrader, C., & Levine, M. (1999). Paraeducators in inclusive settings: Helping, hovering, or holding their own? *Exceptional Children 65*(3), 315–328.

Risley, T. (1996). Get a life! Positive behavioral intervention for challenging behavior through life arrangement and life coaching. In L. K. Koegel, R. L. Koegel, & G. Dunlap (Eds.), *Positive behavioral support: Including people with difficult behavior in the community* (pp.425–437). Baltimore: Paul H. Brookes.

Saunders, R. R., & Saunders, M. D. (1998). Supported routines. In J. K. Luiselli & M. J. Cameron (Eds.), *Antecedent control: Innovative approaches to behavioral support* (pp. 245–272). Baltimore: Paul H. Brookes.

SINGLE-CASE RESEARCH

DESCRIPTION OF THE STRATEGY

A Brief History of Early Single-Case Research in Psychological Science

Although individuals with mental retardation (MR), developmental disabilities, and psychopathology were known to ancient civilizations—in particular, nearly all those born with identifiable congenital defects and likely killed soon thereafter—there were few societal mechanisms by which to accommodate individuals who suffered from these disorders. The earliest clinics in Western civilization were probably founded after the Council of Nicæa met in the 4th century and decreed that Christians provide lodging for those unable to care for themselves. In the 17th century, the largest hospital in Paris, the Hôtel Dieu, was ordered to house individuals with psychopathology or MR. Elsewhere in Europe, however, such individuals were treated either as curiosities and tourist attractions, as they were in England—or worse, demonized and tortured, as they were in France and Germany.

One of the earliest descriptions of adult clinical applications in single cases refers to the mid-18th-century efforts by Jacob Pereira to teach an adolescent deaf-mute to speak. Pereira's individualized approach used, among other things, the sense of touch. His methods were embraced by Edouard Seguin and Jean Itard, the latter of whom attempted to socialize a putatively feral 12-year-old male, Victor of Aveyron. Seguin, a student of Itard's, went on to develop his

own system of individualized instruction, in which each child was evaluated and training exercises developed according to his or her own observed strengths and weaknesses, procedures surprisingly reminiscent of the current techniques used by applied behavior analysts.

Elsewhere in France during the late 18th to early 19th century, Philippe Pinel established new, more humane approaches to the treatment of individuals with mental disorders. In the mid-19th century, Dorothea Dix brought about similar changes in the United States, separating individuals who were mentally impaired from those who were either indigent or criminals. One of the earliest-known applications of a behavioral cure for individuals with psychological disorders was the use of hypnosis, employed during the late 18th to early 19th century by the physician, Antoine Mesmer. Mesmer worked with groups of people, but his student, the Marquis de Puységur, actually hypnotized individuals and, after talking to them during their somnambulant trances, claimed to be able to relieve them of their ailments. Later, Jean Charcot, a neurologist, utilized hypnosis as a therapy with his patients whom he had diagnosed with hysteria to rid them of their somatic symptoms. Sigmund Freud, who learned to use hypnosis from Charcot and initially employed it with his patients as a "talking cure" (catharsis), replaced it with his verbal technique of free association.

Evaluation of individuals and treatment of human disorders was very much a 19th-century phenomenon, particularly the assessment of human development and intelligence. Observational studies of infants by Charles Darwin and other notable figures of the time were published, and individual differences in their patterns of development noted. The first tests of intelligence devised by Alfred Binet and Theodore Simon were used to separate normally developing children from those with special needs. And although trained originally to study maze behavior in the rat, John B. Watson later adapted his stimulus-response behavioral techniques to condition human infants.

The emergence of psychology as its own discipline and the development of laboratories to study psychological phenomena in humans and infrahuman animals came into being during the mid- to late 19th century. The types of subjects evaluated and areas of psychology investigated emerged from several different sources in Germany, England, and the United States. By the early part of the 20th century, psychologists were using both single-subject and group designs to assess behavior. Although Adolphe Quetelet and Francis Galton made use of statistical analyses of groups of individuals in the mid-19th century, the force behind the development of group designs in psychology in the 20th century was R. A. Fisher, the eminent statistician and geneticist. Similarly, single-subject designs were employed by Edward L. Thorndike and Ivan Pavlov early in the 20th century, but the impetus for single-case research in experimental psychology, in humans or infrahuman animals, should probably be attributed to B. F. Skinner, who laid the foundations and presented the epistemological arguments in his text in 1938. Curiously, however, his remarks of what is presumed to be his quarrel with the use of inferential statistics and support for single-subject research designs are limited to the last two pages of that text. Formal arguments against the use of inferential statistics and group studies and in favor of visual inspection of graphed data and single-subject design were elaborated later by Murray Sidman. In his text on how to evaluate experimental data in psychology, Sidman expanded on the need to reduce within-subject variability for each phase of the experiment in order to demonstrate the effects of parameter manipulation across conditions of the experiment. He eschewed the use of inferential statistics as a poor substitute for good experimental control and stipulated that systematic replication was the foundation for an experimental science of behavior.

In the meantime, clinical psychology as an applied discipline within psychology evolved in the mid-19th century, after the Second World War. Much of clinical psychology of that period was influenced by Freud and his method of psychoanalysis. Ironically, almost all clinical psychologists of that period had been trained in the tradition of experimental psychology of the early 20th century. At the time, clinical psychology and psychiatry used the anecdotal case report as their datum. However, there was concern within the clinical community regarding any attempt to make generalizations from the single case. Most clinicians of that era would probably have agreed with M. B. Shapiro, who stated that the primary aim of clinical research was the diagnosis, treatment, and subsequent modification of behavior in the patient with whom the study is performed; and, second, the process of diagnosis and treatment should use the patient as his or her own control. The problem with group studies, as delineated by Chassan, concerned the multidimensionality of psychopathology: that attempts to use statistical

procedures in groups of patients to determine the efficacy of psychopharmacological interventions would be swamped by the large number of outcome measures, the small number of subjects, and the need to adjust the overall Type I error in the wake of multiple comparisons. He too argued for what he called "patient-intensive" designs based on frequent observations of the individual subject over time. Indeed, both Shapiro and Chassan would probably have agreed with Sidman about the use of multiple measures taken during baseline and intervention to establish whether a treatment regimen was effectively changing behavior.

Single-Case Research Designs

As indicated earlier, the ascent of single-subject designs in experimental psychology, particularly among psychologists trained in the experimental analysis of behavior, was facilitated by Sidman's text, *Tactics of Scientific Research,* in 1960. Subsequently, other researchers considered the utility of single-case designs in both basic and applied research, as Hersen and Barlow have noted. Issues regarding group designs, as observed by Sidman and others, concerned the limitations of group studies. In addition to the multidimensionality of psychopathology, the utility of averaging treatment results, psychopharmacological or cognitive-behavioral, across subjects and reporting findings of statistical significance may distort the effect produced on any individual patient. The assumption of homogeneity across subjects in group studies, as Hersen and Barlow noted, is untenable. However, the alternate prospect, intersubject variability, may be so great as to obscure differences between baseline and intervention conditions. Consequently, findings will not appear to be statistically significant if statistical analysis is used to evaluate the outcome, and any robust effects that may occur within individual subjects could be masked. On the other hand, single-case studies making use of naturalistic settings, reminiscent of the studies by Darwin and others in the late 19th and early 20th centuries and unlike the controlled experimental procedures used with infrahuman subjects, lack the power needed to assess the efficacy of any treatment regimen.

The concerns, then, in any science of behavior are the reliability and validity of its findings. An alternate way to view these matters is to examine the circumstances that produce variability in behavior and the generality of any environmental interventions imposed. Variability in behavior may arise from almost any source in a study: the individual subject and his or her history, the experimenter, the subject's environment, and the context in which the study is undertaken. When the sources of variability can de identified and controlled, the effect of any specific intervention may then be observed. Two issues arise. One concerns the external validity of findings obtained under circumstances in which experimental variability is well controlled. As Kazdin observed, if a single-case study removes most heterogeneity within subjects, how generalizable are the findings? A second problem is associated with the observed effects of the intervention or treatment, whether control is obtained experimentally or statistically. That is, is the observed result clinically meaningful?

To examine variability and generalizability in greater detail, we look at each component of the study, beginning with the subject's behavior. Adult clinical studies typically involve some form of psychopathology or cognitive-behavioral impairment, and these behaviors and the factors that produced them are invariably complex. Therefore, a fundamental feature of clinical research is to define the behavior and response class or classes that will be assessed, and these response characteristics must be defined operationally. Response classes may be discrete (e.g., a blow to the head) or continuous (e.g., hyperactivity), and the nature of the response class will determine how responses will be measured. Response classes are typically categorized as topographical or functional, the latter of which may be more relevant to clinical situations. Functional response classes involve observing targeted behaviors, such as self-injury, and attempting to identify the antecedent conditions or events that may have prompted them. Functional response classes may occur as punctuate actions or may extend over intervals of time.

Whereas experimental group research designs depend on the random assignment of subjects into separate arms of a study, in which each arm is administered one intervention or another and at least one treatment group is compared with another (i.e., the control group), single-case designs rely primarily on the individual subject as his or her own control. In clinical settings, studies making use of single-case designs would first take note of individuals' behaviors continually and over a period of time, during which previously stipulated target responses would be observed and recorded. This condition is referred to as the *baseline phase* of the study. Experimental group designs also make use of baseline measures, which are typically composed of group averages and assumed to be comparable across groups in the study as a consequence of some randomization procedure.

At some point after stability of the response measure in baseline has been established, subjects in single-case studies are presented a selected form of treatment or intervention. Intervention or treatment after baseline measurement is also the case for group studies; however, the number of baseline measurements obtained for group studies is typically fewer than those used in single-case designs. Baseline stability in single-case studies is often not specified in advance, but is composed of two elements: (1) variability from one test session to the next and (2) the trend in responding over time. As for session-to-session variability, Sidman suggested that a ratio of standard deviation to mean response (the coefficient of variation) should be small before parameters of the experiment are shifted, although such a standard may be difficult to achieve when working with human subjects in settings such as schools, psychiatric institutions, or group residences, where there are few opportunities to assess baseline behavior, likely under less than optimal conditions. As regards overall baseline stability, the trend across the total number of baseline sessions should be nearly flat. That is, should a best-fitting regression line be computed, its estimated slope calculated from baseline responses should not be significantly different from zero. Behavior analysts determine stability in any phase by visual inspection, a topic that we will return to shortly.

Assuming stability during baseline has been attained, the conditions of the investigation can be modified and some treatment regimen or intervention introduced. These two phases of the design, baseline and intervention, are often referred to schematically as the "A" and "B" conditions, respectively. Many group studies also employ AB designs, but behavior analysts typically insist on an additional phase, return-to-baseline or ABA design, as the minimum number of conditions for a properly designed experiment. Still others would insist on an ABAB format. The concatenation of a second AB pair to the first AB ensures not only that the effect of removing intervention returns the subject to baseline levels of responding, but that the effect of the intervention is replicated also. In some studies, the second "B" may be a different intervention, the intent of which may be to establish which of two treatment regimens or interventions is the more efficacious. For example, one study of attention-deficit/hyperactivity may use a behavioral intervention in the first B phase and a pharmacological one during the second B phase. The ABAB is sometimes referred to as a *family of designs,* and variants can be found in Hersen and Barlow.

A problem posed by an ABA or ABAB variant design in clinical research is that it may be impossible or unethical to implement. For example, if drugs are used to treat depression, the clinician is morally obligated to maintain treatment and not withdraw medication just to ascertain whether the patient will return to his or her previous level of dysfunction. There are other instances, particularly those that involve medical or surgical interventions, where the intervention cannot be removed (e.g., a prosthetic device or a transplanted organ). Hence, there are classes of interventions for which the only design permitted is AB.

One solution to the problem presented by AB-only designs is to employ a multiple-baseline procedure. That is, the intervention is presented to several individuals at different points during baseline or to a given subject at different times in the baseline for several different response measures, thus eliminating the need for a return-to-baseline phase. The replication component of the study is lost, but, as it happens, the power of the multiple-baseline design is greater than that of the ABAB design. Another alternative design involves the use of simultaneous or alternate treatments administered sequentially during the intervention phase to compare the efficacy of different interventions for a particular subject. A third alternative consists of shifting criteria in one direction or another in consecutive stages within the B component to diminish (or increase) the target behavior (e.g., reducing the number of cigarettes permitted for smoking or reducing the number of calories consumed).

DATA ANALYSIS IN SINGLE-CASE DESIGNS

Having completed the study, the collected data are then analyzed. For group designs, simple parametric statistical procedures such as t-tests (between two groups or paired within subjects) or, when more than two groups are studied, analyses of variance (ANOVA) are often employed. Frequently, however, analysis of group data may involve inclusion of additional variables that may also affect the outcome, or data may be missing for one or more subjects in the study, or the data may not conform to the relatively rigorous assumptions associated with the underlying distributions developed by Gossett and Fisher. These and other concerns about the use of statistics are obviated in single-case designs that mainly employ the visual inspection of graphed data.

Visual inspection of graphic information is the standard by which data are analyzed by most behavior analysts. As long as visual inspection was confined to examining well-defined behavioral measures from infrahuman subjects under tight experimental control and within-phase variability was small, response differences across conditions could be readily observed by eye. However, as the principles of behavioral analysis were adapted to more applied settings, such as schools and psychiatric institutions, experimental control of necessity slackened, and subjects with unknown or complex behavioral histories were studied under less than ideal conditions. As a result, about a quarter century ago, attempts were made to introduce statistical procedures into applied behavior analysis.

One problem with introducing statistical procedures to analyze behavioral data concerns the statistical model used. ANOVA is generally inappropriate since in behavioral studies, responses in successive sessions are not independent, but are temporally related to previous outcomes. That is, the data are autocorrelated or serially dependent. Although there are repeated-measures ANOVA procedures that take into account correlations in the covariance structure from one time period to the next, time-series analysis is generally considered a more fitting alternative. Time-series analysis, a stochastic model frequently employed to analyze serially dependent data, requires large numbers of time points that are not usually realized in studies using single-case formats. Since most single-case designs use many fewer points than is demanded by time-series analysis, some investigators have proposed implementing interrupted time-series analysis as an alternative for evaluating serially dependent data. However, the problems associated with any sequence of temporal data, such as trend, nonstationarity, and autocorrelation, will also apply to interrupted time series.

This would suggest that visual inspection should continue to be the choice for analyzing data in single-case settings. However, researchers, among them Fisch and his associates, have shown that visual inspection of graphed data per se can be problematic. Using autoregressive equations to generate point-to-point functions representing behavioral outcomes in AB and ABA designs, Fisch found relatively large-level treatment effects often go unnoticed, even by experienced behavior analysts, although experienced investigators are better able to identify treatment effects than are graduate students. When graphs containing trends within conditions and level treatment effects across conditions are presented, trends are rarely detected and often misinterpreted as level treatment effects, as other investigators have also noted. Trends within conditions are rarely detected, whether they are presented with or without level treatment effects. Surprisingly, level treatment effects across conditions are more readily identifiable when there are relatively fewer data points in either the baseline or intervention phase of the study design.

It would seem that analyses of data from single-case experiments veer between the Scylla of visual inspection and the Charybdis of inferential statistics. On one hand, nearly all clinical researchers using single-case designs adapted to applied settings employ visual inspection of graphed data to infer whether a given treatment has been effective in modifying targeted behaviors. However, session-to-session variability, the scale of the response measure, the number of sessions furnished during the baseline and intervention phases, the lack of experience of the researcher, and other factors may obscure level treatment effects, or trends related to treatments, or both. On the other hand, standard parametric statistical analyses of data may be inappropriate or unfit for data collected from single subjects.

One solution may be to incorporate both visual inspection and nonparametric statistical procedures to strengthen any inferences drawn. Fisch and others have suggested that there are many statistical procedures that may be used as adjuncts to visual inspection. These include the previously mentioned repeated-measures ANOVA, with suitable corrections for large differences in variance (heteroscedasticity) across groups, or nonparametric procedures that make no assumptions about underlying distributions, such as the Kruskal-Wallis, for examining changes in targeted behaviors across experimental conditions. There are also robust parametric methods for analyzing data from study designs that enlist relatively few subjects and employ multiple baselines and differing numbers of points per condition (e.g., hierarchical or mixed-effects linear models). Other nonparametric procedures, such as randomization tests, have long been recommended as an alternative to the parametric statistics employed for group designs. Edgington has published extensively on the use of randomization tests in single-case studies, although these must be constructed carefully, particularly since the number of blocks of sessions that will be permuted will affect the probabilities obtained. The downside to nonparametric tests is that they are often not as powerful as parametric procedures.

APPLICATIONS OF BEHAVIORAL INTERVENTIONS USING SINGLE-CASE DESIGNS IN CLINICAL POPULATIONS

Applied behavior analysis using single-case designs as a technique for modifying behavior has permeated many disciplines, including psychiatry, clinical psychology, education, and counseling. Behavior therapy as a mode of applied behavior analysis has been employed to eliminate maladaptive behaviors or alleviate dysfunctional activities associated with anxiety disorders, depression, substance abuse and addiction, eating disorders, impulsivity, attention-deficit, obsessive-compulsive disorder, posttraumatic stress disorder, sexual dysfunction, daily living skills for and self-injurious behavior by individuals with pervasive developmental disabilities, and/or MR. In some instances (e.g., generalized anxiety disorders), single-subject designs using applied behavior analysis (relaxation therapy) show higher initial rates of recovery than other forms of therapy.

As Krasner and Ullmann noted many years ago, the assumptions made by applied behavior analysts employing single-case designs in behavior therapy are that the laws of behavior derived from infrahuman research using principles of reinforcement are universal and that they can be employed to modify aspects of human behavior. Moreover, after a proper functional analysis of behavior has been made, one can aim at specific target behaviors (e.g., physical aggressiveness, self-injury, grooming, and toileting) and using an appropriate single-case design develop a behavior modification plan that will shape the desired change in behavior.

The *token economy* has been one of the most successful techniques used by behavior analysts and applied to clinical settings. Tokens are generalized reinforcers that in order to be effective must be exchangeable for natural reinforcers. Tokens are typically exchanged for food, drink, or other tangible objects (e.g., toys) or access to certain activities (e.g., movie watching or play time). Behavior therapy that utilizes a token economy requires a fair amount of attention to and supervision of the environment. Typically, token economies are implemented in institutional settings, such as group residences or state hospitals, and would enlist the support and services of a large number of personnel.

Ayllon and Azrin first put a token economy into practice nearly half a century ago, using an ABA design with eight inpatients residing in a psychiatric hospital. Token economies are now commonly used in large facilities, such as state hospitals for long-term patients diagnosed with schizophrenia and/or MR. These programs typically focus on daily living skills, especially personal health care, ward activities, and social competence. They often employ multiple-baseline designs, where staff systematically examine the effect of interventions on target behaviors and their frequency and patients' general level of functioning on and off the ward. Token economies have been shown effective compared with traditional hospital programs. In addition to using their own staff, some residential treatment facilities have employed patients as peers to administer token economies, and both have been shown as effective in managing daily ward behavior, aiding social interactions among patients, and expediting placement into community-based facilities. Using an ABA design, Hersen and his colleagues showed that patients diagnosed as depressed could ameliorate their symptoms by receiving tokens contingent upon eliminating performance of target behaviors associated with depression.

Token economies have also been used for postinstitutional placement but require strategies that coordinate transfer of individuals from hospitals to community-based group homes or day hospitals. Transfer from institution to community residence involves establishing attainable objectives and consistent maintenance of reinforcement contingencies, as well as training the new caregivers with the techniques developed in hospital.

Another often-used application of behavior therapy developed at about the same time as the token economy is *systematic desensitization,* established by Joseph Wolpe. It involves gradually fading out of one (undesirable) behavior or set of behaviors, to be replaced by another (desirable) behavior, whose elements are slowly faded in to the behavioral repertoire. The patient is taught to breathe slowly, visualize something pleasant, and relax. Systematic desensitization as a form of counterconditioning has often been applied to individuals who were unduly fearful of or anxious about going the dentist. In general, it is employed with patients who experience excessive fear or phobias (e.g., fear of flying, agoraphobia, or social phobia). It has also been used with individuals who experience unwarranted stress, as might be the case with someone diagnosed with posttraumatic stress disorder. Biofeedback or relaxation training and visual imagery are used to induce a state of ease and to reduce stress-related responses. Systematic desensitization has been also used to treat delusions in paranoid schizophrenics, albeit with limited success. Indeed, applied behavior analysis has tended to focus more on fear and anxiety, substance abuse, and the eating, mood, sexual, and personality disorders and less on schizophrenia and other forms of psychosis, an issue we shall return to later.

Previously, Hersen and Barlow have written about the application of single-subject designs in clinical settings, particularly those used to modify behaviors such as obsessions and compulsions, phobias, eating disorders, and to some extent, psychoses. More recent single-case studies have shown that patients with refractory obsessive-compulsive disorder (OCD) could be treated effectively at home. Other cognitive-behavioral therapies that attempt to neutralize obsessive thoughts using a variety of nonritualistic coping strategies have reduced distress associated with obsessive-compulsive behavior and improved personal functioning and work-related activities. Muscle tics associated with OCD have been suppressed by introducing competing responses to the tic when individuals with OCD have been made aware of the occurrence of the tic and the antecedent conditions to it. Even an individual diagnosed with Tourette's syndrome, a disorder considered to be genetic in origin, had his vocal tics treated effectively by repositioning his seated body.

In addition to those who display obsessive-compulsive behaviors, applied behavioral techniques have been developed for those who have problems with chemical dependence, such as alcohol and/or drug abuse. Voucher-based reinforcement protocols, like token economies, have been used with cocaine- and heroin-dependent adults to increase abstinence from drug taking; to augment maintenance with other medications, such as naltrexone or methadone employed to reduce chemical dependence; to increase involvement in the treatment process itself; and to improve appropriate verbal interactions with others. Some vouchers are used in exchange for money, while others have been swapped for goods and services. In addition to the amount of the voucher, cocaine-free intervals are affected by voucher schedule parameters (i.e., how frequently vouchers are administered). A client's commitment to treatment may involve many complex behaviors that include attendance at meetings with therapists, showing up for appointments with doctors, or applying for public assistance.

A brief review of published research suggests a greater number of applications and techniques developed for individuals with pervasive developmental disorders and learning disabilities. Applied behavior programs for individuals with autism or autism spectrum disorders have been employed primarily with younger children and have been particularly effective when incidental teaching has been employed to improve language skills. It should be noted that adults with MR have also been trained to use incidental teaching of language to other group home residents diagnosed with developmental disabilities or autism when they were assigned to be peer tutors for them. Individuals with developmental disabilities have been taught social skills involving social interactions, manners, and social confrontations as well.

Applied behavior analysis has been widely employed with adults with MR or learning deficits, the more severely impaired of whom frequently self-injure. Iwata and his colleagues have extensively studied self-injurious behavior (SIB) in MR individuals. Typically, researchers employ a functional analysis of an individual's SIB—identify what the antecedent conditions are that elicit the behavior, and the various response topographies, such as head banging or hand biting, their contexts, and the various reinforcement modalities that maintain them. Often, fading procedures or differential reinforcement for other (DRO) behaviors are employed to eliminate SIB. Occasionally, individuals who have previously self-injured will relapse, often because SIB has become contingent upon stimuli in other contexts. Such cases require further functional analysis, since SIB may be used a form of escape maintenance to avoid meeting with a therapist or engage in other perceived aversive activities. Sometimes, SIB is maintained because individuals move from one setting to another, in which demands may differ, or be assigned a new therapist. Under such circumstances, studies have shown that generalizing compliance to eliminate SIB may prove problematic.

Daily living skills are an important dimension of behavior in training individuals with MR. Employing modeling and prompting procedures, adults with severe or profound MR have been taught to exit their residences rapidly when a fire alarm is sounded. By offering paired-item presentations, adults with profound MR have been given opportunities to make choices and show preferences for food and drink at meals or snack times. Utilizing a multiple-probe design, adults with milder learning problems have been taught to use the personalized system of instruction, a self-paced manual, to learn checking account skills: to write checks, complete deposit slips, and resolve monthly statements.

Job skills are another area in which severely and profoundly MR adults have been successful. Self-instruction statements and correct responses were used to train severely MR adults to package soap for a janitorial supply firm. Using antecedent modeling and quality control checks, adults with mild MR were used as coworker trainers to supervise other mildly MR adults to prepare salads.

Adults who receive head injuries in accidents and subsequently develop severe brain trauma usually form cognitive and behavioral deficits that seriously impact daily living. Typically, these individuals experience chronic unemployment and acquire maladaptive behaviors such as drug or alcohol abuse. Those who, as a result of their injuries, find themselves without careers have found work through programs that establish supported employment intervention, in which behavior analysts provide job placement and training support. Using a multiple-baseline design, researchers found that this program provided success for some of the individuals enrolled. Adults with brain injuries have also been trained to eliminate potential hazards from their living quarters. Having received specific written task analyses with detailed and explicit responses, a multiple-probe technique ascertained that individuals with brain damage showed increases in the proportion of correct responses to items on these lists.

Other forms of brain dysfunction resulting from stroke (Broca's aphasia) or disorders typically associated with old age, such as Alzheimer's disease (AD) have been to some extent amenable to behavior modification techniques. A multiple-baseline design was used to increase conversational interaction in adults with Broca's aphasia. Individuals prompted at the outset of each intervention phase but not trained to a criterion were able to increase the number of subject-initiated topics during intervention and remained above baseline levels during maintenance and follow-up. Moreover, this increase in subject-initiated conversation generalized to individuals familiar with the patients. Persons with AD also experience deterioration in language ability, in addition to memory loss and declines in other daily living skills. Behavior analysts developed a memory aid (book with pictures) for individuals with AD, to be used when relating to their spouses. Studies using an ABAB variant or a multiple-baseline design showed that the number of on-topic conversations increased from baseline to intervention and remained elevated during maintenance and follow-up.

One might argue that philosophically and conceptually, behavior therapy is incompatible with the seemingly verbal strategies employed by psychotherapists to resolve clients' psychiatric disorders. Early use of behavior therapy usually took place with the therapist and within a single session. However, this form of therapy was considered unrealistic, given that the context in which problem behaviors arose was outside the therapist's office and unrelated to the therapeutic environment. Recently, there have been attempts by behavior analysts to bridge the gap, to bring the client's problem back to the therapist in his or her office, particularly for those whose disorders involve personal relationships or who have complicated personal problems.

As described in a series of articles edited by Dougher, clinical behavior analysis attempts to use verbally based interventions to treat psychiatric disorders typically encountered in outpatient settings, disorders such as anxiety, phobias, and depression. As such, it is viewed as form of psychotherapy. Hayes and his colleagues developed a set of techniques based on the experimental analysis of verbal behavior, which they describe as *action and commitment therapy* (ACT). ACT has been used to eliminate the client's tendency to deny his or her symptoms and to avoid engaging behaviors involving commitment to change. Their success has been reported with individuals who would be diagnosed as depressed or dysthymic. Kohlenberg and his colleagues have also developed a technique to manage depression they call

functional analytic therapy (FAP). Unlike ACT, which often attempts to create an atmosphere of confusion from which the client makes a breakthrough, FAP identifies the client-therapist relationship as a social one in which the client benefits optimally when engaging the therapist directly in clinically relevant behavior.

As a form of psychosis, borderline personality disorders (BPD) have often proved less tractable to therapy, due in part to the multifaceted characteristics of the disorder, which include transient delusions. Dialectical behavior therapy (DBT), developed by Linehan, has attempted unravel the complexities associated with BPD by erecting a hierarchy of the client's dysfunctions. DBT assumes that the primary disorder in BPD is generated and maintained in emotionally, biologically sensitive individuals by a pervasive dysregulation of emotional behavior evolving from a disordered family or social environment. This requires the therapist to reinforce functional behaviors when they occur and not to respond when dysfunctional behaviors arise. So, for example, a therapist whose client self-injures may be unwilling to accept emergency telephone calls within 24 hours of the event. When the client is thus motivated to work with the therapist, the therapist would then establish a hierarchy of importance of problems to treat the client's various dysfunctional behaviors.

SUMMARY

Individuals with developmental disabilities and/or psychopathology were probably known to our ancestors, but it has only been relatively recently that attempts have been made to assess and treat these disorders. The emergence of experimental and clinical psychology in the last century has permitted quantitative methodologies and research designs to develop and analyze behavioral dysfunction. Although group studies have also been utilized, the single-case design in applied settings has been particularly successful in evaluating and treating patients with psychological problems. Through a functional analysis of behavior, single-case studies identify and quantify targeted responses, before and during treatment, then again after treatment has been discontinued. This traditional ABA design has been used to establish validity and reliability in single-case studies, although other variants such as ABAB and multiple baselines also attempt to ascertain the effectiveness of interventions. To verify treatment efficacy, statistical analysis is shunned in favor of visual inspection of graphed data of targeted behaviors. However, both statistical analyses and visual inspection have their limitations. Applied behavior analysis has been used in various clinical settings: in schools, state psychiatric facilities, group homes, as well as the behavior therapist's office. Token economies, as applications of behavior analysis using single-case designs, have been used primarily with psychiatric inpatients and individuals with MR who need to develop a variety of daily living skills. Desensitization techniques have also been employed, chiefly to moderate fearful and anxiety-produced behavior. Interventions using single-case methodology have been effectively applied to adults with MR who also self-injure, but applied behavioral programs used to train those who have suffered from brain trauma or Alzheimer's disease have enjoyed limited success. Attempts have been made to broaden single-case applications of behavioral therapy to schizophrenia and various forms of psychosis, but little has been published in this area.

—*Gene S. Fisch*

See also: *Behavioral Case Formulation (Vol. I); Single-Subject Research Design (Vol. III)*

Suggested Readings

Davidson, P. O., & Costello, C. G. (Eds.). (1969). *N = 1: Experimental studies of single cases.* New York: Van Nostrand Reinhold.

Dougher, M. J. (Ed.). (1993). Special section on clinical behavior analysis. Part I. *The Behavior Analyst, 16,* 269–330.

Dougher, M. J. (Ed.). (1994). Special section on clinical behavior analysis, Part II. *The Behavior Analyst, 17,* 287–364.

Fisch, G. S. (1998). Visual Inspection of data revisited: Do the eyes still have it? *The Behavior Analyst, 21,* 111–123.

Hersen, M., & Barlow, D. H. (1976). *Single case experimental designs: Strategies for studying behavioral change.* New York: Pergamon Press.

Hersen, M., & Bellack, A. S. (1999). *Handbook of comparative interventions for adult disorders.* New York: Wiley.

Jayaratne, S., & Levy, R. L. (1979). *Empirical clinical practice.* New York: Columbia University Press.

Johnson, J. M., & Pennypacker, H. S. (1993). *Strategies and tactics of behavioral research* (2nd ed.). Hillsdale, NJ: Erlbaum.

Kazdin, A. E. (1977). *The token economy: A review and evaluation.* New York: Plenum Press.

Kazdin, A. E. (1993). *Research design in clinical psychology* (2nd ed.). Boston: Allyn & Bacon.

Krasner, L., & Ullmann, L. P. (1973). *Behavior influence and personality.* New York: Holt, Rinehart & Winston.

Kratochwill, T. R., & Levin, J. R. (Eds.). (1992). *Single-case research design and analysis.* Hillsdale, NJ: Erlbaum.

Linehan, M. M. (1993). *Cognitive behavior treatment of borderline personality disorder.* New York: Guilford Press.

Neef, N. A. (Ed.). (1994). Special issue on functional analysis approaches to behavioral assessment and treatment. *Journal of Applied Behavior Analysis, 27,* 196–371.

Scheerenberger, R. C. (1982). *A history of mental retardation.* Baltimore: Paul H. Brookes.

Sidman, M. (1960). *Tactics of scientific research.* New York: Basic Books.

Skinner, B. F. (1938). *The behavior of organisms.* Englewood Cliffs, NJ: Prentice Hall.

Wolpe J. (1969). *The practice of behavior therapy.* New York: Pergamon Press.

SKINNER, BURRHUS FREDERIC

Burrhus Frederic (B. F.) Skinner discovered that behavior can be explained not by intention or will or any other "agency" inside a person, but by the moment-to-moment impact of actions within an individual's world. When Skinner began his research, Pavlov had already shown how responses in a reflex could be brought under control of new stimuli. Pairing a previously neutral stimulus with a stimulus that already produced a predictable response enabled the new stimulus to elicit a similar response. Skinner called such behavior "respondent." Therapy with respondents, such as fear or anxiety, thus centers on antecedents, as in systematic desensitization. But not all behavior is part of a reflex. Most of what we think of as uniquely human, such as talking, thinking, or creating, is not part of a reflex. Skinner discovered that the causes of these behaviors lie not in antecedent stimuli, but in postcedent effects. He coined the term "operant" for behavior that operates on the environment and is controlled by its immediate impact. Prior events become important in operant behavior too, but only when they are paired with consequences for responding in their presence or absence. The relationships between actions, consequences, and the context in which behavior occurs Skinner called "contingencies of reinforcement." Changing operant behavior involves altering consequences for client actions in the settings in which they currently live.

EARLY INFLUENCES

B. F. Skinner's life spanned most of the 20th century. He was born in Susquehanna, Pennsylvania, on March 20, 1904, and died on August 18, 1990, in Cambridge, Massachusetts. At the time of Skinner's birth, Susquehanna was a conservative town of about 2,000 inhabitants, and its main business, the railroad, was booming. Skinner's father was a lawyer, his mother a housewife. Frederic and his brother, younger by 2 years, grew up in a stable home. Their parents raised them with a mixture of strictness and leniency. The boys were given stern admonitions about proper social behavior. An improper remark or slouching in a chair would bring a "Tut, tut," from his mother, followed by a warning, "What will people *think?*" But in exploring and constructing things, the young Fred had few constraints. He used his father's hand tools to build things from old planks, scraps of wood, and parts of machinery readily available in the garage. The list of the contraptions the boy built includes a small reading room with shelves and a candle bracket, small houses in the ramshackle back yard complete with cellars dug 6 feet down, a cabin with glass windows, a steam cannon that shot plugs of carrots across the yard when sufficiently fired up, and slides, teeter-totters, merry-go-rounds, and carts. No one taught Skinner how to make things or how to use tools. He mentioned his frustration in trying to screw together two oak planks, not having been told to drill a hole first. He figured out how to do things on his own, an independence that was to serve him well later in graduate school.

EDUCATION

Skinner's early schooling was typical of small-town public schools in the early 20th century. He went through 12 grades in the same building, at a walking distance from his home. In his eighth-grade class, Skinner repeated a remark his father had made that some people thought that Francis Bacon had written the plays attributed to Shakespeare. The teacher dismissed the idea. To bolster his claim, the young student read about Bacon and several of his works. What he read had a lasting impact. Bacon is mentioned in 12 of Skinner's 20 books.

Skinner attended Hamilton College from the fall of 1922 to June of 1926. His first year did not go well, but he made it through with respectable, if not stellar, grades. The remaining years of college went better. He

was asked to tutor the son of the chemistry teacher, Professor Saunders. The Saunders family exposed him to a cultural life that he had never before witnessed. Professor Saunders bred prize-winning peonies, played violin in quartets in the music room, owned and used a telescope, and knew writers such as Ezra Pound. Intellectual activity was always going on at the Saunders's home, and Skinner was invited to many of the afternoon or evening soirees. He remained part of the Saunders's circle for the remainder of his college years.

In his junior and senior years, Skinner became a member of the staff of the college magazine. He began to take writing seriously, majoring in English and attending a writer's workshop at Breadloaf, Vermont, during the summer, where he met Robert Frost. In his senior year, he floated the idea of becoming a writer as a career to his professors and parents but got little encouragement from either. Undaunted, Fred sent Frost a story he had written. The reply, "You are worth twice anyone else I have seen in prose this year," was all Fred needed. He would become a writer.

THE "DARK YEAR"

In the summer of 1926, Skinner moved back home. He set up a study in his parent's third floor, made bookshelves, subscribed to writers' magazines, sharpened pencils, and sat in front of blank pieces of paper. They remained mostly blank. Aside from a few flippant columns for the local newspaper, he published nothing in what he later called his "dark year." Finally, his father gave him a job abstracting legal briefs. The result was a book, *The Digest of Decisions of the Anthracite Board of Conciliation,* coauthored by B. F. Skinner and William A. Skinner.

The abstracts completed, Skinner moved to New York City. A job in a bookstore kept him in touch with literature. He read magazines such as the *Dial,* and it was in the *Dial* that he first read about John B. Watson. In an article called "Is Science Superstitious?" Bertrand Russell mentioned Dr. Watson's Behaviorism as "the spearhead" of science's attack against traditional "superstitious" philosophy. Skinner bought Watson's book and Pavlov's just-translated *Conditioned Reflexes* and Bertrand Russell's *Philosophy.* Skinner decided to study psychology, going to Harvard on the recommendation of a former professor.

GRADUATE SCHOOL AND
THE DISCOVERY OF THE OPERANT

In the fall of 1928, Skinner arrived in Cambridge, Massachusetts, for graduate school. A course taught by Hoagland in the physiology department brought him in contact with William Crozier. The two hit it off right away. As E. A. Vargas put it, "It was a marriage made in heaven; Crozier—caustic, hard-driving and hard-drinking, impatient, contemptuous of what he called organ physiology, an advocate of Loeb in biology and Mach in philosophy; and Skinner—sarcastic, radical and rebellious, impatient, contemptuous of compromisers, and eager to put the investigation of behavior on an independent scientific footing." The chair of the psychology department was Edwin G. Boring, a disciple of the introspective psychology that Watson had attacked in his book. But Boring was on sabbatical that first semester. By the time he returned at midyear, Skinner was working over in physiology. The ambiguity of Skinner's position meant that he had no real supervision, and that suited him well: "In my research courses . . . I worked entirely without supervision. . . . Possibly the psychologists thought I was being counseled by Crozier and Hoagland, and they may have thought that someone in psychology was keeping an eye on me, but the fact was that I was doing exactly as I pleased."

This lack of direction combined with his love of building apparatuses meant that day-to-day research took directions determined by the results of experiments. Skinner began working with rats. Over the course of 3 years, he designed one piece of equipment after another. He was looking for some variable that, when manipulated, had an unambiguous impact on behavior. He started with antecedent stimuli in the tradition of Pavlov, but what he discovered was an entirely different kind of control over behavior. By the end of his third year at Harvard, he had invented the operant chamber known as the "Skinner box" with a "cumulative recorder" that recorded the rat's behavior in real time. The "Skinner box" consisted of an enclosed space with a bar the rat could press and a dispenser that delivered a small pellet of food. The cumulative recorder, a slowly turning drum, had a pen that drew a horizontal line until the bar was pressed, when it moved up a notch. The faster the rat responded, the steeper the slope of the cumulative record. With this equipment, Skinner found that the bar pressing of his rats did not fit within the Pavlovian conditioning model. It was, as he wrote to his best friend, Fred Keller, in the fall of 1931, "an entirely new theory of

learning." Bar pressing was not determined by an *antecedent* stimulus, but by its *postcedent* effect. The action was "emitted" rather than "elicited" by a stimulus. Skinner coined the term "operant" for behavior under control of consequences, to distinguish it from Pavlovian elicited "respondent" behavior.

Of course, the fact that consequences of actions impact future behavior had been known for centuries. Thirty years before, Thorndike had talked of stamping in and stamping out of responses of cats clawing to get out of "puzzle boxes." Thorndike's procedures, however, required "trials," and he recorded only the time it took to escape, finding that it decreased on successive trials. With his apparatus, there was no way to manipulate variables to see their moment-to-moment impact on the rate of behavior, and he had dropped this line of research. It was not until Skinner designed the bar-pressing chamber that a *rate* of responding could be measured and the effect of delivering or not delivering food pellets could be ascertained. Skinner's equipment and early work made possible a science that related the probability of behavior to environmental determinants. His analysis related probability of behavior directly to contingencies of reinforcement.

With 5 years of fellowships, including a 3-year appointment to Harvard's Society of Fellows (1933–1936), Skinner investigated extinction, schedules of reinforcement, delay of reinforcement, amount of reinforcement, and many other postcedent contingencies. He also documented how antecedent stimuli come to control emitted behavior through their connection with the action-consequence relation. He investigated the conditions for "induction" (also called "generalization"), showing the spread of effect from one stimulus to another and one response to another. He looked at the effect of a few behavioral drugs, the first psychopharmacological work using operant techniques. He even developed a kind of auditory Rorschach that he called the "verbal summator" and tried it out with patients at Worchester State Hospital. Playing a series of recorded vowel sounds over and over, he asked patients to report what was being said. As with the Rorschach test, their responses reflected their histories, not anything inherent in the stimuli to which they were responding.

MINNESOTA PROJECT
PIGEON AND *WALDEN TWO*

When Skinner's fellowship ended, life took a different turn. He met Yvonne Blue, and after a short courtship, they got married on November 1, 1936. Skinner took his new bride to St. Paul, Minnesota, where he had been appointed as an assistant professor at the University of Minnesota. Within 2 years, they had the first of two children, Julie. In the same year, his book *The Behavior of Organisms* (1938) came out, documenting his experimental work. The *Behavior of Organisms* did not address human behavior, but by 1939, Skinner was teaching a course on the psychology of literature. Then, World War II broke out.

Project Pigeon

In the early days of the war, radar had not yet been perfected, and there was no way to guide missiles toward a target. Skinner realized that he could train pigeons to do the job. After several attempts, he got funding from General Mills, and set up a top-secret project team. In addition to teaching the birds to peck at images of ships, he and his coworkers researched the impact of deprivation level, kind of grain, pressure of oxygen and carbon dioxide, atmospheric pressure, differing accelerations, prolonged vibration, and noises made to mimic gunshots. They looked at how well pigeons could discriminate specific objects against a variety of backgrounds and in various rotations. Finally, they were ready for full-scale funding, and Skinner took a demonstration bird to Washington. But despite flawless performance from the pigeon even after hours on the train, with the top removed for the first time and strangers peering from above, Washington was not interested.

While Project Pigeon did not further the war effort, it did further the experimental analysis of behavior. As Skinner put it, "It had given rise to a technology," showing an incredible precision of control over behavior. But at the end of Project Pigeon, in the summer of 1944, he turned from experimental work to resume a Guggenheim fellowship he had interrupted for war work. He began a book on verbal behavior. His wife was also pregnant again. Couldn't he put his design skills into improving on the standard crib? Of course he could. Skinner built what he called the "baby tender." It was an enclosed, heated crib. The baby would sleep on a long roll of cotton stretched tightly across a wooden frame. No blankets or sheets were necessary. In August of 1944, he finished the baby tender, just in time for his second daughter. The new baby, Deborah, almost never cried. Though she slept in the baby tender, she spent most of her waking hours outside the bed. Unlike her older sister, Deborah did not have any colds, and Skinner attributed these advantages to the warm, moist air of his new crib. Eager to promote his invention, he wrote his first "popular" article and sent it off to the *Ladies Home Journal*. The editor changed the title to one more likely to attract attention, and the article came out in October of 1945 as "Baby in a Box."

Walden Two

A dinner conversation in the spring of 1945 about servicemen returning from World War II started Skinner thinking about the life to which they would be returning and how cultural practices could be improved. In the summer of 1945, he wrote *Walden Two*. *Walden Two* is a novel about a community based entirely on behavioral principles. The design of the community is revealed to the reader via a visit by "Professor Burris" and his group of visitors. The community is experimental: All procedures, such as the "work credit" system, are based on behavioral principles and are open for testing and adjusting as data indicate. Work credits are set according to the desirability of a job. Gardening earns only a few credits per hour, while cleaning bathrooms earns many. The originator of the community, "Frazier," explains how Walden Two runs and argues vehemently for the advantages of designing cultural practices according to how well they work, rather than letting them occur haphazardly, a theme that would reoccur in Skinner's *Beyond Freedom and Dignity*. One of the visitors, called "Castle," counters all of Frazier's ideas, and Burris weighs each of their arguments. Skinner later realized that using Frazier as a mouthpiece, he was able to propose ideas for cultural design that he was not yet ready to put into print under his own name.

BLOOMINGTON AND THE UNIVERSITY OF INDIANA

In the fall of 1945, the Skinner family moved to Bloomington, Indiana. Skinner had accepted the chair of the Department of Psychology at Indiana University. He began to look for behavioral people for new positions. He hired Sid Bijou, then at Iowa, to head a new clinical program with an experimental orientation. He hired Bill Verplanck as an administrative assistant. The first operant work with a human being occurred at Indiana while Skinner was chair: Using sweet warm milk as a reinforcer, a graduate student, P. R. Fuller, in 1949 shaped and then extinguished arm movements in a "vegetative human organism" who was said to be unable to learn. While behavioral work was not gaining much publicity in psychology, Skinner was becoming known. While at Indiana, the "baby tender" article came out and received a spike of attention in the popular press. Skinner had dozens of letters from parents asking for the special beds and tried to get a business going, only to discover that his partner, the "manufacturer," was taking money for baby tenders but not building or shipping them. Skinner had to refund money from family funds.

Meanwhile, the "experimental analysis of behavior," as Skinner was now calling the field, was growing. In the summers of 1947, 1948, and 1949, conferences were held at which experimental results were shared. Operant researchers continued to interact. Eventually, in 1957, with the suggestion of Skinner and the efforts of Charles Ferster, the Society for the Experimental Analysis of Behavior was formed to publish the *Journal of the Experimental Analysis of Behavior.*

HARVARD UNIVERSITY

In the fall of 1947, at the invitation of Edwin Boring, Skinner was asked to give the William James lectures at Harvard University. He selected verbal behavior as his topic. At the end of the semester, he was invited to join the psychology department. He finished his last semester at Indiana and in the fall of 1948 joined the Harvard faculty as professor in the department of psychology. He was given space for a pigeon lab in the basement of Memorial Hall. Soon, he had an active research lab and graduate students. Between 1955 and 1962, when he stopped experimenting, the department graduated Doug Anger, James E. Anliker, Donald S. Blough, Richard J. Herrnstein, Alfredo V. Lagmay, William H. Morse, Nathan Azrin, Ogden Lindsley, Lou Gollub, Matthew Israel, Harlan Lane, George Reynolds, A. Charles Catania, and Herb Terrace. Much of the research from those years is documented in Ferster and Skinner's 1957 *Schedules of Reinforcement.* This volume is an encyclopedic compendium of cumulative records from more than a million hours of research.

One of Skinner's advisees, Ogden Lindsley, urged Skinner to apply operant techniques with human beings. The back wards of Metropolitan State Hospital housed psychotic human beings for whom no treatment had worked. Why not see what operant conditioning could do? Skinner agreed and found funding for the project. Needing a name for the procedures they were to use, Lindsley coined the term "behavior therapy."

THE BEHAVIOR THERAPY PROJECT

The behavior therapy project began in June of 1953. Small rooms were set up with a chair, an operandum such as a plunger, and a means to deliver reinforcers. Cumulative recorders collected data on 10-inch-wide rolls of paper that cascaded onto the floor as hours of patient records were generated. Different contingencies of reinforcement were set up by changing the wires on panels. Slide projectors enabled the researchers to present a variety of visual images. Pressure panels tracked pacing or other movements of participants, and voice relays recorded vocalizations. It was an impressive setup.

Dozens of studies came out of the behavior research lab as well as new designs for equipment for work with human beings. Lindsley himself published 31 articles between 1953 and 1966. The lab also attracted visitors—nearly 2,000 students and more than 900 professionals in its 12 years. Sid Bijou, Charles Ferster, Nate Azrin, and Lindsley's assistant, Bea Barrett, set up similar labs. Skinner, however, was only intermittently involved. Although giving several talks on behavior therapy, he published little in the field. But his few articles argue that behavior therapists should deal directly with contingencies over behavior instead of inferred mental states.

TEACHING MACHINES AND PROGRAMMED INSTRUCTION

The same year as the behavior therapy lab opened, Skinner entered the field of education. His interest was launched by a visit to his daughter Deborah's math class on Parent's Day in November 1953. Watching a traditional lesson, Skinner suddenly realized that fundamental principles of shaping were not being used. But how could one teacher adapt each step individually to each child's performance level? Over the next 15 years, Skinner designed one teaching machine after another. The first gave only practice, but by 1958, Skinner was talking about *programmed* instruction, which could teach new behaviors using techniques described in

Verbal Behavior. Problems could be randomly presented in the practice machines, but programmed instruction required a careful sequencing of steps. With the help of James G. Holland, Skinner put his own undergraduate course onto machines produced in the Harvard shops, and he and Holland analyzed the thousands of responses written by the students for revisions of the program. Meanwhile, Skinner could not find a company to produce machines commercially, despite tremendous attention from the general public, from whom Skinner was receiving hundreds of letters a month. But although machines were not being produced, programmed instruction in book form swept the country in the early 1960s. Holland and Skinner's own teaching-machine material came out as a book, *The Analysis of Behavior,* in 1961. The book form of programmed instruction did not last, though aspects of programmed instruction, such as "behavioral" or "performance" objectives and "mastery" learning became part of mainstream education. It wasn't until computers were common that programmed instruction had the machine needed for the careful shaping of student repertoires.

BEYOND FREEDOM AND DIGNITY

During the programmed instruction years, Skinner was increasingly sought as a speaker abroad as well as at home. He gave talks in Canada, England, France, Denmark, Austria, Russia, Norway, and Sweden, as well as in dozens of states in the United States. In a diary entry on October 17, 1967, he wrote "Turning down more than 1 invitation a day to speak." As he approached retirement age, he began closing down his lab and reflecting on how the science of behavior could improve cultural practices. The result was *Beyond Freedom and Dignity.* In the book, Skinner argued that no behavior is free. To achieve what we call "freedom and dignity," we must explicitly design cultural practices to produce a better world, instead of leaving the evolution of cultural practices to chance. Design, in turn, would be based upon the science of behavior. The book became a best seller.

LATER LIFE

Skinner's professional activities did not slow down much in the last two decades of his life. He traveled less but continued writing and publishing. He wrote dozens of articles on all kinds of topics, collecting many of them into book volumes. He wrote three volumes of an autobiography, analyzing his own life in terms of the contingencies he had encountered. When experiencing problems associated with old age, he devised strategies to handle them, and with Margaret Vaughan, he wrote his suggestions in *Enjoy Old Age.* Even when diagnosed with leukemia in 1988, he did not decrease his professional activities. Over the last summer of his life, he worked on an article and talk for the American Psychological Association meetings in Boston. Ten days before he died, he delivered, without notes, a 20-minute talk. With cameras rolling, he talked of three kinds of selection: Darwinian, operant conditioning, and cultural selection. To explain or change behavior, one needs an analysis of contingencies, not a search for inferred or physiological processes inside an individual. "Cognitive Psychology," he said, "is the creationism of Psychology."

CONTRIBUTIONS TO BEHAVIOR THERAPY

Although he himself was not a therapist, what Skinner contributed to behavior therapy cannot be overemphasized. Behavioral pharmacology, covert conditioning, and functional analytic psychotherapy (FAP) come directly from Skinner's work. Procedures such as those used in "functional assessment," "token economies," and "mand-before-tact" language training are based upon his writings. Skinner provided a science and an analysis of verbal behavior that could treat clinical problems that Pavlovian techniques did not address. Through hundreds of experiments, he showed how postcedent events in specific settings control operant behavior, with a precision never before seen. He consistently argued against internal "agencies" having any useful role in therapy. An individual is not troubled because he is "psychotic" or "paranoid"—the individual engages in behavior we call "psychotic" or "paranoid." That behavior can be changed if we can control the contingencies that are maintaining it. Skinner gave us a science to find out how.

—Julie S. Vargas

See also: Applied Behavior Analysis (Vols. I, II, III)

Suggested Readings

By B. F. Skinner

The Behavior of Organisms (1938); *Walden Two* (1948); *Science and Human Behavior* (1953); *Schedules of*

Reinforcement (1957), with Charles B. Ferster; *Verbal Behavior* (1957); *Cumulative Record* (1959); *The Analysis of Behavior* (1961), with James G. Holland; *The Technology of Teaching* (1968); *Contingencies of Reinforcement: A Theoretical Analysis* (1969); *Beyond Freedom and Dignity* (1971); *About Behaviorism* (1974); *Particulars of My Life: Part One of an Autobiography* (1976); *The Shaping of a Behaviorist: Part Two of an Autobiography* (1979); *A Matter of Consequences: Part Three of an Autobiography* (1983).

Other Publications

Bjork, Daniel W. (1993). *B. F. Skinner: A Life.* New York: Basic Books.

Richelle, M. N. (1993). *B. F. Skinner: A reappraisal.* Hove, UK: Erlbaum.

Smith, L. D., & Woodward, W. R. (Eds.). (1996). *B. F. Skinner and behaviorism in American culture.* Bethleham, PA: Lehigh University Press.

Todd, J. T., & Morris, E. K. (1995). *Modern perspectives on B. F. Skinner and contemporary behaviorism.* Westport, CT. Greenwood Press.

Vargas, E. A. (1995). Prologue, perspectives, and prospects of behaviorology. *Behaviorology, 3,* 107–120.

Vargas, J. S. (2001). B. F. Skinner's contribution to therapeutic change: An agency-less, contingency analysis. In W. T. O'Donohue, D. A. Henderson, S. C. Hayes, J. E. Fisher, & L. J. Hayes (Eds.), *A history of the behavioral therapies: Founders' personal histories.* Reno, NV: Context Press.

Wiklander, N. (1989). *From laboratory to Utopia: An inquiry into the early psychology and social philosophy of B. F. Skinner.* Goteborg, Sweden: Goteborg Arachne Series.

SOCIAL EFFECTIVENESS TRAINING

DESCRIPTION OF THE STRATEGY

Social phobia is a disorder that affects approximately 2% to 8% of the general adult population. Although many people experience mild anxiety when giving speeches or going on job interviews, those with social phobia experience anxiety so intense that it impairs their functioning, leads to avoidance behavior, and/or results in maladaptive coping strategies. There are two types of social phobia. About 30% of those with social phobia report anxiety and distress only in performance situations, such as giving a speech. Individuals with this rather circumscribed pattern of fear are often referred to as having the *specific,* or *nongeneralized,* subtype. Those with the *generalized* subtype (the other 70%) report distress across a broad range of

social situations, such as giving a speech, meeting new people, and one-on-one social conversation. Behavioral interventions such as exposure or cognitive behavior therapy appear to be most effective in treating the specific subtype of social phobia, but these treatments appear to have a limited effect for the generalized subtype. Social effectiveness therapy (SET) was designed to improve treatment outcomes for the generalized subtype. SET is a unique combination of psychoeducation, social skills training, imaginal and in vivo exposure, and programmed practice. The goals of SET are to reduce social anxiety, improve interpersonal skills, and enhance social functioning.

As noted, SET is a multifaceted approach that utilizes group social skills training and individualized exposure therapy. SET is designed to be flexible. For example, although its social skills component was initially developed as a group intervention, it could be administered in an individual format. Similarly, the exposure component may be conducted using either imaginal or in vivo modalities. Selecting a particular modality may depend upon the patient's unique fear pattern. For some individuals, imaginal exposure may be necessary because of an inability to replicate the individual's core fear in "real life."

The SET protocol consists of 28 treatment sessions that span a 4-month period. During the first 3 months, sessions are held twice a week, once for individual exposure and once for group social skills training. In the fourth month, the frequency of the intervention decreases to once per week, utilizing programmed practice. This component assists individuals in transferring their newly acquired skills to a variety of real-life settings. Below, a brief description of an appropriate assessment strategy for social phobia is presented, and then the components of SET are described.

Social Phobia Assessment Strategy

Determining the presence of social phobia requires a diagnostic interview by a trained clinician. Although the use of a formal standardized diagnostic interview schedule is not necessary, it is important that the clinician inquire about the presence of anxiety across different social situations as well as public performances. In addition to a diagnostic interview, the administration of self-report inventories may assist in documenting the extent and severity of the patient's distress. The Social Phobia and Anxiety Inventory (SPAI), for example, assesses physiological, behavioral, and cognitive symptoms of social phobia. It also assesses social phobia across a range of social situations and addresses distress with a variety of interpersonal partners. The SPAI can provide clinicians with important information regarding specific areas to target in the SET program. In addition to evaluating social distress, it is also important to assess the potential SET participant's level of social skill. If an individual does not possess the verbal and nonverbal components necessary for effective social interaction, interventions designed simply to alleviate social distress will not be effective. Thus, a behavioral assessment designed to measure the individual's verbal and nonverbal social skills functioning is necessary to identify specific skill areas to target in the skills training component of SET.

SET Components

Across the specific treatment components, implementation of SET includes attention to common therapeutic guidelines, including providing a supportive and sympathetic atmosphere, listening to each participant emphatically, and constantly praising participants for accomplishments, both major and minor. Below, a description of each specific SET component is presented.

Educational Information

This first component of SET is addressed in a single group session. During this psychoeducational session, information is presented on the symptomatology, etiology, and treatment of social phobia, the goals of SET, and each of the specific SET components. Thus, prior to conducting any specific therapeutic intervention, the patient gains an understanding of social phobia and the reasons why specific interventions might be effective. Furthermore, the session ensures that the patient understands the goals of SET, the individual components, and the time commitment and energy needed to complete the program. Patients are also informed about how SET differs from traditional group or individual therapy. Group sessions, for example, are not mere discussions of patients' issues, but are active, skill-building interventions. Finally, because those with social phobia often feel that no one understands the intensity of their distress, the psychoeducational session provides an opportunity for participants to meet others who have the same disorder.

Social Skills Training

Deficient social skills are common among many with social phobia, particularly those with the generalized subtype. The skills-training component of SET focuses on three broad areas: social environment awareness, interpersonal skills, and presentation skills. Within each of these areas, specific skills include introducing oneself, starting and maintaining conversations, giving and receiving compliments, being assertive, listening to others, remembering information, and constructing and delivering formal oral presentations. Although many of these components are common content areas for most social skills training programs, two are somewhat unique to SET. First, SET includes instruction in listening and remembering skills. This module was developed because many individuals with social phobia report that during conversations, they are too busy composing the perfect response to attend to the conversation topic. Thus, when it is their turn to talk, they no longer know the specifics of the conversation. Second, SET includes a component on speech construction, because individuals must have the knowledge of what comprises an effective presentation if they are ever to effectively deliver a speech. Because so many of those with social phobia successfully avoid speech classes in high school or college, many have not had the opportunity to acquire these skills. Finally, in addition to verbal content, the nonverbal aspects of social interactions such as eye contact, voice tone and volume, and body posture are also part of the skills addressed in SET.

SET group social skills training is conducted using treatment components traditionally used in all social skills training procedures: instruction, modeling, behavioral rehearsal, corrective feedback, and positive reinforcement. However, additional strategies developed specifically to address unique features of the social phobia syndrome also are included. For example, because of their social withdrawal, many individuals with social phobia are unsophisticated with respect to the nuances of behavioral interactions, and they are often unable to problem solve social situations. For example, many are unable to think creatively about where to meet potential social partners, thus limiting their ability to carry out homework assignments. To respond to this deficit, SET includes flexibility exercises, which are designed to assist participants in generating different ways of approaching the same social task. Thus, SET patients may be required to think of five different ways to greet an old friend or think of five different places where one might meet others with similar leisure time interests. By teaching creative problem solving, SET participants improve their ability to function in a variety of social environments and with a variety of interpersonal partners. Finally, after each social skills session, patients are given homework assignments designed to allow for more practice of the specific skills addressed in the group session.

Exposure Therapy

In SET, exposure therapy is provided through individual weekly treatment sessions for the first 3 months of SET. The content of this exposure sessions is developed conjointly by the therapist and the patient and is designed to tap each patient's unique fears. In SET, exposure typically is conducted using an intensive ("flooding") rather than a graduated paradigm. During exposure sessions, patients maintain contact with the fear-producing situation until their fear dissipates (i.e., until the patient habituates to the fear-producing situation). The SET protocol allows for the use of both imaginal and in vivo exposure strategies in the individual sessions. The selection of in vivo or imaginal exposure often is dictated by the patient's specific fear. In many instances, the individual's fear cannot be replicated in vivo (in "real life"), and thus, imaginal exposure sessions are necessary. Typically, exposure sessions for SET average 90 minutes per session, with the potential to be longer in the earlier treatment sessions and shorter in the later sessions. Because exposure is based on an extinction model, sessions should not be terminated until habituation occurs. Also consistent with the extinction model, coping statements or distraction strategies are not used as part of the exposure sessions. Rather, extinction is achieved while the patient attends to the distressing situation.

Programmed Practice

Programmed practice is the final component of SET, and it is designed to transfer control of the treatment to the patient. Programmed practice facilitates the maintenance of treatment gains and increases the

likelihood of the generalization of skills to a variety of social settings. During this phase, which comprises the final 4 weeks of SET, the therapist and patient develop assignments that require the patient to enter and participate in social activities that formerly were anxiety producing or avoided. Programmed practice assignments are limited only by the creativity of the patient and therapist.

RESEARCH BASIS

The results of controlled research trials have provided considerable evidence that cognitive-behavioral and behavioral treatments are effective in treating adult social phobia. Furthermore, research has identified exposure as the key ingredient. The superiority of exposure in the treatment of social phobia has been reported in numerous controlled studies, substantive reviews, and several meta-analytic studies. Although exposure is a critical element in the treatment of social phobia, exposure alone appears to be more effective for the specific subtype than it is for the generalized subtype. Thus, this research suggests that exposure treatment alone may not be sufficient for achieving optimal outcome for those with the generalized subtype. In analyzing the attenuated treatment response for these patients, they were found to have a more severe and complex symptom pattern at pretreatment than those with the specific subtype. Also, as a group, they were more likely than the specific subtype to have other psychiatric conditions, such as depression. Finally, those with the generalized subtype also appeared to have social skills deficits. In fact, although there was limited empirical evidence at the time of SET's development, there now is an emerging literature that suggests many individuals with social phobia have deficiencies in social skills. Relatedly, research studies have found that social skills training leads to improvement among social phobia patients equal to that obtained by other cognitive-behavioral and behavioral treatments, with the exception of exposure.

A review of this scientific literature led to the development of SET, with its unique combination of two empirically supported intervention strategies: exposure and social skills training. The two-pronged approach of SET is designed to further improve the outcome for the generalized subtype above that obtained through exposure alone. The literature also suggested that cognitive components, such as cognitive restructuring, do not enhance the treatment of social phobia above that achieved with exposure alone. Therefore, a cognitive component such as cognitive restructuring was not included in SET.

The efficacy of SET was tested in a small study of patients with generalized social phobia. In this study, the vast majority of the patients improved to a moderate degree or more. Patient improvement was noted on outcome measures of social anxiety, social skill, and social functioning. These findings are impressive for several reasons. First, the proportion of patients with improved outcomes was substantially greater than that in other studies using exposure alone. Second, the sample consisted of patients who were severely ill in terms of severity and chronicity of the primary disorder as well as the presence of secondary disorders. Third, the treatment was relatively short in duration (i.e., 4 months). In addition, the treatment gains were maintained up to 2 years later.

Although the results of this initial assessment of SET are very promising and SET has been implemented by clinicians in a variety of settings, this treatment approach has not yet been compared with another treatment with demonstrated efficacy. Therefore, SET is currently being evaluated in a large, controlled trial, and the findings will inform conclusions regarding its efficacy. The study compares SET with exposure alone and to a wait-list control. Thus, the study will assess the relative efficacy of SET to the single most efficacious treatment for social phobia, exposure, as well as determine whether the social skills training component is associated with additional improvement in outcomes. In this study, social skills will be assessed directly, and social skill norms will be created that can be used in other studies.

RELEVANT TARGET POPULATIONS AND EXCEPTIONS

SET is appropriate for adults age 18 and over with a primary *DSM-IV* diagnosis of social phobia. SET may be particularly appropriate for those diagnosed with the generalized subtype. Those diagnosed with social phobia who also have comorbid psychiatric disorders appear to benefit from the intervention; however, separate treatment for the comorbid disorders may be necessary after SET is completed. One possible exception to this statement is that those with paranoid personality disorder or severe avoidant personality disorder may have a negative reaction to the intensive exposure (flooding) component of SET. Although the

majority of patients with social phobia understand that intensive exposure to anxiety-producing situations is necessary for treatment success, those with avoidant personality disorder or paranoid personality disorder often interpret intensive exposure sessions as a deliberate attempt by the therapist to personally humiliate them. Therefore, for patients with social phobia who also have avoidant personality disorder or paranoid personality disorder, graduated exposure appears to be a more effective and less distressing approach.

SET is a short-term but intensive intervention requiring twice-weekly sessions for 3 months and once-weekly sessions for the fourth month. Furthermore, homework assignments associated with both the social skills and exposure sessions require additional time on the part of the patient. Given the intensity of the program, patients must be willing to invest the time and energy necessary to effectively participate in the intervention. Although the presence of secondary depression does not necessarily indicate that a patient is not suitable for SET, in cases where the patient's depressed mood results in low energy levels, treatment for depression may be necessary prior to the initiation of SET treatment.

COMPLICATIONS

For exposure treatment to be effective, the imaginal scene or in vivo task must capture the patient's "core fear," including the critical features that trigger and maintain the patient's anxiety and fear and the feared consequences. Although in general, persons with social phobia have fears of negative evaluation by others, the specific parameters of their fears vary markedly across individuals. In addition, the scene or task used in the exposure sessions should include relevant variables that allow the patients to experience the unique physiological and cognitive symptoms associated with their fears. This concept and process may be difficult for beginning clinicians to grasp. Therefore, clinicians who implement exposure therapy must be well trained in basic learning theory and behavioral interventions. Otherwise, the exposure component will be ineffective.

In some instances, patients may find the exposure sessions to be somewhat intensive and distressing. Particularly during imaginal exposure, patients may attempt to minimize their arousal by avoiding the image of the feared stimulus, by imagining themselves coping well (rather than poorly, which would be consistent with their diagnosis of social phobia), or by altering the image so that important anxiety-producing elements are removed. Any and all of these maneuvers interfere with the process of habituation and attenuate the response to the intervention. Therefore, clinicians need to monitor for such cognitive distractions and employ strategies to address them. For example, the clinician can ask the patient to describe the scene out loud in order to identify any coping strategies he or she may be using. Finally, some patients may have difficulty using imaginal exposure, in which case in vivo exposure is recommended.

CASE ILLUSTRATION

"Mary" was a 40-year-old, married, Caucasian female, who described herself as "very nervous" in a range of situations where she had to speak to others. She described herself as "very shy" since early childhood but remembers an intensification of her fears when she entered college. In college, she avoided classes that required group projects, class participation, or formal presentations. When she began working, she actively avoided positions that required frequent interaction with coworkers, meetings, and formal presentations. Indeed, she was working as an accountant from home when she came to our clinic. Mary's social fears also interfered in her personal and social life. To her regret, she declined numerous opportunities to speak at weddings, funerals, retirement parties, and church due to her anxiety. In addition, she reported feeling very nervous in unstructured social situations with her peers, including informal interactions such as talking to a neighbor, as well as more formal events, such as weddings. She avoided many of these situations. For example, she quit the PTA because she was too anxious to give brief updates of her activities at weekly PTA meetings. She also quit being a Brownie group leader because she was too anxious to present badges to the girls in front of other parents. She had few friends, felt very isolated, and rarely engaged in social activities.

A primary diagnosis of social phobia, generalized subtype, was made with the Anxiety Disorders Interview Schedule IV (ADIS-IV), a semistructured interview. Mary did not meet criteria for any personality disorders based on another semistructured interview, the Structured Clinical Interview for *DSM-IV* Personality Disorders (SCID-II-IV). She reported a depressed mood due to the distress and consequences of her social anxiety, but she did not meet criteria for an affective disorder. Other assessment techniques were also used, including self-report, clinician-administered, and behavioral measures. Mary's scores at the time of admittance were consistent with a diagnosis of social phobia. For example, her difference score on the SPAI was a 114, a score indicating severe social anxiety. Public speaking and social skills were assessed through an impromptu speech task and a role play task. In the role play task, she had difficulty asking questions, engaged in long pauses, avoided eye contact, and gave minimal responses to questions. Using a subjective units of distress scale (SUDS) ranging from 0 to 8 (where an 8 is the most anxious a person has ever felt in his/her life), Mary rated her anxiety a 7 and 6 for the speech and role play tasks, respectively.

To treat Mary's generalized social phobia, she participated in SET. The primary treatment goal was to reduce Mary's anxiety and increase her skill in social interactions. SET included 12 group sessions of social skills training, 12 sessions of imaginal exposure, and 4 sessions of programmed practice. A review of the behavioral material indicated that her core fear was a fear that others would view her as unintelligent and insecure. She feared saying something stupid and having others conclude that she was not smart. She also feared that her nervousness would make her look foolish and that others would judge her as weak and unworthy. Ultimately, she feared that these judgments would lead to rejection by her peers, which, in turn, would result in minimal social contact, an inability to participate in important events (e.g., weddings, PTA, etc.), and limited career progression. During the exposure sessions, the imaginal scene evoked Mary's fears by having the feared consequences occur and by including relevant cues, such as the physical symptoms of distress she actually experienced during social encounters. To increase social interactions, Mary was assigned weekly homework. These assignments increased in intensity and difficulty over the course of treatment. They consisted of talking to neighbors on the street, inviting neighbors over for coffee, having lunch with acquaintances, and rejoining the PTA.

During the course of treatment, Mary experienced a marked decrease in social anxiety and social distress. She successfully entered social situations she had previously avoided. She began to enjoy social activities she previously avoided, such as parties and conversations with neighbors. She rejoined the PTA and was planning on volunteering again to be a Brownie leader. She also made several friends with whom she regularly socialized. Based on a posttreatment assessment, Mary no longer met criteria for social phobia. She was able to complete the behavioral assessment tasks with minimal anxiety (SUDS ratings of 0 and 1 on the role play and speech tasks, respectively). Her SPAI difference score was a 41, indicating social anxiety in the nonclinical range. In addition, she reported that the social skills training had helped her in many areas, including positively ending conversations and transitioning between topics. Ratings by independent judges of her social skills indicated an improvement from pre- to posttreatment.

—*Deborah C. Beidel,*
Nancy A. Heiser, and Tyish S. Hall

See also: *Behavior Rehearsal (Vol. I);* *Modeling (Vol. I);* *Social Skills Training (Vol. I)*

Suggested Readings

Beidel, D. C., & Turner, S. M. (1998). *Shy children, phobic adults: Nature and treatment of social phobia.* Washington, DC: American Psychological Association.

Beidel, D. C., Turner, S. M., & Cooley, M. R. (1993). Assessing reliable and clinically significant change in social phobia: Validity of the Social Phobia and Anxiety Inventory. *Behaviour Research & Therapy, 31,* 331–337.

Fedoroff, I. C., & Taylor, S. (2001). Psychological and pharmacological treatments of social phobia: A meta-analysis. *Journal of Clinical Psychopharmacology, 21,* 311–324.

Turner, S. M., Beidel, D. C., & Cooley, M. R. (1995). A multicomponent behavioral treatment for social phobia: Social effectiveness therapy. *Behaviour Research & Therapy, 33,* 553–555.

Turner, S. M., Beidel, D. C., & Cooley-Quille, M. R. (1997). *Social effectiveness therapy: A program for overcoming social anxiety and social phobia.* Toronto, Canada: Multi-Health Systems.

Turner, S. M., Beidel, D. C., & Jacob, R. G. (1994). Social phobia: A comparison of behavior therapy and atenolol. *Journal of Consulting and Clinical Psychology, 62,* 350–358.

SOCIAL SKILLS TRAINING

DESCRIPTION OF THE STRATEGY

Social skills training, often in combination with other methods, has been used to address a wide variety of presenting complaints, including depression, loneliness, employment opportunities, substance abuse, aggressive and explosive behaviors, and obsessive-compulsive behaviors. It has been used to help people make friends, arrange dates, and acquire needed help (e.g., on the part of individuals with learning disabilities). The aim of social skills training is to enhance interpersonal effectiveness in social situations. We may not get a job that we want because we lack the skills to speak up and present ourselves well in a situation. We may not be effective in meeting friends because of a lack of skills in initiating conversations. Lack of effective social skills may result in a variety of maladaptive behaviors. Behaviors, thoughts, and feelings are interrelated. For example, negative thoughts may interfere with acting on our feelings in an effective manner (e.g., initiating conversations, answering questions in class). These thoughts and lack of effective behavior may, in turn, create anxiety or feelings of depression because of a loss of positive consequences or negative consequences. If intervention is successful, anxiety in interpersonal situations decreases and effective responses are used when these are of value in attaining personal and social goals. Assertion training differs from social skills training in emphasizing individual rights and obligations. For example, an advantage of the phrase *assertive behavior* for some groups, such as women, is an emphasis on taking the initiative to enhance social and other opportunities. There is an activist stance. Some consider assertion training one component of social skills training.

Social Skills Training Strategy

Social skills training usually consists of a variety of components, including instruction, model presentation, behavior rehearsal, feedback, programming of change, and homework assignments. Other procedures that may also be used, depending on what is found during assessment, include self-instruction training, relaxation training, cognitive restructuring (e.g., decreasing unrealistic expectations or beliefs), and interpersonal problem-solving training (helping clients to effectively handle challenging situations that arise in social situations, such as reactions of anger that prevent successful use of social skills).

Social skills training should be preceded by a contextual assessment. Exactly what situations are involved, who is involved, and where do relevant exchanges occur? What are the clients' goals? Social behavior is situationally specific in terms of what is effective. A behavior that is effective in achieving a given outcome in one situation may not be successful in another. This highlights the importance of clearly describing situations of concern. Only through a careful assessment can one determine whether a lack of social skills is an issue. That is, clients may have skills but not use them. Clients' entering repertoires should be clearly described. This step requires identifying skills clients already possess. The gap between current skill levels and required skills can then be accurately assessed. Role plays are valuable for this purpose. The behaviors that make up an effective reaction differ in different situations. Definitions of socially effective behavior differ in the extent to which personal outcomes (effects on oneself) as well as social outcomes (effects on others) are considered. Most definitions emphasize providing reinforcing consequences in a way that is socially acceptable and does not harm others. Practice-related literature may offer guidelines about what is effective. Situations of concern as well as effective response options have been identified for many groups, including psychiatric patients, adolescents, the elderly, and individuals with different kinds of physical disabilities. Task analyses of behaviors of interest may be available. These provide an empirically based training guide. Youth residing in a halfway house rated specific staff behaviors on a scale ranging from A to F. Examples of highly rated behavior included joking and doing what was promised. Disliked behavior included criticism and not following through on promises. Normative criteria may be used as a criterion for selection of behaviors to focus on (what most people do in a situation). A concern here is that the norm may not reflect what is desirable. For example, schoolteachers may give low rates of praise and high rates of criticism. Another disadvantage of norm-referenced objectives is lack of information about the specific behaviors required to attain an objective. A task analysis identifying behaviors required to achieve a certain outcome may be required. Obstacles to success should be identified. For example, anxiety or anger may hamper effective use of available skills. Unique socialization patterns may hinder changing behavior in positive directions. Beliefs such as "I must please everyone" may pose an obstacle to acting in new ways.

Selection of intervention methods should flow directly from assessment. This provides information about the nature of clients' current cognitive (what they say to themselves), emotional (what they feel), and behavioral (what they do) repertoires in relation to desired goals and related situations, as well as likely consequences of and options for rearranging the environment. The more outstanding the behavior deficits and need for behavior refinement, the more likely that instructions, model presentation, and rehearsal will be needed. Careful assessment is required to identify skills and relevant situations to determine whether lack of success is due to a discrimination problem regarding when certain behaviors can most profitably used, to identify unrealistic beliefs or expectations that may interfere with effective behavior, and to determine whether negative self-statements or lack of self-management skills get in the way. Sources of assessment data include the interview, self-report measures such as the Assertion Inventory, role playing, and observation in the natural environment. Role playing during assessment (acting out what is usually done as well as what a client thinks he or she should do) may reveal that the client has many effective components of needed skills, and it may be decided that instructions and prompts during rehearsal will be sufficient to develop and refine needed skills. If effective behaviors are not used because of anxiety, intervention may focus on enhancing anxiety management skills. Research suggests that it is exposure that contributes to reducing interfering anxiety reactions. If we speak up and acquire valued consequences in situations in which we were reticent in the past, this makes it easier to act on future occasions because we are less anxious. That is, simply getting into a situation in which we are anxious and performing effectively in that situation seems to be the effective ingredient in decreasing anxiety and encouraging effective social behavior on future occasions. If needed social skills are absent, procedures designed to develop them, such as instructions, model presentation, and practice, may be required. Assessment may reveal that effective behaviors simply have to be placed under new stimulus control (i.e., prompted, perhaps by self-instructions, in certain situations). For example, effective ways of requesting favors from a friend may be of value in work situations but not be used there. Discrimination training is required when skills are available but are not used in situations in which they would result in valued outcomes. This is designed to increase a behavior in situations in which it will be followed by positive outcomes and/or a decrease in situations in which negative outcomes are likely.

Training may be carried out individually or in a group setting. A session may focus on developing effective behavior in one situation or on increasing a specific behavior of value in a range of similar situations (friendly reactions such as smiling). Social skills training may be carried out in groups. A group offers a number of advantages, including a variety of models, multiple sources of support, normalization and validation of concerns, and the availability of many people to participate in role plays. Groups usually include from 5 to 10 sessions, lasting 1 1/2 to 2 hours each. Decisions must be made about how to structure sessions (for example, each session could be structured around a specific social skill). Social skills training in groups has been carried out with a variety of individuals, including students, parents, public welfare clients, and severely disturbed hospitalized patients.

Instructions

Instructions concerning effective behavior may be given verbally or presented in written, audiotape, or filmed form. This is often combined with model presentation and coaching during role plays. Specific behaviors are identified to increase, decrease, stabilize, or vary and their relationship to desired goals described. Instructions may be given concerning only one behavior at a time, which is then role played, or more than one behavior may be reviewed depending on the available skills (entering repertoires) of each client. What not to do (e.g., smile or giggle while requesting a change in an annoying behavior) as well as what to do (look at the person, face the person) is described.

Model Presentation

Instruction, model presentation, rehearsal, and coaching can be used when clients lack requisite behaviors in certain situations or when there is a need to refine behaviors. The need to use modeling will be influenced by the complexity of the skill to be acquired and nature of the entering repertoires (available skills) of clients. The greater the complexity of the skill and the more lacking the initial repertoire, the greater the value of model presentation is likely to be. An advantage of model presentation is that an entire chain of behavior can be illustrated and the client then requested to imitate it. Nonverbal as well as verbal behaviors can be demonstrated and the client's attention drawn to those that are especially important. For example, a client can be asked to notice the model's

eye contact, hand motions, and posture. Models of both effective and ineffective behavior may be presented. The model may verbalize (say aloud) helpful positive thoughts during role plays if effective social skills are hampered by negative thoughts, such as "I'll always be a failure" or "I'll never succeed." At first, appropriate self-statements can be shared out loud by the client when imitating the model's behavior (e.g., "Good for me for taking a chance") and then, by instruction, gradually moved to a covert level. Models who display coping responses (for example, they become anxious and then cope effectively with this) have been found to be more effective than are models who display mastery response (they do not experience any difficulty in a situation).

Effective behaviors may be modeled by the counselor, or written scripts, audiotape, videotape, or film may be used. Essential elements of various responses can be highlighted and written models offered. The advantage of written material is that it can be referred to on an as-needed basis. In addition, the client may be asked to observe people with effective behavior who are in similar roles and to write down the situations, what was done, and what happened. This increases exposure to a variety of effective models, offers examples to use during rehearsal, may increase discrimination as to when to use certain behaviors and when not to do so, and offers opportunities for vicarious extinction of anxiety reactions through observation of positive outcomes following use of social skills (that is, negative emotional reactions decrease via observation of what happens to others). The opportunity to see how negative reactions can be handled may be offered as well. Client observations are discussed, noting effective responses as well as other situations in which certain social behaviors may be usefully employed.

Behavior Rehearsal and Feedback

Following model presentation, the client is requested to practice (rehearse) the modeled behavior. Corrective feedback is offered following each rehearsal. Specific positive aspects of the client's performance are first noted and praised. Praise is offered for effective behaviors or approximations to them, and coaching provided as needed. The focus is on improvements over baseline levels (what a client can do before intervention is initiated). Thus, approximations to hoped-for outcomes are reinforced. Critical comments such as "You can do better" or "That wasn't too good" are avoided. The client is encouraged to develop behaviors that are most likely to result in positive consequences. A hierarchy of scenes graduated in accord with the client's anxiety may be used for role playing. Role playing starts with scenes that create low levels of discomfort. Clients who are reluctant to engage in role playing can be requested to read from a prepared script. As comfort increases, role playing can be introduced. If a client is too anxious to read from a script, relaxation training may be offered as a prelude to role playing. When there are many skills to be learned, one behavior at a time may be targeted. Each role play may be repeated until required levels of skill and comfort are demonstrated.

Models and instructions are repeated as needed, and rehearsal, prompts, and feedback continued until desired responses and comfort levels are demonstrated. Rehearsal alone (without previous model presentation or other instructions) may be effective when skills are available or relevant behaviors are simple rather than complex. Situations used during role playing should be clearly described and closely resemble real-life conditions. Instructions prior to practice or signals during practice can be used to prompt specific responses. Instructions given before a client practices a behavior "prompt" him or her to engage in certain behaviors rather than others. Perhaps a client did not look at her partner during the role play and is coached to look at others while speaking. Checklists may be prepared for clients as reminders about effective behaviors. Covert modeling or rehearsal in which clients imagine themselves acting competently in social situations may be as effective as actual rehearsal if clients possess needed social behaviors (but do not use them) and if social anxiety is low. Home sessions in which clients engage in covert rehearsal can be used to supplement rehearsal in office sessions. Not only does behavior rehearsal provide for learning new behaviors, it also allows their practice in a safe environment and so may reduce discomfort. Rehearsal involves exposure to feared situations. Such exposure is considered to be a key factor in decreasing social anxiety, especially if people remain in the situation even when they are anxious, and act effectively despite their discomfort.

Programming of Change

Specific goals are established for each session. Perhaps only one or two behaviors will be focused on

in a session. Or the initial repertoire might be such that all needed verbal and nonverbal behaviors can be practiced. Assessment of the client's behavior in relation to given situations will reveal available behaviors, and training should build on available repertoires. Hierarchies ranked in terms of the degree of anxiety or anger that different social situations create can be used to gradually establish effective social behavior skills and lessen anxiety. Rehearsal starts with situations creating small degrees of anger or anxiety, and as these are mastered, higher-level scenes are introduced. Thus, introduction of scenes is programmed in accord with the unique skill and comfort levels of each client. Improvements are noted and praised. Praise for improvement should be in relation to a client's current performance levels.

Homework Assignments

After needed skill and comfort levels are attained, assignments, graded in accord with client comfort and skill levels, are agreed on to be carried out in the natural environment. Assignments are selected that offer a high probability of success at a low cost in terms of discomfort. Natural contexts provide many opportunities to enhance valued skills. Careful preparation may be required if negative reactions may occur in real life. A clear understanding of the social relationships in which new behaviors are proposed is needed to maximize the likelihood of positive consequences and minimize the likelihood of negative outcomes when assertive behaviors are used. For example, a parent may become verbally abusive if his son makes certain requests. This possibility should be taken into account (e.g., by encouraging behaviors unlikely to result in abuse or by using some other form of intervention such as family counseling). Coping skills should be developed to handle possible negative reactions before asking the client to carry out new behaviors. With some behaviors, such as making friends, unknown individuals may be involved. Clients can be coached to identify situations in which positive reactions are likely. For example, they can be coached to approach people who look friendly (they smile and greet the client).

When effective social behavior occurs without difficulty in easy situations, more difficult ones are then attempted. Clients are instructed to offer positive self-statements ("I spoke up, and it worked!") for effective behavior. Practice, coaching, and model presentation provide instruction concerning the essential elements of effective behavior, and clients are encouraged to vary their reactions in appropriate ways. As with any other assignment, a check is made at the next meeting to find out what happened. Degree of success in real-life offers feedback about whether relevant skills have been identified and were used and to what effect. Client logs (records) describing relevant behaviors and the situations in which they occurred can be used to provide a daily record of progress and guide selection of new assignments. Information reviewed may include what was said and done, when it was said and done, how the client felt before, during, and after the exchange, whether positive self-statements were provided for trying to influence one's social environment (even though the attempt failed), and what consequences followed the client's behavior. If an ineffective response was given in a situation, clients can be asked to write down one that they think would be more effective. This will provide added practice in selecting effective behaviors. Positive feedback is offered for effective behaviors, additional instructions given as necessary, and further relevant assignments agreed on. Motivation to respond in new ways may be enhanced by encouraging clients to carry out mini-cost-benefit analyses in situations of concern, in which they compare costs and benefits of acting in different ways.

Encouraging Generalization and Maintenance

Generalization refers to the use of social behaviors in situations other than those in which training occurred. *Maintenance* refers to their continued use over time. Planning for generalization and maintenance will be required to increase the likelihood that desired behaviors will occur in relevant situations and will be maintained. Steps that can be taken to increase likelihood of generalization and maintenance of social behaviors include recruiting natural reinforcers (e.g., involving significant others), maximizing the likelihood that new behaviors will be followed by positive consequences, encouraging self-reinforcement for using skills, and using a variety of situations during training. Generalization and maintenance can be encouraged by use of homework assignments and self-monitoring (e.g., keeping track of successes). Situational variations that may occur in real life that influence behavior should be included in practice examples to encourage generalization and maintenance.

For example, a woman may have difficulty refusing unwanted requests in a variety of situations (e. g., with friends as well as supervisors at work). If so, practice should be arranged in these different situations. Self-reinforcement may encourage the development and maintenance of new behaviors. Such reinforcement may be of special relevance in maintaining behaviors that are sometimes followed by punishing consequences. Clients can be encouraged to reward themselves for making efforts to exert more effective influence over their social environments, even though they are not always successful (e.g., if a woman tries to speak up more during a meeting and fails to gain the floor, she should reward herself for trying).

Cognitive Restructuring—Changing What Clients Say to Themselves

Unrealistic beliefs (such as "I must always succeed") and other kinds of thoughts, such as negative self-statements that get in the way of effective behavior, should be identified and replaced by helpful self-statements and beliefs. This process is initiated during assessment and continues during intervention. Thoughts relevant to social behaviors include helpful attributions (causal accounts or behavior), realistic expectations ("I may not succeed; no one succeeds all the time"), helpful rules ("When in doubt, think the best"), self-reinforcement of efforts to improve, and positive consequences, problem-solving skills, and accurate perception and translation of social cues (e.g., noting and accurately interpreting a smile as friendly). In addition, cognitive skills (e.g., distraction) are involved in the regulation of affect (e.g., anger or anxiety). Cognitive restructuring may include altering unrealistic expectations, altering attitudes about personal rights and obligations, and/or self-instruction training in which clients learn to identify negative self-statements related to effective social behavior and to replace them with positive self-statements. Self-management aspects of social behavior include identifying situations in which certain skills will be of value (and when they will not), monitoring (tracking), consequence of behavior, and offering helpful self-feedback. The likelihood of effective social behaviors may be increased by covert (to one's self) questions that function as cues, such as: What's happening? What are my choices? What might happen if . . . ? Which choice is better? How could I do it? How did I do?

Anxiety Reduction Methods

Relaxation training may be included if anxiety interferes with use of social skills. The specific method selected to alter anxiety will depend on the cause(s) of anxiety (e.g., negative thoughts, a past history of punishing consequences because of lack of skills), and/or unrealistic expectations ("Everyone must like me").

RESEARCH BASIS

Both single-case and group designs have been used to evaluate the success of social skills training. Single-case designs are uniquely suited for evaluating progress with individual clients. Here, baseline levels of performance of an individual (prior to intervention) are compared with performance levels of that individual during intervention. Research suggests that social skills training can be effective with a number of different types of clients in pursuit of a number of different outcomes, at least in the short term. Research studies using single-case design suggest that social skills training is effective, as indicated in the case example. With some clients, programs focused on altering cognitions believed to be related to ineffective social behavior have sometimes been found to be as effective as those focused on altering overt behavior, suggesting a similarity of effect across cognitive methods and assertion training. There are some indications that a combination of methods is most effective. However, some studies that purport to show that cognitive methods are as effective as social skills training in enhancing social skills do not include individual assessment of specific entry level skills and do not design individually tailored programs based on this assessment. Such lack may underestimate the potential value of social skills training. Narrative reviews suggest that the efficacy of cognitive-behavioral procedures for students with high-level disabilities is not promising. Reviews with this population suggest that a combination of modeling, coaching, and reinforcement is more effective. These reviews also show that there is a problem in attaining consistent and lasting gains across settings, that there is a relationship between amount of social skills training and effects, and that studies matching skill deficiencies with intervention methods are more likely to be successful. Systematic as well as narrative reviews with this population suggest that such training can result in both small and large effects on social functioning. A number of studies show that instructions alone (without modeling) are not sufficient to develop appropriate social behaviors with psychiatric patients.

Comparison of the effectiveness of social skills training in different studies is often hampered by the use of different criteria for selection of subjects, different training programs, and different criteria for evaluating progress. Evaluation is sometimes limited to changes in self-report or role play measures, leaving the question unanswered as to whether beneficial changes occur in real life. Altering behavior in one kind of situation, such as refusing requests, does not necessarily result in changes in behavior in other kinds of situations, such as initiating conversations. Package programs are often used, leaving the question, "What are the effective ingredients of skills training?" unanswered. Use of package programs may also be a waste of time and effort in including unneeded components. Use of global self-report measures to assess change in specific areas may result in underestimating success of social skills training in relation to behavior in specific situations. Variables that influence success include population characteristics, the degree to which interventions are matched to social skill deficits, the integrity of interventions, assessment issues, and concerns about generalizations.

RELEVANT TARGET POPULATIONS AND EXCEPTIONS

Social skills training is designed to enhance effective social behavior. It is used to "empower" people by increasing their influence over their environments. For example, people with physical disabilities may learn how to request help or to advocate for better services. The main goal of enhancing social skills may be to prevent problems such as acquiring skills in resisting peer pressures to commit criminal offenses (e.g., rob stores) or to take drugs. Social skills training has been used to help clients develop a wide variety of behaviors related to a wide variety of goals. It has been used to enhance the quality of care provided to residents in institutional settings, to enhance friendship skills among women at risk for child maltreatment, to help children to make friends, and to enhance options for youth and adults with developmental disabilities. Examples of behaviors focused on include offering positive feedback to others (empathy and listening), expressing feelings, personal disclosure, requesting behavior changes, negotiating, and refusing requests. Broadly speaking, parent training programs and programs designed to enhance communication among family members can also be viewed in part as social skills training programs because they involve social behaviors. Assertion training is a form of social skills training. Social skills training has been used with "psychiatric" patients, both in hospitals and in the community. In a systematic attempt made to develop and evaluate an interpersonal skills training program for male psychiatric patients, the first step was to obtain a sample of problematic situations that were difficult for this population. Situational contexts reported included dating, making friends, having job interviews, interacting with authorities, interacting with service personnel, and interacting with people viewed as more intelligent or attractive or who appeared in some way different. Behaviors often mentioned included initiating and ending interactions, making personal disclosures, handling conversational silences, responding to rejection, and being assertive.

Social skills training programs are often used in schools, to help people obtain employment, and with prisoners and those on probation. It is often included as one component of a multicomponent package of interventions. It has been used in relation to minimal dating and social contacts in general. With a college population, it has been found that simply arranging a series of practice dates results in a significant increase in dating behavior. Success of such interventions illustrates differences in intervention needed with different individuals. Success achieved by simply arranging practice opportunities suggest that social skills training is not needed when clients possess skills required to gain valued goals. Another exception to use of social skills training includes clients who are unmotivated (they do not possess skills needed to pursue their goals effectively, but cannot be engaged in social skills training). Social skills training is individually focused. It will not redress political, social, and economic inequities that may impede change through this individually tailored route. Clients may have inappropriate goals (those that cannot be met or are met at a high cost, such as social rejection). For example, children who have difficulty making friends may value dominance over cooperation. Poor choice of goals may result in poor choice of social behaviors (those that result in punishing rather than positive consequences).

COMPLICATIONS

Helpers sometimes jump into training too soon without clear descriptions of related situations, client goals, and how to attain them. Social skills training requires a clear description of relevant interpersonal relationships. If this analysis reveals that use of certain social skills would have unavoidable negative effects, as it may, for example, in abusive relationships, this would not be recommended. Other methods must be explored. Clients must be willing to act differently in real-life situations and have the self-management skills to do so (e.g., remind themselves to act differently). Competing behaviors must be addressed that interfere with use of effective skills. Cultural differences as to what behaviors will be effective in certain social situations must be considered. Effective social behavior is situationally specific; what will be effective in one situation may not be in another. There are many ways a training program can go wrong. It may go too fast or too slow. Developing new skills may require a task analysis in which behaviors needed to attain valued goal are identified, including immediate steps. Entering repertoires (what clients can already do) should be described and an "agenda" for change planned. Without finding out what clients can do and what they cannot, necessary steps may be skipped or an agenda may move too slowly. Helping clients acquire new skills requires many skills on the part of the trainer. The more behaviors that must be learned, the more complex they are, and the greater the need for adequate competencies on the part of the trainer. Needed prompts may be difficult to arrange in real-life settings. Homework assignments may be too few or too difficult. A common mistake is spending too much time talking about what do to and not enough time on modeling, practice, and feedback. Valued behaviors may be punished in real-life settings and/or not reinforced. If progress is disappointing, this possibility should be checked. Conducting skills training in a group will require preparation and planning to maximize effectiveness. Special arrangements may be needed to encourage generalization. Shooting from the hip in skill training is not a good idea; it may set clients up for failure.

Multisystem intervention programs in which social skills training is one aspect will often be required to address concerns. Helping people who are depressed often involves multiple interventions guided by assessment. This may include changing environmental stressors as well as thoughts and social behaviors. Programs designed to reduce AIDS risk activities usually comprise a variety of methods, including education, sexual assertion training, self-management training, and enhancing social support. Consider also the community reinforcement approach that Azrin and his colleagues developed to decrease alcohol abuse. This multisystem approach includes attention to family relationships, helping clients to find jobs, establishing a nondrinking social network, and developing recreational opportunities. A buddy system was developed and a social club arranged that provided social opportunities without drinking alcohol. Programs with families often involve multisystem interventions, including social skills training. Helping clients to obtain jobs often requires a multilevel intervention program attending to both individual and environmental characteristics. The same applies to working with youth who belong to gangs. Social skills training will do little to alter political, social, and economic sources of inequity; it is individually focused. There is thus the danger of blaming clients for problems that do not originate with them.

CASE ILLUSTRATION

Richard Eisler and his colleagues Michel Hersen and Peter Miller used social skills training with a 28-year-old house painter admitted to a hospital after he had fired a shotgun into the ceiling of his home. His history revealed periodic rages following a consistent failure to express anger in social situations. His behavior was assessed by asking him to role play in social situations in which he was unable to express anger. These included being criticized by a fellow employee at work, disagreeing with this wife about her inviting company to their home without checking with him first, and his difficulty refusing requests made by his 8-year-old son. An assistant played the complementary role in each situation (wife, son, or fellow employee). The client's reactions were videotaped and observed through a one-way mirror. Review of data collected revealed expressive deficits in four components: (1) eye contact (he did not look at his partner when speaking to him), (2) voice loudness (one could barely hear what he said), (3) speech duration (responses consisted of one- or two-word replies), and (4) requests (he did not ask his partner to change his or her behavior).

Twelve situations that were unrelated to the client's problem areas but that required new social behaviors

were used during training. Each was role played five times in different orders over sessions. Instructions were given to the client through a miniature radio receiver. Instructions related to only one of the four responses at any one time. Thus, during the initial scenes, he was coached to look at his partner when speaking to him, and during the second series, he was coached to increase the loudness of his voice but received no instructions concerning any other response. During the fourth series, he was coached to speak longer, and during the last was instructed to ask his partner for a behavior change. Feedback was provided concerning his performance after each role play. Each response increased after specific instructions regarding this were given and effects generalized to the specific situations that were problematic for this client. Ratings of his behavior were made by reviewing videotapes of his performance.

—*Eileen Gambrill*

See also: *Bellack, Alan S. (Vol. I); Behavioral Treatment in Natural Environments (Vol. I); Social and Interpersonal Skills Training (Vol. II)*

Suggested Readings

Gresham, F. M., Sugai, G., & Horner, R. H. (2001). Interpreting outcomes of social skills training for students with high-incidence disabilities. *Exceptional Children, 67*(3), 331–344.

Meyer, V. J., & Hope, D. A. (1998). Assessment of social skills. In A. S. Bellack & M. Hersen (Eds.), *Behavior assessment: A practical handbook* (4th ed., pp. 232–270). Boston: Allyn & Bacon.

Scott, J. E., & Dixon, L. B. (1995). Psychological interventions for schizophrenia. *Schizophrenia Bulletin, 21*(4), 621–630.

Trower, P. (1995). Adult social skills: State of the art and future directions. In W. O'Donohue & L. Krasner (Eds.), *Handbook of psychological skills training: Techniques and applications* (pp. 54–80). Boston: Allyn & Bacon.

SPOUSE-AIDED THERAPY

DESCRIPTION OF THE STRATEGY

Spouse-aided therapy is defined as any psychological intervention in which the partner of the patient with a psychiatric disorder (e.g., anxiety disorder, depression, substance use disorders) is actively involved in the treatment and the focus of the intervention is on the psychiatric disorder rather than on marital distress. This means that marital therapy directed exclusively to the marital difficulties of the couple without due attention to the specific psychiatric disorder involved is not discussed here. There are several advantages for spouse-aided therapy: (a) The spouse is informed about the psychiatric disorder and the kind of treatment delivered; (b) the spouse can give additional information about symptomatology of the patient and treatment progress; (c) the spouse can be emotionally supported, since living with a patient is often a heavy burden; and (d) the spouse can learn to deal more adequately with disorder-related situations, and in addition, if necessary, general communication between partners can be improved.

Strategies applied vary across the various disorders. In *anxiety disorders,* two different formats of spouse-aided therapy can be distinguished. In partner-assisted exposure, the partner accompanies the patient to each treatment session. The couple receives a treatment rationale in which the focus is on exposing the patient to phobic situations. The partner can assist in making a hierarchy consisting of gradually more difficult exposure tasks. At each session, the patient is given a number of exposure homework assignments. The role of the partner is to stimulate the patient to do these exercises, to help in confronting the phobic situations, to accompany the patient if necessary, and to reinforce the patient in mastering these exposure exercises successfully. Actual presence of the partner is gradually faded out during the exposure exercises. At the beginning of each new session, the patient's performance on the exposure tasks and the assistance of the partner are discussed with the couple, and new homework assignments are given. More difficult tasks are given only if tasks lower in the hierarchy have been performed successfully. The couple determines the pace at which the patient works through the hierarchy. Thus, treatment focuses on the phobia. Relationship problems, if any, are not discussed. Other spouse-aided approaches in anxiety disorders have focused on interpersonal difficulties thought to maintain agoraphobic symptoms. These approaches include communication training and partner-assisted problem solving directed either at phobia-related conflicts or at general life stresses and problems.

Partner-assisted cognitive behavior therapy for *depression* is based on Peter Lewinsohn's and Aaron Beck's individual therapy of depression. It is assumed that depressed individuals do not engage in pleasant activities and hence do not get adequate reinforcement, resulting in mood disturbance. During spouse-aided therapy, partners join all sessions. Treatment focuses on the depression and on ways both partners can deal more adequately with depression-related situations rather than on relationship aspects per se. Therefore, partners are involved in devising reinforcing activities, in stimulating patients to engage in rewarding activities and participate in role playing. Furthermore, partners are asked to attend to the dysfunctional thoughts of the patient and to discuss these with both patient and therapist. In addition, partners are actively involved in designing behavioral experiments to test (irrational) beliefs and are encouraged to take part in challenging the assumptions held by the patient.

Another spouse-aided strategy in depression is *conjoint interpersonal therapy.* In this therapy, the partner is involved in addressing patient-related unresolved difficulties in one of the following domains: loss (e.g., of a child/parent), role disputes, role transitions, and interpersonal deficits. Moreover, five sessions of conjoint communication training are included.

In cases with co-occurring depression and marital discord, conjoint behavioral marital therapy may be applied. Here, the emphasis is not only on the mood disorder but also on the communication between the partners. Generally, in the earlier phase of therapy, problems associated with depression that could hinder a successful application of marital therapy are implemented. Examples of such problems are complicated grief or a low activity level in the depressed patient. Later on, the focus of the therapy is shifted to the training of communication skills in both spouses.

Spouse-aided therapy for *substance use disorders* focuses on behavioral self-control and coping skills to facilitate and maintain abstinence, improving spouse coping with drinking and drug-taking related situations, improving relationship functioning in general, and improving functioning within other social systems in which the couple is currently involved. The degree of emphasis on each of these four domains and on the techniques used to target these domains vary across different treatment protocols. Two well-known protocols for alcohol abuse disorder are the ones used in the Harvard Counseling for Alcoholics' Marriages (CALM) project by Timothy O'Farrell and the Alcohol Behavioral Couple Treatment (ABCT) protocol used by Barbara McCrady. The main differences between these two protocols are that O'Farrell's treatment is designed to be used in conjoint or subsequent to a treatment focusing on cessation of drinking, whereas the treatment developed by McCrady is designed as a stand-alone treatment. Also, part of CALM, treatment is delivered in a group format, while McCrady's treatment is delivered during individual couple sessions.

Some additional techniques often used in spouse-aided therapy in substance use disorder are sobriety contracts to reduce conflict and distrust between the couple, identification of high-risk situations, and teaching both partners alternative skills to cope with these situations. Also, communication between the partners is fostered by using role play to reduce conflict, enhance marital satisfaction, and reduce the chance of relapse.

RESEARCH BASIS

Anxiety Disorders

Theoretically oriented clinicians hold that phobias and other anxiety symptoms have interpersonal meaning in relationships. It was assumed that improvement of the anxious patient would lead to an exacerbation of symptoms in the partner and/or to marital distress.

So far, no convincing evidence has been provided that the partners of patients with anxiety disorders are psychologically abnormal themselves. However, recent empirical studies comparing agoraphobic and obsessive-compulsive couples with healthy control couples suggest there might be some differences as to marital satisfaction, adjustment, and interpersonal problem-solving skills. These differences, though, are usually rather small. Nevertheless, this has given impetus to involving the partners of agoraphobic and obsessive-compulsive patients in the treatment. In contrast to expectations derived from general systems theory, there is no evidence that exposure therapy of the patient with agoraphobia or obsessive-compulsive disorder alone has adverse effects on the relationship or the partner's symptoms. Controlled studies in this area concur that the relationship remains stable or slightly improves, with no exacerbation of symptoms in the partner of the patient. Thus, the empirical evidence does not support the system-theoretic conceptualization of anxiety disorders being a symptom of more serious marital problems.

Studies investigating the effects of spouse-aided therapy in individuals with agoraphobia led to conflicting results. Most studies have evaluated the effects of partner-assisted exposure. Generally, partner-assisted exposure is found to be as effective as treatment by the patient alone. Also, in obsessive-compulsives, no better results are found for partner-assisted exposure compared with exposure of the patient alone. Taking together the results of the studies that have been conducted thus far, there is no need to include the spouse in the exposure treatment of patients with agoraphobia or obsessive-compulsive disorder.

Results of studies that evaluated efficacy of interpersonal skills training interventions are rather mixed, so no general conclusions are allowed. Treatment focusing on general life stress rather than on relationship difficulties was found to be less effective than exposure by the patient alone. In contrast, studies that focused on relationship issues in addition to exposure led to slightly better results, especially at follow-up. Notably, this was also the case in couples who were not maritally distressed. Given the finding that criticism of the spouse may be related to relapse at follow-up, this may require specific attention to communication training in couples with a critical partner.

Depression

Depressed persons are characterized by an aversive interpersonal style to which others respond with negativity and rejection. A lower proportion of positive verbal behavior and a greater proportion of negative verbal and nonverbal behavior have characterized interaction of depressed individuals with their partners. A substantial number of depressed patients presenting for treatment also experience marital distress, whereas in approximately half of the couples who have marital problems, at least one of the spouses is depressed. These data suggest that depression and marital distress are closely linked. Furthermore, marital distress is an important precursor of depressive symptoms. In addition, persons who after being treated for depression return to distressed marriages are more likely to experience relapse. When patients are asked about the sequence of depression and marital distress, most patients hold that marital distress preceded the depressive episode.

To date, a number of controlled studies have shown that *conjoint behavioral marital therapy* in depressed maritally distressed couples may be a good alternative for individual cognitive behavior therapy. Taken together, results of these studies in martially distressed depressed couples show that behavioral marital therapy seems to have an exclusive effect on the marital relationship that is not found in individual cognitive-behavioral therapy. However, it is as effective as cognitive therapy in reducing depressed mood. Not surprisingly, behavioral marital therapy was hardly effective in depressed patients who did not experience marital problems.

Thus far, only one controlled study has investigated the effects of partner-assisted cognitive behavior therapy, and only one has investigated the effects of conjoint interpersonal therapy. Results of partner-assisted cognitive behavior therapy were comparable with those of individual cognitive behavior therapy. Both treatments led to statistically significant improvement on depressed mood, behavioral activity, and dysfunctional cognitions. However, none of the treatment formats affected relationship variables, which comes as no surprise, since couples were not maritally distressed prior to treatment. Thus, partner-assisted cognitive behavior therapy was as effective as individual cognitive behavior therapy. In addition, conjoint interpersonal psychotherapy was equally effective as individual interpersonal psychotherapy on measures of depressive symptomatology. There was some evidence that the conjoint version was slightly more effective than individual therapy on relationship variables. Finally, there is some evidence that treatment focusing on interaction of depressed couples is slightly more effective than antidepressants.

Substance Use Disorders

From a behavioral or social learning perspective, substance use disorders are habitual, maladaptive methods for attempting to cope with the stresses of daily living. Such maladaptive coping is triggered by internal and external cues and reinforced by positive rewards and/or negative punishment. Within this behavioral framework, drinking or drug taking is assumed to have a negative effect on communication between partners; marital satisfaction has also been linked to other issues such as domestic violence and sexual dysfunction. Research has differentiated families of alcoholics from healthier control families, in that the former typically manifest poor communication, organization, problem solving, conflict management, and affect regulation processes. However, comparing alcoholic couples with nonalcoholic but distressed couples revealed that similar dysfunctional processes characterized the latter group as well. Alcoholic couples, however, do differ from nonalcoholic couples in that they report more domestic violence. Even in nonalcoholic couples, more drinking is associated with increased violence.

There is some evidence that specific behaviors of the spouse can function either as a cue or reinforcer in drinking or drug-taking behavior. Furthermore, marital stability is positively related to success of treatment. In studies evaluating alcohol abusers' natural recovery patterns, social support, especially from a spouse, was significantly related to successfully changing the drinking behavior. Finally, there is some evidence that restoring marital satisfaction and reducing conflicts reduce the chance for relapse. Results of these studies suggest that there is a clear need to investigate effectiveness of spouse-aided interventions in substance abuse.

Behavioral couple treatments for substance use disorders other than alcohol are derived from these (and other) alcohol treatment protocols, focus on the same four domains, and use similar behavioral techniques. Another behavioral intervention, in which the spouse is usually involved but also other family members and other individuals from the patient's network, is Azrin's *community reinforcement approach*. Consistent with operant conditioning principles, this treatment is designed to remove reinforcing behaviors by teaching family and friends to ignore drinking and reward nondrinking. Originally designed for treating alcoholics, this treatment has been adapted by Stephen Higgens and colleagues for treating cocaine and drug-abusing patients and their partners.

Contingency Management

Almost all research work done in the last three decades on spouse-aided therapy has focused on alcohol, especially for male alcoholics. Recently, behavioral couple treatment studies have started focusing on other populations, for example, female alcoholics, problem drinkers, and other substance use disorders (cocaine, cannabis, or multiple use). Research suggests that getting a spouse involved in the treatment of alcohol and drug use disorders produces significant reduction in alcohol and/or drug use and improves marital functioning in general. There are some indications that behavioral couple therapy reduces violence in violent alcoholic couples. The amount of violence these couples report after receiving treatment, though, is still elevated compared with the entire alcoholic couple population.

Researchers have started developing new behavioral couple treatment protocols by adding possible new active ingredients, such as Alcoholics Anonymous (AA) attendance or relapse prevention sessions. Although first reports do not suggest additional benefit from combining AA with behavioral couple therapy, adding relapse prevention sessions seems to produce better (long-term) drinking and marital outcomes.

Use of voucher-based reinforcement of abstinence, in combination with community reinforcement, in the treatment of cocaine and other drug abuse has been supported by randomized clinical trials. This treatment seems to be a promising addition in for more severe dependent patients.

RELEVANT TARGET POPULATIONS AND EXCEPTIONS

The relevant target populations are those with panic disorder and agoraphobia, obsessive-compulsive disorder, depression, or substance abuse/dependence who have stable relationships.

COMPLICATIONS

A complicating factor may be a spouse who has also psychological problems. For example, complications arise in couples in which both individuals suffer from the same disorder, such as a couple in which the identified patient suffers from alcohol dependence and her partner also abuses alcohol. Here, spouse-aided therapy is usually of little avail, unless the partner is also motivated to alter his own problem drinking. In other couples, in which both patients have different disorders (e.g., a patient with major depression who has an agoraphobic partner), there are no evidence-based guidelines for how to operate in these cases. A specific, tailored treatment protocol of individual sessions as well as couples sessions may be a promising therapeutic strategy.

CASE ILLUSTRATION

A male patient in his mid-50s was diagnosed at intake with alcohol dependence (with physiological dependence). The patient had been drinking large amounts of alcohol all his adult life. After had he lost his job 6 years prior, he also started drinking during the day, neglecting activities, with concomitant increased marital distress. There was no comorbidity on Axis I. Although the patient's liver functions were poor, he declined the offer of clinical detoxification. Therefore, for several weeks, the therapist had the partners carry out very structured communication exercises. The patient was asked to elaborate about ambivalence regarding changing drinking behavior, and his wife had to express feelings about such ambivalence and the consequences this had on her willingness to continue the marriage. After a few weeks, the wife decided she would no longer tolerate patient's ambivalence and filed for divorce. Although discussed in therapy, this decision still came as a shock to the patient. Three days later, he started an intensive outpatient detoxification program under close supervision of a general practitioner. After 2 weeks, the patient and his wife (re)started behavioral couple therapy (BCT). Treatment focused on maintaining sobriety (recording of craving and discussing strategies to cope with craving) and continued communication training. After 10 sessions of BCT, the client had been sober for 4 months, with no lapses or relapses. Marital satisfaction was still low after treatment but had improved compared with pretreatment.

—Paul M. G. Emmelkamp and Ellen Vedel

See also: *Behavioral Treatment in Natural Environments (Vol. I); Flooding (Vol. I); Systematic Desensitization (Vol. I)*

Suggested Readings

Beach, S. R. H., Fincham, F. D., & Katz, J. (1998). Marital therapy in the treatment of depression: Towards a third generation of therapy and research. *Clinical Psychology Review, 18,* 835–861.

Craske, M., & Zoellner, L. (1996). Anxiety disorders: The role of marital therapy. In N. Jacobson & A. Gurman (Eds.), *Clinical handbook of couples therapy* (pp. 394–410). New York: Guilford Press.

Daiuto, A. D., Baucom, D. H., Epstein, N., & Dutton, S. S. (1998). The application of behavioral couples therapy to the assessment and treatment of agoraphobia: Implications of empirical research. *Clinical Psychology Review, 18,* 663–687.

Emanuels-Zuurveen, L., & Emmelkamp, P. M. G. (1996). Individual behavioural-cognitive therapy versus marital therapy for depression in maritally distressed couples. *British Journal of Psychiatry, 169,* 181–188.

Emmelkamp, P. M. G., & Gerlsma, C. (1994). Marital functioning and the anxiety disorders. *Behavior Therapy, 25,* 407–429.

Emmelkamp, P. M. G., de Haan, E., & Hoogduin, C. A. L. (1990). Marital adjustment and obsessive-compulsive disorder. *British Journal of Psychiatry, 156,* 55–60.

Emmelkamp, P. M. G., Van Dyck, R., Bitter, M., Heins, R., Onstein, E. J., & Eisen, B. (1992). Spouse-aided therapy with agoraphobics. *British Journal of Psychiatry, 160,* 51–56.

Epstein, E. E., & McCrady, B. S. (1998). Behavioral couples treatment of alcohol and drug use disorders: Current status and innovations. *Clinical Psychology Review, 18,* 689–711.

McCrady, B. S., Epstein, E. E., & Hirsch, L. S. (1999). Maintaining change after conjoint behavioral alcohol treatment for men: Outcome at 6 months. *Addiction, 94,* 1381–1396.

O'Farrell, T. J., & Cowles, K. S. (1995). Marital and family therapy. In R. K. Hester & W. R. Miller (Eds.), *Handbook of alcoholism treatment approaches.* Needham Heights, MA: Allyn & Bacon.

Rotunda, J. R., & O'Farrell, T. J. (1997). Marital and family therapy of alcohol use disorders: Bridging the gap between research and practice. *Professional Psychology: Research and Practice, 28,* 246–252

Vedel, E., & Emmelkamp, P. M. G. (in press). Behavioral couple therapy in the treatment of a female alcohol dependent patient with comorbid depression, anxiety and personality disorders. *Clinical Case Studies.*

SQUEEZE TECHNIQUE

DESCRIPTION OF THE STRATEGY

The squeeze technique was introduced as a modification of the earlier behavioral treatment for premature ejaculation, termed the *pause,* or *stop-start* procedure. With both, the partner of the patient is instructed to sit between his legs facing him, and to masturbate him. The patient monitors his arousal and when he feels he is about to ejaculate informs his partner. Unlike the stop-start procedure, when the partner then temporarily ceases stimulation, the partner carries out a penile squeeze. She or he places the first finger on the subject's glans penis, the second fingers just below it, and the thumb under it, and firmly but not painfully squeezes the glans. This inhibits ejaculation and usually results in some loss of erection. The partner then recommences masturbation. It can be helpful if a diagram is used to instruct the partner how to carry out the squeeze. When the patient is maintaining an erection for several minutes before being about to ejaculate, the couple proceeds to have coitus. This is commenced with the patient lying on his back and not thrusting while stimulated by the partner sitting on his penis. If the patient feels about to ejaculate prematurely, he informs his partner. The partner then ceases stimulation by raising herself or himself off the penis and, if necessary, uses the penile squeeze. Alternatively, the partner stops moving, and the patient squeezes the base of his penis. Both the stop-start and the squeeze technique have been reported to be used successfully with self-masturbation by men without partners who had anxieties about premature ejaculation.

RESEARCH BASIS

There is no research demonstrating that the stop-start and squeeze techniques have effects beyond those of suggestion. A significant number of men report an immediate satisfactory response, but it is not established that this is specific rather than due to reduction in anxiety and reassurance equivalent to that which would follow placebo therapy. Also, the techniques are usually employed as part of a cognitive-behavioral approach to treatment of sexual dysfunctions, which includes improvement of the couple's communication about their sexual and emotional relationship. The evidence is substantial that the nature of a couple's communication is much more significant than the presence of sexual dysfunctions in determining sexual satisfaction. Improved communication could lead to the couple finding premature ejaculation no longer a problem. There is as yet no accepted operational definition for premature ejaculation and hence no certainty that subjects treated in research studies have comparable conditions. The *DSM-IV-TR* diagnosis involves persistent or recurrent ejaculation with minimal sexual stimulation before, on, or shortly after penetration. The diagnostician has to take into account factors that could affect the duration of the excitement phase, and the patient must believe the condition causes marked distress or interpersonal difficulty. Premature ejaculation would not be diagnosed in men who report they experience it but do not consider it a problem for themselves or their partners. A representative United States population sample found that 28% of men aged 18 to 59 reported a period of several months or more in the previous year when they came to a climax too quickly. Three-year follow-up studies of men with premature ejaculation reported improvement in about 40% who were not treated and a high relapse rate in those who initially responded to treatment.

Treatment of premature ejaculation reported in the last decade has almost exclusively been with serotonergic drugs. Evidence of their effectiveness in randomized placebo controlled trials or clinical experience has convinced therapists to use them initially rather than stop-start or squeeze techniques.

—Nathaniel McConaghy

See also: *Behavioral Treatment in Natural Environments (Vol. I); Orgasmic Reconditioning (Vol. I); Spouse-Aided Therapy (Vol. I)*

Suggested Readings

Athanasiadis, L. (1998). Premature ejaculation: Is it a biogenic or a psychogenic disorder? *Sexual and Marital Therapy, 13,* 241–255.

Baucom, D. H., Shoham, V., Mueser, K. T., Daiuto, A. D., & Stickle, T. R. (1998). Empirically supported couple and family interventions for marital distress and adult mental health problems. *Journal of Consulting and Clinical Psychology, 66,* 53–88.

McConaghy, N. (1993). *Sexual behavior: problems and management.* New York: Plenum Press.

St. Lawrence, J. S., & Madakasira, S. (1992). Evaluation and treatment of premature ejaculation: A critical review. *Clinical Psychology Review, 22,* 77–97.

STAMPFL'S THERAPIST-DIRECTED IMPLOSIVE (FLOODING) THERAPY

DESCRIPTION OF THE STRATEGY

In the late 1950s, Thomas G. Stampfl developed a new, comprehensive behavioral-treatment approach designed to be used in the treatment of a wide variety of adult clinical psychological symptoms. He based his new approach on the use of established principles of learning developed from laboratory research. The technique he adopted was both unique and controversial. It was unique in that Stampfl was the first therapist to systematically recommend that symptom reduction could be achieved by exposing patients to those fear cues their symptoms were designed to avoid. The goal of his technique was to intentionally elicit within the patient a high level of emotional responding in order to establish the necessary conditions for the unlearning of emotions to these stimuli. At the time, the use of a direct-exposure principle was highly controversial, in large part because of the dominance within the field of psychoanalytic theory, which argued that such a procedure would exacerbate the patient's problem by creating more fear or even producing a psychotic break. This therapists' fear persisted within the psychotherapy community despite the absence of any empirical data to support this concern. Resistance to Stampfl's approach was also generated by clinicians who understandably felt uncomfortable about increasing the fear level of patients who were already overwhelmed by fear.

Nevertheless, Stampfl proceeded in the development of his new approach, which he labeled "implosive therapy" (IT). He borrowed the term *implosion* from physics in order to reflect the inwardly release of affectively stored energy within the brain. Today, some therapists prefer the more behavioral-sounding term of *flooding* to describe a fear cue exposure technique. Although unpublished papers outlining his approach were widely distributed, Stampfl refused to publish his approach for 10 years, until research was conducted to ensure the technique was safe and nonharmful and was applicable to the treatment of a variety of clinical nosologies. IT is characterized as a stimulus-response, dynamic cognitive-behavioral therapy approach.

Implosive theory represents a comprehensive theory of psychopathology, which incorporates a revised version of O. H. Mowrer's two-factor theory of avoidance learning. Maladaptive behavior is conceptualized as a learned behavior resulting from the exposure to past, specific aversive-conditioning experience of considerable intensity. Mowrer adopted Freud's contention that maladaptive behavior represented in the form of clinical symptoms consists of avoidance behavior designed to remove or reduce the presence of previously conditioned aversive cues. Mowrer argued, following extensive research, that avoidance learning or symptom development involves the learning of two response classes. The first response class, which is based on the established laws of classical conditioning, addresses the issue of how fears or anxieties are learned. According to theory, fear and other emotional conditioning results from the contiguity of pairing a nonemotional stimulus in space and time with one inherently primary aversive event producing pain, fear, frustration, or severe states of deprivation. Following sufficient repetition of the "neutral," previously nonemotional stimulus with the biological pain stimulus, the nonemotional stimulus is able to elicit the emotional response of fear in the absence of the biological stimulus. It has been shown that the conditioning events of humans are multiple, involving complex sets of stimuli both internal and external, which are believed to be encoded in long-term memory.

Conditioned fear has been shown to possess drive or motivating properties that set the stage for the development of Mowrer's second response class, avoidance learning, which is governed by the established laws of instrumental conditioning. These laws include both contiguity and drive reduction notions of reinforcement. Avoidance (symptom) behavior is learned because the response results in the termination or reduction in the intensity of the fear response. This reduction in the fear level serves as a reinforcer, which, in turn, strengthens the avoidance behavior.

Fear and Avoidance Unlearning

Mowrer's two-factor theory of avoidance argues that both emotional responding and subsequent avoidance behavior can be readily unlearned via the well-established principle of Pavlovian extinction. This principle states that the repeated presentation of the conditioned fear cues responsible for the development and maintenance of clinical symptoms can be weakened and unlearned (extinguished) by presenting or exposing the patient to the fear cues in the absence of any biological painful stimulation. Although such fear cues will elicit a strong emotional response, repetition should weaken the fear cues to the point the drive properties of the cues are extinguished. Without any motivating state being attached to the fear cues, the ability of the fear cues to elicit and reinforce the avoidance (symptoms) behavior will cease to exist.

Although the avoidance model described is central to conceptualizing psychopathology, it should be understood that maladaptive behavior frequently reflects the presence of a conflict situation involving the pitting of more than one drive state (e.g., feeling of guilt, rejection, anger, frustration and fear), which may be intertwined within the avoided context of cues controlling symptom maintenance.

Symptom Maintenance

Stampfl extended Mowrer's theory to provide resolution of the "neurotic paradox," which addresses the issue of why clinical symptoms are capable of persisting over a lifetime when symptoms reach a point of seriously incapacitating individuals and have long outlived any real justification for their continued maintenance. Stampfl believes that the conceptual resolution of this paradox is critical for any treatment approach to be effective and permanent. To resolve this paradox, he developed his serial conditioned-stimulus (CS) hypothesis. He observed that although fear cues eliciting a given patient's symptomatic behavior do appear to show signs of weakening due to exposure from each symptom occurrence, they are replaced from memory by a new set of previously unexposed fear cues that, upon exposure, secondarily recondition the first set of cues. When the new set of released cues become extinguished from nonreinforced exposure, the stage is set for yet another set of new cues to be released. Thus, according to theory, psychopathology is maintained by a network of historically conditioned events believed to be stored in memory in a serial arrangement along a dimension of stimulus intensity, with the more aversive-conditioned events being least accessible to memory reactivation. Repeated symptom execution has the effect of preventing the release of the next set of cues stored in memory. Patients will even alter the topography of their symptoms or develop new symptoms to prevent release of the most intense complex of fear stimuli stored in the serial arrangement. As a result of the patient's avoidance behaviors, fear (drive) levels to the unexposed fear cues are conserved and capable, until exposed, of maintaining symptomatology over long periods of time.

It would follow from the above theoretical model that if treatment is to be effective, the fear cues controlling patient's symptomatology need to be exposed for the extinction process to take effect. Thus, the fundamental task of the implosive therapist is to repeatedly represent, reinstate, or symbolically reproduce those stimulus situations to which the anxiety response has been learned or conditioned. By exposing the patient to the stimulus complex of fear cues that are being avoided, the patient will be exposed to the full emotional impact of these cues. As a function of repetition, the emotional affect elicited by the presentation of these cues will undergo a weakening or extinction effect, resulting in the elimination of the connection between the ability of the eliciting fear stimulus to generating one emotional response and, in turn, its ability to reinforce symptom behavior.

IT Treatment Strategy

The first task of the therapist is to make an attempt at specifying those historical conditioned stimuli that may be responsible for maintaining the patient's symptomatology. This might seem to be an impossible task. But as Stampfl noted, it is possible for a trained clinician following in-depth clinical interviews to develop hypotheses as to the trend of traumatic events that may have contributed to the origin of the patient's problem. These initial hypotheses represent only first approximations toward the goal of determining the aversive cues controlling the patient's maladaptive behavior. As therapy progresses, new information is obtained as to the validity of these cues, which, in turn, can lead to the generation of new hypotheses. In theory, it is not essential for these hypothesized cues to be completely accurate. If presentation of the hypothesized cues elicits an increase in affect, some effects of emotional unlearning will occur through the established learning principle of generalization of extinction. Of course, the more acute the hypothesized cues are, the greater will be the emotional arousal elicited and, subsequently, the greater the emotional extinction to the cue presented. The goal is to repeat the process until the patient's symptoms are reduced or eliminated. Clinical experience in using this approach indicates it is not uncommon for the presentation of these hypothesized cues to result in a reactivation of the patient's memory of the actual traumatic experience responsible for initial development of the patient's symptoms.

Stampfl's initial attempts in applying his theory to the clinical setting involved the use of the established laboratory procedure of response prevention. The goal of this procedure is to enhance the exposure to the feared cues by preventing the occurrence of the patient's symptom. Stampfl first used this in vivo approach on an obsessive-compulsive patient who for years had engaged in a radio compulsion checking ritual. The patient reported that if he failed to engage in his checking ritual to ensure the radio was turned off, something "catastrophic" might happen. The patient was then instructed not to engage in the checking ritual and to tolerate the level of anxiety experience and confront in imaging his worst possible fear. Numerous fear cues were reactivated, including a number of historical memories that involved a strong elicitation of affect. With repeated exposure to these cues and the continued blocking of the compulsive behavior, the patient's symptom extinguished.

Stampfl recognized that not all patients would be as motivated as this patient and that a directed intervention by the therapist may be required to block the

symptom. Since he recognized that the cues governing psychopathology represent a complex set of cues involving all sensory systems (visual, auditory, tactile, olfactory, and pain), Stampfl concluded that an *imagery technique* rather than an in vivo approach was better suited to represent and reinstate those cues being avoided. Many of the patients' fears involved cognitive thoughts. Although the in vivo approach may result in the activation of these cognitive cues, an imagery approach of introducing them directly by the therapist should represent a more direct and efficient approach given that such fears are stored in the form of images in memory.

Treatment Instructions

For the first two or three sessions, the therapist conducts an intense and thorough diagnostic evaluation of the patient's presenting problem and like history. The rationale and theory behind the technique are then described in detail at a level understandable to the patient. The goal is to illustrate that fears can be overcome by directly confronting them. Most patients readily understand the rationale behind the technique. They are then informed that the procedure being used involves an imagery technique in which they will be asked to imagine various scenes directed by the therapist. At the start of the scene, they are instructed to close their eyes and imagine themselves in the scene described. They are asked, much like an actor or actress, to fully let themselves feel any emotions generated by the therapist's description of the scene. They are told that the events portrayed may never have happened or are not real. Belief or acceptance in a cognitive sense of the theme introduced by the therapist is not requested, nor is any attempt made to secure any admission from the patients that the hypothesis introduced by the therapist actually applies to them. Following the completion of the instructions, the patient is exposed to a neutral imagery practice scene designed to assess the patient's imagery ability to a variety of nonfearful stimulus situations. Once the implosive procedure is started, an attempt is made to encourage the patient to reenact the scenes with genuine emotion and affect. When strong emotions are elicited, the therapist instructs the patient to focus on the full sensory consequence of his or her emotions. The scenes are repeated until the patient's emotional level to the scene is reduced. At the completion of each session, the patient is instructed to repeat the scene introduced at home for at least 20 minutes each day and to record any unusual thoughts or memories reactivated. Experience indicates that compliance with the technique is readily obtained.

Stimulus Cue Categories

As a guide to implementing the therapy, Stampfl has outlined the use of four cue categories, which can be conceptualized along a continuum that ranges from the uses of empirically established cues to hypothetical cues generated by the therapists. The first two cue categories are determined by the patient's behavior, while the second two categories are generated by the therapist's hypothesis. These cue categories and their order of presentation are as follows: (1) symptom-contingent cues, those cues correlated with the onset of the patient's symptoms; (2) reportable internally elicited cues, those verbally reported thoughts, feelings, and physical sensations elicited by presentation of the symptom-correlated cues; (3) unreported cues, hypothesized to be related to the second cue category; and (4) hypothesized dynamic cues, those fear cues associated with unresolved conflict situations usually comprising conflicting emotions (e.g., anger, fear, rejection, and guilt).

Since numerous case illustrations of this procedure already exist in the literature, a simple airplane phobia case will be used to illustrate the above categories. In this case, the symptom-correlated cues would comprise all those external and internal fear cues associated with the making of reservations, going to the airport, boarding the plane, and taking off. An example of a verbally reported cue might be the reported thought that the plane might crash. This cue, in turn, might then result in the generation of the hypothesis that a key component to the patient's fear of flying might relate to his fear of dying. The final cue category might include a dynamic hypothesis that the patient's fear of death, in turn, might be related to unresolved feelings of past guilt, which might result in the fear of being punished in hell for eternity if death occurred. Each of these categories is present in order and repeated until a substantial reduction in anxiety is reported. Not all the cue categories need to be imploded; once the fear level is reduced to the point the patient can fly without intense fear, therapy is terminated.

A key strength of the implosive procedure is that the technique is an operational feedback approach that is self-correcting. If the behavioral and hypothesized

cues introduced into a given scene presentation elicit emotional affects, support for their continual use is obtained. The greater the degree of emotional arousal, the greater the level of support. Cues that do not elicit arousal are abandoned and replaced by new hypothesized cues. This process is continued until the desired emotional affect is obtained and extinguished. Validation of the cues presented is obtained with the establishment of a correlation between the extinction of the emotional affect to these cues and a reduction or removal in the patient symptomatology. Significant changes are usually reported within 1 to 15 1-hour therapy sessions.

RESEARCH BASIS

Perhaps no other behavioral therapy approach has been subjected to such research scrutiny in terms of both theory and practice. More than 50 years of experimental research has been conducted on Mowrer's two-factor theory of avoidance at both the animal and human levels of analysis. Today, extensions of Mowrer's fear theory remain the dominant theory of avoidance within both the experimental and behavioral therapy fields. Experimental support at the animal and human levels has been obtained for Stampfl's attempt to resolve the neurotic paradox via his serial CS hypothesis. Patient conformation for this hypothesis has been developed by the first author's extension in 1985 of Stampfl's therapist-directed IT to a patient-directed IT procedure sometimes referred as "brain release therapy." This latter approach, which is designed primarily for the treatment of adult survivors of sexual abuse, is capable of decoding in great detail the actual traumatic experiences responsible for producing the patient pathology. To date, a data bank of hundreds of decoded traumatic memories have been collected, which are currently being evaluated via behavioral-coding techniques. These data strongly support Stampfl's contention that traumatic memories are encoded in long-term memory, they comprise a complex set of cues, and they are ordered within the brain in the manner he has suggested.

At a treatment outcome level, IT and related fear exposure techniques have also received strong experimental support by patient research. Exposure therapy has been successful in the treatment of a variety of various phobic conditions, obsessive-compulsive behavior, anxiety attacks, hypochondria, anger, agoraphobia, grief, anorexia nervosa, addictions, depression, posttraumatic stress, sexual abuse, and in hospitalized patients who are psychotic or seriously depressed. Follow-up studies confirmed that the therapist's gains were maintained. Finally, the safety of the technique has been confirmed by experimental and survey studies coupled with its continual use for more than 40 years.

RELEVANT TARGET POPULATIONS AND EXCEPTIONS

As reported above, research has confirmed that IT and related exposure techniques have been used successfully on a wide variety of adult nosologies, and some research suggests it may also be useful in treating children's symptoms. Experience indicates that patients are cooperative and rarely drop out of treatment prematurely. However, in a small percentage of patients, their full participation is hindered by too-intense fear levels or intact defenses. In such cases, alternative behavior approaches like systematic desensitization or cognitive-behavioral talk therapy may be more appropriate. Finally, the therapists' own fears in introducing high levels of anxiety may reduce the effectiveness of treatment and recommended use of this procedure. However, the experience of the first author in training therapists in the use of the IT procedure is that the therapist's own fears quickly undergo an extinction effect once therapeutic gains occur.

COMPLICATIONS

Other than the issue raised concerning the therapist's own apprehensions concerning the use of an exposure approach, research has not suggested the presence of any serious complications. However, a medical physical examination should be conducted prior to the start of treatment to ensure no medical complications (e.g., a heart condition) from the exposure of high levels of anxiety are present. Although treatment outcome studies have been conducted on patients who are on psychotropic medication, it is possible certain types of medication may impede the elicitation of the anxiety response. Further research is needed in this area. Therapists should consult with the patient's physician regarding this possibility. Finally, in the treatment of psychotic behavior and borderline personalities, treatment within a hospital setting is recommended unless the therapist has had extensive successful experience in using an exposure approach in an outpatient setting.

CASE ILLUSTRATION

The patient, a 45-year-old male, was psychiatrically diagnosed as having a severe "psychotic" depressive reaction. The patient refused to eat, spoke in a monotone voice, and expressed a desire to kill himself. His suicidal ruminations started 2 years earlier, and he reported he had been recently going down to his cellar daily trying to muster the courage to hang himself. The patient was unable to assert himself appropriately or to express any outward anger. He stated he knew his wife was faithful to him because she was a good Catholic, yet he could not shake the "paranoid" thought that she was secretly having an affair with his brother-in-law. He reported his father was a strict disciplinarian and that he dared not talk back to him. He also reported having difficulty relating to his boss. The first author was given 3 days to treat the patient, who was scheduled to be hospitalized on the fourth day if his depression persisted. The results of the patient's MMPI confirmed the seriousness of this case. Five T-scores on the MMPI (D, Hs, Hp, PD, PT) were elevated in the psychopathological range, with his depression T-score being over 100.

The client was treated for a 2-hour period on each of three successive days. According to Stampfl's treatment model for depression, the patient's depression was conceptualized as an avoidance response blocking cues associated with guilt, rejection, anger, and fear of punishment. The first implosive scene centered on attempts to extinguish the depressive response by having the patient increase his feeling of depression to the point he decided to kill himself. The therapist then described a scene in great detail in which the patient was asked to imagine himself going down to his cellar, putting a rope around his neck, and hanging himself. All the sensory consequences of this act were described in great detail. The patient was then asked to look at his wife as she came down the stairs and saw his dead body. Showing the first strong signs of emotion, the patient spontaneously yelled out, "Now she'll be sorry that I am dead." The therapist said, "No, look again, she has a smile on her face." In fact, she was so happy, she called all her friends and the patient's boss to attend a party around his hanging body. The focus here was to introduce a series of rejection cues in the hopes of releasing the patient's inhibition to expressing anger. At the party, everyone verbalized why they were glad the patient was dead. Although it appeared the rejection cues were having some effect, anger feelings were still inhibited. A scene was then described in which everyone left the party but his wife and brother-in-law. A very detailed scene was then described in which the brother-in-law had sex with the patient's wife in front of his dead body. At this point, it was clear the desired effect was obtained. The patient was told he was wearing a circus collar and was not dead. Spontaneously, the patient's face lit up, he saw himself pulling the rope off his neck, jumping down, and physically attacking his wife and brother-in-law, which was extended by the therapist to include primary-process anger cues. At the end of the first session, it appeared the patient's depression had lifted.

The next two sessions focused on attempts to extinguish the patient's feeling of guilt and fear of punishment. One scene encompassed a courtroom scene in which the patient had to confess his guilt for killing his wife and brother-in-law. Of course, the judge hearing the case found him guilty, and he was condemned to die. Prior to his execution, a scene of the patient's last confession to a priest was described, in which he was refused absolution. A repetition of each of the scenes was presented on the third session in the context of another confession scene after his death, in which he took responsibility for his angry behavior toward himself and others. When God condemned the patient to hell, he yelled out with considerable affect, "God, not hell, purgatory!" This was followed by a punishment scene in hell. At the end of the three treatment sessions, the patient's depression had lifted. A posttest MMPI revealed that all the clinical scales fell with a normal range. A year follow-up of this case revealed the patient's depression did not return, he was able to be appropriately assertive, and his relationship with his wife and work situation were much better. The details of the rationale for the cues introduced in this and other IT cases are described in the article referenced in the Foa and Goldstein handbook listed in the suggested readings.

—Donald J. Levis and Bryan A. Castelda

See also: Flooding (Vol. I); Systematic Desensitization (Vol. I)

Suggested Readings

Boudewyns, P. A., & Shipley, R. H. (1983). Flooding and implosive therapy. New York: Plenum Press.

Levis, D. J. (1980). Implementing the technique of implosive therapy. In A. Goldstein & E. G. Foa (Eds.), Handbook of behavioral interventions: A clinical guide (pp. 92–151). New York: Wiley.

Levis, D. J. (1995). Decoding traumatic memory: Implosive theory of psychopathology. In W. O'Donohue & L. Kramer (Eds.), Theories in behavior therapy (pp. 173–207). Washington, DC: American Psychological Association.

Stampfl, T. G. (1991). Analysis of aversive events in human psychopathology: Fear and avoidance. In M. R. Denny (Ed.), Fear, avoidance, and phobias (pp. 363–393). Hillsdale, NJ: Erlbaum.

STRESS INOCULATION TRAINING

DESCRIPTION OF THE STRATEGY

In recent decades, increased attention has been directed toward understanding the nature of stress, the impact of stress with regard to the etiology of mental illness, and its potentially negative consequences for physical health, individual performance, and productivity in the workplace. Stress generally is defined as a response that occurs when an individual perceives the demands of a particular situation or combination of situations as exceeding his or her coping resources. Stressful responding can include a variety of unwanted physiological, cognitive, behavioral, and interpersonal consequences. For example, chronic-pain patients may experience stress that partially results from an inability to find adequate relief from their ailments. The frequency and intensity of their physical pain may exceed their perceived (or actual) abilities to cope effectively and may subsequently involve increased levels of stress or anxiety, a response that may include heightened autonomic arousal, increased negative cognitions (e.g., worries about finding an adequate treatment, catastrophic thoughts regarding the future), and avoidance behaviors, which might include discontinuation of previously rewarding activities and disengagement in social activities. Unfortunately, such consequences may result in even more escalated levels of stress and also may increase one's vulnerability to a worsening of medical conditions and/or the development of a mental illness such as a mood or anxiety disorder.

Stress can be elicited by a variety of environmental situations (both positive and negative) and may be associated with significant impairment in life functioning. As a consequence of the stress response, for example, employees might exhibit decreased productivity, injured athletes might have an extended recovery time, students might experience a decline in academic performance, and primary caregivers may be less capable of caring for their children. Although minimal to moderate levels of stress may be useful in serving a motivational function and potentially increase performance in some situations, it is evident that significant detrimental consequences can occur when individuals are confronted with overwhelming levels of stress or anxiety. Accordingly, several interventions have been developed to assist individuals in learning the appropriate coping skills necessary to reduce the impact of stressful situations and events. Developed by Donald Meichenbaum, one such treatment is *stress inoculation training* (SIT). This intervention incorporates various treatment strategies designed to increase resistance to stress. For example, clients are taught the transactional nature of the stress and coping process, strategies for self-monitoring thoughts, feelings, and behaviors, as well as problem-solving skills, with subsequent utilization of these skills in both hypothetical and real-life situations. Through these psychoeducational processes, increased self-awareness, and an expanded repertoire of coping skills, clients become "vaccinated," or better prepared to effectively cope with future stressful events or situations.

SIT most commonly consists of three stages: (1) conceptualization and education, (2) coping-skill acquisition and rehearsal, and (3) application and follow-through. The goal of the first stage, conceptualization and education, is to facilitate a more comprehensive understanding of the nature of stress and its consequences. Developing an increased awareness of stress and situations that elicit stressful responding enables the client to form accurate perceptions of situations in which anxiety is experienced and allows for an assessment of ideographic stress responses, as well as clients' resources or strategies to cope effectively with stress. This stage of SIT is in many ways consistent with a functional analytic (A-B-C) approach to conceptualizing stress responses, with a focus on establishing the role of maladaptive cognitions in eliciting stress-related responding and emphasizing that these cognitions can be modified to promote decreased anxiety in stressful situations. As a result of these processes, clients often develop an increased sense of predictability and control about onset of stress and ability to cope with stressful situations, as well as a basic skill repertoire that will allow for exposure and adjustment to future (perhaps novel) stressful events. An equally important objective of the first stage of SIT is for the therapist and client to develop a collaborative relationship, which is crucial insofar as the establishment of rapport may generate client involvement in treatment planning and intervention development, as well as increased motivation, accountability, and compliance with stress reduction strategies.

The objective of the second stage of SIT, coping-skill acquisition and rehearsal, is for the therapist and client to develop a repertoire of coping skills that the client can use to decrease anxiety and increase coping effectiveness. Techniques that are employed in SIT vary systematically according to the nature of the stress-inducing stimulus, individually assessed stress-related symptoms, and patient/therapist preference for certain strategies. Among the most commonly used strategies are cognitive restructuring, generation of coping statements, thought-stopping, and relaxation training. Utilization of cognitive restructuring, coping statements, and thought-stopping procedures assist clients in more effectively regulating negative emotions and distracting thoughts. Relaxation training enhances the client's ability to cope with unwanted physiological responses. These strategies typically are rehearsed during therapy sessions via behavioral role playing or mental imagery techniques and often are incorporated into weekly homework assignments.

The aim of the third stage of SIT, application and follow-through, is to encourage the client to apply the learned skills in situations that induce stress or anxiety. To achieve this goal, the client is exposed to stress-inducing stimuli via imaginal or in vivo procedures (i.e., the natural environment) while simultaneously incorporating cognitive and relaxation strategies previously learned. To facilitate patient progress and initial success, in contrast to more prolonged exposure strategies, clients often are gradually introduced to stress-inducing stimuli in successive approximations. This approach increases perceptions of control and confidence and encourages practice of skills in progressively more threatening situations. Guided imagery and role play procedures initially conducted within the secure confines of the therapeutic environment generally come to be replaced by in vivo exposure to "real-life" situations. As a final component of this stage of treatment, clients often receive training in relapse prevention and are taught to appropriately handle the setbacks that may occur following termination of psychotherapy. High-risk situations for relapse are identified, and strategies for coping with them are rehearsed.

RESEARCH BASIS

A significant body of literature has revealed that SIT is an effective treatment for enhancing resistance to stress in the context of either individual or group psychotherapy. Numerous variations of SIT have been used to address a wide range of presenting problems, such as anger in police officers, posttraumatic stress disorder in rape and assault victims, athletes' post-surgical pain and recovery, interpersonal stress in stepfamilies, dental treatment, fear of flying, teaching and speech anxiety, and job burnout. SIT is considered to be an effective treatment for reducing an individual's performance and state anxiety and for enhancing performance under stress. The outcome of studies investigating the efficacy of SIT generally establish treatment effects comparable, or in some cases superior, to those obtained from prolonged exposure treatments and supportive counseling.

Empirical studies have demonstrated that the effectiveness of SIT generally increases as the number of sessions increases, although some researchers have documented that even a single session of SIT may be beneficial for decreasing performance and state anxiety. Whereas a single session can somewhat improve resistance to stress, more frequent sessions appear to be optimal for obtaining maximum benefits from SIT. For example, between four and seven sessions of SIT appear sufficient for reducing performance and/or state anxiety. In addition, studies have shown that imaginal procedures may be more beneficial than behavioral practice for reducing performance anxiety and behavioral practice may be more effective than imaginal strategies for enhancing performance.

Interestingly, when the efficacy of SIT is examined as a function of provider training, no significant effects are found. That is, experience of the provider does not appear strongly related to the effectiveness of SIT in enhancing clients' abilities to cope with stress and anxiety. Environment of implementation also appears quite flexible, with the benefits of SIT demonstrated in multiple contexts that include both basic and applied research settings. For example, more basic laboratory studies have shown that SIT can reduce research participants' speech anxiety, and more applied work has demonstrated that SIT can benefit job employees coping with burnout or anxious patients dealing with the stress of an upcoming dental procedure.

RELEVANT TARGET POPULATIONS AND EXCEPTIONS

As alluded to earlier, SIT has been adapted for use with a wide variety of clients, including individuals seeking to confront public-speaking situations, control the experience of pain, or manage their reactions to a traumatic experience. SIT also has recently been adapted for use among individuals dealing with inter-personal stressors, such as those encountered in step-families and foster families. Moreover, SIT has been adapted to help clients cope with various forms of on-the-job stress, such as that encountered by law enforcement officers, nurses, social workers, and individuals enlisted in the military.

Although SIT has been adapted for a wide range of presenting problems, SIT may be contraindicated in certain circumstances. Perhaps unsurprisingly, research has shown that SIT may be ineffective when a client exhibits minimal desire to alter resistance to stress. These studies also have indicated that individuals who desire increased control over responses in anxiety-provoking situations and perceive limited control at present may be particularly likely to benefit from an SIT intervention. Therefore, treatments such as SIT are most effective when they correspond to the client's preferred style of coping with stress and when perceptions of control over stress responses are minimal.

COMPLICATIONS

Coexistent psychiatric diagnoses such as clinical depression and personality disorders are likely to interfere with the effectiveness of SIT. It is difficult to ascertain the limitations that these co-occurring disorders may create, however, because much of the research conducted on SIT has excluded individuals with significant psychopathology such as schizophrenia, alcohol or drug dependence, and bipolar disorder. A more systematic program of research needs to be conducted to develop a clearer understanding of the potential complications that may result when clients experience psychological difficulties in addition to overwhelming anxiety and stress.

Insufficient practice or follow-through also can jeopardize the effectiveness of SIT, highlighting the importance of integrating motivational strategies into therapy. It is well-known that SIT may provide immediate and significant relief to clients facing significant stressors, but if clients do not continue to employ SIT strategies following treatment termination, relapse often is the consequence. Finally, it is important that clients practice their newly learned coping strategies outside of the therapeutic context to promote generalization to the natural environment. For this reason, the final phase of SIT should include both in vivo practice exercises and the development of relapse prevention strategies.

CASE ILLUSTRATION

"Billy" was a 32-year-old married Caucasian male, employed as a construction worker. He sought therapy as a consequence of intense episodes of anger that predominantly manifested in the context of driving (i.e., road rage). A recent expression of anger had resulted in a physical confrontation with another driver that was followed by his wife experiencing significant distress about becoming a target of his aggression, as well as the potential for criminal and civil legal action as threatened by the assaulted driver. Although Billy was initially skeptical about the process of psychotherapy, recognizing the potential for litigation and the significant interpersonal problems associated with anger, he consented to treatment.

Initial stages of therapy were designed to promote an increased understanding of the emotional experience of anger. Through psychoeducational means, Billy was informed of the physiological, cognitive, and behavioral components of anger, with emphasis on highlighting those symptoms Billy most commonly experienced. A monitoring exercise was assigned over the following week to facilitate improved therapist and patient understanding of the situations that elicited anger, increased awareness of specific emotional responses, and to assess current coping resources. These data revealed that although driving situations generally elicited the most intense anger, this emotional experience also occurred in contexts where Billy's wife made decisions without his consultation (e.g., home improvement) and when he was "forced" to remain at work longer than scheduled. In such situations, Billy consistently experienced increased autonomic arousal (increased heart and respiratory rate, perspiration), negative cognitions, such as "How dare that person cut me off," "Who do they (e.g., driver, wife, boss) think they are disrespecting me like that," and "I'm gonna teach them I mean business." Anger-related behaviors that included shouting, cursing, inappropriate hand gestures, verbal and physical conflict, honking the horn, and alcohol abuse also were apparent. Adaptive coping resources were all but absent.

Recognizing the coping-skill deficiency and impairment associated with anger, the skills acquisition stage initially consisted of teaching Billy progressive muscle relaxation. Billy was instructed to practice relaxation exercises at a specified time each day, and he exhibited adequate compliance. Based on the rational-emotive model of emotional responding, Billy was also taught the relation among environmental situations and events, mediating cognitions, and subsequent emotional responses and behaviors. Together with the therapist, Billy actively worked toward disputing maladaptive cognitions and identifying appropriate coping statements that would be useful when encountering stressful situations. An anger hierarchy was constructed, with "a driver cutting me off" as the highest item on the hierarchy.

In the application phase of SIT, Billy first engaged in imaginal exposure exercises in the therapeutic context. Progressively moving from the least to most stress-inducing situations, Billy was asked to visualize the stressful experiences. He was instructed to envision scenes as though he were an active participant (rather than external observer), imagining his physiological and cognitive reactions in as much detail as possible as the therapist provided prompts. When Billy signaled to the therapist that he was experiencing elevated levels of stress, he was encouraged to continue to picture the situation as vividly as possible while simultaneously focusing on relaxing his muscles and disputing the maladaptive and anger-eliciting cognitions with self-statements generated in earlier sessions. Following a couple sessions of imaginal exposure, Billy was encouraged to utilize his inoculation skills in the natural environment as situations presented. A relapse prevention session also was conducted to identify other potential anger-provoking situations that might trigger maladaptive responses, as well as reemphasizing the importance of preparing for these situations (when possible), confronting the situations using learned skills, and self-reinforcing when high-risk situations were successfully negotiated.

—Derek R. Hopko and Farrah Hughes

See also: Anxiety/Anger Management Training (Vol. I); Cue-Controlled Relaxation (Vol. I); Mindfulness Meditation (Vol. I)

Suggested Readings

Foa, E. B., Dancu, C. V., Hembree, E. A., Jaycox, L. H., Meadows, E. A., & Street, G. P. (1999). A comparison of exposure therapy, stress inoculation training, and their combination for reducing posttraumatic stress disorder in female assault victims. *Journal of Consulting and Clinical Psychology, 67,* 194–200.

Law, A., Logan, H., & Baron, R. S. (1994). Desire for control, felt control, and stress inoculation during dental treatment. *Journal of Personality and Social Psychology, 67,* 926–936.

Maag, J. W., & Kotlash, J. (1994). Review of stress inoculation training with children and adolescents: Issues and recommendations. *Behavior Modification, 18,* 443–469.

Meichenbaum, D. H. (1985). *Stress inoculation training.* Elmsford, New York: Pergamon Press.

Meichenbaum, D. H. (1993). Stress inoculation training: A 20-year update. In R. L. Woolfolk & P. M. Lehrer (Eds.), *Principles and practice of stress management* (2nd ed., pp. 373–406). New York: Guilford Press.

Meichenbaum, D. H., & Deffenbacher, J. L. (1988). Stress inoculation training. *The Counseling Psychologist, 16,* 69–90.

Saunders, T., Driskell, J. E., Johnston, J. H., & Salas, E. (1996). The effect of stress inoculation training on anxiety and performance. *Journal of Occupational Health Psychology, 1,* 170–186.

SUINN, RICHARD M.

I have been involved with anxiety interventions since the early 1960s, first examining ways of expediting desensitization therapy, then devising the brief-intervention anxiety management training (AMT), applied initially to anxiety treatment, then to anger management.

I was born on May 8, 1933, in Honolulu, Hawaii. I was raised in a multiethnic environment, attended St. Louis High School, and my freshman and sophomore years at the University of Hawaii. Although considering various science or medical majors at the university, the introductory psychology class, experience as a research subject, and volunteer work at the counseling center shifted my interest to psychology.

I was admitted to Ohio State University, arriving there by flying over the ocean, taking a train from the West Coast to the Midwest, then riding a trolley to the campus in Columbus, only to find the dormitories closed. A night's stay in the Ohio State football stadium on a cot may be the source of my later interest in sport psychology and removing stress.

Following the baccalaureate degree from Ohio State in 1955, I was accepted to the doctoral program at Stanford University, where I earned a master's degree in 1957 and the PhD in 1959. During the Stanford years, faculty and speakers were laying the theoretical foundations for behavior therapy, although assessment and intervention techniques had yet to be discovered. Instead, students were expected to learn traditional, nondirective, and psychodynamic approaches, along with acquiring ambivalence about the efficacy of such approaches. The release by Wolpe of his classic book on reciprocal inhibition (basic to desensitization therapy) influenced me to more seriously rely upon the learning theory foundation at Stanford. Later, an inability to provide help to an athlete with performance anxiety became the final precipitant for me to disengage from traditional psychotherapeutic theories or methods and to fully commit to behavioral approaches.

Professional models at Stanford University included C. Lee Winder and Albert Bandura, Leonard Krasner of the psychology department, and John D. Black, of Stanford University Counseling Center, for whom I worked. Brendan Maher was of great help in becoming involved with professional psychology activities, such as doing editorial reviews, serving on American Psychological Association (APA) Divisional committees, and book publishing. A series of personal contacts and readings impressed me with the relevance and value of operant approaches, such as the works of Ted Ayllon and Nate Azrin. Extremely valuable was viewing the use of operant methods for improving children's behaviors at the University of Washington Developmental Psychology Lab, which produced publications by Don Baer, Sid Bijou, Jay Birnbrauer, Todd Risley, and Montrose Wolf. A. Wayne Viney was the head of the Psychology Department at Colorado State University; he interviewed and hired me in 1968 and was my role model when I replaced him as department head. I served in this position for 20 years.

My major contributions include the design and development of anxiety/anger management training, a brief self-control procedure. AMT is unique in being effective for both anxiety and anger, in being applied by patients after termination to other new sources of stress or provocation, and in being useful for focused emotional states such as phobias or conditions where the source is ambiguous, such as in generalized anxiety disorder. AMT has also seen use with diverse populations, ranging from chronic schizophrenics, to medical outpatients, to hypertensive patients or persons facing stressful medical procedures, and to persons seeking to improve their performance by reducing stress, such as Olympic athletes and dance/music performers.

I have also developed ways of speeding up the application of desensitization by reexamining the basic principles and accelerated the treatment. My interests in operant approaches led to the design of a program to train undergraduate paraprofessionals to act as consultants to teachers. During my term as president of the APA in 1999, I called public attention to psychology and cancer and promoted the importance of ethnic minority issues and ethnic minority's strengths and contributions.

In the area of assessment, I produced a scale to measure mathematics anxiety and a scale to measure acculturation levels of Asian Americans, both being among the most used measures by researchers and scholars.

Finally, I was among the first psychologists to provide the foundation for the development of sport psychology training methods. My basic work on visualization remains a cornerstone for practitioners. I also served on the first U.S. Olympic Committee Sport Psychology Committee, which designed and developed sport psychology services for U.S. Olympic athletes.

In 1999, I completed 40 years in academic positions at Whitman College, Stanford University School of Medicine, the University of Hawaii, and Colorado State University, as well as serving as mayor of the city of Ft. Collins, Colorado. I have entered retirement as emeritus professor of psychology and emeritus head of the Department of Psychology at Colorado State University, where I maintain an office. I devote energy as an informal mentor to graduate students, especially ethnic minorities, and continue involvement in the APA.

My future, as my past, is evolving in an unplanful way. In the past, opportunities seem to present themselves, or my latest interest directed exploration of a new avenue. Sometimes research questions required seeking answers, and sometimes social/professional issues demand involvement. I am anticipating that some ventures will appear sometime to guide my future. Meanwhile, I say, "In the winter I ski fanatically, in the spring I play tennis exuberantly, in the summer I fish avidly, and in the fall I am depressed waiting for the winter."

—*Richard M. Suinn*

See also: Anxiety/Anger Management Training
(Vol. I); Association for Advancement of Behavior
Therapy (Vol. I); Behavioral Consultation (Vol. I)

SYSTEMATIC DESENSITIZATION

DESCRIPTION OF THE STRATEGY

Systematic desensitization is a venerable behavior therapy approach developed by Joseph Wolpe for the treatment of fear and anxiety-based disorders. As is described below, treatment with systematic desensitization begins with careful assessment that seeks to describe in detail the objects and/or events that occasion fear. Treatment then continues so as to include three basic procedures. The therapist teaches the patient to relax the voluntary muscles. Concurrently, the therapist and patient develop detailed narrative descriptions of personal encounters with the objects/events that provoke fear, and they arrange the descriptions in order of increasing fearsomeness. Finally, the therapist instructs the patient to visualize the encounters in increasingly fearsome order, while the patient remains fully relaxed. Ordinarily, the therapist also encourages the patient to confront the fearsome objects/events in such a way that the actual confrontations follow relaxed visualization of them.

Wolpe's theory of the effects of systematic desensitization combines concepts borrowed from the famous physiologists Ivan Pavlov, Charles Sherrington, and Edmund Jacobson and the psychologist Clark L. Hull. According to the theory, systematic desensitization reduces fear by causing the cues for fear activation to become cues for fear inhibition. Fear amounts to aversively conditioned sympathetic responsivity to the objects/events of interest and imagery related to them. The sympathetic activation that occurs during fearsome imaging is reciprocally inhibited by the parasympathetic correlates of concurrent muscular relaxation. When sympathetic activation during fearsome imaging is reciprocally inhibited, the act of imaging acquires its own fear-inhibitory capability. This occurs through the action of conditioned inhibition. Hence, Wolpe's explanation of the effects of systematic desensitization appeals to conditioned inhibition of fear activation based on reciprocal inhibition of fear activation. Fearsome images and their real-life referents become conditioned inhibitors of the sympathetic arousal they once excited. Muscular relaxation came to be the reciprocal inhibitor of choice in systematic desensitization, but in principle, reciprocal inhibition of sympathetic activation via assertive behaviors and sexual arousal would serve equally well.

By the late 1960s, systematic desensitization came to be commonly regarded as efficacious and as the treatment of choice for a variety of fear- and anxiety-related disorders. Therefore, psychological theorists were quick to provide post hoc explanations of Wolpe's results using the languages of their own theoretical orientations. By the end of the 1970s, a dozen or so theories of the effects of systematic desensitization had appeared. Some of the theories asserted simply that systematic desensitization was a special case of a more general principle such as habituation, respondent extinction, or counterconditioning. Others of the theories posited the action of change mechanisms such as expectations of therapeutic gain, the therapeutic relationship, and covert self-modeling of fearless behavior. Even psychodynamic explanations of the effects of systematic desensitization appeared. Problematically, the late 1960s and early 1970s saw the emergence of a research literature about systematic desensitization that was large, methodologically heterogeneous, and substantively contradictory. Theorists with diverse doctrinal leanings were able, therefore, to find empirical support for their assertions.

Also during the 1970s, Isaac Marks began popularizing the idea that systematic desensitization is simply a variant of exposure technology. Marks argued that successful fear therapies such as systematic desensitization, flooding, and participant modeling worked for the same reason; they all incorporated imaginal or actual exposure to the cue stimuli for fear. Descriptions of systematic desensitization as a variant of exposure technology are now commonplace, and such a characterization is not without intuitive appeal. However, categorizing systematic desensitization as a variety of exposure technology does little to explain how systematic desensitization works, because the beneficial effects of exposure themselves remain to be explained satisfactorily.

Any effort to explain the action of systematic desensitization is complicated further by contemporary developments such as Peter Lang's bioinformational theory of emotional imagery, Stanley Rachman's related view of emotional processing, revisions in the conceptualization of autonomic regulation, and attempts to integrate anxiety-related phenomena with emotional behaviors such as disgust. To date, there have been only piecemeal efforts to incorporate these and other developments into theoretical explanations of the effects of systematic desensitization.

Assessment

The advent of cognitive behavior therapy has changed our conceptions of fear behavior, our routine modes of assessment, and our behavior change targets. Fear behavior is held to be mediated by catastrophic cognition; assessment is concerned with identifying the content of that cognition and, sometimes, the nature of supporting metacognition; and alteration in cognitive content is a major treatment goal. Systematic desensitization, however, enjoyed its heyday before cognitive theories became influential. It is grounded in the notions that most fear behavior is acquired via aversive Pavlovian conditioning; assessment is concerned with identifying and describing conditioned aversive stimuli and responses; and the goal of treatment is to rid the aversive stimuli of their acquired power to elicit fear behavior.

One purpose of assessment in the context of systematic desensitization is to identify the objects/events (conditioned aversive stimuli) that occasion fear and to describe the elements, dimensions, or abstract themes imbedded in those objects/events that regulate fear intensity. Another purpose of assessment related to systematic desensitization is to characterize the patient's fear experience and fear-related behavior. Face-to-face behavioral interviewing is the most common approach to assessment. Interviewing is often supplemented by some combination of omnibus and special-purpose fear questionnaires, as well as by behavioral tests conducted in the clinic and/or in the natural environment. SUDs scaling (Subjective Units of Discomfort, see below) is also integral to assessment that is related to the use of systematic desensitization.

Some assessment activities are directed toward answering questions related to establishing the patient's suitability for treatment with systematic desensitization. Does the patient report clear, detailed imagery related to the objects/events of interest? Does the patient report or otherwise manifest emotional discomfort while imagining those objects/events? Is there any reason to suspect that the patient will be unable to relax? Is treatment based on actual exposure impossible, inconvenient, or premature? Are there four or fewer fear clusters? Again, face-to-face interviewing usually provides the answers sought.

Relaxation Training

Relaxation training is usually carried out with some variation on the method of progressive relaxation that was developed by Edmund Jacobson during the 1930s. It is guided by instructions for thinking of the skeletal muscles as divided into subgroups, instructions for tensing and relaxing the muscles in each subgroup, and instructions for attending to the different sensations that arise from tension versus relaxation.

Progressive relaxation training typically begins with a transcript that divides the skeletal musculature into 16 muscle groups. Various manuals also provide transcripts that divide the muscles into 8, 6, or 4 groups, so that training can be abbreviated by tensing and relaxing more muscles simultaneously. By the time that systematic desensitization is begun, the patient should be able to relax quickly via abbreviated training.

Hierarchy Construction

In the context of systematic desensitization, preliminary relaxation training typically takes from five to seven sessions. During this time, the therapist and patient construct one or more hierarchies for desensitization, taking care to work on the hierarchies while the patient is not relaxed. Assessment will have provided the requisite information to begin hierarchy construction, including complete and detailed lists of the various objects/events that are feared as well as a provisional arrangement of the objects/events into groups or clusters. Each group of feared objects/events should have a common thread, because it will ultimately be used to arrange a desensitization hierarchy, an increasingly fearsome listing of scenarios that describe personal encounters with the objects/events of interest.

The most common types of desensitization hierarchies are spatiotemporal hierarchies and thematic hierarchies. In spatiotemporal hierarchies, increasingly fearsome scenarios are produced by decreasing the distances and/or times that separate the patient from targeted encounters. For example, the distance to a dentist's office can be reduced from "You're at home in the living room" to "You're a block away from the office, you see . . ." to "You're in the parking lot, you see . . ." to "You're in the waiting room, you see . . ." The time until a dental appointment, in turn, can be decreased from days, to hours, to minutes. In thematic hierarchies, increasingly fearsome scenarios are produced by using successive narratives that capture the themes more and more immediately. For example, if fear of dental treatment rests on a claustrophobic fear of restriction, then the successive scenarios might be "You're in the waiting room, and soon you must be seated in the dental chair;" "You're in the dental chair, the assistant is placing a bib around your neck;" "You're in the dental chair, the dentist is drilling, his face is a foot away from yours."

Forming meaningful fear clusters and developing hierarchies from them sometimes requires creativity. Guidelines for forming fear clusters are available in Wolpe's various books, and groupings can be formed based on factor-analytic studies of omnibus fear inventories. Wolpe, for example, arranged 14 different fears into the categories of acrophobia, agoraphobia, claustrophobia, and fears related to illness. New information that can be brought to bear in forming fear hierarchies for systematic desensitization is, of course, always being produced by the evolving behavior therapy literature. For one example, there is information to the effect that claustrophobia can be broken down into partially independent fears of restriction and of suffocation. The latter fears would make up clusters that differ somewhat from a cluster formed around "claustrophobia."

The most widely used procedure for developing hierarchies for systematic desensitization was developed by Wolpe and is called "SUDs scaling." In SUDs scaling, the patient is first taught to assign a numerical value of 0 SUDs to signify absolute calmness and to assign a value of 100 SUDs to signify the most extreme fear imaginable. Each scenario that might be used in a given hierarchy is then assigned a SUDs value, and the scenarios are ordered so as to be increasingly fearsome. Next, scenarios are dropped and new ones added until the first scenario on the hierarchy is assigned a value near 0 SUDs, the zenithal scenario receives a value near 100 SUDs, and none of those in-between differs by more than 10 to 15 SUDs from those adjacent to it. Ideally, the hierarchy samples the clustered objects/events or themes adequately, and each scene is detailed and concrete or thematically clear.

Pairing Relaxation With Graded Visualization

As noted above, systematic desensitization entails relaxing and visualizing fearsome scenarios in such a way as to remain relaxed. Treatment proceeds typically after five or six sessions of relaxation training, during which the patient has learned to relax quickly. There are two well-established procedures. In the "orthodox" procedure, the patient is first exposed to abbreviated relaxation training. The therapist then instructs the patient to visualize the least aversive hierarchy scenario for 10 to 15 seconds and to signal with an elevated index finger if the visualization is accompanied by discomfort or fear. If fear is not signaled, then the patient is instructed to relax and, later, to visualize the scenario again. If the visualization occasions no fear on this second trial, then a 30- to 60-second period for relaxing follows and the next scenario on the hierarchy is presented for visualization. This process is repeated again and again as progressively more fearsome scenarios are visualized. Should the patient signal that fear is present, he or she is instructed to stop visualizing and relax. After allowing time for relaxation, the scenario is visualized again. If the fear signal recurs, then the therapist repeats the previously desensitized scenario and, after relaxation, repeats the troublesome scene. If the patient still signals the presence of fear, then the therapist and patient spontaneously create a new scenario that stands between the troublesome scenario and the last calmly visualized one. Orthodox imaginal desensitization is complete when the most fearsome scenarios are visualized with no signal of fear.

An "improved" procedure for systematic desensitization begins with abbreviated relaxation practice. Then, the patient is instructed to visualize the appropriate scenario and to signal, by raising an index finger, when the imagery is clear. The therapist allows 10 to 15 seconds after a signal for the patient to continue visualizing fearsome material, then instructs the patient to drop the images and orally report a SUDs rating of the fear experienced during visualization. In this procedure, visualization of each fearsome scenario is repeated until the patient reports 0 SUDs. "Improved" desensitization in imagination is complete

when the patient visualizes the zenithal scenario(s) without reporting any experience of fear.

Beyond the basic techniques (above), there are a number of important considerations at the level of procedure. The following subset of those recommendations demonstrate the flexibility of the approach: (a) multiple hierarchies should be dealt with simultaneously; no more than three or four scenarios in any given hierarchy should be dealt with during a single session; (b) once a particularly troublesome scenario has been visualized calmly, it should be visualized repeatedly before the next one is attempted; (c) throughout desensitization, the patient should be reminded to include himself or herself as a participant in the scenarios; and (d) the patient should be encouraged to participate in the targeted real-life scenarios after they have been imaginally desensitized.

RESEARCH BASIS

There is a very large research literature devoted to systematic desensitization; most of it was produced during the 1960s and 1970s. While many reports can be criticized as showing methodological defects, the clear picture that emerges is that systematic desensitization ameliorates fear behaviors reliably, but consensus does not exist regarding how that happens. Below, the research bases of systematic desensitization are summarized in narratives about animal models, early clinical reports, the first "controlled experiments," and analogue investigations.

Animal Studies

Wolpe reported his pioneering studies of fear reduction via reciprocal inhibition during the late 1940s and early 1950s. He began his research by showing that neurotic behavior in cats (motor responses such as crouching, autonomic responses such as piloerection) could be readily produced by presenting tones followed by high-voltage, low-amperage shocks soon after the animals were placed in a suitable apparatus. The demonstration that signaled shock presentation was sufficient to produce neurotic behaviors convinced Wolpe that the neurotic behaviors were a consequence of aversive Pavlovian conditioning.

Wolpe also dealt with the problem of treating experimental neuroses in cats. First, he tried to extinguish the animals' fear behaviors by unreinforced exposures to the tone and apparatus, that is, exposures without shock. The animals' fear behaviors persisted even after many unreinforced exposures, some with long durations. During the work, he observed that animals did not eat in the presence of apparatus cues even when they were food deprived. Nor would the animals eat after the sounding of the tone that had signaled shock presentation. He reasoned that alimentary responses were being inhibited by conditioned-anxiety responses. He also reasoned that if conditioned anxiety inhibited eating in some circumstances, then eating should inhibit conditioned anxiety if the requisite circumstances were contrived. He then set about to contrive circumstances in which eating would inhibit conditioned anxiety.

Wolpe began by offering food to the animals in the experimental room and on subsequent days offering food in rooms that differed increasingly from the experimental room. When a room was found in which the animal would eat, the animal was fed several meat pellets. As eating continued in that room, anxiety behaviors disappeared gradually. When tested the next day in the same room, the animals showed no anxiety behaviors. When tested that same day in a room that was somewhat more similar to the original experimental room, the animals showed fewer-than-expected anxiety behaviors. On succeeding days, the animals were fed in a series of rooms that were increasingly similar to the room and apparatus used during the original conditioning; care was taken to allow anxiety behaviors to subside in each. Ultimately, the anxiety behaviors that had been conditioned to the apparatus cues were eliminated completely by feeding the animals in the apparatus. Because the tone that had preceded the original shocks still functioned as a conditioned-fear signal, it was necessary to treat responsivity to the tone separately. Again, repeated presentations of the tone without accompanying shock failed to extinguish fear behavior. Fear was eliminated by feeding the animal at progressively shortened distances from ongoing tonal stimuli.

Later work with animal models has shown, of course, that unreinforced exposure to fear signals can by itself eliminate conditioned fear behavior. (One wonders how different the history of behavior therapy might have been had Wolpe's attempts at extinction succeeded.) At the same time, Dennis Delprato and others have shown that fostering competing behaviors in the presence of fear signals can facilitate fear reduction above and beyond the effects of exposure, provided that the competing behaviors do not impede attention to the signals.

Early Clinical Reports

Wolpe began reporting clinical success with systematic desensitization via a series of papers published from 1952 to 1962. Similar reports provided by Arnold Lazarus from 1957 to 1965 shadowed Wolpe's papers. Gordon Paul reviewed these and other reports in 1969.

In his influential 1958 book, *Psychotherapy by Reciprocal Inhibition,* Wolpe reported that nearly 90% of 210 patients were either improved or much improved after being treated with his new methods. Paul later showed that methods other than systematic desensitization were used to treat a number of those 210 patients. He reanalyzed Wolpe's original reports, identified 85 cases that had been exclusively treated with systematic desensitization, and reported success in 78 (92%) of those 85 cases. He also reported that follow-up contacts with 21 patients after periods of 6 to 48 months yielded no report of relapse. The effects of systematic desensitization were gauged, in some cases, by direct observation and by reports from unbiased others. However, "success" was generally defined as improved self-reported responses in the presence of previously anxiety-eliciting stimuli.

Through the first half of the 1960s, Lazarus provided very careful case reports and summaries for a total of 220 patients with whom systematic desensitization had been used. The array of presenting problems included social anxieties, generalized anxiety, panic, and numerous phobias, including agoraphobia. Lazarus counted 190 of these 220 diverse cases as successes based on therapists' Likert-type ratings of patients' functioning in several adaptively significant arenas. He also acquired corroborative reports from referral sources in 70% of his cases.

The successes reported by Wolpe and Lazarus prompted numerous other reports about treating anxiety-related conditions with systematic desensitization. By 1969, Paul was able to locate 51 separate reports of individual cases or clinic series and several reports of systematic desensitization applied in groups. Successful outcomes were not universal in these reports, but there were relatively few failures.

The First "Controlled" Experiments

The earliest behavior therapists sought scientific support for the efficacy of their treatments. Thus, when early experimental work done by Peter Lang and by Paul provided that support, it received unprecedented attention.

In 1963 and again in 1965, Lang and his colleagues reported early experiments in which snake-fearful college students were exposed to standardized forms of systematic desensitization. Altogether, the experiments achieved impressive control over sources of unwanted variance in the dependent-variable measures, and they succeeded in supporting the argument that temporal pairing of muscular relaxation and graded imaging of snake-related scenarios was specifically responsible for observed reductions in avoidance and reported reductions in fear of snakes. They also provided 6-month follow-up data supporting the specific effect of systematic desensitization. Overall, 15 participants who nearly completed the standard course of systematic desensitization improved significantly, by contrast with 10 participants who did not complete the standard course of desensitization, with 10 participants exposed to a procedural control for experimental demand/placebo influences, and with 11 participants who served as untreated controls.

In 1966, Paul reported an experiment that remains a methodological reference point nearly four decades later and that still provides the most convincing available evidence of the specific effectiveness of systematic desensitization. The participants were 96 college students, most of whom would now be diagnosed as having generalized social phobia with particular problems in the domain of public speaking. After extensive assessment, each of 74 participants was assigned to one of four experimental conditions that, taken together, served to compare the effects of systematic desensitization with those of insight-oriented psychotherapy, under conditions that controlled for influence from experimenter (therapist) bias and from major extratherapeutic sources of variance. Fear during a standardized public speaking task was assessed by self-reports, by demonstrably reliable behavioral observation, and by pulse rate and palmar-sweat measures. The group treated with systematic desensitization improved significantly more than did any other group on fear measures in all three domains. Posttreatment differences were maintained as judged by self-reports acquired 2 years later.

Analogue Experiments

By 1970, the behavior therapy movement was growing, and the intellectual tone was optimistic. In this context, the early experiments reported by Lang and his colleagues spawned scores of experiments in which pretreatment and posttreatment measures of fear of snakes among college students were used to evaluate the effects of systematic desensitization. Some of the experiments compared the effects of systematic desensitization with the effects of competing behavior influence packages, notably implosive therapy and imaginal flooding. Most of the experiments compared the effects of systematic desensitization with those of procedural variations that were interesting in one way or another. Many questions were asked. Is muscular relaxation training necessary for fear reduction with systematic desensitization? Must the imaging instructions proceed along a graded, increasingly fearsome hierarchy of scenarios? Can the effects of systematic desensitization be influenced by pretreatment instructions about what outcomes to expect?

Notwithstanding the effort and ingenuity that went into the so-called snake desensitization studies, they afford very little by way of characterizing the clinical efficacy of systematic desensitization. This is true for at least two reasons. First, in the intellectual climate of the day, the efficacy of systematic desensitization was virtually axiomatic; therefore, most of the research was intended to answer other questions, such as questions about the "active ingredients" or causal mechanism(s) that explain the success of the approach. Second, the quality of systematic desensitization research with snake-fearful participants fell off sharply very soon after Lang's original reports; since the early 1970s, the external validity of empirical generalizations based on orthodox "snake desensitization studies" has been suspect.

RELEVANT TARGET POPULATIONS AND EXCEPTIONS

During the past 40 years, clinicians have found numerous and diverse applications for systematic desensitization and assorted procedural variants. The most frequent applications have been to various specific phobias, but applications to social phobia and to other anxiety disorders certainly have not been rare. The specific phobias treated successfully according to case reports have included representatives of all four *DSM* subtypes. A few examples are phobias related to death, injury, cancer, heart attack, injections, sanitary napkins, childbirth, hurricanes, tornadoes, thunder, lightning, atomic holocaust, various animals, birds, insects, reptiles, automobiles, buses, and airplanes. Applications to social phobia have included problems as such shyness, minimal dating, test anxiety, public-speaking anxiety, and authority figures. There have also been creative uses of systematic desensitization in treating anxiety disorders such as obsessive-compulsive disorder and in treating various disorders that are sometimes anxiety-related, such as sexual dysfunctions, asthma, kleptomania, speech disturbances, chronic diarrhea, insomnia, and nightmare behavior.

Notwithstanding early clinical successes based on diverse applications of systematic desensitization, the range of appropriate clinical targets has narrowed markedly over the years. The main factor in such narrowing has been the advent and success of treatment approaches grounded in in vivo exposure coupled with cognitive alteration. The treatment of panic disorder via interoceptive exposure coupled with cognitive restructuring is one example. The treatment of obsessive-compulsive disorder via exposure plus response prevention is another.

Even in cases of specific phobias, in vivo exposure is the treatment of choice when it is feasible. And, in some cases, rapidly effective treatment based on the buildup of positive cognitions about the feared object/event may well replace in vivo exposure as the preferred treatment. Therefore, systematic desensitization is indicated when in vivo treatment is not feasible and possibly when a buildup of positive cognitions is, per se, not expected to be beneficial. Systematic desensitization is useful also as a lead-up to in vivo exposure.

COMPLICATIONS

Some of the complications that can arise in using systematic desensitization are implied in the narrative about assessment. A patient might not have the requisite imagery skills, might not be able to relax, or might have injuries or medical conditions that restrict the muscle-tensing exercises available. Such factors pose problems related to the mechanics of treatment; other "mechanical" problems are discussed in the narrative (above) about the orthodox procedure for pairing imagery with relaxation. Some patients have large numbers of disabling fears, numbers that render systematic desensitization impractical. Creative hierarchy construction often can overcome the problem of multiple fears, but sometimes the patient's problems are best conceptualized and treated in some other way.

Sometimes fear returns after successful treatment, especially when there have been no opportunities for confronting feared objects/events in the natural environment. Return of fear can be disheartening to the patient, so some clinicians prepare patients for that possibility. Booster treatments can be used when fear returns.

CASE ILLUSTRATION

Background

"Jane" was an undergraduate student at a public university in Mississippi. She was engaged to marry "Paul," who was an undergraduate student at the same school. Because of her church affiliation, the couple had participated in premarital counseling. One set of issues that emerged revolved around Paul's interest in guns and hunting and whether guns would be present in the home.

Jane and two sisters were reared in the urban Northeast. Various aspects of childhood and adolescent life had eventuated in Jane's fear of guns. Among these were parental conversations at meal times about gun violence reported in the newspaper and a steady diet of gun violence portrayed in crime- and police-oriented television programs that were watched regularly by the girls' father. In addition, there was one occasion, when Jane was 9 or 10 years of age, on which Jane and her sisters were restricted to their house after a series of drive-by shootings in a neighborhood not far away. There were no guns in the home, and the mother's explanation was that "guns are dangerous."

Paul and his younger brother were reared in Mississippi. The two brothers began playing with toy guns during early childhood and began hunting deer and ducks with their father and grandfather during adolescence. Guns, gun-related magazines, and other outdoor items were a part of everyday life in the home; even when hunting seasons were closed, the guns were regularly dismantled and oiled as a hobby shared by the boys and their father. A loaded revolver was kept in the parents' bedroom; from an early age, the boys were told it was there, it was loaded, and it was not to be touched.

Premarital counseling revealed that Paul was unwilling to give up his guns and related activities and believed strongly that guns were crucial to home safety. Jane agreed, therefore, to try to overcome her fear of guns. Paul, in turn, agreed to do everything possible to minimize gun-related danger. The issue of gun involvement in the lives of forthcoming children was tabled. At that point, the referral for behavior therapy was made.

Assessment

Because the referral had a narrow focus, only cursory attempts were made to characterize Jane in terms of related difficulties or psychopathology. Nothing that was troubling came to light. At the time of this case, there were no diagnostic criteria for specific (then "simple") phobia and no interview structures that were generally recommended. Therefore, the first interview was open-ended, directed mainly to characterizing Jane's fear of guns. As noted earlier, the characteristics of guns that influenced her fear and the nature of the fear itself were of interest.

Two aspects of the appearance of guns that influenced Jane's fear were detected during the interview: Handguns were more frightening than long guns; "black" (blued) guns were more menacing than "silver" guns (nickel-plated, stainless). Pictures of guns were then introduced to aide the interview, and it was determined that handguns with short barrels were more menacing that those with long barrels. Of course, loaded guns were more frightening than were unloaded guns. Subjective dread, perceived breathlessness, and muscle "weakness" typified her self-described fear.

Jane was asked also to recall and report as many details as possible from her last complete mealtime. She reported concrete descriptions, including the colors of the tabletop and dishes and the textures and tastes of some of the foods. Finally, Jane reported significant subjective discomfort during various imagery exercises related to guns and to Paul handling guns in her presence. Taken together, the imagery tests suggested that she was a good candidate for an imagery-oriented treatment such as systematic desensitization.

Enabling arrangements had been made with the campus security office so that Paul was permitted to bring three (disabled) guns to Jane's second interview. The guns were arrayed on tables at the end of a walkway that was then being used for research-related behavioral avoidance tests. Jane was able to traverse the walkway and visually examine the weapons up close; she was not able to touch any of them, and she described the experience as both frightening and disheartening. After a suitable interval, another test was conducted in which Paul sat in a chair at the end of the walkway and held a short-barreled "black" pistol. Jane's walkway behavior was the same.

Relaxation Training and Hierarchy Construction

Treatment commenced on the third visit. Each session began with relaxation training and continued, after three sessions, with activities related to constructing a hierarchy for systematic desensitization. Relaxation training was conducted in a sound-attenuated room and was based on 16, then 4 groups of muscles; it was conducted using transcripts from a widely used manual. There were 7 sessions. 4 sessions were devoted to training based on 16 muscle groups, and 3 sessions were based on 4 muscle groups. All sessions were conducted "live" while Jane was seated in a reclining chair.

After the relaxation portion of the sixth and seventh training sessions, time was devoted to hierarchy construction. In this case, SUDs scaling was not used. Instead, 30 scenes of guns and scenarios involving Paul handling guns were typed on index cards, then used in a paired-comparison procedure. For each pair of scenes/scenarios, Jane rated the image that was most frightening. In two sessions, most of the possible paired comparisons were made several times, and scenes/scenarios were dropped and added until Jane was able to order 22 scenes/scenarios in a smooth gradient of fearsomeness. Among the scenes were, "Thinking about a safe with guns in it in the corner of the living room"; "Seeing Paul just home from hunting holding a long gun in the back yard"; "Seeing Paul sitting at the kitchen table cleaning parts of a silver pistol with a long barrel"; "Seeing Paul handling an unloaded black pistol that has a short barrel"; "Uncovering a loaded pistol in the bedside table."

Systematic Desensitization and Assessment of Treatment

Systematic desensitization was initiated during the 8th session and continued through the 12th. Each session began with four-muscle-group relaxation and continued with the orthodox procedure (above) for systematic desensitization. Each hierarchy item was visualized at least twice consecutively without an anxiety signal before the next was used. Several initially troublesome items were visualized several times after relaxed visualization had been accomplished. New internuncial items were developed as needed during the sessions and were also visualized several times before progress up the hierarchy was continued.

Jane was encouraged to also actually engage in scenarios that had been calmly visualized; Paul was a cooperative assistant vis-à-vis those scenarios that involved his presence. Jane was praised lavishly when she reported success with such in vivo exercises. A second set of behavioral tests, conducted during a 13th session, showed that Jane could handle each of the three test guns briefly without reporting fear and that she could be comfortable when Paul was handling them in her presence. Jane voiced confidence that she was on her way to tolerating guns in the home so long as they were kept and handled safely.

—*F. Dudley McGlynn*

See also: *Classical Conditioning (Vol. I); Relaxation Strategies (Vol. I); Systematic Desensitization With Children and Adolescents (Vol. II)*

Suggested Readings

Goldfried, M. R., & Davison, G. C. (1976). *Clinical behavior therapy.* New York: Holt, Rinehart & Winston.

McGlynn, F. D., Mealiea, W. L., & Landau, D. L. (1981). The current status of systematic desensitization. *Clinical Psychology Review, 1,* 149–179.

Paul, G. L. (1969). Outcome of systematic desensitization I: Background, procedures, and uncontrolled reports of individual treatment. In C. M. Franks (Ed.), *Behavior therapy: Appraisal and status* (pp. 63–104). New York: McGraw-Hill.

Wolpe, J. (1958). *Psychotherapy by reciprocal inhibition.* Stanford, CA: Stanford University Press.

Wolpe, J. (1990). *The practice of behavior therapy* (4th ed.). Elmsford, New York: Pergamon Press.

T

TERMINATION

DESCRIPTION OF STRATEGY

Termination is the ending of therapy. Ideally, it should provide the capstone of an intervention process that has alleviated the client's complaints: a summary of the skills that have been learned, a reminder and rehearsal of how these skills may be used in future situations to prevent a relapse of symptoms, an invitation to return if difficulties arise in future, and a good-bye. In practice, however, termination often does not come at a natural or successful ending of treatment. Some terminations are forced and occur because of external circumstances that may be beyond the control of either therapist or client. For example, insurance companies dictate termination by limiting number of sessions they will cover. Thus, termination must occur after a certain number of sessions, whether or not the participants believe that their work is done. Interns and practicum trainees frequently must leave training sites before clients have met their therapeutic goals. Unexpected events, such as job changes and personal emergencies that bring a premature ending to therapy, can occur in the lives of clients and therapists. Also, sometimes clients just leave treatment unexpectedly, thus precluding any termination wrap-up. This entry discusses the various ways that clients arrive at termination and specifies what termination sessions should address.

Clients typically come to therapy with particular symptoms that they wish to alleviate. Sometimes these are well-delineated problems, such as specific phobias or anxieties. At other times, clients present with more general life problems, such as depression. The initial goal of cognitive-behavioral therapy is to eliminate or greatly reduce these presenting symptoms. In the case of a rather circumscribed problem, such as public-speaking anxiety, for example, therapeutic goals may be highly specific, and thus it is easy to ascertain when they have been reached. For example, a client who experiences debilitating anxiety about public speaking at work may, after desensitization, be able to routinely give presentations to his or her company's clients about the company's new product lines while experiencing relatively little anxiety. In the case of a more general concern, such as depression, cognitive restructuring coupled with homework assignments requiring the client to become more physically active may result in a reduction in depressive symptoms, with the client reporting that he or she is feeling generally happier or more optimistic. Alleviation of these presenting problems may be a time to terminate treatment. Indeed, if insurance coverage is available only for the time it takes to reach these initial goals, there may be no choice but to terminate. But while termination may take place at this juncture, it is not necessarily advisable, nor is it always what clients would like to do.

For many clients, the presenting problem is merely the "tip of the iceberg"—the life problem that caused most concern and drove the client to seek help. The client who sought help for public-speaking anxiety may also have comorbid problems that need therapeutic attention, such as other anxieties, procrastination, marital difficulties, or other problems that affect the quality of life. The person who suffered from depression may have become depressed initially because of a lack of assertiveness with friends and colleagues.

The point is that most clients have comorbid concerns, and cognitive-behavioral therapy can provide clients with strategies (i.e., problem solving, cognitive restructuring, social skills, relaxation, etc.) that can be used to deal successfully with a number of difficulties and life circumstances. Thus, after presenting concerns have diminished, it is appropriate for the therapist to ask about or the client to suggest other issues that could benefit from therapy. Treatment goals should be regularly evaluated and reformulated to address comorbidities and other life issues. In general, the goal of cognitive-behavioral therapy is to teach clients coping skills and help them to recognize which skills can be helpful in what situations, so that they may use these skills independently in their daily lives.

This does not mean that therapy should last many months or years. Cognitive-behavioral therapy is goal oriented, and when goals have been met, it is time to terminate. Thus, clients learn coping skills and apply them to problem situations that occur in their lives, with therapists' prompting and monitoring. Therapists praise the successful application of skills, and clients develop a sense of efficacy regarding the use of these skills as well as the ability to use them independently. At this point, the goals of therapy have been reached. While termination is often a mutual decision, clients frequently take the lead in this process by indicating to therapists that they believe they are able to cope on their own, thus beginning the termination phase of therapy. If it has not happened already, at this point, it is suggested that treatment be phased out by scheduling appointments with greater amounts of time between them. This can also facilitate client self-efficacy by allowing skill application with less therapist monitoring.

During termination sessions, the treatment is reviewed, with particular emphasis on effecting coping skills. Relapse prevention is an important part of termination. Old habits die hard, and it is likely that posttherapy, clients will demonstrate some maladaptive behaviors in response to situations that caused them trouble in the past. Clients should be prepared for these occasions by being instructed to view them as lapses rather than relapses. Because clients have developed coping strategies to deal with problematic situations, lapses are less likely to occur. When they do occur, however, clients are instructed to use strategies that helped relieve the symptoms in the first

place. In termination sessions, clients and therapists anticipate future tricky situations for clients and role-play these. This gives clients the opportunity to practice coping skills for situations that perhaps have not, but might, arise. Clients are given the opportunity to summarize their treatment experience. Therapists extend an invitation for clients to return to treatment in future should the need arise.

Although the relationship between cognitive-behavioral therapists and their clients is not usually as intense as relationships between therapists who subscribe to other orientations that focus more on the association between therapist and client as well as encourage client dependency on the therapist, there is a bonding that comes from having collaborated on the resolution of difficulties that are generally highly personal to clients. Usually, the longer treatment has lasted, the stronger the bond. Also, clients who have sought help for intense interpersonal issues, such as clients with borderline personality disorder, will develop intense connections to their therapists. Termination is a time to lessen these bonds. Therapists should acknowledge the pleasure derived from both the therapeutic collaboration and the knowledge that clients now can apply these coping skills independently. Follow-up visits or phone calls in the more distant future may be scheduled.

When therapy termination is prematurely forced by insurance constraints, relocations, or other situations, therapists should follow the above procedures as closely as possible. When external circumstances will limit the number of sessions, therapists should notify clients of the date that sessions will end and plan the therapy, including termination, accordingly. Thus, if number of sessions allocated allows only enough time for reduction of presenting symptomatology, therapists should confine their work to these symptoms. Therapists should also strongly encourage clients who need further therapy to continue it when circumstances permit. If termination cannot be done in person, a telephone session is advisable. It is important that clients have closure on what has transpired, and a plan for the future.

RESEARCH BASIS

Despite the importance that most therapists place on termination, there has been almost no research on the topic. The few empirical studies that exist have examined what typically takes place during termination and how clients and therapists feel about this. There are no studies linking therapy outcome with termination experiences or comparing terminations by therapists of differing theoretical orientations.

Research indicates that termination occupies about one tenth of treatment sessions. In other words, if therapy were 20 sessions long, 2 of those sessions would be spent discussing termination issues. Clients typically initiate termination, and research suggests that the majority of clients return for therapy at some time in the future. Thus, termination with most clients is a temporary ending to treatment.

For the majority of clients, particularly when therapy has been successful, termination is a relatively pleasant experience. Clients report feelings of accomplishment, excitement, and gratitude but also express some anxiety and sadness at ending a productive working relationship. Clients involved in less successful treatment express more negative feelings at termination. One study found that clients' negative termination feelings were also associated with greater numbers of sessions; thus, the longer the treatment, the more difficult the ending. When therapy has been less successful, clients report more negative reactions. Therapists' feelings over termination tend to mirror those of their clients, with more positive feelings associated with more successful cases and feelings of frustration and anger associated with less successful cases. Termination is harder for clients and therapists who have experienced difficult losses in their lives. Termination is also more difficult when clients have been diagnosed with narcissistic or borderline personality disorders.

The most common activities during termination include summarizing what went on in therapy, assessing goal attainment, sharing feelings about the therapy, and planning for the future. When therapy has been less successful, therapists tend to do less reviewing of the treatment and less examination of clients' feelings about ending treatment than in more successful cases.

RELEVANT TARGET POPULATIONS AND EXCEPTIONS

It is both ethically and therapeutically desirable to provide all clients with a treatment review and a plan for the future. Termination is an integral aspect of cognitive-behavioral therapy. Relapse prevention and continued enhancement of clients' self-efficacy serve to facilitate and sustain treatment gains. Without this

termination activity, temporary lapses of symptoms could become relapses. If outside circumstances dictate that therapy must end suddenly, therapists should make every effort to provide clients with termination sessions. If insurance funds are precipitately cut off, this may mean that therapists see clients for an additional few sessions at greatly reduced rates. If clients must suddenly relocate, termination may be conducted by phone. When otherwise satisfied clients just quit coming for sessions, therapists should contact them to determine why they left and do a termination session or sessions in person or by phone.

The 2002 ethical standards of the American Psychological Association (APA) stipulate that therapists must provide termination wrap-ups "except where precluded by actions of clients." Some dissatisfied clients leave therapy abruptly and angrily, making it clear that they want nothing further to do with treatment. These clients may threaten or initiate lawsuits against their therapists or may make or carry out threats of violence or harassment against therapists. It is not advisable to try to contact these clients for termination sessions. Depending upon the situation, it may be more advisable for therapists in these circumstances to contact their lawyers or law enforcement officials.

COMPLICATIONS

APA ethical standards indicate that therapy should be terminated when a client "is not likely to benefit or is being harmed by continued service." When therapy is not successful, termination should not take the course outlined above. It is not helpful to rehash procedures that did not work, but it is appropriate for clients and therapists to express their regret and frustration that treatment did not go better. In these cases, it is important for therapists to emphasize that just because these particular therapists and coping strategies did not help, it does not mean that these clients would not be helped by other therapists or interventions. It is certainly not desirable for clients who need help to give up on therapy. Therapists and clients should consider what other options for treatment the client finds desirable, and clients should be referred to other service providers. Therapists should follow up to see whether the referrals were satisfactory or whether the clients desire another referral.

As indicated above, clients with diagnoses of borderline or narcissistic personality disorder, who have difficult interpersonal relationships, also tend to be more difficult than other clients to both treat and terminate with. If treatment has been successful, these clients' behaviors may have changed substantially, making the termination process easier. But it should be noted that clients with these diagnoses frequently have trouble ending relationships. Termination with these clients should include coping skills designed to diminish inappropriate relationship-ending symptoms. Because cognitive-behavioral therapists focus on clients' coping strategies, they probably are less likely than are therapists whose theoretical and treatment focus emphasizes transference or client-therapist relationship issues to encounter problematic terminations with clients with these diagnoses.

CASE ILLUSTRATION

"Janet" was a 28-year-old, unmarried graduate student in psychology. She sought help because she continually procrastinated when trying to write her dissertation proposal. She found it easy to distract herself with other things that she needed to do, and days went by without her having written anything. She avoided going to the psychology department, fearing that she would encounter her advisor, who would be upset with her for her lack of progress.

Her therapist had Janet set daily goals involving work on her dissertation, which started off small and got increasingly larger as therapy evolved. She rewarded herself for attaining these goals and kept a chart of her progress. Within a month, she was progressing nicely on her dissertation but mentioned that she feared a relapse of her old behaviors when she visited her highly critical parents during Thanksgiving break. Her father in particular criticized Janet's choice of occupations. He had wanted her to work at his company and take over for him when he retired. As far as he was concerned, Janet had been wasting her time since college graduation by pursuing a degree that he considered useless. Whenever Janet spoke with her parents on the phone, they criticized her career choice, and whenever she visited them, she came away discouraged and depressed. A combination of cognitive restructuring and assertiveness training helped Janet get through her Thanksgiving recess with less distress than usual. After returning to university, Janet continued to use these skills when talking with her parents and when dealing with others who were critical of or placed unfair demands on her.

After another 2 months of treatment, Janet indicated that she felt comfortable using her newly learned skills in a variety of situations. Sessions were decreased to once every other week for three visits. During these sessions, she and the therapist role-played potentially problematic situations that were likely to arise in future, reviewed her coping skills, and pointed to her progress. The therapist told her that she should feel free to return to treatment in future if needed. Janet thanked the therapist, and both acknowledged what had been a productive and fulfilling working relationship.

—*Georgiana Schick Tryon*

See also: *Behavioral Case Formulation (Vol. I); Behavioral Consultation (Vol. I); Behavioral Working Alliance (Vol. I)*

Suggested Readings

Gelso, C. J., & Woodhouse, S. S. (2002). The termination of psychotherapy: What research tells us about the process of ending treatment. In G. S. Tryon (Ed.), *Counseling based on process research: Applying what we know* (pp. 344–369). Boston: Allyn & Bacon.

Goldfried, M. R. (2002). A cognitive-behavioral perspective on termination. *Journal of Psychotherapy Integration, 12,* 364–372.

Marx, J. A., & Gelso, C. J. (1987). Termination of individual counseling in a university center. *Journal of Counseling Psychology, 34,* 3–9.

Quintana, S. M., & Holahan, W. (1992). Termination in short-term counseling: Comparison of successful and unsuccessful cases. *Journal of Counseling Psychology, 39,* 299–305.

THERAPEUTIC RELATIONSHIP

DESCRIPTION OF THE STRATEGY

Psychodynamic and client-centered psychotherapies have a long history of recognizing the importance of the therapeutic relationship. However, this is not the case for behavior therapy. Behaviorism emerged in the 1950s from dissatisfaction with traditional approaches to psychotherapy. Behavior therapists sought to apply techniques derived directly from learning theory and from learning laboratories. It was widely accepted by behaviorists that the application of the established principles of learning was all that was necessary to facilitate change. A number of factors are likely responsible for this omission: (1) In the laboratory, the relationship between scientist and experimental subject was not relevant, so the translation from lab to clinic did not focus on relationship; (2) specifying the therapeutic relationship objectively is quite difficult; and (3) early behavior therapists may have wished to disassociate from less scientific psychotherapeutic approaches and their foci. For these and other reasons, early proponents of behavior therapy de-emphasized the therapeutic relationship.

Emergence of attention to the therapeutic relationship in behavior therapy can be seen in the writings of individual pioneers of the behavior therapy movement. Joseph Wolpe, for example, gave virtually no attention to the therapeutic relationship in his writings from the early 1950s. By the late 1960s, he was suggesting that a nonjudgmental attitude facilitates information gathering and should continue throughout treatment. By the 1980s, Wolpe contended that a therapeutic relationship characterized by warmth and positive regard is a customary component of behavior therapy.

Cognitive-behavioral approaches also tended to expend far more energy describing the intervention strategies than the relationship that would be the context for those interventions. Albert Ellis, founder of rational-emotive behavior therapy, purported that a warm therapeutic relationship was preferable but not necessary for treatment. Aaron T. Beck asserted that cognitive therapists ought to approach treatment as a collaborative effort, in which we treat the client like a colleague. In his description of cognitive therapy, Beck stated that the initial sessions of treatment should focus on initiating a relationship, gathering information, and providing some relief from symptoms. However, he provided few details regarding how to develop the relationship, what interpersonal factors are important, and what is the mechanism by which the relationship facilitates change.

Wide recognition of the importance of the therapeutic relationship in behavior therapy began in the latter part of the 1970s. It was at this time that the possible influence of the therapeutic relationship became more accepted and many behavior therapists came to regard both technical skills and interpersonal sensitivity as important in therapy. Some summary papers and psychotherapy texts published in the late 1970s and early 1980s included detailed descriptions of interviewing methods that would facilitate or enhance the therapeutic alliance. At this time, the client-therapist relationship was commonly described as a "nonspecific"

factor. That is, the relationship was seen as a factor that could reasonably impact the outcome of therapy, although it was not supported as an essential component of treatment.

Current psychotherapy books and treatment manuals include sections on the therapeutic relationship in behavior therapy and address interpersonal considerations more frequently than was common in the past. Furthermore, some contemporary behavior therapies give special attention to the therapeutic relationship, incorporating it as a major component of treatment (e.g., acceptance and commitment therapy, dialectical behavior therapy, functional analytic psychotherapy, integrative behavioral couples therapy).

There is a paucity of systematic empirical investigations examining how the client-therapist relationship facilitates change. Some behaviorally oriented psychologists are attempting to fill this gap by delineating the possible roles that the therapeutic relationship may play in therapy. While theoretically compelling, the validity of each explanation remains uncertain until directly relevant data are available.

For example, a number of behaviorally oriented psychologists assert that the therapeutic relationship is similar to anesthesia for surgery. That is, a positive client-therapist relationship makes the confrontation of painful material less aversive and makes change easier. According to this perspective, the therapeutic relationship should not be the focus of therapy unless it is directly interfering with treatment. Advocates of this viewpoint suggest therapists monitor the client-therapist bond, paying close attention to whether the therapist and the client agree on therapeutic goals and procedures throughout the course of treatment.

Some behavior therapists maintain that the therapeutic relationship functions as a motivator or catalyst: mobilizing client's expectancies, keeping them in therapy, and increasing compliance. They assert that when the client-therapist relationship is collaborative and characterized by respect and regard, the client is more likely to continue with therapy. Others point to the importance of the client-therapist relationship in gathering comprehensive information. They purport that therapy is initially foreign and uncomfortable. Clients may have a number of reservations and be apprehensive to disclose personal information. A therapist that communicates warmth, understanding, and a nonjudgmental attitude will elicit more candid responding. Without rapport, the therapist risks formulating a treatment plan based on incomplete information.

Behaviorists such as Robert Kohlenberg contend that the therapeutic relationship provides useful interpersonal data. They conceptualize the client-therapist interaction as a "sample" of the client's behavior, assuming that a client will engage in behaviors in session that typify his or her interaction or response style outside therapy. The client's in-session behavior, as well as the therapist's reaction to the client, provides valuable information regarding how the client is behaving in his or her natural environment and how others may be reacting.

Some behavior therapists assert that the therapeutic relationship has a larger role in facilitating change. They describe the therapeutic relationship as social reinforcement, a contextual factor important for learning, or as learning itself. From this perspective, the therapist acts as a discriminative stimulus for a variety of client's responses, and therapy is designed to promote generalization of certain responses to situations occurring in the client's natural environment. The goal is for clients to learn more adaptive behaviors and then engage in those behaviors outside of therapy. The therapist modifies the client's behavior using operant techniques during therapy. Clients acquire an additional learning history from interacting with the therapist throughout treatment, and techniques such as modeling and reinforcement of successive approximations shape adaptive behaviors. This new learning history may be especially important for individuals presenting with severe interpersonal difficulties (e.g., clients that meet *DSM-IV* criteria for a personality disorder). Such clients learn how to be more successful interpersonally by being involved in a real relationship.

The interpersonal context of therapy varies considerably from the interactions that take place in the larger social community. A therapeutic relationship that is characterized by positive regard and understanding creates a context in which a client can more directly contact his or her environment and more efficiently learn new ways of responding. The combination of specific interventions and an environment conducive to learning promotes broader and more flexible behavioral repertoires.

RESEARCH BASIS

Although behavioral research on this issue remained minimal until the 1980s, there are early reports of clients improving as a function of the therapeutic relationship. Some behavior therapists have reported instances in which clients who had positive relationships with their therapists improved before the implementation of specific behavioral interventions. Survey research has also emerged indicating that behavior therapists practice techniques that promote the therapeutic alliance and that clients rate such therapists as being high in interpersonal sensitivity. In addition, clients who have been successful in therapy often report the most important part of treatment was the personal interaction with the therapist.

These findings have stimulated investigations of the impact of the therapeutic relationship on therapy outcome. Results have revealed that one of the most reliable predictors of therapy outcome is the relationship between the client and the therapist. Studies have used a variety of means to assess therapeutic relationship, including ratings of the therapeutic relationship made by the therapist and/or client and independent raters who viewed therapy sessions or listened to audiotaped excerpts from therapy. Generally, good therapeutic relationships correlate positively with successful outcome. Many behavior therapists, therefore, currently view psychotherapy outcome as a joint product of specific techniques and client-therapist relationship variables.

Research on the therapeutic relationship with individuals suffering from simple phobias and obsessive-compulsive disorder provides an interesting example. This research is of particular interest given that the most successful behavioral techniques are those designed to treat anxiety disorders. These studies reveal a positive relationship between the outcome of behavior therapy and the client-therapist relationship. That is, clients who had less positive relationships with their therapists were less successful in treatment, despite the use of techniques known to be effective in treating anxiety disorders. This demonstrates that even given the most robust techniques, interpersonal factors may still mediate outcome.

RELEVANT TARGET POPULATIONS

No existing body of data indicates whether the therapeutic relationship is more or less important for specific client groups. Absent data that are directly relevant, a behavior therapist's actions must be guided by logic, theory, and indirect evidence. Three factors suggest that therapists ought to pay attention to therapeutic relationship regardless of client problem or therapeutic approach. First, most modern behavioral and cognitive-behavioral treatment developers suggest that rapport building is important. Second, attention to this feature of therapy does not add a great deal of time or cost to the therapeutic enterprise and so does not increase the cost for the client or the therapist. Finally, the importance of therapeutic alliance has been an extraordinarily robust finding across therapeutic approaches and client populations. Thus, the balance of costs and benefits, along with the best available data, argue that therapists ought to attend carefully to therapeutic relationship with all clients unless contradictory data emerge.

COMPLICATIONS

The empirical investigation of the therapeutic relationship poses many problems, including operationally defining the relationship and determining suitable measures for variables such as warmth and genuineness. Some behaviorists assert that the instruments typically used to measure therapeutic alliance may be inappropriate, since proponents of other theoretical orientations developed many of these measures. Such measures, developed mostly from client-centered therapy, tend to focus on empathetic responses or facilitative comments. Behavioral researchers, interested in the therapeutic relationship, have made efforts to alleviate concern regarding the appropriateness of alliance measures. They have developed scales, such as the Therapist Client Rating Scale, to measure the therapeutic relationship from a behavioral perspective. Behaviorally oriented measures of the therapeutic alliance typically include an assessment of the level of agreement between the therapist and the client regarding the task and treatment goals. This is not usually included in scales developed from other orientations. However, even with adequate measures, the overwhelming majority of data on the therapeutic alliance are correlational. As a result, it is difficult to determine from these data whether clients improve because the relationship is good or whether the relationship is good because the therapy is benefiting the clients.

CASE ILLUSTRATION

The nature of the interpersonal relationship that is cultivated may vary depending upon the particulars of the behavioral theory that drives treatment. The following is a case treated from an acceptance and commitment therapy (ACT) perspective. As suggested above, ACT is a contemporary behavior therapy that pays considerable attention to the therapeutic relationship as a critical context for intervention. "Susan" was a 46-year-old woman suffering from panic disorder with agoraphobia. Although not housebound, Susan's activity was restricted in a variety of ways. She avoided many environments in which escape would be difficult. She was unable to take any public transportation, could not ride elevators, and avoided any setting in which she was likely to encounter a large crowd. Despite these limitations, she was able to fulfill many of her functions as a homemaker. For example, she was unable to tolerate standing in line at the grocery store when more than one or two people got behind her in line. Her solution to this problem was to shop only very late in the evening, when there were few customers in the store.

At the outset of treatment, Susan's goal for treatment was to eliminate panic attacks. After a careful assessment of the phenomenology of her panic attacks, along with avoided situations, the therapist refocused the aims of treatment from symptom remission to moving in a valued life direction.

Therapist: Susan, I can hear such pain in your story. And I have heard hints in your words that you have experienced losses that are much more important to you than the suffering of the panic itself.

Client: I am not sure what you mean.

Therapist: Susan, one thing we could do is treat the panic directly. We could do this by systematically exposing you to the kinds of things you have feared most. Of course, we would do this gradually, and with your permission. But I also recognize that you are more than merely a panic disorder. This panic has cut into your life. For me to be most useful to you, it would help if I could get a sense of your struggle from the inside. Help me to understand the cost in your life. Are there things you have lost or fear you will lose if this goes on?

Client: My daughter, I guess. That is the worst. I remember a time when she was 12. . . . She had a dance recital. I promised her that I would be there. I went, but I just couldn't make myself go in. She was so disappointed, and I felt so ashamed of myself. She is going to graduate from high school in May and I can't even promise her that I will attend. She hasn't even asked me to come.

Therapist: That is perfect, Susan. That is just what I meant. What if this therapy could be about putting you in that auditorium on graduation day? I don't just mean physically there—checking your pulse, looking at the exits constantly, watching for any signs that a panic attack is going to begin. What if this therapy could be about putting you in that room so that when she walked across the stage and looked out into the audience, you would look back at her and truly be with her in that important moment?

Client: I want to be there so badly, but I just don't see how it is possible. I would do anything to be there.

Therapist: Susan, I cannot guarantee that this will happen. I don't know the future, and our best treatments are not 100% effective. However, I can promise a few things. I can promise that this therapy will be very difficult but that we will not do anything that is difficult unless it serves your values. I am inspired by your willingness to experience your fears in the service of your relationship with your daughter. I understand what you are wanting and I am entirely committed to working toward that with you.

In this transcript, the therapist has done several things that are likely to enhance the therapeutic contract. The therapist has reflected the client's description of pain and has asked for a better sense of the cost of the disorder as it extends into important areas of living. The therapist has shown empathy for the client's most deeply held fears and has made a commitment to work toward the client's most deeply held values. Finally, the therapist has placed the exposure work that is to follow into the context of this shared-values-centered work.

—Kelly G. Wilson and Rhonda M. Merwin

See also: *Behavioral Case Formulation (Vol. I); Treatment Compliance in Cognitive Behavior Therapy (Vol. I); Treatment Failures in Behavior Therapy (Vol. I)*

Suggested Readings

Bergin, A. E., & Garfield, S. L. (Eds.). (1994). *Handbook of psychotherapy and behavior change* (4th ed.). New York: Wiley.

Blaauw, E., & Emmelkamp, P. (1994). The therapeutic relationship: A study of the therapist client rating scale. *Behavioural and Cognitive Psychotherapy, 22,* 25–35.

Follette, W. C., Naugle, A. E., & Callaghan, G. M. (1996). A radical behavioral understanding of the therapeutic relationship in effecting change. *Behavior Therapy, 27,* 623–641.

Ford, J. D. (1978). Therapeutic relationship in behavior therapy: An empirical analysis. *Journal of Clinical and Consulting Psychology, 46*(6), 1302–1314.

Hayes, S. C., Strosahl, K. D., & Wilson, K. G. (1999). *Acceptance and commitment therapy: An experiential approach to behavior change.* New York: Guilford Press.

Kohlenberg, R. J., & Tsai, M. (1991). *Functional analytic psychotherapy: Creating intense and curative relationships.* New York: Plenum Press.

Linehan, M. M. (1988). Perspectives on the interpersonal relationship in behavior therapy. *Journal of Eclectic and Integrative Psychotherapy, 7*(3), 278–290.

Linehan, M. M. (1993). *Cognitive behavioral treatment of borderline personality disorder.* New York: Guilford Press.

Rosenfarb, I. S. (1992). A behavior analytic interpretation of the therapeutic relationship. *Psychological Record, 42*(3), 341–355.

Schaap, C., Bennun, I., Schindler, L., & Hoogduin, K. (1993). *The therapeutic relationship in behavioural psychotherapy.* West Sussex, UK: Wiley.

Sloane, R. B., Staples, F. R., Cristol, A. H., Yorkston, N. H., & Whipple, K. (1975). *Psychotherapy versus behavior therapy.* Cambridge, MA: Harvard University Press.

Sweet, A. A. (1984). The therapeutic relationship in behavior therapy. *Clinical Psychology Review, 4,* 253–272.

Wilson, G. T., & Evans, I. M. (1976). *Adult behavior therapy and the therapist-client relationship.* In C. M. Franks & G. T. Wilson (Eds.), *Annual review of behavior therapy: Theory and practice* (Vol. 4, pp. 771–792). New York: Brunner/Mazel.

THOUGHT-STOPPING

DESCRIPTION OF THE STRATEGY

Thought-stopping (TS) was a technique employed by behavior therapists from the 1950s until the 1980s. It was designed to decrease the frequency of unwanted thoughts. It was assumed or hoped that TS would also decrease the ensuing distress or anxiety associated with the thoughts. Although TS was, and to a small extent still is, a common tool in the behavioral therapy toolkit, there is little sound empirical evidence to support its use. Many case studies and case series describe TS as a helpful technique when implemented as the sole intervention technique or as part of a typical cognitive or behavioral treatment package.

Bain introduced TS under the presupposition that thought control is an important aspect of positive mental health. Taylor suggests that an abrupt instigation of an inhibitory behavior (e.g., "Stop!") fosters the conditioned inhibition of a habit (e.g., the insistent train of thought). Although TS is often depicted as a simple technique to apply, a thorough behavioral analysis is necessary for successful implementation. Clinicians can collaboratively prepare a complete hierarchy or record of all the distressing and uncontrollable thoughts. Clinicians should prioritize any thoughts suggesting harmful societal consequences. These thoughts could include anything from vengeance to personal insecurities to a haunting word to classic obsessions.

Targeted intrusive thoughts are collaboratively agreed upon between the clinician and the client, and the rationale for their removal is reviewed. Wolpe and Lazarus suggest that clients be asked to close their eyes and raise a finger once, purposely thinking of the target thought or series of thoughts. When the client raises a finger, the clinician loudly shouts "Stop!" which reliably generates a startle reaction. This response demonstrates for clients that one is unable to think of two things at the same time ("Stop" and the target thought). The clinician is then able to instruct the client in using his or her own voice to subvocally yell "Stop!"

Practice typically continues in the first session for approximately 10 minutes or for 20 rehearsals, until the client is feeling comfortable with the technique. Clients generally discover a gradual but steady decline in the frequency of the target thoughts but only by way of daily practicing the TS technique. Modifications of the procedure can be included on an as-needed basis in successive sessions. These variations might include snapping a rubber band on the wrist, a slight electric shock, substituting another word for "stop," or visualizing a stop sign.

RESEARCH BASIS

There are a number of descriptive case studies suggesting that TS is an effective behavioral technique.

Clients often report initial subjective satisfaction with the technique due to TS's face validity. In actuality, there is very little methodologically sound research to encourage the use of TS. There are no studies on TS with sufficient sample sizes to reliably detect any differences between TS and placebo or other cognitive-behavioral techniques. Another difficulty with assessing the effects of TS is the variety of procedures that have been employed. Many studies offer minimal description of the procedure, use an assortment of TS procedures, and use TS in combination with a variety of other interventions, such as relaxation and self-monitoring.

TS has frequently been applied in the treatment of obsessional difficulties. For example, TS was beneficial for an individual ruminating about his partner's suspected infidelities and reduced the frequency of color obsessions for another individual. TS has facilitated smoking cessation treatment for a number of individuals, treated auditory and visual hallucinations in one client, and eased the symptoms of agoraphobia in two cases. Others have found TS to be unhelpful in treating obsessional difficulties and depressive symptoms.

The effectiveness of TS remains questionable. Rachman and de Silva found that more than 90% of individuals surveyed reported numerous intrusive thoughts, images, and impulses. The results of these and related studies confirm that the experience of unwanted thoughts and images is a natural and normal human phenomenon. Hence, targeting these thoughts through TS or other deliberate suppression and elimination techniques may be ineffectual and frustrating at best—and damaging at worst.

TARGET POPULATIONS

Historically, TS was used in the treatment of obsessions; however, the technique has been used as an intervention in a number of cases and uncontrolled studies for a variety of different disorders. This includes smoking cessation, drug and alcohol abuse or dependence, psychosis, depression, panic, agoraphobia, generalized anxiety, and body dysmorphic disorder.

COMPLICATIONS

Innovative investigations on the impact of thought suppression have transformed our understanding and treatment of obsessive-compulsive disorder (OCD) and other disorders characterized by persistent unwanted thoughts. We now understand that that efforts designed to neutralize distressing thoughts such as distraction, ignoring, and suppression can increase their occurrence. Wegner discovered that individuals asked to not think of a white bear during a 5-minute time period actually thought of a white bear more frequently than another group of participants who were told that it was okay to think of a white bear.

Thought suppression is now thought to function as both a causal and maintaining factor in depression and virtually every anxiety disorder. When offensive thoughts are deliberately suppressed, their frequency and intensity typically increase. Within the OCD literature, the development of obsessions is conceived as being directly linked to active thought suppression and neutralizing. Salkovskis tested students experiencing frequent intrusive thoughts and consequent neutralizing. Their unwanted thoughts were recorded, and they were then asked to either neutralize the thought or distract themselves. When the target thought was presented a second time, those participants who neutralized the thought originally described considerably more anxiety and a greater urge to neutralize and suppress.

A COGNITIVE ALTERNATIVE TO THOUGHT-STOPPING

We now understand TS to be a variation of thought suppression or control, and thus, it may serve to increase the frequency of the unwanted thoughts. For example, clients with OCD will typically express the belief, based on any number of different appraisals, that one must be in control of their thoughts, emotions, and behaviors at all times. Hence, the completely normal and natural experience of unwanted thoughts will produce great levels of anxiety and the desire to control or suppress the thought. Thought control involves various strategies designed to ignore, distract, or suppress the thought. Attempts at thought control focus attention on the thought, which results in noticing the thought more frequently. The increased frequency of unwanted thoughts results in further efforts at thought control and a further narrowing of attention on thoughts, leading to the detection of more unwanted thoughts.

The development of a new technique labeled "come and go" by Whittal and McLean is part of new advances in cognitive-behavioral treatment for OCD. Clients are asked to switch between attempting to control and not control thoughts. On the "come-and-go" day, clients are encouraged to experience the intrusive unwanted thought naturally and without attempts to ignore, suppress, or distract. Unwanted thought frequency and levels of anxiety are predicted a priori for each of the days. Clients consistently predict that letting thoughts come and go will result in higher levels of anxiety and more frequent intrusive thoughts. Clients consistently express surprise at the unexpected results of their current thought control strategies. "Come and go" lessens their anxiety and distress and typically lowers the frequency and intensity of the targeted intrusive thoughts.

The technique of "come and go" works effectively for individuals with OCD concerns. However, it is likely that it would also be helpful for other disorders that feature repetitive unwanted thoughts, such as eating disorders, impulse control disorders, body dysmorphic disorder, and other anxiety disorders.

CASE ILLUSTRATION

"Heather" was a 28-year-old, single, Caucasian woman who worked part-time as a cashier at a retail outlet. She lived in a semirural area and was receiving long-term medication management from a local mental health clinic. She presented with mild symptoms of OCD.

A detailed behavioral analysis revealed that Heather presented with the primary obsessional form of OCD. Her main obsessions were violent in nature and focused on hurting others, particularly her mother and cat. In response to her obsessions, Heather would typically try to ignore or distract herself from the thought. Occasionally, she would pair the negative intrusion with one of her words she considered positive. Otherwise, she had no overt compulsions. Heather had a total Yale-Brown Obsessive-Compulsive Scale (YBOCS) score of 17, with 14 out of a possible 20 points on the obsessions subtotal.

Heather presented to her initial interview at the clinic with an elastic band around her wrist. She had been instructed by one of her mental health team members to snap the band whenever she had an intrusive violent thought and to yell "Stop!" in her mind. She had been using this technique for over a year, and due to the frequency of the obsessional thoughts had large red welts around both wrists. Heather reported no change in the frequency or intensity of her intrusions.

Heather received 12 sessions of cognitive-behavioral therapy for her OCD. Treatment focused on identifying appraisals associated with her intrusive thoughts, conducting thought experiments, and letting thoughts come and go without attempting to control them. In each session, one of the underlying goals was to collaboratively create an alternative story or interpretation for Heather to consider.

With the goal of normalizing intrusive thoughts, Heather and her therapist reviewed the list of intrusive thoughts reported by people with and without OCD. When six thoughts from the clinical and nonclinical samples were read aloud, Heather was unable to determine which thought belonged to which group. She indicated disbelief at the idea of people without OCD having violent thoughts similar to her own. The therapist emphasized that more than 90% of people experience these kinds of thoughts, with OCD sufferers having these thoughts with increased frequency, intensity, and distress. Heather also identified thoughts from the list that occurred infrequently but did not result in distress. For Heather, these nondistressing thoughts were largely sexual in nature and were associated with appraisals such as, "I'm in control of my sexual urges and comfortable with sex and sexuality." To illustrate the importance of the appraisal process, these thoughts and their appraisals were listed alongside their counterparts that did result in distress and the urge to neutralize.

Because Heather was having some difficulty accepting intrusive thoughts as a normal human experience, her therapist had her survey close family and friends to discover the content and frequency of their intrusive thoughts. They also surveyed five random employees from around the hospital. Heather was surprised with the variable results, noting that some people endorsed a great number but that the average tended to be between 4 and 6 intrusive thoughts. The additional evidence gathered from surveying helped facilitate an understanding of these thoughts as more normal for Heather.

Following the thought demonstration on suppression via the "pink elephant," Heather was encouraged to replace the elephant with one of her violent intrusive thoughts. In the first demonstration, she spent 5 minutes dwelling and rationalizing the obsession. This resulted in high anxiety and tearfulness. In the next demonstration, Heather spent 5 minutes allowing the thought to float through her mind, being naturally replaced by another thought. She reported feeling less anxious, as if "a weight had been lifted." The results were dramatically different for Heather. The therapist emphasized the short duration of the experiment and to imagine the result after years of the former technique. For homework, Heather was encouraged to practice the two experiments daily, while gradually shifting to the "come and go" paradigm for longer and longer periods of time. After becoming well versed with "come and go," she began to practice the technique during peak obsession times.

To facilitate an understanding of the role that emotions play in obsessional activity, the therapist had Heather monitor her intrusive thoughts, the appraisal, and any resulting emotions she experienced, including anxiety, annoyance, guilt, anger, or sadness. It became clear during treatment that Heather had strong moral convictions, believing she should always be the nicest and sweetest person. Any overt expression or internal experience of negativity (e.g., anger or guilt) was viewed as inappropriate. If she was anything less than her predetermined standard, she invariably concluded that she was a bad person. These beliefs may have functioned to predispose her to the OCD in that she reacted with horror and extreme guilt when she had normal intrusive thoughts about violence.

A number of behavioral experiments were designed to challenge Heather's "good girl" rules. She was encouraged to test both the reactions of herself and her loved ones when she began swearing, not doing favors for people, and behaving assertively. Adaptive ways for managing anger and annoyance were also practiced.

Heather attended all of the sessions and worked diligently between sessions. She subjectively reported the "come and go" strategy to be extremely helpful in shifting her need to be in control of her thoughts at all times. She felt increasingly confident about her ability to implement the strategy when an obsession began. At her posttreatment interview, Heather reported experiencing 30 minutes of obsessive thoughts per day. The thoughts were occurring a couple of times per hour, with little interference or distress. Her YBOCS resulted in a total score of 5, with a 3 out of 20 for her obsessions subtotal. She was able to begin full-time work and started dating again.

—*Melanie L. O'Neill*

See also: *Response Prevention (Vol. I); Wolpe, Joseph (Vol. I)*

Suggested Readings

Bain, J. A. (1928). *Thought control in everyday life.* New York: Funk & Wagnalls.

Cautela, J. R., & Wisocki, P. A. (1977). The thought-stopping procedure: Description, application, and learning theory interpretations. *The Psychological Record, 2*, 255–264.

Rachman, S. (2003). *The treatment of obsessions.* New York: Oxford University Press.

Rachman, S., & Hodgson, R. (1980). *Obsessions and compulsions* (Century Series). Upper Saddle River, NJ: Prentice Hall.

Taylor, J. G. (1955). The problem of perceptual constancy. *Bulletin of the British Psychological Society, 25,* 41–42.

Tryon, G. S. (1979). A review and critique of thought stopping research. *Journal of Behavior Therapy and Psychiatry, 10,* 189–192.

Wegner, D. M. (1989). *White bears and other unwanted thoughts: Suppression, obsessions, and the psychology of mental control.* New York: Penguin.

Wegner, D. M. (1994). Ironic processes of mental control. *Psychological Review, 101,* 34–52.

Whittal, M. L., & McLean, P. D. (1999). CBT for OCD: The rationale, protocol, and challenges. *Cognitive and Behavioral Practice, 6,* 383–396.

Wolpe, J. (1958). *Psychotherapy by reciprocal inhibition.* Stanford, CA: Stanford University Press.

Wolpe, J., & Lazarus, A. A. (1966). *Behavior therapy techniques: A guide to the treatment of neuroses.* Toronto, Canada: Pergamon Press.

TOKEN ECONOMY

DESCRIPTION OF THE STRATEGY

The token economy was initially developed by Nathan Azrin and Ted Ayllon in the 1960s to motivate mentally ill patients (e.g., schizophrenics) to perform prosocial behaviors. In the token economy, individuals are provided tokens consequent to performing behaviors that are targeted for improvement. Earned tokens may then be exchanged for various reinforcers, which are provided by individuals who maintain the economy (e.g., spouse, staff). Thus, token economies eliminate unnecessary time delays between performance of target behaviors and delivery of reinforcement.

There are several tasks that must be completed before a token economy can be implemented. First, problem behaviors must be identified by observing the patient in "real-world" settings, as well as from interviews with significant others, staff members, and the patient. Without a clear definition of behavior, there is no assurance of proper dissemination of tokens, potentially resulting in a lack of behavioral improvement. Therefore, it is then important to clearly define each target behavior to facilitate agreement of its occurrence among staff and patient. When a group is the focus of behavioral change, similarities and differences in problem behaviors of group members, as well as personal characteristics, must be considered. Generally, it is easiest to employ token economies with groups who share similar problem behaviors.

After target behaviors have been clearly defined, the number of tokens to be delivered to the patient for successful completion of a response must be determined. In general, performance of desired target behaviors that are observed to occur infrequently prior to the token economy should result in more tokens than less desired target behaviors. Other considerations in the specification of token contingencies include the patient's ability. If the patient lacks the ability to perform the target behavior, the individual should first receive tokens for participation in practice exercises to enhance the individual's behavioral repertoire. As skills develop, standards by which the patient may earn tokens should gradually increase. Quite aside from the decision of how many tokens to provide is the issue of whether to consequence negatively occurring behaviors (e.g., hitting a staff member) by taking away tokens (response cost). If the response cost method is employed, the number of tokens deducted must be significantly lower than the number received.

The time interval between token receipt and exchange of reinforcement is also an issue that will need to be considered. Indeed, an effort should be made to deliver the tokens as soon as the target behavior occurs. Similarly, the patient should be provided an opportunity to exchange earned tokens for the various reinforcers as soon as possible. Public posting of tokens earned and rewards exchanged will be helpful in the monitoring process.

Tokens and other materials (e.g., data sheets to record each patient's behaviors, tokens earned, various reinforcers) must be purchased prior to implementing the system. Tokens must be easily transportable and tangible, such as poker chips, stamps, or checks on a chart. They should also not be too large, easily damaged, or easily reproduced by patients. Tokens can be color coded to indicate specified behaviors (e.g., green tokens reflect performance of social skill behaviors, red tokens reflect performance in leisurely activities), allowing staff member to assess what behaviors are being improved and what behaviors still require intervention.

One method of effectively selecting reinforcers to be used in the token economy is to observe their personal preferences in naturally occurring situations (i.e., natural observation of what the individual does when the opportunity for free time exists). Another method is to query the individual's dislikes and likes, including activities that are deemed enjoyable. Last, reinforcers may be selected that have a high probability of occurrence. For instance, there is a high probability that employees will be absent from work if given the choice to attend or be absent. Thus, time off from work would likely be an effective reinforcer. Once a general list of reinforcers has been developed, the individual should be allowed to exchange tokens for reinforcers from the list.

RESEARCH BASIS

Support for the token economy and similar systems that have been derived from the token economy (e.g., point systems, level systems) is extensive. Indeed, within the past 30 years, there have been hundreds of outcome studies that have demonstrated the effectiveness of the token economy and its derivations. In the original research by Ayllon and Azrin, patients were selected for study participation if they were not responding to existing treatments, often being classified as least likely to benefit from treatment and least likely to be released from the hospital. The investigators examined the effect of the treatment procedure for each patient. Target behaviors in this study were positive aspects of patient behavior (e.g., not expressing delusional content). When describing the behaviors, simple terms were used. Reinforcers were identified based on the probability of occurrence. Treatment was evaluated based on the amount of useful or functional behavior the patient engaged in after implementation of the token economy. The investigators found this technique to be extremely useful for increasing various types of positive behaviors.

Interestingly, token reinforcers were shown to be effective in controlled animal research more than three decades before Allyon and Azrin's pioneering work with patients. For instance, in the 1930s, Wolfe and Cowles found tokens were as effective as an immediate food reinforcer. In the late 1950s, Kelleher used tokens with chimpanzees. The chimps pressed a lever to get tokens that could be exchanged for food. Results showed the tokens were effective in maintaining target behavior.

RELEVANT TARGET POPULATIONS

The token economy is commonly employed in group homes, psychiatric and medical hospitals, and classrooms. Although this method has become popular for use with children who evidence behavioral problems, this procedure is frequently initiated to improve prosocial behaviors of adults who evidence mental retardation and severe mental illness (e.g., patients with schizophrenia). Token economies may also be implemented in work settings to improve attendance, decrease off-task behavior, and facilitate a safe work environment.

COMPLICATIONS

Several complications have been identified when implementing the token economy. One of the greatest concerns is diminishing improvements in target behaviors after the economy has been withdrawn. This concern is usually effectively managed by consistently encouraging the patient to perform target behaviors and occasionally providing additional rewards that are not specified in the economy after target behaviors are performed (e.g., praise). In the latter strategy, the noncontingent naturally occurring reinforcers are paired with the contingent rewards such that they become generalized reinforcers for the target behavior.

It is imperative that tokens be delivered as specified in the contingency. Often, persons who are responsible for providing earned tokens (e.g., staff, parents, employers) forget to provide the tokens, or rewards, in a timely manner. This problem is usually managed by establishing regular times to monitor the contingency (e.g., after dinner, 7 a.m.). In the event the patient does not appear motivated to attempt target behaviors, it may be necessary to provide tokens noncontingently for a short duration initially (i.e., reinforcer sampling). In this way, the individual is provided an opportunity to experience benefits of the rewards, which may result in greater motivation to attempt target behaviors when the tokens are later made contingent on performance of the target behaviors.

CASE ILLUSTRATION

"Mr. Johnson" owns a fast-food restaurant and has noticed that one of his hardest working employees, "John," usually arrives late. Mr. Johnson is aware that

John is mentally retarded and decides to implement a token economy to improve his prompt attendance. He clearly defines the attendance behavior as "Being on time for work as scheduled."

He uses specially designed poker chips for tokens and agrees to reward one poker chip for attending each shift. Each token can be exchanged for a favorite meal at the restaurant. To initiate the system, Mr. Johnson gives John a token for free and encourages John to exchange the token for a favorite meal. John chooses a steak sandwich and thanks Mr. Johnson. Mr. Johnson replies, "My pleasure, John. I'd like to do it for you more often. I tell you what. Every day you come to your shift on time, I'm going to give you a token so you can purchase your favorite meal for lunch." John appears surprised but accepts the gesture with a smile. The next day, John arrives to work on time and Mr. Johnson gives him a token immediately, while praising him and giving him a firm handshake. Although John wants to save the token for another day, Mr. Johnson insists that John spend the token that day. In this way, the time interval from delivery of the token to the exchange of the token for the meal is reduced. After a month of using a token economy, John's prompt attendance increases to 95% from 70%.

—*Brad C. Donohue and Valerie Romero*

See also: *Azrin, Nathan H. (Vol. I); Kazdin, Alan E. (Vol. I); Token Economy (Vol. II)*

Suggested Readings

Ayllon, T., & Azrin, N. H. (1968). *The token economy: A motivational system for therapy and rehabilitation.* New York: Appleton-Century-Crofts.

TRAUMA MANAGEMENT THERAPY

DESCRIPTION OF STRATEGY

A *trauma* is defined as an event consisting of actual or threatened death or serious injury, or a threat to the physical integrity of self or others. In addition, the response to the event involves intense fear, helplessness, or horror. Following traumatic life events, individuals exhibit a range of reactions. Many people recover naturally and do not need psychological or psychiatric intervention. For a variety of reasons, other individuals may experience trauma-related responses, marked by psychological distress or some impairment in functioning. Posttraumatic stress disorder (PTSD) and acute stress disorder (ASD) are two diagnoses that describe symptom patterns shown by some individuals following traumatic life events. Studies reveal variable findings for the percentage of individuals who develop PTSD after experiencing a trauma, with the highest rates found for events such as rape, combat, and child abuse. The prevalence of ASD has also been found to vary and depends on the severity and duration of the trauma as well as the degree of exposure to the trauma.

For a diagnosis of PTSD to be appropriate, individuals must first experience, witness, or be confronted with a trauma. Individuals with PTSD experience at least one type of reexperiencing symptom (e.g., intrusive, distressing recollections of the trauma, distressing dreams about the trauma, feeling as if the traumatic event were recurring); at least three types of avoidance symptoms (e.g., avoiding thoughts or feelings associated with the trauma, inability to recall important aspects of the trauma, feelings of detachment from others); and at least two kinds of arousal symptoms (e.g., sleep problems, irritability/anger, difficulty concentrating). These symptoms must be experienced repeatedly, cause distress, and last for at least 1 month for an individual to be diagnosed with PTSD.

Like PTSD, a diagnosis of ASD also includes reexperiencing, avoidance, and arousal symptoms following a traumatic life event. A main difference between ASD and PTSD is that ASD lasts a minimum of 2 days and a maximum of 4 weeks and must occur within 4 weeks of the traumatic event. In addition, individuals with ASD experience three or more kinds of dissociative symptoms during or after the trauma. These include a sense of numbing or detachment, a reduction in the awareness of one's surroundings, an inability to recall important aspects of the trauma, and feelings of unreality regarding one's self or the traumatic situation. Trauma survivors with ASD are at increased risk of developing PTSD.

Of the trauma-focused therapies, many of the cognitive-behavioral therapies have been outlined in detail and have been most thoroughly researched to date. These therapies all utilize some form of exposure-based and cognitive-based interventions. Exposure-based interventions may consist of vividly imagining and describing the traumatic event (imaginal exposure), writing about the event in detail, or actually going to places or performing activities that have been avoided due to anxiety (in vivo exposure). The general rationale for the exposure components of the interventions is to break (or reduce) the connection between stimuli that do not represent realistic threats (e.g., memories of the trauma, nondangerous reminders of the trauma) and the emotional responses they provoke. When clients no longer associate certain thoughts or situations with fear, their avoidance of these cues is typically reduced. Exposure also serves to facilitate the process of recalling and accepting traumatic events.

The main rationale for the cognitive components of the interventions is to identify and explore beliefs associated with the trauma that are interfering with recovery from the event. Through this process, trauma survivors can recognize when their trauma-related cognitions are not realistic appraisals of situations, but rather represent attempts to deny or minimize the trauma or are overexaggerated reactions to the trauma. For instance, one rape survivor may try to deny that the event occurred by saying that it was not really a rape. Another rape survivor may not only accept that what occurred was a rape but also conclude that no man can be trusted and that all social situations are unsafe. A goal of cognitive techniques is to help survivors develop realistic and balanced appraisals of the event and its impact.

Some promising findings have emerged from studies exploring the effectiveness of ASD treatments with regard to reducing symptoms of ASD and preventing the development of PTSD. These treatments generally consist of normalizing reactions to the trauma and challenging any distorted thoughts regarding the trauma. In addition, clients are taught relaxation skills and trained in both imaginal and in vivo exposure. The early interventions that appear to yield the best results have consisted of at least 4 to 5 sessions, rather than single-session debriefings.

Several different approaches to the treatment of PTSD have been studied thus far, with generally equal effectiveness. The major cognitive-behavioral treatments of PTSD include coping-skills training, exposure-based treatments, and cognitive therapy. Stress inoculation training (SIT), prolonged-exposure therapy (PE), and cognitive-processing therapy (CPT) will be described in detail to highlight the specific steps involved in the cognitive-behavioral interventions.

Stress Inoculation Training (SIT)

SIT will be described to illustrate components of a coping-skills approach. The main goals of SIT are to help clients understand and manage their trauma-related fear reactions, resulting in decreased avoidance of fear-producing stimuli. SIT protocols range from 8 to 20 sessions and consist of three phases: education, skill building, and application.

The education phase generally takes place over one to two sessions. Clients are given an explanation of their trauma symptoms and are taught to identify the different modes (channels) in which they respond to fear cues, including emotions, behaviors, physical reactions, and thoughts. They are also provided with an overview of treatment and descriptions of how they will be taught coping skills to address each of the channels.

In the skill-building phase of treatment, clients are usually first taught relaxation skills, including progressive muscle relaxation and imagery techniques. These skills assist clients in identifying body parts in which they carry their stress as well as cues that trigger fear reactions. The relaxation skills provide strategies in three channels of response: physical, emotional, and cognitive. Clients are next taught skills that further focus on the cognitive mode. Thought-stopping, in which clients are instructed to stop anxiety-promoting thoughts and to redirect their thinking, is designed to manage intrusive or obsessional thoughts that promote anxiety and to redirect the client to more productive thought processes. Guided self-dialogue and cognitive restructuring assist clients in replacing irrational, faulty, or maladaptive thinking patterns with more positive and adaptive cognitions. To help clients evaluate potential options to fearful or challenging situations, problem-solving skills are introduced. Finally, to more directly address behavioral modes of responding to fear, role-playing and covert-modeling techniques are used. Both teach the client how to communicate effectively and resolve problems using appropriate social skills.

In the application phase of treatment, clients learn steps to apply these coping skills to daily situations that provoke anxiety. The main steps include assessing the probability of the feared event, managing avoidance behavior and fear reactions, engaging in the feared behavior, and reinforcing oneself for using skills in the feared situation.

Prolonged-Exposure Therapy (PE)

PE is the most extensively researched of the exposure-based interventions. It makes use of repeated, detailed imaginal exposures to the traumatic event. It also involves in vivo behavioral exposures.

PE generally consists of nine 90-minute sessions. The first two sessions involve gathering client information, describing PTSD, and providing explanations of treatment rationale, treatment planning, and breathing retraining. Sessions 3 through 9 consist of both imaginal and in vivo exposures. During the imaginal exposures, clients are asked to close their eyes and to describe the traumatic events they experienced aloud with as much detail as possible. Clients are instructed to include sensory details (sights, smells, sounds, sensations) as well as emotions and thoughts. Depending on the length of the account, the exposure is usually repeated two or three times each session. Clients are instructed to listen to audiotapes of their accounts every day between sessions, along with 45 minutes of in vivo exposure. In vivo exposure consists of the gradual confrontation of safe situations that evoke increasing levels of anxiety. Although they may be conducted alone, it is recommended to clients to conduct the initial in vivo exposures with a person they trust. During both the imaginal and in vivo exposures, clients keep a record of their anxiety levels using Subjective Units of Distress (SUDS) ratings or distress ratings on a scale of 0 to 100. SUDS are expected to be higher during initial exposures and to decrease with repeated exposures.

Cognitive-Processing Therapy (CPT)

CPT is a cognitive-behavioral therapy designed to facilitate the expression of affect surrounding the trauma and the exploration of beliefs regarding the effects of the trauma. CPT generally consists of twelve 60-minute sessions. The first session involves providing clients with information about PTSD and explaining the treatment rationale. For homework, clients are asked to write an impact statement describing what it means to them that the traumatic event happened. In Session 2, clients read their impact statements, and the therapist and client begin to identify problematic beliefs (stuckpoints) that may be interfering with recovery. Clients are also taught to recognize the connection between events, thoughts, and feelings during this session. The assignment following the second session involves recording general as well as trauma-related events, thoughts, and feelings on worksheets. These worksheets are discussed in Session 3, and an emphasis is placed on further identifying

patterns of trauma-related thoughts and feelings. In Sessions 4 and 5, clients read detailed accounts they have written of the traumatic events they experienced. Clients are asked to include thoughts, feelings, and sensory details in these accounts and to reread their accounts daily. Using a Socratic style of therapy, the therapist teaches clients to challenge their maladaptive assumptions and self-statements. In the early stages of therapy, much emphasis is placed on clients' self-blame for the traumatic event or attempts to "undo" the event after the fact. In the final five sessions of therapy, the focus is on exploring and challenging cognitions surrounding common areas of cognitive disruption following traumatic events: safety, trust, control, esteem, and intimacy. Clients are taught how to use worksheets to challenge and replace exaggerated and maladaptive beliefs with more realistic thoughts. In the final session of therapy, clients read a new impact statement on the effects of the trauma on their views of themselves, others, and the world.

RESEARCH BASIS

Numerous studies have shown that cognitive-behavioral treatment interventions are effective in significantly reducing symptoms of PTSD and depression resulting from a variety of traumatic events. No one treatment has been found to be more effective overall than the other treatments. This finding may reflect an actual lack of differences in the effectiveness of the interventions. It is also possible that the similar components between the different treatment approaches may be accounting for these results. Relatively small sample sizes in complex comparison studies may also serve to mask differences in effectiveness.

RELEVANT TARGET
POPULATIONS AND EXCEPTIONS

The majority of the interventions described were designed and tested with adults who experienced traumatic life events and, as a result, developed PTSD or trauma-related depression or anxiety. However, trauma-focused interventions are not appropriate for all individuals experiencing trauma-related symptoms. Trauma-related therapy often evokes painful memories for clients. Clients who are imminently suicidal or homicidal may not be appropriate for this type of therapy. In addition, clients who are undergoing repeated victimization would likely need to develop safety plans to end current traumas prior to processing past traumatic events. The majority of trauma-focused interventions emphasize the importance of feeling one's emotions surrounding the traumatic event as a means to experiencing and habituating to painful feelings associated with the trauma. Clients who are abusing substances would likely not benefit from this aspect of the therapy if they were masking their emotions through substance use.

COMPLICATIONS

It is not uncommon for individuals beginning trauma-focused therapy to initially show a slight increase in symptoms. This may result because the person may have been avoiding thoughts and feelings associated with the trauma until that point. Clients who believe that they cannot cope with their painful memories may avoid therapy by dropping out or not practicing skills in-between sessions. In addition to the feelings that may arise at the start of therapy, engaging in written or verbal accounts of the traumatic events can also evoke painful memories and may be associated with increased avoidance.

Other complications that may arise when conducting interventions include clients who have experienced more than one traumatic event. Focusing on the "worst" trauma or the event that has had the most impact on the client can be a useful approach. At times, however, it may be important to focus on two or more events, such as when it is difficult to determine which event had the greatest impact or when multiple events had strong effects on the client.

Therapy initiation, attendance, and progress can be affected by the messages that trauma victims receive from others about the events they experienced or about the decision to seek professional help. Some family members, friends, or authority figures may give the message that one should "get over" a trauma rather than focus on it. Individuals in one's support system may not be aware of or understand posttrauma reactions and may be unsupportive regarding how a victim is coping with his or her experience. In addition, trauma survivors often receive subtle or direct blaming messages regarding their involvement in traumatic events. It may be important for therapists to explore the messages a client is receiving from others. At times, providing information concerning PTSD to individuals in a trauma survivor's support system can be helpful as well.

CASE ILLUSTRATION

"Laura," a 26 year-old teacher, was referred to a therapist by her general health practitioner. Her physician had inquired about her depressive symptoms and learned that she had been raped by a stranger who followed her home from work 4 months ago. During her initial meeting with the therapist, Laura revealed that she had also been sexually abused by her stepfather between the ages of 12 and 14. Upon further assessment, it became clear that the recent rape had evoked many thoughts and feelings about the sexual abuse she had experienced as a teenager. She said that she had tried to block the abuse out of her mind for years but found herself thinking about it frequently, especially after the rape. Laura was diagnosed with both PTSD and depression.

Cognitive-processing therapy was implemented. When Laura read her impact statement during the second session, it became clear that she felt powerless in her interpersonal relationships and believed that no man could be trusted. Through her written accounts of the sexual abuse, she was able to confront and experience the emotions of shame, sadness, and rage that were associated with the abuse. She was very tearful and angry during her initial readings of the accounts, but after repeated readings, she reported feeling only minimal distress.

The third through fifth sessions were devoted to addressing issues of self-blame in addition to reading and discussing her accounts. Laura believed that she was largely to blame for the abuse because she spent much time with her stepfather before the abuse began and because she did not tell anyone about it. Through the use of Socratic questions, the therapist helped Laura to come to the conclusion that having enjoyed her stepfather's company in no way made her to blame for the abuse. In addition, Laura came to realize that the reason she did not reveal the abuse was because she feared that her stepfather would harm her (as he had threatened to do) and because he told her that nobody would believe her. She was able to acknowledge that it was her stepfather who was solely to blame for the abuse.

Sessions 6 to 11 placed much emphasis on exploring the belief system that Laura had developed during and after the abuse. Attention was also devoted to discussing cognitions related to the recent rape. Cognitive-restructuring techniques were implemented to help her identify which beliefs resulted from realistic appraisals of situations and which beliefs were largely based on unrealistic concerns. For instance, Laura was able to realize that although she felt that no man could be trusted, upon further exploration of her experiences, she actually knew several men who were extremely trustworthy. She also came to the conclusion that she was not completely powerless in relationships. She acknowledged that in some of her relationships, she did have some level of influence and that when she made efforts to assert herself, people were usually attentive to her wishes.

In the 12th and final session of therapy, Laura read a second impact statement. This statement revealed that although the abuse had profoundly affected her life, she did not feel that it precluded her from having healthy relationships in the future. In addition, she acknowledged that the abuse did not "permanently damage" her, but rather helped her realize that she was a strong and successful person who had much to be proud of. At the end of treatment, Laura no longer met criteria for PTSD and major depressive disorder. She continued to be more assertive in her interpersonal relationships and began dating.

—*Patricia A. Resick and Ana A. Sobel*

See also: *Flooding (Vol. I); Paradoxical Intention (Vol. I); Virtual Reality Therapy (Vol. I)*

Suggested Readings

American Psychiatric Association. (1994). *Diagnostic and statistical manual of mental disorders* (4th ed.). Washington, DC: Author.

Bryant, R. A., Moulds, M. L., & Nixon, R. D. V. (2003). Cognitive behaviour therapy of acute stress disorder: A four-year follow-up. *Behaviour Research and Therapy, 41,* 489–494.

Foa, E. B., Dancu, C. V., Hembree, E. A., Jaycox, L. H., Meadows, E. A., & Street, G. P. (1999). A comparison of exposure therapy, stress inoculation training, and their combination in reducing posttraumatic stress disorder in female assault victims. *Journal of Consulting and Clinical Psychology, 63,* 948–955.

Foa, E. B., & Rothbaum, B. O. (1998). *Treating the trauma of rape: Cognitive-behavioral therapy for PTSD.* New York: Guilford Press.

Frank, E., Anderson, B., Steward, B. D., Dancu, C., Hughes, C., & West, D. (1988). Efficacy of cognitive behavior therapy and systematic desensitization in the treatment of rape trauma. *Behavior Therapy, 19,* 403–420.

Kilpatrick, D. G., Veronen, L. J., & Resick, P. A. (1982). Psychological sequelae to rape: Assessment and treatment strategies. In D. M. Dolays, R. L. Meredith, & A. R. Ciminero

(Eds.), *Behavioral medicine: Assessment and treatment strategies* (pp. 473–497). New York: Plenum Press.

Resick, P. A., Nishith, P., Weaver, T. L., Astin, M. C., & Feurer, C. A. (2002). A comparison of cognitive processing therapy, prolonged exposure, and a waiting condition for the treatment of posttraumatic stress disorder in female rape victims. *Journal of Consulting and Clinical Psychology, 70,* 867–879.

Resick, P. A., & Schnicke, M. K. (1993). *Cognitive processing therapy for rape victims: A treatment manual.* Newbury Park, CA: Sage.

Tarrier, N., Pilgrim, H., Sommerfield, C., Faragher, B., Reynolds, M., Graham, E., et al. (1999). A randomized trial of cognitive therapy and imaginal exposure in the treatment of chronic posttraumatic stress disorder. *Journal of Consulting and Clinical Psychology, 67,* 13–18.

TREATMENT COMPLIANCE IN COGNITIVE BEHAVIOR THERAPY

DESCRIPTION OF THE STRATEGY

A distinctive feature of behavioral and cognitive-behavioral therapies is the emphasis on acquisition of new skills and knowledge. Indeed, cognitive-behavioral therapists attempt to teach patients methods they can use throughout their lives to reduce and/or manage a variety of maladaptive behaviors and cognitions. Learning such strategies implies the importance of active participation in therapy assignments on the part of the patient. Such assignments, conducted both within and between sessions (i.e., as homework), are a cardinal feature of cognitive and behavioral therapies and are considered an essential mechanism of therapeutic change.

Consistent with the idea that cognitive-behavioral therapies are instructive is the assumption that therapy outcome is enhanced when the patient complies with the therapists' directives and assignments. Although the relationship between compliance and outcome is an empirical question, there has been only a limited amount of research in this area, most of which has been conducted on cognitive therapy for depression and cognitive-behavioral treatment for anxiety disorders. Most often, investigators have used correlational methods to examine this relationship. That is, some measure of treatment compliance is correlated with scores of pre- to posttest change during treatment. This allows researchers to determine whether patients who exhibit greater compliance with therapy assignments achieve better outcomes than do patients who demonstrate less compliance.

A number of studies suggest that compliance with homework assignments in the cognitive treatment of depression predicts higher rates of improvement. Homework in cognitive therapy typically includes (a) behavioral activation, which involves increasing one's daily activity level; (b) cognitive restructuring, which involves keeping a record of situations in which one feels depressed, using worksheets that assist with identifying and modifying underlying cognitive distortions; and (c) "behavioral experiments," in which patients test out the validity of their modified (functional) beliefs and assumptions. It appears that adherence to instructions to perform specific behavioral experiments may be especially important. However, not all studies have consistently identified a relationship between compliance and treatment outcome in depressed patients.

Researchers have also examined the effects of compliance with behavioral therapy instructions in the treatment of obsessive-compulsive disorder (OCD) using exposure and response prevention (ERP). Therapy assignments in ERP include conducting prolonged and repeated exposure to situations that evoke obsessional anxiety (e.g., entering a public restroom) and resisting urges to perform compulsive rituals (e.g., changing one's clothes in the middle of the day). In addition to in-session practice under the therapist's supervision, patients are given assignments to practice exposure for homework. Studies demonstrate the importance of compliance with ERP both in and outside the treatment session and have shown that both short- and long-term effectiveness of therapy may be affected by compliance. Research on cognitive-behavioral treatment for other anxiety disorders, such as social phobia and panic disorder with agoraphobia, has also indicated that compliance with instructions might be an important variable that influences treatment outcome.

In theory, homework compliance could impact treatment outcome in both specific and general ways. Indeed, the practice of specific treatment procedures is intended to bring about a change in dysfunctional cognition and behavior and develop the patient's skill for modifying such problems. However, nonspecific effects of compliance must also be considered: The completion of any homework assignment may increase a patient's sense of accomplishment and self-worth

and decrease their sense of helplessness, contributing to a reduction in psychological distress. Completing homework assignments may also assist the patient in recognizing the extent of their problem (i.e., self-monitoring), which might motivate further compliance. It is also important to be aware that homework compliance (or failure to comply) may elicit deleterious mood states, such as guilt, self-criticism, anxiety, or hopelessness in some patients. Such effects should be assessed in therapy and processed during the subsequent session.

The importance of the therapist's role in fostering compliance with homework assignments cannot be overstated. Although seemingly straightforward, gaining a patient's compliance with treatment instructions in cognitive-behavioral therapy may be somewhat complicated and is not usually addressed specifically in treatment manuals. There are a number of techniques to promote compliance that may be used when giving assignments as well as when reviewing completed assignments. In assigning homework, the therapist should cultivate collaboration with the patient and include the patient in generating specific assignments. The therapist is also expected to anticipate potential obstacles to carrying out homework tasks, help the patient to identify possible problems, and generate solutions to likely barriers. It is also important to discuss with the patient any thoughts or feelings they have regarding the assigned task(s). Making instructions as clear as possible and putting them in writing will also promote compliance. In-session practice of assigned homework (i.e., completing sample cognitive restructuring forms in session) will build familiarity with the task and increase the likelihood of homework completion.

Cognitive-behavioral therapists can also take advantage of the principles of reinforcement to increase compliance. That is, all work assigned for completion between sessions should be reviewed during the subsequent session (preferably at the beginning) to demonstrate to the patient how such tasks are an important part of therapy. Praise for correctly completed assignments should be generous, whereas problems with compliance should be addressed with care and discretion, as described below.

In assessing the patient's compliance, the therapist should consider both the quality and quantity of homework performed. Whereas *quantity* is somewhat easily determined in terms of the duration of time spent completing homework assignments, *quality* is defined as the degree to which patients completed homework assignments as consistent with the therapeutic instructions. Completion of any homework may be better than no homework at all if doing anything does, in fact, produce favorable nonspecific effects such as increasing awareness or self-efficacy. However, cognitive-behavioral therapy assumes that problem behaviors and cognitions are modified by particular empirically supported treatment procedures.

For example, in the behavioral treatment of OCD, the quality of in vivo exposure homework refers to whether the patient (a) identified a specific exposure task, (b) elicited at least moderate levels of fear during exposure, (c) remained exposed to the stimulus until the fear dissipated, (d) identified avoidance strategies or compulsive rituals, and (e) discontinued the use of rituals. Similarly, for cognitive-restructuring exercises in the treatment of social phobia, quality refers to whether (a) an anxiogenic cognition was appropriately identified, (b) evidence for and against the thought was properly evaluated, (c) an appropriate behavioral experiment was formulated, and (d) the behavioral experiment was executed. Various studies suggest that both quality and quantity are important factors in successful cognitive-behavioral treatment of anxiety disorders. Thus, in reviewing homework, it is important to carefully determine whether the assignments were completed correctly.

While there is no singular solution for noncompliance with cognitive-behavioral therapy (indeed, the reasons for noncompliance may be as broad as the reasons for initiating therapy), some helpful suggestions for managing this difficulty have been identified. First and foremost, therapists need to clearly communicate that compliance with assigned tasks is essential in cognitive-behavioral therapy. Therapeutic tasks (e.g., homework assignments, therapist-assisted exposures) are assigned to help patients learn new habits of thinking and behaving, and noncompliance directly interferes with the acquisition of more adaptive skills. Thus, both the therapist and the patient should take inadequate performance (quality and/or quantity) of assigned therapeutic tasks seriously.

A particularly useful strategy for dealing with noncompliance is to collaboratively identify obstacles to adherence and solutions for overcoming these barriers. Typical barriers to compliance include confusion about how to perform an assigned task, the perception that a task is "busy work" and has little therapeutic value, difficulty with time management, and avoidance

of the effort required by a task (e.g., behavioral activation). Patients can often readily identify reasons for their noncompliance, and awareness of these barriers may suggest potential solutions. Reviewing the cognitive-behavioral explanation of the patient's symptoms and specifying how a given task relates to the patient's improvement may help assignments appear more meaningful. Identifying specific days and times to practice therapeutic tasks can help patients who are particularly busy or have problems managing their time. For patients whose noncompliance is motivated by catastrophic thoughts about the consequences of an assignment, therapists can use cognitive techniques (e.g., examining the evidence) or behavioral techniques (e.g., practicing the assignment together) to demonstrate that the assignment is not as aversive as the patient assumed. The case example below illustrates the use of a number of strategies designed to promote compliance with cognitive-behavioral therapy.

CASE ILLUSTRATION

"Karen" was a 22-year-old medical student with social phobia who was referred by her psychiatrist for cognitive-behavioral therapy. She experienced marked anxiety in most social situations (e.g., attending class, eating in restaurants) and engaged in extensive avoidance to cope with her anxiety. During the initial assessment, a cognitive-behavioral explanation of Karen's symptoms was presented, in which her catastrophic cognitions (e.g., "Other people think I'm stupid") and avoidance behaviors (e.g., skipping classes) were described as the primary contributors to her social anxiety. Cognitive-behavioral therapy was explained as a way to help her acquire new habits of thinking and behaving that would allow her to discover that social situations are not threatening. "Learning new habits of thinking and behaving requires practice," her therapist explained, and Karen was informed that her therapy would particularly include frequent practice in the form of self-monitoring of anxious thoughts and behaviors, identifying and disputing catastrophic thoughts, and confronting feared social situations through in vivo exposure.

Initial therapy sessions focused on educating Karen about social phobia and the role her thoughts and behaviors played in maintaining her social anxiety. Karen read several workbook chapters on social phobia and completed self-monitoring forms, on which she recorded the thoughts, behaviors, and physical sensations she experienced during anxiety-provoking situations. These forms were reviewed at the beginning of each therapy session, and her therapist praised her compliance and hard work. The material Karen recorded was used to illustrate the cognitive-behavioral explanation for her social anxiety, and she developed an understanding of how her habits of thinking and behaving contributed to her problem. A number of subsequent sessions were devoted to identifying and disputing her catastrophic thoughts in social situations. Karen was taught a specific method for challenging her thoughts, and she was asked to complete a cognitive-monitoring form to help her practice this skill. Her therapist modeled how to complete the form before assigning it as homework, and she was provided with a step-by-step instruction sheet to increase her compliance with this task. After conscientiously completing her forms for three weeks, Karen became more adept at challenging catastrophic thoughts in her mind and began to use the forms less often. Her therapist observed that the quality (as opposed to quantity) of her compliance was excellent and reinforced her hard work and growing self-efficacy.

To prepare Karen for confronting feared social situations, her therapist assigned two workbook chapters to read and engaged her in an extensive discussion of the rationale and procedures for exposure. Despite some apprehension about facing her fears, she was able to clearly articulate the value of this approach and agreed to participate in an exposure while accompanied by her therapist. The first exposure required Karen to walk through a crowded hallway and ask people for the time. Shortly before beginning the exposure, Karen became visibly angry with her therapist and refused to participate. Her therapist nondefensively described her anger as a normal reaction to an anxiety-provoking situation but also reminded her of the problematic role of avoidance and the value of exposure. After a brief discussion, Karen agreed to participate in the exposure provided that her therapist first model asking other people for the time. By modeling the exposure for Karen, her therapist not only elicited her compliance but also reinforced the nonthreatening nature of this social situation.

Although Karen's homework for the following week was to practice this same exposure on a daily basis, she arrived to the session without having completed an exposure. She apologetically explained that she had had a busy week and was unable to find time for exposures, though when pressed, she admitted that fear also motivated her noncompliance. Karen's

therapist identified and helped challenge beliefs contributing to her noncompliance (e.g., "My anxiety will be unmanageable"). Her failure to practice exposures was explained as part of a learned pattern of avoidance that she must now work to change. The therapist emphasized that Karen's continued improvement in therapy was highly correlated with her commitment to exposure, and noncompliance was described as more detrimental to her progress than to the therapist's feelings. Karen and her therapist also reviewed her schedule for the upcoming week and identified times for her to schedule planned exposure practices. After a second successful in-session exposure and a week of participating in daily exposure practices, Karen's social anxiety symptoms diminished markedly, and her compliance with therapeutic tasks was excellent for the remainder of therapy.

—*Jonathan S. Abramowitz and Brett J. Deacon*

See also: *Compliance Training (Vol. II); Intensive Behavior Therapy Unit (Vol. I); Effective Learning Environments (Vol. III)*

Suggested Readings

Abramowitz, J. S., Franklin, M. E., Zoellner, L. A., & DiBernardo, C. L. (2002). Treatment compliance and outcome on obsessive-compulsive disorder. *Behavior Modification, 26,* 447–463.

Bryant, M. J., Simmons, A. D., & Thase, M. E. (1999). Therapist skill and patient variables in homework compliance: Controlling an uncontrolled variable in cognitive therapy outcome research. *Cognitive Therapy and Research, 23,* 381–399.

Detweiler, J. B., & Whisman, M. A. (1999). The role of homework assignments in cognitive therapy for depression: Potential methods for enhancing adherence. *Clinical Psychology: Science and Practice, 6,* 267–282.

Edelman, R., & Chambless, D. L. (1995). Adherence during sessions and homework in cognitive-behavioral group treatment of social phobia. *Behaviour Research and Therapy, 33,* 573–577.

Lax, T., Basoglu, M., & Marks, I. M. (1992) Expectancy and compliance as predictors of outcome in obsessive-compulsive disorder. *Behavioural Psychotherapy, 20,* 257–266.

Leung, A., & Heimberg, R. (1996). Homework compliance, perceptions of control, and outcome of cognitive-behavioral treatment of social phobia. *Behaviour Research and Therapy, 34,* 423–432.

Primakoff, L., Epstein, N., & Covi, L. (1986). Homework compliance: An uncontrolled variable in cognitive therapy research. *Behavior Therapy, 17,* 433–446.

Schmidt, N., & Woolaway-Bickel, K. (2000). The effects of treatment compliance on outcome in cognitive-behavioral therapy for panic disorder: Quality versus quantity. *Journal of Consulting and Clinical Psychology, 68,* 13–18.

Woods, C. M., Chambless, D. L., & Steketee, G. S. (2002). Homework compliance and behavior therapy outcome with agoraphobia and obsessive-compulsive disorder. *Cognitive Behavior Therapy, 31,* 88–95.

TREATMENT FAILURES IN BEHAVIOR THERAPY

All clinicians experience treatment failures: The interventions are not successful, and the patient does not improve. Other times, some progress is made, but the patient continues to perform below the level of functioning he or she had prior to the onset of the problem. Therefore, it is important to try to understand the circumstances under which treatment is more likely to fail. Many of these parameters have been identified clinically and supported through research on predictors of treatment outcome for behavior therapy. There are a number of such predictors that elevate risk of poor treatment response, and various strategies are employed to enhance outcome in the face of such predictors. These can be divided into two main categories: patient characteristics and therapist characteristics.

PATIENT CHARACTERISTICS

There are a number of patient characteristics that are related to how well a patient will respond to behavior therapy. These factors include motivation, expectation, severity of symptoms, insight, and comorbidity. Oftentimes, several factors interact within an individual patient, but for clarity's sake, each one is considered separately here.

Motivation

Motivation is a key factor in determining how well a patient will respond to behavior therapy. Motivation is defined by (a) how interested the patient is in making changes in his or her life and (b) how much of an investment the patient is willing to make to make a change. If a patient is brought in by a family member because others are bothered by certain behaviors but the patient does not view the same behaviors as problems worth changing, then the patient will be less likely to engage in treatment and therapy is more likely to fail. More frequently, a patient is interested in changing but may not be willing to endure the distress that it takes to make changes (e.g., not willing to tolerate being anxious during exposure therapy). Thus, a patient who is not both interested in changing and is unwilling to endure the stress of change will more likely fail the treatment.

In behavior therapy for the treatment of anxiety disorders, unwillingness to tolerate the anxiety that accompanies therapy is more frequently the issue. A patient who is suffering from obsessive-compulsive disorder usually does not want to continue to experience the distress of the symptoms, but is sometimes not willing to endure the short-term distress it would take to successfully complete exposure and response prevention. Some researchers have started to examine whether motivational interviewing, a treatment strategy developed to help resistant patients engage in treatments for substance abuse, can assist the patient in deciding to invest in the short-term distress to achieve the long-term gain.

Expectation

Expectancy is defined as how much the patient believes that the therapy will work or how credible the treatment seems to the patient. If a patient believes that he or she is an exception and that behavior therapy will never work for him or her, then the patient is less likely to invest time and energy into the treatment and therefore less likely to improve significantly. Furthermore, if the patient really does not expect that the treatment will help, then motivation to conduct exposures or engage in other behaviors that can cause distress will be low or nonexistent. Depending on the patient, this can lead to either avoidance (e.g., not doing homework, not fully engaging in treatment such as exposures during the session, etc.) or conflict with the therapist (arguments about the treatment rationale, etc.). There are a number of methods that behavior therapists use beyond motivational interviewing to increase patient expectancy. First, because it is founded in empiricism, behavior therapists are able to discuss success rates with their patients. Many behavioral treatments for anxiety disorders suggest that at least 75% of patients will have at least a 50% reduction in their symptoms. This information plus the persuasion of a coherent model of treatment, a good therapeutic alliance, and early change in treatment often help many patients acquire high expectancy of success when they engage in behavior therapy. When these things are not sufficient, the behavior therapist will often work with the patient to determine what factors contribute to low expectancy and attempt to remove the barriers by helping the patient to have positive experiences that are counter to his or her expectations.

Severity

Many patients who have extremely severe symptoms of anxiety or depression can recover through behavior therapy. The issue of severity appears to go beyond simple symptom manifestation to two separate domains: functional impairment (whether the patient is able to be productive in some area of life, such as family, social, work) and distress tolerance (how much the patient is able to cope with bothersome feelings, how likely he or she is to experience such feelings, or how sensitive or reactive he or she is and how easily he or she recovers from such feelings). These two areas may interact with one another but do not necessarily do so.

If a patient is not functioning in any area of life (e.g., unemployed, no social support, no family support, nothing to focus on but illness), it is harder to break him or her out of the maladaptive cycle of behaviors. Patients without any area of positive functioning often present as more demoralized and hopeless: They feel that change is impossible or that the investment needed to change will not be worthwhile. Such patients are less likely to engage fully in treatment (they are less motivated and have lower expectancies) and therefore less likely to improve. In some situations, the behavior therapist will work with the patient to establish specific goals to help gain better functioning in an area of life while simultaneously working on improving any symptoms that would interfere with such goals. This can help instill hope and confidence in the treatment. If the patient is able to engage in one area of functioning, then the therapist can use this to give the patient hope that by changing maladaptive behaviors, more energy can be put into having a more well-rounded, productive life.

If a patient has an extreme inability to tolerate distress, then behavior therapies that involve exposure to feared situations (e.g., exposure therapies for the anxiety disorders) are much more challenging to conduct. This can be addressed by first helping the patient to feel understood while he or she understands the rationale for treatment, and then to work slowly, helping the patient tolerate their experiences while encouraging the patient to experience more anxiety.

Insight

Insight is defined as having an awareness that one's thinking or beliefs are distorted or somehow inconsistent with others' views. Other terms for poor insight include *overvalued ideation, fixed beliefs, delusional thinking,* or *borderline psychotic thinking.* This difficulty is most frequently discussed in the context of obsessive-compulsive disorder, where a patient truly believes that touching doorknobs can cause AIDS despite strong contradictory evidence. In such a case, the patient will often state that other people are wrong to take risks like touching doorknobs and that they probably have AIDS and don't know it. Poor insight can be shown across the emotional disorders, with patients who have panic believing that they really will die from the next panic attack ("The next one is the big one, I know it"), socially anxious patients being sure that they really will be rejected by everyone in the world, and depressed patients being sure that they really will fail at anything they do. While patients on the severe end of poor insight are relatively rare, they are difficult to treat because they believe that they are right. Therefore, the therapist must be wrong to ask the patient to take risks to test a belief. Even though the therapist believes the risk to be low, the patient believes it to be high and too dangerous to test.

To manage poor insight, the therapist will try to find a smaller, related belief on the edge of the patient's fear or core issue that is less fixed (e.g., finding an exercise that the patient does not think is high risk for getting AIDS, but is somewhat concerned that it could lead to cancer) and starting by addressing this issue. Arguing with such patients is counterproductive. Most often, a motivational-interviewing style of reexploring what the patient wants out of treatment and how one might achieve his or her goals is a better approach. However, some patients expect treatment to help them make the world conform to their unrealistic beliefs rather than requiring them to make changes in their behaviors. At such times, treatment is unlikely to work, and waiting to conduct the treatment until the patient can no longer bear the consequences of living with the disorder is sometimes the best solution.

Comorbidity

Comorbidity, defined as co-occurrence of other symptoms or syndromes, can greatly influence treatment outcome. The co-occurrence of depression, panic attacks, personality disorders, and other psychiatric disorders can make treating the target disorder much more challenging. However, several studies have demonstrated that treatment of the primary disorder often leads to a substantial decrease in secondary, or less severe, co-occurring disorders. Therefore, one should not assume that co-occurrence immediately means that one needs to modify his or her treatment strategies. Presence of severe depression, borderline personality disorder, mania, acute psychosis, or a severe eating disorder usually requires stabilization of the syndrome prior to attempting to treat an anxiety or depressive disorder. More controversy surrounds the treatment of patients with comorbid substance dependence or abuse.

In addition, co-occurrence of another disorder should be carefully differentiated from the misdiagnosis of one disorder as another. A number of patients with disorders, such as schizophrenia, autism, and bipolar disorder, can display symptoms that appear to be an anxiety disorder or depression. A number of these patients do, in fact, seem to have co-occurring disorders. However, another group of patients engage in repetitive or ritualistic behaviors, have panic attacks, are socially anxious, are depressed, or are worried, though these symptoms are secondary to psychotic symptoms or other symptoms that characterize the primary disorder. In such cases, trying to treat the apparent anxiety or depressive disorder without careful monitoring of the primary disorder can cause destabilization of the patient. Such cases need to be monitored carefully and should be treated by therapists who are familiar with aspects of all of the disorders being treated.

THERAPIST CHARACTERISTICS

In addition to patient characteristics, the therapist's behaviors can clearly impact treatment outcome positively and negatively. There is less research about such characteristics; however, poor therapist conceptualization of the patient's problems, extreme rigidity or flexibility, criticism, and lack confidence in treatment all may detrimentally influence treatment outcome for behavior therapy.

Conceptualizing the Treatment

Part of the therapist's job in behavior therapy is to provide the patient with a coherent, individualized model of treatment based on theoretical understandings of treatment and how they apply to the individual patient's difficulties. Provision of an all-purpose, general model can make the patient feel as if they are not being listened to and that the therapist does not care about him or her as an individual. More important, without understanding the core fears of the individual patient, the therapist is unable to directly address the fears through treatment procedures such as imaginal and in vivo exposure. For example, if a therapist assumes that every patient with panic disorder has a fear of dying, the therapist may miss the patient's true fear of going crazy. Furthermore, if the therapist assumes that the patient's fear of going crazy means that he or she will be hearing voices, the therapist will not be able to address a patient's specific core fear (e.g., of being paralyzed, etc.). Similarly, in obsessive-compulsive disorder, if a patient reports ritualized hand washing and the therapist immediately assigns a task of putting one's hands in dirt, this may have no significance for the individual patient whose fears could range from a fear of bodily fluids to needing to wash "just right," having nothing to do with dirt. Therefore, it is essential that the therapist gain a clear, detailed understanding of a patient's difficulties in order to be able to effectively address the specific problems that a patient experiences. Furthermore, articulating the conceptualization of the patient's problems provides for a clear rationale for doing exposures and other exercises that may be seen as unusual and/or distressing. The patient is then more likely to feel understood, to be motivated to follow the therapist's treatment plan, and to be hopeful about treatment outcome.

Flexibility and Rigidity

Provision of good behavior therapy requires flexibility on the part of the therapist. If a therapist has a specific treatment plan for a patient and attempts to force the patient to follow it in an unwavering fashion, this would be considered extreme rigidity. Such inflexible execution of treatment will often lead the patient to feel misunderstood and mistreated. It will often evoke arguments, noncompliance, and possibly early termination of treatment by the patient. While many behavior therapies today have been manualized and help the therapist to focus the treatment, a good behavior therapist uses the treatment manuals as a guideline instead of a mandated law for therapy. When patients misunderstand important concepts, have life crises, or are overly distressed by a plan (e.g., a specific exposure), it is important for the therapist to be understanding without losing sight of the treatment plan.

Conversely, some therapists are easily sidetracked, have difficulty in providing structure, and hesitate to pursue the difficult, distressing topics that may be the most beneficial for the patient. Imaginal exposure for posttraumatic stress disorder is a good example of this issue. Many therapists would prefer to provide a supportive environment for the patient and allow them to discuss problems as they arise. This is helpful for some patients, but many will benefit from a structured retelling of the trauma within the supportive environment. If a therapist allows a patient to continuously raise new issues in treatment that postpone exposures, this is ultimately to the patient's detriment and can end up leading the patient to feel that while supported, he or she is not making the desired changes. Thus, a careful balance of structure and flexibility in tailoring the treatment to the patient is necessary in effective behavior therapy.

Criticism

There are many ways for a therapist to provide corrective feedback to a patient. One factor that can undermine treatment is how critical the therapist is when he or she provides such feedback. If a therapist scolds a patient for doing an exercise incorrectly, uses a pejorative tone to discuss noncompliance, or is condescending to the patient when providing information, the patient can feel humiliated, ashamed, and/or angry.

A skilled behavior therapist provides feedback or encourages change through an empathic, unassuming authoritative tone. If a patient is not being compliant with homework, the therapist will inquire as to what barriers are interfering with the successful completion of homework instead of accusingly asking why the patient didn't do what was assigned. If an exercise was conducted incorrectly, the therapist assumes that either the assignment was not articulated clearly (i.e., the therapist's fault for the misunderstanding) or that there were legitimate reasons that interfered with comprehension and completion of the task. If it becomes apparent that the patient is not motivated to

change, then this is openly discussed. Terms such as "laziness" should be replaced with phrases such as "the cost seems to currently outweigh the benefits."

Confidence in Treatment

Therapists can fall on either side of the confidence issue, being either too sure or too insecure. More frequently, it is insecurity that leads to treatment failures. If the therapist is not confident in his or her ability to help the patient, this will come across to the patient in both subtle and not subtle ways. Therapist confidence leads to patient confidence and positive expectations, while therapist insecurity in the treatment makes the patient insecure about the effectiveness of the treatment. The therapist need not only be confident in the treatment as a whole, but needs to project certainty that behavioral tasks assigned to the patient are consistent with the conceptual framework developed to address the patient's core issues. This will allow the therapist to help the patient endure the more distressing situations, such as imaginal exposures.

In contrast, some therapists can express themselves in an overly authoritarian tone, stating that he or she is the expert and that the patient needs to do what the therapist wants if the patient wants to improve. Such a stance can appear arrogant and nonconvincing, which leads to more reluctance to trust the therapist and unwillingness to comply with treatment recommendations.

THERAPEUTIC ALLIANCE

The therapeutic alliance, also known as the *patient-therapist relationship,* is neither a patient or therapist characteristic, but it may impact negatively on outcome. While the alliance has not received as much emphasis in behavior therapy as in some other modalities of therapy, it is clear that a good relationship between the therapist and the patient can facilitate compliance, enhance motivation, and improve treatment credibility. Moreover, a bad or negative relationship is likely to lead to many of the above-mentioned patient and therapist characteristics that lead to treatment failure. Finally, if patient and therapist factors are handled with skill, this may improve the alliance.

SUMMARY

Acknowledging and addressing treatment failures in behavior therapy is a little discussed but extremely important aspect of behavior therapy. Patients' low motivation, low expectations, severity of symptoms, poor insight, and comorbidity and therapists' poor conceptualization of the patient's problems, extreme rigidity or flexibility, criticism, and lack of confidence in treatment are factors that have been identified as potential factors that can lead to treatment failures. By identifying predictors of treatment failure, we can begin to acknowledge limitations of treatment, while working simultaneously to learn new strategies to deal with these factors and further improve outcomes.

—*Jonathan D. Huppert*

See also: *Behavioral Approaches to Gambling (Vol. I); Corporal Punishment (Vol. III); Drug Abuse Prevention Strategies (Vol. II)*

Suggested Readings

Abramowitz, J. S., Franklin, M. E., Foa, E. B., Gordon, P. S., & Kozak, M. J. (2000). Effects of comorbid depression on response to treatment for OCD. *Behavior Therapy, 31,* 517–528.

Beutler, L. E., Machado, P. P., & Neufeldt, S. (1994). Therapist variables. In A. E. Bergin & S. L. Garfield (Eds.), *Handbook of psychotherapy and behavior change* (4th ed., pp. 229–269). New York: Wiley.

Foa, E. B. (1979). Failures in treating obsessive-compulsives. *Behaviour Research and Therapy, 17,* 169–176.

Foa, E. B., & Emmelkamp, P.M.G. (Eds.). (1983). *Failures in behavior therapy.* New York: Wiley.

Frank, J. D., & Frank, J. B. (1993). *Persuasion & healing* (3rd ed.). Baltimore: Johns Hopkins University Press.

Huppert, J. D., & Baker, S. L. (2003). Going beyond the manual: An insiders guide to panic control treatment. *Cognitive and Behavioral Practice, 10,* 2–12.

Keijsers, G. P. J., Schaap, C. P. D. R., & Hoogduin, C. A. L. (2000). The impact of interpersonal patient and therapist behavior on outcome in cognitive-behavioral therapy. *Behavior Modification, 24,* 264–297.

Kozak, M. J., & Foa, E. B. (1994). Obsessions, overvalued ideas, and delusions in obsessive-compulsive disorder. *Behavior Research and Therapy, 3,* 343–353.

Miller, W. R., & Rollnick, S. (2002). *Motivational interviewing: Preparing people for change* (2nd ed.). New York: Guilford Press.

TURNER, SAMUEL M.

I was born in Macon, Georgia, to parents of a rural Georgia background, neither of whom was a college graduate. Although not well educated and not well-off

financially, the family, like many southern African Americans, had a long history of land ownership and relatives in rural areas with substantial farmland. This background of land ownership and family stability provided an atmosphere that fostered independence and upward striving. I attended the segregated schools of the deep South during elementary and high school, schools that, although segregated, were made up of talented African American teachers who provided an unusual nurturing and supportive environment for learning. I did not go directly to college, but instead enlisted in the United States Air Force, where I spent 4 years, one of which was in Thailand during the Vietnam War. My military career did not end there, as I later served as an Army Reserve Officer.

My college career began during military service, and it was my experience with a psychologist who was a former military officer, a Bataan Death March survivor named Grover C. Richards, at a tiny midwestern university in Texas, that fostered my interest in psychology. This professor was a dynamic instructor and ardent behaviorist whose ability to link unusual experiences to behavioral principles and theories was particularly appealing to me. After completing my military obligation, I entered Georgia State University, where I completed the BA degree.

I then started my graduate work at the University of Georgia, a program heavily (but not entirely) influenced by behavioral theory, with a model of training firmly rooted in the scientist-practitioner tradition and a strong integration of clinical and research activities. Influential faculty members in the Georgia program included Rex Forehand, Karen Calhoun, Benjamin Lahey, and Henry Earl Adams, my primary mentor. As a comajor in social psychology, my mentor was Abraham Tesser.

I was fortunate enough to complete internship training at the Mississippi Medical Center, where I was influenced by a highly talented, productive, and influential group of faculty members, as well as trainees. Among the faculty were David H. Barlow, Edward B. Blanchard, Leonard Epstein, Gene Abel, and Richard Eisler. It was there also where I met and was supervised and mentored by Michel Hersen.

Following the successful defense of my dissertation, literally the next day, my family and I left for Pittsburgh, where I would begin my faculty career at what would become one of the most productive psychiatric facilities in the world: Western Psychiatric Institute and Clinic (WPIC) of the University of

Pittsburgh School of Medicine. There, I renewed my association with Michel Hersen and Leonard Epstein and began an association with many illustrious colleagues, including Alan Kazdin, Alan S. Bellack, and Rolf G. Jacob. Following several years of highly productive work with Michel Hersen and Alan Bellack in the area of social skills training for chronic schizophrenic patients, my interest in anxiety disorders solidified, and I began a highly productive research program in the anxiety disorders in collaboration with Deborah C. Beidel. This program of research has focused in particular on social anxiety disorder in children and adults as well as obsessive-compulsive disorder. As director of the Psychology Internship Program at WPIC, I was privileged to be associated with and contribute to the training of an unusually talented group of trainees that included Donald Williamson, Frank Andrasik, Melinda Stanley, Scott O. Lilienfeld, Cynthia Bulik, Michele Cooley, Angela Neal, and Deborah C. Beidel. Following my long tenure at WPIC, I was professor of psychiatry at the Medical University of South Carolina for 7 years. In 1998, I became professor of psychology and director of clinical training at the University of Maryland.

Throughout the course of my career, I have been continually involved in organized psychology and have held a number of positions, including the American Psychological Association Council of Representatives (Division 12), Board of Scientific Affairs, Board of Educational Affairs, and currently serve as the associate editor in chief of the *American Psychologist.* In 1997, I was honored with the American Psychological Association Award for Distinguished Contributions to Knowledge and the Association of Medical School Psychologists Award for Distinguished Contributions to Medical Research.

I have maintained extramural funding for my research continuously since 1978. From this and other research, 140 refereed articles have been published, as well as many chapters and books. Among the books are *Adult Psychopathology and Diagnosis,* edited with Michel Hersen and now in its fourth edition, and *Shy Children: Phobic Adults,* cowritten with Deborah C. Beidel. I expect to continue my career as a clinical scientist, with particular interest in the anxiety disorders. In the future, I hope that I can do something to help further the training of minority psychologists who pursue careers in clinical research and academia.

—Samuel M. Turner

See also: *Behavior Therapy (Vol. II); Behavior Therapy Theory (Vol. I); Behavior Intervention Planning (Vol. III)*

VIDEO FEEDBACK

DESCRIPTION OF THE STRATEGY

Ever since videotaping became financially feasible, psychologists have been interested in its potential use. Broadly speaking, *video feedback* describes any procedure involving showing a participant a videotape of himself or herself in order to provide information from an objective viewpoint. In the 1960s and 1970s, when the technique was first widely researched, applications varied widely, although the explicit or implicit goal of most efforts was to give participants a more realistic sense of their own appearance or behavior. This goal may be understood in a variety of theoretical contexts. A strict behavioral interpretation might hold that viewing the videotape is a form of exposure to a feared but actually harmless stimulus. Alternatively, watching the videotape might be construed as a form of punishment, reinforcement, or general feedback about the behaviors displayed. A more cognitive-behavioral interpretation might hold that video feedback challenges and changes distorted beliefs that have previously given rise to unnecessary distress, dysfunctional behavior, or both.

More recent uses of video feedback have focused primarily on social anxiety, speech anxiety, and, by extension, social phobia. In these contexts, video feedback is thought of as a means to challenge the distorted self-perceptions of socially anxious people who perform adequately despite their beliefs to the contrary. Video feedback has also been suggested as a means of convincing people with social anxiety that their *safety behaviors* (e.g., holding arms rigid to avoid shaking) actually look worse than the visible symptom that is being avoided. Essentially, then, this use of the technique retains the goal of more realistic self-perception.

RESEARCH BASIS

Early research on video feedback found that results differed by context and content of the videotapes. It was suggested that video feedback primarily produces a more accurate self-concept, a conclusion supported empirically and even by those studies that showed a detrimental impact of video feedback on some measures (e.g., self-esteem). As noted by reviewers of this literature, gaining a more realistic self-concept is not necessarily synonymous with immediate elevation in self-esteem, but can still be construed as a positive step if the more realistic self-concept leads to more adaptive behavior.

Although video feedback is reputed to be a strong intervention for social phobia, it has thus far been investigated only in regard to socially anxious participants giving speeches. In this context, video feedback has been shown to be more effective when preceded by a form of cognitive preparation in which participants imagine their speeches in detail and watch the videotape with a detached attitude. There is evidence that when used with the cognitive preparation, the change in self-perception caused by video feedback can last for at least 2 weeks. Although video feedback should theoretically decrease anxiety and avoidance behavior in people with social phobia, research has yet to demonstrate such effects.

RELEVANT TARGET POPULATIONS AND EXCEPTIONS

As described above, the bulk of recent evidence for the effects of video feedback is in regard to social anxiety. More specifically, people who believe they perform inadequately despite the fact that they possess reasonable social skills have the most to gain from video feedback, at least in terms of improved self-perception. People who do not have reasonable social skills may also benefit from video feedback but appear more likely to do so if it is paired with social skills training.

Generally, video feedback may be indicated whenever therapeutic progress will be enhanced by a more accurate self-perception. Thus, its application cuts across diagnostic categories, and its use depends primarily upon the clinical formulation arrived at by the therapist. However, clinicians should be aware that empirical data are limited on the effects of video feedback for any specific disorder other than those relating to social anxiety.

Potential exceptions for video feedback are people with depressive symptomatology, who tend to be more critical of themselves following video feedback. Such individuals may also judge themselves as less able to improve the behavior shown on the videotape, even though they may, in fact, have the required skills. Thus, the clinician should be certain that the benefits outweigh the potential for harm in such cases. Although empirical evidence is otherwise lacking regarding exceptions for video feedback, clinicians should be aware of the possibility that increased self-awareness could result in harm even in people who do not display depressive symptoms. This seems most likely to occur when (a) the videotape reveals flaws or inadequacies that the person was unaware of and (b) the person does not possess the skills to address these problems. Such a situation could result in hopelessness about the situation, which is unlikely to assist therapeutic progress. In such cases, appropriate skills training would probably be a more appropriate choice, at least in the short term.

COMPLICATIONS

One type of complication regarding video feedback would result from participants who refuse to either (a) be videotaped or (b) watch the videotape. In this case, if feedback is felt to be crucial, the focus of treatment may switch to decreasing anxiety in relationship with the video camera or observing the self. As mentioned above, video feedback may be less successful in people displaying depressive symptoms. Otherwise, at present, there are no other known complications for video feedback as a result of diagnostic category or personality variables. Although it has been suggested, for example, that perfectionism should interfere with video feedback, the available evidence suggests it does not. The only consistent finding has been that participants who have a more realistic idea of their performance in giving a speech to begin with are less likely to have an improved self-perception after video feedback. However, it may be that such participants benefit from video feedback in other ways.

—*Thomas L. Rodebaugh*

See also: *Self-Monitoring (Vol. I); Social and Interpersonal Skills Training (Vol. II); Social Competence (Vol. III)*

Suggested Readings

Clark, D. M., & Wells, A. (1995). A cognitive model for social phobia. In R. G. Heimberg, M. R. Liebowitz, D. A. Hope, & F. R. Schneier (Eds.), *Social phobia: Diagnosis, assessment, and treatment* (pp. 69–93). New York: Guilford Press.

Harvey, A. G., Clark, D. A., Ehlers, A., & Rapee, R. M. (2000). Social anxiety and self-impression: Cognitive preparation enhances the beneficial effects of video feedback following a stressful social task. *Behavior Research and Therapy, 38,* 1183–1192.

Hung, J. H. F., & Rosenthal, T. L. (1978). Therapeutic video-taped playback: A critical review. *Advances in Behaviour Research and Therapy, 1,* 103–135.

Kim, H.-Y., Lundh, L.-G., & Harvey, A. (2002). The enhancement of video feedback by cognitive preparation in the treatment of social anxiety. A single session experiment. *Journal of Behavior Therapy and Experimental Psychiatry, 33,* 19–37.

Rapee, R. M., & Hayman, K. (1996). The effects of video feedback on the self-evaluation of performance in socially anxious subjects. *Behaviour Research and Therapy, 34,* 315–322.

Rapee, R. M., & Heimberg, R. G. (1997). A cognitive-behavioral model of anxiety in social phobia. *Behaviour Research and Therapy, 35,* 741–756.

Rodebaugh, T. L., & Chambless, D. L. (2002). The effects of video feedback on the self-perception of speech anxious participants. *Cognitive Therapy and Research, 26,* 629–644.

VIRTUAL REALITY THERAPY

DESCRIPTION OF THE STRATEGY

Virtual reality describes a human-computer interaction that is more than just a multimedia interactive display as the user experiences a sense of presence or immersion in the virtual environment. To illustrate the importance of a sense of presence, imagine seeing a photograph of the Grand Canyon or even a videotape of it. One can get a sense of it but wouldn't feel present at the Grand Canyon. With virtual reality, one feels present in the virtual environment.

The setup for most virtual reality uses includes a computer to run the program and some viewing system. We use desktop computers now that the computing power is so great. Although some virtual reality systems use a series of large screens surrounding the user in a room, most applications in psychiatry and psychology use a head-mounted display. The head-mounted display contains two television screens, one in front of each eye. Sometimes they are programmed to show the same image in each eye, and sometimes they are programmed to show slightly different images in each eye, producing stereoscopic display. There are often headphones, sometimes incorporating directional sound. There is a position tracker and sensor to pick up head movements and change the display in real time so that the user's view changes in a natural way with head and body movements. We have computer scientists, programmers, and graphic designers build the virtual environments. They are three-dimensional environments, and the user can often navigate around them using a joystick or other handheld device. Sometimes we use other props or devices, such as an actual railing that corresponds to a virtual railing or a subwoofer imbedded in the base of the chair or mounted below the chair to produce vibrations consistent with the sounds of the virtual environment. In all the environments, the patient experiences only computer-generated audio and visual stimuli, while "real-world" stimuli are shut out. The therapist communicates with the patient with a microphone connected through the computer to the headphones.

Our group at Virtually Better, Inc., has primarily used virtual reality as a medium for exposure therapy for individuals with anxiety disorders. We began with a virtual glass elevator modeled after the glass elevator at the Marriott Marquis hotel for people with the fear of heights. We also had a series of virtual outdoor balconies and a series of footbridges over a canyon river. Each bridge could be viewed from the other bridges and therefore added to the sensation of height. The revised height virtual environment uses a glass elevator, and the user can get off at floors and walk across a catwalk and look down. The next application

was a virtual airplane we used for people with the fear of flying. It is a virtual passenger cabin of a commercial airplane. Most of the activity occurs out of the window, and the passenger can also view the window on the other side of the aircraft. It begins with the airplane engines off, then engines on, then taxiing to the runway then taxiing down the runway, takeoff, flying in both calm and turbulent weather, and landing. The passenger hears engine noises, the landing gear, the bells signifying the fasten seat belts sign, flight attendant and pilot announcements, thunder and rain during turbulence, and tires screeching upon landing.

We have also created two virtual Vietnam environments for Vietnam veterans with posttraumatic stress disorder (PTSD). For the helicopter ride environment, the patient sits in a special chair, which provides tactile stimuli via a bass speaker integrated in the chair. For the clearing environment, the patient stands on a raised platform surrounded by handrails on all sides and appears to be in a clearing surrounded by jungle, which most of the veterans refer to as a "landing zone." The therapist controls helicopters flying overhead or landing in the clearing. The patient "walks" in the environment by pushing a button on a handheld joystick. The other virtual Vietnam environment is a Huey Helicopter that can fly over different terrain, including jungle, rice paddies, or following a river. Various stimuli are under the therapist's control, such as audio effects (helicopter blades, gunfire, male voices shouting, "Move out! Move out!" and radio chatter and static), including directional sound and visual effects (night or daylight, fog, landing/taking off of the helicopter, helicopters flying nearby, flying over various terrain). The therapist is able to control the apparent closeness of the stimuli with the audio effects and volume control. For the virtual Vietnam, patients are instructed in imaginal exposure to their most traumatic Vietnam memories while immersed in Vietnam stimuli. The therapist attempts to match the virtual stimuli to what the patient is describing.

In the virtual audience environment, designed for people with a fear of public speaking, the patient is surrounded by a computer-generated classroom, including a chalkboard, a window, and a virtual podium, upon which the text of their speeches may be downloaded. The patient may use a handheld puck, similar to a joystick, to scroll forward or backward through their notes on the virtual podium. Directly in front of the patient is a computer-generated curtain. When the curtain opens, the patient is presented with the virtual audience, comprising 5 individuals seated around a conference table (small audience) or of 35 individuals seated in a classroom (large audience). The virtual audience consists of live video of actual people embedded within the virtual environment. During exposure therapy, the therapist controls the audience's reactions, including looking interested, bored, neutral, and applauding.

We also have a virtual thunderstorm environment for people with a fear of thunderstorms. It consists of a living room with a large picture window. The sky starts off blue, with birds chirping and, as the therapist directs, darkens to gray and ominous and develops into a lightning-and-thunder storm. The patient sits in a chair in front of the window and can view the weather outside and hear the thunder claps.

In all of the virtual environments, patients use a SUDs (Subjective Units of Distress/Discomfort) scale, ranging from 0 to 100 to rate anxiety, in which 0 indicates no anxiety and 100 indicates panic-level anxiety, to rate their anxiety approximately every 5 minutes, as in standard in vivo or imaginal exposure therapy. As in standard exposure therapy, they are encouraged to approach the situation, remain at that level until their anxiety decreases, then to gradually increase the exposure. This is repeated until they can approach everything in the virtual environment without undue anxiety. For several problems, virtual reality exposure is a component of a comprehensive treatment program, and treatment may also include training in anxiety management techniques.

RESEARCH BASIS

In the first published controlled study of the application of virtual reality for a psychiatric disorder, virtual reality exposure therapy to virtual heights was significantly more effective than a wait-list control on all measures of anxiety and avoidance. Moreover, 7 out of 10 people who received the virtual reality exposure therapy reported exposing themselves in vivo to real-life, meaningful height situations. In a study comparing exposure to virtual heights versus in vivo heights, both were equally effective. In controlled tests of the virtual airplane for the fear of flying, virtual reality exposure therapy was just as effective as standard exposure therapy using actual airport and airplane, and both were more effective than a wait-list control. In follow-ups months after therapy ended, 93% of treated patients reported flying in real airplanes. In

preliminary open trials using the virtual audiences for individuals with social phobia with a primary fear of public speaking, measures of anxiety and avoidance have decreased, and ease and performance in front of a live audience have increased. In an open clinical trial using the virtual Vietnam for Vietnam veterans with PTSD, significant decreases in PTSD symptoms were noted after treatment and at follow-ups.

RELEVANT TARGET POPULATIONS

Virtual reality has primarily been used with adults with anxiety disorders and has been used when standard exposure therapy would be appropriate. As a very visual and auditory presentation, people without visual or auditory impairments capable of seeing and hearing the virtual reality are appropriate.

Virtual reality has also been used with individuals undergoing painful medical procedures, including burn patients.

COMPLICATIONS

Although it is rare, simulator sickness has been noted with virtual reality. In its extreme form, users can become nauseous and get sick. In milder cases, users can get headaches or feel slightly altered perception after using virtual reality. With better resolution in head-mounted displays, the problem of simulator sickness has been almost nonexistent. Also rare, patients could cognitively avoid by refusing to suspend belief and repeatedly reminding themselves they are just in a virtual environment rather than in the situation they fear.

As with any computer application, computer glitches can interfere with the proper running of a program. The most formidable obstacles to virtual reality are the time, expertise, the expense of constructing appropriate virtual environments, and the expense of the hardware.

CASE ILLUSTRATION, INCLUDING BEHAVIORAL ASSESSMENT

"Ms. N" was a 61-year-old married, Caucasian woman, self-referred for treatment of fear of flying. Ms. N wished to overcome her fear of flying at this time because she had been invited to perform in a musical recital in a large city and hoped to be able to fly there. Ms. N also reported that she would like do more traveling and vacationing in general, especially in light of her recent retirement, and did not want to continue feeling that she and her husband's travel plans had to be limited by her intense fear. Due to her fear, Ms. N had avoided flying her entire life. She had never flown in a commercial airplane and had flown only one time in a small plane in her high school years, which she did not recall to be a negative experience. As Ms. N's performance date was only 4 weeks away, a more intensive brief course of treatment was agreed upon to accommodate her timeline (as opposed to standard weekly sessions). Ms. N also lived out of state from our office; thus, to decrease the amount of travel (by car) to and from the clinic, we agreed to have sessions on 2 consecutive days for 2 consecutive weeks (4 days total).

On Day 1 of treatment, Ms. N completed a psychosocial interview and measures specific to fear of flying and mood and anxiety. The assessment revealed a very high level of fear and avoidance of flying. Anxiety and mood measures indicated a high level of both state and trait anxiety and depressive symptoms at the low-mild range. Ms. N also reported a long history of agoraphobia with panic disorder, for which she had been treated in the past. Although her reported fears were related to the plane crashing, upon discussion, it was revealed that she also feared being in the enclosed space without an escape route. Regarding family history, Ms. N described her mother as "fearing everything" and her father as "a risk taker." She reported having two sisters with panic disorder, a brother with PTSD, and a son with depression. Ms. N was currently in her second marriage and described her husband as very supportive. As per their request, Mr. N participated in and was a beneficial support person to the treatment process.

The session included an orientation to the treatment process and discussion of expectations. Breathing relaxation training was taught, with an explanation of the relationship between panic and hyperventilation and that gaining control of her breathing would help reduce her anxiety symptoms. Breathing was practiced in session, and Ms. N reported experiencing a calming effect from this. At the end of the session, Ms. N was given an article on managing panic symptoms and information regarding many facets of airline travel (e.g., maintenance, pilot and crew training, weather turbulence, and a variety of statistics regarding airplane accidents).

In the next session (Day 2), cognitive restructuring was introduced. Ms. N's fears were often related to

panic, and in completing a thought record in session, she was able to generate effective challenges based on evidence from a prior experience on a boat when she feared she would have a panic attack and did not. Ms. N reported that she had forgotten about this event and felt much better and more optimistic with this event in her mind. Having completed the anxiety management training phase of treatment, Ms. N reported that she felt ready to begin the virtual reality (VR) exposure. Prior to exposure, we developed a hierarchy of fearful situations based on the VR flight scenarios and used a 0 to 100 SUDs scale to assess levels of anxiety. The least anxiety-producing scenarios on her hierarchy included "sitting on the plane" (SUDs = 80) and "taxiing" (SUDs = 90). In VR, beginning with sitting on the plane at the gate, Ms. N became tearful. She stated she was surprised by her strong reaction and had difficulty identifying the contributing thoughts, but did state that the image was "different than she expected" and that she felt scared (recall that Ms. N had not been in a commercial airplane before). She reported a SUDs of 100 and that "looking at the seat in front of her" and "seeing the inner wall of the plane at her side" made her very anxious. Ms. N was supported and guided by the therapist (while remaining in the head-mounted display) through this task. She was encouraged to focus on her breathing and to challenge her anxious thoughts about being on the plane. Ms. N continued to report anxiety and fear in the VR, although her SUDs ultimately came down to an 80 before we agreed to stop the VR for that session. Ms. N described her first VR session as "powerful." She was given thought record sheets and encouraged to continue practicing effective breathing throughout the upcoming week prior to our next sessions.

The next session was devoted to VR exposure. It was decided collaboratively that if Ms. N were able to effectively complete VR exposure in this session, the last session might involve going to the airport for in vivo exposure, as Ms. N has had limited prior airport exposure. At the outset of the session, Ms. N stated that despite the tearful experience of the previous VR session, she found it very beneficial and now felt better knowing what to expect. She had not completed any thought records, but stated that she did actively challenge her thoughts in her head as they arose throughout the week. In VR, Ms. N again started with the scenario of being seated in the plane at the gate, however this time experienced less anxiety. She appeared to focus on her breathing and was able to verbalize rational, fact-based thoughts about her level of safety in the plane. She reported a SUDs of 40 and was able to proceed in VR to the takeoff point, where her SUDs rose to 80. Ms. N was able to successfully complete a full flight from gate to landing. After repeating several takeoffs, her SUDS decreased from 80 to 35. Exposure to turbulence and stormy conditions, the highest scenario on Ms. N's hierarchy, was then incorporated into the VR flight. After repeated exposure of alternating between stormy and calm weather, Ms. N was noticed to use her breathing consistently, her hands were no longer clenched and clammy, and she reported a highest SUDs of 55 in flight, compared with her initial SUDs of 100.

As agreed, our final session consisted of in vivo exposure at the airport. Arrangements were made with airline staff to enable the therapist and Ms. N and her husband to proceed from the terminal, through the security check point, to a gate, and board a plane, without taking a flight. This process enabled Ms. N to experience and get accustomed to the sights, sounds, and feelings associated with being in an airport, as she had never done this before. As we walked through the airport, Ms. N reported enjoying the sights, and her SUDs was a 20. Once we boarded the plane, her anxiety rose considerably, and when seated in the plane, she began to experience shortness of breath. Using her breathing skills, she was able to regulate her breathing. Ultimately, she was able to challenge her thoughts and assure herself that she was not in any danger. Ms. N commented on the likeness of the VR to the interior of the plane and stated that although she was anxious, she felt the VR was good preparation for her flight and now she knew better what to expect. We deplaned and boarded once more and then remained on the plane for several minutes so Ms. N could habituate to the experience. Her breathing was slow and steady, and her SUDs came down to a 35 on the plane. As we exited the airport, Ms. N reported being nervous but optimistic about her upcoming flight. We reviewed her VR exposures and the skills she had learned. Ms. N was given two flight-monitoring sheets to use for her outbound and return flights, on which she could record her SUDs levels at various points prior to boarding the plane, onboard, in flight, and afterward for both her outbound and return flight.

Ms. N completed her flights, and as indicated by her ratings (see Table 1), she experienced much less anxiety overall, particularly on her return flight, evidencing the benefits of continued exposure to flying.

Table 1   SUDs Ratings During Posttreatment Flight

Flight Ratings	Outbound Flight	Return Flight
Pre-board	50	20
Pre-takeoff	75	30
5 min. after takeoff	90	40
5 min. before landing	50	30
Landing	40	20
Post-landing	5	5

SUDs. Subjective Units of Discomfort: 0 = *no anxiety;* 100 = *maximum anxiety*

She described both flights as "great flights," with "some turbulence on the outbound flight," but that "did not bother her," and she was "surprised by her SUDs." She reported that the waiting in the airport was difficult but that she was able to use her breathing "a lot" and once on board the plane began to feel more comfortable. Interestingly, she also reported that she was able to manage a boat ride on her trip much more successfully than she had anticipated and attributed this to the treatment. Ms. N reported that she and her husband were planning their next trip and that her next flight would be soon.

—*Barbara O. Rothbaum*

See also: *Social Competence (Vol. III); Stress Inoculation Training (Vol. I); Virtual Reality Therapy With Children (Vol. II)*

Suggested Readings

Anderson, P. L., Rothbaum, B. O., & Hodges, L. (2001). Virtual reality: Using the virtual world to improve quality of life in the real world. *Bulletin of the Menninger Clinic Supplement, 65,* 4–17.

Anderson, P., Rothbaum, B. O., & Hodges, L. F. (in press). Virtual reality exposure in the treatment of social anxiety: Two case reports. *Cognitive and Behavioral Practice.*

Emmelkamp, P. M. G., Krijn, M., Hulsbosch, L., de Vries, S., Schuemie, M. J., & van der Mast, C. A. P. G. (in press). Virtual reality treatment versus exposure in vivo: A comparative evaluation in acrophobia. *Behaviour Research & Therapy.*

Gershon, J., Anderson, P., Graap, K., Zimand, E., Hodges, L., & Rothbaum, B. O. (2002). Virtual reality exposure therapy in the treatment of anxiety disorders. *Scientific Review of Mental Health Practice, 1,* 78–83.

Rothbaum, B. O., Hodges, L., Anderson, P. L., Price, L., & Smith, S. (2002). 12-month follow-up of virtual reality exposure therapy for the fear of flying. *Journal of Consulting and Clinical Psychology, 70,* 428–432.

Rothbaum, B. O., Hodges, L. F., Kooper, R., Opdyke, D., & Williford, J. (1995). Effectiveness of virtual reality graded exposure in the treatment of acrophobia. *American Journal of Psychiatry, 152,* 626–628.

Rothbaum, B. O., Hodges, L., Ready, D., Graap, K., & Alarcon, R. (2001). Virtual reality exposure therapy for Vietnam Veterans with posttraumatic stress disorder. *Journal of Clinical Psychiatry, 62,* 617–622.

Rothbaum, B. O., Hodges, L., & Smith, S. (1999). Virtual reality exposure therapy abbreviated treatment manual: Fear of flying application. *Cognitive and Behavioral Practice, 6,* 234–244.

Rothbaum, B. O., Hodges, L., Smith, S., Lee, J. H., & Price, L. (2000). A controlled study of virtual reality exposure therapy for the fear of flying. *Journal of Consulting and Clinical Psychology, 68,* 1020–1026.

Rothbaum, B. O., Ruef, A. M., Litz, B. T., Han, H., & Hodges, L. (in press). Virtual reality exposure therapy of combat-related PTSD: A case study using psychophysiological indicators of outcome. *Journal of Cognitive Psychotherapy.*

Zimand, E., Anderson, P. L., Gershon, J., Graap, K., Hodges, L. F., & Rothbaum, B. O. (in press). Virtual reality therapy: Innovative treatment for anxiety disorders. *Primary Psychiatry.*

WOLPE, JOSEPH

One of the seminal figures in behavior therapy, Joseph Wolpe was born in Johannesburg, South Africa, in 1915 and died in Los Angeles in 1997. The grandson of Lithuanian Jews who had fled to South Africa in the late 19th century to escape persecution, Wolpe benefited from a long tradition that valued scholarliness and respect for learning, as well as discipline and hard work. Precocious and bright, he won many scholastic contests as a child and adolescent, even completing college-level chemistry by studying on his own during his high school years.

Wolpe earned his MB (bachelor of medicine, the equivalent of the MD in the United States and other countries) in 1939 and his MD degree (a research degree) in 1948 from the University of the Witwatersrand in Johannesburg, and he served during World War II as a medical officer in the South African army. During this time, he was exposed to what were then called "war neuroses," now termed *posttraumatic stress disorder.* Dissatisfied with the drug and psychoanalytic treatments then available—largely the effort to release repressed memories through injections of sodium pentothal—Wolpe looked for other ways to conceptualize and treat anxiety disorders. He was encouraged and guided by an American psychologist, Leo Reyna, in learning about Clark Hull's theorizing and experimental work in psychology, as well as Pavlov's classical conditioning and the experimental induction of neurotic behavior in animals. While in full-time private practice in Johannesburg, he gave lectures and conducted clinical demonstrations to graduate psychology students, among them Arnold Lazarus and S. J. Rachman, and ended up chairing Lazarus's PhD dissertation.

Wolpe's career took him to the United States in 1956 for a year's study at the Center for Advanced Studies in the Behavioral Sciences in Stanford, California, and then in 1960 to the University of Virginia Medical School as professor of psychiatry. In 1967, he moved to Temple University Medical School. Upon his retirement in 1988, he relocated to Los Angeles and remained active as distinguished professor of psychology at Pepperdine University. A principal focus until his death was as founding editor in 1970 with Reyna of the *Journal of Behavior Therapy and Experimental Psychiatry.*

Throughout his academic career, Wolpe was active as a clinician but especially as a tireless proponent of behavior therapy, traveling and lecturing widely and publishing numerous articles and books, among them *Behavior Therapy Techniques* (in 1966, with Arnold Lazarus), *The Practice of Behavior Therapy* (1969, the fourth edition appearing in 1990), and probably his best-known and most influential work, *Psychotherapy by Reciprocal Inhibition,* in 1958, discussed in greater detail below. His willingness to demonstrate his behavior therapy work in front of live audiences and on film served as an important complement to Carl Rogers's earlier promulgation of audio recordings to open up what goes on in the consulting room and to conduct controlled research to evaluate its effectiveness.

Among Wolpe's many awards was the Distinguished Scientific Award for the Applications of Psychology from the American Psychological Association (APA), in 1979, and in 1995, the Lifetime Achievement Award from the Association for Advancement of Behavior Therapy (AABT), an interdisciplinary interest group that he cofounded in 1966 and for which he served as president in 1967 to 1968. AABT has been the leading force in the United States and elsewhere for the study, development, and promotion of experimentally based psychological interventions for a wide range of mental disorders.

Wolpe's principal conceptual and applied contributions are in the treatment of what used to be called the "neuroses," now referred to as *anxiety disorders.* A closer look at his scholarly work demonstrates the influence he has had in the fields of psychiatry, clinical psychology, and other mental health professions. From 1949 to 1952, he published seven articles in APA's premier theoretical journal, *Psychological Review,* proposing a theory of learning based on Sherrington's early work in neurophysiological systems and on Hull's theory of learning. (This in itself is an astounding feat, for publishing even one paper in this journal over the course of a lifetime is an accomplishment that only a tiny fraction of people achieve.) He extended these and other articles and added considerable clinical detail in his landmark book, *Psychotherapy by Reciprocal Inhibition*, published by Stanford University Press in 1958.

In this seminal book, Wolpe asserted that people learn to become fearful or anxious about inherently innocuous events, people, or objects and can therefore learn to reverse this maladaptive learning. Consistent with the basic assumption of behavior therapy, his overriding concern was that psychotherapeutic procedures be based on experimental research, and he looked to basic learning research with nonhuman animals for findings and methods that could provide a foundation for new, empirically derived techniques to alleviate human psychological suffering.

In his 1958 book, Wolpe proposed a neurophysiological theory of learning based on what was known at the time about learning and about the central nervous system. He also reviewed the experiments with cats that he had conducted at the University of the Witwatersrand in the late 1940s. In these well-known studies, he demonstrated that an effective way to reduce unrealistic fears was to (a) expose the animals to conditioned aversive stimuli in a graduated fashion, beginning with those eliciting the least amount of anxiety, while (b) feeding them. Merely exposing them to the fear cues was not, he concluded, sufficient to eliminate the fear. Rather, following and expanding upon Hull, he reasoned that anxiety, being an autonomic smooth-muscle response, did not generate much reactive inhibition (analogous to fatigue and functioning as a drive state whose reduction could lead to new learning). It was therefore necessary to elicit in the animal a response antagonistic to anxiety so that the resulting reciprocal inhibition could compensate for the inadequate levels of reactive inhibition generated by anxiety and therefore form the basis for conditioned inhibition. When built up enough, this conditioned inhibition would form the basis for extinction of the undesired fear response. The strategy of feeding the cats while gradually exposing them to stimuli associated with their original fears did indeed eliminate the cats' conditioned fears.

From these experiments, Wolpe articulated his famous principle of reciprocal inhibition: "If a response antagonistic to anxiety can be made to occur in the presence of anxiety-evoking stimuli so that it is accompanied by a complete or partial suppression of the anxiety responses, the bond between these stimuli and the anxiety responses will be weakened."

Sometimes referred to as *counterconditioning,* this approach was actually based on earlier work by Mary Cover Jones in 1924, who reduced a child's fear of rabbits by feeding him over successive occasions while a rabbit was brought very gradually closer to the child. Care was taken by Jones, as it was years later by Wolpe, to titrate exposure to the aversive stimulus such that the child's eating was not disrupted by the growing presence of the animal.

Taking a page from some clinical reports by Andrew Salter in his 1949 book, *Conditioned Reflex Therapy,* Wolpe began to extrapolate from his cat experiments to his therapy work with anxious adults. He looked to Edmund Jacobson's classic work in the 1920s on deep muscle relaxation for a response that could be the functional equivalent of the pleasures of eating. And because many of the anxiety problems his patients had could not easily, if at all, be brought live into the consulting room—for example, fear of speaking up in a group or asserting oneself to an authority figure—he relied on the ability of human beings to visualize anxiety-provoking situations. In this way, Wolpe was able to pair the anxiety-competing effects of muscle relaxation with the anxiety-provoking effects of aversive imagery. The result was his renowned technique of systematic desensitization.

Systematic desensitization entails teaching a person to relax his or her muscles via various exercises while imagining increasingly bothersome situations. These situations are drawn from what Wolpe called an "anxiety hierarchy." This list of fearsome situations is drawn up over several sessions by the therapist and the patient and represents a sampling from the universe of things that the patient is anxious about and that the patient and the therapist believe should not elicit anxiety. For example, "You return home with groceries, and your partner comments that you have bought the wrong kind of bread." Then, once the hierarchy is developed, the therapist helps the patient over the course of subsequent sessions to become deeply relaxed and has him or her imagine items one at a time, beginning with the least anxiety provoking and moving slowly up the hierarchy. The aim is to tolerate each increasingly challenging item without feeling anxious. Should anxiety arise during an imaginal exposure, overriding the relaxed state that the patient is in, the item is withdrawn and the patient's attention diverted while a relaxed state is reinduced. The goal is for the patient to imagine the aversive scene without being bothered by it. When a given item is mastered, the next scene on the anxiety hierarchy is introduced. It is assumed that having successfully confronted an easier item in imagination without becoming anxious, the next item in the hierarchy will be relatively easy to deal with.

The following fanciful analogy may clarify the essence of desensitization. Think of being afraid of heights and having to climb a ladder. Stepping onto the first rung makes one a little bit anxious, but relaxing while one is on this rung enables one to be there without feeling anxious. When one then lifts the foot to step onto the next higher rung, this is not overly daunting, because one was able to stand on the first rung without becoming anxious. One can think of the first rung having been removed, sawed off, if you will. In this way, one climbs up the ladder without actually being more than a few inches from the ground at any given moment. One learns to respond to the higher rungs and ultimately to the top of the ladder with as little anxiety as one originally had when standing on the first rung, before relaxation was paired with the experience of being on the ladder.

Scores of controlled studies confirm the effectiveness of systematic desensitization in reducing a wide variety of unwanted fears, ranging from specific phobias, like fear of heights, to more complex sensitivities, like social anxiety. Wolpe also proposed responses other than relaxation that under certain circumstances could serve as more appropriate

sources of reciprocal inhibition. For example, with people uncomfortable or fearful of sexual activities, sexual arousal could compete with anxiety if the patient approached sex in a very gradual, nonthreatening way; this work anticipated the innovations of Masters and Johnson in the late 1960s. Also, unassertive patients could, following Salter, be taught and encouraged to express themselves when dealing with others, the assumption being that such emotional openness would compete with (reciprocally inhibit) the anxiety elicited by interpersonal situations.

In his many articles, chapters, and books, Wolpe energetically promoted desensitization and a variety of other anxiety reduction procedures as direct, effective, and efficient ways to help people unburden themselves from unwarranted fears. But the resistance Wolpe and his contemporaries (e.g., Andrew Salter, H. J. Eysenck, Arnold Lazarus, Cyril Franks) encountered from the psychoanalytic establishment cannot be overstated. In the early days of behavior therapy, roughly the late 1950s and throughout the 1960s, concerns were expressed that "symptomatic" treatment of people's anxieties was either impossible or, worse still, would lead to symptom substitution, relapse, and possibly a general worsening of the patient's psychological condition. This often strongly worded caveat arose from the assumption in psychoanalytic theory that the problems people take to therapists are but surface manifestations of underlying, repressed conflicts and that, moreover, these symptoms serve an adaptive function for the person, namely, protecting the psyche from being overwhelmed by unresolved unconscious forces. The clinical reports of Wolpe and others, and especially the early controlled desensitization experiments of researchers (e.g., Peter Lang, Gordon Paul, Gerald Davison) demonstrated that not only did symptom substitution and relapse seldom occur, but that relieved of their anxieties, most patients showed generalized improvement in other areas of their lives.

Throughout his life, Wolpe remained a purist in the sense that he decried efforts to import into behavior therapy techniques or concepts that were not rooted in learning principles. Furthermore, he resisted to the very end what he saw as the unwelcome intrusion of cognitive theory and research as exemplified in the writings of Albert Ellis, Aaron Beck, and his former student Arnold Lazarus. He regarded these developments as a regrettable reversion to the kind of mentalism that had, he believed, been rightly displaced by learning-theory-based innovations such as the ones he and others had developed, like the aforementioned Andrew Salter. While doubt has been cast on some of his theorizing—Hullian learning theory, for example, has been shown to have several inconsistencies, and the acquisition of unrealistic fears and their therapeutic elimination have been shown to be more complicated than Wolpe hypothesized—Wolpe's legacy is secure: More than any single clinician or experimentalist, with the possible exception of B. F. Skinner, Wolpe ushered in a virtual paradigm shift in how human psychopathology is conceived of and especially how many psychological disorders can be treated.

—Gerald C. Davison

See also: *Stimulus Control (Vol. III); Systematic Desensitization (Vol. I); Systematic Desensitization With Children and Adolescents (Vol. II)*

Suggested Readings

Poppen, R. (1995). *Joseph Wolpe.* Thousand Oaks, CA: Sage.

Salter, A. (1949). *Conditioned reflex therapy.* New York: Creative Age Press.

Wolpe, J. (1958). *Psychotherapy by reciprocal inhibition.* Stanford, CA: Stanford University Press.

Wolpe, J. (1990). *The practice of behavior therapy* (4th ed.). New York: Pergamon Press.

Bibliography

Abel, G. G., & Blanchard, E. B. (1976). The measurement and generation of sexual arousal in male sexual deviates. In M. Hersen, R. Eisler, & R. M. Miller (Eds.), *Progress in behavior modification* (Vol. 2, pp. 99–133). New York: Academic Press.

Abernathy, W. B. (2000). *Managing without supervising: Creating an organization-wide performance system.* Memphis, TN: PerfSys Press.

Abramowitz, J. S., Franklin, M. E., Foa, E. B., Gordon, P. S., & Kozak, M. J. (2000). Effects of comorbid depression on response to treatment for OCD. *Behavior Therapy, 31,* 517–528.

Abramowitz, J. S., Franklin, M. E., Zoellner, L. A., & DiBernardo, C. L. (2002). Treatment compliance and outcome on obsessive-compulsive disorder. *Behavior Modification, 26,* 447–463.

Addis, M. E., & Jacobson, N. S. (2002). A closer look at the treatment rationale and homework compliance in cognitive-behavioral therapy for depression. *Cognitive Therapy and Research, 24,* 313–326.

Ader, R., Felten, D., & Cohen, N. (2001). *Psychoneuroimmunology* (3rd ed., Vols. 1 & 2). San Diego, CA: Academic Press.

Agostinelli, G., Brown, J. M., & Miller, W. R. (1995). Effects of normative feedback on consumption among heavy drinking college students. *Journal of Drug Education, 25,* 31–40.

Agras, W. S. (1982). Behavioral medicine in the 1980's: Nonrandom connections. *Journal of Consulting and Clinical Psychology, 50,* 797–803.

Agras, W. S., Kazdin, A. E., & Wilson, G. T. (1979). *Behavior therapy: Toward an applied clinical science.* San Francisco: W. H. Freeman.

American Medical Association Council on Scientific Affairs. (1987). Aversion therapy. *Journal of the American Medical Association, 258,* 2562–2566.

American Psychiatric Association. (1994). *Diagnostic and statistical manual of mental disorders* (4th ed.). Washington, DC: American Psychiatric Association.

American Psychological Association. (2002). Ethical principles of psychologists and code of conduct. *American Psychologist, 57*(12), 1060–1073.

Anderson, C. M., & Warzak, W. J. (2000). Using positive behavior support to facilitate the classroom adaptation of children with brain injuries. *Proven Practice: Prevention and Remediation of School Problems, 2,* 72–82.

Anderson, P. L., Rothbaum, B. O., & Hodges, L. (2001). Virtual reality: Using the virtual world to improve quality of life in the real world. *Bulletin of the Menninger Clinic Supplement, 65,* 4–17.

Anderson, P., Rothbaum, B. O., & Hodges, L. F. (in press). Virtual reality exposure in the treatment of social anxiety: Two case reports. *Cognitive and Behavioral Practice.*

Anton, R. F., & Swift, R. M. (2003). Current pharmacotherapies of alcoholism: A U.S. perspective. *American Journal on Addictions, 12,* S53–S68.

Antoni, M., Schneiderman, N., Fletcher, M., Goldstein, D., Ironson, G., & Laperriere, A. (1990). Psychoneuroimmunology and HIV-1. *Journal of Consulting and Clinical Psychology, 58,* 38–49.

Antonuccio, D. O., Boutilier, L. R., Ward, C. H., Morrill, G. B., & Graybar, S. R. (1992). The behavioral treatment of cigarette smoking. In M. Hersen, R. M. Eisler, & P. M. Miller (Eds.), *Progress in behavior modification.* Dekalb, IL: Sycamore.

Antonuccio, D. O., Thomas, M., & Danton, W. G. (1997). A cost-effectiveness analysis of cognitive behavior therapy and fluoxetine (Prozac) in the treatment of depression. *Behavior Therapy, 28,* 187–210.

Antony, M. M., & Barlow, D. H. (2002). Specific phobias. In D. H. Barlow (Ed.), *Anxiety and its disorders: The nature and treatment of anxiety and panic* (2nd ed., pp. 380–417). New York: Guilford Press.

Antony, M. M., & Barlow, D. H. (Eds.). (2002). *Handbook of assessment and treatment planning for psychological disorders.* New York: Guilford Press.

Antony, M. M., & Swinson, R. P. (2000). *Phobic disorders and panic in adults: A guide to assessment and treatment.* Washington, DC: American Psychological Association.

Antony, M. M., Craske, M. G., & Barlow, D. H. (1995). *Mastery of your specific phobia.* Albany, NY: Graywind.

Antony, M. M., Orsillo, S. M., & Roemer, L. (Eds.). (2001). *Practitioner's guide to empirically based measure of anxiety.* New York: Kluwer Academic/Plenum.

Appelbaum, P. S. (1997). Informed consent to psychotherapy: Recent developments. *Psychiatric Services, 48,* 445–446.

Ardila, R., et al. (Eds.). (1998). *Manual de análisis experimental del comportamiento* [Handbook of experimental analysis of behavior]. Madrid, Spain: Biblioteca Nueva.

Ardila, R. (1980). *Terapia del compotamiento, fundamentos, técnicas y aplicaciones* [Behavior therapy, foundations, techniques, and applications]. Bilbao, Spain: Desclée de Brower.

Arena, J. G., & Blanchard, E. B. (2001). Biofeedback therapy for chronic pain disorders. In J. D. Loeser, D. Turk, R. C. Chapman, & S. Butler (Eds.), *Bonica's management of pain* (3rd ed., 1755–1763). Baltimore, MD: Williams & Wilkins.

Arena, J. G., & Blanchard, E. B. (in press). Assessment and treatment of chronic benign headache in the primary care setting. In W. O'Donohue, N. Cummings, D. Henderson, & M. Byrd (Eds.), *Behavioral integrative care: Treatments that work in the primary care setting.* New York: Allyn & Bacon.

Ascher, L. M. (1989). *Therapeutic paradox.* New York: Guilford Press.

Athanasiadis, L. (1998). Premature ejaculation: Is it a biogenic or a psychogenic disorder? *Sexual and Marital Therapy, 13,* 241–255.

Ayllon, T., & Azrin, N. (1968). Reinforcer sampling: A technique for increasing the behavior of mental patients. *Journal of Applied Behavioral Analysis, 1,* 13–20.

Ayllon, T., & Azrin, N. H. (1968). *The token economy: A motivational system for therapy and rehabilitation.* New York: Appleton-Century-Crofts.

Azrin, N. H. (1976). Improvements in the community-reinforcement approach to alcoholism. *Behavior Research and Therapy, 14,* 339–348.

Azrin, N. H., & Besalel, V. A. (1980). *A Job Club counselor's manual: A behavioral approach to vocational counseling.* Austin, TX: Pro-Ed.

Azrin, N. H., & Nunn, R. G. (1973). Habit reversal: A method of eliminating nervous tics and habits. *Behaviour Research and Therapy, 11,* 619–628.

Azrin, N. H., & Nunn, R. G. (1977). *Habit control in a day.* New York: Simon & Schuster.

Azrin, N. H., & Philip, R. A. (1979). The Job Club method for the job-handicapped: A comparative outcome study. *Rehabilitation Counselors Bulletin, 25,* 144–155.

Azrin, N. H., Nunn, R. G., & Frantz-Renshaw, S. (1980). Habit reversal treatment of thumbsucking. *Behaviour Research & Therapy, 18,* 395–399.

Azrin, N. H., Philips, R. A., Thienes-Hontos, P., & Besalel, V. A. (1981). Follow-up on welfare benefits received by Job Club clients. *Journal of Vocational Behavior, 18,* 253–254.

Azrin, N. H., Philips, R. A., Thienes-Hontos, P., & Besalel, V. A. (1980). A comparative evaluation of the Job Club program with welfare recipients. *Journal of Vocational Behavior, 16,* 133–145.

Babcock, J. C., & LaTaillade, J. J. (2000). Evaluating interventions for men who batter. In J. P. Vincent & E. N. Jouriles (Eds.), *Domestic violence: Guidelines for research-informed practice* (pp. 37–77). London: Jessica Kingsley.

Babkin, B. P. (1949). *Pavlov.* Chicago: University of Chicago Press.

Babor, T. F., & Del Boca, F. K. (Eds.). (2003). *Treatment matching in alcoholism.* Cambridge, UK: Cambridge University Press.

Baer, D. M., Wolf, M. M., & Risley, T. R. (1987). Some still current dimensions of applied behavior analysis. *Journal of Applied Behavior Analysis, 20,* 313–328.

Baer, L., & Minichiello, W. E. (1998). Behavior therapy for obsessive-compulsive disorder. In M. A. Jenike, L. Baer, & W. E. Minichiello (Eds.), *Obsessive-compulsive disorders:*

Practical management (3rd ed., pp. 337–367). Boston: Mosby.

Bain, J. A. (1928). *Thought control in everyday life.* New York: Funk & Wagnalls.

Baird, S., & Nelson-Gray, R. O. (1999). Direct observation and self-monitoring. In S. C. Hayes, D. H. Barlow, & R. O. Nelson-Gray (Eds.), *The scientist-practitioner* (2nd ed., pp. 353–386). New York: Allyn & Bacon.

Bakeman, R., & Gottman, J. M. (1997). *Observing interaction: An introduction to sequential analysis* (2nd ed.). New York: Cambridge University Press.

Baltes, M., Neumann, E., & Zank, S. (1994). Maintenance and rehabilitation of independence in old age: An intervention program for staff. *Psychology and Aging, 9*(2), 179–188.

Bandura, A. (1977). *Social learning theory.* Englewood Cliffs, NJ: Prentice Hall.

Bandura, A. (1986). *Social foundations of thought and action: A social cognitive theory.* Englewood Cliffs, NJ: Prentice Hall.

Bandura, A. (1997). *Self-efficacy: The exercise of control.* New York: Freeman.

Barkley, R. A. (1997). *Defiant children: A clinician's manual for assessment and parent training* (2nd ed.). New York: Guilford Press.

Barlow, D. H. (1988). *Anxiety and its disorders: The nature and treatment of anxiety and panic.* New York: Guilford Press.

Barlow, D. H. (1996). Health care policy, psychotherapy research, and the future of psychotherapy. *American Psychologist, 51,* 1050–1058.

Barlow, D. H. (2001). *Anxiety and its disorders* (2nd ed.). New York: Guilford Press.

Barlow, D. H. (2001). *The clinical handbook of psychological disorders* (3rd ed.). New York: Guilford Press.

Barlow, D. H. (Ed.). (2001). *Clinical handbook of psychological disorders: A step-by-step treatment manual* (3rd ed.). New York: Guilford Press.

Barlow, D. H., & Craske, M. G. (2000). *Mastery of your anxiety and panic: Client workbook for anxiety and panic* (3rd ed.). Boulder, CO: Graywind.

Barlow, D. H., & Hersen, M. (1984). *Single case experimental designs: Strategies for studying behavior change* (2nd ed.). New York: Pergamon Press.

Barlow, D. H., Gorman, J. M., Shear, M. K., & Woods, S. W. (2000). Cognitive-behavioral therapy, imipramine, or their combination for panic disorder: A randomized controlled trial. *Journal of the American Medical Association, 283,* 2529–2536.

Barlow, D. H., Gorman, J. M., Shear, M. K., & Woods, S. W. (2000). Cognitive-behavioral therapy, imipramine, or their combination for panic disorder: A randomized controlled trial. *Journal of the American Medical Association, 283,* 2529–2536.

Barlow, D. H., Hayes, S. C., & Nelson, R. O. (1984). *The scientist-practitioner: Research and accountability in clinical and educational settings.* New York: Pergamon Press.

Barlow, D. H., Raffa, S. D., & Cohen, E. M. (2002). Psychosocial treatments for panic disorders, phobias, and generalized anxiety disorder. In P. E. Nathan & J. M. Gorman (Eds.), *A guide to treatments that work* (2nd ed.). New York: Oxford University Press.

Barnes-Holmes, Y., Hayes, S. C., Barnes-Holmes, D., & Roche, B. (2001). Relational frame theory: A post-Skinnerian account of human language and cognition. In H. W. Reese & R. Kail (Eds.), *Advances in child development and behavior* (Vol. 28, pp. 101–138). New York: Academic.

Barratt, P. M. (1998). Group therapy for childhood anxiety disorders. *Journal of Clinical Child Psychology, 27,* 459-468.

Basco, M. R., & Rush, A. J. (1966). *Cognitive-behavioral therapy for bipolar disorder.* New York: Guilford Press.

Baucom, D. H., Shoham, V., Mueser, K. T., Daiuto, A. D., & Stickle, T. R. (1998). Empirically supported couple and family interventions for marital distress and adult mental health problems. *Journal of Consulting and Clinical Psychology, 66,* 53–88.

Baum, W. M. (1974). On two types of deviations from the matching law. *Journal of the Experimental Analysis of Behavior, 22,* 231–242.

Beach, S. R. H., Fincham, F. D., & Katz, J. (1998). Marital therapy in the treatment of depression: Towards a third generation of therapy and research. *Clinical Psychology Review, 18,* 835–861.

Beahrs, J. O., & Gutheil, T. G. (2001). Informed consent to psychotherapy. *American Journal of Psychiatry, 158*(1), 4–10.

Beck, A. T. (1999). *Prisoners of hate: The cognitive basis of anger, hostility, and violence.* New York: HarperCollins.

Beck, A. T., Freeman, A., & Associates (1990). *Cognitive therapy of personality disorders.* New York: Guilford Press.

Beck, A. T., Rush, A. J., Shaw, F. B., & Emery, G. (1979). *Cognitive therapy of depression.* New York: Guilford Press.

Beck, J. S. (1995). *Cognitive therapy: Basics and beyond.* New York: Guilford Press.

Beck, R., & Fernandez, E. (1998). Cognitive behavior therapy in the treatment of anger: A meta-analysis. *Cognitive Therapy and Research, 22,* 63–75.

Beidel, D. C., & Turner, S. M. (1998). *Shy children, phobic adults: Nature and treatment of social phobia.* Washington, DC: American Psychological Association.

Beidel, D. C., Turner, S. M., & Cooley, M. R. (1993). Assessing reliable and clinically significant change in social phobia: Validity of the Social Phobia and Anxiety Inventory. *Behaviour Research & Therapy, 31,* 331–337.

Bellack, A. S., & Hersen, M. (1998). (Eds.). *Behavioral assessment: A practical handbook.* Boston: Allyn & Bacon.

Bellack, A. S., Gold, J. M., & Buchanan, R. W. (1999). Cognitive rehabilitation for schizophrenia: Problems, prospects, and strategies. *Schizophrenia Bulletin, 25,* 257–274.

Bellack, A. S., Hersen, M., & Kazdin, A. E. (Eds.). (1990). *International handbook of behavior modification and therapy* (2nd ed.). New York: Plenum Press.

Bellack, A. S., Morrison, R. L., Mueser, K. T., Wade, J. H., & Sayers, S. L. (1990). Role play for assessing the social competence of psychiatric patients. *Psychological Assessment: A Journal of Consulting and Clinical Psychology, 2,* 248–255.

Bellack, A. S., Mueser, K. T., Gingerich, S., & Agresta, J. (1997). *Social skills training for schizophrenia: A step-by-step guide.* New York, NY: Guilford Press.

Benson, H. (1975). *The relaxation response.* New York: William Morrow.

Bergan, J. (1977). *Behavioral consultation.* Columbus, OH: Merrill.

Bergen, A. E., & Garfield, S. L. (Eds.). (1994). *Handbook of psychotherapy and behavior change* (4th ed.). Oxford, UK: Wiley.

Bergin, A. E. (1991). Values and religious issues in psychotherapy and mental health. *American Psychologist, 46,* 394–403.

Bergin, A. E., & Garfield, S. L. (Eds.). (1994). *Handbook of psychotherapy and behavior change* (4th ed.). New York: Wiley.

Bernstein, D. A., & Borkovec, T. D. (1973). *Progressive relaxation training.* Champaign, IL: Research Press.

Bernstein, D. A., & Carlson, C. R. (1993). Progressive relaxation: Abbreviated methods. In P. M. Lehrer & R. L. Woolfolk (Eds.), *Principles and practice of stress management* (2nd ed., pp. 53–87). New York: Guilford Press.

Beutler, L. E., Clarkin, J. F., & Bongar, B. (2000). *Guidelines for the systematic treatment of the depressed patient.* Oxford, UK: Oxford University Press.

Beutler, L. E., Machado, P. P., & Neufeldt, S. (1994). Therapist variables. In A. E. Bergin & S. L. Garfield (Eds.), *Handbook of psychotherapy and behavior change* (4th ed., pp. 229–269). New York: Wiley.

Bezchlibnyk-Butler, K. Z., & Jeffries, J. J. (Eds.). (2001). *Clinical handbook of psychotropic drugs.* Kirtland, WA: Hogrefen & Huber.

Bickel, W. K., & Etzel, B. C. (1985). The quantal nature of controlling stimulus-response relations as measured in tests of stimulus generalization. *Journal of the Experimental Analysis of Behavior, 44,* 247–270.

Binet, A. (1888). Le fetichisme dans l'amour. *Études de Psychologie Expérimentale,* 1–85.

Birchler, G. R., Fals-Stewart, W., & Magana, C. (2003). Marital dyads. In M. Hersen & S. M. Turner (Eds.), *Diagnostic interviewing* (3rd ed.). New York: Kluwer/Plenum.

Bjork, Daniel W. (1993). *B. F. Skinner: A Life.* New York: Basic Books.

Blaauw, E., & Emmelkamp, P. (1994). The therapeutic relationship: A study of the therapist client rating scale. *Behavioural and Cognitive Psychotherapy, 22,* 25–35.

Blanchard, E. B. (1982). Behavioral medicine: Past, present, and future. *Journal of Consulting and Clinical Psychology, 50,* 795–796.

Blanchard, E. B., & Andrasik, F. (1985). *Management of chronic headaches.* New York: Pergamon Press.

Blaszczynski, A. (1998). *Overcoming compulsive gambling: A self-help guide using cognitive-behavioral techniques.* London: Robinson.

Blumenthal, J., Babyak, M. A., Moore, K. A., Craighead W. E., Herman S., Khatri, P., et al. (1999). Effects of exercise training on older patients with major depression. *Archives of Internal Medicine, 159,* 2349–2356.

Boersma, K., den Hengst, S., Dekker, J., & Emmelkamp, P. M. G. (1976). Exposure and response prevention in the natural environment: A comparison with obsessive-compulsive patients. *Behaviour Research and Therapy, 14,* 19–24.

Bond, F. W., & Dryden, W. (2002). *Handbook of brief cognitive behaviour therapy.* New York: Wiley.

Borkovec, T. D., & Whisman, M. A. (1996). Psychosocial treatment for generalized anxiety disorder. In M. R. Mavissakalian & R. F. Prien (Eds.), *Long-term treatments of anxiety disorders* (pp. 171–199). Washington, DC: American Psychiatric Press.

Bornstein, P. H., Hamilton, S. B., & Bornstein, M. T. (1986). Self-monitoring procedures. In A. R. Ciminero, K. S. Calhoun, & H. E. Adams (Eds.), *Handbook of behavioral assessment* (2nd ed., pp. 176–222). New York: Wiley-Interscience.

Bottomley, A., Hunton, S., Roberts, G., Jones, L., & Bradley, C. (1996). A pilot study of cognitive-behavioral therapy and social support group interventions with newly diagnosed cancer patients. *Journal of Psychosocial Oncology, 14,* 65–83.

Boudewyns, P. A., & Shipley, R. H. (1983). *Flooding and implosive therapy.* New York: Plenum Press.

Bourne, E. J. (1995). *The anxiety and phobia workbook.* Oakland, CA: New Harbinger.

Brady, J. V. (1975). Toward a behavioral biology of emotion. In L. Levi (Ed.), *Emotions—Their parameters and measurement* (pp. 17–45). New York: Raven Press.

Braksick, L. W. (2000). *Unlock behavior, unleash profits.* New York: McGraw-Hill.

Bray, G. A., Bouchard, C., & James, W. P. T. (Eds.). (1998). *Handbook of obesity.* New York: Marcel Dekker.

Breslin, F. C., Zack, M., & McMain, S. (2002). An information-processing analysis of mindfulness: Implications for relapse prevention in the treatment of substance abuse. *Clinical Psychology: Science and Practice, 9,* 275–299.

Brown, M. A., & Lewinsohn, P. M. (1984). *Participant workbook for the Coping With Depression Course.* Eugene, OR: Castalia.

Brown, P. L., & Jenkins, H. M. (1968). Autoshaping of the pigeon's key-peck. *Journal of the Experimental Analysis of Behavior, 11,* 1–8.

Brown, R. A., & Lewinsohn, P. M. (1984). A psychoeducational approach to the treatment of depression: Comparison of group, individual, and minimal contact procedures. *Journal of Consulting and Clinical Psychology, 52,* 774–783.

Brown, R. A., & Ramsey, S. E. (in press). Addressing comorbid depressive symptomatology in alcohol treatment. *Professional Psychology: Research and Practice.*

Brown, R. A., Kahler, C. W., Niaura, R., Abrams, D. B., Sales, S. D., Ramsey, S. E., et al. (2001). Cognitive-behavioral treatment for depression in smoking cessation. *Journal of Consulting and Clinical Psychology, 69,* 471–480.

Brownell, K. D., & Barlow, D. H. (1976). Measurement and treatment of two sexual deviations in one person. *Journal of Behavior Therapy and Experimental Psychiatry, 7,* 349–354.

Brunswig, K. A., & O'Donohue, W. (2002). *Relapse prevention for sexual harassers.* New York: Kluwer Academic/Plenum.

Bryant, M. J., Simmons, A. D., & Thase, M. E. (1999). Therapist skill and patient variables in homework compliance: Controlling an uncontrolled variable in cognitive therapy outcome research. *Cognitive Therapy and Research, 23,* 381–399.

Bryant, R. A., Moulds, M. L., & Nixon, R. D. V. (2003). Cognitive behaviour therapy of acute stress disorder: A four-year follow-up. *Behaviour Research and Therapy, 41,* 489–494.

Burgio, K. L, Locher, J. L., Goode, P. S., Hardin, J. M., McDowell, B. J., Dombrowski, M., et al. (1998). Behavioral versus drug treatment for urge urinary incontinence in older women: A randomized controlled trial. *Journal of the American Medical Association, 280,* 1995–2000.

Burish, T. G., & Jenkins, R. A. (1992). Effectiveness of biofeedback and relaxation training in reducing side effects of cancer chemotherapy. *Health Psychology, 11,* 17–23.

Burns, D. D. (1999). *The feeling good handbook* (Rev. ed.). New York: Plume.

Buse, L., & Pawlik, K. (2001). Ambulatory behavioral assessment and in-field performance testing. In J. Fahrenberg & M. Myrtek (Eds.), *Ambulatory assessment: Computer-assisted psychological and psychophysiological methods in monitoring and field studies* (pp. 29–50). Kirkland, WA: Hogrefe & Huber.

Butcher, J. (Ed.). (1994). *International adaptations of the MMPI-2: Research and clinical applications.* Minneapolis: University of Minnesota Press.

Calloway, C. J., & Simpson, R. L. (1998). Decisions regarding functions of behavior: Scientific versus informal analyses. *Focus on Autism and Other Developmental Disabilities, 13*(3), 167–175.

Campos, P. E. (Ed.). (2002). Special series: Integrating Buddhist philosophy with cognitive and behavioral practice. *Cognitive and Behavioral Practice, 9,* 38–78.

Carlson, C. R., & Bernstein, D. A. (1995). Relaxation skills training: Abbreviated progressive relaxation. In W. T. O'Donohue & L. Krasner (Eds.), *Handbook of psychological skills training: Clinical techniques and applications.* Boston: Allyn & Bacon.

Carlson, J. G., Chemtob, C. M., Rusnak, K., Hedlund, N. L., & Muraoka, M. Y. (1998). Eye movement desensitization and reprocessing for combat-related posttraumatic stress disorder. *Journal of Traumatic Stress, 11,* 324.

Carnap, R. (1953). Testability and meaning. In H. Feigl & M. Brodbeck (Eds.), *Readings in the philosophy of science* (pp. 47–92). New York: Appleton-Century-Crofts.

Carney, N. C., Maynard, H. M., & Patterson, P. H. (1999). Effect of cognitive rehabilitation on outcomes for persons with traumatic brain injury: A systematic review. *Journal of Head Trauma Rehabilitation, 14*(3), 277–307.

Carr, E. G., Doolabh, A., Horner, R. H., Marquis, J. G., McAtee, M. L., McLaughlin, D. M., et al. (1999). *Positive behavioral support for people with developmental disabilities.* Washington, DC: American Association on Mental Retardation.

Carr, J. E., Coriaty, S., Wilder, D. A., Gaunt, B. T., Dozier, C. L., Britton, L. N., Avina, C., et al. (2000). A review of "non-contingent" reinforcement as treatment for the aberrant behavior of individuals with developmental disabilities. *Research in Developmental Disabilities, 21,* 377–391.

Carroll, K. M. (1996). Relapse prevention as a psychosocial treatment approach: A review of controlled clinical trials. *Experimental and Clinical Psychopharmacology, 4,* 46–54.

Carroll, K. M., & Nuro, K. F. (2002). One size cannot fit all: A stage model for psychotherapy manual development. *Clinical Psychology: Science and Practice, 9,* 396–406.

Carstensen, L. (1988). The emerging field of behavioral gerontology. *Behavior Therapy, 19,* 259–281.

Carter, M., & Barlow, D. H. (1993). Interoceptive exposure in the treatment of panic disorder. In *Innovations in clinical practice: A source book* (Vol. 12, pp. 329–336). Sarasota, FL: Professional Resource Exchange.

Cassidy, E. L., & Sheikh, J. I. (2002). Pre-intervention assessment for disruptive behavior problems: A focus on staff needs. *Aging & Mental Health, 6,* 166–171.

Catania, A. C. (1971). Reinforcement schedules: The role of responses preceding the one that produces the reinforcer. *Journal of the Experimental Analysis of Behavior, 15,* 271–287.

Cautela, J. (1990). The shaping of behavior therapy: A historical perspective. *The Behavior Therapist, 13,* 211–212.

Cautela, J. R. (1966). A behavior therapy treatment of pervasive anxiety. *Behavior, Research, and Therapy, 4,* 99–109.

Cautela, J. R. (1966). Treatment of compulsive behavior by covert sensitization. *Psychological Record, 16,* 33–41.

Cautela, J. R. (1967). Covert sensitization. *Psychological Record, 20,* 459–468.

Cautela, J. R. (1969). A classical conditioning approach to the development and modification of behavior in the aged. *The Gerontologist, 9*(Part 1), 109–113.

Cautela, J. R. (1971). Covert conditioning. In A. Jacobs & L. B. Sachs (Eds.), *The psychology of private events: Perspectives on covert response systems* (pp. 109–130). New York: Academic Press.

Cautela, J. R., & Kearney, A. (1986). *The covert conditioning handbook.* New York: Springer.

Cautela, J. R., & Kearney, A. J. (1990). Behavior analysis, cognitive therapy, and covert conditioning. *Journal of Behavior Therapy and Experimental Psychiatry, 21,* 83–90.

Cautela, J. R., & Wisocki, P. A. (1977). The thought-stopping procedure: Description, application, and learning theory interpretations. *The Psychological Record, 2,* 255–264.

Cautela, J., & Kastenbaum, R. (1967). A reinforcement survey schedule for use in therapy, training, and research. *Psychological Reports, 20,* 1115–1130.

Cautela, J., & Kearney, A. (1986). *The covert conditioning handbook.* New York: Springer.

Chambless, D. L., Baker, M. J., Baucom, D. H., Beutler, L. E., Calhoun, K. S., Crits-Christoph, P., et al. (1998). Update on empirically validated therapies, II. *The Clinical Psychologist, 51,* 3–16.

Chambless, D. L., Sanderson, W. C., Shoham, V., Bennett-Johnson, S., Pope, K. S., Crits-Chiristoph, P., et al. (1996). An update on empirically validated therapies. *The Clinical Psychologist, 49,* 5–18.

Chappell, M. N., & Stevenson, T. I. (1936). Group psychological training in some organic conditions. *Mental Hygiene, 20,* 588–597.

Chemtob, C. M., Novaco, R. W., Hamada, R., & Gross, D. (1997). Cognitive-behavioral treatment for severe anger in posttraumatic stress disorder. *Journal of Consulting and Clinical Psychology, 65,* 184–189.

Cicerone, K. D., Dahlberg, C., Kalmar, K., Langenbahn, D. M., Malec, M. F., Bergquist, T. F., et al. (2000). Evidence-based cognitive rehabilitation: Recommendations for clinical practice. *Archives of Physical Medicine and Rehabilitation, 18*(12), 1596–1615.

Clark, D. A., & Beck, A. T. (with Alford, B. A.). (1999). *Scientific foundations of cognitive theory and therapy of depression.* New York: Wiley.

Clark, D. M., & Fairburn, C. G. (Eds.). (1997). *Science and practice of cognitive behaviour therapy.* New York: Oxford University Press.

Clark, D. M., & Wells, A. (1995). A cognitive model for social phobia. In R. G. Heimberg, M. R. Liebowitz, D. A. Hope, & F. R. Schneier (Eds.), *Social phobia: Diagnosis, assessment, and treatment* (pp. 69–93). New York: Guilford Press.

Clark, H. B., & Davis, M. (2000). *Transition to adulthood: A resource for assisting young people with emotional or behavioral difficulties.* Baltimore: Paul H. Brookes.

Clarke, G. N., Hawkins, W., Murphy, M., Sheeber, L. B., Lewinsohn, P. M., & Seeley, J. J. (1995). Targeted prevention of unipolar depressive disorder in an at-risk sample of high school adolescents: A randomized trial of a group cognitive intervention. *Journal of the American Academy of Child and Adolescent Psychiatry, 34*(3), 312–321.

Cohen-Mansfield, J., & Werner, P. (1997). Management of verbally disruptive behaviors in nursing home residents. *Journal of Gerontology: Medical Sciences, 52A,* M369–M377.

Collins, R. L., Morsheimer, E. T., Shiffman, S., Hufford, M. R., Shields, A. L., Shiffman, S., et al. (1998). Ecological momentary assessment in a behavioral drinking moderation training program. *Experimental and Clinical Psychopharmacology, 6*, 306–315.

Cone, J. D. (1999). Introduction to the special section on self-monitoring: A major assessment method in clinical psychology. *Psychological Assessment, 11*, 411–414.

Constantino, M. J., Castonguay, L. G., & Schut, A. J. (2002). The working alliance: A flagship for the "scientist-practitioner" model in psychotherapy. In G. S. Tryon (Ed.), *Counseling based on process research: Applying what we know* (pp. 81–131). Boston: Allyn & Bacon.

Coon, D. W., & Gallagher-Thompson, D. (2002). Encouraging homework completion among older adults in therapy. *Journal of Clinical Psychology, 58*, 549–563.

Cormier, S., & Cormier, B. (1998). *Interviewing strategies for helpers: Fundamental skills and cognitive-behavioral interventions.* Pacific Grove, CA: Brooks/Cole.

Corrigan, P. W., & Jakus, M. R. (1994). Behavioral treatment. In J. M. Silver & S. C. Yudofsky, et al. (Eds.), *Neuropsychiatry of traumatic brain injury* (pp. 733–769). Washington, DC: American Psychiatric Association.

Costello, E., & Borkovec, T.D. (1992). Generalized anxiety disorder. In A. Freeman & F. M. Dattilio (Eds.), *Comprehensive casebook of cognitive therapy.* New York: Plenum Press.

Craske, M. G., & Barlow, D. H. (2000). *Mastery of your anxiety and panic: Client workbook for agoraphobia* (3rd ed.). Boulder, CO: Graywind.

Craske, M. G., Barlow, D. H., & Meadows, E. A. (2000). *Mastery of your anxiety and panic: Therapist guide for anxiety, panic, and agoraphobia* (3rd ed.). Boulder, CO: Graywind.

Craske, M., & Zoellner, L. (1996). Anxiety disorders: The role of marital therapy. In N. Jacobson & A. Gurman (Eds.), *Clinical handbook of couples therapy* (pp. 394–410). New York: Guilford Press.

Critchley, J. A., & Capewell, S. (2003). Mortality risk reduction associated with smoking cessation in patients with coronary heart disease: A systematic review. *Journal of the American Medical Association, 290*, 86–97.

Cuijpers, P. (1998). A psychoeducational approach to the treatment of depression: A meta-analysis of Lewinsohn's "Coping With Depression" course. *Behavior Therapy, 29*, 521–533.

Curtis, R. H., & Presley, A. S. (1972). The extinction of homosexual behaviour by covert sensitization: A case study. *Behavior Research and Therapy, 10*, 81–83.

Cuvo, A. J., & Davis, P. K. (1998). Establishing and transferring stimulus control: Teaching people with developmental disabilities. In J. K. Luiselli & M. J. Cameron (Eds.), *Antecedent control: Innovative approaches to behavioral support* (pp. 347–372). Baltimore: Paul H. Brookes.

D'Zurilla, T. J., & Nezu, A. M. (1999). *Problem-solving therapy: A social competence approach to clinical intervention* (2nd ed.). New York: Springer.

D'Zurilla, T. J., Nezu, A. M., & Maydeu-Olivares, A. (2002). *Social Problem-Solving Inventory-Revised (SPSI-R): Technical manual.* North Tonawanda, NY: Multi-Health Systems.

D'Zurilla, T. J., Nezu, A. M., & Maydeu-Olivares, A. (in press). What is social problem solving? Meaning, measures, and models. In E. C. Chang, T. J. D'Zurilla, & L. J. Sanna (Eds.), *Social problem solving: Theory, research, and training.* Washington, DC: American Psychological Association.

Daiuto, A. D., Baucom, D. H., Epstein, N., & Dutton, S. S. (1998). The application of behavioral couples therapy to the assessment and treatment of agoraphobia: Implications of empirical research. *Clinical Psychology Review, 18*, 663–687.

Dana, R. H. (Ed.). (2000). *Handbook of cross-cultural and multicultural personality assessment.* Mahwah, NJ: Erlbaum.

Daniels, A. C. (1989). *Performance management: Improving quality productivity through positive reinforcement.* Tucker, GA: Performance Management Publications.

Daniels, A. C. (1994). *Bringing out the best in people.* New York: McGraw-Hill.

Daniels, A. C. (2001). *Other people's habits.* New York: McGraw-Hill.

Dattilio, F. M. (2002). Homework assignments in couple and family therapy. *Journal of Clinical Psychology, 58*, 535–547.

Davidson, P. O., & Costello, C. G. (Eds.). (1969). *N = 1: Experimental studies of single cases.* New York: Van Nostrand Reinhold.

Day, W. F. (1969). On certain similarities between the philosophical investigations of Ludwig Wittgenstein and the operationism of B. F. Skinner. *Journal of the Experimental Analysis of Behavior, 12*, 489–506.

De Jongh, A., Ten Broeke, E., & Renssen, M. R. (1999). Treatment of specific phobias with eye movement desensitization and reprocessing (EMDR): Protocol, empirical status, and conceptual issues. *Journal of Anxiety Disorders, 13*, 69–85.

Deffenbacher, J. L., & Michaels, A. C. (1981). Anxiety management training and self-control desensitization: 15 months later. *Journal of Counseling Psychology, 28*, 459–462.

Deffenbacher, J. L., & Michaels, A. C. (1981). Two self-control procedures in the reduction of targeted and non-targeted anxieties: A year later. *Journal of Counseling Psychology, 27*, 9–15.

Deffenbacher, J. L., & Stark, R. S. (1992). Relaxation and cognitive-relaxation treatments of general anger. *Journal of Counseling Psychology, 39*, 158–167.

Delprato, D. J. (1989). A paradigm shift in behavior therapy: From external control to self-control. In W. A. Hershberger (Ed.), *Volitional action: Conation and control* (pp. 449–467). Amsterdam: North Holland.

Delprato, D. J. (1995). Interbehavioral psychology: Critical, systematic, and integrative approach to clinical services.

In W. O'Donohue & L. Krasner (Eds.), *Theories of behavior therapy: Exploring behavior change* (pp. 609–636). Washington, DC: American Psychological Association.

Delprato, D. J. (2003). J. R. Kantor's interbehavioral psychology and humanism. *The Psychological Record, 53,* 3–14.

Dempster, R. J., & Hart, S. D. (2002). The relative utility of fixed and variable risk factors in discriminating sexual recidivists and nonrecidivists. *Sexual Abuse: A Journal of Research and Treatment, 14,* 121–138.

Detweiler, J. B., & Whisman, M. A. (1999). The role of homework assignments in cognitive therapy for depression: Potential methods for enhancing adherence. *Clinical Psychology: Science and Practice, 6,* 267–282.

Dickerson, F. B. (2000). Cognitive-behavioral psychotherapy for schizophrenia: A review of recent empirical studies. *Schizophrenia Research, 43,* 71–90.

Dickinson, J. (1977). *A behavioral analysis of sport.* Princeton, NJ: Princeton Book Company.

DiClemente, C. C., Prochaska, J. O., Fairhurst, S. K., Velicer, W. F., Velasquez, M. M., & Rossi, J. S. (1991). The process of smoking cessation: An analysis of precontemplation, contemplation, and preparation stages of change. *Journal of Consulting and Clinical Psychology, 59*(2), 295–304.

Division 12 Task Force. (1995). Training in and dissemination of empirically validated psychological treatments: Report and recommendations. *The Clinical Psychologist, 48,* 3–23.

Dobson, K. S. (1989). A meta-analysis of the efficacy of cognitive therapy for depression. *Journal of Consulting and Clinical Psychology, 57,* 414–419.

Donahoe, J. W. (1997). The necessity of neural networks. In G. E. Stelmach & P. A. Vroon (Series Eds.), J. W. Donahoe & V. P. Dorsel (Vol. Eds.), *Advances in psychology: Vol. 121. Neural-network models of cognition: Biobehavioral foundations* (pp. 1–19). Amsterdam: Elsevier.

Donahoe, J. W., & Palmer, D. C. (1989). The interpretation of complex human behavior: Some reactions to parallel distributed processing (J. L. McClelland, D. E. Rumelhart, & the PDP Research Group, Eds.). *Journal of the Experimental Analysis of Behavior, 51,* 399–416.

Donahoe, J. W., & Palmer, D. C. (1994). *Learning and complex behavior* (pp. 37–49). Boston: Allyn & Bacon.

Donahoe, J. W., & Wessells, M. G. (1980). *Learning, language, and memory* (pp. 176–189). New York: Harper & Row.

Donahoe, J. W., Burgos, J. E., & Palmer, D. C. (1993). Selectionist approach to reinforcement. *Journal of the Experimental Analysis of Behavior, 58,* 17–40.

Donahoe, J. W., Crowley, M. A., Millard, W. J., & Stickney, K. A. (1982). A unified principle of reinforcement. *Quantitative models of behavior* (Vol. 2, pp. 493–521). Cambridge, MA: Ballinger.

Donnellan, A. M., LaVigna, G. W., Negri-Shoultz, N., & Fassbender, L. L. (1988). *Progress without punishment.* New York: Teachers College Press.

Donohue, B., Acierno, R., Hersen, M., & Van Hasselt, V. B. (1995). Social skills training for depressed, visually impaired older adults. *Behavior Modification, 19,* 379–424.

Dougher, M. J. (2000). *Clinical behavior analysis.* Reno, NV: Context Press.

Dougher, M. J. (Ed.). (1993). Special section on clinical behavior analysis. Part I. *The Behavior Analyst, 16,* 269–330.

Dougher, M. J. (Ed.). (1994). Special section on clinical behavior analysis, Part II. *The Behavior Analyst, 17,* 287–364.

Dougher, M. J., Crossen, J. R., Ferraro, D. P., & Garland, R. (1987). The effects of covert sensitization on preference for sexual stimuli. *Journal of Behavior Therapy and Experimental Psychiatry, 18,* 337–348.

Dowd, E. T. (1995). Cognitive career assessment: Concepts and applications. *Journal of Career Assessment, 3,* 1–20.

Dowd, E. T. (2000). *Cognitive hypnotherapy.* Livingston, NJ: Jason Aronson.

Dowd, E. T. (2002). History and recent developments in cognitive psychotherapy. In R. L. Leahy & E. T. Dowd (Eds.), *Clinical advances in cognitive psychotherapy.* New York: Springer.

Dowd, E. T., & Courchaine, K. E. (2002). Implicit learning, tacit knowledge, and implications for stasis and change in cognitive psychotherapy. In R. L. Leahy & E. T. Dowd (Eds.), *Clinical advances in cognitive psychotherapy.* New York: Springer.

Downing, J. E., & Perino, D. M. (1992). Functional versus standardized assessment procedures: Implications for educational programming. *Mental Retardation, 30*(5) 289–295.

Driskell, J., Copper, C., & Moran, A. (1994). Does mental practice enhance performance? *Journal of Applied Psychology, 79,* 481–492.

Dryden, W. (Ed.). (2003). *Rational emotive behaviour therapy theoretical developments.* East Sussex, UK: Brunner-Routledge.

Dryden, W., & DiGiuseppe, R. (1990). *A primer on rational-emotive therapy.* Champaign, IL: Research Press.

Dubbert, P. M. (2002). Physical activity and exercise: Recent advances and current challenges. *Journal of Consulting and Clinical Psychology, 70,* 526–536.

Dush, D. M., Hirt, M. L., & Schroeder, H. E. (1983). Self-statement modification with adults: A meta-analysis. *Psychological Bulletin, 94,* 408–422.

Dush, D. M., Hirt, M. L., & Schroeder, H. E. (1989). Self-statement modification in the treatment of child behavior disorders: A meta-analysis. *Psychological Bulletin, 106,* 97–106.

Edelman, R., & Chambless, D. L. (1995). Adherence during sessions and homework in cognitive-behavioral group treatment of social phobia. *Behaviour Research and Therapy, 33,* 573–577.

Edinger, J. D., & Wohlgemuth, W. K. (1999). The significance and management of persistent primary insomnia: The past, present and future of behavioral insomnia therapies. *Sleep Medicine Reviews, 3,* 101–118.

Einstein, A., & Infeld, L. (1938). *The evolution of physics.* New York: Simon & Schuster.

Elkin, I., Shea, M. T., Watkins, J. T., Imber, S. D., Sotsky, S. M., Collins, J. F., et al. (1989). NIMH treatment of depression collaborative research program. I: General effectiveness of treatments. *Archives of General Psychiatry, 46,* 971–983.

Elksnin, L. K., & Elksnin, N. (1991). The school counselor as job search facilitator: Increasing employment of handicapped students through job clubs. *School Counselor, 38,* 215–220.

Elliot, A. J., Miltenberger, R. G., Kaster-Bundgaard, J., & Lumley, V. (1996). A national survey of assessment and therapy used by behavior therapists. *Cognitive and Behavioral Practice, 3,* 107–125.

Ellis, A. (1994). *Reason and emotion in psychotherapy: Revised and updated.* Secaucus, NJ: Birch Lane Press.

Ellis, A., & Dryden, W. (1987). *The practice of rational emotive therapy.* New York: Springer.

Emanuels-Zuurveen, L., & Emmelkamp, P. M. G. (1996). Individual behavioural-cognitive therapy versus marital therapy for depression in maritally distressed couples. *British Journal of Psychiatry, 169,* 181–188.

Emmelkamp, P. M. G. (1990). Anxiety and fear. In A. S. Bellack, M. Hersen, & A. Kazdin (Eds.), *International handbook of behavior modification and therapy.* (2nd ed., pp. 283–305). New York: Plenum Press.

Emmelkamp, P. M. G. (1994). Behavior therapy with adults. In A. E. Bergin & S. L. Garfield (Eds.), *Handbook of psychotherapy and behavior change: An empirical analysis.* New York: Wiley.

Emmelkamp, P. M. G., & Gerlsma, C. (1994). Marital functioning and the anxiety disorders. *Behavior Therapy, 25,* 407–429.

Emmelkamp, P. M. G., & Walta, C. (1978). The effects of therapy-set on electrical aversion therapy and covert sensitization. *Behaviour Therapy, 9,* 185–188.

Emmelkamp, P. M. G., de Haan, E., & Hoogduin, C. A. L. (1990). Marital adjustment and obsessive-compulsive disorder. *British Journal of Psychiatry, 156,* 55–60.

Emmelkamp, P. M. G., Krijn, M., Hulsbosch, L., de Vries, S., Schuemie, M. J., & van der Mast, C. A. P. G. (in press). Virtual reality treatment versus exposure in vivo: A comparative evaluation in acrophobia. *Behaviour Research & Therapy.*

Emmelkamp, P. M. G., Van Dyck, R., Bitter, M., Heins, R., Onstein, E. J., & Eisen, B. (1992). Spouse-aided therapy with agoraphobics. *British Journal of Psychiatry, 160,* 51–56.

Emmelkamp, P. M. G., van Linden-van den Heuvell, C., Rüphan, M., & Sanderman, R. (1989). Home-based treatment of obsessive-compulsive patients: Intersession interval and therapist involvement. *Behaviour Therapy and Research, 27*(1), 89–93.

Emmelkamp. P. M. G., & Wessels, H. (1975). Flooding in imagination versus flooding in vivo. A comparison with agoraphobics. *Behaviour Research & Therapy, 13,* 7–16.

Epstein, E. E., & McCrady, B. S. (1998). Behavioral couples treatment of alcohol and drug use disorders: Current status and innovations. *Clinical Psychology Review, 18,* 689–711.

Epstein, N. B., & Baucom, D. H. (2002). *Enhanced cognitive-behavioral therapy for couples: A contextual approach.* Washington, DC: APA Books.

Ervin, R. A., Radford, P. M., Bertsch, K., Piper, A. L., Ehrhardt, K. E., & Poling, A. (2001). Descriptive analysis and critique of the empirical literature on school-based functional assessment. *School Psychology Review, 30*(2), 193–210.

Espie, C. A. (2002). Insomnia: Conceptual issues in the development, maintenance and treatment of sleep disorder in adults. *Annual Review of Psychology, 53,* 1–44.

Estes, W. K., & Skinner, B. F. (1941). Some quantitative properties of anxiety. *Journal of Experimental Psychology, 29,* 390–400.

Evans, J. R., & Abarbanel, A. (Eds.). (1999). *Introduction to quantitative EEG and biofeedback.* New York: Academic Press.

Evans, M. D., Hollon, S. D., DeRubeis, R. J., Piasecki, J. M., Grove, W. M., Garvey, M. J., et al. (1992). Differential relapse following cognitive therapy and pharmacotherapy for depression. *Archives of General Psychiatry, 49,* 802–808.

Fairburn, C. G. (1995). *Overcoming binge eating.* New York: Guilford Press.

Fairburn, C. G., Cooper, Z., & Shafran, R. (2003). Cognitive behaviour therapy for eating disorders: A "transdiagnostic" theory and treatment. *Behavior Research and Therapy, 41,* 509–528.

Fairburn, C. G., Marcus, M. D., & Wilson, G. T. (1993). Cognitive-behavioral therapy for binge eating and bulimia nervosa: A comprehensive treatment manual. In C. G. Fairburn & G. T. Wilson (Eds.), *Binge eating: Nature, assessment, and treatment* (pp. 383–418). New York: Guilford Press.

Falk, J. L. (1977). The origin and functions of adjunctive behavior. *Animal Learning and Behavior, 5,* 325–335.

Falk, J. L. (1992). Drug abuse as an adjunctive behavior. *Drug and Alcohol Dependence, 52,* 91–98.

Fals-Stewart, W., Marks, A. P., & Schafer, J. (1993). A comparison of behavioral group therapy and individual behavior therapy in treating obsessive-compulsive disorder. *The Journal of Nervous and Mental Disease, 181,* 189–193.

Farne, M. A., & Jimenez-Munoz, N. (2000). Personality changes induced by AT practice. *Stress Medicine, 16*(4), 263–268.

Farrell, A. D. (1992). Computers and behavioral assessment: Current applications, future possibilities, and obstacles to routine use. *Behavioral Assessment, 13,* 159–179.

Favell, J. E. (Chairperson), Azrin, N. H., Baumeister, A. A., Carr, E. G., Dorsey, M. F., Forehand, R., et al. (1982). The treatment of self-injurious behavior (Monograph). *Behavior Therapy, 13,* 529–554.

Fay, A., & Lazarus, A. A. (1993). On necessity and sufficiency in psychotherapy. *Psychotherapy in Private Practice, 12,* 33–39.

Febbraro, G. A. R., & Clum, G. A. (1998). Meta-analytic investigation of the effectiveness of self-regulatory components in the treatment of adult problem behaviors. *Clinical Psychology Review, 18,* 143–161.

Fedoroff, I. C., & Taylor, S. (2001). Psychological and pharmacological treatments of social phobia: A meta-analysis. *Journal of Clinical Psychopharmacology, 21,* 311–324.

Feindler, E. L., & Ecton, R. B. (1986). *Adolescent anger control: Cognitive therapy techniques.* New York: Pergamon Press.

Ferguson, J., Marquis, J., & Taylor, C. B. (1977). A script for deep muscle relaxation. *Diseases of the Nervous System, 38,* 703–708.

Ferster, C. B. (1967). Arbitrary and natural reinforcement. *The Psychological Record, 22,* 1–16.

Ferster, C. B., & Skinner, B. F. (1957). *Schedules of reinforcement.* New York: Appleton-Century-Crofts.

Finch, A. J., Nelson, W. M., & Ott, E. S. (1993). *Cognitive-behavioral procedures with children and adolescents: A practical guide.* Boston: Allyn & Bacon

Fiore, M. C., Bailey, W. C, Cohen S., et al. (2000). *Treating tobacco use and dependence: Clinical practice guidelines.* Rockville, MD: U.S. Department of Health and Human Services.

Fiore, M. C., Smith, S. S., Jorenby, D. E., & Baker, T. B. (1994). The effectiveness of the nicotine patch for smoking cessation: A meta-analysis. *Journal of the American Medical Association, 271*(24), 1940–1947.

Fisch, G. S. (1998). Visual Inspection of data revisited: Do the eyes still have it? *The Behavior Analyst, 21,* 111–123.

Fisher, J. E., Swingen, D. N., & Harsin, C. M. (2001). Agitated and aggressive behavior. In B. Edelstein (Ed.), *Clinical geropsychology.* Oxford, UK: Elsevier Science.

Fishman, D. B., & Franks, C. M. (1997) The conceptual evolution of behavior therapy. In P. L. Wachtel & S. B. Messer (Eds.), *Theories of psychotherapy: Origins and evolution* (pp. 131–180). Washington, DC: American Psychological Association.

Fishman, S. T., & Lubetkin, B. S. (1983). Office practice of behavior therapy. In M. Hersen (Ed.), *Outpatient behavior therapy: A clinical guide.* New York: Grune & Stratton.

Fluharty, G., & Glassman, N. (2001). Use of antecedent control to improve the outcome of rehabilitation for a client with a frontal lobe injury and intolerance for auditory and tactile stimuli. *Brain Injury, 15*(11), 995–1002.

Foa, E. B., & Emmelkamp, P.M.G. (Eds.). (1983). *Failures in behavior therapy.* New York: Wiley.

Foa, E. B. (1979). Failures in treating obsessive-compulsives. *Behaviour Research and Therapy, 17,* 169–176.

Foa, E. B., & Franklin, M. E. (2001). Obsessive-compulsive disorder. In D. H. Barlow (Ed.), *Clinical handbook of psychological disorders* (3rd ed., pp. 209–263). New York: Guilford Press.

Foa, E. B., & Rothbaum, B. O. (1998). *Treating the trauma of rape: Cognitive-behavioral therapy for PTSD.* New York: Guilford Press.

Foa, E. B., Dancu, C. V., Hembree, E. A., Jaycox, L. H., Meadows, E. A., & Street, G. P. (1999). A comparison of exposure therapy, stress inoculation training, and their combination for reducing posttraumatic stress disorder in female assault victims. *Journal of Consulting and Clinical Psychology, 67,* 194–200.

Foa, E. B., Dancu, C. V., Hembree, E. A., Jaycox, L. H., Meadows, E. A., & Street, G. P. (1999). A comparison of exposure therapy, stress inoculation training, and their combination in reducing posttraumatic stress disorder in female assault victims. *Journal of Consulting and Clinical Psychology, 63,* 948–955.

Foa, E. B., Wilson, R., & Wilson, R. R. (2001). *Stop obsessing: How to overcome your obsessions and compulsions* (Rev. ed.). New York: Bantam Doubleday Dell.

Fodor, J. (1968). *Psychological explanation: An introduction to the philosophy of psychology.* New York: Random House.

Follette, W. C., & Callaghan, G. M. (1995). Do as I do, not as I say: A behavior-analytic approach to supervision. *Professional Psychology: Research and Practice, 26,* 413–421.

Follette, W. C., Naugle, A. E., & Callaghan, G. M. (1996). A radical behavioral understanding of the therapeutic relationship in effecting change. *Behavior Therapy, 27,* 623–641.

Ford, J. D. (1978). Therapeutic relationship in behavior therapy: An empirical analysis. *Journal of Clinical and Consulting Psychology, 46*(6), 1302–1314.

Foster, S. L., Laverty-Finch, C., Gizzo, D. P., & Osantowski, J. (1999). Practical issues in self-observation. *Psychological Assessment, 11,* 426–438.

Fox, P., & Emerson, E. (2002). *Positive goals: Interventions for people with learning disabilities whose behavior challenges.* Cheapside, Brighton, UK: Pavllion.

Frank, E., Anderson, B., Steward, B. D., Dancu, C., Hughes, C., & West, D. (1988). Efficacy of cognitive behavior therapy and systematic desensitization in the treatment of rape trauma. *Behavior Therapy, 19,* 403–420.

Frank, J. D., & Frank, J. B. (1993). *Persuasion & healing* (3rd ed.). Baltimore: Johns Hopkins University Press.

Frankl, V. E. (1975). Paradoxical intention and dereflection. *Psychotherapy: Theory, research and practice, 12,* 226–237.

Frankl, V. E. (1985). Logos, paradox, and the search for meaning. In M. J. Mahoney & A. Freeman (Eds.), *Cognition and psychotherapy.* New York: Plenum Press.

Franks, C. M. (1987). Behavior therapy and AABT: Personal recollections, conceptions, and misconceptions. *The Behavior Therapist, 10,* 171–174.

Franks, C. M. (1998). Forward: The importance of being theoretical. In J. J. Plaud & G. H. Eifert (Eds.), *From behavior theory to behavior therapy* (pp. ix–vxiii). Boston: Allyn & Bacon.

Frederiksen, L. W. (Ed.). (1982). *Handbook of organizational behavior management.* New York: Wiley.

Freeman, A., & Rosenfield, B. (2002). Modifying therapeutic homework for patients with personality disorders. *Journal of Clinical Psychology, 58,* 513–524.

Freeman, K. A., Anderson, C. M., & Scotti, J. R. (2000). A structured descriptive methodology: Increasing agreement between descriptive and experimental analyses. *Education and Training in Mental Retardation and Developmental Disabilities, 35,* 55–66.

Freud, S. (1917). *Completed psychological works: Vol. 14. Mourning and melancholia* (J. Strachey, Ed.). New York: Hogarth Press.

Fuller, P. R. (1973). Professors Kantor and Skinner: The "grand alliance" of the 40's. *The Psychological Record, 23,* 318–324.

Gaggioli, A., Mantovani, F., Castelnuovo, G., Wiederhold, B., & Riva, G. (2003). Avatars in clinical psychology: A framework for the clinical use of virtual humans. *Cyberpsychology and Behavior, 6*(2), 117–126.

Gaither, G. A., Rosenkranz, R. R., & Plaud, J. J. (1998). Sexual disorders. In J. J. Plaud & G. H. Eifert (Eds.), *From behavior theory to behavior therapy* (pp. 152–171). Boston: Allyn & Bacon.

Gambrill, E. (1995). Behavioral social work: Past, present and future. *Research on Social Work Practice, 5,* 460–484.

Gambrill, E. (1999). *Helping clients: A critical thinker's guide.* New York: Oxford University Press.

Garb, H. N. (1996). *Studying the clinician: Judgment research and psychological assessment.* Washington, DC: American Psychological Association.

Garfield, S. L. (1996). Some problems associated with "validated" forms of psychotherapy. *Clinical Psychology: Science and Practice, 3,* 218–229.

Garner, D. M., Vitousek, K., & Pike, K. (1997). Cognitive-behavioral therapy for anorexia nervosa. In D. M. Garner & P. E. Garfinkel (Eds.), *Handbook of treatment for eating disorders* (pp. 94–144). New York: Guilford Press.

Garssen, B., & Goodkin, K. (1999). On the role of immunological factors as mediators between psychosocial factors and cancer progression. *Psychiatry Research, 85,* 51–61.

Geller, E. S. (1998). *Applications of behavior analysis to prevent injuries from vehicle crashes.* Concord, MA: Cambridge Center for Behavioral Studies.

Gelso, C. J., & Woodhouse, S. S. (2002). The termination of psychotherapy: What research tells us about the process of ending treatment. In G. S. Tryon (Ed.), *Counseling based on process research: Applying what we know* (pp. 344–369). Boston: Allyn & Bacon.

Gershon, J., Anderson, P., Graap, K., Zimand, E., Hodges, L., & Rothbaum, B. O. (2002). Virtual reality exposure therapy in the treatment of anxiety disorders. *Scientific Review of Mental Health Practice, 1,* 78–83.

Gilbert, T. F. (1978). *Human competence: Engineering worthy performance.* New York: McGraw-Hill.

Goldfried, M. R. (1971). Systematic desensitization as training in self-control. *Journal of Consulting and Clinical Psychology, 37,* 228–234.

Goldfried, M. R. (2002). A cognitive-behavioral perspective on termination. *Journal of Psychotherapy Integration, 12,* 364–372.

Goldfried, M. R., & Davison, G. C. (1976). *Clinical behavior therapy.* New York: Holt, Rinehart & Winston.

Goldfried, N. M. R., & Goldfried, A. P. (1977). Importance of hierarchy content in the self-control of anxiety. *Journal of Consulting and Clinical Psychology, 45,* 124–134.

Goldiamond, I. (1973). A diary of self-modification. *Psychology Today, 7*(6), 95–102.

Goldiamond, I. (1975). Alternative sets as a framework for behavioral formulations and research. *Behaviorism, 3*(1), 49–86.

Goldiamond, I. (2002). Toward a constructional approach to social problems: Ethical and Constitutional issues raised by applied behavior analysis. *Behavior and Social Issues, 11*(2), 108–197. (Original work published 1974, *Behaviorism, 2,* 1–85)

Goldstein, E. B. (1994). Basic learning processes. In *Psychology* (pp. 220–271). Pacific Grove, CA: Brooks/Cole.

Gomez, E. J., Caceres, C., Lopez, D., & Del Pozo, F. (2002). A Web-based self-monitoring system for people living with HIV/AIDS. *Computer Methods and Programs in Biomedicine, 69,* 75–86.

Goss, A. E. (1961). Early behaviorism and verbal mediating responses. *American Psychologist, 16,* 285–298.

Gottman, J. M. (1999). *The marriage clinic: A scientifically based marital therapy.* New York: Norton.

Gould, R. A., Otto, M. W., & Pollack, M. H. (1995). A meta-analysis of treatment outcome for panic disorder. *Clinical Psychology Review, 15*(8), 819–844.

Graham, D. T., Kabler, J. D., & Lunsfors, L. (1961). Vasovagal fainting: A diphasic response. *Psychosomatic Medicine, 23,* 493–507.

Granvold, D. K. (1994). *Cognitive and behavioral treatment: Methods and applications.* Pacific Grove, CA: Wadsworth.

Greenberg, P. E., Stiglin, L. E., Findelstein, S. N., & Berndt, E. R. (1993). The economic burden of depression in 1990. *Journal of Clinical Psychiatry, 54,* 405–418.

Greenberger, D., & Padesky, C. A. (1995). *Mind over mood: Change how you feel by changing the way you think.* New York: Guilford Press.

Gresham, F. M., Sugai, G., & Horner, R. H. (2001). Interpreting outcomes of social skills training for students with high-incidence disabilities. *Exceptional Children, 67*(3), 331–344.

Gross, B. H. (2001). Informed consent (for psychotherapeutic treatment). *Annals of the American Psychotherapy Association, 4*(5), 24.

Gunaratana, H. (2002). *Mindfulness in plain English* (Updated and expanded ed.). Boston: Wisdom Publications.

Haley, J. (1973). *Uncommon therapy: The psychiatric techniques of Milton H. Erickson, M.D.* New York: Norton.

Hamberger, L. K. (1997). Cognitive-behavioral treatment for men who batter their partners. *Cognitive and Behavioral Practice, 4,* 147–169.

Hank, P., & Schwenkmezger, P. (2001). Computer-assisted versus paper-and-pencil based self-monitoring: An analysis of experiential and psychometric equivalence. In J. Fahrenberg & M. Myrtek (Eds.), *Ambulatory assessment: Computer-assisted psychological and psychophysiological methods in monitoring and field studies* (pp. 85–99). Kirkland, WA: Hogrefe & Huber.

Hanson, H. M. (1959). Effects of discrimination training on stimulus generalization. *Journal of Experimental Psychology, 58,* 321–334.

Hanson, R. K., Gordon, A., Harris, A. J. R., Marques, J. K., Murphy, W., Quinsey, V. L., et al. (2002). First report of the collaborative outcome data project on the effectiveness of psychological treatment for sex offenders. *Sexual Abuse: A Journal of Research and Treatment, 14,* 169–194.

Harvey, A. G., Clark, D. A., Ehlers, A., & Rapee, R. M. (2000). Social anxiety and self-impression: Cognitive preparation enhances the beneficial effects of video feedback following a stressful social task. *Behavior Research and Therapy, 38,* 1183–1192.

Haugen, N. S. (2000). The effect of autogenic relaxation on hostility and cardiovascular reactivity in African-American women. *Dissertation Abstracts International: Section B: The Sciences and Engineering,* 61(6-B0, 2988).

Hawton, K. (1993). *Sex therapy.* Oxford, UK: Oxford University Press.

Haydn-Smith, P., Marks, I., Buchaya, H., & Repper, D. (1987). Behavioral treatment of life threatening masochistic asphyxiation: A case study. *British Journal of Psychiatry, 150,* 518–519.

Hayes, L., Austin, J., Houmanfar, R., & Clayton, M. (Eds.). (2001). *Organizational change.* Reno, NV: Context Press.

Hayes, S. C., Barlow, D. H., & Nelsen-Gray, R. O. (1999). *The scientist practitioner: Research and accountability in the age of managed care* (2nd ed.). Boston: Allyn & Bacon.

Hayes, S. C., Barnes, D., & Roche, B. (Eds.). (2001). *Relational frame theory: A post-Skinnerian account of human language and cognition.* New York: Plenum Press.

Hayes, S. C., Brownwell, K. D., & Barlow, D. H. (1978). The use of self-administered covert sensitization in the treatment of exhibitionism and sadism. *Behavior Therapy, 9,* 283–289.

Hayes, S. C., Jacobson, N. S., Follette, V. M., & Dougher, M. J. (Eds.). (1994). *Acceptance and change: Content and context in psychotherapy.* Reno, NV: Context Press.

Hayes, S. C., Strosahl, K. D., & Wilson, K. G. (1999). *Acceptance and commitment therapy: An experiential approach to behavior change.* New York: Guilford Press.

Hayes, S. C., Wilson, K. G., & Gifford, E. V. (1999). A contextualistic perspective on consciousness and private events. In B. A. Thyer (Ed.), *The philosophical legacy of behaviorism* (pp. 153–187). Dordrecht, Netherlands: Kluwer.

Haynes, S. N. (2001). Clinical applications of analogue behavioral observation: Dimensions of psychometric evaluation. *Psychological Assessment, 13,* 73–85.

Haynes, S. N., & Heiby, E. M. (Eds.). (2003). *Behavioral assessment.* New York: Wiley.

Haynes, S. N., & O'Brien, W. H. (1990). Functional analysis in behavior therapy. *Clinical Psychology Review, 10,* 649–668.

Haynes, S. N., & O'Brien, W. H. (2000). *Principles and practice of behavioral assessment.* New York: Kluwer.

Hays, P. A. (1995). Multicultural applications of cognitive-behavior therapy. *Professional Psychology: Research and Practice, 26,* 309–315.

Heimberg, R. G., & Becker, R. E. (2002). *Cognitive-behavioral group therapy for social phobia.* New York: Guilford Press.

Hempel, C. (1980). The logical analysis of psychology. In N. Block (Ed.), *Readings in the philosophy of psychology* (Vol. I, pp. 14–33). Cambridge, MA: Harvard University Press.

Herman, S. M. (1991). Client-therapist similarity on the Multimodal Structural Profile Inventory as predictive of psychotherapy outcome. *Psychotherapy Bulletin, 26,* 26–27.

Herman, S. M. (1998). The relationship between therapist-client modality similarity and psychotherapy outcome. *Journal of Psychotherapy Practice and Research, 7,* 56–64.

Herman, S., & Koran, L. M. (1998). In vivo measurement of obsessive-compulsive disorder symptoms using palmtop computers. *Computers in Human Behavior, 14*(3), 449–462.

Herrnstein, R. J. (1970). On the law of effect. *Journal of the Experimental Analysis of Behavior, 13,* 243–266.

Hersen, M. (Ed.). (2002). *Clinical behavior therapy: Adults and children.* New York: Wiley.

Hersen, M., & Barlow, D. H. (1976). *Single case experimental designs: Strategies for studying behavior change.* New York: Pergamon Press.

Hersen, M., & Bellack, A. S. (1999). *Handbook of comparative interventions for adult disorders.* New York: Wiley.

Hersen, M., Bellack, A. S., & Himmelhoch, J. M. (1980). Treatment of unipolar depression with social skills training. *Behavior Modification, 4,* 547–556.

Hersen, M., Eisler, R. M., & Miller, P. M. (Eds.). (1990). *Progress in behavior modification.* Newbury Park, CA: Sage.

Hersen, M. (Ed.). (2002). *Clinical behavior therapy: Adults and children.* New York: Wiley.

Higgins, S. T., Wong, C. J., Badger, G. J., Ogden, D. E. H., & Dantona, R. L. (2000). Contingent reinforcement increases cocaine abstinence during outpatient treatment and 1 year of follow-up. *Journal of Consulting and Clinical Psychology, 68,* 64–72.

Hillenberg, B., & Collins, F. (1982). A procedural analysis and review of relaxation training research. *Behavior Research and Therapy, 20,* 251–260.

Hoffart, A. (1995). A comparison of cognitive and guided mastery therapy of agoraphobia. *Behavior Research and Therapy, 33,* 423–434.

Hoffart, A. (1998). Cognitive and guided mastery therapy of agoraphobia: Long-term outcome and mechanisms of change. *Cognitive Therapy and Research, 22,* 195–207.

Holburn, S., & Vietze, P. M. (2002). *Person-centered planning: Research, practice, and future directions.* Baltimore: Paul H. Brookes.

Holder, H. D., Cisler, R. A., Longabaugh, R., Stout, R. L., Treno, A. J., & Zweben, A. (2000). Alcoholism treatment and medical care costs from Project MATCH. *Addiction, 95,* 999–1013.

Hollon, S. D. (2001). Behavioral activation treatment for depression: A commentary. *Clinical Psychology: Science and Practice, 8,* 271–274.

Hollon, S. D., DeRubeis, R. J., Evans, M. D., Wiemer, M. J., Garvey, M. J., Grove, W. M., et al. (1992). Cognitive therapy and pharmacotherapy for depression. *Archives of General Psychiatry, 49,* 774–781.

Hollon, S. D., Muñoz, R. F., Barlow, D. H., Beardslee, M. D., Bell, C. C., Bernal, G., et al. (2002). Psychosocial intervention development for the prevention and treatment of depression: Promoting innovation and increasing awareness. *Biological Psychiatry, 52,* 610–630.

Hopko, D. R., Lejuez, C. W., LePage, J., McNeil, D. W., & Hopko, S. D. (in press). A brief behavioral activation treatment for depression: A randomized pilot trial within an inpatient psychiatric hospital. *Behavior Modification.*

Hopko, D. R., Lejuez, C. W., Ruggiero, K. J., & Eifert, G. H. (in press). Contemporary behavioral activation treatments for depression: Procedures, principles, and progress. *Clinical Psychology Review.*

Horvath, A. O., & Bedi, R. P. (2002). The alliance. In J. C. Norcross (Ed.), *Psychotherapy relationships that work: Therapist contributions and responsiveness to patients* (pp. 37–69). New York: Oxford.

Howard, K. I., Moras, K., Brill, P. L., Martinovich, Z., & Lutz, W. (1996). Efficacy, effectiveness, and client progress. *American Psychologist, 51,* 1059–1064.

Hudson, J. L., & Kendall, P.C. (2002). Showing you can do it: Homework in therapy for children and adolescents with anxiety disorders. *Journal of Clinical Psychology, 58,* 525–534.

Hughes, J. (1998). Harm-reduction approaches to smoking. The need for data. *American Journal of Preventive Medicine, 15,* 78–79.

Hughes, J. R., Shiffman, S., Callas, P., & Zhang, J. (2003). A meta-analysis of the efficacy of over-the-counter nicotine replacement. *Tobacco Control, 12,* 21–27.

Hughes, J. R., Stead, L. F., & Lancaster, T. (2001). Antidepressants for smoking cessation (Cochrane Review). *The Cochrane Library, 4.*

Hughes, R. C. (1977). Covert sensitization treatment of exhibitionism. *Journal of Behavior Therapy and Experimental Psychiatry, 8,* 177–179.

Hume, D. (1973) *A treatise of human nature* (A. Selby-Bigge, Ed.; Book 3, Pt. 1, Sec. 1. L.). Oxford, UK: Clarendon Press.

Hung, J. H. F., & Rosenthal, T. L. (1978). Therapeutic videotaped playback: A critical review. *Advances in Behaviour Research and Therapy, 1,* 103–135.

Huppert, J. D., & Baker, S. L. (2003). Going beyond the manual: An insiders guide to panic control treatment. *Cognitive and Behavioral Practice, 10,* 2–12.

Hurt R. D., Sachs, D. P., Glover, E. D., Offord, K. P., Johnston, J. A., Dale, L. C., et al. (1997). A comparison of sustained-release buproprion and placebo for smoking cessation. *New England Journal of Medicine, 337,* 1195–1202.

Hurt, R. D., Krook, J. E., Croghan, I. T., Loprinzi, C. L, Sloan, J. A., Novotny, P. J., et al. (2003). Nicotine patch therapy based on smoking rate followed by bupropiron for prevention of relapse to smoking. *Journal of Clinical Oncology, 21,* 914–920.

Hussian, R. A. (1981). *Geriatric psychology: A behavioral perspective.* New York: Van Nostrand.

Hussian, R. A., & Davis, R. L. (1985). *Responsive care: Behavioral interventions with elderly persons.* Champaign, IL: Research Press.

Hyman, R. B., Feldman, H. R., Harris, R. B., Levin, R. F., & Malloy, G. B. (1989). The effects of relaxation training on clinical symptoms: A meta-analysis. *Nursing Research, 38*(4), 216–220.

Iwata, B. A., Smith, R. G., & Michael, J. (2000). Current research on the influence of establishing operations on behavior in applied settings, *Journal of Applied Behavior Analysis, 33,* 411–418.

Iwata, B. A., Sung Woo, K., Wallace, M. D., & Lindberg, J. S. (2000). The functional analysis model of behavioral assessment. In J. Austin & J. E. Carr (Eds.), *Handbook of applied behavior analysis.* Reno, NV: Context Press.

Jackson, J. L. (1999). Psychometric considerations in self-monitoring assessment. *Psychological Assessment, 11,* 439–447.

Jackson, Y., Dietz, W., Sanders, C., Kolbe, L. J., Whyte, J. J., Wechsler, B. S., et al. (2002). Summary of the 2000 Surgeon General's listening session: Toward a national action plan on overweight and obesity. *Obesity Research, 10,* 1299–1305.

Jacobs, E. (1984). A skills-oriented model facilitating employment among psychiatrically disabled persons. *Rehabilitation Counseling Bulletin, 28,* 87–96.

Jacobson, E. (1977). The origins and development of progressive relaxation. *Journal of Behavior Therapy and Experimental Psychiatry, 8,* 119–123.

Jacobson, E. (1929). *Progressive relaxation: A physiological and clinical investigation of muscular states and their significance in psychology and medical practice.* Chicago: University of Chicago Press.

Jacobson, E. (1938). *Progressive relaxation* (2nd ed.). Chicago: University of Chicago Press.

Jacobson, E. (1970). *Modern treatment of tense patients.* Springfield, IL: Charles C Thomas.

Jacobson, E. (1978). *You must relax* (4th ed.). New York: McGraw-Hill.

Jacobson, N. (Ed.). (1987). *Psychotherapists in clinical practice: Cognitive and behavioral perspectives.* New York: Guilford Press.

Jacobson, N. S., & Margolin, G. (1979). *Marital therapy: Strategies based on social learning and behavior exchange principles.* New York: Brunner/Mazel.

Jacobson, N. S., Dobson, K. S., Truax, P. A., Addis, M. E., Koerner, K., Gollan, J. K., et al. (1996). A component analysis of cognitive-behavioral treatment for depression. *Journal of Consulting and Clinical Psychology, 64,* 295–304.

Jacobson, N. S., Martell, C. R., & Dimidjian, S. (2001). Behavioral activation treatment for depression: Returning to contextual roots. *Clinical Psychology: Science and Practice, 8,* 255–270.

Jamison, R. N., Raymond, S. A., Levine, J. G., Slawsby, E. A., Nedeljkovic, S. S., & Katz, N. P. (2001). Electronic diaries for monitoring chronic pain: 1-year validation study. *Pain, 91,* 277–285.

Jaspers, K. (1963). *General psychopathology.* Manchester, UK: Manchester University Press.

Jayaratne, S., & Levy, R. L. (1979). *Empirical clinical practice.* New York: Columbia University Press.

Jenkins, H. M., & Harrison, R. H. (1962). Effect of discrimination training on auditory generalization. *Journal of the Experimental Analysis of Behavior, 5,* 434–441.

Jenkins, H. M., & Moore, B. R. (1973). The form of the auto-shaped response with food and water reinforcement. *Journal of the Experimental Analysis of Behavior, 20,* 163–181.

Johnson, C., Mawhinney, T. C., & Redmon, W. (Eds.). (2001). *Handbook of organizational performance: Behavior analysis and management.* Binghamton, NY: Haworth Press.

Johnson, J. M., & Pennypacker, H. S. (1993). *Strategies and tactics of behavioral research* (2nd ed.). Hillsdale, NJ: Erlbaum.

Johnson, R. E. (1980). Memory-based rehearsal. In G. Bower (Ed.), *The psychology of learning and motivation* (Vol. 14, pp. 263–307). New York: Academic Press.

Johnson, W. B., Ridley, C. R., & Nielsen, S. L. (2000). Religiously sensitive rational emotive behavior therapy: Elegant solutions and ethical risks. *Professional Psychology: Research and Practice, 31*(1), 14–20.

Johnston, P., Hudson, S. M., & Marshall, W. L. (1992). The effects of masturbatory reconditioning with nonfamilial child molesters. *Behaviour Research and Therapy, 30,* 559–561.

Joseph, A. M., & Antonuccio, D. O. (1999). Lack of efficacy of transdermal nicotine in smoking cessation. *New England Journal of Medicine, 341,* 1157–1158.

Kabat-Zinn, J. (1990). *Full catastrophe living: Using the wisdom of your body and mind to face stress, pain, and illness.* New York: Dell.

Kabat-Zinn, J. (1994). *Wherever you go, there you are: Mindfulness meditation in everyday life.* New York: Hyperion.

Kadden, R. M. (2001) Behavioral and cognitive-behavioral treatments for alcoholism: Research opportunities. *Addictive Behaviors, 26*(4), 489–507.

Kahng, S. W., & Iwata, B. A. (1998). Computerized systems for collecting real-time observational data. *Journal of Applied Behavior Analysis, 31,* 253–261.

Kamin, L. J. (1969). Predictability, surprise, attention, and conditioning. In B. A. Campbell & R. M. Church (Eds.), *Punishment and aversive behavior* (pp. 279–296). New York: Appleton-Century-Crofts.

Kanfer, F. H., & Gaelick-Buys, L. (1991). Self-management methods. In F. H. Kanfer & A. P. Goldstein (Eds.), *Helping people change: A textbook of methods* (4th ed., pp. 305–360). New York: Pergamon Press.

Kanter, N. J., & Goldfried, M. R. (1979). Relative effectiveness of rational restructuring and self-control desensitization in the reduction of interpersonal anxiety. *Behavior Therapy, 10,* 472–490.

Kantor, J. R. (1953). *The logic of modern science.* Chicago: Principia Press.

Kantor, J. R. (1959). *Interbehavioral psychology.* Granville, OH: Principia Press.

Kantor, J. R. (1969). *The scientific evolution of psychology* (Vol. 2). Chicago: Principia Press.

Kantor, J. R., & Smith, N. W. (1975). *The science of psychology: An interbehavioral survey.* Chicago: Principia Press.

Kapche, R. (1974). Aversion-relief therapy: A review of current procedures and the clinical and experimental evidence. *Psychotherapy: Theory, Research, and Practice, 11,* 156–162.

Karel, M., Ogland-Hand, S., & Gatz, M. (2002). *Assessing and treating late-life depression: A casebook and resource guide.* New York: Basic Books.

Karoly, P. (1995). Self-control theory. In W. O'Donohue & L. Krasner (Eds.), *Theories of behavior therapy: Exploring behavior change* (pp. 259–285). Washington, DC: American Psychological Association.

Kasman, G. S., Cram, J. R., Wolf, S. L., & Barton, L. (1998). *Clinical applications in surface electromyography: Chronic musculosketal pain.* Gaithersberg, MD: Aspen.

Kazantzis, N. (1999). Psychologists' use of homework assignments in clinical practice. *Professional Psychology: Research and Practice, 30,* 581–585.

Kazantzis, N., & Lampropoulos, G. K. (2002). Reflecting on homework in psychotherapy: What can we conclude from research and experience? *Journal of Clinical Psychology, 58,* 577–585.

Kazantzis, N., Deane, F. P., & Ronan, K. R. (2000). Homework assignments in cognitive and behavioral therapy: A meta-analysis. *Clinical Psychology: Science and Practice, 7,* 189–202.

Kazdin, A. (1994). *Behavior modification in applied settings* (5th ed.). Pacific Grove, CA: Brooks/Cole.

Kazdin, A. E. (1977). Assessing the clinical or applied importance of behavior change through social validation. *Behavior Modification, 1,* 427–451.

Kazdin, A. E. (1977). *The token economy: A review and evaluation.* New York: Plenum Press.

Kazdin, A. E. (1978). *History of behavior modification: Experimental foundations of contemporary research.* Baltimore: University Park Press.

Kazdin, A. E. (1982). *Single-case research designs: Methods for clinical and applied settings.* New York: Oxford University Press.

Kazdin, A. E. (1993). *Research design in clinical psychology* (2nd ed.). Boston: Allyn & Bacon.

Kazdin, A. E. (1994). *Behavior modification in applied settings* (5th ed.). Pacific Grove, CA: Brooks/Cole.

Kazdin, A. E. (2000). *Psychotherapy for children and adolescents: Directions for research and practice.* New York: Oxford University Press.

Kazdin, A. E. (2001). *Behavior modification in applied settings* (6th ed.). Belmont, CA: Wadsworth/Thomson Learning.

Kazdin, A. E. (2003). *Research design in clinical psychology* (4th ed.). Needham Heights, MA: Allyn & Bacon.

Kazdin, A. E. (Ed.). (2000). *The encyclopedia of psychology* (Vols. 1–8). New York/Washington, DC: Oxford University Press/American Psychological Association.

Kazdin, A. E. (Ed.). (2003). *Methodological issues and strategies in clinical research* (3rd ed.). Washington, DC: American Psychological Association.

Kazdin, A. E., & Weisz, J. R. (Eds.). (2003). *Evidence-based psychotherapies for children and adolescents.* New York: Guilford Press.

Kazdin, A. E., & Wilson, G. T. (1978). *Evaluation of behavior therapy: Issues, evidence, and research strategies.* Cambridge, MA: Ballinger.

Kegel, A. H. (1948). Progressive resistance exercise in the functional restoration of the perineal muscles. *American Journal of Obstetrics and Gynecology, 56,* 238–248.

Keijsers, G. P. J., Schaap, C. P. D. R., & Hoogduin, C. A. L. (2000). The impact of interpersonal patient and therapist behavior on outcome in cognitive-behavioral therapy. *Behavior Modification, 24,* 264–297.

Kenardy, J., & Taylor, C.B. (1999). Expected versus unexpected panic attacks: A naturalistic prospective study. *Journal of Anxiety Disorders, 13,* 435–445.

Kendall, P. C., & Chambless, D. L. (Eds.). (1998). Empirically supported psychological therapies [Special section]. *Journal of Consulting and Clinical Psychology, 66,* 3–167.

Kendall, P. C., Holmbeck, G., & Verduin, T. (2004). Methodology, design, and evaluation in psychotherapy research. In M. J. Lambert (Ed.), *Bergin & Garfields's handbook of psychotherapy and behavior change* (5th ed., pp. 16–43). New York: Wiley.

Kendrick, S. R., & McCullough, J. P. (1972). Sequential phases of covert reinforcement and covert sensitization in the treatment of homosexuality. *Journal of Behavior Therapy and Experimental Psychiatry, 3,* 229–213.

Kenford, S. L., Fiore, M. C., Jorenby, D. E., Smith, S. S., Wetter, D., & Baker, T. B. (1994). Predicting smoking cessation: Who will quit with and without the nicotine patch. *Journal of the American Medical Association, 271*(8), 589–594.

Kerr, M. M., & Nelson, C. M. (1998). Stereotypic behaviors. In *Strategies for managing behavior problems in the classroom* (3rd ed., pp. 307–311). Englewood Cliffs, NJ: Prentice Hall.

Khan-Bourne, N., & Brown, R. G. (2003). Cognitive behaviour therapy for the treatment of depression in individuals with brain injury. *Neuropsychological Rehabilitation, 13*(1–2), 89–107.

Kiecolt-Glaser, J. K. (1999). Stress, personal relationships, and immune function: Health implications. *Brain, Behavior, and Immunity, 13,* 61–72.

Kilpatrick, D. G., Veronen, L. J., & Resick, P. A. (1982). Psychological sequelae to rape: Assessment and treatment strategies. In D. M. Dolays, R. L. Meredith, & A. R. Ciminero (Eds.), *Behavioral medicine: Assessment and treatment strategies* (pp. 473–497). New York: Plenum Press.

Kim, H.-Y., Lundh, L.-G., & Harvey, A. (2002). The enhancement of video feedback by cognitive preparation in the treatment of social anxiety. A single session experiment. *Journal of Behavior Therapy and Experimental Psychiatry, 33,* 19–37.

Kincaid, D. (1996). Person-centered planning. In L. K. Koegel, R. L. Koegel, & G. Dunlap (Eds.), *Positive behavioral support: Including people with difficult behaviors in the community* (pp. 439–465). Baltimore: Paul H. Brookes.

King, M. B. (1990). Sneezing as a fetishistic stimulus. *Sexual and Marital Therapy, 5,* 69–72.

Klein, S. (1987). *Learning: Principles and applications.* New York: McGraw-Hill.

Kleinknecht, R. A. (1994). Acquisition of blood, injury, and needle fears and phobias. *Behaviour Research and Therapy, 32*(8), 817–823.

Klesges, R. C., Ward, K. D., & DeBon, M. (1996). Smoking cessation: A successful behavioral/pharmacologic interface. *Clinical Psychology Review, 16*(6), 479–496.

Koerner, K., & Linehan, M.M. (2000). Research on dialectical behavior therapy for borderline personality disorder. *The Psychiatric Clinics of North America, 23*(1), 151–167.

Kohlenberg, R. J., & Tsai, M. (1991). *Functional analytic psychotherapy: A guide for creating intense and curative therapeutic relationships.* New York: Plenum Press.

Kohlenberg, R. J., & Tsai, M. (1994). Functional analytic psychotherapy: A behavioral approach to treatment and integration. *Journal of Psychotherapy Integration, 4,* 175–201.

Kohlenberg, R. J., & Tsai, M. (1994). Improving cognitive therapy for depression with functional analytic psychotherapy: Theory and case study. *The Behavior Analyst, 17,* 305–320.

Kohlenberg, R. J., & Tsai, M. (1995). I speak, therefore I am: A behavioral approach to understanding the self. *The Behavior Therapist, 18,* 113–116.

Kohlenberg, R. J., & Tsai, M. (1998). Healing interpersonal trauma with the intimacy of the therapeutic relationship. In

F. R. Abueg, V. Follette, & J. Ruzek (Eds.), *Trauma in context: A cognitive-behavioral approach.* New York: Guilford Press.

Kohlenberg, R. J., Kanter, J. W., Bolling, M. Y., Parker, C. R., & Tsai, M. (2002). Enhancing cognitive therapy for depression with functional analytic psychotherapy: Treatment guidelines and empirical findings. *Cognitive and Behavioral Practice, 9,* 213–229.

Koocher, G. P., & Keith-Spiegel, P. (1998). *Ethics in psychology: Professional standards and cases* (2nd ed.). New York: Oxford University Press.

Korotitsch, W. J., & Nelson-Gray, R. O. (1999). An overview of self-monitoring research in assessment and treatment. *Psychological Assessment, 11,* 415–425.

Kozak, M. J., & Foa, E. B. (1994). Obsessions, overvalued ideas, and delusions in obsessive- compulsive disorder. *Behavior Research and Therapy, 3,* 343–353.

Kozak, M. J., & Foa, E. B. (1997). *Mastery of obsessive-compulsive disorder: A cognitive-behavioral approach.* San Antonio, TX: The Psychological Corporation.

Kozak, M. J., & Montgomery, G. K. (1981). Multimodal behavioral treatment of recurrent injury-scene-elicited fainting (vasodepressor syncope). *Behavioral Psychotherapy, 9,* 316–321.

Krasner, L. (1971). Behavior therapy. *Annual Review of Psychology, 22,* 483–532.

Krasner, L., & Ullmann, L. P. (1973). *Behavior Influence and personality.* New York: Holt, Rinehart & Winston.

Kratochwill, T. R., & Levin, J. R. (Eds.). (1992). *Single-case research design and analysis.* Hillsdale, NJ: Erlbaum.

Kratochwill, T. R., Bergan, J. R., & Bergan, J. R. (1990). *Behavioral consultation in applied settings: An individual guide.* Cambridge, MA: Perseus.

Kuiken, D., Bears, M., Miall, D., & Smith, L. (2001–2002). Eye movement desensitization reprocessing facilitates attentional orienting. *Imagination, Cognition, and Personality, 21*(1), 3–20.

Lam, D. H., Jones S. H., Hayward P., & Bright J. A. (Eds.). (1999). *Cognitive therapy for bipolar disorders: A therapist's guide to concepts, methods, and practice.* New York: Wiley.

Lambert, M. J. (2001). Psychotherapy outcome and quality improvement: Introduction to the special section on client-focused research. *Journal of Consulting and Clinical Psychology, 69,* 147–149.

Lambert, M. J., & Ogles, B. M. (2004). The efficacy and effectiveness of psychotherapy. In M. J. Lambert (Ed.), *Bergin & Garfield's handbook of psychotherapy and behavior change* (5th ed., pp. 139–193). New York: Wiley.

Lamontagne, Y., & Lesage, A. (1986). Private exposure and covert sensitization in the treatment of exhibitionism. *Journal of Behavior Therapy and Experimental Psychiatry, 17,* 197–201.

Langer, E. J., & Moldoveanu, M. (2000). The construct of mindfulness. *Journal of Social Issues, 56,* 1–9.

Last, C. G., & Hersen, M. (1985). Clinical practice of behavior therapy. In M. Hersen & C. G. Last (Eds.), *Behavior therapy casebook.* New York: Springer.

LaVigna, G. W., & Donnellan, A. M. (1986). *Alternative to punishment: Solving behavior problems with non-aversive strategies.* New York: Irvington.

LaVigna, G. W., & Willis, T. J. (in press). Episodic severity: An overlooked dependent variable in the application of behavior analysis to challenging behavior. *Journal of Positive Behavior Interventions.*

Law, A., Logan, H., & Baron, R. S. (1994). Desire for control, felt control, and stress inoculation during dental treatment. *Journal of Personality and Social Psychology, 67,* 926–936.

Laws, D. R. (1995). A theory of relapse prevention. In W. O'Donohue & L. Krasner (Eds.), *Theories of behavior therapy: Exploring behavior change.* Washington, DC: American Psychological Association.

Laws, D. R. (1995). Verbal satiation: Notes on procedure, with speculations on its mechanism of effect. *Sexual Abuse: A Journal of Research and Treatment, 7,* 155–166.

Laws, D. R. (Ed.) (1989). *Relapse prevention with sex offenders.* New York: Guilford Press.

Laws, D. R., & Marshall, W. L. (1991). Masturbatory reconditioning with sexual deviates: An evaluative review. *Advances in Behaviour Research and Therapy, 13,* 13–25.

Laws, D. R., & O'Donohue, W. (Eds.). (1997). *Sexual deviance: Theory, assessment, and treatment.* New York: Guilford Press.

Laws, D. R., Hudson, S. M., & Ward, T. (Eds.). (2000). *Remaking relapse prevention with sex offenders: A sourcebook.* Thousand Oaks, CA: Sage.

Lax, T., Basoglu, M., & Marks, I. M. (1992) Expectancy and compliance as predictors of outcome in obsessive-compulsive disorder. *Behavioural Psychotherapy, 20,* 257–266.

Lazarus, A. A. (1966). Behavior rehearsal vs. nondirective therapy vs. advice in effecting behavior change. *Behaviour Research and Therapy, 4,* 209–212.

Lazarus, A. A. (1992). Multimodal therapy: Technical eclecticism with minimal integration. In J. C. Norcross & M. R. Goldfried (Eds.), *Handbook of psychotherapy integration* (pp. 231–263). New York: Basic Books.

Lazarus, A. A. (1997). *Brief but comprehensive psychotherapy: The multimodal way.* New York: Springer.

Lazarus, A. A. (2000). My professional journey: The development of multimodal therapy. In J. J. Shay & J. Wheelis (Eds.), *Odysseys in psychotherapy.* New York: Irvington.

Lazarus, A. A. (2001). From insight and reflection to action and clinical breadth. In M. R. Goldfried (Ed.), *How therapists change* (pp. 163–181). Washington, DC: American Psychological Association.

Lazarus, A. A. (2001). Multimodal therapy in clinical psychology. In N. J. Smelser & P. B. Baltes (Eds.), *Encyclopedia of the social and behavioral sciences* (pp. 10193–10197). Oxford, UK: Elsevier Press.

Lazarus, A. A. (2002). Behavior rehearsal. In M. Hersen & W. Sledge (Eds.), *Encyclopedia of psychotherapy* (Vol. 1., pp. 253–257). New York: Academic Press.

Lazarus, A. A. (2002). Client readiness for change, cultural concerns, and risk taking: A multimodal case presentation. *Clinical Case Studies, 1,* 39–48.

Lazarus, A. A., & Lazarus, C. N. (1991). *Multimodal life history inventory.* Champaign, IL: Research Press.

Lazarus, C. N., & Lazarus, A. A. (2002). EMDR: An elegantly concentrated multimodal procedure? In F. Shapiro (Ed.), *EMDR as an integrative psychotherapy approach* (pp. 209–223). Washington, DC: American Psychological Association.

Leahy, R. L., & Holland, S. J. (2000). *Treatment plans and interventions for depression and anxiety disorders.* New York: Guilford Press.

Legostaev, G. N. (1996). Changes in mental performance after voluntary relaxation. *Human Physiology, 22*(5), 637–638.

Lehrer, P. M., Carr, R., Sargunaraj, D., & Woolfolk, R. L. (1994). Stress management techniques: Are they all equivalent or do they have specific effects? *Biofeedback and Self-Regulation, 19,* 353–401.

Leiblum, S. R., & Rosen, R.C. (2000). *Principles and practice of sex therapy.* New York: Guilford Press.

Lejuez, C. W., Hopko, D. R., & Hopko, S. D. (2002). *The brief behavioral activation treatment for depression (BATD): A comprehensive patient guide.* Boston: Pearson.

Lejuez, C. W., Hopko, D. R., LePage, J., Hopko, S. D., & McNeil, D. W. (2001). A brief behavioral activation treatment for depression. *Cognitive and Behavioral Practice, 8,* 164–175.

Leon-Carrion, J. (1997). Rehabilitation of memory. In J. Leon-Carrion (Ed.), *Neuropsychological rehabilitation: Fundamentals, innovations, and directions.* Delray Beach, FL: GR/St. Lucie Press.

Leung, A., & Heimberg, R. (1996). Homework compliance, perceptions of control, and outcome of cognitive-behavioral treatment of social phobia. *Behaviour Research and Therapy, 34,* 423–432.

Levis, D. J. (1980). Implementing the technique of implosive therapy. In A. Goldstein & E. G. Foa (Eds.), *Handbook of behavioral interventions: A clinical guide* (pp. 92–151). New York: Wiley.

Levis, D. J. (1995). Decoding traumatic memory: Implosive theory of psychopathology. In W. O'Donohue & L. Kramer (Eds.), *Theories in behavior therapy* (pp. 173–207). Washington, DC: American Psychological Association.

Lewinsohn, P. M, Hoberman, H. M., & Rosenbaum, M. (1988). The Coping With Depression course: Review and future directions. *Canadian Journal of Behavioural Science, 21,* 470–493.

Lewinsohn, P. M. (1974). A behavioral approach to depression. In R. M. Friedman & M. M. Katz (Eds.), *The psychology of depression: Contemporary theory and research.* New York: Wiley.

Lewinsohn, P. M., Antonuccio, D. O., Steinmetz-Breckenridge, J. L., & Teri, L. (1984). *The Coping With Depression course: A psychoeducational intervention for unipolar depression.* Eugene, OR: Castalia.

Lewinsohn, P. M., Clarke, G. N., Rohde, P., Hops, H., & Seeley, J. R. (1996). A course in coping: A cognitive-behavioral approach to the treatment of adolescent depression. In E. D. Hibbs & P. S. Jensen (Eds.), *Psychosocial treatments for child and adolescent disorders: Empirically based strategies for clinical practice.* Washington, DC: American Psychological Association.

Lewinsohn, P. M., Munoz, R. F., Youngren, M. A., & Zeiss, A. M. (1986). *Control your depression.* New York: Prentice Hall.

Lewinsohn, P. M., Muñoz, R. F., Youngren, M. A., & Zeiss, A. M. (1992). *Control your depression* (2nd ed.). Englewood Cliffs, NJ: Prentice Hall.

Lewinsohn, P. M., Weinstein, M., & Alper, T. (1970). A behavioral approach to the group treatment of depressed persons: A methodological contribution. *Journal of Clinical Psychology, 26,* 525–532.

Liberman, R. P., Wallace, C. J., Blackwell, G., Eckman, T. A., Vaccaro, J. V., & Kuehnel, T. G. (1993). Innovations in skills training for the seriously mentally ill: The UCLA Social and Independent Living Skills Modules. *Innovations and Research, 2,* 43–60.

Lichstein, K. L. (1988). *Clinical relaxation strategies.* New York: Wiley.

Lichstein, K. L., & Hung, J. H. F. (1980). Covert sensitization: An examination of covert and overt parameters. *Behavioral Engineering, 6,* 1–18.

Lichstein, K. L., & Morin, C. M. (2000). *Treatment of late-life insomnia.* Thousand Oaks, CA: Sage.

Lichtenstein, E. (2002). From rapid smoking to the Internet: Five decades of cessation research. *Nicotine & Tobacco Research, 4,* 139–145.

Linden, W. (1994). AT: A narrative and quantitative review of clinical outcome. *Biofeedback and Self-Regulation, 19*(3), 227–264.

Linehan, M. M. (1988). Perspectives on the interpersonal relationship in behavior therapy. *Journal of Eclectic and Integrative Psychotherapy, 7*(3), 278–290.

Linehan, M. M. (1993). *Cognitive behavior treatment of borderline personality disorder.* New York: Guilford Press.

Linehan, M. M. (1993). *Skills training manual for treating borderline personality disorder.* New York: Guilford Press.

Linehan, M. M. (1997). Validation and psychotherapy. In A. Bohart & L. Greenberg (Eds.), *Empathy reconsidered: New directions in psychotherapy* (pp. 353–392). Washington, DC: American Psychological Association.

Linehan, M. M. (1998). Development, evaluation, and dissemination of effective psychosocial treatments: Stages of disorder, levels of care, and stages of treatment research. In M. D. Glantz & C. R. Hartel (Eds.), *Drug abuse: Origins and interventions.* Washington, DC: American Psychological Association.

Linehan, M. M., Armstrong, H. E., Suarez, A., Allmon, D., & Heard, H. L. (1991). Cognitive-behavioral treatment of chronically parasuicidal borderline patients. *Archives of General Psychiatry, 48,* 1060–1064.

Lonner, W. J., & Malpass, R. S. (1994). *Psychology and culture.* Boston: Allyn & Bacon.

Lopez Viets, V. C., & Miller, W. R. (1997). Treatment approaches for pathological gamblers. *Clinical Psychology Review, 17,* 689–702.

Lucyshun, J. M., Olson, D. L., & Horner, R. H. (1999). Building an ecology of support for a young woman with severe problem behaviors living in the community. In J. R. Scotti & L. H. Meyer (Eds.), *Behavioral intervention: Principles, models, and practices* (pp. 269–290). Baltimore: Paul H. Brookes.

Luiselli, J. K., & Cameron, M. J. (Eds.). (1998). *Antecedent control: Innovative approaches to behavioral support.* Baltimore: Paul H. Brookes.

Luthans, F., & Kreitner, R. (1985). *Organizational behavior modification and beyond.* Glenview, IL: Scott, Foresman.

Maag, J. W., & Kotlash, J. (1994). Review of stress inoculation training with children and adolescents: Issues and recommendations. *Behavior Modification, 18,* 443–469.

Maier, S. F., & Watkins, L.R. (1998). Cytokines for psychologists: Implications of bidirectional immune-to-brain communication for understanding behavior, mood, and cognition. *Psychological Review, 105,* 83–107.

Maletzky, B. M. (1985). Orgasmic reconditioning. In A. S. Bellak & M. Hersen (Eds.), *Dictionary of behavior therapy techniques* (pp. 157–158). New York: Pergamon Press.

Maletzky, B. M. (1991). *Treating the sexual offender* (pp. 102–109). Newbury Park, CA: Sage.

Maletzky, B. M. (2003). A serial rapist treated with behavioral and cognitive techniques and followed for 12 years. *Clinical Case Studies, 1,* 1–27.

Maletzky, B. M., & George, F. S. (1973). The treatment of homosexuality by "assisted" covert sensitization. *Behavior Research and Therapy, 11,* 655–657.

Maletzky, B. M., & Steinhauser, C. (2002). A 25-year follow-up of cognitive/behavioral therapy with 7,275 sexual offenders. *Behavior Modification, 26,* 123–147.

Malott, R. W. (1984) Rule-governed behavior, self-management, and the developmentally disabled: A theoretical analysis. *Analysis and Intervention in Developmental Disabilities, 4,* 199–209.

Malott, R. W. (1986). Self-management, rule-governed behavior, and everyday life. In H. W. Reese & L. J. Parrott (Eds.), *Behavioral science: Philosophical, methodological, and empirical advances* (207–228). Hillsdale, NJ: Erlbaum.

Malott, R. W. (1989). The achievement of evasive goals: Control by rules describing contingencies that are not direct-acting. In S. C. Hayes (Ed.), *Rule-governed behavior: Cognition, contingencies, and instructional control* (pp. 269–322). New York: Plenum Press.

Malott, R. W., & Harrison, H. (2003). *I'll stop procrastinating when I get around to it.* Kalamazoo, MI: DickMalott.com.

Malott, R. W., Malott, M. E., & Trojan, E. A. (2000) *Elementary principles of behavior* (4th ed.). Upper Saddle River, NJ: Prentice Hall.

March, J. S., & Mulle, K. (1998). *OCD in children and adolescents: A cognitive-behavioral treatment manual.* New York: Guilford Press.

March, R. E., & Horner, R. H. (2002). Feasibility and contributions of functional behavioral assessment in schools. *Journal of Emotional & Behavioral Disorders, 10*(3), 158–170.

Marks, I. (1999). Computer aids to mental health care. *Canadian Journal of Psychiatry, 44*(4), 548–555.

Marks, I. M. (1987). *Fears, phobias, and rituals: Panic, anxiety, and their disorders.* Oxford, UK: Oxford University Press.

Marks, S. U., Schrader, C., & Levine, M. (1999). Paraeducators in inclusive settings: Helping, hovering, or holding their own? *Exceptional Children 65*(3), 315–328.

Marlatt, G. A. (1998). *Harm reduction: Pragmatic strategies for managing high-risk behaviors.* New York: Guilford Press.

Marlatt, G. A., & Gordon, J. R. (1985). *Relapse prevention: Maintenance strategies in the treatment of addictive behaviors.* New York: Guilford Press.

Marlatt, G. A., Larimer, M. E., Baer, J. S., & Quigley, L. A. (1993). Harm reduction for alcohol problems: Moving beyond the controlled drinking controversy. *Behavior Therapy, 24,* 461–504.

Marshall, W. L. (1979). Satiation therapy: A procedure for reducing deviant sexual arousal. *Journal of Applied Behavior Analysis, 12,* 377–389.

Marshall, W. L., Anderson, D., & Fernandez, Y. M. (1999). *Cognitive behavioural treatment of sexual offenders.* Chichester, UK: Wiley.

Martell, C. R., Addis, M. E., & Jacobson, N. S. (2001). *Depression in context: Strategies for guided action.* New York: Norton.

Martin, D. J., Garske, J. P., & Davis, K. M. (2000). Relation of the therapeutic alliance with outcome and other variables: A meta-analytic review. *Journal of Consulting and Clinical Psychology, 68,* 438–450.

Martin, G. L., & Hrycaiko, D. (Eds.). (1983). *Behavior modification and coaching: Principles, procedures, and research.* Springfield, IL: Charles C Thomas.

Martin, G., & Pear, J. (1999). *Behavior modification. What it is and how to do it* (6th ed.). Upper Saddle River, NJ: Prentice Hall.

Martin, G., & Pear, J. (2002). *Behavior modification: What it is and how to do it* (7th ed.). Englewood Cliffs, NJ: Prentice Hall.

Marx, J. A., & Gelso, C. J. (1987). Termination of individual counseling in a university center. *Journal of Counseling Psychology, 34,* 3–9.

Mateer, C. A., & Raskin, S. A. (1999). Cognitive rehabilitation. In M. Rosenthal, E. R. Griffith, J. S. Kreutzer, & B. Pentland (Eds.), *Rehabilitation of the adult and child with traumatic brain injury* (3rd ed., pp. 254–270). Philadelphia: F. A. Davis.

Matson, J. L., Bamburg, J. W., Mayville, E. A., Pinkston, J., Bielecki, J., Kuhn, D., et al. (2000). Psychopharmacology and mental retardation: A 10-year review (1990–1999). *Research in Developmental Disabilities, 21,* 263–296.

Mattaini, M. A. (1997). *Clinical practice with individuals.* Washington, DC: National Association of Social Worker's Press.

Maxfield, L., & Hyer, L. A. (2002). The relationship between efficacy and methodology in studies investigating EMDR treatment of PTSD. *Journal of Clinical Psychology, 58,* 23–41.

McConaghy, N. (1977). Behavioral treatment in homosexuality. In M. Hersen, R. M. Eisler, & P. M. Miller (Eds.), *Progress in behavior modification* (pp. 309–380). New York: Academic Press.

McConaghy, N. (1983). Agoraphobia, compulsive behaviours and behaviour completion mechanisms. *Australian and New Zealand Journal of Psychiatry, 17,* 170–179.

McConaghy, N. (1993). *Sexual behavior: problems and management.* New York: Plenum Press.

McConaghy, N. (1998). Assessment of sexual dysfunction and deviation. In A. S. Bellack & M. Hersen (Eds.), *Behavioral assessment: A practical handbook* (4th ed., pp. 315–341). Boston: Allyn & Bacon.

McConnaughy, E. A., DiClemente, C. C., Prochaska, J. O., & Velicer, W. F. (1989). Stages of change in psychotherapy: A follow-up report. *Psychotherapy: Theory, Research, Practice, Training, 26*(4), 494–503.

McCrady, B. S. (1994). Alcoholics Anonymous and behavior therapy: Can habits be treated as diseases? Can diseases be treated as habits? *Journal of Consulting and Clinical Psychology, 62,* 1159–1166.

McCrady, B. S., Epstein, E. E., & Hirsch, L. S. (1999). Maintaining change after conjoint behavioral alcohol treatment for men: Outcome at 6 months. *Addiction, 94,* 1381–1396.

McDermut, W., Miller, I. W., & Brown, R. A. (2001). The efficacy of group psychotherapy for depression: A meta-analysis and review of the empirical research. *Clinical Psychology: Science & Practice, 8*(1), 98–116.

McGill, P. (1999). Establishing operations: Implications for the assessment, treatment, and prevention of problem behavior, *Journal of Applied Behavior Analysis, 32,* 393–418.

McGinn C. (1993). *The problem of consciousness.* London: Blackwell.

McGlynn, F. D., Mealiea, W. L., & Landau, D. L. (1981). The current status of systematic desensitization. *Clinical Psychology Review, 1,* 149–179.

McGuigan, F. J. (1993). Progressive relaxation: Origins, principles, and clinical applications. In P. M. Lehrer & R. L. Woolfolk (Eds.), *Principles and practice of stress management* (2nd ed., pp. 17–52). New York: Guilford Press.

McGuire, R. J., Carlisle, J. M., & Young, B. G. (1965). Sexual deviation as conditioned behavior. *Behavior Research and Therapy, 2,* 185–190.

McInnis, T., Himelstein, H., Doty, D., & Paul, G. (1974). Modification of sampling-exposure procedures for increasing facilities utilization by chronic psychiatric patients. *Journal of Behavior Therapy and Experimental Psychiatry, 5,* 119–127.

McLean, P. D., & Woody, S. R. (2001). *Anxiety disorders in adults: An evidence-based approach to psychological treatment.* New York: Oxford University Press.

McLean, P. D., Whittal, M. L., Thordarson, D. S., Taylor, S., Söchting, I., Koch, W. J., et al. (2001). Cognitive versus behavior therapy in the group treatment of obsessive-compulsive disorder. *Journal of Consulting and Clinical Psychology, 69*(2), 205–214.

McLean, P. E., Woody, S., Taylor, S., & Koch, W. J. (1998). Comorbid panic disorder and major depression: Implications for cognitive-behavioral therapy. *Journal of Consulting & Clinical Psychology, 66*(2), 240–247.

McLeod, P., Plunkett, K., & Rolls, E. T. (1998). *Introduction to connectionist modeling of cognitive processes.* New York: Oxford University Press.

McMullin, R. E. (1986). *Handbook of cognitive therapy techniques.* New York: Norton.

McNally, R. J., & Lukach, B. M. (1991). Behavioral treatment of zoophilic exhibitionism. *Journal of Behavior Therapy and Experimental Psychiatry, 22,* 281–284.

Medalia, A., & Revheim, N. (1999). Computer assisted learning in psychiatric rehabilitation. *Psychiatric Rehabilitation Skills, 3,* 77–98.

Meichenbaum, D. (1977). *Cognitive-behavior modification.* New York: Plenum Press.

Meichenbaum, D. H. (1985). *Stress inoculation training.* Elmsford, New York: Pergamon Press.

Meichenbaum, D. H. (1993). Stress inoculation training: A 20-year update. In R. L. Woolfolk & P. M. Lehrer (Eds.), *Principles and practice of stress management* (2nd ed., pp. 373–406). New York: Guilford Press.

Meichenbaum, D. H., & Deffenbacher, J. L. (1988). Stress inoculation training. *The Counseling Psychologist, 16,* 69–90.

Metcalfe, J., & Mischel, W. (1999). A hot/cool system analysis of delay of gratification: Dynamics of willpower. *Psychological Review, 106,* 3–19.

Meyer, V. J., & Hope, D. A. (1998). Assessment of social skills. In A. S. Bellack & M. Hersen (Eds.), *Behavior assessment: A practical handbook* (4th ed., pp. 232–270). Boston: Allyn & Bacon.

Meyers, R. J., & Smith, J. E. (1995). *Clinical guide to alcohol treatment: The community reinforcement approach.* New York: Guilford Press.

Miller, C. A. (2002). Informed consent. In M. Hersen & W. Sledge (Eds.), *Encyclopedia of psychotherapy* (pp. 17–24). New York: Academic Press.

Miller, C. M. (2002). Flooding. In M. Hersen & W. Sledge (Eds.), *Encyclopedia of psychotherapy* (Vol. I, pp. 809–813). New York: Academic Press.

Miller, W. R. (Ed.). (1999). *Enhancing motivation for change in substance abuse treatment* (Treatment Improvement Protocol Series, No. 35). Rockville, MD: Center for Substance Abuse Treatment.

Miller, W. R. (Ed.). (1999). *Integrating spirituality into treatment: Resources for practitioners.* Washington, DC: American Psychological Association.

Miller, W. R. (in press). Motivational interviewing in the service of health promotion. *American Journal of Health Promotion.*

Miller, W. R., & Mount, K. A. (2001). A small study of training in motivational interviewing: Does one workshop change clinician and client behavior? *Behavioural and Cognitive Psychotherapy, 29,* 457–471.

Miller, W. R., & Rollnick, S. (2002). *Motivational interviewing: Preparing people for change* (2nd ed.). New York: Guilford Press.

Miller, W. R., Leckman, A. L., Delaney, H. D., & Tinkcom, M. (1992) Long-term follow-up of behavioral self-control training. *Journal of Studies on Alcohol, 53,* 249–261.

Miller, W. R., Zweben, A., DiClemente, C. C., & Rychtarik, R. G. (1992). *Motivational enhancement therapy manual: A clinical research guide for therapists treating individuals with alcohol abuse and dependence* (Vol. 2, Project MATCH Monograph Series). Rockville, MD: National Institute on Alcohol Abuse and Alcoholism.

Miltenberger, R. G. (2001), *Behavior modification: Principles and procedures.* Belmont, CA: Wadsworth/Thomson.

Miltenberger, R. G. (2001). Habit reversal treatment manual for trichotillomania. In D. Woods & R. Miltenberger (Eds.), *Tic disorders, trichotillomania, and other repetitive behavior disorders: Behavioral approaches to analysis and treatment* (pp. 171–196). Norwell, MA: Kluwer.

Miltenberger, R. G., Fuqua, R. W., & Woods, D. W. (1998). Applying behavior analysis to clinical problems: Review and analysis of habit reversal. *Journal of Applied Behavior Analysis, 31,* 447–469.

Moergen, S. A., Merkel, W. T., & Brown, S. (1990). The use of covert sensitization and social skills training in the treatment of an obscene telephone caller. *Journal of Behavior Therapy and Experimental Psychiatry, 21,* 269–275.

Moore, D. W., Prebble, S., Robertson, J., Waetford, R., & Anderson, A. (2001). Self-recording with goal-setting: A self-management programme for the classroom. *Educational Psychology, 21,* 255–265.

Moore, J. (1980). On behaviorism and private events. *The Psychological Record, 30,* 459–475.

Morin, C. M., & Espie, C. A. (2003). *Insomnia: A clinical guide to assessment and treatment.* New York: Kluwer/ Plenum.

Morin, C. M., Hauri, P. J., Espie, C. A., Spielman, A. J., Buysse, D. J., & Bootzin, R. R. (1999). Nonpharmacologic treatment of chronic insomnia. *Sleep, 22,* 1134–1156.

Morris, E. K. (1992). ABA presidential address: The aim, progress, and evolution of behavior analysis. *The Behavior Analyst, 15,* 3–29.

Mount, B. (1987). *Person futures planning: Finding directions for change* (Doctoral dissertation, University of Georgia). Ann Arbor, MI: UMI Dissertation Information Service.

Mount, B., & Zwernick, K. (1988). *It's never too early, it's never too late: An overview on personal futures planning.* St. Paul, MN: Governor's Council on Developmental Disabilities.

Mowrer, O. H. (1960). *Learning theory and behavior.* New York: Wiley.

Muñoz, R. F., Ying, Y. W., Bernal, G., Perez-Stable, E. J., Sorensen, J. L., & Hargreaves, W. A. (1995). Prevention of depression with primary care patients: A randomized

controlled trial. *American Journal of Community Psychology, 23*(2), 199–222.

Murtagh, D. R. R., & Greenwood, K. M. (1995). Identifying effective psychological treatments for insomnia: A meta-analysis. *Journal of Consulting and Clinical Psychology, 63,* 79–89.

Nakamura, N. (2000). The new applicative fields of AT. *Japanese Journal of Autogenic Therapy, 18*(2), 64–67.

Nathan, P. E., & Gorman, J. M. (2002). *A guide to treatments that work* (2nd ed.). New York: Oxford University Press.

Nathan, P. E., & Gorman, J. M. (Eds.). (1998). *A guide to treatments that work.* New York: Oxford University Press.

Nathan, P. E., & Gorman, J. M. (Eds.). (2002). *A guide to treatments that work* (2nd ed.). New York: Oxford University Press.

National Heart, Lung, and Blood Institute. (1998). Clinical guidelines on the identification, evaluation, and treatment of overweight and obesity in adults: The evidence report. *National Institutes of Health Obesity Research 6*(Suppl. 2), 51S–209S.

National Institute on Alcohol Abuse and Alcoholism. (2003). *Helping patients with alcohol problems* (NIH Publication No. 03-3769). Bethesda, MD: National Institute on Alcohol Abuse and Alcoholism.

Neef, N. A. (Ed.). (1994). Special issue on functional analysis approaches to behavioral assessment and treatment. *Journal of Applied Behavior Analysis, 27,* 196–371.

Newman, M. G., Kenardy, J., Herman, S., & Taylor, C. B. (1995). The use of handheld computers as an adjunct to cognitive-behavioral therapy. *Computers in Human Behavior, 12,* 135–143.

Nezu, A. M. (in press). Problem solving and behavior therapy revisited. *Behavior Therapy.*

Nezu, A. M., Nezu, C. M., & Lombardo, E. R. (2001). Managing stress through problem solving. *Stress News, 13,* 11–14.

Nezu, A. M., Nezu, C. M., & Perri, M. G. (1989). *Problem-solving therapy for depression: Theory, research, and clinical guidelines.* New York: Wiley.

Nezu, A. M., Nezu, C. M., Felgoise, S. H., McClure, K. S., & Houts, P. S. (in press). Project Genesis: Assessing the efficacy of problem-solving therapy for distressed adult cancer patients. *Journal of Consulting and Clinical Psychology.*

Nezu, A. M., Nezu, C. M., Friedman, S. H., Faddis, S., & Houts, P. S. (1998). *Helping cancer patients cope: A problem-solving approach.* Washington, DC: American Psychological Association.

Nezu, A. M., Ronan, G. F., Meadows, E. A., & McClure, K. S. (Eds.). (2000). *Practitioner's guide to empirically based measures of depression.* New York: Kluwer Academic/ Plenum.

Nielsen, S. L. (2001). Accommodating religion and integrating religious material during rational emotive behavior therapy. *Cognitive and Behavioral Practice, 8*(1), 34–39.

Nielsen, S. L., Johnson, W. B., & Ellis, A. (2001). *Counseling and psychotherapy with religious persons: A rational-emotive behavioral therapy approach.* Mahwah, NJ: Erlbaum.

Nielsen, S. L., Johnson, W. B., & Ridley, C. R. (2000). Religiously sensitive rational emotive behavior therapy: Theory, techniques, and brief excerpts from a case. *Professional Psychology: Research and Practice, 31*(1), 21–28.

Notarius, C., & Markman, H. (1993). *We can work it out: Making sense of marital conflict.* New York: Putnam.

Novaco, R. W. (1986). Anger as a clinical and social problem. In R. Blanchard & C. Blanchard (Eds.), *Advances in the study of aggression* (Vol. 2, pp. 1–67). New York: Academic Press.

Novaco, R. W. (1997). Remediating anger and aggression with violent offenders. *Legal and Criminological Psychology, 2,* 77–88.

Novaco, R. W., & Chemtob, C. M. (2002). Anger and combat-related posttraumatic stress disorder. *Journal of Traumatic Stress, 15,* 123–132.

O'Brien, J., Mount, B., & O'Brien, C. (1990). *The personal profile.* Lithonia, GA: Responsive Systems Associates.

O'Brien, R. M., Dickinson, A. M., & Rosow, M. P. (Eds.). (1982). *Industrial behavior modification.* New York: Pergamon Press.

O'Brien, W. H. (1995). Inaccuracies in the estimation of functional relations using self-monitoring data. *Journal of Behavior Therapy and Experimental Psychiatry, 26,* 351–357.

O'Donohue, W. T., & Plaud, J. J. (1994). The conditioning of human sexual arousal. *Archives of Sexual Behavior, 23,* 321–344.

O'Farrell, T. J., & Cowles, K. S. (1995). Marital and family therapy. In R. K. Hester & W. R. Miller (Eds.), *Handbook of alcoholism treatment approaches.* Needham Heights, MA: Allyn & Bacon.

O'Leary, A. (1990). Stress, emotion, and human immune function. *Psychological Bulletin, 108,* 363–382.

Oakley-Browne, M. A., Adams, P., & Mobberly, P. M. (2002). Interventions for pathological gambling (Cochrane Review). *The Cochrane Library, 4,* 1–23. Oxford, UK: Update Software.

Olton, D. S., & Noonberg, A. R. (1980). *Biofeedback: Clinical applications in behavioral medicine.* Englewood Cliffs, NJ: Prentice Hall.

Onken, L. S., Blaine, J. D., Genser, S., & Horton, A. M. (1997). Treatment of drug-dependent individuals with comorbid mental disorders. *NIDA Research Monograph, 172.* Rockville, MD: National Institute on Drug Abuse.

Organista, K. C., & Munoz, R. F. (1996). Cognitive-behavioral therapy with Latinos. *Cognitive and Behavioral Practice, 3,* 255–270.

Öst, L. G. (1992). Blood and injection phobia: Background and cognitive, physiological, and behavioral variables. *Journal of Abnormal Psychology, 101*(1), 68–74.

Öst, L. G., & Sterner, U. (1987). Applied tension: A specific behavioral method for treatment of blood phobia. *Behaviour Research and Therapy, 25*(1), 25–29.

Öst, L. G., Sterner, U., & Lindahl, I. L. (1984). Physiological responses in blood phobics. *Behaviour Research and Therapy, 22,* 109–177.

Overholser, J. C. (1990). Passive relaxation training with guided imagery: A transcript for clinical use. *Phobia Practice and Research Journal, 3,* 107–122.

Overskeid, G. (1992). Is any human behavior schedule-induced? *Psychological Record, 42,* 323–340.

Palmer, S., & Lazarus, A. A. (2001). In the counselor's chair: Multimodal therapy. In P. Milner & S. Palmer (Eds.), *Counselling: The BACP counselling reader* (pp. 94–98). London: Sage.

Paradis, C. M., Friedman, S., Hatch, M., & Ackerman, R. (1996). Cognitive-behavioral treatment of anxiety disorders in Orthodox Jews. *Cognitive and Behavioral Practice, 3,* 271–288.

Pargament, K. I. (1997). *The psychology of religion and coping: Theory, research, practice.* New York: Guilford Press.

Park, N. W., Conrod, B., Hussain, K. J., Rewilak, D., & Black, S. E. (2003). A treatment program for individuals with deficient evaluative processing and consequent impaired social and risk judgement. *Neurocase, 9*(1), 51–62.

Parrott, L. J. (1984). Listening and understanding. *The Behavior Analyst, 7,* 29–39.

Patelis-Siotis, I. (2001). Cognitive-behavioral therapy: Applications for the management of bipolar disorder. *Bipolar Disorders, 3,* 1–10.

Patterson, T. L., Moscona, S., McKibbin, C. L., Davidson, K., & Jeste, D. V. (2001). Social skills performance assessment among older patients with schizophrenia. *Schizophrenia Research, 48,* 351–360.

Paul, G. L. (1966). *Insight vs. desensitization in psychotherapy.* Stanford, CA: Stanford University Press.

Paul, G. L. (1966, May). *The specific control of anxiety: Hypnosis and conditioning.* Paper presented at the meeting of the American Psychological Association, New York.

Paul, G. L. (1969). Outcome of systematic desensitization I: Background, procedures, and uncontrolled reports of individual treatment. In C. M. Franks (Ed.), *Behavior therapy: Appraisal and status* (pp. 63–104). New York: McGraw-Hill.

Paul, G. L. (2001). The active unconscious, symptom substitution, & other things that went "bump" in the night. In W. T. O'Donohue, D. A. Henderson, S. C. Hayes, J. E. Fisher, & L. J. Hayes (Eds.), *A history of the behavioral therapies: Founders' personal histories* (pp. 295–336). Reno, NV: Context Press.

Paul, G. L., & Lentz, R. J. (1977). *Psychosocial treatment of chronic mental patients: Milieu versus social-learning programs.* Cambridge, MA: Harvard University Press.

Pavlov, I. P. (1906). The scientific investigation of psychical facilities or processes in the higher animals, *Science, 24,* 610–619.

Pavlov, I. P. (1927). *Conditioned reflexes.* New York: Oxford University Press. (Reprinted, New York: Dover, 1960)

Pavlov, I. P. (1941). *Conditioned reflexes and psychiatry.* New York: International Publishers.

Pear, J., & Martin, G. L. (2002). *Behavior modification: What it is and how to do it* (7th ed.). Upper Saddle River, NJ: Prentice Hall.

Pearpoint, J., O'Brien, J., & Forest, M. (1996). *Planning alternative tomorrows with hope: A workbook for planning possible and positive futures.* Toronto, Canada: Inclusion Press.

Perkins, B., & Rouanzoin, C. (2002). A critical evaluation of current views regarding eye movement desensitization and reprocessing (EMDR): Clarifying points of confusion. *Journal of Clinical Psychology, 58,* 77–97.

Perrez, M., & Reicherts, M. (2001). A computer-assisted self-monitoring procedure for assessing stress-related behavior under real life conditions. In J. Fahrenberg & M. Myrtek (Eds.), *Ambulatory assessment: Computer-assisted psychological and psychophysiological methods in monitoring and field studies* (pp. 51–67). Kirkland, WA: Hogrefe & Huber.

Perri, M. G., & Corsica, J. A. (2002). Improving the maintenance of weight lost in behavioral treatment of obesity. In T. A. Wadden & A. J. Stunkard (Eds.), *Handbook of obesity treatment* (pp. 357–379). New York: Guilford Press.

Persons, J. (1989). *Cognitive therapy in practice: A case formulation approach.* New York: Norton.

Persons, J. B., Davidson, J., & Tompkins, M. A. (2001). *Essential components of cognitive-behavioral therapy for depression.* Washington, DC: American Psychological Association.

Petrila, J. (2003). The emerging debate over the shape of informed consent: Can the doctrine bear the weight? *Behavioral Sciences and the Law, 21,* 121–133.

Petry, N. M., & Armentano, C. (1999). Prevalence, assessment, and treatment of pathological gambling. *Psychiatric Services, 50,* 1021–1927.

Plaud, J. J., & Eifert, G. H. (Eds.). (1998). *From behavior theory to behavior therapy.* Boston: Allyn & Bacon.

Plaud, J. J., & Gaither, G. A. (1997). A clinical investigation of the possible effects of long-term habituation of sexual arousal in assisted covert sensitization. *Journal of Behavior Therapy and Experimental Psychiatry, 28,* 281–290.

Plaud, J. J., & Martini, J. R. (1999). The respondent conditioning of male sexual arousal. *Behavior Modification, 23,* 254–268.

Poppen, R. (1995). *Joseph Wolpe.* Thousand Oaks, CA: Sage.

Poppen, R. (1998). *Behavioral relaxation training and assessment* (2nd ed.). Thousand Oaks, CA: Sage.

Premack, D. (1959). Toward empirical behavioral laws: I. Positive reinforcement. *Psychological Review, 66,* 219–233.

Primakoff, L., Epstein, N., & Covi, L. (1986). Homework compliance: An uncontrolled variable in cognitive therapy research. *Behavior Therapy, 17,* 433–446.

Project MATCH Research Group (1997). Project MATCH secondary a priori hypotheses. *Addiction, 92,* 1671–1698.

Project MATCH Research Group. (1997). Matching alcoholism treatments to client heterogeneity: Project MATCH post-treatment drinking outcomes. *Journal of Studies on Alcohol, 58,* 7–29.

Project MATCH Research Group. (1998). Matching alcoholism treatment to client heterogeneity: Treatment main effects and matching effects on drinking during treatment. *Journal of Studies on Alcohol, 59,* 631–639.

Propst, R., Ostrom, R., Watkins, P., Dean, T., & Mashburn, D. (1992). Comparative efficacy of religious and nonreligious cognitive-behavioral therapy for the treatment of clinical depression in religious individuals. *Journal of Consulting and Clinical Psychology, 60*(1), 94–103.

Purdon, C. (1999). Thought suppression and psychopathology. *Behaviour Research and Therapy, 37,* 1029–1054.

Quine, W. V. (1972) Methodological reflections on current linguistic theory. In D. Davidson & G. Harman (Eds.), *Semantics of natural language.* (pp. 442–454). Dordrecht, Netherlands: D. Reidel.

Quintana, S. M., & Holahan, W. (1992). Termination in short-term counseling: Comparison of successful and unsuccessful cases. *Journal of Counseling Psychology, 39,* 299–305.

Rachlin, H. (1976). *Introduction to modern behaviorism.* San Francisco: W. H. Freeman.

Rachlin, H. (2000). *The science of self-control.* Cambridge, MA: Harvard University Press.

Rachman, S. (1961). Sexual disorders and behavior therapy. *American Journal of Psychiatry, 118,* 235–240.

Rachman, S. (2003). *The treatment of obsessions.* New York: Oxford University Press.

Rachman, S., & Hodgson, R. (1980). *Obsessions and compulsions* (Century Series). Upper Saddle River, NJ: Prentice Hall.

Ramsay, M. C., Reynolds, C. R., & Kamphaus, R. W. (2002). *Essentials of behavioral assessment.* New York: Wiley.

Randall, E. J. (1994). Cultural relativism in cognitive therapy with disadvantaged African American women. *Journal of Cognitive Psychotherapy: An International Quarterly, 8,* 195–207.

Rangaswamy, K. (1987). Treatment of voyeurism by behavior therapy. *Child Psychiatry Quarterly, 20,* 73–76.

Rapee, R. M., & Hayman, K. (1996). The effects of video feedback on the self-evaluation of performance in socially anxious subjects. *Behaviour Research and Therapy, 34,* 315–322.

Rapee, R. M., & Heimberg, R. G. (1997). A cognitive-behavioral model of anxiety in social phobia. *Behaviour Research and Therapy, 35,* 741–756.

Rapoport, M., McCauley, S., Levin, H., Song, J., & Feinstein, A. (2002). The role of injury severity in neurobehavioral outcome 3 months after traumatic brain injury. *Neuropsychiatry, Neuropsychology, & Behavioral Neurology, 15*(2), 123–132.

Raskin, S. A. (2000). Cognitive remediation of mild traumatic brain injury in an older age group. In S. A. Raskin & C. A. Mateer (Eds.), *Neuropsychological management of mild traumatic brain injury* (pp. 254–268). New York: Oxford University Press.

Raskin, S. A. (2000). Memory. In S. A. Raskin & C. A. Mateer (Eds.), *Neuropsychological management of mild traumatic brain injury* (pp. 93–112). New York: Oxford University Press.

Ray, A. L., & Zbik, A. (2001) Cognitive behavioral therapies and beyond. In C. D. Tollison, J. R. Satterthwaite, & J. W. Tollison (Eds.), *Practical pain management* (3rd ed., pp. 189–208.). Philadelphia: Lippencott.

Ray, R. D., & Delprato, D. J. (1989). Behavioral systems analysis: Methodological strategies and tactics. *Behavioral Science, 34,* 81–112.

Rector, N. A., & Beck, A. T. (2001). Cognitive-behavioral therapy for schizophrenia: An empirical review. *Journal of Nervous and Mental Disease, 189,* 278–287.

Rehm, L. P. (1977). A self-control model of depression. *Behavior Therapy, 8,* 787–804.

Rehm, L. P. (1985). A self-management therapy program for depression. *International Journal of Mental Health, 13*(3–4), 34–53.

Rehm, L. P., & Sharp, R. N. (1996). Strategies in the treatment of childhood depression. In M. Reinecke, F. M. Dattilio, & A. Freeman (Eds.), *Comprehensive casebook on cognitive behavior therapy with adolescents* (pp. 103–123). New York: Guilford Press.

Rehm, L. P., Fuchs, C. Z., Roth, D. M., Kornblith, S. J., & Romano, J. (1979). A comparison of self-control and social skills treatments of depression. *Behavior Therapy, 10,* 429–442.

Rehm, L. P., Kaslow, N. J., & Rabin, A. S. (1987). Cognitive and behavioral targets in a self-control behavior therapy program for depression. *Journal of Consulting and Clinical Psychology, 55,* 60–67.

Rehm, L. P., Kornblith, S. J., O'Hara, M. W., Lamparski, D. M., Romano, J.M., & Volkin, J. I. (1981). An evaluation of major components in a self-control therapy program for depression. *Behavior Modification, 5,* 459–490.

Renaud, P., Rouleau, J. J., Granger, L., Barsetti, I., & Bouchard, S. (2003). Measuring sexual preferences in virtual reality: A pilot study. *Cyberpsychology and Behavior, 5*(1), 1–10.

Renwick, S. J., Ramm, M., Black, L., & Novaco, R. W. (1997). Anger treatment with forensic hospital patients. *Legal and Criminological Psychology, 2,* 103–116.

Rescorla, R. A. (1967). Pavlovian conditioning and its proper control procedures. *Psychological Review, 74,* 71–80.

Rescorla, R. A. (1991). Associative relations in instrumental learning: The eighteenth Bartlett Memorial Lecture. *Quarterly Journal of Experimental Psychology, 43B,* 1–23.

Rescorla, R. A., & Wagner, A. R. (1972). A theory of Pavlovian conditioning: Variations in the effectiveness of reinforcement and nonreinforcement. In A. H. Black & W. F. Prokasy (Eds.), *Classical conditioning II* (pp. 64–99). New York: Appleton-Century-Crofts.

Resick, P. A., & Schnicke, M. K. (1993). *Cognitive processing therapy for rape victims: A treatment manual.* Newbury Park, CA: Sage.

Resick, P. A., Nishith, P., Weaver, T. L., Astin, M. C., & Feurer, C. A. (2002). A comparison of cognitive processing therapy, prolonged exposure, and a waiting condition for the treatment of posttraumatic stress disorder in female rape victims. *Journal of Consulting and Clinical Psychology, 70,* 867–879.

Reynolds, W. M., & Coats, K. I. (1986). A comparison of cognitive-behavioral therapy and relaxation training for the treatment of depression in adolescents. *Journal of Consulting and Clinical Psychology. 54*(5), 653–60.

Rice, D. P., & Miller, L. S. (1993). The economic burden of mental disorders. *Advances in Health Economics and Health Services Research, 14,* 37–53.

Richard, D. C. S., & Bobicz, K. (2003). Computers and behavioral assessment: Six years later. *The Behavior Therapist, 26*(1), 219–223.

Richard, D. C. S., & Lauterbach, D. L. (2003). Computers in the training and practice of behavioral assessment. In M. Hersen, S. N. Haynes, & E. Heiby (Eds.), *Comprehensive handbook of psychological assessment: Vol. 3. Behavioral assessment.* New York: Wiley.

Richelle, M. N. (1993). *B. F. Skinner: A reappraisal.* Hove, UK: Erlbaum.

Riley, A. L., & Wetherington, C. L. (1989). Schedule-induced polydipsia: Is the rat a small furry human? (An analysis of an animal model of human alcoholism). In S. B. Klein & R. R. Mowrer (Eds.), *Contemporary learning theories: Instrumental conditioning theory and the impact of biological constraints on learning* (pp. 205–236). Hillsdale, NJ: Erlbaum.

Risley, T. (1996). Get a life! Positive behavioral intervention for challenging behavior through life arrangement and life coaching. In L. K. Koegel, R. L. Koegel, & G. Dunlap (Eds.), *Positive behavioral support: Including people with difficult behavior in the community* (pp.425–437). Baltimore: Paul H. Brookes.

Robb, H. (2001). Facilitating rational emotive behavior therapy by including religious beliefs. *Cognitive and Behavioral Practice, 8,* 29–34.

Robb, H. B. III. (2002). Rational emotive behavior therapy and religious clients. *Journal of Rational-Emotive & Cognitive-Behavior Therapy, 20*(3/4), 169–200.

Robin, M. W., & DiGiuseppe, R. (1997). Shoya Moya ik Baraba: Using REBT with culturally diverse clients. In J. Yakura & W. Dryden (Eds.), *Special applications of REBT: A therapist's case book* (pp. 39–67).

Robinson, T. R., Smith, S. W., Miller, M. D., & Brownell, M. T. (1999). Cognitive behavior modification of hyperactivity-impulsivity and aggression: A meta-analysis of school-based studies. *Journal of Educational Psychology, 91,* 195–203.

Rodebaugh, T. L., & Chambless, D. L. (2002). The effects of video feedback on the self-perception of speech anxious participants. *Cognitive Therapy and Research, 26,* 629–644.

Roemer, L., & Orsillo, S. M. (2002). Expanding our conceptualization of and treatment for generalized anxiety disorder: Integrating mindfulness/acceptance-based approaches with existing cognitive-behavioral models. *Clinical Psychology: Science & Practice, 9*(1), 54–68.

Rogers, S., & Silver, S. M. (2002). Is EMDR an exposure therapy?: A review of trauma protocols. *Journal of Clinical Psychology, 58,* 43–59.

Rokke, P. D., Tomhave, J. A., & Jocic, Z. (2000). Self-management therapy and educational group therapy for depressed elders. *Cognitive Therapy & Research, 24*(1), 99–119.

Rollnick, S., Mason, P., & Butler, C. (1999). *Health behavior change: A guide for practitioners.* New York: Churchill Livingstone.

Rose, S. D. (1989). *Working with adults in groups.* San Francisco: Jossey-Bass.

Rose, S. D. (1998). *Group therapy with troubled youth: A cognitive-behavioral interactive approach.* Thousand Oaks, CA: Sage.

Rosenberg, H. (1993). Prediction of controlled drinking by alcoholics and problem drinkers. *Psychological Bulletin, 113,* 129–139.

Rosenfarb, I. S. (1992). A behavior analytic interpretation of the therapeutic relationship. *Psychological Record, 42*(3), 341–355.

Rosqvist, J., Thomas, J. C., Egan, D., & Willis, B. S. (2002). Home-based cognitive-behavioral treatment of chronic, refractory obsessive-compulsive disorder can be effective: Single case analysis of four patients. *Behavior Modification, 26*(2), 205–222.

Rossello, J., & Bernal, G. (1996). Adapting cognitive-behavioral and interpersonal treatments for depressed Puerto Rican adolescents. In E. Hibbs & P. S. Jensen (Eds.), *Psychosocial treatments for child and adolescent disorders* (pp. 157–185). Washington, DC: American Psychological Association.

Rossello, J., & Bernal, G. (1998). Treatment of depression in Puerto Rican adolescents. *Journal of Consulting and Clinical Psychology, 67,* 734–745.

Rothbaum, B. O., & Ninan, P. T. (1999). Manual for the cognitive-behavioral treatment of trichotillomania. In D. J. Stein, G. A. Christenson, et al. (Eds.), *Trichotillomania* (pp. 263–284). Washington, DC: American Psychiatric Association.

Rothbaum, B. O., Hodges, L. F., Kooper, R., Opdyke, D., & Williford, J. (1995). Effectiveness of virtual reality graded exposure in the treatment of acrophobia. *American Journal of Psychiatry, 152,* 626–628.

Rothbaum, B. O., Hodges, L., & Smith, S. (1999). Virtual reality exposure therapy abbreviated treatment manual: Fear of flying application. *Cognitive and Behavioral Practice, 6,* 234–244.

Rothbaum, B. O., Hodges, L., Anderson, P. L., Price, L., & Smith, S. (2002). 12-month follow-up of virtual reality exposure therapy for the fear of flying. *Journal of Consulting and Clinical Psychology, 70,* 428–432.

Rothbaum, B. O., Hodges, L., Ready, D., Graap, K., & Alarcon, R. (2001). Virtual reality exposure therapy for Vietnam Veterans with posttraumatic stress disorder. *Journal of Clinical Psychiatry, 62,* 617–622.

Rothbaum, B. O., Hodges, L., Smith, S., Lee, J. H., & Price, L. (2000). A controlled study of virtual reality exposure therapy for the fear of flying. *Journal of Consulting and Clinical Psychology, 68,* 1020–1026.

Rothbaum, B. O., Ruef, A. M., Litz, B. T., Han, H., & Hodges, L. (in press). Virtual reality exposure therapy of combat-related PTSD: A case study using psychophysiological indicators of outcome. *Journal of Cognitive Psychotherapy.*

Rotter, J. B. (1954). *Social learning and clinical psychology.* Englewood Cliffs, NJ: Prentice Hall.

Rotunda, J. R., & O'Farrell, T. J. (1997). Marital and family therapy of alcohol use disorders: Bridging the gap between research and practice. *Professional Psychology: Research and Practice, 28,* 246–252

Rubio, G., Manzanares, J., Lopez-Munoz F., Alamo, C., Ponce, G., Jimenez-Arriero, et al. (2002). Naltrexone improves outcome of a controlled drinking program. *Journal of Substance Abuse Treatment, 23,* 361–366.

Rummler, G. A., & Brache, A. P. (1995). *Improving performance: How to manage the white space on the organization chart* (Rev. ed.). San Francisco: Jossey-Bass.

Rushall, B. S. (2003). *Mental skills training for serious athletes.* Available at http://members.cox.net/brushall/mental/index.htm.

Rushall, B. S. (2003). *Mental skills training for sports* (3rd ed.). Spring Valley, CA: Sports Science Associates.

Rushall, B. S. (2003). *Sport psychology consultation system* (3rd ed.). Spring Valley, CA: Sports Science Associates.

Rushall, B. S., & Siedentop, D. (1972). *The development and control of behavior in sports and physical education.* Philadelphia: Lea & Febiger.

Russell, R. K., & Sipich, J. F. (1973). Cue-controlled relaxation in the treatment of test anxiety. *Journal of Behavior Therapy and Experimental Psychiatry, 4,* 47–49.

Russell, R. K., & Sipich, J. F. (1974). Treatment of test anxiety by cue-controlled relaxation. *Behavior Therapy, 5,* 673–676.

Russell, R. K., Miller, D. E., & June, L. N. (1974). Group cue-controlled relaxation in the treatment of test anxiety. *Behavior Therapy, 5,* 572–573.

Ryle, G. (1949). *The concept of mind.* New York: Barnes & Noble.

Salter, A. (1949). *Conditioned reflex therapy.* New York: Creative Age Press.

Sandberg, G. G., & Marlatt, G. A. (1991). Relapse prevention. In D. A. Gravlo & R. I. Shader (Eds.), *Clinical manual of dependence.* Washington, DC: American Psychiatric Press.

Sarrazin, M. S. V., Hall, J. A., Richards, C., & Carswell, C. (2002). A comparison of computer-based versus pencil-and-paper assessments of drug use. *Research on Social Work Practice, 12*(5), 669–683.

Sato, Y., & Matanuga, I. (2002). Examination of "method learning of autogenic training" and "the clinical effects depending on it": The difference between "the direct clinical effects by the way of AT" and "the clinical effects moving it to the place." *Japanese Journal of Autogenic Therapy, 21*(1–2), 16–23.

Saunders, R. R., & Saunders, M. D. (1998). Supported routines. In J. K. Luiselli & M. J. Cameron (Eds.), *Antecedent control: Innovative approaches to behavioral support* (pp. 245–272). Baltimore: Paul H. Brookes.

Saunders, T., Driskell, J. E., Johnston, J. H., & Salas, E. (1996). The effect of stress inoculation training on anxiety and performance. *Journal of Occupational Health Psychology, 1,* 170–186.

Schaap, C., Bennun, I., Schindler, L., & Hoogduin, K. (1993). *The therapeutic relationship in behavioural psychotherapy.* West Sussex, UK: Wiley.

Schatzberg, A. F., Cole, J. O., & DeBattista, C. (2003). *Manual of clinical psychopharmacology.* Washington, DC: American Psychiatric Publishing.

Scheerenberger, R. C. (1982). *A history of mental retardation.* Baltimore: Paul H. Brookes.

Schmidt, N., & Woolaway-Bickel, K. (2000). The effects of treatment compliance on outcome in cognitive-behavioral therapy for panic disorder: Quality versus quantity. *Journal of Consulting and Clinical Psychology, 68,* 13–18.

Schoenfeld, W. H. (1950). An experimental approach to anxiety, escape, and avoidance behavior. In P. H. Hoch & J. Zubin (Eds.), *Anxiety* (pp. 70–99). Oxford, UK: Grune & Stratton.

Schultheis, G. M. (1998). *Brief therapy homework planner.* New York: Wiley.

Schultz, J. H., & Luthe, W. (1969). *Autogenic therapy: Vol. I. Autogenic methods.* New York: Grune & Stratton.

Schultz, W. (1997). Adaptive dopaminergic neurons report the appetitive value of environmental stimuli. In J. W. Donahoe & V. P. Dorsel (Eds.), *Neural-network models of cognition: Biobehavioral foundations* (pp. 317–325). Amsterdam: Elsevier Science Press.

Schwartz, B. K., & Cellini, H. R. (Eds.). (1995, 1997, 1999, 2002). *The sex offender* (Vols. 1, 2, 3, 4). Kingston, NJ: Civic Research Institute.

Schwartz, G. E. (1982). Testing the biopsychosocial model: The ultimate challenge facing behavioral medicine. *Journal of Consulting and Clinical Psychology, 50,* 1040–1053.

Schwartz, G. E., & Weiss, S. M. (1978). Behavioral medicine revisited: An amended definition. *Journal of Behavioral Medicine, 1*(3), 249–251.

Schwartz, G. E., & Weiss, S. M. (1978). Yale Conference on Behavioral Medicine: A proposed definition and statement of goals. *Journal of Behavioral Medicine, 1*(1), 3–12.

Schwartz, M., & Andrasik, F. (Eds.). (2003). *Biofeedback: A practitioners guide.* New York: Guilford Press.

Scott, D. S., & Rosenstiel, A. K. (1975). Covert positive reinforcement studies: Review, critique., and guidelines. *Psychotherapy: Theory, Research, and Practice, 12,* 374–384.

Scott, J. (2001). Cognitive therapy as an adjunct to medication in bipolar disorder. *British Journal of Psychiatry, 178*(4), s164–s168.

Scott, J. E., & Dixon, L. B. (1995). Psychological interventions for schizophrenia. *Schizophrenia Bulletin, 21*(4), 621–630.

Segal, Z. V., Williams, J. M. G., & Teasdale, J. D. (2002). *Mindfulness-based cognitive therapy for depression: A new approach to preventing relapse.* New York: Guilford Press.

Seligman, M. E. P. (1995). The effectiveness of psychotherapy: The *Consumer Reports* study. *American Psychologist, 50*(12), 965–974.

Shapiro, D. A., Rees, A., Barkham, M., Hardy, G., Reynolds, S., & Startup, M. (1995). Effects of treatment duration and severity of depression on the maintenance of gains after cognitive-behavioral and psychodynamic interpersonal psychotherapy. *Journal of Consulting and Clinical Psychology, 63,* 378–387.

Shapiro, F. (2001). *Eye movement desensitization and reprocessing: Basic principles, protocols, and procedures* (2nd ed.). New York: Guilford Press.

Shapiro, F. (2002). *EMDR as an integrative psychotherapy approach: Experts of diverse orientations explore the paradigm prism.* Washington, DC: American Psychological Association Books.

Shapiro, F. (2002). EMDR twelve years after its introduction: Past and future research. *Journal of Clinical Psychology, 58,* 1–22.

Sharpe, T. L., & Koperwas, J. (2000). *Software assist for education and social science settings: Behavior evaluation strategies and taxonomies (BEST) and accompanying qualitative applications.* Thousand Oaks, CA: Sage-Scolari.

Sharpe, T. L., & Koperwas, J. (2003). *Behavior and sequential analyses: Principles and practice.* Thousand Oaks, CA: Sage.

Sharpe, T. L., Hawkins, A., & Lounsbery, M. (1998). Using technology to study and evaluate human interaction: Practice and implications of a sequential behavior approach. *Quest, 50,* 389–401.

Sharpe, T. L., Hawkins, A., & Ray, R. (1995). Interbehavioral field systems assessment: Examining its utility in preservice teacher education. *Journal of Behavioral Education, 5,* 259–280.

Sheridan, S. M., Bergan, J. R., & Kratochwill, T. R. (1997). *Conjoint behavioral consultation: A procedural manual.* Cambridge, MA: Perseus.

Shimp, C. P. Optimal behavior in free-operant environments. *Psychological Review, 76,* 97–112.

Shull, R. L., & Scott, L. P. (1998). Reinforcement: Schedule performance. In K. A. Lattal & M. Perone (Eds.), *Handbook of research methods in human operant behavior* (pp. 95–129). New York: Plenum Press.

Sidman, M. (1960).*Tactics of scientific research.* New York: Basic Books.

Siegman, A. W., & Smith, T. W. (1994). *Anger, hostility, and the heart.* Hillsdale, NJ: Erlbaum.

Silagy, C., Lancaster, T., Stead, L., Mant, D., & Fowler, G. (2003). Nicotine replacement therapy for smoking cessation (Cochrane Review). *The Cochrane Library, 3,* 2003.

Skinner, B. F. (1938). *The behavior of organisms.* Englewood Cliffs, NJ: Prentice Hall.

Skinner, B. F. (1938). *The behavior of organisms.* New York: Appleton-Century-Crofts.

Skinner, B. F. (1945). The operational analysis of psychological terms. *Psychological Review, 42,* 270–277.

Skinner, B. F. (1948). "Superstition" in the pigeon. *Journal of Experimental Psychology, 38,* 168–172.

Skinner, B. F. (1953). *Science and human behavior.* New York: Free Press.

Skinner, B. F. (1974). *About behaviorism.* New York: Knopf.

Sloane, R. B., Staples, F. R., Cristol, A. H., Yorkston, N. H., & Whipple, K. (1975). *Psychotherapy versus behavior therapy.* Cambridge, MA: Harvard University Press.

Smith, J. C. (1985). *Relaxation dynamics: Nine world approaches to self-relaxation.* Champaign, IL: Research Press.

Smith, J. C. (1989). *Relaxation dynamics: A cognitive-behavioral approach to relaxation.* Champaign, IL: Research Press.

Smith, J. W., & Frawley, P. J. (1990). Long-term abstinence from alcohol in patients receiving aversion therapy as part of a multimodal inpatient program. *Journal of Substance Abuse Treatment, 7*(2), 77–82.

Smith, L. D., & Woodward, W. R. (Eds.). (1996). *B. F. Skinner and behaviorism in American culture.* Bethleham, PA: Lehigh University Press.

Smull, M. (1997). *A blueprint for essential lifestyle planning.* Napa, CA: Allen, Shea & Associates.

Sobell, M. B., & Sobell, L. C. (1978). *Behavioral treatment of alcohol problems: Individualized therapy and controlled drinking.* New York: Plenum Press.

Sobell, M. B., & Sobell, L. C. (1995). Controlled drinking after 25 years: How important was the great debate? *Addiction, 90,* 1149–1153.

Sohlberg, M. M., & Mateer, C. A. (2001). *Cognitive rehabilitation: An integrative neuropsychological approach.* New York: Guilford Press.

Solyom, L. (1971). A comparative study of aversion relief and systematic desensitization in the treatment of phobias. *British Journal of Psychiatry, 119,* 299–303.

Solyom, L. (1972). Variables in the aversion relief therapy of phobics. *Behavior Therapy, 3,* 21–28.

Sorbi, M. J., Honkoop, P. C., & Godaert, G. L. R. (2001). A signal-contingent computer diary for the assessment of psychological precedents of the migraine attack. In J. Fahrenberg & M. Myrtek (Eds.), *Ambulatory assessment: Computer-assisted psychological and psychophysiological methods in monitoring and field studies* (pp. 403–412). Kirkland, WA: Hogrefe & Huber.

Spiegler, M. D, & Guevremont, D. C. (2003). Stimulus control and reinforcement therapy. In *Contemporary behavior therapy* (4th ed., pp. 113–120). Belmont, CA: Wadsworth.

Spiegler, M. D., & Guevremont, D. C. (1993). Brief/graduated exposure therapy: Systematic desensitisation and in vivo exposure. In *Contemporary behavior therapy* (2nd ed., pp. 194–225). Pacific Grove: Brooks/Cole.

Spiegler, M. D., & Guevremont, D. C. (1993). Prolonged/intense exposure therapy: Flooding and implosive therapy. In *Contemporary behavior therapy* (2nd ed., pp. 226–250). Pacific Grove: Brooks/Cole.

Spiegler, M. D., & Guevremont, D. C. (2003). Modeling therapy and skills training. In *Contemporary Behavior Therapy* (4th ed.). Belmont, CA: Thomson-Wadsworth.

Spielman, A. J., & Glovinsky, P. B. (1991). The varied nature of insomnia. In P. J. Hauri (Ed.), *Case studies in insomnia* (pp. 1–15). New York: Plenum Press.

Speigler, M. D., & Guevremont, D. C. (1998). *Contemporary behavior therapy.* Belmont, CA: Brooks/Cole.

St. Lawrence, J. S., & Madakasira, S. (1992). Evaluation and treatment of premature ejaculation: A critical review. *Clinical Psychology Review, 22,* 77–97.

Stampfl, T. G. (1991). Analysis of aversive events in human psychopathology: Fear and avoidance. In M. R. Denny (Ed.), *Fear, avoidance, and phobias* (pp. 363–393). Hillsdale, NJ: Erlbaum.

Stanley, M., Beck, J., Novy, D., Averill, P., Swann, A., Diefenbach, G., & Hopko, D. (2003). Cognitive-behavioral treatment of late-life generalized anxiety disorder. *Journal of Consulting and Clinical Psychology, 71*(2), 309–319.

Stark, K. D., Reynolds, W. M., & Kaslow, N. J. (1987). A comparison of the relative efficacy of self-control therapy and a behavioral problem-solving therapy for depression in children. *Journal of Abnormal Child Psychology. 15*(1), 91–113.

Stava, L., Levin, S. M., & Schwanz, C. (1993). The role of aversion in covert sensitization treatment of pedophilia: A case report. *Journal of Child Sexual Abuse, 2,* 1–13.

Steketee, G. (1999). *Therapist protocol: Overcoming obsessive-compulsive disorder: A behavioral and cognitive protocol for the treatment of OCD.* Oakland: New Harbinger.

Stickgold, R. (2002). EMDR: A putative neurobiological mechanism of action. *Journal of Clinical Psychology, 58,* 61–75.

Stith, S. M., Rosen, K. H., & McCollum, E. E. (2002). Domestic violence. In D. H. Sprenkle (Ed.), *Effectiveness research in marriage and family therapy* (pp. 223–254). Alexandria, VA: American Association for Marriage and the Family.

Stokes, T. F., & Baer, D. M. (1977). An implicit technology of generalization. *Journal of Applied Behavior Analysis, 10,* 349–367.

Stone, A. A., & Shiffman, S. (1994). Ecological momentary assessment: Measuring real world processes in behavioral medicine. *Annals of Behavioral Medicine, 16,* 199–202.

Stricker, G., & Trierweiler, S. J. (1995). The local clinical scientist: A bridge between science and practice. *American Psychologist, 50*(12), 995–1002.

Stuart, R. B. (1980). *Helping couples change.* New York: Guilford Press.

Sue, D. W., & Sue, D. (1999). *Counseling the culturally different: Theory and practice* (3rd ed.). New York: Wiley.

Sue, S. (1999). Science, ethnicity, and bias: Where have we gone wrong? *American Psychologist, 54,* 1070–1077.

Suinn, R. M. (1990). *Anxiety management training: A behavior therapy.* New York: Plenum Press.

Suinn, R. M., & Deffenbacher, J. L. (1988). Anxiety management training. *The Counseling Psychologist, 16,* 31–49.

Sweet, A. A. (1984). The therapeutic relationship in behavior therapy. *Clinical Psychology Review, 4,* 253–272.

Takaishi, N. (2000). A comparative study of AT and progressive relaxation as methods for teaching clients to relax. *Sleep and Hypnosis, 2*(3), 132–136.

Tarrier, N., Pilgrim, H., Sommerfield, C., Faragher, B., Reynolds, M., Graham, E., et al. (1999). A randomized trial of cognitive therapy and imaginal exposure in the treatment of chronic posttraumatic stress disorder. *Journal of Consulting and Clinical Psychology, 67,* 13–18.

Task Force on Promotion and Dissemination of Psychological Procedures. (1995). Training in and dissemination of empirically validated psychological treatments: Report and recommendations. *The Clinical Psychologist, 48,* 3–23.

Taylor, I., & O'Reilly, M. F. (1997). Toward a functional analysis of private verbal self-regulation. *Journal of Applied Behavior Analysis, 30,* 43–58.

Taylor, J. G. (1955). The problem of perceptual constancy. *Bulletin of the British Psychological Society, 25,* 41–42.

Taylor, S. (2000). *Understanding and treating panic disorder: Cognitive and behavioral approaches.* New York: Wiley.

Telch, F., Agras, W., Rossiter, E., Wilfley, D. T., & Kenardy, J. (1990). Group cognitive-behavioral treatment for the nonpurging bulimic: An initial evaluation. *Journal of Consulting and Clinical Psychology, 58,* 629–635.

Thagard, P. (2000). *Coherence in thought and action.* Cambridge: MIT Press.

Thomas, J. C., & Hersen, M. (Eds.). (2003). *Understanding research in clinical and counseling psychology.* Mahwah, NJ: Erlbaum.

Thyer, B., & Hudson, W. W. (1987). Progress in behavioral social work: An introduction. *Journal of Social Service Research, 10,* 1–6.

Timberlake, W., & Allison, J. (1974). Response deprivation: An empirical approach to instrumental performance. *Psychological Review, 81,* 146–164.

Tincani, M. J., Castrogiavanni, A., & Axelrod, S. A. (1999). Comparison of the effectiveness of brief versus traditional functional analyses. *Research in Developmental Disabilities, 20*(5), 327–338.

Todd, J. T., & Morris E. K. (1995). *Modern perspectives on B. F. Skinner and contemporary behaviorism.* Westport, CT. Greenwood Press.

Tompkins, M. A. (2002). Guidelines for enhancing homework compliance. *Journal of Clinical Psychology, 58,* 565–576.

Toogood, S., & Timlin, K. (2000). The functional assessment of challenging behaviour: A comparison of informant-based, experimental and descriptive methods. *Journal of Applied Research in Intellectual Disabilities, 9*(3), 206–222.

Tracey, T. J. G. (2002). Stages of counseling and therapy: An examination of complementarity and the working alliance. In G. S. Tryon (Ed.), *Counseling based on process research: Applying what we know* (pp. 265–297). Boston: Allyn & Bacon.

Trower, P. (1995). Adult social skills: State of the art and future directions. In W. O'Donohue & L. Krasner (Eds.), *Handbook of psychological skills training: Techniques and applications* (pp. 54–80). Boston: Allyn & Bacon.

Truax, C. B. (1966). Reinforcement and non-reinforcement in Rogerian psychotherapy. *Journal of Abnormal Psychology, 71,* 1–9.

Tryon, G. S. (1979). A review and critique of thought stopping research. *Journal of Behavior Therapy and Psychiatry, 10,* 189–192.

Tryon, G. S. (2002). Engagement in counseling. In G. S. Tryon (Ed.), *Counseling based on process research: Applying what we know* (pp. 1–26). Boston: Allyn & Bacon.

Tryon, G. S., & Winograd, G. (2002). Goal consensus and collaboration. In J. C. Norcross (Ed.), *Psychotherapy relationships that work: Therapist contributions and responsiveness to patients* (pp. 109–125). New York: Oxford.

Tryon, W. W. (1986). The convergence of cognitive behaviorism and ego-psychology. *Theoretical and Philosophical Psychology, 6,* 90–96.

Tryon, W. W. (1991). *Activity measurement in psychology and medicine.* New York: Plenum Press.

Tryon, W. W. (1995). Neural networks for behavior therapists: What they are and why they are important. *Behavior Therapy, 26,* 295–318.

Tryon, W. W. (1998). Behavioral observation. In M. Hersen & A. S. Bellack (Eds.), *Behavioral assessment: A practical handbook* (4th ed., pp. 79–103). Boston: Allyn & Bacon.

Tryon, W. W. (1998). Physical activity. In M. Hersen & B. B. Van Hasselt (Eds.), *Handbook of clinical geropsychology* (pp. 523–556). New York: Plenum Press.

Tryon, W. W. (1999). A bidirectional associative memory explanation of posttraumatic stress disorder. *Clinical Psychology Review, 19,* 789–818.

Tryon, W. W. (1999). Behavioral model. In M. Hersen & V. B. Van Hasselt (Eds.), *Advanced abnormal psychology* (pp. 93–123). New York: Plenum Press.

Tryon, W. W. (2002). Activity level and *DSM-IV*. In S. Turner & M. Hersen (Eds.), *Adult psychopathology and diagnosis* (4th. ed., pp. 547–577). New York: Wiley.

Tryon, W. W. (2002). Expanding the explanatory base of behavior analysis via modern connectionism: Selectionism as a common explanatory core. *The Behavior Analyst Today, 3,* 104–118.

Tryon, W. W., & Williams, R. (1996). Fully proportional actigraphy: A new instrument. *Behavior Research Methods Instruments & Computers, 28,* 392–403.

Tucker, M., Sigafoos, J., & Bushell, H. (1998). Use of noncontingent reinforcement in the treatment of challenging behavior. *Behavior Modification, 22,* 529–547.

Turner, S. M., Beidel, D. C., & Cooley, M. R. (1995). A multicomponent behavioral treatment for social phobia: Social effectiveness therapy. *Behaviour Research & Therapy, 33,* 553–555.

Turner, S. M., Beidel, D. C., & Cooley-Quille, M. R. (1997). *Social effectiveness therapy: A program for overcoming social anxiety and social phobia.* Toronto, Canada: Multi-Health Systems.

Turner, S. M., Beidel, D. C., & Jacob, R. G. (1994). Social phobia: A comparison of behavior therapy and atenolol. *Journal of Consulting and Clinical Psychology, 62,* 350–358.

Turner, S. M., Beidel, D. C., & Long, P. J. (1992). Reduction of fear in social phobics: An examination of extinction patterns. *Behavior Therapy, 23,* 389–403.

Twamley, E. W., Jeste, D. V., & Bellack, A. S. (in press). A review of cognitive training in schizophrenia. *Schizophrenia Bulletin.*

U.S. Department of Health and Human Services. (2000). *Therapy manuals for drug addiction: A cognitive-behavioral approach: Treating cocaine addiction.* Bethesda, MD: National Institute on Drug Abuse.

van den Hout, M., Emmelkamp, P., Kraaykamp, H., & Griez, E. (1988). Behavioral treatment of obsessive-compulsives: Inpatient vs. outpatient. *Behaviour Therapy and Research, 26*(4), 331–332.

Vandercook, T., York, J., & Forest, M. (1989). The McGill Action Planning System (MAPS): A strategy for building the vision. *Journal of the Association for Persons With Severe Handicaps, 14,* 205–215.

Vargas, E. A. (1995). Prologue, perspectives, and prospects of behaviorology. *Behaviorology, 3,* 107–120.

Vargas, E. A. (1996). Explanatory frameworks and the thema of agency. *Behaviorology, 4,* 30–42.

Vargas, E. A. (1999). Ethics. In B. A. Thyer (Ed.), *The philosophical legacy of behaviorism* (pp. 89–115). London: Kluwer.

Vargas, J. S. (2001). B. F. Skinner's contribution to therapeutic change: An agency-less, contingency analysis. In W. T. O'Donohue, D. A. Henderson, S. C. Hayes, J. E. Fisher, & L. J. Hayes (Eds.), *A history of the behavioral therapies: Founders' personal histories.* Reno, NV: Context Press.

Vedel, E., & Emmelkamp, P. M. G. (in press). Behavioral couple therapy in the treatment of a female alcohol dependent patient with comorbid depression, anxiety and personality disorders. *Clinical Case Studies.*

vom Saal, W., & Jenkins, H. M. (1970). Blocking the development of stimulus control. *Learning and Motivation, 1,* 52–64.

Vriezen, E. R., & Pigott, S.E. (2002). The relationship between parental report on the BRIEF and performance-based measures of executive function in children with moderate to severe traumatic brain injury. *Child Neuropsychology, 8*(4), 296–303.

Wahler, R. G., & Dumas, J. E. (1989). Attentional problems in dysfunctional mother-child interactions: An interbehavioral model. *Psychological Bulletin, 105,* 116–130.

Walen, S. R., DiGiuseppe, R., & Dryden, W. (1992). *A practitioner's guide to rational-emotive therapy* (2nd ed.). New York: Oxford University Press.

Wampold, B. E. (1992). The intensive examination of social interactions. In T. R. Kratochwill & J. R. Levin (Eds.), *Single-case research design and analysis: New directions for psychology and education* (pp. 93–131). Hillsdale, NJ: Erlbaum.

Ward, T., & Hudson, S. (1996). Relapse prevention: A critical analysis. *Sexual Abuse: A Journal of Research and Treatment, 8,* 177–199.

Ward, T., Hudson, S. M., & Laws, D. R. (Eds.). (2003). *Sexual deviance: Issues and controversies.* Thousand Oaks, CA: Sage.

Warzak, W. J., & Anhalt, K. (2003). Facilitating the psychosocial recovery of youth and adolescents with traumatic brain injury. In K. Hux (Ed.), *Assisting survivors of traumatic brain injury: The role of speech/language pathologists.* New York: Pro Ed Press.

Watson, D. L., & Tharp, R. G. (2001). *Self-directed behavior: Self-modification for personal adjustment* (8th ed.). Monterey, CA: Brooks/Cole.

Watson, D. L., & Tharp, R. G. (2002). *Self-directed behavior: Self-modification for personal adjustment* (8th ed., chap. 3.) Belmont, CA: Wadsworth.

Watzlawick, P., Weakland, J., & Fisch, R. (1974). *Change: Principles of problem formulation and problem resolution.* New York: Norton.

Webster-Stratton, C., & Hammond, M. (1997). Treatment of children with early-onset conduct problems: A comparison of child and parent training interventions. *Journal of Consulting and Clinical Psychology, 65,* 93–109.

Weeks, G. R., & L'Abate, L. A. (1982). *Paradoxical psychotherapy: Theory and practice with individuals, couples, and families.* New York: Brunner/Mazel.

Wegner, D. M. (1989). *White bears and other unwanted thoughts: Suppression, obsessions, and the psychology of mental control.* New York: Penguin.

Wegner, D. M. (1994). Ironic processes of mental control. *Psychological Review, 101,* 34–52.

Weigle, K. L., & Scotti, J. R. (2000). Effects of functional analysis information on ratings or intervention effectiveness and acceptability. *Journal for the Association of Persons with Severe Handicaps, 25,* 217–228.

Weisz, J. R., Hawley, K. M., Pilkonis, P. A., Woody, S. R., & Follette, W. C. (2000). Stressing the (other) three R's in the search for empirically supported treatments: Review procedures, research quality, relevance to practice, and the public interest. *Clinical Psychology: Science and Practice, 7,* 243–258.

Wells, A. (1997). *Cognitive therapy of anxiety disorders: A practice manual and conceptual guide.* New York: Wiley.

Wesolowski, M. D., & Zencius, A. H. (1994). *Critical issues in neuropsychology: A practical guide to head injury rehabilitation: A focus on postacute residential treatment.* New York: Plenum Press.

Wetherington, C. L. (1981). Is adjunctive behavior a third class of behavior? *Neuroscience and Biobehavioral Reviews, 6,* 329–350.

Whittal, M. L., & McLean, P. D. (1999). CBT for OCD: The rationale, protocol, and challenges. *Cognitive and Behavioral Practice, 6,* 383–396.

Wiklander, N. (1989). *From laboratory to Utopia: An inquiry into the early psychology and social philosophy of B. F. Skinner.* Goteborg, Sweden: Goteborg Arachne Series.

Williams, L., & Zane, G. (1989). Guided mastery and stimulus exposure treatments for severe performance anxiety in agoraphobia. *Behavior Research and Therapy, 27,* 237–245.

Williams, L., Dooseman, G., & Kleifield, E. (1984). Comparative effectiveness of guided mastery and exposure treatments for intractable phobias. *Journal of Consulting and Clinical Psychology, 53,* 237–247.

Williams, L., Turner, S., & Peer, D. (1985). Guided mastery and performance desensitization treatments for severe acrophobia. *Journal of Consulting and Clinical Psychology, 52,* 505–518.

Willis, B. S., Rosqvist, J., Egan, D., Baney, D., & Manzo, P. (1998). Inpatient and home-based treatment of obsessive-compulsive disorder. In M. A. Jenike, L. Baer, & W. E. Minichiello (Eds.), *Obsessive-compulsive disorders: Practical management* (3rd ed., pp. 570–591). Boston: Mosby.

Wilson, G. T., & Evans, I. M. (1976). *Adult behavior therapy and the therapist-client relationship.* In C. M. Franks & G. T. Wilson (Eds.), *Annual review of behavior therapy: Theory and practice* (Vol. 4, pp. 771–792). New York: Brunner/Mazel.

Wilson, G. T., & Fairburn, C. G. (2002). Treatments for eating disorders. In P. E. Nathan & J. M. Gorman (Eds.), *A guide to treatments that work* (pp. 559–592). Oxford, UK: Oxford University Press.

Wilson, K. G., & Hayes, S. C. (2000). Why it is crucial to understand thinking and feeling: An analysis and application to drug abuse. *The Behavior Analyst, 23,* 25–43.

Wing, R. R. (2002). Behavioral weight control. In T. A. Wadden & A. J. Stunkard (Eds.), *Handbook of obesity treatment* (pp. 301–316). New York: Guilford Press.

Wisocki, P. A. (1970). Treatment of obsessive-compulsive behavior by covert sensitization and covert reinforcement: A case report. *Journal of Behaviour Therapy and Experimental Psychiatry, 1,* 233–239.

Wisocki, P. A. (1973). A covert reinforcement program for the treatment of test anxiety: A brief report. *Behavior Therapy, 4,* 264–266.

Wisocki, P. A. (1973). The successful treatment of a heroin addict by covert conditioning techniques. *Journal of Behavior Therapy and Experimental Psychiatry, 4,* 55–61.

Wisocki, P. A. (1976). A behavioral treatment program for social inadequacy: Multiple methods for a complex problem. In J. Krumboltz & C. Thoresen (Eds.), *Counseling methods* (pp. 287–301). New York: Holt, Rinehart & Winston.

Wisocki, P. A. (1993). The treatment of an elderly woman with orofacial tardive dyskinesia by relaxation and covert reinforcer sampling. In J. R. Cautela & A. J. Kearney (Eds.), *Covert conditioning casebook* (pp. 108–115). Pacific Grove, CA: Brooks/Cole.

Wisocki, P. A., & Telch, M. (1980). Modifying attitudes toward the elderly with the use of sampling procedures. *Scandinavian Journal of Behavior Therapy, 9,* 87–96.

Wittgenstein, L. (1953). *Philosophical investigations.* New York: Macmillan.

Wolpe, J. (1969). *The practice of behavior therapy.* New York: Pergamon Press.

Wolpe, J. (1958). *Psychotherapy by reciprocal inhibition.* Stanford, CA: Stanford University Press.

Wolpe, J. (1990). *The practice of behavior therapy* (4th ed.). Elmsford, New York: Pergamon Press.

Wolpe, J., & Lazarus, A. A. (1966). *Behavior therapy techniques: A guide to the treatment of neuroses.* Toronto, Canada: Pergamon Press.

Wolpe, J., Salter, A., & Reyna, L. J. (Eds.). (1964). *The conditioning therapies.* New York: Holt, Rinehart & Winston.

Woods, A., Smith, C., Szewczak, M., Dunn, R. W., Cornfeldt, M., & Corbett, R. (1993). Selective serotonin re-uptake inhibitors decrease schedule-induced polydipsia in rats: A potential model for obsessive-compulsive disorder. *Psychopharmacology, 112,* 195–198.

Woods, C. M., Chambless, D. L., & Steketee, G. S. (2002). Homework compliance and behavior therapy outcome with agoraphobia and obsessive-compulsive disorder. *Cognitive Behavior Therapy, 31,* 88–95.

Woods, D. W. (2001). Habit reversal treatment manual for tic disorders. In D. Woods & R. Miltenberger (Eds.), *Tic disorders, trichotillomania, and other repetitive behavior disorders: Behavioral approaches to analysis and treatment* (pp. 33–52). Norwell, MA: Kluwer.

Woods, D. W. (2001). Habit reversal treatment manual for tic disorders. In D. W. Woods & R. G. Miltenberger (Eds.), *Tic disorders, trichotillomania, and other repetitive behavior disorders: Behavioral approaches to analysis and treatment* (pp. 97–132). New York: Kluwer Academic.

Woods, D. W., & Miltenberger, R. G. (1995). Habit reversal: A review of applications and variations. *Journal of Behavior Therapy and Experimental Psychiatry, 26*(2), 123–131.

Woods, D. W., & Miltenberger, R. G. (1996). A review of habit reversal with childhood habit disorders. *Education and Treatment of Children, 19*(2), 197–214.

Wright, J. H., & Davis, D. (1994). The therapeutic relationship in cognitive-behavioral therapy: Patient perceptions and therapist responses. *Cognitive and Behavioral Practice, 1,* 24–45.

Wykes, T., & Van der Gaag, M. (2001). Is it time to develop a new cognitive therapy for psychosis–cognitive remediation therapy (CRT)? *Clinical Psychology Review, 21,* 227–256.

Yerkes, R. M., & Margulis, S. (1909). The method of Pavlovian animal psychology. *Psychological Bulletin, 6,* 257–273.

Young, J. E. (1999). *Cognitive therapy for personality disorders: A schema-focused approach* (3rd ed.). Sarasota, FL: Practitioner's Resource Series.

Young, J. E., Klosko, J. S., & Weishaar, M. E. (2003). *Schema therapy: A practitioner's guide.* New York: Guilford Press.

Yudkin, P., Hey, K., Roberts, S., Welch, S., Murphy, M., & Walton, R. (2003). Abstinence from smoking eight years after participation in randomized controlled trial of nicotine patch. *British Medical Journal, 327,* 28–29.

Zimand, E., Anderson, P. L., Gershon, J., Graap, K., Hodges, L. F., & Rothbaum, B. O. (in press). Virtual reality therapy: Innovative treatment for anxiety disorders. *Primary Psychiatry.*

Zuckerman, E. L. (1997). *The paper office* (2nd ed.). New York: Guilford Press.

Zuercher-White, E. (1999). *Overcoming panic disorder and agoraphobia.* Oakland, CA: New Harbinger.

Index